CLASSICAL AND MEDIEVAL LITERATURE CRITICISM

Guide to Gale Literary Criticism Series

For criticism on	Consult these Gale series
Authors now living or who died after December 31, 1999	*CONTEMPORARY LITERARY CRITICISM (CLC)*
Authors who died between 1900 and 1999	*TWENTIETH-CENTURY LITERARY CRITICISM (TCLC)*
Authors who died between 1800 and 1899	*NINETEENTH-CENTURY LITERATURE CRITICISM (NCLC)*
Authors who died between 1400 and 1799	*LITERATURE CRITICISM FROM 1400 TO 1800 (LC)* *SHAKESPEAREAN CRITICISM (SC)*
Authors who died before 1400	*CLASSICAL AND MEDIEVAL LITERATURE CRITICISM (CMLC)*
Authors of books for children and young adults	*CHILDREN'S LITERATURE REVIEW (CLR)*
Dramatists	*DRAMA CRITICISM (DC)*
Poets	*POETRY CRITICISM (PC)*
Short story writers	*SHORT STORY CRITICISM (SSC)*
Black writers of the past two hundred years	*BLACK LITERATURE CRITICISM (BLC)* *BLACK LITERATURE CRITICISM SUPPLEMENT (BLCS)*
Hispanic writers of the late nineteenth and twentieth centuries	*HISPANIC LITERATURE CRITICISM (HLC)* *HISPANIC LITERATURE CRITICISM SUPPLEMENT (HLCS)*
Native North American writers and orators of the eighteenth, nineteenth, and twentieth centuries	*NATIVE NORTH AMERICAN LITERATURE (NNAL)*
Major authors from the Renaissance to the present	*WORLD LITERATURE CRITICISM, 1500 TO THE PRESENT (WLC)* *WORLD LITERATURE CRITICISM SUPPLEMENT (WLCS)*

ISSN 0896-0011

Volume 43

CLASSICAL AND MEDIEVAL LITERATURE CRITICISM

Excerpts from Criticism of the Works of World Authors from Classical Antiquity through the Fourteenth Century, from the First Appraisals to Current Evaluations

Elisabeth Gellert
Jelena O. Krstović
Editors

Detroit
New York
San Francisco
London
Boston
Woodbridge, CT

STAFF

Janet Witalec, Lynn M. Spampinato, *Managing Editors, Literature Product*
Kathy D. Darrow, *Product Liaison*
Elisabeth Gellert, Jelena Krstović, *Editors*
Mark W. Scott, *Publisher, Literature Product*

Mary Ruby, *Technical Training Specialist*
Deborah J. Morad, Kathleen Lopez Nolan, *Managing Editors, Literature Content*
Susan M. Trosky, *Director, Literature Content*

Maria L. Franklin, *Permissions Manager*
Edna Hedblad, *Permissions Specialist*
Julie Juengling, *Permissions Assistant*

Victoria B. Cariappa, *Research Manager*
Tracie A. Richardson, *Project Coordinator*
Andrew Guy Malonis, Barbara McNeil, Gary J. Oudersluys, Maureen Richards, Cheryl L. Warnock, *Research Specialists*
Tamara C. Nott, *Research Associate*

Dorothy Maki, *Manufacturing Manager*
Stacy L. Melson, *Buyer*

Mary Beth Trimper, *Composition and Prepress Manager*
Gary Leach, *Composition Specialist*

Randy Bassett, *Image Database Supervisor*
Robert Duncan, *Imaging Specialist*
Mike Logusz, *Graphic Artist*
Pamela A. Reed, *Imaging Coordinator*
Kelly A. Quin, *Imaging Editor*

Library of Congress Catalog Card Number 88-658021
ISBN 0-7876-5059-5
ISSN 0896-0011
Printed in the United States of America

10 9 8 7 6 5 4 3 2 1

Contents

Preface

Since its inception in 1988, *Classical and Medieval Literature Criticism* (*CMLC*) has been a valuable resource for students and librarians seeking critical commentary on the works and authors of antiquity through the fourteenth century. The great poets, prose writers, dramatists, and philosophers of this period form the basis of most humanities curricula, so that virtually every student will encounter many of these works during the course of a high school and college education. Reviewers have found *CMLC* "useful" and "extremely convenient," noting that it "adds to our understanding of the rich legacy left by the ancient period and the Middle Ages," and praising its "general excellence in the presentation of an inherently interesting subject." No other single reference source has surveyed the critical reaction to classical and medieval literature as thoroughly as *CMLC*.

Scope of the Series

CMLC provides an introduction to classical and medieval authors, works, and topics that represent a variety of genres, time periods, and nationalities. By organizing and reprinting an enormous amount of critical commentary written on authors and works of this period in world history, *CMLC* helps students develop valuable insight into literary history, promotes a better understanding of the texts, and sparks ideas for papers and assignments.

Each entry in *CMLC* presents a comprehensive survey of an author's career, an individual work of literature, or a literary topic, and provides the user with a multiplicity of interpretations and assessments. Such variety allows students to pursue their own interests; furthermore, it fosters an awareness that literature is dynamic and responsive to many different opinions. Early commentary is offered to indicate initial responses, later selections document changes in literary reputations, and retrospective analyses provide the reader with modern views. The size of each author entry is a relative reflection of the scope of the criticism available in English.

An author may appear more than once in the series if his or her writings have been the subject of a substantial amount of criticism; in these instances, specific works or groups of works by the author will be covered in separate entries. For example, Homer will be represented by three entries, one devoted to the *Iliad,* one to the *Odyssey,* and one to the Homeric Hymns.

CMLC continues the survey of criticism of world literature begun by Gale's *Contemporary Literary Criticism* (*CLC*), *Twentieth-Century Literary Criticism* (*TCLC*), *Nineteenth-Century Literature Criticism* (*NCLC*), *Literature Criticism from 1400 to 1800* (*LC*), and *Shakespearean Criticism* (*SC*).

Organization of the Book

A *CMLC* entry consists of the following elements:

- The **Author Heading** cites the name under which the author most commonly wrote, followed by birth and death dates. Also located here are any name variations under which an author wrote, including transliterated forms for authors whose native languages use nonroman alphabets. If the author wrote consistently under a pseudonym, the pseudonym will be listed in the author heading and the author's actual name given in parenthesis on the first line of the biographical and critical information. Uncertain birth or death dates are indicated by question marks. Single-work entries are preceded by a heading that consists of the most common form of the title in English translation (if applicable) and the original date of composition.

- The **Introduction** contains background information that introduces the reader to the author, work, or topic that is the subject of the entry.

- A **Portrait of the Author** is included when available.

- The list of **Principal Works** is ordered chronologically by date of first publication and lists the most important works by the author. The genre and publication date of each work is given. In the case of foreign authors whose works have been translated into English, the list will focus primarily on twentieth-century translations, selecting those works most commonly considered the best by critics. Unless otherwise indicated, dramas are dated by first performance, not first publication. Lists of **Representative Works** by different authors appear with topic entries.

- Reprinted **Criticism** is arranged chronologically in each entry to provide a useful perspective on changes in critical evaluation over time. The critic's name and the date of composition or publication of the critical work are given at the beginning of each piece of criticism. Unsigned criticism is preceded by the title of the source in which it appeared. All titles by the author featured in the text are printed in boldface type. Footnotes are reprinted at the end of each essay or excerpt. In the case of excerpted criticism, only those footnotes that pertain to the excerpted texts are included. Criticism in topic entries is arranged chronologically under a variety of subheadings to facilitate the study of different aspects of the topic.

- A complete **Bibliographical Citation** of the original essay or book precedes each piece of criticism.

- Critical essays are prefaced by brief **Annotations** explicating each piece.

- An annotated bibliography of **Further Reading** appears at the end of each entry and suggests resources for additional study. In some cases, significant essays for which the editors could not obtain reprint rights are included here. Boxed material following the further reading list provides references to other biographical and critical sources on the author in series published by Gale.

Cumulative Indexes

A **Cumulative Author Index** lists all of the authors that appear in a wide variety of reference sources published by the Gale Group, including *CMLC*. A complete list of these sources is found facing the first page of the Author Index. The index also includes birth and death dates and cross references between pseudonyms and actual names.

Beginning with the second volume, a **Cumulative Nationality Index** lists all authors featured in *CMLC* by nationality, followed by the number of the *CMLC* volume in which their entry appears.

Beginning with the tenth volume, a **Cumulative Topic Index** lists the literary themes and topics treated in the series as well as in *Nineteenth-Century Literature Criticism, Twentieth-Century Literary Criticism,* and the *Contemporary Literary Criticism* Yearbook, which was discontinued in 1998.

A **Cumulative Title Index** lists in alphabetical order all of the works discussed in the series. Each title listing includes the corresponding volume and page numbers where criticism may be located. Foreign-language titles that have been translated into English are followed by the titles of the translation—for example, *Slovo o polku Igorove* (*The Song of Igor's Campaign*). Page numbers following these translated titles refer to all pages on which any form of the titles, either foreign-language or translated, appear. Titles of novels, dramas, nonfiction books, and poetry, short story, or essay collections are printed in italics, while individual poems, short stories, and essays are printed in roman type within quotation marks.

Citing *Classical and Medieval Literature Criticism*

When writing papers, students who quote directly from any volume in the Literary Criticism Series may use the following general format to footnote reprinted criticism. The first example pertains to material drawn from periodicals, the second to material reprinted from books.

T. P. Malnati, "Juvenal and Martial on Social Mobility," *The Classical Journal* 83, no. 2 (December-January 1988): 134-41; reprinted in *Classical and Medieval Literature Criticism,* vol. 35, ed. Jelena Krstović (Farmington Hills, Mich.: The Gale Group, 2000), 366-71.

J. P. Sullivan, "Humanity and Humour; Imagery and Wit," in *Martial: An Unexpected Classic* (Cambridge University Press, 1991), 211-51; excerpted and reprinted in *Classical and Medieval Literature Criticism,* vol. 35, ed. Jelena Krstović (Farmington Hills, Mich.: The Gale Group, 2000), 371-95.

Suggestions are Welcome

Readers who wish to suggest new features, topics, or authors to appear in future volumes, or who have other suggestions or comments are cordially invited to call, write, or fax the Managing Editor:

Managing Editor, Literary Criticism Series
The Gale Group
27500 Drake Road
Farmington Hills, MI 48331-3535
1-800-347-4253 (GALE)
Fax: 248-699-8054

Acknowledgments

The editors wish to thank the copyright holders of the excerpted criticism included in this volume and the permissions managers of many book and magazine publishing companies for assisting us in securing reproduction rights. We are also grateful to the staffs of the Detroit Public Library, the Library of Congress, the University of Detroit Mercy Library, Wayne State University Purdy/Kresge Library Complex, and the University of Michigan Libraries for making their resources available to us. Following is a list of the copyright holders who have granted us permission to reproduce material in this volume of *CMLC*. Every effort has been made to trace copyright, but if omissions have been made, please let us know.

COPYRIGHTED EXCERPTS IN *CMLC*, VOLUME 43, WERE REPRODUCED FROM THE FOLLOWING PERIODICALS:

Classical Philology, v. 73, 1978. Copyright © 1978 by The University of Chicago. Reproduced by the permission of The University of Chicago./ v. XL, January, 1945. Copyright © 1945, renewed 1973 by The University of Chicago . Reproduced by permission of The University of Chicago.—*Harvard Studies in Classical Philology,* v. 86, 1982. Copyright © 1982 by the President and Fellows of Harvard College. All rights reserved. Reproduced by permission of Harvard University.—*Latomus: Revue D'Etudes Latines,* v. XLIII, April-June, 1984; v. XLVIII, January-March, 1989. Copyright © 1984, 1989 by Latomus: Revue D'Etudes Latines. Reproduced by permission.—*Leeds Studies in English,* v. 8, 1975. Copyright © 1975 by School of English University of Leeds. Reproduced by permission.—*Neuphilogische Mitteilungen,* v. LXXIV, 1973. Reproduced by permission.—*Proceedings of the British Academy,* v. 41, 1955. Copyright © 1955 British Academy. Reproduced by permission.—*Speculum,* v. 13, October, 1938; v. 20, October, 1945; v. 22, April, 1947. Copyright © 1938, renewed 1966; Copyright © 1945, renewed 1973; Copyright © 1947, renewed 1975 by the Medieval Academy of America. All reproduced by the permission of the Medieval Academy of America.—*Studies in Philology*, v. LXXII, January, 1975. Copyright © 1975 by The University of North Carolina Press. Reproduced by permission.—*University of Toronto Quarterly,* v. XXXVII, October, 1967. Copyright © 1967 by University of Toronto Press. Reproduced by permission of University of Toronto Press Incorporated.

COPYRIGHTED EXCERPTS IN *CMLC*, VOLUME 43, WERE REPRODUCED FROM THE FOLLOWING BOOKS:

Barnish, S. J. B. From an introduction to *The "Variae" of Magnus Aurelius Cassiodorus Senator.* Edited by S. J. B. Barnish. Liverpool University Press, 1992. Copyright © 1992 S. J. B. Barnish. Reproduced by permission.—Benson, Larry D. From "Originality of 'Beowulf,'" in *Old English Poetry: Fifteen Essays.* Edited by Robert P. Creed. Brown University Press, 1967. Reproduced by permission of Harvard University.—Benson, Larry D. From "The Pagan Coloring of 'Beowulf,'" in *Old English Poetry: Fifteen Essays.* Edited by Robert P. Creed. Brown University Press, 1967. Reproduced by permission.—Bosworth, A.B. From an introduction to *A Historical Commentary on Arrian's History of Alexander.* Oxford at the Clarendon Press, 1980. Copyright © 1980 by Oxford University Press. Reproduced by permission of the Oxford University Press, Clarendon.—Davidson, Olga M. From *Poet and Hero in the Persian Book of Kings.* Cornell University Press, 1994. Copyright © 1994 by Cornell University Press. All rights reserved. Reproduced by permission of Cornell University Press.—Devine, A. M. From "Arrian's 'Tactica,'" in *Aufstieg und Niedergang der rominschen Welt.* Edited by Wolfgang Hasse and Hildegard Temporini. Walter de Gruyter, Berlin, 1993. Copyright © 1993 by Walter de Gruyter & Co. Reproduced by permission of the publisher.—Evans, Stephen S. From *The Heroic Poetry of Dark-Age Britain: An Introduction to Its Dating, Composition, and Use as a Historical Source.* University Press of America, 1997. Copyright © 1997 by University of America Press, Inc. Reproduced by permission of the publisher.—Ferdowsi, Abolqasem. From *The Epic of the Kings:Shah-Nama, the National Epic of Persia* by Ferdowsi. Routledge and Kegan Paul, Ltd., 1967. Copyright © The Royal Institute of Publication of Teheran, 1967. Reproduced by permission of Taylor & Francis Books, Ltd.— From *In the Dragon's Claws: The Story of Rostram and Esfandiyar from the Persian Book of Kings by Abolqasem Ferdowsi.* Mage Publishers, 1999. Copyright © 1999 by Mage Publishers. All rights reserved. Reproduced by permission.— From *Suhrab and Rustam: A Poem for the "Shah Namah" of Firdausi.* Scholars' Facsimiles and Reprints, 1972. Translated by James Atkinson. Copyright © 1972 Scholars' Facsimiles and Reprints, Inc. All rights reserved. Reproduced by permission.—Dick Davis. From *The Legend of Seyavash* by Ferdowski. Penguin Books, 1992. Copyright © Dick Davis, 1992. All rights reserved. Reproduced by permission of Penguin Books, a division of Penguin Putnam Inc. —From

Arrian
c. 95?-c. 175?

(Full name Flavius Arrianus) Greek historian, philosopher, biographer, and treatise writer.

INTRODUCTION

Although he was of Greek descent, Arrian inherited Roman citizenship from his father, and as a Roman citizen, Arrian was able successfully to pursue a political and military career. The highest office he attained was the imperial governorship of Cappadocia. His military experiences informed a variety of historical writings, including his history of Alexander the Great, the *Anabasis Alexandri,* which is probably the best known of his writings. Little had been written concerning military life on the Roman frontier, and Arrian has been praised for his original approach to historical writing.

BIOGRAPHICAL INFORMATION

Aside from the dates of his political offices, the facts concerning Arrian's life are sketchy. Scholars conjecture that he was born in the 90s in Nicomedia, in Bithynia. He served as consul during the reign of the emperor Hadrian and from about 130 through 137 he held the post of governor of Cappadocia, defending the province against an attack by the Alans, a Germanic tribe. After travelling extensively on imperial business, Arrian retired to Athens. There, he held a civic office from 147 to 148. Biographers estimate that he died around the year 175.

MAJOR WORKS

Pursuing his interest in philosophy, Arrian studied under the Stoic philosopher Epictetus. He published the notes he had taken during Epictetus's lectures as *Discourses,* or *Diatribes,* and also completed a summary of the philosopher's teaching, *Encheiridion,* or *Manual.* Later, Arrian wrote the *Periplus Ponti Euxini,* a guide to the circumnavigation of the Black Sea. The work incorporated official reports he had written during his governorship. Another work composed at this time was the *Tactica,* or *Techne Taktike (Tactical Manual),* written in 136, which focuses on Roman military exercises. Arrian also prepared a report for Hadrian on the *Order of Battle against the Alans.* After retiring to Athens, Arrian composed a treatise on hunting, *Cynegetica,* as well as biographies of Dion, Timoleon of Syracuse, and a bandit named Tilloborus. These biographical works are no longer extant. Arrian's most famous biographical endeavor was his history of Al-

exander. The title, the *Anabasis,* is uncertain, as scholars point out. The work examines the reign and military campaigns of Alexander the Great and is based heavily on the writings of Ptolemy, as well as on those of Aristobulus. Arrian supplemented the *Anabasis* with a historical discussion of India known as the *Indica.* Two other histories, the *Bithynica* and *Parthica,* have been lost.

CRITICAL RECEPTION

Modern scholars have shown an interest in Arrian because his works provide a rare glimpse into the life and experiences of the Roman army on its frontier borders. Critic H. F. Pelham has surveyed Arrian's military writings, those he composed prior to his retirement. In discussing *Tactica,* the *Order of Battle against the Alans,* and the *Periplus,* Pelham praises Arrian's versatility, his graceful writing, and intellectual acuity, as well as his strong grasp of Roman military affairs. Ronald Syme has likewise examined the military career of Arrian and the probable order in which he composed his works. Other critics have focused on the *Tactica* alone. Philip A. Stadter explains that there are two sections of the work: the first closely follows traditional tactical manuals, and the second is an original discussion of contemporary Roman military exercises. Stadter focuses his study on the first portion of the work, noting that, while he makes heavy use of traditional material, Arrian makes significant contributions in clarifying often abstract ideas by citing historical and contemporary Roman experiences. Like Stadter, A. M. Devine analyzes the *Tactica,* noting as well that the second portion of the work is the more original. Devine describes the work as detailed and colorful, and asserts that, in its comprehensiveness, it is one of the most significant extant Hellenistic tactical manuals.

Many critics have concentrated their efforts on Arrian's histories rather than his military writings. J. R. Hamilton fas focused on the *Anabasis,* noting that Arrian intended the work to be his masterpiece. Hamilton reviews the use Arrian made of his sources, Ptolemy and Aristobulus, and praises Arrian's keen understanding of human affairs, as well as his patience in addressing his subject. Yet the work is flawed, Hamilton maintains, by Arrian's sometimes "narrow" approach to the topic and lacks a sense of appreciation for larger issues. A. B. Bosworth has also examined the *Anabasis,* studying Arrian's use of his source materials and his accuracy as a historian. Bosworth states that while Arrian uses source documents in a complex manner, his selection of source material and his own historical knowledge is questionable. Bosworth praises Arrian's conciseness, his adept use of figurative language, and his sophistication as a stylist. Philip A. Stadter offers a discussion of those histories composed by Arrian which have since been lost, including his history of his native Bithynia, a history of Parthica, and another work, *Events after Alexander,* which describes the power struggles of Alexander's successors after his death. These works, argues Stadter, demonstrate the variety of Arrian's interests and secure his position as the preeminent writer of his generation.

PRINCIPAL WORKS

Anabasis Alexandri [also known as *Anabasis of Alexander* and *Campaigns of Alexander*] (history)
Bithnica [also rendered as *Bithynica*] (history)
Cynegetica [*Treatise on Hunting*] (treatise)
Discourses (philosophical notes)
Encheiridion (philosophical summary)
Events after Alexander (history)
Indica (history)
Order of Battle against the Alans [also known as *Expedition against the Alans*] (military field report)
Parthica (history)
Periplus Ponti Euxini (maritime guide)
Tactica [also known as *Techne Taktike*] (tactical manual)
  136

Principal English Translations

Arrian: "Anabasis of Alexander" and "Indica" (translated by E. I. Robson) 1929
Arrian: "The Campaigns of Alexander" (translated by A. de Selincourt, revised by J. R. Hamilton) 1971
Arrian: "History of Alexander" and "Indica" (translated by P. A. Brunt) 1976

*Dates uncertain.

CRITICISM

H. F. Pelham (essay date 1896)

SOURCE: "Arrian as Legate of Cappadocia," in *The English Historical Review,* Vol. XLIV, October, 1896, pp. 625-40.

[*In the essay below, Pelham surveys Arrian's works, noting ways in which Arrian's military experience informed his writings.*]

That Arrian, the historian of Alexander the Great and the disciple of Epictetus, was also for a time governor of the important frontier province of Cappadocia is a fact which,

though long known as well established, has received much less attention than it deserves. Yet it is remarkable enough that a Greek philosopher and man of letters should have been entrusted by a Roman emperor with a first-rate military command. It was, indeed, no uncommon thing, in the second century A.D., for Greeks to find admission into the Roman senate, and to be decorated with a consulship. More rarely a distinguished Greek was given some administrative post in a peaceful province, such as Asia.[1] But I know of no other instance, before the third century, in which the command of Roman legions and the defence of a Roman frontier were placed in Greek hands. And the significance of Arrian's appointment becomes greater when it is remembered that it was the doing of Hadrian, the emperor who, though by temperament and policy a lover of Greeks, was of all the Caesars the most solicitous for the efficiency both of the imperial army and of the frontier defences.

The interest attaching to Arrian's legateship does not, however, stop here. What we know of Roman frontier life and of the duties and difficulties of Roman frontier officers is mainly derived from the monuments, for it is a subject on which the literature is provokingly silent. Unless startled into attention by some serious reverse or brilliant success the world of letters knew little and cared less about what was passing in the distant camps and forts where the imperial troops kept constant watch and guard against the outside barbarians. To this prevailing indifference Arrian was naturally an exception, and he has given us from his own pen a unique glimpse of Roman frontier life, and of a Roman frontier force in the first half of the second century of the Christian era, at a period which marked an epoch in the history of the Roman frontier system. Nor is this all; Arrian was not only a trusted officer, but the intimate friend of Hadrian, and in the writings of Arrian the character and policy of Hadrian are reflected almost as clearly as the character and policy of Trajan in the letters of the younger Pliny.

We have no means of knowing how Arrian's appointment to Cappadocia (131 A.D.) was received in official circles, but some explanation of Hadrian's choice is supplied by what is known both of Arrian himself and of Hadrian's policy. The literary materials for a biography of Arrian are somewhat scanty, and have until quite recently been very badly used.[2] They consist chiefly of incidental notices in Arrian's own writings, in those of his friend and protégé Lucian, and in Dio Cassius, and of the meagre summaries of his career supplied by Photius and Suidas. A few additional facts and some important dates are furnished by inscriptions.

It should be noticed in the first place that Arrian, though by descent a Greek, and of a good family at Nicomedia, in Bithynia, where, as he tells us, he was born and bred, was also a Roman citizen, and that not, as is constantly stated, by the grace of Hadrian, but by birth. Both his *nomen,* Flavius, and his *cognomen,* Arrianus, are Roman, and the former proves that the Roman franchise came into his family as the gift not of Hadrian, but of one of the Flavian emperors. Now Domitian, the last of the Flavii, died in 98 A.D., when Arrian, who did not become legate of Cappadocia till 131 A.D., and who was still living in 171 A.D.,[3] must have been a mere boy in his father's house at Nicomedia. It must therefore have been Arrian's father who received citizenship, possibly from Vespasian. It is moreover conceivable that Arrian not only inherited the Roman citizenship, but had Roman blood in his veins. His *cognomen,* Arrianus, certainly suggests the conjecture that his mother was a Roman lady belonging to the *gens* Arria,[4] a family famous in the annals of Roman Stoicism. Such a connexion may well have influenced Arrian's philosophic views, and would certainly have been of service to him in his official career. In any case no one can read Arrian without being struck by the unusual combination in him of Roman and Greek. With the versatility, grace, and intellectual keenness of the latter he unites a genuinely Roman sobriety and capacity for affairs.

The boyhood and youth of the future legate were passed at Nicomedia. Like his favourite hero, Xenophon, he was already devoted to hunting, to the art of war, and to study,[5] a combination of tastes which no doubt aided him in winning the favour of Hadrian. Of hunting, as practised by himself and his companions, and of a favourite hound, he tells us something in his treatise on hunting, which, though rewritten in later life, seems to have been partly at least composed in his younger days. It is possible too that his interest in the adventures and exploits of a famous Mysian brigand, whose history, according to Lucian, he afterwards wrote, may date from this period of his life.[6] From Nicomedia Arrian passed, after the fashion of his day, to complete his education by a course of philosophic study. In going to Nicopolis and to the lecture room of Epictetus he was not improbably influenced by the traditions of his mother's family. His teacher, who had seen his sect persecuted, and had lived to see it patronised by the Caesars, was the most prominent representative of a Stoicism in which very little remained of the impracticable arrogance and contumacy of the days of Thrasea, and which aimed only, to quote Arrian's description of Epictetus's discourses, at raising men to better things.[7] How long Arrian remained at Nicopolis it is impossible to say, but long enough certainly to become known as the most devoted and loyal of Epictetus's disciples. It may well have been during this period that he became a familiar figure at Athens, and it was conceivably by the wits of Athens that he was christened the younger Xenophon, a nickname of which he was evidently proud, and which was certainly justified by the strong similarity in tastes and accomplishments which existed between the disciple of Socrates and the disciple of Epictetus.

So far Arrian's career had differed but little from that of other young provincials of good family and fortune. As a Roman citizen, and probably of equestrian rank, he no doubt looked forward to a term of military service, and then to the customary round of municipal duties and honour in his native town. But at some date which cannot be precisely fixed an event occurred which altered his whole prospects in life. His introduction to Hadrian probably took place early in that emperor's reign—certainly several years before Arrian's consulship in 130 A.D. It was the beginning of a close friendship between the two men, and Hadrian's favour opened to Arrian a new career. As a Roman knight he might have risen to high place in the household of Caesar as a procurator or prefect. But the ancient magistracies of the state, and the great provincial commands to which they led, were reserved for men of senatorial rank, the *homines laticlavii* ('the men of the broad stripe'). Senatorial dignity was not Arrian's by right of birth, and he must have received it from Hadrian. He may have been granted the *ius lati clavi,* and thus enabled to offer himself as a candidate for the quaestorship, an office through which the ordinary road lay to a seat in the senate and to the higher *honores,* or he may have been directly admitted to the senate with quaestorian rank (*allectus inter quaestorios*). In either case his promotion was assured and seems to have been rapid, though of his official career up to 130 A.D. no record remains. That he held the praetorship may be taken for granted, and he very probably gained useful experience as a legate of a legion and legate of a praetorian province. He obtained the consulship, as *consul suffectus,* in 130 A.D.,[8] and in 131 A.D.,[9] was made legate of the consular province of Cappadocia, a post which he held for at least seven years.

The new legate had unquestionably much in common with his master. Both were enthusiastic sportsmen, and zealous students of military tactics. That Hadrian, in pursuance of his policy of strengthening the defences of the empire, was bent on increasing the efficiency of the frontier troops is well known, and the combination in Arrian of scientific knowledge with practical ability may well have marked him out as a valuable ally in the work. Arrian moreover was a student of philosophy, a scholar, and a connoisseur. Hadrian at least aspired to be all three. But, apart from this congeniality in tastes and pursuits, there may have been weightier reasons for Arrian's appointment. Hadrian aimed above all things at the consolidation of the empire. He was consequently opposed not only to ambitious schemes for its expansion, but to the old-established view of the empire as a federation of allied communities under the leadership of Rome. The differences of race and political status, which the federal theory helped to keep alive, Hadrian did his best to sink in a sense of common citizenship. It was a policy which has often been called cosmopolitan, but which might more properly be described as imperialist. With such aims before him Hadrian would naturally welcome the chance of promoting to high office a man who was in many ways the ideal citizen of a united empire, a man who was Greek by descent, but born a Roman citizen, and probably with Roman blood in his veins.

In a legate of Cappadocia this mixture of the Greek and the Roman was especially appropriate, and indeed few provinces of the empire demanded a greater variety of qualifications in their governor For the Cappadocia of 131 A.D. was by no means the Cappadocia which on its annexation in 16 A.D. had been relegated to the care of an imperial procurator. Arrian's province included not only the ancient kingdom of Archelaus, but also the entire district lying between the northern boundary of that kingdom and the Black Sea and in addition the seaboard eastward from Trapezus to Dioscurias. The area was wide, and the population heterogeneous, comprising as it did the scattered pastoral inhabitants of the Cappadocian uplands, the dwellers in the Greek or half Greek towns of Pontus, and then unruly neighbours the tribes of the hills. Cappadocia, again, in 131 A.D. was a frontier province, with legions and legionary camps, and with a chain of frontier stations garrisoned, as elsewhere, by auxiliary troops. The duty of keeping both camps and garrisons in a high state of efficiency was not the least important of the legate's duties, especially under the rule of Hadrian. But on the Upper Euphrates the care of the frontier required more than the strict discipline and constant vigilance which was as a rule sufficient on such frontiers as those of the Rhine or the Danube, where no more serious danger was to be feared than a marauding raid by some restless, half savage tribe. For in this quarter of the empire the frontier question was political as well as military. It was necessary for the legate of Cappadocia to keep a watchful eye on Rome's great rival, Parthia, to check Parthian intrigue in Armenia, and to take care that none of the smaller potentates beyond the frontier, such as the Iberian king, did anything disrespectful to the majesty of the Roman people, or likely to disturb the Roman peace. Nor was this all. As the chief political officer in the near East he was bound to keep himself and his master informed of the movements of the restless peoples beyond the Caucasus, and even, as the *Periplus* shows, of the attitude and temper of the tribes and princes bordering the Black Sea. A threatened descent of Alans, or the death of a powerful ruler, such as the king of the Cimmerian Bosporus, was equally an event with which the legate of Cappadocia had to deal. In Arrian's own case both the political and military difficulties of the position had been increased by the unsettling effect produced by Trajan's momentary conquest beyond the Euphrates, and by Hadrian's prompt return to a defensive policy.

Three of Arrian's extant works belong to the period of his legateship—the *Periplus of the Euxine Sea,* the fragment styled *The Expedition against the Alans,* and the treatise on *Tactics.* The *Periplus,* as the reference to the death of King Cotys proves, was written in 131 A.D.—in the first year, that is, of his command. It is a unique specimen of a report made by a Roman frontier officer to his master, the emperor, and ranks with the letters of Pliny to Trajan as a document of the first importance for the history of provincial administration under the Caesars. The *Expedition against the Alans* describes the composition and marching order of the expeditionary force led by Arrian against the Alans, in 135 A.D., on the occasion of their invasion of Armenia, when, as Dio tells us, they retired 'through fear of Flavius Arrianus, governor of Cappadocia.'[10] It stands alone as a contemporary account by a Roman commanding officer of a Roman frontier force. The treatise on *Tactics* was written, as its author states, in the twentieth year

of Hadrian's reign (137-8 A.D.) and the last year of Arrian's legateship. Its chief value consists in the fact that it is an exposition by one of Hadrian's most trusted officers of the cavalry tactics in use at the time on the frontiers, and of the reforms introduced by Hadrian himself. Outside these three important documents we possess only a few isolated references to Arrian's command. Dio mentions the Alan invasion; a rescript of Hadrian, addressed to Arrian, is quoted in the 'Digest,'[11] and a single inscription records a dedication to Hadrian by the city of Sebastopolis 'during the legateship of Flavius Arrianus.' The date is 137 A.D.[12] We may, lastly, with some confidence assume that Arrian was the governor of Cappadocia who supplied Lucian with an escort when he went to expose the false prophet Alexander,[13] a task which would command Arrian's sympathy both as a Roman official and as a man of letters. Lucian speaks of the governor in question as 'my friend,' and nothing is more likely than that the brilliant young provincial, whose native place, Samosata, was on the borders of Arrian's own province, should have sought and won the patronage of a Greek scholar, whom Lucian himself describes characteristically as 'a foremost man among the Romans.'[14]

The process of creating a 'scientific frontier' along the line of the Upper Euphrates seems to have been gradual. As early as the reign of Nero the imperial government had realised that, for the protection of Eastern Asia Minor, no less than for effective action in Armenia, some nearer base of operations than Syria was needed;[15] and the annexation of Pontus and Lesser Armenia, towards the close of Nero's reign, rendered possible the drawing of a continuous frontier line up to the Black Sea. Vespasian took the important step of permanently stationing a legion on the Upper Euphrates,[16] and the legionary camp at Melitene probably dated from his time. The roads which, according to an inscription, were made under Domitian in Cappadocia, Lesser Armenia, and Pontus,[17] presumably included the frontier road from Samosata northwards to Trapezus, along which Hadrian seems to have travelled in 124, and the line of the road was no doubt guarded by military stations. By the time of the accession of Hadrian a second legionary camp had been formed at Satala,[18] and the entire frontier from Samosata to Trapezus, together with the Euxine coast as far as Dioscurias, had been placed under the command of a legate of consular rank. When, therefore, Hadrian visited the frontier, some seven years before Arrian's appointment, he must have found the frontier system fairly well developed. He travelled along the frontier northwards to Trapezus, and possibly visited also some of the Black Sea stations. Here, as on other frontiers, he reviewed the frontier force, the 'army of Cappadocia;'[19] and inspected the military stations; existing forts were remodelled and new forts constructed.[20] The *Periplus,* as will be seen, indicates that Hadrian's reforming activity left its mark on the Cappadocian no less than on the German, British, and African frontiers.

Arrian followed in his master's steps, and evidently inaugurated his command by a tour of inspection along the frontier. Of the earlier part of this tour we have no record, for the *Periplus* begins at the moment when, on nearing Trapezus from the south, he caught sight of the sea from the spot whence 'both that other Xenophon and you' viewed it. The results of the entire tour he embodied in an official report to Hadrian, written, as etiquette required, in Latin. He alludes to it as τα 'Ρωμαικα γραμματα.²¹ The *Periplus* itself is part of a supplementary report, and deals primarily with the Black Sea stations from Trapezus to the limits of the Roman empire at Sebastopolis (Dioscurias). It contains, in addition, a summary account of the estuaries and harbours along the shores of the Black Sea, and especially along the northern coast, such as would give Hadrian the information necessary to enable him to act with vigour should any crisis in these quarters call for Roman intervention. The *Periplus* was clearly a less formal document than the Latin report. Arrian is writing in his native Greek, and he writes as a friend to a friend, as one man of letters to another, rather than as a legate to his *imperator*. Consequently together with reports on forts and harbours we get a good deal of lively chat about the weather, the antiquities, the traditions, and the scenery. Arrian is never long-winded or rhetorical; but his Greek discursiveness and keen curiosity temper pleasantly the military brevity of the Roman officer.

The first place noticed by Arrian is the ancient Greek sea-port of Trapezus, the emporium and chief town of eastern Pontus. In Pliny's lists²² it appears as a free town, and that it was still free at the time of Arrian's visit may be inferred from the fact that he makes no reference to the presence of any imperial garrison²³ there, and that the hoplites from Trapezus, who marched with Arrian against the Alans, are classed with the native allies, not with the legions and auxiliaries of the regular army. The importance of Trapezus as a centre for the neighbouring tribes, and as a port where supplies and troops for the frontier could be landed, had evidently been appreciated by Hadrian, for when Arrian visited the place a new harbour was in process of construction by Hadrian's orders;²⁴ till then, it would seem, there had been only an open roadstead. Another memorial of Hadrian's visit is described by Arrian. On the high ground whence the older Xenophon first caught sight of the sea, a statue of Hadrian and altars had been set up. Both were probably connected with the official worship of Caesar. Trapezus still called itself a Greek city, but its Hellenism was clearly somewhat corrupt, for Arrian comments on the barbarous Greek of the inscriptions on the altars, as well as on the inferior workmanship of the statue.²⁵ Life in these remote Greek towns was not altogether peaceful even under Roman rule. In the highlands near Trapezus dwelt a Colchian tribe, the Sauni.

> 'To this day,' writes Arrian, 'they are most warlike, and live at deadly feud with the people of Trapezus. They dwell in strongholds and have no king, and though long tributary to the Romans they are not punctual in paying their tribute, being engaged in robbery and pillage. Now, however, they shall pay regularly, or, with the help of God, we will root them out.'²⁶

It would seem, however, that here, as in other parts of the empire, these marauding highlanders maintained their ground, for the description given of them by Procopius²⁷ differs little from that just quoted.

On leaving Trapezus—not without sacrificing in the temple of Hermes, and offering a prayer for the welfare of his benefactor Hadrian—Arrian started on a cold and stormy voyage along the coast eastward, touching in turn at each of the military stations, which, as on the coasts of Britain, were situated at the mouths of the rivers, and performed the double duty of guarding the river mouth and protecting the trading settlements against attacks from the hill-sides of the interior. The first station visited was at the mouth of the Hyssus. The garrison consisted of infantry, 'as you are aware,' adds Arrian significantly, with twenty mounted spearmen, the latter being apparently intended to assist in foraging for supplies. The infantry were put through their exercises, and even the spearmen were obliged to show that they could use their weapons. It is worth noting, as characteristic of the permanence of the Roman frontier arrangements, that in the 'Notitia Dignitatum'²⁸ 'Ysiportus' was still garrisoned by a regiment of infantry, the 'Cohors Apuleia Civium Romanorum,' which may possibly have been the one which Arrian reviewed.²⁹ Proceeding eastward, Arrian and his staff were detained for two days by stress of weather at a lonely little harbour, with a ruinous fort, which bore, however, the name of Athens. 'We were not permitted,' he remarks, 'to sail past even Athens in Pontus as if it were some deserted and nameless harbour.'

The next station of importance was Apsarus, on a river of the same name. Pliny³⁰ mentions a fort there, called 'in faucibus,' evidently from its position in a narrow valley. In 131 A.D. Apsarus was a considerable military station, with a garrison of unusual strength. '*The five cohorts*,' as Arrian calls them, implying that Hadrian knew all about them, as about the infantry at Hyssi portus, constituted a much larger force than was usual in frontier stations. Possibly the reason is to be found in the close proximity of the important valley of the Acampsis, leading, as it did, for a long distance into the interior. Arrian paid the troops and inspected the fort, examining not only the walls and fosse, but the hospital and granary. The results of his inspection he had, unfortunately for us, already given in the Latin report.

From Apsarus Arrian sailed along the coast to the Phasis. As he entered the mouth of the river he saw on his left hand the colossal statue of the Phasian goddess. She was represented seated on a throne supported by lions, and holding a cymbal in her hands. Clearly here, as at Arrian's own city of Nicomedia, and at a hundred other places in Asia Minor, the 'Great Mother' was the supreme protecting deity. But it was for relics of Jason and his Argonauts that Arrian most eagerly inquired. None, however, were to be found, with the exception of some fragments of a stone anchor, which might possibly have belonged to the good ship Argo. An iron anchor was also shown to him, but he rightly assigned it to a much later date than the time of Jason. From antiquarian gossip Arrian passes to matters more directly connected with the main object of his journey, and his account of the Roman station on the Phasis is of especial interest. The garrison consisted of 400 'picked soldiers.' These . . . *milites singulares,* were a somewhat recent invention, probably dating from Trajan. They were auxiliaries, but differed from the ordinary auxiliary cohort or squadron in being composed of picked men of different nationalities, and possibly selected from different auxiliary corps. A regiment of *equites singulares* was included in the force which Arrian led against the Alans, but whether the garrison on the Phasis consisted of cavalry or infantry we are not told. The fort is described as occupying a position of great natural strength, and well adapted for the protection of vessels entering the river. It had originally been inclosed in the old way, by an earthen *vallum,* with wooden towers and probably a wooden palisade. But when Arrian visited the place these old-fashioned defences had been replaced by walls and towers of brick, with solid foundations, and carrying a sufficient equipment of military engines. Such reconstruction was probably common enough at the time, and may safely be connected with Hadrian's visit to the Cappadocian frontier in 124 A.D.

No less interesting, as illustrating a characteristic feature of Roman frontier life, is the account which Arrian gives of the civil settlement which was growing up near this, as near most other frontier stations. The evidence furnished by inscriptions and by the actual remains discovered in Germany, Africa, Britain, and elsewhere has thrown much light on the origin and character of these *canabac,* some of which developed into important towns and obtained the status of colonies or *municipia.* Ancient literature, however, says as little about them as about any other institution of Roman frontier life. Arrian's brief notice is, therefore, all the more valuable, and is in complete agreement with our other evidence. The fort on the Phasis was protected by a double fosse. Arrian decided to dig a third, for the better protection of the settlement, which had planted itself between the fort and the river. This settlement, which he describes as consisting partly of retired soldiers and partly of traders,[31] was probably of comparatively recent date. A more important settlement of the same class was the one near the camp of the 12th legion at Melitene, which it would seem had already attained to the dignity of a municipality.[32]

From the mouth of the Phasis Arrian passed on rapidly to Sebastopolis, with only a brief halt at the mouth of the Chobus. The reason for this halt, and 'what we did there, you will learn,' he says, 'from the Latin report.' Sebastopolis, anciently known as Dioscurias, marked the extreme limit of the Roman empire and of Arrian's province in this direction. Commercially it was important as the centre to which the polyglot tribes of the Caucasus came down for purposes of trade. In the time of the elder Pliny the old Greek town had been deserted, but he implies that a considerable business was done with the natives by Roman merchants.[33] It was probably to the later settlement that the name Sebastopolis was given, and the fort which Pliny

mentions and which Arrian inspected may have been built for its protection. Arrian, however, mentions only the fort, which at the time was clearly a regular military station, with walls and fosse, hospital and granary.[34] The garrison consisted of cavalry, or possibly mounted infantry. In the 'Notitia' the regiment stationed at Sebastopolis was the *Cohors I. Claudia equitata.* From near Sebastopolis Arrian got a view of the higher peaks of the Caucasus, and one peak in particular was pointed out as that to which Prometheus was bound.

In addition to his brief reports on the military stations along the coast Arrian supplies information, such as a modern Anglo-Indian 'political' would be expected to furnish, as to the native chiefs and tribes inhabiting the neighbouring hill country. The settlement of this *Hinterland* had been, it seems, the work of Trajan and Hadrian, and the majority of the chiefs are described as holding their 'kingships' from one or other of these emperors. But the political interests of Rome and her sphere of influence extended here, as elsewhere, beyond the actual frontiers of her empire round the northern shores of the Black Sea, and it was the duty of the legate of Cappadocia to keep his master duly informed of any important event in these remote regions. Such, for instance, was the death of Cotys, king of the Cimmerian Bosporus, of which Arrian heard, while at Sebastopolis.[???] Cotys, like his predecessors, held his crown from the emperor, and his successor would have to be, in his turn, formally recognised by Rome. It is improbable that Hadrian contemplated any change in the old-established relations between the Roman government and this prosperous vassal state; nevertheless Arrian thought it proper to supply Hadrian with such a brief sketch of the northern seaboard of the Euxine as might enable the latter to act with effect if action were considered necessary. The sketch is highly business-like, but its monotony is relieved, after Arrian's manner, with antiquarian digressions, and in one place[36] by a picturesque account of the Island of Achilles, near the mouths of the Danube, with its ancient temple, tended only by countless sea birds.

The fragment entitled . . . ***The Expedition against the Alans*** shows us the legate of Cappadocia engaged, not in the inspection of the frontier forts and garrisons, but in preparing to meet and repel a threatened invasion of his province. The invaders were the Alans from the plains beyond the Caucasus, who once already in the reign of Vespasian had invaded Armenia, and who now, according to Dio, came at the invitation of the Iberian king Pharasmanes. The same historian tells us that the invasion came to nothing. The Parthian king purchased immunity for his own territories by gifts, while their invasion of Armenia was checked by fear of Flavius Arrianus, the legate of Cappadocia. Arrian seems to have promptly advanced to meet the enemy with a considerable force, and it is with the composition of this force, with its order of march, and with the tactics to be employed when face to face with the enemy, that the ***Expedition against the Alans*** is concerned.

The troops which Arrian led against the Alans belonged to the standing army of Cappadocia, the *exercitus Cappa-*

docicus, to use the territorial designation which came into fashion under Hadrian. What proportion of the entire army was called out for the expedition is not clear. We learn, however, that of the two available legions one, the 12th, was represented only by a detachment, and the same was the case with some of the auxiliary regiments. The probability is that Arrian, who may be supposed to have been making for northern Armenia, composed his force, as far as possible, of the troops nearest at hand. Hence the presence in full strength of the 15th legion, whose camp at Satala would be a convenient base of operations, while Melitene, the headquarters of the 12th legion, was a long way to the southward. For the same reason, no doubt, the native levies present were those belonging to the northern half of the province, to Lesser Armenia and Pontus. But the strength of the expeditionary force was very considerable. In addition to the 15th legion, and a substantial portion of the 12th, it included the whole or part of eighteen regiments of auxiliaries. Unless therefore the auxiliaries in the Cappadocian army were more numerous than in other frontier armies at the time, very few auxiliary corps can have been entirely unrepresented. The army of Upper Germany, for instance, consisted in 116 A.D. of two legions and nineteen auxiliary regiments, that of Britain in 146 A.D. of three legions and fourteen auxiliary corps. To the legions and auxiliaries must be added the native levies, of whom there were clearly a considerable body. These local troops were not a part of the regular army, but were called out, if necessary, to repel a threatened invasion. They were, with the exception of the hoplites from Trapezus, light troops, and both on the march and when the line of battle was formed were brigaded with a regiment of regulars.

Returning to the auxiliaries as the most characteristic and interesting element in the expeditionary force, we notice at once the predominance of cavalry over infantry, there being twelve cavalry and only five infantry regiments, a predominance which recurs in the army of Africa, whereas in Germany and Britain the proportion is reversed. Both cavalry and infantry were largely composed of archers, as we should expect to be the case in an army on the eastern frontier, and indeed the majority of the auxiliaries belonged to the eastern rather than the western half of the empire. Spain and Gaul were represented by one regiment each, Raetia by two, Dacia by one. On the other hand the African provinces supplied four, and there were also infantry from the Thracian Bosporus and cavalry from Cappadocia, Ituraea, and Arabia Petraea. It is noteworthy that among the officers mentioned are several Greeks. Such were the commander-in-chief himself, Daphnes, of Corinth, commanding the 4th Raetian cohort, Demetrios, commanding a cavalry brigade composed of four regiments, one being the 1st Raetian cohort, and Lamprocles, who commanded the infantry regiment from the Bosporus.

The army of Cappadocia was not of such old standing as some of the other frontier armies, and its definite organisation was probably the work of Trajan and Hadrian. The 12th legion, indeed, had been stationed at Melitene by Vespasian some sixty years before Arrian came out as legate, but it was not before Trajan's time that the 15th was established at Satala. As to the auxiliaries, both the Dacian cavalry and the mounted archers from Arabia Petraca must be subsequent to Trajan's Dacian and eastern campaigns. We know from an inscription[37] that the Spanish regiment in Arrian's army, the *Ala Auriana,* bore the title 'Ulpia,' and was therefore either raised by Trajan or served under him with distinction. The 1st Raetian cohort was certainly on the Danube in 108 A.D.,[38] and probably followed Trajan to the east. On the other hand the evidence of the 'Notitia'[39] proves that not only the legions but some at least of the auxiliaries of the army of Cappadocia remained there as immovably as did the legions and auxiliaries in Britain. The *dux Armeniae* had altogether 26 corps under his command, and among them were several which formed part of Arrian's army. The 12th and 15th legions were still at Melitene and Satala; in addition we find still on the Cappadocian frontier the 4th cohort of Raetians, the Spanish *ala Auriana,* the *ala Colonorum,* a cohort from the Bosporus, an *ala Dacorum,* an *ala Gallorum,* and a *cohors Petracorum.* Nor is it unlikely, when we remember the permanence of Roman military stations when once the frontier defences had been organised, that the stations assigned to these corps in the 'Notitia' were those which they occupied in the time of Arrian. These stations, with one exception, that assigned to the *Ala II. Gallorum,* lay along the frontier line between the two legionary camps at Satala and Melitene, and are given in the Antonine 'Itinerary' as stations on the frontier road which led from Samosata past Melitene and Satala to Trapezus, a road certainly as old as the reign of Hadrian. Two other stations mentioned by Arrian in the ***Periplus*** reappear in the 'Notitia.' At Hyssi portus the latter places a *cohors Apuleia civium Romanorum.* In Arrian's time the garrison consisted of infantry, and in the expeditionary force was a regiment of Πεζοι 'Απλανοι, who were brigaded on the march with the native levies from Trapezus, Rizus, and Colchis, and may well, therefore, have come from Hyssi portus. They were commanded by a Roman officer, and when the line of battle was formed they occupied a position on the left wing corresponding to that of the 'Italian cohort' on the right. The other station is Sebastopolis, where the cavalry garrison mentioned by Arrian may possibly have been the *cohors I. Claudia equitata* of the 'Notitia.' . . .

Both the order of march and the line of battle to be adopted in face of the enemy were evidently prescribed with reference to the peculiar tactics of the Alan horsemen and the danger of a sudden attack in a difficult country. The flanks and rear of the column were protected by light cavalry, while in advance of it rode the . . . the 'guides' or 'scouts,' a class of auxiliary troops best known under their Latin name of *exploratores.* The column was formed of three main divisions, corresponding to the three elements of which the force was composed. In the first were the auxiliary cavalry and infantry, with the mounted archers from Arabia Petraea at their head. In the second, forming the centre of the column, were the legions, preceded by two picked cavalry corps, the *equites singulares* and the *equites legionarii,* and by the artillery of the period. In the third division were the native levies and the baggage train, protected, as has been said, by a cavalry regiment from Dacia. The fighting order was clearly intended, in the first place, to resist the charge of the dreaded light horsemen of the east, and secondly to defeat any attempt on the part of the enemy to outflank the Roman force. On the extreme right and left, but on rising ground, were posted the native levies, mostly archers; in front of them, but at a lower level, Arrian placed some of his heavy auxiliary infantry. The local militia were thus protected against the enemy's charge, while able to shoot freely over the heads of the protecting infantry. In the centre were the legions drawn up eight deep, and behind them the rest of the auxiliary infantry. In the rear of the whole line were the cavalry. When the enemy attacked they were to be received with a might shout, and a discharge of missiles from the whole line. If this fire failed to check the charge of the Alans, which it is assumed would be directed against the centre, then, says this general order 'let the front ranks of the legions prepare to receive the charge kneeling, shoulder to shoulder, with locked shields and levelled pikes.' If the charge is thus repelled the cavalry are to follow up the retreating enemy, the infantry, after opening their ranks to let the cavalry pass, advancing to support them. At this point Arrian notes and provides for the likelihood that the enemy would rapidly wheel round and endeavour to outflank one of the wings. To meet this manuvre the wings should be extended as far as possible. Should it, however, succeed, then the cavalry are to wheel round and charge the enemy on the flank, engaging them at close quarters, and using their broadswords and axes with deadly effect upon riders and horses unprotected by defensive armour. Here the fragment ends.

The third of the three of Arrian's extant works belonging to this period of his career has only an indirect bearing on his Cappadocian command. The treatise on 'Tactics' was written, as its author tells us, in the 20th year of Hadrian's reign (137-8), and it is closely connected with one part of Hadrian's frontier work, his endeavour to render the frontier troops as efficient as possible in the field. In this work Arrian was keenly interested, as a life-long student of tactics. He had written, he tells us, a treatise on infantry tactics for the benefit and probably at the suggestion of the emperor. The existing treatise is a popular exposition of cavalry tactics, with especial reference to the reforms introduced by Hadrian. Throughout Arrian impresses upon his readers the readiness with which the tactics of all the various peoples included within the empire, and of many outside it, had been adopted by Rome, so that the imperial army anticipated that political fusion which Hadrian of all the Caesars was most anxious to bring about. The treatise is in fact, a good commentary not only on the brief statement of Hadrian's biographer[40] as to his military reforms, but on the fragments of the speech addressed by Hadrian himself to the army of Africa, when just established in their new headquarters at Lambresis.[41] Of its general drift no better summary can be given than is furnished by Ar-

rian himself in the closing chapter. 'The king,' as in the Greek fashion he styles Hadrian,

> has obliged his soldiers to practise barbaric movements, both those of the mounted archers of Parthia and the rapid evolutions of Sarmatians and Celts. They have been obliged also to learn the native war cries proper to such movements—those of the Celts, and the Dacians, and the Raeti. They have been trained also to leap their horses across trenches and over ramparts. In a word, in addition to their ancient exercises they have learnt all that has been invented by the king tending to grace or speed, or calculated to strike terror into the enemy, so that the words once applied to ancient Lacedaemon seem to me to apply to this present monarchy which Hadrian now holds for the 20th year, 'where the strength of the young flourishes, and the clear-voiced muse, and broad justice, the helper of noble deeds.'

The close of Arrian's legateship preceded his master's death by a year at the most.[42] With his retirement or recall from Cappadocia Arrian's official career seems to have ended, and it is not my business here to follow him in his later literary labours. I hope, however, that I have been able to give some idea of the value of the glimpse which Arrian allows us to get of an eastern frontier province at a critical moment in the history of the imperial frontiers.

Notes

1. Herodes Atticus was for a time *corrector civitatum liberarum* in the province of Asia.

2. The biography of Arrian in the new edition of Pauly's *Real-Encyclopädie* contrasts most favourably with all previous ones. It is more complete, and it is free from the blunders which disfigure, for instance, the article in Smith's *Dictionary of Greek and Roman Biography.*

3. *Corp. Inscr. Attic.* iii. 1032.

4. In older times such a cognomen would have indicated that Arrian was by birth an Arrius, and by adoption a Flavius. But in the first two centuries A.D. the cognomen frequently indicated the family of the mother, *e.g.* in the case of the emperor Vespasianus.

5. *Cyneget.* ii.

6. Lucian, *Alexander,* i.

7. *Dissert.* praef. i.

8. The date is fixed by stamps on bricks (Borghesi, iv. 157). The *Dict. of Biogr.* wrongly places Arrian's consulship after the Cappadocian legateship.

9. Arrian was already legate at the time of the death of Cotys II, king of the Cimmerian Bosporus, which took place in 131 A.D. (see *Periplus,* 17, and Liebenam, *Legaten,* p. 124).

10. Dio, 69, 15.

11. *Digest,* 49, 14, 2.

12. Liebenam, *Legaten,* p. 124.

13. Lucian, *Alexander,* 54.

14. *Ibid.* i.

15. Tacitus, *Annals,* xiii. 7.

16. Suetonius, *Vespas.* 8; Joseph. *Bell. Jud.* 7, 3. 1.

17. *C. I. L.* 3, 312.

18. See below, p. 636 *seq.*

19. Cohen, *Médailles,* ii. p. 153.

20. Dio, 69, 9.

21. *Periplus,* 6.

22. Pliny, *Nat. Hist.* vi. 11.

23. At a later period Trapezus was the headquarters of 'Legio I. Pontica' (*Notit. Dig. Or.* 38).

24. *Periplus,* 16.

25. *Ibid.* 1.

26. *Ibid.* 11.

27. Procop. *De Aedif.* iii. 6.

28. *Not. Dig. Or.* 381. . . .

31. *Periplus,* 11.

32. Procopius, *De Aedif.* iii. 5, states that under Trajan Melitene attained to πολεως αξιωμα. He refers not to the camp but to the civil settlement. . . .

37. *C. I. L.* 3, Suppl. 6743.

38. *Ibid.* 3.

39. *Not. Dia. Or.* 38

40. *Vita Hadriani,* 10.

41. *C. I. L.* viii. 2532.

42. Liebenam, *Legaten,* p. 124.

J. R. Hamilton (essay date 1971)

SOURCE: An introduction to *The Campaigns of Alexander,* by Arrian, translated by Aubrey de Sélincourt, rev. ed., Penguin Books, 1971, pp. 13-40.

[*In the essay below, Hamilton offers an overview of Arrian's* Anabasis Alexandri, *discussing the way Arrian used his sources as well as the style and tone of the work.*]

Arrian is remembered today only as the author of ***The Campaigns of Alexander*** and as the pupil of the philosopher Epictetus who preserved his master's teachings from oblivion. Yet he was a famous man in his own time. ***The Campaigns of Alexander*** was only one of a number of substantial historical works, while he held the chief magistracies at Rome and Athens and governed for a lengthy period an important frontier province of the Roman empire.

LIFE OF ARRIAN

Flavius Arrianus Xenophon, to give him his full name,[1] was a Greek, born at Nicomedia, the capital of the Roman province of Bithynia, probably a few years before A.D. 90.[2] His family was well-to-do, and Arrian himself tells us that he held the priesthood of Demeter and Kore in the city. Like other wealthy Greeks, Arrian's father had received the Roman citizenship, evidently from one of the Flavian emperors, most probably Vespasian. Hence Arrian became at birth a Roman citizen with the prospect, if he wished it and possessed the requisite ability, of a career in the imperial service.

Arrian's boyhood and youth were spent in his native city, where he presumably received the customary upperclass Greek education in literature and rhetoric. Then, like many other young Greeks of similar social standing who planned a career in the imperial service, Arrian decided to complete his education by studying philosophy. He went about the year 108 to Nicopolis in Epirus, where the Stoic philosopher Epictetus had founded a school after the general expulsion of philosophers from Rome by Domitian in A.D. 92/3.[3] This remarkable man, a former slave, concerned himself mainly with ethics, and his teachings with their emphasis on the need for the individual to concern himself with his soul and their contempt for wealth and luxury had certain affinities with Christianity. Indeed, they have sometimes been thought, though wrongly, to have been influenced by the new religion. Like Socrates, Epictetus wrote nothing for publication, but fortunately he made such an impression on the young Arrian that he took down his master's words in shorthand and later published them in eight books of ***Discourses.***[4] Four of these still survive to give us a vivid portrait of a striking personality. Also extant is the ***Manual*** or ***Handbook*** (***Encheiridion***) in which, for the benefit of the general public, Arrian combined the essentials of Epictetus' teaching. In the Middle Ages it enjoyed great popularity as a guide of monastic life. It is clearly from Epictetus that Arrian derived the high moral standards by which he judges Alexander. Epictetus, too, warmly commends repentance after wrongdoing, an attitude which finds an echo in Arrian's praise for Alexander's conduct after the murder of Cleitus. Since Epictetus drew on his experience of life in Rome under Domitian to illustrate his teachings, it is possible that Arrian's comments on 'the bane of monarchs', the courtier, have their origin in the same source.

Of Arrian's career in the imperial service until he reached the consulship in 129 or 130 we know only that he served on the Danube frontier and possibly in Gaul and Numidia. Arrian's career may have been forwarded by the philhellenism of Hadrian, the 'Greekling' as he was nicknamed, who succeeded Trajan as emperor in A.D. 117. But his appointment, in the year following his consulship, to the governorship of Cappadocia, it is safe to say, recognised his military and administrative abilities; for there is no evidence that Hadrian allowed sentiment to imperil the security of the empire. At this time the large and important frontier province of Cappadocia extended northwards to the Black Sea and along its eastern coast from Trapezus as far as Dioscurias, and Arrian commanded two Roman legions and a large body of auxiliary troops, a rare, perhaps unexampled, command for a Greek at this period. It was an unsettled time 'produced by Trajan's momentary conquests beyond the Euphrates, and by Hadrian's prompt return to a defensive policy.'[5] In 134 the Alans from across the Caucasus threatened to invade Cappadocia and although they did not cross the frontier Arrian is recorded to have driven the invaders out of Armenia. The extant work of Arrian, **The Formation against the Alans,** describes the composition of his force, with its order of march and the tactics to be followed. Two other works dating from the period of his governorship are extant, the **Circumnavigation of the Black Sea (Periplus Ponti Euxini)** and a **Tactical Manual,** the latter dated precisely to 136/7 A.D. It is concerned only with cavalry tactics; for Arrian tells us he had already written a work on infantry tactics. The **Circumnavigation** is an account, based on the official report (in Latin) which he, as governor, submitted to the emperor, of a voyage from Trapezus to Dioscurias combined with two other passages to form an account of the whole Black Sea coast. This voyage took place at the beginning of his office—he mentions hearing of the death of king Cotys in 131/2 in the course of it—in order to inspect the defences of his area.

Arrian is attested as governor of Cappadocia in 137, but he retired or was recalled before the death of Hádrian in June 138. He seems not to have held any further office, for reasons we can only guess at, but to have taken up residence at Athens and to have devoted the remainder of his life to writing. He became an Athenian citizen and in 145/6 held the chief magistracy, the archonship. We last hear of him in 172/3 as a member of the Council, and in 180 the satirist Lucian refers to him in terms which reveal that he was already dead.

The writings of Arrian's Athenian period are numerous and varied. The order in which they were composed cannot be determined with certainty, but we may with confidence place early in his stay his biographies of Dion of Syracuse and Timoleon of Corinth, and possibly a life of Tilliborus, a notorious bandit who plagued Asia Minor. Of these no trace remains. In his writings he frequently refers in a spirit of rivalry to his namesake, the Athenian Xenophon, and a short work on hunting forms a supplement to the older writer's book on the same topic. By choosing the same title, **On the Chase (Cynegeticus),** Arrian stresses the connexion and challenges comparison. Indeed, he writes that he had from his youth onwards the same interests as the Athenian Xenophon—hunting, tactics, and philosophy. His major historical works came later. Apart from **The Campaigns of Alexander (Anabasis Alexandri),** whose title and division into seven books are clearly modelled on Xenophon's *Anabasis,* he wrote the still extant **Indica,** an account of the voyage of Alexander's fleet from India to the Persian Gulf (based on Nearchus' book) prefaced by a description of India and its people. Of his **Events after Alexander** in ten books we have virtually only the narrative of the first two years. The rest has perished—undoubtedly the greatest loss among the works of Arrian. We possess only fragments of his other works, a **Parthian History** dealing with Trajan's campaigns in seventeen books, and a **History of Bithynia** which traced the story of his native land from mythical times down to 74 B.C., when the last king, Nicomedes IV, bequeathed his kingdom to Rome.

THE CAMPAIGNS OF ALEXANDER

This book was intended to be Arrian's masterpiece, his lasting claim to fame. How important it was to him, his own words (I.12) make clear:

> I need not declare my name—though it is by no means unheard of in the world; I need not specify my country and family, or any official position I may have held. Rather let me say this: that this book is, and has been since my youth, more precious than country and kin and public advancement—indeed, for me it *is* these things.

He had, he felt, a splendid subject, and a splendid opportunity. No one had had more written about him than Alexander, yet no one, poet or prose-writer, had done him justice. The real Alexander was hidden behind a mass of contradictory statements, while the works of earlier writers contained downright error. They could not even get right the location of the decisive battle against Darius; they did not know which men had saved Alexander's life in India. Not to speak of Achilles' good fortune in having Homer relate his exploits, lesser men, such as the Sicilian tyrants, had fared better than Alexander. Arrian's book was intended to end this state of affairs. Such is the importance of Alexander that he will not hesitate to challenge the great historians of Greece.

For this task Arrian possessed substantial advantages. We cannot say with any certainty when he began his book, but a date before the middle of the second century would seem highly unlikely. Arrian, therefore, was probably in his sixties; he had read widely in the Alexander-literature and was thoroughly familiar with the classical historians, Herodotus, Thucydides, and Xenophon; he had written a considerable amount, although perhaps nothing as ambitious as this; he had at least some philosophical training and considerable military and administrative experience; finally, and not least important, he possessed, it is evident, a good deal of common sense.

But he faced formidable difficulties, difficulties he shared with the other extant writers on Alexander. Of these the earliest is the Sicilian Greek Diodorus, who almost exactly three hundred years after Alexander's death, devoted the 17th Book of his *Universal History* to his reign. The Latin writer Quintus Curtius wrote his *History of Alexander* in the first century A.D., while early in the next century the Greek biographer Plutarch wrote a *Life of Alexander* which provides a useful supplement to Arrian. The *Philippic Histories* of the Romanised Gaul Pompeius Trogus, who wrote a little earlier than Diodorus, is extant only in the wretched summary of Justin (3rd cent. A.D.).[6] All these authors were faced with the problem of choosing from a multiplicity of conflicting sources. For Arrian does not exaggerate the mass of material that confronted the historian of Alexander. Much of this has perished almost without trace, but enough remains, in the shape of 'fragments' embedded in extant writers, to confirm his statement that many lies were told about Alexander and many contradictory versions of his actions existed.

Many of those who accompanied Alexander wrote of the expedition and its leader from their particular standpoint.[7] Callisthenes, Aristotle's nephew, acting as Alexander's 'press-agent' composed for Greek consumption—for Alexander's allies were by no means enthusiastic—an account of the expedition in which the king, who surely 'vetted' Callisthenes' narrative, bore a distinct resemblance to the 'heroes' of legend. This official version was necessarily broken off when its author was arrested, and later executed, on suspicion of treason. The last event certainly dealt with was the battle of Gaugamela. Chares, the royal chamberlain, wrote a book of anecdotes, valuable when he is dealing with events at court, otherwise useless, while Onesicritus, Alexander's chief pilot, who had been a pupil of Diogenes, created a dangerous blend of truth and falsehood with a Cynic flavour. For him Alexander was the 'philosopher in arms', a man with a mission. Nearchus, who commanded Alexander's fleet on its voyage from India to the Persian Gulf, followed with a more sober account, beginning, unfortunately, only with the start of his voyage. Lastly, to mention only the most important of the contemporary accounts, we have the histories of Ptolemy, who after Alexander's death became ruler and later king of Egypt, and of Aristobulus, apparently an engineer or architect. With these I shall deal later. But the history of Alexander which enjoyed the greatest popularity in succeeding centuries—Caelius, the friend of Cicero, read it—was written by a man who was not a member of the expedition, Cleitarchus, who wrote at Alexandria at the end of the fourth century, or perhaps even later. He portrayed Alexander as 'heroic', as Callisthenes had done, and (somewhat incongruously) as the possessor of the typical virtues of a Hellenistic king. But the main attraction of his book was almost certainly the vivid descriptions and the sensational incidents it contained—the Greek courtesan Thais leading Alexander, the worse for drink, in a Bacchic revel to set fire to the palace at Persepolis, Alexander's wholesale adoption of Persian luxury and practices, including a harem of 365 concubines, the week-long revel in Carmania, the poisoning of Alexander—to mention but a few.

All or much of this Arrian will have read. He will doubtless have been familiar, too, with the criticisms of the philosophical schools, particularly the Stoics, and the rhetoricians.[8] These found a congenial theme in Alexander's drunkenness, his conceit, his lack of self-control erupting into murderous violence, and his divine aspirations.

Faced with this mass of evidence Arrian decided, very sensibly, to use the histories of Ptolemy and Aristobulus as the basis of his narrative. Where their versions tallied, he

tells us, he accepted their consensus as true. Where they differed, he sometimes gives both versions; more often, one suspects, he followed Ptolemy. Certainly for military matters Ptolemy is his principal source. His reasons for his choice, admittedly, do not inspire confidence. Since Alexander was dead when they wrote, neither, he claims, had anything to gain by not telling the truth, while it would be disgraceful for a king, as Ptolemy was when he wrote, to tell lies. It is not difficult to think of reasons why Aristobulus and, especially, Ptolemy might not care to tell the truth, at least the whole truth. But it would seem reasonable to suppose that Arrian had come to the conclusion, after long study of the available material, that these authors provided the most honest and most reliable accounts of Alexander. To supplement their works Arrian includes the 'stories' of other writers, such as Callisthenes and Chares, where these appeared 'worth relating and reasonably reliable'.

So far as we can judge, Arrian's choice of Ptolemy as his main source was fully justified, particularly as he concerned himself largely with military matters. For Ptolemy was an experienced soldier who had taken a part, although not at first a prominent one, in many of the operations he describes. His accounts of Alexander's major battles, as we see them through Arrian's eyes, are by no means free from problems, perhaps because of the difficulty a participant has in obtaining an overall view of the fighting. We should remember too that Ptolemy was not promoted to 'the Staff' until late in 330. The other military operations, particularly those in which Ptolemy took part, are reported with admirable clarity, although Ptolemy's tendency to exaggerate his personal contribution seems well established.[9] This is understandable, and unimportant. Less excusable is the apparently systematic denigration of Perdiccas, his bitter enemy in the struggle for power after Alexander's death.[10] The main fault of his book, it seems, lies elsewhere, in his reticence about some of the more controversial, and perhaps discreditable, episodes in Alexander's career. Arrian does not cite him as a source for his narrative of the murder of Cleitus, although it is difficult to believe that Ptolemy did not mention the tragedy, while neither he nor Aristobulus is the basis of Arrian's account of Alexander's attempt to introduce the ceremony of prostration (*proskynesis*). It would seem that Ptolemy said no more than he had to about these incidents. The same is probably true of the 'plot' of Philotas and the conspiracy of the Pages, although he asserted the guilt of Philotas and Callisthenes.

Aristobulus' book provided a useful supplement to Ptolemy, since he was, it seems, more interested in geography and natural history. Most of the geographical and topographical detail in the *Campaigns* comes from Aristobulus and it was he who described Alexander's measures to improve the canal system of Babylonia and the navigation of the River Tigris. Aristobulus was ordered by the king to restore the tomb of Cyrus near Pasargadae which had been plundered by robbers, and it is to him that we are indebted for the description of the tomb before and after it was robbed, a description that modern archaeology has confirmed. It is probable that the vivid narrative of the march through the Gedrosian desert with its valuable botanical observations comes from the same source. It is Aristobulus too who related the exploration of the coasts of Arabia and the plans which Alexander had made for its conquest. One of Alexander's motives for the expedition, Aristobulus tells us—we learn this from Strabo, for Arrian does not mention the name of his source—was the expectation that the Arabians would recognize him as a god.

But it is on the personal side that Aristobulus' account is open to question. Whereas Ptolemy had been content to pass over the less pleasant aspects of Alexander's character, Aristobulus' book seems to have had a distinctly 'apologetic' character which earned him in antiquity the soubriquet of 'flatterer' (*kolax*). He justifiably stressed the generosity of the king towards the captured Persian royal family, and put forward the tenable view that Cleitus asked for trouble, but although he asserted the guilt of Philotas and Callisthenes he was apparently as reticent as Ptolemy about the reasons for his judgement. Then his statement that the king was not a heavy drinker, but remained long at banquets only for the sake of the conversation, must provoke a smile. The murder of Cleitus alone disproves it. In fact, it represents an excessive reaction from the quite indefensible view that Alexander was habitually drunk. Many writers depicted the king towards the end of his life as a prey to superstitious fear. According to them Alexander, on the advice of his seers, put to death the sailor who had worn the royal diadem and the man who had sat upon the royal throne. Aristobulus, however, stated that the sailor was merely flogged and then let go and that the second man was tortured to reveal his motive, implying, it would seem, that he suffered nothing worse. But, as the man was a scapegoat, this seems doubtful. On the other hand, Aristobulus relates that he learned from the seer Peithagoras himself that Alexander had treated him with great favour because he had told the king the truth, namely that his sacrifices had disclosed impending disaster for him.

Arrian brought to his task patience, common sense, and a shrewd knowledge of human affairs, as well as considerable military and administrative experience. In military matters his adherence to Ptolemy produced good results. Here he followed a first-rate source well up in the inner circle of the Macedonians, whom he seems almost always to have understood. We might be tempted to depreciate Arrian by saying that he did little more than summarize Ptolemy's narrative. To do so would be unfair. We have only to compare his account of Issus or of Gaugamela with that of Quintus Curtius, who certainly had access to Ptolemy's book at first or second hand, to see his achievement. This is not to say that his account of military operations is everywhere satisfactory or that he tells us all we would like to know about the Macedonian army. We do not know, for example, what the soldiers in the various units were paid, and, more important, we hear almost nothing of the logistics of the army. Again, at Gaugamela Arrian fails to explain how a messenger from Parmenio could

reach Alexander after he had begun the pursuit of Darius. Only occasionally does he appear to misunderstand Ptolemy, for it is unlikely that the Macedonian supposed that Alexander, after crossing the Hydaspes, rode ahead with his cavalry in the expectation that he could defeat Porus' entire army with it alone. On the other hand he offers sensible criticism of Aristobulus' statement that Porus' son was sent with only 60 chariots to oppose Alexander's crossing of the R. Hydaspes, and rightly commends Alexander for refusing to risk attacking the Persians by night at Gaugamela, as Parmenio advised. Moreover, Arrian nearly always uses technical terms correctly, an immense help to the student of military history, and takes care to name the commanders of the various units. His use of *taxis* ('unit') as a utility word and of 'Companions' (*Hetairoi*) to refer either to the Companion cavalry or to Alexander's 'Peers' does give rise to difficulties, but for this Arrian can hardly be held responsible. The same painstaking attention to detail is evident in administrative matters. Appointments of governors are duly mentioned, and throughout his book Arrian is careful to give the father's name in the case of Macedonians, e.g. Ptolemy son of Lagus, and in the case of Greeks their city of origin. One can imagine the confusion that would have resulted had he not done so, in view of the shortage of Macedonian proper names and the resultant abundance of Ptolemys and Philips.

We must regret, however, that Arrian has interpreted his subject in a somewhat narrow fashion, perhaps because his model, Xenophon, had concentrated on *his* expedition. Unlike Polybius, he does not discuss *why* Alexander invaded Asia—he might, however, have said that this was a matter for the historian of Philip and that Alexander never thought of not continuing an operation already begun—nor does he mention previous operations in Asia or the existence of a Macedonian force in Asia in 334. His account of the events of 336, which determined Alexander's relations with the Greek states, formally at least, are dealt with so summarily as to be barely intelligible. Consequently the reader, I suspect, is in the dark when, without having heard of the League of Corinth, he is told of 'the resolutions of the Greeks'. In fact, Alexander's relations with the Greek states and events in Greece during the expedition are almost entirely neglected. This is to some extent understandable and justifiable, although Persian hopes of transferring the war to Greece in 333 are not fully intelligible without the background of Greek discontent. Indeed, Arrian's preoccupation with Alexander leads him to treat this important, though admittedly abortive, episode in the war very sketchily. Again, the reader must be curious, one would think, to learn what happened to King Agis of Sparta who vanishes from the pages of Arrian after receiving 30 talents and 10 ships from the Persians, even if we regard the Spartan revolt in 331, as Alexander is said to have regarded it, as 'an affair of mice'.

Arrian clearly made no attempt to give a comprehensive account of the war, or of its antecedents. We hear only incidentally of the troubles in the Persian empire that preceded Darius' accession in 336, and every reader must have asked himself the question: 'Why did the Persians allow Alexander's forces to cross into Asia unopposed?' Even after the start of the expedition we hear what the Persians have been planning and doing only when they come into contact with Alexander. It is only on the eve of Issus in November 333 that we are told of Darius' plans in the preceding months. Arrian deliberately chose to disregard the Persian background, as Professor Brunt has proved.[11] He was not ignorant of Persian matters; but his method 'was to follow the movements and describe the activities of Alexander himself'.

Arrian's portrait of Alexander is in general more open to criticism than his narrative of military operations, partly through his reliance on Ptolemy and Aristobulus. Yet Arrian's portrait is more than the sum of his sources; for he possesses a distinct personality of his own which we can detect most clearly in his attitude to religion and morals. Many of the characteristics of his Alexander are undeniably true. We can see clearly the qualities which enabled Alexander to maintain for so many years his hold upon his men, the dashing leadership which was expected of a general in his day—although Arrian does not conceal the fact that his officers thought that the king sometimes went too far in hazarding his life—the confidence (seldom disappointed) of success, with which he inspired his troops, and his care for their welfare. We remember how after the victory at the Granicus Alexander 'showed much concern about the wounded, visiting each, examining their wounds, asking how they were received, and encouraging each to relate, and even boast of, his exploits'. We recall his determination and persistence in many sieges, notably in the face of the desperate resistance by the Tyrians for seven long months, and his courage in adversity, exemplified by his 'noblest deed', the refusal to drink the helmetful of water, too little for his troops to share, in the burning heat of the Gedrosian desert—a proof, as Arrian remarks, of his endurance and his generalship. Arrian, too, rightly praises his generous treatment of the defeated Indian rajah Porus—although this was not altogether disinterested—and his compassion for the captured Persian royal family. There are many instances of Alexander's affection for his friends, particularly his *alter ego* Hephaestion, and his trust in them is portrayed in the celebrated scene with his doctor Philip, while Arrian warmly commends his repentance after his murder of Cleitus.

It is when Arrian's imagination is kindled by incidents such as these that he raises the pitch of his narrative and achieves eloquence. For the most part he is content to let the story speak for itself. Certainly he deliberately avoided sensationalism and he explicitly denied the truth of such favourite stories as the visit of the Amazon queen or the week-long revel through Carmania. Perhaps no passage better illustrates Arrian's admiration for his hero and the heightened tone of his narrative than that in which he describes the king's return to his army after his recovery from the wound which so nearly caused his death. I quote the end of the passage:

> Near his tent he dismounted, and the men saw him walk; they crowded round him, touching his hands, his knees, his clothing; some, content with a sight of him standing near, turned away with a blessing on their lips. Wreaths were flung upon him and such flowers as were then in bloom.

But Arrian's evident admiration for Alexander and his achievements did not prevent him from criticizing his hero where he failed to reach the high standard which, as a Stoic, Arrian felt a king ought to attain. In particular, Alexander is censured several times for his excessive ambition. Arrian does not know, and commendably will not speculate about, Alexander's future plans, but he is convinced that he would never have rested content with his conquests. The Indian wise men are expressly commended for their view that 'each man possesses just so much of the earth as he stands on', and Alexander, despite his applause of this sentiment, is said to have acted always in a way completely opposed to it. It is clear that for Arrian Alexander's conquests are merely an expression of Alexander's insatiable appetite for fame. There is some truth in this, but it is not the whole story. It is, however, entirely to Arrian's credit that he wholeheartedly condemns Alexander's letter to Cleomenes, the governor of Egypt (7.23.6-7), in which the king offers to pardon him for his past misdeeds and to give him a free hand in the future if he erects temples in Egypt for the dead Hephaestion. The historian's understanding and humanity is apparent in his attitude to the murderer of Cleitus. Alexander's act excites in him pity for the man who has given way to two grave vices, passion and drunkenness. The king has failed to achieve that self-mastery which, as Arrian has remarked a little earlier, is necessary before one can be happy. A similar sentiment occurs in the speech of Coenus at the River Hyphasis when he says to Alexander 'when things go well with us, the spirit of self-restraint is a noble thing'—surely Arrian's own view, whether or not it was shared by Coenus.

The main weaknesses in Arrian's portrait of Alexander seem to me two-fold—a tendency, which he derives from his sources, to gloss over the less attractive side of the king's character, and a failure to appreciate Alexander's intentions, especially with regard to the Persians.

The first of these is apparent before the expedition gets under way. The slaughter of the Thebans, perhaps rightly, and the destruction of the city and the enslavement of the survivors is blamed on the Greek allies of Alexander. Nothing is said of his responsibility for permitting them, as in fact he did, to pass this sentence. Yet even Plutarch, whom no one could accuse of hostility to Alexander, implicitly holds him responsible; as he saw, Alexander's intention was to terrify the other Greek states into submission. At the battle of the Granicus Arrian relates without comment the massacre of the Greek mercenaries, nearly 18,000 according to his own account; he does not remark on the cruelty or the inadvisability of the massacre. In the same way at Massaga in India the massacre of 7,000 Indians passes without comment. Nor should we guess from Arrian that some writers had doubts about the involvement of Philotas in a plot against the king. He is content to accept Ptolemy's statement, although the 'manifest proofs' of his guilt adduced by him do not amount to much. Again, the burning of the palace at Persepolis is very briefly referred to with no mention of the alternative tradition that it was set on fire during a drunken revel. On the other hand, Arrian gives a much more balanced account of the murder of Cleitus than Aristobulus seems to have done, and he is obviously reluctant to accept the statements of Ptolemy and Aristobulus that Callisthenes was involved in the conspiracy of the Pages.

What the modern reader misses in Arrian's book is an appreciation of the larger issues. Alexander emerges as a great leader, a great conqueror possessed of boundless ambition, a man who reached the height of human prosperity and who, if he committed great crimes, had the magnanimity to repent of them. Certainly the conquest of the Persian Empire was his most lasting achievement, but what we want to know is whether he was more than the supreme conqueror. What plans did he have for his empire? What part did he intend the conquered peoples to play in it? Amid a great deal that is obscure about Alexander, one thing is certain, that he was very much in earnest about what modern writers have called his 'policy of fusion'. The clearest expression of this policy is his prayer at Opis—a prayer that Arrian records without comment—that Macedonians and Persians might live in harmony and jointly rule the empire. This was a revolutionary idea, not shared by his Macedonians, nor, we can be sure, by many Greeks either. For the most distinguished of Alexander's many teachers, the eminent philosopher Aristotle, who inspired him with a love of Greek literature and particularly of Homer, is said by Plutarch to have written to Alexander advising the young king to behave towards the Greeks as a leader but towards the 'barbarians' as a master. This contemptuous attitude towards 'barbarians' was no doubt widespread. But Alexander, who may have felt doubts about it even before the expedition—Artabazus and other leading Persians lived as exiles at Philip's court when Alexander was a boy—soon came to reject it. After Gaugamela we find him appointing Persians as governors, certainly not through a lack of suitable Macedonians.

Arrian clearly shared Aristotle's prejudice against 'barbarians' and had no conception of Alexander's vision of a partnership between the two peoples. In the characterisation of Alexander at the end of his book he sees Alexander's adoption of Persian dress and his introduction of Persian troops into the Macedonian army as a mere 'device', designed to render him less alien to his Persian subjects. Indeed, Arrian has earlier (4.7) condemned his adoption of oriental dress as a 'barbaric' act not so different from his 'barbaric' punishment of the pretender Bessus. Both acts, in Arrian's view, indicate a deterioration of Alexander's character. Even in the case of Bessus Arrian does not see that the punishment was a Persian punishment inflicted on him by Alexander in his position as 'Great King'. Elsewhere, he refers to Alexander 'going some way towards "barbarian" extravagance', and his com-

ment on the king's marriage to Roxane, the Bactrian princess, is illuminating. 'I approve', he writes, 'rather than blame'. This 'policy of fusion' with the adoption of Persian dress and Persian court ceremonial was bitterly resented by the Macedonians, as Arrian is well aware. Drink led Cleitus to give utterance to grievances which were deeply felt and widely shared, while the extent of the Pages' conspiracy leads one to think that their motives were not so much personal as political. Yet Arrian does not ask himself whether Alexander would have persisted in a policy so universally detested if it were nothing more than a 'device' to win Persian favour.

Plutarch, perhaps exaggerating, puts the number of cities founded by Alexander at seventy. In his *Campaigns* Arrian mentions fewer than a dozen foundations; not a cause for complaint, for he was not compiling a catalogue. But we are not told what Alexander's motives were, military or economic or, as some scholars believe, part of his mission to spread Greek culture throughout Asia. It is from the *Indica* that we learn that cities were established among the conquered Cossaeans to encourage them to forsake their nomadic habits and become a settled people.

Alexander took his religious duties very seriously indeed, as the account of his last days makes plain. Arrian frequently records that the king offered sacrifice or made drink-offerings, and the prophecies made by his seers, notably Aristander, are faithfully reported. Only once, before the siege of Tyre, is he provoked to sarcasm; 'The plain fact', he writes, 'is that anyone could see that the siege of Tyre would be a great undertaking'. But Arrian's hostile or sceptical attitude to the ruler cult of his day—an attitude he shares with Plutarch and the historian Appian—prevents him from doing justice to Alexander's divine aspirations. That Alexander believed himself to be the son of Ammon-Zeus, as his ancestor Hercules was son of Zeus, is very probable, although admittedly not susceptible of proof. Arrian will have none of this. Alexander set out for Siwah 'hoping to learn about himself more accurately, or at least *to say that he had so learnt*'. For him Alexander's claim was merely another 'device', to impress his subjects. He displays the same sceptical attitude towards Alexander's divinity. In 324 the Greek states, probably in response to a 'request' from the king himself, sent *theoroi* (envoys sent on sacred missions) to crown him with a golden crown at Babylon. That the envoys were *theoroi* admits of no doubt; the fact that they themselves wore crowns proves it. If Arrian writes that 'they came as *theoroi* forsooth', using a Greek particle implying disbelief or sarcasm, he is suggesting that Alexander, as a mortal, could never be a god. Gods were immortal, men were not, and 'after all', as Arrian drily comments, 'Alexander's death was near'.

Arrian set out to produce the best and most reliable account of Alexander's expedition, avoiding the exaggerations of his predecessors and correcting their errors. That he succeeded few will dispute. The histories of Diodorus and Curtius and, particularly, the biography of Plutarch throw light (and sometimes darkness) on the character of Alexander and occasionally even on his military exploits, but Arrian's book is the basis of our knowledge. It impresses one as the work of an honest man who has made a serious and painstaking attempt to discover the truth about Alexander—a task perhaps impossible by his time—and who has judged with humanity the weaknesses of a man exposed to the temptations of those who exercise supreme power. We need not deny the limitations of the work, but it is proper to remember that Alexander's idea of an empire in whose rule conquering Macedonians and conquered Persians were to share perished with him. To spare the conquered was one thing, to associate them with one in government was another, an idea that was not to reach fulfilment until long after Alexander's death.

ALEXANDER'S ARMY[12]

In the spring of 334 Alexander set out from Macedonia, leaving Antipater with 12,000 infantry and 1,500 cavalry to defend the homeland and to keep watch on the Greek states. The size of the army with which he crossed the Hellespont has been variously reported, totals ranging from 30,000 to 43,000 for infantry and 4,000 to 5,500 for cavalry. But the detailed figures given by Diodorus (17.17), 32,000 infantry and 5,100 cavalry, agree essentially with the totals in Arrian (Ptolemy), and may be taken as substantially correct. The size and composition of the force holding the bridgehead at Abydos—there surely must have been some troops there in 334—is not known, but the likelihood is that it was small and consisted mainly of mercenary infantry.

The backbone of the infantry was the Macedonian heavy infantry, the 'Foot Companions', organized on a territorial basis in six battalions (*taxeis*) of about 1,500 men each. In place of the nine-foot spear carried by the Greek hoplite, the Macedonian infantryman was armed with a pike or *sarissa* about 13 or 14 feet long, which required both hands to wield it. The light circular shield was slung on the left shoulder, and was smaller than that carried by the Greek hoplite which demanded the use of the left arm. Both Greek and Macedonian infantry wore greaves and a helmet, but it is possible that the Macedonians did not wear a breastplate.[13] The *phalanx* (a convenient term for the sum total of the Macedonian heavy infantry), like all the Macedonian troops, had been brought by Philip to a remarkable standard of training and discipline. Unlike the phalanx which the Romans encountered over a century later, Alexander's phalanx was capable of rapid movement and was highly manoeuvrable, as one can see from a reading of the first half-dozen chapters of Arrian's book.

In battle the right flank of the phalanx was guarded by the *Hypaspists* or 'Guards'. These were an élite corps, consisting of a Royal battalion (*agema*) and two other battalions, each of approximately 1,000 men. Alexander used them frequently on rapid marches and other mobile operations, often in conjunction with cavalry and light-armed troops. This suggests, although it does not prove, that they were

more lightly armed than the heavy infantry; but if they were less heavily armed, we do not know where the difference lay.

The member states of the Corinthian League contributed 7,000 heavy infantry, while 5,000 Greeks served as mercenaries. The remainder of Alexander's infantry consisted of 7,000 Thracian and Illyrian light troops armed with javelins and two bodies of archers from Crete and Macedonia respectively. The outstanding unit among the light troops was the Agrianians, 1,000 strong, who have been well compared in their relation to Macedon and in their quality to the Gurkhas of the Indian army. Alone of the allies they served throughout the campaign and Arrian mentions them almost fifty times. With the archers and the Guards they took part in all the reconnaisances and skirmishes as well as fighting superbly in the set pieces.

Pride of place among the cavalry was held by the Macedonian 'Royal Companions', originally 1,800 troopers divided into 8 squadrons or *Ilai,* all under the command of Parmenio's son, Philotas. Among them the Royal Squadron, consisting of perhaps 300 men, was Alexander's own bodyguard, which spearheaded the devastating cavalry charge in the major battles. Their position was on the immediate right of the Guards, who had the task of maintaining contact between the Companions and the phalanx. The counterpart of the Companions on the left of the phalanx was the Thessalian cavalry, also 1,800 strong at the start of the expedition. Under the general command of Parmenio, they had the difficult task at Issus and Gaugamela of holding much superior forces of Persian cavalry while Alexander delivered the decisive blow on the right. The Greek allies furnished 600 horsemen, and the remaining 900 were made up of Thracians, Paeonians, and 'Scouts' (*Prodromoi*) who were also called 'Lancers' (*Sarissophoroi*) since they were armed with the *sarissa,* presumably shorter than those carried by the infantry which required the use of both hands. Whether these light cavalry were Macedonians or Thracians is not clear; certainly they were distinct from 'the Thracians'. Finally, although Diodorus does not mention mercenary cavalry in his list of forces, Alexander may have had some from the beginning. By Gaugamela at least he had perhaps 1,000 of these.[14]

Despite the need for garrisons in Asia Minor and Egypt, Alexander's army at Gaugamela numbered 40,000 infantry and 7,000 cavalry. The only substantial reinforcements of Macedonian and allied troops recorded by Arrian reached Gordium early in 333, and there is no good reason to suppose that Alexander received any worthwhile number of Macedonians or allies apart from these before Gaugamela. For Quintus Curtius, who after 331 records the arrival of many reinforcements not mentioned by Arrian, mentions reinforcements only of mercenaries in this period. Indeed, it is clear that the increase in the number of Alexander's troops was due principally to the recruitment of mercenaries from Greece and to the enlistment of mercenaries who had fought for Persia. Alexander had begun by treating the latter as traitors, but finding that this merely encouraged desperate resistance decided within a few months to change this unsuccessful policy. Many of the garrisons doubtless consisted in large part of mercenaries.

Soon after Gaugamela Alexander received strong reinforcements of Macedonian troops, no fewer than 6,000 infantry and 500 cavalry. This enabled him to create a seventh battalion of infantry, which was certainly operating early in 330.[15] The other battalions must have remained over strength for some time. This is the last draft of Macedonians he is known to have received until he returned to the west after his Indian campaign, and there is no compelling reason to think that he received any others. In 330 the allied troops from the Greek states and from Thessaly were discharged at Ecbatana. Many, we are told, chose to re-enlist as mercenaries. Increasing use was made of Greek mercenaries, and the garrisons of the many cities founded by Alexander in the eastern satrapies consisted of them together with the native inhabitants and some unfit Macedonians. Presumably few of the 10,000 infantry and 3,500 cavalry left behind to protect Bactria in 327 were Macedonians.

After Gaugamela the pattern of warfare changed. In Bactria and Sogdiana Alexander found himself faced with a national resistance which, under the leadership of Bessus and then of Spitamenes, wisely avoided major conflicts and concentrated on widespread guerrilla activity. It was probably to cope with this altered mode of fighting that in 329 Alexander made an important change in the organization of his Companion cavalry. We no longer hear of eight squadrons (Ilai), but of (at least) eight regiments (Hipparchiai), each consisting of two, or perhaps more, squadrons. Some of these squadrons, it seems likely, now included or consisted of the excellent Persian cavalry.[16] Certainly Alexander made use of Persian cavalry outside the Companions. As early as 330 we hear of a unit of Persian mounted javelin-men (3.24), and at the battle of the River Hydaspes in 326 he had in his army a body of Daae, mounted archers, as well as horsemen from Bactria, Sogdiana, Scythia, Arachotia, and the Parapamisus, or Hindu Kush, region.

At Massaga in India Alexander is said to have attempted to enlist Indian mercenaries in his army, but when they attempted to desert to have massacred them. No further recruitment of Indian mercenaries is recorded, and the only Indian troops that we hear of in his army are those provided by the rajahs Taxiles and Porus and the city of Nysa, some 11,000 in all. However, if Nearchus is correct in saying (**Indica** 19.5) that at the start of the voyage down the River Hydaspes Alexander had 120,000 fighting men with him (a figure given by Curtius (8.5.4) for the army at the start of the Indian campaign and by Plutarch (Alexander 66.4) for the (Infantry) force with which Alexander left India), Alexander must have had a great many Indian troops in his army. But their presence was only temporary, since there is no indication that any Indians returned to the west with him.

Among the grievances of the Macedonians in 324 Arrian (7.6.4) mentions the (recent) creation of a fifth cavalry regiment consisting, if we accept Professor Badian's emendation of Arrian's text,[17] almost entirely of Iranians. This means that the division of the Companion cavalry into eight regiments had been abandoned and that for a brief period after the return from India there were only four. It is sometimes said that the change reflects the losses sustained in the march through the Gedrosian desert. This need not be the case. Hephaestion's command is described (7.14.10) as a 'Chiliarchy', a group of 1,000 men, and, although it is true that he was 'Chiliarch' or 'Vizier', it is not self-evident that the preservation of his *name* required that his unit be called 'the chiliarchy of Hephaestion' rather than 'the regiment of Hephaestion'. It is probable, it seems to me, that the new regiments were (nominally) 1,000 strong. If this is so, the change will have been a change in organization, a consolidation of the cavalry into fewer and stronger units.

In 324 the 30,000 young Persians (the 'Successors'), who had been undergoing training in Macedonian fashion for the last three years, joined Alexander at Susa. Later in the same year, after the mutiny at Opis, Alexander sent home those Macedonians who were unfit or past the age for service, about 10,000 infantry and perhaps 1,500 cavalry, probably the bulk of his Macedonian forces. In 323 strong reinforcements reached Babylon. Philoxenus brought an army from Caria and Menander one from Lycia, while Menidas came with the cavalry under his command. It is likely that, as Brunt suggests,[18] these were fresh drafts from Macedon to replace the veterans now on their way home; Alexander had not drawn on the manpower of the homeland since 331 and it is not likely that he wished the Macedonian element in his army to be reduced to negligible proportions. In addition, Peucestas brought 20,000 Persian archers and slingers, as well as a considerable force of Cossaean and Tapurian troops, presumably infantry. Alexander now carried out his last reform. The Persians were integrated into Macedonian units in such a way that each platoon consisted of 4 Macedonian NCOs and 12 Persians, each armed in their national fashion.

For the future, then, or at least for the immediate future, the army in Asia was to consist predominantly of Iranian troops. The only indication of the size of the Macedonian component is given in a speech in Quintus Curtius purporting to have been delivered by Alexander but certainly the historian's own composition. There (10.2.8) the king mentions an army of 13,000 infantry and 2,000 cavalry, surely all Macedonians, excluding the garrisons already in being.

Notes

1. Philip A. Stadter (*Greek, Roman and Byzantine Studies* 8, 1967, 155ff) has shown that Xenophon was not merely a nickname, but part of the historian's name.

2. Arrian was suffect consul in 129 or 130 A.D., and in his day it was usual for a man to hold the consulship at about the age of 42; see *JRS* 55 (1965), p. 142 n. 30.

3. We do not know why Arrian chose to study under Epictetus rather than, as we should have expected, at Athens. In an important article on Arrian's governorship in the *English Historical Review* 1896 (reprinted in his *Essays*, ed. F. Haverfield, Oxford, 1906), Professor H. F. Pelham has suggested that Arrian was probably influenced by the traditions of his mother's family, the 'gens' Arria, famous in the history of Roman Stoicism. He conjectures that the *cognomen* Arrianus indicates the family of the historian's mother, as *cognomina* often did in the first and second centuries A.D.

4. In a letter to a Lucius Gellius Arrian gives his reasons for publishing them. We now know that this Gellius was an eminent citizen of Corinth, L. Gellius Menander, who with his son, L. Gellius Iustus, set up an inscription in honour of Arrian at Corinth; see G. W. Bowersock in *Greek, Roman and Byzantine Studies* 8 (1967), 279-80.

5. The quotation is taken from page 218 of Pelham's article mentioned in n. 3.

6. Diodorus' 17th Book is translated (with useful notes) by C. Bradford Welles in the Loeb Classical Library, Curtius by J. C. Rolfe in the same series, and Justin (with Cornelius Nepos and Eutropius) in Bohn's Library. Plutarch's *Alexander* has been frequently translated (usually with a number of other Lives), most recently by Ian Scott-Kilvert in *The Age of Alexander* (Penguin Books).

7. These authors are the subject of detailed study by Lionel Pearson, *The Lost Histories of Alexander the Great* (New York, 1960).

8. On these see my *Plutarch* Alexander: *A Commentary* (Oxford, 1969), lx-lxii.

9. See the convincing analysis by C. B. Welles, 'The reliability of Ptolemy as an historian', in *Miscellanea . . . A. Rostagni* (Turin 1963) 101ff. Curtius, who had the advantage of reading Ptolemy's book, presumably refers to this aspect of Ptolemy's writing when he describes him (9.5.21) as a man 'who was certainly not inclined to depreciate his own glory'.

10. R. M. Errington, 'Bias in Ptolemy's History of Alexander', in *CQ* 1969, 233ff., gives several instances of misrepresentation by Ptolemy. He considers that Aristonous was deprived of the credit for helping to save Alexander's life, but he contests the usual view that Antigonus' hard-fought victories over the survivors of Issus were ignored by Ptolemy, because of his rivalry with Antigonus in the years following 314.

11. See his 'Persian Accounts of Alexander's Campaigns' in *CQ* 1962, 141ff. The quotation which follows is taken from p. 141.

12. For details of Alexander's troops see especially Major-General J. F. C. Fuller, *The Generalship of Alexander the Great* (London, 1958); E. W. Marsden, *The Campaign of Gaugamela* (Liverpool, 1964), Appendices I and II; A. R. Burn, 'The Generalship of Alexander', in *Greece and Rome* 1965, 140-54.

13. See G. T. Griffith, *Proceedings of the Cambridge Philological Association,* 4 (1956/7), pp. 3ff.

14. P. A. Brunt, 'Alexander's Macedonian Cavalry', in *JHS* 83 (1963), 27-46 discusses the many problems concerning Alexander's cavalry.

15. As R. D. Milns has demonstrated in *Greek, Roman and Byzantine Studies* 7 (1966), 159-166.

16. On the Hipparchies see Appendix A.

17. E. Badian in *JHS* 85 (1965), 161.

18. *JHS* 83 (1963), 39.

Abbreviations

AJP: American Journal of Philology.

CQ: Classical Quarterly.

Ehrenberg Studies: Ancient Society and Institutions. Studies presented to Victor Ehrenberg, edited by E. Badian (Oxford, 1966).

Fuller: Major-General J. F. C. Fuller, *The Generalship of Alexander the Great* (London, 1958).

JHS: Journal of Hellenic Studies.

Tarn, *Alexander:* Sir William Tarn, *Alexander the Great,* 2 Vols. (Cambridge, 1948).

Tod: M. N. Tod, *A Selection of Greek Historical Inscriptions,* vol. 2 (Oxford, 1948).

Wilcken, *Alexander:* Ulrich Wilcken, *Alexander the Great,* translated by G. C. Richards (London, 1932); reprinted with an introduction to Alexander studies, notes, and a bibliography by Eugene N. Borza (New York, 1967).

Philip A. Stadter (essay date 1978)

SOURCE: "The *Ars Tactica* of Arrian: Tradition and Originality," in *Classical Philology,* Vol. 73, No. 2, 1978, pp. 117-28.

[*In the essay below, Stadter examines the use Arrian made of traditional tactical manuals in composing his* Ars Tactica, *arguing that even though his work is a close reflection of his sources, Arrian made a significant contribution to tactical writing through his discussion of contemporary Roman experience.*]

The sense of tradition and the rhetorical principle of *imitatio* were so fundamental to Greek literary production in the imperial period that it is frequently difficult to determine the contribution of an individual writer. Such is the case with Arrian of Nicomedia. Arrian's major work, the **Anabasis,** is heavily influenced by literary models, such as

Herodotus and Xenophon, and is immediately dependent on the historical writings of Aristobulus and Ptolemy. How much can we expect Arrian to have modified the presentation and point of view of his sources? One means of attacking the problem is to analyze Arrian's practice in a quite different genre. The *Ars tactica* . . . gives valuable clues about Arrian's handling of earlier material.

Knowledge of the military organization of Greek and Hellenistic armies was passed down from generation to generation by a series of manuals on tactics, of which three have survived, by Asclepiodotus, Aelian, and Arrian.[1] It is the nature of manuals, especially those on technical subjects, to repeat themselves, and these are no exception.[2] The two by Aelian and Arrian echo each other so closely that Hermann Köchly, the first to study the problem in detail, concluded that they were actually two recensions of the same work.[3] Both this hypothesis and the theory subsequently advanced by Richard Förster,[4] that Arrian used Aelian's treatise as a source for his own, have been shown to be false by Alphonse Dain.[5] Aelian and Arrian, as well as an anonymous lexicon of military terms (the *Glossarium militare,* or *Definitiones*), derive independently from a common source. Asclepiodotus' treatise is distinct but closely related. The common source is not preserved, but we can guess its author. The Asclepiodotus who wrote on tactics was probably the same man as the follower of Posidonius mentioned by Seneca; and since Posidonius' lost treatise on tactics is mentioned by Arrian and Aelian, it is likely that all these works go back, directly or through an intermediary, to Posidonius' book.[6]

To the writers of the manuals before Arrian, Hellenistic military practice was an abstract study, not directly related to contemporary usage. Therefore each author followed his exemplar, with only minimal changes. Aelian, in his dedication addressed to the emperor Trajan, freely admitted that he had no military experience, no knowledge of Roman military practice (*praef.* 1-2). Like Posidonius and Asclepiodotus before him, he wrote as a philosopher, whose duty and privilege it was to consider systematically every branch of knowledge. The consular Frontinus had encouraged Aelian to write, showing an interest in the "theoretical learning of the Greeks" . . . ; and the philosopher expresses the hope that the work will please as "Greek theory and refined inquiry" . . . , and considers the index of contents which precedes the treatise a major contribution, permitting rapid consultation of the desired topics (*praef.* 6-7).[7]

Arrian's situation was quite different. At the time of composition of the *Tactica,* in A.D. 136/37,[8] Arrian was commander of two Roman legions and numerous auxiliary troops as governor of Cappadocia.[9] Unfortunately the beginning of Arrian's treatise was lost when a folio was torn out of our archetype,[10] so that we do not know whether he there mentioned his experience, explained his decision to write, or described his intended audience. The book itself shows that he had a double purpose: in the first part he describes Macedonian tactics (1-32), in the second contemporary Roman cavalry exercises (33-44). His audience, then, would have been men interested in both the theory and the practice of war. The major difference from Aelian is not in the first part, the description of Macedonian tactics, but in Arrian's recognition that a manual such as Aelian's was not enough, and in his decision to complement it with the second section on contemporary Roman exercises. The combined work, therefore, reflects a spirit far different from that of Aelian.

Moreover, the *Ars tactica* was not Arrian's first work on military matters. At *Tactica* 32. 3 he writes, "I have already explained the infantry exercises [performed by the Romans] in a treatise I wrote for the emperor himself." The *Tactica* was a sequel and complement to his earlier booklet on contemporary Roman infantry exercises (*gymnasia*). This second work developed the thought of the first in two different directions: first, historically, by giving his version of the standard account of Macedonian and Hellenistic military practice (both infantry and cavalry); second, practically, by completing his description of contemporary military exercises through a treatment of the Roman cavalry. Seen in this perspective, the historical section of the *Tactica* (1-32) is only a part of a larger work directly concerned with the military practice of his day. The contemporary Roman army is also the subject of a third work by Arrian, the *Acies contra Alanos* or *Ectaxis*. While governor of Cappodocia, Arrian had to defend this province against the marauding Alans. Later, he wrote a semi-literary version of the plan of march and battle which he used. The *Acies* is preserved in the same archetype manuscript as the *Tactica,* and immediately follows it. Arrian may well have appended it to the *Tactica* as a practical example of the use of some of the formations described there. A didactic purpose would explain the style of the *Ectaxis,* which, while preserving some of the flavor of an order of the day (notably in the constant use of the third person imperative and infinitive with imperative force), is far removed in choice of vocabulary from military usage. It would also account for the presence of explanatory phrases which would not be necessary in an actual order of battle (e.g., *Ect.* 16, explaining the meaning of *kontophoroi*).[11]

The booklet on Roman infantry exercises which preceded the *Tactica* was dedicated to Hadrian (*Tact.* 32. 3). The author's familiarity with the emperor, as revealed in his *Periplus Ponti Euxini* (chap. 1 and passim) written five years before, and all we know of Hadrian's efforts to renew the army assure us that Hadrian would have read the *Tactica* with interest, too, even if he had not specifically requested it. However, the *Tactica* is addressed not to Hadrian but to some unknown figure, as is apparent from the use of the third person to name the emperor at *Tactica* 32 and 44. 2-3.

The practical and contemporary direction of Arrian's writings on military subjects had its effect even on the first and traditional portion of the *Tactica,* as can be discovered by a systematic comparison of the texts of Aelian and Arrian. Although Arrian is not derived directly from Aelian, but from a common source, Aelian (supplemented by Asclepiodotus and the *Glossarium militare*) gives us an excellent indication of the contents of the common source. This paper will explore as precisely as possible Arrian's use and modification of traditional material in the first half of the *Tactica.* The second half, Arrian's detailed presentation of Hadrian's reforms in cavalry training, has been recently studied with great care by Franz Kiechle.[12]

The outline of the traditional section of the *Tactica* follows the procedure of subdivision and explanation standard in such manuals.[13]

	ARRIAN	AELIAN
I.	Introduction (1)	1. 1-3
II.	Basic divisions of warfare (2)	2. 1-6
III.	Description of combatants by equipment used (3-4)	2. 7-13
	1. Infantry (3)	2. 7-10
	2. Cavalry (4)	2. 11-13
IV.	Organization of the army (5-10)	3-10
	1. Need for organization (5. 1-3)	3
	2. The *lochos* (5. 4-6. 6)	4–5
	3. Combinations of *lochoi* (7-8)	6-7. 3
	4. Light-armed troops and cavalry (9. 1-2)	7. 4-6
	5. The ideal number for an army (9. 3-6)	8
	6. Army units from the *lochos* to the full army of 16,384 men (10)	9
V.	Formations and use of troops in battle (11-19)	11–23
	1. The phalanx (11-12)	11. 1-4, 13-14
	a. Formations (11)	11. 1-4
	b. Different ranks (12. 1-5, 10-11)	13-14
	c. Spacing and the use of the *sarissa* (12. 6-10)	—
	2. Light-armed troops (13-14)	15-16
	3. Archers and spearmen (15)	17
	4. Cavalry (16-18)	18-20
	5. Chariots and elephants (19)	22-23
VI.	Movements (20-27)	24-35
	1. Names (20)	24
	2. Descriptions of turns, etc. (21-25)	25-29
	3. Shapes of the phalanx (26)	30-31
	4. Relaying commands to the army (voice, signal, trumpet) (27)	35
VII.	Marches (28-30)	36-39
	1. Order of the army (28)	36
	2. Formations on the march (29)	37-38
	3. Baggage (30)	39
VIII.	Manner of issuing commands (31-32)	40–42

The scheme followed here is the same as that of Aelian, and the content almost equivalent, as was seen by Köchly.[14] The modern reader is surprised to discover that even the introductory section, which reviews earlier writers of tactical manuals, contains the same names as Aelian, in the same order (*Tact.* 1. 1 = Ael. 1. 2).[15] Both Aelian and Ar-

rian complain that earlier writers have written for experts and not explained the technical terms, and assert that they will remedy this obscurity (*Tact.* 1. 2 = Ael. 1. 3). In the body of the *Tactica,* passages of technical explanation are frequently almost verbatim equivalents of those in Aelian. . . .

Less scientific passages are handled with slightly more freedom. An example is the simile at *Tactica* 12. 2, comparing the front rank of the phalanx to the edge of a sword. . . .

The comparison with Aelian reveals that even such a "literary" device as this simile was taken over by Arrian from his source.[16] Recognizing the suitability and didactic value of the sword simile here, Arrian rewrote the passage for greater clarity and effectiveness, but did not hesitate to borrow the idea itself, and much of the presentation of it.

In another passage, *Tactica* 31, we might expect that the series of quotations from Homer on silence in the army would reflect the Nicomedian's own literary inclinations. Not so: all the quotations, in the same order, are found in Aelian 41, and thus derive from the common source. Aelian had begun his treatise with a quotation from Homer (1. 1), and since he cites Homer as the first writer on military matters, we may presume that, from the earliest manuals on the subject, the poet was regularly quoted.[17] Comparison of the parallel chapters in the two authors does show, however, that Arrian makes stylistic changes, as he had with the simile in *Tactica* 12. Less important lines are paraphrased, reducing the eighteen lines of Homer quoted by Aelian to nine. Aelian's first citation of *Iliad* 3. 8-9 is omitted, because it will appear again only a few sentences later. A false line had been added in Aelian's quotations before *Iliad* 4. 428 and a false ending to *Iliad* 4. 431 to complete the sense; Arrian's paraphrase eliminates these.[18] Thus the long blocks of quotations in Aelian[19] are broken into smaller and more cogent units, and the whole passage becomes smoother and more effective.

Arrian treats these two passages (*Tact.* 12. 2 and 31) individually, preserving the content of his source while substantially altering the verbal presentation. The author's skill with words is evident. Unfortunately, a stylistic analysis of the first half of the *Tactica,* although it would reveal Arrian's general superiority in clarity and felicity of expression to the average contemporary writer of Greek prose, would not give us a certain indication of Arrian's own contributions. Since both Aelian and Arrian drew from a common source, there would still remain the unknown factor of Aelian's own stylistic modifications, which are much less easy to define than his minor additions of content.[20] We may note, however, that while Aelian has a marked aversion to hiatus, Arrian here, as in his other works, makes no attempt to avoid it.

Arrian, then, takes over the contents and frequently the words of the tactical manual he used as a source. Nevertheless, significant differences in content reveal his active contribution. The abstract categories of the manual he clarifies with examples, from both history and contemporary Roman experience.[21] In one case, after his description of hoplite armor according to the traditional manual, Arrian adds:

> For the complete heavy hoplite outfit, a helmet is added too, or Laconian or Arcadian caps,[22] and shinguards, as the ancient Greeks did, or a single shinguard for the knee which is put forward in battle, as the Romans did,[23] and corselets, some of scale, some overlapped with fine iron chains.
>
> [*Tact.* 3. 5]

In describing cavalry weapons he supplements and clarifies the traditional material with references to the Romans and their opponents (the italicized passages are not found in the other manuals):

> δορατοφοροι are those who draw near to the ranks of the enemy and fight with spears . . . , *or push with lances . . . in their onslaught, as do the Alans and Sarmatians;* ακροβολισται are those who use missiles from a distance, *like the Armenians and those of the Parthians who do not carry lances.*
>
> [*Tact.* 4. 3]

Note that Arrian had had direct experience with the Alans and the Armenians as governor of Cappadocia, and that the Parthians, just across the Euphrates frontier, would also have become known to him then, if he had not already seen them in action years before during Trajan's Parthian campaigns.

At the end of the same section Arrian adds his own information on Roman cavalry equipment:

> With the Romans, some cavalry carry lances . . . , and attack in the manner of the Alans and the Sarmatians, while others carry spears. . . . A wide and flat sword is hung from their shoulders, and they carry flat oblong shields, an iron helmet, a woven corselet, and small shinguards. They carry spears . . . for both purposes, both to hurl from a distance, when there is need, and to hold in the hand when fighting close in; and, if it is necessary to lock together in hand to hand combat, they fight with their swords. Some have also small axes (maces?) with points all around in a circle.[24]
>
> [*Tact.* 4. 7-9]

Arrian supplements the standard account of the use of a deep phalanx by citing the tactics of Epaminondas at Leuctra and Mantinea (cf. Xen. *Hell.* 6. 4. 12 and 7. 5. 21-22), and he adds that the deep phalanx is necessary "if one has to repel onrushing troops, as for instance against the Sarmatians and the Scythians" (*Tact.* 11. 1-2).[25] He followed his own precepts in his formation against the Alans, drawing up his phalanx eight deep and close together (. . . , *Ect.* 15). In the same passage of the *Tactica* he also describes the peculiarly Roman formation called *testudo* (which he calls by its Greek name, . . .) as a particular example of the close formation called συνασπισμς (*Tact.*

11. 4-6). In his account of cavalry units, he notes that the hipparchy of 512 men is called ειλη by the Romans (*Tact.* 18. 3). He is thinking of the Roman *ala quingenaria* of 500 men, which he regularly calls ειλη in his battle plan against the Alans (*Ect.* 1 and passim).[26]

The methodical scheme of the original manual furnished the occasion for a remarkable discussion of the use of chariots and elephants (*Tact.* 19). Arrian had already revealed an interest in the subject at the beginning of his work, where he had enriched the standard reference to elephants with a specific statement on their use by the Indians, Ethiopians, Macedonians, Carthaginians, and Romans (2. 2).[27] In the same chapter he had also explicitly contradicted the traditional opinion as we know it from Aelian. The latter states that both elephant and chariot warfare is of one type only (Ael. 2. 6). Arrian begins by agreeing, at least about elephants, but then has second thoughts. Exceptions exist: some elephants carry howdahs or towers . . . ; others are trained to fight with tusks fitted with metal.[28] Chariots are even more subject to variation:

> Chariot warfare was multifold: one could fight with unarmed chariots, like the ones in the Trojan War, or with scythe-bearers like the Persian ones later, or with horses either armored or not, and with [chariots having] one pole, or two, or even many poles.
>
> [*Tact.* 2. 5][29]

Considering this unusual interest in these two methods of fighting, we are surprised to discover Arrian saying at *Tactica* 19. 1 that it is futile . . . to give the names of the elephant and chariot units, since their use had been abandoned long ago, and the Romans never fought with chariots in any case. In the parallel passage, Aelian (22. 1) defends his decision to record these names, "for completeness' sake," and goes on to record conscientiously the various units: "two chariots are called a zygarchy," etc. (Ael. 22-23).[30] Arrian omits these useless names, but in their place furnishes a précis on chariots in warfare.

> The barbarians in Europe did not use chariots either, except those of the so-called British isles, outside the great sea. These used two-horse chariots, with small, bad horses. Their light, two-wheeled chariots . . . are well adapted to running across all sorts of terrain and the wretched horses to enduring hardships.[31] Of the Asians, the Persians long ago practiced the use of scythe-bearing chariots and armored horses, beginning in the time of Cyrus, and even before this the Greeks with Agamemnon and the Trojans with Priam used chariots with unarmored horses. The Cyrenians also for some time fought from chariots.[32] But now all these practices have been abandoned, as has the use of elephants for warfare, except by the Indians and the upper Ethiopians.
>
> [*Tact.* 19. 2-6][33]

Thus the author gives the reader some sense of the variety of types of military chariots, rather than a bare list of obsolete titles.

Certain other additions by Arrian also reflect his desire to make the book significant to the contemporary reader: thus his notes differentiating Clearchus and Iphicrates, the writers of earlier tactical manuals, from the homonymous and more famous generals;[34] and the note identifying the Scipio who was friend of Polybius (*Tact.* 1. 1). Other additions describe with greater precision the weapons of the hoplites[35] and cavalry,[36] Xenophon's use of the word ενωμοτια,[37] the importance of the ουραγος (the last man of a file),[38] and the use of light-armed troops.[39] He notes that, besides the standard bowmen and javelin men, slingers are very useful,[40] and in general is more precise and descriptive of the use of missiles than is the standard presentation known from Aelian or Asclepiodotus.[41] Arrian's respect for this branch of his army is real, for when he was planning his confrontation with the Alans, he was certain that a heavy shower of missiles would be sufficient to repel the Alan cavalry, before there was any real contact (*Ect.* 25-26). He explains the effectiveness of the wedge formation of cavalry,[42] and is well aware of the dangers of changing formation when close to the enemy.[43]

A number of omissions, on the other hand, reveal a desire not to overburden the reader with useless information passed down in the manuals. Besides the obsolete names of elephant and chariot units already mentioned, Arrian omits the whole section in Aelian 10 on where the best phalangarchs should be placed, and also the sections on the density and weapons of the phalanx (Ael. 11. 2, 5-6; 12). His idea seems to be to avoid going into unprofitable detail, whether on cavalry formations,[44] certain kinds of troop movements,[45] or types of commands.[46]

Deliberate or unconscious distortion of the original, as opposed to additions or omissions, is difficult to establish. In several places where Arrian differs from Aelian, one cannot be certain whether it is Aelian or Arrian who deviates from the source. The only clear example of Arrian's changing content is at *Tactica* 12. 7-10, on the use of the *sarissa* by the phalanx. Arrian states that the *sarissa* was sixteen feet long, of which four feet were needed to hold it, and that the ranks stood two feet behind each other, so that six rows of *sarissae* would project distances of twelve, ten, eight, six, four, and two feet beyond the front line. Aelian, on the other hand, explains that the *sarissa* was originally sixteen cubits long (1 cubit = 1½ feet), but in practice was fourteen cubits, of which four cubits were used for holding the *sarissa;* and that the ranks were two cubits behind one another, allowing five rows of *sarissae* to project ten, eight, six, four, and two cubits beyond the front line. Aelian here echoes precisely the statements of Polybius in describing the Macedonian phalanx (18. 29-30. 4), and we may conclude that the manuals from Polybius on gave Aelian's figures.[47] Asclepiodotus (5) is slightly different, giving the length of the *sarissa* as between ten and twelve cubits, but since he calculates on the basis of a ten-cubit projection (i.e., a twelve-cubit *sarissa*, with two cubits for holding), his conclusion is the same as that of Aelian and Polybius, that there were five ranks of *sarissae* projecting, each two cubits behind the other. It is apparent that Arri-

an's substitution of feet for cubits represents his own correction of his predecessors.[48] Modern writers have frequently questioned Polybius' figures on the length of the *sarissa,* disturbed by the weight of the weapon and its consequent awkwardness in use (European pikes in medieval and modern times have been fifteen feet or less) and by Theophrastus' casual comment that Macedonian *sarissae* were twelve cubits long (supported by the passage in Aelian just referred to). We must suppose that Arrian shared these doubts, and that he not only questioned the figures but changed them, changing as well the interval between the ranks and thus preserving the same overall situation. His use of sixteen units rather than fourteen is apparently an attempt at compromise, using the larger figure given with a smaller unit, and results in his six projecting ranks rather than the standard five. Arrian's correction, as far as can be determined, was mistaken: Polybius' figures apparently are reliable, although it is difficult to imagine how the twenty-one-foot *sarissa* was manipulated in battle.[49]

In sum, then, the raw material of the first half of Arrian's *Tactica* is a manual of Hellenistic military practice, but in preparing his work he has introduced significant modifications. Building upon the traditional form and content, he has incorporated it into a larger scheme of works on Hadrianic military practice, the lost booklet on the infantry, *Tactica* 33-44 on the cavalry, and the *Acies contra Alanos.* Furthermore, he has added historical and contemporary examples relating the definitions of the standard manual to specific events and practices and has indicated Roman parallels to Hellenistic usage. With the contemporary reader in mind, he omits, or, as in the case of elephant and chariot warfare, substitutes for, material of value only to theoreticians or antiquarians. Where he believes his source mistaken, on the length of the *sarissa,* he is ready to correct it.

On the whole, Arrian has achieved an unusual synthesis. While conscious that he is repeating a technical manual . . . , his is not an exercise in pedantry. An active soldier, who is intimately involved with the Hadrianic military reforms—as is evident from the close relationship of Hadrian's address to his troops at Lambaesis and *Tactica* 33-44[50]—Arrian tries always to make the principles of Hellenistic practice comprehensible and relevant to his contemporaries. He draws on his own experience with the Alans and the Parthians, and on his reading of Roman history (British chariots) and of Greek history (Epaminondas' phalanx). Style also, as far as is possible in such matters, he adapts to fit the needs and expectations of his readers. The final work represents a combination of traditional knowledge and original intelligence which reflects the spirit of the Hadrianic age. Arrian himself sounds the keynote: "[The Romans] do not love so much their own traditional ways that they do not select the best from every quarter and make it their own."[51] Arrian has brought his military experience and literary skill to the task of re-editing a military manual, revealing even in a work that is necessarily derivative his capacity as an original writer.

Notes

1. Asclepiodotus has been edited with Aeneas Tacticus by W. A. Oldfather and the Illinois Greek Club for the Loeb Classical Library (London-New York, 1923); Arrian's treatise is in *Flavii Arriani Quae exstant omnia*, vol. 2: *Scripta minora et fragmenta*[2] (Leipzig, 1968), ed. A. G. Roos, with additions by G. Wirth. Aelian has not been re-edited since the edition of H. Köchly-W. Rüstow, *Griechische Kriegsschriftsteller*, vol. 2.1 (Leipzig, 1855). On Aelian and Asclepiodotus, see the articles by K. K. Müller, s.v. "Aelianus (10)," *RE* 1 (1894): 482-86, and s.v. "Asclepiodotus (10)," *RE* 2 (1896): 1637-41.

2. Note that the title in the manuscripts of a similar work on artillery is Ηορωνος Κτηςιου Βελοποι ικα, Heron's edition of Ctesibius' *Belopoeica*. I learned Latin composition from Bradley's Arnold, edited by Mountford, again a single work successively revised. For a general discussion of ancient handbooks, see M. Fuhrmann, *Das systematische Lehrbuch* (Göttingen, 1960). Works on tactics are considered on pp. 181-82. Various studies exist of particular traditions: see, e.g., H. Plommer, *Vitruvius and Later Roman Building Manuals* (Cambridge, 1973); and O. A. W. Dilke, *The Roman Land Surveyors* (New York, 1971).

3. See his *De libris tacticis, qui Arriani et Aeliani feruntur, dissertatio*, Index lectionum (Zurich, 1851), reprinted in *Opuscula academica*, vol. 1 (Leipzig, 1853). In his edition (*Griechische Kriegsschriftsteller*, 2.1:218-471) he printed the texts of Aelian and Arrian in parallel columns.

4. R. Förster, "Studien zu den griechischen Taktikern, I: Über die Tactica des Arrian und Aelian," *Hermes* 12 (1877): 426-49. Förster demolished Köchly's theory of the single work in two recensions.

5. A. Dain, *Histoire du texte d'Élien le tacticien* (Paris, 1946), pp. 26-40.

6. On the identity of Asclepiodotus, see Müller, s.v. "Asclepiodotus (10)," cols. 1637-41. The only fragments of Posidonius' *Tactica* are the citations by Aelian and Arrian (F 80 and 81 in L. Edelstein and I. G. Kidd [eds.], *Posidonius*, vol. 1; *The Fragments* [Cambridge, 1972]). In Dain's reconstruction (see his stemma, *Histoire*, p. 39), Aelian and Arrian are derived from a common source; this lost source and Asclepiodotus are in turn both derived from Posidonius. The differences which separate Asclepiodotus from Aelian and Arrian Dain attributes to changes in the lost work. However, a simpler stemma is also possible, according to which all three authors used Posidonius directly, but Asclepiodotus introduced a number of modifications. The text of the *Glossarium militare* is in Köchly-Rüstow, *Griechische Kriegsschriftsteller*, 2.2:219-33.

7. See the analysis of Aelian's preface by Dain, *Histoire*, pp. 15-21, and the comments on Aelian's purpose by F. Kiechle, "Die 'Taktik' des Flavius Arrianus," *BRGK* 45 (1964): 109 and 113-14. Frontinus himself wrote a *De re militari*, now lost, as well as the extant *Strategemata*, *De aquis urbis Romae*, and a book on measuring land preserved in fragments. Since Frontinus was active as a commander of troops, his book may have been less theoretical than Aelian's. On Frontinus as a writer of handbooks, see Fuhrmann, *Lehrbuch*, pp. 98-104.

8. The *Tactica* is dated by the reference to Hadrian's twentieth regnal year at *Tact*. 44. 3.

9. See especially H. F. Pelham, "Arrian as Legate of Cappadocia," *EHR* 11 (1896): 625-40 = *Essays* (Oxford, 1911), pp. 212-33; K. Hartmann, *Flavius Arrianus und Kaiser Hadrian*, Progr. Augsburg, 1907; and A. B. Bosworth, "Arrian and the Alani," *HSCP* 81 (1977): 217-55. For a brief summary of the contribution of recently discovered inscriptions to our knowledge of Arrian's career, see W. Eck, s.v. "L. Flavius Arrianus," *RE*, suppl. 14 (1974): 120. See also Bosworth, "Arrian's Literary Development," *CQ*, n.s. 22 (1972): 163-185.

10. On the loss of one folio at the beginning of the *Tactica* and another at the end of the *Acies contra Alanos* as well as elsewhere in the archetype (Laur. 55.4), see Dain, *Histoire*, p. 375. The pages were ripped out not for their illumination, as suggested by Holstein, and repeated by Bandini and Roos, but for empty or half-empty parchment pages. One side of a page in Laur. 55.4 equals about forty lines in the Teubner edition. In Laur. 55.4, the text of Aeneas Tacticus ends at f. 181[v]. Since the next page (181*a*) was ripped out, the recto must have been blank, or more likely, carried a diagram so pale that the sheet could be reused (the folio lost between ff. 145 and 146 is similar: Dain, *Histoire*, p. 187). In this case Arrian's *Tactica* would have begun at the top of f. 181*a*[v]. Allowing space for the title, about thirty-five Teubner lines would be lost before our present text begins at 182[r].

11. The style of the *Acies* makes it most unlikely that it is a fragment of the *Alanike*, a lost history of the Alans, as suggested by F. Jacoby, (*FGrHist*, comm. to 156 F 12) and others. Most of the *Acies* has recently been translated by A. Dent, "Arrian's Array," *HT* 24 (1974): 570-74.

12. Kiechle, "Die 'Taktik' des Flavius Arrianus," pp. 87-129, demonstrates that the cavalry exercises described by Arrian are indeed contemporary and incorporate the reforms of Hadrian known from other sources, notably the Lambaesis inscription (*CIL*, 8. 2532; *ILS* 2487; E. M. Smallwood, *Documents Illustrating the Principates of Nerva, Trajan, and Hadrian* [Cambridge, 1966], no. 328).

13. The chapters listed in the right-hand column give an indication of the parallel passages in Aelian. The many omissions and additions are only apparent from inspection of the parallel texts in the Köchly-Rüstow edition.

14. The relation is set out in the parallel presentation in Köchly-Rüstow and in the tables in Förster, "Studien, I," pp. 431-32. Förster also demonstrates their similarity to the scheme of Asclepiodotus. The parallel with the *Glossarium militare* is clear from the apparatus in Roos's edition of Arrian. See also W. A. Oldfather and J. B. Titchener, "A Note on the *Lexicon militare*," *CP* 16 (1921): 74-76, and Dain, *Histoire*, pp. 26-40.

15. See the parallel texts of Köchly-Rüstow and Dain, *Histoire*, pp. 27-28. The equivalent of nine Teubner lines has been lost in Arrian, paralleling the first part of this chapter in Aelian. Arrian's own preface would thus have run about twenty-six Teubner lines (cf. n. 10). At the end of his list of names, Arrian omits the "many others, who published introductions, like Bryon, or particular treatises" mentioned by Aelian.

16. The simile also appears briefly in Asclep. 3. 5. Xenophon had used a slightly different version at *Eq. mag.* 2. 3.

17. Note also Polybius' irrelevant quotation of Homer in his account of the phalanx at 18. 30.

18. Both Aelian and Arrian seem to imply that *Il.* 4. 436-37 followed immediately upon 2. 459-63. This combination of two Homeric passages into one unit to illustrate a point was common in antiquity: e.g., Plato's combination of *Il.* 3. 8 and 4. 431 at *Rep.* 389E.

19. Ael. 41. 1 quotes *Il.* 4. 428-31, prefixed with an additional line and, after και, 3. 8-9; 41. 2 quotes *Il.* 2. 459-63 followed immediately by 4. 436-37; 41. 3 quotes *Il.* 3. 1-2, 8-9. In all, there are three blocks of seven, seven, and four lines respectively.

20. On the style of Arrian in this part of the *Tactica*, see Förster "Studien, I," pp. 439-41 and H. R. Grundmann, *Quid in elocutione Arriani Herodoto debeatur* (Ph.D. diss., Leipzig; Berlin, 1884), pp. 83-88 = *Berliner Studien* 2 (1885): 263-68. Both Förster and Grundmann demonstrate the presence of typical features of Arrian's style in the *Tactica*. The problem of drawing conclusions about modifications from the common source is illustrated by *Tact.* 29. 8. The reference to Xenophon there is absent from Aelian, and might be thought to be an addition by Arrian; but it is found also in the *Glossarium militare* and therefore belongs to the common source. Similarly, for the reference to the frightening aspect of the phalanx at *Tact.* 12. 6, cf. Asclep. 5. 2.

21. Contrast Asclepiodotus, of whom Oldfather writes in the Loeb edition, "There is not a single illustration drawn from either history or from experience" (p. 232). The same could be said of Aelian.

22. On ancient Greek military caps . . . , see J. K. Anderson, *Military Theory and Practice in the Age of Xenophon* (Berkeley-Los Angeles, 1970), pp. 29-37.

23. The Romans had taken over from the Samnites the practice of using only one greave, although by Arri-

an's day greaves had been abandoned except for parade dress. See F. Lammert, s.v. "Ocreae," *RE* 17.2 (1937): 1778, and note the use of the singular προκνημις in Polyb. 6. 23. 8. Some gladiators continued to use the single greave in imperial times: see G. Lafaye, s.v. "Gladiator," Dar.-Sag., vol. 2², figs. 3573 and 3576.

24. This passage is quoted and related to the evidence from Trajan's column by G. Webster, *The Roman Imperial Army of the First and Second Centuries A.D.* (London, 1969), p. 151. Unfortunately, he does not distinguish the Hellenistic material from Arrian's contemporary additions. We have no other evidence for the greaves which Arrian says the armored horsemen wore. The last weapon described is called an axe with a curved blade by Webster, but it seems more like a mace, such as those illustrated by E. Saglio, s.v. "Clava," Dar.-Sag., vol. 1², figs. 1581-83. Cf. also the mace of rather different shape described by F. Cumont, "Le sacrifice du tribun romain Terentius," *MMAI* 26 (1923): 35 and fig. 5.

25. The whole passage from κατα βαθος δε το χρν ταττειν appears to be Arrian's addition. The use of εμβολον here and in Xenophon for the Theban formation is confusing, since Arrian uses εμβολον elsewhere in the sense of "wedge": see J. K. Anderson, *Military Theory and Practice*, pp. 326-27.

26. ειλη is Arrian's normal spelling for ιλη in these works: see Roos's apparatus to *Ect.* 1. The explanation of the Roman use of the term is desirable because just before Arrian had explained that (in Hellenistic usage) the ειλη consisted of sixty-four men (*Tact.* 18. 2).

27. *Tact.* 2. 2. . . .

28. H. H. Scullard, *The Elephant in the Greek and Roman World* (Ithaca, 1974), pp. 240-45, describes the towers or platforms used on elephants in ancient times. There is no certain evidence for the use of platforms before the time of Pyrrhus, but Arrian may be thinking of the various traditions which linked their use with the Indians and the first successors. For the use of sharpened tusks, Scullard's closest parallel is the reference to spears fastened to tusks in Silius Italicus 9. 581-83 (pp. 239-40). Arrian himself remarks that he had seen elephants dancing and playing cymbals (*Ind.* 14. 5-6); can he be thinking of some kind of exhibition or spectacle in this case, too?

29. The notion of many-poled chariots seems to reflect Arrian's reading of Xenophon's *Cyropaideia*. The chariot of Abradatas in that work had four poles: *Cyr.* 6. 1. 51, 6. 4. 2. Anderson, *Military Theory and Practice*, p. 179, suggests that this type of chariot is "probably a product of Xenophon's imagination." At *Cyr.* 6. 1. 52, Cyrus decides to make an οκταρρυμον carriage for moving towers. For general comments on the multiplicity of military uses of chariots in ancient times, see Anderson, "Homeric, British, and

Cyrenaic Chariots," *AJA* 69 (1965): 349-52, and "Greek Chariot-Borne and Mounted Infantry," *AJA* 79 (1975): 175-87. On chariots in general, see T. G. E. Powell, "Some Implications of Chariotry," in I. L. Foster and L. Alcock (eds.), *Culture and Environment: Essays in Honour of Sir Cyril Fox* (London, 1963), pp. 153-169.

30. Cf. also Asclep. 8-9.

31. The Britons' use of chariots to harass his troops in the invasions of 55 and 54 B.C. was described by Caesar, *BG* 4. 33, 5. 15-16; cf. Sheppard Frere, *Britannia* (Cambridge, Mass., 1967), p. 35. Plautius encountered them again in A.D. 43; see Dio 60. 20. 3 and Frere, p. 64. Incidentally, Plautius brought elephants on this expedition (Dio 60. 21. 2).

32. The statement that Cyrus originated the use of the scythe-chariot is no doubt based on Xen. *Cyr.* 6. 1. 30. Xenophon also refers to Trojan and Cyrenian chariots, *Cyr.* 6. 1. 27-28. Cf. Anderson, "Homeric, British, and Cyrenaic Chariots," p. 352; "Greek Chariot-Borne and Mounted Infantry," pp. 176-77.

33. On Ethiopian elephants, see Scullard, *The Elephant,* pp. 134 and 207, and (quoting Pliny), pp. 216 and 218. In the next century the Sassanids continued to use elephants in their battles with Rome: see Scullard, pp. 200-206.

34. Both generals, Clearchus and Iphicrates, had been made famous by Xenophon, the former in the *Anabasis,* the latter in the *Hellenica.*

35. *Tact.* 3. 2. . . .

36. *Tact.* 4. 1. . . .

37. *Tact.* 6. 3 . . . , referring to Xen. *Anab.* 4. 3. 26. On the problem of λόχοι and Ηνωμοαι in Sparta, see Anderson, *Military Theory and Practice,* pp. 225-51, esp. 226-27, and p. 297, n. 17.

38. *Tact.* 6. 5 . . . Xenophon's Socrates had long before noted the importance of the last man in the file (*Mem.* 3. 1. 8). See also *Eq. mag.* 2. 3 (the last man in a cavalry file), *Cyr.* 3. 3. 41-42, and the comments of Anderson, *Military Theory and Practice,* pp. 174-76. More is said on the ουραγός at Arr. *Tact.* 12. 11 (cf. Ael. 14. 8).

39. *Tact.* 9. 1 . . . ; 9. 2. . . .

40. *Tact.* 15. 1 . . . ; 15. 2. . . .

41. Contrast *Tact.* 15 with Ael. 17 and Asclep. 7. 1.

42. *Tact.* 16. 8. . . .

43. *Tact.* 25. 7. . . .

44. Cf. Ael. 19. 2-4 on the necessity of keeping the proper distance when in formation, and on the various types of rhomboid formations, either with ranks, or files, or both, or neither; 19. 6-13 on the formation of the wedge, which Arrian dismisses in a few words: "the wedge is half of a rhombos, so that I have explained the scheme of the wedge at the same time"

(*Tact.* 17. 3). Cf. also Asclep. 7. 6-9. Aelian had used diagrams to illustrate the cavalry formations described (see Ael. 1. 5, 18. 1, and Dain, *Histoire,* pp. 48-52); none appear or are mentioned in Arrian's text. Arrian may have omitted them because they were not in his source, because he did not understand them (in Aelian they are very confused), or because he expected that his readers would not.

45. Cf. Ael. 25. 3-4 on the difference of a . . . about-face toward or away from the enemy and 32-34 on turns executed by whole . . . 256 men.

46. Arr. *Tact.* 32 gives only eighteen of the forty-four commands found in Ael. 42, chiefly because Arrian does not repeat commands already listed in another context. Thus for a turn Arrian gives, "Left face. Right face. Forward march. Halt. Front face." He combines two separate sets of orders; whereas Aelian keeps left and right face as two sets of commands, and adds left and right about-face, thus listing thirteen commands to Arrian's five. Asclep. 12. 11 strikes a middle ground with twenty-seven commands.

47. Note that both Ael. 1. 2 and Arr. *Tact.* 1. 1 cite Polybius as an earlier writer on *tactica.* Posidonius continued Polybius' history, and it is likely that he reworded Polybius' *Tactica* for his own treatise, the probable source of Aelian and Arrian.

48. It is possible but unlikely that the change represents an error in the manuscript tradition.

49. On the question of the Macedonian *sarissa,* see F. Lammert, s.v. "Sarisse," *RE* 1A (1920): 2515-30, esp. 2517 on Arrian; F. W. Walbank, *Commentary to Polybius,* vol. 2 (Oxford, 1967), pp. 586-87 on 18. 29. 1-30. 4; M. Andronicos, "Sarissa," *BCH* 94 (1970): 91-107; and M. M. Markle III, "The Macedonian Sarissa, Spear, and Related Armor," *AJA* 81 (1977): 323-39. It would be incorrect to emend Arrian's πόδας to πηχεις as Walbank suggests. The mistake—or correction—is Arrian's. Markle suggests that Arrian may have wished to give an average dimension for the *sarissa,* which he estimates to have been between fifteen and eighteen feet long.

50. On the close ties between Arrian's treatise and the training of the cavalry under Hadrian, see Kiechle, "Die 'Taktik' des Flavius Arrianus," pp. 123-27, and R. W. Davies, "Fronto, Hadrian and the Roman Army," *Latomus* 27 (1968): 88-91. See also K. Hartmann, *Über die "Taktik" des Arrian,* Progr. Bamberg, 1895, on the relation of the *Tactica* to Arrian's *Acies contra Alanos.*

51. *Tact.* 33. 2; cf. 44. 1-2. Arrian's book on hunting, *Cynegeticus,* in a similar way reveals his combination of dependence on an earlier author (in that case Xenophon's *Cynegeticus*) and original contributions. See my "Xenophon in Arrian's *Cynegeticus,*" *GRBS* 17 (1976): 157-67.

A. B. Bosworth (essay date 1980)

SOURCE: An introduction to *A Historical Commentary on*

Arrian's "History of Alexander," Volume I: Commentary on Books I-III, Clarendon Press, 1980, pp. 1-41.

[*In the excerpt below, Bosworth studies several critical issues concerning Arrian's composition of his history of Alexander, focusing on the controversy surrounding the title and dating of the work; the historical method Arrian employed in writing the work; and Arrian's style. Bosworth concludes that while Arrian was a "sophisticated stylist," his abilities as a historian were somewhat flawed.*]

. . . 2. THE HISTORY OF ALEXANDER

Arrian's major work, the history of Alexander, is universally known by the title **Anabasis Alexandri**. The title occurs in the *codex Vindobonensis*, the known archetype of Arrian, as well as in excerpts from Stephanus of Byzantium . . . and the 'Suda'. . . . But the ancient testimonia are not consistent. The majority of later writers, in particular Photius, refer to the work in more general terms, as τα περὶ Ἀλεξάνδρου.[1] Arrian himself gives little hint of the true title, merely referring to it as his 'history concerning Alexander' (vii 3. 1). Now this divergence does not occur in the companion work, the **Indica**, whose title is twice given by Arrian and is repeated in the manuscript tradition and later testimonia without significant variation.[2] The divergence in the case of the Alexander history is troublesome. Krüger took it as axiomatic that **Anabasis** was the original title and assumed that the variants arose from a desire to provide a companion work (and title) for Arrian's **History of the Successors**. . . . That seems hardly compelling, and there is at least an equal possibility that the title **Anabasis** is a fiction of late antiquity. Commentators meeting a work in seven books by a man purporting to be the New Xenophon might well have given it a spurious Xenophontean title. Certainly Arrian's work on Alexander is not notably influenced by Xenophon. His stylistic debts are rather to Herodotus and Thucydides, and his direct references to Xenophon's work are sparse and perfunctory,[3] a sharp contrast to the **Cynegeticus**, a work which *is* explicitly modelled upon Xenophon and which constantly, both implicitly and explicitly, echoes the subject-matter and phraseology of the master.[4] The ancient critics were only too aware of the relationship, and on the title-page of the **Cynegeticus** Arrian's name has been deleted and replaced by 'Xenophon of Athens, the second'.[5] They might easily have been dissatisfied with a title as unassuming as τα περὶ Ἀλεξάνδρου and fabricated a second **Anabasis** for their second Xenophon.

The date of the work is as controversial as its title. There is both an early date, some time in the reign of Hadrian, and a later date, towards the end of the reign of Antoninus Pius or even in Marcus' reign.[6] The theories to some extent depend on the view of Schwartz (above p. 4) that Arrian only devoted himself to serious historical inquiry after his retirement from public life, but the arguments which are crucial rest upon the internal evidence of the text and the extant testimonia about the relative order of Arrian's historical works. What is certain is that Arrian has completed confidence in his abilities as a writer. He invites comparison with all extant histories of Alexander, claiming that he is fully competent to do justice to the greatness of his subject, and the success of his work will cement his pre-eminence in Greek letters.[7] The language presupposes a good deal of earlier publication—and successful publication, if not necessarily in the sphere of historical studies. Such indications as we have suggest that the Alexander history came relatively early in the sequence of historical works. In his digest of the *Bithyniaca* Photius summarizes Arrian's apology for the late appearance of this history of his native province;[8] he mentioned other works, monographs on Timoleon and Dion, which preceded the **Bithyniaca,** and Photius claims that the **Bithyniaca** was Arrian's fourth historical effort, succeeding the history of Alexander and the two monographs.[9] The subject-matter seems generally derived from Arrian; and, even if the statement about the relative order of the works comes from Photius himself, he must have had some grounds for the statement. Later works are also quoted and excerpted, the seventeen books of the **Parthica** and the ten books of the **History of the Successors.** They were not mentioned in the preface to the **Bithyniaca** and presumably followed it in the sequence of Arrian's works. There is some corroboration in the literary echoes of the Alexander history which we find in the **Parthica.** The fragments dealing with Trajan's voyage down the Tigris are strikingly reminiscent of the description of Alexander's voyage down the Hydaspes[10] and the character-study of Arsaces echoes the wording of Arrian's celebrated encomium upon Alexander.[11] As far as the evidence goes, it suggests a definite pattern in Arrian's historical development. He began with biographical monographs, culminating in the Alexander history, and then turned to more complex composite works, covering more extended and variegated periods of time.

An absolute date is a more difficult task. Citations in later datable authors give merely a *terminus ante quem,* and it is rare that we can be sure that Arrian is in fact cited directly. The supposed satire in Lucian's treatise on historiography (c. 165) is not only anonymous; its association with actual passages of Arrian's history of Alexander is very tenuous and depends upon free use of the imagination.[12] It is hardly a basic dating criterion. Similarly Appian's use of the Alexander history in his *Syriaca* and Book II of the Civil Wars,[13] even if it is proved, gives no more than the most general indication of date (before 161-3). The relative chronology of Arrian's own work is more helpful. There seem to be echoes of his work on Alexander in the **Parthica,** and, since that work concluded with Trajan's Parthian Wars of 114-17,[14] there is every reason to assume that it was published before the victories of Lucius Verus in 165/6. The Alexander history appeared some considerable time before, with the **Bithyniaca** published in the interval, and we must surely go back at least to the middle years of Pius' reign. More significant, however, is the **Order of Battle against the Alani,** the literary report of Arrian's engagement with the Alani while he was governor of Cappadocia. I have tried to prove that in this opuscule Arrian cast himself in the role of Alexander, and borrowed from his description of Alexander's defeat of the Saca nomads in 329.[15] In any case he uses Macedonian terminology for the Roman army of the 130s A.D. describing legions as phalanxes, his infantry headquarter corps as ςωματοφονλακες.[16] Arrian was certainly familiar with Macedonian military institutions and, in all probability, when he wrote the ***Order of Battle*** he had the Alexander history already behind him. Now it is probable that the ***Order of Battle*** was composed in the aftermath of the engagement with the Alani, as a literary adjunct to his official report, some time around A.D. 135. If the Alexander history preceded it, it cannot be dated after Hadrian's reign and almost certainly pre-dated the legateship of Cappadocia.

The dating criteria which can be extracted from the body of the Alexander history are largely arguments from silence. It is a feature of Arrian's work that he draws upon his own experience to illustrate or expand material from his sources. The information is provided even where it is not directly relevant, as in the case of the contemporary location of the statue-group of the tyrannicides.[17] Yet there are instances where Arrian ignores experiences which are attested elsewhere in his literary *corpus*. Ignorance of Cappadocia is particularly striking. His discussion of the location of Prometheus' cave is a case in point. Arrian is aware that the subject is controversial and he explicitly criticizes his sources (***Anab.*** v 3. 1-4). Yet he had been shown Prometheus' purported place of punishment in the Caucasus during his inspection tour of 131/2 (***Periplus*** 11. 5). His experience was materially relevant, but he fails to adduce it. There is also ignorance of the most elementary facts of Armenian geography, which is astounding in a man who had worked and fought in Cappadocia and Lesser Armenia.[18] There is a prima facie case for dating the work before the legateship. But Arrian seems ignorant of Rome also. His interest in the tyrannicide-group at Athens contrasts with his lack of interest in Lysippus' statue-group, which had been removed from Dium in 148 B.C. and transferred to Rome, where it became a noted monument, stationed outside the *porticus Octaviae* in the southern part of the Campus Martius (i 16. 4 n.). Arrian speaks as though the group were still at Dium—a startling oversight, if he had already held office in Rome. Even the location of the tyrannicide-group at Athens may be imprecise; Arrian seems to have placed it at the wrong point along the Sacred Way (cf. iii 16. 8 n.). If so, it is an error hard to credit in a permanent resident of Athens; it presumably derives from Arrian's faulty recollection of the procession of the initiates, which he will have participated in as a visitor to Athens. Finally the digression on Heracles in the West also contains inaccuracies and a surprising lack of knowledge about the antiquities of Gades, which must be familiar to him after his proconsulate in Baetica (cf. ii 16. 4 n.). The argument from error and omission is cumulative, and it suggests a date of composition before 125, when Arrian was in his thirties.

There is one strongly autobiographical passage, where Arrian proudly conceals his name and career, claiming that his works are paramount. In the context he claims that he has no need to write his name, nor his homeland, nor the offices he has held εν τη εμαυτον. The reference to offices can only denote offices held in Arrian's homeland, Bithynia (cf. i 12. 5 n.); certainly not Rome, for there is no instance of Greek authors of the second century AD describing Rome as the πατρις of a citizen of eastern extraction. Italy was merely a land of temporary domicile.[19] Now the omission of his senatorial *cursus* is important in the context. The point Arrian is making is most emphatic; his offices are of secondary importance to his literary themes. It would be most strange if he chose to omit the prestigious senatorial offices and concentrated on the much less distinguished local magistracies. The evidence as a whole suggests a relatively early date of composition. Arrian was a mature writer with a successful record of publication, but not primarily in the area of historical studies. What his earlier works were can only be guessed at, but there is a tradition of specifically philosophical works, portions of which have survived in the meteorological fragments preserved in Stobaeus. Arrian was specifically commemorated as a philosopher in his own lifetime (above p. 5) and it is perfectly possible that his notes on the ***Diatribae*** of Epictetus were followed by a series of philosophical dialogues and treatises. Arrian's interest in history, as he claims in his Alexander work and the later ***Cynegeticus,*** dates back to his extreme youth,[20] but he did not embark on historiography until he was a relatively experienced writer.

Arrian's work on Alexander was the third of a series of biographical monographs. Nothing is known of the earlier works on Dion and Timoleon, but both belonged to a background of philosophical history and *exempla* which might have rendered them congenial subjects. But there is more. All three individuals had been the subjects of biographies by Plutarch, and the biographies are so interconnected by cross-references that Mewaldt argued that the three pairs were issued simultaneously.[21] The theory is plausible in itself and has found some acceptance.[22] If so, it is hardly coincidental that Arrian produced three successive monographs on figures whose biographies appeared conjointly in Plutarch's publications; and, since Plutarch's biographies (at least the three in question) appeared before 116,[23] there is every possibility that they provided Arrian with his direct inspiration. It was an inspiration to emulate. Arrian harps constantly on the deficiencies of previous histories of Alexander, and, if he knew Plutarch's work, he included it in the general censure. The same will have applied to the lives of Dion and Timoleon. The appearance of Plutarch's work could have given Arrian the stimulus to improve upon it.[24] There is no direct influence in the work on Alexander. Arrian worked from different sources, used a different arrangement of material, and is never, it seems, influenced by Plutarch's style or phraseology. Plutarch seems merely to have supplied the theme and the element of literary rivalry. Arrian himself gave a similar stimulus to later writers. A certain Amyntianus dedicated a work on Alexander to Marcus Aurelius and he promised to give an account worthy of Alexander's deeds, language that irresistibly recalls Arrian's own boasts (cf. i 12. 4, vii 30. 3).

The classic of one generation became something for the next to surpass.

Arrian's interest in the figure of Alexander certainly went deeper than mere literary emulation of his predecessors. The programmatic statement at i 12. 5 suggests that his involvement with his literary themes goes back at least to his youth. What is more, his generation had witnessed an increasing emphasis on the positive aspects of Alexander's figure. As is well known, the complex and contradictory personality of the Macedonian king made him an obvious source of examples for every type of moral theory; he was a bottle into which could be poured any and every vintage.[25] The character of the king was debated in the philosophical schools of the Hellenistic period, but the tradition is too sparse and ambiguous for any clear picture to emerge. There are modern theories of canonical and hostile Stoic or Peripatetic views of Alexander, but those views are largely constructs from scattered passages in later writers, predominantly Cicero, passages which are rarely, if ever, securely derived from a Hellenistic original.[26] It is safer to say that the actions of Alexander could be separated into widely different compartments, each compartment serving as an illustration for theories upon monarchy. Certainly there was a tradition of hostile criticism with its keynote Alexander's lack of moderation. Cicero could castigate Alexander for pride, cruelty, and lack of moderation and rate his *humanitas* far lower than that of his father, a view which Seneca continued more emphatically and consistently, regarding Alexander at best as the victim of his passions and at worst as the type of the cruel tyrant.[27] Certain episodes lent themselves to this stock portrait: the murder of Cleitus and execution of Callisthenes, the excess of grief at the death of Hephaestion, the adoption of Persian dress and court protocol, and the claims to be son of Ammon.[28] The result was a caricature, but a caricature designed to serve as an *exemplum*. There were of course other portraits. Alexander the world-conqueror was the symbol which inspired his military imitators—Pompey, Augustus, or Trajan; and in the hands of a Dio Chrysostom Alexander could be portrayed as a defender and emulator of the ideal Homeric kingship.[29] It was largely the literary form which determined the treatment for good or ill, and the same incident might be used in very different ways. The adoption of Persian dress could be used either as a sign of pride or immoderation or as an example of conscious stimulation of unity of feeling within the empire.[30] Dio Chrysostom varied his treatment of Alexander in his orations on kingship. In the fourth Alexander appears as a youthful interlocutor of Diogenes, basically sound but in need of Cynic deflation. In the second he is the defender and advocate of Homeric virtues, while in the first oration, a general treatise on the ideal king, he appears briefly as a type of the immoderate ruler (*Orat.* 1. 1). Even in Seneca, whose treatment of Alexander is almost uniformly hostile, there is an inconsistent anecdote: his trust in Philip the Acarnanian is praised as a classic example of moderation (*De Ira* ii 23. 2 f.).

The literary treatment of Alexander must have continued to be multifaceted and contradictory, but the literature which has survived from the late first and early second centuries is largely encomiastic. The young Plutarch produced two rhetorical speeches *On the Fortune or Virtue of Alexander* which are undiluted rhapsodies upon the perfection of the king; their object is rhetoric and there is no streak of dark in the entire picture.[31] Similarly Dio Chrysostom had written an eight-volume treatise on the virtues of Alexander, which was on a much more extended scale than Plutarch's work, but no less encomiastic.[32] It was a work which should have influenced his fellow countryman Arrian, and it may have stimulated him as much as did Plutarch's *Life*. The literary climate was encomiastic and so was the political climate. Trajan's personal interest in Alexander is well attested. He sacrificed to the Macedonian king in the ruins of Babylon and boasted to the senate that in 116 he had advanced further than Alexander.[33] Given such a background Arrian could hope for both official and public approval.

Arrian's emphasis is clear from the outset. It is Alexander's ἔργα, the *res gestae* of the reign, which primarily concern him; they have never been adequately commemorated in prose or verse (i 12. 2-4). Arrian is emphatically declaring that his function is to give a record of action and achievement; and there may be an implicit contrast with Plutarch's declaration at the beginning of his *Life of Alexander,* the statement that the magnitude of Alexander's deeds precludes an exhaustive enumeration of them (*Al.* 1. 1-2). Arrian, on the contrary, claims to give a full history of his hero and he makes it plain from the outset that its aim will be encomiastic. The stress is upon recording fact, and there is relatively little attempt to use the events of Alexander's life as material for moral discussion. Arrian is of course aware of the role of the historian as moral critic (vii 30. 3), and in Isocratean fashion he inveighs against Alexander at the standard points where his behaviour was used for philosophical *exempla*. The clearest example is at iv 7. 4, where Arrian is clearly shocked by the barbaric mutilation of Bessus and digresses to give a sermon on the necessity for moderation. Elsewhere he adverts naïvely on the incongruity of Alexander's revenge motive (iii 18. 12, vi 30. 1). But the criticism of Alexander himself is generally muted. When he discusses the Cleitus affair he strongly condemns Cleitus for his contumacy but pities Alexander for falling victim to anger and drunkenness, and he praises the depth of Alexander's repentance (iv 9. 1-2; cf. vii 29. 1). Similarly he condemns Callisthenes for his intransigence and agrees that Alexander had every reason for his hostility (iv 12. 6 f.). The criticism may be muted in other ways. Arrian condemns various aspects of Alexander's grief for Hephaestion (vii 14. 2-7), but he presents the offensive behaviour as reports from untrustworthy authorities, which he himself discounts. Again, Arrian cites with approval the gymnosophists' criticism of Alexander's lust for conquest (vii 1. 5-6), but he adds that Alexander himself approved the criticism, even though he could not resist his ambitions (vii 2. 1-2); and the passage begins with a rapturous description of Alexander's will to conquer, which tends to nullify the criticism. The positive side of Alexander's achievement is presented without qualification. Whereas he uses the unreliability of the sources to discount criticism, he can be quite sophistical where praise is involved. The story of the reception of Sisygambis might be apocryphal, but Alexander deserves praise for having inspired it (ii 12. 8). The cutting reply to Parmenion is similarly presented as a subsidiary report . . . , but Arrian gives no opinion about its authenticity and praises Alexander for his reasoning and his self-confidence (iii 10. 1-4). The final character study epitomizes the entire tendency of the work (vii 28-30). It begins with an impassioned eulogy, framed in superlatives, and then turns to the various statements of reprobation, which Arrian mitigates firstly by stressing the saving grace of repentance (vii 29. 1-2) and then by suggesting that both his claim to divine filiation and the adoption of Persian dress were ςοφιςματα, stratagems to influence the subject peoples (vii 29. 3-4). Finally he says categorically that Alexander's faults are insignificant in comparison with his achievements, and even implies that the critic of Alexander is himself reprehensible (vii 30. 1).

The bias towards encomium explains much of Arrian's work. It is basically a narrative of achievement, with a favourable verdict built into the texture of the narrative (cf i 17. 12, ii 4. 11). Indeed one of the principal reasons why Arrian preferred Ptolemy and Aristobulus as narrative sources may well have been their very favourable attitude to the king (see below p. 30). It also explains the comparative dearth of moral comment. Arrian's verdict was presupposed, and the main function of his comments was to mitigate the criticisms traditionally levelled at the figure of Alexander. He could therefore devote himself to the composition of a laudatory account of Alexander's *res gestae* and concentrate on the stylistic presentation.

3. ARRIAN'S HISTORICAL METHODS

In the **Praefatio** Arrian supplies information about his use of sources which is almost unique in ancient works of non-contemporary history. That information concerns both his principles of selecting material from his sources and the reasons for his choice of two basic sources for his historical narrative. The principles of selection come first, and it is best to begin the discussion with them. Arrian states that where Ptolemy and Aristobulus give a consistent account he will follow their consensus as wholly true; where they disagree he will adopt the version he considers the more worthy of credence and the more memorable (*praef.* 1). One is therefore tempted to assume that Ptolemy and Aristobulus are considered of equal weight and used alternately. But it is clear that Ptolemy is the more important authority. At vi 2. 4 Arrian explicitly singles him out as his principal source . . . , and it seems that he placed him above Aristobulus in the same way that he places Ptolemy and Aristobulus together above the subsidiary sources (cf. v 7. 1, vii 15. 6). Passages like the account of the Danubian campaign seem extracted *in toto* from Ptolemy with no additional material added from other sources (cf. i 1. 4, i 4. 6 nn.). The narrative core of Arrian's history is generally agreed to be Ptolemy, but it re-

mains controversial to what degree Aristobulus is used as a control source. There exist speculative analyses by Hermann Strasburger and Ernst Kornemann, but they depend on supposed general characteristics of the lost works, extrapolated from the scanty extant fragments.[34] There is rarely any concrete ground for a positive source attribution, and Arrian's text is usually a safer basis for reconstruction than one's impressions of a vanished original source.

Direct citations give some assistance. Like most historians of antiquity Arrian refers to his sources primarily in order to dissociate himself from some particular statement. He may signal a source-conflict by naming his authorities but he also marks out specific statements in the sources which strike him as suspicious by noting the author's name. In the early books it is almost always Ptolemy who is singled out in this way. His figures for the Macedonian casualties at the Lyginus (i 2. 7) and his statement that Perdiccas began the attack on Thebes (i 8. 1) are the only direct citations in Book i and in both cases the detail singled out is an integral part of the context. The surrounding narrative may be attributed to Ptolemy with reasonable confidence. There is no named reference to Aristobulus before Book ii, and, when he is adduced, it is usually to note some aspect of his account which is discrepant from the general tradition.[35] Few passages before the end of Book vi can be attributed to Aristobulus by the method of citation,[36] whereas whole chapters can be singled out for Ptolemy with relative ease. There is a good example in Book v, where Arrian mentions in passing that the Acesines was the only river whose breadth was noted by Ptolemy (v 20. 8); the narrative continues in an unbroken flow with the crossing of the Hydraotes and the siege of Sangala, culminating with an engagement led by Ptolemy himself (v 23. 7-24. 3). The combination of direct citation and autobiographical material led Jacoby to attribute the entire extended passage to Ptolemy (*FGrH* 138 F 35), and he was certainly right to do so.[37] There is some temptation to infer that Arrian followed the procedure Klotz attributed to Livy,[38] namely excerpting Ptolemy's narrative without comment and using Aristobulus as a control source. But Arrian's procedure is certainly more sophisticated. There are passages like the account of the journey to Siwah (iii 3. 3-6) which juxtapose material from Ptolemy and Aristobulus in a way that suggests that material from the two authors was blended in a composite narrative. It clearly made a difference whether an incident was recounted with similar but complementary details or retailed in two different contradictory versions. In the one case Arrian might use the two sources together, selecting material alternately as it appealed to his taste, but in the other he would be tempted to select one version and either suppress the other or note the variants.

Internal inconsistencies also help to isolate the contributions of the two sources. There are variations, and significant variations, in Arrian's use of geographical terms. The people of modern Süstan are termed Drangae or Zarangae, and the alternation of names twice helps to isolate the separate traditions in Arrian.[39] Similarly the Tapurians of the Elburz are referred to either as Τόπειροι or Ταπουροι (cf. iii 8. 4 n.), and the form Τόπειροι occurs in the Persian army list taken from Aristobulus (iii 11. 4). The different forms suggest different authors. There are also variations in the military terminology, which may also be indicators of the different sources. The battle of the Granicus is a particularly useful test case. The cavalry under the command of Amyntas son of Arrhabaeus is termed both πρόδρομοι and σαρισσοφόροι in passages which are widely spaced,[40] and the account of the Macedonian battle line at i 14. 1-3 has the striking incongruity that the phalanx battalions are termed φάλαγγες, not τάξεις, the term used in all the other major battle narratives. There is a strong presupposition to identify the source as Aristobulus, for there is no doubt that Arrian's principal source for the battle narratives was Ptolemy. But variations of this nature are infrequent and, when they occur, there is often no means of deciding which variant should be attributed to which author.

Citations in other authors are also a help. Strabo's excerpt of Ptolemy's account of the Danubian campaign confirms that the parallel passage of Arrian is also derived from Ptolemy (cf. i 4. 6 n.), and his excerpts from Aristobulus' version of events at Pasargadae and in Babylonia supplies excellent material for comparison with Arrian's text.[41] But once again the available material is not extensive and there are dangers. It is only too easy to gloss over significant differences and make an attribution on general similarity of narrative. The digression on the Sardanapallus monument has been attributed to Aristobulus on the basis of the parallel descriptions in Athenaeus and Strabo even though the central feature of the description is markedly different (cf. ii 5. 3 n.). The truth is that Arrian's use of his major sources is intricate and varied, and there is no single reliable method to isolate their relative contributions. In the Commentary I have attempted as far as possible to refer specific passages to specific sources, but it must be admitted that the attributions are largely conjectural.

Arrian's use of his major sources is complex but his technique is far from infallible, as one would expect in the first extended work of his historical corpus. There are a number of errors resulting from inefficient conflation or insufficiently close reading of his sources.[42] On occasion he accepts one tradition but inadvertently combines it with the variant he has rejected. The result can be perplexing. At iii 11. 9 Philippus intrudes as the patronymic of Amyntas son of Andromenes, an error which seems only explicable if Arrian had in mind the name of Philippus, son of Balacrus, who the variant tradition names as the commander of Amyntas' battalion at Gaugamela. Similarly the double placing of Craterus' battalion at the Granicus (i 14. 2-3) is best explained on the assumption that his two sources located it at different points in the battle line and Arrian unwittingly combined the two versions. Occasionally his sources are so divergent that he gives both versions independently without noticing that they refer to the same event. This may occur on a minor scale, as in the case of the double reference to the passage of Drangiana

(iii 27. 4-28. 1), but there are also quite serious doublets where the same event is narrated twice at different points in the narrative. The arrival of Phrataphernes and Stasanor is narrated in the winters of both 329/8 and 328/7 (iv 7. 1, 18. 1), and the march of Craterus' column through central Iran is described at two different stages of the journey down the Indus (vi 15. 5, 17. 3).

The occurrence of doublets and conflations inevitably raises a wider question: how careful was Arrian in his use of primary sources? Since neither Ptolemy nor Aristobulus is an extant author, we have little scope for direct comparison. But there is another work, the **Cynegeticus,** where Arrian was operating with an extant source, the *Cynegeticus* of Xenophon, and the accuracy of his reproduction can there be checked.[43] It is quite clear that Arrian is capable of reproducing his original almost *verbatim* with only the most insignificant variations of wording (**Cyneget.** 30. 2; cf. Xen. 7. 3), and in the Alexander history he includes an extremely faithful quotation of Herodotus (iii 30. 8 = Hdt. iv 57). But at other times Arrian merely gives a free paraphrase.[44] He may distort the sense slightly by variation of expression—and the slightest change in word-order and construction can produce a genuine difference in sense.[45] What is more, he can superimpose ideas of his own upon his original; from his citation of the exordium of the περὶ ιππικης (**Cyneget.** 1. 5) one would assume that Xenophon disclaimed all considerations of rivalry with Simon but wrote for reasons of general utility. Neither motive in fact occurs in the original. There are obvious repercussions for our assessment of Arrian's use of source material in the Alexander history. We can never be sure how true Arrian is to the wording of his original—and in the case of Ptolemy and Aristobulus he may well have allowed himself freer range than when he adapted the classical masters of prose style. More significantly, he may always alter the original meaning of his source by stylistic reinterpretation or superimpose his own views. The Alexander history is of course far longer than the **Cynegeticus** and the use of sources is more complex. Arrian is not commenting upon and adding to a single text, but working up a historical narrative from two major sources and a number of subsidiary works. The scope for variation is accordingly greater as is the mass of source material, and there are a number of instances where Arrian can plausibly be argued to have misunderstood his original. These slips range from relatively venial errors such as the placing of the Macedonian Olympia at Aegae instead of Dium (cf. i 11. 1 n.) to serious distortions of historical fact, such as (I believe) the statement that Alexander visisted Ecbatana in 330 (cf. iii 19. 5 n.). The conclusions must impose caution. We cannot usually separate the contributions of Ptolemy and Aristobulus with any degree of certainty. The traditions may be intertwined and intertwined in a misleading fashion. Nor can we be sure that Arrian even in direct citations reproduces the exact wording of his sources or that his reproduction of the original factual material is unerringly accurate. All this may well seem depressingly negative; but the tendency of modern historians is to regard Arrian as a direct reflecting mirror of Ptolemy and his own characteristics as historian and stylist have been relegated to the background—or, more often, ignored altogether. A corrective is both salutary and urgently needed.

Arrian also refers to his subsidiary sources in the *Praefatio*. There is material from historians other than Ptolemy and Aristobulus which strikes Arrian as memorable and not unconvincing and he has included it under the heading of tales told about Alexander. . . . The motif recurs repeatedly in the body of the narrative,[46] and it is tempting to infer that whenever an incident is introduced by a formula like λεγεται it is a detail extracted from Arrian's subsidiary sources. But, once again, Arrian's usage is more sophisticated than it first appears. The formula has a wider purpose, to mark out a detail which Arrian does not find wholly convincing and does not wish to relate on his own authority. Such detail may well come from his principal sources.[47] At vii 20. 1 he introduces the information about the gods of the Arabians with the sceptical formula λογος δι κατεχει, but it is clear from Strabo (xvi 1. 11 (741)) that the material comes directly from Aristobulus. Again, it seems certain that the narrative of the Danubian campaign is taken directly from Ptolemy, yet it proceeds in *oratio obliqua* for some eight lines before reverting to direct narrative (i 1. 4-5). In this case the introductory λεγεται δο does not express scepticism; it seems to be a conventional introductory formula (cf. i 1. 1 n.). At other times the λεγουσι-formula is used in a general sense to indicate passages of general agreement and to prepare the way for variants. At ii 12. 3 he begins the story of the Persian captives with a general reference to the statements of some Alexander historians; at 12. 5 he identifies those sources as Ptolemy and Aristobulus and adds a *logos* from his subsidiary sources dealing with the confusion between Alexander and Hephaestion. Similarly at vi 24. 1-2 Arrian first refers to the general tradition . . . and then singles out Nearchus' unique story of rivalry with Cyrus and Semiramis. True *logoi* are relatively rare and they illustrate Arrian's methods of selection. The stories of Hephaestion's actions at the tomb of Patroclus pave the way to the *logos* of Alexander envying Achilles his Homer, which in turn leads naturally to Arrian's famous piece of self-advertisement (i 12. 1 with notes); the *logoi* are chosen to lead naturally to the justification for the history.[48] Again, the *logos* at ii 12. 6-8 is explicitly introduced to illustrate the virtues of Alexander and the story of Parmenion's advice to launch a night attack leads to an appreciation of Alexander's generalship (iii 10. 2-4). Other stories are included for pure sensationalism, like the Bacchic procession through Carmania, which Arrian is at pains to deny—in true Herodotean manner.[49]

Arrian's procedure is, as always, flexible. In the *Praefatio* he says merely that he will present material from his subsidiary sources as *legomena*. That does not exclude his using *oratio obliqua* to present material from his principal sources. Indeed there is every reason to believe that Arrian followed Herodotus in referring to his source material, as he followed him generally in matters of style. Now Herodotus has a rich variety of constructions in *oratio obliqua*,

designed to indicate reservations towards his subject matter.[50] His method centres on constructions with the infinitive; and infinitives may intrude in subordinate clauses, follow sequentially in a clause introduced by οτι/ως, or even do duty for indicatives in narrative passages. Arrian uses the narrative intrusive infinitive, notably in the account of the happenings at Nysa, and the usage appears Herodotean.[51] His deployment of intrusive infinitives is nowhere near as sophisticated as Herodotus', and often accusative and infinitive constructions alternate with οτι-clauses, with no motive apparent other than desire for variation.[52] But the alternation is occasionally more complex. At iii 26. 1 he begins his account of the Philotas affair with the joint account of Ptolemy and Aristobulus, presented as a οτι-construction. But when he presents Ptolemy's story alone the construction switches to accusative and infinitive—with a single vivid clause in the indicative underlining the ground of Philotas' conviction (iii 26. 3). At iii 27. 1 the joint account resumes, beginning with accusative and infinitive, but changing to *oratio recta* after the first clause. The most elaborate instance is the extended passage beginning with the Cleitus affair (iv 8 ff.). Arrian first states that he will narrate the episode out of chronological sequence and plunges immediately into an extended construction in *oratio obliqua*, with a single outburst into direct speech introduced for dramatic effect (iv 8. 8). Now it is clear that the story is not taken in its entirety from Arrian's subsidiary sources, for he cites an apologetic variant from Aristobulus (iv 8. 9). The *oratio obliqua* occurs because Arrian wishes to distance himself from his material; it was a stock negative *exemplum* hardly congenial to his encomiastic purposes (above p. 14), and Arrian is reluctant to retail it as fact on his own authority. Accordingly he switches to an infinitival construction and distances himself from the narrative. We cannot therefore infer from the construction that the episode was not recounted by Ptolemy; it is perfectly possible that he gave the story much as Arrian tells it.[53]

Arrian's citations of his source material are complex and varied, but there is no reason to doubt what the *Praefatio* implies, that the majority of his narrative was built upon the works of Ptolemy and Aristobulus. It remains to see how justifiable that choice was. Such an investigation properly requires detailed examination of all the extant fragments together with detailed study of the general characteristics of Arrian's narrative. That clearly lies outside the scope of an Introduction, and in what follows I can only distil the arguments expounded at greater length in the body of the Commentary.

Ptolemy's history is almost entirely known from citations in Arrian.[54] Arrian provides all but four of the fragments which Jacoby accepts as genuine; and of those four one is a piece of comic romance preserved by Synesius,[55] another is at best a second-hand citation by Stephanus of Byzantium, the third a passing reference to his figure for Alexander's invasion army, cited by Plutarch in a list of variants, and finally Strabo's brief reference to the story of the Celtic embassy.[56] It is a reasonable assumption that Ptolemy's work was ignored and largely unknown in antiquity. It was Arrian's service to exhume his work, and modern scholars have been unstinting in their gratitude. But, even so, the outlines of Ptolemy's work remain vague. We have no idea of the number of books or how the material was distributed. More seriously we have no information when Ptolemy wrote, except for Arrian's statement that the history appeared after Alexander's death. It is commonly believed that the work fell after 305/4, when Ptolemy assumed the title of king, but we cannot assume that Arrian's reference to him as a king is taken from Ptolemy's preface or is even strictly accurate for the time of writing. Arrian may have regarded him in timeless terms, the kingship a permanent characteristic. Nor can it seriously be alleged that Ptolemy had no time for serious writing until he abdicated in favour of his son in 285;[57] such an argument would make it *a priori* impossible for, say, Caesar to have written his *Commentarii* or Augustus his *Autobiography*. It would help if it could be proved that Ptolemy knew Aristobulus' work, for that author wrote after 301 in his old age (see below), but the hypothesis is at best unprovable. The key passage (v 14. 5) is not evidence for direct criticism of Aristobulus. Arrian merely places Aristobulus and Ptolemy side by side and (for once) explains his preference for Ptolemy; the formula αλλα . . . γαρ marks the return to Ptolemy's statement about the forces with Porus' son, after an anticipatory argument justifying the figures (and rejecting those of Aristobulus) on grounds of general probability.[58] Nothing seriously suggests a late date of composition, but there are certain positive and negative aspects of the work which suggest a period close to Alexander's death. The strongly autobiographical character of many of the attested fragments indicates a period when it was in Ptolemy's interest to emphasize his closeness to Alexander, and the well-known polemical bias against Perdiccas and his associates suggests a period not too far removed from Perdiccas' death during the invasion of Egypt in 321.[59]

The characteristics of Ptolemy's narrative are equally hard to grasp. His traditional reputation rests largely on the assumption that he preserved in his narrative archival material derived from the *Ephemerides* or *Court Journal* of Alexander himself. This is a timehallowed theory[60] but impossible to sustain. The *Ephemerides* as such are cited in the sources six times in all—once for Alexander's hunting habits, three times for his excessive drinking, and most extensively in the reports of Alexander's last illness, which Arrian and Plutarch take from the *Ephemerides* with varied and sometimes inconsistent details.[61] It seems most probable that Arrian's extract is in fact taken indirectly from Ptolemy and/or Aristobulus. He concludes his digest of the *Ephemerides* with the observation that Ptolemy and Aristobulus took their narratives no further (. . . vii 26. 3). The alternative interpretation, that their account was not substantially different from that of the *Ephemerides,* is most unlikely.[62] Arrian is delaying mention of his principal sources (as at ii 12. 3-6); he begins with a reference to the account of the *Ephemerides* (vii 25. 1), repeats it at vii 26. 1, and then ends his report of the official version with a re-

mark that Ptolemy and Aristobulus take the story no further. He can then add the vulgate story of the bequest 'to the strongest' (vii 26. 3). The account provided by the *Ephemerides* was recounted by Ptolemy (or Aristobulus) as the prime source for Alexander's death; but the document is not cited outside the context of the last illness and it is a reasonable assumption that the information it provided did not extend beyond the last months of Alexander's life.[63] But even if the *Ephemerides* were, as some have supposed, a complete day-to-day record of the official business of the reign, the fact that Plutarch refers to them proves that they were not unique to Ptolemy and the variants in his account suggest that they existed in several recensions—and were not necessarily an unimpeachable source of fact.

Nor is the so-called archival material unique to Ptolemy's narrative, as reproduced by Arrian. The 'vulgate' tradition of Diodorus and Curtius Rufus provides details of appointments, promotions, arrival of reinforcements, and reception of embassies which often corroborate the material in Arrian and not infrequently supplement it.[64] There seems to be a central core of information about the public business of Alexander's court which was available to all sources. It may stem originally from some document like a court journal, but there is no positive evidence for the supposition and equally nothing to controvert the suggestion that the 'archival' material was transmitted first by contemporary historians like Callisthenes, recording events from their own experience, and then used by subsequent writers as basic fact. Ptolemy's only advantage over the other sources is that he was closer to Alexander and presumably had more direct experience of events at court, but it remains conjectural whether his memories and files were any more accurate or detailed than Callisthenes' contemporary account of events as they happened. Perhaps the most seductive (and certainly the most fallacious) argument is based on the 'diary-like' style of Arrian, which is thought to reflect—at two removes—the dry, factual record of the original court journal. But, if anything is certain about Arrian as a writer, it is that his style is his own, and, if his narrative has lucid clarity and an apparent diary-style, that is a carefully contrived result and contrived by Arrian himself. There are passages in Thucydides which are as dry and detailed as any in Arrian, but nobody would claim (I hope) that the style is based on some official chronicle of the war which he copied out.[65]

There is another hypothesis that Ptolemy wrote 'to set the record straight', that is, to correct the extravagant fantasies of earlier writers by presenting a sober record of fact. Once more there are some serious difficulties. In the first place there is no evidence that Ptolemy indulged in polemics against other writers. The two passages of Arrian which might be adduced under this heading are the criticism of Aristobulus' figure for the forces with Porus' son (v 14. 3-6) and the criticism of the vulgate tradition that Ptolemy saved Alexander's life at the Malli town (vi 11. 7-8), but in both cases the criticism is Arrian's own; he places Ptolemy's statement against the other tradition and uses it in an argument from probability. If, then, Ptolemy's critique of Alexander historians was not explicit, it was implicit, leaving his readers to draw their own conclusions from his unvarnished record of fact.[66] Such a hypothesis is difficult either to support or subvert. If Ptolemy's narrative differs from the rest of the tradition it is indeed possible to argue that he was attempting to correct it—but it is also possible that the majority tradition is correct and that Ptolemy had motives for altering the record. The question can only be answered by continuous detailed analysis of the tradition such as attempted in the Commentary, and even then the results are ambiguous. There are cases like the treatment of Parmenion (cf. i 13. 2, iii 15. 1 nn.) where Ptolemy does seem to be implicitly rebutting some aspect of the received tradition, but there is not sufficient evidence to single out such implicit criticism as a primary reason for his writing. More often when his version is discrepant there appear to be personal or propagandist motives at work. Nor can it be seriously argued that Ptolemy reacted against the romantic, novel-like aspects of earlier writers. It seems difficult to maintain that he avoided all excursuses on natural history, for the Elder Pliny names him alongside such authors as Onesicritus and Ephippus as an authority on exotic types of trees.[67] His account of Issus included the romantic picture of a ravine choked with enemy dead (cf. ii 11. 8 n.), and it is difficult to accept his story of guidance to Siwah by snakes as anything more than romantic fiction (iii 3. 5 n.).

What, then, can be deduced about the characteristics of Ptolemy's history? In the first place it was strongly autobiographical. Ptolemy laid great emphasis on his services under Alexander and wrote them up in vivid and elaborate detail, particularly in the section dealing with the Indian expedition.[68] What is more, he certainly exaggerated his role, particularly in his earlier appearances; his command at the Persian Gates is apparently distorted in respect of its importance and function (iii 18. 9 n.) and his role in the capture of Bessus is built up into a full-scale repetition of Alexander's pursuit of Darius (iii 30. 5 n.). Such an emphasis is only natural in a survivor of the campaigns (one need only think of Nearchus);[69] and it had an immediate purpose in the period of the Successors, when prestige was enhanced and positions were cemented by reference to services rendered under Alexander.[70] But natural though the emphasis is, it should put us on our guard against the idea that Ptolemy is an unsullied repository of historical fact. There are also occasions where a hostile bias can be demonstrated. Ptolemy's treatment of Perdiccas is particularly vulnerable in this respect. Perdiccas' achievements are omitted (iii 15. 2 n.), particularly his promotion in 324 to the vacant chiliarchy of Hephaestion, and there is a degree of calumny, notably in the allegation that the Macedonian reverse at Thebes was caused by an unauthorized attack on his part (i 8. 1 n.). The same bias can be detected in Ptolemy's treatment of the lieutenants of Perdiccas, particularly Aristonous who is almost totally ignored in Arrian[71] and the younger sons of Andromenes, who are portrayed in a most invidious light (cf. iii 11. 9, 14. 5, 27. 2 nn.). Antigonus' achievements in Phrygia are also omitted,

but in this case there is no detectable malice (cf. i 29. 3 n.). Once again the bias has an immediate explanation in the period after Alexander's death; Ptolemy was suppressing services rendered by his political enemies and suggesting that their role was harmful. But the bias is again an obvious warning against accepting every detail from Ptolemy as the literal truth. The assessment of the rest of the narrative is a more intricate problem, since what we have is an amalgam of Ptolemy and Aristobulus; but that amalgam has certain general characteristics which can be analysed and appreciated. The appreciation must, however, follow consideration of Arrian's use of Aristobulus.[72]

Aristobulus' work appeared relatively late, after the battle of Ipsus in 301 (vii 18. 5); and according to the pseudo-Lucianic *Macrobioi* he stated in his preface that he began writing in his 84th year.[73] He is also described as a citizen of Cassandreia,[74] founded in 316 B.C. on the site of Potidaea, and it seems very probable that he wrote in Macedonia after the death of Cassander (298). Details of his life are very sparse, and we know only that he served with Alexander. In what function is uncertain. The supposition that he was an architect and/or engineer[75] rests on his commission to restore the pillaged tomb of Cyrus (vi 29. 4-11; cf. Strabo xv 3. 7 (730)), but that was largely a cosmetic operation; the only feature requiring anything like engineering skills was the sealing of the door (cf. vi 29. 10). His other commission in India is totally obscure (Strabo xv 1. 19 (693)). All that can be said is that Aristobulus served as an under-officer, close enough to Alexander to receive direct commissions but outside the immediate court entourage.

In antiquity Aristobulus was much better known than Ptolemy. Outside Arrian there are citations in Plutarch, Athenaeus, and Strabo. Strabo in particular seems to have used him as a primary source for his description of India. Even so the content of his work is most imperfectly known. No book-number survives and there is no indication how the narrative was distributed. Various characteristics appear in the surviving fragments, but it is conjectural how prominent they were in the non-extant parts of the work; Aristobulus is cited by name for divergent or sensational details, and it is unsafe to extrapolate from them characteristics of the whole work. There seems an interest in botanical curiosities. Aristobulus described the oaks of Hyrcania (F 19), the asafoetida of the Hindu Kush (iii 28. 5-7 = F 23) and the plants of the Gedrosian desert (vi 22. 4-8 = F 49). Rivers are also prominent in the extant fragments. Aristobulus noted the course of the Oxus (F 20), the phenomenon of the disappearing rivers of Central Asia (F 28), the monsoon floods in the Punjab (F 35), the fauna of the Nile (F 39), and the drainage system of Mesopotamia (vii 21; cf. F 56). Such preoccupations were not unique to Aristobulus; Onesicritus gave a detailed (and inaccurate) description of the banyan trees of India[76] and the monsoons are a common feature of Alexander historians. But the citations of Aristobulus' data about natural history come from a variety of sources, both from Strabo and Arrian; and botanical and geographical excursuses are likely to have been a recurrent feature of his work. We can go further. Some of Aristobulus' information is given by other sources in different contexts. Aristobulus mentioned asa-foetida as a natural curiosity of the Hindu Kush, but an-other source, excerpted by Strabo (xv 2. 10 (725)), in-cludes a description of the plant in an account of the hardships suffered during the transit of the passes (cf. iii 28. 6 n.). Similarly the description of the monsoon rains is presented as a catalogue of natural phenomena with no at-tempt to trace their effect (which was devastating) upon the Macedonian troops.[77] Again Aristobulus' description of the flora of the Gedrosian desert is a bland survey of curi-osities—even the giant thorns being portrayed as more comic than dangerous (vi 22. 7-8), whereas in Strabo's parallel account (probably from Nearchus) the desert plants are described as poisonous, contributing to the fearful hardships suffered during the desert journey.[78] There seems a tendency to shy away from descriptions of hardships and to concentrate on the curiosities of the march. That ten-dency was not unique to Aristobulus. One of Hermann Strasburger's great services has been to call attention to a series of reports of hardships ('Strapazenberichte') which are totally ignored by Arrian,[79] and the most obvious and plausible explanation is that they were omitted by both his primary sources. Stories of suffering and casualties on the march did not apparently suit the taste either of Ptolemy or of Aristobulus.

An associated tendency of Aristobulus' work is his incli-nation towards apologetic, to exculpate or mitigate aspects of Alexander's behaviour which were susceptible to criti-cism. This tendency has often been noted, perhaps too em-phatically;[80] we know too little of what happened at Gor-dium or at the Cydnus to be sure that his variant stories are apologetic in nature (cf. ii 3. 7, 4. 7 nn.). But some things are indisputable. Aristobulus unequivocally made Cleitus alone responsible for his murder (iv 8. 9) and de-nied that Callisthenes was ever executed (iv 14. 3). He also reacted against the contemporary allegations that Al-exander drank himself to death and maintained that the king did not drink excessively but kept late hours for con-versation's sake.[81] This apologetic tendency was noted in antiquity. Some of the references are of late and weak au-thority and may be discarded,[82] but it is hard to see how Lucian's story of Alexander's rebuke to Aristobulus (de hist. conscr. 12=T 4) could have taken shape unless his history was commonly thought to be a highly flattering one.[83] Clearly Arrian was aware of the reputation of his source but he thought the bias justified. Because Aristobu-lus wrote after Alexander's death he wrote what he did without fear or favour; if, then, his work has a bias to-wards eulogy, it is a bias justified by the facts. The argu-ment may be naïve and simplistic, but it does not disprove the view that Aristobulus' work was adulatory and apolo-getic. Again Ptolemy shared the tendency, to some degree at least. The tendency to exculpate is sharply illustrated by their common account of the trial of Philotas, which both treat as a clear-cut case of treason and even, it seems, ad-duce admissions extracted by torture as historical fact (iii

26. 1 n.); and they state unequivocally that Callisthenes was involved in the Pages' conspiracy (iv 14. 1).

There was clearly much material common to both Ptolemy and Aristobulus. Their joint account is sometimes referred to, as are joint omissions (cf. ii 12. 6, iii 26. 1, iv 14. 1, v 7. 1, vi 11. 5, vi 28. 2, vii 13. 3). Occasionally variants are cited which are so trivial that they suggest that the two ac-counts were otherwise unanimous (cf. iv 3. 5, v 20. 2). It has even been argued that Aristobulus drew upon Ptolemy,[84] but it is hard to see why he should have followed the same general lines and chosen the most trivial points for dis-agreement. It seems more probable that both authors fol-lowed a common tradition which diverged in detail. Arrian may even have chosen to report only those variants which he was unable to decide between and in other cases made his own selection without noting the variants. The dis-agreements may well have been wider and more radical than the text of Arrian implies. But even so, the narrative of Arrian has certain general characteristics which were certainly common to both sources. Arrian's narrative can be placed alongside the so-called vulgate tradition, the tra-dition common to Diodorus xvii, Curtius Rufus, and Jus-tin, which in all probability derives from the first-generation historian Cleitarchus;[85] and from critical comparison of the two traditions various traits emerge.

Firstly, it is undeniable that there is a strong encomiastic trait in Arrian, a trait that depicts both the king and his army as invincible and virtually superhuman. The cam-paign narrative reads as an unbroken catalogue of success, and contrasts sharply with the more chequered record of the vulgate. There is little or no record of setback and losses—and what defeats occur tend to be attributed to others. The reverse outside Thebes is laid at the door of Perdiccas (i 8. 1) and the disaster in Sogdiana attributed to the incompetence of other officers (iv 5. 7-6. 2). Alexander is uniformly successful, except in the first assault at Tyre (ii 22. 6-7 with notes) and the first advance on the Persian Gates (iii 18. 3 n.), and these comparative failures are given the briefest coverage, with no suggestion that casu-alties were widely sustained. In the large-scale siege de-scriptions, particularly those of Halicarnassus, Tyre, and Gaza, the selection of episodes is overwhelmingly biased towards reports of Macedonian successes, particularly those led and inspired by Alexander himself,[86] and there are significant instances where reverses sustained are trans-formed into victories for the attackers.[87] They are not merely victories but effortless victories. There is an addi-tional tendency. Alexander is made to accept every chal-lenge offered him. At the Granicus he accepts at once the challenge of the Persian defence along the river bank (i 13. 2 n.) and at Issus the whole tenor of the narrative is that Alexander moved at high speed to attack the Persians on their chosen position at Sochi; there is no hint of the ri-val tradition that Alexander deliberately forced the Per-sians into his chosen ground in the coastal defiles (ii 6. 1 n.). Natural obstacles also presented challenges to be over-come, and the motif is epitomized in the comment about the 'impregnable' position of Gaza (. . . ii 26. 3; cf. iv 21.

3, 28. 3-4). There are also exaggerations of the natural difficulties, notably the absurd figures for the height of the walls of Tyre (ii 21. 4 n.) and the description of the citadel at Celaenae (i 29. 1 n.). Alexander conquers against all obstacles and conquers effortlessly with the favour of the gods. That tendency is perhaps best illustrated by the brief narrative of the passage of Mt. Climax (i 26. 2 n.), but the presentation of Arrian as the favourite of heaven is recurrent and consistent (cf. i 17. 6, ii 3. 8, 6. 6, 7. 3, 14. 7, iii 3. 4). The king fought with the gods on his side and was naturally invincible, as the casualty figures strikingly demonstrate. Nowhere else in the extant sources is so much carnage wrought upon the enemy at such trivial cost as in Arrian's narrative (cf. i 16. 4, ii 11. 8, 24. 4, iii 15. 6 with notes).

The encomiastic aspect of Arrian's narrative is patent, as are the distortions it produced, and it seems that much of the tradition was already provided by Alexander's first historian, Callisthenes of Olynthus.[88] Callisthenes' work was notoriously eulogistic and flattering to the king, and some of the known features of his work recur in Arrian. His description of the phenomena encountered in the journey to Siwah was repeated more or less completely by Ptolemy and Aristobulus (iii 3. 4 n.). More significantly Arrian's account of Issus not only follows the main lines of Callisthenes' narrative (in so far as it can be restored from Polybius' critique) but reproduces and even improves upon the encomiastic distortions which it contained (ii 10. 1, 11. 8nn.). The motif of divine favour is also likely to derive from Callisthenes, who depicted the Pamphylian sea offering *proskynesis* to Alexander (F 31; cf. i 26. 2n.), portrayed him as son of Zeus (F 14 a), and reported his prayer at Gaugamela—which was duly answered (F 36=Plut. *Al.* 33. 1-2). The eulogistic bias is entirely explicable, since Callisthenes was broadcasting the king's achievements from court, and the emphasis upon invincibility had an obvious propaganda value at a time when there was serious unrest in the Greek world. Nor is it surprising that Ptolemy used and improved upon the distortions in Callisthenes. He was the custodian of the mummified body of Alexander, and his regime dependent upon Alexander's right of conquest. Not only that. Survivors of Alexander's campaigns were well represented in his armies, and he had some interest in stressing that they had been invincible.[89] Aristobulus' bias is less easy to explain. It is usually argued that he was influenced by genuine friendship and admiration for Alexander, and that may be true. If so, his experiences under Cassander may have had some effect. Cassander was bitterly hostile to the memory of Alexander, annihilated his family, and ceremoniously restored Thebes.[90] The negative aspects of Alexander's reign will have been stressed in the propaganda of his reign, and Aristobulus may well have been left with an obsession to correct the emphasis at all costs. If he were looking back at Cassander, his tendency to apologetic is perfectly explicable.

It would be wrong to claim that the tradition of Ptolemy and Aristobulus is worthless. As one would expect in the writings of first-generation historians with access to contemporary materials, there is a great deal of uncontroversial factual material—details of itineraries, embassies, appointments, and the like. But the information is not unique; the vulgate tradition often confirms and sometimes corrects. Above all there is a constant bias to encomium which needs the constant corrective of the vulgate tradition. It therefore needs to be asked why Arrian chose precisely these two sources and did not adduce other contemporary historians, notably Cleitarchus who also participated in the campaigns (it seems) and wrote after the king's death. His work is usually stigmatized as rhetorical and romantic, and Arrian has received many compliments for his preference for the supposedly sober and factual narrative of Ptolemy. But it is now clear that Ptolemy's narrative was as romantic as any other—and Arrian was far from averse to romance.[91] His account of Parthian pre-history is both sensational and romantic and contrasts most unfavourably with the alternative tradition preserved in Strabo and Justin/Trogus.[92] It is more likely to have been the over-all view of Alexander which attracted him. His task was to commemorate Alexander's *res gestae,* and the material provided by Ptolemy and Aristobulus, a virtually unbroken catalogue of success, was particularly adapted to his purposes.

Arrian did occasionally use sources other than Ptolemy and Aristobulus in his narrative portions, particularly in the sections on India which overlap his work in the *Indica.* His geographical material seems taken from Eratosthenes (cf. v 3. 1-4, v 5. 1, 6. 2), but significantly Eratosthenes seems not to have been used before Book v, for Arrian uses the new material to correct an earlier inaccuracy (cf. iii 28. 5n.). Nearchus is also used from the beginning of Book vi both as a narrative source and a control source.[93] An appreciation of his material is out of place here and must be reserved for the second volume, but once again it must be stressed that there is no trace of Nearchus before the Indus journey. Arrian only used the portions of his work which were relevant for the *Indica.*

The sources for the *logoi* are wholly uncertain. Arrian only once mentions specific authors; the supposed Roman embassy is reported according to the accounts of Aristus and Asclepiades (vii 15. 5). Both authors are obscure, Asclepiades totally so. Aristus was known to Strabo as a historian much later than Aristobulus and Onesicritus, resident in Salamis in Cyprus.[94] A handful of citations survive, none of any significance—apart from the report of the Roman embassy, and nothing can be inferred of the content of his work—or even of its date, beyond the fact that it appeared before Strabo and long after Alexander's reign. The possibilities remain open. Arrian could have selected the accounts of Aristus and Asclepiades because they gave the fullest version of the Romans' reception. Alternatively he could have used a later work which singled out Aristus and Asclepiades as sources. The latter is probably the case. There is little trace of intensive investigation of sources elsewhere in Arrian, and he seems to imply, wrongly, that only Aristus and Asclepiades referred to a

Roman embassy; had he researched the matter closely he must have found the reports in Cleitarchus which were known to Pliny.[95] Similarly the subsidiary report of the introduction of *proskynesis* runs exactly parallel in substance and language to Plutarch's narrative excerpted from Chares of Mitylene.[96] Plutarch is not used directly, for Arrian has a little additional detail;[97] but the similarity of wording is so close that we must accept that the two authors either used Chares direct or drew on precisely the same intermediary source. There is no other valid evidence. The rest of the *logoi* have little in common. Some are frequently attested throughout the tradition (e.g. ii 12. 6f., iii 10. 1), while others reflect a variant or even unique version (e.g. i 12. 1, iii 2. 1). The variety of sources at Arrian's disposal was far greater than the number known to us, whether extant or attested, and he could logically have used any of them in any combination. All that we can say with any confidence is that *logoi* are not likely to have been taken from a large number of direct sources.

Arrian's qualities as a historian can be called into question both in his selection of sources and in his use of them. It may also be doubted how extensive his historical knowledge was. He had none of the encyclopaedic erudition of Polybius, and when he leaves the narrow confines of Alexander and his chosen sources the knowledge displayed is at best superficial. The excursus on the fall of Thebes is based almost entirely on the two great classics, Thucydides and Xenophon; and Arrian's presentation is neither wholly accurate nor wholly lucid (cf. i 9. 3nn.). Whatever originally stood in his sources, the double attribution of the Peace of Antalcidas to the reign of 'Darius' shows scant appreciation of the facts of fourth century history (cf. ii 1. 4n.). His final character-study of Darius shows total ignorance of his reign, where its history did not impinge on the actions of Alexander (iii 22. 2n.), and refers casually to the battle 'at Arbela', despite the fact that he devotes an excursus to correcting that very error (iii 8. 7, 22. 4nn.). The combination of carelessness and lack of erudition is startling in a writer who has been regularly praised for his reliability and who himself claimed to be composing a definitive factual history (cf. vi 11. 2, 8).

4. ARRIAN'S STYLE AND POPULARITY

Arrian prides himself on his style above all, and he claims that the success of his history of Alexander will win him primacy in the sphere of Greek letters (i 12. 5nn.; cf. *praef.* 3). Half a millennium later his claims were fully justified by Photius, who ended his précis of the *History of the Successors* with a glowing appreciation of his style (cod. 92: 72[b]40ff. = Roos, *Arriani Scripta Minora* lxvif.): 'this man is inferior to none of the best writers of history'. He is praised for his conciseness and avoidance of newly coined vocabulary. Photius admires his skilful use of figures to vary his narrative and states explicitly that it is in the composition of the narrative that his innovations lie. The result of his writing, he thinks, is a happy mixture of stylistic virtuosity and conventional vocabulary, which produces an impression of lucid clarity. That is fair com-

ment. Anyone who examines an extensive passage of Arrian's narrative, such as the review of the armies before Gaugamela (iii 11. 3-12. 5), will be immediately struck by the complex variation of word-order, construction, and vocabulary. Even in the most lengthy catalogue the construction is so subtly arranged that it is rare for two consecutive clauses to match each other in language. What in particular impresses Photius is Arrian's use of ellipse; he does not omit periods, rather individual words—and it is stylistically impossible to provide a supplement. Modern historians, more concerned with fact than style, might be less charitable in their reactions to Arrian's ellipses, which can pose baffling problems of interpretation,[98] but Photius' judgement remains a valuable corrective. Arrian was no slavish copier of sources, as modern scholars have tended to suppose, but a very expert and sophisticated stylist in his own right.

Arrian's prose is a very personal and artificial creation. It has been described as Attic, but it is far removed from the academic Atticism of the second century A.D. There is a strong trend towards archaism; Arrian uses compounds in ξυν-, the reflexive pronouns ου and ϛφεις, and the archaic Attic plural-ης.[99] Some usages contravene the strict canons of Attic prose; αιχμαλωτισθεϛαν was a notorious inelegancy (cf. iii 22. 4n.), καιτοι is used with the participle instead of καπερ, and πριίν with the infinitive occurs after a negative main clause.[100] Significantly the last two usages, like many other departures from strict Attic, have parallels in Herodotus, and it cannot be too strongly emphasized that Arrian's chief stylistic debt is to Herodotus.[101] Most of the particular characteristics of the Ionian historian are reproduced in Arrian's style. There is the same superfluity of expression,[102] the same use of epanalepsis,[103] the same use of resumptive clauses at the end of key stages of the narrative.[104] There is the same looseness of construction, which Demetrius characterized as λεξις ειρομενη; clauses are strung together by connecting particles with little or no binding from subordinate clauses[105] and anacoloutha occur frequently, the construction often changing in mid sentence.[106] Equally striking is a wide range of vocabulary shared between the two authors and often not attested elsewhere in Greek prose usage.[107] One can speak of Arrian's style as literary reconstruction of Herodotus. The borrowing is of course explicit in the *Indica* where Arrian resurrects the Ionic dialect but it is implicit throughout most of his other work; the Ionicisms are eliminated but the style is distinctively Herodotean.

Arrian has debts to other authors, not least Thucydides. There are repeated echoes of Thucydides, particularly in speeches or historical excursuses. The comment on the fall of Thebes is strongly Thucydidean in phrasing; not surprisingly, since most of the examples chosen are based on his work (i 9. 1-3 with notes). But Thucydides can appear less intrusively; the debate at Miletus (i 18. 6-9) contains reflections of the speeches before the battle in the Great Harbour,[108] and Alexander's speech before Gaugamela is virtually a piece of free composition in Thucydidean style (cf. iii 9. 6n.). Key phrases from Thucydides also occur at appropriate points in Arrian's work (cf. i 12. 2 and vi 11. 8 with Thuc. i 97. 2). But Thucydides is a more occasional influence than Herodotus, who is an all-pervasive influence on style and vocabulary, and, perhaps surprisingly, Xenophon is even less obtrusive. Admittedly the opening of the narrative proper seems modelled upon the *Cyropaedia* (cf. i 1. 1 n.), but the stylistic debt to Xenophon is not pronounced. His characteristic use of καὶ with a demonstrative pronoun referring to the antecedent clause occurs frequently enough in Arrian[109] as do his temporal conjunctions . . . and the repetition of a subordinate verb as the main verb of the following clause.[110] There is also some imitation of Xenophon's vocabulary,[111] but at a much lower level than his imitation of Herodotus.

These remarks might give the impression that Arrian's style is a pastiche. That would be unfortunate. Arrian had an artificial style, it is true, and the elements which constitute it can be isolated, but his work displays none of the flagrant parody such as is found in the passages of the 'histories' of Verus' Parthian Wars which are stigmatized by Lucian.[112] On the contrary, his style is unitary, and, even though it is dominated by Herodotus, the effect is one of re-creation not crude borrowing. It is, if anything, a tribute to him that modern historians have so often been misled by the seeming simplicity of the style, and treated his carefully constructed narrative as an excerpt at two removes from Alexander's archives. Arrian might not enjoy the pre-eminence in Greek prose writing that he and Photius claim for his work, but he is without a doubt a most accomplished and sophisticated stylist and he should be treated as such.

Arrian regarded his work as definitive (vi 11. 2), and he seems to have been regarded as a model historian in antiquity. Lucian refers to him as a precedent for his attempt to write up the career of Alexander of Abonuteichos:[113] even Arrian, a leading Roman and a life-long devotee of culture, wrote a history of the brigand Tillorobus. Nothing is known of this work, but, since the brigand in question ranged over Mysia and Mt. Ida, there is a fair probability that it formed part of the *Bithyniaca* or was issued as a supplementary opuscule like the *Indica*.[114] Lucian's formal justification lies in the rank and literary prestige of Arrian, but there are wider implications. He begins his work with a contrast between Alexander of Abonuteichos and Alexander son of Philip; the one was as pre-eminent in vice as the other in virtue. The reference to Alexander no doubt evoked the name of Arrian, and, Lucian implies, if the leading historian of that paragon of virtue could stoop to the biography of a brigand, there was every justification for his description of the career of the prophet of Abonuteichos. Lucian's remark in its context is ample evidence of Arrian's prestige immediately after his lifetime, as is the fact that Appian drew directly upon him for material on Alexander and the mysterious Amyntianus parodied his claims to literary supremacy.[115] So far the evidence deals with the reign of Marcus Aurelius and its immediate sequel. But Arrian's reputation remained high in the third century. His fellow countryman, Claudius Cassius Dio

Cocceianus,[116] wrote a life of 'Arrian the philosopher', commemorated his achievements in Cappadocia, and used his *Parthica* as the primary source for Trajan's Parthian Wars.[117] That emphasis was to be expected in a native of Bithynia, but Arrian's prestige stood high elsewhere, notably in his adopted city, Athens. About the middle of the third century the Athenian historian P. Herennius Dexippus wrote a history of events after Alexander's death. Photius gives a summary of his version of the Babylon settlement, which follows very closely his summary of Arrian and adds the note that the rest of the work likewise agreed largely with Arrian.[118] Dexippus clearly used his *History of the Successors* as a primary source for his own work; it must have been the definitive treatment of the subject.

In the fourth century the influence of Arrian is less explicit but it is none the less detectable. Themistius writing in 384 was well acquainted with the facts of Arrian's career and adduces him as a celebrated example of a philosopher active in public life.[119] More importantly there exists from the time of Constantius II (340) an anonymous tract named the *Itinerarium Alexandri*.[120] It was composed at the beginning of Constantius' Persian expedition and purports to give the *itinerarium* of two earlier conquerors, Alexander and Trajan. The portion relating to Trajan has been lost, and what remains concerns Alexander alone. It is a brief and scrappy history, carelessly written and, despite the author's protestations, very rhetorically presented. But it is clear that the bulk of it (chs. 16-109) is extracted almost wholly from the first four books of Arrian's history of Alexander (thereafter the *Itinerarium* reverts to the tradition of the Alexander Romance). The selection of material is capricious and sporadic but there is no doubt that Arrian was used, however carelessly, as a direct source (cf. *Itin.* 18 with i 11. 3-5; *Itin.* 42 with ii 20. 1-2; *Itin.* 48 with iii 1. 1-5). Indeed there are peculiar additions which suggest that the text used was different from that of our archetype (see the notes to ii 14. 3, iii 2. 1). But, whatever minor divergences occur, the main fact is clear that the *Itinerarium* is a derivative of Arrian, and the author makes it clear that he has followed the sources whose reputation traditionally stood highest.[121] It seems unavoidable that the reputation of Arrian and his Alexander history was undiminished in the fourth century.

Arrian remained a classic in the Byzantine period.[122] Stephanus drew on his historical works, particularly the *Bithyniaca* and the *Parthica,* but also to a lesser degree the Alexander history. In the mid ninth century Photius read the Alexander history, the *Bithyniaca,* the *Parthica,* and the *History of the Successors,* and, as we have seen, placed Arrian in the first rank of historians. Arrian's works were a mine for the compilers of florilegia and commentaries. The 'Suda' refers repeatedly to all the historical works (with the exception of the *Bithyniaca*), and the *Parthica* is largely reconstructed from the fragments so provided. The same liberal use of Arrian persists as late as Eustathius in the latter part of the twelfth century AD; Eustathius drew upon the *Bithyniaca* and to a lesser extent the Alexander history in his commentaries on the *Iliad* and

Odyssey and Dionysius Periegetes. However harshly we may judge Arrian's talents as a historian, his works were undoubtedly used and admired as classics for a millennium after his death. . . .

Notes

1. Phot. *Bibl.* cod. 58: 17ᵃ24; cod. 91: 67ᵇ23; cod. 93: 73ᵇ12. See also Eustath. *ad Dion. Per.* 907, 976; *Anecd. Bekkeri* i p. 129. 27; Schol. *ad* Procl. *Comm. in Timaeum* (i 469 Diehl). . . .

2. Arr. v 6. 8; vi 16. 5. Cf. Phot. cod. 91: 68ᵇ1; Steph. Byz. s.v. Μασσακα.

3. i 12. 3, ii 7. 8, ii 8. 11 (see my notes ad locc.), vii 13. 4. Herodotus is far more to the forefront of his work.

4. See the excellent discussion by P. A. Stadter, *GRBS* xvii (1976) 157-67. In the Alexander history the echoes of phraseology are confined to Herodotus (cf. iii 30. 8 with Hdt. iv 57).

5. Cf. Roos, *Arriani Scripta Minora* xii; Stadter, *GRBS* viii (1967) 157.

6. The *locus classicus* for the late dating is E. Schwartz, *RE* ii 1230-6. See also G. Wirth, *Historia* xiii (1964) 209-45; *Studii Clasice* xvi (1974) 188-209, esp. 199f.; E. Bowie, *Past and Present* xlvi (1970) 24-7. For the early date see F. Reuss, *Rh. Mus.* liv (1899) 446-65; A. B. Bosworth, *CQ* xxii (1972) 163-85, and 'Arrian and Rome', section iv.

7. i. 12. 2-5 (see the notes ad loc.); cf. *praef.* 3, vi 11. 2; vii 30. 3.

8. Phot. *Bibl.* cod. 93: 73ᵃ32ff. = *Bithyniaca* F 1. For the interpretation see Bosworth, *CQ* xxii (1972) 178-80 (*contra* Wirth, *Studii Clasice* xvi (1974) 199 n. 128).

9. . . .

10. *Parthica* F 60-3 (Roos) = vi 3. 3. The alternative suggestion (Wirth, *Philologus* cvii (1963) 298), that Arrian excerpted both passages from Nearchus, gives too little credit for stylistic originality.

11. *Parthica* F 19 = vii 28. 1-3.

12. For the supposed echoes see C. E. Gleye, *Philologus* liii (1894) 442-8; Wirth, *Historia* xiii (1964) 232-45.

13. App. *Syr.* 56. 285-91 = vii 22. 5; App. *BC* ii 152. 639f. = vii 18. 1-4; *BC* ii 153. 642-44 = vii 16. 5-17. 2; 21. 1-22. 1. Cf. Bosworth, *CQ* xxii (1972) 176-8.

14. *Parthica* F 1. 2-3 (Roos). The seventeenth (and last) book apparently dealt with the siege of Hatra in 117 (F 17).

15. Bosworth, *HSCP* lxxxi (1977) 247-55. The most convenient and accurate text of the *Order of Battle* is in Roos, *Arriani Scripta Minora*, pp. 177-85. For the parallels with Alexander's engagement see Bosworth, op. cit. 252.

16. *Ectaxis* 5-6; 15 (phalanxes); 22. . . . Cf. Bosworth 248-51.

17. Cf. iii 16. 8 with note.

18. At vii 16. 3 he refers to majority opinion for the simple fact that the river Araxes flows into the Caspian (contrast Strabo xi 16. 3 (527)), and there is no hint of autopsy in his reference to the domicile of the Amazons along the Thermodon (vii 13. 4-6; cf. *Periplus* 15. 3).

19. Dio F 1. 3; cf. F. Millar, *Cassius Dio* 10.

20. . . . i 12. 5; *Cyneget.* 1. 4. The *Cynegeticus* speaks only of interest in σοφια, but the term was general enough to include history, and some regarded history as its most important component (cf. Dio xxxviii 28. 1).

21. J. Mewaldt, *Hermes* xlii (1907) 564-78. *Dion* 58. 10 refers to the *Timoleon*, whereas *Timoleon* 13. 10 and 33. 4 refer to the *Dion. Brutus* 9. 9 refers to the *Caesar*, whereas *Caesar* 62. 8 and 68. 7 refers to the *Brutus.*

22. Mewaldt's thesis was attacked extensively by C. Stolz, *Zur relativen Chronologie der Parallelenbiographien Plutarchs* (Lund 1929), but he failed to shake the arguments for the interrelation of the *Dion* and *Timoleon* and the *Caesar* and *Brutus.* Cf. P. A. Stadter, *Plutarch's Historical Methods* 32 n. 1; C. P. Jones, *JRS* lvi (1966) 66 f.; J. R. Hamilton, *Plut. Al.* xxxv ff.

23. Cf. C. P. Jones, *JRS* lvi (1966) 69; Hamilton, *Plut. Al.* xxxvii.

24. It need not have been an immediate stimulus. Literary rivalry with Plutarch persisted throughout the second century. Appian, *BC* ii 149-54. 619 ff, supplies a comparison between Caesar and Alexander, which Plutarch had omitted; and Amyntianus also wrote parallel lives of figures omitted by Plutarch (Phot. *Bibl.* cod. 131 = *FGrH* 150).

25. The metaphor of A. Heuss, *Antike und Abendland* iv (1954) 102, developed by E. Badian in *Alexandre le Grand: image et réalité* 280 ff. (with respect to modern interpretations).

26. The theory of Peripatetic hostility to Alexander is based on interpretation of Theophrastus' lost work, *Callisthenes* (cf. Schwartz *RE* iv 1899; Tarn ii 319), and its supposed derivatives in later literature. But nothing is known of the content or economy of the *Callisthenes,* and the other passages cited cannot be referred to specific Peripatetic sources. Cf. Badian, *CQ* viii (1958) 153 ff.; E. Mensching, *Historia* xii (1963) 274 ff.; Bosworth, *Historia* xix (1970) 407 f. The Stoic portrait was a construct of J. Stroux, *Philologus* lxxxviii (1933) 222-40, and its foundations have been recently undermined by J. R. Fears, *Philologus* cxviii (1974) 113-30. See further P. A. Brunt, *Athenaeum* lv (1977) 30-48.

27. Cic. *de Off.* i 26. 90; *ad Att.* xiii 28. 3; Sen. *de Ben.* i 13. 2-3, ii 16. 1-2, v 6. 1, vii 2. 5-6 (cf. Lucan x 20 ff.); on Seneca see Heuss (above n. 25) 88 f.

28. For a typical exposition see Livy ix 18. 3-5.

29. Dio Chrys. *Orat.* 2; for discussion see Heuss 92 f.

30. Cf. Livy ix 18. 3-4; Curt. vi 6. 4; Justin xii 3. 8 f. (negative); Plut. *Al.* 45. 1; *de Al. f.* i 8, 330 A (positive). Arrian seems to espouse both views: iv 7. 4 f., vii 29. 4.

31. See the analysis by Hamilton, *Plut. Al.* xxiii-xxxiii.

32. 'Suda' *s.v.* Διων ο Πασικρατους = *FGrH* 153 F 6.

33. Dio lxviii 29. 1, 30. 1. Cf. W. Weber, *Untersuchungen zur Geschichte des Kaisers Hadrianus* (Leipzig 1907), 8 ff.; F. A. Lepper, *Trajan's Parthian War* (Oxford 1948), 193 ff.; G. Wirth, in *Alexandre le Grand: image et réalité* 197 ff.

34. H. Strasburger, *Ptolemaios und Alexander* (Leipzig 1934); E. Kornemann, *Die Alexandergeschichte des Königs Ptolemaios I. von Ägypten* (Leipzig 1935). Of the two Strasburger's scheme is the more flexible, and he begins with an analysis of Arrian as a historian (8 ff.), but the explicit 'Ausgangspunkt' is appreciation of the extant fragments of Ptolemy (16 ff.), and much depends on subjective presuppositions of the contents of the lost original (e.g. 'Spuren seines Stils finden sich nicht': 40). Kornemann's work is far more schematic and operates on the assumption that Arrian had no style of his own and largely copies Ptolemy. For appreciations see Strasburger's review, *Gnomon* xiii (1937) 483-92; Pearson, *LHA* 195 f.; Wirth, *RE* xxiii 2467 f.

35. e.g. ii 3. 7, 4. 7, iii 30. 5, iv 6. 1-2, 8. 9.

36. From the end of Book vi Aristobulus becomes dominant: cf. vi 22. 4-8, 28. 3-4, 29. 4-11, vii 17. 5-22. 5.

37. Cf. Pearson, *LHA* 202-4; Seibert, *Untersuchungen zur Geschichte Ptolemaios' I.* (Munich 1969), 23-5.

38. A. Klotz, *Livius und seine Vorgänger* (Leipzig/Berlin 1940-1); cf. P. G. Walsh, *Livy* (Cambridge 1963), 138 ff.

39. iii 25. 8, 28. 1, vi 15. 5, 17. 3. See further *CQ* xxvi (1976) 128 f.

40. i 12. 7, 14. 1, 14. 6; see the notes ad locc.

41. Strabo xv 3. 7 (730) = vi 29. 4-11; xvi 1. 11 (741) = vii 20.

42. For a fuller exposition see *CQ* xxvi (1976) 117-39.

43. See the excellent discussion of P. A. Stadter, *GRBS* xvii (1976) 159-67.

44. For examples see Stadter 161.

45. Cf. Arr. 2. 2 with Xen. 5. 29; Arr. 31. 2 with Xen. 7. 5.

46. Cf. ii 12. 8, iii 2. 1, vii 15. 6.

47. The classic discussion is by Schwartz, *RE* ii 1240-3; see also Kornemann 21-30 (much oversimplified).

48. Compare the discussion of the Amazons at vii 13. 2-6, where the *logos* is a peg for an antiquarian excursus.

49. See also the discussion of Alexander's reaction to the death of Hephaestion (vii 14. 2-8).

50. See the detailed analysis by Guy L. Cooper, *TAPA* civ (1974) 23-80.

51. v 1. 4 . . . ; 2.2 . . . ; 2.5. . . . In all these cases the intrusive infinitive follows directly after a genuine accusative and infinitive construction, and the closest parallel seems to be Hdt. i 59. 3 (cf. Cooper 72).

52. Cf. iii 2. 3-6, iii 10. 1, etc.

53. Similarly we cannot assume that he omitted the stories of the Gordian Knot and Philip the Acarnanian (ii 3. 8, 4. 7 notes).

54. The fragments are printed by Jacoby, *FGrH* 138. For a survey of literature see Seibert, *Alexander der Grosse* 19-21; note particularly the discussions of Pearson, *LHA* 188-211 (with Badian, *Studies* 256-8) and G. Wirth, *RE* xxiii 2467-84.

55. F 11. Cf. E. Rohde, *Rh. M.* xxxviii (1883) 301-5; Jacoby, *FGrH* ii D. 504; Pearson, *LHA* 189.

56. F 5, 4, 2. Curt. ix 5. 21 refers to Ptolemy's statement that he was not at the Malli town (more fully in Arrian vi 11. 7-8 = F 26a) and Plutarch, *Al.* 46. 2 includes Ptolemy in a list of sources not mentioning the Amazon queen (more fully in Arrian vii 13.2-3 = F 28[b]).

57. Cf. Kornemann 7 f.; Tarn ii 43; Pearson, *LHA* 193.

58. So Hamilton, *PACA* iv (1961) 19 n. 24; Badian, *Studies* 257, against Pearson, *LHA* 172 f., following the traditional view (cf. Schwartz, *RE* ii 916; Kornemann 13-15).

59. So R. M. Errington, *CQ* xix (1969) 241.

60. Adumbrated by Droysen i² 2. 383-6 and established as a canon by Wilcken, *Philologus* liii (1894) 84-126. I have examined the theory briefly in *Alexandre le Grand: image et réalité* 3-6. See also Brunt, *Arrian* xxiv-xxvi.

61. The extant fragments are printed by Jacoby, *FGrH* 117. For analysis of the reports of the illness, with the variants, see Pearson, *Historia* iii (1955) 432-4; cf. also Bosworth, *CQ* xxi (1971) 120 f.

62. For a review of opinions see Pearson, art. cit. 438 n. 37 (add Jacoby, *FGrH* ii D. 507; Strasburger 48 f.). Like Herodotus Arrian uses πορρω in a spatial sense, even when he is metaphorical; so iv 11.5 . . . = 'further than is sufficient' (cf. v 20. 10: . . . = 'not far from the truth'; Strabo xv 1. 35 . . .). 'Far from this' in the sense of 'different from' is unlikely and one would expect some explanatory qualification. Elsewhere Arrian tends to be explicit; cf. iv 14. 1. . . .

63. For hypothetical explanations of these peculiarities see A. E. Samuel, *Historia* xiv (1965) 1-12; Bosworth, *CQ* xxi (1971) 117-23. Pearson 432-9 argues that the so-called document is in fact a Hellenistic forgery.

64. Note the records of arrangements in Babylon and Susa (iii 16. 4 and 9-10 with notes). For a baffling case of disagreement over what must have been officially recorded and widely known see the variant reports of Greek embassies at the Persian court in 333 and 330 (ii 15. 2 n.).

65. There are obvious similarities with Wilamowitz's famous theory that the entire framework of Athenian local history was provided by an official chronicle of the *exegetai*. Cf. Jacoby, *Atthis* (Oxford 1949) *passim*, esp. 5: 'an ingenious thesis . . . which moreover begins with the monstrosity in method that the first Atthidographer must be eliminated from Atthidography'.

66. 'So ist sein Werk Korrektur und Polemik durch Darstellung und Stillschweigen' (Strasburger 55); 'silence was Ptolemy's method of dealing with untrue stories; he never explicitly rejects or argues' (Tarn ii 268).

67. Pliny *NH* i 12-13 (T 2); cf. Badian, *Studies* 256; *CW* lxv (1971) 38.

68. See, in general, the survey by C. B. Welles in *Miscellanea Rostagni* (Turin 1963), 101-16; his arguments are challenged and modified by Seibert, *Untersuchungen zur Geschichte Ptolemaios' I.* 4-26, but the conclusions reached are similar.

69. For the bias of Nearchus see Pearson, *LHA* 131-9, and most recently Badian, *YCS* xxiv (1975) 147-70.

70. See the independent observations by Bosworth and Errington in *Alexandre le Grand: image et réalité* 14-16, 159-62. Cf. also Seibert, *Untersuchungen . . .* 152-6.

71. See the cogent analysis by Errington, *CQ* xix (1969) 235 f.

72. Fragments of Aristobulus may be found in Jacoby, *FGrH* 139, and a survey of modern opinion in Seibert, *Alexander der Grosse* 21-3. See most recently, P. A. Brunt, *CQ* xxiv (1974) 65-9.

73. [Luc.] *Macrob.* 22 = T 3. Brunt, art. cit. 65, suggests that the author may have been deceived by a manuscript corruption; that seems improbable.

74. T 2, F 6, F 47 (Plutarch and Athenaeus).

75. The assumption is well-nigh universal; cf. Jacoby, *FGrH* ii D. 508; Berve no. 121; Pearson, *LHA* 151; Hamilton, *Plut. Al.* liv.

76. *FGrH* 134 F 22; cf. T. S. Brown, *Omesicritus* (Berkeley 1949), 81 ff.; Pearson, *LHA* 100 f.

77. Cf. Diod. 94. 1-3; Strabo xv 1. 27 (697). Nearchus also described the Acesines in flood, and Strabo significantly connects his account with the effects on the Macedonians: they were forced to move camp (xv 1. 18=*FGrH* 133 F 18).

78. Strabo xv 2. 7 (723) with Theophr. *HP* iv 4. 13. The fundamental treatment of the passage is by H. Strasburger, *Hermes* lxxx (1952) 461-5. His attribution of the variant account to Nearchus has not gone unchallenged (cf. Pearson, *LHA* 178 n. 151; Badian *CW* lxv (1971) 50), but it should be clear that the passage on the poison plants does not come from Aristobulus.

79. Strasburger, art. cit. 470-3. The most striking of these instances is the death march to the Oxus (cf. iii 29. 2 n.).

80. Cf. Schwartz, *RE* ii 917 f.; Strasburger 13 f.; Pearson, *LHA* 150, 157 ff. Tarn (ii 37-43, 131 f.) protested in favour of Aristobulus, but his own taste for apologetic was remarkably similar.

81. For the contemporary propaganda see Bosworth, *CQ* xxi (1971) 114-16 and for a possible additional example of Aristobulus' apologetic see below i 9. 1-8 n.

82. Cf. Brunt, *CQ* xxiv (1974) 65 ff., disposing successfully of the evidence from the Byzantine epitome on rhetoric (T 5), which most likely does not refer to the historian Aristobulus.

83. Brunt 68 f. attacks the content of Lucian's story as romantic fabrication. That is no doubt true, but it is significant that the romance was attached explicitly to Aristobulus. It is a counsel of desperation to suggest that it was wrongly fastened to him in later tradition.

84. Cf. Strasburger 15 f., cautiously approved by Badian, *Studies* 257.

85. The existence of a common source has long been known and it is an incontrovertible fact, acknowledged as such since at least the first edition of de Sainte-Croix, published in 1770 (cf. Seibert, *Alexander der Große* 26-8; and for a revealing list of parallels see Schwartz, *RE* iv 1873 f.). The identification of that source as Cleitarchus is still contested (cf. E. N. Borza, *PACA* ii (1968) 25-45; P. Goukowsky, *RÉA* lxxi (1969) 320), but there seems no other viable contender and the identification has been strongly pressed in recent years (cf. Schachermeyr[2] 658-62; J. R. Hamilton in *Greece & the E. Mediterranean* 126-46). The dating of Cleitarchus' work is controversial and depends in part on intricate arguments of borrowings which at times border on the metaphysical. I would accept with great caution the arguments lately adduced which would place his work in the vicinity of 310 B.C.; cf. Schachermeyr, *Alexander in Babylon* 211-24; Badian, *PACA* viii (1965) 1-8; Hamilton, *Historia* x (1961) 448-58.

86. Cf. i 21. 5, ii 4. 4, ii 10. 3, ii 22. 4, 23. 5, iii 14. 3, etc.

87. Cf. i 21. 3, 22. 2, ii 22. 6 with notes ad locc.

88. For the fragments of Callisthenes see Jacoby, *FGrH* 124. The foundation article is still that by Jacoby in *RE* x 1674-1707. See also T. S. Brown, *AJP* lxx (1949) 225-48; Pearson, *LHA* 22-49; Hamilton, *Plut. Al.* liii f.; Seibert, *Alexander der Große* 11 f.

89. This argument is expanded in *Alexandre le Grand: image et réalité* 25-9.

90. Diod. xix 52. 4-5, 53. 2 ff.; cf. Errington, in *Alexander le Grand: image et réalité* 151 f.

91. Cf. v 5. 1: a major heading of the *Indica* is to be ατοπα ξωα.

92. *Parthica* F 1; cf. Strabo xi 9. 2 (515); Justin xli 4. 4-10 with the excellent analysis of J. Wolski, *Berytus* xii (1956/7) 35-52.

93. vi 13. 4, 24. 2, vii 3. 6, 20. 9. Cf. Schwartz, *RE* ii 1239.

94. Strabo xiv 6. 3 (682), xv 3. 8 (730) = *FGrH* 143 T 1, F 1. For a brief description of the fragments see Pearson, *LHA* 254 f.

95. Pliny, *NH* iii 57 = *FGrH* 137 F 31. Cf. Schachermeyr, *Alexander in Babylon* 218 ff.

96. iv 12. 3-5 = Plut. *Al.* 54. 4-6 (Jacoby prints both versions as *FGrH* 125 F 14).

97. He gives the father's name of Demetrius (Pythonax); Plutarch 54. 6 gives his pseudonym Pheidon.

98. Note particularly vii 6. 4-5, where Arrian's extremely elliptical phrasing totally obscures the crucial question how far barbarian cavalry had been drafted into the ranks of the *hetairoi*: cf. P. A. Brunt, *JHS* lxxxiii (1963) 43 f.; E. Badian, *JHS* lxxxv (1965) 161.

99. The archaic form only occurs sporadically in the manuscripts of Arrian, but it appears unambiguously in the second-century papyrus fragment of the *History of the Successors* (*PSI* xii 2. 1284, col. 82. 5; cf. K. Latte, *Kleine Schriften* (Munich 1968), 597).

100. For a convenient list of non-Attic usages see the edition of K. Abicht, 16-18. For the divergent uses of καιτοι and πριν compare Hdt. viii 53. 1, i 165. 3 (cf. Powell, *Lexicon to Herodotus* 317).

101. See particularly the excellent dissertation by H. R. Grundmann, 'Quid in elocutione Arriani Herodoto debeatur', *Berliner Studien* ii (1886) 181-268. This work supplements and largely supersedes earlier dissertations by E. Meyer, *De Arriano Thucydideo* (Rostock 1887) and C. Renz, *Arrianus quatenus Xenophontis imitator sit* (Rostock 1879).

102. Dozens of examples collected by Grundmann 200-2.

103. Cf. ii 10. 4 . . . ; iii 18. 12 . . . See further Grundmann 206 ff.

104. Cf. i 19. 11, 20. 7, 25. 10, iii 12. 1, etc. Further examples Grundmann 211.

105. Good examples at i 1. 1 and ii 11. 5. Full discussion Grundmann 214 ff.

106. Cf. iv 4. 4 with the further examples in Grundmann 230 ff. For a particularly striking use of anacolouthon see the imitation of the Herodotean nominative absolute at i 9. 5 (cf. my note ad loc.). The Herodotean intrusive infinitives (above p. 21) should also be included in this category.

107. Note particularly πόθος λαμβάνει αοτόν (i 3. 5 n.) and ονδεν αχαρι παθεν (i 17. 9 n.), both phrases

which have been claimed for Ptolemy. See also the notes on the Herodotean verb . . . (iii 2. 1-2). For a full and impressive list of such borrowings see Grundmann 248-56.

108. Cf. Thuc. vii 62. 2, 67. 2.

109. i 12. 7, 16. 4-5, 21. 2, etc. Full list of instances in Grundmann 184-6.

110. i 10. 6, 17. 2, etc. See further Grundmann 186.

111. Perhaps most strikingly at ii 10. 3. . . . See further the far from impressive list in Grundmann 191.

112. Cf. Luc. *de hist. conscr.* 15 (Creperius Calpurnianus and Thucydides); 18 (copying from Herodotus in bogus Ionic). See the commentary by H. Homeyer, *Lucian: Wie man Geschichte schreiben soll* (Munich 1965).

113. Luc. *Alexander* 2 = T 24 (Roos). The work was written after the death of Marcus in 180 (cf. *Al.* 48).

114. Tillorobus is only known from the reference in Lucian. There is no way of dating him and his depredations may well have occurred before the Romans annexed Bithynia—the terminal point of Arrian's *Bithyniaca*.

115. See the references above pp. 12.

116. For the full nomenclature see *AÉ* 1971. 430.

117. For the biography see 'Suda' s.v. . . . (T 1) with G. Wirth, *Klio* xli (1963) 221-33; Bosworth, *CQ* xxii (1972) 166; for Arrian in Cappadocia see Dio lxix 15. 1 with Bosworth, *HSCP* lxxxi (1977) 218 ff.; for the use of the *Parthica* see A. G. Roos, *Studia Arrianea* (Leipzig 1912); K. Hartmann, *Philologus* lxxiv (1917) 73-91; Lepper, *Trajan's Parthian War* 1 ff.; Wirth, *Studii Clasice* xvi (1974) 194 ff.

118. Phot. cod. 82: 64ᵃ21 ff. = *FGrH* 100 F 8. For the life and background of Dexippus see F. Millar, *JRS* lix (1969) 12-29.

119. Themistius 34. 8 = T 13. Cf. Bosworth, *HSCP* lxxxi (1977) 229 ff.

120. For general discussion see Kubitschek, *RE* ix 2363-6. The most accessible (though far from satisfactory) text is that following Müller's edition of Ps.-Callisthenes in the appendix to Dübner's Arrian (Didot 1846: pp. 154-67). The edition of D. Volkmann (Programm Schulpforta 1871), which is allegedly a great improvement, has unfortunately not been accessible to me. . . .

121. *Itin.* 2: *nec . . . vilibus usus auctoribus, sed quos fidei amicissimos vetus censura pronunciat.*

122. For documentation see the painstaking indexes of Roos (*Anabasis* xxxvi-xli; *Scripta Minora* 315-20).

Abbreviations and Bibliography of Short Titles

AAA: . . . *Athens Annals of Archaeology*

Abh. Berl. Akad.: Abhandlungen der preußischen Akademie der Wissenschaften, phil.-hist. Abteilung

ABSA: The Annual of the British School of Archaeology at Athens

AE: L'Année épigraphique

AHR: American Historical Review

AJA: American Journal of Archaeology

AJP: American Journal of Philology

Alexandre le Grand: image et réalité: Alexandre le Grand: image et réalité, Entretiens sur l'Antiquité classique xxii (Fondation Hardt, Geneva 1976)

Andreotti: *Il problema politico* R. Andreotti, *Il problema politico di Alessandro Magno* (Parma 1933)

'Αρχ. 'Εφ.: 'Αρχαιολογικη 'Εφημερις

Ath. Mitt.: Mitteilungen des deutschen archäologischen Instituts: athenische Abteilung

AS: Antike Schlachtfelder in Griechenland, ed. J. Kromayer and G. Veith (4 vols.: Berlin 1903-31)

ATL: The Athenian Tribute Lists, by B. D. Merritt, H. T. Wade-Gery, and M. F. McGregor (4 vols.: Cambridge and Princeton 1939-53)

Badian, *Anc. Soc. & Inst.:* E. Badian, 'Alexander & the Greeks of Asia' in *Ancient Societies and Institutions: Studies presented to V. Ehrenberg* (Blackwell, Oxford 1966)

Badian, *Studies:* E. Badian, *Studies in Greek and Roman History* (Oxford 1964)

BCH: Bulletin de Correspondance hellénique

BE: J. and L. Robert, *Bulletin Épigraphique* (published initially in *REG* and reprinted as a series with indexes, Paris 1972-)

Bellinger: A. R. Bellinger, *Essays on the Coinage of Alexander the Great* (Numismatic Studies xi: New York 1963)

Beloch: K. J. Beloch, *Griechische Geschichte* (2nd edn.: 4 vols.: Strassburg-Berlin and Leipzig 1912-27)

Bengtson, *Strategie:* H. Bengtson, *Die Strategie in der hellenistischen Zeit* (Münchener Beiträge, vols. xxvi [1937]; xxxii [1944]; xxxvi [1952])

Berve: H. Berve, *Das Alexanderreich auf prosopographischer Grundlage* (2 vols.: Munich 1926)

BMC Arabia: G. F. Hill, *Catalogue of the Greek Coins of Arabia, Mesopotamia and Persia.* British Museum Catalogue (London 1922)

BMC Caria: B. V. Head, *Catalogue of the Greek Coins of Caria, Cos, Rhodes, etc.,* British Museum Catalogue (London 1896)

BMC Phoenicia: G. F. Hill, *Greek Coins of Phoenicia,* British Museum Catalogue (London 1910)

Briant, *Antigone le Borgne:* P. Briant, *Antigone le Borgne: les débuts de sa carrière et les problèmes de l'assemblée macédonienne* (Paris 1973)

Brunt, *Arrian"* P. A. Brunt, *Arrian* i (Loeb Classical Library: Cambridge and London 1976)

Busolt-Swoboda *GS:* G. Busolt and H. Swoboda, *Griechische Staatskunde* (3rd edn.: Munich 1920-6)

Casson, *Ships and Seamanship:* L. Casson, *Ships and Seamanship in the Ancient World* (Princeton 1971)

CIL: Corpus Inscriptionum Latinarum

CIS: Corpus Inscriptionum Semiticarum

Cook, *Troad:* J. M. Cook, *The Troad: an archaeological and topographical study* (Oxford 1973)

Corinth: Corinth; results of excavations conducted by the American School of Classical Studies at Athens (Cambridge and Princeton 1929-)

C. Phil.: Classical Philology

CQ: Classical Quarterly

CRAI: Comptes rendus de l'Académie des inscriptions et belles-lettres

CW: The Classical World

Delbrück: H. Delbrück, *Geschichte der Kriegskunst im Rahmen der politischen Geschichte* (3rd edn.: Berlin 1920)

Denkschr. Akad. Wien: Denkschriften der Akademie der Wissenschaften in Wien

Droysen: J. G. Droysen, *Geschichte des Hellenismus* (2nd edn.: Gotha 1877-8)

Ehrenberg: *Al. & the Greeks* V. Ehrenberg, *Alexander and the Greeks* (Blackwell, Oxford 1938)

Ellis: *Philip II* J. R. Ellis, *Philip II and Macedonian Imperialism* (London 1976)

FGrH: F. Jacoby, *Die Fragmente der griechischen Historiker* (Berlin and Leiden 1923-)

Fuller: J. F. C. Fuller, *The Generalship of Alexander the Great* (London 1958)

Gomme: *HCT* A. W. Gomme, *A Historical Commentary on Thucydides* (vols. i-: Oxford 1945-)

Grazer Beitr.: Grazer Beiträge: Zeitschrift für die klassische Altertumswissenschaft

GRBS: Greek, Roman and Byzantine Studies

Greece & the E. Mediterranean: Greece and the Eastern Mediterranean in History and Prehistory, Studies Presented to Fritz Schachermeyr, ed. K. H. Kinzl (Berlin 1977)

Grundmann: H. R. Grundmann, *Quid in elocutione Arriani Herodoto debeatur* (Berliner Studien II [1886])

Habicht, *Gottmenschentum*[2]: Chr. Habicht, *Gottmenschentum und griechische Städte* (Zetemata XIV: 2nd edn.: Munich 1970)

Hamilton, *Al.*: J. R. Hamilton, *Alexander the Great* (London 1973)

Hamilton, *Plut. Al.*: J. R. Hamilton, *Plutarch, Alexander: a Commentary* (Oxford 1969)

Hammond, *Epirus*: N. G. L. Hammond, *Epirus: The Geography, the Ancient Remains, the History and the Topography of Epirus and Adjacent Areas* (Oxford 1970)

Hammond, *Macedonia*: N. G. L. Hammond, *A History of Macedonia* i (Oxford 1972)

Head, *HN*[2]: B. V. Head, *Historia Numorum* (2nd edn., Oxford 1911)

HSCP: *Harvard Studies in Classical Philology*

HZ: *Historische Zeitschrift*

IG: *Inscriptiones graecae* (1st edn. Berlin 1873—2nd edn. Berlin 1913-)

IG: *Bulgaria Inscriptiones Graecae in Bulgaria Repertae*, ed. G. Mihailov (4 vols.: Sofia 1958-70)

IGR: *Inscriptiones graecae ad res romanas pertinentes*

ILS: *Inscriptiones latinae selectae*, ed. H. Dessau (Berlin 1892-1916)

Inschr. Magn.: O. Kern, *Die Inschriften von Magnesia am Maender* (Berlin 1900)

Inschr. Priene: F. Hiller von Gaertringen, *Die Inschriften von Priene* (Berlin 1906)

Instinsky: H. U. Instinsky, *Alexander der Groβe am Hellespont* (Godesberg 1949)

Ist. Mitt.: *Mitteilungen des deutschen archäologischen Instituts: Abteilung Istanbul*

Janke: A. Janke, *Auf Alexanders des Groβen Pfaden* (Berlin 1906)

JDAI: *Jahrbuch des deutschen archäologischen Instituts*

JHS: *The Journal of Hellenic Studies*

JKF: *Jahrbuch für kleinasiatische Forschung*

JÖAI: *Jahreshefte des österreichischen archäologischen Instituts*

Jones, *CERP*[2]: A. H. M. Jones, *The Cities of the Eastern Provinces* (2nd edn.: Oxford 1971)

JRAS: *Journal of the Royal Asiatic Society*

JRS: *The Journal of Roman Studies*

Julien: P. Julien, *Zur Verwaltung der Satrapien unter Alexander dem Groβen* (Diss. Leipzig 1914)

Kaerst: J. Kaerst, *Geschichte des Hellenismus* (2 vols.: Leipzig 1927 [vol. i, edn. 3] and 1926 [vol. ii edn. 2])

Kirchner: *PA* J. Kirchner, *Prosopographia Attica*, 2 vols. (Berlin 1901-3)

Kornemann: E. Kornemann, *Die Alexandergeschichte des Königs Ptolemaios I von Aegypten* (Leiptzig 1935)

Kromayer-Veith: J. Kromayer and G. Veith, *Heerwesen und Kriegführung der Griechen und Römer* (Munich 1928)

Lanckoroński: K. Graf Lanckoroński, *Städte Pamphyliens und Pisidiens*, unter Mitwerkung von G. Niemann und E. Petersen (2 vols.: Vienna 1890-9)

Lane Fox: R. Lane Fox, *Alexander the Great* (London 1973)

Larsen: *GFS* J. A. O. Larsen, *Greek Federal States* (Oxford 1968)

Launey, *Recherches*: M. Launey, *Recherches sur les armées hellénistiques* (2 vols.: Paris 1949-50)

Leuze, *Satrapieneinteilung*: O. Leuze, *Die Satrapieneinteilung in Syrien und in Zweistromland von 520-320* (Schriften der Königsberger Gelehrten Gesellschaft: Geisteswiss. Klasse xi [1935])

LSJ[2]: H. G. Liddell, R. Scott, and H. S. Jones, *A Greek-English Lexicon* (rev. ed. Oxford 1968)

Magie, *RRAM*: D. Magie, *Roman Rule in Asia Minor to the end of the Third Century after Christ* (Princeton 1950)

Marsden: E. W. Marsden, *The Campaign of Gaugamela* (Liverpool 1964)

Mederer: E. Mederer, *Die Alexanderlegenden bei den ältesten Historikern* (Stuttgart 1936)

Meiggs/Lewis: R. Meiggs and D. Lewis, *A Selection of Greek Historical Inscriptions to the end of the Fifth Century B.C.* (Oxford 1969)

Meyer, *Forschungen*: E. Meyer, *Forschungen zur alten Geschichte* (2 vols.: Halle 1892-9)

M. Helv.: *Museum Helveticum*

Milet: *Milet: Ergebnisse der Ausgrabungen und Untersuchungen seit dem Jahre 1899* (Berlin 1906-)

Miscellanea Rostagni: *Miscellanea di studi alessandrini in memoria di Augusto Rostagni* (Turin 1963)

Moretti: L. Moretti, *Iscrizioni storiche ellenistiche* (Florence 1967-)

Müller, *GGM*: C. Müller, *Geographi graeci minores* (2 vols.: Paris 1855-61)

NC: *Numismatic Chronicle*

OGIS: *Orientis graeci inscriptiones selectae*, ed. W. Dittenberger (2 vols., Leipzig 1903-5)

PACA: *Proceedings of the African Philological Association*

PCPS: Proceedings of the Cambridge Philological Society

PdP: La parola del passato

Pearson, *LHA:* L. Pearson, *The Lost Histories of Alexander the Great* (Philological Monographs XX: Am. Phil. Ass. 1960)

PIR²: Prosopographia imperii romani, saec. I, II, III, 2nd edn., ed. E. Groag, A. Stein, L. Petersen (Berlin and Leipzig 1933-)

P. Oxy.: Oxyrhynchus Papyri, ed. B. P. Grenfell and A. S. Hunt (London 1898-)

PSI: Papiri greci e latini (Pubblicazioni della Società Italiana per la ricerca dei papiri greci e latini in Egitto)

P. Tebt.: Tebtunis Papyri, ed. B. P. Grenfell, A. S. Hunt, J. G. Smyly, E. J. Goodspeed (3 vols.: London-New York-California 1902-38)

RE: Realencyclopädie der classischen Altertumswissenschaft, ed. Pauly, Wissowa, Kroll (Stuttgart 1893-)

REA: Revue des études anciennes

REG: Revue des études grecques

RFIC: Rivista di filologia e di istruzione classica

Rh. Mus.: Rheinisches Museum für Philologie

Robert, *Études anatoliennes:* L. Robert, *Études anatoliennes: recherches sur les inscriptions grecques de l'Asie Mineure* (Paris 1937)

Robert, *Hellenica:* L. Robert, *Hellenica, recueil d'épigraphie, de numismatique et d'antiquités grecques* (vols. i-: Paris 1940-)

Rostovtzeff, *SEHHW:* M. Rostovtzeff, *The Social and Economic History of the Hellenistic World* (3 vols.: Oxford 1941)

RSI: Rivista storica italiana

SB Berlin: Sitzungsberichte der preußischen Akademie der Wissenschaften, phil.-hist. Klasse

SB Heidelberg: Sitzungsberichte der Heidelberger Akademie der Wissenschaften, phil.-hist. Klasse

SB Munich: Sitzungsberichte der bayerischen Akademie der Wissenschaften, phil.-hist. Abteilung

Schachermeyr²: F. Schachermeyr, *Alexander der Große: das Problem seiner Persönlichkeit und seines Wirkens* (Sitzungsberichte der österreichischen Akademie der Wissenschaften, phil.-hist. Klasse, cclxxxv [1973])

Schachermeyr, *Alexander in Babylon* F. Schachermeyr, *Alexander in Babylon und die Reichsordnung nach seinem Tode* (Sitzungsberichte der österreichischen Akademie der Wissenschaften, phil.-hist. Klasse, cclxviii. [1970])

Schaefer: A. Schaefer, *Demosthenes und seine Zeit* (2nd edn.: Leipzig 1886)

Schwyzer: W. Schwyzer, *Dialectorum graecarum exempla epigraphica potiora* (Leipzig 1923)

SEG: Supplementum Epigraphicum Graecum

Seibert, *Alexander der Große:* J. Seibert, *Alexander der Große* (Erträge der Forschung X: Darmstadt 1972)

SGDI: Sammlung griechischer Dialekt-Inschriften, ed. H. Collitz and F. Bechtel (4 vols.: Göttingen 1884-1905)

SIG³: Sylloge inscriptionum graecarum, ed. W. Dittenberger (3rd edn.: Leipzig 1915-24)

Staatsverträge: Die Staatsverträge des Altertums, ii: *Die Verträge der griechischrömischen Welt von 700 bis 338 v. Chr.,* ed. H. Bengtson (Munich 1962), iii: *Die Verträge der griechisch-römischen Welt von 338 bis 200 v. Chr.* ed. H. H. Schmitt (Munich 1969)

Strasburger: H. Strasburger, *Ptolemaios und Alexander* (Leipzig 1934)

TAM: Tituli Asiae Minoris

TAPA: Transactions of the American Philological Association

Tarn: W. W. Tarn, *Alexander the Great* (2 vols.: Cambridge 1948)

Tod: M. N. Tod, *A Selection of Greek Historical Inscriptions,* vol. ii (Oxford 1948)

von Schwartz: F. von Schwartz, *Alexanders des Großen Feldzüge in Turkestan* (Munich 1893: 2nd ed. 1906)

Walbank, *Philip V:* F. W. Walbank, *Philip V of Macedon* (Cambridge 1940)

Walbank, *Polybius:* F. W. Walbank, *A Historical Commentary on Polybius* (vols. i-iii: Oxford 1957-79)

Welles, *Diodorus: Diodorus of Sicily,* vol. viii, ed. C. B. Welles (Loeb Classical Library: Cambridge and London 1963)

Welles, *RC:* C. B. Welles, *Royal Correspondence of the Hellenistic Age* (Yale 1934)

Wilcken: U. Wilcken, *Alexander the Great,* with Introduction and Notes by E. N. Borza (New York 1967)

Wilcken, *Berliner Akademieschriften:* U. Wilcken, *Berliner Akademieschriften zur alten Geschichte und Papyruskunde (1883-1942)* (2 vols.: Leipzig 1970)

Wilcken, *Grundzüge:* L. Mitteis and U. Wilcken, *Grundzüge und Chrestomathie der Papyruskunde* (4 vols.: Leipzig-Berlin 1912)

Wilcken, *UPZ:* U. Wilcken, *Urkunden der Ptolemäerzeit* (2 vols.: Berlin 1922-37)

Wüst, *Philipp II:* F. R. Wüst, *Philipp II von Makedonien und Griechenland in den Jahren 346 bis 338* (Munich 1938)

YCS: Yale Classical Studies

ZPE: Zeitschrift für Papyrologie und Epigraphik

N.B. References to the ancient sources follow the standard conventions. Where Diodorus Siculus is cited by chapter and section alone the reference is to Book xvii.

Philip A. Stadter (essay date 1980)

SOURCE: "The Lost Histories," in *Arrian of Nicomedia,* University of North Carolina Press, 1980, pp. 133-63.

[*In the essay below, Stadter surveys several of Arrian's no-longer-extant historical works, maintaining that these compositions demonstrate his wide range of interests and reveal him as a writer virtually unrivalled among his contemporaries.*]

The *Anabasis of Alexander* and the *Indike* reveal the clarity and competence of Arrian as a writer and historian, his straightforward narrative, and his judicious selection of sources. But for a true evaluation of the breadth of his interests, the variety of his works, and his preeminence among the writers of his generation we must examine also those works no longer preserved, but which were equally well known in antiquity and the Middle Ages, and whose quantity and excellence established his reputation. The *Bithyniaca* in eight books, the *Parthica* in seventeen books, the *Events after Alexander* in ten books, the *Alanike, Dion, Timoleon, Tillorobus*—an impressive mass of history on the most disparate subjects, treated with an extraordinary virtuosity according to a variety of historical genres. Three works are longer than the *Anabasis* and reveal a perspective quite different from that apparent in an Alexander history. The *Parthica* in seventeen books considers the relations between Rome and Parthia, a question of vital interest to the empire in Arrian's time, giving special consideration to the most recent Roman expedition under Trajan. Here there is no glorification of the Greek past, but a historical exploration of significant contemporary events. The *Bithyniaca* falls at the other extreme. Its eight books were devoted to the glorification of Arrian's native land, with emphasis on its mythical and legendary past. Somewhere between excursuses on myth and contemporary wars we may place the ten books of the *Events after Alexander,* a dense account of the first years after Alexander's death, when Perdiccas strove for control of the empire against the other generals. Such variety defies classification. Felix Jacoby's decision in his *Fragmente der griechischen Historiker* to place Arrian's fragments among the historians of the period of the Successors in II B is justifiable, but arbitrary, since they could as well be grouped with the writers of *Bithyniaca* or *Parthica* in III C. The scope of Arrian's interests requires that each work be considered separately before a synthetic view can be attempted.

These three major histories, the *Parthica,* the *Events after Alexander,* and the *Bithyniaca,* although now lost, survived well into the Byzantine period, and enough is preserved in summaries, quotations, and paraphrases by Byzantine scholars (some 180 fragments) to allow us a glimpse of their individual qualities.[1] The ninth-century scholar Photius, later patriarch of Constantinople, summarized each of these histories, along with the *Anabasis,* in his *Library.*[2] Later, as part of the vast collection of historical excerpts made under various headings for the emperor Constantine Porphyrogenitus, selections were made from the *Anabasis,* the *Parthica,* and the *Events after Alexander.*[3] Although most of this collection has also been lost, it was used in the great literary-historical encyclopedia, the *Suda,* which thus preserves numerous bits and pieces, usually frustratingly short and difficult to locate in the context of a work or even to ascribe with certainty to a given work.[4] Later still, Eustathius, before being appointed bishop of Thessalonica in 1174/75, cited the *Bithyniaca* frequently and often at length in his commentaries on Homer and on the geographer Dionysius Periegetes.[5] These three sources provide us the bulk of our information, though a few citations come from other writers.[6]

For both the *Parthica* and the *Events after Alexander,* Photius' summaries are our best guide. Nevertheless, they must be used with caution. Photius composed his summaries from notes, often made long before, and his memory; normally he did not have the works themselves before him. In summarizing, he occasionally adds his own comments or modifies the original order. He feels free to add material from marginal notes or scholia.[7] The summary of the *Anabasis* provides a useful sample of his work: the coverage is uneven (e.g., *Anab.* 1-3.22 in fifteen lines, 6.29-7.30 in forty lines); there are many omissions (such as the campaigns in Europe, the sieges of Tyre and Gaza, the Egyptian campaign); the mutilation of Bessus is described out of order, immediately after his capture; he states that the Indus was bridged by boats, although Arrian expressly says he does not know how it was bridged; and he refers to the "seven wounds" of Alexander, although Arrian never gives the number of his wounds. Thus, although generally accurate in reporting facts, these summaries are not always so useful in preserving the author's presentation or interpretation.

In all cases, the particular interest of these Byzantine writers is responsible for the type of fragments which are preserved, and this fact must be considered when attempting to construct a picture of these works.

THE PARTHICA

The *Parthica,* as the longest work and one with strong personal relevance to Arrian, may be considered first. The Parthians had begun as one tribe among many in the vast empire of the Seleucids, who inherited what they could of Alexander's eastern conquests.[8] Profiting from Seleucid weakness, the Parthians established their independence and gradually extended their sovereignty westward from their homeland in northeastern Iran and southern Turkmenistan. By the time of Sulla, when the Romans first encountered them, they ruled a vast territory extending from Mesopotamia to the frontiers of India. How much the triumvir Crassus knew of the Parthians when he set out in 54 B.C. to conquer them is not known, but the annihilation of his army at Carrhae (Harran) in the following year made an indelible impression on the Roman consciousness.[9] From an obscure kingdom on the frontiers of the empire Parthia became for the Romans a menacing power, challenging Rome's rule of the world. From that date until the eventual collapse of the Parthian kingdom in the third century A.D., Parthia was Rome's leading opponent in the East, and a major thrust of Roman foreign policy was the establishment of suitable relations between the two countries, whether by war or negotiation. Major expeditions were launched by Mark Antony, Nero, and Trajan, the peaks in the continuous tension between Rome and Parthia.

When Arrian decided to write on Parthia, therefore, various possibilities were open to him.[10] He could write a historical ethnography of Parthia and the Parthians, designed to acquaint Romans more exactly with their opponents. According to the canons of this well-established genre, he would describe the geography and climate of the country, give a general account of the people, their origins, traditions, customs, religion, and diet, and then narrate the most interesting facts concerning their kings and wars. The type is best represented by Herodotus' book on Egypt but was followed with variations by Herodotus in other digressions and by many famous writers, such as Ctesias in his *Persica,* Manetho in his *Egyptiaca,* and Berosus in his *Babylonica* (*FGrHist* 688, 609, 680). Arrian followed a compressed version of this scheme in the ***Indike,*** 1-17. Such apparently were the *Parthica* of Apollodorus of Artemita and Seleucus of Emesa (*FGrHist* 779 and 780).[11] Or he could have written a monograph on one of the Seleucid or Roman campaigns against Parthia, a detailed treatment of a single military venture, such as that of Crassus or Corbulo. The works of Julius Polyaenus and Q. Dellius on the campaigns of Ventidius and Mark Antony (*FGrHist* 196 and 197) seem to follow this pattern. Again there is a long tradition of such works (collected by Jacoby in *FGrHist* II B), including not only the historians of Alexander but writers on the Italian campaign of Pyrrhus of Epirus, the Hannibalic War, or, closer to Arrian, the swarm of writers on the Parthian war of Lucius Verus mocked by Lucian (*FGrHist* 203-10) and the rhetor Cornelius Fronto, who promised Verus a history of the war.[12] If, as I believe, Arrian took part in Trajan's expedition, he might have written memoirs of his own experiences, following the good Roman examples of Sulla, Lucullus, Caesar, and Cicero, although considering his youth, he may have been more inclined to write an encomiastic account of Trajan's triumphs.

Arrian's final decision combined certain elements of each of these types of history into a new framework. Photius tells us, and he is supported by our other fragments, that Arrian "in this work narrates the wars which the Romans and Parthians fought" (P1 = F30). Arrian attempted to put the Roman-Parthian conflict into some kind of historical

perspective by tracing its course through the one hundred seventy years from Crassus to Trajan, from the disaster of Carrhae to the crowning by a Roman emperor of a Roman client-king in Ctesiphon.[13] Arrian's initiative resembles to a degree the attempt of Appian to treat Roman history as a series of external and internal conflicts, named according to Rome's chief opponents, but differs in presenting an exhaustive treatment of a single enduring tension over a period of almost two centuries.[14] Considering the disproportion between the history of the earlier campaigns and the ten books devoted to Trajan, the earlier history of the attempts to deal with the Parthians should probably be regarded as historical background meant to reveal the magnitude of Trajan's task in finally conquering Parthia.[15]

Arrian intended to combine detail with broad scope, and thus created his longest work, in seventeen books. The fragments tell us little about the organization of the material, other than confirming the natural hypothesis that the campaigns were taken in chronological order: Book II for Crassus' expedition of 54 B.C. (P2 = F33), Book IV for Antony's of 36 (P3 = F34), Book VI for Corbulo's in A.D. 53 (P4 = F35). Ten books, over half of the whole, were given over to the campaign of Trajan, 113-17, with which the work ended.[16]

The first book was reserved for an account of the Parthians before their first encounter with Rome in the time of Sulla.[17] Here, if at all, would have been found the usual ethnographical material on religion, customs, and geography, but none of this is preserved. Arrian did trace their origin back to the distant past, when their Scythian ancestors were reported to have migrated from the north into the satrapy of Parthia in the northeast of the Persian empire at the time of the invasion of Asia by Sesostris of Egypt and the return attack of the Scythian king Iandyses. The derivation of the Parthians from a migrant Scythian tribe was common, and is probably correct,[18] but Arrian also places it in the Hellenic framework of the great military campaigns which in legendary times were said to have swept from one continent to another.[19]

The emergence as an independent nation appears in Photius' summary as follows: "[The Parthians] had long before been enslaved by the Macedonians, at the time when the Persians were conquered, but they revolted for the following reason. Arsaces and Tiridates were two brothers, Arsacids, the descendants of Phriapitus the son of Arsaces. When Pherecles,[20] who was appointed satrap of their country by Antiochus Theos [261-246 B.C.], shamefully tried to violate one of the brothers, these Arsacids did not endure the insult but killed him. Then, joining with five other comrades they led their tribe in revolt from the Macedonians and ruled independently" (P1 = F30). The story, as given here by Photius and with minor variations by Syncellus (P1b = F31), is in the Herodotean tradition. Actions are seen as resulting not from the discontents of a people or a ruling class, nor from contrasts in ways of thinking or from interests of power, but from direct personal involvement. The origin of Parthian freedom, like that of Athens and innumerable other cities in Greece, began with the violent erotic impulses of a tyrant. Arrian accepts the Parthians' attempt to legitimize their rule by tracing the Arsacid to an Achaemenid, Arsaces, whose throne name was Artaxerxes II (king 404-358 B.C.).[21] The association of five other men in the conspiracy is a striking parallel to the seven conspirators who put Darius the Great on the throne (Hdt. 3.71ff.). "Thus does Arsaces I conform to the 'legend' of the founder of a dynasty in Iran."[22] Syncellus continues Arrian's narrative of the brothers, telling us that the one brother, Arsaces, ruled for two years, then died and was succeeded by his brother Tiridates, who ruled for thirty-seven years. Although the story has been challenged and Tiridates dismissed as an invention, it may be true.[23]

The fragments of Books II-VI are meager and tell us little. Arrian portrays Antony as "ruined by his love for Cleopatra" (P23) and not interested in negotiating (P28), but sees the victory of Ventidius in 38 B.C. as counterbalancing the defeat of Crassus fifteen years before (P24). Books VIII-XVII, Trajan's Parthian war, furnish the bulk of our fragments.[24] These are sufficient to preserve a dim outline of Arrian's presentation of this expedition, so important in terms of the number of men involved, the area overrun if not subdued, and the risk to the empire. They also raise questions as difficult to resolve as they are interesting. What was Arrian's attitude toward Trajan? What were his sources? When did he write? What is the relation of this work to the *Anabasis of Alexander*? Two points should be noted at once. Arrian devoted ten books to the Roman conqueror as against seven to the Macedonian, although Trajan's campaigns occupied little more than three years, and Alexander's almost twelve. Moreover, although basically favorable to Alexander, Arrian was ready to admit that he had weaknesses. He may have seen weaknesses in Trajan as well.

Despite the negative bias of some modern assessments of the war and its results, there is no doubt that Arrian conceived of it as a success. Photius ends his summary, "The emperor of the Romans, Trajan, humbled the Parthians by force and left them under treaty, having himself crowned a king for them" (P1 = F30). Arrian shared the vision of the expedition that had been heralded on Trajan's coins with the slogans "Parthia capta" and "Rex Parthis datus."[25] He appears to have felt that Trajan's establishment of Parthamaspates as king represented a respectable achievement which was not rendered meaningless by any of the actions subsequently taken by Hadrian to stabilize the eastern frontier after Trajan's unexpected death. Although Arrian does consider the revolts of 116-17, which seriously undermined Trajan's conquests, Lepper has shown that he treated them only in Book XVII, in which were compressed both these revolts and Trajan's final retreat. The account of these difficulties was not allowed to overwhelm the narrative of Trajan's victories, as had previously been supposed.[26]

The focus of these ten books was Trajan: his actions, decisions, and feelings. The extant fragments do not discuss the problem of the causes of the war, which Dio Cassius reduced to a desire for personal glory (*doxs epithymia*, 68.17.1), and modern writers to a need to control the caravan route to the East or "regularize" the eastern frontier.[27] Arrian does tell us that the war was begun after an attempt at peace: "He decided not to leave the opportunity untried, if Osroes in some way would admit his mistake and submit to the just demands of the Romans and himself" (P33 = F126). He defends the assassination of the Armenian king Parthamasirus after his deposition, reporting Trajan's words that "as far as Parthamasirus is concerned, the decision was not Axidares' to take, but his own, since Parthamasirus was the first to break the agreement, and received his punishment" (P40 = F51). Someone, probably Trajan, is quoted giving the Roman position: "There seems to me to be no question that Axidares should rule Armenia" (P37 = F120).[28] We may ask, however, whether Arrian ever really felt it necessary to explore the deeper causes of the war. He carefully avoids doing so in the *Anabasis,* where he treats Alexander's desire to conquer Persia as a simple fact, not requiring explanation, and presents the expedition as a series of military campaigns without attempting to motivate them. Far from questioning the war, these books were laudatory. Trajan's operations were successful, and his motives honest. On a personal level as well Trajan was admirable. As a good general he was in close contact with his troops. "Trajan lightened the toil of the troops by sharing in the work" (P41), and showed sympathy with their distress: "Many of the Romans were killed, and Trajan was angry at what had been done" (P82).[29]

Both to contemporaries and to posterity Trajan's expedition was comparable to Alexander's. The image of Alexander the great conqueror was always present in the Roman mind, prompting many to assert, as Livy did (9.17-19), that Alexander would have met his match in Rome, or to compare his achievements with those of Roman conquerors, notably Pompey and Caesar.[30] Thus Trajan as emperor and successful general could readily be compared with Alexander, as Dio Chrysostom does by implication in his second and fourth discourses on kingship. The resemblance was all the more apparent when Trajan mounted a war against the Parthians, the successors of the Persians. Every rhetor, every educated man would naturally think of Alexander. This being the case, it is remarkable how little actual testimony we have of Trajanic *imitatio* of Alexander.[31] There seems to be no suggestion of Alexander on the coins, which rather emphasize the labors and virtue of Heracles.[32] The extant fragments of Arrian's *Parthica* makes no direct reference to Alexander.

Dio Cassius' history, on the other hand, even in its lacerated form, suggests the parallel at several points. Describing the moment when Trajan arrived at the head of the Persian Gulf, Dio writes, "When he had seen a ship sailing to India, he said, 'I should certainly have crossed over to India, too, if I were still young.' For he began to think about the Indians' affairs, and counted Alexander a lucky man" (68.29.1-2). Dio goes on to say that nevertheless Trajan boasted that he had gone further than Alexander, although in fact "he could not hold the territories he had subdued." He was honored with the highest honors but never reached Rome to enjoy them (68.29.2-4). Trajan visited Babylon, Dio adds, "because of Alexander, to whom he offered sacrifice in the room where he had died" (68.30.1). The comparison with Alexander in these passages is melancholy, not glorifying either emperor but rather commenting on their ultimate defeat by death.

Dio apparently depended heavily on Arrian's *Parthica* for his account of this war,[33] and this presentation of Trajan might be derived from Arrian. True, Dio, from the perspective of several generations and of other wars against the Parthians, might more easily evaluate Trajan's achievements objectively than Arrian. Yet there are close associations between Dio's account and the picture presented by Arrian of Alexander's visit to the Persian Gulf and his plans there (*Anab.* 7.1). Roos argues that P73 (= F131), "those who write not only the deeds but also the plans of Trajan," belongs to the same scene on the Persian Gulf, when Arrian would have treated the plans of Trajan.[34] In the *Anabasis*, Arrian, like Dio in the case of Trajan, used the consideration of Alexander's plans to introduce his most extensive philosophical evaluation of the desire for conquest (*Anab.* 7.1-3). If, as seems likely, Dio derives from Arrian, then we may conclude that Arrian, the student of Epictetus, could not resist making some observations on the contrast between Trajan's urge to conquer and his defeat by sickness and death, the ultimate enemy. Such comments, as in the case of Alexander, would have heightened the heroic presentation of Trajan's achievements and been congenial to Hadrian, the intellectual and admirer of Epictetus. Death remains the final boundary of mortal achievement.[35]

There are other possible grounds for comparison with Alexander which might have been exploited by Arrian. Dio, in describing Trajan's conquest of Adiabene, recalls that this district includes Gaugamela (68.26.4), where Alexander defeated Darius. In describing Trajan's character, Dio remarks that he drank heavily yet remained sober (68.7.4), perhaps a silent comparison with Alexander's drunken murder of Clitus. Arrian may therefore have made an implicit or explicit comparison with Alexander, and even raised questions about the value of an unlimited desire for conquests and the glory they bring. But as with Alexander, whatever his reservations, the final picture drawn by Arrian of Trajan and the Parthian expedition as we see it in the fragments is favorable. Trajan was the great leader who humbled the Parthians.

The contents of the *Parthica*, as far as we can tell, were political and military events, with little attention given to other matters which might make the history more novelistic or exploit the exotic aspects of a campaign far beyond the imperial boundaries. In military matters, as in the *Anabasis*, the coverage is careful. It includes the planning before an engagement: "[The Parthians] had decided that when the Moors should rush against them, the troops facing them would flee as if terrified, but those stationed on

either side would attack on the flanks of the pursuers" (P53 = F140). There are numerous descriptions of the operations themselves: a march against a hostile country (P55), the flight of a king (P56 = F167), the bridging of the Tigris (P57 = F165), a defensive action against invaders (P21). Noteworthy in the *Parthica* is the vivid treatment of numerous embassies to Trajan. The reason for the large number of fragments of this sort lies in part with one of our intermediate sources, the Constantinian excerpts *On Embassies*, but also in the real situation in Parthia, which was not a strongly centralized state but a collection of petty kingdoms ruled by men who were vassals to the Parthian King of Kings.[36] The success of the campaign depended on whether Trajan could win some of these vassals to the Roman cause, and negotiations thus represented an important part of his total activity. Unlike the faceless embassies we find in the *Anabasis*, the kings and princes who came before Trajan are described as individuals: Arsaces (P19), Arbandes, "handsome and tall and in the bloom of youth" (P43), Sanatruces (P77), and others whose names are lost (P89 = F123, P99 = F157). Although the fragment is not explicitly ascribed to Arrian, the description of Sanatruces is worth quoting: ". . . the king of Armenia, who was moderate in stature, but extraordinary in judgment toward everything, not least toward military matters. He seemed to be a careful guardian of what was right and in his way of life as restrained as the best of the Greeks and Romans." Here again we see Arrian the student of Epictetus, admiring the man, although a barbarian, for his self-control. On the other hand, the judgment of the unknown leader in P89 (= F123) brings out the weaknesses of a bad leader, "a man reckless because of his youth, foolish because of his inexperience of affairs, persuasive to the multitude because of his physical strength and rashness in battle. He wanted plans about even the most important matters to be deliberated in the whole crowd rather than among a few of those who especially showed forethought, and desired that those who opposed too long should be bound, and yet should follow in their bonds."

When Arrian does describe Parthian ways, it is usually because they have a military relevance, as when he describes Parthian armor (P20; cf. the descriptions of foreign military dress in his *Tactics*), the native use of snowshoes made of willow withes to cross sixteen-foot snow (P85 = F153), and the native wild horses (P88 = F138). The description of Semiramis' tomb, which was seen by Trajan in Babylon (P74), was no doubt introduced as part of the continuing comparison of Trajan with great conquerors of the past.[37]

The narrative of embassies and battles was relieved by a number of orations and letters. Some fourteen fragments appear to belong in this category, most of them not direct quotations but indirect reports of what someone wrote or spoke. Of those reported directly, several appear to be only a line of dialogue introduced into the narrative, rather than a fragment of a full oration. This technique, also found in the *Anabasis*, is well exemplified in P46: "Trajan said to Augarus' son [Arbandes], 'You were wrong not to have come sooner to join my expedition and share my efforts, and for this reason I would gladly pull off one of these earrings of yours,' and at the same time he grasped one of his ears. Both of Arbandes' ears were pierced, and gold earrings hung from both."

In the preface to the **Anabasis,** Arrian writes that he intends to rely on Aristobulus and Ptolemy, because they seem more trustworthy in that both accompanied Alexander on the expedition, yet wrote only after his death, when there was neither need nor profit in writing other than as it occurred. Since the Parthian war only ended with the death of Trajan in 117, there is no doubt that Arrian also wrote after the death of his protagonist. Moreover, he had almost certainly been a participant in the Parthian war.[38] The frequent argument that P73 (= F131), "Those who write not only the deeds of Trajan but his plans as well," proves that Arrian had no personal experience in the war but derived his knowledge from earlier authors[39] has little to recommend it. The use of written sources is not incompatible with autopsy. Lucian's comments on the writers of Verus' Parthian war show us, first of all, that many histories of such wars were produced almost at once, so that we may presume that as early as 125 there were a number of memoirs, reports, and monographs on the war which could have been used by Arrian, without prejudicing in the slightest his capacity to write on the basis of his own experience. On the other hand, there is the notice by Johannes Lydus (T14 Roos, P6 = F37), found after his discussion of the Caspian Gates (the Darial Pass): "Such is the account in the Roman writers concerning the Caspian Gates. Arrian in the **Alanike Historia** and especially in the eighth book of the **Parthica** describes them quite accurately, inasmuch as he himself was commander of the area, since he was in charge of that region under Trajan the Excellent."

The reference to the **History of the Alans** and a command in the area might naturally lead one to think of Arrian's governorship of Cappadocia under Hadrian. Arrian is said to have settled affairs in Iberia after warding off the Alans in 135,[40] and could have seen the Darial Pass at that time. If the reference is in fact to Arrian's governorship, then the name Trajan in Johannes Lydus is a mistake for Hadrian. However, the second reference, to **Parthica** Book VIII, places us firmly in Trajan's reign, since Arrian also referred to Elegeia in that book (P5 = F36), no doubt to describe Trajan's stay there in 114. If Arrian described the Darial Pass in the same book, the more probable conclusion is to trust Lydus' date and understand him to refer to a command in the area of the Darial Pass held by Arrian at the time of Trajan's expedition, when Trajan was at Elegeia and wanted to protect his northern flank from a surprise attack by the Alans through the pass. Such a mission beyond the frontiers of the empire into the territory of client kings was not uncommon; especially relevant is the presence of Roman garrisons in Iberia in the vicinity of Tbilisi and Baku under the Flavian emperors. Iberia supported Trajan's war; an Iberian prince died fighting at Nisibis. An early assignment to guard the Darial Pass, perhaps as military tribune, would have given Arrian experience in the area, a factor which would influence Hadrian when he later made him governor of the province.[41] There is no problem of age or rank; Arrian would have been in his late twenties, and depending on his career he could have served in various capacities with Trajan's army. In our fragments of the **Parthica** Arrian makes no statements of the sort "I have seen and know" found with reference to the Inn and Save (**Ind.** 4.15) or throughout the **Periplus.** Certain fragments, however, suggest autopsy without guaranteeing it: P46, the story of Trajan and the earring of Arbandes, quoted above; P77, the description of Sanatruces, also quoted above; and P85 (= F153), the description of native snowshoes. The weight of the evidence inclines towards Arrian's participation in the expedition.[42]

The time of composition of the **Parthica** remains a puzzle. Given his success in recording his years with Epictetus, Arrian may have begun taking notes for the Trajanic section of his history even during the course of the expedition. Lucian describes how the authors writing histories of Lucius Verus' Parthian war were writing as the war took place—and even described Verus' triumph before the war was over! Although it is thus possible that the **Parthica** was one of Arrian's early works, Arrian's presentation of Trajan as a great conqueror bound to die suggests a certain perspective on events, and Parthia and the wars with Parthia were of immediate interest in the Roman world throughout Arrian's lifetime. If Trajan's war was not the immediate occasion of the **Parthica,** Arrian might have been encouraged to write by his experience on the frontier in Cappadocia in the 130s, or even by the war led by Lucius Verus in 160-164.[43]

The **Parthica,** then, appears to have been an extensive review of Roman-Parthian relations, prefaced by a brief account of the rise of the Parthian nation and focusing especially on the recent campaign of Trajan. Trajan was portrayed as a successful general and emulator of Alexander, accomplishing his objective in humbling the Parthians despite the revolts of 116-17. Although Trajan's desire for conquest probably was viewed from a moralistic and philosophical standpoint, the overall presentation was laudatory. The general tone suits the policy of Hadrian, which was to honor the memory of Trajan and his operations against Parthia, while making no attempt to continue to hold Trajan's conquests.[44]

THE EVENTS AFTER ALEXANDER

The second major work, known as **Ta meta Alexandron** or the **Events after Alexander,**[45] narrated the first struggles among the successors of Alexander. This title is probably not Arrian's, although it is used by Photius and an anonymous Byzantine work on syntax. Photius refers to the **Anabasis** as Ta kata Alexandron (*The Events during Alexander's Lifetime*) and the anonymous Byzantine scholar cites the same work as Ta peri Alexandrou (*Concerning Alexander*). The title which we receive from the Byzantines, then, need not reflect the purpose or conception of Arrian, but the long summary of the whole work given by Photius (S1 = F9, 11) provides a basis from which Koehler, Reitzenstein, Roos, and Jacoby have been able to reconstruct its contents.[46]

When Alexander died in Babylon on 10 June 323, he left no clear successor to his empire; on his deathbed he is reported to have said that he was leaving his kingdom "to the strongest." Although he gave Perdiccas his ring, he was not able to give him his authority. The generals who had been held in check by Alexander's charm, ruthlessness, ability, and ascendancy over the soldiers each began to assert themselves in the power vacuum left by Alexander's death. It would take two generations before a stable pattern of power could be established, but the first and most important decisions were made by 320 B.C., when at the settlement of Triparadisus any real hope for keeping the empire a unity was given up. In the period between June 323 and Triparadisus the major events involve this wrestling for power: the first division of offices in Babylon immediately after Alexander's death; the quelling of revolts by various peoples, including the uprising in Greece called the Lamian War; and the attempt of Perdiccas by marriages and force to convert his regency for the two young kings, Alexander IV and Philip Arrhidaeus, into absolute rule over Alexander's empire. Perdiccas was supported by the Greek Eumenes, but opposed by Antipater, Craterus, and Ptolemy, and after an unsuccessful battle with the latter in Egypt, he was killed by his own troops in May 320. His death opened the way for the new accord of Triparadisus.[47] . . .

Considering the short period covered, the length of the work is surprising; Diodorus, our fullest extant account, treats the same period in half of Book XVIII. The history falls easily into the genre of the monograph on a specific period. Even as such, however, it stands out for its length—the general rule is that contemporary histories are long, but later monographs short. Some sense of the detailed narrative which is implied by ten books on three and a half years is discoverable in two fragments which preserve Arrian's own words for more than the few phrases usual in the citations of the *Suda*. Two palimpsest folios copied in the tenth century preserve part of Book VII (S24-25). The first begins at the end of Ptolemy's successful attempt to bring Alexander's body to Egypt despite Perdiccas' opposition. Perdiccas reacts to this by a series of moves: he marches from Asia Minor through Cilicia toward Egypt, deposes on his way the satrap of Cilicia for being too friendly to Craterus, and sends Docimus to Babylon, with instructions to depose Archon the satrap of Babylon if possible. The narrative briefly follows Docimus as he confronts Archon and takes his place. Perdiccas meanwhile is engaged with dissident kings in Cyprus, against whom he gathers a fleet, marines, and cavalry under the combined command of Aristonous, once a bodyguard of Alexander. Here the first folio of the palimpsest ends. In these two pages Arrian describes with greater precision than any other author the feverish activity of Perdiccas as

he is being challenged on all sides. The theft of Alexander's body is well known, but the removal of Philotas from Cilicia recurs only in a phrase of Justin (13.6.16: "Cilicia is taken from Philotas and given to Philoxenus"), and the events in Babylon and Cyprus are completely new to us. One notes also a delight in specifics: "He prepared many merchant ships, and had about 800 mercenaries and about 500 horses go on board. He appointed Sosigenes of Rhodes admiral, Medius the Thessalian commander of the mercenaries, and Amyntas commander of the cavalry, while Aristonous the bodyguard of Alexander was general of the whole force" (S24, lines 22-28).

The second folio of the palimpsest (S25) reveals Arrian's care in following the diplomatic maneuvering connected with Antigonus' crossing into Asia Minor, the ill-feeling of Menander, the satrap of Lydia, toward Eumenes, Cleopatra, and Perdiccas, and how Cleopatra's timely advice saved Eumenes from being ambushed by Menander. Again the narrative, insofar as it is legible, is particular and clear, explaining both the thoughts and the actions of the various actors.

A recently identified papyrus fragment from Oxyrhynchus (*PSI* XII, 1284)[48] preserves a passage from the battle of Eumenes against Neoptolemus. We know from Plutarch that Eumenes was defeated in the infantry battle, but routed Neoptolemus' cavalry and captured his baggage train. With this advantage, he was able to make the infantry surrender.[49] But this fragment reveals that Arrian knew much more. The papyrus preserves part of a unique account of Eumenes' parleying with the opposing Macedonian soldiers through a certain Xennias, a Greek who spoke the Macedonian dialect. Eumenes was able to persuade Neoptolemus' troops that although their phalanx could resist a frontal attack, his cavalry could harass them and keep them from food-gathering, so that it was best to surrender to him.

Such fragments are evidence of the generally high quality of Arrian's history, a quality due in no small degree here as in the *Anabasis* to a discriminating choice of sources. The general plan of the *Events after Alexander* is almost exactly that of the equivalent section of Diodorus;[50] the congruence with Diodorus suggests that they both used the same source, Hieronymus of Cardia.[51] But some caution is necessary, since Hieronymus' history spanned the period 323 to 272 (if not further), some fifty-two years, and although the number of books is not known, it appears extremely unlikely that he, despite his general reliability as a historian, provided anywhere as much detail as Arrian. Few other candidates present themselves as authors whom Arrian might have used to supplement Hieronymus. Nymphis of Heraclea's twenty-four books *On Alexander, the Successors, and Their Followers* (*FGrHist* 432 F17) and an anonymous History (*FGrHist* 155) are the only known historians of the period who precede Arrian; his only successor, Dexippus of Athens, seems to have used Arrian's account. I suggest that Arrian used together with Hieronymus an author he found invaluable in writing the *Anaba-*

sis: Ptolemy. We know nothing of the scope of Ptolemy's narrative. All the extant fragments refer to Alexander, but it is in fact very likely that Ptolemy would have chosen to present not merely his view of Alexander, but also of the struggles among the generals, especially the discreet and moderate role he had played.[52] Arrian had used the narrative of Nearchus in the *Anabasis* and then presented it more fully in the *Indike;* there may be a similar use of Ptolemy in the *Anabasis* and the *Events after Alexander.* Errington, following Badian, has argued that Ptolemy published his book not late in life, as regularly supposed, but quite early, soon after 320.[53] He may therefore have taken as his stopping point the decisions at Triparadisus and the return of Antipater to Europe, and thus set the example for Arrian, who broke off his history at that point.

Alongside such reliable sources as Hieronymus and, if my hypothesis is accepted, Ptolemy, Arrian would have used less trustworthy accounts. In the preface to the *Anabasis* he justifies using such material, which he qualifies as hearsay (*legomena*), if it is sufficiently interesting. An example of his use of *legomena* in the *Events after Alexander* occurs in the fragment describing the battle of Eumenes and Craterus: "Eumenes *is said* to have found Craterus still alive. He jumped down from his horse and lamented over him, testifying to Craterus' courage, intelligence, excessive gentleness and unaffected response to friendship . . ." (S26 = F177). The source of this anecdote is unknown; Plutarch (*Eumenes* 7) reports the story with no allusion to where he found it. Arrian clearly liked the picture of a general praising his fallen opponent on the battlefield but did not wish to treat it as undoubtedly authentic, and so presented it as hearsay.

Arrian in this work, like Diodorus and Hieronymus, divides the action into campaign years, completing the account of one year before beginning the next. On only two occasions does the Photian summary suggest that this principle is violated: (1) after the deaths of Demosthenes and Hyperides in Book VI, Arrian follows the later history of those responsible, recalling Demades' execution in 319 and Archias' ultimate poverty and disgrace; and (2) before describing Thibron's attempt to gain control of Cyrene, Arrian, like Diodorus (18.19.1), finds it necessary to backtrack a bit to give the background of the story. The transition from Demosthenes and the anti-Macedonians to Thibron (Photius has one follow the other in his summary) may have been facilitated by the fact that both Demosthenes and Thibron were involved with Harpalus and the treasure stolen from Alexander. On the other hand, even these exceptions may be distortions by Photius of Arrian's narrative.[54]

Concerning the partition of books we know from Photius only the divisions between Books V and VI and IX and X. Book X appears as a neat unit, covering events in Asia Minor from Eumenes' discovery of Perdiccs' death to Antipater's return to Europe. At the end of Book IX, Antipater had completed the reorganization of the empire at Triparadisus and had set out for home. Book X backtracks

to treat Eumenes' activity while the others were at Triparadisus and then follows Antipater on his way through Asia Minor, noting his troubles with his troops, with Cleopatra, and with Cassander and Antigonus, who insisted on quarreling. The noteworthy fact about the division of Books V and VI, on the other hand, is the continuity of action. Book V ends with the battle of Crannon and its immediate aftermath, the Greek acceptance of Macedonian terms. In Book VI, Arrian turns to the specific problem of Athens and the city's reaction to this final proof that its days of liberty were gone forever. Apparently the author wished to get maximum value from a dramatic moment by treating it in two halves, first the battle, then the Athenian aftermath. A somewhat similar technique is used in the *Anabasis,* where Alexander arrives at Gordion and receives new troops at the end of Book I, but cuts the Gordian knot at the beginning of Book II.

There are a number of omissions in Photius' summary, most notably the revolt of the Greeks whom Alexander settled in Bactria (Diodorus 18.7) and the two phases of the Macedonian-Aetolian war (Diodorus 18.24-25, 38). At least the Aetolian war would be an integral part of the struggle between Perdiccas and Antipater, so we may credit the omission to Photius rather than to Arrian. The papyrus and palimpsest fragments remind us how much Photius necessarily left out, and we must be on our guard not to limit Arrian only to what Photius reports.

Arrian's chief interest in writing the history, one gathers from the extant fragments, was to describe the military encounters which were so frequent in this period, and the diplomatic maneuvering which preceded them. No period in history was richer in important battles or boasted more illustrious generals. The team of brilliant and ruthless men whom Alexander by charm and force of will had kept under control had broken up, and each now had his own army and his own ambition and was ready to fight against native rebellions and his own ex-comrades to win a position for himself in the world Alexander had left. Some died quickly—Leonnatus, Neoptolemus, Craterus, Perdiccas—and new men took their places. The fragments show, as we have seen, a keen interest in troop movements and dispositions, siege works, and the tactics which meant victory for one side or the other.[55] Any biographical interest which Arrian might have had in these figures was secondary to their military activity, as we find time and again in the biographical notices which the *Suda* preserves from his history. The description of the impetuosity of Leosthenes (S17 = F179) or of the sense of superiority of Perdiccas (S27 = F180)[56] is directly linked to other reasons for their deaths, and not pure character portrayal. Leonnatus' long connection with Alexander and his own high opinion of himself would be an integral part of the narrative of his attempt to assert himself, with the support of the Macedonian cavalry, in the first days after Alexander's death, the apparent context of the characterization in S12 (= F178).[57] Nor do the two passages on Craterus preserved in the *Suda* biography follow the Xenophontic manner of recording brief notices and evaluations of a general after his death. The first (S19 = F177a) elaborates the contrast in character between Antipater and Craterus which was to play an important part in determining the outcome of the Lamian war and in all their relationships; the second (S26 = F177b) considers Craterus' death in the light of the Macedonians' respect for his outstanding qualities and of Eumenes' honorable treatment of his body.[58]

Diplomatic negotiations and secret intrigues were an important part of the struggle for power, and as such were described with care. Besides the account in the Vatican palimpsest of the activity of Antigonus, Menander, Eumenes, and Cleopatra (S25 = F10B), we may note Arrian's narrative of the various marriage alliances (S1 = F9, sect. 21-23, 26), the schemings of Eurydice (S1 = F9, sect. 31, 33) and Cleopatra (S1 = F9 and 11, sect. 21, 26, 40), and the quarrel and reconciliation of Cassander and Antipater (S1 = F11, sect. 42-43).

For a man with as abiding an interest in generalship as Arrian, the peculiar opportunities for military history in this period may be a sufficient explanation for his decision to write the **Events after Alexander.** We have no information either external or internal as to the time of composition of the work, so we cannot even say that it was composed as a continuation of the **Anabasis.** It is not an obvious or natural sequel, being different in scope and in the kind of material handled, as well as in size. Unlike the **Indike,** the **Events** is never mentioned or alluded to in the **Anabasis,** suggesting that Arrian had not even conceived it at the time of the **Anabasis.** It is possible, of course, for a historian to treat an earlier period after a later one, as we learn from the examples of Sallust and Tacitus. Nevertheless, it is more reasonable to assume that Arrian's interest in this period was first aroused by the figure of Alexander and that he turned to the **Events** sometime after he completed the **Anabasis.** It is natural to connect this work with Arrian's lifelong interest in Asia Minor. Asia Minor was the major theater of action in the period covered by the **Events,** and Eumenes, one of the leading figures of Hieronymus' account and apparently of Arrian's, remained there continuously. Finally, the subject of the history, the problem of succession to imperial power, was not without contemporary interest. Hadrian on his accession may not have approved, but certainly found useful, the action of those in Rome who ordered the immediate execution of four leading generals; if Perdiccas had been able to do the same, Alexander's empire might have remained intact. The decision to end the history with Antipater's return to Europe is not so arbitrary as some have argued. With the deaths of Neoptolemus, Craterus, and Perdiccas, Ptolemy's successful defense of Egypt as an independent unit, and Antipater's decision to return to Macedonia as his home province, any immediate hopes for a continuation of the empire of Alexander as a unit were crushed. The separatist tendency had won out, and the way was open for the establishment of the various Hellenistic kingdoms.[59] Thus Cappadocia and Armenia could be independent, and Bithynia become the sovereign state whose history Arrian recorded in the **Bithyniaca.**

THE *BITHYNIACA*

The eight books of Arrian's **Bithyniaca**[60] represent local history, a different genre from his other writings. The historical sense of the Greeks had been built especially by great works of "national" history—first and foremost the poems of Homer, which for the Greeks preserved a historical reality, though expressed in poetry; then the histories of Herodotus, Thucydides, Xenophon, Ephorus, and Theopompus. In these works the world of Greece was conceived as a unit, and the author attempted to portray the events of the Greek world as a whole. Yet this world was composed of individual city-states, each with its own history, its own cults, and its own heroes, and by a natural reaction to the panhellenism of the monumental histories there arose the genre of local history, which celebrated the past of city-states or regions.[61] These writings began at least as early as Herodotus and were regularly composed by native sons—witness the *Chronicles of Lampsacus* by Charon (*FGrHist* 262) and the *Foundation of Chios* by Ion (*FGrHist* 392). One of the main objects of these histories was to trace the beginnings of their respective cities back to the earliest events of prehistoric times, and to relate the tradition of the particular state to the larger Hellenic history recorded by Homer, Herodotus, and later writers. Genealogy, one of the formative elements of the Greek historical tradition, played an important part in this process of integrating the local history into the general Hellenic history.

In the second century A.D. there was a revival of interest in local history,[62] part of the general renewed confidence and self-assertion of the Greek world. Arrian, who in his writings and career was a major representative of this Greek renaissance, shared as well the desire to celebrate his native land and try his pen at the ancient genre of local history. The notice of Photius (B1 = T4, F14) gives us an idea of the purpose and content of the work:

> He wrote the **Bithyniaca,** presenting as a gift to his native land its heritage [*ti patridi dōron anapherōn ta patria*]. For in this work he specifies that he was Nicomedian by family, that he was born, raised, and educated in Nicomedia, and was a priest there of Demeter and Persephone, to whom the city is dedicated. . . . From the time when he began to have some capacity for writing, he had wanted to undertake to compose this work, but the preparation needed to remedy his deficiencies stretched out the time. He himself gives this explanation for his slowness in the matter. It begins, as has been said, from mythical times, and goes down to the death of the last Nicomedes. . . .

Photius certainly derived the above material, with the exception of the last sentence, from Arrian's preface, where the author would have placed himself in the series of those who narrated the traditions of their native land. The fact that Nicomedia had been founded relatively recently in Greek terms (ca. 265 B.C.), and by the king of Bithynia, would have led him to write the history of that region, rather than of his own city, which had no independent history.[63] This same emphasis on the history of a free state, a fundamental feature of Greek historiography, dictated that the work must end with the end of Bithynian independence, in 75 or 74 B.C., when Nicomedes IV left his kingdom in his will to the Roman people.[64]

Arrian's statement in his preface that his own deficiency delayed the work must refer not to literary weakness—the volume of his works suggests a facility with the pen from his youth—but lack of knowledge. The source problem for any local history, but especially for *Bithyniaca,* was potentially much more complicated than for Arrian's other histories. The *Anabasis,* once Arrian made the decision to follow chiefly Aristobulus and Ptolemy, presented itself as a relatively straight-forward problem in historical narration, and apparently treatment of the *Events after Alexander* and the *Parthica* were similar. But to write *Bithyniaca,* a conscientious author would wish to become familiar with at least some of the writers who had attempted to relate Bithynian place and tribal names, cults, and migrations to Hellenic history. Moreover, Bithynia was a neighbor of Troy, and its history had to be integrated with the information found in Homer and other poets of the epic cycle. Not only local historians but Homeric scholars had been fighting for centuries over passages such as the catalogue of Troy's allies (*Iliad* 2.816-77): Demetrius of Scepsis (a city in the Troad) found it necessary to write thirty books to elucidate these sixty-two lines![65] Without pretending to suggest that Arrian tried to attain a scholar's knowledge of the problems,[66] it is clear that anyone who approached the task seriously would find he needed to do a lot of reading. Arrian's familiarity with Bithynia, its geography, cults, and customs, would no doubt have helped him, but the book in the nature of things is chiefly the product of reading and not original research and autopsy.

We do not know anything useful about earlier writers of *Bithyniaca.* Asclepiades of Myrleia (*FGrHist* 697), the earliest of whom any notice has been preserved, wrote in the first century B.C., apparently to satisfy the curiosity connected with Bithynia's change of status from kingdom to Roman province, composing perhaps ten books, of which we have six fragments. Parthenius borrowed from Asclepiades two love stories, of the kind which were common in the narration of the relations between Greek colonists and the indigenous population, for his *Amatory Narratives* (F1-2).[67] In the same period Alexander Polyhistor (*FGrHist* 273) devoted one of his many books to Bithynia and composed others on related subjects—the Black Sea, Paphlagonia, and Phrygia. Two centuries later a contemporary of Arrian, Nicander of Chalcedon, produced a book called *The Changes of Fortune of the Bithynian Kings* (*FGrHist* 700). Of four other authors who cannot be dated (*FGrHist* 698-99, 701-702) the most interesting is Demosthenes of Bithynia, who wrote an epic poem in ten books entitled *Bithyniaca,* which was used by Stephanus of Byzantium for information on place names.[68] These bits and pieces suggest a continuing interest in Bithynia but tell us little about how Arrian might have handled his material.

Nor do the extant fragments, of which only five record the book from which they are taken. Four of these are short geographical notices from Stephanus of Byzantium, giving no clue as to the contents of the respective books. The arrangement may have been topographical, chronological, or some combination. We would expect the history of the Bithynian kings to be treated chronologically, but the mythical and Homeric period could have been treated more freely. Only one fragment can be certainly fixed to a historical narrative,[69] and that is preserved not in Arrian's words but in the verse narrative of the Byzantine polymath Tzetzes:

> The Nicomedes who founded Nicomedia . . . had a very large dog, a Molossian and very faithful to him. Once, the queen, the wife of Nicomedes, whose name was Ditizele, a Phrygian by birth, was playing with the king, and the dog, thinking she was an enemy, closed his jaws over her right shoulder and pulled it away, grinding her flesh and bones with his teeth. She died in the arms of the king, and was buried at Nicomedia with great honor, in a gilded stone tomb. . . . The story has it that the dog, having fallen out of the king's favor, died from love of the king and grief for his wife. Arrian writes the story in the *Bithyniaca.*

(B63 = F29)

The story is striking, and so was preserved. A love for unusual anecdotes such as this is a standard feature of Greek historiography, even in serious writers. Arrian may have been especially attracted to this story as a dog lover, for what it showed of this dog's faithfulness and affection. Nevertheless, it is disappointing that this is our sole fragment for the Hellenistic period. We could wish that we had some idea whether Arrian gave a serious account of the efforts of Nicomedes and his dynasty to maintain the independence of Bithynia among the conflicting pressures of the Hellenistic world.

Thanks to the twelfth-century Byzantine scholar Eustathius we are much better informed on Arrian's treatment of the earliest periods of Bithynian legendary history.[70] The *Bithyniaca* survived so long no doubt because since the foundation of Constantinople Bithynia had become one of the most flourishing and central parts of the empire, and Arrian's clarity of presentation and clear Attic style made it valuable for individual or school use. Eustathius quotes the *Bithyniaca* frequently in his commentaries on Homer and on the geographical work of Dionysius Periegetes, not only for historical information but even for grammatical points,[71] so that his most recent editor suggests that Eustathius may have taught the *Bithyniaca* in his school in Constantinople.[72] Eustathius' quotations are frequently verbatim[73] and thus provide a welcome occasion to evaluate, if only piecemeal, Arrian's work. Allowance must be made, of course, for Eustathius' own interests in considering the content and emphases of Arrian's history.

The material on the early period in the *Bithyniaca* was apparently usually introduced to explain names of places and tribes. This conclusion is undoubtedly influenced by

Eustathius' selection, which was itself on this basis, but it fits into the general pattern of Hellenistic scholarship as well. Thus on the name Bosporus we find two explanations quoted by Eustathius (B36 = F20b):

> Arrian states the following: "The crossing at Chalcedon and Byzantium was once called Mysian, because the Mysians once lived opposite Thrace, but was later called Bosporus [Cow-ford] on account of the misfortune of Io, who, the myths have it, was driven by a gadfly because of the anger of Hera and coming to these regions crossed at this point." But the same man [Arrian] says that according to some the Bosporus got its name not from this cow, but from another, "which when the Phrygians were attacking jumped fearlessly into the sea and crossed without injury the Chalcedon-Byzantium Bosporus. In this way she became a guide for those men, according to a prophecy which ordered them to make a cow their guide for the route. This they did, and crossed safely. A bronze cow is set up as a memorial of this crossing, erected at some later time by the Chalcedonians. Perhaps because of this cow a certain place there is called Damalis [Heifer] to this day."

In this story we find the standard aetiological explanation of the name Bosporus, referring to Io, cautiously ascribed to "the myths," and beside it a rationalized explanation connected with early tribal migrations and confirmed by a monument and another place name. Finally, even before Io, the crossing had been named Mysian because of their onetime location near it, although in later times Mysia was further south. Other fragments indicate this same desire to historicize mythological events.[74] The tendency is apparent also in the *Anabasis,* e.g., 2.16.5-6 on Heracles and the cattle of Geryon.

Not only god-driven mortals, but the gods themselves appear, as in the following explanation of why Ares was called Enyalios (B14 = F103): "On coming into Thrace, where Enyalios had his home, Ares wished to be entertained. But Enyalios did not wish to receive him, saying that he would not entertain anyone who was not stronger in war than himself. And he, 'It is time for you to entertain me, since I assert that I am stronger in war than you.' When Enyalios denied this, they fought and after a long battle Enyalios was killed by Ares, struck by his weapon, the broad Thracian sword. Therefore since Ares accomplished this great deed as a young man, he was called because of it Enyalios." Here, besides the unusual feature of calling Ares' opponent Enyalios rather than Enyos, we note the use of a brief direct quote to increase the vividness of the scene. Both this and the use of historical presents (*erchetai, piptei*) is typical of Arrian's narrative style in his other works. On another occasion—presumably while describing the laurel over the tomb of the Bebrycian king Amycus at Daphne near Byzantium—he mentions "the laurel [*daphn*] which some say to have sprung from the ground because of Daphne, the daughter of Ladon, who while fleeing from her lover Apollo prayed that she might disappear under the earth, and received the answer to her prayer" (B40 = F87). This laurel is shown, Arrian tells us, at Daphne near Antioch, although we have no assurance that he actually saw it.

Two examples of Arrian's treatment of Homeric names will suffice for an idea of his technique in explaining them:

> The Eneti, having been hard pressed in battle by the Assyrians, and having crossed into Europe, dwelt by the Po River and in the native language are called Veneti to this day instead of Eneti, and Venetia is the name of their land.

(B46 = F63)

> Those whom Homer in the Catalogue of Ships calls "Halizones, whom Hodius and Epistrophus ruled," were Bithynians. And Alybe, which he says was the "birthplace of silver" is [still] pointed out, and one can see an unfaded record [there], the works of the silver mines which are left. These men are called Halizones because they are closed in on all sides by the sea, on the north and east by the Black Sea, on the south by the bay of Astacus, the one by Nicomedia, and on the west by the Propontis and the Bosporus, so that the greater part of their territory is not far from being a peninsula, and it is quite fair to say that they are embraced by the sea [*hali zōnnysthai*].

(B22 = F97)

Both the Eneti and the Halizones in Homer's catalogue of Trojan allies were problematic, because neither name was known in historical times. The Eneti were early on associated with the Veneti at the head of the Adriatic Sea, as here. Arrian's Assyrians, here and in B51 (= F74), must be taken to be the White Syrians, whom Strabo places on the south coast of the Black Sea, in what was later called Pontus. The question of the Halizones and Alybe, also unknown, was never satisfactorily settled. An indication of the problems Arrian may have encountered in the composition of the *Bithyniaca* is given by Strabo, who devotes eight chapters (12.3.20-27) to the Halizones, reviewing the opinions of Ephorus, Apollodorus, and others. Since Strabo argued particularly from the absence of silver mines anywhere east of the territory of the Chalybes that Alybe was a corruption of Chalybe, Arrian's comment (from autopsy?) on traces of silver mining in a Bithynian Alybe is noteworthy. Strabo lists many alternate suggestions, including Ephorus' emendation of Alizones to Amazones. Arrian's identification was not new (it is reported also by Pliny the Elder, *NH* 5.143, and uses standard Greek etymological practices), but must be seen as part of a long tradition of scholarship and speculation.

This is one of Arrian's more reasonable etymologies. In general he is given to deriving geographical names—of cities, tribes, rivers—from an eponymous hero, invented by Arrian or his source for this purpose.[75] Occasionally the etymologies are more complicated, as in B3 (= F16), where Deucalion establishes an altar to Zeus Aphesios because he was saved (*apheith*) from the flood, and the name Nemea is derived from the word for pasture (*nemein*), because the animals of Argos were pastured there, or in B36 (= F20), the passage on the Bosporus quoted above. On some occasions he permits a name to be taken over by another person, as in the case of Enyalios and Ares (B14 = F103; cf. also B15 = F102) or notes a change in name (B22 = F98).

Arrian, of course, as every local historian, gave special attention to narratives of the foundation of a city. One apparently verbatim account shows that these stories could be quite short (B55 = F71): "Phanagoria, which Phanagoras the Teian founded, fleeing from the arrogance of the Persians. And again Hermonassa, named after Hermonassa the wife of a certain Semandros of Mytilene. When he led some men from the Aeolian cities to found a colony, and then died while founding the city, his wife became ruler of the city and gave her own name to it." Was there also a novelistic element in the story of the woman founder-queen? If so, the fragment does not suggest it. On the contrary, if Eustathius is quoting accurately, the fragment implies that Arrian gave a list of towns, with brief comments on each. The brevity may be explained by the distance from Bithynia of Phaenagoria and Hermonassa, which were on the straits of the Cimmerian Bosporus. Yet one gets the same impression from a notice on Zeleia in the Troad (B34 = F96): "Zeleia or Lycia: Apollo too [is called] Lycius because of this Lycia. For this reason also the father of Pandarus [is named] Lycaon, which name is not much different from that of this race." Perhaps Arrian did not attempt a narrative treatment of this kind of material but presented it in catalogue form, somewhat as he does the cities and rivers described in parts of his *Periplus*.

A trace of the familiar romantic foundation narrative, such as those told by Asclepiades of Myrleia or reported in Parthenius, can be found in the story of Crocodice, paraphrased by Eustathius (B39 = F61c): "[Arrian says] that Crocodice, an expert on drugs, while she was distributing wine group by group to her father's army, threw roots into the mixing bowls, drugs producing sleep and forgetfulness; so that they lay half-dead from the potion. Thus they were killed by the enemy because of love for the youth Prieneus." Crocodice presumably was the daughter of the native chieftain where Prieneus was attempting to found Priene. She fell in love with him, and weakened her father's troops so that the Greeks could found their city.[76]

With so many heroes, genealogy is an essential element of history, especially useful to correct erroneous stories which do not sufficiently show the importance of Bithynia in the heroic world. The family of the nymph Electra and her son Dardanus were preeminent, as one might expect in northwestern Asia Minor (B31 = F64, B32 = F95, B33 = F107), but others were considered as well.[77] Arrian distinguishes two Sarpedons (B29 = F58), knows the Amazons by name (B48 = F85), and can provide a nymph mother for every hero.[78]

A few fragments show that Arrian shared the local historian's interest in religion and customs, hardly surprising in one who also attempted more exclusively ethnographical works such as the *Indike* and the *Alanike*.[79]

The treatment of the early history, then, reflects the standard methodology of local history: use of mythological information, though rationalized to make a more "historical" account, explanation by etymology and aetiology, and in

general a desire to fit Bithynia into the larger world of Hellenic saga. The vivid treatment of the death of the wife of Nicomedes I (if not completely due to Tzetzes) suggests that Arrian did not entirely avoid occasions to enliven his history with novelistic touches. Although he concentrated on Bithynia,[80] in his treatment of movements and migrations of peoples he was able to enlarge his focus, to touch Crete (B57 = F65), the Nile (B61 = F57), Babylon (B53 = F90), Gades (B62 = F64bis), Salamis (B59 = F66), Delos (B60 = F69), Melos (B58 = F70), and especially the Black Sea area—the cities of Phanagoria and Hermonassa on the Cimmerian Bosporus (B55 = F71), the Chalybes in Pontus (B52 = F73), the Iris River (B47 = F75), the Cappadocians of Pontus Polemoniacus (B51 = F74), the Cimmerians (B19 = F60, B43-44 = F76), Thracians (B14 = F103, B15 = F102, B16 = F68bis), and the nomadic Scythians (B47 = F75, B54 = F72). Arrian's description of the Scythians in the last mentioned fragment perhaps gives us the best example of stylistic craftmanship found in this work, an account of how the Scythians, under pressure from their enemies, abandoned a settled life in Thrace and became wanderers: "Once they ate bread and farmed, lived in houses and had cities, but when they received this blow from the Thracians, they changed their former ways and swore great oaths never to build a house or to break the ground with a plow or to build cities or to possess a treasured possession, but to make wagons their homes, wild game their food, milk their drink, to possess only animals which they could drive as they moved from one land to another. And thus from being farmers, they became nomads."

This larger view of the Bithynian past seems to confirm the observation of Rostovtzeff that in historical times Bithynia was deeply involved with the whole Black Sea area. Arrian related the early history of Bithynia to the movements of barbarian tribes like the Thracians and Scythians and to the progress of Greek colonization around the Black Sea. Bithynia was a crossroads in the migrations between Europe and Asia and between the Aegean and the Black Sea. All the peoples, Greek and barbarian, of the Black Sea littoral had their place in an account of the noble part that Bithynia had played in history before it had become a part of the Roman world-state.

DION, TIMOLEON, TILLOROBUS, AND THE ALANIKE

The three major works survived to Byzantine times, and thus some idea of their content has reached us. Of four other lesser works of a historical nature we know hardly more than the names. Photius tells us that Arrian wrote works on Timoleon and Dion which were mentioned in the preface to the *Bithyniaca* (B1 = T4): "[One work] narrates what was done by Timoleon of Corinth in Sicily; the other whatever deeds worth narrating were accomplished by Dion of Syracuse when he freed the Syracusans and all Sicily from Dionysius II, the son of Dionysius I, and from the barbarians, whom Dionysius had introduced so that he could more firmly rule as a tyrant." Dion of Syracuse (408-354 B.C.), the brother-in-law of Dionysius I and friend of Plato, was exiled by Dionysius II. In 357 B.C. he returned and drove the tyrant from Syracuse, then in the following years lost and regained control of the city, and was finally murdered in 354 B.C. His biography by Plutarch is built around his double role of philosopher and general, and as such he is set parallel to Brutus, with whom he compared favorably as general. It was presumably this double-faceted life which appealed also to Arrian, himself a philosopher-general. Photius' reference to deeds worth narrating (*axiaphgta erga*) recalls Arrian's preface to the **Anabasis**, where he promises to select whatever is more believable and more worth narrating (*axiaphgtotera*) whenever Ptolemy and Aristobulus disagree. If the words which describe Dion's deeds reflect Arrian's own comments and are not Photius' addition, the narrative would have been favorable to Dion as liberator of Sicily from tyranny.

Much the same could be said of Timoleon. Timoleon was a Corinthian sent to Sicily in 345 to help the Syracusans against Dionysius II, who had installed himself once more as tyrant. Timoleon, a bold general and clever diplomat, was able to liberate Syracuse and began a crusade against tyrants in other cities, and in 341 won a great victory against the Carthaginians in Sicily. Although he had setbacks as well as successes, he was able to make peace with Carthage, crush the tyrants, and open a new period of prosperity for Greek Sicily. Timoleon as a successful general would naturally have appealed to Arrian. Moreover, the Stoic teaching against tyranny could make the tyrant-hater Timoleon into something of a philosopher.

Thus in some respects the studies of Dion and Timoleon form a pair and may in fact represent one book rather than two. These were the sole works in which Arrian turned his pen away from eastern affairs. Perhaps the composition of these works—whether monographs or biographies—may be connected with a tour of duty in Sicily. It is likely that he was still a young man, perhaps a quaestor, since the overt interest in philosophy (in the case of Dion) and the geographical theater so far removed from his mature works, as well as the context of Photius' statement, suggest that they were early works.

Lucian preserves our only notice of a third work. In defense of his decision to write on the false prophet Alexander, a contemporary figure whom he considered a charlatan, Lucian cites the case of Arrian: "For Arrian, the disciple of Epictetus, one of the most prominent of the Romans and one who lived with literature all his life, would defend us, since he suffered something similar; he thought it was worthwhile to write a life of Tillorobus the bandit. But we are writing of a much more fierce robber, who robs not in woods and mountains, but in the cities, not ravaging Mysia alone or Mount Ida, or pillaging a few of the more desert parts of the province of Asia, but filling the whole of the Roman empire, so to speak, with his robbing" (*Alex.* 2 = T24 Roos, F52 Jacoby). Tillorobus the bandit is otherwise unknown, although the name is found on inscriptions from Termessus and Apollonia in Pisidia. Lucian's last sentence, however, appears to contrast Alex-

ander and Tillorobus and implies that the latter harried Mysia and the province of Asia, working from a base in the hills. As such his life could have been interesting to Arrian for two reasons: militarily, as a contemporary example of the tactics employed by mountain-based guerillas and the countertactics suitable against them; and also for the local interest of an episode in the contemporary history of Mysia, an area not far from Nicomedia and which he treated in his **Bithyniaca**.[81]

For none of these three works do we know the size or method of presentation. Presumably they were all short—twenty to thirty pages—and more likely historical monographs than lives in the Plutarchean manner.

Our notices of a book on the Alans, the **Alanike** or **Alanike historia**, are equally unsatisfactory. Photius mentions it (P1 = T2) as one of Arrian's works ("He composed also the affairs of the Alans [*ta kata Alanous*], which he entitled **Alanike**") but probably it did not survive to his time. Johannes Lydus mentions it (P6 = F13) and it was perhaps used by Procopius (p. 286 Roos = F109), although Jacoby assigns that fragment to the **Bithyniaca**. The name implies a geographical and ethnographical work like the **Indike**, describing to the Romans this tribe which continued to invade their territory. It possibly contained an account of Arrian's confrontation with the tribe when it attacked Cappadocia in 135, although Jacoby is mistaken in ascribing to it the **Battle Formation against the Alans** (F12), which as we have seen is written in a style unsuitable for a history, preserving the imperatives and infinitives of a genuine order of battle. The **Alanike** was undoubtedly composed as a result of the Alan attack.

Despite the fact that they are preserved only in fragments and short notices, the lost works of Arrian serve to fill out the picture of their author. The **Anabasis**, in the light of these other works, is not a fluke of literature, the happy inspiration of a retired general, nor the wistful backward look of a Greek afraid to face the Roman present, but one of a series of intelligently conceived and smoothly executed histories by a man who was a professional both as soldier and as writer.

Notes

1. The fragments of Arrian's lost histories were collected and printed almost simultaneously by two outstanding scholars, by Felix Jacoby as no. 156 in *FGrHist* II B (Berlin 1929), with a separate volume of commentary (Berlin 1930), and by A. G. Roos, *Flavius Arrianus* II (Leipzig 1928) 197-290. Roos attempted to gather all the fragments, including the many anonymous notices he recognized in the *Suda* and elsewhere, and arrange them in the order in which they might have occurred in Arrian. Jacoby restricts himself to named fragments of Arrian and includes references to other material in his commentary. Jacoby arranges all fragments not assigned to books according to the author by whom they are quoted. I here cite first the number from Roos, and

then, if Arrian is named, the fragment (F) of Jacoby. Occasionally, reference is made to the material in Jacoby's commentary in *FGrHist* II B.

2. Photius, *Bibl.* cod. 58, 91, 92, 93. For the text see now the edition by R. Henry, I (Paris 1959) 51-52, and II (Paris 1960) 16-34.

3. On these excerpts, see Cohn, *RE* s.v. Constantinus 16, IV, 1 (1901), esp. 1037-39 and the earlier bibliography cited there; A. Dain, "L'Encyclopédisme de Constantin Porphyrogénète," *Lettres d'humanité* 12 (1953) 64-81, esp. 71-75; Gyula Moravcsik, *Byzantinoturcica*² (Berlin 1958) I, 359-61.

4. On the *Suda* see A. Adler, *RE* s.v. Suidas 1, IV A 1 (1931) 675-717, especially on the use of the Constantinian excerpts, cols. 700-705. See also A. G. Roos, *Studia Arrianea* (Leipzig 1912) 2-4.

5. For Eustathius see the discussion below of the *Bithyniaca.*

6. Stephanus of Byzantium uses Arrian's lost works twenty-eight times (*Parthica* nineteen, *Bithyniaca* nine) as sources for geographical names. He and an anonymous Byzantine grammarian (*peri syntaxeos*) who makes ten citations from the *Events* are especially valuable because they assign the quotations to the individual books within the works.

7. On Photius, see in general K. Ziegler, *RE* s.v. Photios 13, XX, 1 (1941) 667-737, esp. 684-727 on the *Bibliotheca,* and R. Henry's introduction to his edition. Antonio Nogara provides a recent and thorough study of the debated question of Photius' method, with copious bibliography: "Note sulle composizione e la struttura della Biblioteca de Fozio, Patriarca de Constantinopoli, I," *Aevum* 49 (1975) 213-42. See also Thomas Hägg, *Photios als Vermittler antiker Literatur* ("Acta Univ. Upsaliensis, Studia Graeca Upsaliensia," 8; Uppsala 1975), and "Photius at Work: Evidence from the Text of the *Bibliotheca,*" *GRBS* 14 (1973) 213-22 (on his account of Philostratus' *Vita Apollonii*); Henri Tonnet, "Les notes marginales et leur transmission dans quelques manuscrits d'Arrien," *Revue d'histoire des textes* 3 (1973) 39-55; and Friedrich Lenz, "La tradizione indiretta dei discorsi di Aristide nella 'Bibliotheke' di Fozio," *St Ital* 14 (1937) 203-25, 261-79.

8. For modern accounts of Parthia, see Malcolm A. R. Colledge, *The Parthians* (New York and Washington 1967); Richard N. Frye, *The Heritage of Persia* (London 1962) 178-206; Roman Ghirshman, *Iran, from the Earliest Times to the Islamic Conquest* (Harmondsworth 1954) 243-88; and Nelson Carel Debevoise, *A Political History of Parthia* (Chicago 1938).

9. On the impression made by the disaster at Carrhae, see Dieter Timpe, "Die Bedeutung der Schlacht von Carrhae," *MusHelv* 19 (1962) 104-29. Before this the Romans showed no particular fear, as is demonstrated by Josef Dobias, "Les premiers rapports des Romains avec les Parthes et l'occupation de la Syrie, "*Archiv Orientalni* 3 (1931) 215-56.

10. Writers of *Parthica* are collected by Jacoby in *FGrHist* III C, nos. 779-82. See the succinct and useful comments of Arnaldo Momigliano, *Alien Wisdom* (Cambridge 1975) 139-41. Arrian is by far the best preserved of any author of *Parthica.*

11. The *Parthian Stations* of Isidore of Charax is a bare list of names of cities, with occasional landmarks, on the caravan route from Zeugma on the Euphrates to Kandahar. The text is in Karl Müller, *Geographi graeci minores* (Paris 1855) 244-54, *FGrHist* 781 F2, and, with map and commentary, in W. H. Schoff, *The Parthian Stations of Isidore of Charax* (Philadelphia 1914). A story from Isidore's *Periegesis of Parthia* is preserved in Athenaeus (*FGrHist* 781 F1).

12. On Lucian see, besides Jacoby, *FGrHist* 203-10, G. Avenarius, *Lukians Schrift zur Geschichtsschreibung* (Meisenheim/Glan 1956); and *Lukian, Wie man Geschichte schreiben soll,* ed. Helene Homeyer (Munich 1965). For Fronto, see *Epistulae M. Cornelii Frontonis,* ed. M. P. J. van den Hout (Leiden 1954) 125 (letter of Verus to Fronto) and 191-200 (*Principia Historiae,* a rhetorical comparison of the Parthian wars of Trajan and Verus); translation by C. R. Haines in the Loeb edition of Fronto (London 1920) II, 195-97, 199-219. Dio of Prusa, an older contemporary of Arrian from Bithynia, wrote a book on the Getai, *Getica,* later used by Jordanes, the sixth-century historian (*FGrHist* 707). Dio (*Or.* 36.1) speaks of wishing to visit the Getai while in exile at Olbia on the Black Sea (ca. 82-96). The fragments in Jordanes refer only to earlier times, but Dio may have brought his history down as far as the Dacian wars of Trajan. On the other hand, we know that the *Getica* of a certain Crito, who was on Trajan's Dacian campaign, described the war (*FGrHist* 200). This history would have furnished a recent model for Arrian's *Parthica.*

13. In this design he appears to have been imitated almost a century later by Asinius Quadratus in his nine books of *Parthica* (*FGrHist* 97).

14. The problem of genre is especially important in considering lost works, because our attempts at reconstruction are dependent in large part on our conception of the literary form of the work. It is misleading to call the *Parthica* "narrative ethnography," as Jacoby did in his early classification in "Über die Entwicklung der griechischen Historiographie und den Plan einer neuen Sammlung der griechischen Historikerfragmente," *Klio* 9 (1909) 80-123 at 107 = *Abhandlungen zur griechischen Geschichtschreibung* (Leiden 1956) 16-64 at 47. In *FGrHist* II B, comm., 566, Jacoby places it somewhat more accurately with the "type of ethnography already beginning in the oldest *Persica* and *Sicelica,* in which pre-history and description of land and peoples forms only an introduction to political history, which here is mostly

military history." However, the fragments give no indication that Arrian attempted to write a political history of Parthia.

15. We may compare the account of the people of Britain and the Roman attempts to pacify the island in Tacitus *Agricola* 10-17, which serves as prelude to the narrative of Agricola's conquest of the island (*Agr.* 18-38). Cf. Sir Ian Richmond and R. M. Ogilvie, *Cornelii Taciti De Vita Agricolae* (Oxford 1967) 15, and Ronald Syme, *Tacitus* (Oxford 1958) I, 121-22.

16. See Jacoby, *FGrHist* II B, comm., 566-67; Roos, *Studia,* 1-64.

17. Roos, *Studia,* 4-10; Jacoby, *FGrHist* II B, comm., 567-71.

18. Cf. Frye, *Persia,* 180.

19. See the parallels cited by Roos to P1 (p. 226, lines 12ff.), and the traditions of intercontinental warfare recalled by Herodotus, 7.20.

20. Agathocles in Syncellus' parallel version.

21. On this claim see W. W. Tarn, "Queen Ptolemais and Apama," *CQ* 23 (1929) 138-141 at 140.

22. Frye, *Persia,* 181.

23. Józef Wolski, "Arsace II," *Eos* 41 (1946) 160, castigates the story as invention, but its potential veracity is defended by Frye, *Persia,* 181; Ghirshman, *Iran,* 243; Colledge, *Parthians,* 26; and Debevoise, *Parthia,* 9. Wolski makes a firm rejoinder in "Untersuchungen zur frühen parthischen Geschichte," *Klio* 58 (1976) 439-57. It is doubtful whether other fragments are correctly ascribed to Book I by Roos (P18-21): see Jacoby *FGrHist* II B, comm., 567-68.

24. On this war see Debevoise, *Parthia,* 213-47; R. P. Longden, "Notes on the Parthian Campaigns of Trajan," *JRS* 21 (1931) 1-35 and *CAH* XI (1936) 239-50; Julien Guey, *Essai sur la guerre parthique de Trajan (114-117)* ("Bibliothèque d'Istros," 2; Bucharest 1937); F. A. Lepper, *Trajan's Parthian War* (London 1948); Marie Louise Chaumont, "L'Arménie entre Rome et l'Iran," in *ANRW,* II, 9, 1 (1976) 71-194, esp. 130-43; and Maria Gabriella Angeli Bertinelli, "I Romani oltre l'Eufrate nel II secolo d.C.," ibid., 3-45, esp. 5-23.

25. On these coins see Paul L. Strack, *Untersuchungen zur römische Reichsprägung des zweiten Jahrhunderts* (Stuttgart 1931) I, 224-25.

26. See Lepper, *Parthian War,* 128.

27. See especially Guey, *Guerre parthique,* 17-35, and Lepper, *Parthian War,* 156-204.

28. Compare the words here, "There seems to be no question," with the identical phrase in *Anab.* 7.22.5, "There seems to be no question that Seleucus was the greatest king of those coming to power after Alexander."

29. One is reminded of the virtues ascribed to Agricola by Tacitus (cf. Richmond and Ogilvie, *Vita Agricolae,* 20). The list of the virtues proper to a general was traditional.

30. See on this subject the works cited in chapter 5, n. 14. On the Livy passage see also Hans Rudolf Breitenbach, "Der Alexanderexkurs bei Livius," *MusHelv* 26 (1969) 146-57. In the time of Trajan, it should be remembered, Dio Chrysostom wrote *On the Virtues of Alexander* in eight books, now lost, and Plutarch wrote the parallel lives of Caesar and Alexander as well as a pair of speeches, *On the Fortune or Virtue of Alexander.*

31. Trajan's generosity to the oracle of Apollo at Didyma may have reflected an imitation of Alexander: see C. P. Jones, "An Oracle given to Trajan," *Chiron* 5 (1975) 406. Tacitus may possibly have been thinking of Trajan in comparing Germanicus with Alexander: see Syme, *Tacitus* II, 770-71. Cf. also Gerhard Wirth, "Alexander und Rom," in *Alexandre le Grand: image et réalité* ("Entretiens Hardt," 22; Geneva 1975) 181-221 at 197-200.

32. A Heracles type appears in 100 A.D. and continues with variations throughout Trajan's reign: see Harold Mattingly, *Coins of the Roman Empire in the British Museum* (London 1936) III, lxvii-lxviii; Strack, *Untersuchungen,* 95-104. The Heracles portrayed is usually Heracles Gaditanus, in whose temple at Gades there was a statue of Alexander—the very one which had brought Julius Caesar to tears in 68 B.C. See Suetonius *Divus Julius* 7 and Jean Gagé, "Hercule-Melqart, Alexandre et les Romains à Gadès," *REA* 42 (1940) 425-38. In general on Trajan and Heracles see G. W. Bowersock, "Greek Intellectuals and the Imperial Cult in the Second Century A.D.," in *Le Culte des souverains dans l'empire romain* ("Entretiens Hardt," 19; Geneva 1973) 179-212 at 193-94.

33. See Roos, *Studia,* 39; Karl Hartmann, "Über das Verhältnis des Cassius Dio zur Parthergeschichte des Flavius Arrianus," *Philologus* 74 (1917) 73-91; Jacoby *FGrHist* II B, comm., 567; and Gerhard Wirth, "Arrian und Traian—Versuch einer Gegenwartsdeutung," *Studii Clasice* 16 (1974) 169-209, esp. 202-7. Fergus Millar, *A Study of Cassius Dio* (Oxford 1964), does not consider the question.

34. *Studia,* 54.

35. Wirth, "Arrian," 169-209, gives a rather different assessment of the Alexander-Trajan parallel in the *Parthica.*

36. For a survey of the vassal kingdoms in Parthia, see Frye, *Persia,* 187-90; and Geo Widengren, "Iran, der grosse Gegner Roms: Königswalt, Feudalismus, Militärwesen," in *ANRW* II, 9, 1, 291-306, esp. 263ff.

37. Cf. the references to the tombs of Sardanapalus and Cyrus in *Anab.* 2.5.3 and 6.29.4.

38. Arrian's presence with the Roman army on the Parthian expedition has in the past been variously af-

firmed—Henri Doulcet, *Quid Xenophonti debuerit Flavius Arrianus* (Paris 1882) 9; Alfred von Domaszewski, "Die Phalangen Alexanders und Caesars Legionen," *SBHeid* 16 (1925/26) Heft 1, p. 5 (as an equestrian officer); Gerhard Wirth, "Anmerkungen zur Arrianbiographie," *Historia* 13 (1964) 228—and denied—Jacoby, *FGrHist* II B, comm., 567 and 575; Lepper, *Parthian War,* 2. Caution is in order, but there is no chronological difficulty, despite Syme's hesitancy: "Too old (it would appear) to serve as a *laticlavius* at that time, too young to command a legion" (*Historia* 14 [1965] 354 = *Danubian Papers* [Bucharest 1971] 236).

39. E.g., Schwartz, *RE* s.v. Arrianus, 1236, and Jacoby, *FGrHist* II B, comm., 567.

40. See the treatment of this question in connection with the *Ectaxis* in chapter 3.

41. Lepper, *Parthian War,* 7 and 128, notes this fragment but does not attempt to explain what exactly Trajan wanted to do at the Caucasian Gates. Wirth, "Arrian," 189, also sees P6 as evidence that Arrian was given a command by Trajan in this area.

42. Wirth, "Arrian," 189 n. 79, sees a number of other fragments from the *Parthica* as evidence of autopsy.

43. See also appendix 5.

44. Trajan was honored as a victor by Hadrian, who permitted him a post-humous triumph, regularly celebrated *ludi Parthici,* and continued to use *Parthicus,* the name the emperor had been voted in 116, in Trajan's official nomenclature: see Guey, *Guerre Parthique,* 144.

45. The modern use of *Successors* or *History of the Successors* is concise but misleading, since Arrian's work covers so little of the period of the Diadochi.

46. Ulrich Koehler, "Über die Diadochengeschichte Arrians," *SBBerl* 1890, 557-88; Ricardus Reitzenstein, "Arriani *ton met' Alexandron* libri septimi fragmenta," *Breslauer philologische Abhandlungen* 3, 3 (1888); Roos, *Studia,* 65-75; and the editions of Roos and Jacoby.

47. The extant sources for this period are Curt. 10.6-10 (restricted to the first division of power at Babylon), Diod. 18.1-39, Justin 13.1-8, and Plutarch *Eumenes.* For modern accounts, see W. W. Tarn, *CAH* VI (1927) 461-504; Julius Beloch, *Griechische Geschichte*² (Berlin and Leipzig 1927) IV, pt. 2, 623-39; M. J. Fontana, "Le Lotte per la successione di Alessandro Magno," *Atti della Accademia di scienze lettere e arti di Palermo,* ser. 4, 18, 2 (1957-58); the review of Fontana by E. Badian, *Gnomon* 34 (1962) 381-87 = *Studies in Greek and Roman History* (Oxford 1964) 262-70; Edouard Will, *Histoire politique du monde hellénistique (323-30 av. J.-C.)* Pt. I ("Annales d'Est," memoire no. 30, 1966) 19-35; and R. M. Errington, "From Babylon to Triparadeisos: 323-320 B.C.," *JHS* 90 (1970) 49-77. Unfortunately, Pierre Briant, *Antigone le Borgne: les débuts de sa*

carrière et les problèmes de l'assemblée macédonienne ("Annales littéraires de l'Université de Besançon," 152; Paris 1973), became available too late for me to use for this section. Perdiccas' death and Triparadisus can now be dated in 320, not 321: see Errington, 75-77, following Eugenio Manni, "Tre note di cronologia ellenistica," *Rendiconti dell'Accademia nazionale dei Lincei,* ser. 8, 4 (1949) 53-61. I use these dates, but the traditional dating makes no significant change in the interpretation of Arrian's history.

48. *Editio princeps* by V. Bartoletti, "Frammenti di storia di Diadochi (Arriano?)," *PSI* XII, 2 (1951) 158-61, no. 1284, identified as Arrian by Kurt Latte, "Ein neues Arrianfragment," *NachGöttingen* 1950, 23-27 = *Kleine Schriften* (Munich 1968) 595-99; see also Gerhard Wirth, "Zur grossen Schlacht des Eumenes 322 (*PSI* 1284)," *Klio* 46 (1965) 283-88, and A. B. Bosworth, "Eumenes, Neoptolemus, and *PSI* XII 1284," *GRBS* 19 (1978) 227-37. The text is printed by Wirth in the second edition of Roos II, 323-24. Bartoletti argued that the fragment referred to the battle of Eumenes against Craterus, but Bosworth has demonstrated that the earlier battle with Neoptolemus must be meant.

49. Plutarch *Eumenes* 5.5. Simple notices of the battle are found in Diod. 18.29.5, Justin 13.8.4-5, and Photius' summary of Arrian, S1, 27.

50. See the comparative table in Jacoby, *FGrHist* II B, comm., 554-55.

51. On Diodorus' use of Hieronymus see E. Schwartz, *RE* s.v. Diodorus 38, V, 1 (1905) 685 = *Griechische Geschichtschreiber* (Leipzig 1959) 68; Jacoby, comm. to *FGrHist* 154, II B, pp. 544-45.

52. For a trenchant analysis of Ptolemy's purposes and bias in writing his narrative, see R. M. Errington, "Bias in Ptolemy's History of Alexander," *CQ,* n.s. 19 (1969) 233-42. Errington notes that it was important for Ptolemy to establish the "correct" view of Alexander and his relation to Perdiccas in the years immediately after 323.

53. "Ptolemy's History," 241. The prevailing view of the date of composition of Ptolemy's narrative was first attacked by E. Badian, in his review of Pearson's *Lost Histories, Gnomon* 33 (1961) 666 = *Studies,* 258. Cf. the discussion of Ptolemy's history in chapter 5.

54. Note that Photius in his summary of the *Anabasis* narrates the mutilation of Bessus and Alexander's capture of Pasargadai out of order (*Bibl.* cod. 93, 67b 36-37, 39).

55. See besides Photius' summary S14, S17 = F179, S21 = F124, S24-25 = F10, S26 = F177b, S31 = F117, and *PSI* XII, 1284.

56. The contrast with Alexander was present, but hardly explicit. *Suda* s.v. Alexandros, which Koehler, "Dia-

dochengeschichte," 585, relates to this because of the similarity of diction, is taken from *Anab.* 3.10.2, not *Events.*

57. See Roos, *Studia,* 71; Jacoby, comm. to 156 F178. Neither of the two passages united by the *Suda* seems to be related to Leonnatus' death in the Lamian War (cf. S1 = F1, 9).

58. I am very doubtful that the encomium of Demosthenes preserved by the *Suda* (S23) is from Arrian.

59. Ptolemy's history may also have stopped at the same point, and for much the same reason, as argued above.

60. Despite Roos II, xxix n. 1, the correct form of the title is probably *Bithyniaca* and not *Bithynica.* Eustathius, who used the work most frequently, regularly calls it *Bithyniaca.* Jacoby uses throughout *Bithyniaca,* Roos *Bithynica.*

61. For the place of local history in Greek historiography see Jacoby, "Entwicklung"; Lionel Pearson, *Early Ionian Historians* (Oxford 1939). See also the bibliography by W. Spoerri in *Der kleine Pauly* 3 (1969) s.v. Lokalchronik, Lokalgeschichte, 715-17. Histories of Greek cities are collected by Jacoby in *FGrHist* III B. Histories of Bithynia are found in III C, with histories of non-Greek lands and peoples, but because of the Greek settlements there, are more closely akin to the histories of Greek states than to the historical ethnography found in *Persica* or *Aegyptiaca.*

62. On the revival of local history see Walter Spoerri in *Lexikon der alten Welt* (Zürich and Stuttgart 1965) s.v. Geschichtsschreibung, griechische, cols. 1070-71. On Greek attitudes to their past, see E. L. Bowie, "Greeks and Their Past in the Second Sophistic," *Past and Present* 46 (1970) 3-41. Bowie does not realize, however, in his treatment of local history (19-22) and his comment on Arrian's *Bithyniaca* (27), that the fact that local histories terminated with the advent of Roman rule is not evidence of a rejection of the Roman present but simply a characteristic of the genre: all local histories, and ethnographies as well, end with the subjection of the state to another power.

63. Contrast the several known histories of Heraclea, *FGrHist* 430-34, as well as others on Byzantium, Ilium (Troy), Cyzicus, and Lampsacus.

64. Greek historiography always presumed an independent state or states as the object of its interest. The history of a city or country ceased with its subjection to another power—one reason for our ignorance of Greece under Roman domination.

65. Strabo 13.1.45. On Demetrius see E. Schwartz in *RE* s.v. Demetrios 78, IV, 2 (1901) 2807-13 = *Griechische Geschichtschreiber* (Leipzig 1959) 106-14; Rudolf Pfeiffer, *History of Classical Scholarship from the Beginnings to the End of the Hellenistic Age* (Oxford 1968) 249-51.

66. Still less that it was Arrian's *Lebenswerk,* for which the *Anabasis* and other books were practice exercises, as argued by E. Schwartz, *RE* s.v. Arrianus, 1236. See the corrective remarks by Jacoby, *FGrHist,* comm. to 156, II B, p. 552. The date of composition of the *Bithyniaca* is not certain, since the only outside evidence, the notice in Photius, is variously interpreted. See appendix 5.

67. Other stories of this type taken from local histories may be found in Parthenius and in Plutarch's *Brave Deeds of Women,* nos. 7 and 18 (*Mor.* 246D-247A, 255A-E). See Philip A. Stadter, *Plutarch's Historical Methods* (Cambridge, Mass. 1965) 57-58, 97-101.

68. The fragments of Demosthenes are in *FGrHist* 699 and Iohannes U. Powell, ed., *Collectanea Alexandrina* (Oxford 1925) 25-27.

69. The first part of B36 (= F20b) contains the statement "he marched to Chrysopolis, then during the night crossed the Bosporus," which apparently forms part of a historical narrative, but the subject is not known. Arrian reported that Libyssa, the city in Bithynia where Hannibal died, was called *ta Boutiou* (B65 = F28), but this may have been in a gazetteer, not a historical narrative. The passage relating that Pharnabazus castrated Chalcedonian boys and sent them to Darius (B37 = F79) is more possibly from a historical narrative, though it may belong to an ethnographical section, reporting the custom among the Chalcedonians of treating the twenty-first of each month as unlucky.

70. Eustathius has no less than sixty-seven of the eighty-two citations of the *Bithyniaca.* Stephanus of Byzantium is next with nine, and the rest have one each.

71. Grammatical points: B20b = F77b, B23 = F22, B24 = F23, B31 note = F91, B41 = F101, B67 = F119b, B70 = F89a, B72 = F99.

72. Marchinus van der Valk, *Eustathii Commentarii ad Homeri Iliadem pertinentes* (Leiden 1971) I, L.

73. Verbatim citations: B9 = F82, B14 = F103, B20 = F77b, B21 = F83, B22 = F97, B28 = F173, B31 note = F91, B33 = F67, B34 = F96, B36 = F20, B38 = F81, B40 = F87, B43 = F76a, B46 = F63, B47 = F75?, B52 = F73, B54 = F72, B55 = F71, B57 = F65, B70 = F89a.

74. B29 = F58 (Europa carried off by Tauros, king of Crete), B31 = F64 (Cadmus and Harmonia), B33 = F107 (Iasion was an enthusiast of Demeter, not her lover), B35 = F92 (Briareus as a king ruling the sea, *thalattokrator*).

75. See B5 = F26, B7 = F17, B11 = F59, B12 = F110, B13 = F61a, B16 = F68bis, B18 = F27, B20 = F77, B21 = F83, B30 = F86, B32 = F95, B33^2 = F67, B35^1 = F92, B37^1 = F78, B38 = F81, B40 = F87, B47 = F75, B49 = F84, B51 = F74, B55 = F71, B56 = F68, B57 = F65, B58 = F70, B59 = F66. Note the criticism of those deriving the name of the Nile from Neilasios (B61 = F57). In B39^1 = F61c we may assume that Prieneus is the eponym of Priene. At B10 (= F106) the name of the dance *sikinnis* is derived from an otherwise unknown homonymous nymph.

76. Other foundation notices are listed in n. 75 above. Note that as often in local historians, the historical foundation is antedated by a mythological one: thus Astacus (later moved and refounded by Nicomedes I as Nicomedia) was founded according to Arrian by Astacus the son of Poseidon, long before its colonization by Megarians ca. 712 B.C. (B5 = F26). Cf. also the story of the foundation of Chalcedon (B37[1] = F78). The story of Crocodice is similar to others which have become more distinctly mythological, such as that of Nisus and Scylla, as told by Ovid *Met.* 8.1.151.

77. Cf. B20 = F77, B21 = F83, B31 = F64.

78. Cf. B11 = F59, B13[1] = F61a, B18 = F27, B21 = F83.

79. Religion: B3 = F16, B9 = F82, B10 = F106, B23 = F22, B24 = F23, B33[1] = F107, B37[2] = F79, B37[3] = F80. Custom: B25 = F100, B27 = F108, B66 = F104.

80. Note the patriotic bias of B10 = F106, B22[1] = F97, B26 = F94, and B42 = F88.

81. Mount Olympus in Mysia was heavily wooded and furnished a haven for brigands: cf. Strabo 12.574. The proper form of the name is Tillorobus, not Tilliborus, as we learn from inscriptions from Termessus: see M. L. Radermacher, "Nochmals der Räuber Τιλλοροβος," *Anzeiger Akademie Wien,* Ph.-hist. Kl. 73 (1936) 8; and Louis Robert, *Études Anatoliennes* (Paris 1937) 98 n. 3. F. Zimmermann, "Ein Bruchstück aus Arrians Τιλλιβορον βιος," *Archiv für Papyrusforschung* 11 (1935) 165-75, attempted to assign *POxy* 416 to Arrian's *Tillorobus,* but the style seems quite different from Arrian's and the identification has not been accepted.

Abbreviations

Arrian's works and the abbreviations used for them are listed in Appendix 1. The extant works, except for those about Epictetus, are cited according to the edition of A. G. Roos, *Flavii Arriani quae extant omnia:* I, *Alexandri Anabasis* (Leipzig 1907) and II, *Scripta Minora et Fragmenta* (Leipzig 1928); reprinted with additions and corrections by G. Wirth (Leipzig 1968). The fragments of lost works are cited both by the number in Roos II and by the fragment in Felix Jacoby, *Fragmente der griechischen Historiker* II B (Berlin 1929-1930), no. 156. The fragments in Roos are numbered separately by work: B = Bithyniaca, P = Parthica, S = Events after Alexander, C = On the Nature, Composition, and Appearances of Comets. The fragments in Jacoby are numbered consecutively and identified by an F preceding the number. Thus the citation P1 = F30 refers to *Parthica* fragment 1 in Roos, which is the same as Arrian fragment 30 in Jacoby. Testimonia to the life of Arrian are collected by both Roos (vol. II, pp. LVIII-LXV) and Jacoby. They are cited by T followed by the number and, if necessary, the name of the editor. The Epictetian works are cited from the edition by Henricus Schenkl, *Epicteti Dissertationes ab Arriani Digestae*[2] (Leipzig 1916).

AAA: Athens Annals of Archaeology

ABSA: Annual of the British School at Athens

AE: L'Année Épigraphique

AJA: American Journal of Archaeology

AJP: American Journal of Philology

AnatSt: Anatolian Studies

ANRW: Aufstieg und Niedergang der römischen Welt, ed. Hildegard Temporini (Berlin and New York 1972-)

AntCl: L'Antiquité classique

ArchDelt: Archaiologikon Deltion

AthMitt: Mitteilungen des deutschen archäoligischen Instituts, Athenische Abteilung

BCH: Bulletin de correspondance hellénique

BEFAR: Bibliothèque des écoles françaises d'Athènes et de Rome

BibO: Bibliotheca Orientalis

CAH: Cambridge Ancient History

CIL: Corpus Inscriptionum Latinarum

ClMed: Classica et Mediaevalia

CP: Classical Philology

CQ: Classical Quarterly

CR: Classical Review

CW: Classical World

EHR: English Historical Review

FGrHist: Fragmente der griechischen Historiker, ed. Felix Jacoby

GRBS: Greek, Roman and Byzantine Studies

HSCP: Harvard Studies in Classical Philology

IG: Inscriptiones Graecae

IGRR: Inscriptiones Graecae ad Res Romanas Pertinentes, ed. R. Cagnat

ILS: Inscriptiones Latinae Selectae, ed. H. Dessau

IRT: The Inscriptions of Roman Tripolitania, ed. J. M. Reynolds and J. B. Ward Perkins

IstMitt: Mitteilungen des deutschen archäologischen Instituts, Abteilung Istanbul

JHS: Journal of Hellenic Studies

JRS: Journal of Roman Studies

MusHelv: Museum Helveticum

NachGöttingen: Nachrichten der Akademie der Wissenschaften in Göttingen, phil.-hist. Klasse

NJbb: Neue Jahrbücher für Philologie und Pädagogik

PIR: Prosopographia Imperii Romani

ProcBritAc: Proceedings of the British Academy

PSI : Papiri greci e latini, pubblicazioni della società italiana per la ricerca dei papiri greci e latini in Egitto

RE: Real-Encyclopädie der classischen Altertumswissenschaft, ed. A. Pauly, G. Wissowa, and W. Kroll

RE s.v. Arrianus: Eduard Schwartz, *RE* s.v. Arrianus 9, II (1896), 1230-47, repr. in Schwartz, *Griechische Geschichtschreiber* (Leipzig 1959), 130-55.

REA: Revue des études anciennes

REG: Revue des études grecques

RhM: Rheinisches Museum für Philologie

SBBerl: Sitzungsberichte der deutschen Akademie der Wissenschaften zur Berlin, Klasse für Philosophie, Geschichte, Staats-, Rechts- und Wirtschaftswissenschaften

SBHeid: Sitzungsberichte der Heidelberger Akademie der Wissenschaften, phil.-hist. Klasse

SBWien: Sitzungsberichte der österreichischen Akademie der Wissenschaft in Wien, phil.-hist. Klasse

SEG: Supplementum Epigraphicum Graecum

SIG: Sylloge Inscriptionum Graecarum, ed. G. Dittenberger

StItal: Studi italiani de filologia classica

VDI: Vestnik Drevnej Istorii

YCS: Yale Classical Studies

ZPE: Zeitschrift für Papyrologie und Epigraphik

Ronald Syme (essay date 1982)

SOURCE: "The Career of Arrian," in *Harvard Studies in Classical Philology,* Vol. 86, 1982, pp. 181-211.

[*In the following essay, Syme offers an account of Arrian's career as a public official, analyzing the order in which Arrian possibly composed his writings and commenting on Arrian's literary and intellectual development.*]

I

When senators compose history they are not always eager to obtrude their occupations or any travels in foreign parts. Erudite enquiry has to seek after hints or traces in the writings, a seductive pastime but often hazardous and liable to deceive.

Arrian excites curiosity on various counts. It is baffled by problems of dating, which extend to the lost works. In his manifold productivity two opuscules belong to the period when under Hadrian he governed the military province of Cappadocia (?131-137). Next, he indited the treatise on hunting and the *Discourses of Epictetus* after he had retired to Athens early in the next reign, becoming an honorary citizen and holding the archonship. For the rest, and notably for his history of Alexander (the *Anabasis*), disputation goes on.

A tradition obtained, and a recurrent phenomenon. The senator turns to history when reaching high office—or rather when employment lapsed, writing for consolation and sometimes for revenge. In consonance therewith the bulk of Arrian's works was consigned to the late season of a long life. Weighty authority commended the notion.[1]

Brief reflection dissuades. In the happy epoch of the Antonines performance in oratory or letters led notoriously to public honor, as witness Herodes Atticus and Cornelius Fronto, consul and consul suffect in 143. Arrian, so he affirmed, had been devoted from early years to the study of warfare and philosophy as well as hunting.[2] Official duties whether at Rome or in a province were never as exacting as the ingenuous fancy. They conveyed the need or the excuse for recreation. A scholar could take a provision of books to far Cappadocia—or find them there.

That region, which bore a sad name for bleak and rural retardation, had cities such as Mazaca (now styled Caesarea) and primeval Tyana. Cappadocia had already anticipated the epoch of the sophists with Apollonius, the magician and charlatan. Perhaps an isolated figure. Yet Cappadocia was soon to exhibit the orator Pausanias, a pupil of Herodes Atticus, and young Diodotus, cut off before his prime.[3]

Arrian's writings interlock with his official career. They ought to stand in some relation, so it is presumed. Apart from recourse to internal evidence, sundry experiences might be invoked, or the impact of notable transactions.

Arrian's major work narrated the wars between the Romans and the Parthians. Of the seventeen books of his *Parthica,* no fewer than ten were devoted to the campaigns of Trajan (114-117). Whether or no Arrian himself saw service, the Imperator evoked the conquering Macedonian.

Alexander, it is true, finds no mention in any fragment of the *Parthica.* The theme and parallel was not lost on Cassius Dio.[4] Like Arrian's *Parthica,* the *Anabasis* might fall in the sequel to Trajan's war, at no long interval.

Hesitations are enjoined. Authors do not always respond with due and prompt alacrity or leave clues for guidance. The governor of Africa Nova is not disclosed by Sallust's second monograph; and when Flaubert came back from his tour in the Orient it was not for the exotic *Salammbo.* His choice went to rural and bourgeois Normandy.

In the recent time preoccupation with Alexander has issued in a spate of writing: penetrating and subversive as well as erudite or fluent. Arrian suffered neglect, raw material for the industry or ending as a by-product. Compensation accrues from two recent studies of author and writings. A thorough investigation puts the *Anabasis* in the early years of Hadrian, not later than the year 125.[5] By contrast, an excellent book stands by a later dating.[6]

Interest in Arrian's person is now stimulated by three epigraphic discoveries, in close sequence. First, a fragmentary inscription at Corinth registers a legate of Cappadocia, styling him a philosopher. Second, at Athens the *praenomen* of Flavius Arrianus emerges as "Lucius." Third, at Corduba Arrianus, a proconsul of Baetica, makes a dedication to Artemis in Greek verse.[7]

The present disquisition will eschew as far as possible the nature and content of Arrian's writings, their order of composition, the author's intellectual development. The design is to furnish a framework. Emphasis will concentrate on ages and stages in the service of the Caesars, on types and prospects of advancement, on comparison with other senators among Arrian's coevals.

II

Entering the Senate by the quaestorship at the age of twenty-five, the *novus homo* normally attains the *fasces* when forty-two. Two tiles with the stamp "Arriano et Severo" assign Arrian's consulship to either 129 or 130.[8] A provisional device to facilitate the conduct of the enquiry may assume the former year and put his birth about 86.

Senators from the eastern provinces, that is a large theme and attractive, a long story.[9] They arrive sooner than might be expected, and more numerous. In the first place from the veteran colonies and from cities favored by the Italian diaspora. Close behind follow the native aristocracies, promoted already by the Flavian rulers and on conspicuous show under Trajan with a whole cluster of consular magnates.

Bithynia's first senator was an equestrian officer adlected by Vespasian: he came from Apamea, a *colonia*.[10] Furthermore, Apamea (or perhaps Nicaea) is now claimed as the *patria* of a man who rose to abnormal eminence, namely L. Catilius Severus (suff. 110, cos. II 120).[11] The *nomen* "Catilius" is very rare, even in Italy, and not borne by any previous senator.[12]

Arrian's city was Nicomedia, where he held a priesthood; and he wrote a history of the Bithynian kingdom. Nicomedia, despite its rank and strategic advantages, shows few traces of Italian settlement.[13] As for Arrian's family, their Roman citizenship may go back a long way. The nomenclature "L. Flavius Arrianus" invites conjecture, although the *nomina* "Flavius" and "Arrius" are common and indistinctive. With the latter nothing can be done, but attention goes to L. Flavius, consul suffect in 33 BC, at that time with Marcus Antonius in the eastern lands.[14] For parallel, observe the *cognomen* "Cocceianus," later on splendid attestation with Dio, the sophist of Prusa, and with the consular historian Cassius Dio from Nicaea. As partisans of Antonius both C. Cocceius Balbus (suff. 39) and M. Cocceius Nerva (cos. 36) held commands and earned the title of "imperator."[15]

Along with the historian, Bithynian Cassii evoke Cassius Asclepiodotus, whose funeral monument stands outside Nicaea.[16] Also, and relevant to the present theme, the fragmentary inscription of a senatorial "[Cas]sius" who may be identical with Cassius Agrippa (or Agrippinus), consul suffect in 130.[17]

Young Arrian is first discovered at Nicopolis of Epirus, attending the lectures (or rather dialogues) of Epictetus. He wrote them up many years later. One incident he reports gives the season of his sojourn. A certain Maximus turned up, on his way to an appointment in Hellas as *diorthotes* (that is, *corrector*). Maximus, of the Epicurean persuasion, was enticed or forced into an interchange with the relentless sage (*Diss.* 3.7).

Now Pliny happens to address a friend called Maximus, departing "ad ordinandum statum liberarum civitatum" (*Epp.* 8.24.2). The letter belongs to 107 or 108. Persons of that name cause perplexity, but an attractive identification is to hand: Sex. Quinctilius Maximus, who in 99/100 had been an exemplary quaestor in the province Bithynia-Pontus.[18]

This man was in fact one of the better sort at the *colonia* Alexandria in the Troad. That Pliny should equip him with copious admonishment about the way to behave toward Greeks is no impediment. The artful orator was emulating Cicero's epistle to his brother Quintus, proconsul in Asia.

Next, Delphi. An inscription yields five members of a Roman governor's *consilium*, among them "Fl. Arrianus."[19] The governor, C. Avidius Nigrinus, is styled "leg. Aug. pro pr."[20] Caesar's legate has thus replaced the proconsul in Achaea, as did Pliny and Cornutus Tertullus in Bithynia-Pontus. Like them, Nigrinus (suff. 110) should be presumed a consular, his post falling somewhere between 111 and 114.[21] He went on to govern Dacia, where he was superseded in 117 by the illustrious Pergamene C. Julius Quadratus Bassus (suff. 105).

There is an advantage in having Nigrinus in Achaea in 112 or 113. He belonged to a cultivated and philhellenic family—and he was a close friend of Hadrian. An anecdote asserts that Hadrian intended Nigrinus for his successor.[22] At first sight dubious—but the item may go back to an apologia in that emperor's autobiography. Nigrinus was one of the Four Consulars put to death in the early months of the reign, for a conspiracy not plausible.

In 112 Hadrian was elected archon at Athens. The ardent addict to all things Greek would hardly fail to grace the city with his presence. So far as known, he had never been previously in Achaea—and escape from Rome was welcome for one whose personality was not wholly congenial to the Imperator, apart from an uneasy kinship and prospects at the mercy of hazard.

Going eastward or returning, many Romans put in at Nicopolis, from veneration of the sage long established there, or from curiosity.[23] Hadrian, averse from pomp and rank, was drawn to the unconventional philosopher who had once been a slave; and Epictetus, although a Stoic, had marked affinities with Cynics through his sharp criticism of society and government.[24]

The *Historia Augusta* transmits a precious item, deriving from the basic source: "in summa familiaritate Epictetum et Heliodorum philosophos habuit" (*Hadr.* 16.10). Heliodorus, otherwise C. Avidius Heliodorus, Prefect of Egypt at the end of Hadrian's reign, was an Epicurean.[25] These casual facts, it may be noted in passing, go far toward invalidating much that has been alleged and written about the beliefs of Hadrian.

III

Arrian is attested at Delphi in the company of Avidius Nigrinus. Delphi evokes Plutarch of Chaeronea, holder of a priesthood and assiduous at the sanctuary. Also sundry friends of Plutarch, among whom the Avidii had been conspicuous.[26]

Arrian knew other cities, in the first place Corinth, a Roman colony and seat of the provincial governor. Lucius Gellius carries the dedication of the books devoted to Epictetus—and one of the new inscriptions reveals L. Gellius Menander as a friend of Arrian.[27] This person already stood on record as a fancier of Roman officials: dedications in honor of three imperial procurators.[28]

Likewise much in evidence at Corinth was Cn. Cornelius Pulcher, of an old Epidaurian family.[29] He paraded a collection of priesthoods and ceremonial titles.[30] Topics of varied interest radiate from this pretentious character. Pulcher became procurator in Epirus, a post created by Nero (in 67, when Hellas was liberated) or by Vespasian.[31] Nothing debars identity with the unnamed procurator whose ostentatious comportment at Nicopolis drew condign censure from Epictetus (*Diss.* 3.3). Pulcher, it is suitable to add, earned a treatise from Plutarch—on the technique for getting benefit from personal enemies.

IV

So far the private existence of L. Flavius Arrianus. A larger theme unfolds, namely the season and the manner in which he made the transit to senatorial status. Various paths offered. Brief clarification may be useful.

When assuming the *toga virilis* with the broad stripe a senator's son duly enters the "amplissimus ordo." To other youths Caesar grants the *latus clavus* either at once (before minor magistracy and military tribunate) or just before the quaestorship. The first senator in a family tends to suppress the change of status. Few specify as did Quinctilius Maximus, "lato clavo exornatus" by Nerva.[32] The negative side illustrates, since "dignitas senatoria" can be discarded or refused. Thus Valerius Macedo declined when Hadrian offered "latum clavum cum quaestura."[33]

Some new men came to the quaestorship from equestrian service. Their acquisition of the *latus clavus* may be expressed by the periphrasis "adlectus in amplissimum ordinem." Thus Ti. Claudius Quartinus (suff. 130) after a tribunate in the legion III Cyrenaica.[34] In most cases the quaestorship follows at once on military posts, without explanation. Thus Aemilius Arcanus of Narbo, after three tribunates—and also after all the local magistracies.[35]

Some of those promoted equestrians thus became quaestors well above the normal age. The striking and peculiar example is Statius Priscus (cos. 159): after five military charges and a procuratorship.[36]

In sharp contrast stand adlections to rank in the Senate. Admissions were conducted by the Caesars when censors (Claudius and Vespasian), by censorial powers (Domitian), by imperial prerogative (later rulers). By this device officers, procurators, or local worthies enter the Senate without having previously belonged to the "amplissimus ordo."

V

It has been expedient to register these distinctions and variations. Misconceptions about Arrian's early career still occur.[37] Furthermore, emphasis on uncertainties all through. If Arrian was born in 86, and if he advanced by the quaestorship, he would be a senator in 112 or 113—when he is merely a member of a governor's *consilium*. Again, on the same hypothesis about Arrian's age, he would be too old for *tribunus laticlavius* in Trajan's Parthian War (114-117), too young for legate of a legion.

Equestrian service seems the answer. Here again there is a danger of misconceptions, fostered by the existence of a "militia equestris" with a regular sequence of three posts. Ages of entry varied, likewise a man's tastes or his prospects.[38] Some, not ambitious for higher or civilian employment, might rest content with a single post. Municipal men looked to travel and exotic experiences, to acquiring a patron or local prestige.[39] Specimens abound in the western lands, to mention only Junius Columella, the Gaditane agronome, tribune in VI Ferrata.[40] For the context of Arrian, Cornelius Pulcher avails, tribune in IV Scythica.[41]

For Arrian himself the great war in the Orient may have marked a new turn in his fortunes as well as an incentive to authorship. His participation has been doubted or denied it is true.[42] The evidence is imperfect. According to a passage in Johannes Lydus, Arrian in his ***Historia Alanica,*** in Book 8, gave precise information about the Caspian Gates, having been put in charge of the region by Trajan.[43]

Some infer a military command, exercised in the direction of the Caucasus. Others disallow, supposing a confusion with the Cappadocian governorship under Hadrian. The item may be allowed to lapse.

A number of fragments from the **Parthica** have been adduced that appear to disclose special knowledge or autopsy.[44] Caution is prescribed. Arrian was composing the ample narration of a contemporary war, with a wide theatre of operations. Whether or no present himself at some of the actions, the author needed much information from eye-witnesses.

If Arrian had not yet become a senator, the hypothesis is reasonable that he saw service as an equestrian officer in this period, and precisely in Trajan's campaigns. It would be a pleasing diversion to adduce persons whose acquaintance Arrian now made or reinforced, whose reminiscences he was able to exploit in the sequel.[45]

Most of the fragments are brief and tell little. One, of larger compass, concerns a general called "Broutios." Facing snow sixteen feet deep, he rescued his force through help from native guides and the use of snowshoes.[46] Identity was patent: Bruttius Praesens, the epigraphic record of whose career shows him commander of VI Ferrata.[47] Nor is the date and occasion beyond conjecture. Snowshoes employed on Mount Masius and in Atropatene are mentioned by Strabo.[48] Therefore Praesens in the winter of 114/5 brought troops southward across the high Taurus that separates Armenia from the upper valley of the Tigris.[49]

After the charge of a minor road in Italy (the Via Latina) Praesens is discovered as governor of Cilicia when Trajan died at Selinus in August of 117. His long life and notable career was crowned by a second consulship in 139. There is something else, a small and neglected fact—he wrote a history of his own times.[50]

In the written record of the campaigns one name finds no mention: the heir-apparent whom the Imperator left in command of the army in Syria.[51] Imagination or fiction fills out his previous occupations. On one estimate, Hadrian had been the chief of staff.[52] On another, he resided at Antioch.[53]

It fell to the new emperor to conduct back to Europe troops from the failed war. Ancyra and Nicomedia lay on his path. At Ancyra the Galatian magnate C. Julius Severus had generously facilitated the passage of armies to the seat of war.[54] Arrian, it is supposed, may have played a similar role in his city, either then or when they returned in the autumn of 117.[55] That is, if then resident at Nicomedia.

Arrian's friendship with Hadrian, which turns out to be closer and more congenial than conveyed by the word "amicus" (at an early date it had become a kind of title), may go back several years. In any event, let it be conjectured that he was adlected to the Senate either during the Parthian war or in 118. That is well before Hadrian's first journey which took him to Gaul and Germany in 121, to Britain in the next year. There is no reason for retarding Arrian's admission.

If adlected "inter praetorios" Arrian stood in fair prospect of a consulship when ten or twelve years had elapsed. Not without employment by Caesar, at the minimum the command of a legion. The equestrian officers whom Vespasian promoted in 69 and 73 furnish useful parallels.[56] None happen to be available for the first quinquennium of Hadrian's reign.

VI

For Arrian the only sign points toward a senatorial province. At Corduba a proconsul of Baetica called Arrianus consecrates a Greek poem to Artemis, declaring his gift better than gold and silver, better than the products of hunting.[57] None other than the author of the **Cynegetica,** the notion is highly attractive. A long way from home and from familiar lands, it is true. For that matter, the Pergamene historian Claudius Charax was to visit Britain about the year 140, to command the legion II Augusta.[58]

Arrian's writings lend no support. It is not safe to use the long digression in the **Anabasis** which, devoted to the Tyrian Heracles, happens to mention the shrine of Hercules "at Tartessus" (i.e., Gades).[59]

Again, the age knew other senators of the name, such as Arrianus Severus, a *praefectus aerarii* under Trajan or Arrianus, a *curator operum publicorum* (epoch not determinate).[60]

Nor is it certain that one can claim for Arrian the small fragments of a Hadrianic governor of Cappadocia, who was curator of the Tiber.[61] The inscription carries the word "H]ispa[niae." That might, however, be supplemented to give the legion IX Hispana.

If the dedicant at Corduba is held to be Flavius Arrianus (suff.?129) the date might invite curiosity. Sortition for proconsulates comes five years after the praetorship. In Arrian's case perhaps toward the year 124. A predecessor (perhaps immediate) would then be Tullius Varro, who after commanding XII Fulminata in Cappadocia brought VI Victrix from the Rhine to Britain (presumably in 122); and who, after Baetica, proceeded by the charge of the *Aerarium Saturni* to a suffect consulship in 127.[62] Hadrian, it will suitably be recalled, departing from Britain to Gaul and Spain, spent the winter of 122/3 at Tarraco but omitted a visit to his *patria* in Baetica.

Engaging speculations are curtailed by the chance of a later date. By anomaly a proconsulate can come late, after an imperial governorship that was leading straight to the *fasces*. After a legion and Lusitania both Oppius Sabinus and Javolenus Calvinus became proconsuls of Baetica. Their consulates can be assigned c. 140 and c. 143.[63] Earlier specimens can be discovered, and various reasons might be canvassed.

Of double relevance to Fl. Arrianus is the Cassius of the fragmentary inscription at Nicaea. After commanding a legion (XX Valeria Victrix, in Britain) he was proconsul of Baetica before the consulship. As indicated, perhaps the *suffectus* of 130, Cassius Agrippa (or Agrippinus).[64]

As happens elsewhere, a new document can engross interest beyond its value for history. Let Corduba recede.[65] A proconsulate in Baetica has diverted attention from posts of another character likely to be held by a man who goes on as consular to one of the ten military commands in the portion of Caesar.[66]

VII

The evidence about senatorial careers is so abundant as to constitute a subject in itself; and while system is to be deprecated (being liable to be overridden by social rank, by capacity, by patronage), types and patterns emerge. Even in the four minor magistracies a kind of predestination can be discovered.[67] The *tresviri capitales* have slender prospects, whereas patricians claim almost a monopoly among the *monetales*. Furthermore, under the Antonine rulers patricians are seldom *tribuni militum,* legionary legates or governors of praetorian provinces. The rare exceptions are noteworthy.[68]

For a man's advancement and success, posts subsequent to the praetorship are crucial. One significant pattern takes shape under the Flavian emperors: the legionary command followed by the governorship of an imperial province, in some cases the sole praetorian posts, and with access to the *fasces* four or five years short of the standard age. The prime specimen is Julius Agricola (suff. 77), with XX Valeria Victrix and Aquitania; and there are good instances under Trajan.[69]

Although most consuls had commanded a legion, education and social gifts rather than military training opened the path to high honors; and a consular's experience with the armies had seldom been continuous and prolonged. Trajan numbered among his marshals men of high cultivation such as Licinius Sura and Sosius Senecio (the most eminent friend of Plutarch).

A recent survey of consular legates, putting emphasis on diversities, goes all the way from 70 to 235.[70] A shorter span during which stability and routine obtained is more manageable and might prove more instructive. That is, the forty-four years from the death of Trajan to the accession of Marcus Aurelius.[71] Confined to those limits, the catalogue that was furnished is reduced to twenty-eight names.[72]

Three should be added, viz.:

> Ti. Claudius Quartinus (suff. 130). *PIR*², C 990. He held a legionary command in 123; his governorship of Lugdunensis, deduced from *CIL* XIII 1802, is now confirmed by an inscription at Lugdunum (*AE* 1976, 427).

> (L.?) Valerius Propinquus (?132). *CIL* II 6084 (Tarraco), cf. G. Alföldy *RIT* (1975) 149. After the praetorship he had VI Victrix and either Arabia or Aquitania.

> T. Flavius Longinus Marcius Turbo (c. 150). *PIR*², F 305. He had in succession I Adiutrix and Lugdunensis: his sole praetorian posts.

In this total of thirty-one all except four commanded a legion. Each is exceptional in various fashions.

> C. Popilius Carus Pedo (suff. 147). *ILS* 1071. Appointed to command X Fretensis (in Judaea), "a cuius cura se excusavit." His service as a military tribune had been passed in the same country with decorations from Hadrian, "ob Iudaicam expeditionem."

> P. Salvius Julianus (cos. 148). *ILS* 8973. He acceded to the *fasces* after holding both treasury posts. Salvius was the great jurist of the age.

> L. Dasumius Tullius Tuscus (suff. 152). *ILS* 1081 (Tarquinii). A legionary command may have been omitted from the inscription. Otherwise Tuscus is left with a single praetorian post.

> T. Pomponius Proculus Vitrasius Pollio (?c. 150). *ILS* 1112. This man was a patrician: also married to Annia Fundania Faustina, a cousin of Marcus Aurelius. It is indeed an anomaly to find him governing Moesia Inferior, where he is attested in 157
>
> (*AE* 1937, 247).

Next, the posts that qualify for the consulate. The total of praetorian provinces in the portion of Caesar, eight under the Flavians, had now risen to twelve; and in three of them the governor was at the same time commander of a legion.[73] Of the thirty-one senators here under review, twenty reached the consulate by this path.

The remainder may be summarily catalogued. For the patrician Vitrasius Pollio, a post was not requisite or normal; and Lollius Urbicus (suff. c. 135) had a staff appointment during the Jewish War (*ILS* 1065). No fewer than nine held the prefecture of the *Aerarium Saturni*, in a collegiate pair with a tenure normally triennial.[74] Like Salvius Julianus, Catilius Severus (suff. 110) had the two treasuries. His career is noteworthy for lack of promise until the vicinity of 107, when, so it may be conjectured, he married an heiress and attached himself to the potent Hispano-Narbonensian group, being known in the sequel as a "great-grandfather" to Marcus Aurelius.[75]

Finally, three *curatores* in charge of the Via Flaminia or the Via Appia, combined with the charge of the *Alimenta*.[76] These posts clearly rank as equivalents to the praetorian province or the *Aerarium Saturni*.

For posts of this kind it would be superficial to postulate special aptitudes. While not such sinecures as the minor roads or the office of *praefectus frumenti dandi* (seldom found in epigraphical careers of the successful), they denote a patent privilege. Some of Caesar's friends thus dispense with a province and enjoy a spell at the capital after the legionary command.

A similar explanation may avail for the *cura operum publicorum,* held in this period immediately after the consulate. The tenure might be assumed biennial.[77] Both Bruttius Praesens (suff. 118 or 119) and Metilius Secundus (123) were *curatores* before going to a province.[78] A collegiate pair is not on direct attestation until Ti. Julius Julianus and M. Ma[, dated to the consulate of Q. Insteius Celer (?128).[79]

Statistics combine helpfully. Of sixteen *curatores* between the years 136 and 161, no fewer than twelve proceed to consular provinces. Seven of them had been *praefecti Aerarii Saturni.*[80]

Some students of the Principate are prone to set a high value on administration. The Romans did very little of it. It is a question how arduous were the functions of the various *curatores.* When Julius Frontinus was put in charge of the aqueducts he took his duties seriously, and even compiled a technical handbook. Its accidental survival should not mislead. Several of the earliest *curatores* held the office for life. Further, Cocceius Nerva spent six years on the island Capreae, and (under Claudius) Didius Gallus went away for some years to be legate of Moesia.[81] After as before, experts of lower station did the work. After the reign of Trajan the government may have allowed the *cura aquarum* to lapse.[82]

VIII

On the evidence presented by thirty-one consular legates in office under Hadrian and Pius, it would be premature and harmful to deny Arrian the command of a legion; and he may well have governed one of the twelve praetorian provinces. It will be of use to register ten of his coevals by their modes of access to consulships during a quinquennium.

> Sex. Julius Maior (suff.?126). Numidia. *PIR*[2], J 397.
>
> Ti. Julius Julianus (?126). Arabia, attested in 125. *AE* 1976, 691.
>
> Sex. Julius Severus (127). Dacia, from 120 (or rather 119) to 126. *PIR*[2], J 576.
>
> Q. Tineius Rufus (127). Thrace, in 124. *CIL* III 14207[35] (a milestone).
>
> P. Tullius Varro (127). *Aerarium Saturni. ILS* 1047.
>
> A. Egrilius Plarianus (128). *Aerarium Saturni. AE* 1955, 173.
>
> M. Acilius Priscus Egrilius Plarianus (c. 130). *Aerarium Saturni. AE* 1955, 171.[83]
>
> L. Aurelius Gallus (c. 130). *Aerarium Saturni. ILS* 1109.
>
> Q. Fabius Catullinus (cos. 130). Numidia. *PIR*[2], F 25.
>
> Ti. Claudius Quartinus (suff. 130). Lugdunensis, cf. above.

So far as known, five of the ten proceeded to consular provinces.[84] In contrast to the whole reign of Antoninus Pius, the Hadrianic evidence is capricious and defective. For example, for a whole decade (120 to 130) not one of the legates governing two of the four major commands (with garrisons of three legions) is on record, namely Pannonia Superior and Syria.

These ten consuls are heterogeneous. Various in origins as in attainments, they reflect the cosmopolitan recruitment of the upper order; the first two eastern, two of the others perhaps from the western provinces, while Julius Severus had for *patria* the colony of Aequum in Dalmatia.[85]

IX

The limits have been indicated within which speculation should operate when discussing Arrian's employments anterior to his consulship. Turning to inferences from the writings, primary value adheres to a passage that describes the Indian rivers, with comparison of the Danube (***Ind.*** 4.15f.).

The author mentions two tributaries of the Danube, namely the Inn and the Save. He had seen them both. The Inn, he says, flows into the Danube in the border territory of Noricum and Raetia. A senator was not likely to see those provinces, which were governed by equestrian procurators.

Next, so Arrian states, the place where Save and Danube unite is called Taurunum. Compare the valuable notice in Pliny: "Taurunum ubi Danuvio miscetur Savus" (*NH* 3.148). It may appear peculiar that Arrian should specify Taurunum (the modern Zemun) as the confluence of the two rivers rather than Singidunum (Belgrade), which in his time was the camp of the legion IV Flavia. Taurunum was a port on the bank of the Danube; and, seen from Belgrade, the broad Danube flows gently into the rushing Save.

The facts about Taurunum were worth registering, whether to support or to deny autopsy. Taurunum was the boundary station of Pannonia Inferior. Not, however, valid to encourage a notion that Arrian had been governor of that province c. 126-129.[86]

For the rest, appeal has been made to certain items about hunting.[87] Arrian in the ***Cynegetica*** refers in general terms to a variety of regions (23.2). About two he is specific. He describes the practices of the Gauls (3.19f., cf. 34). Further, when governor of Cappadocia he was able to compare the Caucasus (seen from the coast at Dioscurias) with the Celtic Alps (*Peripl.* 11.5).

Next, "a sight like nothing else," the African nomads hunting on horseback (24.3). In the year 128 Hadrian visited the African provinces. There is no call, however, to suppose that the friend was in his company, admiring the technical skill that informed the imperial discourse to the troops at Lambaesis—and notably some remarks about cavalry.[88] As concerns the African nomads, Arrian might somewhere have seen in their recreations the Moorish horsemen led by their chieftain Lusius, active in both the Dacian and Parthian campaigns.[89]

Nor will other peregrinations of the Emperor be with safety invoked, although Arrian (if with him in 121) might have contemplated the Alps and visited Raetia. It is better to re-nounce—or fall back on experiences gathered by an equestrian officer, wider than what befell most senators.

X

A "dira cupido" or conscientious endeavor attempts to wrest from ancient writers information they had no mind to furnish; and disputation of any kind about authorship and dates finds excuse or earnest commendation.

The other chronicler of Alexander is a palmary example, namely Q. Curtius Rufus. Dates have ranged from the Augustan age to the fourth century, with much ingenuity and industry expended in the controversy.[90] Meanwhile some historians were content to acquiesce in the belief that the historian of Alexander is identical both with the *rhetor* named by Suetonius (*De rhet.* 9) and with the legate of Germania Superior, to whose paradoxical destiny Tacitus devoted a delightful digression (*Ann.* 11.21).

Tacitus declined to state what he knew about the squalid origin of the consular, a gladiator's son, so some alleged: "neque falsa prompserim, et vera exsequi pudet."[91] It is no scandal, no surprise that the Roman annalist chose to sup-press the existence of the ten books entitled "Historiae Alexandri regis Macedonum."

By good fortune the latest investigation comes as close to proof as can reasonably be expected. It puts the compiler of the work under Caligula and Claudius—and Caligula's admiration for the Macedonian furnished an incentive.[92]

The praenomen of Rufus and his consular year (43) are now confirmed.[93] A thoroughgoing enquiry could hardly refrain from some speculation about the man's career. Rufus received the *latus clavus* while serving in the "militia equestris," so it is suggested.[94] That notion is discountenanced by the language of Tacitus. After frequenting the quaestor in Africa, Rufus "acri ingenio quaesturam . . . adsequitur" (11.21.1).

The disquisition failed to allude anywhere to posts between praetorship and consulate. Even the low born orator Eprius Marcellus (suff. 62) had commanded a legion.[95] Further, he was legate of Lycia—Pamphylia, proconsul of Cyprus.[96]

Praetorian posts, that question concerns occupations surmised both for Arrian and for another literary gentleman, M. Cornelius Fronto (suff. 143). This African *novus homo* is the subject of a recent monograph, comprehensive yet admirable in its economy.[97]

Fronto in a letter to Marcus says that he has never governed provinces or commanded an army.[98] It therefore becomes expedient to devise for him some suitable employments at the capital or in Italy. For example, one might think of one of the roads, which (combined with the *Alimenta*) conveyed three senators to the consulship in the period 136-142.[99]

Instead is advocated the *Aerarium militare* followed by the *Aerarium Saturni*. For parallel, Pliny and Salvius Julianus are adduced, an orator and a jurist. Further, for Fronto's tenure the *sexennium* 126-131 is proposed.[100]

That proposal engenders a problem. Fronto should then have come straight to the *fasces*. How account for the long delay? Fronto, it is argued, was born c. 95, hence about five years beyond the standard age when he finally became consul, in 143.[101]

Fronto, it is a noteworthy fact, speaks of Hadrian with distaste and acerbity.[102] One could evoke the dark years before the ruler's decease. Hence a marked setback for the orator.[103]

XI

Caesar's friend from Nicomedia was not likely either to suffer retardations (at least when well launched on the senatorial career), or, on the other hand, to benefit from abnormal favor. It is not easy to verify *novi homines* reaching the consulship under Hadrian before the age of forty.[104] After the praetorship and the command of a legion Sex. Julius Severus (suff. 127) passed seven years as governor of Dacia.[105] The promoted equestrian can take longer. Ti. Claudius Quartinus (130) was legate in Asia and *iuridicus* of Tarraconensis before the death of Trajan.[106]

Arrian was consul in 129 or 130 with a Severus for colleague. While that *cognomen,* along with "Maximus" among the six most common, deters any identification, a thought has gone to Herennius Severus, the patron of Philo of Byblos.[107]

In these pages the year 129 has been accorded a convenient preference. If consul in 129, Arrian might have been *curator operum publicorum* before his appointment to Cappadocia.[108] The post was attractive, as has been indicated. By the same token, Caesar might take pleasure if congenial friends or favored adherents remained in the capital. Hadrian, however, after the African tour in 128 went eastward on peregrinations that lasted for six years.

On any count Arrian's governorship falls between the limits of 130 and 138. There are three fixed points. First, while Arrian was inspecting the coast of the eastern Euxine he learned at Dioscurias that Cotys, the ruler of the Bosporan kingdom, was no longer among the living (*Peripl.* 17.3): the last coins of Cotys were struck in 131/2.[109] Second, the dedication made to Hadrian by Sebastopolis (in Galatian Pontus), dated to the year 137, under the imperial legate Fl. Arrianus (*ILS* 8801). Third, the successor Burbuleius Ligarianus (suff. c. 134), after holding the *cura operum publicorum,* arrives before the decease of Hadrian (*ILS* 1066). Hadrian died in July of 138.

One scholar has Arrian's tenure begin in 130, another assigns 138-141 to Burbuleius.[110] No harm is done or deception entailed if one allocates to Arrian the *sexennium* 131-137.

Along with Cappadocia, the large command embraced Armenia Minor, Pontus Polemoniacus—and also Pontus Galaticus, with the cities of Amaseia, Zela, and Sebastopolis. On the Euxine littoral Roman posts went eastward beyond Trapezus across the river Phasis as far as Dioscurias beneath the mountain of Caucasus. The kingdom of Bosporus, however, fell under the supervision of the legate governing Moesia Inferior.

Caesar's legate in Syria had charge of relations with the Parthians, to face an intermittent threat of war or to conduct negotiations, and he was sometimes invested with special authority. The role of the Cappadocian command (instituted by Vespasian) should not be neglected.[111] Two legions, stationed at Melitene and at Satala, commanded the routes for invading Armenia. The governor had also a diplomatic function: not only Armenia but the vassal states behind Armenia toward Caucasus.

Pharasmanes the Iberian had been recalcitrant, refusing to meet Hadrian when he appeared on the frontier in 129.[112] The prince, who controlled the Darial Pass, is under incrimination. In 135 he incited the Alani. They came through the Caucasus, harried Armenia and Media, menacing (so it seemed) the zone of the Roman frontier.[113]

Arrian mustered his army and deterred the Alani.[114] No battle ensued; and there is no sign that Arrian seized the opportunity to march through Armenia and approach the defiles of Caucasus.[115]

The governor has left a detailed account of the order of battle for deployment against the Alani. The ***Ectaxis*** is variously instructive. The legion at Satala, XV Apollinaris, is in prominence, and its legate Vettius is named.[116] XII Fulminata had the left wing: the eagle is mentioned, and the legion was under the command of its tribunes.[117] No word, however, of the legate, or of the *laticlavius* in either legion, although four commanders of auxiliary regiments earn a mention. Two years later the *laticlavius* of XV Apollinaris happens to be on record, namely M'. Acilius Glabrio (cos. 152). It is highly peculiar for a patrician to hold this appointment anywhere, let alone at bleak Satala on the edge of the Roman world. Hence legitimate curiosity.[118]

XII

Anomalies crop up anywhere. They are recognized as such through regularities observed when evidence is abundant, as for example about the governors of several praetorian provinces under Hadrian and Pius.[119]

Cappadocia presents a welcome contrast to certain other consular provinces. After Catilius Severus who held the command from 114 to 117 (with Armenia briefly annexed), before proceeding to Syria and a second consulship in 120, there is a gap for three or four years. Then, thanks to recent accretions, there follows a complete run for two decades:

> ?121-124. C. Bruttius Praesens (suff. 118 or 119). For his *cursus, IRT* 545; *AE* 1950, 66.
>
> 127/8 (L.?) Statorius Secundus (suff. ?c. 123). *AE* 1968, 504 (nr. Sebastopolis).
>
> 129 T. Prifernius Paetus Rosianus Geminus (?125). *AE* 1976, 675 (Archelais).
>
> ?131-137 L. Flavius Arrianus (?129).
>
> 138 L. Burbuleius Optatus Ligarianus (c. 134). *ILS* 1066.

Statorius Secundus is only a name. The others illustrate varieties of age and experience. Bruttius Praesens, a *laticlavius* with military decorations as early as 89, is found living at ease in Campania about the year 107, gently rebuked by Pliny for his Epicurean tastes (*Epp.* 7.3). His exploit in 114/115 and his governorship of Cilicia have already been noted. After the *cura operum publicorum* Praesens proceeded to Cappadocia: governor there when Hadrian in 123, breaking off his tour of the western provinces, came to the east and had a satisfactory interview on the Euphrates with the Parthian monarch.[120]

Prifernius Paetus, son by adoption to a consular, had been Pliny's quaestor in the year 100, under the name of "Rosianus Geminus," as emerges from a petition of Pliny on his behalf a decade later (10.26). Nothing more is heard of the man until he becomes proconsul of Achaea c. 123 and survives to be proconsul of Africa in 141/2.[121] The surprise is to learn from an inscription that this unpromising person, coeval with Hadrian (q. 101), should have a military province in his middle fifties.

Burbuleius Ligarianus began as *triumvir capitalis.* This *novus homo* engages interest by the slow process of his career: no fewer than half a dozen praetorian posts (mostly minor) before acceding to the *fasces* in 134 or 135. He came from Africa, so it may be argued.[122] Comparable in certain ways is Ti. Claudius Quartinus (suff. 130), whose first post was equestrian. His tribe, the "Palatina" may indicate libertine origin ultimately.[123]

Consular legates tend to be drawn from nonconsular or equestrian families. Of some appointed by Hadrian, such as Praesens and Prifernius, one suspects that they had failed to win approval from his predecessor.

Other friends of the deceased Pliny may furnish instruction. About the prospects of Erucius Clarus, Pliny, who had got him the *latus clavus* and the quaestorship (?99), was moved to express some disquiet (2.9.2). Still only a legionary legate in 116, a vigorous exploit in Mesopotamia elevated him to a consulate the next year.[124] Erucius was the nephew of Septicius Clarus, whom Hadrian in 119 appointed to command the Guard as colleague of Marcius Turbo; and about the same time Suetonius Tranquillus (a diffident character in the letters of Pliny) became the secretary *ab epistulis*.[125]

XIII

A hostile tradition impugns Hadrian for ingratitude toward friends and allies. The indictment embraces a whole catalogue (*HA, Hadr.* 15). Late in the year 136 Hadrian turned against his kinsfolk, choosing Ceionius Commodus as heir and successor, with dire consequences for old Julius Servianus and for the youth Pedanius Fuscus, the grandson of Hadrian's sister.

Hadrian had a propensity to omniscience (15.8). Conflicts with scholars and men of letters are duly reported—in some instances with manifest exaggeration.[126] Arrian had no further occupation after Cappadocia, so far as known. He is next discovered in retirement, archon at Athens.[127] Estrangement from the capricious ruler has been surmised.[128] Some may (or may not) have wondered about the attitude of Antoninus Pius. Bland but percipient, Pius could not quite suppress a distrust of sophists and philosophers.[129]

Before leaving Cappadocia Arrian wrote his *Tactica*. The manual divides sharply into two parts. The second, after a full exposition of cavalry tactics, praises military innovations due to the Emperor and concludes with a reference to his *vicennalia* (44.3) That is, the anniversary falling in 136/7. The language conveys an unobtrusive solicitation for further employment, so it has been supposed.[130]

In fact, Arrian may have become legate of Syria not long after. According to Lucian, the notorious Peregrinus Proteus was once released from prison by a governor of Syria who delighted in philosophy (*Per.* 14). Why not Arrian? The notion finds some favour.[131] It has also been deprecated.[132] However, to have Syria after Cappadocia is a natural and easy promotion, attested for Burbuleius Ligarianus and for others before or after.[133] Faint support may accrue from the new inscription at Corinth that designates Arrian as "the philosopher." Thus Arrian has recently been assigned Syria, c. 138-141.[134]

That dating concerns other governors of Syria. Sex. Julius Severus (suff. 127), legate of Judaea and earning the *ornamenta triumphalia* for quelling the rebellion, proceeded to Syria. His inscription shows him there before the decease of Hadrian.[135] Account must also be taken of a fragment at Palmyra, bearing a date in April of 138 and disclosing the names of Bruttius Praesens and Julius Maior.[136] The former had been proconsul of Africa (133/4 or 134/5), the latter is attested as legate of Moesia Inferior in 134 and is further a known legate of Syria.[137] The two consulars, it can hardly be denied, were in succession governors of Syria in the last epoch of Hadrian.[138] Brief tenures are no bar. A senior consular like Bruttius Praesens, possessing diplomatic tal-ents and eastern experience, may have been charged with negotiations with the Parthians.

XIV

A threat of hostilities is on record soon after the accession of Antoninus Pius, dispelled by a missive he sent to the Parthian monarch (*HA, Pius* 9.6). Not before it provoked a display of energy from the tranquil ruler, as a casual piece of evidence proves. A legionary legate called Neratius Proculus was instructed to conduct reinforcements to Syria "ob bellum Parthicum" (*ILS* 1076). Proculus, after holding the *Aerarium militare,* was promoted to the consulate.

The "prudentes," the men who know history and assess policy on a long view, may not have expected a war with a power that was normally not aggressive. Yet it ensued early in the next reign, perhaps through miscalculations on both sides, the first action being the disaster incurred by a legate of Cappadocia, Sedatius Severianus (suff. 153), whom Lucian styled "that silly Celt": a friend of the false prophet, a devotee of the sacred snake (*Alex.* 25).

The date of Arrian's *Parthica* now comes in again. As indicated, an easy assumption looks to the near aftermath of Trajan's war. Contemporary history is a hazardous enterprise, as Arrian stated in the exordium to the *Anabasis.* None the less, a loyal senator and a discreet expositor might be equal to the double challenge—the Imperator a great and glorious general, yet no disparagement of the actions and policy of Hadrian who renounced conquests that had already been lost or abandoned.

Later dates have been advocated, the question regarded as open. The *Parthica* might be a by-product of the Cappadocian governorship—or evoked by the Parthian War (162-166) which Lucius Verus conducted, or rather supervised.[139] The latter notion entailed for the historian a survival longer than most now contemplate. Moreover, a thought should have been spared for the crisis at the beginning of Pius' reign.

To sum up. On the hypothesis of a late dating, the *Parthica* might be regarded as comparable in some fashion to the *Discourses of Epictetus,* being in part recollection of a man's earlier years, especially if he had fought in Trajan's campaigns. On the other hand, those seventeen books were a major work of history—and the longest that Arrian wrote.[140]

Uncertainty also envelops the termination of Arrian's official employment. The chance has been noted that he was governor of Syria. Reflection may import a fairly strong doubt. Julius Maior may have continued there for several years or have been replaced by Julius Severus before the death of Hadrian.[141]

Again, about the year 143 Arrian would become eligible for the sortition for the proconsulates in Asia or Africa. For Asia the tenure 143/4 is available, preceding Claudius Quartinus (suff. 130) and (?Claudius) Julianus (?130).[142]

For Africa, a long gap follows Tullius Varro (suff. 127), who should go in 142/3.[143] For the man of Nicomedia, Africa might appear less suitable. Not but that Africa rather than Asia may be the proconsulate of Julius Maior (suff.?126), whose family was domiciled at Nysa and who traced a descent from Polemo, the king of Pontus, and Antonia Pythodoris.[144]

Some "viri militares" neither needed nor wanted a proconsulate—and a discreet hint from Caesar's friends could counsel withdrawal from the sortition. Again, age or health might deter. Cornelius Fronto, awarded Asia, hesitated before going there—and may never have left the shores of Italy.[145]

The proconsulates have been adduced, since they were the peak of a senator's ambition. Before that point Arrian may have made his decision. There are no grounds for attributing his Athenian retreat to supersession or frustration. After a sexennium in Cappadocia (double the normal tenure) either the senator or Caesar might conceive that he had had enough.

XV

Parading as the modern Xenophon and even styling himself "Xenophon" when governor of Cappadocia, Arrian in this reincarnation combines the author and the man of action.[146] He likewise exemplifies the double aspect of the times. The Hellenic renascence of letters, adumbrated by Plutarch and by Dio of Prusa, came to full bloom under Hadrian and Pius, producing the age of the sophists. The political aspect preceded. It exhibits eastern consuls of native stock, from Sardis and Pergamum, before the end of the Flavian dynasty.

Conventional history, built up largely on the biographies of emperors, was content for a long time to assign the main role and initiation to Hadrian. Facts emerging combine to declare a process, actions accelerated by accidents; and much credit is transferred from Hadrian to his martial predecessor. Trajan's reign is adorned by a group of four consulars, advertised on the inscription of their cousin Julius Severus of Ancyra, the descendant of kings and tetrarchs.[147] The conspicuous members of the nexus are A. Julius Quadratus, consul for the second time in 105, and the consul suffect C. Julius Quadratus Bassus. The latter, who commanded an army corps in Trajan's second war beyond the Danube, went on to govern Cappadocia, Syria, Dacia (dying on campaign in the winter of 117/8).[148]

Not all of the eastern magnates claim comparable splendor or merit. By lineage, in the forefront was C. Julius Antiochus Philopappus, grandson of the last ruler of Commagene (and with Seleucid ancestry), whose sepulchral monument stands on the Hill of the Muses.[149] A citizen of Athens, and archon, Philopappus was adlected to the Senate by Trajan and given a consulship in 109. Of active employment, no sign. Curiosity is aroused (and perhaps quenched) by the fact that Philopappus belonged to the priestly fraternity of the *Arvales*.[150]

The opulence and ostentation of these invaders may well have excited resentment, with enmity and feuds ensuing. Not even vestiges appear to survive. As elsewhere, the sparsity of the written sources has to be taken into account—and not least its character. To a satirist devoted to the Roman tradition the magnates of Asia would be an attractive target. Juvenal directs his shafts against the dead or the fictitious. Nor is illumination to be expected from Pliny. Approving of Greek culture with conventional and disciplined enthusiasm, he nowhere alludes to the eastern origin of any member of the "amplissimus ordo."

Hadrian himself, at divergence from Trajan in so many of his tastes and habits, may not have shared Trajan's liking for the descendants of kings and tetrarchs. There is a peculiar fact concerning the Galatian aristocrat C. Julius Severus (suff.?138): late entry to the Senate through adlection "inter tribunicios" about the year 125.[151]

Hadrian's sympathies (it may be conjectured) went rather to Athens, to old Hellas, to the more modest and useful city aristocrats. Not that any sharp antithesis existed. Galatian tetrarchs had links with Pergamum long since; and Italian immigrants intermarried with dynastic families.[152]

A dearth of evidence about consuls impedes the estimate. Apart from the years 127 and 128 (complete thanks to the *Fasti Ostienses*) hardly any *suffecti* are on record after 122 and before 138. Again, few governors of certain military provinces during the twenties.

Of the easterners, about ten consuls can be rounded up, a mixed bag. No *ordinarius* is among them, unless perhaps M. Antonius Rufinus (131) and M. Antonius Hiberus (133); and no *consul bis* apart from Catilius Severus in 120. By contrast, observe under Trajan the pair Julius Quadratus and Julius Candidus introducing the year 105.[153]

Hadrian paid special honor and deference to the Roman Senate, so it is averred. One of the proofs alleged is a mass of iterations in the *fasces*.[154] The facts refute.

After deplorable transactions in the first months (much worse than the dubious adoption) the new ruler stood in sore need of allies. It was also expedient to conciliate the whole senatorial order. By paradox, one method was to avoid exalting too many of the eminent with second consulates. Another would be to insist on regularity in the senatorial *cursus*.

In fact, Hadrian made no scandalous promotions, such as Trajan had—a Guard Prefect, Attius Suburanus, consul suffect in 101 and *ordinarius* two years later. Toward the end occurred other acts of flagrant favoritism, such as Terentius Gentianus, consul in 116 before he reached the age of thirty and Lusius Quietus, the Moorish chieftain, abruptly elevated in 117.[155]

Philhellenism has various and even contrasted facets—and so had the ruler himself: "varius multiplex multiformis."

While certain features in Hadrian's conduct may disturb or repel, such as his infatuation with Antinous, the fact that he chose for friend a disciple of Epictetus acquires emphasis. Arrian, governor of Cappadocia and historian, is an attractive phenomenon in an age dominated by the sophists and paying homage to the pompous and verbose, to persons like Antonius Polemo, Aelius Aristides, Herodes Atticus.

XVI

Arrian selected Athens for domicile. That does not betoken estrangement either from Rome and the Empire or from Nicomedia. Adequate reasons explain a predilection for Athens, and he had been away from Nicomedia for a long time.

It was to honor his *patria* that Arrian wrote about the antiquities and legends of Bithynia, the annals of the kingdom down to its annexation by Rome. Were it not for clear evidence in a passage of Photius, a temptation might have insinuated to suppose the **Bithyniaca** a late testimony of gratitude from an expatriate.[156]

Along with the **Bithyniaca,** the monographs on Dion and Timoleon are recognized among the earliest compositions of the polygraph.[157] If they concern Sicily, no special and personal interest in that island. Those biographies reflect rather the experience at Nicopolis, they bear upon the relationship between philosophical studies and the life of a general or a statesman.

Different avenues and complex motives lead to the writing of history. Not all authors begin with biography or local antiquities—and some go no further.

Soon or late in the reign of Antoninus Pius Arrian published the **Discourses of Epictetus.** When the elderly sage ended his days is beyond ascertainment: late or confused notices prolong his existence unduly.[158]

Unauthorized circulation of the books induced Arrian to publish at last, as an apologia explains in the letter addressed to L. Gellius Menander.[159] Another letter about Epictetus happens to be on record, to the address of "Messalinus."[160] That is, a personage of some eminence although known only from inscriptions: C. Prastina Pacatus Messalinus, the consul of 147.[161]

Friends of Arrian in the aristocracy of the consulars would be worth knowing. Speculation is legitimate but unproductive. Let it suffice to call up in passing Julius Maior (suff.?126) or Julius Severus (?138), each of illustrious birth in Asia.

Matrimony created or reinforced alliances, some local, others transcending a province or a whole region in the world empire. No clue leads to the wife or wives of Fl. Arrianus. There was issue, on record at Athens.[162]

While Hadrian made a painful exit during the ominous sixty-third year of life, Arrian enjoyed length of days and continuing productivity. Although not earning admittance to the intellectuals registered in Lucian's catalogue of "Macrobii," he may have lived on into the reign of Marcus and Verus, reaching or surpassing the age of eighty. If outdoor pastimes contribute to longevity (that is a common belief), there is something to be said for addiction to polite studies, in defiance of sloth or mere recreation. Sustenance derives from writing—or even from compilation.

Estimates of Arrian's birth have exhibited a wide range, from 85 to 95.[163] The later year was never plausible. Better, between 85 and 90.[164] So far the present disquisition has operated with the year 86, for the manifest and avowed convenience of the "suus annus" for a senator consul in 129. It was a further assumption (duly to be recalled) that Arrian entered the Senate during the Parthian War or soon after, by adlection.

The argument falls short of proof (and a retarded quaestorship is not excluded). There is something else. Parallel instances of promoted equestrians (whatever the mode of entrance), show them acceding to the *fasces* some years later than the standard age. A suspicion subsists that Arrian saw the light of day as early as 82 or 83.

Arrian's sojourn at Nicopolis in 107 or 108 will no doubt continue to be invoked—a student aged about eighteen, hence born about 89. That is, "iuvenis admodum" to adopt the parlance of the Latins, referring to a *laticlavius* just before the military tribunate.[165] In that season a youth was liable to be captivated by teachers (or by doctrines and fashions), whether in oratory or in philosophy.[166]

Julius Agricola, when "prima in iuventa," embraced philosophy with more ardor than was suitable in a Roman and a senator.[167] A vigilant mother curbed his ingenuous aspirations. Others may have had a retarded approach to the hazards of conversion, among them the country gentleman from Nicomedia who was devoted to horses and dogs. A rapid allegiance was not forsworn in the sequel although perhaps impaired by a senator's life and by experience of men and government.

Notes

1. E. Schwartz, *RE* II 1231, cf. 1234.

2. Arrian, *Cyneg.* 7-4.

3. Philostratus, *Vit. Soph.* 593f.; 617. The latter is now disclosed as M. Acilius Diodotus (*Pergamum* 8.3, no. 35). For his name and his kinsfolk, *Chiron* 10 (1980) 429f.

4. Dio 68.29.1; 30.1.

5. A. B. Bosworth, "Arrian's Literary Development," *CQ* 22 (1972) 163ff. For a firm pronouncement see his commentary I (Oxford 1980) 6: "The Alexander history, which demonstrably comes early in the sequence of his historical works, was composed when Arrian was in his thirties."

6. P. Stadter, *Arrian of Nicomedia* (1980) 184: "after his consulship, in Cappadocia or in Athens."

   Observe also G. Wirth, *Historia* 13 (1964) 209ff. (subsequent to the year 147); E. L. Bowie, *Past and Present* 46 (1970) 24ff. (in the early years of Marcus).

7. *AE* 1968, 473; 1971, 437; 1974, 370.

8. *CIL* XV 244; 252. Cf. *PIR*² F 219.

9. For the full statement and catalogue, H. Halfmann, "Die Senatoren aus dem östlichen Teil des Imperium Romanum bis zum Ende des 2. Jh. n. Chr." *Hypomnemata* 58 (1979).

10. Halfmann, no. 18. That is, "]atilius L. f. Clu. Longus" (*CIL* III 335, as emended by W. Eck). In Halfmann's view probably a Catilius. Add, also at Apamea, the slave of a Cn. Catilius Atticus (III 337).

11. Halfmann, no. 38. For his full nomenclature and cursus, *ILS* 1041 (Antium); I.l. d'Afrique 43 (Thysdrus). The latter document furnishes the tribe, generally supplemented as "[Cla]u." (cf. *PIR*² C 558): better "[Cl]u.," cf. Halfmann.

12. *TLL*, Onom. That repertory yields Κατιλλια Γαυριανη Νεικαηνη *IG* XIV 790: Naples). Add further P. Catilius Macer from Nicaea (*SIG*² 836: Delphi, dated to the year 125).

13. In apparent contrast to Nicaea, cf. J. Hatzfeld, *Les trafiquants italiens dans l'Orient hellénique* (1919) 134; 172f. However, for rare names at Nicomedia, see K. F. Dörner, *Inschriften und Denkmäler aus Bithynien* (1941), no. 28 ("Numisienus"); 53 ("Ampilius"); 60 ("Tuccius" and "Poppaeus"); 101 ("Oclatius").

14. Dio 49.44.3.

15. *PIR*² C 1214; 1224.

16. *PIR*² C 486. See further on Cassii F. Millar, *A Study of Cassius Dio* (1964) 8f.

17. *AE* 1950, 251 (Nicaea). Strong doubts about identity are expressed by W. Eck, *RE* Suppl. XIV, 86f.; and this man has no separate entry in Halfmann, who notes him under no. 123 (M. Cassius Apronianus, the parent of the historian). Cassius was admitted among the proconsuls of Baetica by G. Alföldy, *Fasti Hispanienses* (1969) 168.

18. *ILS* 1018 (Alexandria Troadis), cf. Pliny, *Pan.* 70.1. Doubt is voiced by Sherwin-White in his commentary (1966) on *Epp.* 8.24.6.

19. *SIG*³ 827. For the names see the revised text of A. Plassart, *Fouilles de Delphes* III 4 (1970) no. 290.

20. As on an Athenian inscription, published in *Hesperia* 32 (1963) 4.

21. Similarly L. Aemilius Juncus (suff. 127), cf. Halfmann, no. 55.

22. *HA, Hadr.* 7.1.

23. Epictetus was among the philosophers banished by Domitian (Gellius 15.11.5). That is, in 93.

24. See the illuminating paper of F. Millar, "Epictetus and the Imperial Court," *JRS* 55 (1965) 141ff.

25. *PIR*² A 1405 = H 50.

26. For the Avidii, C. P. Jones, *Plutarch and Rome* (1971) 51ff. Heliodorus presumably derives his Roman name from this family.

27. *AE* 1968, 473 (Corinth), cf. G. W. Bowersock, *GRBS* 8 (1967) 279f.

28. *PIR*² G 132.

29. *PIR*² C 1424; Pflaum, *Carrières,* etc. (1960), no. 81. Add now *AE* 1974, 593 (Athens). At Corinth he was honored by Justus, the son of L. Gellius Menander (*IG* IV 1601).

30. In those predilections Pulcher had a rival in another Epidaurian, Q. Alleius Epictetus (*IG* IV 691 = *AE* 1977, 775).

31. The earliest procurator is patently Sex. Pompeius Sabinus (Pflaum no. 53). Next, after Pulcher, A. Ofillius Macedo (no. 112), to be presumed Hadrianic.

32. *ILS* 1018 (Alexandria).

33. *ILS* 6998 (nr. Vienna).

34. *CIL* XIII 1802 (Lugdunum): with, anomalously, "splendidissimus" instead of "amplissimus." For the normal term, *ILS* 1064.

35. *ILS* 1064 (Narbo).

36. *ILS* 1092 (Rome).

37. Thus in P. Stadter (above, n. 6) 6f. Arrian (he suggests) may have "served several years in his early twenties in the equestrian military career." After being commander of a cohort he may have been a *tribunus militum angusticlavius.* Then, after receiving the *latus clavus,* "Arrian could have gone on as *vigintivir,* one of twenty minor administrative officials at Rome, then as *tribunus militum laticlavius.*" That process lacks parallel.

38. E. Birley, *Roman Britain and the Roman Army* (1953) 135ff.

39. As emphasized through Spanish examples in *HSCP* 73 (1969) = *Roman Papers* (1979) 748.

40. *ILS* 2923 (Tarentum).

41. *IG* IV 795 (Troezen).

42. Firmly denied by E. Schwartz, *RE* II 1236; and "unlikely" for F. A. Lepper, *Trajan's Parthian War* (1948) 2. On the other hand, "little reason to doubt" for P. Stadter (above, n. 6) 9, cf. 142ff.

43. Lydus, *De mag.* 1.36 = Arrian, *Parthica* fr. 6 (ed. A. G. Roos, *Arrianus* II [1928]).

44. G. Wirth, *Studii Clasice* 16 (1974) 189f. Not so many are admitted by Stadter (above, n. 6) 144.

45. Notably Catilius Severus, who governed Cappadocia along with the newly annexed Armenia from 114 to 117, when he took over Syria (*ILS* 1041). Catiliu was still extant in 138 (*HA, Hadr.* 24.6).

46. *Parthica* fr. 85.

47. *IRT* 545 (Lepcis); *AE* 1950, 66 (Mactar).

48. Strabo XI, p. 506.

49. For this deduction, *Historia* 18 (1969) 352 = *Roman Papers* (1979) 774. Strabo in three other passages defined as "Masius" the range north of Nisibis (522; 527; 747). That is, the Tur Abdin: not very high.

50. Nothing precludes identity with the Bruttius who according to Christian writers mentioned a Domitianic persecution (*PIR*² B 159). Praesens suffered retardation in his earlier career; and the language of Pliny shows him an Epicurean (*Epp.* 7.3).

51. Hadrian's epigram about Trajan's dedication on Mount Casius (*Anth. Pal.* 6.332) is quoted in fr. 36.

52. W. Weber, *CAH* 11 (1936) 299. Indeed, "he was at the nerve-centre of all action."

53. M. Yourcenar, *Mémoires d'Hadrien* (1951) 80ff. (allegedly appointed governor of Syria in 112).

54. *OGIS* 544 (Ancyra).

55. Thus A. B. Bosworth in his commentary on the *Anabasis* I (1980) 2. Hadrian might have spent the winter of 117/118 at Nicomedia or Byzantium.

    Bosworth adds "Hadrian also passed through Nicomedia and Nicaea on his first journey of 119-121 (Magie 613f.)." To be discarded: Hadrian sojourned at Rome until spring or summer of 121.

56. W. Eck, *Senatoren von Vespasian bis Hadrian* (1970) 103ff.

57. *AE* 1974, 370.

58. *AE* 1961, 320.

59. *Anab.* 2.16.4, with Bosworth's note. Stadter however sets value on the notice (above, n. 6, 10).

60. *Dig.* 49.14.42; *CIL* VI 31132. The former may be the consul Arrianus Aper Veturius Severus (XIV 3587: Tibur). Nothing further is known about C. Statius Capito Arrianus, boy ministrant to the Arvales in 117 and 118 (*CIL* VI 2076; 2078). The nomen "Arrius" is extremely common (about forty entries in *PIR*² A).

61. From Caesarea Mazaca. Recalled by W. Eck, *RE* Suppl. XIV 120, from *Mélanges Beyrouth* 5 (1911) 309.

62. *ILS* 1047 (Tarquinii).

63. *ILS* 1059 (Firmum); 1060 (Tusculum).

64. *AE* 1950, 251, cf. G. Alföldy, *Fasti Hispanienses* (1969) 168. Also above, p. 184 n. 17. This senator might be a son of M. Cassius Agrippa, procurator in Baetica (*CIL* II 2212: Corduba).

65. Nine periodical articles are listed by Stadter (above, n. 6, 195f.), terminating with L. Koenen, "Cordoba and no End," *ZPE* 24 (1977) 35ff.

66. Ten, omitting Dalmatia, consular but lacking a legion since 85.

67. For this, and for some other matters see E. Birley, "Senators in the Emperor's Service," *Proc. Brit. Ac.* 39 (1953) 197ff.

68. Thus the consul of 152, M'. Acilius Glabrio (*ILS* 1072). On whom see "An Eccentric Patrician," *Chiron* 10 (1980) 427ff.

69. *Tacitus* (1958) 650.

70. B. Campbell, "Who were the 'Viri Militares,'" *JRS* 65 (1975) 11ff., with a catalogue of seventy names and three Incerti. One of the three (*ILS* 1057) is identical with no. 37, viz. Cn. Julius Verus, cf. *ILS* 8974. Further, to that rubric should accrue the Ignotus of Nemausus (*CIL* XII 3169), early Trajanic, with consular decorations; and likewise the acephalous cursus of a governor of Syria (*CIL* XIII 2662; Augustodunum), which should be assigned to the Flavio-Antonine period.

    The argument concludes that "in general there are no clearly discoverable patterns of promotion" (23). For temperate criticism of that thesis, G. Alföldy, *Konsulat und Senatorenstand unter den Antoninen* (1977) 375f.

71. For the detail see G. Alföldy, *Konsulat und Senatorenstand,* etc. (1977).

72. It includes, be it noted, five legates in office when Trajan died, viz. Julius Quadratus Bassus (suff. 105); Minicius Natalis (106); Aelius Hadrianus (108); Pompeius Falco (108); Catilius Severus (110).

73. Viz. Numidia, Arabia, Pannonia Inferior. Judaea had been elevated to consular status, perhaps from 117.

74. For the detail, M. Corbier, *L'Aerarium Saturni et l'Aerarium Militare* (1974).

75. If Catilius married the widow of Cn. Domitius Tullus (suff. II 98), who is attested in Pliny (*Epp.* 8.18.8), he would become a step-great-grandfather to the boy Marcus. For this conjecture, *Historia* 17 (1968) 95f. = *Roman Papers* (1979) 692f.; *HSCP* 83 (1979) 305.

76. Namely Minicius Natalis (*ILS* 1061); Cluvius Maximus Paullinus (*AE* 1940, 99); Julius Severus (*ILS* 8829). Natalis was consul suffect in 139, Cluvius c. 141, Severus the ordinarius of 155.

77. Annual tenure was assumed by G. Alföldy (above, n. 17) 26, cf. 289.

78. Praesens to Cappadocia (*IRT* 545), Metilius to a province missing from the inscription (*ILS* 1053), inspection of which (*CIL* XI 5718) might suggest Judaea.

79. *AE* 1973, 36, cf. Halfmann, no. 53. Julianus had been legate of Arabia, attested in 125 (*AE* 1976, 691: Gerasa). The colleague baffles ascertainment.

80. For these statistics, *Historia* 14 (1965) 358f. = *Danubian Papers* (1971) 241f.

81. *History in Ovid* (1978) 124 (discussing the tenure of Messalla Corvinus).

82. At least no curator on record between Neratius Marcellus under Trajan (*ILS* 1032) and Caesonius Macer under Severus Alexander (1182).

83. For the supplementing of that inscription see F. Zevi, *MEFR* 83 (1970) 301. The Egrilii of Ostia have caused much perplexity. For a clear statement, M. Corbier (above, n. 74) 164ff., with a stemma.

84. Namely Julius Maior (Moesia Inferior and Syria); Julius Severus (Moesia Inferior, Britannia, Judaea, Syria), Tineius Rufus (Judaea); Tullius Varro (Moesia Superior); Claudius Quartinus (Germania Superior).

85. *AE* 1904, 9; 1950, 45.

86. Space is vacant well before L. Attius Macro (suff. 134), attested as cos. des. by *AE* 1937, 213 (Aquincum).

87. P. Stadter (above, n. 6) 16: "Arrian seems to imply that he has been in both Gaul and Numidia."

88. Thus words of encouragement for cavalrymen attached to a cohort: "difficile est cohortales equites etiam per se placere," etc. (*ILS* 2487); praise for the *ala Pannoniorum* (9134).

89. *PIR*² L 439.

90. Nineteen scholars are cited by J. E. Atkinson in his recent commentary on Books 3 and 4 (Amsterdam 1980) 19ff. Add the Augustan dating preferred to Vespasianic by Tarn, *Alexander the Great* II (1948) 113f.

91. One could adduce a Q. Curtius Rufus, *duumvir* at Arausio in Narbonensis (*CRAI* 1951, 238)—but the nomenclature is not distinctive.

92. J. E. Atkinson (above, n. 90) 19ff.

93. *AE* 1975, 366 (a small fragment of the Fasti Ostienses).

94. Atkinson (above, n. 90) 52.

95. *AE* 1956, 186 (Paphos).

96. Tacitus, *Ann.* 13.33; *ILS* 992 (Capua).

97. E. Champlin, *Fronto and Antonine Rome* (1980).

98. Fronto, *Ad M. Caesarem* 1.3.4 = Haines I 86.

99. *ILS* 1061 (Minicius Natalis); *AE* 1940, 99 (Cluvius Maximus Paullinus); *ILS* 1069, cf. *AE* 1957, 135 (Caesernius Macedo). Compare later C. Julius Severus, the consul of 155 (*ILS* 8829).

100. E. Champlin (above, n. 97) 80f., cf. 164. Observe that M. Acilius Priscus Egrilius Plarianus (suff. c. 130) also held the two prefectures in succession c. 125-128 (M. Corbier (above, n. 74) 169ff.).

101. Champlin (above, n. 97) 97, cf.; 81.

102. Champlin (above, n. 97) 94ff.

103. That depends upon the conjecture about the two prefectures—which not all may be disposed to find attractive.

104. The two Caesernii, Macedo (*ILS* 1069) and Macrinus (1068) became consuls early in the next reign. For the careers of this favored pair, G. Alföldy, *Konsulat u. Senatorenstand* (1977) 347ff.

105. *PIR*² J 576.

106. *CIL* XIII 1802 (Lugdunum), cf. II 2959 (Pompaelo, dated to 119).

107. *PIR*² H 130.

108. The Arrianus of *CIL* VI 31132 defies dating. The collegiate pair Ti. Julius Julianus (suff.?126) and the enigmatic M. Ma[is attested by *AE* 1973, 36: probably of the year 128, cf. above, p. 195 n. 79.

109. *PIR*² F 219.

110. W. Eck, *Senatoren*, etc. (1970) 204; C. Alföldy (above, n. 104) 220.

111. On which see A. B. Bosworth, "Vespasian's Reorganization of the North-East Frontier," *Antichthon* 10 (1976) 63ff.

112. *HA, Hadr.* 13.9. Furthermore, he visited the coast of Pontus before Arrian's arrival, cf. *Peripl.* 1.1 (Trapezus); 5.2. Presumably not in 129 but in 131.

113. Dio 69.15.1.

114. E. Ritterling, *Wiener Studien* 24 (1902) 359ff.; A. B. Bosworth, *HSCP* 81 (1977) 217ff.

115. As argued by Bosworth (above, n. 55, 229f.) on the basis of a passage in Themistius (*Or.* 34.8 = test. 13 Roos).

116. *Ect.* 5. That is, M. Vettius Valens (*CIL* XI 383: Ariminum).

117. *Ect.* 6; 15; 24.

118. *Chiron* 10 (1980) 427ff. (discussing *ILS* 1072).

119. *Historia* 14 (1965) 342ff. = *Danubian Papers* (1977) 225ff.

120. *HA, Hadr.* 12.8.

121. *ILS* 1067 (the cursus of his son-in-law Pactumeius Clemens).

122. *Historia* 27 (1978) 597.

123. *CIL* XIII 1802 (Lugdunum), cf. XIV 4473 (Ostia). Puteoli shows a *duumvir* of that name (X1782f.).

124. Dio 68.32.5.

125. For the date of Turbo's appointment, recently contested, see *JRS* 70 (1980) 71f.

126. G. W. Bowersock, *Greek Sophists in the Roman Empire* (1969) 51ff.; R. Syme, *JRS* 70 (1980) 74.

127. In 145/6 (*IG* II² 2055).

128. E. Schwartz, *RE* II 1231.

129. W. Williams, *JRS* 66 (1976) 75.

130. G. L. Wheeler, *GRBS* 19 (1978) 351ff.

131. W. Hüttl, *Antoninus Pius II* (1933) 156, following the opinion of G. A. Harrer.

132. By A. Stein in *PIR*² F 219.

133. *JRS* 67 (1977) 46.

134. G. Alföldy (above, n. 104) 238f.: "mit grosser Wahr-scheinlichkeit."

135. *ILS* 1056 (Burnum). The governorship of Syria (following "Syria Palaestina") was unfortunately neglected in *PIR*² J 576.

136. *AE* 1938, 137.

137. *PIR*² J 397. Syria is certified by *IG* IV² 454 (Epidaurus).

138. As assumed in *Historia* 9 (1960) 575 = *Roman Papers* (1979) 490f. See further *ZPE* 37 (1980) 10f., which registers different views about the position of Praesens and Maior.

139. Thus P. Stadter (above, n. 6) 144. He there came to no conclusion, regarding the date of the *Parthica* as a puzzle. In a later place the early date is preferred (183).

140. For a full and excellent appraisal, P. Stadter (above, n. 6) 135ff.

141. There is a better solution. As follows. Severus died not long after passing from Judaea to Syria in 134 or 135. Hence the anomalous appointment of Bruttius Praesens. Julius Maior soon succeeded, holding Syria until 140 or 141. He was replaced by Burbuleius Ligarianus: "in quo honor. decessit," as the inscription states (*ILS* 1066).

    For mortality in the insalubrious province see "Governors Dying in Syria," *ZPE* 41 (1981) 125ff.

142. For those proconsuls, G. Alföldy, *Konsulat u. Senatorenstand* (1977) 212. The second of them is probably a Claudius Julianus rather than (as Alföldy) Ti. Julius Julianus.

143. *ZPE* 37 (1980) 5 (the proconsuls from 136/7 to 142/3).

144. For that problem (Africa or Asia) see *ZPE* 37 (1980) 13f. Maior had been legate of Numidia, attested in 125 (*AE* 1950, 58) and in 126 (1954, 49).

145. *Ad Antoninum* 8 = Haines I 236. Champlin, though cautious, inclines to believe that Fronto in fact went to Asia (above, n. 97, 164).

146. The name is conveyed or implied already in *Peripl.* 1.1; 12.5; 25.1. That is, perhaps a sign that he had already published the *Anabasis*.

147. *OGIS* 544 (Ancyra).

148. *PIR*² J 508.

149. *ILS* 845.

150. As attested by the inscription—but no presence on the protocols of 101, 105, 110. Cf. *Some Arval Brethren* (1980) 113.

151. *ILS* 8826 (Ancyra).

152. As notably the Plancii of Perge, cf. S. Mitchell, *JRS* 64 (1974) 27ff.

153. The latter, so it now appears, came from western Asia. Cf. Halfmann, no. 11; R. Syme, *Some Arval Brethren* (1980) 50f.

154. *HA, Hadr.* 8.4: "tertio consules, cum ipse ter fuisset, plurimos fecit, infinitos autem secundi consulatus honore cumulavit."

155. *ILS* 1046a, inscribed on one of the Pyramids (Gentianus); Dio 68.32.3 (Lusius).

156. Photius, reproduced in Roos II 197f. For the early date, A. B. Bosworth, *CQ* 22 (1972) 179ff.; P. Stadter (above, n. 6) 182f.

157. Stadter (above, n. 6) 162.

158. For the evidence, H. v. Arnim, *RE* VI 127f.

159. Reproduced in Roos II 196.

160. Roos, test. 4.

161. This important and enigmatic person, known only from inscriptions, was legate of Moesia Inferior soon after his consulship. For the problems of his nomenclature and career, *Dacia* XII (1968) 336 = *Danubian Papers* (1971) 219f.

162. Halfmann, no. 88.

163. He was put "c. 95-175" in *CAH* 11 (1936) 688.

164. Stadter suggests "born about A.D. 89, although perhaps as early as 85, or as late as 92" (above, n. 6, 3). Cf., in the chronological table (173), "ca. 89"; and he is assumed to be about eighteen when with Epictetus at Nicopolis (5).

165. Thus Cornelius Tacitus in *Dial.* 1.2 (assuming the year 75 as the dramatic date).

166. Observe Helvidius Priscus: "ingenium inlustre altioribus studiis iuvenis admodum dedit" (*Hist.* 4.5).

167. *Agr.* 4.3.

A. M. Devine (essay date 1993)

SOURCE: "Arrian's *Tactica*," in *Aufstieg und Niedergang der röminschen Welt*, edited by Wolfgang Hasse and Hildegard Temporini, Walter de Gruyter, 1993, pp. 312-37.

[*In the following essay, Devine examines Arrian's treatise on the military tactics of the Roman army,* Tactica, *discussing the content, originality, and textual history of the work.*]

I. L. FLAVIUS ARRIANUS: THE AUTHOR AND HIS CAREER

Of all the ancient tactical authors, the career and personal history of Arrian is by far the best known, even though much of his early military career has to be conjectured from geographical or historical allusions in his surviving works. Lucius Flavius Arrianus was born and educated at Nicomedia (Izmit), the capital of the province of Bithynia in north-western Asia Minor. Although the date of his birth is not attested, the fact that he held the consulship around 130 implies that he was born between A. D. 85 and 90, the normal age for the supreme magistracy in this period being around forty-two.[1] His family had apparently acquired Roman citizenship through the patronage of L. Flavius, an adherent of M. Antonius the Triumvir and himself suffect consul of 33 B. C. (Cass. Dio 49.44.3).[2] Around A. D. 108, Arrian attended the lectures of the celebrated Stoic philosopher, Epictetus, at Nicopolis in Epirus. Our author may have served in the Roman army as an equestrian *praefectus cohortis* or *tribunus angusticlavus* in *legio VII Claudia* during Trajan's Dacian Wars. Although he reported the emperor's Eastern Wars in his 'Parthica', there is no unimpeachable evidence that he saw active service in the Armenian and Mesopotamian campaigns of 114-17. However, he does seem to have made the acquaintance of the future emperor Hadrian before 112/13. In the *Periplus,* the literary account of his tour of inspection in the Black Sea (131/32), Arrian addresses the emperor in familiar, even intimate, terms (2.4). Arrian seems to have been adlected to the senate *inter praetorios* soon after Hadrian's accession, and then to have served as *legatus legionis* in a Danubian province during the early 120s. He was proconsul of the unarmed public province of Baetica in Spain around 125, before becoming suffect consul in 129 or 130, the first Bithynian to hold the consulship. From 130/31 to 137/38, he served as governor of the key frontier province of Cappadocia in eastern Asia Minor, repulsing an invasion by the nomadic Alani and driving them northward through the Caucasus in 135 (Cass. Dio 69.15.1). No official recognition for this campaign is attested, and it is possible that no recognition was merited, since the battle described in Arrian's *Ectaxis contra Alanos* (hereafter *Ectaxis*) is a tactical plan, rather than the account of an actual battle. And, in fact, no major battle between the Alani and Arrian's army can be proved.[3] In 136 Arrian published his principal tactical treatise, . . . *Tactica*), his own revision and adaptation of a pre-existing Hellenistic tactical manual. Around 137/38 he retired to Athens, where he received honorary citizenship and was eponymous archon in 145/46, dying probably in the 160s.[4]

Arrian's best-known work, the *Anabasis Alexandri* (composed after 115 but before 125),[5] is the fullest and most reliable surviving source for the reign and campaigns of Alexander the Great, beginning with those of 335 B. C. It is based on the Alexander-histories of Ptolemy, one of Alexander's most prominent generals and later king of Egypt, and Aristobulus, a Greek technical expert of some kind in Alexander's entourage. Arrian's account of Alexander is supplemented by the *Indica,* published at about the same time as the *Anabasis* and expanding on the details of Alexander's invasion of India as given in book V of the larger work.[6]

Although modern scholarship knows Arrian exclusively as a historian, in his own day his reputation was primarily that of a philosopher. This apparent paradox is due in part to the much broader conception, in the Hellenistic and Roman imperial period, of what a philosopher was and did.

As also in the case of Aelian . . . writing on tactics and other technical topics counted as philosophy. Aristotle's writings on marine biology and Theophrastus' botanical treatise, to name only two instances, were certainly viewed in antiquity as philosophy. Indeed, two contemporary inscriptions are explicit in describing Arrian as a philosopher.[7] Some of his reputation as such derived from his publication of his own summaries of Epictetus' lectures, but fragments of an Arrianic treatise on meteorology, a standard 'philosophical' topic, survive in Stobaeus. Arrian's strictly philosophical writings, if they ever existed, were lost by the time of Photius, the great Byzantine bibliographer who was twice Patriarch of Constantinople (858-867 and 878-886) and who excerpted many subsequently lost Arrianic works (cf. Photius, Bibl. cod. 58.5).

Linked with Arrian's philosophical ambitions was his conscious imitation of Xenophon, who in late antiquity was likewise more famous as a philosopher than a historian.[8] Indeed, in two of his late works, the *Cynegeticus* and the *Ectaxis* (ca. 135/36), Arrian goes so far as to call himself Xenophon. The Byzantine biographical tradition, stemming from Heliconius of Byzantium, maintained that Arrian was actually called the New Xenophon in his lifetime. Works of the period allude to Xenophon the Elder, and a contrast with a younger aspirant to the name is implied. The device of usurped nomenclature is not, however, present in the *Anabasis Alexandri,* which title, evocative as it is of the Elder Xenophon's best-known work, is first attested by Stephanus of Byzantium and need not be Arrian's own: a second Xenophon would naturally be credited with a second 'Anabasis'. Although Xenophon is undoubtedly a source of inspiration for the Alexander-history, there is no indication there that Arrian is casting himself in the role of the new Xenophon to the new Cyrus and his march up-country. The emulation is, however, explicit in the *Periplus* and the *Cynegeticus,* not to mention the *Ectaxis,* and probably only came quite late in Arrian's public life. Then, as the authoritative biographer of Epictetus, and himself a noted Stoic philosopher, prolific historian and geographer, successful military commander, and huntsman, Arrian convincingly resembled the real Xenophon. His close relationship to Hadrian could be seen to parallel that of Xenophon to Agesilaus III the Great of Sparta. The adoption of the Xenophontean name thus came late, and the nomenclature of Neos Xenophon may well have been conferred on Arrian as a title of honour, rather like those of the New Homer and the New Themistocles as conferred by the Athenians on C. Julius Nicanor.[9]

II. THE DATE AND OCCASION OF ARRIAN'S
TACTICA

Unfortunately, the beginning of the *Tactica* was lost when a folio (181a) was torn out of the Codex Laurentianus gr. 55.4, the prototype of the entire manuscript tradition. Stadter[10] argues convincingly that a total equivalent of 35 Teubner lines has thus disappeared, of which 26 would have constituted the formal preface. The size of the missing portion (at least 200 words) makes it almost certain that the lost preface would, by analogy with the extant one of Aelian, have contained a statement of Arrian's qualifications for writing such a treatise, a description of the intended audience, and a formal dedication of the work to the emperor.[11]

The publication of the *Tactica* can, nevertheless, be precisely dated from the reference to Hadrian's *vicennalia* at Tact. 44.3, where the work's concluding lines and the verses of Terpander (frg. 6 Bergk = frg. 4 Diehl) quoted there indicate its ostensible purpose. It was meant as an occasional composition to commemorate the emperor's *vicennalia*, which, according to a calendar of the imperial cult (P. Oslo 3.77, lines 15-16), seems to have been celebrated on 13 December, A. D. 136. Hadrian's *vicennalia*, the first achieved since that of Tiberius in A. D. 34 (and, incidentally, the last until that of Diocletian in 304), was a highly apposite occasion for glorifying the emperor and his regime, and Arrian embellishes the latter part of his work with glowing references to Hadrianic policy and the themes of the reign.

While in the first part (1-32.2) of the *Tactica* Arrian gives a detailed but conventional account of the minor tactics and drill of the Hellenistic armies, in the second part (32.3-44.3) he produces, in overt compliment to Hadrian, a colourful, first-hand description of the parade-ground exercises of the Roman cavalry of his own day. This affords an opportunity, at *Tact.* 44.1-2, to list and praise Hadrian's cavalry reforms, while carefully noting their consistency with the *mos maiorum*. It may be noted, nonetheless, that the cavalry exercises described at *Tact.* 34-43 actually predate Hadrian.

At the time of composition Arrian was serving as *legatus Augusti pro praetore* in Cappadocia, and his frequent allusions to the Sarmatians and the Alani seem to be an attempt to draw attention to his own Transcaucasian campaign of 135. Moreover, at *Tact.* 42.1 our author portrays himself as "the good commander" conscientiously following the emperor's drill instructions. Arrian's governorship of Cappadocia appears to have ended in 137 or at least before Hadrian's death in the following year, and the underlying motive for the *Tactica* would thus have been one of inducing the emperor to continue the author in his command there or in some other armed province.[12]

III. The Form and Content of Arrian's Tactica

1. The Hellenistic Elements

Arrian's 'Τεχνη τακτικη' is, after Aelian's 'Τακτικη θεωρία' and Asclepiodotus' 'Τεχνη τακτικη', the fullest and most important of the surviving Hellenistic tactical manuals, the study of which is effecting a revolution in our understanding of the military techniques of both the Hellenistic states and the Romans, as well as even those of the Persians and the Carthaginians.

Comparison of Arrian's *Tactica* with the cognate tactical manuals of Asclepiodotus (first century B. C.) and Aelian

(published ca. A. D. 106-113) is instructive.[13] Of the three treatises, that of Aelian is the longest at 10,913 words (in the obsolete edition of the 'Short Recension' made by Köchly and Rüstow[14]), and that of Asclepiodotus, at 7,002 words (in the edition prepared by W. A. Oldfather for the Loeb Classical Library), is the shortest. Nonetheless, while the text of Arrian's *'Tactica'* (in the Teubner edition of Roos and Wirth) runs to 9,460 words, of this approximately 2,600 words (327 lines in the Teubner edition) belong to the second, exclusively Roman, part of Arrian's treatise. This fact actually makes Arrian's Hellenistic section the shortest of the three Hellenistic tactical manuals. It should be noted, however, that the issue is complicated by the occurrence of a lacuna of indeterminate, though obviously not of very great, length (represented by a space of seven or eight letters in the prototypical Codex Laurentianus gr. 55.4) at *Tact.* 32.3 (in the bridge passage between the Roman and Hellenistic sections of the work). Moreover, part of section 1.1 (= 1.1K and part of 1.2K) is lost, and there are further lacunae at 10.1 (= 9.2K), 10.3 (i. e., at the beginning of 9.4K) and 29.2 (= 37.2K and 37.3K), and also possibly at 20.3 (= 24.3K) and 24.3 (= 28.3K).

A comparison of the beginning of Aelian's treatise with what remains of the opening of Arrian's reveals, despite some notable points of difference, a remarkable similarity of approach. In the *Prooimion* and the first section of his main text, Aelian explains his reasons for composing the 'Τακτικη θεωρια', freely admitting that he has no personal experience of warfare and no real knowledge of Roman military practice (praef. 1-2). Instead, he writes, like most of his predecessors, as a philosopher (and a perpetuator of the Stoic tradition, as we will see), expressing the hope that his efforts will find favour as "a Greek theoretical work and a polished dissertation" (praef. 6). In line with contemporary literary convention, Aelian justifies his undertaking by stressing his own erudition and ability, which transcends that of earlier writers on tactics (praef. 1 and 4-5). Arrian voices analogous sentiments in his "delayed introduction" to the *Anabasis Alexandri* (1.12.4-5), and their appearance in the lost introduction to the *Tactica* is a high probability. An authority on the Roman art of war through long personal experience (in contrast to Aelian), and a successful military commander like his model Xenophon, Arrian likewise saw himself writing primarily as a philosopher.[15] And tactics, especially the tactics of a bygone age, was an appropriate subject for abstract discussion by a philosopher, which is the only interpretation that the unoriginal Hellenistic part of Arrian's treatise will bear. Both Aelian and Arrian complain that earlier tactical authors have written for a readership already familiar with tactical matters and have failed to explain their terminology (*Tact.* 1.2 = 1.3K; cf. Aelian 1.3). Arrian's express intention, like that of Aelian, is to combat the obscurantism and lack of clarity of these earlier tactical writers (*Tact.* 1.2-3 = 1.3-4K; cf. Aelian 1.4, 1.7). But Arrian (*Tact.* 1.4 = 1.3-4K) goes so far as to claim that he is the first to use his knowledge to correct the sheer obscureness of these antecedent authors. The same claim made implicitly by

Aelian (1.4) suggests that both are in fact appropriating and adapting a claim from a common source—Poseidonius, probably, or perhaps even Polybius.

Further, Aelian considers the table of contents (the 113 'Headings of the Book') which he prefixes to the 'Τακτικη θεωρια' a major contribution to the genre (praef. 7). Arrian's *Tactica*, like those of both Asclepiodotus and Aelian, to begin with probably had an index of section-headings prefixed to it. Arrian's failure to refer to his subsequently suggests that it was a somewhat more rudimentary affair than Aelian's, much more like the twelve headings with which the text of Asclepiodotus opens. Like his misguided and spurious claim of originality, it is certainly evidence that Arrian was unacquainted with Aelian's treatise and its superior model index.

Again, as autopsy of the Codex Laurentianus gr. 55.4 shows, Arrian also diverges from the mainstream tradition represented by Aelian and Asclepiodotus by failing to illustrate his treatise with diagrams—a deficiency which renders his text more difficult to follow—especially when he is describing such unusual formations as the cavalry εμβολος (*Tact.* 16.6-8 = 18.4K) and the Thessalian ρομβος (*Tact.* 16.3-5 [= 18.1-3K] and 17.1-3 [= 19.1-2K and 19.5K]). As, apparently, in the case of the prefixed index or table of contents, Arrian's failure to imitate the more comprehensive and lucid approach of Aelian and Asclepiodotus argues for his lack of familiarity with their rival productions.

Finally, it is in the addition of a major appendix, of a non-Hellenistic character, that Arrian diverges most radically from the rest of the tradition. But while the second part of the *Tactica* (32.2-44.3) is devoted to a tendentious account of the parade-ground exercises of contemporary Roman auxiliary cavalry (discussed below), the first part (1-32.2), as per convention, describes in detailed but generalized terms the minor tactics, drill, arms and equipment, tactical organization, and commands of the Hellenistic armies (rather than of the Macedonian army of Philip II and Alexander the Great).

And, indeed, as a section by section comparison of the three treatises reveals, the order of contents adopted by Arrian in the first part of the *Tactica* follows the pre-existing convention very closely. This order is as follows:[16]

I. Introduction (*Tact.* 1.1-3; cf. Aelian, praef. and 1.1-3).

II. Basic divisions of warfare (*Tact.* 2; cf. Aelian 2.1-5D [= 2.1-6K]; Asclep. 1.1).

III. Description of troops in terms of the equipment used (*Tact.* 3-4; cf. Aelian 2.6-11D [= 2.7-13K]; Asclep. 1.2-3).

1. Infantry (*Tact.* 3; cf. Aelian 2.6-8D [= 2.7-9K]; Asclep. 1.2).

2. Cavalry (*Tact.* 4; cf. Aelian 2.9-11D [= 2.11-13K]; Asclep. 1.3).

IV. Organization of the army (*Tact.* 5-10; cf. Aelian 3-10; Asclep. 1.4-3.4).

1. The need for organization (*Tact.*5.1-3; cf. Aelian 3; Asclep. 1.4).

2. The λοχος (*Tact.*5.4-6.6; cf. Aelian 4-5; Asclep. 2.1-3).

3. Combinations of λοχοι (*Tact.* 7-8; cf. Aelian 6-7.3; Asclep. 2.4-5).

4. Light-armed troops and cavalry (*Tact.* 9.1-2; cf. Aelian 7.4-6).

5. The ideal number for the phalanx (*Tact.* 9.3-6; cf. Aelian 8; Asclep. 2.7).

6. The units of the army (*Tact.* 10; cf. Aelian 9; Asclep. 2.8-10).

V. Formations and the use of troops in battle (*Tact.* 11-19; cf. Aelian 11-23; Asclep. 3.5-9).

1. The phalanx (*Tact.* 11-12; cf. Aelian 11.1-4, 13-14; Asclep. 4.2, 5.1, 3.5-6).

a. Formations (*Tact.*11; cf. Aelian 11.1-4; Asclep. 4.2).

b. Arms and equipment (omitted; cf. Aelian 12; Asclep. 5.1).

c. The different ranks (*Tact.* 12.1-5, 12.10-11; cf. Aelian 13-14; Asclep. 3.5-6).

d. The spacing of the troops and the use of the *sarissa* (*Tact.* 12.6-10; cf. Aelian 14.2-6; Asclep. 5.1-2).

2. Light-armed troops (*Tact.* 13-14; cf. Aelian 15-16; Asclep. 6).

3. Archers and javelin-men (*Tact.* 15; cf. Aelian 17).

4. Cavalry (*Tact.* 16-18; cf. Aelian 18-20; Asclep. 7).

5. Chariots and elephants (*Tact.* 19; cf. Aelian 22-23; Asclep. 8-9).

VI. Movements (*Tact.* 20-27; cf. Aelian 24-35; Asclep. 10.1-21, 12.10).

1. Their names (*Tact.* 20; cf. Aelian 24; Asclep. 10.1).

2. Description of movements (*Tact.* 21-25; cf. Aelian 25-29; Asclep. 10.2-20).

3. Formations taken up by the phalanx (*Tact.* 26, cf. Aelian 30-31; Asclep. 10.21).

4. Means of relaying commands to the army (*Tact.* 27; cf. Aelian 35; Asclep. 12.10).

VII. Marches (*Tact.* 28-30; cf. Aelian 36-39; Asclep. 11.1-6, 11.8).

1. Order of the army (*Tact.* 28; cf. Aelian 36; Asclep. 11.1-2).

2. Formations on the march (*Tact.* 29; cf. Aelian 37-38; Asclep. 11.3-6).

3. The baggage-train (*Tact.* 30; cf. Aelian 39; Asclep. 11.8).

VIII. The manner of issuing commands (*Tact.* 31-32.2; cf. Aelian 40-42; Asclep. 12.11).

Detailed comparison with Aelian also reveals what Arrian omits: Aelian's more extended diatribe against previous tactical writers, and his declaration that he will illustrate his text with diagrams (1.4-6); his claim that tactics is the most useful of all the sciences, and his citation, in support of this contention, of Plato, *Laws* 626a to the effect that "all cities by their very nature wage undeclared war against all other cities" (1.7); Aelian's inclusion of fighting on rivers in the category of naval warfare, and his (unfulfilled) promise to discuss naval tactics later (2.1); the definitions of tactics advanced by Aeneas ("the science of military movements") and Polybius ("whenever anyone takes an unorganized crowd, organizes it, divides it into files and, grouping these together, gives them a practical training for war") (3.4); the information that the last man in a file is called the ουραγος (5.1 ad fin.), and that the commander of a τελος is called a τελαρχης (9.7 ad fin.); the description of the arrangement within the phalanx of the phalangarchies, merarchies, tetrarchies, and syntagmata in terms of the proportionality of the fighting qualities of their commanders (10.1-4); the information that πεκνωσις permits the individual soldiers to face about (11.3), while ςυναοπιομος permits neither withdrawals nor individual turns to right or left (11.4); the description of the standard-issue Macedonian shield and—with the present author's emendation[17]—the ten cubit (= 15 foot) *sarissa* (12; cf. Asclep. 5.1); the information that the men in the sixth and subsequent ranks of the phalanx do not extend their *sarissai* beyond the bodies of the men in the front rank—instead Arrian claims that the phalangites of the sixth rank extend their *sarissai* two feet beyond the front rank and modifies all the dependent statistics in the tradition accordingly (14.4-6, contradicting also Asclep 5.1-2); the information that some commanders have the troops posted in the rear equipped with longer spears than those in front, so that the weapon-heads of those stationed as far back as the third or fourth rank will project just as far (14.7); the observation that it is a great source of strength to a unit to have a senior commander posted not just in front but also in the rear (14.9); the file-closer . . . from the list of supernumerary men attached to each hekatontarchy (16.2, contradicting also Asclep. 6.3); the observations that whenever the number of the horses in the length (i. e. front) of a cavalry formation is equal to that of those in the depth, a square of number will be achieved but the shape of the formation will be an oblong rectangle with the depth greater than the length, and that whenever the shape of the squadron is square, the number of horsemen in rank will differ from that of those in file (18.9); the explanation of why the horses on the left and right sides and rear of the rhomboid-formation have to be stationed at a distance from each other (19.2); the observation that some authorities draw up the cavalry in a rhomboid-formation by both rank and file, others by neither rank nor file, some by file but not by rank, some by rank but not by file (19.3); the information that in drawing up a ρομβος by rank and file, the middle rank in the formation is assigned an odd number of horsemen, and that this number is diminished by two per rank as the formation narrows down towards both the front and the rear (19.4); the manner of drawing up the ρομβος by neither rank nor file, to make wheeling and riding through easier (19.6); the details of the positioning of the ilarch and the remaining horsemen in this way of drawing up the ρομβος (19.7); the position of the zygarch or rank-commander (19.8); the formation of the rearward half of the ρομβος (19.9); Polybius' ideal 64-man *ile* or squadron (19.10); the formation of the ρομβος by file (19.11); the drill for facing about "spearward" and "reinward" by the horsemen in the ρομβος (19.12); the drawing up of the squadron by rank (19.13); [Aelian's reference to one of his own illustrative diagrams (20.1)]; the exhortation to try out in the daily drills all the cavalry formations described, in order to determine which are the most useful and appropriate for actual fighting (21.1-3); the list of chariot-corps units—the zygarchy, syzygia, episyzygia, harmatarchy, keras, and phalanx (22.2); the division of chariots into "light-armed" and scythe-bearing (22.3; but cf. *Tact.* 2.5 = 2.6K); the nomenclature for the various elephant-corps unit-commanders and units—zoarch, therarch and therarchy, epitherarch and epitherarchy, ilarch and ilarchy, elephantarch and elephantarchy, keratarch or merarch and keratarchy, phalangarch and phalanx (23); the injunction that commands should be given in terms of fixed terminology, introducing the catalogue of terms for the various infantry manuvres (24.1); explanation of the terms . . . "insertion", . . . "supporting-position", and . . . "forward position" (24.3); the remark that the tactical writers differ from one other as regards this terminology (24.4); the use of the movement called κλιοις to repel flank-attacks and for making counterattacks (25.1); the definition of the kinds of . . . "about-face", "spearward" or "away from the enemy" and "shieldward" or "towards the enemy" (25.2-4); the promise to explain how the . . . "quarter-turn" is used (25.6); the qualification that the οηνταγμα in making an επιοτροφη resumes close-order on its completion (25.7); the information that being drawn up by rank involves the individual soldier keeping himself equidistant from his comrades in both file and rank (26.1); the description of countermarches by row . . . , that is, the exchange of positions between the right and left within the row (28.4); the doubling of place occupied by a phalanx by depth, by means of half the men in each file countermarching to the rear (29.7D = 29.9K); the reversal of the countermarch, by means of the recall of those inserted as rear-rank men in the original files to their own separate files (29.8D = 29.10K); the account of the ορθια φαλαγξ (30.2); the statement that in νποταξις the formation has the shape of a triple gate (31.4); the extended description of the various kinds of "wheel"—the "quarter-turn spearward", "quarter-turn shieldward", "half-turn spearward", "half-turn shieldward", and the reversal of each of these, the "three-quarter turn, spearward or shieldward" (32.1-9); the "compacting" . . . of the phalanx—on the right wing, on the left wing, and in the centre, and the reversal of each of these manuvres (33.1-5); the injunctions that spears be held upright whenever "wheelings" are made in compact order, and that the light-armed infantry should be trained in the same drill (33.6); the observation that the commands for "facing-about", "quarter-turns", "half-turns", "three-quarter turns", and "resuming first position" are useful for confronting sudden approaches by the enemy, whether they appear on the right or the left, in front or in rear of the army's line of march, and that the same holds good for countermarches (34.1); the information that the Macedonians are said to have invented the Macedonian countermarch and the Spartans the Laconian countermarch (34.2); the claim that Philip II of Macedonia and Alexander the Great both preferred the Laconian countermarch, and only used the Macedonian variety when forced to do so by circumstance (34.3); the explanation that, in the Macedonian countermarch, sudden attacks on the rear tend to produce great disorder, thus increasing the danger of panic and enemy pursuit, since the troops are being marched around from the rear to a position behind the file-leaders—a manœuvre resembling flight, which emboldens the enemy (34.4); the claim that the Laconian countermarch has the opposite effect in the case of an attack on the rear, since the troops advance towards the enemy through their own formation (34.5); the comment that it is sometimes hard to find signals for all purposes, as critical moments present new circumstances to which the troops are unaccustomed, but since it is unlikely that all the various kinds of difficulties will arise simultaneously, distinct orders can still be given either by voice or visual signal (35.5D = 35.6K); the list of march-formations to be described (36.6D = 36.7K); the qualification that in the infantry . . . wedge-formation it is the file-leaders that end up actually engaging the enemy, and likewise in the . . . "hollow-wedge" (37.6-7); the definition of . . . "attenuation" as the reduction of the depth of a phalanx in terms of the number of ranks, the full phalanx-depth of sixteen being given as the example (38.3); the observation that those receiving commands given in haste must be on their guard against ambiguity, lest some do one thing, and others the opposite (40.1); the injunction that, in commands, the specific term precede the general term, to reduce the possibility of ambiguity (40.2, but cf. *Tact.* 31.3 = Aelian 40.3); the repetition of the injunction to put the specific term before the general (40.4); the quotation of Iliad 3.8-9 and the beginning and end of the preceding quotation of Iliad 4.428-431 (41.1); the last three lines of the quotation of Iliad 2.459-463 (41.2); the quotation of Iliad 3.1-2 (41.3); twenty-six of the listed commands (42.1); and the concluding comments on the principles utilized by the tactician (42.2; cf. Asclep. 12.11 ad fin.).

Some of the items omitted by Arrian, like the purely mathematical observation on the square of the number of horsemen in the front of an oblong cavalry formation, are of course of doubtful value for the understanding of Hellenistic minor tactics, though they are precisely the sort of thing that a 'philosopher' would be expected to reflect upon. But much of the omitted material, such as the progression of tactical units and the hierarchy of unit-commanders (notably in the elephant- and chariot-corps) and details regarding phalangite equipment (e. g. the standard-issue Macedonian shield), is of some importance for reconstructing the day-to-day practice and command-structure of the Hellenistic armies.

In view of the fact that Arrian had published a major work of military history, the **Anabasis Alexandri** (with a length of 80,714 words in the Roos-Wirth Teubner edition), some twelve to twenty-two years prior to the composition of his **Tactica,** the absence from the latter of any significant reference to, or example or illustrative material drawn from, the career of Alexander the Great or his opponents is remarkable. Were it not an established fact that both works derive from the pen of a single author, arguments based on the difference in content and the lack of any kind of intertextuality between them could be adduced in support of ascriptions to two separate writers.

A notable example of this apparent divergence is to be found in Arrian's failure, in discussing the term in the **Tactica** to recall his own use of εμβολος or εμβολον to describe the formation taken up by the Macedonian phalanx at the battle of Pelion during Alexander's Illyrian campaign in 335 B. C. (**Anab.**1.6.3), a Persian cavalry formation at the battle of the Granicus (**Anab.** 1.16.7), and the grand tactical formation into which Alexander threw his Companion cavalry and part of his infantry phalanx at the crisis of the battle of Gaugamela (**Anab.** 3.14.2).[18] 'νεμβολος, instead, appears in the **Tactica** as an instantiation of πυκνωσις: . . .

> "(1) The phalanx is drawn up . . . depthwise . . .[19] where a more compact order is required, as when it is necessary to dislodge the enemy by sheer compactness and force—(2) just as when Epaminondas at Leuctra drew up the Thebans themselves, and at Mantineia all the Boeotians, making, as it were, a wedge and leading it against the Spartan formation—or, again, where it is necessary to beat off those making a charge, just as when we have to take up a formation against the Sarmatians and the Scythians. (3) And 'compacting' . . . is the contracting from a more open to a more compact order as regards both rank and file, that is, in both length and depth"
>
> (*Tact.* 11.1-3 = 11.1-3K).

The parallel passage in the authentic text or "Short Recension" of Aelian (11.3-5), preserved in the Cod. Laurentianus gr. 55.4, is more succinct, and devoid of such tactical examples: . . .

> "(3) It is 'compact order' . . . whenever from a more open order the intervals are reduced so as to contract the formation as regards both rank and file, that is, as regards both length and depth, while still permitting the troops to face about . . . (5) 'Compacting' . . . is used whenever the general wishes to lead the phalanx against the enemy".

Arrian' illustration is, however, closely paralleled in the interpolated or 'Long Recension' of Aelian (47.3-4 [= Dain L3-L4]):[20] . . .

> "(3) Opposed to this [sc. the cavalry square-formation] is the infantry formation called the 'wedge' (εμβολος), which has all of its sides made up of heavy infantry. This type of formation is derived from the cavalry wedge, but whereas in the case of the cavalry wedge

one man is enough to lead the attack, three are required in that of the infantry wedge, one not being enough to engage the enemy alone. (4) By this device, Epaminondas the Theban, fighting the Spartans at Leuctra, defeated a very large force by compacting his army into a wedge".

Arrian's reference to Epaminondas and the infantry εμβολος indicates that this material, while not appearing in the authentic 'Short Recension' of Aelian, does nonetheless belong to the same, authentic Hellenistic tactical manual tradition, i.e. it is not merely an unjustified Byzantine interpolation, but derives ultimately from Poseidonius or even Polybius himself.[21] Conversely, the interpolated 'Long Recension' of Aelian (39.4 [= Dain D4]) mentions the Sarmatians and Alani in a related context, which suggests derivation from Arrian.

Although Arrian's account of the cavalry wedge (*Tact.*16.6-8 = 18.4K)—from which, according to the interpolated passage of Aelian (47.3) quoted above, the infantry wedge is derived—is virtually identical with that of Aelian (18.4), our author does add a brief amplification: . . .

". . . but the formation which is pointed, even if it advances drawn up in depth, yet, by wheeling with its leading point within a small arc, renders the entire formation easy to manuvre"

(*Tact.* 16.8).

Arrian interpellates another, much more generalized, example at *Tact.* 11.4 (= 11.6K): . . .

"It is 'locked-shield order' . . . whenever from an existing 'compact order' . . . the formation is contracted still further, so that on account of the closeness of the troops it is not possible to turn the formation in either direction. And it is by means of such a locking of shields that the Romans form the 'tortoise' . . .".

Although Arrian's account of the *testudo* is briefer and less informative than that of Cassius Dio (49.30.1-4), it is, after all, adduced only as an instance of ουναοπιομος. The later reference to the *testudo* . . . at *Tact.* 36.1, as being the name of both the Roman infantry formation produced by *synaspismos* and an analogous Roman cavalry formation, is clearly intended to provide a link between the Hellenistic and Roman divisions of Arrian's treatise, and to indicate their interdependence.

But this stress on the interdependence of the two parts is somewhat artificial and the connections are a little contrived. This is evident from further instances where Arrian attempts to up-date or Romanize the content of the Hellenistic tactical manual he is adapting. Thus, while Aelian 2.10-11D (= 2.12-13K), for example, defines "spear-bearing cavalry" and "cavalry-skirmishers" as follows: . . .

"(10) Spear-bearing cavalry . . . are those which engage the enemy at close quarters and fight hand-to-

hand on horseback with spears . . . (11) Of the cavalry those which fight from a distance with missiles are called skirmishers . . .",

Arrian, who had had first-hand experience of the Alani and Armenians as governor of Cappadocia, and also probably of the Parthians earlier during Trajan's Parthian War, expands on Aelian's definitions, doubtless on the basis of autopsy: . . .

"Spear-bearing cavalry . . . are those which close with the enemy formation and fight with spears . . . or push with lances . . . in their onslaught, as do the Alani and the Sarmatians. Skirmishers . . . are those which fight from a distance with missiles, like the Armenians and those of the Parthians who are not lance-bearing"

(*Tact.* 4.3 = 2.12K).

Arrian, moreover, concludes this section on the various types of cavalry by adding information on Roman cavalry arms and equipment: . . .

"(7) Among the Romans, some cavalry carry lances . . . and charge in the manner of the Alani and the Sarmatians, while others carry javelins. . . . (8) A long, flat broadsword is suspended from their shoulders, and they bear flat oblong shields, an iron helmet, a woven corselet, and small greaves. (9) They bear javelins . . . for both purposes, both to throw from a distance, when required, and to hold in the hand when fighting at close quarters. And, if it is necessary to come together in hand-to-hand fighting, they fight with their broadswords. Some also carry small double-headed axes [or maces] with spikes set all around in a circle"

(*Tact.* 4.7-9 = 2.14K).

The subject of chariot-fighting, however, brings out the antiquarian in Arrian. In contrast to Aelian (22.2), Arrian omits the names of the various units of the chariot-corps, adding instead, at *Tact.* 2.5 (= 2.6K), a reference to many-poled . . . chariots, which he derives from the 'Cyropaedia' of his favourite model Xenophon (6.1.51-52, 6.4.2): . . .

"(4) Chariot-fighting is more diverse: (5) for there are light-armed chariots, such as those used in the Trojan War, or scythe-chariots like those used later in the Persian War, or those with the chariot horses either armoured or unarmoured, or chariots with one pole or two or even many-poled"

(*Tact.* 2.4-5 = 2.6K).

Roman originality in this regard lies in never having used chariots in battle: . . .

"(2) For the Romans have not at any time practiced fighting from chariots. Nor did the barbarians in Europe use chariots either, aside from those of the so-called British Isles, beyond the Great Sea. (3) These often used two-horse chariots, with small, poor-quality horses. Their two-man chariots (διφροι) are well adapted for running over all kinds of terrain and their ponies to enduring hardships. (4) Of the Asians, the

Persians in ancient times practiced the use of scythe-bearing chariots and armoured horses, beginning in the time of Cyrus, (5) and before this the Greeks with Agamemnon and the Trojans with Priam used chariots with unarmoured horses. The Cyrenians also for some time fought from chariots. (6) But now all these practices have been abandoned, as has the use of elephants for warfare, except by the Indians and the Upper Ethiopians"

(*Tact.* 19.2-6 = 22.2-6K).

Arrian's excursus on the scythe-chariots of Asia again derives from Xenophon's 'Cyropaedia', which likewise credits Cyrus with the introduction of scythe-chariots (6.1.29-30) drawn by armoured houses (6.1.50), and claims that these superseded the unarmoured chariots utilized in the Trojan War (6.1.27) and in contemporary Cyrene (6.1.27). Xenophon recapitulates his account at 6.2.17 and 8.8.24.

Elephants, however, are patient of a more contemporaneous treatment. At 2.2 (= 2.3K), Arrian notes that elephants were used by Indian and Ethiopian armies, and later by the Macedonians and the Carthaginians, and occasionally even by the Romans, adding that some elephants are equipped with fighting-towers (2.4 = 2.5K).

Likewise, at *Tact.*18.4 (= 20.2K), Arrian, in describing the hierarchy of Hellenistic cavalry-units, adds that the Romans call the equivalent of a Hellenistic hipparchy (a unit of 512 horsemen) an . . . *ala.*

A similar attempt at up-dating and Romanizing Hellenistic material appears in Arrian's account of phalangite equipment: . . .

"For the full heavy infantry equipment, a helmet is also added, or Spartan or Arcadian conical caps . . . , and greaves, as with the ancient Greeks, or, as with the Romans, a single greave for the leg that is put forward in battle, and breastplates, some covered with plate-mail, some with fine iron chain-mail"

(*Tact.*3.5 = 2.10K).

The parallel passage in Aelian (2.6D = 2.7K) is more succinct, and omits the mention of Spartan and Arcadian πιλοι; and there is of course no reference to Roman practice.

Arrian's additions are often gratuitous and laboured, as at *Tact.* 27.4-5 (= 35.3-4K), where, to Aelian's mention of uneven ground as an obstacle to visible tactical signals, he adds a reference to hills. At *Tact.* 25.9 (= 29.7K), Arrian uses υπερφαλαγγειν instead of υπερκεραοειν (as in the parallel passages in Aelian 29.5D [= 29.7K] and Asclep. 10.18) merely for the sake of stylistic variation, thereby obscuring the original specific sense of the passage. Occasionally, indeed, Arrian's interpellations are totally irrelevant, as at 6.3 (= 5.3K), where he quotes Xenophon (*Anab.* 4.3.26) verbatim to show that the ενωμοτια contained less than half the number of troops in the λοχος. In the passage cited, however, Xenophon is in fact speaking

of the hundred-man Spartan λοχος (3.4.21), not the basic sixteen-man unit of the Hellenistic period.

A major difference between Arrian and the other tactical writers of the same tradition—although in this case having no bearing upon our author's tendency towards the Romanization and up-dating of his source-material—concerns the length of the Macedonian *sarissa*. At *Tact.* 12.7 (= 14.2K), Arrian gives the length of the *sarissa* as 16 feet. According to Polybius 18.29.2 and Aelian 14.2, however, the *sarissa* was 16 cubits (24 ft.) long as regards the original design but in actuality only 14 cubits (21 ft.) long. Polyaenus (Strat. 2.29.2), indeed, credits the Eddessans at Cleonymus of Sparta's siege of their city (ca. 300 B.C.) with the use of sixteen-cubit (24 ft.) *sarissai*. But Asclepiodotus, on the other hand, says that the *sarissa* was not more than 12 cubits (18 ft.) and not less than 10 cubits (15 ft.) in length, a statement corroborated by (the emended text of) Aelian 12.[22] The contemporary Aristotelian philosopher Theophrastus (370-288/85 B.C.) also claims that the "longest" *sarissa* was 12 cubits (Hist. Pl. 3.12.2). Since the entire Arrianic passage *Tact.* 12.7-9 (= 14.2-4K) is punctuated by measurements in feet . . . , it is probable that the variant is no mere scribal error, but goes back to the author's holograph. . . .

Similarly, Arrian contradicts Aelian (14.5) and Asclepiodotus (5.1) on the number of *sarissai* that extend beyond the front rank of the phalanx: . . .

"Therefore for each of the front-rank-man six *sarissai* project, in a semicircle, one behind another, so that each soldier is hedged about by six *sarissai* and pushes forward reinforced with the strength of six men, with which they are able to press heavily on"

(*Tact.* 12.10 = 14.5K).

To this may be compared the parallel passage in Aelian (14.5): . . .

"Therefore for each of those stationed in front rank five *sarissai* project, presenting a forbidding aspect to the enemy, and thus each man is hedged about by five *sarissai* and pushes forward reinforced with the strength of five, as can easily be seen".

Since the only significant point of divergence here is a factual one, the remarkable verbal similarity suggests a common source, from which Arrian himself has chosen to differ for reasons which can no longer be reconstructed. Certainly no other surviving work of this tradition provides any support or justification for Arrian's modification.

Arrian's description of the arrangement of the *sarissai* in the Macedonian phalanx as overlapping "in a semi-circle, one behind another" is problematic. Arrian apparently visualizes the weapon-heads of the *sarissai* of the first six ranks as forming an arc in profile, with the shafts of the rearmost *sarissai* being held at 90° to the foremost, which would of course be an extremely difficult arrangement to sustain in a tactical advance. But the choice of the words "in a semi-circle" . . . is suspect, and the expression may in fact be gratuitously borrowed from the description of the cavalry wedge at *Tact.*16.6-8 (= 18.4K),[23] where it applies to the perimeter of the formation: . . .

> ". . . this formation . . . seems useful because the leaders are posted in a semi-circle . . . , and the front narrowing down to a point makes it easy to break through every enemy formation, while permitting rapid wheeling and withdrawing movements"
>
> (16.7).

A similar, less ambiguous, use of ἐν κύκλω to mean "the perimeter" of a formation occurs in Arrian's Romanizing description of the formation of the infantry variant of the *testudo:*

> "(4) [The *testudo*] often takes the form of a square, or, where required, it advances as an oval . . . or an oblong. (5) Those troops on the perimeter . . . of the brick-formation . . . or drawn up in circular formation . . . hold their large oblong shields before them, while those deployed alongside them hold theirs over their heads, one shield overlapping the other"
>
> (*Tact.* 11.4 - 5 = 11.6K).

One valuable contribution that Arrian does make to the Hellenistic tactical tradition is his definition, at *Tact.* 2.3 (= 2.4K), of the type of cavalry called ἀμφίπποι, which occurs, for example, in Antigonus Monophthalmus' order-of-battle at the battle of Paraitacene in 317 B.C. (Diodorus 19.29.2):[24]

> ". . . some cavalry are ἀμφίπποι. Some cavalrymen use only one horse, but ἀμφίπποι are those who tie together a pair of unsaddled mounts, so that they can leap from the one to the other".

It is not surprising to find this obscure passage reproduced virtually verbatim in the 'Suda' (Suidas) and the Byzantine 'Glossarium militare' ('Definitiones') 25.

2. The Roman Elements

It is only in the second, or Roman, section of the *Tactica* that we can discern any real originality on Arrian's part. Here, in general contrast to the Hellenistic section of his treatise, he is writing about subjects he knows from personal experience. Given the conditions that obtained on the eastern frontier of the Roman empire in the early second century, where the highly effective cavalry of the Parthians, Armenians, and Alani loomed large in the Roman military consciousness, it is not surprising that Arrian should decide to focus his attention on the drilling of auxiliary cavalry.

In marked contrast to his handling of Hellenistic tactical terminology, where Arrian is doing little more than merely plagiarizing the minute detail of the written tradition, technical terms are conspicuous by their absence from his account of the Roman cavalry exercises. Only four new terms are introduced—πέτρινος (37.4), ξύννημα (42.4),

τολόντεγον (43.2), and the attack called Κανταβρικν (40.1, 40.6)—the first three Celtic, the last Spanish in origin.

The πέτρινος, which Arrian claims is the most difficult of the basic cavalry exercises (37.4), surprisingly enough never reappears in the text of the *Tactica* after its original citation. The ξύννημα, which seems to be an elaboration of the πέτρινος, may by contrast have originated as genuine battle-drill, since Arrian specifies that it is to be performed after the troopers have changed into their field uniforms, including breastplates (41.1). Both exercises are to be carried out while the rider is in the course of wheeling to the right (37.4, 42.2-3), i.e. the javelin is hurled across the front of the rider's body. In the case of the ξύννημα, the final throw is made at an angle to the line of advance, and is preceded by two or three earlier throws while riding in a straight line. The τολόντεγον is a manuvre that involves the horseman raising his shield over his head to protect his back from one opponent's strike and swinging his lance around to confront another opponent (43.2). The "Cantabrian attack" involves aiming a heavy spear, without an iron weapon-head, at an opponent's shield while making a full wheel around him (40.1-6).

In describing the Roman cavalry exercises, Arrian is at pains to stress that the emperor's specifications are being followed, actually noting this fact no less than three times (42.2, 42.4). And, indeed, the three Celtic drills are adduced primarily in support of an encomium of Roman and especially Hadrianic eclecticism. This approach is recapitulated in the treatise's concluding paean in praise of Hadrian for adapting the military techniques of the empire's barbarian enemies, in pursuance of the sound Roman tradition of appropriating excellence whatever the source (42.2, 42.4, 44.1). The cavalry drill of the Middle Empire is represented as a prime example of such commendable eclecticism, with, as we have seen, manuvres borrowed from the Gauls and Spaniards, and further innovations from the West introduced by Hadrian himself. Indeed, Arrian's account of the cavalry drills seems to be intended to evoke Hadrian's imperatorial address at Lambaesis (ILS 9134, 2487). There is a striking agreement in content: both, for example, mention the "attack from concealment" (*e tecto*) and the "Cantabrian attack" (35.1, 40.1).

Despite Arrian's extensive personal acquaintance with Roman practice, his description of the auxiliary cavalry exercises is disappointing. Devoid of any didactic utility, his account is written from the standpoint of "top brass" judging a military display from the reviewing stand. Accordingly, he stresses the importance of good visibility and the need for the javelin-throwers to maintain proper intervals between their successive waves, so that good and bad performers can be distinguished and appropriate praise or blame can be awarded (38.2-6). The focus is on the outstanding performers, N.C.O.s like the *decuriones, duplicarii, sesquiplicarii* (42.1), and the *draconarii*, who carried the serpent standards and who, like all standard-bearers in all armies, had to be expert in the entire repertoire of drill (40.8-12). The average trooper, trained merely to follow the standards, is largely ignored (35.6). Arrian does, however, disparage display for its own sake (40.12), specifying twenty throws as the most any rider can make without cheating (40.11). Each trooper in each *decuria* is to perform individually, and the reviewing commander is to single out for particular commendation the *decuria* that contains the most troopers who excel in javelin-throwing, which Arrian extols as "practise for the actuality of combat" (42.5; cf. Aelian 21.2). But Arrian's object is clearly that of describing a mere festive display, not of instructing his readers in the mechanics of cavalry drill. His descriptions are occasionally obscure (as at 38.1 and 40.2), often degenerating into mere summaries of the proceedings, especially towards the end of the treatise (as at 43.1-4), where it is the inferior second-line squadrons that carry out the exercises, including the attack καντβρικη, albeit at a lower level of expertise and using slings and hand-thrown stones. Rather than stressing tactical utility, Arrian extols the beauty, elegance, astonishing qualities, and sheer splendour of these manuvres (34.2, 34.4, 34.5, 35.1, 36.4, 38.2-4, 40.7, 40.12, 44.2).[25]

Bosworth contends that the *Tactica* is intended to serve larger purposes than the essentially self-ingratiating plagiarism suggested above. According to him, "it provides a stylistically improved manual of Hellenistic tactics, emphasising the manuvres which could be developed by contemporary commanders, and describes the training which inculcated the technical skills to carry them out".[26] This is to see too much in it, since there is actually very little in the first part of the *Tactica* that can be divorced from Hellenistic military organization, arms, and equipment. Moreover, Arrian's main parallels—like that between Epaminondas' use of the grand tactical *lambda*-shaped infantry εμβολος at Leuctra and Mantineia and the minor tactical Roman *testudo*—are hardly compelling. And, as the work and protestations of Aelian indicate, lightly reworking a tactical manual for dedication to someone like a militarily-successful or -interested emperor, though reprehensible in terms of the modern canons of originality, seems to have been a commonplace activity in the Middle Empire period. Arrian's superficially Romanized manual is thus a conventional, 'philosopher's' way of ingratiating himself with the reigning emperor, rather than an attempt at genuine originality or the production of a tactical guide of practical utility to contemporary commanders.

IV. THE SOURCES OF ARRIAN'S *TACTICA*

As is evident from the earlier comparison, the three tactical treatises of Arrian, Aelian, and Asclepiodotus are very closely related. H. Köchly[27] in fact believed that Arrian and Aelian were merely two recensions of the same treatise and printed them in parallel columns in his edition,[28] omitting altogether those sections of Arrian with a purely Roman content (i.e. 33.1-44.3 in the edition of Roos and Wirth). This view and the hypothesis subsequently advanced by R. Förster,[29] that Arrian drew on Aelian for his

own *Tactica,* were decisively refuted by A. Dain.[30] Dain argued that Aelian and Arrian were independently derived from a common (lost) source, which, together with Asclepiodotus, in turn derived from a tactical treatise (also lost) by the Stoic philosopher Poseidonius of Rhodes (mentioned by both Arrian, *Tact.* 1.1 and Aelian 1.2). On this view, the differences which separate Asclepiodotus from Aelian and Arrian are the result of changes in the lost intermediate source. Stadter,[31] however, argues that all three authors used Poseidonius directly, but Asclepiodotus introduced a number of modifications. The fact that Arrian's immediate source was either the Stoic Poseidonius or a known follower would explain his attraction for our author, the first part of whose *Tactica* should thus be interpreted as a fairly conventional retailing of an aspect of the Stoic philosophical tradition. Since Arrian (*Tact.* 1.1) and Aelian (1.2) both imply that Poseidonius' treatise was, like those of Asclepiodotus and Arrian, entitled 'Τεχνη τακτικη', the title itself was clearly part of the tradition (a change of title possibly being another modest attempt at originality on the part of Aelian).

Poseidonius himself is known to have continued the 'Histories' of Polybius, and it is probable that Polybius' own (lost) tactical treatise (Arrian, *Tact.* 1.1; Aelian 1.2) provided the basis for the Stoic's 'Τεχνη τακτικη'. Certainly the striking resemblance between Polybius 18.29.2-5 and 18.29.1-30.4, on the one hand, and Aelian 14.2-6, Arrian, *Tact.* 12.6-10, and Asclepiodotus 5.1-2, on the other, argues very strongly for Polybius' position as the principal source for the entire tradition.

V. THE MANUSCRIPT TRADITION

The manuscript tradition of Arrian's *Tactica* is unitary and the number of manuscripts very limited.[32] Only one, the Codex Laurentianus graecus 55.4, is of any independent value.

—Index siglorum [Dain] of known manuscripts:

F: Cod. Laurentianus gr. 55.4, saec. X.

B: Cod. Bernensis gr. 97, saec. XVI.

W: Cod. Parisinus gr. 2446, saec. XVII.

Cod. Parisinus suppl. gr. 270 (folios 169-181), saec. XVII.

Cod. Parisinus gr. 2539, saec. XVII.

C: Cod. Barberinianus gr. 59.

D: Cod. Barberinianus gr. 200.

e: Cod. Barberinianus gr. 245.

—Codex Laurentianus graecus 55.4.:

The "prototype"[33] of the entire manuscript tradition of Arrian's *Tactica,* like those of Aelian and Asclepiodotus, is to be found in the celebrated Cod. Laurentianus gr. 55.4, folios 182^r to 195^v, now in the Biblioteca Medicea-Laurenziana in Florence.[35] The Laurentianus is a parchment codex of 405 folios, each 32.5 cm. × 26 cm., dating from the time of the Byzantine emperor Constantine VII Porphyrogenitus (reigned a.d. 912-959). At the beginning of the fifteenth century it belonged to one Demetrius Lascaris Leontarios, who utilized the blank folios for family records (down to the death of his mother in 1450). In 1491 it passed into the possession of Lorenzo the Magnificent (died 1492) and thereafter (1508) into that of the Medici Pope Leo X, who finally deposited it in the Monastery of St. Laurence in Florence in 1521. It contains three separate collections of almost exclusively tactical works. They are as follows:

First Collection (Byzantine):

1^r: Constantine Porphyrogenitus, 'Praecepta imperatori'

3^r: [Mauricius] Urbicius III, 'Strategicon'

68^r: 'De militari scientia'

76^v: 'Hypotheseis (ex Polyaeno)'

103^v: 'De Re strategica'

131^r: 'Praecepta e Mauricio'

Second Collection (Hellenistic and Classical):

132^r: Asclepiodotus, 'Techne tactica'

143^r: Aelian, 'Tactica theoria'

159^v: Aeneas Tacticus, 'Commentarius poliorceticus'

182^r: Arrian, 'Techne tactica'

196^r: Arrian, 'Ectaxis contra Alanos'

198^r: Onasander, 'Strategicus'

Inserted between the Second and Third collections:

216^r: 'Rhetorica militaris'

230^r: Sextus Julius Africanus, 'Cestorum fragmenta'

Third Collection (Byzantine):

253^r: Leo VI, 'Problemata'

281^r: Leo VI, 'XVIII Tacticae Constitutiones'

379^r: Leo VI, 'De Incursionibus necopinatis'

387^r: Leo VI, 'De Obsidionibus'

394^r: Leo VI, 'De navali pugna'

401^r: 'Quomodo Saracenis debelletur' (paraphrase of Leo VI)

403^r: Constantine Porphyrogenitus, 'De moribus diversarum gentium'

The codex has suffered extensively from damp and mildew during the eleven centuries of its history, and the text is almost completely illegible in places, especially towards the left-hand margin of each page near the spine of the present sixteenth-century binding. This difficulty is compounded by the fact that the ink has, to varying degrees, come through the individual folios, as on folio 159^r where the last three lines of the text of Aelian are largely obscured by the ornamental band marking the beginning of the text of Aeneas Tacticus at the top of folio 159^v, which has also imprinted itself on the opposing page, folio 160^r. Here and there folios have been torn out, as in the case of 145a and, more significantly, 181a. The recto of 181a was either blank or carried a diagram like the series of five or six diagrams illustrating the text of Aelian, now largely obliterated (in five spaces on folios 151^v, 152^v, 153^r [three]), or the earlier sequence illustrating the text of Asclepiodotus (on the folios 136^v, 137^v, 138^v, 139^r, 139^v, 140^r, 140^v, 141^r [three]).

The text of the codex, 32 lines per each full page, is written throughout in an elegant miniscule hand current prior to the middle of the tenth century, and, where not faded or obscured, is relatively easy to read. It is, however, far from immune to minor scribal mistakes, although the overall standard of accuracy is fairly high. But comparison of Aelian 12 with Asclepiodotus 5.1 reveals an important instance of *saut du même au même*. The third sentence of Aelian 12 . . . corresponds to the second sentence of Asclepiodotus 5.1. . . .[35]

VI. EDITIONS OF ARRIAN'S *TACTICA*

Although the *editio princeps* of Aelian was published by Francesco Robortello (1516-1567) in Venice as early as 1552 under the title 'Aeliani de militaribus ordinibus instruendis more graecorum liber a Francisco Robortello Utinensi nunc primum graece editus multisque imaginibus, et picturis ab eodem illustratus', the cognate treatise of Arrian had to wait almost a century for publication. The *editio princeps* of Arrian's **'Tactica'** was published in Upsala in 1644 by Joannes Schefferus (Scheffer), together with Mauricius' (i. e. Urbicius III's) 'Strategicon', under the title 'Arriani Tactica et Mauricii artis militaris libri duodecim omnia numquam ante publicata', pp. 1-121. A second edition, based on *Manuscripta ex Bibliotheca Claudii Salmasii* (Cl. Salmasius, 1588-1653), was published by Nicolaus Blancardus (Blankaert) in Amsterdam in 1683 in 'Arriani Ars Tactica, Acies contra Alanos. Periplus Ponti Euxini. Maris Erythraei. Liber de Venatione, etc. . . . Cum Interpretibus Latinis', pp. 1-97. Subsequent editions were published in Paris in 1792-1811 and in 1845 (the Didot edition by Karl Müller).

The first critical edition of the **Tactica** was that of Köchly in H. Köchly and W. Rüstow, Griechische Kriegsschriftsteller 2.1. (Leipzig, 1855) 201-552. The Köchly edition was based primarily on two poor-quality copies of the Codex Laurentianus gr. 55.4, namely the sixteenth-century Codex Bernensis 97 and the seventeenth-century Codex Parisinus gr. 2446. Unfortunately, Köchly's work is vitiated by his failure to utilize or even consult directly the famous Codex Laurentianus. A. G. Roos' critical edition (1928) of Arrian was, however, based on the Florentine codex and, with G. Wirth's revision (1968), seems to approximate the author's holograph. No new critical edition is required.

VII. Translations of the *Tactica*

Although a German translation of Aelian accompanies the Köchly edition, Köchly and Rüstow declined to translate those passages of Arrian that are not paralleled in the text of Aelian. Arrian's **Tactica** was, however, finally translated into German by Franz Kiechle, 'Die Taktik' des Flavius Arrianus, Bericht der Röm.-Germ. Kommission 45 (1964) 87-129. Charles Theophile Guischardt translated the first (i. e. Hellenistic) part of Arrian's **Tactica** in: Mémoires militaires sur les Grecs et les Romains 2 (Lyon, 1760). There is to date no published English translation.

Notes

All references here will be in terms of the Roos-Wirth (Teubner) edition of Arrian, unless indicated by the addition of K for the Köchly-Rüstow edition, the forthcoming Devine edition of Aelian (indicated by D as required), and the Oldfather edition of Asclepiodotus in the Loeb Classical Library.

1. Sir Ronald Syme, Tacitus, vol. 2 (Oxford, 1958) 653-656.

2. Sir Ronald Syme, The Career of Arrian, Harvard Studies in Classical Philology 86 (1982) 181-211, at 184 (= Idem, Roman Papers, vol. 4, ed. A. R. Birley [Oxford, 1988] 21-49, at 24).

3. E. L. Wheeler, The Occasion of Arrian's *Tactica*, Greek, Roman, and Byzantine Studies 19 (1978) 351-365, at 352.

4. A. B. Bosworth, From Arrian to Alexander: Studies in Historical Interpretation (Oxford, 1988) 17-24; Idem, Arrian and Rome: the Minor Works, above in this volume (ANRW II.34.1) 226-275, esp. 253-264.

5. A. B. Bosworth, A Historical Commentary on Arrian's History of Alexander (Oxford, 1980) 8-11, esp. 11: "a date of composition before 125"; Bosworth (above, note 4) 29-37, esp. 37: "we can date the work sometime towards the end of Trajan's reign"; and Bosworth, Arrian's Literary Development, Classical Quarterly N.S. 22 (1972) 163-185, esp. 185. Cf. Wheeler (above, note 3) p. 355, note 19.

6. Bosworth (above, note 4) 28.

7. AE 1968. 473 (from Corinth): on which see G. W. Bowersock, Greek, Roman and Byzantine Studies 8

(1967) 279-280; and AAA 3 (1970) 377-380 (= AE 1971.437) (from Athens).

8. The evidence is summarized in Bosworth (above, note 4) 25, Bosworth, A Historical Commentary on Arrian's History of Alexander (Oxford, 1980) 5-6, and Idem., Arrian and Rome etc., above in this same volume (ANRW II.34.1) 272-275 (V. 'The New Xenophon'). Cf. A. Silberman, Arrien 'Périple du Pont Euxin': Essai d'interprétation et d'évaluation des données historiques et geographiques, above in this volume (ANRW II.34.1) 302 n. 147 and 303 n. 155.

9. Bosworth (above, note 4) 26-27; Bosworth (above, note 8) 6-7.

10. Classical Philology 73 (1978) 117-128, at p. 121, note 15.

11. Cf. Wheeler (above, note 3) p. 355, note 18.

12. Wheeler (above, note 3) 364-365.

13. For the date of Asclepiodotus, see W. A. Oldfather and C. H. Oldfather in: The Illinois Greek Club, Aeneas Tacticus, Asclepiodotus, Onasander (Loeb edition: Cambridge, Mass. and London, 1923) 230-237; and A. Dain, edited posthumously by P. Lemerle, Les Stratégistes Byzantins, Travaux et Mémoires 2 (1967) 317-392, at 326. For the date of Aelian, see A. Dain, Histoire du texte d'Élien le tacticien (Paris, 1946) 15-21, esp. 18-19; and A. M. Devine, Aelian's 'Manual of Hellenistic Military Tactics': A New Translation from the Greek with an Introduction, The Ancient World 19 (1989) 31-64, at 31. The *Prooimion* or preface to Aelian's 'Τακτικη θεωρια' is addressed to the reigning emperor, and although our surviving manuscripts all give the name of this emperor as "Hadrian" (praef. 1), it is obvious, from the reference (praef. 3) to the emperor's "deified father Nerva" (reigned A.D. 96-98), that the received text is corrupt and that Trajan (reigned 98-117) is the princeps addressed. The name of the distinguished consular Sextus Julius Frontinus, who encouraged Aelian's study of Hellenistic tactics in conversations during the author's stay in Formiae, also appears in this section (praef. 3). Frontinus was himself well-known, not only as a successful military commander (who had conquered the Silures in Britain in 78), but also as the author of two military treatises, the 'Strategemata' and the (lost) 'De re militari', and Aelian mentions him (1.2) in his catalogue of tactical writers (1.1-2). Frontinus died in 103, and the notice in the *Prooimion* does seem to suggest that the great consular was no longer writing at the time the 'Tactica theoria' was being composed. Aelian's allusions to the emperor's military prowess, though attended by hyperbole, provide us with a slightly later *terminus post quem*. At praef. 4 Aelian speaks of the emperor excelling "all the other generals who have ever been", and at praef. 6 he alludes to his having "commanded in such great wars". The plural in the latter case, together with the transcendent strategic status

accorded the emperor, indicates the end of the Second Dacian War in 106 as the *terminus ante quem non* for Aelian's dedication. Trajan was in Rome from 106 or 107 until 113, when he departed the capital to begin the series of wars in Parthia and Armenia that occupied his attention until his death in 117. The publication of Aelian's 'Tactica theoria' can thus be plausibly assigned to these six or seven years of victorious peace, during which time Roman public interest in military affairs would have stood very high.

14. On the 'Short' and 'Long' (i. e. interpolated) Recensions, see A. Dain, Histoire du texte d'Elien le tacticien (Paris, 1946), passim, esp. 77-115; Devine (above, note 13), esp. 33-39 and 59-64.

15. See above, note 8.

16. The comparative method adopted here owes much, despite significant points of disagreement, to P. A. Stadter, The *Ars Tactica* of Arrian: Tradition and Originality, Classical Philology 73 (1978) 117-128, at 120.

17. Devine (above, note 13) 35 and 48, see also below, section V, ad fin.

18. On the various tactical senses of the term, see A. M. Devine, EMBOΛON: A Study in Tactical Terminology, Phoenix 37 (1983) 201-217, esp. 213-216 (for the Alexandrine instances).

19. Added by Roos on the basis of the parallel passage in Aelian.

20. Dain (above, note 14) 98.

21. On the historical authenticity of the passage and its content, see Devine (above, note 18) 203-210.

22. Anrw ii 34.1. See below, section V, ad fin.

23. On the cavalry wedge, see Devine (above, note 18) 201-202.

24. See further, A. M. Devine, Diodorus' Account of the Battle of Paraitacene, The Ancient World 12 (1985) 75-86, at 79-80; N. G. L. Hammond, A Cavalry Unit in the Army of Antigonus Monophthalmus: ASTHIPPOI, Classical Quarterly N.S. 28 (1978) 128-135, esp. 134.

25. Wheeler (above, note 3) 354-361, esp. 357. In general, A. B. Bosworth, Arrian and Rome etc., above in this volume (ANRW II.34.1) pp. 226-275, esp. 253-264, vastly overestimates Arrian's value and originality as a source for Roman and even Hellenistic tactics.

26. Bosworth, Arrian and Rome etc., above in this volume (ANRW II.34.1) p. 259.

27. H. Köchly, De libris tacticis, qui Arriani et Aeliani feruntur, dissertatio, Index lectionum (Zurich, 1851).

28. In H. Kochly and W. Rüstow, Griechische Kriegsschriftsteller 2.1 (Leipzig, 1855) 270-470.

29. Hermes 12 (1877) 426-449.

30. Histoire du texte d'Élien le tacticien (Paris, 1946) 26-40 (especially 39: stemma).

31. Classical Philology 73 (1978) 117-118.

32. Select bibliography: A. Dain, Les manuscrits des traités tactiques d'Arrien, Mélanges Bidez I, pp. 160-194 = Annuaire de l'Institut de philologie et d'histoire orientale 2 (Bruxelles, 1934) 157-184; ID., Le Parisinus gr. 2522, Revue de Philologie 67 (1941) 21-28.

33. To use the later terminology of Dain, not the "archetype", as Roos-Wirth and Bosworth call it.

34. Select Bibliography: A. M. Blandini, Epistola de celeberrimo codice Tacticorum Bibliothecae Laurentianae (Florence, 1761) = ID., Catal. cod. Manuscriptorum graecorum Bibl. Laurentianae 1 (Florence, 1768) col. 218-238; R. Förster, Studien zu den Griechischen Taktikern, Hermes 12 (1877) 426-471, esp. 427-430 and 459-461; The Illinois Greek Club, Aeneas Tacticus, Asclepiodotus, Onasander (Loeb edition: Cambridge, Mass. and London, 1923) esp. 18-19, 240-243, and 363-365; A. Dain, Histoire du texte d'Élien le tacticien (Paris, 1946) passim, esp. 183-202 and 375-377; ID., Les manuscrits d'Énée le tacticien, REG 48 (1935) 1-32, esp. 6-10; ID., edited posthumously by P. Lemerle, Les stratégistes Byzantins, Travaux et Mémoires 2 (1967) 317-392, esp. 382-385; A. G. Roos, revised by G. WIRTH, Flavii Arriani Quae extant omnia, Teubner edition, vol. 2: Scripta minora et fragmenta (Leipzig, 1968) xx-xxiv; A. B. Bosworth, Arrian and the Alani, Harvard Studies in Classical Philology 81 (1977) 217-255, esp. 217 and 251; P. A. Stadter, The *Ars Tactica* of Arrian: Tradition and Originality, Classical Philology 73 (1978) 117-128, esp. 118-119.

35. Devine (above, note 13) 35.

FURTHER READING

Criticism

Bosworth, A. B. "Arrian and the Alani." *Harvard Studies in Classical Philology* 81 (1977): 217-55.
    Studies Arrian's account of the attack on Cappadocia by the Germanic Alani tribe in *Order of the Battle against the Alani.*

————. *From Arrian to Alexander: Studies in Historical Interpretation.* Oxford: Clarendon Press, 1988, 225 p.
    Analysis of Arrian's treatment of Alexander, including a discussion of Arrian's historical method and his utilization of his sources.

————. "Arrian and Rome: The Minor Works." *Aufstieg und Niedergang der Romische Welt* 34, No. 1 (1993): 226-75.

Examines Arrian's *Cynegeticus, Periplus, Tactica,* and *Order of Battle against the Alani.* Bosworth also reviews the influence of the philosopher Xenophon on Arrian's writing.

Falconer, William. "A Geographical Dissertation." In *Arrian's Voyage Round the Euxine Sea,* pp. 23-91. Oxford, 1805.

Detailed discussion of the specifics of Arrian's geographic work.

Hammond, N. G. L. "Arrian's Sources for the *Anabasis Alexandrou.*" In *Sources for Alexander the Great: An Analysis of Plutarch's "Life" and Arrian's "Anabasis Alexandrou,"* pp. 189-312. Cambridge: Cambridge University Press, 1993.

Studies Arrian's historical methodology and discusses his use of sources for each portion of Alexander's life as covered in the *Anabasis.*

Hyland, Ann. *Training the Roman Cavalry: From Arrian's "Ars Tactica."* Phoenix Mill, U.K.: Alan Sutton Publishing, 1993, 197 p.

Explores various aspects of the military training and experience of the Roman army as described in Arrian's writings.

Schepens, Guido. "Arrian's View of His Task as Alexander-Historian." *Ancient Society* 2 (1971): 254-68.

Reviews the critical debate over whether Arrian's intentions were more historical or literary in composing the *Anabasis,* and argues that Arrian's choice of subject was informed by his Stoic outlook on life and his belief in divine providence.

Stadter, Philip A. "Flavius Arrianus: The New Xenophon." *Greek, Roman and Byzantine Studies* 8, No. 2 (1967): 155-61.

Compares the literary activities of Xenophon and those of Arrian, and comments on the influence of Xenophon on Arrian's writings.

Wheeler, Everett L. "The Occasion of Arrian's *Tactica.*" *Greek, Roman and Byzantine Studies* 19 (1978): 351-65.

Investigates Arrian's purpose in writing *Tactica,* suggesting that he intended to use the work "as an ecomium on the occasion of Hadrian's *vicennalia.*"

Beowulf

Old English poem, circa eighth century. For further discussion of *Beowulf*, see *CMLC*, Vol. 1.

INTRODUCTION

Hailed as the first major poem in English literature, *Beowulf* relates the adventures of its Scandinavian hero, at the same time presenting a detailed description of the life and mood of the age during which it was written. Little is known for certain regarding the author, the date, motivation, or method of the poem's composition. Modern critics continue to debate such issues, focusing on the Christian and pagan elements of the poem, its concern with heroic values, and its formulaic structure. The question of whether the poem's composition was contemporary with the creation of the only known manuscript is also a hotly debated issue among scholars.

TEXTUAL HISTORY

The original *Beowulf* manuscript dates from 975 to 1000, and is included in a volume containing a total of five works in Old English. Basing this view on historical, linguistic, and stylistic evidence, many critics agree that the poem was composed in the eighth, or perhaps the ninth century, with the extant manuscript representing a later version of the poem. It has also been suggested that a written version may predate the eighth-century poem, with a possible composition date of 685 to 725, and that an oral version of the poem may have been composed even earlier. In 1731, after joining the manuscript collection of Sir Robert Cotton, the *Beowulf* manuscript was damaged in a fire. A gradual deterioration of letters and words began, although it was stemmed in the nineteenth century. Two transcriptions were made from the manuscript in 1786-87 by Icelander Grímur Jónsson Thorkelin, and are considered invaluable, as they capture portions of the text later lost. These transcriptions served as the basis of the first printed edition of *Beowulf* and are incorporated in modern versions of the poem.

PLOT AND MAJOR CHARACTERS

Although the narrative of *Beowulf* is not linear and contains long digressions concerning Geatish and Danish history, the plot of the poem is easily summarized. Beowulf, nephew to the King of the Geats, Hygelac, learns that a monster known as Grendel regularly raids Heorot, the Danish hall of King Hrothgar. Along with his men, Beowulf travels by sea to Denmark in order to rid the land of

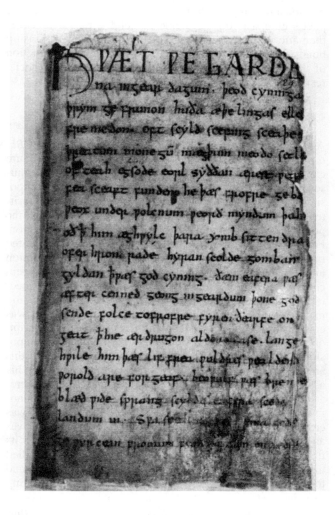

the dangerous beast Grendel. Beowulf succeeds, but Grendel's mother then resumes her offspring's attacks on the Danes. After traveling to the monster's underwater lair, Beowulf slays Grendel's mother and is generously rewarded with Danish treasure and acclaim. He then returns to the court of King Hygelac, goes to war with the Geats, and is eventually made king. Having served fifty years as the Geatish ruler, Beowulf defends the Geats from the attacks of a firedrake. Abandoned by his men, Beowulf nevertheless pursues the dragon, finally killing it with the help of his loyal retainer, Wiglaf. Beowulf discovers the dragon's treasure, then dies of his wounds. His people raise a funeral pyre, and the poem ends with the praising of the hero.

MAJOR THEMES

Scholars have identified numerous themes in *Beowulf*, many related to the portrayal of the Germanic *comitatus* relationship, a code of social behavior stressing the reciprocity enjoyed between a lord and his thanes. In return for protection provided by the lord, the thanes owe service and loyalty. Such themes as order versus chaos and reward and revenge are dramatized through the depiction of this relationship. The role of the monsters also underscores the poet's emphasis on the theme of good versus evil. Other thematic concerns include the role of women in kinship bonds, the use of treasure as a societal bond, the function of the narrator in poem, the nature of heroism and social responsibility, and the purpose of the quest motif.

CRITICAL RECEPTION

A number of questions surrounding the composition of *Beowulf* still inspire modern critical debate. Paull F. Baum examines several of these issues, arguing that the manuscript's date being so much later than the original composition, combined with the fact that the manuscript is written in a different dialect from the original, indicate that the poem lacks a continuous history of reading or recitation. Furthermore, while many believe that *Beowulf* was recited rather than read, the poem's length makes this assumption unlikely. Baum insists that the evidence suggests a poem composed for the enjoyment of its author, with the expectation that others might also take pleasure in it. While many scholars, including Baum, hold that the poem was composed much earlier than the date of the manuscript, others contend that the manuscript and the poem's composition are contemporaneous. Kevin S. Kiernan makes this argument, citing historical and linguistic evidence for his assertion that both the poem and the manuscript were created in the early eleventh century. Another issue surrounding the poem's composition is the method by which it was created. Some critics maintain that the original poem was an oral composition, while others believe that it made its first appearance in written form. Alain Renoir has studied the motifs of *Beowulf*, including the underwater fight and the monster's attack on a human dwelling, demonstrating that the poet's use of these devices shows that he was familiar with the traditional methods of oral-formulaic composition. Renoir stresses that this familiarity does not necessarily indicate that the poem was composed orally. J. D. A. Ogilvy similarly comments that it is improbable that *Beowulf*—as a whole, or even in smaller units—was composed orally. Stephen S. Evans, on the other hand, asserts that an oral form (dating from 685 to 725) of the poem preceded a written version. The original pagan poem was extensively modified, Evans argues, by Christian oral poets sometime between 625 and 700 in order to create a work better suited to a Christian audience.

Like Evans, many critics have explored the Christian aspects of the poem, particularly the juxtaposition of Christian and pagan elements. Larry D. Benson notes that although some critics appear certain that *Beowulf* is the work of a Christian author, rather than a pagan work later modified by a Christian scribe, the question is far from settled. The pagan elements of the poem, including Beowulf's funeral ship, the observance of omens, and the practice of cremation, seem to create an inconsistent tone in the poem. Benson maintains that this apparent contradiction stems from modern assumptions about the poet's attitude toward paganism. The Christian Englishmen of the time, assures Benson, viewed the Germanic pagan with interest, and the sympathetic treatment of the pagan values in *Beowulf* provides a framework that allowed the Christian to admire the pagan. Likewise, Stanley B. Greenfield suggests that the Christian author of *Beowulf* viewed the poem's heroic world with kindness and sympathy and even lauded the ethical and social values of that world. Greenfield feels that Beowulf and his world are presented as flawed in an effort to humanize them and elicit a more emotional response from the audience. Margaret E. Goldsmith takes a different approach in explaining the coexistence of Christian and pagan symbols in the poem, contending that the poet was cognizant of the ambivalence of the symbolism used, especially Heorot and the treasure. The great hall and the treasure seem to embody grandeur and wealth, the hero's reward, while to the Christian audience they exemplify man's pride and are to be viewed as costly and worthless. Bernard Felix Huppé similarly emphasizes the poem's Christian message, maintaining that *Beowulf* may have been used as a Christian apologetic, highlighting the error of English ancestral ways.

While some critics continue to be interested in the Christian attitudes of the poem and the poet's possible motivation, others focus on the style and structure of the poem. Eric Gerald Stanley praises the poet's vocabulary, word choice, and manipulation of complex sentences. In Stanley's view, *Beowulf*'s superiority rests on the "concord between the poet's mode of thinking and his mode of expression." John Leyerle studies the poem as a poetic analogue to Anglo-Saxon art–characterized by interlace designwork notable for its complexity– contemporary with the poem's composition. Leyerle marshals ample evidence to demonstrate that interlace designs had stylistic and structural literary parallels in England, and argues that the function of various episodes in *Beowulf* becomes apparent only when the likelihood of analogous design is accepted. The themes of the poem, argues Leyerle, are threaded together to form an intricate interlace that cannot be undone without losing the design of the whole poem. Like Leyerle, Kathryn Hume recognizes the poem's interlace structure and suggests that this structure supports the creation of moral and thematic juxtapositions, rather than a simple heroic narrative. J. D. A. Ogilvy analyzes the formulaic structure of the poem, noting in particular the use of traditional epithets and phrases, its sentence formula, its use of larger rhetorical patterns, and the formulaic elaboration of the poem's various themes.

PRINCIPAL WORKS

Principal English Editions

Beowulf, the Oldest English Epic (translated by Charles W. Kennedy) 1940

Beowulf: A Verse Translation into Modern English (translated by Edwin Morgan) 1952

Beowulf (translated by David Wright) 1957

Beowulf (translated by Burton Raffel) 1963

Beowulf: A New Translation (translated by E. Talbot Donaldson) 1966

Beowulf (translated by Mark Alexander) 1973

Beowulf: A Dual Language Edition (translated by Howell D. Chickering, Jr.) 1977

Beowulf (translated by Albert W. Haley) 1978

Beowulf: A Verse Translation with Treasures of the Ancient North (translated by Marijane Osborn) 1983

Beowulf (translated by Kevin Crossley-Holland) 1984

Beowulf: A New Verse Translation (translated by Seamus Heaney) 2000

CRITICISM

Paull F. Baum (essay date 1960)

SOURCE: "The *Beowulf* Poet," in *Philological Quarterly*, Vol. XXXIX, No. 4, October, 1960, pp. 389-99.

[*In the essay below, Baum explores the possible audience for which* Beowulf *was composed and argues that internal evidence suggests the poet intended to create a "quasi-heroic" poem for his own enjoyment, with the hope that others might also be pleased with his work.*]

Some years ago (1936) Professor Tolkien, in his British Academy lecture, created an academic stir with his complaints that the scholars had been too busy about their own concerns and had neglected the criticism of *Beowulf* as a poem.[1] Latterly, Miss Whitelock (1951) attempted to recreate the 'audience' of *Beowulf* in the interests of bringing forward its date from the early to the late eighth century.[2] Though the two subjects are not closely related, one may be used to throw light on the other.

Tolkien was attacked and defended, but the questions are still open—and little wonder, for the critical handicaps are forbidding. The language of the poem is difficult, partly owing to the state of the text and partly because the poet chose to make it so. Very few, even of the specialists, can pretend to such a feeling for style as we bring to the appreciation of later English poets; and the others are dependent on translations of uncertain merit and fidelity. Knowing so little about whom the poet addressed, we cannot easily estimate the responses he expected: what seems re-

mote to us may well have seemed simple to them. It would help a good deal if we knew whether he wrote to please himself, to satisfy an inner need, or for recitation to a listening audience capable of following with pleasure and understanding his often cryptic language and his often intricate plan of narrative, his ironies, and his exhilarating methods of reticence and indirection. Moreover, *Beowulf* is unique. Being the first of its kind in the vernacular, it has an honored position, but it exists, for us, in a kind of literary vacuum without historical perspective. Nothing is certainly known of its author or of his 'audience.' And its survival in a single manuscript and a different dialect some two and a half centuries after its original composition tells us little; it does not signify a continuous history of recitation or reading.

I

There are really two poems: one about Beowulf and the Danes, the other, roughly half as long, about Beowulf and the Geats. They have in common the same hero, first as a youth then as an old man, overcoming first two water-monsters and later a fire-drake. The earlier victories appear to be successful, though in delivering the Danes from Grendel and his Mother the hero has left them a prey to subsequent disaster; he has established his renown, which was paramount, but as the savior of a nation in distress his achievement was only temporary. His later victory has also a tragic irony: it brings his own death and so opens the way to disaster for his own people. Thus the two poems, or parts of the same poem, share a single theme: that beyond the hero's bravery there are forces which he cannot subdue. Valor is vanity in the end. So much any reflective reader may see.

The plan of Part I looks simple: the Danish setting, the hero's journey and reception, his fight and the celebration of his victory, his second fight and the following celebration, his return home and report of his adventures. But such is the poet's chosen method that he disguises the symmetry by making his concluding point (Hroðgar's plan to heal a feud with the Heaðobards) look like an irrelevance. This is the result of pursuing two themes at once, the plight of the Danes and their deliverance by the hero—with the necessary interchange of background and foreground. For the rest, having not much story to tell and meaning to tell none *as* story, the poet took his raw materials from the old 'lays,' and combining them with history and with folklore created something new, not exactly a heroic poem, (for there is less of that sheer delight in man-to-man fighting than we expect in heroic poems; compare the tone of the Finnsburgh Fragment with the poet's treatment of the same situation) and certainly not an epic, but a modification or adaptation to suit himself—a mixture of pagan matter treated in a somewhat non-pagan manner and of heroic matter from the legendary and historic past along with court ceremonies as he understood them. The actual fighting, including Beowulf's recapitulation, occupies less than one-tenth of the whole.

Part II, with less than a thousand lines, is another poem with the same hero. No significant differences in vocabulary, syntax, style, or meter have been found, and in the face of an improbable assumption of two men writing at about the same time in the same, or almost the same, manner, it must be taken for granted that both poems are by the same author. There are small linkages, but the subject and planning of the two Parts are different; there is a wholly new cast of characters, the emphasis is shifted, the polarity is altered. Part I had a beginning, a middle, and an end. Part II is less simple, it is more confused, the so-called digressions occupy relatively much more space (besides being more puzzling to the modern reader), and the whole is more gloomy, not only with the hero's death but also with the presage of disaster for his race.

II

One of the 'intentions' attributed to the poet is the portrayal of a virtuous pagan who might be said to manifest some of the high qualities inculcated by the new religion; and this might imply, or even signify, a semi-didactic purpose. Perhaps, as some have thought, he felt the zeal of a new convert; but if so, one would have expected him to go further. Or perhaps, as Gang conjectures, "*Beowulf,* so far from being a Christianized epic, is an attempt at a sort of secular Saints' Life," as though to prove that the heathen legends contained, latent, "a great deal of sound doctrine and Christian morality." Perhaps; or, since the divine guidance of the world, though prepotent, evidently—from the turn of events among Danes, Swedes, and Geats—leaves room for family and dynastic distress (*gyrn æfter gomene*), the poet's aim might be a warning to his contemporaries, pointing a deadly parallel to the local wars he saw all about him and their inevitable outcome. Or, even more narrowly, he might mean to show that the supernatural forces which threaten mortal man can be overcome— Grendel driven off and finally beheaded, his Mother killed in her hidden haunt, the Dragon tumbled lifeless over the cliff—but the human conflicts, treachery and cowardice against loyalty and bravery, bring ineluctable doom. But if so, the poet has left these inferences to our ingenious interpretation. He was too much the artist to certify a "palpable design."

The symbolic or parabolic interpretations have a distinguished history. They go back at least to Grundtvig and they seem now to be taken for granted.[3] They are only suspect when they are applied to raise the epic level of the poem and to dignify the monsters—otherwise crude and merely folklorish—by assuming that they stood *in the poet's mind* for the dark forces of evil which oppress mankind and thus acquire in the reader's mind a Satanic stature. This "usury of our own minds" should not be allowed to crystallize into dogma.

Nor need we stop with the monsters. For example, if Hroðgar thought it necessary to warn Beowulf against pride, it is a short step to discovering a psychic disturbance in his own predicament. He himself has been guilty; he has erected his splendid meadhall and God is punishing him with Grendel. Grendel is specially irritated by the revelry and the sound of the harp. And Beowulf? Unbidden—or so we may suppose, though the poet is not altogether perspicuous on this point—he has crossed the seas and freed Heorot of its plague, and has thus interfered with divine justice and punishment, just as he did later when he became entangled with the accursed hoard. Moreover, Hroðgar's warning goes unheeded, for Beowulf at the end of a long and prosperous reign interferes again and stubbornly insists on fighting the Dragon in spite of his advanced age. Pride must have its fall and he is punished both by the humiliation of having to depend on Wiglaf and by his own death.

Moreover, the poem may be read not as an exaltation of manly valor and fortitude but a lament for the hopelessness of the human lot—"an heroic-elegiac poem" (Tolkien), beginning with a burial, ending with a cremation, and all that seemed so heroic in between coming to naught. But then, by superimposing a Christian orientation on those noble heathens, the poet compromised his Christian faith in God's goodness; or perhaps one should say he acknowledged the pessimism latent in Christian doctrine, a resignation to the evils of the world, without being able to hold out the hopes of relief and salvation in another life.[4] Thus as critical latitude broadens, puzzling difficulties deepen.

One might go further. *Beowulf* is, as Chambers said, a poem of ambiguities; and in every ambiguity may lurk a secret meaning. For example, Beowulf encounters in Part I the evils of water (especially with Grendel's Mother) and in Part II the evils of fire (the fire-drake and his cremation). With this there is a chiastic balance which ought to be significant; for in Part I Heorot's destruction by fire is prophesied and in Part II the Dragon is pushed over into the sea. And, assuming a little different position, one notes that Grendel is the agent, not the enemy of God; he was sent to punish the Danes and the poet was only adding his touch of cunning subtlety when he said *Godes yrre bær.*

One more speculation. Taking a leaf from Samuel Butler, one could argue that the poet was a woman, a learned abbess inspired, say, by Hild's success with Cædmon—or why not Hild herself? Feminine authorship would account for many things in the poem: the absence of gory fighting and lust of battle; the vagueness of detail in the wrestling match with Grendel and in the encounter with his Mother and in the final contest with the Dragon, so much interrupted by Beowulf's speeches; the touches of pathos here and there, the implied sympathy with Hildeburh, and with the Dragon; the praise of queen Hugd and queen Wealhþeow; in general, "the poet's sympathy with weak and unfortunate beings" (Klaeber); Beowulf's interest in the gold ornaments from the hoard; the feeling for harsh landscape on the way to Grendel's mere; the delicate reticence about the parentage of Fitela; the absence of gluttony and lechery (though there is abundance of mead and the duguð get drunk, drunkenness leads to nothing worse than noise and some reckless talk); the celebrations of victory in Part I by singing and racing, with none of the grosser indulgences; the pervasive manner of indirection;

the extraordinary amount of talking and the tendencies to 'digress'; the pessimistic judgment on men's inability to rule successfully at home and abroad (the hero's long reign is only an apparent exception; it was far from peaceful); the crowning attribute of mildness in Beowulf; and much more. An enthusiast could write convincingly on this topic.

These, and other such hypotheses, do no harm if they are not taken too seriously. They testify to our critical industry and also—which is the point here—to our uncertainty about the fundamental criteria of the poem. They emphasize its enigmas.

III

A poem assumes readers, but since in the eighth century the *Beowulf* poet could hardly expect any considerable number of readers and since then poetry was commonly recited, read aloud with some sort of musical accompaniment—

> þær wæs hearpan sweg,
> swutol sang scopes—

it is usually taken for granted that the *Beowulf* poet cast himself in the role of *scop* and both recited his poem to a group of listeners and hoped that others would do the same. Miss Whitelock has computed that the poem "could easily be delivered in three sittings," and it only remains to inquire who the listeners would be. This question she has faced with courage and great learning; she presents her case with shrewd caution, avoiding over-confidence: "it would be unsafe to argue that any part of England was in the eighth century insufficiently advanced in intellectual attainments for a sophisticated poem like *Beowulf* to have been composed there and appreciated." Most admirable caution, though one might have hoped for a more positive conclusion. "The audience," she says, "would doubtless consist of both veterans and young men" in the royal retinue, as well as "an audience of sportsmen." They would probably be Christians. Remembering Alcuin's *Quid Hinieldus cum Christo,* she seems not to have included a monastic audience. (One wonders how much Alcuin knew about Ingeld. Saxo's spelling is Ingellus.) The men on the mead-bench are slightly disguised as veterans and young men: they would have to be more temperate than the celebrants in Heorot.

For such an "advanced" audience two requisites must be met: one, a group both interested in the fearless exploits of a heathen hero, modified for Christian ears, who fought ogres and a dragon in the long ago, and sufficiently familiar with Geatish and Swedish feuds and with continental legends and sagas—Sigemund and Heremod, Hengest and the Heaðobards, and so forth—to be able to absorb easily and with pleasure the poet's somewhat abrupt allusions; and secondly, a group capable of the concentrated attention necessary to follow, while listening, a narrative as involved and circuitous ("circumambient," "static" with the illusion of forward movement), in a style as compressed

and often cryptic, as that of *Beowulf.* The reasoning assumes not only a group of listeners knowledgeable on all the many topics to which the poet points and passes, as well equipped as the poet himself, and sufficiently able to fill in all that he leaves out or hints at, but *a fortiori* nimble-minded enough ("alert") *while listening* to, say, three sequences of about 1000 lines each, to pick up and drop at need the several allusions historical and traditional without losing the main pattern, to adjust and readjust their attention in rapid alternation to diverse matters without sacrificing their interest in the principal concern. Could such a listening audience ever have existed? Did ever a poet before or since ask so much of one?

The 'argument' was succinctly put, long ago, by Gummere: "The style of reference to the death of Hæthcyn shows how familiar the whole story must have been."[5] Miss Whitelock elaborates this. At every turn she insists that the poem would not be intelligible unless the audience was well informed—on Christian doctrine, for example, to understand a Biblical reference (the giants of *Exodus*), or on the subsequent history of Hroðgar's strife with his own son-in-law to catch the hint of *þenden* (1019), and so on. "To an audience that did not know that Hrothulf killed Hrethric, the whole section [1164 ff.] would be pointless." She dwells at length on the fourfold account of Hygelac's Frisian raid. It would ask a good deal for the audience to pick up the second hint eleven hundred and forty lines after the first unless they were well acquainted with Frankish tradition and Geatish history. It assumes "the likelihood that the poet could rely on his hearers' previous knowledge of the Geatish kings as on that of the Danish kings, and could leave it to them to supply more than he chose to tell them"—while they listened for what was coming next. And finally, "if even a few of the claims I have made are true, we must assume a subtle and sophisticated poet, and an alert and intelligent audience" later than the age of Bede.

Those elements of the minstrel style which the poet made use of, and his picture of the improvising scop at Hroðgar's court will not have deceived him, or us. He was not composing an enlarged tripartite 'lay.' "The first concern of heroic poetry," says Bowra, "is to tell of action, . . . bards . . . avoid . . . not merely moralizing comments and description of things and places for description's sake, but anything that smacks of ulterior or symbolic intentions"; "the listening audience requires single moods and effects, without complications." A bard has to hold the audience's attention, "to make everything clear and interesting."[6] This hardly describes the **Beowulf** poet and his work. The "discontinuity of action" (Tolkien) and the calculated double movement of Part II especially, with its rapid interchange of present (Beowulf and the Dragon) and the historical past is the last thing a scop would submit to a group of listeners. Miss Whitelock's "we must assume" is therefore circular: if the poet wrote for an audience, the audience must have been waiting.

Who will, may hear Sordello's story told.

IV

We are still in the dark about the poet's intentions. If we knew anything precise about those lost 'lays' we might guess a little about his originality. Did he invent Grendel's Mother, for instance? and why did he give her no name? The supernatural elements were, one assumes, in the 'lays' and he accepted them; they are the folklore coefficient of heroic saga. The Scandinavian settings were, one assumes also, in his 'lays' and he had to accept them and try his best to make them interesting to his Anglian 'audience.' He would celebrate a hero whose life was dominated by a (pagan) desire for fame, who won fame by overcoming superhuman opponents, and whose last act was to order a burial mound on a conspicuous headland as a monument to his fame, and whose epitaph was *lofgeornost*. But he would raise what might seem like a tale of adventure "above mere story telling"; he would make it a *poem* and load every rift with ore. So he avoided continuous narrative, intercalated fragments of story with recondite, enriching, sometimes teasing, allusions and with forward and backward glances into the historical backgrounds, and arrayed it all in a highly ornate, alembicated style, with some vestiges of the minstrel formulas to set it off. These have an odd look alongside his methods of "syntactic correlation, parallel and antithetic structure, parenthesis, and climactic progression" (Klaeber). His *style* is one of the poet's glories—and impediments. It makes his poem a tour de force, which he must have enjoyed writing and hoped others would enjoy—enjoy the peculiar strain he put upon language and relish the tension of keeping pace with his structural convolutions. But this combination is so curious, so original, in the sense of being contrived, that the whole seems more like an artifact than a poem created out of the artist's experience.

When, finally, one thinks of the modern reader, *Beowulf* suffers the drawbacks of all subjects drawn from Northern myth and legend. The Greek and Roman world is too much with us. The subject of the poem is unsympathetic to our taste and the cultivation of a taste for it is a burden. Its people are alien to us. The tribal conflicts of sixth-century Danes and Swedes have no recognizable place on our stage of history. Their names have no familiar associations; and for our confusion there are twenty-six personal names beginning with H———. We have some acquaintance with literary dragons, but our imagination can do little with ogres and trolls; and what is more, none of the characters in the story makes an empathic appeal to us. Only by intervals is there a touch of human feeling or anything that speaks directly to us. There is no conception of character tested in significant human situations or any clear sense of tragic conflict, man against man or man against fate, with a catharsis which ennobles the victim through his sacrifice and the reader through contemplation of victory in death. (The hero's end is confused, for the reader, by his involvement with the heathen hoard.) The divided spirit of Hroðgar; the plight of that terrible old Ongenþeow, his queen captured and rescued and his death at the hands of a young man; the graciousness of Wealhþeow; the pathos of Hildeburh and the indecision of Hengest; the little comedy (if it be comedy) of Unferð—these seem to us undeveloped possibilities. We can see them but they are offered in passing. Like the tragic glimpses of Heremod and young Ðryð, and all the so-called digressions, they are absorbed into the main 'narrative'—smaller or larger pieces of color, purple or crimson or black—with little attention to their emotional or psychological interest. Whether functional or decorative or both at once, they appear suddenly and are gone quickly, and one hardly has time to enjoy them. The poet evidently set great store by them, but his touch-and-go use of them robs them of their power. The one major character for whom we are invited to feel sympathy is the Dragon.

All this and more would make for the dulness and dimness which the late Middleton Murry saw in the poem.[7] But dulness and dimness are relative terms, and it is worth recalling that to some Racine is dull, his characters a seeming vehicle for rhetorical declamation. To your French critic Shakespeare is chaos. Even *Prometheus Bound* is a strange work unless one brings to it the right kind of sympathetic understanding; Prometheus on his rock and the Oceanides singing would be, if we were not brought up on them, as remote as Hroðgar and his trolls or Beowulf and his Dragon. The language of Aeschylus is as difficult, until one has learned it, as the language of *Beowulf*.

As literature, said Mr. Murry, *Beowulf* is "an antediluvian curiosity," and Professor Gilbert Highet, speaking as a classicist, says that "artistically *Beowulf* is a rude and comparatively unskilled poem."[8] Well, it must be conceded that *Beowulf* is a foreign masterpiece, as foreign to modern taste in subject and manner as in language. It has, however, affinities with much of Donne and some of Browning, and it looks forward, curiously, to the very modern handling of time-sequence. But it cannot be translated into our idiom because we have no language corresponding to its ideas and emotions and we have no ideas and emotions to fit its peculiar language. The poet seems to have created many of his own difficulties. He had, one surmises, his own taste of chaos and in his fashion revived it, recreated it, while at the same time he looked back to a time of ideal loyalties and heroism. Simplicity, clarity, and elegant organization were luxuries he could not afford if he was to communicate what he felt the need of expressing. Why did he try? He could expect few silent readers in his own day. He adopted a tense crowded style and a convoluted method of narration, the very antithesis of a minstrel's, most unsuited for oral recitation, and if he looked for an audience of listeners he was extraordinarily, not to say stubbornly, sanguine. But all the signs point (they can hardly be called evidence but they are all we have) to a very individual man, a serious and gifted poet, steeped in the older pagan tradition from the continent, moved perhaps by a pious desire to compromise his two religions, and above all delighting in his unusual skill with language (as all poets do)—all the signs point to such a poet sitting down to compose a quasi-heroic poem to please himself, in the quiet expectation of pleasing also just that "fit audience though few." Shelley said of *Prometheus Unbound* that it was "never intended for more than five or six persons." It may seem odd to picture such an ivory-towered poet in the eighth century, but **Beowulf** is unique in every sense, and in the balance of probabilities the scales incline to even this unlikely assumption: a poet as individual and apart as his style, his plan, and his subject.

Notes

1. J. R. R. Tolkien, "Beowulf: the Monsters and the Critics," *Proc. of the British Academy,* XXII (1936), 245-295. This has been called a "masterful defence of the monsters against the critics." It was attacked by T. M. Gang, "Approaches to *Beowulf,*" *RES,* III (1952), 1-12, and defended by A. Bonjour, "Monsters Crouching and Critics Rampant," *PMLA,* LXVIII (1953), 304-312. Cf. also Arthur G. Brodeur, "The Structure and Unity of *Beowulf,*" *PMLA,* LXVIII (1953), 1183-95. Also cf. J. R. Hulbert, "The Genesis of *Beowulf:* a Caveat," *PMLA,* LXVI (1951), 1168-76, which shows how far we are from agreement on even the essential points, and warns against the dangers of "a new orthodoxy."

2. Dorothy Whitelock, *The Audience of Beowulf* (Oxford, 1951).

3. Cf. H. V. Routh, *God, Man and Epic Poetry* (Cambridge, 1927), I, 13, 17, 21; Malone, *English Studies,* XXIX (1948), 161-72; Klaeber, 1, li; Tolkien *passim;* Arthur T. DuBois, *PMLA,* XLIX (1934), 374-405 and *ibid.,* LXXII (1957), 819-822.

4. The poet shows some knowledge of the Old Testament (which aligns him with Cædmon) but none of the New (which distinguishes him from Cynewulf). The Sermon on the Mount and the Epistles of Paul have not touched him. The doctrines and dogmas of the Church—sin and redemption, revelation, a future life—have left little mark on his poem; at least he found no place for them. For obvious reasons there are no miracles; but the friends of Bede would have cleansed Heorot with Holy Water and vanquished the Dragon with a sign of the Cross. Beowulf seems to have followed St. Paul's exhortation to avoid women—thereby unfortunately leaving the succession open.

5. *The Oldest English Epic* (New York, 1910), p. 129.

6. C. M. Bowra, *Heroic Poetry* (London, 1952), pp. 48, 55, 215.

7. J. Middleton Murry, a review of the translation by C. K. Moncrieff, in *The Nation and the Athenum,* 22 October 1921.

8. Gilbert Highet, *The Classical Tradition* (Oxford, 1949), p. 24.

Eric Stanley (essay date 1966)

SOURCE: "Beowulf," in *Continuations and Beginnings: Studies in Old English Literature,* edited by Eric Gerald Stanley, Thomas Nelson and Sons Ltd., 1966, pp. 104-41.

[*In the essay below, Stanley offers an overview of the poem's style and imagery, and attempts to discern the way in which Anglo-Saxons may have regarded* Beowulf.]

We have no traditional approach to **Beowulf**.[1] We are entirely ignorant of the author's intentions except for what we may claim to be able to infer from the poem itself. Even the subject and the form of the poem are in doubt; words like epic and elegy are applied to it, epic because it is heroic, early and fairly long, and elegy because it commemorates and mourns men who were honoured in their generations and were the glory of their times. Some have seen the poem in its entirety as an *exemplum* in illustration of Hrothgar's great 'sermon' (lines 1700-84); others have held that the poem celebrates a dynasty of kings, gloriously founded by Beowulf son of Ecgtheow, a Wægmunding like his successor Wiglaf, whose nobility of purpose was, as the poet tells us (lines 2600f.), such that nothing could make him turn aside the claims of kinship.

We are ignorant of the reception the poem had among the Anglo-Saxons, how widely it was known or how highly it was regarded. Those modern readers who see in Beowulf the personification of the Anglo-Saxon heroic ideal must be surprised that, as far as our evidence goes, only a couple of Anglo-Saxons bore his name. There is some evidence that **Beowulf** may to some extent have served one other Old English poet, the poet of *Andreas,* as a model.

If we wish, we can compare **Beowulf** with other Old English poems. We may find that **Beowulf** is not only longer but also better than the others. That is not necessarily high praise; we may try to turn this relative praise into something more nearly absolute by protesting that the poem is the product of a great age, the age of Bede, an age which knew artistic achievements of the kind buried at Sutton Hoo, an age in which art and learning were united to produce great gospel books like the Lindisfarne Gospels, now in the British Museum, and the Codex Amiatinus, now at Florence. Even so, we cannot tell how good *Beowulf* was compared with the best works of that age. Is it not possible that at a time when the country was full of poems, no longer extant, of the stature of *Paradise Lost,* **Beowulf** (which happens to survive) had the standing roughly of Davenant's *Gondibert* or Cowley's *Davideis?* Or are we to believe that some special dispensation preserves the best of every age? That, surely, is a romantic superstition: from the thirteenth century to the sixteenth, and after, Old English was not sufficiently understood for an Old English text to be preserved deliberately because of its literary merit.[2] And more particularly, the fire which on 23 October 1731 raged in the Cotton Library at Ashburnham House in Westminster is not likely to have held back from doing worse harm to MS Vitellius A xv, the **Beowulf** Manuscript, than to scorch its edges, merely because the first taste the fire got of the poem convinced it of the excellence of **Beowulf** as a work of literature.

The evidence of the Anglo-Saxons' own interest in the poem lies chiefly in the manuscript itself. It is of the late tenth or early eleventh century, a long time after the composition of the poem, which is usually thought to have taken place no later than the eighth century. Several copyings (probably made in different parts of England where different dialects of Old English were spoken) lie between the only extant manuscript and the author's original. Of course, we cannot be sure what in each case made them copy the poem; as far as the extant manuscript is concerned, however, it seems that a finer sense of its value as poetry was less to the fore than its associations with monsters. The manuscript contains also some prose texts. One of them is a life of the dog-headed St Christopher, in the course of which we learn that the saint was twelve fathoms tall—twelve cubits, or roughly eighteen feet, in the Latin source—and he is treated and behaves accordingly. Another text in the manuscript is about *The Wonders of the East;* the monsters there are so numerous and so varied that strangely tall men are among the lesser marvels.[3]

. . .

A third text in the manuscript, *Letter of Alexander the Great to Aristotle,* has its monsters too; though it is disappointing to find that where the Old English text has a great battle between men and water monsters, *nicras,* the Latin source reads something like *hippopotami* for the Old English *nicras.*

Now a dragon and water monsters belong to the Beowulf story, and in England Beowulf's king, Hygelac of the Geats, was renowned because he was exceptionally tall. In a book, probably roughly contemporary with *Beowulf,* called *Liber Monstrorum* or *De Monstris et de Belluis* ('Book of Monsters' or 'Of Monsters and Wild Beasts') the following passage occurs:

> And there are monsters of wonderful size; such as King Higlacus who ruled the Getæ and was killed by the Franks, whom from his twelfth year no horse could carry. His bones are preserved on an island in the Rhine, where it flows forth into the ocean, and are shown to those who come from afar as a miracle.[4]

It has been shown that the *Liber Monstrorum* is English in origin. It preserves a reasonably good form of Hygelac's name and a form of the name of his people, the Geats, not remembered otherwise (as far as our evidence goes) on the Continent at that time. It is not an unreasonable speculation to think it possible that the centre which produced the *Liber Monstrorum* would have been interested in the subject-matter of *Beowulf;* the direction of that interest runs parallel with that shown by those who put together (long after the composition of the poem[5]) the material in our *Beowulf* Manuscript. A dragon, monsters, strangely tall men, these excited the Anglo-Saxons and seem to have done so over a long period. Nothing more literary than that is needed to explain the preservation of the poem.

All this need not redound to the glory of *Beowulf* as a literary masterpiece. It might seem rather to confirm the most cynical opinions about the intolerably naive views of the Anglo-Saxons, who delighted in those parts of the poem of which many modern apologists are most ashamed, and that includes the dragon.

Dragons are a common occurrence in the Bible; and in the Vulgate the word *draco* comes not only on the numerous occasions when the Authorised Version has *dragon,* but also often when the Authorised Version has *serpent.* It is not difficult to find in the Bible confirmation for the view that the dragon (or the serpent) is in league with the devil. Revelation 20:2 makes the dragon one with the devil: 'And he laid hold on the dragon, that old serpent, which is the Devil, and Satan, and bound him a thousand years.' The dragon in *Beowulf,* however, does not seem at all like that; it is very much more like the dragon of another book of the Bible, that of the story of Bel and the Dragon in the Book of Daniel.[6] Daniel among the Babylonians has destroyed their brass and clay idol, Bel. Verses 23-7 tell the next event, an historical event:

> And in that same place there was a great dragon, which they of Babylon worshipped. And the king said unto Daniel, Wilt thou also say that this is of brass? lo, he liveth, he eateth and drinketh; thou canst not say that he is no living god: therefore worship him. Then said Daniel unto the king, I will worship the Lord my God for he is the living God. But give me leave, O king, and I shall slay this dragon without sword or staff. The king said, I give thee leave. Then Daniel took pitch, and fat, and hair, and did seethe them together, and made lumps thereof: this he put in the dragon's mouth, and so the dragon burst in sunder: And Daniel said, Lo, these are the gods ye worship.

The dragon in *Beowulf* is more like that: lo, he liveth, he eateth and drinketh, and can be destroyed, by Daniel's trick or by the courage of men like Beowulf and Wiglaf— suitably protected by a flame-proof shield. And when dragons perish they may burst in sunder like that of Babylon or melt in their own heat like that slain by Sigemund (*Beowulf* 897). The dragon slain by Beowulf (as much as that slain by Daniel) is an evil adversary; but the words used by the poet to describe it, *niððraca* (2273), *se laða* (2305), *manscaða* (2514), *inwitgæst* (2670), and the like, seem less definitely links with hell than the words used by the poet of the fiendish brood of Grendel and his mother. The killing of the dragon is described as a terrible exploit from which men who at other times bear themselves valiantly may shrink: their fear is of a real being, a monstrously powerful creature—mercifully rare on this earth.[7]

It seems inconceivable that the poet of *Beowulf* should have intended to sublimate his evil dragon into draconity, making what has reality in the Bible into something abstract or symbolic, something acceptable to a twentieth-century audience willing to swallow monsters only as myths or symbols. Moreover, however we ourselves may wish to read *Beowulf,* of one thing we can be pretty sure on the evidence of the manuscript: the Anglo-Saxons read the poem as an account of Beowulf the monster-slayer, and preserved it with other accounts of monsters.

Nevertheless, it would be a highly imperceptive reading of *Beowulf* which finds in it nothing except monster-slaying.

We may not go all the way with Klaeber when he says, 'The poet would not have selected so singular a fable if it had not been exceptionally well-suited to Christianisation';[8] yet that judgment points in the right direction. Most of us now think tales of monsters a low order of literature, unless redeemed in the handling. The poet of *Beowulf* handles his story with literary artistry; he has made the story rich with spirituality. That has led some modern critics to look away from the reality of the monsters, to make them *be* wholly the powers of darkness towards which they *tend* (and from which Grendel's race is derived).

It is worth considering at the very outset one clear example of the poet's great skill in handling the customary material of Old English verse. Jacob Grimm, writing of Old English poetry with particular reference to *Elene*, said:

> The way in which battles and war, the favourite occupation of our antiquity, are described deserves our attention before all else. There is something glorious in every battle-scene. Wolf, eagle and raven with joyous cry go forward in the van of the army, scenting their prey.[9]

In Old English poetry the wolf, the eagle and the raven occur as satellites of battle some sixteen times in all. Wherever they come they convey the expectation of slaughter. The lean wolf leaves the forest for that, and the wings of eagle and raven, dark and glistening with dew, seem to reflect impending carnage. The *Beowulf* poet uses the same imagery at the end of the speech which near the end of the poem foretells the destruction of the Geatish nation now that Beowulf is dead:

>   Forðon sceall gar wesan
> monig morgenceald mundum bewunden,
> hæfen on handa, nalles hearpan sweg
> wigend weccean, ac se wonna hrefn
> fus ofer fægum fela reordian,
> earne secgan, hu him æt æte speow,
> þenden he wið wulf wæl reafode.
>
>   3021-7[10]

In no other poem is an attempt made to establish a relationship between the beasts of battle: they are attendants of carnage operating singly though pursuing the same end. In *Beowulf* they are more than that: there is on the one hand the grim conversation between the birds, and on the other the cadaverous eating match. The purposeful combination of the beasts of battle expresses effectively the certainty that the Geats shall be extirpated:[11] the three will have much to tell of things to their liking.

Other poets may refer to the beasts of battle to convey lustily the impending downfall of an enemy; the poet of *Beowulf* invokes them when friends must fall. If, as may well be, the beasts of battle first had a place in poems exulting in the overthrow of an enemy, like that of the Danes in *The Battle of Brunanburh* (60-5) and of the Assyrians in *Judith* (204-12, 294-6), the formulas turn sour in the hands

of the poet of *Beowulf,* who uses them to call up all that is most abhorrent to warriors. There is deliberate artistry in that.

It would be pleasant to think that the poet's art did not remain unrecognised in Anglo-Saxon times. There is, outside the context of the *Beowulf* Manuscript itself, only one point which might provide evidence of how the Anglo-Saxons themselves regarded the poem: there seems to be some connection between *Beowulf* and one other of the longer Old English poems, *Andreas.* Klaeber surveys the material in the introduction (pp. cx ff.) of his edition of *Beowulf* and so does Mr K. R. Brooks, the most recent editor of *Andreas,* in the introduction to his edition. Parallels have been adduced between *Beowulf* and Old English poems other than *Andreas,* but they seem less striking than those with *Andreas,* nothing that cannot be readily explained as arising from the fact that *Beowulf* and *Andreas* share their poetic traditions with other Old English poems.[12] Often traditional phrases were available to an Old English poet for subjects occurring frequently in traditional poetry. Some of the details which *Andreas* shares with *Beowulf* can be ascribed to that cause. For example, Heorot, the Danish hall in *Beowulf* (82), like the Temple of Jerusalem (*Andreas* 668), is described as *heah ond horngeap.* There are *stræte stanfage* in *Andreas* (1236) and *stræt wæs stanfag* in *Beowulf* (320). Such parallels do not provide evidence of indebtedness; after all, if 'lofty and wide-gabled' represents an ideal in a hall and if roads paved with stones in the Roman manner are an impressive sight it is not very surprising that two suitable and alliterating epithets should be used of a hall in a number of Old English poems and that *stræt* should come in collocation with *stanfah* in more places than one.

Nevertheless, when due allowance has been made for what may be derived independently from the common poetic heritage of the nation, there remain one or two parallels that do seem to be the result of one poet imitating the other. It should be possible to deduce from this special relationship between *Beowulf* and *Andreas* something that might help us to evaluate how *Beowulf* was regarded by at least one other Anglo-Saxon.

Perhaps the clearest of the parallels connecting *Beowulf* and *Andreas* are the words *ealuscerwen* (*Beowulf* 769) and *meoduscerwen* (*Andreas* 1526) and the opening lines of the two poems. The *Beowulf* poet's use of the word *ealuscerwen* almost certainly implies the image of Death's bitter cup.[13] In his use of the word the image lies all in the word *ealuscerwen* itself. Literally *ealu* means 'ale' and *meodu* means 'mead', and *scerwen* probably means 'dispensing' or possibly 'privation' (though the meaning 'privation' would not fit the context of *meoduscerwen* in *Andreas* at all well). The words do not occur except here. In the *Beowulf* context *ealuscerwen* refers to disaster: ale is a bitter drink. When the poet of *Andreas* uses the word *meoduscerwen* he labours away at the image. He applies it to a sea-flood overwhelming a multitude. The bitterness implicit in the *Beowulf* image is made explicit in *Andreas* as a *biter beorþegu* (1533), 'bitter beer-drinking', and he further exploits the metaphor by a reference to a *sorgbyrþen* (1532), 'brewing of sorrow'. Unfortunately for the image, when the *Andreas* poet was introducing the idea expressed by the *Beowulf* poet as *ealuscerwen,* he happened to be writing a second half-line, following a first half-line which used *m*-alliteration, *myclade mereflod,* 'the sea-flood increased'; and so forgetting that mead (unlike the ale of *ealuscerwen*) is a sweet honey-drink quite unconnected with brewings of sorrow and bitter *beer*-drinking, he wrote *meoduscerwen.* If his use of that word is indebted to *Beowulf* it is clear that he bungled what he borrowed. A skilful versifier would have found no difficulty in producing a first half-line with vocalic alliteration to allow the use of the *Beowulf* word *ealuscerwen* in the second half-line: that word is presumed in the clumsy exploitation of the image in *Andreas.*

A comparison of the opening lines of *Beowulf* with those of *Andreas* reveals further similarities which it would be difficult to explain simply by reference to their common poetic inheritance:

> Hwæt, we Gardena   in geardagum,
> þeodcyninga   þrym gefrunon,
> hu ða æþelingas   ellen fremedon!
>
>   *Beowulf* 1-3
>
> Hwæt, we gefrunan   on fyrndagum
> twelfe under tunglum   tireadige hæleð,
> þeodnes þegnas.   No hira þrym alæg . . .
>
>   *Andreas* 1-3[14]

The opening word *hwæt* is common as the opening word of many Old English poems, and that both *Beowulf* and *Andreas* begin with the same word is of no special significance. The formula *we (. . .) gefrunon* is also a common one in Old English verse, but the two poets handle it quite differently. In the *Beowulf* opening the two verbs *gefrunon* and *fremedon* play no part in the alliteration of the lines in which they come. The complex alliterative scheme rests on nouns: *Gar* alliterates with *gear, dena* with *dagum,* both second elements of compounds; *þeod* alliterates with *þrym,* and the initial vowels of *æþelingas* and *ellen* alliterate. The sense requires Spear-Danes and days of yore, the glory of a nation's kings, princes and deeds of valour to be stressed. The metre requires those syllables to be stressed which are emphasised also by the sense, and the alliteration reinforces the stress. By its positioning, the subject *we* at the beginning of the clause and the verb *gefrunon* at the end, the phrase *we . . . gefrunon* frames the glory of the Spear-Danes' royal dynasty in days of yore, and leads on to the next clause. It is quite different in *Andreas.* His word-order is pedestrian; his statement merely asserts, first, the apostles' existence, secondly, their glory. Without in any way complicating the alliteration the poet tells us that he has heard tell of twelve glorious heroes under the stars in distant days, the Lord's retainers; the word *þrym* comes in the next sentence: their glory did not fail. The ingredients of the two openings are similar, but they have been used with differing degrees of skill. The devices

available to Anglo-Saxon poets are used together in *Beowulf* to produce that harmony of sense and metre which it is possible for Old English poets to achieve if they know how to exploit the relative freedom of word-order permitted in verse. There is nothing wrong with *Andreas*—unless it is wrong for the opening of a poem to lack every distinction.

It is not always profitable to look for modern analogies and to transfer subjective judgments of poems of one age to poems of another. It is not possible to say how high in absolute terms *Beowulf* is to be rated, where it might be allowed to stand in relation to *Paradise Lost,* for example. Even so, it is perhaps possible to discern that the poet of *Beowulf* achieved something that was achieved also in the opening of *Paradise Lost;* and that the difference between the opening of *Beowulf* and that of *Andreas* (whatever its *degree*) is something of the *kind* of difference between the opening which begins 'Of Man's first Disobedience' and:

> I sing the *Man* who *Judah's Sceptre* bore
> In that right Hand which held the *Crook* before;
> Who from best *Poet,* best of *Kings* did grow;
> The two chief *Gifts Heav'n* could on *Man* bestow.

That is the opening of Cowley's *Davideis.* It was published earlier than *Paradise Lost,* so that there can be no question of Cowley's being indebted to Milton—and there is of course not much similarity. There is similarity between the opening of *Beowulf* and that of *Andreas,* and to assume indebtedness is a likelier explanation than any other that might explain the similarity.

The dating of Old English poems is tricky. *Andreas* is generally held to be later than *Beowulf.* The possibility that *Andreas* is imitated in *Beowulf* is unlikely; the fact that *ealuscerwen* fits its context in *Beowulf* well whereas *meoduscerwen* fits its context in *Andreas* badly may be regarded as sufficient evidence that (if there is indebtedness at all) the borrowing is from *Beowulf* into *Andreas.* It seems inconceivable also that the successfully ornate opening of *Beowulf* should owe anything to the indifferent opening of *Andreas.* There are, of course, instances of a better poet borrowing from a worse. Thus, Lord Lyttleton's line

> Poured forth his unpremeditated strain

(from James Thomson's *Castle of Indolence,* Canto I, stanza lxviii) does seem to have contributed something to the opening stanza of Shelley's *To a Skylark,* written in 1820, nearly three-quarters of a century later:

> That from heaven or near it
> Pourest thy full heart
> In profuse strains of unpremeditated art.

But the line from *The Castle of Indolence* is sufficiently competent for it to have jingled in Shelley's mind even if the possibility of conscious borrowing were to be ruled out by those who know about Shelley. It is difficult to believe that the mind of the **Beowulf** poet was chiming with memories of *Andreas.*

It seems likely, therefore, that one Old English poet, the poet of *Andreas,* drew on **Beowulf.** Can we base anything on such borrowing in our attempt to establish whether or not **Beowulf** was highly regarded by the Anglo-Saxons? A first reaction, to base nothing on what a poetical dunderhead like the poet of *Andreas* may happen to choose as his models, should probably be rejected as too hasty. An inferior versifier's critical acumen may well be better than his practice, not merely on account of the general principle that one need not be a hen to know if an egg is rotten, but rather on account of the particular principle that many who do not themselves excel in an art nevertheless make sensitive critics of other practitioners, their failure having given them better insight into what success is possible. There is something in the view that imitation implies admiration; the imitation of **Beowulf** in *Andreas* is testimony to the regard in which one Anglo-Saxon, whose own efforts made him a competent judge of what we now call Old English literature, seems to have held the poem. We have a right to show greater faith in him, for all his faults as a poet, than in the monster-mongers who preserved the poem. It is poor evidence of the original reception of the poem: we have no better evidence.

If we have little to go on in assessing the original reception of the poem, we have still our own judgment to tell us that in **Beowulf** certain details of poetic expression are put to better use than in other poems of the Old English period. In this kind of comparative analysis we cannot be sure that the details we single out for praise would, in fact, have been among things considered important by the Anglo-Saxons themselves.

The superior use made by the poet of **Beowulf** of the beasts of battle has been cited already as an example of the poet's special skill. The poet uses the traditional material of Old English verse with an aptness which makes it often seem the fresh product of his mind. His skill shows itself in his exploitation of the resources of the Old English poetic vocabulary, in his manipulation of complicated sentences, and in his use of the alliterative metre to convey his meaning effectively. These particulars are in the first place aspects of the poet's art of expression and therefore only less immediately aspects of what is being expressed. We have no means of knowing how these things were valued by the Anglo-Saxons themselves, and we may find that if we value these accomplishments of poetic expression highly and turn to them as criteria for judging the merits of Old English verse we may come to think less well of such pieces as *The Battle of Maldon, The Dream of the Rood,* and *The Later Genesis,* however good these may be at communicating pathos and passion.

Comparison must occupy an important place in any analysis of the poetic art of **Beowulf.** But there is a limit to what can be subjected to comparison. This is especially true of Old English poetic vocabulary, the greatest glories of which may well be the coinages: they were created to fill a special need and cannot for that reason be compared. In the **Beowulf** passage which ends in the figure of the beasts of battle, for example, the word *morgenceald* (3022[15]) 'morning-cold' demonstrates what can be done with words in Old English verse. The adjective applies to the hand-gripped spear, and satisfactorily communicates the clammy fear of the Geatish warriors as they wake to their last battle. The substantival and adjectival compounds used by the **Beowulf** poet have often been singled out for their excellence.[16] G. Storm's careful discussion of a small group of adjectives, including words like 'lordless', 'joyless', 'soulless', well illustrates the poet's skill with words. Thirty years before Storms's analysis of words ending in *-leas* Hoops discussed compounds beginning with *ær-*. He suggested convincingly that in words like *ærgod* (the first element of which means 'previously' and the second means 'good') the prefix *ær-* means 'old and venerable', so that the compound *ærgod,* for example, means 'excellent as things were formerly'; it does not mean 'formerly good, but not so good now'. Weohstan, Wiglaf's father—a most important personage if the poem should in any way be thought of as celebrating a dynasty—is described (line 2622) as *ærfæder.* The meaning of the word is 'father, old and venerable'—not 'a good old man but a little senile' like Goodman Verges in Dogberry's eyes. The poet describes ancient treasure as *ærgestreon, ærgeweorc, ærwela;* and we know from descriptions of ancient treasure in **Beowulf** that it was admired for excellence, presumably because some of the skill that made the treasure in former times was not to be found among the poet's contemporaries. From the poet's use of the prefix *ær-* we can see his attitude to *le temps perdu* some part of which may be recalled as the hand touches the hilt of an ancient sword great in associations and glorious in workmanship (cf. 1677-98).

These are detailed points, and **Beowulf** is rich in such points. Compounds are a common occurrence in the poem. On average there is a compound every other line of the poem. This very high frequency is, of course, of some interest in itself. It would be of greater interest if we could tell which of them the poet coined. Klaeber, in the excellent glossary to his edition of the poem, indicates by means of a double dagger those words which do not occur outside the poem. It is likely enough that the poet made up many of these compounds, but we can never be sure that any particular compound which we think bears the stamp of his individuality, *morgenceald* for example, might not have been more widespread. Too much has been lost. In a few cases we know that a word only found in **Beowulf** must have had wider currency in English at one time. Thus the adjective *niðhedig* (3165), 'hostile thinking', only comes in **Beowulf;** but the cognate *niðhugdig* occurs in Old Saxon (*Heliand* 1056). Similarly the word *nydgestealla* (882), 'companion in need', occurs in **Beowulf** alone of extant Old English texts; but Old High German forms of the word (e.g. *notgistallo,* Otfrid's *Evangelienbuch* IV, xvi, 4) are not uncommon. It is best, therefore, not to praise the *Beowulf* poet's originality in coining words. We must content ourselves with praising that he used words aptly.

The way in which the poet manipulates complicated sentences distinguishes his work among Old English poets (though other Old English poems also contain long sentences). If we take the *Beowulf* Manuscript as our starting-point, the organisation of ideas can be discerned to some extent from the rudimentary punctuation and sporadic capitalisation, rudimentary and sporadic, that is, when compared with modern editions. Except for that, no help is given to the reader, who has to rely on his familiarity with the alliterative metre to guide him to correct metrical phrasing, and in Old English verse metrical phrases correspond to meaningful phrases. Since the poem is written continuously like prose (that is, not in lines of verse) it is obvious that the Anglo-Saxon readers of the manuscript must have been helped by the metre to a meaningful reading of the poem.

In selecting the passage which covers lines 864 to 886 for the following discussion the hope is that, though perhaps no individual passage can be called typical of *Beowulf,* nothing atypical will have been chosen. In Klaeber's edition the lines are printed as follows (ignoring the macrons and other diacritics he uses):

> Hwilum heaþorofe　　　hleapan leton,
> on geflit faran　　　fealwe mearas,
> ðær him foldwegas　　　fægere þuhton,
> cystum cuðe.　　　Hwilum cyninges þegn,
> guma gilphlæden,　　　gidda gemyndig,
> se ðe ealfela　　　ealdgesegena
> worn gemunde,　　　word oþer fand
> soðe gebunden;　　　secg eft ongan
> sið Beowulfes　　　snyttrum styrian,
> ond on sped wrecan　　　spel gerade,
> wordum wrixlan;　　　welhwylc gecwæd,
> þæt he fram Sigemunde[s]　　　secgan hyrde
> ellendædum,　　　uncuþes fela,
> Wælsinges gewin,　　　wide siðas,
> þara þe gumena bearn　　　gearwe ne wiston,
> fæhðe ond fyrena,　　　buton Fitela mid hine,
> þonne he swulces hwæt　　　secgan wolde,
> eam his nefan,　　　swa hie a wæron
> æt niða gehwam　　　nydgesteallan;
> hæfdon ealfela　　　eotena cynnes
> sweordum gesæged.　　　Sigemunde gesprong
> æfter deaðdæge　　　dom unlytel,
> syþðan wiges heard . . .[17]

In the manuscript the following punctuation is used. *Hwilum* (864) is preceded by a punctuation mark and the word begins with a capital. There is a mark of punctuation after *wiston* (878), but the mark is less prominent than that preceding *Hwilum* (864) and *fæhðe* (879) has no initial capital. There is again a prominent mark of punctuation after *gesteallan* (882) and the next word, *Hæfdon* (883), begins with a capital. The next mark of punctuation, again prominent, comes after *unlytel* (885), and the next word, *Syþðan* (886), begins with a capital.

A comparison of the manuscript punctuation with Klaeber's shows that, though there is some correspondence, the manuscript punctuation is insufficient to enable a modern reader to grasp the meaning at the kind of speed needed for reading the poem to an audience. Yet there is nothing unusual about the punctuation of this passage or of the rest of the poem. It is not known if the punctuation of the manuscript goes back to the poet; there is no need to claim authorial authority for the punctuation for the present purpose, which is to consider how an Anglo-Saxon reader of the manuscript would have understood the text before him in spite of the sparseness of marks of punctuation, and how the author's characteristic style might be particularly well suited for the kind of reading which an Anglo-Saxon reader used to alliterative verse might have achieved.

An Anglo-Saxon reader of the poem had to rely on the metrical phrasing for a meaningful delivery. We may assume him to have been familiar with alliterative verse, and for that reason he can have had no difficulty in splitting up the text into the units we call half-lines and lines. The poet's syntax depends on the metre for its clarity, so that his art of discourse is poetic not only in his exploitation of the vocabulary available to him, but poetic also in the more prosaic virtue of clarity. This is not lowering the dignity of the word *poetic:* what is involved is the characteristic sentence paragraph of the *Beowulf* poet; that is, the poet depends on the metre for his ability to formulate his ideas at length and for his complexity of utterance.[18] It may well be that those Old English prose writers, ælfric and Wulfstan among them, who at times wrote metrical prose, did so partly because they gained in clarity of expression, but mainly because metrical phrasing would more easily enable their readers to achieve meaningful delivery; however, the use to which metre is put in Old English prose has only an indirect bearing on the present discussion.

In all Old English verse, words which have the function of joining phrases or clauses or sentences (that is, metrically unstressed connectives) precede the first stressed syllable of the half-line in which they come. This is simply the result of the fact that the beginning of phrases, clauses and sentences must coincide with the beginning of metrical phrases: a break within a half-line is not tolerated. As in any other passage of Old English verse, the connectives, e.g. *hwilum* (867), *buton* (879), *þonne* (880), come in the initial dip of the half-line. *Hwilum* at line 864 is (or, at least, could be) stressed; that is borne out by the alliteration of the line, *h*-alliteration, in which *Hwilum* shares. The word does so also at line 2107, and at line 2020 it takes part in cross-alliteration. It follows that *hwilum,* though not always stressed, is stressable; and stressable particles when they are in fact not stressed must come in the first dip (i.e. unstressed position) of the clause.[19] When, as at line 867 for example, the stressable particle (here *hwilum*) is a connective it must come in the dip which precedes the first stress of the clause.

Though there are exceptions,[20] the vast majority of clusters of three or more unstressed syllables come in the position between the last stress of a half-line and the first stress of the following half-line. Not more than one unstressed syllable may end a half-line (except insofar as an additional unstressed syllable may be required for resolution of the last stressed syllable of the half-line). It follows that an Old English reader who comes upon a cluster of syllables consisting of words (or parts of words) which are unstressable and particles which are occasionally stressed will recognise that he is very probably at the beginning of a clause, even though he is reading a manuscript which, by modern standards, is insufficiently punctuated and not split up into lines and half-lines of verse.

Unstressed syllables in clusters may be regarded as signals to tell the reader how the construction of the sentence continues. The dip at the beginning of a half-line is a signalising position, especially clear when it is used in excess of the minimum requirements of the metre.[21] All this applies to all Old English verse. There is every reason for thinking that the poets knew what syntactical advantages were to be derived from the regularity of metre.

The method of composition in **Beowulf** is usually additive and annexive. That is not to say that the poet simply tacks phrase to phrase without premeditation. Though sentences in which the subordinate clauses precede their main clause are not very common in the poem there are enough of them (examples occur at lines 1368-72 and 1822-30) to show that the poet's complexity of utterance is premeditated. Other examples of complex sentence structure include the embedding of one clause within another, as occurs, for instance, at lines 867-71, where (however we may relate *word oðer fand/soðe gebunden* to what precedes it) the relative clause *se ðe ealfela ealdgesegena/ worn gemunde* comes between *cyninges þegn,* the subject, and its verb. Other examples are to be found at lines 731b, 1613b, 1831b, and 2855b. Nevertheless the commonest shape of long sentences in the poem begins with the main clause, and clauses and phrases are added and annexed one after the other.

Correlatives enable Old English poets to construct their very long sentences. Modern editors not infrequently punctuate passages containing a pair of correlatives as two separate sentences, each beginning with a correlative. An example is provided by Klaeber's punctuation of lines 864ff., where he has two sentences each beginning with *Hwilum.* Modern writers on the whole prefer a set of logically connected short sentences to a single long sentence containing them all, and Klaeber's punctuation accords well with their practice. His punctuation is unexceptionable, as long as we remember that the reference of the correlative at each of its two occurrences is not identical: at its first occurrence the reference of *hwilum* is forward, at its second occurrence it refers back. The meaning of *hwilum* at its first occurrence is 'at certain times (which are to be given)', at its second occurrence 'at other times (than those already named)'. When the word first occurs the reader or listener cannot know if there is going to be another occurrence of the word; for *hwilum* does exist in

constructions other than correlative constructions (just as 'at certain times' does). An Anglo-Saxon reader or listener would know the way in which the word *hwilum* could be used. The first occurrence would alert him for any second occurrence. At both occurrences here the word comes at the beginning of the clause, in the dip at line 867 and in what could be the dip (if we knew more about the rules of double-alliteration involving particles) at line 864. The initial dip of a clause is a signalising position. At line 916, fifty-odd lines away from the first occurrence of *hwilum* the word comes again, also in the signalising position:

Hwilum flitende   fealwe stræte
mearum mæton.

There is good reason for thinking that *hwilum* here (though Klaeber makes it begin a new paragraph) refers back to the two earlier occurrences of the word. They introduce related ideas (though the use of *hwilum* at line 916 is not strictly correlative)—and we cannot call the whole passage from lines 864 to 917 one single sentence, because the passage consists of an organism greater than is covered by our concept of a sentence, a concept for practical purposes defined by practical rules of permissible punctuation. By utilising the initial dips of clauses, occupying them with connectives—*hwilum,* for example—the poet is able to embark on a complex idea, extending it over one sentence or two or more, without losing lucidity, even if (as in the case of Anglo-Saxon manuscripts) the punctuation is only rudimentary.

The device of variation acts in the same direction, though not at such length. Variation, as usually defined, is prosodically of stressed units only: it does not include personal pronouns, for example. In the passage under discussion the subject *cyninges þegn* (867) is varied by *guma gilphlæden* (868), which adds to the description of the king's retainer, and is varied further by *secg* (871), which continues the idea, lucidly enabling the reader to follow the sense of the passage without the help of punctuation; and *secg* is taken up by the pronoun *he* (875), though that is not strictly 'variation'.

There is more to the sentence than that. The word *gemyndig* (868) is echoed paronomastically by *gemunde* (870); the adjective *gilphlæden* is varied and made explicit by *gidda gemyndig* (868), and the word *gidda* dependent on *gemyndig* is varied by *ealfela ealdgesegena/worn* (869f.) dependent on *gemunde.* Whatever it may mean, the phrase *word oþer fand* (870) is answered across Klaeber's semicolon by *wordum* (874); *wordum,* a dative plural used adverbially, goes with the infinitive *wrixlan,* and is parallel to *snyttrum* (872) which goes with the infinitive *styrian.* It would not be difficult to go on: there is more to the passage; and almost every passage in the poem can be analysed in this way. Of course, it is not likely that the original audience would have apprehended these interweavings at a first hearing. Their effect is twofold: these interweavings enable the poet to proceed in an additive and annexive progress, which is far from simple and can nevertheless be understood; and they give to his verse a peculiar density of texture, only rarely found in Old English verse outside **Beowulf.**

It is pleasing to trace in the totality of the poem the patterns which we discern in a small part of it. Conversely, it is pleasing to find in a short passage of the poem the patterns which seem to underlie the structure of the poem as a whole. Professor J. R. R. Tolkien has said that '**Beowulf** is indeed the most successful Old English poem because in it the elements, language, metre, theme, structure, are all most nearly in harmony'.[22] But the overall pattern which he selects in illustration of this statement is balance: that is, the static principle which to his mind governs the total structure of the poem as much as it governs the individual lines with their 'opposition between two halves of roughly equivalent phonetic weight, and significant content, which are more often rhythmically contrasted than similar'.[23] There are many ways of regarding the poem. If there is a balance either in the smaller units or in the total structure of the poem it is perceived only on looking back. As the poem advances, as it is read or heard, it is surely a continuum: the listening ear strains for what is to come. The adding of bit to bit in that continuum and the diversity of the means by which the continuity is attained provide evidence of the poet's art.

The passage under discussion is a good example of the poet's skill in sentence structure. It is also an excellent example of how he uses an additive and annexive method of progression for a much larger unit. The general statement of what the king's retainer does (867-77), with its specific statement (868-71) about the traditional nature of what he sings, is followed by a statement (871-4) that Beowulf is the subject still in the account of Sigemund the dragon-slayer and his fame; and that Beowulf is still the subject of the song even when it proceeds to speak of Heremod, the Saul-like king of the Danes, is made clear when at line 913 the singer reverts to Beowulf.[24] The modern reader (waylaid and beset by linguistic difficulties and background notes of exceptional length) thinks the transitions sudden. The forward-listening members of the original audience, told at the beginning of the song that it is of Beowulf, make the connection and apprehend the unity. It is of great importance for an understanding of how the poem compares with other Old English poems to realise that it is unusual in Old English verse other than **Beowulf** to attempt such long organisms. In **Beowulf** the attempt is successful because the poet exploits all the devices of Old English versification (including the syntax peculiar to Old English verse) to prepare the listener for long units and to give them clarity.

Twice in the course of **Beowulf** the poet gives expression to a poetic ideal, once in the passage some aspects of which have been discussed already, lines 867-74, and once at lines 2105-14. The former is a difficult passage: we are not sure what is meant by the two half-lines *word ofer fand/soðe gebunden;* but its beginning is clear. The other passage, lines 2105-14 is easier:

> Þær wæs gidd ond gleo;   gomela Scilding,
> felafricgende   feorran rehte;
> hwilum hildedeor   hearpan wynne,
> gomenwudu grette,   hwilum gyd awræc
> soð ond sarlic,   hwilum syllic spell
> rehte æfter rihte   rumheort cyning;
> hwilum eft ongan   eldo gebunden,
> gomel guðwiga   gioguðe cwiðan,
> hildestrengo;   hreðer inne weoll,
> þonne he wintrum frod   worn gemunde.[25]

A comparison of these two passages shows that they have much in common. The singer tells a wondrous tale, *syllic spell,* true and sad, *soð and sarlic.* And in both passages the emphasis is on the memory. In the first passage the phrase *soðe gebunden* may refer to the technicality of alliteration, 'truly linked'; on the other hand, *soð ond sarlic* of the second passage may lead us to prefer the translation 'bound in truth' for *soðe gebunden.* The phrase *æfter rihte* in the second passage should probably be regarded as a vague statement, meaning 'according to what is right', rather than a specific reference to accurate alliteration. The best explanation of the words *wordum wrixlan* does seem to be[26] to regard it as a reference to the 'weaving of words' in the rhetorical devices of variation, specifically, and paronomasia, more generally.

There is good reason for taking the two passages together, for they both refer to the same occasion. The first is the poet's account of the festivities at Heorot after Beowulf's defeat of Grendel, the second is Beowulf's own account to Hygelac, his king, of what is presumably a later stage of the same festivities. It is an ideal picture of a society deeply rooted in its traditions, recalling past events to provide fit comparison for present deeds of glory.

The crux *word oðer fand* (870) has sometimes been interpreted in contradistinction to *ealdgesegen* (869); that is, 'he composed *new* words' in contradistinction to 'he remembered a great multitude of *old* traditions'. That view is not accepted by Professor Else von Schaubert in her edition of the poem, and the reasons of syntax which led her to reject it (and which led Klaeber to follow her in the second supplement (p. 466f.) of his edition) seem convincing. In any case, there is nothing that might lead one to the view that old traditions in new words represents an ideal among the Anglo-Saxons; and, even if it were possible to parallel in Old English the meaning 'new' for *oþer,* that alone would make one doubt the interpretation. This is the value of Professor F. P. Magoun's application to Old English poetry of the theories relating to preliterate poetic composition, and this, as Professor C. L. Wrenn has shown,[27] is one important aspect of the miracle of Cædmon: that Old English had only one form of poetic utterance; it was aristocratic and traditional whatever the subject and whatever the mood. According to Bede, Cædmon was the first in England to take Christian themes as subjects for that traditional poetry. Since traditional diction is as much a part of the definition of Old English verse as the use of regular rhythms and the use of regular alliteration, Christ, Lucifer, the saints and the Patriarchs appear as Germanic liege-lords with their retainers. That is the reason for the Germanisation of the Orient, as Heusler called it. The audience expected what they were used to, and the poet supplied it: there was no other way of telling in verse of the deeds of men.

So far we have considered the means of poetic expression and the use made of them by the poet of *Beowulf.* The passage selected for closer analysis contains a statement of the poet's ideal in poetry, the singing of a song about deeds performed that day. The singer in Heorot is the poet's fiction, part of his picture of the society of the past. Before we consider that picture as a whole we must take issue with the application to *Beowulf* of theories which may help to explain some of the characteristics of oral poetry such as is found in the Balkans. That poetry makes use of a stock of formulas traditionally associated with it. Old English verse, like the verse of related Germanic tribes, for example the Old Saxons, is formulaic. Formulas found again and again in different Old English poems, a seemingly unique phrase found in the same or a very similar form in some other poem, all confirm that Old English poets draw not merely on an ancient hoard of poetic words, but also on an ancient hoard of whole poetic phrases when they wish to give expression to something already expressed in a set formula. No doubt, very often the availability of a formula will influence poets to make use of it.

As we have seen, in descriptions of battles poets introduce in traditional terms something on the beasts of battle. The traditional formulaic element is available for a very wide range of ideas, at times for an absence of ideas, as when they introduce some tag like *heard under helme,* 'strong under his helmet', to describe—very vaguely—some hero, or *under heofones hwealf,* 'under the arch of heaven', to localise—very vaguely—some action. The origin of the use of such phrases may well lie in the characteristics of oral poetry, the product of an extemporising singer. This has been the opinion of scholars for a long time. It is sufficient to quote A. F. C. Vilmar's view of a hundred and twenty years ago:

> These formulas, which rest as much on ancient tradition as they characterise oral tradition, create the refreshing impression that what we are concerned with here is nothing invented, nothing artificial or fictive, no mere book-learning, but rather a living tale which wholly fills the teller and stands at all times at his command.[28]

Vilmar distinguishes the traditional origin of the formulas of Germanic verse, and their connection with oral poetry, from the *impression* given by their use. That is an important distinction to be borne in mind when we come to *Beowulf;* that poem survives in written form only: whether we think it the work of an extemporising poet or of a man who composes pen in hand depends on our response to the *impression* made on us by the poem.

Professor F. P. Magoun's discussion[29] of oral-formulaic versification has deepened our understanding of the kind of poetry that underlies the Old English poetry surviving in such manuscripts as have been preserved. To understand the use of tags and set phrases, whole half-lines of verse used repeatedly, it is useful to know about some kinds of preliterate composition. But we should not necessarily assume that what applies to the poetry of a genuinely preliterate society has an immediate and direct bearing on the elaborately literate poetry of the Anglo-Saxons. When we come to *Beowulf,* I agree with Professor Kemp Malone: 'The *Beowulf* poet was no minstrel, strumming a harp and composing verse as he strummed.'[30] Though the devices of sense and sound, variation and paronomasia, could in themselves be explained as the vehicles of an associative imagination working *extempore,* when they come, as in *Beowulf,* in combination with the careful exploitation of every aspect of what was available to an Old English poet, it seems more likely that this highly wrought poem is the product of a lettered poet, or at least of a slow, non-extemporising poet.

In his analysis of Old English verse Professor Magoun has made crucial use of the example of Cædmon.[31] It may be worth considering Cædmon again to see if we are really presented by Bede with 'the case history of an Anglo-Saxon oral singer' in the sense in which Magoun and his school interpret that phrase. We have the authority of Bede for the fact that Cædmon was illiterate. Except for the nine lines of his *Hymn* none of his poems survives. Even so, we know from Bede's account that he recited his orally composed verses to his teachers who acted as scribes. We are told also that they were long poems. However, nothing in Bede's account suggests that Cædmon composed *extempore* before an audience; nothing suggests even that he composed harp in hand; nothing suggests that he composed long poems other than bit by bit. Bede's famous phrase that Cædmon composing was like a clean beast ruminating, *quasi mundum animal ruminando,* calls to mind slow and deliberate, many-stomached digestion, remouthing again and again the same material. This does not support Magoun: not even the case of Cædmon, the illiterate neat-herd. We have no account of how the *Beowulf* poet went about his work. Nevertheless, the product of his art, with its sophisticated interweaving of devices, and the mechanics of elaborate, long, sentence-like structures composed with metrical precision, all aptly matching a subtle and complex set of ideas, makes one doubt that *Beowulf* should have been the work of an oral singer.

Magoun makes a distinction between good and bad oral verse, by saying that 'a good singer is one able to make better use of the common fund of formulas than the indifferent or poor singer'.[32] This is obvious enough: the putting together is part of the art. Aptness and organisation make suitable criteria for judging a poem. More recently a disciple of Magoun's, writing 'On the Possibility of Criticizing Old English Poetry', has told us,

> Our praise is misplaced when we would offer it to the poet for the *wording* of a verse or line, as much misplaced as if we should praise Yeats for *inventing the words* of his poems.[33]

This seems misguided. The *wording* is not the same as the *words*. There is a degree of contrivance and invention in putting together words and phrases from the hoard of oral formulas. There is invention in the use of compounds, and we can judge that invention by the criteria of aptness and organisation. We are not in a position to know which individual phrase or compound is new, but we are in a position to detect good use made of traditional language. In *Beowulf* good use is made of it; in *Andreas* less so. Regardless of whether the technique of composition is fully *extempore,* or slow composition refined by revision, or even written composition painfully corrected, putting together words from the customary poetic vocabulary of the nation, making use of customary compounds and phrases can lead to good poetry or bad.

As we have seen, the *Beowulf* poet himself twice gives expression to a poetic ideal: the creative activity of the singers thought by him worth the attention of heroes in Heorot consists in the memory of ancient strife recalled in language that lies beyond the tickle of novelty. These idealised singers belong to the glorious past, to which oral poetry also belonged.

The poet does not advert to this ideal *simpliciter,* but uses the scop's song to bring out also certain ulteriors, perhaps the crimes of Sigemund (879), perhaps the hopes men had of Heremod (909-13). The *Beowulf* poet is sophisticated: his art cannot be identified with the scop's. The scop sings *extempore* a song in praise of Beowulf. So the poet imagines him as he peoples the heroic past; but that in no way implies that he, like his creature, Hrothgar's singer, also sings *extempore.*[34]

When we consider the *Beowulf* poet's treatment of Hrothgar's scop we should perhaps distinguish two phases in the use of formulaic poetry: the oral and the written. The oral stage, that of the scop in Heorot, is well described by Magoun. It is fully *extempore;* the minstrel as he stands before his audience composes with the use of ready-made formulas. Sometimes he introduces old tags, virtually meaningless; much of the time he describes traditional happenings, battles or feasting for example, in traditional words and phrases. Sometimes a minstrel working in the oral-formulaic tradition coined a phrase, for every phrase must have been new before it grew old, and one man can coin a multitude of phrases for use by himself at first and later for use by others in admiring imitation. Nevertheless, tradition is tenacious and change slow in that kind of literature; and in any case we have no means of knowing what is new.

Much has been said of the singers, and less of the audience. For a hearer (as for a reader) there are many ways of feeling pleasure in poetry; but, at one level of appreciation at least, a great part of the pleasure seems to lie in pleasurable recognition of the expected and pleasurable surprise at the unexpected. An audience used to formulaic verse is presumably conditioned to feeling pleasure in recognition of the familiar.[35] It is characteristic of the secondary stage in the use of formulaic poetry that it still draws on the formulas descended from the primary, the extemporising stage of poetic composition, partly because there is no other conception of poetry and partly because the audience demands the traditional. The Christian poetry of the Anglo-Saxons may well have been written to supply a audience's craving for what they had always had.

Gregory the Great wrote for the guidance of St Augustine that well-constructed pagan temples in England should not be destroyed but dedicated to the glory of Christ, so that the nation, seeing their temples preserved, might gather with a new spirit more familiarly in the places to which they were accustomed. In the extant Anglo-Saxon verse we see the customary poetic formulas of the nation deliberately, artificially even, put to a new use. Tags like *heard under helme* 'strong under his helmet', *ecg wæs iren* 'its blade was of iron', *maðma mænigeo* 'a multitude of treasures', serve as reminders of an old order, and as such have new meaning. In origin they may have been the *hums* and *haws* of hesitating poetic extemporisation: in their new context they have become living tokens of a heroic past which the Christian present still wears among its ornaments.

A long time ago Adolf Ebert wrote of the Anglo-Saxons:

> The quick acceptance and ready assimilation of the civilisation of Latin Christianity, assimilation moreover which soon turned into prolific learned activity in Latin, was not merely a consequence of the great talent of this Germanic nation: it presupposes a higher degree of indigenous refinement. This refinement, of course, was not of a scholarly nature; but rather a refinement of disposition, a refinement of the affections, and a refinement of the imagination.[36]

It would perhaps be too fanciful to say that Gregory sensed this refinement when he saw the English slave-boys for sale in Rome, and took to punning on angels and Angles. We know, however, that he thought their outward appearance so full of grace that he lamented the darkness of their souls; and he must have thought them capable of responding to missionary efforts. The conversion of the English became the object of his special zeal; he laboured to fill the minds and altars of the nation with a different spirit; he condemned in them only that they were pagan. It is not likely that when the English neophytes looked back they would condemn and despise the past which had nurtured them and given them a mind to apprehend the new faith. Their past did not lack nobility, and when they came to sing of God and his saints they turned to the past to furnish them with the means of expression. In the vernacular they had no other means.

It goes deeper than that. When the Anglo-Saxons turned to their language to express their thoughts they would have found, if they had been capable of such Humboldtian reasoning, that it had been at work already, and had shaped not merely their thoughts but also the mode of perception that underlay them. There is a statement of Wilhelm von

Humboldt's which seems highly pertinent to the study of Old English literature:

> Since languages, or at least their constituent parts . . . , are transmitted by one age to the next, and since we can speak of incipient languages only by going right outside the range of our experience, it follows that the relationship in which the past stands to the present reaches down into the uttermost depths of all that shapes the present.[37]

We delude ourselves if we believe that we can catch a nation in its infancy and hear its first babblings. When in the fifth century the Anglo-Saxon tribes left their Continental homes they brought with them a group of closely related, ancient dialects including the tribes' poetic word-hoard, their oral-formulaic stockpile. Centuries earlier, Tacitus, writing of the Germanic tribes in general, refers to song as the vehicle of their tribal memory, that is, of their history. We have evidence that some memory of the origin of the nation in northern lands was preserved, and survived to be recorded in definite form by Bede and in the genealogies of the English royal dynasties.

Beowulf, both as a young man and as king, is represented as embodying the traditional ideals of the nation. The language in which this ideal is expounded is the traditional diction in the traditional metre of the English. Of course, the poem owes a great deal to Christianity, but it does not owe everything to Christianity; the language in which the ideal is expressed and the mode of perception by means of which the Anglo-Saxons were able to grasp the ideals of the new faith, relating them to their indigenous ideals, go back to the pagan past.

In the passage we have been considering (lines 864-915) the ideal seems absolute. Beowulf has triumphed against an evil being, has deserved the gratitude of a good and wise king, and his merit calls forth a song of praise from a panegyrist filled with the memory of ancient traditions. The poet presents the scop to us as singing the hero's praise in the traditional manner in the traditional poetic medium. *Secg eft ongan/sið Beowulfes snyttrum styrian* (871-2), we are told; surely, we may expect something about Beowulf himself. Instead we get the ideal which is embodied in Beowulf expressed in terms of Sigemund and Heremod. The relevance of Sigemund, the dragon-slayer, is not made explicit, it is too obvious to need explanation; but how love fell to Beowulf whereas iniquity took possession of Heremod is clearly stated. It would be going too far to claim that a traditionalist, such as the *Beowulf* poet imagines Hrothgar's minstrel to be, could only have praised Beowulf by borrowing some of the actual words which belong to the praise of men like Sigemund or to the dispraise of men like Heremod. All that we have the right to claim is that the merit of Beowulf, however it might have been expressed, could only have been perceived in terms which had their application to earlier heroes. There is a special directness in the *Beowulf* poet's adduction of Sigemund and Heremod. The poet's associative habit of mind working in the same direction as his annexive syntax, which is in part based on the devices of the alliterative metre, leads him to take for granted the transitions. Without expressing the transitions he puts down directly the whole of the circumstances of a comparable or contrasting personage or situation. Other poets might have stripped the parallel of some of the words in which it is expressed and taken them over for their own use. The poet of *Beowulf* takes over the parallel whole, perhaps because he is conscious that he perceives the hero of his poem at this point as being all that, in descriptions known to him, made Sigemund glorious and all that Heremod was not.

A number of the passages in the poem referred to by critics of *Beowulf* as 'digressions and episodes' owe their place to the poet's habit of mind. Far from being intrusions or excrescences they are the result of his directness of expression. The sorrow to be experienced by Wealhtheow, Hrothgar's queen, who presumably lives to see the treacherous enmity of Hrothulf to her poor sons, is expressed, not by telling us proleptically how *she* suffered, but how her parallel, Hildeburh suffered when her son and brother and later her lord were slain (lines 1063-1191). The poet makes it appear by his use of Hildeburh's manifold sorrows that she is the *locus classicus* of a queen's suffering in intestine strife. There is, of course, a strong element of foreboding in all this: as Hildeburh mourned, so shall Wealhtheow. The poet shapes his account of the wars between Finn (Hildeburh's husband) on the one hand and Hnæf (Hildeburh's brother) and Hengest (who succeeds Hnæf) on the other to bring out to the full the misery of Hildeburh.

At the first appearance of Hygd, Hygelac's young and gracious queen, she is described chiefly by the device which the poet had used when he drew on the evil Heremod to expound the virtues of Beowulf. The mind of Modthryth, the untamed shrew, was disgraced by every opposite of Hygd's many graces (lines 1925-62, especially 1929-43). Here, as in the case of Heremod, the transition is abrupt, the connection is not made explicit, so that some of the best critics of the poem suspect (unnecessarily, it seems to me) a gap.[38] Once again, the abruptness is the result of the directness with which the poet habitually lays the past under contribution to set forth the present: his mode of perception of the present is as much part of his heritage as the language in which he expresses it. It has been suggested[39] that the reference in this passage to Offa, the legendary king of Angle, may be in the nature of a compliment to Offa of Mercia, his historical descendant. Offa of Angle is praised in a very similar way in the Old English poem *Widsith*. If, as seems very likely, this is the correct analysis of why Offa of Angle is twice praised in Old English verse, it follows that two Old English poets at least, and Offa of Mercia too if he understood their praise, were accustomed to direct reference to the glorious past for an exposition of the present; those not very close kinsmen of the then reigning king of Mercia who gave the new-born Offa his name must have looked back similarly (as royal families do in name-giving). In *Beowulf,* however, this is not just an occasional device for a graceful compliment:

the poem is about the past and is furnished with instances drawn from the past.

It is not to be inferred from all this that the *Beowulf* poet, going to his nation's word-hoard, has come away with something equivalent to the Elgin Marbles, where his fellow poets were content to pick up bits and pieces the size of acanthus leaves or vine-leaf scrolls. Whatever the poet of *Beowulf* takes over, little units and large ones, he moulds and modulates to suit his specific purpose. In the same way as he makes apt use of the smaller units and organises them well, so he does not leave the larger units strewn about unhewn and unaltered in his work like a scatter of erratic boulders.

We know, merely through the poet's choice of subject, that he resembles the ideal minstrel whom he presents to us on two occasions in this, that he too delights in the exercise of a well-stored memory deeply imbued with traditions, enshrined also in some of the genealogies of the Anglo-Saxons by which their kings appear as descendants of Scyld. The genealogies contain some of the Danish names in the poem: Beow,[40] Scyld, Sceaf, and Heremod. It seems likely that before these names, all appearing as ancestors of Woden, were incorporated in the genealogies, Woden must have been euhemerised (as he is explicitly in the *Chronicle* of æthelweard, almost certainly a member of the West Saxon royal house living in the tenth century). This act of euhemerisation is clear evidence that members of the royal families took these genealogies seriously, even in Christian times. The extension of the genealogies beyond Woden, though presumably quite unhistorical, shows that they wished to associate these figures, of whom they knew (*Beowulf* is witness to that), with their own royal dynasties. *Beowulf* could well have been written late enough for at least some of the Danes mentioned in the poem to have been regarded by the poet and his audience as ancestors of Anglo-Saxon kings in England.[41]

It is likely that the rulers who knew of their ancient descent were stirred by the memory of glorious deeds of those men from whom they were descended. The use to which the *Anglo-Saxon Chronicle* puts Offa's genealogy in the annal for the year of his accession (in 757) seems to indicate a deliberate exploitation of the list of kings going back to Woden as contributing to the glorification of Offa. If, as is natural, Anglo-Saxon rulers delighted in the ancient nobility of their dynasty their retainers must have been aware of these traditions also. The beginning of the poem with its piece of Danish history is relevant to England, to English kings and therefore to their retainers, as much as the Trojan origins of the British dynasty relevantly introduce poems, like *Sir Gawain and the Green Knight*, on British themes.

There is evidence that there was in Anglo-Saxon England a considerable knowledge of the legends of the Germanic heroic age. Interest in these legends is not likely to have been swiftly reduced when Christianity came, and the poet of *Beowulf* was able to rely on his audience's familiarity

with the ancient traditions to such an extent that he introduced allusive references and not fully coherent accounts of feuds, apparently without needing to fear that he would not be understood. The Finn Episode (lines 1063-1159) could not be understood by an audience not already familiar with the facts; perhaps the original audience was familiar with these events because (if the Hengest of the Episode was identified with the Hengest of the Anglo-Saxon Settlement) the feud was held to belong to proto-Kentish history.[42] The wars between the Geats and the Swedes are not told by the poet in chronological sequence, but allusively and selectively. In lines 2177-89 praise of Beowulf and a reference to his ignominious youth encloses an allusion to Heremod, who had been trusted in his youth: change came to both of them. The allusion is missed by anyone who fails to seize on Heremod as one pattern of evil in a king.

As the poet's ideal minstrel relates Beowulf's merit, gained from present exploits in Denmark, to the merit of past figures, Sigemund and Heremod, so the poet analyses a Christian ideal, appropriate to the English audience for whom he is writing, in terms of an ideal figure of the past: Beowulf. The language which he uses, the traditional poetic vocabulary of the Anglo-Saxons, with many formulas expected by the audience to whom no other language seemed fit for poetry, has led the poet to seek his material outside Christian story in the Germanic traditions to which his language had had its first, its most direct application. His habit of mind which finds expression in an annexive syntax, such as goes well with the alliterative metre, is associative. He does not always make explicit how his associations are linked to his main theme, no more than the minstrel does in Heorot who fails to make explicit why in singing the praise of Beowulf he should recall what he heard tell of Sigemund's exploits and the tyranny of Heremod.

The excellence of the poem is in large measure due to the concord between the poet's mode of thinking and his mode of expression. An associative imagination works well in annexive syntax: each is the cause of the other's excellence. At the same time, he is good with the smaller units, the words and formulas which all Anglo-Saxon poets had to handle. Perhaps there is a deeper reason why *Beowulf* is satisfactory. The Christian poet chose to write of the Germanic past. His ideal king is Beowulf the monster-slayer, whom he compared, not with Daniel, but with Sigemund, and contrasted, not with Saul, but with Heremod.

His success lies in that choice. The elements of Old English poetic diction, the words and the traditional phrases feel at home in the world which they first celebrated in song.[43] Old English poetic diction is retrospective: it looks back to the civilisation that gave it shape and which in turn it helped to shape. Heusler[44] said rightly of the Germanisation in Old English verse of Genesis and of Exodus, of the legends of St Andrew and of St Helena's Invention of the Cross, of Christ even (of whom *The Dream of the Rood* (lines 39-41) reports 'that the young hero armed himself, strong and fierce of mind he mounted the high gallows, brave in the sight of many'), that all this Germanisation was not taken seriously. But the language of his poetry is something a poet must feel serious about. The Germanisation of biblical narrative is a good device only where its spirit can be accepted as part of a fuller transformation. In the account of the Crucifixion in *The Dream of the Rood* the ideal raised by the Germanising language clashes with the idea of the Crucifixion.

There are good things in Old English verse, in the Elegies especially, but also in some of the saints' lives, the second part of *Guthlac,* for example; but it is difficult to see how the inapposite application of the Germanic battle-style to Christian themes could ever have called forth critical praise. The beginning of *Andreas* reads in rough translation:

> Lo, we heard tell of twelve in far-off days under the stars, glorious heroes, the Lord's retainers. Their glory did not fail in warfare, whenever banners clashed . . . They were men famous on earth, eager leaders of nations, men active in the army, warriors renowned whenever in the field of assault buckler and hand defended the helmet on the plain of destiny.

Here is a poet who can do the big bow-wow like any man going. But he was writing of those twelve whom Christ ordained with the words, 'Behold, I send you forth as sheep in the midst of wolves' (Matthew 10:16).

The *Beowulf* poet avoided that mistake.

So far we have been less concerned with *what* the *Beowulf* poet says than with *how* he says it. The poem is obviously about the past. In Professor Tolkien's words:

> When new *Beowulf* was already antiquarian, in a good sense, and it now produces a singular effect. For it is now to us itself ancient; and yet its maker was telling of things already old and weighted with regret, and he expended his art in making keen that touch upon the heart which sorrows have that are both poignant and remote.[45]

The sadness of the poem lies in that. But there is glory in it too, such as is proper to a noble society presented as an ideal. Beowulf himself is of heroic stature. His strength and valour, made manifest in every exploit, his wisdom, his regard for the etiquette of an aristocratic society, his long victorious reign, the assurance of his speeches and the nobility of his intentions, all these are the proper ingredients of heroism; and that the heroic ideal embodied in Beowulf goes deeper still follows from his loyalty to Hygelac, his king, and to Heardred, Hygelac's son (2373-9), from his mildness, praised by his survivors (3180-2), and from the speech, modestly expressed, in which, surveying a world of deceit and murderous perfidy, he finds himself at the end of his days unperjured and guiltless of the blood of kinsmen (2736-43). He is the ideal ruler of a society held together by bonds of love and service. Though less fashionable now as a theme for literature, strength is

emphasised in the poem and is gloried in. Beowulf brought strength to Hrothgar, the aged king of the Danes, bowed down with care for his people; and with strength he survived the proud Frisian raid in which Hygelac was slain; with strength also he kept the Swedes out of the land of the Geats.

It seems as if the poet's intended audience looked back to the nation's past (as adumbrated in the royal genealogies), and took pleasure in it. The poet gratifies his audience's idealising love of the Germanic past. The opening of the poem by means of its specific references to the ancestors of kings in England plays on an audience's memory of the past. There is in the poem a strong element of regret for a noble order which will never come back.

I have said elsewhere[46] that it seems to me that, though the poet presents the heroic ideal of his people lovingly, he presents it as ultimately unavailing and therefore not worth ambition. Perhaps there is a hint even that Beowulf, being a pagan too eager in the hour of his death for posthumous fame and the sight of gold—what else *can* pagans think about when they die?—will not, for all his virtues, be saved from everlasting damnation in hell. Once the modern reader feels that hint he ceases to read the poem simply as the Germanic heroic ideal presented elegiacally. What is implied is that the poet is aware of the fact that the pagan heroic ideal stands in conflict with the ascetic ideal of Christianity, as it was known in the English monasteries of the poet's time. By the standards of that higher ideal the heroic ideal is insufficient. The poet, however, nowhere states unambiguously (except at lines 175-88) that the pagan ideal he presents is insufficient, and some readers will be reluctant to read the poem in that way (especially if they first delete lines 175-88 as an interpolation).

We have no means of telling who the poet's first audience was: perhaps in some royal hall, where the lord and his men still delighted in the ancient nobility of the dynasty; or perhaps in some monastery to which a king retired, as we know King Sigebeht of East Anglia did when he gave up his throne in the second quarter of the seventh century, and as King Ethelred of Mercia did in 704, and Ceolwulf of Northumbria in 737, and Eadberht of Northumbria in 758. Kings like these proved by their abdication that they thought the pagan glory of pledging in the hall, of victory in the field, of treasure-giving and of loyalty to an earthly throne, a vain ideal. A poet might have written a poem like *Beowulf* for one of many courts, to teach a king wisdom, or for some monastery whose refectory contained a man descended from a line of Spear-Danes and not contemptuous of that ancestry. It is only a guess; but that is the kind of original audience that would have heard *Beowulf* with understanding.

Notes

1. I wish to thank Professors Randolph Quirk and Geoffrey Shepherd for reading this essay in typescript, and for their help and criticism.

2. Two pieces of evidence, neither of them conclusive, that Old English verse may have ceased to be fully understood as early as the twelfth century are Simeon of Durham's misunderstanding of *Bede's Death Song* (cf. M. Förster, *Archiv* 135 (1917), 282-4) and a possible misunderstanding of *The Battle of Maldon* in the *Liber Eliensis* (cf. Camden Society, 3rd Series, 92 (1962), 134f., footnotes). Cf. also K. Sisam, *The Structure of* Beowulf, 1965, pp. 70f.

3. 'There are dragons born which are a hundred and fifty feet long. They are as big as great stone pillars. On account of the size of those dragons no man can easily travel into that land.' EETS os 161, 59.

4. Quoted from Dorothy Whitelock, *The Audience of Beowulf*, p. 46. Professor Whitelock's discussion of the relationship between the *Liber Monstrorum* and *Beowulf* is of fundamental importance in this connection.

5. See the important discussion by Kenneth Sisam, 'The Compilation of the Beowulf Manuscript', in *Studies*, 1953.

6. In the Authorised Version the story is relegated to the Apocrypha, for excellent textual reasons.

7. Cf. W. W. Lawrence, *Beowulf and Epic Tradition*, p. 207; T. M. Gang, *RES* NS 3 (1952), 6ff.; K. Sisam, *RES* NS 9 (1958), 128-40, and also his *The Structure of* Beowulf, 1965, p. 25.

8. *Anglia* 36 (1912), 195.

9. *Andreas und Elene*, 1840, p. xxvii. For recent discussions of the beasts of battle, considered from widely different points of view, see F. P. Magoun, Jr., *Neuphilologische Mitteilungen* 56 (1955), 81-90, E. G. Stanley, *Anglia* 73 (1956), 442f., A Bonjour, *PMLA* 72 (1957), 563-73 (and *Twelve Beowulf Papers*, 1962, ch. X). For Grimm's discussion see E. G. Stanley, *Notes and Queries* 209 (1964), 244.

10. 'Therefore many a morning-cold spear must be gripped, raised by the hand; not the sound of the harp shall awaken the warriors, but the black raven, eager in pursuit of doomed men, shall speak of many things, tell the eagle how he prospered at the feast when in competition with the wolf he despoiled the slain.' R. Quirk (in *Early English and Norse Studies Presented to Hugh Smith*, 1963, p. 166) also selects this passage (3014-27) to demonstrate the excellence of *Beowulf*: 'We see here the use of incongruous collocations to form a critical undercurrent of a kind which notably enriches *Beowulf* from time to time and which is prominent among the features making it a great poem.'

11. For a different view, see K. Sisam, *The Structure of* Beowulf, 1965, pp. 54-9.

12. Cf. A. F. C. Vilmar, *Deutsche Altertümer im Heliand*, etc., Marburg 1845, 'Epische form' (pp. 3ff. of the edition of 1862); and, more recently, F. P. Magoun, Jr., *Spec.* 28 (1953), 446-67. See also H. Schabram, '*Andreas* und *Beowulf*', *Nachrichten der Giessener Hochschulgesellschaft* 34 (1965), 201-18.

13. See G. V. Smithers, *English and Germanic Studies* 4 (1952), 67-75.

14. See p. 137 below for a translation.

15. See p. 109 above.

16. An excellent account of the diction of *Beowulf* is provided by A. G. Brodeur, *The Art of Beowulf*, 1959, ch. I. See also G. Storms in *Studies in Old English Literature in Honor of Arthur G. Brodeur*, 1963, pp. 171-86, and J. Hoops, *Beowulfstudien*, 1932, pp. 20-24. Among earlier studies, O. Krackow, *Die Nominalcomposita als Kunstmittel im altenglischen Epos*, 1903, is still useful.

17. 'At times men famed in battle made their bay horses gallop, run races where paths seemed suitable, known for their excellence. At times the king's retainer, a man filled with high rhetoric, with the memory of songs, who remembered a multitudinous wealth of ancient traditions, came upon other words (?) bound in truth (?). The man did then tell with art the exploit of Beowulf, set forth with happy skill a well-told tale, weaving words; he said all that he heard tell of Sigemund's deeds of valour, much of things unknown, the Wælsing's strife, distant exploits, of such things, hostility and crimes, as the sons of men knew little of, had Fitela not been with him whenever he wished to tell something of such a matter, uncle to nephew, friends in need as they were at all times in every enmity. They had laid low a numerous race of giants with their swords. No little glory came to Sigemund after his hour of death when bold in battle. . . .'

18. See A. Campbell's important 'The Old English Epic Style', in *English and Medieval Studies Presented to J. R. R. Tolkien*, 1962, especially in this connection pp. 19f.

19. See H. Kuhn, *Beiträge* 57 (1933), 1-109 (summarised in English by D. Slay, *TPS* 1952, 1-14).

20. Cf. E. Sievers, *Altgermanische Metrik*, 1893, §82; an example of an exceptionally long multisyllabic medial dip (given by Sievers) is *sealde þam þe he wolde* (*Beowulf* 3055).

21. Cf. J. Ries, *Die Wortstellung im Beowulf*, 1907, pp. 72-5, who rightly insists on the similarity of verse and prose in this respect. The difference lies in the greater regularity and, therefore, predictability of verse. For a discussion, not always convincing, of the style and syntax of *Beowulf*, cf. S. O. Andrew, *Syntax and Style in Old English*, 1940, and the same author's *Postscript on Beowulf*, 1948. The earlier book is especially good on co-ordinate clauses in *Beowulf*; ch. VIII (on asyndetic co-ordinate clauses) deals with an important aspect of the additive style of *Beowulf*, a characteristic uncommon elsewhere in Old English verse, as Andrew notes.

22. *Beowulf: The Monsters and the Critics*, 1936, p. 31 (*PBA* 22 (1936), 273).

23. Tolkien, loc. cit.

24. See J. Hoops, *Beowulfstudien*, 1932, pp. 52-5.

25. 'There was singing and revelry: the aged Scylding, a man of wide learning, told of far-off things; at times the man brave in battle touched his joyful, pleasure-giving harp of wood; at times he set forth a song true and sad; at times the magnanimous king told a wondrous story according to what is right; at other times the aged warrior, in the grip of years, did lament his youth, his strength in battle; his heart within him was moved whenever he, old in years, recalled a multitude of memories.'

26. But cf. the use of the phrase at line 366 (and elsewhere in verse), where the meaning is quite unspecifically 'to converse'.

27. 'The Poetry of Cædmon', *PBA* 33 (1946).

28. Op. cit., 1862 ed., p. 5.

29. *Spec.* 28 (1953), 446-67.

30. *ESts.* 41 (1960), 5 (quoted by A. Bonjour, *Twelve Beowulf Papers*, 1962, p. 149). See also A. G. Brodeur, *The Art of Beowulf*, 1959, ch. I.

31. F. P. Magoun, Jr., 'Bede's Story of Cædman: The Case History of an Anglo-Saxon Oral Singer', *Spec.* 30 (1955), 49-63.

32. Op. cit., p. 447.

33. R. P. Creed, *Texas Studies in Literature and Language* 3 (1961), 98.

34. For a different view, cf. R. P. Creed, *Studies in Old English Literature in Honor of Arthur G. Brodeur*, 1963, pp. 44-52.

35. Cf. in this connection R. Quirk's important paper 'Poetic language and Old English metre' in *Early English and Norse Studies Presented to Hugh Smith*, 1963, pp. 150-71.

36. *Allgemeine Geschichte der Literatur des Mittelalters im Abendlande*, III (1887), p. 3.

37. *Sprachphilosophische Werke*, ed. H. Steinthal, 1883, p. 225.

38. Among others, K. Sisam, *Studies*, p. 41 (reprinting *RES* 22 (1946), 266); D. Whitelock, *The Audience of Beowulf*, 1951, pp. 58ff.; E. von Schaubert (in the *Kommentar* to her edition (1961), pp. 114f.) has a fuller list of critics who suspect a gap here.

39. By D. Whitelock, loc. cit.

40. For the view that the name *Beowulf* at lines 18 and 53 is probably an error for *Beow* see A. J. Bliss, *The Metre of Beowulf*, 1958, p. 58, as well as the editions.

41. For a comprehensive and fundamental account of the genealogies, see K. Sisam, *PBA* 39 (1953), 287-348.

42. Cf. K. Sisam, *Studies*, p. 136.

43. F. P. Magoun (in *Studies in Medieval Literature in Honor of A. C. Baugh*, ed. by MacEdward Leach,

1961, pp. 280-2) suggests that the merits, which, he claims, all readers of Old English poetry see in *The Battle of Maldon*, are grounded on the harmony of subject matter and diction in that poem.

44. *Die altgermanische Heldendichtung*, 1926, p. 140:

45. *Beowulf: The Monsters and the Critics*, pp. 35f. (277f.).

46. *Studies in Old English Literature in Honor of Arthur G. Brodeur*, ed. by Stanley B. Greenfield, 1963, pp. 136-51.

Select Bibliography

Extensive bibliographies are to be found in Klaeber's edition of the poem and in Chambers's *Beowulf: An Introduction*. The following list of books and articles has therefore been kept very brief. Most of what is included must be regarded as indispensable for an understanding of the aspect of the poem under which it is listed.

THE MANUSCRIPT

K. Malone, *The Nowell Codex*, EEMF XII, 1963.

J. Zupitza and N. Davis, *Beowulf Reproduced in Facsimile*, EETS 245 (1959).

Max Förster, 'Die Beowulf-Handschrift', *Berichte der Sächsischen Akademie der Wissenschaften*, 71 (1919).

K. Sisam, *Studies*, 61-96, 288-90.

EDITIONS

F. Klaeber, *Beowulf and the Fight at Finnsburg*, 3rd ed. with supplements, 1951.

E. V. K. Dobbie, *Beowulf and Judith*, ASPR IV, New York 1953 (London 1954).

E. v. Schaubert, *Beowulf*, 17th ed., 1958-9.

C. L. Wrenn, *Beowulf with the Finnesburg Fragment*, 2nd ed., 1958.

TRANSLATIONS

J. R. Clark Hall, *Beowulf and the Finnesburg Fragment*, new edition by C. L. Wrenn, with Prefatory Remarks by J. R. R. Tolkien, 1950.

E. Morgan, *Beowulf: A Verse Translation*, 1952 (paperback 1962).

IMPORTANT BOOKS ON THE POEM

R. W. Chambers, *Beowulf: An Introduction to the Study of the Poem*, 3rd ed. with a supplement by C. L. Wrenn, 1959.

D. Whitelock, *The Audience of Beowulf*, 1951.

A. G. Brodeur, *The Art of Beowulf*, 1959.

THE METRE OF *BEOWULF*

E. Sievers, *Beiträge* 10 (1884), 209-314, 451-545.

J. C. Pope, *The Rhythm of* Beowulf, 1942.

A. J. Bliss, *The Metre of* Beowulf, 2nd ed., 1962.

There is a useful *Anthology of Beowulf Criticism,* ed. by L. E. Nicholson, 1963, which includes some various pieces of early and recent criticism; other pieces, including the full text of Margaret E. Goldsmith's 'The Christian Perspective in *Beowulf*' are to be found in *Studies in Old English Literature in Honor of Arthur G. Brodeur,* ed. by S. B. Greenfield, 1963. Stanley B. Greenfield's *A Critical History of Old English Literature,* New York 1965, surveys some older and more recent *Beowulf* scholarship in a chapter devoted to 'Secular Heroic Poetry'. Kenneth Sisam's *The Structure of* Beowulf, Oxford 1965, is referred to in footnotes added in proof.

Abbreviations

Anglia Beiblatt: Beiblatt zur Anglia

Archiv: Archiv für des Studium der neueren Sprachen und Literaturen

ASPR: The Anglo-Saxon Poetic Records, edited by G. P. Krapp and E. V. K. Dobbie

Beiträge: Beiträge zur Geschichte der deutschen Sprache und Literatur

BM Add.: British Museum Additional Manuscript

BN: Bibliothèque Nationale

CCC: Corpus Christi College

CCCC: Corpus Christi College, Cambridge

Chadwick Mem. Sts.: The Early Cultures of North-West Europe (H. M. Chadwick Memorial Studies), edited by Sir Cyril Fox and Bruce Dickins, Cambridge 1950

CL: Comparative Literature

EEMF: Early English Manuscripts in Facsimile, edited by B. Colgrave, Kemp Malone and K. Schibsbye

EETS: Early English Text Society

EETS OS: Early English Text Society, Original Series

EETS ES: Early English Text Society, Extra Series

EHD: English Historical Documents, edited by D. C. Douglas

EHR: English Historical Review

EIC: Essays in Criticism

ESts.: English Studies

Grein-Wülker, *Prosa:* Bibliothek der angelsächsischen Prosa, edited by Ch. W. M. Grein, R. P. Wülker, *et al.*

JEGP: Journal of English and Germanic Philology

JTS: Journal of Theological Studies

Ker, N. R., *Catalogue:* Catalogue of Manuscripts Containing Anglo-Saxon, by N. R. Ker, Oxford 1957

Mæ: Medium ævum

Med. & Ren. Sts.: Medieval and Renaissance Studies

Methuen's OE. Lib.: Methuen's Old English Library, edited by A. H. Smith and F. Norman

Migne, *PL:* J. P. Migne, *Patrologia Latina*

Migne, *PG:* J. P. Migne, *Patrologia Graeca*

MLN: Modern Language Notes

MLQ: Modern Language Quarterly

MLR: Modern Language Review

MP: Modern Philology

PBA: Proceedings of the British Academy

PMLA: Publications of the Modern Language Association of America

Polity: Wulfstan's *Institutes of Polity, Civil and Ecclesiastical* (edited by K. Jost in *Swiss Studies in English,* vol. 47)

PQ: Philological Quarterly

Q & F: Quellen und Forschungen zur Sprach- und Culturgeschichte der germanischen Völker

RES: Review of English Studies

RES NS: *Review of English Studies,* New Series

Rolls Series: Rerum Britannicarum Medii ævi Scriptores or Chronicles and Memorials of Great Britain and Ireland during the Middle Ages

Sisam, K., *Studies: Studies in the History of Old English Literature,* by K. Sisam, Oxford 1953

SP: Studies in Philology

Spec.: Speculum

TPS: Transactions of the Philological Society

Trad.: Traditio

Wanley, *Catalogue: Antiquæ Literaturæ Septentrionalis Liber Alter seu Humphredi Wanleii Librorum Vett. Septentrionalium, qui in Angliæ Bibliothecis extant . . . Catalogus Historico-Criticus,* Oxford 1705

YSE: Yale Studies in English

John Leyerle (essay date 1967)

SOURCE: "The Interlace Structure of *Beowulf,*" in *University of Toronto Quarterly,* Vol. XXXVII, No. 1, October, 1967, pp. 1-17.

[*In the following essay, Leyerle argues that the structure of* Beowulf *is analogous to the patterns of interlace decorative art common in Anglo-Saxon art of the seventh and eighth centuries. When the likelihood of this parallel is ac-*

cepted, Leyerle states, the function of otherwise confusing episodes of the poem becomes apparent.]

In the time since Norman Garmonsway [On February 28, 1967, Norman Garmonsway, Visiting Professor of English at University College in the University of Toronto, died suddenly. This paper, in a slightly different form, was read on March 30 in West Hall of the College in place of a lecture on Canute that Professor Garmonsway was to have delivered on that day.] died I have reflected about what I could say that would not embarrass the spirit of the man I wish to honour. He was reticent about himself and I shall be brief. I rarely heard him refer to his distinguished career at King's College, London, for when he spoke of his work, it was always of what lay ahead. His characteristic manner was understatement, like that of the early literature of the north that he knew so well and loved. He was a man who preferred to listen rather than to talk, but he was quick to praise and encourage. He had the virtues of Chaucer's Clerk of Oxenford mixed with a gentle humour.

> Noght o word spak he moore than was neede,
> And that was seyd in forme and reverence,
> And short and quyk and ful of hy sentence;
> Sownynge in moral vertu was his speche,
> And gladly wolde he lerne and gladly teche.

Toronto is a better place for his having lived and worked among us. This paper concerns material he was teaching this year, the relation between early art and poetry in England. I should like to dedicate it to his memory.

I

Beowulf is a poem of rapid shifts in subject and time. Events are fragmented into parts and are taken with little regard to chronological order. The details are rich, but the pattern does not present a linear structure, a lack discussed with distaste by many.[1] This lecture will attempt to show that the structure of *Beowulf* is a poetic analogue of the interlace designs common in Anglo-Saxon art of the seventh and eighth centuries. *Beowulf* was composed in the early eighth century in the Midlands or North of England, exactly the time and place where interlace decoration reached a complexity of design and skill in execution never equalled since and, indeed, hardly ever approached. Interlace designs go back to prehistoric Mesopotamia; in one form or another they are characteristic of the art of all races.[2]

The bands may be plaited together to form a braid or rope pattern, a design that appears, for example, on borders of the Franks Casket, a whalebone coffer made in Northumbria about the year 700. Interlace is made when the bands are turned back on themselves to form knots or breaks that interrupt, so to speak, the linear flow of the bands. The south face of the Bewcastle Cross from Cumberland has three panels of knot work; this cross is dated before 710.[3] The bottom panel . . . has two distinct knots formed by two bands and connected together, a pattern that is identical to that on folio 94[v] of the Lindisfarne Gospels. . . .[4]

There are about a thousand separate pieces of stone surviving from pre-Norman Northumbrian crosses. One need only leaf through W. G. Collingwood's *Northumbrian Crosses of the Pre-Norman Age* (London, 1927) to be struck by the appearance of one interlace design after another, despite the fact that such patterns are relatively difficult to execute in stone, especially when there is any undercutting.

When the bands are cut, the free ends are often elaborated into zoomorphic heads, seen in a very simple stage of development on the Abingdon Brooch . . . , dated in the early seventh century.[5] In more complex designs the stylized heads take on a pronounced zoomorphic character, often derived from eagles or wolves; the bodies of these creatures extend into curvilinear ribbon trails that form the interlace design. The heads often bite into the bands or back on to a free end, as on the seventh-century Windsor dagger pommel which has an open design with clear separation between the bands. . . . When the bands are drawn together more tightly, the pattern becomes harder to follow, as on the great gold buckle from Sutton Hoo, also of the seventh century. . . . The interlace on the buckle is not symmetrical. The weave is drawn tighter and the zoomorphic heads are less prominent than on the Windsor dagger pommel.

In further development of the zoomorphs, the ribbon trails develop limbs on their serpentine bodies. These limbed lacertines have a coiled and woven appearance and look very like dragons even when they have no wings and have canine heads. The abundant appearance of lacertines in early Anglo-Saxon design may well have reinforced belief in the existence of dragons, thought of as uncommon creatures not met with every day, much as we might think of a hippopotamus or iguana. An example of vigorous treatment of such lacertines may be seen on folio 192[v] of the Book of Durrow . . . ; this manuscript is generally dated in the middle or second half of the seventh century and is often ascribed to Iona. The design is similar to that found on the hilt of the Crundale sword, found in Kent; it dates from the early seventh century. . . . A detail from the seventh-century pins from Witham, Lincolnshire . . . , shows a similar design, although the zoomorphs are distinctly canine. In the lacertine design on folio 110[v] of the St. Chad Gospels, which were probably written between the Severn and the Welsh marches in the late seventh or early eighth centuries . . . , the zoormorphs are clearly derived from birds, despite the ears. Designs over an entire folio are called carpet pages after their resemblance to woven tapestries. Perhaps the finest carpet pages are found in the Lindisfarne Gospels of about 700; in the later years of the Anglo-Saxon period it was thought to have been the work of angels since no mortal could execute such complex designs so faultlessly. Folio 94[v] is reproduced in Plate VIII. The entire design of the knot work is done with only two ribbons. The generally circular pattern is elaborated with intricate weaving, but the circular knots—which might be thought of as episodes, if I may look forward for a moment—are tied with relatively long straight bands that bind these knots together in the total pattern of the page. With patience and a steady eye one can follow a band through the entire knot-work design of this page. Occasionally the lacertines become recognizable dragons as on the Gandersheim Casket. It is carved from walrus teeth and probably was made at Ely in the second half of the eighth or early ninth century. . . . The casket is small and the skill shown in carving on such miniature scale is impressive.

From the early Anglo-Saxon period there are thousands of interlace designs surviving in illuminations of manuscripts, in carving on bone, ivory and stone, and in metal work for weapons and jewellery. They are so prolific that the seventh and eighth centuries might justly be known as the interlace period. In one artifact after another the complexity and precision of design are as striking as the technical skill of execution. Recognition of this high level of artistic achievement is important for it dispels the widely held view, largely the prejudice of ignorance, that early Anglo-Saxon art is vigorous, but wild and primitive. As the interlace designs show, there is vigour to be sure, but it is controlled with geometric precision and executed with technical competence of very high order. Apart from such direct analogies as the one presented in this lecture, study of Anglo-Saxon art is most useful as an aid to the reassessment of early English literature because it is an important reminder that the society was capable of artistic achievements of a high order which can be looked for in the poetry as well.

II

The pervasive importance of interlace designs in early Anglo-Saxon art establishes the historical possibility that a parallel may be found in poetry of the same culture. The historical probability for the parallel, a rather more important matter, can be established from seventh- and eighth-century Latin writers in England. There is ample evidence that interlace design has literary parallels in both style and structure.

Stylistic interlace is a characteristic of Aldhelm and especially of Alcuin. They weave direct statement and classical tags together to produce verbal braids in which allusive literary references from the past cross and recross with the present subject.[6] The device is self-conscious and the poets describe the technique with the phrases *fingere serta* or *texere serta,* "to fashion or weave intertwinings." *Serta* (related to Sanscrit *sarat,* "thread" and to Greek ϛειρα, "rope") is from the past participle of *serere,* "to interweave, entwine, or interlace." The past participle of *texere,* "to weave, braid, interlace," is *textus,* the etymon of our words text and textile. The connection is so obvious that no one thinks of it. In basic meaning, then, a poetic text is a weaving of words to form, in effect, a verbal carpet page.

The passage in **Beowulf** about the scop's praise of Beowulf describes a recital in which a literary past, the ex-

ploits of Sigemund and Heremod, is intertwined with the present, Beowulf's killing of Grendel. This episode is extended and might equally be considered as an example of simple structural interlace. The scop is said to *wordum wrixlan,* "vary words" (874); the verb *wrixlan* is found elswhere in this sense, for example in Riddle 8 of the Exeter Book. Klaeber calls such variation "the very soul of the Old English poetical style" (lxv); it involves multiple statement of a subject in several different words or phrases, each of which typically describes a different aspect of the subject. When variation on two or more subjects is combined, the result is stylistic interlace, the interweaving of two or more strands of variation. This may be what Cynewulf refers to in *Elene* when he writes *ic . . . wordcræftum wæf,* "I wove words" (1236-7). An example from **Beowulf** will serve to illustrate stylistic interlace:

> No þæt læsest wæs
> hondgemot[a]   þær mon Hygelac sloh,
> syðdan Geata cyning   guðe ræsum,
> freawine folca   Freslondum on,
> Hreðles eafora   hiorodryncum swealt,
> bille gebeaten.
>
> [2354-9]

Although awkward in modern English, a translation following the original order of phrases shows the stylistic interlace.

> That was not the least
> of hand-to-hand encounters where Hygelac was killed,
> when the king of the Geats in the rush of battle,
> the beloved friend of the people, in Frisia,
> the son of Hreðel died bloodily,
> struck down with the sword.

Hygelac, Geata cyning, freawine folca, and *Hreðles eafora* make one strand; *mon . . . sloh, hiorodryncum swealt,* and *bille gebeaten* make a second strand; *þær, guðe ræsum,* and *Freslondum on* make the third. The three strands are woven together into a stylistic braid. This feature of style is familiar to readers of Anglo-Saxon poetry and is the literary counterpart for interlace designs in art that are decorative rather than structural. Designs on a sword, coffer or cross are decoration applied to an object whose structure arises from other considerations.

At a structural level, literary interlace has a counterpart in tapestries where positional patterning of threads establishes the shape and design of the fabric, whether the medium is thread in textile or words in a text. Unfortunately cloth perishes easily and only a few fragments of Anglo-Saxon tapestry survive although the early English were famous for their weaving and needle work which was referred to on the continent simply as *opus Anglicum* with no other description. Since tapestry examples are lost, decorative interlace must serve here as graphic presentation of the principle of structural interlace, a concept difficult to explain or grasp without such a visual analogue.

Rhetoricians of the classical period distinguished between natural and artificial order, but emphasized the former as being especially effective for oral delivery since they were chiefly concerned with the orator. In the *Scholia Vindobonensia,* an eighth-century commentary on the *Ars Poetica* of Horace, there is a passage on artificial order of great interest to the subject of interlace structure in Anglo-Saxon poetry. The authorship of the *Scholia* is unknown, but its editor attributes it to Alcuin or one of his school.[7] The passage is a comment on four lines of the *Ars Poetica.*

> Ordinis haec virtus erit et venus, aut ego fallor,
> ut iam nunc dicat iam nunc debentia dici,
> pleraque differat et praesens in tempus omittat,
> hoc amet, hoc spernat promissi carminis auctor.

> [42-5]

> Of order, this will be the excellence and charm, unless I am mistaken, that the author of the long-promised poem shall say at the moment what ought to be said at the moment and shall put off and omit many things for the present, loving this and scorning that.

The commentator was particularly interested in the last line, which he regards as having the force of an independent hortatory subjunctive; he takes *hoc . . . hoc* in the strong sense of "on the one hand . . . on the other" which would have been expressed by *hoc . . . ille* in classical Latin.

> *Hoc,* id est, ut nunc dicat iam debentia dici quantum ad naturalem ordinem; *amet auctor promissi carminis,* id est, amet artificialem ordinem. *Hoc,* id est, contrarium ordinis artificialis, id est, ordinem naturalem *spernat auctor promissi carminis;* hoc breviter dicit. Nam sententia talis est: quicunque promittit se facturum bonum carmen et lucidum habere ordinem, amet artificialem ordinem et spernat naturalem. Omnis ordo aut naturalis aut artificialis est. Naturalis ordo est, si quis narret rem ordine quo gesta est; artificialis ordo est, si quis non incipit a principio rei gestae, sed a medio, ut Virgilius in Aeneide quaedam in futuro dicenda anticipat et quaedam in praesenti dicenda in posterum differt.[8]

> *Hoc,* that is, he should say now what ought to have been said before according to natural order; *amet auctor promissi carminis,* that is, should love artificial order. *Hoc,* that is, the opposite of artificial order, that is, *spernat auctor promissi carminis* natural order; Horace says this briefly. For the meaning is as follows: whoever undertakes to make a good poem having clear order should love artificial order and scorn natural order. Every order is either natural or artificial; artificial order is when one does not begin from the beginning of an exploit but from the middle, as does Virgil in the *Aeneid* when he anticipates some things which should have been told later and puts off until later some things which should have been told in the present.

This comment extends the source into a doctrine on the suitability of artificial order for poetry concerned with martial material (*res gesta*) and takes an epic (the *Aeneid*) as an example. What I have called interlace structure is, in more general terms, complex artificial order, with the word complex in its etymological sense of woven together. Interlace design is a dominant aspect of eighth-century Anglo-Saxon visual art and the *Scholia Vindobonensia* present convincing evidence that the same design principle was applied to narrative poetry.

Alcuin's two lives of St. Willibrord provide instructive examples of natural and artificial order.[9] The prose version begins with an account of Willibrord's parents and gives a chronological account of the Saint's life, death, and the subsequent miracles at his tomb. The poem, on the other hand, plunges *in medias res* with an account of Willibrord's visit to Pippin; the details of the Saint's early life are placed at the end. The poem is in simple artificial order, and in the Preface Alcuin states that it is for private study but that the prose version is for public reading. The same logic is followed in Alcuin's *Disputatio de Rhetorica* which deals only with natural order since it is intended for instruction in public oral discourse.[10] On the basis of this preference for natural order in work intended for oral delivery, an argument might be made that **Beowulf** was meant for private study since it has complex artificial order.

Before I turn to the poem, a brief summary of my argument thus far may be helpful. In the visual arts of the seventh and eighth centuries interlace designs reached an artistic perfection in England that was never equalled again. Interlace appears so regularly on sculpture, jewellery, weapons, and in manuscript illuminations that it is the dominant characteristic of this art. There is clear evidence that a parallel technique of word-weaving was used as a stylistic device in both Latin and Old English poems of the period. Finally there is the specific statement of the *Scholia Vindobonensia* that artificial order was preferred for narrative poetry. Such artificial order I have called interlace structure because the term has historical probability and critical usefulness in reading **Beowulf.**

III

Beowulf is a work of art consistent with the artistic culture that it reflects and from which it came, eighth-century England. It is a lacertine interlace, a complex structure of great technical skill, but it is woven with relatively few strands. When **Beowulf** is read in its own artistic context as an interlace structure, it can be recognized as a literary work parallel to the carpet pages of the Lindisfarne Gospels, having a technical excellence in design and execution that makes it the literary equivalent of that artistic masterpiece.

Examples of narrative threads, intersected by other material, are easy to perceive in the poem once the structural principle is understood. The full account of Hygelac's Frisian expedition is segmented into four episodes, 1202-14, 2354-68, 2501-9 and 2913-21, in which chronology is ignored. The poet interlaces these episodes to achieve juxtapositions impossible in a linear narrative. In the first episode the gift of a precious golden torque to Beowulf for killing Grendel is interrupted by an allusion to its loss years later when Hygelac is killed. Hygelac's death seeking Frisian treasure foreshadows Beowulf's death seeking the dragon's hoard. The transience of gold and its connection with violence are obvious. In the second episode Beowulf's preparations to face the dragon are intersected by another allusion to Hygelac's expedition; each is an example of rash action and each ends in the death of a king. The third episode comes as Beowulf recalls how he went in front of Hygelac

> ana on orde,   ond swa to aldre sceall
> sæcce fremman,   þenden þis sweord þolað.
>
> [2498-9]
>
> alone in the van and so will I always
> act in battle while this sword holds out.

He had needed no sword to crush Dæghrefn, the slayer of Hygelac; against the dragon his sword Nægling fails. The pattern is the same as for the fights with Grendel whom he had killed with his hands and with Grendel's mother against whom the sword Hrunting fails. Beowulf's trust in a sword against Grendel's mother had nearly cost him his life; against the dragon it does. The last episode comes in the speech of the messenger who states that the fall of Beowulf will bring affliction to the Geats from their enemies. Among them, the messenger warns, are the Frisians seeking revenge for Hygelac's raid years before. Hygelac's death led to the virtual annihilation of his raiding force; Beowulf's death leads to the virtual annihilation of all the Geats. The four Hygelac episodes, like all the narrative elements in the poem, have positional significance; unravel the threads and the whole fabric falls apart. An episode cannot be taken out of context—may I remind you again of the etymology of the word—without impairing the interwoven design. This design reveals the meaning of coincidence, the recurrence of human behaviour, and the circularity of time, partly through the coincidence, recurrence, and circularity of the medium itself—the interlace structure. It allows for the intersection of narrative events without regard for their distance in chronological time and shows the interrelated significances of episodes without the need for any explicit comment by the poet. The significance of the connections is left for the audience to work out for itself. Understatement is thus inherent in interlace structure, a characteristic that fits the heroic temper of the north.

The Hygelac episodes contribute to what I believe is the major theme of *Beowulf*, "the fatal contradiction at the core of heroic society. The hero follows a code that exalts indomitable will and valour in the individual, but society requires a king who acts for the common good, not for his own glory."[11] Only two periods in Beowulf's life are told in linear narrative; they are the few days, perhaps a week, when he fights Grendel and his mother and the last few days when he fights the dragon. This treatment emphasizes Beowulf's heroic grandeur, his glorious deeds, and his predilection for monster-fighting. However, this main narrative is constantly intersected by episodes which present these deeds from a different perspective. The Hygelac epi-

sodes show the social consequences of rash action in a king and they become more frequent as the dragon fight develops. Hygelac's Frisian raid was a historical event; the history of this age provides many parallels. In 685 Ecgfrid, King of Northumbria, led a raiding party against the advice of his friends deep into Pictish territory. Caught in mountainous narrows at a place called Nechtanesmere on May 20, he and most of his army were killed, a disaster that ended English ascendency in the north. The main theme of *Beowulf* thus had relevance to a major recent event in the society that most probably produced it. Ecgfrid's brother Aldfrid, a man famed for his learning and skill as a poet, ruled from 685 to 704; Bede says that he re-established his ruined and diminished kingdom nobly,[12] a stable reign that made possible the learning and scholarship of eighth-century Northumbria, the golden age of Bede and Alcuin.

At first the episodes give little more than a hint that Beowulf's heroic susceptibility may have calamitous consequences for his people. The references to Sigemund and Heremod after Beowulf kills Grendel foreshadow Beowulf's later career as king. He kills a dragon, as Sigemund did, and leaves the Geats to suffer national calamity, as Heremod left the Danes to suffer *fyrenðearfe* (14), "terrible distress."[13] In the second part of the poem Beowulf's preparations to fight the dragon are constantly intersected by allusions to the Swedish wars, ominous warnings of the full consequences to the Geats of Beowulf's dragon fight. In this way the poet undercuts Beowulf's single-minded preoccupation with the dragon by interlacing a stream of more and more pointed episodes about the human threats to his people, a far more serious danger than the dragon poses. Beowulf wins glory by his heroic exploit in killing the dragon, but brings dire affliction on his people, as Wiglaf quite explicitly states.

> Oft sceall eorl monig   anes willan
> wræc adreogan,   swa us geworden is.
>
> [3077-8]
>
> Often many men must suffer distress
> For the willfulness of one alone, as has happened to us.

Of particular interest to my subject is the way in which the interlace design, in and of itself, makes a contribution to the main theme. Because of the many lines given to the monsters and to Beowulf's preparations to fight them, they are the largest thread in the design, like the zoomorphs on the Windsor dagger pommel or the dragons on the Gandersheim casket. Monster-fighting thus pre-empts the reader's attention just as it pre-empts Beowulf's; the reader gets caught up in the heroic ethos like the hero and easily misses the warnings. In a sense the reader is led to repeat the error, one all too easy in heroic society, hardly noticing that glorious action by a leader often carries a terrible price for his followers.

The monsters are the elongated lacertine elements that thread through the action of the poem making symmetrical patterns characteristic of interlace structure. Beowulf's fights against Grendel's mother and against the monsters in the Breca episode are clear examples. During the swimming match Beowulf, protected by his armour, is dragged to the ocean floor. Fate gives him victory and he kills *niceras nigene* (575), "nine water monsters," with his sword; this prevents them from feasting on him as they intended. After the battle, light comes and the sea grows calm. This is almost a *précis* of the later underwater fight against Grendel's mother; the pattern is the same, though told in greater detail.

Once the probability of parallel design is recognized, the function of some episodes becomes clearer. The Finnesburh lay, for example, is probably a cautionary tale for the Danes and Geats. Beowulf and his Geats visit Hroðgar and his Danes in Heorot to assist in defending the hall against an *eoten*, Grendel. During the first evening they share the hall Unferð issues an insulting challenge to which Beowulf makes a wounding reply stating that Unferð had killed his own brothers. This deed associates him with Cain, the archetypal fratricide, and Cain's descendant, Gendel. The defence of the hall is successful and Grendel is killed. At the victory celebration the scop recites a lay about the visit of Hnæf and his Half-Danes to Finn and his Frisians in Finnesburh. They fall to quarrelling and slaughter each other. In this episode the word *eoten* occurs three times in the genitive plural form *eotena* and once in the dative plural *eotenum*. These forms are often taken as referring to the Jutes, although no one can say what they are doing there or what part they play. More likely the references are to monsters. At line 1088 the Frisians and Danes surviving from the first battle are said each to control half of the hall *wið eotena bearn*, which probably means "against the giants' kin." Quite possibly the Half-Danes go to Finnesburh to help the Frisians hold their hall against monsters, a situation which would explain why Finn did not burn out the Half-Danes when the fighting started. The hall was their joint protection against the monsters. After the lay Wealhþeow makes two moving pleas (1169-87 and 1216-31) for good faith and firm friendship in Heorot, especially between the Geats and the Danes. She clearly takes the scop's lay as a warning and fears being afflicted like Hildeburh. Just before she speaks, Unferð is described as sitting at Hroðgar's feet; he is a figure of discord as shown by his name, which means "mar-peace", and by his behaviour. The queen might well be concerned lest insults between Dane and Geat be renewed and lead to fighting. From all this emerges an interesting connection. In *Beowulf* monsters are closely associated with the slaying of friends and kinsmen.[14] They function in part as an outward objectification and sign of society beset by internecine slaughter between friend and kin.

The Finnesburh episode and the situation in Heorot are part of another theme that forms a thread of the interlace design of *Beowulf*—visits to a hall. A guest should go to the hall with friendly intent and be given food and entertainment of poetry by his host. Grendel inverts this order. He visits Heorot in rage, angered by the scop's song of creation, and makes food of his unwilling hosts. Hroðgar cannot dispense men's lives in Heorot, but Grendel does little else. He is an *eoten*, or "eater," and swallows up the society he visits almost as if he were an allegorical figure for internecine strife. In a similar way Grendel's mother visits Heorot and devours æschere; in return Beowulf visits her hall beneath the mere, kills her, and brings back the head of Grendel. The Heaþobard episode concerning Ingeld and the battle that breaks out when the Danes visit his hall is another appearance of this thematic thread. Hroðgar gives his daughter Freawaru to Ingeld in marriage, hoping to end the feud between the two tribes, but an implacable old warrior sees a Dane wearing a sword that once belonged to the father of a young Heaþobard warrior. He incites the youth to revenge and the feud breaks out again; in the end the Heaþobards are decimated and Heorot is burnt. Other hall visits may be noted briefly. A slave visits the hall of the dragon and steals a cup; the dragon burns halls of the Geats in angry retribution, a token of the fate in store for Geatish society soon to be destroyed by war. Beowulf attacks the dragon who dies in the door of his hall fighting in self-defence.

Another theme of the poem is that of women as the bond of kinship. The women often become the bond themselves by marrying into another tribe, like Wealhþeow, Hildeburh, and Freawaru. This tie often has great tension put on it when the woman's blood relations visit the hall of her husband and old enmities between the tribes arise, as happens in the Finnesburh and Heaþobard episodes. The marriage then gives occasion for old wounds to open, even after an interval of years, and produces a result exactly opposite to its intent. On the other hand, women can be implacable in revenge as Grendel's mother is. Þryð (or Modþryð) is also implacable at first in resisting marriage; she causes her would-be husbands to be killed. Afterwards her father sends her over the sea as wife to Offa who checks her savage acts and she becomes a *freoðuwebbe*, "peace-weaver," knitting up her kinsmen rather than refusing all ties. In general the women are *cynna gemyndig*, "intent on kinship," as the poet says of Wealhþeow (613). They preserve the tie of kin or revenge it when given cause.

Another tie that binds society is treasure, especially gold; but, like kinship, it is also a cause of strife. Treasure is not sought for selfish avarice, but to enable a hero to win fame in gaining treasure for his lord and his lord to win fame dispensing it as a *beaga bryttan*, a "dispenser of treasure," from the *gifstol*, "gift throne." The gift and receipt of treasure are a tie between a lord and his retainer, an outward sign of the agreement between them. The strength and security of heroic society depend on the symbolic circulation of treasure. A lord offers support and sustenance to his retainer who agrees in turn to fight unwaveringly for his lord, a bond of contractual force in heroic society. Injury or slaughter of a man had a monetary price and could be atoned by *wergild*, "man payment." The monsters are outside this society; for them treasure is an object to be hoarded under ground. They receive no gifts and do not dispense them. The poet states ironically that none need expect handsome recompense for the slaughter that Grendel inflicts. Hroðgar is the one who pays the *wergild* for the Geat, Hondscio, killed by Grendel in the Danish cause. The relation of the monsters to *gifstolas* presents an interesting parallel in the interlace design. The dragon burns the *gifstol Geata* (2327), an act that implies his disruption of the entire social order of Beowulf's *comitatus*. The full extent of this disruption appears when all but one of Beowulf's chosen retainers desert him in his last battle. Grendel, on the other hand, occupies Heorot, but he is not able to cause complete disruption of Hroðgar's *comitatus*, however ineffective it is against him. The sense of lines 168-9, a much disputed passage, thus seems likely to be that Grendel cannot destroy Hroðgar's *gifstol* (168), thought of as the objectification of the Danish *comitatus*.

The poem is also concerned with a society's gain of treasure as well as its loss. When a king seeks treasure himself, the cost may be ruinous for his people. Hygelac's Frisian raid and Beowulf's dragon fight are examples. Although Grendel's cave is rich in treasure, Beowulf takes away only a golden sword hilt and the severed head of Grendel; his object is to gain revenge, not treasure. Hroðgar's speech to Beowulf after his return contains warnings on pride in heroic exploits and on the ease with which gold can make a man stingy, hoarding his gold like a monster; either way the *comitatus* is apt to suffer. Heremod, who ended *mid eotenum,* is an example. When treasure passes outside the society where it is a bond, it becomes useless. The treasure in Scyld's funeral ship, the golden torque lost in Frisia, the lay of the last survivor, and the dragon's hoard buried with Beowulf are examples. Treasure had some positive force in heroic society, but it casts a baleful glitter in the poem because it is associated with monsters, fighting, the death of kings, and funerals.

These various themes are some of the threads that form the interlace structure of **Beowulf.** Often several are present together, as in the Finnesburh episode or in the final dragon fight. The themes make a complex, tightly-knotted lacertine interlace that cannot be untied without losing the design and form of the whole. The tension and force of the poem arise from the way the themes cross and juxtapose. Few comments are needed from the poet because significance comes from the intersections and conjunctions of the design. To the **Beowulf** poet, as to many other writers, the relations between events are more significant than their temporal sequence and he used a structure that gave him great freedom to manipulate time and concentrate on the complex interconnections of events. Although the poem has to be lingered over and gives up its secrets slowly, the principle of its interlace structure helps to reveal the interwoven coherence of the episodes as well as the total design of the poem in all its complex resonances and reverberations of meaning. There are no digressions in **Beowulf.**

The structural interlace of **Beowulf,** like the visual interlace patterns of the same culture, has great technical excellence, but is not to be regarded as an isolated phenomenon. The term is specifically applied to literature in the late middle ages. Robert Manning states in his *Chronicle* (1338) that he writes in a clear and simple style so that he will be readily understood; others, he says, use *quante Inglis* in complicated schemes of *ryme couwee* or *strangere* or *enterlace*.[15] *Entrelacement* was a feature of prose romances, especially those in the Arthurian tradition, as Eugène Vinaver has recently shown.[16]

The term interlace may be taken in a larger sense; it is an organizing principle closer to the workings of the human imagination proceeding in its atemporal way from one associative idea to the next than to the Aristotelian order of parts belonging to a temporal sequence with a beginning, middle, and end. If internal human experience of the imagination is taken as the basis, the Aristotelian canon of natural order as moving in chronological progression is really *ordo artificialis,* not the other way around as the rhetoricians taught. The human imagination moves in atemporal, associative patterns like the literary interlace. *Don Quixote* presents a useful illustration. The Don, supposedly mad, is brought home in a cage on wheels at the end of Part I. He could be taken as the interlacing fecundity of the associative mind, caught in the skull-cage, reacting with complex atemporal imagination, weaving sensory impressions with literary experience. The Canon of Toledo who rides along outside mouthing Aristotelian criticism of romances is, as his name suggests, an uncomprehending set of external rules, or canons, sent to bedevil and torment the poetic imagination.

There is a substantial amount of literature having interlace structure, if I may extend the term without presenting evidence here. Mediaeval dream poetry, such as *Le Roman de la Rose* and *Piers Plowman,* is largely a mixture of literary and imaginative experience with an atemporal interlace structure as are many complex romances, especially those with allegorical content like the *Faerie Queene*. The allegorical impulse in literature is often presented with an interlace structure because it is imaginative, literary and atemporal. Stream-of-consciousness novels frequently have something like interlace structures as well, for the same reasons.[17]

Like the poem, this lecture will make an end as it began. Scyld's glorious accomplishments and ship funeral at the opening of the poem mark the start of a dynasty and a period of prosperity for the Danes after the leaderless affliction they suffer following the death of Heremod. The funeral in the Finnesburh episode begins the period of affliction of the Half-Danes and presages the destruction of Finn's dynasty. At the end of the poem Beowulf's death begins a period of affliction for the Geats. The poem ends as it began with a funeral, the return of the interlace design to its start. The sudden reversals inherent in the structure as one theme intersects another without regard to time give to the whole poem a sense of transience about the world and all that is in it as beginnings and endings are juxtaposed; this is the much-remarked elegiac texture of

Beowulf. Scyld's mysterious arrival as a child is placed beside his mysterious departure in death over the seas. A description of Heorot's construction is followed by an allusion to its destruction. The gift of a golden torque, by its loss. Beowulf's victories over monsters, by his defeat by a monster. With each reversal the elegiac texture is tightened, reminding us of impermanence and change, extending even to the greatest of heroes, Beowulf, a man mourned by those who remain behind as

> manna mildust   ond mon(ðw)ærust,
> leodum liðost   ond lofgeornost.
>
> [3181-2]
>
> the most gentle and kind of men,
> most generous to his people and most anxious for praise.

A bright and golden age of a magnanimous man vanishes, even as it seems hardly to have begun.

> The jawes of darkness do devoure it up:
> So quicke bright things come to confusion.
>
> [*Mids.* I. i. 148-9]

Notes

1. For example, see F. P. Magoun, Jr., "*Beowulf* A[1]: A Folk-Variant," *ARV: Tidskrit för Nordisk Folkminnesforskning,* XIV (1958), 95-101, or *Beowulf and the Fight at Finnsburg,* ed. Fr. Klaeber, 3rd edition (Boston, 1950), li-lviii. All quotations are from this edition.

2. For an account of the origin of these designs, see Nils Åberg, *The Occident and the Orient in the Art of the Seventh Century,* Part I, The British Isles, Kungl. Vitterhets Historie och Antikvitets Akademiens Handlingar, Del. 56:1 (Stockholm, 1943). An admirable account of such designs is given by R. L. S. Bruce-Mitford in *Codex Lindisfarnensis,* ed. T. D. Kendrick, *et al.* (Olten and Lausanne, 1956-60), II, iv, vii-x, 197-260.

3. Lawrence Stone, *Sculpture in Britain* ([London], 1955), 13.

4. I wish to thank Professor Michael Sheehan of the Pontifical Institute of Mediaeval Studies at Toronto for helping me assemble the slides used in the lecture and Miss Ann Hutchison of the University of Toronto for help in assembling the prints used to make the plates.

5. Ronald Jessup, *Anglo-Saxon Jewellery* (London, 1950), 116.

6. See Peter Dale Scott, "Alcuin as a Poet," *UTQ,* 33 (1964), 233-57.

7. *Scholia Vindobonensia ad Horatii Artem Poeticam,* ed. Josephus Zechmeister (Vienna, 1877), iii. I wish to acknowledge my considerable debt to Paula Neuss of the University of Kent at Canterbury for research assistance in eighth-century Latin authors and for constructive criticism throughout the work for this lecture.

8. Zechmeister, 4-5, repunctuated.

9. *De Vita Sancti Willibrordi Archiepiscopi,* ed. B. Krusch and W. Levison, *MGH, Scriptores Rerum Merov.* (Hanover and Leipzig, 1919), VII, 113-41; this is the prose version. *De Vita Willibrordi Episcopi,* ed. E. Dümmler, *MGH, Poetarum Latinorum Medii Aevi,* I (Berlin, 1881), 207-20.

10. Ed. and trans. Wilbur S. Howell (Princeton, 1941), Section 22.

11. John Leyerle, "*Beowulf* the Hero and the King," *Medium ævum,* 34 (1965), 89.

12. *Historia Ecclesiastica,* ed. C. Plummer (Oxford, 1896), IV, xxiv, Vol. I, 268. See F. M. Stenton, *Anglo-Saxon England,* 2nd edition (Oxford, 1950), 85-9.

13. See "*Beowulf* the Hero and the King," 101.

14. Heremod's story fits this context, too, for he kills his table companions and dies *mid eotenum* (902).

15. Ed. F. J. Furnivall (London, 1887). See lines 71-128.

16. "Form and Meaning in Medieval Romance," The Presidential Address of the Modern Humanities Research Association (1966).

17. Interlace structure in later texts will be the subject of a larger work now in preparation. I wish to thank Mrs. Medora Bennett of the University of Toronto for help in the final preparation of this article for press.

Larry D. Benson (essay date 1967)

SOURCE: "The Pagan Coloring of *Beowulf,*" in *Contradictions: From "Beowulf" to Chaucer; Selected Studies of Larry D. Benson,* edited by Theodore M. Andersson and Stephen A. Barney, Scolar Press, 1995, pp. 15-31.

[*In the essay below, originally written in 1967, Benson studies the apparent conflict in* Beowulf *between Christian and pagan elements, observing that modern assumptions concerning the attitude of the Christian poet and his audience toward paganism are incorrect. Benson goes on to argue that understanding the relationship between Christian Englishmen and Germanic pagans allows us to view the poem as a framework within which Christians could contemplate the idea of the "good pagan."*]

The old theory that ***Beowulf*** is an essentially pagan work only slightly colored with the Christianity of a later scribe has now been dead for many years, and critics today generally agree that the poem is the unified work of a Christian author.[1] Indeed, most of the elements in ***Beowulf*** that once supplied arguments for its essential paganism—the function of Wyrd, the emphasis on the comitatus, the duty of revenge—are now recognized not as pagan but as secular values that were easily incorporated into the framework of Anglo-Saxon Christianity.[2] Likewise, though the stories of Beowulf and the monsters probably originated in pagan times, it is now generally acknowledged that they have been assimilated into a Christian world view with the monsters allied with the devil and Beowulf (or so Friedrich Klaeber and others have held) fitted to the pattern of Christ himself.[3] Yet the ghost of the old pagan-versus-Christian dispute still lingers, for along with the Christian and Christianized secular elements the poem does contain some indisputably pagan features that have remained intractable to modern criticism. Moreover, the knockings of that spirit have become steadily more insistent, for the more deeply Christian the meanings of *Beowulf* are discovered to be, the more difficult become the still-unanswered questions raised by H. M. Chadwick in 1912: "If the poem preserves its original form and is the work of a Christian, it is difficult to see why the poet should go out of his way in v. 175 ff. to represent the Danes as offering heathen sacrifices. . . . Again why should he lay Beowulf himself to rest with heathen obsequies, described in all possible detail . . . ?"[4] Why, one must ask, should the poet's whole representation of the Danes and Geats include all the other details that Chadwick notes—the funeral ship (27 ff.), the observation of omens (204), and the use of cremation (1108 ff., 2124 ff., 3137 ff.)?[5]

The intrusion of these pagan elements into an otherwise completely Christian work presents more difficult problems than the simple matter of factual inconsistency. Certainly the poet is inconsistent in first showing us the Danes listening to the Christian account of the Creation and then, a few lines later, telling us that they knew nothing of God and sacrificed to idols. That is only the sort of historical inaccuracy that one expects in medieval poetry; Chaucer and Shakespeare confused pagan and Christian elements in much the same way.[6] Poets (especially medieval poets) are responsible for total aesthetic effect rather than documentary accuracy. The difficulty in *Beowulf* is that the pagan elements seem to confound the aesthetic effect, to destroy the consistency of tone. Instead of casually mixing pagan and Christian, as so many medieval poets do, the *Beowulf* poet goes out of his way to draw our attention to the Danes' heathen sacrifices. Furthermore, the paganism that he describes is not simply literary or historical; it was a still strong and threatening force in his own day. For him to present his characters as heathens is, so we assume, to show them in the worst of possible lights. Alcuin, in his famous letter to the monks at Lindisfarne, defines for us the Christian Englishman's attitude toward the pagans: *Quid Hinieldus cum Christo? Angusta est domus: utrosque tenere non poterit. Non vult rex celestis cum paganis et perditis nominetenus regibus communionem habere* "what has Ingeld to do with Christ? Narrow is the house; it cannot hold both. The King of Heaven wants no fellowship at all with pagan and damned kings."[7] Given this attitude toward the heathens, our poet's insistence that his characters are both emphatically pagan and exceptionally good seems self-contradictory, and that apparent contradiction has seemed to many critics a touch of feebleness at the very heart of the poem, so feeble that even his warmest admir-

ers have been forced either to fall back on the old theory of scribal tampering or to conclude that the poet simply blundered.[8]

The blunder may be our own, for the apparent contradiction arises, not from the poem itself, but from our assumptions about the meaning of paganism to the poet and his audience. These assumptions have been based on our knowledge of one letter by Alcuin, written in a spirit of reforming zeal at the end of the eighth century, and scattered comments by Bede, who is not quite so inflexible in his attitude toward pagans as his doctrinal pronouncements make him seem.[9] The extreme distaste for everything pagan that these comments exhibit is not typical of the age to which the composition of *Beowulf* is usually assigned; beginning in the last years of the seventh century and extending throughout the eighth, the dominant attitude of Christian Englishmen toward the Germanic pagans was one of interest, sympathy, and occasionally even admiration. This was the period during which the English church was engaged in an intense missionary activity on the Continent, sending missionaries in significant numbers first to the Frisians and Danes and then to the Old Saxons and the tribes in central Germany. This major undertaking, the great interest that it aroused in England, and the attitude it fostered toward pagandom has received relatively little attention from students of *Beowulf;* yet it can shed considerable light on the problems raised by the pagan elements in the poem, revealing artistry where we thought we detected blunders.

I

The missionary activity of the English church began by accident when Wilfred, on his way to Rome to protest his deposition as Bishop of York, landed in Frisia to avoid falling into the hands of his political enemies and spent the winter of 678-79 as guest of the pagan king Aldgisl.[10] He preached the gospel to the heathens, apparently with some success, and then traveled on to Rome. He returned to England, where he occupied a number of sees during his contentious career, but evidently he always maintained an interest in the missionary work in Frisia. In 697 he consecrated a bishop, Suidbert, for the Frisian mission, and the founder of the most successful mission there was Willibrord, who had been Wilfred's student at Ripon and whom Wilfred visited when he again passed through Frisia in 703.

The next missionary effort came from English monks living in Ireland. As Bede tells it, the mission began with the plan of Egbert, who *proposuit animo pluribus prodesse; id est, inito opere apostolico, verbum Dei aliquibus earum quae nondum audierant gentibus evangelizando committere: quarum in Germania plurimas noverat esse nationes, a quibus Angli vel Saxones qui nunc Brittaniam incolunt, genus et originem duxisse noscuntur; unde hactenus a vicina gente Brettonum corrupte Garmani nuncupantur. Sunt autem Fresones, Rugini, Danai, Hunni, Antiqui Saxones, Boructuari: sunt alii perplures eisdem in partibus populi paganis adhuc ritibus servientes . . .* "set his mind on doing good to many; that is, by undertaking the apostolic work, to preach to some of those peoples that had not yet heard the word of God; he knew that there were several such nations in Germany, from which the Angles or Saxons who now inhabit Britain are known to have taken their stock and origin; hence, by the neighboring race of the Britons they are to this day corruptly called 'Garmani.' There are the Frisians, the *Rugini,* the Danes, the Huns, the Old Saxons, the *Boructuari;* there are many other peoples in these same parts still in servitude to pagan rites. . . ."[11] Egbert was deterred from this undertaking by a series of visions and a shipwreck. Yet he had established the plan, basing it on the idea of the kinship between the insular and Continental "Garmani" that was to remain a basic motivation of this missionary work. One of his disciples, Wictbert, took up the task next and preached for two years, though without success, to the Frisians and to their king Rathbod.[12]

The next year, 690, Willibrord, who had spent several years in Ireland as a pupil of Egbert after his studies at Ripon, set out for Frisia with a company of twelve English missionaries.[13] Shortly thereafter, two more English priests, both named Hewald (known as "White" and "Black" Hewald, from the colors of their hair), journeyed to the Continent and met martyrdom among the Old Saxons (whose alderman, though a pagan, was incensed at this murder and avenged their deaths).[14] But despite this setback the mission flourished. Suidbert, one of Willibroard's twelve helpers, was consecrated bishop by Wilfred and carried the mission to the *Boructuari,* and Willibrord received the pallium at Rome and extended his work in Frisia. He carried the gospel even to the Danes, whose king, Ongendus, received him with "every mark of honor" but was unimpressed by his preaching.[15] Nevertheless, Willibrord brought back with him from Denmark thirty Danish youths whom he instructed in the Christian faith, and on his return journey he visited and desecrated the famous pagan shrine at Heligoland. At the time Bede was writing, Willibrord still lived among his converted flock in Frisia, one of the heroes of the English church.

The next and greatest stage in the movement was the mission of Boniface.[16] With two companions he sailed with a trader from London to Frisia in 716. He spent the winter among the Frisians and, meeting with no success, returned to England. After a trip to Rome he went again to Frisia, preaching in places as yet untouched by missionaries. He succeeded Willibrord as leader of the movement and turned his attention to the Old Saxons. From Britain an "exceedingly large number of holy men came to his aid, among them readers, writers, and learned men trained in the other arts."[17] In his last years he went back to Frisia and, pushing farther into heathendom, was martyred near the border of Denmark in 754. He was succeeded by Lull, another Englishman, and the missionary effort of the English church continued unabated throughout the eighth century; the later intellectual expeditions of scholars such as Alcuin were only extensions of the movement that Wilfred and Willibrord began.

One of the most remarkable features of these missions was the close relation that they all maintained with the homeland. We have already noted Wilfred's continuing interest in Frisia and the fact that Suidbert returned to England to be consecrated a bishop at Wilfred's hands. We also know that another of Willibrord's helpers visited Lindisfarne, and in general, even though Willibrord's correspondence does not survive, there is evidence of frequent intercourse between his mission and England.[18] Likewise, it is probable that a good many other Englishmen joined him, for the missionary expeditions were fairly large, involving not one or two wandering preachers but the mission *suorum tantum stipatus clientum numero* 'accompanied only by a number of servants,' including armed soldiers.[19] Boniface's letters do survive, as do those of his successor, Lull, and beginning with the first quarter of the eighth century, we have ample evidence for Levison's assertion that "the continental mission was regarded as a national undertaking of the whole English people. . . ."[20] It was to England that Boniface looked for advice, books, and the help of prayer, and his correspondents included clergy and laymen alike from Thanet to Lindisfarne. On one occasion he addressed a letter, which we shall shortly examine, to the entire English nation. The nation responded by turning its eyes to the pagan Continent—hoping for the conversion of the heathen, for the prayers of the missionaries, or like King Ethelbert of Kent, for a pair of falcons of the sort that Boniface had sent along with shields and spears as a gift to the king of Mercia.[21]

II

The extent and intensity of this traffic with the Continent has long been known, but this knowledge has had little effect on the study of *Beowulf.* This is largely because the English missions have been considered only in relation to the history of the plot. As early as 1816 Outzen proposed that the missions in Frisia supplied the route by which the story of Beowulf reached the poet.[22] The more recent discovery of the possible English origin of the *Liber Monstrorum* with its account of Hygelac, which probably came to England by way of Frisia, has led critics to reflect anew that a good many Englishmen of the late seventh and eighth centuries must have seen or heard of Hygelac's grave on that island in the mouth of the Frisian Rhine.[23] It does seem likely that English travelers would have brought home some tales of Hygelac and Hrothgar, of Finn, and perhaps even of Beowulf—if not the tales our poet used, at least some related tales that helped kindle new interest in the old materials. Likewise, the Frisians, that "great trading people of the North" who dealt with Christian London on the west and pagan Scandinavia on the east,[24] are the most likely means by which tales of the Swedes and stories of Sigmund would have reached England. We know that the Frisians had a recognized class of minstrels,[25] and it would be surprising if their store of songs did not include at least some of the tales used in *Beowulf.* Yet this is only conjecture, and critics have rightly set aside the impossible task of tracing the exact sources of the plot and have turned their attention elsewhere.

Unfortunately, in turning away from the Continent as a contemporary source for the poet's plot, they have also turned away from it as a source of the poet's knowledge of heathen customs, such as the burials in **Beowulf.** The study of **Beowulf** has been needlessly complicated by a search of the English past for the possible hints and memories upon which the poet could have based his accounts of pagan funerals. Even the Sutton Hoo discovery has been of little help; but on the Continent, where the English missionaries were working, pagan burials both by cremation and by interment in mounds continued throughout the eighth century, as we know from laws directed against anyone who *corpus defuncti hominis secundum ritum paganorum flamma consumi fecerit et ossa eius ad cinerem redierit* "has had the body of a deceased man consumed by flame and returned his bones to ashes according to the rite of the pagans" or who buried the dead *ad tumulus paganorum* "at pagan grave-mounds."[26] Likewise, such practices as augury and sacrificing to idols might reflect a memory of England's own past but are more likely based on some knowledge of the Germanic pagans themselves, for throughout the Continent divination and idol-worship were widely and persistently practiced.[27] That Christians of this period were interested in learning about such practices is shown by the contemporary references to pagan beliefs that have survived,[28] and certainly some information of this sort must have been a common subject of conversation whenever a cleric or trader returned to England with news of the missions. We cannot be sure that any of the poet's plot reached him by this route, but we can be positive that he had at his disposal a good deal of information about the pagans that he chose to celebrate.

More important to the student confronted with the problem of the poet's characterization of his pagans is the attitude toward the Germanic heathen which the missionaries maintained and encouraged among their supporters in England. They had none of Alcuin's disdain, and from Egbert to Lull one of the prime motives for the missions was the sympathy fostered by the kinship between the English and *nostra gens,* the Germanic tribes on the Continent.[29] This sympathy appears in Bede's account of Egbert's decision to become a missionary, quoted above, and it is stated even more emphatically in the celebrated letter that Boniface wrote in 738 to the whole English nation, from the bishops to the laymen, *immo generaliter omnibus catholicis* "indeed, to all Catholics in general": *Fraternitatis vestrae clementiam intimis obsecramus precibus . . . ut deus et dominus noster Iesus Christus, 'qui vult omnes homines salvos fieri et ad agnitionem Dei venire,' convertat ad catholicam fidem corda paganorum Saxonum, et resipiscant a diabuli laqueis, a quibus capti tenentur, et adgregentur filiis matris ecclesiae. Miseremini illorum, quia et ipsi solent dicere: 'De uno sanguine et de uno osse sumus'* "We implore the mercy of your brotherhood with deepest prayers [that you pray] . . . that God and Our Lord Jesus Christ, 'who wants all men to be saved and to come to the knowledge of God,' may turn the hearts of the pagan Saxons to the Catholic faith, and that they may repent of the devilish snares by which they are held captive, and be joined to the sons of Mother Church. Have mercy upon them, for they themselves are accustomed to say, 'We are of one blood and one bone.'"[30] The tone of this letter, its certainty that the pagan Saxons are damned if they are not converted, and its intense sympathy with their plight is almost the same as that which we find in one of the most difficult passages in **Beowulf,** the poet's overt comment on the Danes' idol worship:

> Swylc wæs þeaw hyra,
> hæþenra hyht;   helle gemundon
> in modsefan,   Metod hie ne cuþon,
> dæda Demend,   ne wiston hie Drihten God,
> ne hie huru heofena Helm   herian ne cuþon,
> wuldres Waldend.   Wa bið þæm ðe sceal
> þurh sliðne nið   sawle bescufan
> in fyres fæþm,   frofre ne wenan,
> wihte gewendan!   Wel bið þæm þe mot
> æfter deaðdæge   Drihten secean
> ond to Fæder fæþmum   freoðo wilnian![31]
>
> (178-88)

Such was their custom, the hope of the heathens; they remembered hell in their minds, they did not know the Ruler, the Judge of Deeds, nor did they know the Lord God, nor indeed did they know how to praise the Protector of Heaven, the Ruler of Glory. Woe be to him who must, in terrible affliction, thrust his soul into the embrace of fire, expect no consolation, no change at all! Well is it for him who, after the day of death, can seek the Lord and ask for peace in the embrace of the Father!

Critics have often suggested that these lines must refer to some relapse into idolatry, but the remarkable quality of this passage is its tone of compassion, and a return to idolatry is a sin for which compassion is not the appropriate emotion.[32] To describe such relapses even the gentle Bede employs the conventional image of the "dog returning to his own vomit."[33] It is to those who have not had a chance to know of God, *ne wiston hie Drihten God,* that one can be compassionate. Their sin, as the missionaries repeatedly tell us, is "ignorance." They are "blundering in the darkness," ensnared in devilish errors through no fault of their own. The poet's insistence on the Danes' ignorance of God (*ne wiston, ne cuþon*) places them clearly with those blameless and pitiful heathens of whom Boniface speaks.

The poet's sudden shift from the past tense, which he uses to refer to the Danes, to a more generalized present provides an even more important link between his fictional pagans and those real pagans still living on the Continent in his own time. If there is a "Christian excursus" in **Beowulf,** it is not in the account of the sacrifices themselves but in the lines beginning *Wa bið þæm,* for the changed tense shows that the object of the poet's compassion includes not only those long-dead Danes in his poem but also those heathens who exist at the moment he is speaking and who are compelled—*sceal*—through ignorance to thrust their souls *in fyres fæþm.* Their plight is made even sadder by the parallel consideration of those—perhaps their kinsmen—whose lot is the happier because they may *Drihten secean.* Marie P. Hamilton has suggested that "by presenting Scandinavian men of good will as looking in the main to the governance of God he [the poet] might bring them within the sympathetic ken of their English cousins."[34] This is true enough, but given the English attitude toward Continental heathens, it may also be that the poet engages his audience's sympathy for his characters by emphasizing their very paganism. Certainly in this "excursive" passage he seems to step aside from the course of his narrative to draw attention to the similarity between the Danes in *Beowulf* and the real Danes whose salvation had become a matter of widespread concern.

The characters in *Beowulf* are men of good will, despite their paganism, and this has seemed to most critics the central contradiction in the poem. In the face of the attitude represented by Alcuin the only way out of this dilemma seems to be that proposed by Charles Donahue: the possibility that the poet was touched by the Pelagian heresy, which taught that pious heathens could be saved for their natural goodness and thus made it possible for a Christian to admire a native heathen hero.[35] Donahue shows that in early medieval Ireland some native heroes were regarded as having lived under the "natural law," virtuous even though heathen and eligible for salvation because they were born outside the Judaic and Christian dispensations. Yet in England and on the Continent, as Donahue also shows, a strict Augustinian orthodoxy prevailed. Bede, writing an attack on the Pelagian heresy, states flatly that even the great philosophers *nullam veram virtutem nec nullam veram sapientiam habere potuerunt. In quantum vero vel gustum aliquem sapientiae cujuslibet, vel virtutis imaginem habebant, totum hoc desuper acceperunt* "could have no true virtue or knowledge of God. Indeed, insofar as they had any taste of knowledge or image of virtue, they received it from above."[36] The second sentence seems to grant that the pagans may have some virtue after all, but even so Bede affirms that all those born outside the Judaeo-Christian law are damned, even those born between Adam and Moses, *quia regnavit mors ab Adam usque Moysen, etiam in eos qui non peccaverunt* "since Death ruled from Adam until Moses, even over those who had not sinned."[37] This was the attitude the missionaries upheld. In the famous near-baptism of Rathbod a touch of Pelagianism would have saved that "Scourge of Christians" and made the conversion of Frisia much easier, but when Rathbod, with one foot in the water, turned to ask Bishop Wulfram whether he would meet his ancestors in heaven, Wulfram said they were in hell, Rathbod withdrew his foot, and the great chance was lost.[38] Boniface was as orthodox as Wulfram and Bede, and when it came to his attention that a Celtic bishop named Clement was teaching that Christ brought all from hell, "believers and unbelievers, those who praised God and the worshippers of idols," he lost no time in bringing the matter to the attention of Rome, where the "folly" was roundly condemned in 745.[39] The fact that Boniface and Bede paid so much attention to this heresy may indicate that Pelagianism was more widespread than is usually thought. The lives of the early missionaries, who were trained in Ireland, show that relations between the English and Celtic churches were quite close despite their differences, and the works of Pelagius himself were circulating in England (some even under the name of Augustine).[40]

However, we need not hunt for heresy to explain the poet's presentation of his heroes as both virtuous and pagan, for despite the Pelagian dispute (which turns really on the functions of nature and grace) even the most orthodox eighth-century churchmen could regard the pagans as quite virtuous, following the natural law and lacking only the knowledge of God necessary for salvation. The *Translatio Sancti Alexandri* puts this most clearly in its account of the Saxons: *Legibus etiam ad vindictam malefactorum optimis utebantur. Et multa utilia atque secundum legem naturae honesta in morum probitate habere studuerunt, quae eis ad veram beatitudinem promerendam proficere potuissent, si ignorantiam creatoris sui non haberent, et a veritate culturae illius non essent alieni* "indeed, they made use of excellent laws for the punishment of wrongdoers. And they were diligent to maintain in their conduct a very useful and, according to the law of nature, decent probity, which would have helped them to a truly deserved blessedness, if they had not been ignorant of their Creator and were not alien to true religion."[41] The praise for Germanic institutions in this work is drawn from Tacitus, and among early Latin writers—Horace, Tacitus, Martianus Capella—there was a slender tradition of idealizing the Germanic pagans for their good morals and institutions.[42] As early as the fifth century one finds Christian writers employing this idealized view. Salvianus writes of the Goths and Vandals who were attacking the Empire: *tantum apud illos profecit studium castimoniae, tantum seueritas disciplinae, non solum quod ipsi casti sunt, sed, ut rem dicamus nouam, rem incredibilem, rem paene etiam inauditam, castos etiam Romanos esse fecerunt* "so much did the zeal for chastity prevail among them, so great was the severity of their discipline, that not only were they chaste themselves, but—to say a new thing, a thing incredible, a thing almost unheard of—they made even the Romans chaste."[43]

In addition to the weight of this minor tradition of the "honest Germanic pagan," some of the missionaries must have been led to accept the idea that virtue can exist among the pagans simply from meeting an occasional good heathen, like this Frisian nobleman of the early eighth century: *qui quamvis fidem sanctae Trinitatis nondum sciret, erat tamen adiutor pauperum, defensor oppressorum, in iuditio quoque iustus* "though he did not yet know the faith of the Holy Trinity, he was nevertheless a helper of paupers, a defender of the oppressed, and also just in pronouncing judgments."[44] Such decent men, of the sort that exist in all societies, often performed acts of kindness to the missionaries, even when they refused the chance to be converted, and they must frequently have impressed the English priests with their natural goodness.[45] They thus exemplified the most important source of the idea that pagans observe the natural law, the statements in the Bible itself, which taught that the gentiles "show the work of the law written in their hearts, their conscience also bearing witness, and their thoughts the mean while accusing or else excusing one another" (Rom. 2:15).

Boniface drew on all three sources—the literary tradition represented by Tacitus, his own knowledge, and the Bible—in what must have been the most famous use of natural law in the eighth century, his letter to King Ethelbald of Mercia. Ethelbald's loose sexual conduct had become an international scandal, and it was a matter of concern to English churchmen (and probably laymen) on both sides of the Channel. Finally (around 745-46), Boniface wrote directly to the king, rebuking him for his sin: *Quod non solum a christianis, sed etiam a paganis in obprobrium et verecundiam deputatur. Quia ipsi pagani verum Deum ignorantes naturaliter, quae legis sunt et quod ab initio Deus constituit, custodiunt in hac re . . . Cum ergo gentiles, qui Deum nesciunt et legem non habent iuxta dictum apostoli, naturaliter ea quae legis sunt faciunt et ostendunt opus legis scriptum in cordibus suis. . . .* "which not only by Christians but even by pagans is held in shame and contempt. For these pagans, ignorant of the true God, by nature maintain in this matter those things which are lawful and what God established in the beginning. . . . When thus the gentiles, who do not know God and have no law according to the word of the apostle, do by nature what is lawful and show the work of the law written in their hearts. . . ."[46] Since Boniface himself, the persecutor of the heretical Clement, held this opinion, we need have no lingering doubts about the theological respectability of admiring the virtues of the pagans. Even Bede, despite his doctrinal rigidity, found some admirable pagans in the course of his history, and he held that at least one unbaptized pagan had been saved.[47] Certainly the author of *Beowulf,* even if he was a cleric addressing a clerical audience, would have encountered no difficulty in presenting his characters as both virtuous and pagan.

III

In the light of what we now know of attitudes toward the pagans in the late seventh and eighth centuries, it appears that the paganism of the poet's characters may have been a positive advantage to him rather than the insuperable difficulty that it seemed to early critics. Those critics assumed that *Beowulf* was originally and essentially pagan, and what pagan elements the poem contains were therefore most easily explained as mere undigested lumps of primitive matter. We are still accustomed to think of the pagan elements as part of the original essence of the poem, the Christian elements as additions—beautifully integrated, but additions nevertheless. Yet our reading of the poem does not accord with our theory. Christianity is part of the very fabric of *Beowulf;* the pagan elements are not. When we examine those elements that are actually pagan rather than secular, references to practices that ceased altogether or became criminal with the introduction of Christianity— augury, cremation, the worship of idols—we find that they are few in number and easily isolable. Their removal

would harm but not destroy the poem (which may explain why good critics have wanted to take some of them out), for one cannot imagine *Beowulf* in anything like its present state without its Christian basis, but one can easily conceive of it without its few touches of paganism. Without them, it would simply be a more ordinary medieval poem, a narrative in which the past is seen through the eyes of the present, as Chaucer viewed Troy in *Troilus* or Shakespeare ancient Denmark in *Hamlet*. The tales that the poet used must have come to him in that more ordinary state, originally created in pagan times but insensibly altered to fit the requirements of new audiences by each succeeding generation of oral poets.[48] Probably it was the *Beowulf* poet who deepened the Christian meanings when he reshaped the inherited material; but probably it was also he who added the "pagan coloring," drawing on contemporary information about the Germanic pagans and on the prevalent attitude toward them to add both interest and a new dimension of meaning to his materials.

The most obvious advantage that the poet gained by his use of pagan materials is that of "local color." He was able to capitalize on the general interest in pagandom that the missions had aroused, and by providing vivid, even sensational, accounts of rites such as cremation of which his audience had only heard, he was able to engage their attention for his more important purposes. For those more sober members of his audience who, like the later Alcuin, could see no good in stories of pagan kings, the very reminders that the kings in *Beowulf* are pagan serve to build interest and sympathy, for the poem functions as a kind of proof of the missionaries' reports that the heathens are indeed virtuous, while the pagan elements have something of the same function as Boniface's letter to the English nation, emphasizing the perilous condition of these good heroes and thus appealing for a compassionate, serious consideration of their state. Perhaps that is why the "Christian excursus" comes so early in the poem, providing the framework within which the good Christian can ponder the deeds of the good pagans.

There must have been a good many more in the poet's audience who, like the monks at Lindisfarne, simply enjoyed a good secular tale, and for them most of all the touches of paganism are means of building interest and sympathy in the dual purpose of this poem. *Beowulf* is now recognized as a skillful blend of secular and religious values; it is simultaneously a celebration of the ideal Germanic warrior and a statement of Christian morality.[49] These values were not necessarily opposed, as poems like *The Dream of the Rood* show, but they were nevertheless quite different. Aldhelm apparently recognized this, for we are told that he would stand at crossroads, singing the old songs until he had gathered crowds for his more edifying discourses.[50] The *Beowulf* poet seems to employ his secular materials in the same way, using his tales of monster killing as an occasion for a meditation on life and on the meaning of victory and defeat. For those who were drawn to listen primarily to hear again the deeds of heroes, the insistence on the paganism of those heroes provided the larger context of that present day, helping to reinforce the point of Hrothgar's sermon that strength alone is not enough and to state the further requirement that even that "intelligent monotheist" cannot meet, that to strength and natural piety must be added the New Law of Christ. In this way the touches of paganism in **Beowulf** place the fictional ironies and tragedy of the poem within the dimension of the real irony and tragedy of Germanic history as it was viewed by an eighth-century audience newly aware of the sad condition of their Continental kinsmen to whom the gospel had not yet been preached. Thus the poet builds a link between the doomed heroes of his poem and the sad but admirable pagans of his own time, whose way of life seemed likewise fated to disappear before the apparently certain victory of the Church.

The final irony of **Beowulf** is that which Wyrd visited on the poet himself, when the pagans he celebrated swept down to destroy their Christian kinsmen in England. After the burning of Lindisfarne in 793, it would be another two centuries before English missionaries would again set out for the Continent and the attitude toward pagandom expressed in **Beowulf** would again be appropriate. We can only speculate, but it may be that we owe the survival of the poem to its touches of paganism, for the only manuscript in which it survives was written at that other moment in English history, around the year 1000, when English churchmen were again concerned with the fate of their heathen kinsmen in northern Europe.[51]

Notes

1. William Whallon, "The Christianity of *Beowulf*," *Modern Philology* 60 (1962): 81-94, argues that the poet is a very naive Christian who knows little except for the tales of the Old Testament, but this is as close as critics today come to assuming a pagan author. For a full discussion see E. G. Stanley, "The Search for Anglo-Saxon Paganism," *Notes and Queries,* N.S. 11 (1964): 205-9, 242-50, 282-87, 324-33, 455-63, and 12 (1965): 9-17, 203-7, 285-93, 322-27, especially 11: 326-31.

2. On Wyrd see, for example, Alan H. Roper, "Boethius and the Three Fates of *Beowulf*," *Philological Quarterly* 41 (1962): 386-400; on revenge see Dorothy Whitelock, *The Audience of Beowulf* (Oxford: Clarendon, 1951), pp. 13-17; the comitatus is, of course, found throughout Old English religious poetry (e.g., *Andreas*).

3. *Beowulf and the Fight at Finnsburg,* ed. Friedrich Klaeber (3rd ed.; Boston: D. C. Heath, 1950), cxxi: "in recounting the life and portraying the character of the exemplary leader . . . he [the poet] was almost inevitably reminded of the person of the Savior. . . ."

4. *The Heroic Age* (Cambridge, Eng.: Cambridge University Press, 1912), 53.

5. *Ibid.,* 52-53; I have included Scyld's funeral ship, although it seems to represent the departure of a legendary hero, as Klaeber suggests, rather than a real burial like that of Baldr.

6. Marie P. Hamilton, "The Religious Principle in *Beowulf*," *PMLA* 61 (1946): 309-31; reprinted in *An Anthology of Beowulf Criticism,* ed. L. E. Nicholson (Notre Dame, Ind.: University of Notre Dame Press, 1963), 125; in *The Knight's Tale* Chaucer shows his essentially Christian characters worshipping in pagan shrines.

7. Alcuin, *Albini Epistolae,* ed. E. L. Dümmler, in *Monumenta Germaniae Historica, Epistolae* (Berlin: Weidmann, 1895), 4, letter 124, 183.

8. For example, J. R. R. Tolkien, "*Beowulf:* The Monsters and the Critics," *Proceedings of the British Academy* 22 (1937): 245-95; reprinted in *An Anthology of Beowulf Criticism* (note 6), 101-2. In his edition of *Beowulf and the Fight at Finnsburg,* note to ll. 175-88, Klaeber holds that the poet "failed to live up to his own modernized representation of [the Danes]."

9. Chadwick, *The Heroic Age,* 73; his work is still the most recent full discussion of the problem, and it has been accepted without question.

10. Eddius Stephanus, *Vita Wilfridi Episcopi,* cap. 28, in *Rerum Britannicarum Medii Aevi Scriptores,* ed. James Raine (The Historians of the Church of York and Its Archbishops, vol. 1 [London, 1879]), 71:38. For a full account of the missions in Frisia see Wilhelm Levison, *England and the Continent in the Eighth Century* (Oxford: Clarendon, 1946): 45-69. Translations of some of the relevant materials are provided in *The Anglo-Saxon Missionaries in Germany,* ed. and trans. C. H. Talbot (New York: Sheed and Ward, 1954).

11. *Historia Ecclesiastica Gentis Anglorum,* V, ix, in *Opera Historica,* trans. John Edward King (New York: W. Heinemann, 1930), 2:234; the translations of Bede in this essay, however, are mine.

12. *Ibid.,* 238-40.

13. *Ibid.,* V, x-xi, pp. 240-52; Alcuin, *Vita Willibrordi,* ed. Wilhelm Levison, in *Monumenta Germaniae Historica, Scriptores Rerum Merovingicarum* (Hanover: Hahn, 1919) 7:81-141.

14. Bede, *Historia Ecclesiastica Gentis Anglorum,* V, x (2:244).

15. *The Anglo-Saxon Missionaries in Germany* (note 10), p. 9, notes that this king has been identified with Ongentheow in *Beowulf,* but I can find no basis for the identification.

16. Levison, *England and the Continent* (note 10), 70-93. Willibald, *Vita S. Bonifacii,* ed. G. H. Pertz, in *Monumenta Germaniae Historica, Scriptores* (Hanover: Hahn, 1829), 2:331-53.

17. Willibald, *Vita S. Bonifacii,* cap. 6 (340-42), trans. Talbot, in *The Anglo-Saxon Missionaries in Germany,* 47.

18. Levison, *England and the Continent* (note 10) 61.

19. Hermann Lau, *Die angelsächsische Missionsweise im Zeitalter des Bonifaz* (Kiel: J. M. Hansen, 1909), 39.

20. *England and the Continent,* 92.

21. *Die Briefe des heiligen Bonifatius und Lullus,* ed. Michael Tangl, in *Monumenta Germaniae Historica, Epistolae Selectae* (Berlin: Weidmann, 1916),1, letter 105; trans. Ephraim Emerton, in *The Letters of St. Boniface* (Records of Civilization: Sources and Studies 31 [New York: Columbia University Press, 1940]), 177-79.

22. See *Beowulf and the Fight at Finnsburg,* ed. Klaeber, p. cxvi, n. 1, for a summary of early scholars' views on this question.

23. Antoine Thomas, "Un manuscrit inutilisé du *Liber Monstrorum,*" *Bulletin du Cange: Archivum Latinitatis Medii Aevi* 1 (1925): 232-45; Whitelock, *The Audience of Beowulf,* 50; Kenneth Sisam, *Studies in the History of Old English Literature* (Oxford: Clarendon, 1953), 288-90.

24. Matts Dreijer, *Häuptlinge, Kaufleute, und Missionare im Norden vor Tausend Jahren* (Skrifter Utgivna av Ålands Kulturstiftelse 2 [Mariehamn, 1960]), 71-80.

25. Cf. Bernlef who joined St. Liudger's retinue and was "loved by his neighbors because he was of an open and free nature, and would repeat the actions of the men of old and the contests of kings, singing to his harp," *Vita Liudgeri,* ed. G. H. Pertz, in *Monumenta Germaniae Historica, Scriptores* 2: 403; cited and trans. W. P. Ker, in *The Dark Ages* (New York: New American Library, 1958), 57.

26. On Sutton Hoo in relation to the burials in *Beowulf* see the Supplement by C. L. Wrenn, "Recent Work on *Beowulf* to 1958," especially p. 513, in R. W. Chambers, *Beowulf: An Introduction* (3d ed.; Cambridge, Eng.: Cambridge University Press, 1959); for the Continental sources quoted in the text see *Capitulatio de Partibus Saxoniae* in *Texte zur germanischen Bekehrungsgeschichte,* ed. Wolfgang Lange (Tübingen: Niemeyer, 1962), 154-55, nos. 7, 22. This text dates from about 789.

27. They are frequently mentioned in the texts collected in *Texte zur germanischen Bekehrungsgeschichte,* ed. Lange; e.g. *Dicta Pirmini* (written between 718 and 724), 90-91.

28. In the ninth century more extended accounts of the pagans were written, such as the *Translatio Sancti Alexandri,* ed. G. H. Pertz, in *Monumenta Germaniae Historica, Scriptores* 2 (note 16), 673-81, and the *Indiculus Superstitionum et Paganiarum,* ed. G. H. Pertz, in *Monumenta Germaniae Historica, Leges* (Hanover: Hahn, 1835) 1: 19-20.

29. Lau, *Die angelsächsische Missionsweise im Zeitalter des Bonifaz,* 3, quotes an Englishman, Wigbert, writing to Lull (*Die Briefe des heiligen Bonifatius und Lullus,* letter 137).

30. *Die Briefe des heiligen Bonifatius und Lullus,* letter 46.

31. The text is from *Beowulf and the Fight at Finnsburg,* ed. Klaeber.

32. For example, Whitelock, *The Audience of Beowulf,* 78-79.

33. *Historia Ecclesiastica Gentis Anglorum* (note 11), II, v (1:228): *Quo utroque* [Eadbald and his wife] *scelere occasionem dedit ad priorem vomitum revertendi* 'by both crimes [Eadbald and his wife] he gave occasion for returning to the previous vomit.' Cf. Caesarius of Arles, *Sermones,* in *Texte zur germanischen Bekehrungsgeschichte,* ed. Lange, 61; Prov. 26:11.

34. "The Religious Principle in Beowulf," in *An Anthology of Beowulf Criticism* (note 6), 125.

35. "Beowulf, Ireland, and the Natural Good," *Traditio* 7 (1949-51): 263-77.

36. *In Cantica Canticorum,* in *The Complete Works of the Venerable Bede,* ed. J. A. Giles (London, 1844): 9:197. The *desuper* is a reminder that even a pagan like Ongendus (see n. 45) or Beowulf can be touched by grace.

37. *Ibid.,* 199.

38. *Annales Xantenses,* in *Monumenta Germaniae Historica, Scriptores* (note 28), 2: 221.

39. *Die Briefe des heiligen Bonifatius und Lullus,* letter 59.

40. Sister M. Thomas Aquinas Carroll, *The Venerable Bede: His Spiritual Teachings* (Catholic University of America Studies in Medieval History, N.S. 9 [Washington, D.C.: Catholic University of America Press, 1946]), 95. For a further discussion of this doctrine in relation to *Beowulf* see the suggestive article by Morton Bloomfield, "Patristics and Old English Literature: Notes on Some Poems," *Comparative Literature* 14 (1962): 36-43; reprinted in *Studies in Old English Literature in Honor of Arthur G. Brodeur,* ed. Stanley B. Greenfield (Eugene, Ore: University of Oregon Books, 1963), 36-43, and in *An Anthology of Beowulf Criticism* (note 6), 367-72. In writing the present article, I have had the benefit of Bloomfield's suggestions and criticisms.

41. *Monumenta Germaniae Historica, Scriptores* (note 16), 2: 675.

42. Horace *Odes* III.xxiv (referring to *Getae*); Tacitus *Germania;* Martianus Capella, *De Nuptiis Philologiae et Mercurii,* ed. F. Eyssenhardt (Leipzig: Teubner, 1866), 227-28, 240. Adam of Bremen takes the references in Horace and Martianus to refer to the Danes and the Geats: see *History of the Archbishops of Hamburg-Bremen,* trans. F. J. Tschan (Records of Civilization: Sources and Studies 53 [New York: Columbia University Press, 1959]), 195, 199, 204.

43. *De gubernatione Dei,* in *Texte zur germanischen Bekehrungsgeschichte,* ed. Lange, 16. Bede takes a

somewhat similar view when he (following Gildas) speaks of the Saxon invaders as agents of God's just vengeance for the crimes of the Celtic Christians: *Historia Ecclesiastica Gentis Anglorum* (note 11), 1, xiv-xv (1: 64-74).

44. *Vita S. Liudgeri* (note 16), II, 405.

45. See, for example, the alderman who avenged the two Hewalds (see n. 14), the Danish king Ongendus who, though a pagan, "nevertheless, through divine intervention, received the herald of truth with every mark of honour" (trans. Talbot, in *The Anglo-Saxon Missionaries in Germany,* 9), the pagans who spare the lives of St. Lebuinus (ed. G. H. Pertz, *Monumenta Germaniae Historica, Scriptores* [note 16], 2: 363) and of St. Willehad (2: 381), those pagans *prudentia naturali* 'with natural wisdom' reported in the *Historia Translationis Sanctae Pusinnae* (ibid., 2: 681) and the pagan Frisians who honorably received Wilfred: *Cujus loci incolae, nondum imbuti fide Christi, solo humanitatis affectu eos obvii benigne suscepere, et relevantes lassitudinem ipsorum quaeque necessitas exigebat gratis obtulere* "the inhabitants of this place, not yet filled with the faith of Christ, moved by human kindness alone, received them kindly along the way and, relieving their weariness, brought them freely whatever necessity required," *Breviloquium Vitae S. Wilfridi,* (note 10) 71:231 (cf. *Vita Wilfridi,* cap. 26-27, pp. 37-58, in the same volume).

46. *Die Briefe des heiligen Bonifatius und Lullus,* letter 73. In parts of the letter not quoted Boniface draws on Tacitus for his account of the pagans' attitude toward adultery, and he draws on his own experience by extending that account to cover also the Wends; in the passage quoted Boniface cites the Bible.

47. *Historia Ecclesiastica Gentis Anglorum* (note 11), I, vii: a pagan who refuses to execute St. Alban is himself executed, *de quo nimirum constat, quia etsi fonte baptismatis non est ablutus sui tamen est sanguinis lavacro mundatus* "of whom it is clearly apparent that though he was not bathed in the baptismal font yet he was cleansed by the washing of his own blood" (1: 43). Likewise, Edwin before his baptism is described as a man of "extraordinary sagacity" (II, ix).

48. Cf. Albert B. Lord, *The Singer of Tales* (Cambridge, Mass.: Harvard University Press, 1960), 100: "I believe that once we know the facts of oral composition we must cease trying to find an original of any traditional song. From one point of view each performance is an original."

49. Arthur G. Brodeur, *The Art of Beowulf* (Berkeley, Calif.: University of California Press, 1959), demonstrates that Beowulf and Hrothgar are "exemplars of an ideal and a course of conduct in harmony with both the best traditions of antiquity and the highest ideal of Christian Englishmen" (185).

50. However, William of Malmesbury is our only authority for the story.

51. Cf. Adam of Bremen, *History of the Archbishops* (note 42), 80-93; Dreijer, *Häuptlinge, Kaufleute, und Missionare im Norden vor Tausend Jahren* (note 24), 199-207.

Margaret E. Goldsmith (essay date 1970)

SOURCE: "The Marriage of Traditions in *Beowulf:* Secular Symbolism and Religious Allegory," in *The Mode and Meaning of "Beowulf,"* The Athlone Press, 1970, pp. 60-96.

[*In the essay that follows, Goldsmith examines the ways in which the influence of Christianity accounted for a shift in the function of heroic poetry and altered the meaning of the secular symbols traditionally used in heroic poetry generally, and in* Beowulf *in particular.*]

My attention has so far been given to the Christian climate of thought revealed in writings made in religious centres in early Anglo-Saxon England. It is now time to consider what kinds of poetic expression and what theories of the nature of poetry could have been at the disposal of the maker of **Beowulf,** and how far these were compatible with the attitudes inculcated in the Latin learning of the schools.

It must be admitted from the start that all statements made about native Germanic poetry anterior to **Beowulf** are inferential. The 'Germanic heroic epic' is an academic construct, since there are no direct, and, what is more important, no uncontaminated sources of information about pagan oral poetry. Of early evidence, there is the brief mention by Tacitus of the *carmina antiqua* which served as oral historical records among the *Germani,* and the battle-songs of 'Hercules' which they chanted before fighting.[1] The custom of preserving in verse the memory of the gods and kings and their great battles is reasonably presumed to have continued right up to the period when written annals and lettered poetry took their place—save that the pagan gods were replaced by the Lord of Hosts. The long memories of the poets could perpetuate the names of kings and heroes for three or four hundred years, as is proved by the two surviving fragments of early secular heroic verse, *The Fight at Finnsburh* and *Waldere,* and the two scopic songs *Widsith* and *Deor,* which, though not themselves heroic lays, include the names of ancient legendary heroes. All these short pieces now survive in late tenth-century manuscripts, but are thought to have been composed by the eighth century, *Widsith* and *Finnsburh* perhaps being older than **Beowulf.**[2] These poems are characterized by formulaic diction, a basically similar metrical form, a highly allusive style and a narrow range of subject-matter. Only the fragments of *Waldere* by their style give reason to think that in its entirety this was a poem of some length. But in this longer poem there are references to the Christian God,[3] which suggests that *Waldere,* like **Beowulf,** is of mixed ancestry. We therefore have no evidence at all that the unlettered Anglo-Saxon poets composed songs of epic length and complexity. The one surviving secular piece from Germany, the *Hildebrandslied,*[4] is a short self-contained lay which does nothing to contradict the impression given by the English corpus that longer poems were first made upon Latin models, or at least by educated men familiar with Latin poetry.

This impression is strengthened by the results of modern studies of living oral poetry and the techniques used by oral poets today. One might quote on this point Professor F. P. Magoun, who certainly cannot be accused of bias in favour of a literary *Beowulf,* since the article quoted is an attempt to explain away the fact that *Beowulf* presents an abnormal structure for an oral composition:

> Seldom if ever does a folk-singer, composing extemporaneously without benefit of writing materials, compose a cyclic poem, that is, sing in a single session or series of sessions a story which he or she feels is a unit dealing with several consecutive events in a character's life. . . . In view of a general lack of cyclic composition in oral singing the apparent cyclic character of the Beowulf material in Brit. Mus. MS Cotton Vitellius A. XV is *a priori* immediately suspect . . .[5]

Magoun's explanation of the curious form of 'the Beowulf material' is that it was put together from separate lays with transition verses 'by some anthologizing scribe'. It will be evident, however, that if one begins with the hypothesis of a lettered poet working with inherited verse-material about Beowulf, there is no abnormality to be explained.

The studies mentioned by Magoun have added further evidence to conclusions earlier drawn from the Homeric poems and other ancient compositions. These indicate that at a certain stage of cultural development, illiterate societies produce, and preserve in oral form, public poetry which acts as a stabilizing factor in the political and social life of the group. It incorporates religious myths, dynastic history, and customs and moral values admired by the society. (Later, when the ruling classes have become literate, oral poetry becomes the prerogative of folk entertainers and the songs become more romantic in type.) It has often been observed that some parts of the Old Testament have the mythic and social qualities I have mentioned. To find something similar today, one must turn to the emergent countries, where warrior societies built upon the clan system still produce such poetry. Recent research into living poetry among the tribes of the Congo by Dr Jan Vansina[6] reveals some very interesting resemblances to the remnants of Germanic tribal poetry, and may help us to realize that primitive poetry of this sort is far from plain or simple in its modes of expression, though simple enough in its message. It seems to me that some of Vansina's informed generalizations about the nature of oral poetry correct some current opinions derived from vestigial folk-singing among more developed nations. In the first place, Vansina finds no marked difference between written and oral literature except for a greater frequency of repetition in oral compositions. He comments on the formal structures in-

herent in a given literary category, and the conventions of style, which include allusions, stock phrases and many kinds of rhetorical device. He particularly notes: 'Dans les cultures illettrées, une des figures de style les plus appréciées est l'expression symbolique.'[7] His comments on 'symbolic statements' and 'poetic allusion', in primitive socieities generally, may incline us to believe that the obscurities, veiled allusions and dramatic ironies found in *Beowulf* by modern critics are natural to poetry dependent on such an oral tradition as has been described, and should certainly not be dismissed as figments of over-subtle modern criticism.

> Voiler sa pensée est dans beaucoup de cultures et pour beaucoup d'auteurs un artifice de style très apprécié. Déjà le symbolisme n'est au fond qu'une technique pour exprimer par circonlocutions une pensée qu'on ne veut pas traduire directement. Mais en dehors des cas de symbolisme que tous les participants à la culture peuvent comprendre il existe une série d'artifices, les allusions poétiques, qui restent incompréhensibles pour tous ceux qui ne connaissent pas à l'avance une partie ou la totalité des faits dont le témoignage rend compte.[8]

Vansina gives illustrations from Rwanda poetry, which he says are by no means exceptional.

> Dans presque toutes les cultures on pourrait citer des exemples analogues. Il résulte de l'emploi des allusions poétiques, que pour les comprendre il faut disposer de traditions historiques parallèles au poème qui en sont un commentaire explicatif.[9]

The familiar sound of all these statements to students of Germanic heroic poetry needs no underlining. Vansina also discusses stock phrases and stereotyped motifs in the African oral texts, and again the similarity with Germanic poetry is striking. His explanation of the use of these devices is germane to my general argument about the nature of *Beowulf:* 'Les lieux-communs à proprement parler apparaissent dans des textes qui traduisent des idéaux culturels acceptés par tous les tenants de la culture.'[10] The complex stereotypes form the motifs of episodes; one thinks of the washing ashore of an infant in a boat as probably such a motif in *Beowulf.* Vansina explains the inclusion of such motifs:

> Il semble bien que ces clichés complexes ne soient que des procédés purement littéraires pour expliquer un fait historique connu, pour colorer le récit ou pour rendre compte d'un événement désagréable du passé sans choquer les valeurs et les idéaux culturels du moment.[11]

Vansina's study brings out very clearly that an initiated illiterate audience can accept and enjoy in poetry much that is obscure and allusive or symbolic in expression. If one supposes that the Anglo-Saxon nobility enjoyed similar qualities in the secular poetry recited to them, not only is the style of *Beowulf* what one would expect, but the obscurity and ambiguity of some other Old English poems such as *The Seafarer* and *Exodus* becomes less remarkable in works composed for laymen. Altogether, the apparent ease with which biblical and exegetical symbolism was absorbed by the Anglo-Saxons is much more understandable if the secular poetic tradition contained the elements Vansina mentions.[12] My purpose in this chapter is to demonstrate the fundamental way in which the change of cultural ideals at the Conversion altered the function of heroic poetry, and at the same time inevitably changed the meaning of traditional secular symbols. In gaining a spiritual dimension, such poetry became potentially, almost necessarily, allegorical.[13]

In the learned tradition, Virgil's *Æneid* was the great model for a heroic poet. The *Æneid,* though vastly more sophisticated, fulfils the secular functions I have been speaking of. It upholds the ruler by celebrating his predecessors and by showing that the gods destined him to reign. It presents in its ancient heroes a pattern of moral conduct. In many respects it would seem to be a fitting model for a Christian epic poet. But it has, inescapably, a pagan religious foundation, which early Christian scholars naturally found repellent, though they could not bring themselves to reject the *Æneid* from the educational curriculum. Instead, they followed the lead of the pagan commentators Servius and Macrobius in discovering symbolic meaning in the more superstitious passages of the epic, so that the *Æneid* came to be read in the Christian schools as a historical epic with allegorical elements.[14]

It would scarcely be an exaggeration to say that every literate poet in Europe from the fourth century onwards was influenced by Virgil, yet though Christian epic poems in Latin appeared, there were no secular epics by Christian authors at that time. The reason is not far to seek. Christendom as a realm on earth to be upheld and defended was a concept not yet formed, and the heroes whose memories were perpetuated in Christian poetry were either the Old Testament *figuræ* of Christ, or the Lord and his apostles, or those famous later disciples who renounced wordly honours and fought their battles with the invisible hosts of the Enemy. A secular Christian epic would have been a contradiction in terms in a cultural environment dominated by the monastic ideal, but the way was still open for the advancement of God's kingdom through allegory. In England and the Germanic countries generally, there was the further obstacle that the ancestral heroes were pagan; again, allegorical treatment would permit the celebration of their nobility and valour, because it could be believed that the good men of the past also fought the Enemy. In fact, since there could not be a legitimate marriage between the politico-social heroic poetry of the secular tradition and the epic saint's Life which celebrates a hero of the invisible Kingdom, the product of such a strange union must, like *Beowulf,* laud a hero who inhabits two worlds, and is not quite at ease in either.

Sulpicius Severus, author of the influential *Vita S. Martini,* plainly states the contrast between the aims of secular and religious writers, the one celebrating great men, the other, the saints. He speaks of the examples of great men whose memory is preserved in literature, but he regards the reading of such secular work as profitless: . . .

for, in truth, those who evaluate life by present actions have given their hope to fables and their souls to tombs . . . hence it seems to me that I shall make a work of some worth, if I write the life of a very holy man which will be an example for others in the future: through which readers will be inspired towards true wisdom and heavenly warfare and divine virtue. In this we are also thinking of our own advantage, as thus we may look for, not worthless remembrance by men, but eternal reward from God.[15]

The above passage may have influenced the writer of a discourse on Psalm 52: 1-4 once attributed to Bede: the work begins with a short statement of his purpose in writing: . . .

When I marked many clerics established in places of learning giving so much time to the acquisition of knowledge of secular compositions, which studiously teach their hearers to desire carnal things and to strive for worldly glory . . . I decided that I myself would collect those literary works through which I might encourage some people towards the pattern of the holy faith, towards concern for the love and fear of God, towards the purity of spiritual life, towards devotion to humility and charity, towards penance for wrongdoers and amendment of their ways.[16]

This purpose is served by a discourse made up of a string of biblical parables, similitudes and exempla taken from the common stock, their inclusion justified by the doctrine that God is to be seen in his creation: . . .

For since the visible things were created by God such that *any understanding or seeking God* can easily be taught in these to recognise the invisible, to *inquire* (of God) is to test someone subtly through those same visible things, to discover whether he loves and fears him by obeying his commandments, or whether he serves his own pleasure by accepting diabolical illusions.[17]

The *Beowulf* poet quite probably knew the *Vita S. Martini,* which Colgrave groups with the *Vita S. Pauli,* the *Vita S. Antonii* and Gregory's *Dialogi* as works 'which had much influence on all writers of saints' lives of the seventh, eighth and later centuries'.[18] And I do not doubt that he also knew material like that assembled in the Ps.-Bede discourse. It will now, I think, be plain that *Beowulf,* if the religious element were removed, would fall into Sulpicius's category of secular works which offer the examples of great men for emulation and celebrate worldly glory. Beowulf himself earns and receives that *inanem ab hominibus memoriam* which Sulpicius contrasts with the *æternum præmium* which those who follow the example of the saints may hope to gain. Without the religious element, the poem would most surely teach its audience *pro obtinendi mundi gloria contendere* but with its 'Christian colouring' it seems to me to lead them *ad veram sapientiam et cælestem militiam divinamque virtutem.* How is this done? Obviously not by an added and extraneous condemnation of everything that the narrative has extolled, but instead by the more subtle use of the ambiguities and ironies which the two scales of values generate when the audience is brought to look *through* the one at the other. I believe that Beowulf is shown being tested as Ps.-Bede describes, through a 'diabolical illusion': the treasure hoard. The poet achieves this effect by exploiting the plurality of meanings which inheres in symbols and the essential irony of the *visibilia*, that 'what appears is so unlike what is'.[19] No sceptical reader need think that a use of symbols in the manner I have described would be alien to the mind of an Anglo-Saxon author. It seems to me quite congruent with the treatment of persons, objects and events in commentaries upon the Bible, remembering the arbitrary and occasionally antithetical meanings which may be attached to a single symbolic word or event.

At this point, some theoretical discussion is required to explain the nature of the symbolism we are concerned with and its relation to the allegory I have postulated. Vansina's use of the word symbol needed no explanation: it implied simply the substitution of a veiled term for a literal one.[20] Some of the substitutions he quotes are quite trivial, others would deserve the name of symbolism on almost any definition: for example, the rumbling of a storm as sign of the coming of a king in war (the king being the tribal rainmaker), or the loss of a tribal drum signifying the break-up of a kingdom.[21] The latter example brings to mind Mrs Winifred Nowottny's statement on symbolism in her book *The Language Poets Use:*

> It is as though . . . the poet were trying to leap out of the medium of language altogether and to make his meaning speak through objects instead of through words. Even though he does not tell us what the object X stands for, or even that it does stand for anything, he makes us believe that it means, to him at least, something beyond itself.[22]

This statement will serve very well as a point of departure. It will be recalled that my explanation of the purpose of Aldhelm's riddles in Chapter 2 involved this 'speaking through objects', and my examples of the symbols used in religious teaching could be so described. There is, I need hardly say, a profound difference between Aldhelm's speaking universe and a drum which speaks of a tribal kingdom, in respect of their philosophical implications, but as literary devices they can be classified together. Because of this, a social and political poem which uses symbolism of the latter sort can be enlarged to include religious symbolism without much violence to its surface literary integrity. This, I believe, is what happened in the making of *Beowulf.*

Augustine's literary theory in *De doctrina christiana* makes no fundamental distinction between secular and sacred symbols; he divides them into *signa naturalia* (such as smoke signifying fire) and *signa data* (which include all kinds of communication through sound or gesture, picture or object).[23] Among his illustrative examples are the dragon-standards of the army which *per oculos insinuant voluntatem ducum* 'indicate to the eye the generals' intent', the perfumed ointment poured over Christ's feet, and the woman touching the hem of his garment.[24] These,

which nowadays would probably be called symbolic objects or symbolic gestures, he uses to illustrate the various ways in which meaning can be conveyed, before he introduces the reader to the obscurities and ambiguities of Scripture. Augustine also warns his readers that similitudes in the Bible may sometimes have contrary meanings, one good, the other bad, as in the example of the lion, which signifies Christ in the Apocalypse 5: 5, and the Devil in 1 Peter 5: 8.[25] He moves on from figures to tropes, with a special mention of *allegoria, ænigma* and *parabola,* and a special paragraph on *hironia.*[26] It is evident from this classification and also from his explanation of *allegoria* in *De Trinitate,*[27] that 'allegory' for him was a general term for a literary device *aliud ex alio significare,* which included in its sub-classes both irony and enigma, the latter being an obscure allegory. A student brought up on *De doctrina christiana* would therefore have a very different conception of allegory from the modern student, who tends to think primarily in terms of personification allegory and the clothing of an abstract theme in a fictional dress.[28] Bede agrees with Augustine in regarding *allegoria* as a class of tropes including irony and enigma. He also rather unsuccessfully tries to find a theoretical category into which to fit the famous 'four senses' found in Scripture; his difficulty, of course, is that these *multiplex* tropes do not identify themselves by any formal sign and completely resist rhetorical classification.[29] (He puts them, quite wrongly, under *asteismus;* Augustine is content to include them under *ænigma.*)

In view of the attitudes to literary composition revealed here, one would not expect an allegorical work composed in Bede's time or thereabouts either to identify itself by formal signs or to preserve consistent levels of meaning. Allegory to these scholars was not a literary form, but, in the convenient phrase adopted by Angus Fletcher, 'a symbolic mode' of thinking and writing.[30] It is quite clear from the works I have just quoted that there was no theoretical separation of symbol and allegory; an allegorical work was simply one in which there was a great deal of hidden or obscure meaning conveyed in parable, enigma, proverb or almost any kind of metaphorical or ironic statement. When allegory is conceived in this way, the distinction between allegorical interpretation (of Scripture or of pagan writers) and allegorical creation (in new compositions) dissolves away. Fletcher, though in another context, makes a penetrating statement on this point:

> The modern question as to how we relate the interpretative and the creative activities could not arise before a break-up of the medieval world-view. Modern empirical science, on the other hand, depends in part on the disjunction of creative (imaginative and synthetic) and interpretative (empirical and analytic) mind, a major intellectual shift which might explain the modern distaste for allegory.[31]

A great deal of modern argument about the possible existence of allegorical meaning in Old English secular compositions has developed simply from confusion of terms and failure to accept allegory as a literary mode rather than a form.

Much confusion has been caused by the existence of the 'four senses' or 'planes of meaning' in scriptural interpretation. The first point to be noted is that though the great exegetes recognized the coexistence of different kinds of meaning in scriptural passages, they were not always sure how to differentiate these kinds, and in practice they might find two, three or four planes of meaning in some verses, and only literal meaning in others. For example, Augustine in the *De utilitate credendi* distinguishes four senses which he calls historical, ætiological, analogical and allegorical, covering respectively the actual Old Testament event, its cause, its agreement with the doctrine of the New Testament, and its figurative meaning. (His example is Abraham's two wives signifying the two covenants.)[32] As to the existence of these senses in a given text, he suggests the proper direction of scholarly enquiry in a series of rhetorical questions in the tract *De vera religione:*

> Do some [scriptural stories] signify visible events, others the motions of the mind, others the law of eternity, or are some found in which all these are to be discovered?[33]

Gregory, explaining his own method in the dedicatory letter to the *Moralia,*[34] has a slightly different system; he distinguishes historical, typological, and moral-allegorical kinds of interpretation, which may be applicable severally or in conjunction. Bede in his commentaries compiles from the work of his predecessors; in his homilies, which are based on New Testament texts, he recognizes historical, moral, and spiritual or mystical meaning.[35]

In one homily, Bede makes an unusually clear distinction between the different ways in which a story can be understood. He uses the changing of the water into wine at the Marriage at Cana as an allegory of the transformation of the meaning of the Old Testament stories by the significance of the life of Christ. The six vessels are six Old Testament stories from which the Jews drew, and any man can draw, moral lessons: this is the water. From the same six vessels the Christian can draw a more precious spiritual nourishment: this is the wine.[36] The spiritual meaning comes from the typological relationship between the acts of Noah, Isaac and the other *figur* in the stories and the acts of Christ himself:[37] the kind of prophetic symbolism already mentioned above as the subject of pictures brought by Benedict Biscop from Rome to Jarrow. There are of course two kinds of symbolism involved in Bede's homily. Each of the Old Testament stories is symbolic in its own right, and it teaches a moral lesson, as the religious pictures might. But each in conjunction with a New Testament story reveals typological symbolism and teaches a spiritual lesson.

Beowulf, I suggest, is a symbolic history from which one can draw the refreshing water of moral lessons; some critics have been tempted to suppose that one might also draw wine, by treating Beowulf as *figura* or 'type' of Christ like Noah or Isaac. They are, I believe, mistaken. Beowulf and Hrothgar are quite probably modelled on Old Testament characters, and are, like them, moral examples. But this resemblance does not make them a part of prophetic sacred history. Typological interpretation in the strict sense has no certain place outside of the inspired Scriptures.[38] It might, I suppose, be legitimately extended to poems in which Christ himself is the hero, such as the Old English *Phoenix,* or to a paraphrase of part of the Old Testament in which the *figura* occurred in the source. It could only be extended to the acts of a man living in the Christian era by someone who had an incomplete grasp of the theory of typological interpretation. There is, I believe, an intended relationship between Beowulf and the warrior-Christ, but it is not a direct and simple one.[39]

It is true that no line was drawn at that period, as in modern times, between the mythical and legendary parts of the Old Testament narrative and later history properly so called, as witness, for example, the *Chronica*[40] of Sulpicius Severus, whose views on the purpose of literature have been quoted above. His compact history of the world includes Cain's murder of Abel, the miscegenation which spawned the giants, and the Flood, just as the 'historical' poem of ***Beowulf*** does, and proceeds through such events—to take a few at random—as the burning of Rome under Nero, the finding of the Cross by Helena, and several notable synods of the Church, down to doctrinal controversies in his own day. This work was not intended to be a church history; it is a Christian's view of the history of mankind; and though there is no separation of biblical history and later events there is a line of demarcation between the era of prophecy which led up to the Incarnation and the Christian era which followed. Typology in the patristic sense of the word belongs only to the era of prophecy. There is in the holy men of the world before Christ a partial revelation of the pattern of perfection; after the life of Christ the witness of holy men is *imitation* of Christ; the word 'type' in its narrow exegetical sense can no longer apply.

Christian literature is naturally full of reminiscences of New Testament incidents and sayings. To recognize these is not the same thing as to discover *figuræ Christi* in the heroes of the works concerned. I quote in support of this contention that great student of medieval symbolism, Rosemond Tuve, who has discussed this question in relation to Guyon in *The Faerie Queene.* She speaks of Spenser's use of allegorical images to indicate

> that we are to read them with this reach into ultimate questions. We recognise them as instruments for the discussion of just such matters—but able to speak in the present of the timeless, and locally of the universal. I do not mean that images repeat the story they told in the past. It does not turn Guyon into a 'Christ-figure' when in Canto vii. 9 Spenser directs us to see the parallel with Christ's three temptations. Rather, this indicates the amplitude of the issue and states a doctrine about the relation between all human temptations and Christ's.[41]

This quotation seems to me to point to the right way to read Beowulf's descent into the world of his demonic adversaries, which recalls Christ's descent into hell in rather the same way as Guyon's temptations recall the temptations of Christ. It indicates the allegorical amplitude of the issue, but it does not turn Beowulf into a 'type' of Christ.

If we put aside typological significance as inappropriate to *Beowulf*, we are left with the other kinds of allegorical meaning, the moral and the spiritual. One might distinguish these as appertaining to right conduct upon earth, and that conduct viewed in the perspective of eternal life and man's relationship with God. I think that the *Beowulf* poet is intermittently writing on both these planes.

It should by now be evident that when I speak of *Beowulf* as an allegory of the life of man I mean something rather different from what C. S. Lewis had in mind when he said of Fulgentius's *Expositio Virgilianae continentiae*, 'The whole story of the *neid* is interpreted as an allegory of the life of man'.[42] Fulgentius's interpretation of the *neid* calls for a far greater degree of abstraction than I find in *Beowulf*, and all the incidents are treated as images in the progress of a life. Whether Fulgentius was available to the *Beowulf* poet remains uncertain. There is no positive evidence that the *Mitologiae* and the *Virgilianae continentia* were known in England before the ninth or tenth century.[43] An instance in Bede of the Fulgentian method, namely, his allegorizing of the fabled nature of Cerberus, merely demonstrates a similar approach to the pagan myths, since Bede does not follow Fulgentius in his interpretation of the monster's three heads.[44] One might deduce that Bede would have found the work of Fulgentius congenial in some respects; his lack of reference to the mythographer's books is therefore significant. Aldhelm, who uses allegorical beasts as symbols of the vices,[45] would undoubtedly have been interested in Fulgentius had he known his compositions, but he betrays no acquaintance with them. On the whole, it seems unlikely that Fulgentius had direct influence on the Anglo-Saxon poets; those who were able to read the *neid* probably found latent symbolic significance in particular objects or actions rather than a continuous didactic underthought. neas's descent into the underworld had received particular attention from religious writers;[46] this could have provided a model for the allegorical treatment of Beowulf's descent into the hellish depths of the mere. It must, however, be said that the supposed Virgilian reminiscences in this part of *Beowulf* are rather dubious.

A minor but interesting question which pertains to the Beowulf poet's conception of allegory is whether or not he employs personification allegory in his poem. Virgil provides a model for the occasional appearance of abstractions in living form, notably in the vices which cluster round the portals of Hades.[47] There is nothing quite of this kind in *Beowulf*, but as Professor Bloomfield has pointed out, the names Unferth and Hygd could suggest that these characters were invented to fill the role the names connote.[48] It seems to me rather more in keeping with the poet's general practice to suppose that the characters had a traditional part to play and the names were perhaps modified to underline the nature of that part. Personified vices

in beast form, on the other hand, such as appear in the battle with the vices at the end of Aldhelm's *De virginitate*,[49] might well have guided the poet to awareness of the allegorical potential of Beowulf's monster-fights.

I have now, I hope, shown that *allegoria* in Bede's time was not a category of formal structure, but a mode of figurative writing which might inhere only intermittently in a given work, and that it involved moral and spiritual symbols and figurative passages. The allegory in *Beowulf*, as I believe, is intermittent and concerns only one aspect of man's life, the contest with the Enemy. Though the poet quite probably knew the *neid* with its accompanying symbolic commentaries, there are no signs that he was influenced by it except in the most general way; for the kind of subject he was interested in, the saint's Life, the Bible as read by the commentators, and perhaps the *psycho-machia* type of allegory, would provide him with sufficient models for the religious aspect of his composition.

In a rather different respect, the way in which the *æneid* was read may have offered the *Beowulf* poet a pattern. It provided an authoritative warrant for the composition of a historical epic with moral and philosophical symbolism and with divine intervention. Whether or not *Beowulf* can be called an epic depends entirely on whether one sets up a theoretical category distinguished by certain formal requirements. It is of course much shorter and more restricted in its range than the classical epic, but I suppose that by the standard of the time it would have been included in the epic genre. Its shortness would hardly have been a bar, since Homer's reputation was perpetuated in Western Europe through the *Ilias Latina,* a first-century Latin abridgment of the *Iliad* in 1070 lines.[50] According to the definitions given by Isidore of Seville, which Bede used in his own brief literary treatise, *Beowulf* would belong to the *heroica species* of the *genus commune* (i.e. that in which both poet and characters speak). Our poet performs his function well according to Isidore's definition of the poet's task:

> A poet's function lies in this, that he presents things which have actually taken place transformed into other images through oblique and figurative modes of expression, adding beauty.[51]

I now turn more particularly to the means by which the poet transforms the *gesta* in *Beowulf* and gives the historical narrative a new significance.[52] It will be useful to return to Rosemond Tuve's criticism of the *Faerie Queene*. She speaks of Spenser's employment of classical symbols, such as the golden apples, which

> evoke all those sad stretches of human history when men's concupiscence, for power of all kinds, had brought all the great typical 'ensamples of mind intemperate' to their various eternities of frustrated desire. He uses what he calls 'the present fate' of these long-dead persons to tell the powerful who have *not* yet left their mortal state for that other, 'how to use their present state'; this is evidence that he wishes us to read allegorically of the relations between a virtue Tem-

perance and what can happen to a soul, and not merely morally of a character Guyon and his confrontation of covetous desires.[53]

One cannot press the analogy with the *Faerie Queene* very far, but some of Tuve's observations appear to me also appropriate to *Beowulf*. The poem is undoubtedly addressed to the powerful and is designed to warn them of the dangers attendant upon power; I believe that the hero's 'confrontation of covetous desires' when he fights for the buried hoard is to be read as an image of the soul's struggle and not merely morally of a character Beowulf. Tuve reminds us that the images carry their history with them, to deepen the conviction 'that all things though fully present to the senses are meaningful beyond what sense reports'.[54] The dusty gold of Mammon's cave has a long line of predecessors, among which I do not think it wrong to place the rust-eaten treasures for which Beowulf fought. The modern reader is unhappily ill-equipped with material in which to trace the history of the images used by the *Beowulf* poet, but some of the associations of dragon and treasure in classical and Christian writings can be recovered so as to deepen their meaning for us.

Tuve also recognizes that a poet writing in this mode must sometimes guide his readers by 'outright conceptual statement.' She cites 'Here is the fountaine of the worldes good' (*F.Q.* 7, 38).[55] The equivalent in *Beowulf* is the blunt observation,

> Sinc eaðe mæg,
> gold on grund(e),   gumcynnes gehwone
> oferhigian,   hyde se ðe wille.
>
>   (2764-6)

The audience has been prepared for this by the didactic matter in Hrothgar's admonition, which by reaching 'into the area . . . of man's metaphysical situation'[56] requires the hearer to think of Beowulf's subsequent life in terms of the *bellum intestinum*. Thus Beowulf's dragon-fight can be read as an image of the interior struggle of the king with the Enemy. The symbolic significance of Beowulf's great contests will require a separate chapter: in what remains of this, I shall examine the purely secular symbols which the poet makes the instruments of his purpose.

It is rather obvious that the rhythmic, alliterative, and syntactic frames within which an Anglo-Saxon poet has to work inhibit precise utterance; the compound word is more useful to him than the corresponding phrase, and inevitably less specific; a range of interchangeable words is required by the metre, so that fine distinctions are worn away; and the traditional vocabulary is relatively small. All these handicaps notwithstanding, a satisfying communication is apparently achieved; and this can only be through the lighting-up of part of the spectrum of associations shared by poet and audience. As Vansina's observations showed, traditional oral poetry is one means by which a people preserves its social stability and its cultural ideals. The associations of the stylized diction are familiar

and predictable, and necessarily so. This was presumably true of the oral poetry of the heathen Anglo-Saxons. But upon their conversion to Christianity, they did not discard their inherited poetry. A very strange state of affairs is thus brought about when the traditional diction serves both the old and the new ideals. It is not simply that the vocabulary has to be enlarged and adapted; more curious and interesting is that it has to accommodate the paradoxes of Christianity: that man's home is *elþeodigra eard,*[57] that the strong are weak and the rich poor, that the tangible sword snaps and the helmet splits, but the invisible shield of faith endures. The trappings of life remain as before and the poets retain the words for them, but their significance as symbols becomes ambivalent. In general, symbols of magnificence and grandeur will take on connotations of pride and mutability, and symbols of military prowess connotations of strife and vainglory. In addition, the old vocabulary is analogically stretched to provide a language for the invisible and eternal world. Words like *woroldcyning, wuldorfull, dream* and *dom* take on two aspects, changing as the poet shortens or lengthens his focus. *Beowulf* as a poem about the departed world has its own particular ambivalence.

There are, I suggest, a number of objects, persons and actions in the narrative to which the term symbol (in Nowottny's sense) can be applied, because they are given prominence in a manner not actually called for by the movement of the plot: such objects as Scyld's funeral boat, Grendel's hand, Hrethel's sword, such persons as Heremod and Hama, such actions as the arming of Beowulf.[58] For convenience in discussing them, it will be useful to class these symbols according as they have primarily religious, mythic,[59] social, or contextual significance. The categories are not, of course, exclusive: the second may impinge on the first, and the fourth embraces the others. The first three are probably inherited by the poet with his source material, the last comes as near as this public poetry allows to revealing the personal concerns of the poet. His interests are indicated by the selection and disposition of the material to hand; the relative importance accorded to the life of Sigemund and the funeral of Hnæf, for example, can be taken as evidence of particular preoccupations of the author, since neither is demanded by the action. I take for granted that once the Creator is introduced into the narrative, a perspective is opened through the whole history of the created world; the natural elements may speak of their Maker and the historical events speak of his purposes.

The poem opens with praise of the might of the Danes *in geardagum,* represented through the symbolic person of Scyld.[60] It is remarkable that the mysterious and exciting life of this royal hero is so slightly treated in comparison with his obsequies. The episode of the child in the boat, which as an ancient mythic, or social, symbolic motif may have recorded in a veiled form a profound change in the Danish way of life, is used by the poet chiefly to illustrate the power of God in effecting reversals of fortune and bringing comfort to the afflicted. The reversal of fortune is pointed by the contrast of the two boats, but of the two only the funeral ship is fully described, so that Scyld's mysterious origins and subsequent prosperity are quite overshadowed by the scene of his death. The *heiti* for God, *Liffrea* (*auctor vit*),[61] places emphasis on the fact that the provision of an heir for Scyld and the continuation of the royal line were signs of God's care for the unhappy nation; the second name, *wuldres Wealdend* (17),[62] may have the double aspect I have spoken of, praising the Lord who dispensed earthly glory to Scyld as well as the Lord who rules in Glory in his heavenly Kingdom. The effect of the two phrases in conjunction is like that of the prayer *Deus, et temporalis vit auctor et tern, miserere. . . .*[63] In birth and in death, man lies in God's hand: this is the affirmation made by the poet as he surveys the pagan king's prosperous career and magnificent parting from life. By this simple means he opens the perspective of eternity, and the brilliant foreground picture of Scyld's costly foreign spoils shades from a symbol of magnificent power into a symbol of transience.

The funeral ship is one of the most memorable secular symbols of the poem: *isig and utfus* (33), it gathers into itself the human feelings which accompany death. Both epithets have figurative meaning, icy coldness evoking misery, the readiness for a journey figuring the parting from life; nevertheless it would be wrong, I think, to empty them of literal meaning;[64] the boat shining with ice and straining at the mooring-ropes is beautiful, as the treasure is brilliant, because the poet is keenly aware of the beauty of the created world and the works of men's hands. It is the great strength of **Beowulf** as a poem that it does not become abstract. What more does the poet achieve with the boat-symbol? Some of its potency depends perhaps on its universal significance; it is not simply a reminiscence of an ancient custom (which a Christian poet could hardly wish to revive for its own sake), but as Cope says,

> The boat is a universal symbol connected with both birth and death—cradle and coffin are alike special cases of a boat. We are reminded of such diverse examples as the boat-crib of Moses and the ship-burials of Germanic peoples right back to the Bronze Age.[65]

As universal symbols framing a life, Scyld's two boats form a brilliant contrast between the destitution of the child and the wealth of the old man. But even here there are ironic undertones. The use of litotes (43-4) sets up in the mind two opposed possibilities; the words assert what the syntax denies, that Scyld in death was no better furnished than the destitute child. The reader of The Book of Job who remembers the words, *Nudus egressus sum de utero matris meæ, et nudus revertar illuc* 'Naked came I out of my mother's womb, and naked shall I return thither' (Job 1: 21) will be well aware that the treasure passed into the sea's keeping; though Scyld remained *on Frean wære* (27). This latter phrase seems deliberately chosen to stress God's continuous governance of mankind without introducing the issue of salvation.[66]

Other ships appear in the course of the narrative, the return of a treasure-laden keel serving as a sign of victory and the victor's reward in the stories of Sigemund and Hengest as well as the story of Heorot. The faint memory of the loading of Scyld's treasure-ship may intrude its shadow in these other scenes; it is very striking that the piling of the treasure round the dead man is much more fully treated than Scyld's death, and of actual funeral rites there is nothing at all. The ships in the poem are not described objectively; like Scyld's cold and deathly funeral ship, the others reflect some of the emotions of the seamen. Beowulf's ship beginning the adventure presses on eagerly, and Hengest's ship is the prisoner of winter.[67] Of itself, Scyld's funeral ship could hardly act as *memento mori* in the way I have suggested, but the dark shadow is soon reinforced by other scenes in which the splendour of gold is accompanied by the thought of death.

The second great symbol of the poem is the royal hall which Scyld's descendant Hrothgar caused to be built. The narrative moves with great economy through the king's ancestry and his early successes in war, so that the building of Heorot becomes the dominant feature of the king's life-story. Hrothgar conceives the idea of having his men build the largest hall in the world, where he will hold court and dispense his bounty (67-73). The huge project needs the labours of craftsmen from many nations, and when it is finished it is a towering landmark (81 f.). He names it *Heorot,* and lives liberally and in convivial splendour within, at the centre of his great court. Heorot is a monument to Hrothgar's power, success and wealth. He is a good and generous ruler, and as a social symbol Heorot reflects nothing but the greatness of the king. Its name 'Hart' appears to connote royalty,[68] the descriptive terms *horngeap* (82) and *hornreced* (704), whatever their literal meanings, help to build an image of the majestic beast with wide-curving antlers, *hornum trum* (cp. 1369). That the name Heorot has some symbolic significance we cannot doubt, for no other hall is given a name. I am inclined to relate that significance to the associations given to the beast by the Latin fabulists and later woven into the Bestiaries, because these associations consort remarkably well with what I take to be the **Beowulf** poet's view of splendid palaces. Some years ago, C. S. Lewis offered the suggestion that a fable by Phædrus perhaps had something to do with Beowulf's dragon.[69] The evidence concerning the dragon is discussed in Chapter 4. I do not wish to anticipate that argument here, because the connection is at best unproven, but if the one fabled beast is acceptable, so perhaps is the other. In any case, the moral meaning which Phædrus and later fabulists found in the hart is one which any hunter of a reflective turn of mind might independently reach when he came upon a stag caught in a thicket. The animal's stance suggests pride in his spreading antlers, and when he is trapped by them, the moralist would find it hard to resist the thought that his pride was his undoing.[70] Is it too far-fetched to suppose that Heorot's towering gables drew Grendel to its doors and so brought death among the Danes?

It is convenient here to mention in passing that the hart as a Christian religious symbol deriving from Psalm 41: 2,

Sicut cervus desiderat ad fontes aquarum ita desiderat anima mea ad te Deus 'As the hart panteth after the fountains of waters, so my soul panteth after thee, O God', seems to me to be unrelated to Heorot. The hard-pressed hart of line 1369 is more problematical. An Anglo-Saxon educated as I have described could not fail to know this symbol for the thirsting soul, but it is not drawn into the allegory of Beowulf.[71]

What I am suggesting is that the symbolism of the name Heorot could reinforce the moral attitude conveyed by the poet's juxtaposition of its building and its coming ruin (74-85). It was regal and magnificent, and as durable as good craftsmen could make it (cp. 770-82) but the poet reminds his hearers that within the lifetime of the builders it was maliciously destroyed by fire (cp. 781 f.). Thus the social symbol summing up the magnificence of a line of great kings is altered by a single stroke into a symbol of *þeos læne gesceaft* in which nothing endures. It may also, as I have suggested elsewhere, act as an eschatological symbol, bringing to mind a subject zealously treated by Anglo-Saxon poets, namely the destruction of the cities of earth and the engulfing of the wealth of kings by the devouring fire which was expected to bring the world to an end in some not distant time.[72]

Contextually, Heorot acts as an image of the Danish court, first in its splendour, then in its uselessness during Grendel's persecution of the Danes. At the conclusion of the Grendel story, the hall bears the marks of Grendel's ferocious strength (997-1000). The cracks and breaks are partly masked by gold hangings which are brought out for the feast of celebration. On the surface, the court at Heorot is brilliant and splendid, but half-hidden enmities are hinted (1017-19) and as the company assembles for the feast, the author, in a rather longer moral statement than he usually permits himself, speaks of death:

> No þæt yðe byð
> to befleonne,   fremme se þe wille,
> ac gesecan sceal   sawlberendra,
> nyde genydde,   niþða bearna,
> grundbuendra   gearwe stowe,
> þær his lichoma   legerbedde fæst
> swefeþ æfter symle.

(1002-8)

By his brilliant placing of two quite commonplace images, escaping from death and sleeping after the feast of life,[73] the poet makes his hearers aware that just as Grendel vainly ran away from death over the wastes, and now after his monstrous feasting lies asleep in death, so the Danes, sitting now at the table, rejoicing that the shadow has been lifted from Heorot with the defeat of Grendel, have not escaped death after all, because the feud is not over (cp. 1251-5). And the Grendel feud has its echo in the bloody thoughts of Hrothulf which at a later time end Hrothgar's renewed hopes of a settled time of peace ahead. The cracks in the fabric of Heorot are an image of the treacherous hatreds which are already—to judge by the setting and tone

of Wealhtheow's speech (1162-91)—making rifts in the concord of the kinsmen.

The other royal halls which appear in the poem have no recognizable identity. The Geatish royal hall is burnt down by the dragon without any preliminary description of it or prophecy of its destruction. These facts make the emphasis on Hrothgar's hall more striking and justify my inclusion of it among the symbols of the poem. The furnishings of the hall consist of ornamental hangings, a high seat, benches, beds and pillows, and drinking-cups. Some of these may be inferred to have symbolic significance, since the poet does not describe them as objects interesting in themselves and there is no detailed account of feasting or ceremonial. For example, the passing of the cup honours the king's guests, and with this piece of social ritual the poet succeeds in giving an impression of civilized conviviality.

Deeper meaning seems possible in two particular objects belonging to social life, namely the *gifstol* of line 168, and the *fæted wæge* of line 2282, which was brought from the dragon's hoard. I postpone discussion of the *gifstol* to Chapter 4, because the interpretation of the word has bearing upon the poet's conception of Grendel. The gilded cup could have come into the story simply as the cause of contention between the dragon and the Geats, but the symbolism of the cup in religious writing seems to indicate an allegorical significance; I believe it to be a reminder of Adam's *poculum mortis* and, as such, a symbol of cupidity. My reasons for looking upon it in this way are bound up with exegetical interpretation of the war with the Serpent-Dragon, which is treated apropos of Beowulf's contest in Chapter 7.

Swords and armour have an important place in the poem. Their costly materials and fine workmanship are often praised by the poet, and he records, without adverse comment, that Beowulf's mail-coat was Weland's work and that three of the swords were forged by the giants; he also describes the boar-images which surmounted the warriors' helmets as protective talismans. One may guess that these three elements were more prominent in his source-material, since they smack of heathen superstition and magic, if not of pagan worship. They add an exciting air of antiquity to the story and there is no sign that the poet himself believed in their magical power. His obvious veneration for great craftsmanship is a very different matter, enhancing the stature of the heroes and magnifying the perilous adventures in which even these stout accoutrements failed those who bore them.

The poet's attitude to the boar-figures which adorned his warriors' helmets has some interest for his handling of a remnant of pagan superstition in the poem. Beowulf's own helmet, rather fully described in the careful preparations for his dive into the mere, had boar-figures round its crown:

> swa hine fyrndagum
> worhte wæpna smið,   wundrum teode,

besette swinlicum,   þæt hine syþðan no
brond ne beadomecas   bitan ne meahton.

(1451-4)

The ancient smiths believed in the protective power of the
boar, but if one looks rather closely at the poem, one observes that nowhere in the action does the wearing of such
a helmet affect the course of events. There is instead a
mute denial of the power of the boar in the scene of
Hnæf's funeral, where the slain men's gold-adorned helmets lie on the pyre:

t þæm ade wæs   eþgesyne
swatfah syrce,   swyn ealgylden,
eofer irenheard,   æþeling manig
wundum awyrded;   sume on wæle crungon.

(1110-13)

Shields are surprisingly unimportant in *Beowulf,* until one
remembers that Beowulf prefers to wrestle, and there are
otherwise very few of the conventional cut-and-thrust combats of battle in the poem. The one memorable shield is
the huge device which protected both Beowulf and Wiglaf
from the dragon's fire (2675-7). Its function was to give
cover to Beowulf until he was near enough to strike at the
dragon, and this it did, but, like his sword, it failed him at
the last (2570-2). I have already published[74] the opinion
that the great shield represents the strongest human defence a man can make, and that its meaning in the allegory is that without spiritual defences (*scutum fidei*)[75] no
man can successfully oppose the Dragon. The development of this religious aspect of the poem is treated in
Chapters 6 and 7 below.

The sword is a potent symbol of varying significance in
Beowulf. In the society depicted, a good sword is a sign
of the prowess of the wearer; such are Unferth's Hrunting,
lent to Beowulf in recognition that the Geat was the better
man, and the sword of Hrethel presented to the hero on his
triumphant return from Heorot. Probably also traditional is
the use of a sword as signal of a re-kindling feud: such are
the sword which roused Hengest, the sword which incited
Ingeld's man to kill his father's slayer, and the sword *Eanmundes laf* which Wiglaf bore. This last example is contextually used to very subtle effect, drawing together the
scattered incidents which had marked the progress of the
Geatish feud with the Swedes during Beowulf's lifetime,
and representing—in something the same fashion as the
cracks in the walls of Heorot—at the moment when the
dragon is felled, the imminent strife with the Swedes which
will make an end of the tribe.

The swords which Beowulf possesses all fail him, and my
observations on the iron shield in the allegory would apply
also to the sword. In a quite different category is the sword
which Beowulf found in the underwater hall. With this
giant-made sword he beheaded his giant adversaries, and
in so doing destroyed the sword, save for the curiously-
patterned hilt which he took back to Heorot. I regard this
as an important element in the allegory. As a symbol of

Beowulf, about to slay Grendel.

the prowess of the giants, its wasting away in the corro-
sive blood of the slain Grendel kin has an obvious significance, but the enduring hilt brought back to the world of
men has a much more complex story to tell. The ramifica-
tions of this story of the feud of the giants with God will
be explored in my next chapter.

The giant sword is not said to have had magical power,
nor is magical immunity offered as a reason for Hrunting's
failure to bite on the giantess's hide.[76] The audience is left
to think that the extraordinary weight of the ancient
weapon gave Beowulf's blow the necessary force. The description of its melting blade merits special notice: the
poet has focused attention upon it by his simile of the
melting of icicles in the spring. The simile, beautiful and
apt as it is for the change that comes over the hard iron, is
remarkable in another respect. The presence of God in this
dark infernal place *under gynne grund* (1551) is gradually
manifested, first by the line,

rodera Rædend hit on ryht gesced,

(1555)

then by the appearance of light as bright as day,

> efne swa of hefene   hadre scined
> rodores candel.[77]

(1571 f.)

Then, with the simile I have mentioned, thought of the Father's control over all times and seasons turns the mind away from the curious wonder of the melting blade to the annual miracle of melting ice, and the giant sword and the power of the giant race become small in the comparison.

Beowulf carries the hilt of the wonderful sword to Heorot, together with Grendel's head, and in presenting these trophies to Hrothgar he ascribes his escape from the monster to God's protection (1658) and his sight of the giant weapon to God's favour (1661-2). The hilt is described: it is decorated with serpentine patterning and runic letters. Thus an aura of mysterious and malevolent antiquity is created about it, and at its centre is the engraved picture of God's retribution on the giants in the days of Noah. I pass over for the present the meaning of this backward extension of the feud with the giants into Old Testament times, to show the complex of symbolic meaning given to the giant sword, which is for the Danes a symbol of victorious revenge in the feud, for Beowulf a symbol of God's protective care for those who fight in his battles, and for the audience a symbol of the enduring cosmic war in which Beowulf's contests are brief incidents.

Weapons and armour, being costly and valued possessions, also appear in the poem as a species of wealth. Like the *beagas* which are prized as much for the status they confer upon the wearer as for their intrinsic value, the splendid accoutrements are symbols of social relationships in the society depicted. They signal the munificence of the royal giver as much as the worth and deserts of the great warrior who receives them. The poet openly approves the ancestral custom of dispensing rich gifts from the throne,[78] and considerable attention is given to the princely gifts which were conferred on Beowulf in recognition of his triumphs.[79] To a Christian poet, riches were the means through which a man could exercise the virtue of charitable giving and therefore were not invariably evil, but as the cupidity of man was potent for harm, great treasures were a source of danger. The evil which treasure could beget was both moral and spiritual, as causing violent quarrels for possession, and as contaminating the soul of the possessor. The *Beowulf* poet treats all these aspects of treasure while not losing sight of its social importance, principally by emphasizing the brevity of a man's possession of costly objects, and by making them the focal point in stories of bloodshed and death. The spiritual danger inherent in accumulated wealth is a major theme in the latter part of the poem.

Standing out among the regal gifts described in the tale of Heorot is the *healsbeah* (1195) which Queen Wealhtheow gave to Beowulf. Like the sword *Eanmundes laf* (2611) in the later story of the Geats, it acts as a linking symbol in a series of historical incidents. The necklace stands as a symbol for treasure as plunder, in the way that Eanmund's sword stands as a symbol of fraternal strife.

The necklace given to Beowulf reflects nothing but glory on the hero; in the social sphere it speaks of his preeminent achievements, in the moral sphere it shows him untouched by personal vanity or covetousness, since he does not try to keep it for himself. Hygelac later received it, and wore it on the plundering expedition which cost him his life. His premature death set in train the events which led to the death of Eanmund and the resurgence of Swedish power and enmity which Beowulf's own reign could only temporarily hold back. At the level of historical narrative therefore, the necklace serves as a useful means of uniting the histories of the Danes and the Geats. At the moral level it points the contrast between Beowulf and Hygelac. It is also made to act as a symbol of the vanity of human life. Between the queen's presentation (1192-6) and the applause of the company (1214) are sandwiched two stories of robbery and death[80] which dim the brightness of the jewel in just the way that the prophecy of consuming flame casts the shadow of death over gold-adorned Heorot (80-5).

The first of these interposed stories remains very obscure, since the incident of the necklace does not occur in any of the legends concerning Hama which survive in later German and Norse epic and saga.[81] The allusion is made still more obscure by the vagueness of the two phrases *to þre byrhtan byrig* (1199) and *geceas ecne rd* (1201). The identity of the *burg* is quite unknown, and the meaning of the latter phrase is doubtful. In the present state of knowledge, one can only conjecture what the poet intended by the reference to Hama. Comparison with the structurally rather similar treatment of Sigemund and Heremod (874-915) suggests that some contrast between Hama and Hygelac is intended; the line

> syþdan he for wlenco wean ahsode

(1206)

implies an adverse judgment on the king's action, which would support any interpretation of Hama as an admirable person in spite of his carrying off the Brosings' (Brísings'?) necklace. The unpleasant word *searonidas* (1200) alienates sympathy from the wronged Eormenric, and the phrase *geceas ecne rd* seems to imply that he made a good end.[82] Whatever the lost details of the story, the effect of the two interposed incidents is undoubtedly to remind the hearers that man's possession of wealth is short-lived in the perspective of eternal reward. I think it can be seen that the poet deliberately created this effect, because he has separated the matter of the robbing of Hygelac's corpse on the battlefield from Beowulf's reminiscent account of his revenge on the despoiler (2503 f.). In the more natural later position, the incident would have enhanced Beowulf's reputation as an ideal retainer and winner of treasure rather better than in its present place: one cannot avoid the conclusion that the notes of tragic irony in the happy scene at

Heorot were integral to the poet's theme, and that praise of Beowulf was only one element in that theme.

I come now to the last of the great secular symbols of the poem, and the most controversial in significance: the burial mound with its hidden treasure-hoard. There are only two such monuments in the poem, the one inhabited by the dragon, and the other raised over Beowulf's ashes as his memorial. This fact is in itself worth remarking. The other heroes whose death is recorded have no memorial; for Hnæf and his kinsmen there is no compensatory ritual of remembrance, only the ugly bursting of their bodies in the flame, and their epitaph: *ws hira bld scacen* (1124). Beowulf's *bld* would be remembered as long as the mound remained on *Hronesness* (cp. 2800-8), and in a secular society that is the most that a man could ask or deserve. The poet's interest in funerals does not involve him in repetitions; each is different in conception and effect. Scyld's passing speaks of the mystery of the unknown otherworld, Hnæf's pyre is a frightening image of physical destruction, Beowulf's funeral fire is blotted out by the great beacon of earth which is his grave and his glory.

The feature common to all three funeral descriptions is the placing of treasure with the dead, and the Christian poet does not censure the practice. He speaks through the treasure itself. Scyld's vast wealth goes into unknown hands (50-2), Hnæf's treasure is swallowed up in the devouring fire (1122-4). Only of Beowulf's hard-won gold does the poet say in his own voice,

> forleton eorla gestreon   eorðan healdan,
> gold on greote,   þær hit nu gen lifað
> eldum swa unnyt   swa h(it ær)or wæs.
>
> (3166-8)

This is a kind of epitaph upon the treasure; consigned to earth, it is seen at the last to be intrinsically worthless, though a man should give his life for it.

The burial of a treasure within the new-made tomb which the dragon afterwards made his lair is an incident which belongs to a different imaginary world from the rest of the poem. The other funeral-treasures belong to the heroic world as it was remembered; the Sutton Hoo burial might have been within living memory when *Beowulf* was composed,[83] and other less elaborately furnished graves were possibly known to the poet and those he wrote for; *gold on greote* was no imaginary thing. Though the Sutton Hoo deposit appears to have been a cenotaph, it is presumed that the grave goods were intended for the use of their royal owner in the next world. The burial of the treasure which became the dragon's hoard is, in contrast, a motive-less gesture, irrational in a different way from the second burial of the same treasure, since among the pagan Geats such an action could be thought to honour their king.

My justification for taking this view of the burial of the dragon's hoard lies in the nature of the character who commits it to the grave. He does not exist as a quasi-historical person like the other characters in the poem. His nearest kin is the nameless old man who grieves for his hanged son (2444 ff.). The nameless father can be absorbed into the narrative, because he exists only in a simile. He is a literary device and pretends to be nothing more. But the man who buries the treasure inhabits the same world as the exile and the wise man in *The Wanderer.*[84] They are faceless speakers invented by the poets to give utterance to some universal human feeling. Each is a *persona* of the poet, given no more individuality than his condition requires—in this they differ sharply from dramatic characters who speak in soliloquy, or the central figures in dramatic monologues. The uncomfortable truth about the man who buries the hoard is that he too is a literary device, but he needs to be more than this, because the story of the rifled hoard begins with him. He has to be believed in, like Scyld or Sigemund, as a remote historical person, but the poet has here allowed his theme to take charge of the narrative, and the beautiful elegy almost blinds one to the unreality of the whole episode.

The ritual action has no other celebrants, and no social or religious significance. Professor Smithers has interestingly argued that this scene is the garbling of a pagan story in which the last owner of the treasure was himself transformed into a dragon—as happened to several Norsemen in similar circumstances, according to the sagas.[85] But one has to admit that the *Beowulf* poet has altogether erased any possible former connection between man and dragon, and the critical problem remains. The burial of the treasure of a lost tribe is the improbable excuse for the lament *Heald þu nu hruse . . .* (2247-66). Man must return the treasure to earth because no other has claim upon it. It is an image signifying that the worth of gold-plated sword and goblet, helmet and armour derives from their use by men. When the heroes are dead, their treasures begin to decay. Inert, tarnished and crumbling, the buried treasure becomes for the poet a focal symbol for the transience of the material world. A critic may carp, but the bold device succeeds. Before Beowulf sets out to win the hoard, the poet has planted doubt as to whether it is worth the winning. In the outcome, his victory does not ameliorate the lot of anyone concerned, and the second burial of the treasure symbolically re-enacts the tragedy of the lost race.

The hoard, as I see it, is from the outset conceived as a symbol of transience. Another element in the conception is indicated by the epithet *hðen* (2216, 2276). The word is elsewhere applied to Grendel and to the idolatrous Danes; the use of it for the treasure might be an oblique condemnation of the pagan custom of burying grave goods, but it undoubtedly gives a general atmosphere of evil to the hoard.

I come now to the most curious aspect of the treasure-hoard as symbol, the curse upon it. The oddity about the curse is that the poet makes no good use of it, and it becomes a literary blemish. Without it, there is a satisfying moral sequence; with it, there is a conflict of causes which obscures the circumstances of Beowulf's end. I have shown that this hoard was from the first mention associated with death; the imagined owner, with a sentimental attachment to his possessions which the Anglo-Saxon audience might find understandable, made a grave for the treasure of his dead tribe. The consequence of his act was the appearance of the dragon, and ultimately Beowulf's death and the ruin of the Geatish people stem from the burial of the hoard. The curse, as it is reported, sealed up the gold in the tomb until God should grant the power to touch it to some man of his choosing (3051-7). It looks as though the poet was working with intractable material, since his faith required an affirmation of God's power to break the ancient spell, but his moral and his religious theme are considerably weakened by the existence of the spell, and even more by the proviso that God could prevent its dire effect. One may wonder why he kept the curse in the story at all. Two reasons suggest themselves: the first, that the heathen *þeodnas mre,* by invoking evil powers to protect their hoard (3069 f.), were thought to have called the dragon into being; the second, more prosaic, possibility is that the curse was a well-known feature of the given story which the poet felt obliged to include. Having brought it in, he could make no effective use of it, since if Beowulf was estranged from God it needed no curse to consign him to hell-bonds, and if on the other hand he remained uncorrupted by the gold, he retained his Lord's favour and would be divinely protected from the curse. An operative curse belongs to a poem of a different kind, in which the characters are unwitting victims of fate, and such a conception could not be harmonized with the doctrine of God's watchful care for mankind expressly affirmed more than once in **Beowulf.**

The inconsistency between the *þeodnas mre* who sang the incantation and the lone survivor who buried the hoard is a very clear sign that in this part of the poem the author's thoughts were dominated by his theme, to the detriment of the narrative. Uppermost is the doctrine that the burial of the hoard was itself a wrong action. The lone survivor's imagined gesture and the curse upon despoilers each sprang from men's desire to store up possessions even when they have no use for them. This is the characteristic desire of the dragon of European fable, as will be shown in the next chapter. Every pile of gold is potentially dangerous to mankind, as readers of St Antony's Life were reminded, for when the saint found gold in his path he passed by as though going over fire, knowing it for another temptation of the Enemy.[86]

I think it is fair to conclude from the transformation of the secular materials I have described that the poet was very much aware of the ambivalence of his symbols, which reflect the paradox of earthly life as it was then understood. The two great symbols, Heorot and the treasure, embody the magnificence and the wealth which are a hero's reward. But in the longer perspective they can be seen to be the images of man's pride and cupidity, the two fundamental sins which tie the carnal man to earth. To their possessors they seem to be durable; to the Christian audience they are presented as brilliant and destructible, costly and without worth.

Notes

1. Tacitus, *Germania,* c. 3; quoted by Wrenn, *OE Literature,* pp. 74-5.

2. For a convenient summary of their contents and scholarly opinion on the dating, see Wrenn, op. cit., pp. 76-83 and pp. 85-90.

3. Wrenn, op. cit., p. 87, says 'Its definitely Christian references to God . . . would seem, perhaps, to point to a clerical maker'.

4. Edited by E. von Steinmeyer, *Die kleineren althochdeutschen Sprachdenkmäler* (Leipzig, 1916).

5. F. P. Magoun, '*Béowulf B:* a Folk-Poem on Béowulf's Death', in *Early English and Norse Studies presented to H. Smith,* ed. A. Brown and P. Foote, pp. 128-9. His observation that one finds no cyclic poem in Old Icelandic (p. 129) is also pertinent.

6. Jan Vansina, *De la tradition orale.*

7. ibid., p. 63.

8. ibid., p. 64.

9. ibid., p. 65.

10. ibid.

11. ibid., p. 67.

12. Apart from *Beowulf* itself, the remains of Germanic secular poetry are too short to provide a clear general picture, but the allusive style is very marked in *Deor* and *Widsith.*

13. I use the word 'allegorical' here in a very broad sense, which could be defined as 'saying one thing in order to mean something beyond that one thing' (cp. Angus Fletcher, *Allegory: the Theory of a Symbolic Mode,* p. 4). For further definition of the kinds of allegory and symbolism in *Beowulf,* see below, pp. 68 ff.

14. cp. D. P. A. Comparetti, *The Study of Vergil in the Middle Ages,* trans. E. F. M. Beneke (London, 1895), especially pp. 57 and 59. For details of the symbolic meanings found in *æneid* VI, see P. Courcelle, 'Les Pères devant les Enfers. Virgiliens', *Archives d'Histoire Doctrinale et Littéraire du Moyen Age.*

15. Sulpicius Severus, *Vita S. Martini,* ed. C. Halm, 110 f.

16. *PL* 93, 1103.

17. *PL* 93, 1109; cp. Ps. 52: 3 and p. 52, above.

18. B. Colgrave, *Felix's Life of Saint Guthlac,* p. 16.

19. The phrase is from Christopher Fry. *A Phoenix too Frequent* (Oxford, 1946), p. 31.

20. See p. 63

21. One is reminded of the loss of *meodosetla* signifying the end of tribal independence in *Beowulf* (5).

22. W. Nowottny, *The Language Poets Use,* p. 175.

23. Augustine, *De doctrina christiana,* ed. W. M. Green, p. 34.

24. Augustine, ibid., p. 35.

25. ibid., p. 100. Had he not been writing for beginners in biblical study, he might have included also St Peter's ambivalent symbols which mean one thing to the faithful and something quite other to the unbeliever, viz., the corner-stone which is the foundation of a spiritual edifice to the Christian and a stumbling-block to the unbeliever (1 Pet. 2: 7-9), and the Flood-waters which prophesy baptism and salvation to the former and destruction to the latter (1 Pet. 3: 20-2); cp. Jean Daniélou, *Bible et Liturgie* pp. 89-104.

26. Augustine, op. cit., p. 103.

27. Augustine, *De Trinitate, PL* 42, 1068, on the text 1 Cor. 13: 12. Here he compares *in ænigmate* with *in allegoria* (Gal. 4: 24), explaining that translators who did not wish to use the Greek word have employed the circumlocution *which signify one thing by another.*

28. Personification allegory was of course also known to the Anglo-Saxons from Virgil's use of it and from Prudentius's *Psychomachia.* The last part of Aldhelm's verse *De virginitate* is written in this mode; see *MGH AA* xv, pp. 452-71.

29. Bede, *De schematibus et tropis sacræ scripturæ, PL* 90, 184-6. His definition is as follows:

> *Allegoria est tropus quo aliud significatur quam dicitur.*

> Allegory is a trope in which something other is signified than what is said.

Among the kinds, he brings in the four senses thus:

> Item allegoria verbi, sive operis, aliquando historicam rem, aliquando typicam, aliquando tropologicam, id est moralem rationem, aliquando anagogen, hoc est sensum ad superiora ducentem, figurate denuntiant.

> In like manner they intimate in a figure allegory of word or deed, sometimes a historical matter, sometimes a prefiguration, sometimes a tropological matter (that is, a moral concern), sometimes an anagogical relation (that is the sense guiding us to things above).

30. Fletcher, op. cit., pp. 2-3, takes very much Augustine's general view based on the linguistic process involved in making an allegory: 'In the simplest terms, allegory says one thing and means another. It destroys the normal expectation we have about language, that our words "mean what they say" . . . In this sense we see how allegory is properly considered a mode: it is a fundamental process of encoding our speech. For the very reason that it is a fundamental process of encoding our speech. For the very reason that it is a radical linguistic procedure it can appear in all sorts of different works . . .'

31. Fletcher, op. cit., p. 135.

32. Augustine, *De utilitate credendi,* ed. J. Zycha, 1, 70.

33. Augustine, *De vera religione,* ed. W. M. Green, pp. 7 f.

34. Gregory, *Moralia, PL* 75, 513:

> Sciendum vero est, quod quædam historica expositione transcurrimus, et per allegoriam quædam typical investigatione perscrutamur; quædam per sola allegoricæ moralitatis instrumenta discutimus; non nulla autem per cuncta simul sollicitus exquirentes, tripliciter indagamus.

> It is to be recognized that we hasten over some things in a historical exposition and we scrutinize some by the use of allegory in search of typological significance; some we discuss only as instruments of moral allegory; on the other hand, some we explore in three ways, carefully looking for all these senses together.

35. Bede, *Homeliæ, CCSL* 72, passim.

36. ibid., *Liber Primus, Homelia* 14, pp. 95-104. There is further complexity in the homily in that each of the O.T. stories represents one of the Ages of the World. The homilies also include a good deal of incidental symbolism. One example contrasts dove and raven, which could conceivably shed light upon the raven who wakes the men of Heorot:

> Habent autem oscula et corvi, sed laniant, quod columba omnino non facit: significantes eos *qui loquuntur pacem cum proximo suo, mali autem sunt in cordibus eorum.* Ravens too have kisses, but they tear with them, which the dove never does, signifying those *who speak peace with their neighbour but evil thoughts are in their hearts.* (*Hom.* 1, 15, p. 107). One remembers the hints of hidden hostility in lines 1164 and 1015 ff. of the poem.

37. For a clear explanation of the theory of *figura,* see E. Auerbach, *Mimesis,* trans. W. R. Trask (Princeton, 1953), pp. 73-5.

38. Auerbach, op. cit., sees 'figural thinking' in Dante's view of the universal Roman monarchy as the earthly anticipation of the Kingdom of God. 'An event taken as a figure preserves its literal and historical meaning' (p. 196). As I have sai elsewhere (*Neophil.* 1964, p. 67) an Augustinian view of history perhaps underlies the symbolic treatment of events in *Beowulf.* But it is difficult to believe that an Anglo-Saxon poet saw the wars of the Swedes and Geats as part of the divine plan of salvation, or that he disregarded the fact that Beowulf lived after the Incarnation, from which the *figuræ Christi* take their meaning.

39. For further discussion of this matter, see pp. 241 ff., below.

40. Sulpicius Serverus, *Opera,* ed. cit., pp. 1-105.

41. Rosemond Tuve, *Allegorical Imagery,* pp. 32-3. Professor Tuve makes a clear distinction between a moralization and an allegory in discussing late medieval and Renaissance texts. I do not think such a distinction is valid for Old English poetry, and I have not used 'allegory' in Tuve's more precise sense, follow-

ing her own principle: 'It is as well to repeat periodically that we do not seek to define allegory as if it were some changeless essence, and then in turn use the definition to admit or shut out poems from the category. We seek something quite limited and historical—what was involved in reading allegorically to certain writers at a given time, and for reasons we can trace.' (ibid., p. 33).

42. C. S. Lewis, *The Allegory of Love: a study in medieval tradition,* pp. 84 f.

43. Alcuin's catalogue of authors in the library at York includes the name Fulgentius, but it is by no means certain that the mythographer was intended. For discussion of the extant works ascribed to Fulgentius and argument against identifying the mythographer and the Bishop of Ruspe, see M. L. W. Laistner, 'Fulgentius in the Carolingian Age', in *The Intellectual Heritage of the early Middle Ages,* ed. C. G. Starr (New York, 1957), pp. 202-15.

44. Fulgentius had related the three heads to three kinds of contention in the world (*Opera,* ed. R. Helm, Leipzig, 1898, pp. 20 and 98 f.); Bede interprets the Dog of Hell as *Avaritia,* and its three heads as the three kinds of concupiscence in 1 Jo. 2: 16. (*Ep. Ecg.,* Plummer 1, 422 f.).

45. cp. pp. 76 and 135, below.

46. See P. Courcelle, op. cit., for the patristic treatment of the scene.

47. *æneid* VI, 273-89.

48. M. W. Bloomfield, '*Beowulf* and Christian Allegory, An Interpretation', *Traditio* 7 (1949-51), 410-15. He suggests that Unferth = *Discordia,* as in Prudentius's *Psychomachia.* As Prudentius is thinking in terms of schism and heresy within the Church, the connection is not very likely.

49. Aldhelm, *De virginitate, MGH AA* xv, 452-471, lines 2446-2914; see also p. 135, below.

50. E. Curtius, *European Literature and the Latin Middle Ages,* p. 49.

51. Isidore, *Etymologiae,* ed. W. M. Lindsay; *De Poetis,* Book 8b, 7.

52. I do not of course imply that he was working with raw historical material; no doubt a good deal of transformation had been effected by the oral poets who transmitted the matter.

53. Tuve, op. cit., pp. 32 f. See my observations above, p. 74, n. 1, on her use of the word 'allegory'.

54. Tuve, ibid., p. 32.

55. ibid.

56. ibid., p. 17.

57. cp. *The Seafarer* (38) where the paradox is exploited by the poet. See also the discussion of the phrase by P. L. Henry in *The Early English and Celtic Lyric*

(Belfast, 1966), pp. 195 ff., following up a suggestion by Professor C. L. Wrenn.

58. Of the objects and persons mentioned, Grendel's greedy and grasping hand and Hrethel's symbol of prowess require no special comment; for Heremod, cp. pp. 184 ff., for Hama, p. 91, for Beowulf's weapons and armour, pp. 86 f.; Scyld's funeral boat is treated here.

59. I use the word *mythic* here in the sense 'pertaining to an anonymous story telling of origins and destinies'; cp. R. Wellek and A. Warren, *Theory of Literature,* 3rd ed. (Peregrine Books, 1963), p. 191. Under this definition both Scyld and Cain are mythic symbolic persons.

60. *In geardagum* (1) is to be noted, as clearly placing the story in remote time.

61. For Latin equivalents to the OE names for God, see F. Klaeber 'Die Christlichen Elemente im *Beowulf*'. He draws upon the liturgy and Latin hymnaries and the earlier work of J. W. Rankin, 'A Study of the Kennings in Anglo-Saxon poetry'.

62. Rankin, op. cit. notes the parallel development of Latin *gloria* in Christian use.

63. The prayer quoted is among *Orationes tempore belli* in *The Gelasian Sacramentary* (ed. H. A. Wilson, London, 1893, pp. 275 f.). It reads:

> *Deus, et temporalis vitae auctor et aeternae, miserere supplicium in tua protectione fidentium, ut per virtute brachii tui omnibus qui nobis adversantur revictis, nec in terrenis nec a caelestibus possimus excludi.*

> O God, author of life both temporal and eternal, have mercy upon the suffering of the faithful within thy protection, that we, having conquered through the strength of thine arm all who oppose us, may not be hindered in things earthly nor from things heavenly.

It is not possible to establish whether this particular prayer was in use where the *Beowulf* poet was educated, but rather similar prayers also occur in *The Gregorian Sacramentary* revised by Alcuin (ed. H. A. Wilson, London, 1915). In both prayer-books the enemy attacks are attributed to the sins of the nation. (e.g. *Gelasian,* p. 273, *Gregorian,* pp. 198 f.) For the circulation of these two prayer-books, see Deanesly, *Pre-Conquest Church,* pp. 156-9. My point is that such prayers represent a current attitude towards God's giving or withholding success in war which is relevant to the whole of *Beowulf.*

64. E. G. Stanley, in 'OE poetic diction and the interpretation of *The Wanderer, The Seafarer,* and *The Penitent's Prayer*', *Angl.* 73 (1955) 441, suggests that *isig* (*Beow.* 33) is the equivalent of *winterceald,* figuratively evocative of sorrow. However, there seems no good reason also to reject the literal 'icy', since the season of Scyld's death is not otherwise men-

tioned, and the beginning of spring with its breaking-up of the ice would fit the circumstances.

65. Gilbert Cope, *Symbolism in the Bible and the Church,* p. 36.

66. The word *wær* is used of God's covenant with Abraham in the OE *Genesis* (2204); apart from its general sense of 'protection' here it may therefore have associations suggesting a pre-Christian man's relationship with God.

67. Wind and weather likewise mirror the feelings of men, as for example in the struggle with the sea (545-8) followed by the peace and brightness of morning (569-72); when Beowulf voyages, the wind is with him (217, 1907-9).

68. Wrenn calls attention to the bronze stag found in the Sutton Hoo deposit, apparently designed to be carried as a standard (*Beowulf,* p. 314). The use of *hornas* in *Finnsburh* (7) shows that a derived sense 'gable' had developed, but the name 'Heorot' would surely recall the older meaning of *horn.* The epithet *banfag* (780) also brings the stag to mind.

69. C. S. Lewis, *The Discarded Image,* p. 152.

70. See *The Fables of Phaedrus,* ed. C. H. Nall (London, 1895), pp. 7 f., *Cervus ad Fontem.*

71. As Augustine's examples showed, a biblical scholar had no difficulty in accepting contrary meanings for the same symbol in different contexts. D. W. Robertson finds in the hunted hart a symbol of the faithful soul which will not enter the waters of cupidity; for discussion of Robertson's argument, see pp. 120 f., below.

72. cp. The Judgment scene in *Christ* II, especially 811-14 (*ASPR* III, 25), also *Phoenix* 500-8 (ibid., p. 108).

73. A variant of the same image is used of the sea-beasts cheated of their supper and put to sleep by the sword in lines 562-7. (The *Andreas* poet also uses it of the dead cannibals (1002 f.), perhaps in imitation of *Beowulf.*)

74. In 'The Christian Perspective in *Beowulf*', *Brodeur Studies,* p. 85.

75. cp. Eph. 6: 16.

76. The swords of Eofor and Wiglaf are also described as *eotenisc* (2616, 2979), so the word obviously carried no necessary connotation of magical properties—for Eofor at least fought in ordinary human wars. Grendel had put a spell upon swords (804), but he uses no magical arts against Beowulf, so he is hardly more of a magician than the ancient princes who wove a spell about the hoard (3051 ff. and 3069 ff.). That Anglo-Saxons of the period believed in the power of incantations may be inferred from the Act of the synod of *Clofesho* (747) which commands the bishop to travel about his diocese forbidding pagan observances, including incantations. (cited by Whitelock, *Audience,* p. 79.)

77. The significance of the light in the allegory is further discussed in Chapter 8.

78. See, for example, line 80 f. and cp. 20 f.

79. The whole passage from line 1020 to 1055 describes the rewards given to Beowulf and his men.

80. It is likely that some of the poet's audience would sympathize with the plundering. Guthlac's early life was spent in such enterprises, and his biographer Felix shows no disapproval (since he gave back a third part of his booty), *Vita Guthlaci,* ed. cit., p. 80. The author of *Guthlac* A, on the other hand, describes how the saint's evil angel incites him to join a raiding band,

> swa doð wræcmæcgas
> þa þe ne bimurnað monnes feore
> þæs þe him to honda huþe gelæded
> butan hy þy reafe rædan motan.
>
> (129-32)

It was presumably one of the tasks of the early Anglo-Saxon church to dissuade young princes from taking up a life of pillage.

81. For a general survey of the references to Hama in early literature, see R. W. Chambers, *Widsith* (Cambridge, 1912), pp. 52-7. The sources seem to be agreed that Hama lived by plunder and that he acquired treasure; in *Widsith* he rules with Wudga over a people (129-30), which may suggest, as Chambers thinks (p. 223), that 'the bright city' of *Beowulf* (1199) was his own stronghold.

82. The phrase is discussed with similar phrases in Chapter 5, pp. 167 ff., below.

83. For a convenient survey of articles on the Sutton Hoo Ship-Burial, see the Supplement by C. L. Wrenn to R. W. Chambers, *Beowulf: An Introduction,* 3rd edition.

84. See p. 2, above.

85. G. V. Smithers, *The Making of Beowulf,* p. 11; see also p. 103, below.

86. Athanasius, *Vita S. Antonii, PG* 26, 862.

Abbreviations

The following shortened forms of titles of books, periodicals, etc. are used throughout the footnotes and the practice of the notes generally is to omit details of publication if the work cited is listed in the Select Bibliography.

ASPR: Anglo-Saxon Poetic Records Series

ASS: Acta Sanctorum Bollandiana

(Bede) *HE: Historia ecclesiastica gentis Anglorum*

(Bede) *Ep. Ecg.: Epistola Bedae ad Ecgbertum Episcopum*

Beiträge: Beiträge zur Geschichte der Deutschen Sprache und Literatur

Brodeur, *Art:* A. G. Brodeur, *The Art of Beowulf*

Brodeur *Studies: Studies in Old English Literature in honor of Arthur G. Brodeur*

CSEL: *Corpus Scriptorum Ecclesiasticorum Latinorum*

CL: *Comparative Literature*

CCSL: *Corpus Christianorum Series Latina*

Continuations: Continuations and Beginnings: Studies in Old English Literature, ed. E. G. Stanley

Deanesly, *Pre-Conquest Church:* Margaret Deanesly, *The Pre-Conquest Church in England*

Dobbie, *Beowulf:* E. v. K. Dobbie, ed. *Beowulf and Judith, ASPR* IV

Donahue, *Traditio,* 1949-51: Charles Donahue, 'Beowulf, Ireland and the Natural Good', *Traditio,* 7 (1949-51)

Donahue, *Traditio,* 1965: Charles Donahue, 'Beowulf and Christian Tradition: a reconsideration from a Celtic Stance', *Traditio,* 21 (1965)

Godfrey, *AS Church:* J. Godfrey, *The Church in Anglo-Saxon England*

Gregory, *Moralia: Sancti Gregorii Magni Moralium Libri, sive Expositio in Librum B. Job*

Kenney, *Sources:* J. F. Kenney, *The Sources for the Early History of Ireland,* vol. 1, *Ecclesiastical*

Klaeber, *Angl.* 1912: F. Klaeber, 'Die Christlichen Elemente im *Beowulf*', *Anglia,* 35 and 36 (1912)

Klaeber, *Beowulf:* F. Klaeber, ed., *Beowulf and the Fight at Finnsburg*

Laistner, *Thought:* M. L. W. Laistner, *Thought and Letters in Western Europe, A.D. 500-900*

Magoun Studies: Medieval and Linguistic Studies in honor of Francis P. Magoun, Jr.

MGH: *Monumenta Germaniae Historica*

MGH AA: *Auctores Antiquissimi*

MGH Ep.: *Epistolae*

MGH Ep. Kar.: *Epistolae Karolini Aevi*

MGH Ep. Mer.: *Epistolae Merowingici et Karolini Aevi*

MGH Poet.: *Poetarum Latinorum Medii Aevi*

Ogilvy, *Anglo-Latin Writers:* J. D. A. Ogilvy, *Books known to Anglo-Latin Writers from Aldhelm to Alcuin*

PG: J. P. Migne, ed. *Patrologia Graeca*

PL: J. P. Migne, ed. *Patrologia Latina*

Rankin, *JEGP,* 1909: J. W. Rankin, 'A Study of the Kennings in Anglo-Saxon Poetry', *JEGP,* 8 (1909) and 9 (1910)

von Schaubert, *Beowulf:* Else von Schaubert, ed. *Heyne-Schückings Beowulf*

Sisam, *Structure:* Kenneth Sisam, *The Structure of Beowulf*

Sisam, *Studies:* Kenneth Sisam, *Studies in the History of Old English Literature*

Tolkien, *Monsters:* J. R. R. Tolkien, *Beowulf: The Monsters and the Critics*

Whitelock, *Audience:* Dorothy Whitelock, *The Audience of Beowulf*

Wrenn, *Beowulf:* C. L. Wrenn, ed. *Beowulf*

Wrenn, *OE Literature:* C. L. Wrenn, *A Study of Old English Literature*

Gwyn Jones (essay date 1972)

SOURCE: "Hero with Monsters," in *Kings, Beasts, and Heroes,* Oxford University Press, 1972, pp. 3-26.

[*In the essay below, Jones investigates the folklore motifs which support the epical and heroic nature of* Beowulf.]

The old english poem **Beowulf** is one of the most precious relics of the early literature of England, and justly prized for a number and variety of reasons. For a start it is unique, in that no other poem of its size and kind has survived either in Old English or in the other Germanic literary languages to which English is related. Had it somewhere in its manuscript history succumbed to those perils of age, neglect, and fire to which we know it has been exposed, we should be left to speculate whether in fact the poets of any branch of the Germanic people were capable of composing a long sustained poem on a theme drawn from the world of pre-Christian Germanic tradition. In the light of such phenomena as the Sigurd lays of the Poetic Edda, the Latin *Waltharius,* the upturned horn of story which is Saxo's Danish History, and the Christian witness of the Old English *Andreas,* we might assume that they were, yet always be uneasy in the assumption. So the manuscript in which **Beowulf** is preserved, British Museum, Cotton Vitellius A 15, is a primary document not only for the English, but for the Germans, the Scandinavians, and their descendants in the New World as in the Old, with its proof that their ancestors had mastered the art of prolonged verse narrative and attempted that elevated mode of poetry which for the moment we may be content to describe as epic.

Moreover, this is a poem with claims on our regard far beyond its power of manuscript survival. It is most easily described as a poem of an epical and heroic nature, and in respect of its incident and action provides a notable synthesis of Germanic heroic legend and international wondertale as this latter was viewed in a Germanic context. Some have read it as pagan myth, others as Christian allegory, while some consider that its story remembers myth though its poet did not. Though not a true history, it touches closely on the matter of history, the triumphs and tribulations of kings, the winning of wars and loss of a kingdom, and has been pressed into service as a 'Gesta Danorum, Sveorum, Gothorumque', for the first half of the sixth century. Structurally, to a modern eye, it is less than perfect; even so its story of a young hero is compelling, of an old hero moving. It offers a noble picture of an age, its assumptions and behaviour, its hierarchical bases, and the gold-decked splendour of its warrior class. It conducts its protagonist through diverse settings and episodes, by land and sea, at court and in battle, in contests with monsters and courtesies with his peers. And our poet has time for much more than adventures and monster-riddings. He was conscious, like other Anglo-Saxon poets, of the world's lack of duration. Life, he knows, is fleeting; all things are hastening to their end. Warrior and corslet crumble side by side, fair maiden moulders in her fair array; the steed that paws the stronghold yard, the falcon winging through the hall, must falter and fall; rust frets and earth devours the toil of giants and works of wondrous smiths. Also, he was deeply concerned with values: the bonds that prevented society flying apart, heroic conventions, the claims of piety, a warrior's worth and woman's excellence, the qualities of good kingship, the means to fame. In the aged Hrothgar's words to Beowulf, we like the poem's hero are bidden: 'Know what manly virtue is.' In short, *Beowulf* is a poem of multiple source and episode, which combines the attractions of a brave tale with high moral seriousness, and offers a reading of life and experience. And finally, it is by any standards a good, even a fine poem; and there have been many to think it a great one—less for its movement and action, or fable, than because they find it a statement about human life and values by an artist who—by virtue of his technical ability, his command of words and metre, his power to present narrative, argument, reflection, mood, and feeling in verse—has given lasting significance to the thing he wrote, which is now the thing we read. Which means that *Beowulf* is worthy of our esteem for the reasons, no more, no less, for which we esteem all fine poetry.

We have by implication described *Beowulf* as a long sustained poem. To be precise, its length is 3,182 lines of Old English alliterative verse. There is so marked a break before line 2,200 that some scholars have thought that the concluding 983 lines, with their account of the Geat-Swedish wars, Beowulf's fight with a dragon, his death and funeral obsequies, were not part of the poet's original design, and either grew out of his ruminations during the writing of what we will call Part One, to which some such descriptive subtitle as 'Beowulf's Youthful Exploits' or 'Young Beowulf in Denmark' is commonly applied, or were added to Part One by a different poet. The first idea is possible but unprovable; the second appears altogether unlikely. Since we know nothing of the author as a person, and next to nothing of him as an author, and since we stand in ignorance of when and where and how and in what circumstance he composed his poem, we are of necessity confined to conjecture in respect of the poem's

structure, and in modesty bound to admit that even the best conjecture may be wide of the mark. What we do know is that *Beowulf* is preserved in a manuscript copied about the year 1000, and that from what we know of the history of Old English alliterative verse it could hardly have been composed before the very late seventh century. The likeliest speculations have been in favour of the age of Bede (*c.* 680-730) in Northumbria; the reign of king Offa (757-96) in Mercia; and—since the discovery in the Sutton Hoo ship burial or cenotaph in East Anglia of a rich range of Vendel-style artefacts, helmet, sword, standard, shield, gold ornaments, all strongly reminiscent of artefacts described in *Beowulf*—the reign of an East Anglian king in the late seventh or early eighth century. There is no way of settling between these three claims, and we are left to conclude that some time in or near the eighth century an unknown person to whom for convenience sake we accord the title of 'author', composed, or put together, or in some way set his seal on the poem we call *Beowulf,* and that this poem was to all intents and purposes the one copied down in Cotton Vitellius A 15, alongside three pieces of Old English prose and a fragment of the poem known as *Judith.* Essentially, that is, we are considering the one and only surviving manuscript version of *Beowulf,* and this because no other course makes sense.[1]

If this by formal definition is what *Beowulf* is, we may now ask ourselves, What is it about? Or if that is a question which invites a too complex answer just now let us replace it with, What story does it tell? In essence, the following.

A young man in the kingdom of the Geats, Beowulf by name, learns that a famed but ageing king of the Danes, whose name is Hrothgar, is denied the use of his royal hall Heorot by a monstrous creature called Grendel. He goes to Heorot with some companions, and fatally injures Grendel when he next attacks the hall by night.

The following night the hall is attacked by a second monster, Grendel's Mother, while Beowulf is sleeping elsewhere. He pursues her to her lair, which is at the bottom of a mere, kills her, and cuts off the head of the first monster, whom he finds lying there dead. He receives a rich reward from Hrothgar, and returns to his own home in triumph.

In later days, when Beowulf has become king of the Geats and ruled them well for fifty years, their land is ravaged by a dragon. Beowulf kills this dragon with the help of a companion, but dies of his injuries.

The immediate virtue of a summary as spare and undeviating as this is that it shows how Beowulf's first two exploits are linked together, while the third is removed in time, place, and also in kind. The first two are found in lines 1-2199, the third in lines 2200-3182. For convenience sake we will identify them by the titles (unknown to the scribe) of 'Young Beowulf in Denmark' and 'Beowulf's Fight with the Dragon'.

As we have indicated, and will show in more detail later on, the basic story of Part One is enlarged, dignified, diversified, and often obscured by other story-material. For example, there is a pseudo-historical or, if the adjective is preferred, legendary preamble about the royal house of the Danes and the mysterious origin of the Scyldings. There is also a small amount of firm historical information about the Geats, their kings, and their warrings. There are several elaborately retailed scenes at the Danish court, in one of which Beowulf is verbally assailed by an enigmatic courtier named Unferth, and defends himself with a 'gab' or *gilp* about his skill and endurance as a swimmer and killer of sea-beasts, and in another of which the feasters in hall are regaled with the disaster-laden story of Finn the Frisian, Hnaef the Half-Dane, and the lady Hildeburh, wife of the one, sister of the other, and destined to forfeit them both, and her sons along with them. Elsewhere a minstrel tells of Sigemund son of Waels, Sigmund the Volsung, how he killed a dragon, so that he won fame and treasure, and of Heremod, a king among the Danes, how he was a burden to his people, so that they drove him away. There is a fairly determined retelling, in the guise of a foretelling, of the story of the Heathobard prince Ingeld's ill-fated marriage to Hrothgar's daughter Freawaru, and an interpolation even more intrusive when the poet elusively and puzzlingly tells of the vindictiveness of the lady Thryth (Modthrytho) and how she grew kinder after her marriage to king Offa. There is an old man's homily on the dangers of excessive pride addressed by Hrothgar to Beowulf, and warnings aplenty against faithlessness, impiety, cowardice, and greed. We are freely advised of the world's mutability and the transitoriness of all created things. But despite the interest and importance of all these matters, the basic story of **Beowulf,** Part One, is that set out above; and since Panzer's decisively documented but not overwarmly welcomed *Studien zum germanischen Sagengeschichte: I. Beowulf* appeared in 1910, we have been aware that its origins lie not in early Germanic heroic tradition, and certainly not in nature myths, but in the world of wondertale or popular story. And since the publication of Antti Aarne and Stith Thompson's *The Types of the Folktale,* 1928 and 1961, and Stith Thompson's *Motif-Index of Folk-Literature,* 1932-6 and 1955-8, we know from which airt and region of that world.

The essential primitive story-material of the first part of **Beowulf** is that comprised in the folktale-type listed by Aarne and Thompson as 'The Three Stolen Princesses'. The apparent unlikeliness of the connection in the light of the title alone is a tax we must pay on the two scholars' immense and beneficial ordering of what had earlier been seen as an almost ungraspable mass of oral and written popular story. Unfortunately for the student of **Beowulf** their essay in scientific classification led them to abandon the title 'The Bear's Son' (under which earlier scholars including Panzer and Chambers had grouped the cognate folktale material), so that in *The Types of the Folktale* the Bear's Son motifs must be sought under the main head of 'The Three Stolen Princesses', Type 301, and to a considerably lesser extent under 'Strong John', Type 650A. There

are interesting resemblances between the opening sections of these two, but unless in combination with the somewhat similar 301A (see A-T pp. 92-3) 'Strong John' does not include the hero's pursuit of a monster underground, his adventures there, and the circumstances attendant on his return to the upper world. That 'The Three Stolen Princesses' is an elaborate and complicated type of folktale, incorporating a great many motifs and episodes, and tolerating a considerable choice of alternatives by the story-teller without losing its story line, is immediately apparent when we read not only the analysis printed in *The Types of the Folktale* (2nd revision, Helsinki, 1961), but the motif-analysis supplied by Stith Thompson so as to display the 'anatomy of the tale'. These are transcribed in full so that what is taken over from story and motifs and what is omitted may be seen in perspective and proportion.

THE THREE STOLEN PRINCESSES.

I. *The Hero is of supernatural origin and strength: (a) son of a bear who has stolen his mother; (b) of a dwarf or robber from whom the boy rescues himself and his mother; (c) the son of a man and a she-bear or [d] cow; or (e) engendered by the eating of fruit, (f) by the wind or (g) from a burning piece of wood. (h) He grows supernaturally strong and is unruly.*

II. *The Descent. (a) With two extraordinary companions (b) he comes to a house in the woods,* or (b¹) a bridge; *the monster who owns it punishes the companions but is defeated by the hero, (c)* who is let down through a well into a lower world.—Alternative beginning of the tale: (d) *The third prince, where his elder brothers have failed, (e) overcomes at night the monster who steals from the king's apple-tree, and (f) follows him through a hole into the lower world.*

III. *Stolen Maidens.* (a) Three princesses are stolen by a monster. (b) The hero goes to rescue them.

IV. *Rescue. (a) In the lower world, with a sword which he finds there, he conquers several monsters and rescues three maidens. (b) The maidens are pulled up by the hero's companions and stolen.*

V. *Betrayal of Hero. (a) He himself is left below by his treacherous companions, but he reaches the upper world* through the help of (b) a spirit whose ear he bites to get magic power to fly or (c) a bird, (d) to whom he feeds his own flesh; or (e) he is pulled up.

VI. *Recognition.* He is recognized by the princesses when he arrives on the wedding day. (b) He is in disguise and (c) sends his dogs to steal from the wedding feast; or (d) he presents rings, (e) clothing, or (f) other tokens, secures the punishment of the impostors and marries one of the princesses.[2]

However, in thus digging for the deepest roots of Beowulf's story it is important not to fall into ancient error or new superstition. Demonstrably **Beowulf** is *not* 'The Three Stolen Princesses' retold in Old English verse. There are no stolen princesses, as in section III, so none can be rescued and wed; much of section V and practically all of section VI is consequently missing; and in section II we must manage without an apple-tree. This need not discomfit us: our concern is with those elements of the story which entered *Beowulf,* not those that fell by the story-teller's wayside. More than 600 versions or variants of 'The Three Stolen Princesses' have been recorded, a small proportion of them as void of princesses as *Beowulf,* and others where it is not the king's apple-tree but his palace which is prey to a monster who is injured and pursued by the hero. 'The Three Stolen Princesses' is itself an enor-mously variable complex of story-telling, and in addition it is far from being the complete story material of our poem. If then we now attempt a further summary of the first part of *Beowulf,* it is not in order to restore the rightly discarded view of earlier critics that the poem is a 'wild folktale' (which emphatically it is not), but to show how much of its subject matter, and how much of what is dis-tinctive in the story it tells, must be related to a well-known, widespread, and many times reshaped and retold popular wondertale, and that unless we allow for this we shall not always know why our poet is doing what he is, nor fairly assess how well he is doing it. With an eye to the Aarne-Thompson analysis of 'The Three Stolen Princesses', we may now expand our earlier summary of Part One thus:

A hero of noble origin and superhuman strength, with the name of a bear (if, as appears likely, Beowulf = *Beo-wulf,* the Wolf or Foe of Bees, i.e. the Bear), the attributes of a bear, and the troublesome boyhood typical of the Bear's Son, goes with his companions to cleanse a king's hall which is under night-attack by a monster. The monster kills one of the hero's companions, but the hero fatally in-jures him by tearing off his arm. In the morning a band of warriors follow his bloody tracks to a mere whose waters they see are stained with his life's blood. They return home rejoicing.

That night, while the hero is sleeping elsewhere, a second monster attacks the hall, and a second time a companion is slain. With a number of companions the hero pursues the new monster's tracks to a mere whose waters are stained with blood, and in an underground hall, with a sword which he finds there, he overcomes a she-monster and cuts off the head of the male monster he had fatally injured be-fore. Some of his companions do not wait for his return; without good reason they leave the scene; but he gets safely up again with a precious swordhilt and the male monster's severed head. He receives his promised reward and returns to his own home in triumph.

But a tale's strength is in its telling, and its success regis-ters not by summary but in the heart of a hearer. At this point we need to know something of how well and by what means the *Beowulf* poet has managed his story so far.

The poem's opening is formal and stately. We shall not meet our hero for a while, and even our first monster must stand expectant in the wings. For the beginning of the poem is antecedent to the beginning of its story. We have a prologue to traverse, whose concern is with Scyld, the legendary founder of the Danish Scylding (that is, Skjöldung) dynasty, who came from over the water a help-less child, to wax and thrive and cheer a troubled people, and at his life's end returned to the unknown source of his being. The relevance of this prologue to the rest of the poem has been contested: some see in its account of the funeral of an aged and beloved king a sad and distanced foreshowing of the funeral of another aged and beloved king at the poem's end; but this assumes a long memory, and most readers, one imagines, enjoy it separately and for its own sake, as a notable set-piece in the epic tradition, lofty in tone, elegiac in quality, and burthened with its proper mystery.

> Then Scyld departed at the appointed hour, a great and mighty prince, to fare into the Lord's keeping. His be-loved comrades carried him to the seaflood, as he had himself requested when the Scyldings' friend still ruled with his word. A well-loved leader of his country, he had held power for a long time. A ship waited there at the landing-place, icy and eager to be away, the king's own vessel, and they laid down their treasure-giver in her bosom, their glorious lord by the mast. There was many a treasure there, ornaments fetched from afar. I have never heard of a ship more handsomely decked with weapons of war and armour, swords and corslets. A multitude of precious things lay on his breast, which must make a far journey with him into the sea's do-minion. For indeed they did not furnish him with lesser gifts and national treasures than those others did who sent him forth in the beginning over the sea alone, when he was still a child. Further, they set a golden standard high above his head, let the sea take him, gave him to the ocean. Their hearts were sad within them, their minds laden with grief. None can tell for sure, counsellors in hall or heroes under heaven, who received that freight

(26-52).

If Prologue there must be (and ours is the first age of read-ers to be dubious of such courtesies) this can hardly be bettered; and once it is over we soon reach the three requi-sites of the basic wondertale of the first part of *Beowulf:* a royal hall, a monster who plagues it, and a hero who ar-rives to cleanse it. It was a hall built for magnificence and joy, the bestowal of gifts and drinking of wine, the sound of the harp and the minstrel's clear song. The monster was a creature of darkness, exiled from happiness and accursed of God, the destroyer and devourer of our human kind. Like the Norse *draugr* or animated corpse, he is in human form but devoid of humanity, though his size, shape, ap-pearance, are what we make of them. Some *draugar* have a horrible smell, are rough-coated, or catlike, prodigal of blood and vomit; but of Grendel we are informed only that a horrid light most like to flame shone from his eyes, that it would require four strong men to carry his severed head, that the fingers of his torn-off arm were shod with long nails hard as steel—and that steel would not bite on him. When he first raids Hrothgar's hall, the antlered Heorot (Hart), he kills or carries off thirty fighting-men and eats them in his lair. Later we are told how he carried a glove or pouch at his belt to hold the victims. The hero who destroys him is a gallant young prince from far off, with thirty men's strength in his handgrip, and furbished in mind as in body for the task he undertakes. His very chivalry and pride, excessive as Byrhtnoth's at Maldon, serve their wondertale purpose, for he dispenses with sword and shield against an enemy who bears neither, and engages with him on his own terms, hand to hand—the only terms, as it happens, on which success may be won.

> Then came Grendel stalking off the moor under the misty hill-slopes; he bore God's anger. . . . He came on under the clouds until he clearly recognized the wine-chamber, the gold-hall of men, shining with beaten gold. . . . The warlike creature, bereft of joy, came journeying to the hall. Though secured with forged bands the door sprang wide on the instant, as soon as he touched it with his hands. With havoc in mind, all swollen with rage, he dashed open the hall-entrance.

> Swiftly then the fiend stepped on to the coloured floor, moved forward in anger. A horrid light shone from his eyes, most like to fire. Inside the hall he saw many warriors, a band of kinsmen sleeping all together, a brotherhood of fighting-men. His heart laughed within him; the loathsome creature planned before day came to part each one of them life from limb, now that he could hope to eat his fill.

> But it was no longer his fate that he should devour more of mankind after that night. Hygelac's mighty kinsman was watching how this foul adversary would set about his brusque assault. The monster had no mind to delay, but promptly seized one sleeping man for a start, tore him unhindered, bit into his flesh, drank blood from his veins, swallowed him mouthful by mouthful, and had soon devoured the entire corpse, feet, hands, and all. He advanced still nearer, reached with his hands for the brave-hearted man where he lay, the fiend stretched out his claws towards him. Beowulf gave him a brisk and hostile welcome, propped himself on his arm. That pastmaster of wickedness soon realized that never in all this world, in any corner of earth, had he met with a stronger grip from any other man. He felt fear in head and heart, but might escape none the sooner for that. He longed to be gone, make tracks for his hiding-place, seek the noisy swarming-place of devils. His situation here was something he had never met with before in all the days of his life. And now Hygelac's brave kinsman remembered his evening's talk; he drew himself upright, and embraced him hard. His fingers burst: the giant was striving to get out, the hero pressed forward. If only he might, the infamous creature wanted to get farther into the open and flee to his fen-refuge. He knew that the power of his fingers was in the grip of a fierce foeman. It was a sorry journey that pernicious foe made to Heorot . . .

> . . . A din arose, and was ever renewed. Terrible fear filled the North-Danes, every man of them that heard the wailing from the wall, God's adversary yelling his frightful lay, his song void of victory, hell's captive lamenting his hurt. He had him firmly in hand who was strongest in might of all men in that day and age. . . . His parting from life in this world and time was to be wretched; the alien spirit must travel a far way into the power of fiends. For now God's adversary, who before

with joyful heart wrought so much violence on mankind, discovered that his bodily frame could not help him, but that Hygelac's brave thane had him in hand. So long as life was in him each was hateful to the other. The horrid creature suffered a hurt in his body; a widening wound grew visible at his shoulder; the sinews sprang apart, the tendons burst. Glory in battle was ordained for Beowulf. Grendel, hurt to death, must take flight away from there into the fen-refuges, seek his joyless dwelling. He knew only too well that he had reached the end of his life, his count of days

(710-823).

The poet shows the same intense and steady purpose in his tale of Grendel's Mother, when after the joy and feasting that celebrated her son's death she arrived at Heorot, rescued the bloody trophy of Beowulf's success, killed a retainer where he lay sleeping, and left his severed head on the sea-cliff near her underwater home. Much care is given both to the scene and fashion of Beowulf's second exploit: the stony approach with its tall crags and narrow paths; the gloomy mere described in advance by king Hrothgar (see p. 57 below); the water burdened with sea-dragons and the shore from which beasts and monsters plunged sullenly away from the warhorn's challenge. Likewise Beowulf's preparations: his woven mailshirt, shining helm and glittering sword; his lordly speech commending his men and treasure to Hrothgar's care, his warblade to its owner should death be his lot; his vow to win fame or perish in pursuit of it. Then, his preparations made and farewells taken, he dives down through the water for a long while of day. As soon as he reaches the bottom he is grappled with by its repulsive tenant. She fails to hurt his body with her sharp fingers, as do the seamonsters with their tusks as she drags him to her dwelling. There, free from the flood as in a water-spider's bubble, he finds that his sword, brave blade that it is, will not bite on her; they wrestle and he flings her to the ground, but her strength is too great, he takes a fall, she throws herself upon him and seeks his vitals with her stabbing knife. In vain—God and his corslet protect him, he gets back on his feet, and sees then 'amid the armour a blade blessed with victory, an old sword made by etins, doughty of edge, the glory of warriors; it was the choicest of weapons, save that it was bigger than any other man could carry into battle, good and splendid, the work of giants.' With this he struck her so fiercely on the neck that her bones broke and the huge blade sheared through her body. A light shone forth, and by it he saw where Grendel lay dead, so struck off his head.

Meanwhile the Danes on the cliff above, observing the waters stained with blood, despaired of his life and rode sorrowfully for home. The Geats, sick at heart, stayed on, expectant of woe. Far below Beowulf observed a great marvel. The swordblade with which he had destroyed his foes began to melt away 'in battle icicles', long drips of gore, till only the ornamented hilt was left. It was with this and Grendel's head that he swam back up to daylight and met his rejoicing comrades.

The wondertale central to the first part of **Beowulf,** we have said, is that of the hero who rids the king's hall of the monster that plagues it, pursues it into some kind of lower world, and there is involved with another monster or monsters. The wondertale central to the second part of **Beowulf** is that of the dragon-killer. For the bases of Part Two, 'Beowulf's Fight with the Dragon', no extensive documentation is necessary. That a man fights a dragon is a commonplace of story, and appears in medieval literature as myth, folktale, heroic legend, saint's life, onomastic anecdote, romance, and quasi-history. So many heroes over so many centuries killed so many dragons, from Frotho and Fridlevus to Ragnarr Hairybreeks, and from Sigurd to St George, that the presence of one, or even two, dragons in a poem inclined to monsters excites no surprise. In general the dragon of north Germanic story is a creature of such ill presage, so steeped in evil, hell-bent on mayhem, and deeply involved with a treasure of gold, that on any one of these counts, much less all three, it must prove an adversary worthy of Sigemund early in the poem and of Beowulf nearer its close. It was a boast of king Volsung as of Hrolf Kraki, of Bothvar Bjarki as of Starkad the Old, that they never fled from fire or iron, and the flaming spew of a fire-drake was fire at its most legendary and horrendous. Our poet might have found a fitter and more consummatory foe for Beowulf's last adventure, because more famous, baleful, or legend-fraught, but it is hard to think of one. Bear, boar, *draugr,* a Swedish dreng or Frankish kemper, would all appear less primal and less awful. A man is a man, and a beast is a beast, but a dragon is a dragon is a dragon.

Is, not necessarily *was.* A number of scholars are coming to believe that Beowulf's three folktale exploits are in their nature closely connected: not two plus one, but an integrated three, either bound together by their not infrequent attribution to this or that member of a monster-slaying family; or by the recurrence in northern sources of apparent trinities of man-monster, woman-monster, and dragon-monster in human or animal shape; or by the identification of dragon with *draugr* (plural *draugar,* the animated dead), so that Beowulf's fight with the dragon is merely a variant on his fight with that other *draugr* Grendel and his Mother.[3] Some of this could be true, and more of it can be argued at length, with analogues, parallels, and a little pleading to help. That a number of Norse stories reveal affinities and relationships between *draugr,* dragon, and a woman-troll is demonstrable, and as more and more stories are read with this in mind the demonstration will strengthen. Equally there is no doubt that Beowulf's closest parallels in Germanic wondertale fought with adversaries showing a family likeness to Beowulf's best known foes. Bothvar Bjarki, declaredly a Bear's Son, fought with the living dead (maybe with one, the enigmatic Agnarr, certainly with an army of them at Lejre); with a winged monster at a foreign king's court (which he kills); and at a pinch he may be considered to have fought with a woman troll, Skuld, who at a further pinch may be considered to have killed *him*—matters dealt with in the third part of this book. Grettir, the hero of the fourteenth-century Ice-

landic *Grettis Saga Ásmundarsonar,* fought with *draugar* twice and with a trollwoman; he also went down into a cave under a waterfall and was betrayed by a helping companion whose task it was to safeguard the rope which should bring him back up again. The correspondences between those parts of **Beowulf** which tell of Beowulf's fight with Grendel and Grendel's Mother at Heorot in Denmark, and those parts of *Grettis Saga* which tell of Grettir's fight with Glam in Forsæludal and with the trollwife at Eyjardalsá in Bardardal in Iceland, are impressively close and universally acknowledged, and a further substantial body of analogues has been discovered in medieval saga and romance.[4] For example, *Bósa Saga ok Herrauds, Hálfdans Saga Eysteinssonar, Harðar Saga ok Hólmverjar, Gullþóris Saga, Orms þáttr Stórólfssonar,* and *Samsons Saga Fagra* in the North, and the romance *Wigalois* farther south, all supply parallels sometimes close, sometimes not. Expectedly, when we are dealing with a widespread and enduring wondertale, partial reminiscence and residual detail will be found frequently and in many places.

But to stay with **Beowulf:** its author was seized of a body of wondertale (some of its features likewise observable in myth) whose shape and features and general development in a Germanic context we readily discern, and craftsman that he was he made good use of this to help produce the poem which is his masterpiece. That is, he committed himself to a hero who as a young man achieved two related monster-killings at the court of a foreign king, and as an old man achieved a monster-killing in his own and native land. This last achievement brought about his own death. His foe was a dragon, and that this *draca* had physical affinities with *draugr* or *ketta* is not indicated.[5] Admittedly one would be troubled to draw the dragon in any detail,[6] but as much can be said of Grendel and Grendel's Mother. For a man who cannot have seen an original our poet does very well indeed. And the hero-monster confrontation is perfect. The dragon was in his right place, fulfilling his proper function (*Draca sceal on hlwe, frod, frtum wlanc:* 'A dragon shall live in a mound, old and proud of his ornaments'). So too was Beowulf, the people's guardian. That such dread veterans of the wars prove fatal to each other was a thing foredoomed, and the deaths of man and creature conclude a heroic story with heroic propriety.[7]

The fight and its preliminaries, as is usual with our poet, are formally deployed and heavily embellished. There is a deal of historical reference to hostilities between Geats and Swedes, Geats and Franks, whose significance is touched on below (see p. 33ff.); the deeply-troubled king discourses with an old man's wisdom of past events, present intentions, and future prospects; at a fitting time he delivers his *gilp,* his vaunting speech, as a hero should; we hear much of the dragon's treasure-hoard, its origins in sorrow and its enduring uselessness to men; and the Geat comitatus, that band of the king's chosen comrades who should rightly have died for him, is brought grievously to prominence by its cowardice and disloyalty. Conversely we watch a young hero, Beowulf's successor to the gift-stool of the Geats, bearing himself as a brave man should. The fight itself is soon over. With a huge iron shield made specially for the occasion the still mighty king, swelling with rage, shouts his challenge to the dragon inside his mound; the foe, three hundred years gold's guardian, quickly emerges, and the fight takes place in three desperate rounds. In the first Beowulf is forced to give ground; in the second he is so obviously getting the worse of it that his retainers flee to the shelter of a wood, and only Wiglaf hurries down to help his hard-pressed lord. In the third his sword snaps, the dragon bites him mortally in the neck, but Wiglaf pierces the dragon's unarmoured underbelly, and with the last of his strength the old man draws his sax and severs him at the middle. This is a handsome apportioning of glory for veteran and bachelor, nor is the firedrake without lurid splendour in life and a stricken majesty in death.

> Beowulf's slayer lay there too, the dread earth-dragon, emptied of life and whelmed in ruin. No longer might the coiled serpent reign over his hoard of treasure, but the edges of swords, hard, battle-notched, offspring of hammers, had demolished him, so that the far-flier sank to the ground near his treasure hall, stilled by his wounds. Not now did he wheel sporting in air at midnight, reveal his face exulting in riches, but he fell to earth through the might of the war-leader's hand
>
> (2824-35).

If we were now to summarize the story and substance of *Beowulf* along lines different from those of wondertale and Germanic heroic legend, and show that its bases and controls lay elsewhere, in myth (a task many times embarked on with results between the unlikely and the impossible),[8] or in northern history (a venture notoriously self-defeating), we should at least answer the well-known stricture of some well-known critics that the *Beowulf* poet was so little the master of his material that he placed the irrelevancies (the monsters) at the poem's centre, and the serious things (the historical, pseudo-historical, and legendary elements) on its outer edges. The monsters are at the centre because the centre is their proper place. Granted that our author saw Beowulf as a king, and hero of a heroic poem, we cannot fail to see that behind this conventionally-accoutred figure falls the long shadow of the strong hero of folktale, wave-piercer, scourge of sea-beasts, cleanser of a house, grappler with a monstrous arm, finder of a wondrous sword, destroyer of giants and merewife, to say nothing of dragon-slayer later. It follows that we must accept *Beowulf* for what it is, and judge it by the canons of criticism appropriate to it. Had its author proposed to write an epic after the fashion of Homer, to withstand a summary after the fashion of Aristotle, he would have chosen a different hero, from a different milieu, and set him to different adventures. Had he proposed to recount a myth of a divine being performing cosmic tasks he would not have made his god into a man achieving non-cosmic adventures. Had he proposed to write a historical poem, and we accept under that head historical tradition and legendary history, he would not have given his poem up to fabulous monsters and the achievement of non-historical tasks.

That said, we repeat that it was not our author's intention to repeat a folktale in folktale manner. Not only is our ignorance complete as to what version or versions of the monster stories counted most with him, but we cannot be sure to what extent he recognized the monster stories as different in kind from legendary and historical tradition. However, unless we are to assume without a shred of evidence that some utterly vanished predecessor had already produced an utterly vanished version of the same story, and that our author merely retold it as he knew it—and a more arbitrary and unhelpful assumption could hardly be devised—unless we wander after will-o'-the wisps like this, it seems reasonable to conclude that he gratefully accepted the guiding lines of well-established folktales and the freedom to add non-folktale episodes and dissertations; established his story within the boundaries of a carefully portrayed heroic society, with the decisive changes of emphasis and tone sequent on such a transfer; for reasons we can guess at provided his hero with a geographical and historical setting; and gave story and hero a moral significance beyond the requirements or tolerance of folktale. So that if we at last proceed to summarize the poem as it presently exists we have the following:

I. LINES 1-2199. YOUNG BEOWULF IN DENMARK

The poem opens with the story of Scyld, the eponymous founder of the Danish Scylding dynasty, who came from over the sea a helpless child, and was returned to it after a glorious reign. His great-grandson king Hrothgar builds a mighty hall Heorot for magnificence and joy, but it is invaded by a monster in giant human form called Grendel, who kills no fewer than thirty men in each of his opening assaults, and by his continuing malignancy denies Hrothgar the use of his hall by night for twelve long years. Danish wisdom and valour alike avail nothing.

News of the king's affliction comes to the ears of Beowulf, the nephew of Hygelac, king of the Geats, and with the approval of his peers he makes a sea-journey to Heorot with fourteen chosen companions. Beowulf has, we are told, the strength of thirty men in his handgrip. In Denmark he declares his purpose, and is given an honourable welcome, excpet that during the feast that follows a Danish courtier named Unferth calls his skill and valour in question. By way of reply Beowulf tells how he outswam Breca in a seven-day swimming contest and slew nine monsters with his drawn sword. He vows that this time again he will conquer or die. And conquer by strength alone, without shield or sword.

As the shadows thicken the Danes retire from the hall, leaving its defence to Beowulf and his Geats. All save Beowulf fall asleep. He alone, when Grendel came stalking off the moors, sees him enter and devour a sleeping warrior.[9] He reaches for Beowulf, and they fight hand-to-hand until Beowulf tears the monster's arm off at the shoulder, and Grendel must flee, dying, to his fen-refuge. Men followed his tracks there the next morning, and as they returned the minstrel sang to them the contrasting tales of the hero Sigemund and his nephew Fitela and of the cruel and unhappy king Heremod. At Heorot all are joyful as they survey Beowulf's bloody trophy; there is oratory and feasting and a hero's reward for his deed. A minstrel tells the tragic tale of Finn. Queen Wealhtheow gives Beowulf precious gifts, including the torque which we are told king Hygelac the Geat would wear on his fatal expedition to Frisia. That evening the Danish chivalry re-occupies the hall.

Disastrously. This time Heorot is raided by Grendel's Mother, who in a night-scene of anguish and uproar carries off a Danish retainer and recovers her son's arm. Beowulf, who has been sleeping elsewhere, is summoned to the royal presence, heartens the Danes, and promises to track down the she-monster. He does so, accompanied by his Geats and a troop of Danes led by Hrothgar, and when they reach the blood-stained mere he plunges down alone to find her. He is attacked, but vainly, by sea-beasts as she grapples with him and drags him to her dwelling. The struggle in her underwater hall is hard and long; his sword, a choice weapon lent him by his earlier detractor Unferth, will not bite on her, and it is only when he has resort to a wondrous sword reposing in the lair itself that he prevails and kills her. He sees Grendel lying dead and cuts off his head. Meantime the discouraged Danes, seeing blood come up through the waters of the mere, take themselves off.[10] His own men stay on, sick at heart. He makes a safe return with Grendel's head and the hilt of the wondrous sword, whose blade had melted away after contact with Grendel's venomous blood, and they make their way to Heorot with these spoils. Hrothgar makes a long descant on mutability and moderation, and the next morning Beowulf receives his promised reward and takes his leave.

Down at the shore the Geats load their ship with horses, weapons, and treasures, hoist sail, and proceed to their own country, their king Hygelac, and his queen Hygd. The poet discourses of Thryth (Modthrytho), who appears to have been a perilous maiden before marriage and a gracious queen thereafter. Beowulf tells Hygelac about his adventures, and is led to speculate on what must be the ill consequences of a proposed dynastic marriage between Hrothgar's daughter Freawaru and Froda's son, the Heathobeard prince Ingeld. He then bestows on Hygelac and Hygd the gifts he had received from king Hrothgar and queen Wealhtheow. Despite the doubts suggested by his unprofitable youth (which we now hear mentioned for the first time) he has shown himself glorious, and Hygelac rewards him with his own father's sword, a vast estate, a hall, and a princely throne.

II. Lines 2200-3182. Beowulf's Fight with
the Dragon

After the death in battle of Hygelac and his son Heardred, Beowulf became king over the Geats and ruled them well for fifty years, till one of his subjects stole a precious cup from a dragon's treasure-hoard and the dragon visited his vengeance upon the country-side.

Old now, troubled in mind, yet valiant as ever, Beowulf determines to protect his people and meet the dragon in single combat. He has a shield of iron (it would require the strength of thirty men to manage it) made to this end, and while he awaits battle reviews past history: the slaughter of Hygelac and his Geats on a raid into Frisia, from which Beowulf alone escaped by a stupendous feat of swimming; the death of Heardred at the hands of the Swedes, and of king Haethcyn before him; the cruel mishaps which had brought Hygelac to the throne in the first place; Beowulf's role as Hygelac's champion; his clash with Grendel. He tells his eleven companions that this time too he will win fame or death.

He now challenges the dragon to come out and fight. It is a sore encounter. One only of his companions comes to his aid, young Wiglaf; despite his reminding them of the obligations owed to loyalty, gratitude, reputation, and love, the other ten flee into the forest. Beowulf and Wiglaf kill the dragon when he makes his third onset, but Beowulf is hurt to death. He has just time to see the dragon's treasure before he dies.

Wiglaf announces his death to the cowards and bitterly reproves them a second time. A messenger reminds the main body of the Geats of the ill-will existing between them and the Franks since Hygelac's time, and surveys the long history of the Geat-Swedish wars. Nothing but disaster lies ahead for the Geat people. At Wiglaf's command they prepare Beowulf's funeral pyre, celebrate his obsequies, and erect a mighty barrow over their well-loved king.

Notes

1. (*a*) 'With all this, however, the poem continues to possess at least an apparent and external unity. It is an extant book, whatever the history of its composition may have been; the book of the adventures of Beowulf, written out by two scribes in the tenth century; an epic poem, with a prologue at the beginning, and a judgement pronounced on the life of the hero at the end; a single book, considered as such by its transcribers and making a claim to be so considered' (W. P. Ker, *Epic and Romance*, p. 158).

   (*b*) 'I deal with the structure of the poem as it stands in MS. Vitellius A. xv, copied round about the year 1000, assuming that its text represents approximately the form given to the story by one man—original poet, or poet-editor, or accomplished reciter able to adapt and vary existing stories in verse' (K. Sisam, *The Structure of Beowulf*, p. 2).

2. The motifs are given with their reference to Stith Thompson, *Motif-Index of Folk-Literature*, 6 vols., Copenhagen and Bloomington, Indiana, 1955-8. The italics here as in the story-analysis above have been supplied by the present writer.

   I. *L114. Hero (heroine) of unpromising habits. F610. Remarkably strong man. B631. Human offspring from marriage to animal. B635.1. The Bear's Son. Human son of woman who marries a bear acquires bear characteristics.* F611.1.1. Strong man son of bear who has stolen his mother. F611.1.2. Strong man son of woman and dwarf. F611.1.5. Strong man son of man and she-bear. F611.1.6. Strong man son of man and mare. F611.1.8. Strong hero engendered by eating fruit. F611.1.9. Strong hero engendered by the wind. F611.1.10. Strong hero engendered from burning brand. F611.2.1. Strong hero suckled by animal. *T615. Supernatural growth. L114.3. Unruly hero.*

II. *F601. Extraordinary companions. A group of men with extraordinary powers travels together. G475.1. Ogre attacks intruders in house in woods. G475.2. Ogre attacks intruders on bridge. H1471. Watch for devastating monster. Youngest alone successful.* F451.5.2. Malevolent dwarf. *F102.1. Hero shoots monster (or animal) and follows it into lower world. N773. Adventure from following animal to cave (lower world). F92. Pit entrance to lower world. Entrance through pit, hole, spring or cavern. F96. Rope to lower world. F80. Journey to lower world.*

III. R11.1. Princess (maiden) abducted by monster (ogre). H1385.1. Quest for stolen princess.

IV. R111.2.1. Princess(es) rescued from lower world. *F601.3. Extraordinary companions betray hero.* K1935. Impostors steal rescued princess.

V. *K1931.2. Impostors abandon hero in lower world.* K677. Hero tests the rope on which he is to be pulled to upper world. K963. Rope cut and victim dropped. K1932. Impostors claim reward (prize) earned by hero. K1933. Impostor forces oath of secrecy. D2135.2. Magic air journey from biting ear. B542.1.1. Eagle carries men to safety. *F101.3. Return from lower world* on eagle. B322.1. Hero feeds own flesh to helpful animal. The hero is carried on the back of an eagle who demands food. The hero finally feeds part of his own flesh.

VI. K1816.0.3.1. Hero in menial disguise at heroine's wedding. T68.1. Princess offered as prize to rescuer. T161. Year's respite from unwelcome marriage. N681. Husband (lover) arrives home just as wife (mistress) is to marry another. H151.2. Attention drawn by helpful animal's theft of food from wedding table; recognition follows. *H83. Rescue tokens. Proof that hero has succeeded in rescue. H80. Identification by tokens.* H94. Identification by ring. H111. Identification by garment H113. Identification by handkerchief. Q262. Impostor punished. L161. Lowly hero marries princess.

3. J. Fontenrose, *Python, A Study of Delphic Myth and its Origins,* California, 1959, Appendix 5, 'The Combat in Germanic Myth and Legend', pp. 524-34, sees Grendel as 'the Thanatos of German pagans' and his Mother as 'the old Chaos-Hag almost intact'. He considers the second part of the poem to be in large measure a parallel of the first.

'The dragon need not detain us as long as Grendel did; for the tale runs parallel in many respects. Be-

owulf is now an aged man who dies in the moment of victory, protecting his own Geatish land this time against the destroyer. The *Beowulf* poet's purpose resembles that of the *Gilgamesh* poet: the mightiest hero cannot finally conquer death, but must in the end succumb to destiny. But the poet's creation belongs to literature; the tale that he used belongs to myth. Wiglaf, Beowulf's kinsman, the last of his house, who stood beside the hero in this combat, was truly victor in the fray; for he plunged his sword into the dragon's soft underbelly, delivering a mortal wound; then Beowulf, now near death from a poisoned wound, drew his knife and cut the monster in two. Beowulf, dying, gave his armor to Wiglaf as to a son; for he had no sons of his own. Therefore I place this combat under subtype II, wherein it is the slain god's son who fights and kills the monster.

'The dragon coincides fairly closely with the Grendel pair, and his tale with theirs, in the following respects. (1) He raided at night, spreading death and devastation far and wide among the Geats, and had to get back to his lair before dawn. (2) He lived in a dark cavern underground, beneath a burial mound on a rocky promontory beside the sea. (3) There he guarded an immense treasure. (4) He was huge of size, fifty feet long, and (5) he breathed forth blasts of flame. (6) Beowulf went to the barrow's rocky mouth to meet Firedrake, as we shall henceforth call him. (7) His companions fled, all except Wiglaf; much as years before his comrades at the mere's edge thought him dead and went back to Heorot. (8) Firedrake was fought and killed, and (9) his body was cut into two parts and cast into the sea. (10) The victor Wiglaf wielded a marvellous sword that giants had forged. Recalling the preceding discussion we can see some correspondence also in that (11) the victor succeeded to the throne, and (12) the Geats mourned the dead Beowulf.'

This seems to me unconvincing on two chief counts. First, Professor Fontenrose's demonstration of myth reads still more like a demonstration of wondertale and heroic legend. Second, the correspondences between the two stories are too general to be impressive. Nos. 2, 3, 4, 5, and 6 lack all urgency; nos. 8 and 12 would appear unavoidable in a story involving the deaths of two such protagonists; no. 7 I would relate to such heroic convention as we find in the *Battle of Maldon* rather than to folktale, much less myth; and no. 10 is a commonplace. This leaves no. 1, for which see the reference to the *Anglo-Saxon Chronicle* on p. 33 below; no. 9, whose second half is unremarkable; and no. 11, which requires special pleading.

Undoubtedly we need to widen our view of the structure of *Beowulf* if we accept that its two parts are variant expressions of the same myth. But I see no sign that such identification was ever in the poet's mind. For him Grendel and Grendel's Mother were one traditional set of supernatural adversaries, and the Dragon a different kettle of fish altogether.

4. For translations see in particular G. N. Garmonsway and Jacqueline Simpson, *Beowulf and its Analogues*, 1968. See too G. V. Smithers, *The Making of Beowulf*, 1961, and Nora K. Chadwick, 'The Monsters and Beowulf', in *The Anglo-Saxons*, edited by Peter Clemoes, 1959, pp. 171-203.

5. G. V. Smithers in *The Making of Beowulf* argues strongly on different grounds from Professor Fontenrose that the dragon is a variant of the *draugr* or 'creature who haunts a grave-mound after death', and that in story-terms he is to be identified with the 'last survivor' who laid up in a mound the treasure he would henceforth watch over in the shape of a dragon. But the poem distinguishes between these two absolutely:

> So the sad-hearted man proclaimed his sorrows, lone survivor of them all, and wandered joyless day and night till death's tide touched at his heart. The old foe of the half-light found the joyous hoard standing open, he who seeks out barrows all afire, flies by night a naked nithdrake wrapped in flame—dwellers round about fear him greatly. He must seek a treasure in the earth where ancient in years he watches over the heathen gold—and is none the better off for it.

(2267-77)

Professor Smithers accepts that 'To the author of *Beowulf* it was no longer clear that the dragon was identical with the "last survivor" and therefore had been a human being.' Either the poet misunderstood this part of his story material or it was already blurred for him. I would put it more strongly: in *Beowulf* the last survivor is the last survivor, the dragon is a dragon, and the poet sees neither as anything else at any time. For him the dragon is not a *draugr*, and the second part of his poem is not a variant on Part One.

I offer two (I fear) unfairly brief comments on Professor Smithers' remarks on the unity of the poem (p. 12). That *Beowulf* is 'genetically' a unity follows, I think, from the circumstance that one and the same hero undertakes wonder-tale ridding-tasks against supernatural adversaries, whether we consider Grendel, Grendel's Mother, and the Dragon as *draugar* or not. The poem can be an 'aesthetic' unity only in so far as its unity is aesthetic, that is, apparent in terms of its own art form, and this, I suspect, cannot be demonstrated by finding a significance in the second part of the poem of which its poet was unaware.

6. It is likely that the Germanic dragon owed something to the horse, and the representation of his head to a shrilling, grinning horsehead. His body seems to have been thought of as narrow and serpentlike. Our *Beowulf* dragon has been given one canine characteristic—the way in which from time to time he turns back into the barrow looking for his vanished trea-

sure just as a dog turns back from time to time to where he knows he left his vanished bone (2293-300).

7. This is one of several contexts where the inquirer will be both wiser and better-informed if he re-reads J. R. R. Tolkien's 'Beowulf: The Monsters and the Critics' (Sir Israel Gollancz Memorial Lecture, British Academy, 1936).

8. The most memorable lines of approach have been, I think, these:

(1) The Beow of the Anglo-Saxon genealogies, son of Scyld or Sceldwa and descendant of Sceaf (*beow*, grain, barley: *sceaf*, sheaf), was apparently a god of agriculture and fertility. The first Beowulf of our poem (18-57 only), son of Scyld, a descendant of Scef, and father of Healfdene, may be identified with Beow. The stories of this Beow-Beowulf's struggles with monsters are the myths proper to a god of agriculture and fertility, and have in a manner unknown, a place unmarked, and a time unrecorded, been transferred to Beowulf son of Ecgtheow, who may therefore be seen as a divine person established in myth.

(2) The same Beow conducts as before to Beow-Beowulf, and so to the hero of our poem who is to be seen as a divine protector of mankind from the destructive forces of nature. Grendel is the spoiling sea, or more specifically the in-rushing spring-tides of the North Sea or, more recently, the Baltic; his Mother is the sea's hostile depth; the Dragon represents the onset of fierce weather towards winter, inimical and deathly. Or the nature-myths may be of marsh, swamp and fen, or the terror-haunted darkness of the northern night, tamed or defeated by sky-god, sun-god, weather-god, or such other god as Beowulf can be identified with.

(3) As vegetation-god and sun-god grow victims of our modern contagion of disbelief and fade from field and sky, the esoteric interpreters of *Beowulf* have taken fresh heart and new bearings, this time in the fields of pagan (Germanic) or Christian mythology. The reference points are Heorot-Asgard-Eden; Grendel's kin-the Jotuns-Moral Evil; Beowulf-Thor-Christ; Dragon-Midgarthsormr-Satan; with such additions as are yielded by Herebeald-Balder, Hama and the Brosinga mene, and the like. For a precise allegorical Christian interpretation see the footnote on p. 40 below, and for a comment p. xxiii above and pp. 48-9 below.

(4) There remains the detailed summary of *Beowulf* Part One, and the equation of *Beowulf* Part Two with *Beowulf* Part One (see pp. 16-17 n. above), made by Fontenrose, who sees Beowulf's fights with Grendel and Grendel's Mother, and thereafter his fight with the Dragon, as variants of a subtype of the combat myth which he traces through the ancient world in Europe and Asia from his starting-point in the Homeric Hymn to Apollo which records that Apollo fought with a she-dragon, and in Simonides and the

pseudo-Julian which record that Apollo killed a he-dragon named Python. We can be grateful to Professor Fontenrose for so eruditely displaying the Apollo-Python story as a possible area of reference for Germanic myth and wondertale; and once more we may agree that husks and sheddings of myth are discoverable in our poem; but his summary of *Beowulf* as myth seems to me on the whole to show that it is heroic legend and wondertale with remote and largely forgotten mythical antecedents for some of its features. Also there are numerous places where we do not read the poem in the same way.

9. That the companions shall fall sound asleep, and Beowulf make no move to prevent the devouring of his follower, are incidents inexplicable in the context of a heroic poem unless we recognize them for what they are: gaunt and unassimilable folktale motifs which the *Beowulf* poet found he could neither reject nor rationalize.

10. Here, unlike the residual grotesqueries of the companions falling asleep at Heorot, and Beowulf watching Grendel devour his friend and retainer Hondscio, the poet has neatly rationalized, or used a rationalization of, the folktale motif of the deserting companions.

Elisabeth M. Liggins (essay date 1973)

SOURCE: "Revenge and Reward as Recurrent Motives in *Beowulf*," in *Neuphilologische Mitteilungen,* Vol. LXXIV, No. 2, 1973, pp. 193-213.

[*In the essay below, Liggins argues that the pattern of reference to vengeance and reward—both earthly and divine—in* Beowulf *emphasizes the poem's sense of order. She stresses however, that there is a dearth of evidence indicating that the poet intended to convey this sense of order. Rather, the poet's interest in the "duty of vengeance" imbues the poem with an internal orderliness.*]

In the Introduction to his edition of *Beowulf,* C. L. Wrenn discusses the parallels between the Finn Episode and the tale of Ingeld, of which one is that"they both treat of the supreme necessity of vengeance for a slain leader to be taken by a faithful member of his *comitatus*",[1] and he also suggests that one purpose of the Finn Episode may be to illustrate"the great Germanic duty of vengeance for a slain leader of one's *comitatus*" which"is not at all fully illustrated by the events of the hero's life dealt with in *Beowulf*".[2]

The treatment of vengeance in these two episodes is very powerful, both within the scope of each tale itself and in its bearing on the poem as a whole. The opening lines of the Finn Episode are not concerned with the moral duty of vengeance, but they pick out the other elements of violence and poignancy as they might appear in the case of the warriors and then in the situation of Hildeburh: sudden

disaster (*se fær*), death at the decree of inexorable fate (*feallan scolde* and *hie on gebyrd hruron*), treachery (*Ne huru Hildeburh herian þorfte / Eotena treowe*), the injustice of suffering and the loss of kindred (*unsynnum weard / beloren leofum . . . bearnum ond broðrum*).[3] The tragedy of Hildeburh, whose happiness and security are destroyed in the conflict between the two groups with whom she has ties of the deepest affection and loyalty as both kinswoman and subject, is summarized in a phrase which concentrates on her sorrow, without reference to moral issues, and which, moreover, is itself almost impersonal in tone, *þæt wæs geomuru ides*. A variation of *þæt wæs god cyning,* the comment expresses no overt sympathy, and assumes that her dignity will remain constant, however deep are her sufferings. Indeed, the next reference to Hildeburh shows her giving orders at the cremation:

> Het ða Hildeburh   æt Hnæfes ade
> hire selfre sunu   sweoloðe befæstan,
> banfatu bærnan,   ond on bæl don
> eame on eaxle
>
> (1114-17).

Only when that has been attended to is she permitted to display her emotions and even then the expression of her grief becomes a part of the formal ceremony:

> Ides gnornode,
> geomrode giddum
>
> (1117-18).

The details of the fighting are of much less importance in the poem than the emotions of the protagonists, and, particularly, than those of Hengest, whose situation and temperament make him one of the most complex and interesting of all the heroic figures in *Beowulf.* His dilemma, as a partner to the compact with Finn[4] and as the one upon whose shoulders falls the duty of avenging the leader, is one incapable of easy solution. It is brilliantly suggested in the passage of atmospheric writing (lines 1127 ff.), in which the poet divides his attention between the brooding, turbulent-spirited leader and the bleak, violent weather of winter, which both echoes his own mood and in large measure causes it by the inactivity it forces upon him. Man and nature are brought together violently in the opening lines, with the strongly evocative epithet for winter:

>   Hengest ða gyt
> wælfagne winter   wunode mid Finne
> [ea]l unhlitme
>
> (1127-29).

His thoughts of home are in part nostalgic (and to some extent, perhaps, emotional memories of the dead leader whose duty had been to defend his land have been transmuted to longings for the land itself), and in part, perhaps, very practical, in Hengest's awareness of the impossibility of travel either for those who would be able to return after the battle with Finn or, if we accept one suggestion,[5] for reinforcements of Danes to come to his aid before the battle:

> eard gemunde,
> þeah þe ne meahte   on mere drifan
> hringedstefnan,—   holm storme weol,
> won wið winde,   winter yþe beleac
> isgebinde

> (1129-33).

The coming of spring both brings with it the possibility of action which alone can lift Hengest's depression and also symbolizes the lightening of his spirit. (The dual significance here resembles that in the case of winter.) It is only after the poet has marked the change of season and implied the joy which this usually brings to mankind that he turns to Hengest. In *his* case, the beauty of spring for its own sake means nothing, but the relief he feels comes from the opportunity to take positive action at last, to purge his feelings of guilt by performing his duty of vengeance:

> Da wæs winter scacen,
> fæger foldan bearm;   fundode wrecca,
> gist of geardum;   he to gyrnwræce
> swiðor þohte   þonne to sælade,
> gif he torngemot   þurhteon mihte,
> þæt he Eotena bearn   irne gemunde

> (1136-41).

His feelings of relief and the overwhelming force of the memory of Hnæf perhaps obliterate any last thoughts of the temporary, and hated, bond with Finn. The poet gives no hint, though in his attitude towards the Frisian leader there is a certain ambivalence. His own approbation is unqualified for Hengest and for the Danish viewpoint that, no matter how honourable are the terms offered by the Frisians, an alliance with them is no substitute for independence and for a single bond of loyalty to their own leader, but his sympathy for Finn comes through very clearly in

> Swylce ferhðfrecan   Fin eft begeat
> sweordbealo sliðen   æt his selfes ham

> (1146-47),

just as it had been implied earlier in his account of Finn's generous treatment of the Danes after the first battle and in his reference to Hildeburh's happy married life. Finn's appreciation of the difficult and galling situation of the Danes is implied in his willing agreement to the condition that his own men should never, through enmity or malice (*þurh inwitsearo*) remind the visitors of their subjection to the slayer of their lord, and that any Frisian who transgressed should be immediately put to death.

But the poet's sympathy seems to vanish suddenly as he summarizes the report of Guthlaf and Oslaf, and the death of Finn is hurried over in half a dozen words (though this of course is in agreement with the scant attention paid in the Episode to physical action). The ethics of the last attack are ignored, perhaps because the poet had no wish to commit himself, perhaps because he saw no problem there.

Within the framework of the whole poem, the Finn Episode emphasizes the point that tragedy and death are never far away. The happiness of Hildeburh cannot last, and the triumph of Beowulf will eventually be replaced by at least partial defeat and by death. The tale of Finn is told as part of *healgamen* and the tragic outcome is given in the opening lines. There may possibly be word-play between the *gid oft wrecen* (1065) by Hrothgar's scop as he entertains the warriors at this feast of triumph and the very different kind of *gid* uttered beside Hnæf's pyre (1118), and also between the sense of *mænan* in l. 1067,

> ðonne healgamen   Hroþgares scop
> æfter medobence   mænan scolde,

and that in which it is applied to the two Danes of old,

> siþðan grimne gripe   Guðlaf ond Oslaf
> æfter sæside   sorge mændon,
> ætwiton   weana dæl

> (1148-50).

Beyond this, one may perhaps see a contrast between the faithfulness of the Danes to their dead lord and the cowardice of the Geats of the last part of the poem, who, with the shining exception of Wiglaf, desert their living leader in his time of desperate need.

The Ingeld story is concerned with vengeance for a slain parent, not specifically with that for a leader, and it is apparently not Ingeld, the bridegroom, who makes the first move. However, the prince is named separately when Beowulf speaks of the resentment of the Heathobards against the Danish nobles who so tactlessly wear the arms of those whom they had overcome:

> Mæg þæs þonne ofþyncan   ðcodne Heaðo-Beardna
> ond þegna gehwam   þara leoda,
> þonne he mid fæmnan   on flett gæð:
> dryhtbearn Dena,   duguða biwenede

> (2032-35).

Both here and in the Finn Episode, the warrior who actively begins the second stage of the quarrel is urged on by somebody else. Here it is an *eald æscwiga* (2042) who makes an inflammatory speech. Lines 1142-44 have been interpreted in a number of different ways, but the most widely accepted one sees the laying of the sword in Hengest's lap as a symbolic act reminding him of his duty. There is something especially appropriate in this (apparently) silent reminder to the introspective leader. It is as though his thoughts are suddenly given visible form. Whether by chance or by the poet's deliberate design this is more subtly powerful in these particular circumstances than a speech could have been. The Heathobard's action is more hotheaded, provoked by the sight of the thoughtless or arrogant visitors and by the beer at the feast, whereas there is an implication of cooler and more deliberate action by Hengest and his party, but in both cases the memory of the earlier battle is bitter and the desire for vengeance strong. In both episodes, the dead man is avenged, though subsequent events are different: whereas the Finn tale is brought to an end with a second fight leading to the destruction of the leader and his men and the lady's return to her own people, in that of Ingeld there is clear reference only to a single encounter. (However, mention of the breaking of the *aðsweord* (2064) seems to imply further bloodshed and there are suggestions of more reprisals at a still later date when Ingeld's love for his wife has cooled in his grief for the slaughter of his men.)

Although it is in these two episodes that the duty of vengeance appears most strongly, it is important in a number of other interludes. Moreover, in most of the exploits of Beowulf, it is used in a new way, in his struggles with non-human creatures: with the sea-monsters, with Grendel, Grendel's mother and finally the dragon. Sometimes the poet uses words that specifically mean "vengeance", "avenge", "revenge". At other times he does not do so, but, while nothing can be proved, it seems highly probable that in any counter-attack upon an enemy who had previously been victorious, the notion of revenge or of vengeance would play an important part. That the desire was very long-lived is shown by Wiglaf's reference to the threat which the Franks and Frisians will offer once the news of Beowulf's death has become known: the memory still rankled of the raids which the Geats had made upon the Franks more than half a century before. In them Hygelac, after initial victories, was slain (lines 2913 ff); however, his death was itself followed by an act of vengeance, for Beowulf, fulfilling a double obligation, as kinsman and as thane, had at once killed Dæghrefn, who may well have been the actual slayer of Hygelac (lines 2501 ff). The Swedes, too, says Wiglaf, may be expected to renew their ancient feuds (ll. 2922-23, 2999-3007).

The complicated story of the wars between Geats and Swedes is a pattern of revenge (and its concomitant, reward for the loyal service of thanes). The attack made upon the Geats at Hreosnabeorh by the arrogant Swedes, after the death of Hrethel, is followed by the vengeance of the Geats, who raid Sweden and capture Ongentheow's queen. In reprisal, Ongentheow again engages with his enemies at Ravenswood, kills Hæthcyn, the son of Hrethel, releases his wife, and pursues the leaderless Geats. He besieges them all night long, with threats of wholesale destruction in the morning. At daybreak Hygelac, Hæthcyn's younger brother, arrives with reinforcements, and the battle is resumed. Ongentheow's powers of resistance are already lowered by his knowledge of Hygelac's prowess, and the Geat, for his part, is inflamed by his desire to avenge the one who was both his near kinsman and his lord:

> Þæt mægwine   mine gewræcan,
> fæhðe ond fyrene,   swa hyt gefræge wæs
>
> (2479-80).

In this case Hygelac does not personally slay the Swedish ruler but, in his capacity as new leader of the Geats, is responsible for seeing that this is done. It is the brothers Eofor and Wulf who actually engage Ongentheow. Wulf strikes the first mighty blow, and, despite its effect, the Swede immediately repays it with even more violence:

> Næs he forht swa ðeh,
> gomela Scilfing,   ac forgeald hraðe
> wyrsan wrixle   wælhlem þone,
> syðdan þeodcyning   þyder oncirde
>
> (2967-70).

Wulf is too badly wounded to return the blow,

> Ne meahte se snella   sunu Wonredes
> ealdum ceorle   ondslyht giofan
>
> (2971-72),

and the responsibility for retaliation therefore passes to his brother Eofor, who now has the double duty of avenging his leader's death and his brother's wounding. Having slain Ongentheow, he strips him of byrnie, sword and helmet and hands the armour to Hygelac. On their return home, Hygelac rewards the brothers for their services with magnificent gifts and to Eofor he also gives the hand of his only daughter. The pattern has been completed, with the aggressors punished and services recompensed. There is no bitterness and the bravery of Ongentheow is fully acknowledged. The fighting is very much a pitting of the strength of one man against another. Eofor takes no part until his brother has been disabled.

Years later, the Geats and Swedes again become involved in a fierce quarrel, when the young Geatish king, Heardred, gives shelter at his court to the Swedish princes Eanmund and Eadgils, who had fled when their uncle, Onela, seized the throne. Seeking revenge for this unfriendly act (at this stage the Geats do not seem to have been directly involved in the quarrel), Onela invades Geatland, killing both Heardred and Eanmund. A couple of years later, Eadgils with Geatish support marches against his uncle, in retaliation for Onela's seizing of the throne, killing of Eanmund and exile of himself:

> he gewræc syþðan
> cealdum cearsiðum,   cyning ealdre bineat
>
> (2395-96).

The crime of usurpation has been punished at last. But the seeds of further trouble between Swedes and Geats have been sown.

On many occasions, the poet refers to Beowulf's fights with the various monsters in terms appropriate to the code of revenge. This conception appears in Beowulf's account of his struggle with the sea-beasts, which is a kind of self-recommendation to Hrothgar and which serves as a prelude to his later and even more desperate encounters. He concludes the brief tale of his victory over the giants and water-demons with the comment

> wræc Wedera nið   —wean ahsodon—,
> forgrand gramum
>
> (423-4),

which transforms his actions from mere deeds of bravado and turns them into a sacred duty, concerning not only the safety of his people but also their honour. He thus establishes his right to ask for the privilege of fighting Grendel, not in the role of an adventurer but in that of a saviour, of one who, if the Lord wills it, may be able to "cleanse" Heorot (and the same word, *fælsian,* is used by the poet after he has succeeded (825)). It is probably significant that he offers himself in this role only to Hrothgar; in his earlier speech to the coastguard he says simply:

> Ic þæs Hroðgar mæg
> þurh rumne sefan   ræd gelæran,
> hu he frod ond god   feond ofers wyðeþ
>
> (277-79),

and he tells Wulfgar that he will declare the real purpose of his journey to the prince alone:

> Wille ic asecgan   sunu Healfdenes,
> mærum þeodne   min ærende,
> aldre þinum . . .
>
> (344-46).

In Beowulf's reply to Unferth's taunting speech, there is a strong suggestion that Grendel's attacks on the Danes may be a direct consequence of Unferth's treachery, but I shall return later to the matter of Divine Vengeance.

The revenge theme comes out strongly in the case of Grendel's mother. The first reference to her when she attacks Heorot is in the role of avenger and it is interesting that this motive is immediately ascribed to her by the Danes and Geats; in fact, she is called a *wrecend* before she is identified in any other way, by name, sex, or relationship to Grendel:

> Þæt gesyne wearþ,
> widcuþ werum,   þætte wrecend þa gyt
> lifde æfter laþum
>
> (1255-57).

Grendel may be *laþ,* but he is still entitled to an avenger. And when the poet returns to her again fourteen lines later, after an interpolation dealing with Cain, the origins of the evil spirits and a brief recapitulation of the fight between Beowulf and Grendel, he makes the same point:

> Ond his modor þa gyt
> gifre ond galgmod   gegan wolde
> sorhfulne sið,   sunu deoð wrecan
>
> (1276-78).

Even though Hrothgar is filled with grief for æschere, and although Grendel's mother is to him *wælgæst wæfre* and *atol æse wlanc,* he still thinks of her action in similar terms, and even, to some extent, sees Beowulf's defeat of Grendel from her point of view:

> Heo þa fæhðe wræc,
> þe þu gystran niht   Grendel cwealdest
> þurh hæstne had   heardum clammum,
> forþan he to lange   leode mine

> wanode ond wyrde.   He æt wige gecrang
> ealdres scyldig,   ond nu oþer cwom
> mihtig manscaða,   wolde hyre mæg wrecan . . .
>
> (1333-39).

(Here, Beowulf's action is seen as the result and the punishment of Grendel's long series of raids, but the poet's "sympathy" seems to be more with the bereaved mother who for the moment is raised to human dignity.) At the climax of the underwater struggle, when Grendel's mother sits on top of Beowulf and draws her knife, the poet pauses briefly to add *wolde hire bearn wrecan, / angan eaferan* (lines 1546-47). Despite the fact that he happens to be the one who first attracts the attention of the creature when she realizes that she is discovered, there is perhaps a certain ironic justice in the slaying of æschere:

> Se wæs Hroþgare   hæleþa leofost
> on gesiðes had   be sæm tweonum
>
> (1296-97).

The death of a son has been avenged by the death of a specially beloved thane. But even if the choice of this victim is only the working of chance, the poet is specific enough, a few lines later, in drawing up a balance sheet in terms of the obligations of the code of revenge:

> Ne wæs þæt gewrixle til,
> þæt hie on ba healfa   bicgan scoldon
> freonda feorum!
>
> (1304-06).

Beowulf sees the coming struggle with Grendel's mother as an act of vengeance (and so accords her a certain human dignity by implying that she is to be considered as the offending party in a feud) when he takes the situation which follows the death of æschere as a particular example of a common case:

> Selre bið æghwæm,
> þæt he his freond wrece,   þonne he fela murne
>
> (1384-85).

In his later account of the underwater fight, the slaying of the female and the beheading of Grendel are regarded as acts of vengeance, not for the killing of any one man but for the long series of deeds of violence and destruction:

> fyrendæda wræc,
> deaðcwealm Denigea,   swa hit gedefe wæs.
>
> (1669-70).

Beowulf's report to Hygelac also presents both sides of the operation of the code of revenge. In the opening lines he gives the gist of the news that his lord is anxious to hear, when, after a reference to the many sorrowful deeds done by Grendel to the Danes, he says *ic ðæt eall gewræc* (line 2005). Later he can afford to be generous to his adversaries and even to spare a thought for the sorrow of the monstrous woman as she goes about her duty of revenge:

þa wæs eft hraðe
gearo gyrnwræce   Grendeles modor,
siðode sorhfull;   sunu deað fornam,
wighete Wedra.   Wif unhyre
hyre bearn gewræc,   beorn acwealde
ellenlice;   þær wæs æschere,
frodan fyrnwitan   feorh uðgenge

(2117-23).

The emphasis is laid upon her grief and even upon her courage and the reference to æschere is almost cursory.

The theme of vengeance appears several times in the story of the dragon. When he is disturbed by the fugitive, the dragon at once plans revenge:

wolde guman findan,
þone þe him on sweofote   sare geteode

(2294-95),

and when he discovers the theft of the flagon, he at once begins to ravage the countryside:

wolde se laða   lige forgyldan
drincfæt dyre

(2305-06).

As soon as Beowulf learns of his depredations, he plans revenge (lines 2335-36). Up to this point, vengeance has been taken (by the dragon) for the breach of privacy and for the theft of valuable objects and planned (by Beowulf) for widespread destruction of property. The crimes have been of increasing gravity and each is met by a punishment, not by a closely-matching act of vengeance. In the last case the progression continues, and now it is life that is at stake. To save his country and his people Beowulf attacks the dragon and quickly wounds him. But the dragon fights back until each mortally wounds the other and the feud between dragon and humans is brought to an end. Wiglaf had played his part in aiding his leader, but ascribes the credit to Beowulf alone, in words that once more use the language of the code of revenge:

hwæðre him God uðe,
sigora Waldend,   þæt he hyne sylfne gewræc
ana mid ecge,   þa him wæs elnes þearf

(2874-76).

It is fitting that he should have avenged himself. The implication is that no other was able to do so, for Wiglaf lacked experience and the other Geats had fled from the scene. For Wiglaf to have succeeded alone when his leader had failed would perhaps have detracted from Beowulf's own glory, and would moreover have been out of harmony with the poet's prophecy of the impending collapse of the Geats. It is a part of Beowulf's supremacy that even in old age and close to death he alone can avenge himself.

Forming a variation on the theme of vengeance are the cases in which, for different reasons, such action is impossible and the grief of the relatives is accordingly exacer-

bated. Twice, in the course of a speech made near the end of his life, does Beowulf refer to the accidental slaying of Herebeald by his younger brother Hæthcyn and to the impossibility of seeking compensation, either by money or by human life:

Þæt wæs feohleas gefeoht,   fyrenum gesyngad,
hreðre hygemeðe;   sceolde hwæðre swa þeah
æðeling unwrecen   ealdres linnan

(2441-43).

The somewhat generalized statement here is replaced by one of greater poignancy in the second reference, when Beowulf is concerned with the grief and helplessness of the old father, who finds relief only in death (lines 2462-71). The intervening lines (2444-62) picture the sorrow of the man whose son has been hung, and who has to bear the weight of his death in circumstances where there can be no vengeance and who has also to suffer the knowledge of his guilt. Both this nameless father and Hrethel are isolated from men by their impotence even more than by their grief; neither can put into practice the advice which Beowulf as a young man had offered to Hrothgar in Heorot:

Ne sorga, snotor guma!   Selre bið æghwæm,
þæt he his freond wrece,   þonne he fela murne

(1384-85).

(This third case of an old man unable to take vengeance for the death of one who, though not his son, was specially dear to him, presents a number of contrasts with the other two. Here he is prevented from taking action not because of any legal restrictions but because of old age and physical inability. Here the foe is a supernatural one whose power no ordinary man could expect to overcome. But here there is a champion at hand, a man of another race but one who owes Hrothgar a debt for the protection the Danes had given to his own father, Ecgtheow, in bygone years, and, though the chance of success seems slight, vengeance is at least possible.) Another variation is found in a brief reference in lines 2618-19:

no ymbe ða fæhðe spræc,
þeah ðe he his broðor bearn   abredwade.

Wihstan has slain Eanmund, the nephew of Onela, but he is rewarded by the uncle, not punished, since Eanmund, as an exile, has forfeited all his natural rights. Rebellion against his ruler cancels out family ties.

The alternative method of settling a feud—by a money payment—appears several times in the poem, both in the main action and in episodes. Hrothgar cannot avenge the death of Hondscio, but, at the celebration banquet which follows the fight with Grendel, he not only rewards the living Geats but also promises to make a money payment on behalf of the dead one:

þone ænne heht
golde forgyldan,   þone ðe Grendel ær
mane acwealde

(1053-55).

Hrothgar had settled Ecgtheow's feud with the Wylfings by means of money (lines 470-72). Such payments were intended to put a stop to violence and, from being a substitute for revenge, they could easily become a means of buying off a would-be attacker. Grendel's blood-lust is not to be satisfied, however:

> sibbe ne wolde
> wið manna hwone   mægenes Deniga,
> feorhbealo feorran,   fea þingian
>
> (154-56).

Finn's offer that the Danes should share in the use of a hall and in the distribution of treasure rather than that the battle should continue between the two weakened sides is a further variation in methods of compounding a dispute.

The poet sometimes applies the terminology of the civil law code to cases where the methods are much more direct:

> Ne wæs þæt gewrixle til,
> þæt hie on ba healfa   bicgan scoldon
> freonda feorum
>
> (1304-06),

where the "purchasers" are Hrothgar and Grendel's mother. Grendel's death at the hands of Beowulf is seen as a just punishment:

> He æt wige gecrang
> ealdres scyldig
>
> (1337-38),

though he is given a curious dignity when his planned snatch-and-run raid is seen as *wig,* or when Beowulf vows:

> ond nu wið Grendel sceal,
> wið þam aglæcan   ana gehegan
> ðing wið þyrse
>
> (424-26).

The cycle of acts of vengeance between warring tribes could also be brought to an end—at least temporarily—by a marriage alliance. Freawaru's betrothal to Ingeld was an act of expediency, by which Hrothgar calculated

> þæt he mid ðy wife   wælfæhða dæl,
> sæcca gesette
>
> (2028-29).

The reference to the *bongar* two lines later confirms that this has been a blood-feud, and Beowulf comments on the frequency with which the strong instinct to reopen the feud in active fighting quickly prevails (lines 2029-31).

When Beowulf arrives at Heorot, both Hrothgar's answer to Wulfgar (the first speech we have heard from the king) and his reply to Beowulf's greeting begin with a reference to Ecgtheow and then pass on to the depredations of Grendel. Although reminiscence is natural enough in an old man trying to construct a framework of familiar material into which he can fit a new acquaintance, and although there is no specific reference[6] to a return by Beowulf for services rendered to his father in the past, there is at least a strong implication that Beowulf is partly motivated by this awareness of a debt which can only be paid by his own actions. The concept of return for services, in the form either of material rewards or of further service, is closely allied to that of vengeance, and is a basic one in the organization of Germanic society.

There are frequent references to the generosity of a leader and some also to the lack of it (for example, to the meanness of Heremod—lines 1719-20). The remuneration may or may not be related to a specific act on the part of the recipient; it is when it is so related that it is most clearly the obverse of vengeance. In general, the ruler rewards his thanes with gold, with treasures and occasionally with armour, while the thane repays his lord with loyal service. But a special obligation may carry a special reward. When Beowulf kills Grendel and saves the Danes from threatened destruction, Hrothgar takes him into his own family:

> Nu ic, Beowulf, þec,
> secg betsta,   me for sunu wylle
> freogan on ferhþe;   heald forð tela
> niwe sibbe
>
> (946-49).

In his emotion, this is what the old king mentions first and, in one sense, the material gifts are thought of as a consequence of this relationship:

> Ne bið þe [n]ænigre gad
> worolde wilna,   þe ic geweald hæbbe.
>
> (949-50)

Sometimes a promise of reward is made in advance of the service, as when Hrothgar, before he sees Beowulf for the first time, tells Wulfgar, the messenger:

> Ic þæm godan sceal
> for his modþræce   madmas beodan
>
> (384-85),

and this promise is repeated to Beowulf himself, in lines 660-61. The fulfilment of the promise is narrated in lines 1020-49 and 1193-96 (while in 1173-74 Wealhtheow urges Hrothgar to be generous in his gifts to the company of Geats as a whole). Later, Beowulf speaks of it again in his report to Hygelac (lines 2101-04). Similarly, before Beowulf's struggle with Grendel's mother Hrothgar promises a further reward of gold and treasures if the young man survives (lines 1380-82, and again 2134, when Beowulf reports to Hygelac). This time there is no narrative of the celebration feast and we hear of the actual bestowal of the gifts from Beowulf's lips (lines 2142-43 and 2145-47). Hygelac rewards Eofor and Wulf with great treasures for their service in slaying Ongentheow (lines 2989ff.) and Ongentheow's son, Onela, rewards Wihstan with helmet,

byrnie and famous sword for his action in killing Eanmund. It is not only for martial deeds that rewards are
given: the gentle Wealhtheow implores Beowulf not to ex-
cite her young sons too much, and promises a reward,
which may or may not be monetary (lines 1219-20).

To receive a reward for services already rendered does
not, as it were, finalize the account. On the contrary, a new
cycle of obligation is begun. Beowulf tells how he with
his shining sword repaid Hygelac for the treasures and
land given by the prince (lines 2490-93). The fullest development of this theme of the retainers' duty to requite
the generosity of their lord is found in the last five hundred lines of the poem, in the contrast between the behaviour of Wiglaf and that of the rest of the Geats. As Beowulf and the dragon come together in the second stage of
their encounter, the hero's plight is briefly and dramatically described. Though encircled by flames, he takes heart
in the thought of his responsibility to his people. In violent
contrast with this is the action of his followers, who, with
one exception, flee to the woods to save their own lives:

> nearo ðrowode
> fyre befongen   se ðe ær folce weold.
> Nealles him on heape   handgesteallan,
> æðelinga bearn   ymbe gestodon
> hildecystum,   ac hy on holt bugon,
> ealdre burgan
>
> (2594-99).

(And the point is made again in lines 2882-83). The poet
dwells much longer on what we may call the positive side,
on the immediate response of the faithful Wiglaf:

> geseah his mondryhten
> under heregriman   hat þrowian.
> Gemunde ða ða are,   þe he him ær forgeaf
> wicstede weligne   Wægmundinga,
> folcrihta gehwylc,   swa his fæder ahte
>
> (2604-08),

and on some of the details of his fight. Having shown his
own valour, and in a pause in the battle, Wiglaf expresses
his grief in a speech whose whole theme is the obligation
of the thanes to the lord who has given them rings and
treasures and the disgrace of abandoning him in his time
of need:

> Ic ðæt mæl geman,   þær we medu þegun,
> þonne we geheton   ussum hlaforde
> in biorsele,   ðe us ðas beagas geaf,
> þæt we him ða guðgetawa   gyldan woldon,
> gif him þyslicu   þearf gelumpe,
> helmas ond heard sweord
>
> (2633-38),

and

> Nu is se dæg cumen,
> þæt ure mandryhten   mægenes behofað,
> godra guðrinca . . .
> . . . God wat on mec,

> þæt me is micle leofre,   þæt minne lichaman
> mid minne goldgyfan   gled fæðmie
>
> (2646-52).

When Beowulf is dead, the last offices are seen as the final
opportunity for his men to repay the gifts of their lord:

> Nu is ofost betost,
> þæt we þeodcyning   þær sceawian,
> ond þone gebringan,   þe us beagas geaf,
> on adfære
>
> (3007-10).

Though it is in the last part of the poem that the theme of
the thane's obligations to his lord is developed most fully,
the mutual relationship is epitomized in the moralizing
sentiments of the introductory fitt when the poet interrupts
his account of Scyld and his son to comment

> Swa sceal geong guma   gode gewyrcean,
> fromum feohgiftum   on fæder bearme,
> þæt hine on ylde   eft gewunigen
> wilgesiþas,   þonne wig cume,
> leode gelæsten;   lofdædum sceal
> in mægþa gehwære   man geþeon
>
> (20-25).

In the last clause the duties of lord and of thane are neatly
drawn together. The bond of loyalty must be proved by
deeds on each side.

The obligation of one who is both relative and thane is expressed—ironically as events prove—by Wealhtheow, in
her speech of confidence in Hrothulf (lines 1180-87).

For the most part we see Beowulf receiving rewards for
his exceptional services to the Danes with whom his bond
is a somewhat loose one, but in a long reminiscing speech
he recalls how he repaid the generosity of his own lord,
Hygelac, in a normal lord-thane situation:

> Ic him þa maðmas,   þe he me sealde,
> geald æt guðe,   swa me gifeðe wæs,
> leohtan sweorde;   he me lond forgeaf,
> eard eðelwyn
>
> (2490-93).

Sometimes the lord's generosity takes the form not of gifts
but of protection or of other services to his thanes or to
members of other tribes who have come to his court. So
Beowulf, before going out to his encounter with Grendel's
mother, can ask Hrothgar to assume responsibility for the
young Geats, if he himself should not return:

> gif ic æt þearfe   þinre scolde
> aldre linnan,   þæt ðu me a wære
> forðgewitenum   on fæder stæle.
> Wes þu mundbora   minum magoþegnum,
> hondgesellum,   gif mec hild nime;
> swylce þu ða madmas,   þe þu me sealdest,
> Hroðgar leofa,   Higelace onsend
>
> (1477-83).

And, after his return, Hrothgar reaffirms his gratitude:

> Ic þe sceal mine gelæstan
> freode, swa wit furðum spræcon
>
> (1706-07).

Beowulf, by his generous treatment, makes amends to Eadgils for the losses he has suffered:

> Se ðæs leodhryres   lean gemunde
> uferan dogrum,   Eadgilse weard
> feasceaftum freond
>
> (2391-93).

Rewards may be given, too, for slighter services faithfully performed, as when Beowulf, in his capacity as leader of the band of adventurers, gives a sword, bound with gold, to the Danish *batweard* who has guarded the Geatish ship (lines 1900-01).

Allied to the idea of reward is that of compensation for injuries or ill-fortune suffered, as in the military successes of Scyld Scefing which the poet sees as atoning for his destitute childhood (lines 4-11), or the good fortune which was brought to the Danes by Scyld's son, the first Beowulf,

> . . . þone God sende
> folce to frofre;   fyrenðearfe ongeat,
> þe hie ær drugon   aldorlease
> lange hwile;   him þæs Liffrea,
> wuldres Wealdend   woroldare forgeaf
>
> (13-17).

In a small group of examples, the notion of "reward" is ironically applied to the struggle between Beowulf and the Grendel-kin. Once the payment is made by Grendel's mother, when Beowulf has thrown her to the floor:

> Heo him eft hraþe   andlean forgeald
> grimman grapum   ond him togeanes feng
>
> (1541-42).

When Beowulf decapitates Grendel's body, the poet comments that this is in return for the monster's depredations, *He him þæs lean forgeald* (line 1584), and Beowulf reports his success to Hrothgar in similar terms:

> To lang ys to reccenne,   hu ic ðam leodsceaðan
> yfla gehwylces   ondlean forgeald
>
> (2093-94).

In line 1577 the verb *forgyldan* alone is applied to Beowulf's actions:

> . . . he hraþe wolde
> Grendle forgyldan   guðræsa fela
> ðara þe he geworhte   to West-Denum
> oftor micle   þonne on ænne sið
>
> (1576-79),

while Beowulf

> forgeald hraðe
> wyrsan wrixle   wælhlem þone
>
> (2968-69).

The "reward" for evil is, thus, vengeance.

Both rewards and retribution may be dispensed also by superhuman forces, either by Wyrd or by God. The act of repayment may be implied, as in the maxim,

> Wyrd oft nered
> unfægne eorl,   þonne his ellen deah!
>
> (572-73),

or Hrothgar's confident assertion to Beowulf that, despite his ravages, Grendel may eventually be overcome:

> God eaþe mæg
> þone dolsceaðan   dæda getwæfan!
>
> (478-79).

(Similarly with lines 106-110 (of Cain), 168-69 (of Grendel), 587-601 (of Unferth, whose act in slaying his brother is claimed by Beowulf to be the cause of Grendel's continued depredations), 977-79 (of Grendel on Judgment Day), 1263-65 (of Cain), which all concern punishments, and with 1553-56 (which tell how Beowulf, having once displayed his strength and determination, receives divine assistance). In lines 1724-27 the poet speaks of the lavishness of God which far exceeds mere human deserts:

> Wundor is to secganne,
> hu mihtig God   manna cynne
> þurh sidne sefan   snyttru bryttað,
> eard ond eorlscipe.

In some places, the direct vocabulary of reward is used, either literally, as in Hrothgar's wish for Beowulf,

> Alwalda þec
> gode forgylde,   swa he nu gyt dyde!
>
> (955-56),

or ironically, as in the two references to the giants,

> swylce gigantas,   þa wið Gode wunnon
> lange þrage;   he him ðæs lean forgeald
>
> (113-14),

and

> . . . syþðan flod ofsloh,
> gifen geotende   giganta cyn,
>   . . . . .
> . . . him þæs endelean
> þurh wæteres wylm   Waldend sealde
>
> (1689-93).

Most of the references to divine vengeance and rewards are found in the first part of the poem. The dragon has, in fact, no theological connections; however, Beowulf's first thought is that the series of raids are intended as a punishment for some offence he himself has committed against the Lord:

> wende se wisa,   þæt he Wealdende
> ofer ealde riht   ecean Dryhtne
> bitre gebulge
>
>   (2329-31).

Occasionally, retribution is exacted by somebody who does not appear to have any natural right to do so. So Wiglaf prophesies that the cowardice of the Scyldings will be quickly followed by the seizing of all property and the removal of the privileges normally enjoyed by a landowner,

>   syþðan æðelingas
> feorran gefricgean   fleam eowerne,
> domleasan dæd
>
>   (2888-90),

though here the implication of punishment is doubtless combined with that of opportunism when the weakness of a once powerful tribe has become apparent. The ambivalent role of Grendel appears in Beowulf's reference to Unferth's fratricide, when the creature who is elsewhere depicted as the enemy of God seems to become the instrument of His vengeance. One can only conjecture whether the poet is indulging in a subtle piece of theology or whether he is merely being inconsistent.

The poet's brief recapitulation of the story of the dragon's crime and punishment neatly stresses the moral by concluding the summary with the retribution, even though to do this means a disturbance of the chronology of the earlier full narrative of the battle:

> Þa wæs gesyne,   þæt se sið ne ðah
> þam ðe unrihte   inne gehydde
> wræte under wealle.   Weard ær ofsloh
> feara sumne;   þa sio fæhð gewearð
> gewrecen wraðlice
>
>   (3058-62).

There is, of course, no evidence to prove that the poet thought in terms of any overall purpose apart from that of the main narrative of two principal episodes in Beowulf's career, and allusions to revenge are natural enough in heroic tales of the age. But at the same time, the references to revenge taken or not taken, to conflicting loyalties in blood-feuds, to vengeance for crimes, and to rewards for loyalty are so frequent in the main narrative, in all the major episodes and in several of the briefer ones that they help to give the poem a continuity and a pattern just as much as do the many references to Hygelac or to such things as the contrasts between good and evil or joy and sorrow, to *sapientia et fortitudo,* or to the pattern of Beowulf's three great fights against the monsters.[7] The poet may or may not have planned or recognized this, but his own keen interest in situations involving the duty of ven-

geance helped to give his poem a certain internal orderliness and shape apart from the parallelisms within its central narrative.

Notes

1. C. L. Wrenn, *Beowulf, with the Finnesburg Fragment,* revised and enlarged ed. (London, 1958), p. 74.

2. Ibid., p. 75.

3. All quotations are from F. Klaeber, *Beowulf and the Fight at Finnsburg,* 3rd. ed. (Boston, 1950).

4. The problems involved in the treaty are not relevant to my subject, and hence are not discussed.

5. F. Klaeber, *Beowulf and the Fight at Finnsburg* (1st ed.), p. 220; R. A. Williams, *The Finn Episode in Beowulf,* (Cambridge, 1924), pp. 101 f.; K. Malone, *JEGPh* XXV, 169, *ELH* X, 282f.; and A. G. Brodeur, *Essays and Studies* (University of California Publications in English, Vol. XIV), p. 27.

6. There would, of course, be such a reference if MS *fere fyhtum* (457) is a mistake for *for gewyrhtum,* as suggested by Trautmann, followed by Chambers and Klaeber.

7. See, for example, A. E. Du Bois, 'The Unity of *Beowulf'*, *PMLA* XLIX, 374-405; A. G. Brodeur, 'The Structure and Unity of *Beowulf'*, *PMLA* LXVIII, 1183-95; Kemp Malone, 'Beowulf', *English Studies* XXIX, 169-72; H. G. Wright, 'Good and Evil; Light and Darkness; Joy and Sorrow in *Beowulf'*, *RES,* N. S. VIII, 1-11; R. E. Kaske, 'Sapientia et Fortitudo* as the Controlling Theme of *Beowulf'*, *Studies in Philology* LV, 423-56; H. L. Rogers, 'Beowulf's Three Great Fights', *RES,* N.S. VI, 339-55.

Ramond J. S. Grant (essay date 1975)

SOURCE: "*Beowulf* and the World of Heroic Elegy," in *Leeds Studies in English,* Vol. 8, 1975, pp. 45-75.

[*In the essay that follows, Grant asserts that* Beowulf *cannot be viewed as an entirely Christian poem because it also embraces pagan values, and it is by these values that* Beowulf *is ultimately judged. The fact that the poet finds these values inadequate, Grant states, generates the elegiac tone of the poem.*]

Beowulf has justifiably attracted much critical opinion, some of which is valuable, some irrelevant, some absorbing, some tedious. I should like now to give some further reconsideration to the poem itself as it survives in BM MS Cotton Vitellius A. xv. I propose to discuss the text as a unified work of art by one poet and with a Christian colouring which is no mere interpolation. By "the poet" I mean the author who gave the poem its present form and heroico-elegiac tone.

The excavations at Sutton Hoo in 1939 and the subsequent work of numismatists dated the ship-burial as about 650-60 AD (although following re-excavation the current dating is somewhat earlier, around 625-30),[1] and this strengthened the impression that the poem was written in the age of Bede (c. 672-735). Dorothy Whitelock[2] has shown that Lawrence, Tolkien, Chambers, Klaeber and Girvan all argue for a date around 700; she herself, however, argues persuasively that a date in the eighth century, even in the late eighth century, is to be preferred on cultural, religious and historical grounds. A compromise such as c. 750 serves my purposes well enough. Although scholarly disagreements also centre round the poem's sources, origin, dialect, textual readings and historicity of persons,[3] these are irrelevant to the poem as a work of literature.

Looking at the text itself, *Beowulf* takes us back to an age of heroes and valiant deeds. We behold a hero in action, moving on an elemental plane, combatting the powers of darkness, seeking to define his existence as a human being, performing deeds of valour with an epic grandeur that is nevertheless described in elegiac mood. Beowulf is a Geat, a hero set in the heroic past of the Anglo-Saxons in their original homeland among their Germanic forebears, yet there is little point in a map of seventh-century Scandinavia, for the background against which symbolic heroic deeds are performed is an equally symbolic one—Middaneard, Middle Earth. The main action concerns Beowulf's slaying of two supernatural beings, Grendel and his Dam, in Denmark, and later, in his old age, of the fire-dragon in his own kingdom. The poet alludes also to many other stories from the heroic age, two of which, the Scylding dynastic struggles and the Geats' wars with the Swedes and Franks, are given especial prominence, *but* the main action, which is to be viewed against a traditional, heroic, pseudo-historical background, is fantastic, elemental and primal, and can also be viewed artistically and philosophically against the archetypal backcloth of Middle Earth.

The cosmology of *Beowulf* is the normal Germanic one of the human world as an enclosure defended against Chaos. In Norse sources, better preserved than Old English ones on this point,[4] we read of the human Miðgarðr, contrasted with Ásgarðr, the citadel of the æsir rising in the centre of the circle of Miðgarðr, and with Útgarðr, the outer circle, the icy barrier of the world, the home of the giants, one remove from Niflheimr and the gulfs of Chaos. In *Beowulf,* the work of a Christian poet, there is no Ásgarðr, but we deal with the same Middle Earth of man and listen with the heroes to the sea crashing on the rocks and the surges of Chaos booming on the dykes of the world. As J.R.R. Tolkien[5] wrote:

> . . . we may still, against his great scene, hung with tapestries woven of ancient tales of ruin, see the *hæleð* walk. When we have read his poem, as a poem, rather than as a collection of episodes, we perceive that he who wrote *hæleð under heofenum* may have meant in dictionary terms 'heroes under heaven', or 'mighty men upon earth', but he and his hearers were thinking of the *eormengrund*, the great earth, ringed with *gar-*

secg, the shoreless sea, beneath the sky's inaccessible roof; whereon, as in a little circle of light about their halls, men with courage as their stay went forward to that battle with the hostile world and the offspring of the dark which ends for all, even the kings and champions, in defeat. That even this 'geography', once held as a material fact, could now be classed as a mere folk-tale affects its value very little. It transcends astronomy. Not that astronomy has done anything to make the island seem more secure or the outer seas less formidable.

This is the primal world of nature, and early interpretations of *Beowulf* were along the lines of nature myth. K. Müllenhof[6] tells us that Grendel and his Dam represent the North Sea flooding the coastal regions in the spring while Beowulf represents a friendly divinity who seeks to combat their onslaughts; summer peace is seen in Beowulf's long reign over the Geats, the attacks of autumn are seen in the fire-dragon and the cold of winter is seen in the hero's death. Chaos then is come again.

While it is too simplistic to view the poem thus purely as nature myth, there is no doubt that primitive myths of creation and of the cosmic battle between Chaos and Righteousness are behind some of the symbolic patterns of *Beowulf*. F. Klaeber[7] points us to the landscape of *Beowulf* in his introduction:

> Elements of nature are introduced as a background for human action or as symbols of sentiment. Nightfall, dawn, the advent of spring signalize new stages in the narrative. The storm on the wintry ocean accompanies the struggle of the courageous swimmers. The swirl of the blood-stained lake tells of deadly conflict (847 ff., 1422, 1593 ff.). The funeral ship is covered with ice (33), and frost-bound trees hang over the forbidding water (1363). The moors of the dreary desert, steep stone-banks, windy headlands, mist and darkness are fit surroundings for the lonely, wretched stalkers of mystery. 'Joyless' (821) is their abode. Strikingly picturesque and emotional in quality is the one elaborate landscape picture representing the Grendel lake (1357 ff.), which conveys all the horror of the somber scenery and forcefully appeals to our imagination—a justly celebrated masterpiece of English nature poetry.

In *Beowulf,* then, Chaos and Unreason are represented by images of fire, the sea, and darkness, all encroaching upon the land and the light, upon the created human world.

Let us first consider the image of fire. In Old Norse and Germanic mythologies, the Ragnarøkr or Götterdämmerung—the Twilight of the Gods—is attended by fire; Surtr, the fire-god, raises his flaming sword, and the earth and the heavens are consumed by discreating fire.[8] In the Christianized *Beowulf*, fire stands for hell-fire and the Apocalypse; we are told of the Danes:

> Wa bið þæm ðe sceal
> þurh sliðne nið   sawle bescufan
> in fðres fæþm,   frofre ne wenan
> wihte gewendan!

(ll. 183-6)

When Grendel arrives in Heorot to devour the sleeping Geats, fire flares in his gaze:

> Raþe æfter þon
> on fagne flor　　　feond treddode,
> eode yrre-mod;　　　him of eagum stod
> ligge gelicost　　　leoht unfæger.

(11. 724-7)

By defeating Grendel, Beowulf purges Heorot of the forces of destruction, if only for a while—we are made conscious that Heorot will eventually be consumed by flames in the fatal feud with the Heathobards (11. 81-5). In the underwater cave of Grendel and his Dam, a flame burns perpetually, by the light of which Beowulf perceives Grendel's mother (11. 1516-17); the dragon slain by Sigemund (1. 897) melts in its own fiery heat, and Beowulf's final enemy, who wounds him mortally, is a fire-dragon. Finally, Beowulf himself is consumed by flames—the forces of Chaos which he was able to stave off for so long finally have their way with the hero:

> Him ða gegiredan　　　Geata leode
> ad on eorðan　　　unwaclicne,
> helm[um] behongen,　　　hilde-bordum,
> beorhtum byrnum,　　　swa he bena wæs;
> alegdon ða tomiddes　　　mærne þeoden
> hæleð hiofende,　　　hlaford leofne.
> Ongunnon þa on beorge　　　bæl-fyra mæst
> wigend weccan　　　*wudu*-rec astah
> sweart ofer swioðole,　　　swogende leg,
> *woþe* bewunden　　　—wind-blond gelæg—
> oðþæt he ða ban-hus　　　gebrocen hæfde,
> hat on hreðre.

(ll. 3137-48)

The next archetypal image is the sea, which is inhabited by Grendel and his mother, by vicious sea-monsters and by the giants who were destroyed in the Flood of *Genesis* (cf. vi. 4, 12, 17), reference to which is made in the inscription engraved on the blade of the ancient sword which Beowulf brings from the cave of Grendel's Dam:

> Hroðgar maðelode,　　　hylt sceawode,
> ealde lafe.　　　On ðæm wæs or writen
> fyrn-gewinnes,　　　syþðan flod ofsloh,
> gifen geotende,　　　giganta cyn;
> frecne geferdon;　　　þæt wæs fremde þeod
> ecean Dryhtne;　　　him þæs ende-lean
> þurh wæteres wylm　　　Waldend sealde.

(ll. 1687-93)

It is in the waters that Beowulf fights monsters in the company of Breca. Unferth,[9] whose name means "Unpeace", "Discord", is here a Chaos figure, giving a false acount of Beowulf's swimming-contest with Breca (ll. 506-24). Beowulf, in a long description (ll. 530-81), gives the correct version of the story and tells how he slew sea-monsters by night. Beowulf thus establishes his credentials as a hero and is accorded the hero-worship he deserves, just as in the *Odyssey* Book VIII Odysseus, the guest of the Phaeacians, is insulted on purpose by Euryalus while observing an athletic contest and is thus given an opportunity of showing his mettle.[10]

It is, then, the duty of heroes in this mythical, archetypal world to combat evil beasts in the waters. Beowulf battles with the sea-beast, Grendel's Dam, in the mere; the wounded Grendel goes home to the waters; Hrothgar's guards watch the sea, for it is thence attacks come, not from the land. And when Beowulf is buried after being consumed by fire, it is beside the sea.

The third archetypal image of Chaos is darkness. When we first meet Grendel, we are given a description of his origin from Cain, the original murderer and begetter of giant broods, then see him setting off for Heorot in the darkness (ll. 115-17), he keeps up his attacks for twelve years, in the night (ll. 159-63). In like manner, the fire-dragon, infuriated by the theft of a goblet from his barrow, waits for night in order to take vengeance:

> Hord-weard onbad
> earfoðlice,　　　oððæt æfen cwom.
> Wæs ða gebolgen　　　beorges hyrde,
> wolde *se laða*　　　lige forgyldan
> drinc-fæt dyre.　　　Þa wæs dæg sceacen
> wyrme on willan;　　　no on wealle læ[n]g
> bidan wolde,　　　ac mid bæle for,
> fyre gefysed.

(ll. 2302-09)

These evil and monstrous deeds have to take place at night, for such evil cannot stand the light of common day, the light of God.

Light is used throughout the poem as an image of creation. Immediately after the building of Heorot, the scop sings a song of creation, a song about God's rescuing of Middle Earth from the waters and lighting it with the sun and the moon to create life:

> Da se ellen-gæst　　　earfoðlice
> þrage geþolde,　　　se þe in þystrum bad,
> þæt he dogora gehwam　　　dream gehyrde
> hludne in healle　　　þær wæs hearpan sweg,
> swutol sang scopes.　　　Sægde, se þe cuþe
> frumsceaft fira　　　feorran reccan,
> cwæð þæt se lmihtiga　　　eorðan worh*te*,
> wlite-beorhtne wang,　　　swa wæter bebugeð:
> gesette sige-hreþig　　　sunnan ond monan
> leoman to leohte　　　land-buendum,
> ond gefrætwade　　　foldan sceatas
> leomum ond leafum;　　　lif eac gesceop
> cynna gehwylcum,　　　þara ðe cwice hwyrfaþ.

(ll. 86-98)

This is the usual picture of the Anglo-Saxon world, painted by means of images of light and of warmth, fire under control. It is a commonplace to compare this passage with the famous passage in the Old English translation of Bede's *Ecclesiastical History*[11] containing the description of life presented to Edwin of Northumbria by one of his thegns in 627 in favour of the new religion being preached by Paulinus:

Þyslic me is gesewen, þu cyning, þis andwearde lif
manna on earðan to wiðmetenesse þære tide, þe us un-
cuð is, swylc swa þu æt swæsendum sitte mid þinum
ealdormannum 7 þegnum on wintertide, 7 sie fýr
onælæd 7 þin heall gewyrmed, 7 hit rine 7 sniwe 7
styrme ute; cume an spearwa 7 hit þus þurhfl-
leo, cume þurh oþre duru in, þurh oþre ut gewite. Hwæt
he on þa tid, þe he inne bið, ne bið hrinen mid þy
storme þæs wintres; ac þæt bið an eagan brythm 7 þæt
læsste fæc, ac he sona of wintra on þone winter eft
cymeð. Swa þonne þis monna lif to medmiclum fæce
ætyweð; hwæt þær foregange, oððe hwæt þær æfter-
fylige, we ne cunnun. Forðon gif þeos lar owiht cuðli-
cre 7 gerisenlicre brenge, þæs weorþe is þæt we þære
fylgen.

So, in Heorot, light, warmth and a hymn of creation stand for a human society attuned, for a brief while at least, to cosmic order and God's will. Heorot is splendid, decked with gold; its radiance now gleams over many lands. It is a Jerusalem on earth, such as is described in *Solomon and Saturn;* similar descriptions of Biblical cities occur in *Genesis A, Judith* and *Andreas.*[12] In *Beowulf,* the treasure shines; the standard which Wiglaf takes from the fire-dragon's barrow to the dying Beowulf, reminiscent of that first standard by which Scyld is buried, shines as an image of kingship giving light to men. Irving[13] points to the use of light as an image of human life and hall-joy in *The Wanderer,* and the archetypes of such images are those in *Genesis* i., 3, 4, 9 and 10.

Let us consider how these images of Chaos and Order operate throughout *Beowulf.* The circle of light representing human life is constantly under attack by Chaos—there is frost on the funeral boat that is to carry Scyld back to the waters whence he came; there is frost on the bough of the tree by the mere; Grendel, his Dam and the fire-dragon attack the land and the hall of light in the darkness, trying to extend the field of influence of Chaos; Grendel's Dam drags Beowulf down into the depths of the mere; the episode of Finn has treachery in the dark; winter and storm oppress Hengest and prevent his taking action; and the battle of Ravenswood traps the lordless Geats for a long, miserable night.

Beowulf's first journey to Denmark and his return thence are both easy because they take place during the day, on the *surface* of the water; the hero is described as *lau-cræfti mon* (l. 209) nevertheless. The land reached after the first voyage is a splendid one, with a fine road leading to the shining Heorot.

In the Breca episode, Beowulf is assailed by sea-monsters, storm, wind, and darkness:

> Ða wit ætsomne　　on sæ wæron
> fif nihta fyrst,　　oþþæt unc flod todraf,
> wado weallende,　　wedera cealdost,
> nipende niht,　　ond norþan wind
> heaðo-grim *ond*hwearf.　　Hreo wræon yþa.

> (ll. 544-8)

Note the images of cold, darkness and tumultuous ocean, followed by the description of victory:

> ac on mergenne　　mecum wunde
> be yð-lafe　　uppe lægon,
> swe*ordum* aswefede,　　þæt syþðan na
> ymb brontne ford　　brim-liðende
> lade ne letton.　　Leoht eastan com,
> beorht beacen Godes;　　brimu swaþredon
> þæt ic sæ-næssas　　geseon mihte,
> windige weallas.

> (ll. 565-72)

The sun comes up, *after* the battle, and the seas calm.

Similarly, the mere where Grendel and his mother dwell (ll.1357-76) is worth nothing,[14] with its impression of water, wind and darkness, with fire glowing under the water; the hart (OE *heorot*) will not enter the waters—the light of the hall (Heorot) or of God will not yet penetrate Chaos. When Beowulf jumps in, he is assailed by all sorts of sea-beasts seeking to rend him, the worst of them all being, of course, Grendel's Dam. When Beowulf slays her, however,

> Lixte se leoma　　leoht inne stod,
> efne swa of hefene　　hadre scined
> rodores candel.

> (ll. 1570-2)

When Beowulf swims back up through the waters, they are ordinary waters once more and now purged of monsters. The whole picture of the mere is reminiscent of the lake of Hell in the apocryphal *Visio Pauli* (and in the vernacular version of the *Visio Pauli* contained in the seventeenth Blickling Homily of the tenth century)[15] and the parallel confirms the interpretation of this part of *Beowulf*—Beowulf has harrowed Hell.

> wæron yð-gebland　　eal gefælsod,
> eacne eardas,　　þa se ellor-gast
> oflet lif-dagas　　ond þas lænan gesceaft.

> (ll. 1620-2)

To emphasize this, we learn:

> 　　　　　　　　Þa þæt sweord ongan
> æfter heaþo-swate　　hilde-gicelum,
> wig-bil wanian.　　Þæt wæs wundra sum,
> þæt hit eal gemealt　　ise gelicost,
> þonne forstes bend　　Fæder onlæteð
> onwindeð wæl-rapas,　　se geweald hafað
> sæla ond mæla;　　þæt is soð Metod.

> (ll. 1605-11)

When Beowulf and the Geats ride back from the mere after Grendel's flight, morning joy pervades the poem, and when Beowulf sails home again to the land of the Geats, the sun again shines brightly.

In this dark world of *Beowulf,* then, the function of a hero is to aid God in his maintenance of creation. God's powers are strangely limited in this poem; we have references to the Old Testament, but not to the New Testament except for the *Apocalypse.* D. Whitelock has argued that such a limited position is unlikely since conversions usually begin with the major doctrines of New Testament Christianity and pass later to the detailed stories of the Old Testament. Yet **Beowulf** does not mention Christ at all, let alone the great Christian dogmas of the Incarnation, Passion, Crucifixion, Resurrection and Salvation of Mankind.[16] K. Sisam has pointed out that the Old English taste was for the Old Testament and *Revelations;* Bede tells us that when Caedmon sang the first-ever Anglo-Saxon religious poem at Whitby, he sang further of *Genesis* and of the future judgment as well as of the life of Christ.[17] It is to the point to consider to which parts of scripture the **Beowulf** poet has restricted himself, and why.

The Anglo-Saxons were almost obsessed, in their homiletic writings and poems, with the Day of Judgment and the ways of death of men who have gone before. Lines 80-4 of *The Wanderer,* for example, list the ways of death, and similar passages occur in four Old English homilies.[18] They are all based on the Biblical account of the Apocalypse:

> And the sea gave up the dead that were in it, and death and hell gave up their dead that were in them; and they were judged every one according to their works.
>
> [*Apocalypse* xx. 13]

The New Testament continues with a note of hope:

> And God shall wipe away all tears from their eyes: and death shall be no more, nor mourning, nor crying, nor sorrow shall be any more, for the former things are passed away.
>
> [*Apocalypse* xxi. 4]

But until that Day, the powers of darkness will prevail, and it is precisely these powers mentioned in the *Apocalypse* that Beowulf must combat. The circle of light that is human life is constantly under attack by the powers of Chaos and darkness, and the hero fends them off as well as he can, purging Heorot and Grendel's mere, fighting monsters in the waters, harrowing Hell in order that God's light may shine the more clearly upon His creation.

But man appears on earth, almost by accident, for a short time only. At the end of the poem, the images of Chaos all turn upon Beowulf: a fire-dragon flying by night brings fire to the land, fire which eventually devours the hero's corpse; the only light comes from the treasure of an earthly king and will not succour the dying hero; and the land he dies on is a headland near the sea. In a world where God is little more than *wyrd,* nothing is left for the hero save death.[19] Beowulf's last action is to command that his barrow be built on the headland as a beacon to guide other mariners across the ocean.

In a world which knows not the Christ who walks upon the waters, who preaches peace and mercy, who makes gentle jokes about little sparrows or the lilies of the field, life is brief and transitory—*lif is læne.* This is the true theme of the poem, and underlies its entire elegiac aspect. For example, in the Finnsburg episode, the reference to the return of spring is not trite, but vital:

> holm storme weol,
> won wið winde;   winter yþe beleac
> is-gebinde,   oþðæt oþer com
> gear in geardas,   swa nu gyt doſiſð.
>
> (ll. 1131-34)

Whatever men do in the slaughter-stained winter, the cycle of the seasons is not at all disturbed. The regular order of nature is not affected by monsters *or by men*—that is the pity of it.

It is, I think, valuable in studying this poem of monsters and men to consider their functions in turn, to view them against the background of the heroic world I have delineated and then attempt a final assessment of the poem.

Any study of the archetypal imagery of **Beowulf** must come to grips with the problem of the monsters and what they represent. The poem has come under attack in the past because of its concentration on monsters when in actual fact monsters are precisely what the poet chose to write on. The attack was launched by W.P. Ker:[20]

> In construction it is curiously weak, in a sense preposterous; for while the main story is simplicity itself, the merest commonplace of heroic legend, all about it, in the historic allusions, there are revelations of a whole world of tragedy, plots different in import from that of **Beowulf,** more like the tragic themes of Iceland. Yet with this radical defect, a disproportion that puts the irrelevances in the centre and the serious things on the outer edges, the poem of **Beowulf** is unmistakably heroic and weighty. The thing itself is cheap; the moral and the spirit of it can only be matched among the noblest authors.

Tolkien quotes the charge made by R.W. Chambers[21] in his discussion of the Ingeld allusion:

> Nothing [Chambers says] could better show the disproportion of **Beowulf** which 'puts the irrelevances in the centre and the serious things on the outer edges', than this passing allusion to the story of Ingeld. For in this conflict between plighted troth and the duty of revenge we have a situation which the old heroic poets loved, and would not have sold for a wilderness of dragons.

C. S. Lewis,[22] too, seizes on this point:

> Hengest, who ought to have been the Aeneas of our epic if the poet had had Virgil's notion of an epic subject, is mentioned only parenthetically.

All such critics seem to regret the fact that the **Beowulf** poet has not told some of the heroic tales mentioned in *Widsith or Deor* instead of talking at length about monsters. Their question is, 'Why did he not tell the whole

Scylding story and not put the irrelevant monsters to the outer edges?' To sum up, they assume, of course, that what is important to them was what was important to the poet; the real problem, surely, is to decide what the *poet's* purpose was.

Tolkien's famous paper is very important in this regard, for it was the first strong claim that the main theme of *Beowulf* is the important one and that the background has been kept, quite correctly, in the background. One must suspend disbelief in monsters when reading *Beowulf* and accept that the poet is *not* telling a fairy-story but treating of a theme worth taking trouble over. In a world lacking our modern communications and our scientific knowledge, and which seems to be centred on a tiny explored area surrounded by forests and wastes, the Anglo-Saxons might well peer fearfully into the darkness and imagine all sorts of monsters lurking in the shadows.

Once again, the Old English translation of Bede's *Ecclesiastical History*[23] is helpful. In Book III, thelwald of Northumbria gives Bishop Cælin land on which to erect a monastery:

> Þa gefultmode se biscop þæs cyninges willan, 7 him stowe geceas mynster to getimbrigenne in heawum morum uppe, in þæm wæs má gesegen sceaðoena deagolnesse 7 wildeora fernisse þonne monna eardungstow. Ða æfter Esaies witedome, in þæm cleofum, þe ær dracan eardodon, wære úpyrnende grownes hreodes 7 rixa: þæt is to ongeotonne, þætte acende wæron wæstmas godra dæda, þær ær oðþe wildeor eardedon oððe mæn wunedon wildeorlice lifigan.

This is allegory, but a less sophisticated people would take it literally. Similarly, in Felix's mid-eighth-century Latin *Life of St. Guthlac,* translated into Old English in the 11th century, Guthlac goes to the fens on the Granta River near Cambridge in emulation of the Christian martyrs setting off into the desert, and he is assaulted by portents and terrors of unknown shape, by monsters and the phantoms of demons; men could not inhabit an island there 'on account of the unknown monsters of the wasteland and terrors of diverse shapes'.[24] Conversion to Christianity did not kill belief in monsters, but then, why should it?[25] It is not education so much as the spread of settlements that eventually killed belief in monsters. The poet probably set his tale in Denmark and the land of the Geats to lend verisimilitude to his monsters through distance in the same way as later ages were able to conceive of Dracula and Frankenstein in places remote from civilisation such as Transylvania.

It is worth considering for a few moments the contents of the *Beowulf* manuscript, BM Cotton Vitellius A. xv.[26] It starts with the latter part of a homily on St. Christopher, who is described in the Latin original as twelve cubits high and in the Anglo-Saxon version as twelve fathoms! He is not only a giant, but a monster with a dog's head. The *Old English Martyrology*[27] tells us that 'he had a dog's head, and his locks were extraordinarily long, and his eyes gleamed as bright as the morning star, and his teeth were as sharp as a boar's tusks.'

Christopher is thus described as one of the race of dog-headed cannibals, the Cynocephali, and the *healfhundingas* are also dealt with in the next two (prose) works in the manuscript, *The Wonders of the East* and *Alexander's Letter to Aristotle.*[28] A lively interest in monsters is therefore continued in *Beowulf.* The history of Beowulf's lord, Hygelac, in the (eighth-century?) *Liber Monstrorum*[29] helps to confirm this conjecture:

> Concerning King Huiglaucus of the Getae, and his amazing hugeness.
>
> Now there are also these monsters of amazing hugeness, namely, King Huiglaucus, who ruled the Getae and was slain by the Franks. Even when he was twelve years old, no horse could carry him. His bones are preserved on an island in the Rhine, where it flows into the sea, and are shown as a prodigy to people who come from afar.[30]

It would distort *Beowulf* to take this idea of Hygelac as a monster too far, but there is surely in BM MS Cotton Vitellius A. xv and in this description of Hygelac sufficient to suggest that the manuscript was compiled by someone interested in the theme of monsters.

Granted the suspension of disbelief and granted a genuine belief in monsters by the audience of *Beowulf,* one must ask, 'Why are there monsters and dragons in a divinely-created world?' The poet is surely attempting to answer the one great problem of philosophy—the existence of evil in the world.

The Cotton gnomic poem[31] tells us:

> Draca sceal on hlæwe,
> frod, frætwum wlanc.
> þyrs sceal on fenne gewunian
> ana innan lande.

The *Beowulf* dragon thus runs true to type, for he is old, likes treasure and stays in a barrow. On the other hand, Grendel is a *þyrs* and also runs true to type, living in the fens and feeling alone. The poet of a Christian era would have to explain to his audience how such animals came about in a Christian creation, and it is therefore no accident that early in the poem, just after the introduction relating who the Scyldings were, the scop sings a song of creation in Heorot. Human happiness of this sort would annoy any self-respecting monster, for spirits who lurk in darkness envy human happiness, but we notice that Grendel does not simply attack Heorot because he is the archetypal party-pooper; he attacks when he hears a song of creation. This is quite deliberate on the part of the poet; other bards in the poem sing of the heroes of the past, but this scop sings of creation, thus indicating that the Danes are Christians and and that it is *this* that annoys Grendel:

> Ða se ellen-gæst   earfoðlice
> þrage geþolode,   se þe in þystrum bad,
> þæt he dogora gehwam   dream gehyrde
> hludne in healle;   þær wæs hearpan sweg,
> swutol sang scopes.   Sægde, se þe cuþe

frumsceaft fira   feorran reccan,
cwæð þæt selmihtiga   eorðan worh*te*,
wlite-beorhtne wang,   swa wæter bebugeð:
gesette sige-hreþig   sunnan ond monan
leoman to leohte   land-buendum,
ond gefrætwade   foldan sceatas
leomum ond leafum;   lif eac gesceop
cynna gehwylcum,   þara ðe cwice hwyrfaþ.

(ll. 85-98)

This is based ultimately on the Vulgate version of *Genesis* i. 20 and 30, and this is the question stated directly—God made all creatures that move alive and thought it good; the monsters are not good, so God did not make them. Where, then, did they come from?

The early English church offered three answers to the problem. The first is based on an early interpretation of *Genesis* vi. 2 by Justin Martyr, who took the words *filii dei* to refer to the fallen angels. According to this view, the fallen angels produced demons and evil broods; the Flood destroyed their bodies, but their spirits lived on. In *Guthlac A* the saint struggles with demons in his fenland retreat, and the demons are described as the descendants of Lucifer, the warriors of the ancient enemy, who had been using the area as a rest-home. In *Guthlac B* the saint's tormentors are devils, sometimes in the form of beasts, sometimes in human form, sometimes dragons.[32] This explanation, however, it not used by the *Beowulf* poet.

The second, the view of the *Beowulf* poet, is that the monsters were the brood of Cain, the archetypal murderer. This was the view of the Irish church, and it was Irish monks who first converted the English in the north.[33] So, having introduced us to the story of *Genesis* and creation in the song sung in Heorot, the poet introduces us to the first villain of the poem, Grendel:

Wæs se grimma gæst   Grendel haten,
mære mearc-stapa,   se þe moras heold,
fen ond fæsten;   fifel-cynnes eard
won-sæli wer   weardode hwile,
siþðan him scyppen*d*   forscrifen hæfde
in Caines cynne—   þone cwealm gewræc
ece Drihten,   þæs þe he abel slog.
Ne gefeah he þære fæhðe,   ac he hine feor for-
wræc,
Metod for þy mane,   man-cynne fram.
no he þone gif-stol   gretan moste,
maþðum for Metode,   ne his myne wisse.
Þanon untydras   ealle onwocon,
eotenas ond ylfe   ond orcne-as,
swylce gig*antas*,   þa wið Gode wunnon
lange þ*rage;*   he him ðæs lean forgeald.

(ll. 102-14, 168-9)[34]

The poet backs up this descent from Cain by referring to it again when Hrothgar finds the tale of the ancient strife when flood destroyed the race of giants written on the sword which Beowulf brings up from the mere (ll. 1687 ff.). The other specific reference to Cain occurs in the passage which introduces us to Grendel's Dam:

Grendles modor,
ides, aglæc-wif   yrmþe gemunde,
se þe wæter-egesan   wunian scolde,
cealde streamas,   siþðan Ca*in* wearð
to ecg-banan   angan breþer,
fæderen-mæge;   he þa fag gewat,
morþre gemearcod,   man-dream fleo[ha]n,
westen warode.   Þanon woc fela
geosceaft-gasta;   wæs þæra Grendel sum
heoro-wearh hetelic,   se æt Heorote fand
wæccendne wer   wiges bidan.

(ll. 1258-68)

The *Beowulf* poet would seem to assume that his hearers are familiar with Biblical stories just as much as they are familiar with heroic legends. This belief in the monsters' descending from Cain is based upon another interpretation of *Genesis* vi. 2: 'The sons of God seeing the daughters of men, that they were fair, took to themselves wives of all which they chose.' This was taken to refer to the union of the descendants of Seth with those of Cain, and *Genesis* vi. 4, 'Now giants were upon the earth in those days', implied that the giants destroyed by the flood were to be identified with the descendants of Cain. Only the giants were destroyed by the flood, and the evil broods of sea-monsters lived on; a flood, after all, would not particularly distress Grendel and his Dam. This interpretation of *Genesis* is given in Bede's commentary on *Genesis*[35] and in the Old English poem *Genesis*.[36]

The third answer is that Noah's wicked son Ham was the first person to be cursed after the flood; Irish sources suggest that he then gave birth to all the monsters. The deluge drowned the descendants of Cain, but then the monsters descended from Ham were conceived. This descent from Ham is not, as I have shown, the view of the *Beowulf* poet, but it seems to have been the view of the *Beowulf* scribe, for both of the references in the poem to Cain are blundered; 1. 107 reads *caines*, altered from *cames*, and 1. 1261 reads *camp*—obviously the scribe was familiar with the Ham theory.[37]

The poet, then, has the minstrel in Heorot sing of creation, partly to raise this matter and partly to illustrate the theme that creation is God's. The monsters 'were not coeval with God; they did not exist before the creation of the world; they were not part of that creation; they were the offspring of sinful humanity, the progeny of the first murderer'.[38] Heroes like Beowulf do God's work by combatting such monsters:

Þær him aglæca   ætgræpe wearð;
hwæþre he gemunde   mægenes strenge,
gim-fæste gife   ðe him God sealde,
ond him to Anwaldan   are gelyfde,
frofre ond fultum;   ðy he þone feond ofercwom,
gehnægde helle-gast.

(ll. 1269-74)

Tolkien[39] points out that:

At this point new Scripture and old tradition touched and ignited. It is for this reason that these elements of

Scripture alone appear in a poem dealing of design with the noble pagan of old days. For they are precisely the elements which bear upon this theme. Man alien in a hostile world, engaged in a struggle which he cannot win while the world lasts, is assured that his foes are the foes also of Dryhten, that his courage noble in itself is also the highest loyalty: so said thyle and clerk.

Grendel is described in terms used elsewhere to describe the devil, for example, *ʒodes andsaca, se ellenʒæst, wiht unhælo, feond mancynnes, helle hæfton, atol aʒlæca, deorc deaþscua, helruna, synscaða, manscaða.* This does not, of course, mean that he *is* the devil, for that would make Beowulf Christ and we know where that can lead. Grendel is simply the enemy of God and the antithesis of Beowulf.

Grendel's Dam is of the same order of evil as her son, but she is not described in such terms of theological guilt as Grendel. She comes to Heorot to take revenge for her son's death when she carries off the Danish counsellor æschere, and this gives her a small excuse. She is to be regarded as a monster too, representing evil and descended of Cain, as we are specifically reminded. Beowulf has more trouble dispatching the female of the species as one might expect, and artistically a worse battle is required to avoid anticlimax.

The problem is the dragon. Tolkien[40] seems to think all three monsters are of a similar order and kindred significance. T.M. Gang[41] objects that the dragon is of a different order altogether from Grendel and his Dam; the dragon is never specifically named as the enemy of God, rather he is a figure of impending doom at the end of the poem. The vexed question is whether or not the dragon is an *untydre,* whether or not he, too, is descended of Cain. Sisam points out that in some passages of Scripture and Christian writings the devil is represented by a dragon, but the fire-dragon is not very like the dragon of the Apocalypse; Sisam[42] draws our attention to Augustine of Hippo's view that the devil is represented by the lion *propter impetus* and by *draco propter insidias,* thinking of the traditional wiliness of the serpent rather than the fiery breath of the ***Beowulf*** dragon.

Tolkien[43] maintains that the conception of the dragon approaches *draconitas* rather than *draco. Pace* Tolkien, the dragon here is *draco* rather than *draconitas,* for the dragon is simply the animal dragon of the Cotton gnome. After the poignant lay of the last survivor and the burial of the treasure of the ancient people, the dawn-flier finds the barrow and settles on it as he should by his very nature. The dragon is all animal in ***Beowulf;*** his feelings and emotions are not analysed as in the cases of Grendel and his mother, for he has not thoughts, only animal behaviour. Look how he acts when he wakes and finds the thief's footprints:

> Hord-weard sohte
> georne æfter grunde, wolde guman findan,
> þone þe him on sweofote sare geteode;
> hat ond hreoh-mod hlæw oft ymbe-hwearf,
> ealne utanweardne; ne ðær ænig mon
> on þære westenne; hwæðre *wiges* gefeh,
> bea*duwe* weorces; hwilum on beorh æthwearf,
> sinc-fæt sohte.
>
> (ll. 2293-2300)

This is a dog who has lost his bone.

When considering the use of monsters in ***Beowulf,*** I am not at all convinced that the study of parallels in other Germanic literatures[44] is particularly relevant or helpful, for none of them are of the same date as the ***Beowulf*** poem and in none of them are the monsters what W.P. Ker would call 'in the centre.' For example, the dragon-slayings in the O.H.G. *Nibelungenlied* and the corresponding O.N. sources do describe Sigurðr (Siegfried) gaining an immense treasure by killing a dragon, but the heroes are not renowned principally for the dragon-control service they offer—that emphasis comes only with Wagner. Nothing of import is gained by a consideration of Sigurðr's fights in *Fáfnismál, Völsunga saga, Þiðreks saga* or Snorri's *Edda,* of Ragnar's matter-of-fact serpent slaying in *Ragnars saga Loðbrókar* or of Frotho's exploits in Saxo's *Gesta Danorum.* It is similarly a critical commonplace to compare the Grendel fight with Grettir's struggle with Glam in *Grettis saga* or the parallel battles of Orm, Böðvarr Bjarki, Þorstein, Gull-þórir or Samson. Yet even with the closest parallel from a much later century, we see that the fight with Glam is *not* central to *Grettis saga* as the fights *are* in ***Beowulf*** and that Grettir is cursed for his success where Beowulf is praised for a task seen in quite a different light. The best thing to do is to rely on the descriptions of the monsters given us in ***Beowulf*** itself.

It might be objected that the poet's descriptions of the monsters are rather vague, but, after all, the early mediaeval taste was for conceptualisation rather than for visualisation along the lines of the Renaissance poets. Closeness of detail helps one to visualise the monsters in Spenser,[45] Sin and Death in *Paradise Lost,* Ariosto's Hippogriff, Drayton's monsters in *PolyAlbion,* and so forth, monsters influenced perhaps by the art of the Renaissance in heraldry, emblem books or the paintings of Giotto. The Renaissance response becomes an intellectual one where the ***Beowulf*** poet by his deliberate lack of such detail elicits an emotional response; he leaves the monsters vague, suggesting that in the primal darkness one may see two weird creatures of damnation in human shape and a fire-dragon breathing flame—the rest is left to the imagination of an audience that believes implicitly in monsters and their monstrosity.

The function of the monsters is, I think, now clear. We can answer the question 'Why does the ***Beowulf*** poet not have his hero fight other champions of other nations to get glory?' The answer is that the poet wants him to fight monsters and dragons. The monsters represent the offspring of Cain and are Chaos figures, belonging to the sea and the darkness, so a hero has no alternative but to aid God in the maintenance of His creation by opposing such creatures of damnation; the dragon, a fire image of Chaos, represents the final enemy, death, which no-one, not even Beowulf, can defeat. He is not Christ. As Tolkien[46] has put it:

> We do not deny the worth of the hero by accepting Grendel and the dragon. Let us by all means esteem the old heroes: men caught in the chains of circumstance or of their own character, torn between duties equally sacred, dying with their backs to the wall. But *Beowulf*, I fancy, plays a larger part than is recognized in helping us to esteem them . . . But though with sympathy and patience we might gather, from a line here or a tone there, the background of imagination which gives to this indomitability, this paradox of defeat inevitable yet unacknowledged, its full significance, it is in *Beowulf* that a poet has devoted a whole poem to the theme, and has drawn the struggle in different proportions, so that we may see man at war with the hostile world, and his inevitable overthrow in Time. The particular is on the outer edge, the essential in the centre.

C.S. Lewis[47] also gets to the heart of the matter:

> The fall of Virgil's Troy is a catastrophe, the end of an epoch. *Urbs antiqua ruit*—"an ancient city, empress of long ages, falls." For Homer it is all in the day's work. *Beowulf* strikes the same note. Once the king is dead, we know what is in store for us: that little island of happiness, like many another before it and many another in the years that follow, is submerged, and the great tide of the Heroic Age rolls over it . . . In Homer the background of accepted, matter-of-fact despair is, after all, a background. In *Beowulf* that fundamental darkness comes out into the foreground and is partly embodied in the monsters. And against those monsters the hero fights. No one in Homer had fought against the darkness.

Thus the world of *Beowulf* is a tiny circle of light on land surrounded by darkness and the restless, relentless ocean, an island universe rescued from Chaos by creation but only temporarily, an uneasy equilibrium between the forces of evil, represented by images of the sea, darkness and discreating fire, and the forces of good, represented by the land, the light and the warmth of the hearth-fire, an unstable stability, a fixity that is infixity, a portion of time wrested from eternity and thereby made miserable.

The God of the poem, the God only of the Old Testament and the Apocalypse, does not seem to care particularly about man, an experiment gone wrong which should, perhaps, be abandoned. The function of a hero (as mentioned more briefly above) is to aid the limited power of God in the maintenance of creation by battling against God's adversaries, the Chaos monsters Grendel and his Dam, and inevitable death in the shape of the fire of the fire-dragon and of the funeral pyre. In this mighty endeavour, a hero gets himself no real reward and ultimately no real success; *lif is læne: eal scæced leoht and lif somod,* 'life is transitory: light and life together all hasten away'.[48] The tone is aptly dignified, for the poem is an elegy.

J.C. Maxwell[49] tells us that *King Lear* is 'a Christian play about a pagan world'; the setting and the actions are pa-

gan, but the values are Christian. King Lear, morally blind and spiritually depleted at the beginning of the play, learns sanity through madness and gains the Christian values of humility, brotherhood, love and mercy. In Marlowe's phrase, he is, at the end of the play, 'on the way to heaven'. He is permitted to learn Christian patience through suffering. *Beowulf* is also a Christian work of a Christian poet about a pagan world, but here the values of the poem are pagan. The God of the New Testament is missing from the poem, so Beowulf cannot learn Christian patience; yet, since the poem is Christian in that we have in it the God of the Old Testament and of the Apocalypse, Beowulf is denied even stoic patience. All that is left for him is pessimism and death after a heroism of uncertain value.

Throughout the poem we are given to understand that beyond the instability of this world there is stability, outside time there is eternity. After the fearful winter at Finnsburg, spring returns as usual, *swa nu gyt do[i]đ* (l. 1134). Compare also

	Metod eallum weold
gumena cynnes,	swa he nu git do[i]đ
	(ll. 1057-8)
Wolde dom Godes	dædum rædan
gumena gehwylcum,	swa he nu gen do[i]đ
	(ll. 2858-9)

and Beowulf's last words—'Ic him æfter sceal!'

Those critics who try to insist that *Beowulf* is purely a Christian poem point to the following facts. The universe is God's, and men on earth recognize this. The Danes in the newly-built Heorot listen to a song of creation (ll. 90-100); Beowulf, in the Breca episode, calls the sun *beorht beacen Godes* (l. 570); a son Beowulf is sent to Scyld by God (l. 13); glory in fight is granted to Beowulf against Grendel by God (l. 819); and Hrothgar's speech points out that Heremod was given strength by God but misused the gift (ll. 1716-20). This long speech of Hrothgar's to Beowulf is often with justification referred to as Hrothgar's sermon. Gazing on the sword-hilt Beowulf brings from Grendel's cave, with its message about the giants drowned in the flood of *Genesis,* Hrothgar proceeds to a mediaeval *exemplum* in which comparison with Sigemund praises the hero, comparison with Heremod warns him about the dangers of pride (ll. 1761-8).

The poet himself preaches us a sermon when the Danes pray to idols for help against Grendel. We have seen the Danes listen to a song of creation, and we have heard Christian speeches from the coast-guard, Wealtheow and Hrothgar, referring to a God they now seem not to know:

Hwilum hie geheton æt *hærg-trafum*	
wig-weorþunga,	wordum bædon,
þæt him gast-bona	geoce gefremede
wið þeod-þreaum.	Swylc wæs þeaw hyra,
hæþenra hyht;	helle gemundon
in mod-sefan,	Metod hie ne cuþon,
dæda Demend,	ne wiston hie Drihten God

ne hie huru heofena Helm   herian ne cuþon,
wuldres Waldend.

(ll. 175-88)

Such reversion to heathen habits by Christians sometimes happened in times of stress; compare, for example, the following account from the Old English version of Bede's *Ecclesiastical History*[50] of the relapse to paganism of the East Saxons during a pestilence in AD 665:

Seo ilce mægð þa Eastseaxna mid þy heo wæced wæs mid þy wæle þære foresprecenan deaðlicnesse, ða Sighere mid þy dæle his folces, þe he heold, forlet þa gerynu þæs Cristnan geleafan 7 to hæðenisse wæs gehwyrfed. Forðon þe se seolfa cyning 7 his aldormen 7 monige of his folce lufodon þis deaðlice líf 7 þæt towearde ne sohton, ne þæt furðum gelefdon, þæt hit ó wære. Þa ongunnon heo þa heargas edniwian, þa ðe ær forlætene wæron, 7 deofolgild weorþian 7 gebiddan, swa swa heo þurh þas þing meahton from þam woole 7 fram þære deaþlicnesse gescilde beon.

Trust in God and gratitude to Him is expressed several times in the poem. The coast-guard entrusts Beowulf and his companions to God (ll. 316-18), and Hrothgar's immediate reaction to the news of the hero's arrival is that Beowulf must have been sent by God to aid the West Danes. Wealhtheow, Hygelac, Wiglaf, and Beowulf (during his escape from the mere) make similar remarks. All these observations might be dismissed as merely the commonplace of conversation, but it is not so easy to dismiss Beowulf's speech before his fight with Grendel (ll. 685-8), telling us that the holy God may decree the triumph to whichever side seems meet to him, or his speech after the battle (ll. 977-9), pointing out that God will sentence Grendel at the Last Judgment.

Beowulf does not make as many references to God as Hrothgar does until the second part of the poem when he is himself the leader of a people facing disaster. He wonders what he has done to so sorely anger the Almighty (ll. 2329-32) in much the same way as the Old English homilists lfric and Wulfstan were to do later. Such instances could be multiplied easily, for the poet tells his audience quite clearly that Beowulf, Hrothgar and their peoples are Christians and that what one does in this world determines one's fate in the next. Klaeber[51] even argues that Beowulf is a Christ figure and others tell us that the poem is a psalm about redemption in which Beowulf is Christ and Grendel is the Devil.[52] Such critics in my opinion go to absurd lengths to examine only part of the evidence supplied in the poem on this matter; for an allegorical Christ, Beowulf surely does and says some very strange things! Here, we are told, we have a Christian poem written for Christians by a Christian poet and including frequent references to God in the person of the poet and in the speeches of the characters, a psalm about creation, a sermon about heathenism from the poet and a sermon on pride from Hrothgar.

I maintain, however, that **Beowulf** cannot be interpreted as a Christian poem in the fullest sense, for its values are pa-

gan; by these values Beowulf is judged, and it is these values that are found wanting and lend the poem its elegiac tone. The poem equates the pagan idea of Fate, of Wyrd, with Old Testament Christianity, which it would be quite impossible to do with New Testament Christianity. Admittedly there is a stability and order in eternity, but not here on earth; whatever takes place on earth, in Heorot, in Grendel's cave, in Finnsburg, does not affect the divine order one way or another. Men and monsters may do as they may—the universe shrugs. There is a song of creation, but it is Grendel, not God, who hears it. Light from God shines on the waters after the Breca episode and light lances through the waters of Grendel's mere after the slaying of his mother, but only *after* Beowulf has done all the work; there is not yet a Christ to harrow Hell—man has to do it himself. There is not yet a Christ to conquer death.

Again, Hrothgar preaches a sermon against pride and urging humility, but these values are not specifically Christian. They are part of the gnomic wisdom of the comitatus. I have already pointed out that such a list of ways of death is Apocalyptic and may be paralleled in several Judgment Day homilies and Biblical passages, and also that a similar list is contained in the Old English elegy, *The Wanderer.* Tolkien points to a parallel in another elegy, *The Seafarer,*[53] and this so-called *sum* figure is developed in great elaboration in *The Fates of Men*[54] in the Exeter Book, a terrifying *danse macabre* in which we have listed for us all the possible ways of death—falling from a tree, war, plague, murder, old age, being torn by the wolf or the eagle, being burned on the funeral pyre or drowned at sea, being hanged for a crime, and so on. These I regard also as the gnomic wisdom of the comitatus. Beowulf himself, towards the end of the poem, in an elegiac passage just before his final battle, considers the feelings of the bereaved father looking on the hanging body of his son (ll. 2444-59). Hrothgar's sermon exhorts the hero to accept knowledge of human limitation, as signalled by death. In the *Iliad,* Achilles goes out at last to avenge Patroclus by killing Hector, knowing he will thus bring about his own early death; Beowulf sets off to face the fire-dragon knowing he will die—what makes him heroic is the fact that he still goes, not any knowledge of pride.

It is common practice to regard the poet's sermon about the Danes' lapse from Christianity to paganism as an interpolation; both Tolkien and Whitelock adopt this solution.[55] But I take it to be an expression of the fact that the Danes cannot really distinguish between God and Wyrd. Their song of creation and their prayers to God have not dispatched Grendel, so why not try an appeal in another court, at another shrine? Scarcely encouraging Christianity is the fate of one of Beowulf's men; the hero's troop go to sleep in Heorot, secure in their faith in the protection of God, yet Grendel enters and devours Hondscio without any objection from the Deity or his representative, Beowulf.

Finally, it is true that Beowulf and the other characters in the poem make frequent references to God and utter Christian gnomes, but they utter an equal number of gnomes about Wyrd and see no contradiction therein. For them, Wyrd and God are the same thing. For example, Beowulf tells Hrothgar,

> ðær gelyfan sceal
> Dryhtnes dome   se þe hine deað nimeð.

> (ll. 440-1)

and later:

> Gæð a wyrd swa hio scel!

> (l. 455)

Beowulf refers to the sun as *beacen Godes,* 'the beacon of God', then utters a pagan gnome:

> Leoht eastan com,
> beorht beacen Godes;   brimu swaþredon
> þæt ic sæ-næssas   geseon mihte,
> windige weallas.   Wyrd oft nereð
> unfægne eorl,   þonne his ellen deah.

> (ll. 569-73)

Beowulf attributes his victory over the sea-monsters to fate, saying, *Hwæþere me gesælde,* Yet it was granted me . . . (l. 574), and in telling Hygelac about his survival in Grendel's mere remarks, *næs ic fæge þa gyt,* 'I was not doomed as yet' (l. 2141). The poet himself comments on the man who escaped the dragon:

> Swa mæg unfæge   eaðe gidigan
> wean ond wræc-sið,   se ðe Waldendes
> hyldo gehealdeþ.

> (ll. 2291-3)

This is in a world in which God and Wyrd are equated; this is Christianity, but without Christ. Therefore, in this sense, *Beowulf* is *not* a Christian poem. 'What is it, then?', one might ask, and my reply must be Tolkien's; it is a heroic elegy.

Despite incidents, speeches and motifs which bring to mind corresponding parts of the epics of Homer and Virgil, *Beowulf* is not an epic. The scale is correct, the speeches are long enough in all conscience, and we follow the fortunes of a hero with whose destiny that of an entire people is inseparably linked, but we have no gods and goddesses, no divine intervention, no romantic interest; for example, Beowulf is not given a hero's reward by Wealhtheow. Above all, we do not have battles between armies or champions as the main theme. Nor is the poem heroic in the usual sense of the word, for the same reasons. Our hero's monster fights are central to the poem where they would normally be mere incidents in a long list of battles. The heroic world is present, but only in the background (the family strife within the Scylding dynasty, the wars between the Geats and the Swedes, the wars between the Geats and the Franks, the story of Sigemund, the stories of

Heremod, Finnsburg, Ravenswood) and this is what differentiates *Beowulf.*

The things that are heroic, however, are vitally important—the social structure based on the comitatus, the exaggerated rituals of courtesy, the traditional knowledge of the people and their values, the concept of the hero. We first read of the comitatus in chapters 14 and 15 of Tacitus' *Germania,*[56] and it is the basis of all Germanic heroic societies. The king or chieftain gives the gesiths and geneatas of his comitatus rings, food, shelter and protection; *hlaford* derives from *hlafweard,* 'the protector/provider of the bread.' In return for these bounties, the thanes of the comitatus serve their lord in time of war, honour his name, and die by his side if they must; Byrhtnoth's men stand firm at Maldon, Harold's at Senlac Hill. So in *Beowulf* Hrothgar is the lord of the Danes, the protector of earls, the giver of rings. Hygelac, then Beowulf, perform the same function among the Geats. Gnomes throughout the poem point to the concept of the comitatus:

> Swa sceal *geong g*uma   gode gewyrcean,
> fromum feoh-giftum   on fæder *bea*rme,
> þæt hine on ylde   eft gewunigen
> wil-gesiþas,   þonne wig cume,
> leode gelæsten;   lof-dædum sceal
> in mægþa gehw*æm*   man geþeo[ha]n.

> (ll. 20-5)

And when Beowulf has killed the fire-dragon, the poet remarks:

> Swylc sceolde secg wesan,
> þegn æt ðearfe!—

> (ll. 2708-9)

Absence of the comitatus is a common motif in elegy; *The Ruin, The Wanderer, The Seafarer* are all put on the lips of those who are outside their comitatus, and *Beowulf* includes the lay of the last survivor who is bereft of his comitatus. Grendel has no such comitatus, since God threw Cain far from mankind, so when he is referred to in terms usually reserved for exiles the poem has great irony; when the figure of Chaos takes over Heorot, we similarly get an inversion pattern—he cannot approach the throne, he will not pay wergild for those he has slain, but when he controls Heorot he is ironically described as *healðegen* (l. 142).

Beowulf's comitatus accompanies him over the sea to Denmark and his thanes try uselessly to aid their lord against Grendel. During the second fight, they simply wait for Beowulf by the mere, and during the third battle they desert Beowulf altogether. The only person to help him against the dragon is Wiglaf, who is bound to him also by the bond of kinship. Wiglaf's speeches to the deserters show how the comitatus *should* have behaved (ll. 2633-91) while his second speech ends with a gnome:

> Dead bið sella
> eorla gehwylcum   þonne edwit-lif!

> (ll. 2890-1)

Anglo-Saxon verse has two collections of such gnomes in the Cotton manuscript and the Exeter Book. These pieces of traditional wisdom record the knowledge of the comitatus and define its values. The names of things are important; when you can name something, you can say something about it and add to the store of knowledge. The Norse god Óðinn hung nine days and nine nights over the gulf of Chaos for knowledge; he stole the mead of poetry from the giants; he gave his right eye to Mimir to drink from her well of knowledge, and in the guise of the Wanderer he travelled the earth in search of knowledge and a true love. The *Völuspá*, or *Prophecy of the Sibyll*, which tells of the Ragnarøkr, the Doom of the Gods, has the refrain, *Vitu þér enn eða hvat*? 'Know ye more, or what?'[57]

So in *Beowulf* the gnomes define the poet's world. The gnomes about the nature of a *draca* or a *þyrs* explored earlier showed that the dragon and Grendel and his Dam fitted the Cotton definitions. We can see now that Beowulf and Hrothgar fill the definitions of a good king, the comitatus does not meet the definition of a true comitatus, and so on. Towards the climax of the poem, gnomes come thick and fast:

> swa sceal æghwylc mon
> alætan læn-dagas.
>
> (ll. 2590-1)
>
> Sinc eaðe mæg,
> gold on grunde,   gum-cynnes gehwone
> oferhigian   hyde se ðe wylle!
>
> (ll. 2764-6)
>
> swa hit ge*defe* bið
> þæt mon his wine-dryhten   wordum herge,
> ferhðum freoge,   þonne he forþ scile
> of lic-haman   *læded* weorðan.
>
> (ll. 3174-7)

Gnomes and genealogies put together give us the heroic code and define the roles of heroes and kings and their elaborate behaviour. When Beowulf and his men arrive in Denmark, they have to declare their lineage to the coast-guard, who shows them the way to Heorot. There they have to declare their lineage to Wulfgar to ask permission to enter when surely there is nothing Hrothgar wants more then the coming of a hero. Beowulf and his thanes must leave their spears and shields outside the hall, but are permitted to take their short swords with them into the presence. Hrothgar finds it necessary now to point out that he was a benefactor of Ecgtheow, father of Beowulf, and the ruffled feathers of Unferth, the local champion who has failed to fight Grendel, have to be soothed. To save Hrothgar's face, Hrothgar is described as a valiant battle warrior, most famous of fighters. When Wealhtheow later brings in the cup of beer, she offers it first to Hrothgar, for she is *cynna gemyndig* (l. 613), 'mindful of courtly etiquette'.

Based on all these points, the code of the comitatus is quite clear and simple—be mindful of the obligations of kin and of comitatus. Loyalty and bravery are valued above all else. Since death comes to all but the gnomes tell no more that is certain, an honourable death is the highest morality of the heroic honour-value. The gnomes of the *Battle of Maldon* give this code its finest expression:

> Hi3e sceal þe heardra, heorte þe cenre,
> mod sceal þe mare, þe ure mæ3en lytlað.[58]

These gnomes express the limit of the knowledge of the Anglo-Saxon comitatus, and its honour-value was capable of turning the greatest of defeats, death itself, into a virtue. In this connection Tolkien[59] quotes in part W.P. Ker on the code of the Vikings:

> The last word of the Northmen before their entry into the larger world of Southern culture, their last independent guess at the secret of the Universe, is given in the Twilight of the Gods. As far as it goes, and as a working theory, it is absolutely impregnable. It is the assertion of the individual freedom against all the terrors and temptations of the world. It is absolute resistance, perfect because without hope. The Northern gods have an exultant extravagance in their warfare which makes them more like Titans than Olympians; only they are on the right side, though it is not the side that wins. The winning side is Chaos and Unreason; but the gods, who are defeated, think that defeat is not refutation.

But applied to *Beowulf* this is a distortion. This is where Tolkien starts to go wrong, for the Old Norse *Völuspá* ends with the coming of a new earth, Gimle, and all the gods will live again with men in a new Paradise. Beowulf dies alone, without gods or men by his side, and cannot hope for any such future Elysium.

This is where the heroic poem shades into elegy, for all the heroic matters discussed fail Beowulf in the end. Just as the archetypal images of water and fire turn on him as he is burnt on a headland within sight of the sea and with Wiglaf ironically bathing his face with water, so all the values of the comitatus desert Beowulf. His men let him down and will not fight the dragon alongside him; he turned up as a hero to help Hrothgar, but no hero is at hand to help him in his extremity.[60] The gnomes tell him that he must die, and that earthly glory must pass away, but no more than that. His ancestral weapon lets him down, for his sword snaps as he smites the dragon. Genealogy lets him down, for he has no son; he must die childless since succession on earth would be a substitute for that immortality which belongs to elegy:

> Nu ic suna minum   syllan wolde
> guð-gewædu,   þær me gifee swa
> ænig yrfe-weard   æfter wurde,
> lice gelenge.
>
> (ll. 2729-32)

Further, Wiglaf is the last of the race, paralleling the last survivor of the previous human race:

> þu eart ende-laf   usses cynnes,
> Wægmundinga;   ealle wyrd forspeon

```
mine magas        to metodsceafte,
eorlas on elne;        ic him æfter sceal.
```

(ll. 2813-16)

This is the final gnome Beowulf has to tell.

Beowulf pathetically asks to see and touch the dragon's treasure, but he can do this only for an instant, and it is a sign of the frailty of mortality and the vanity of human wishes in any event. His honour-value as a person is intact but valueless if the context for it, the comitatus, is finished. For Beowulf there will be no Gimle; this brave man, dying for a comitatus that does not appreciate him, has nothing left. Faced with the onrush of the powers of darkness and the relentless flood of Chaos, all he can do is face death with dignity.

This is the very stuff of heroism, but no-one in the poem knows what heroism is. We learn of Beowulf's unhappy life when his special qualities were not appreciated (ll. 2177-89). This man, who is the strongest of men in might in this life's day, who is so powerful that he breaks every sword he uses, is no ordinary man—he has to go where the clarion call of glory summons him. Hygelac does not understand this, however:

```
Hu lomp eow on lade,        leofa Biowulf,
þa du færinga        feorr gehogodest
sæcce secean        ofer sealt wæter,
hilde to Hiorote?        Ac ádu Hroðgare
wid-cuðne wean        wihte gebettest,
mærum deodne?        Ic dæs mod-ceare
sorh-wylmum seað,        side ne truwode
leofes mannes.        Ic de lange bæd,
þæt du þone wæl-gæst        wihte ne grette,
lete Suð-Dene        sylfe geweorðan
guðe wið Grendel.        Gode ic þanc secge,
þæs de ic de gesundne        geseon moste.
```

(ll. 1987-98)

But Beowulf has to go. His final battle, however, is for his people, not for glory; the concept of the hero itself is now out of date. The whole poem ends ironically:

```
Swa begnornodon        Geata leode
hlafordes hryre,        heorð-geneatas;
cwædon þæt he wære        wyruld-cyninga,
manna mildust        ond mon-þwærust,
leodum liðost        ond lof-geornost.
```

(ll. 3178-82)

'The most eager for fame'—they simply do not understand. Beowulf has to die, as he has done everything else, alone. As Tolkien puts it, 'He is a man, and that for him and many is sufficient tragedy'.[61]

If this is the stuff of heroism, it is also the stuff of elegy, heroic elegy. The opening of the poem sets the tone of dignity and elegy for the whole. The funeral of an ancestor, surrendered once again to the Chaos whence he came for a brief sojourn, looks forward to the end of the poem,

to the funeral of Beowulf himself. Scyld's name means 'shield', and Beowulf is the 'shield of his people' against the fire-dragon; to emphasize this, he makes a special shield of metal for the combat.[62] Further, Scyld is buried beneath a standard, and from the dragon's barrow Wiglaf brings Beowulf a standard. To clinch matters, the half-line formula describing Scyld Scefing, 'þæt wæs god cyning' (l. 11), is repeated of Beowulf before his final battle (l. 2390).

To summarize my previous arguments, we are constantly reminded how transitory is earthly glory. Heorot, the moment it is built, is described being destroyed by flames. When Beowulf slays Grendel, a minstrel sings of the death of Sigemund, the dragon-slayer; when Beowulf kills Grendel's Dam, Hrothgar preaches him a sermon on the theme 'remember thou art mortal!' Costly treasure, symbol of mortality, is given to Beowulf after both victories, and before the final battle we have the interlude of the lay of the last survivor burying treasure no longer of use to his race:

```
Heald þu nu hruse,        nu hæled ne mostan,
eorla æhte.        Hwæt hyt ær on de
gode begeaton.        Gud-dead fornam,
feorh-bealo frecne,        fyra gehwylcne
leoda minra,        þara de þis [lif] ofgeaf,
gesawon sele-dream;        nah, hwa sweord wege
odde feormie        fæted wæge,
drync-fæt deore        dugud ellor scoc.
```

(ll. 2247-54)

Once this tone has been set, it is maintained for the last part of the poem until it finally comes to rest after Beowulf's funeral:

```
þa ymbe hlæw riodan        hilde-deore,
æþelinga bearn,        ealra twelfe,
woldon ceare cwiðan,        kyning mænan,
word-gyd wrecan        ond ymb wer sprecan.
```

(ll. 3169-72)

But this is not just the funeral of one hero; it is also the funeral of what he represents—a secular society or at least a Christian society that knows not Christ. It is a Ragnarøkr without Oðinn; an Apocalypse without a God of love; an elegy for man. Thus the world of ***Beowulf*** comes to an end with elegiac dignity and a reminder that *lif is læne*.

Notes

Throughout, quotations from *Beowulf* are taken from the edition by C.L. Wrenn (London, 1953, rev. 1958, reprint 1959).

1. See R. Bruce-Mitford, *The Sutton Hoo Ship-Burial: A Handbook* 2nd ed., (London, 1972), pp. 54-9.

2. *The Audience of Beowulf* (Oxford U.P., 1951, reprint 1967), pp. 22 ff. See also Wrenn, *Beowulf*, pp. 32-7, and R.W. Chambers *Beowulf—An Introduction* with a supplement by C.L. Wrenn 3rd ed., (Cambridge U.P., 1963), pp. 486 ff., 531 ff.

3. On, for example, the historicity, see Wrenn, *Beowulf,* pp. 47-9.

4. For a convenient diagram of Norse cosmography, see E.V. Gordon, *An Introduction to Old Norse,* 2nd ed., (Oxford, 1957, reprint 1966), p. 196. More detailed information may be found in E.O.G. Turville-Petre, *Myth and Religion of the North* (London, 1964).

5. "*Beowulf*—the Monsters and the Critics", *Proceedings of the British Academy* 22 (1936), 245-95; (O.U.P. reprint 1958, 1960), p. 3. Reprinted also in *The Beowulf Poet,* ed. D.K. Fry, (Englewood Cliffs, N.J., 1968), pp. 8-56, and *An Anthology of Beowulf Criticism,* ed. L.E. Nicholson, (Notre Dame U.P., 1963, reprint 1971), pp. 51-103.

6. *Beovulf: Untersuchungen über das angelsächsische Epos und die älteste Geschichte der germanischen Seevölker* (Berlin, 1889).

7. *Beowulf and the Fight at Finnsburg* (3rd ed., Boston, 1922, reprint 1950), p. lx.

8. See Gordon, *An Introduction to Old Norse,* pp. 17-20 for the relevant portions of *Voluspá* as quoted by Snorri in *Gylfaginning,* the first part of his Prose Edda of 1223. For a modern English translation, see *The Prose Edda of Snorri Sturluson,* trans. J.I. Young, (Berkeley and Los Angeles, 1966), pp. 86-90.

9. Some uncertainty attends the etymology of the name 'Unferth' and the role of *þyle;* see, for example, J.L. Rosier, "Design for Treachery: The Unferth Intrigue", *P.M.L.A.* 77 (1962), 1-8; N.E. Eliason, "The *Thyle* and *Scop* in *Beowulf*", *Speculum* 38 (1963), 267-84; J.L. Baird, "Unferth the *þyle*", *Medium Evum* 39 (1970), 1-12; F.C. Robinson, "Personal Names in Medieval Narrative and the Name Unferth in *Beowulf*", in *Essays in Honor of Richebourg Gaillard McWilliams,* ed. H. Creed, *Birmingham-Southern College Bulletin* 63, (1970), 43-8; and M.W. Bloomfield, "*Beowulf* and Christian Allegory: An Interpretation of Unferth", *Traditio* 7 (1949-51), 410-15.

10. This parallel between Beowulf and Odysseus is noted by E.B. Irving, Jr., *A Reading of Beowulf* (Yale, 1968), pp. 67-8. On this and other parallels between the two heroes, see A.B. Lord, "Beowulf and Odysseus", *Franciplegius: Medieval and Linguistic Studies in Honor of Francis Peabody Magoun, Jr.,* ed. J.B. Bessinger, Jr., and R.P. Creed (New York U.P., 1965), pp. 86-91.

11. *The Old English Version of Bede's Ecclesiastical History of The English People,* ed. T. Miller, EETS, OS 95 (1890, reprint 1959), I., i., pp. 134-7.

12. See D.K. Crowne, "The Hero on the Beach—An Example of Composition by Theme in Anglo-Saxon Poetry", *Neuphilologische Mitteilungen* 61 (1960), 362-72, and G. Clark, "The Traveler Recognizes his Goal: A Theme in Anglo-Saxon Poetry", *J.E.G.P.* 64 (1965), 645-59.

13. *A Reading of Beowulf,* pp. 204-5, quoting *The Wanderer,* 11. 94-6.

14. Such an extended description of landscape is rare in Old English poetry; that of the Happy Land in *The Phoenix* comes to mind as the only parallel. It is also rare in Old Norse literature, where the one example I can think of is Grettir's sojourn in winter beneath the Geitland glacier in ch. 61 of *Grettis saga.* For editions of *Grettis saga* see R.C. Boer, *Altnordische sagabibliothek* (Halle, 1900) and G. Jónsson, *Íslenzk Fornrit 7* (Reykjavik, 1936); and translation by G.A. Hight, *The Saga of Grettir the Strong* (London 1914, reprint 1929).

15. See Wrenn, *Beowulf,* p. 210.

16. *Audience,* pp. 6 ff.

17. *The Structure of Beowulf* (Oxford, 1965, revised ed. 1966), pp. 75 ff.

18. See the list of passages in J.E. Cross, "On *The Wanderer* Lines 80-84", *Vetenskaps-Societetens i Lund Arsbok* (1958-9), 85 ff., and add the unpublished homily in praise of St. Michael in the margins of pp. 402-17 of Cambridge, Corpus Christi College MS 41. One stanza relevant here reads, in part: "7 wonne arisað ealle ða deadan ðe eorðe forsweal, oððe sæ bescente, oððe fir forbærnde, oððe wildeor abiton, oððe fulas on lande tobæren, oððe wirmas on eorðan fræten. I hope to publish this homily in full. See also M.R. James, *The Apocryphal New Testament* (Oxford, 1924), p.512, the Ethiopic *Apocalypse of Peter* and the following, more extended passage on p. 522 from *The Second Book of the Sibylline Oracles* of the late second or third century and, according to James, based on the *Apocalypse of Peter:* "Then shall the great angel Uriel break the monstrous bars framed of unyielding and unbroken adamant, of the brazen gates of Hades, and cast them down straightway, and bring forth to judgment all the sorrowful forms, yea, of the ghosts of the ancient Titans, and of the giants, and all whom the flood overtook. And all whom the wave of the sea hath destroyed in the waters, and all whom beasts and creeping things and fowls have feasted on: all these shall he bring to the judgment seat; and again those whom flesh-devouring fire hath consumed in the flames, them also shall he gather and set before God's seat".

19. For a less pessimistic view than my own, see B. Mitchell, "'Until the Dragon Comes . . .' Some Thoughts on *Beowulf*", *Neophilologus* 47 (1963), 122-38, especially 131-3. The joys of which Mitchell speaks are certainly present in the poem but for me render it more poignant. I can see only one conclusion to draw and only one interpretation of the final word of the poem, *lofgeornost;* the heroic *summum bonum* of the impermanent bubble reputation comes a poor second to Christian eternal life.

20. *The Dark Ages* (Edinburgh and London, 1923), p. 253.

21. *Widsith: A Study in Old English Heroic Legend* (Cambridge, 1912), p. 79.

22. *A Preface to Paradise Lost* (London, 1942, 9th impression 1956), p. 28.

23. Miller, *Old English Bede,* I, ii., pp. 230-1.

24. See *Audience,* pp. 75-6, for the quotation from B. Colgrave, *Felix's Life of St. Guthlac,* (p. 88).

25. There are plenty of Biblical references to monsters; the Apocalypse, the story of Jonah and the whale, Behemoth, the Leviathan, and so on. I am grateful to a colleague, Dr. Jean MacIntyre, for bringing to my attention *Job* xxxi: 21-2, which contains an interesting parallel to the fight with Grendel: "Si levavi super pupillum manum meam, etiam cum viderem me in porta superiorem: Humerus meus a junctura sua cadat, et brachium meum cum suis ossibus confringatur". "If I have lifted up my hand against the fatherless, even when I saw myself superior in the gate: Let my shoulder fall from its joint, and let my arm with its bones be broken." For the inability of modern science to help *Beowulf* scholars with the monsters see S.M. Garn and W.D. Block, "The Limited Nutritional Value of Cannibalism", *American Anthropology* 72 (1970), 106.

26. See *Audience,* p. 51, and Sisam, "The Beowulf Manuscript" in *Studies in the History of Old English Literature* (Oxford U.P., 1953, reprint 1962), pp. 65-8, detailed description by N.R. Ker, *Catalogue of Manuscripts Containing Anglo-Saxon* (Oxford, 1957), pp. 281-3.

27. Ed. G. Herzfeld, EETS, OS 116 (1900), p. 66 and note (p. 229).

28. See *Three Old English Prose Texts in MS. Cotton Vitellius A xv,* ed. S. Rypins, EETS, OS 161 (1924) for editions of *The Letter of Alexander the Great to Aristotle* (pp. 1-50), *The Wonders of the East* (pp. 51-67) and *The Life of St. Christopher* (pp. 68-76).

29. See *Audience,* pp. 46-53. The history of Hygelac may also be found in Saxo Grammaticus' *Danish History* (c. 1200), Snorri Sturluson's *Heimskringla* (c. 1223-35), *Ynglinga saga* in Old Norse and two other earlier Frankish works—Gregory of Tours's (d. 594) *History of the Franks,* the *Book of the History of the Franks (Gesta Francorum)* c. 727. For the relevant extracts from these works, see *Beowulf and its Analogues,* ed. G.N. Garmonsway and J. Simpson, (London and New York, 1968), pp. 112-15.

30. Garmonsway and Simpson, *Beowulf and its Analogues,* p. 113.

31. *Sweet's Anglo-Saxon Reader,* rev. D. Whitelock, (Oxford, 1967), p. 175, ll. 26-7, 42-3.

32. See *Audience,* pp. 80-1. In Felix's Latin *Life of St. Guthlac* the saint addresses his tormentors as 'the seed of Cain', but the Old English poems omit this reference altogether.

33. On the Irish tradition, see further O.F. Emerson, "Legends of Cain, especially in Old and Middle English", *P.M.L.A.* 21 (1906), 831-929, especially 878-

83, 888-94, 916-26, and J. Carney, "The Irish Elements in *Beowulf*", *Studies in Irish Literature and History* (Dublin, 1955), pp. 102-12.

34. I accept the suggestion of Wrenn, *Beowulf,* p. 69, that ll. 168-9 are out of place and I follow him in inserting them between ll. 110 and 111.

35. *Venerabilis Bedae Commentaria in Scripturas—Sacras Genesis,* ed. J.A. Giles, I., p. 92, and *In Pentateuchum Commentarii,* Migne, *Patrologia Latina,* XCI, cols. 210 ff, 219 ff.

36. *Genesis A* in *The Junius Manuscript,* ed. G.P. Krapp, The Anglo-Saxon Poetic Records 1 (New York, Columbia U.P., 1931, reprint 1964), pp. 39-40, ll. 1248-62.

37. Wrenn misses the error in l. 107 (Klaeber, *Beowulf,* p. 5). On the *Cham/Cain* confusion, see further Emerson, "Legends", 925, who discusses Alcuin's *Interrogationes et Responsiones in Genesin* and other examples.

38. *Audience,* p. 77.

39. "Monsters and Critics", p. 27. On pp. 36-8, Tolkien gathers the epithets for Grendel and discusses them fully. See also J.L. Baird, "Grendel the Exile", *Neuphilologische Mitteilungen* 67 (1966), 375-81.

40. "Monsters and Critics", p. 33.

41. "Approaches to *Beowulf*", *R.E.S.* N S 3 (1952), 1-12.

42. Sisam, *Structure,* p. 25, n.l. For the most recent extensive argument for aligning the *Beowulf* dragon and the Christian dragon-devil see M.E. Goldsmith, *The Mode and Meaning of 'Beowulf'* (London, 1970), pp. 124-45.

43. "Monsters and Critics", p. 17.

44. The relevant extracts from the parallels cited in this paragraph may be found in R.W. Chambers, *Beowulf—An Introduction,* and in Garmonsway and Simpson, *Beowulf and its Analogues.*

45. Compare, for example, Spenser's description of the dragon in *The Faerie Queene,* ed. J.C. Smith and E. de Selincourt (Oxford U.P., London, 1912, reprint 1959), p. 58, I., xi., 10-12, and his descriptions of Corflambo, Orgoglio, Discord, Lust, Error, Duessa stripped.

46. "Monsters and Critics", pp. 17, 18.

47. Preface to *Paradise Lost,* pp. 29, 30.

48. Quoted by Tolkien, "Monsters and Critics", p. 18. I am grateful to Professor Whitelock for identifying his source for me as *Widsith,* ll. 141-2.

49. "The Technique of Invocation in *King Lear*", *M.L.R.* 45 (1950), 142.

50. Miller, *Old English Bede,* I., ii., pp. 250-1.

51. *Beowulf,* pp. cxx-cxxi.

52. For the most extreme views, see G.G. Walsh, *Medieval Humanism* (New York, 1942), pp. 54 ff.; A. Ca-

baniss, "*Beowulf* and the Liturgy", *J.E.G.P.* 54 (1955), 195-201; M.B. McNamee, S.J., "*Beowulf -* An Allegory of Salvation?", *J.E.G.P.* (1960), 190-207.

53. "Monsters and Critics", pp. 39-40, Appendix B. See further J.E. Cross, "'Ubi Sunt' Passages in Old English—Sources and Relationships", *Vetenskaps-Societetens i Lund Arsbok* (1956), 26-44.

54. *The Exeter Book,* ed. G.P. Krapp and E.V.K. Dobbie, The Anglo-Saxon Poetic Records 3 (New York, Columbia U.P., 1936), pp. 154-5, ll. 10-63.

55. "Monsters and Critics", pp. 45-7, Appendix C, and *Audience,* pp. 78-9.

56. Cornelii Taciti, *De Origine et Situ Germanorum,* ed. J.G.C. Anderson (Oxford, 1938, reprint 1970), pp. 12-13. See also L.L. Schüucking, "Das Konigsideal im *Beowulf*", *Englische Studien* 67 (1932), 1 ff.

57. See Gordon, *An Introduction to Old Norse,* p. 19.

58. Ed. E.V. Gordon (London, 1937, reprint 1967), p. 61, ll. 312-13.

59. "Monsters and Critics", p. 21.

60. True, Wiglaf comes to his aid, but his action is in no way similar to Beowulf's coming from overseas to take over the fighting completely from Hrothgar. That concept of the hero is now out of date, and Wiglaf's heroism is certainly not of the same order.

61. "Monsters and Critics", p. 18.

62. See Irving, *A Reading of Beowulf,* p. 217, on the parallels between Beowulf and Scyld and the play on *Scyld/scyld.*

Kathryn Hume (essay date 1975)

SOURCE: "The Theme and Structure of *Beowulf*," in *Studies in Philology,* Vol. LXXII, No. 1, January, 1975, pp. 1-27.

[*In the following essay, Hume maintains that* Beowulf's *construction emphasizes the author's concern with theme, rather than with the hero or the action. The major thematic issue of the poem, Hume states, is the threat to social order.*]

I

What is *Beowulf* about? Ever since Turner, Conybeare, and Grundtvig impressed Beowulf's name on this titleless poem, the natural answer has been "Beowulf, the hero." This assumption, so simple and inevitable as to be almost unconscious, lies behind most subsequent criticism, and is responsible for much that makes it contradictory and unsatisfactory. Actually, the author's handling of Beowulf and his selection of events neither suggest nor suit a hero-centered design.

No *Heldenleben* could overlook the steps in the *edwenden* from *sleac, unfrom* youth to monster queller; at the very least we might expect to be told as much about the transformation as appears in *Viga-Glum's Saga.* The author could hardly fail to make much of the rise to kingship, particularly since it was complicated by moral dilemmas concerning Heardred and Onela of a sort which would have delighted later saga writers. An ordinary celebration of a hero would probably have dilated upon the vengeance Beowulf exacted for the death of Hygelac, his beloved uncle and king.[1] Sherman Kuhn is correct in stating that the facts for a coherent life of Beowulf are present,[2] but the information appears in allusive and fragmented form— interlaced—and interlace narrative technique is better suited to the creation of juxtapositions of a moral or thematic nature than for simple heroic narrative.[3]

Were the poem centered on Beowulf himself, we would expect to learn something about him as a person. Instead, we hear his public pronouncements and watch his attempts to deal with three monsters. Virtually nothing else is given us: few private thoughts or personal hopes or misgivings; no characterizing features except extraordinary strength. Beowulf does not even have a striking possession used by the author to build our sense of his heroic presence. His helmet has boars on it (l. 1453), but so do those of his men (l. 303).[4] His corselet is *Welandes geweorc* (l. 455), but except for a later testimonial to its efficacy, nothing is made of that fact. His sword is of so little import that he does not use it in the first two fights and breaks it in the third. Beowulf's relations with other people are all public and formal; and though we infer deep feeling for Hygelac, we witness no more personal an exchange than might take place between any staff commander and scout. We do not know if Beowulf ever married. He is his actions in three fights and their immediate contexts, and little else besides.

If one argues that the piece is not really hero- but rather action-oriented, other objections have to be met. The notorious lack of suspense is not consonant with adventure for its own sake. Nor can an action-centered reading explain the long passages describing Swedish wars or the elegiac digressions on the old man and last survivor. Moreover, a sad ending is so foreign to the adventure-story pattern that anyone treating the poem purely as an entertaining tale would have to consider whether something more were not hinted at in the melancholy of the conclusion.

Assumptions of hero- or action-orientation underlie many readings of the poem despite the complete inability of either approach to account for the poem's structure. There are three fights, each occupying one third of the whole; however, they take place at only two stages in Beowulf's life, in two countries, and involve only two kinds of monster. That critics should disagree over whether the structure has two parts or three is hardly surprising. Those concentrating on the hero tend to see two, those on action usually prefer three.[5] But neither camp has produced a structural analysis which does not, by implication, damn the poet for gross incompetence, or leave the critic with a logically awkward position. Tolkien, for instance, who considers the structure one of the work's most admirable strengths, believes the poem to reflect "two moments in a great life, rising and setting . . . youth and age."[6] But if the poet meant to play life's extremes against each other, balancing them like verse half-lines, why are the two movements not more similar in length and plot-construction? Is the Grendel's mother episode anything but an excrescence in a youth/age dichotomy, or indeed in any two-part reading? If, on the other hand, the poet was more concerned with the monsters in a three-part action than with the hero, why should the first two antagonists be so similar? No critic of either persuasion has succeeded in explaining the nature and sequence of the monsters. Why are two so alike? Why does a dragon come last? Why three? Concentration on hero or action reduces the antagonists to mere folktale monstrosities, and to inexplicability.

Because nothing of Beowulf's life is presented in detail except his attempts to deal with monsters; because of the author's suppressions and omissions (exceedingly odd by any biographical standard); and because the three antagonists bulk so large in the poem, logic suggests that the poem's concern will be determined by whatever significance the poet assigns to the monsters, and that the poet's interest in Beowulf is not in him as a person, however heroic, but in his stand against his adversaries. Every feature of the poem's construction supposes concern with a theme rather than hero or action, and the clue to the theme seems to lie in the prominence and nature of the monsters.

The thematic approach to **Beowulf** is not new, though critics using it rarely seem aware of the changes in perspective which their stance demands, or of the corollaries such changes suggest. A representative spread of proposed themes would include the offerings of Schücking (*Königsideal*), Gradon (exemplary heroic action and the influence of Fortune's mutability), Kaske (*sapientia* and *fortitudo*), Goldsmith (pride and covetousness), Lee (hell's possession of middle-earth), Leyerle (the fatal contradiction at the core of heroic society), Kahrl and O'Loughlin (feuding), and Halverson (order versus chaos).[7] Such thematic interpretations share, to a greater or lesser degree, one drawback: they tend to rest for supportive evidence on relatively few lines, and consequently the resultant readings, as can be seen, are wildly varied—indeed are often mutually exclusive—and none has gained general acceptance. Most students of the poem would agree that such readings are useful for sensitizing us to the poem's nuances, but that they are weak on broader issues. By failing to explain the role of Grendel's mother or the Swedish wars, or to account for the number, kind, and ordering of the monsters, most such readings have greatly lessened their claims to consideration as total and self-sufficient interpretations.

Because the logical objections to hero- or action-orientation are so strong, it seems unlikely that they can offer more light on the poem. The thematic approach however is not thus limited on theoretical grounds, and indeed idea-orientation seems called for by such features as the interlace-style. I will attempt, therefore, to establish a thematic reading able to withstand the objections just raised. The controlling theme of the poem, I believe, is *threats to social order.* Specifically, these threats are troublemaking, revenge, and war—problems inescapably inherent in this kind of heroic society, yet profoundly inimical to its existence. The poem's structure is simply the progressive sequence of these threats, each embodied in a suitable monster. In Beowulf's conduct, we see the best responses possible within this society. Stated so bluntly, such a reading sounds over-schematic and indifferent to the poem's emotional complexity. Indubitably too, "threats to social order" lacks the catchy appeal of *sapientia* and *fortitudo,* or youth and age, or man versus death. But this concept of the subject can greatly sharpen our grasp of the interrelation of the poem's parts and assist in explaining the function of apparently extraneous details.

II

If we examine the monsters in terms of their motives and the effects they have on those humans unfortunate enough to cross them, a definite pattern emerges. Grendel is driven by two intertwined motives. The first is a kind of envy—the envy of one *dreamum bedæled* for those living in *wynn,* of the dweller in darkness for those in light, of one from the lonely moors for those of the hall. He may envy their more harmonious relations with the Creator, even as Cain envied Abel. Such differences fill him with a lust to destroy. The second motive, less easily described but arguably more important, is the twist of character which leaves him untouched by all the usual social restraints and inhibitions against violence toward others. Not only does he kill freely, he even enjoys the act: his eyes light up (ll. 726-7), *his mod ahlog* (l. 730), *he lust wigeð* (l. 599).[8] For whatever reasons of heredity or environment, he has the killer mentality which characterizes most of the deliberate troublemakers in heroic narrative. Thjostolf and Hrapp in *Njal's Saga* systematically say and do the unforgivable, and enjoy the results. So too does Egil Skallagrimsson, albeit successfully. Many a king's berserk or arrogant man-at-arms in the sagas conforms to the type. So apparently does Unferth.

Being a larger-than-life embodiment of the Cain-principle, Grendel's effect is proportionately hyperbolical. A troublemaker in a hall makes a sham of all expressions of brotherhood and solidarity. He undermines his lord's power and control. He causes bad feeling with his insults and taunts, and eventually he starts quarrels which lead to somebody's death. Grendel does all this and more. He literally makes hollow the hall and all its promise of social joy by rendering it uninhabitable at night. He undercuts Hrothgar's rule until only a feeble travesty of royal power remains, and of course he murders retainers at will. Though he must, by virtue of his monstrous nature, operate from outside, his symbolic equivalence to a force normally found within society is underlined by his human shape and by the author's ironic treatment of him as a *healðegn.*[9] Like Cain, Grendel is an originator of feuds. Feuds do not start unless some interested party has a streak of unreasonableness, whether as aggressor or as injured party unwilling to accept fair compensation. Grendel, in his mentality, his descent from Cain, and his effect, is a personification of such unreason.

Grendel's mother represents the sequent force which complicates a feud once it is started. As is generally recognized, she has one simple motive—revenge. This too is often an unreasoning emotional drive. To everyone else, Grendel is a vicious killer whose death was an unmixed blessing. The lady of the mere only knows that her son is dead. The revenge principle cannot come into play until a feud has been initiated, but once invoked, can carry on and extend the scope of the violence indefinitely. In a typical saga act of vengeance, she comes when totally unexpected, falls upon those sleeping, and kills a man who bears no direct responsibility for her son's death. What makes vengeance so uncontrollable and tragic is the fact that it is directed by the same laudable forces which help create and ensure social order in a violent world—the desire to conserve and protect kin or allies. Exercised blindly, without regard for higher justice, however, this desire destroys social harmony as surely as does the troublemaker.

Folktales, because of their rapid pacing, can repeat an event or figure, and the incremental effect will be pleasing. What works in the Bear's Son Tale because description is minimal, however, is aesthetically clumsy in *Beowulf.* Grendel and his mother are simply too like each other for the good of the narrative, despite the pains the author took to vary them. Their similarity upsets our sense of the poem's structure; the later shift to a dragon is made to seem more of a discontinuity than is warranted just because of his differing species. This flaw has to be recognized and admitted. If my reading of the monsters' significance is correct, however, we can at least explain how the author got himself boxed into this corner. If the second adversary is to represent the revenge-principle, then Beowulf must do something which would incur vengeful retaliation. Were the second monster from a different land and period in his career, the author would have had to construct an elaborate setting to account for Beowulf's deserving such enmity, and would, moreover, have been hard pressed to concoct one in which Beowulf was as guiltless of wrongful aggression as here. The evidence of the analogues suggests that the author found ready to hand a monstrous relation living with the Grendel-counterpart, and decided that a mother would be ideally suited to the economical development of his thematic pattern.[10] She qualifies as an avenger precisely because she is Grendel's relative and is naturally therefore very like him.

Reasons for the third monster not being just another of Grendel's kin lie in the typical interests and weapons of dragons. *Draca sceal on hlæwe, / frod, frætwum wlanc.*[11] The desire to possess gold motivates him, and his reaction when robbed is to exact appalling retribution by burning Beowulf's great hall as well as the lesser buildings of the land. If, judged by motive and effect, Grendel is the origi-

nator of feuds and his mother an unreasoning wreaker of vengeance, the dragon represents war,[12] more specifically the sort of war which can upset the balance of social order. Civil war has that effect; so does fighting on home territory against an invader. Even an unsuccessful foreign venture like Hygelac's rash Frisian raid may also prove so costly in important lives that it too can be said to upset the balance. The dragon behaves like an invader, firing the countryside and burning buildings. Since such national wars often followed as extensions of smaller feuds, the dragon logically comes third in this progression of threats to social order.

The author does not seem to have counted successful foreign fighting as evil in quite the same way as he does these other types of war. A king had to extract wealth from someone if he was to maintain order in his own realm. Without rings to give, he could not hope to keep his retainers loyal. The fatal flaw in heroic social theory may not have been the code of individual honor[13] (which was in theory subject to reason and higher justice), but the necessity of waging wars to replenish a kingdom's coffers with immediate spoil and future tribute. Such wars may not bring instant trouble to the victor, but they lay it up for the future. Beowulf managed through his long reign to keep others from preying on his people—*næs se folccyning, / ymbesittendra ænig ðara, / þe mec guðwinum gretan dorste* (ll. 2733-5)—and apparently gained enough gold to keep his kingdom prosperous and peaceful, but he and his predecessors incurred such envy and hatred from neighboring lands that the messenger expects invasion once news of the king's death spreads.

If a good man and the abstraction "troublemaking" are given heroic shapes and matched in contest, we expect the good man to win, for troublemaking is not a sin likely to overcome him. Likewise, with luck and God's grace, he may avoid being swept up by the wild dictates of revenge. Undoubtedly he will have to undertake occasional revenges, even as Beowulf agreed to face Grendel's mother, but he will act decisively and without malice, and without unreasonable obstinacy. But the good man cannot avoid taking part in war. He cannot, within heroic society, eradicate this threat to order; at best he can hope to minimize the possible miseries to his own people, and no nation can expect to succeed in war forever. Hence Beowulf's attempt to root out the third threat to society is a kind of stand off: as king, he has kept war from disturbing the harmony of his society, so he can rightfully defeat the dragon. But success at expense of rival nations is self-limiting. Too much of it, and envious neighbors will band together to gain revenge and plunder. Beowulf is overcome at the height of his triumph, precisely as his realm will be. But his death is no personal defeat, as we can sense from the magnificence of his last effort. Tolkien is surely right when he insists that the dragon is aesthetically "the right end for Beowulf" (p. 276). Had Beowulf been killed by one of the monsters while yet a young man, his death would have been tragic; that he should die so when old, especially when taking his antagonist with him and leaving treasure for his people, is the highest blaze of glory achievable within the heroic framework, Or, in terms of his motives and effects, *þæt wæs god cyning*.

III

Judged by their deeds, the monsters appear to represent the three forces most inimical to heroic social order. Even in physical shape and sequence, they fit a pattern: the two threats usually offered by single individuals within a society are given man-like form and are related, as befits the logical tie between instigation and revenge. That war should succeed feuding conforms to actual practice: Ecgtheow was refused refuge by the Geats lest he bring war on his protectors. Though the dragon's differing species is initially disconcerting, we can admit his extraordinary aptness to his role. Not only are his tactics those of war, but so is his concern with wealth. He is even encased in armor.

But the poem is not reducible to its three fights alone. Interpreters must also examine the other strands of narrative. "Historical" episodes are interwoven with the contests, some being mentioned only once; others, like Hygelac's raid, recurrently. And there are a number of set pieces whose contextual relevance is problematical: Hrothgar's sermon, the old man's lament, the lay of the last survivor. Allusions to other heroes form another body of referential matter. To be taken at all seriously, a thematic interpretation must account for the presence of such material. Most thematic interpreters have not even tried to be thorough. Halverson (order versus chaos) and Kahrl and O'Loughlin (feuding) are best able to be so because of the broad applicability of their themes, and obviously this reading resembles theirs. But I believe that more precise distinctions and arrangements are actually present, that the subsidiary material in each movement is specifically relevant to the monster.

The poem's first movement is preceded by the Scyld episode, generally considered a prelude to the total work, a variant equivalent to Beowulf's own life pattern rather than a narrowly relevant introit to the Grendel story. But it functions as both. The activity most important to Scyld's winning the poet's accolade *þæt wæs god cyning* seems to be his successful foreign fighting: he drove away or subjugated his neighbors and milked tribute from them. He also brought internal order after an interregnum, and left an heir of age to rule the realm. His people appreciated this combination of luck, policy, and success, and gave him a splendid funeral; thanks to him, they could afford such a gesture. His treasury, which his heirs increased through war (l. 64), led to the construction of Heorot and the subsequent envy of Grendel. If envy breeds feud on the personal level and war on the national, then we get in the Scyld passage the evidence we need to see the inevitability of the progressive rise to success and fall to misery which will occupy the Danes from Scyld's appearance to the Heathobard's burning of Heorot. The social problems, as well as the overall life pattern, are indeed the same for Scyld and Beowulf, but Scyld's deeds are also important to the precarious state in which Beowulf finds Denmark.

Cain's relevance to Grendel has already been mentioned. Both originate feuds for no defensible reason: Cain the first to distress the harmony of creation, Grendel the first to challenge successfully the Danish prosperity founded by Scyld. And within the hall, Unferth, brother-slayer and troublemaker, sits at the feet of the Lord of the Scyldings, his presence boding ill for the future. Another referential figure apparently akin to these is Ecgtheow. Hrothgar wishes to interpret Beowulf's arrival as a gesture of thanks, not of pity, and so reminds the hero *Gesloh þin fæder fæhðe mæste* (l. 459)—Ecgtheow started a feud with the Wilfings and made the peninsular regions too hot to hold him. Hrothgar takes credit for sheltering Beowulf's father and composing the feud. Sigemund and Heremod are two other outside figures the poet seems to bring into this pattern. The Sigemund allusion can be justified purely on grounds of immediate local relevance: as part of celebrating Beowulf's exploit, the harper sings of another killer of monsters and *eotena cynnes* (l. 883). Despite the generally favorable nature of the reference, the author attributes to the harper songs concerning divers *fæhðe ond fyrena* (l. 879) not generally known. This may imply that the harper knew of traditions attributing feud-starting crimes to Sigemund, for the same phrase, *fæhðe ond fyrene*, is used of Grendel (l. 137). The Heremod passage can also be justified on aesthetic grounds, but the import of the accusing description is that Heremod became a problem, an *aldorcearu* or a threat to the very lives of his people, and therefore may be said to exemplify the willingness to kill and the unreason which characterize other external figures alluded to in the Grendel movement. All the currents and undercurrents of the poem's first movement concern the starting of trouble; Beowulf works to eradicate it. Specifically, in real-life terms, he meets and bests a quarrelsome drunken troublemaker without indulging in complementary violence; and in the heightened terms of the heroic *agon*, he defeats the feud originator Grendel.

If the poet was indeed fitting his material thematically to three monsters, we might expect abrupt and aesthetically awkward shifts as he passed from one to the next. He seems, however, to have forestalled the difficulty by providing two intermodulatory set pieces: the Finn story and Beowulf's prediction concerning Danish-Heathobard relations. That which transposes the thematic key from starting feuds to revenge, the Finnsburg story, is told as hall entertainment after Grendel's defeat and before his mother's foray. The first steps in the Finnsburg clash are unclear; all we can determine is that a solemn treaty was made, that the exigencies of winter kept the two parties penned together, and that Hengest, as spring approached, decided to seek revenge for his fallen lord despite his oaths. That the story has other artistic purposes has long been recognized. Wealtheow's joy is as doomed as Hildeburgh's, for she and her old husband are blindly determined, against custom and reason, that their young son shall inherit the Scylding throne despite the presence of

Hrothulf, an adult and ambitious prince.[14] The episode serves more than one function, but by the author's choice of details—little on the origins of the strife, much on the treaty and Hengest's change of mind—the revenge motif is insinuated into our thoughts before the second monster arrives, and her appearance is therefore a satisfaction to our halfroused expectations, not an awkward surprise.

Trouble is more easily checked before revenge complicates the picture than after. A good man can curb his behavior and avoid starting feuds, but he may not be able to avoid being sucked into quarrels through the actions of his relatives. Moreover, treacherous slaughter can make even a mild man thirst for vengeance if its victim is a beloved son or brother. For reasons such as these, any figure signifying revenge ought to be more difficult to overcome than one representing troublemaking. Simply within oneself, the latter is easier to control than the former. Beowulf is very hard pressed by the *merewif*, but with luck and God's grace he accomplishes his task. Because there are no close relatives left, the feud he has undertaken on another's behalf is ended for good. In terms of his own conduct, Beowulf is completely successful: it is not his fault (as Kahrl observes) that though he can rescue the Danes from monsters, he cannot save them from themselves.

The main action in this second movement is uncomplicated. What is problematical is the series of remarks Hrothgar makes while handling the hilt Beowulf has presented to him. The speech is clearly relevant to interpretations centered on ideal kingship, and indirectly to the theme of *sapientia* and *fortitudo*. It can be treated as a warning by those who consider Beowulf's fight with the dragon proof that his judgment has been twisted by *ofermod*. The words may be read as a device of characterization: the old man retreats to minatory moralizing when this embodiment of youth, strength, valor, and wisdom makes him feel his own shortcomings. The sentiments do not, however, have any direct bearing on troublemaking, revenge, or war, as I freely admit. However, Hrothgar five times touches on a complementary concern—the giving of gold. After a few words of formal praise, he says to Beowulf *Ic þe sceal mine gelæstan / freode, swa wit furðum spræcon* (ll. 1706-7). Given Hrothgar's notions of kingly gratitude and the phrase *swa wit furðum spræcon*, the implication is that Hrothgar wishes to tell Beowulf that fit gifts will be forthcoming, for their last two exchanges prior to Beowulf's descent into the mere concerned just this matter of treasure. Hrothgar promised reward for this second, unanticipated fight (ll. 1380-2) and later Beowulf asked for assurance that should he die, the treasure would be sent to Hygelac (ll. 1482-7).

Following the rhetorical convention of contrast, Hrothgar mentions Heremod, and it becomes clear that he was indeed a Cain- and Grendel-like figure who killed often and unreasonably—*breat bolgenmod beodgeneatas, / eaxlgesteallan* (ll. 1713-4). However, another characteristic emerges also: *nallas beagas geaf / Denum æfter dome* (ll. 1719-20). Hrothgar underlines the enormity of this niggardliness and of Heremod's consequent suffering by exclaiming *Đu þe lær be þon, / gumcyste ongit!* (ll. 1722-3).

Then Hrothgar expatiates on the ruler who is given everything by a beneficent God. After describing the hypothetical ruler's blessings and the degeneration of outlook which gradually darkens his mind, Hrothgar gets down to specific results and the first is *nallas on gylp seleð / fætte beagas* (ll. 1749-50). Ultimately, Hrothgar points out, someone else will inherit *se þe unmurnlice madmas dæleþ, / eorles ærgestreon* (ll. 1756-7). Again, Hrothgar admonishes *Bebeorh þe ðone bealonið, Beowulf leofa* (l. 1758).

The substance of his disquisition on the fates of men and the reference to his own experience seems to be his insistence that for one who has faithfully dealt out treasure, help will come should trouble arise. Naturally such help comes because of a man's reputation for generous dealing. Hrothgar ends his speech with yet another assurance that payment will be forthcoming: *unc sceal worn fela / maþ ma gemænra, siþðan morgen bið* (ll. 1783-4). Gold giving is not Hrothgar's only theme by any means, but it plays a more central part than is generally realized among all the warnings about failing strength, pride, and the inevitability of death. He states the cardinal commandment enjoined upon a king by his position and the customs of the time. Just as a dragon must guard a hoard, *Cyning sceal on healle / beagas dælan.*[15] This imperative—reward good conduct fittingly—helps a king overcome trouble and feuds, and thus strengthen social order. The same laudable rule, however, involves him in wars to win the wealth to give rewards.

Just as the first and second movements are bridged by an intermodulatory set piece—the Finnsburg Episode—the second and third are similarly spanned, this time by Beowulf's prediction concerning Danish-Heathobard relations. The former charts the development from uneasy treaty to revenge; Beowulf's prophecy takes the two nations from fragile truce to war. The fight is sparked, appropriately enough, by a piece of war-spoil. Though details of the enmity are difficult to untangle, lines 81-5 imply that ultimately the Heathobard Ingeld sets Heorot to the torch, the quintessential act of war, since it destroys the symbolic heart of a nation. Beowulf's forecast raises fairly definite expectations of the theme the author wishes next to consider.

The third movement gives the impression of separateness. Beowulf has changed. From being young, he is now exceedingly old. From being the king's nephew, he has risen through tragedy and political confusion to be king. He is not in Denmark (mostly an island-nation with natural boundaries) but in Sweden, where there are no easily defensible territorial divisions, and where neighbors are hereditary foes. Moreover, the monsters differ in the two locales. If my reading is correct, the three sections should seem more equivalent. What accounts for the separation of the third part?

The change in location presumably follows from two traditions: the author seems to have known some story of

Swedish wars and either found Beowulf part of the tale, or decided to graft him into it. Also inherited in all probability was a form of the Bear's Son Tale localized in Denmark, perhaps some progenitor of the Bothvar Bjarki story. That Beowulf should prove his heroism away from his native land upsets none of our aesthetic assumptions; in folktale (and, later, romance) such a test archetypally takes place in a distant or special realm. We would feel no unease at two adventures, one Danish and one Swedish (AB), nor at three in three separate lands (ABC), nor at the Danish sequence followed by a homecoming but no dragon (aBa). What the author has given us—AAB—is unsymmetrical. But the related nature of troublemaking and vengeance, and the necessity of Beowulf's attracting a vengeful attack without reproach to his conduct, make it expedient and economical to tie the first two thematic concerns together.

As for Beowulf's being old and a king, those developments are also logically explicable. The ruler, not the hero, is the figure who decides whether to make war or not, fends off invasions, and has to concern himself with the state of his treasury. If he is to keep the loyalty and praise of his retainers, he must always be on the watch for wealth which can be obtained with as little loss to his men as possible, and must choose whether to risk battle for the gold or not. Beowulf's being advanced to lordship for a thematic consideration of war is virtually necessary, but being king at the beginning would have precluded his rightfully risking his life to free some other realm of its monsters. Goldsmith and Leyerle even argue that his foray against the dragon is improper for a king. By the tenets of later social theories, that is correct; but I question whether the logic of the later theories applies to Beowulf and to primitive kingship. The protection that Beowulf's name affords his people against hostile neighbors will last only as long as he proves powerful. A dragon unchecked in its ravages would invite invasion as readily as news of his death. Even had Beowulf failed to kill the beast, his willing gift of his life for his realm must be counted to his credit, and since he manages to kill his adversary, he seems to me to deserve nothing but admiration. Leyerle disagrees; but I would say that Beowulf cuts a much better figure than Hrothgar in a similar situation.

Beowulf's shift in age seems best explained by reference to audience response. Had Beowulf died young, or even in his prime, the effect produced would have been that of pathos, of lament for potential unfulfilled. We would feel pity for the hero and our thoughts would center on this personal tragedy. Beowulf's dying as he does reduces the pathetic and personal element to negligible proportions. To die heroically instead of in his bed is no loss to him.[16] He is very old, and any span hypothetically left to his frame is borrowed time. He is spared the frustration of living beyond his power—and even granting Hrothgar all dignity and virtue, the Danish king is a man who has outlived his usefulness.[17] Beowulf's dying old transfers our focus from the personal aspects of his death to larger problems—social order, the unstable nature of earthly good, dilemmas of conduct, and other such general concerns.

The dragon harms the Geat nation as a war would, with hall burning and fire raising. His reason for invading is one of the usual reasons for belligerence: some of his wealth has been stolen. Once he is pulled into the quarrel, Beowulf's concerns are those of any conscientious king—protecting his people and winning treasure for his realm. The very partial nature of his success and the messenger's foreboding concerning the fate of the nation all fit the interpretation of the dragon's symbolizing war. The pattern of episodic allusions confirms this impression, for the referential layer persistently draws our attention to the endless national bickerings between Swedes and Geats. Interpretative problems arise not concerning this main action, but rather in peripheral matters: the treasure, the lay of the last survivor, and the old man's lament. The first is a major crux, the latter two are passages of great emotional power, but sufficiently removed from the subject proposed here to deserve commentary.

The hoard is morally problematical. Those critics taking an ascetic Christian stance can condemn treasure as evil. Those willing to grant positive virtues to the *wynn* and *dream* which it can be used to support will see in what Beowulf wins the potentiality for great good. The meaning of the whole poem turns on the significance of the treasure, for Beowulf must be either praised or damned for his attitude toward it.

How we are meant to view the treasure is difficult to determine for two reasons. The first is the validity of strict Christian evaluation; the second, the poet's obscure and possibly contradictory statements about the hoard's origins and the curse laid upon it. That Beowulf is extremely eager to see what he has won is undeniable. His state of mind is revealed in lines 2747-51, when he tells Wiglaf to bring some of the gold out, and lines 2794-801, where he thanks God *þæs ðe ic moste minum leodum / ær swylt-dæge swylc gestrynan,* and talks about bartering his life for the gold. In a monkish context, such sentiments would indeed suggest grave spiritual shortcomings, even imminent damnation. But if gold is handled here as it seems to be in the rest of the poem, then Beowulf's concern does not condemn him. The social theory he has lived by is flawed logically as well as by the standards of *caritas,* but he himself has done admirably in upholding and extending its best features, and his joy at winning treasure whose acquisition has lost his people so few lives is in keeping with his ideal behavior throughout.[18]

The curse on the treasure complicates the picture. Former owners demanded *þæt se secg wære synnum scildig, / hergum geheaðerod, hellbendum fæst, / wommum gewitnad, se þone wong strude* (ll. 3071-3). The absoluteness of this curse is mitigated by three factors. The first concerns the murkiness with which religion is portrayed in the poem; whatever Beowulf's spiritual status may be, the curse is purely pagan, placed on gold that is several times referred to as heathen. Whether the Christian author would have believed such a spell to have power over so virtuous a man as Beowulf is uncertain, and even if he did, we should not read into *hellbendum* the Christian Hell. Secondly, the author himself has left Beowulf a loophole: *ðam hringsele hrinan ne moste / gumena ænig, nefne God sylfa, / sigora Soðcyning sealde þam ðe he wolde / —he is manna gehyld—hord openian* (ll. 3053-6). This seems to suggest that no man would be able to get to (*hrinan*) the treasure unless he had God's favor; by implication, Beowulf's success means that he had divine support, and since the author describes the condition in his own narrative voice, he is granting to Beowulf aid from the Christian God, which might be thought to be more than enough to offset a heathen curse. Finally, there is Scandinavian precedent for heroes plundering tomb-hoards, most of which were presumably bespelled, without thereby being damned for desecration.[19] Perhaps risking his life in struggle with the resident *draugr* gives a hero a right to the wealth which is denied to the mere grave robber. Very possibly, the curse of former owners does not condemn Beowulf to Hell, and indeed may not even be responsible for his death, as Smithers and Goldsmith argue. That an old man dies in a dragon fight does not mean that God has forsaken him; he cannot live forever.

The lay of the last survivor tells us something of the treasure's earlier history. War, *guðdeað*, has carried off all his people. The echoing emptiness, both physically of the hall and spiritually of the mind, is feelingly expressed. There is no social joy, and as death approaches, he puts the treasure in the earth, perhaps to help prevent its falling into the hands of his nation's foes. Later, when war threatens to destroy the Geats, Wiglaf prescribes the same measure, and the wealth is once again consigned to earth, possibly to prevent the anticipated invaders from making off with it. We see in this passage an unhappy awareness, couched in lyric-lament terms, that war cannot always be carried out successfully, a topic which recurs as a mournful motif whenever Hygelac's Frisian raid comes up. Allusions to that appear throughout the poem, not just in the war-movement. They remind us of how one foolish move can work toward the destruction of a society, even though that society's continued well-being demanded the action.

The old man's lament (ll. 2444-62) is actually not a monologue but an epic simile, a hypothetical portrait tangentially relevant to Hrethel. The amount of time Beowulf spends musing aloud on Hrethel, one of whose sons killed another, and on an old man whose son is hanged, is difficult to explain on logical grounds. Neither has any bearing on the dragon or on Swedish wars. True, the lamenting tone is appropriate for one whose mind is feeling *wæfre ond wælfus* (l. 2420), but both vignettes are more illuminating if viewed as an expression by Beowulf of the frustration an old man feels when that which he cares for is taken from him. The man whose son is hanged feels that the hall is silent, the wind whistles through the rafters, and that no harp can pierce the shell of his grief. The dragon may have taken lives, some possibly dear. Beowulf's great hall is a charred shell through whose scorched, broken beams the wind sighs. No harp can gladden. Were Beowulf like Hrethel, he might very well pine and die from

sorrow. He might live in the past like the last survivor, and withdraw to nurse his grief. He might, like Hrothgar, live out a travesty version of his once great power. But Beowulf is determined to act, and is lucky in having an external foe.

IV

As this reading suggests, the poem never moves away from its pervasive concern with the maintenance of stability in an heroic society. Most of the seemingly extraneous referential material is actually directly relevant to the action of the movement in which it appears. The exceptions are minor. The concerns of Hrothgar's sermon are very natural coming from a king, regardless of immediate context. Recurring references to Hygelac's Frisian raid are justifiable both because of its importance to Beowulf's career and thematically as a many-sided negative example. Hygelac is mindless *fortitudo* to Hrothgar's strengthless *sapientia,* while Beowulf combines both. Hygelac is the overreaching king who wastes his life without profit to his realm, the ruler who loses treasure (his torque) rather than gaining it. He is not evil, as is Heremod, the other king to be mentioned several times in similar fashion. Rather, he represents the mistakes a good heroic king can make. These two and Hrothgar all serve to make plain the superiority of Beowulf's modes of conduct in each of the crises he faces.

A number of questions remain: they cannot be answered with certainty, but must be acknowledged. Would an Anglo-Saxon audience react positively or negatively to this picture of a flawed heroic society? Should we presume powerful Christian presuppositions in the poem's original audience? Was the composition of the poem so non-literary as to make elaborate literary interpretation misguided? What would make an Anglo-Saxon poet take up the subject of threats to social order?

Because the heroic society is portrayed as flawed, is the poem meant as a Christian treatise of rejection? A number of recent readers have taken this stand.[20] The objections to such a conclusion are forceful. The worlds of harp and hall, of gold-giving, of love between lord and retainer, are too feelingly and attractively rendered to provoke sweeping condemnation. Flawed these joys may be, and insecure, but nonetheless they are real, and within the context of the poem, they are all that stands between man and the outer darkness. For the story's characters, as for Bede's sparrow, the hall is shelter from the lashing storm, and the society in it is better than the alternative chaos. The most likely audience reaction seems to me to be at least moderate admiration. We may consider, too, that the society of the original audience, heroic in its assumptions but undistinguished and unstable-seeming to one living in it, would tell against rejection of a more glamorous and satisfactory heroic society which supposedly existed in the past.

Conceivably, the author's desire was to provoke rejection of all secular societies, past or present. He would expect the audience to know what ideal Christian life should be like. A critic espousing this general approach will stress the "tragic," "hopeless," "doomed" tone of the ending. But Beowulf's death need not be interpreted as tragedy. His people are due for a fall; but the fall is no more absolute than their triumph. Winning general condemnation of a way of life is better done in bleaker terms than the *Beowulf*-poet has used, terms which elicit less respect and admiration, less sense that the men portrayed in the story were greater in distress, as well as in joy, than their descendants.

Could religious presuppositions have overridden the natural reaction? Possibly; but it is one thing to say that men in the eighth and ninth centuries were good Christians, and quite another to assume an elaborately learned and exegetical habit of response to works not patently religious. To such an audience, gold may be invariably evil; Heorot may be Babel or Babylon; Beowulf may be covetous, or proud, or simply damned because pagan. The audience may have had at its command obscure details from the apocryphal *Book of Enoch* concerning the descendants of Cain, but if that was the standard of response which could be expected, why, as Halverson observes, does the author keep reminding us that Cain slew his brother Abel, and why did the scribe keep mispelling the name?[21] Can the intellectual background for complex exegesis be expected from any but a few churchmen, who might in any case have agreed with Alcuin that Ingeld had nothing to do with Christ? Was this patently heroic poem written for such churchmen, or for laymen and those monks Alcuin was rebuking? The nation may well have been obedient to the physical demands of Christianity—church attendance, fasts, and penance—without achieving much expertise in theological profundities. Perhaps the dragon should be read as Satan and Beowulf's interest in the treasure construed as avarice, but such readings seem basically to distort the poem's natural heroic strain.

The kind of thematic reading proposed here can account for the content and structure of the poem as we have it, whereas few of the passages read exegetically by recent critics are unambiguously theological—an argument for caution in exegesis. But the thematic reading is open to challenge on external grounds by the ultra-conservative and the oral formulaicist alike. If the story was originally assembled from independent works and handed down with little but minor alterations from one generation of scop to the next, then we would not expect an ideaorientation. The *Liedertheorie,* by denying single, self-conscious authorship, explodes assumptions of artistic and thematic unity, and my interpretation's aptness to the poem would be coincidental. Even if the poem were composed by oral formulaic means, we would expect action- or hero-orientation to dictate the inherited story-line. But if either variety of non-literary composition was employed, then most *Beowulf*-criticism is invalid, just as it may be if a strict Christian outlook was expected to control the audience response. But whether educated monks would have been as reverently determined to preserve unlettered composition

precisely as delivered is a question worth considering. The acrostic games of Cynewulf suggest that poetry imitating or using oral stylistic conventions could be literarily composed, and most of the Christian poetry is clearly not the product of generations of court scops. To adherents of either approach, one may also observe that the presence of complex and subtle *thematic* relationships is seldom an accident if they are consistently handled at every stage and level of a long poem.

Unless the themes and connections traced here and by a host of other critics are wholly imaginary, *Beowulf* has a great deal of deliberate literary artistry. My argument has been that the controlling interest behind that artistry is threats to social order. Better than any other yet proposed, that subject seems able to account for the nature and sequence of the monsters. *Sapientia* and *fortitudo* or *Königsideal* are better viewed as incidental or subsidiary interests within the broader concern of social order than as central and controlling subjects. "Order versus chaos" and "feuding" overgeneralize the point of the poem. What, though, of the semi-thematic dichotomies given prominence by Tolkien and his followers: man and his inevitable overthrow in time, or man against death; man against evil; the soul against its adversaries; youth and age?[22] These seem logically wanting. There are deaths more horrible and destructive of self-respect than being rent and bitten in heroic strife, and worse tragedies than taking a dragon with you when over seventy. The contrast between youth and age can hardly be central if the change does not significantly diminish a man's ability to fight monsters.[23] Are we to feel pity and terror over Beowulf's demise? There is an extremely powerful elegiac strain in the poem, and a definite sense of the threat of death, but to my mind it is death by unnecessary violence, death in futile and petty wars, death falling on unsuspecting and innocent revelers which haunts the author, not death in the abstract. His sadness seems directed at the impossibility of realizing the ideal pattern of heroic society indefinitely, not at the limitations of this ideal from a Christian point of view or at life in general.

If we ask why the author should have been so concerned with social harmony, the answer is not far to seek: "from the close of Bede's *History* in 731 down to the decisive victory of Egbert over Mercia in 829, is the darkest and most barren century in the history of Christian England. The interminable strife between kingdoms and the feuds between rival claimants within the kingdoms seem . . . to be as futile as they are wearisome."[24] The chronicles occasionally mention small feuds and large, even a stand in a hall reminiscent of Finnsburh.[25] However, most of the bloodshed recorded was politically motivated and would have appeared to those on the periphery sordid, selfish, unnecessary, and profitless.

Periods of civil strife may be exceedingly unpleasant to live in, but they do seem to be conducive to composition in the heroic mode. Many of the Icelandic family sagas were produced within long memory of a particularly nasty period of civil strife. Much later in English literature, the War of the Roses produced a similar response; indeed, Malory and the *Beowulf*-poet seem to me startlingly similar in method. Neither was recreating a genuine past; nor were they seeking mythical golden ages. Rather, they each took a system of values which was the theoretical ideal reflected in ruling class entertainment but not put into practice—the heroic and the chivalric codes of behavior. They created "past" worlds by giving life to these theories, and then tried to understand the forces which could have caused such societies to fail, or to degenerate to what they themselves lived in. Both were successful at visualizing the specific vices which would logically and naturally have flourished within their chosen codes: the *Beowulf*-poet's three types of violence, Malory's conflicts between allegiances to Church, state, and woman. Both seem haunted, partly by a melancholy recognition that these refined and heightened forms of their own societies would be incapable of survival because of inherent flaws, and partly by a sense that even with the faults, such societies were more attractive than what they had to live with. Both the *Morte Darthur* and *Beowulf* lament the non-existence of a pattern of living because it is possessed of the memorability, the worthiness, and the significance not found in the authors' own daily acts. We know nothing about the *Beowulf*-poet, and so these last observations are speculative, but they seem entirely consonant with the tone of the poem he has left to us.

Notes

1. This is all the more true if, as Arthur G. Brodeur and Lawrence E. Fast have argued, Hygelac is a unifying or centripetal force in *Beowulf*: see respectively *The Art of Beowulf* (Berkeley, 1959), pp. 79-87, and "HYGELAC: A Centripetal Force in 'Beowulf'," *AnM*, XII (1971), 90-9. Our sense that we might have expected more concerning the rise to kingship, for instance, is expressed by Dorothy Whitelock in *The Audience of Beowulf* (Oxford, 1951), p. 97, when she says "The poet must deliberately have refrained from enlarging on this incident."

2. "*Beowulf* and the Life of Beowulf: A Study in Epic Structure," *Studies in Language, Literature, and Culture of the Middle Ages and Later*, ed. E. Bagby Atwood and Archibald A. Hill (Austin, 1969), pp. 243-64.

3. For discussions of the poem's interlacement of narrative strands, see John Leyerle, "The Interlace Structure of *Beowulf*," *UTQ*, XXXVII (1967), 1-17, and "Beowulf the Hero and the King," *Mæ*, XXXIV (1965), 89-102; John A. Nist, "The Structure of Beowulf," *PMASAL*, XLIII (1958), 307-14; and E. Carrigan, "Structure and Thematic Development in Beowulf," *Proceedings of the Royal Irish Academy*, LXVIc (1967), 1-51.

4. All references are to Frederick Klaeber's *Beowulf and the Fight at Finnsburg*, 3rd ed. (Boston, 1950).

5. Most of these critics insist that the poem is unified, but some of those who picture the author as having

stitched two movements together into a whole include Arthur G. Brodeur (n. 1); E. Carrigan (n. 3); R. W. Chambers (*Beowulf: An Introduction*, 3rd ed. [Cambridge, England, 1959], pp. 112 ff.); Charles Donahue ("*Beowulf* and Christian Tradition: A Reconsideration from a Celtic Stance," *Traditio*, XXI [1965], 55-116); George J. Engelhardt ("On the Sequence of Beowulf's *geogoð*," *MLN*, LXVIII [1953], 91-5); Margaret E. Goldsmith (n. 12); Robert E. Kaske (n. 7); W. P. Ker (*Epic and Romance* [1897; rpt. New York, 1957], pp. 158 ff.); Frederick Klaeber (n. 4); Kemp Malone ("Beowulf," *ES*, XXIX [1948], 161-72); and J. R. R. Tolkien (n. 6). Those who think in terms of triptych construction include Adrien Bonjour ("Grendel's Dam and the Composition of *Beowulf*," *ES*, XXX [1949], 113-24); Nora K. Chadwick (n. 10); Jack Durant (n. 8); John Gardner ("Fulgentius's *Expositio Vergiliana Continentia* and the Plan of *Beowulf*: Another Approach to the Poem's Style and Structure," *PLL*, VI [1970], 227-62); Bruce Mitchell (n. 22); John A. Nist (n. 3); H. L. Rogers ("Beowulf's Three Great Fights," *RES*, n.s. VI [1955], 339-55); and Kenneth Sisam (n. 23).

6. "*Beowulf*: The Monsters and the Critics," *Proceedings of the British Academy*, XXII (1936), 245-95. Quotation from p. 271.

7. Levin L. Schücking, "Das Königsideal im Beowulf," *MHRA Bulletin*, III (1929), 143-54; Pamela Gradon, *Form and Style in Early English Literature* (London, 1971), pp. 127-31; R. E. Kaske, "*Sapientia et Fortitudo* as the Controlling Theme of *Beowulf*," *SP*, LV (1958), 423-57; Margaret E. Goldsmith, "The Christian Perspective in *Beowulf*," *Studies in Old English Literature in Honor of Arthur G. Brodeur*, ed. Stanley B. Greenfield (Eugene, Oregon, 1963), pp. 71-90; Alvin A. Lee, *The Guest-Hall of Eden* (New Haven, 1972), p. 171; John Leyerle, "Beowulf the Hero" (n. 3); Stanley J. Kahrl, "Feuds in *Beowulf*: A Tragic Necessity?" *MP*, LXIX (1972), 189-98; J. L. N. O'Loughlin, "*Beowulf*—Its Unity and Purpose," *Mæ*, XXI (1952), 1-13; John Halverson, "The World of *Beowulf*," *ELH*, XXXVI (1969), 593-608.

8. Jack Durant analyzes this "diabolic joy" in "The Function of Joy in *Beowulf*," *TSL*, VII (1962), 61-9.

9. See Edward B. Irving, Jr., "*Ealuscerwen*: Wild Party at Heorot," *TSL*, XI (1966), 161-8, especially p. 164.

10. For discussions of the analogues, see Nora K. Chadwick, "The Monsters and *Beowulf*," *The Anglo-Saxons: Studies in some Aspects of their History and Culture Presented to Bruce Dickins*, ed. Peter Clemoes (London, 1959), pp. 171-203; G. V. Smithers, *The Making of Beowulf* (Durham, England, 1961), and Larry D. Benson, "The Originality of *Beowulf*," *The Interpretation of Narrative: Theory and Practice*, ed. Morton W. Bloomfield, Harvard Studies in English 1 (Cambridge, Mass., 1970), pp. 1-43.

11. Maxims II, ll. 26-7, *The Anglo-Saxon Minor Poems*, ed. Elliott Van Kirk Dobbie, *Anglo-Saxon Poetic Records*, vi (New York, 1942), p. 56.

12. Examining the third movement from different premises and perspectives, Arthur E. DuBois hints at much the same explanation of the dragon's significance; see "The Dragon in *Beowulf*," *PMLA*, LXXII (1957), 819-22. Other interpretations include *malitia* (Kaske); death (Lee, who points out [p. 217] that "worms" devour corpses); Beowulf's "fate" (Irving, in *A Reading of Beowulf* [New Haven, 1968], p. 216); and Leviathan (Goldsmith, *The Mode and Meaning of "Beowulf"* [London, 1970], p. 143).

13. Leyerle, in "Beowulf the Hero," interprets the poem as a study of the "fatal contradiction at the core of heroic society," which he diagnoses as the demand for a personal heroism that causes a king like Beowulf to risk his life and thus harm his kingdom.

14. Wealtheow's hopes are unrealistic, whether measured by the little we know of the continental tribes of the fifth and sixth centuries, or by the later standards of Christian England of the seventh through ninth centuries. (See R. H. Hodgkin, *A History of the Anglo-Saxons,* 2 vols., 3rd ed. [London, 1952], II, 407-8.) Particularly when the maintenance of national wealth and stability depended on a king's waging successful foreign wars, the rule of a minor would have been as disastrous to his realm as it was unpalatable to his older uncles and cousins.

15. Maxims II, ll. 28-9, *ASPR,* vi, p. 56.

16. This stand is well argued by John C. Pope in "Beowulf's Old Age," *Philological Essays: Studies in Old and Middle English Language and Literature in Honour of Herbert Dean Meritt,* ed. James L. Rosier (The Hague, 1970), pp. 55-64.

17. Without subscribing to his notions of ritual royal sacrifice, I think Charles Moorman, in "The Essential Paganism of *Beowulf*," *MLQ,* XXVIII (1967), 3-18, is substantially correct in viewing Hrothgar as having outlived his capacity to fulfill the demands of a primitive kingship. Having done so, Hrothgar is not really maintaining order, but is prolonging an unstable political configuration, and causing pressures to mount.

18. For a well-argued antidote to the harshly Christian views of the hoard, see Michael D. Cherniss, "The Progress of the Hoard in *Beowulf*," *PQ,* XLVII (1968), 473-86.

19. See Smithers, pp. 8 ff., for a discussion of heroic grave-plundering. In *Egilssaga einhendar ok Ásmundar,* for instance, a grave is robbed with impunity.

20. Goldsmith and Lee tend to believe a negative response is demanded. So does E. G. Stanley, "Hæthenra Hyht in *Beowulf*" (Brodeur *Festschrift,* pp. 136-51).

21. "*Beowulf* and the Pitfalls of Piety," *UTQ,* XXXV (1966), 260-78, especially p. 268.

22. All these are suggested by Tolkien. Man against death is given special prominence by Bruce Mitchell, "'Until the Dragon Comes . . .': Some Thoughts on *Beowulf*," *Neophil.,* XLVII (1963), 126-38.

23. Kenneth Sisam makes this point in *The Structure of Beowulf* (Oxford, 1965), p. 24.

24. Hodgkin, II, 383-4.

25. See the "story of Cynewulf and Cyneheard" in the Laud and Parker MSS under the year 755.

Kevin S. Kiernan (essay date 1981)

SOURCE: *An Introduction to "Beowulf" and the "Beowulf" Manuscript,* Rutgers University Press, 1981, pp. 3-12.

[*In the essay below, Kiernan reviews historical and linguistic evidence which he contends indicates that* Beowulf *is contemporary with the extant manuscript.*]

It may well be surprising that a study of **Beowulf** in conjunction with its unique MS represents a radical departure from all previous approaches to the poem. In fact, the **Beowulf** MS has scarcely been studied at all. It still holds a wealth of undiscovered paleographical and codicological evidence, which, under ordinary circumstances, textual scholars would have uncovered and weighed long ago, as a matter of course, for the purpose of founding a reliable text. This evidence has remained safely hidden away because most editors of the poem have relied on photographic FSS of the MS, and, often enough, modern transcriptions of the FSS, rather than on the MS itself. Their tacit justification for this decidedly unorthodox procedure is that the MS cannot possibly hold any relevant textual evidence that FSS would not show as well. For, however variegated and contentious **Beowulf** studies are in all other respects, there was until very recently complete unanimity in the view that **Beowulf** is an early Anglo-Saxon poem preserved in a late Anglo-Saxon MS. The chronological gulf between the poem and the MS is usually reckoned to be two to three centuries. Under these circumstances, we are lucky to have an extant MS at all, but still rather unlucky to have such a late one. Surely, the broad paleographical features of a MS that ends an untraceably ancient transmission of the archetype are not textually vital. *Beowulf and the Beowulf Manuscript* challenges the unproven premise that **Beowulf** is an early poem. It argues instead, ultimately on the basis of extraordinary paleographical and codicological evidence, that the poem is contemporary with the MS.

The argument of the book is presented in three main stages. The first stage reconsiders the historical and linguistic evidence that has seemed to justify the neglect of the MS, and concludes that, historically and linguistically, both the poem and the MS could have been created in the early 11th century. The second stage is an extensive physical description of Cotton Vitellius A. xv., the composite codex in which the **Beowulf** MS now resides. The immediate relevance of this description is that it affords a clear view of the construction of the *Beowulf* MS, in relation to the construction of contiguous texts, and leads to the conclusion that the poem could have been copied in the early 11th century as a separate codex. The third stage studies the *Beowulf* MS as a contemporary MS of the poem. A variety of paleographical and codicological evidence shows that the poem may have been still undergoing revision while the MS was being copied, and that it was again undergoing revision later in the 11th century. In short, the evidence suggests that the actual creation of *Beowulf,* as we now know it, is partially preserved in the MS that has come down to us.

This relatively straightforward argument is necessarily embedded in a long and complicated train of subsidiary arguments that can be fruitfully summarized here. Part 1, "The Poem's Eleventh-Century Provenance," argues that the paleographical dating of the MS, roughly between 975 and 1025, can be safely placed on historical grounds after 1016. Anglo-Saxon scriptoria during the reign of æthelred Unræd (978-1016) would not have copied a poem that praised the Danish Scylding dynasty, while the latest Scyldings, led by Swein Forkbeard, plundered and murdered throughout the country. By 1016 the Danes had conquered England. Swein's son, Cnut the Great, soon made England the center of his dynasty, and by the way provided a suitable historical context for copying a poem like *Beowulf.* But Cnut's reign (1016-1035) also provided an excellent environment for the creation of the poem, and we must not neglect the exciting possibility that the poem is contemporary with the extant MS. Until now, the origin of the poem has nearly always been restricted to the 8th century or earlier on the rough historical grounds that a poem eliciting sympathy for the Danes could not have been composed by Anglo-Saxons during the Viking Age of the 9th and 10th centuries. Historically, at least, there is a better argument for an 11th-century, post-Viking origin of the poem, since an 8th-century poem would still have to be transmitted by Anglo-Saxons through the Viking Age.

The great problem of accepting an early 11th-century provenance of *Beowulf* is linguistic, not historical. On closer scrutiny, the linguistic arguments for an early date (or against a late date) are by no means decisive. The specific linguistic tests of the poem's antiquity are especially weak: the syntactical tests magnify the occurrence in *Beowulf* of some acknowledged archaisms found in unquestionably late verse; the phonetic-material tests are based on subjective interpretations of the meter that require sweeping, yet inconsistently selective emendations to unrecorded, early, linguistic forms; and the lonely phonetic-morphological-orthographical test is based on a MS "ghost." The most compelling linguistic evidence that *Beowulf* is an early poem that has endured a long and complex transmission is its rich mixture of linguistic forms. The language of the extant MS is basically Late West Saxon, but this base is permeated with apparent non-West Saxonisms and, more significantly, with earlier linguistic forms, all of which would seem to prove that the poem had passed

through many dialect areas on the way to its present form. There are, however, other explanations for this mixture of forms that do not rule out an 11th-century provenance, and do not even require a linguistically diverse transmission of the text.

Late West Saxon was a standard literary dialect used throughout England in the early 11th century. Complete orthographical uniformity, however, even in West Saxon territory, cannot be expected in an age before printing and formal dictionaries, and all Late West Saxon texts exhibit a natural mixture of forms, including some early forms. If the *Beowulf* MS was copied in non-West Saxon territory, there would be good reason to expect the occasional intrusion of late, non-West Saxon spellings in the text, as indeed is the case. The mixture of forms in the poem is further complicated by the fact that Anglo-Saxon poets of all periods shunned the language of prose, and consciously employed an artificial, archaic, poetic diction, whose roots were in Anglian territory. This fact explains the persistent occurrence of certain early, non-West Saxon forms beside the basically Late West Saxon language of the MS as a whole. Finally, if the poet and his two scribes each spoke a slightly different dialect, a confusing mixture of occasional spellings in the MS might well have been inevitable. An 11th-century convergence of all of these factors in *Beowulf* explains the mixture of forms, and accordingly eliminates the need to presume a long and complicated transmission of the text. The 11th-century provenance of *Beowulf* is historically and linguistically possible.

Part 2, "The History and Construction of the Composite Codex," prepares the way for a close analysis of the *Beowulf* MS. The composite codex, known as British Library MS Cotton Vitellius A. xv., to which the *Beowulf* MS belongs, has never been fully described in English, and a full description is desperately needed. The only existing study (in German) is not only out of date and rather inaccessible; it is also demonstrably inaccurate in dating, foliation, and collation. Moreover, it is rendered practically worthless as a reference, because among its many other errors it mistakenly uses a foliation of the codex that was abandoned in 1884, thirty-five years before the description of the codex was published. But a complete description of Cotton Vitellius A. xv. is needed for another, even more urgent reason. What is now the official foliation of the *Beowulf* MS is inaccurate, and it cannot be corrected without discussing Cotton Vitellius A. xv. as a whole. A new description of the entire codex, then, has the practical advantage of facilitating references to the *Beowulf* MS.

At present, it is very difficult indeed to make clear references to folios in the *Beowulf* MS, because a single, acceptable foliation has not been established. Thus, one FS uses the official foliation, a second FS uses a foliation written on the MS leaves, and a third FS uses the same MS foliation, while acknowledging the technical rectitude of the official foliation. As a result, it is not possible simply to refer, for example, to fol. 133 of the *Beowulf* MS, for it will not be clear which foliation it belongs to: fol. 133 is the second leaf of the **Beowulf** MS in the official foliation, but the fourth leaf in the MS foliation. Even those scholars who accept the official foliation have not been able to ignore the MS foliation because of the FSS, and because the different numbers on the MS leaves always need to be explained. Consequently, those who accept the official foliation still use the MS foliation in tandem with it, so that fol. 133 is normally referred to as fol. 133(130). Obviously, a complicated system of reference like this vitiates the purpose of a foliation. What makes matters even worse is that the official foliation, in addition to perpetuating some of the errors of the MS foliation, has been pervasively wrong since a flyleaf that it counts was removed from the codex. All of these difficulties are easily resolved by abandoning the confusing official foliation and by correcting the MS foliation in the few places where it is wrong. Except for two numbers, the foliation written on the **Beowulf** MS is accurate. For convenience of reference it needs to be reinstated as the official foliation.

The inadequacy of the current official foliation is best explained by discussing the flyleaves of Cotton Vitellius A. xv., which account for the marked discrepancies between the official and the MS foliations. A description of these prefixed leaves is useful in itself, for they have not been fully or accurately represented before, but a knowledge of their contents helps justify a return to the MS foliation. In addition, one of the leaves contains a scrap of new information about the state of the **Beowulf** MS before the fire of 1731. This subject is further investigated in a separate section on the history of the multiple foliations of the composite codex. Until now, scholars have mistakenly thought that the composite codex was not foliated in its entirety until after the fire. The discovery of two distinct foliations before the fire provides startling proof that the **Beowulf** MS was missing a folio at the time. A study of the various foliations (six different ones are documented and dated) shows precisely how three different folios from **Beowulf** were shifted from place to place from the early 17th century to the late 18th century.

To an extent, then, it is necessary to study Cotton Vitellius A. xv. as a whole in order to establish a simple and accurate foliation for the **Beowulf** MS. The utter confusion in the current system of foliation, and the history of the many abortive efforts to provide a correct foliation, are good indications of the astonishing lack of interest scholars have shown in Cotton Vitellius A. xv. and the MSS that comprise it. The rest of Part 2 is devoted to describing the physical makeup of the various MSS, and to defining their relation to the codex as a unit. To begin with, in Cotton Vitellius A. xv. Sir Robert Cotton artificially combined two totally unrelated codices, a 12th-century collection known as the Southwick Codex, and an 11th-century collection (which includes **Beowulf**) known as the Nowell Codex. This basic construction of Cotton's codex is self-evident. What is far more interesting, but not at all self-evident, is the basic construction of the Southwick and Nowell codices. The evidence shows that both are themselves composite codices. The original construction of the Southwick and Now-

ell codices has remained somewhat obscure to scholars because the fire of 1731 destroyed the threads and folds of the gatherings, reducing books to a stack of separate leaves. To recreate the Anglo-Saxon genesis of the book in which **Beowulf** was actually written, it is necessary to deduce the most probable construction of the original gatherings.

The task is comparatively simple in the case of the Southwick Codex, though no one before has ever deduced from the evidence at hand that the Southwick Codex is a Middle English composite of two late Old English MSS, copied by the same scribe at different times in his life. The original gatherings of these two MSS can be confidently reconstructed on the basis of sheet and quire signatures that were made in late Middle English times when the new book was rebound from old MSS. But there are no sheet or quire signatures on the leaves of the Nowell Codex, and the job of reconstructing the original gatherings is considerably more complicated. Strangely, the most reliable method of reconstruction has been used to identify only one gathering. Each vellum sheet has, of course, a hair and a flesh side, and the difference in color and texture between them is noticeable. Gatherings can be identified, usually with virtual certitude, by collating the hair and flesh sides of separate folios, to see if two leaves that are presumed to be two halves of the same folded sheet are in fact conjugate. The method is not infallible, because the pattern of hair and flesh sides occasionally permits alternative gatherings, but usually there is other paleographical evidence that confirms one description over another. Moreover, the method can eliminate as impossible some established descriptions of the original gatherings; it can prove beyond doubt that some falsely paired folios are nonconjugate, and so could not once have been a single, folded sheet of vellum.

A close study of the original gatherings of the Nowell Codex leads to a revolutionary view of the **Beowulf** MS. The usual view is that **Beowulf** was copied as the fourth item in a basically prose codex. The traditional description of the gatherings seems to confirm this view by showing that the scribe began copying **Beowulf** within the last prose gathering, making the **Beowulf** MS an inextricable part of the prose codex. But a close analysis of the hair-and-flesh patterns throughout the Nowell Codex reveals that the scribe could have begun copying the **Beowulf** MS on a new gathering, while distinct differences in format and in execution indicate that the prose codex and the **Beowulf** MS were originally copied as separate books. It now seems that the Nowell Codex became a composite codex in two stages: first, the **Beowulf** MS was combined with the prose codex, probably soon after **Beowulf** was copied; then, undoubtedly, the *Judith* fragment was added on in early modern times at the end of this composite codex by ripping out a sheet from the **Beowulf** MS and using it as a cover for the late accretion.

The discovery that **Beowulf** was probably copied as a separate codex strengthens the argument that **Beowulf** is an 11th-century poem preserved in an 11th-century MS. Certainly, it suggests that *Beowulf* was important to the scriptorium in which it was copied, and that it had an 11th-century audience who understood it and appreciated its merits. Textual scholars have always assumed that the poem was mechanically copied by scribes who, since they were largely ignorant of its meaning, were consequently lazy and inattentive. Yet one of the most striking indications that *Beowulf* at first existed as a separate codex emerges from the scribes' manifest efforts to provide an accurate copy of the poem. The first scribe carefully proofread his part of *Beowulf*, but did not proofread the prose texts; the second scribe carefully proofread his own part of *Beowulf*, and the first scribe's part, but again not the prose texts. Thus, the scribal proofreading of *Beowulf* alone strongly implies that the *Beowulf* MS once existed as a separate codex. More important, it is eloquent testimony that the scribes were neither lazy nor inattentive in copying the poem; on the contrary, they understood and appreciated it enough to want an accurate copy. In any case, *Beowulf* was obviously a special poem in the early 11th century, and all the indications are that it was intelligently copied in our extant MS as a separate codex.

Part 3, "The *Beowulf* Codex and the Making of the Poem," studies the MS as a separate codex from the entirely new perspective that the MS and the remarkable poem it preserves share the same 11th-century origin. A belief in the absolute textual and paleographical authority of the MS has, to be sure, revolutionary implications for the study of the poem. Until now, it has been impossible to see the MS as anything other than a very late transcript of a very early poem, and this limited view has not only justified many scores of needless emendations, but has made the conscious neglect of paleographical and codicological evidence appear to be a sound editorial principle. By this view, the 11th-century scribes are so hopelessly distant from the archetype, and separated by so many intermediate copies, that they cannot have had any better knowledge of it than we do today. These assumptions are invalidated by postulating a contemporary MS. If *Beowulf* had no appreciable transmission at all, the degree of corruption reflected in all current editions must be challenged, for the causes of deep-seated corruption are gone. Moreover, the fresh conviction that the MS has a good chance of being right where it was always perceived to be wrong has a liberating effect on the most intractable cruces. At the same time, a rigorous textual conservatism becomes an exciting means of discovering new and intriguing variations in alliterative and metrical patterns, most of which have gone unnoticed in *Beowulf* because of the doubtful assumption that an early poet would adhere mechanically to standard patterns. Only by rejecting those emendations and interpolations based solely on an arid application of "rules" can the individual style of a late, traditional poet be studied.

The theoretical authority of the *Beowulf* MS is most effectively vindicated by the quality and extent of the scribal proofreading. There can be no doubt whatever that the MS was subjected to thorough and intelligent scrutiny, by both scribes, while the copying was in progress and after it was done. The nature of the proofreading firmly establishes the authority of the MS. The two scribes' written corrections and erasures unequivocally identify the kinds of errors each scribe was prone to make, and frequently show, as well, how alert the scribe was in the act of copying, for many corrections were made at the moment of the incipient error. The erasures (all of which were studied under ultraviolet light) are particularly informative in this respect, because the erased material can be used to recreate the causes of scribal error. All previous studies of scribal error in *Beowulf* are founded on editorial emendations, but this reasoning is circular, and hence untrustworthy. In most cases a conjectural emendation is only presumptive evidence of an error, and even when an error is certain, an emendation without the aid of another text is at best only a good guess at what the correct reading might have been. The scribes, on the other hand, have identified unquestionable errors, and have presumably corrected them on the authority of the exemplar.

The vast evidence of scribal proofreading clearly illustrates the importance of a close paleographical investigation of the MS. Surely, no valid assessment of the reliability of the scribes (or the authority of the MS) can afford to ignore the scribes' written corrections and erasures, and yet no editor has ever taken them into account. On the contrary, there are several cases in all editions of the poem where a scribal correction has itself been subjected to a conjectural emendation. In such cases we can be sure that the MS reading, however difficult it may be, is right, and the emendation is wrong. Paleographical study of the scribes' work also reveals that the second scribe's connection with the MS was not limited to copying and proofreading. Apparently the MS remained in the second scribe's possession, presumably as part of a monastic library, for this scribe continued to work with the MS long after he had originally copied it. He has restored readings that were later damaged through accident or by ordinary wear and tear, most notably on the last page of the MS, where he freshened up a badly faded text. But the most extraordinary instance of his later work is that he made a palimpsest of an entire folio, and copied on it a new text.

The palimpsest provides startling paleographical evidence that *Beowulf* was revised in the course of the 11th century, long after the original text was copied. It is certain that the entire folio, containing lines 2207-2252, was scraped and washed down after the binding of the MS, for the palimpsest is part of the outside sheet of a gathering, yet the vellum's surface contrasts sharply with its conjugate leaf. Scholars have long believed that all of the original text on the folio in question was freshened up by a later hand, but a recent study has shown that the handwriting is still in fact the second scribe's, in a later stage of development. In any event, there is no credible reason for the palimpsest other than revision. A full paleographical and codicological investigation supports this conclusion in various ways. An objective transcription of the new text on the folio discloses a number of anomalous linguistic forms, which can be interpreted as signs of later attrition in the standard literary dialect, a process that accelerated as the 11th century advanced. A closer look at the badly damaged condition of the text, particularly at the textual lacunas, shows that the revised text was shorter than the original text, that parts of the revised text were erased for some reason, and that a full restoration *of the revised text* was never carried out.

The incipient state of the text on the palimpsest, and the fact that it contains in any case a late revision, opens the possibility that the *Beowulf* MS is in effect an unfinished draft of the poem. As incredible as it may seem, there is considerable paleographical and codicological support for the view that the *Beowulf* MS actually preserves the last formative stages in the creation of the epic. Three lines of text thematically related to the new text on the palimpsest have been imperfectly, but deliberately, deleted on the next folio, verso. The erasing was never finished, though it seems likely that the vellum was being prepared for a new text, as well. Presumably, both folios are part of the same revision. An analysis of the construction of the *Beowulf* MS provides a possible explanation for the purpose of this revision. The palimpsest begins a self-contained unit of the MS. It is the first leaf of the last two gatherings. The number of sheets in these last two gatherings, the manner in which the sheets are arranged, and the number of rulings to the sheets, are unique in the *Beowulf* MS. It is possible, then, that this part of the MS formerly existed separately, and was artificially appended to the extant MS. If so, the revised text on the palimpsest may have been written to provide a smoother, more natural transition between the two, originally distinct, and perhaps even totally unrelated MSS.

The theory is based on paleographical and codicological grounds, and it is defended with other paleographical and codicological facts. But it is surprisingly corroborated as well by the three-part structure of the poem:

1. Beowulf's fights in Denmark with Grendel and Grendel's dam;
2. His homecoming, and report to Hygelac;
3. His fight with the dragon and his death in Geatland.

Indeed, many critics have argued that the first and last parts once existed as separate poems, or oral narratives, and that the homecoming was composed at a later stage to link the Danish and Geatish narratives.

The paleographical and codicological evidence leads to precisely the same conclusion. The palimpsest is the first folio of the dragon episode. And there is paleographical and codicological proof that the gathering immediately preceding the palimpsest, which holds the text of Beowulf's homecoming, was copied by the second scribe *after* he had copied the last two gatherings of the MS. The obvious conclusion is that the Danish and Geatish exploits of Beowulf were first brought together in the extant MS by the second scribe. The aesthetic fusion of these parts does not reflect a dim, romantic view of a non-Anglo-Saxon past, but rather a vivid imaginative response to chilling contemporary events. The fall of a great and noble hero, and the imminent extinction of the race he ruled, was well understood by this 11th-century Anglo-Saxon who had recently seen the fall of Alfred's house and the subsumption of his homeland in the Danish empire. The second scribe begins to look like "the last survivor of a noble race," while the *Beowulf* MS, the treasure he continued to polish after the death of his old lord, no longer looks like a reproduction.

J. D. A. Ogilvy (essay date 1983)

SOURCE: "The Formulaic Style of *Beowulf*," in *Rereading "Beowulf": An Introduction to the Poem, Its Background, and Its Style,* edited by J. D. A. Ogilvy and Donald C. Baker, University of Oklahoma Press, 1983, pp. 137-58.

[*In the following essay, Ogilvy surveys the formulaic methods used by Old English poets and examines the ways in which such methods—including the use of traditional epithets and phrases which probably originated in orally composed and transmitted poetry—are utilized in* Beowulf.]

The student of Old English poetry will no doubt have remarked the popularity during the past twenty years of "oral-formulaic" studies, especially among American scholars. Beginning with F. P. Magoun's famous article in 1953,[1] a growing body of scholarship has attempted to prove that much of Old English poetry, including *Beowulf,* was composed orally, extemporaneously, from the traditional stock of formulas with which the scop was provided in his word hoard, or poetic vocabulary. The case for oral composition is, at best, not proven. In our opinion it is most improbable that *Beowulf* was composed orally, even in smaller units, but a scrupulous analysis of the evidence beyond our scope here.[2] There can be no doubt, however, that the controversy has been helpful in calling renewed attention of students to the technical characteristics of *Beowulf.* That the poem is formulaic—i.e., constructed of traditional epithets and phrases that must have had their origin in a poetry orally composed and transmitted—is obvious. An appreciation of how the formulaic materials are used in Old English poetry is of the first importance to the reader who wishes to deal with *Beowulf* in its original language, or even in a competent modern version.

Our discussion has two parts. First, we survey the formulaic material used by Old English poets, and, second, we consider the peculiar characteristics of the kind of poetry that the formulaic tradition produced.

THE EPITHET AND MODIFYING FORMULA

The formulaic materials may usefully be considered in four groupings: (1) the epithet and brief modifying formula, (2) the sentence formula, (3) the larger rhetorical patterns that employ formulas in their construction, and (4) the formulaic elaboration of themes.

One kind of epithet, the kenning, is the best known of the formulas.[3] It is a condensed metaphor or simile, for example, "hron-rad" (whale road) for the sea, "sund-wudu" (sea wood) for a ship, "isern-scur" (iron shower) for a flight of arrows, "hildegicelum" (battle icicle) for a sword, and "hædstapa" (heath stepper) for a deer. Other noun epithets verge on the kenning, but many are literal descriptions. All of them share the characteristics of being compounds, and they most frequently occupy an entire half line of verse. They form by far the greater part of the "building-block" material of Old English poetry.

One can scan the glossary of Klaeber's third edition of *Beowulf* and find the nature of the noun epithet amply illustrated. A good place to begin is under the letter *h* with the "hilde-" (battle) compounds. We find "hilde-bord" (battle shield), "hilde-cumbor" (battle banner), "hilde-mece" (battle sword), "hilde-ræs" (battle rush), and twenty others. The difference between these straightforward compounds and the kennings is made clear when one compares "hilde-mece" (battle sword) with a kenning for sword, "hilde-leoma" (battle light). All are formulaic in that they are repeated, in *Beowulf* and elsewhere, and many have their counterparts in similar metrical patterns under different alliterative heads. Battle was one of the richest sources of formulas in Old English poetry; a number of words besides "hilde" convey the idea: "beado," "gud," "wæl," and so on. For "hilde-mece" (sword) we have "beado-mece." For "hilde-rinc" (warrior) we have "beado-rinc," and so on. They do not necessarily mean exactly the same thing; usually there are distinctive nuances. They provide the variation that is essential to a poetic based upon repetition.[4] Most of the equivalent epithets, as one would expect, reflect the concerns of a warrior culture: the attributes of the warrior and his weapons and the nature of his lord and his companions.

In *Beowulf* each person or important thing has its characteristic epithets, as in the Homeric poems, but with considerably more variety of choice for the poet.[5] The proper names are themselves epithets, like Beowulf (probably "bee-wolf," or bear), Hrothgar (glory spear), Unferth (mar peace). Beowulf's most common epithet is "bearn Ecgdeowes" (son of Ecgetheow), but with different alliteration and meter—and a different function for the hero—he is also "lidmanna helm" (protector of the seamen, line 1623) when he leads his men ashore in Denmark. Hrothgar is variously "Helm Scyldinga" (protector of the Scyldings, line 371), "wine Scyldinga" (friend of the Scyldings, line 30), "maga Healfdenes" (kinsman of Half-Dane, line 189), and "Deniga frean" (Lord of the Danes, line 271). Grendel is the "grimma gæst" (grim guest, line 102) and the "mære mearcstapa" (mighty wanderer of the wastes, line 103). Heorot, the famous hall built by Hrothgar, is "beahsele beorhta" (bright ring hall, i.e., hall where treasure is dispensed, line 1177). And so the list goes.

The Anglo-Saxon poet was thus capable of considerable variation and precision in his epithets for things and people. An unanswered question concerns the extent to which he may have indulged in irony in this respect, for certainly he was elsewhere fond of irony. The use of such an ordinary epithet as "helm Scyldinga" (protector of the Scyldings) for Hrothgar in line 1322, when Hrothgar is weeping and pouring out his troubles to Beowulf after Grendel's mother has killed æschere (and there are examples of such seeming inappropriateness elsewhere) certainly appears to the modern eye as ironic. But we must be cautious in assigning modern intention and reaction to a poet who was telling his story twelve hundred years ago.

Adjectival epithets are frequently found in alliterative pairs in *Beowulf,* filling the half-line unit, as do their noun counterparts. Grendel is "grim ond grædig" (grim and greedy, line 121), and this family trait is observed also in his mother in the second episode, where she is "gifre ond galgmod" (greedy and gallows-minded, line 1277) as well. Heorot is "heah ond horngeap" (high and horn-gabled, line 82) and "geatolic ond goldfah" (splendid and gold-adorned, line 308). The dragon is "hot ond hreohmod" (hot and fierce in spirit, line 2296). Formulaic adjectives are otherwise normally paired alliteratively with nouns, as in "sigoreadig secg" (victorious warrior, line 1311), creating the half-line unit.

The adverbial formula is found in both phrase and clause forms. A common phrase pattern is the half-line time formula, e.g., "in geardagum" (in days of yore, line 1) and "lange hwile" (for a long while, line 16), likewise the general-place formula, "under wolcnum" (under the heavens, line 8), "ofer hronrade" (beyond the whale road or sea, line 10), and "geond þisne middangeard" (throughout this world, line 75). Phrases of purpose, or truncated clauses, are frequently half-line formulas as well: "folce to frofre" (as an aid to the people, line 14). Very occasionally an adverbial formula may occupy a whole line, as in line 197: "on þæm dæge þysses lifes" (in that time of this life). Adverbial clauses of purpose and result are also found among half-line formulas, e.g., "þæt ic þe sohte" (that I should seek you, line 417). A common formula of time is "sydþan morgen (aefen) cwom" (after morning or evening came), and there are many others.

THE SENTENCE FORMULA

The sentence formula, both simple and complex, is obviously of great importance in the word hoard of the scop. Such sentences provide the necessary summaries and transitions and are the backbone of formulaic rhetoric. Many of them are short, half-line formulas. The best-known type is of the "þæt wæs god cyning" (that was a good king, line 11) sort; others are "ic þæt eall gemon" (I recall all that, line 2427) and "swa sceal mon don" (so shall man do, line 1172). Sentence formulas provide the usual means by which the poet expresses a variety of things. One person speaks to another in an almost invariable pattern: "Hrodgar maþelode, helm Scyldinga" (Hrothgar spoke, protector of the Scyldings, line 371); the passage of life is expressed in a sentence like "weox under wolcnum" (he waxed under the heavens, line 8); physical progression is normally a sentence formula, e. g., "wod under wolcnum" (he moved beneath the skies, line 714). The effect of weapons is usually expressed in short formulas, e.g., "Hra wide sprong" (The corpse rebounded far, line 1588).

In addition to the sentence formulas that are repeated verbatim or nearly so, there are many sentence patterns that serve the poet as outlines to be filled in, as it were, and that are used frequently enough to be considered formulaic. A negative, contrasting pattern beginning "not at all" or "not only" and containing "but," "after," "until," or "then" clauses is often employed in the ironic understatement that is so characteristic of the Anglo-Saxon poetic mode. Of Hildeburh in the Finn episode we read (lines 1076-79a, italics ours):

> *Nalles* holinga   Hoces dohtor
> meotodsceaft bemearn,   *syþdan* morgen com,
> da heo under swegle   geseon meahte
> morþorbealo maga,

(*Not at all* without cause did the daughter of Hoc bemoan the decree of Fate *after* morning came, when she might see under heaven the slaughter of kinsmen.)

Describing the cowardly thanes who deserted Beowulf in his fight against the dragon, the poet tells us (lines 2596-98, italics ours):

> *Nealles* him on heape   handgesteallan
> ædlinga bearn   ymbe gestodon
> hildecystum,   *ac* hy on holt bugon,

(*Not at all* did his comrades in arms, the children of warriors, stand about him [Beowulf] in martial glory, *but* they fled into the forest,)

Another common transitional pattern is "It was not long . . . until . . . ," describing ironically an immediate result (lines 2591b-92):

> *Næs* da long to don,
> þæt da aglæcean   hy eft gemetton.

(It was not long thence that the deadly fighters came together again.)

The clauses of the "when . . . then" and "since" and "until . . . that" patterns are frequently transitional in function and serve the poet as a means of encapsulating a brief bit of history that has a bearing on the immediate concern or of anticipating action to follow within the poem (or subsequent history outside the poem). The clauses allow rapid and rhetorically effective juxtaposition and bear much of the burden of the paralleling and contrasting technique that is a hallmark of the Anglo-Saxon style. An example of the first sort of use is seen in the introduction of Grendel (lines 102-108, italics ours):

> wæs se grimma gæst   Grendel haten,
> mære mearcstapa,   se þe moras heold,
> fen ond fæsten;   fifelcynnes eard
> wonsæli wer   weardode hwile,

> *siþdan* him Scyppend   forscrifen hæfde
> in Caines cynne—   þone cwealm gewræc
> ece Drihten,   þæs þe he Abel slog;

(The grim guest was called Grendel, the mighty stepper of the marches, who held the moors, the fens, and the fastnesses; the hapless one dwelt a while in the home of the monster race, *since* the Creator had cursed him, in the race of Cain—he avenged that murder, the eternal Lord, whereby Cain slew Abel;)

The "siþdan" (since) clause gives us the origin of Grendel and the reason that he bore the wrath of God, to which the poet refers later. A similar construction is subsequently used in describing the mother of Grendel (lines 1261-63).

The "oþ þæt" (until . . . that) clause has a similar function in that it allows for a brief summary but, of course, looks ahead. Of Beowulf's reign over the Geats, we learn (lines 2208-10, italics ours):

> he geheold tela
> fiftig wintra   —wæs da frod cyning,
> eald eþelweard—,   *od dæt* an ongan
> deorcum nihtum   draca rics[i]an,

(he ruled well for fifty winters—he was a wise king, the old guardian of his people—*until* in the dark nights a dragon began to rule,)

The double function of summary and contrast—here powerful in its stark simplicity—could not be better illustrated.

Larger Rhetorical Patterns

The kinds of larger rhetorical structures that can be built from individual formulas and sentence patterns can be seen in the opening lines of **Beowulf.** To see how these structures are indeed formulaic, it will be necessary to look at introductions to other Old English poems as well.

Beowulf (lines 1-11, italics ours):

> *Hwæt,* we Gar-Dena   *in geardagum,*
> þeodcyninga   þrym gefrunon,
> *hu da æþelingas   ellen fremedon!*
> Oft Scyld Scefing   sceaþena þreatum,
> monegum mægþum   meodosetla ofteah,
> egsode eorl[as],   *syddan ærest weard*
> feasceaft funden;   he þæs frofre gebad,
> *weox under wolcnum*   weordmyndum þah,
> od þæt him æghwylc   ymbsittendra
> ofer hronrade   hyran scolde,
> gomban gyldan;   þæt wæs god cyning!

(*Hark, we have learned of the glory* of the princes of the Spear-Danes *in days of yore, how the chiefs wrought mighty deeds.* Oft Scyld Scefing took the mead seats from troops of enemies, from many peoples; he terrified the earls, *after he first was found helpless*—he survived to be recompensed for that—*he grew under the heavens,* enjoyed high honor, *until* each of his neighbors over the whale road should obey him and pay tribute; that was a good king!)

The *Fates of the Apostles* (lines 1-8, italics ours):

> *Hwæt!* Ic þysne sang   *sidgeomor fand*
> on seocum sefan,   *samnode wide*
> *hu þa ædelingas*   *ellen cyddon,*
> torhte ond tireadige.   Twelfe wæron
> dædum domfæste,   dryhtne gecorene,
> *leofe on life.*   *Lof wide sprang,*
> miht ond mærdo,   *ofer middangeard,*
> þeodnes þegna,   þrym unlytel.[6]

(Lo! I this song, *weary of wandering* and sick in spirit, *made and put together from far and wide, of how the heroes,* bright and glorious, *made their courage known.* They were twelve in number, famed in deeds, chosen by the Lord, *beloved in life. Praise sprang wide,* the might and the fame, *throughout the world, of the Prince's thanes*—no small glory.)

Andreas (lines 1-6, italics ours):

> *Hwæt! we gefrunan   on fyrndagum*
> *twelfe under tunglum   tireadige hæled,*
> *þeodnes þegnas.*   No hira þrym alæg
> camprædenne   þonne cumbol hneotan,
> *syddan hie gedældon,*   swa him dryhten sylf,
> heofona heahcyning,   hlyt getæhte.[7]

(Lo! *We have heard, in days gone by, of the twelve under the stars,* glorious heroes, *the Lord's thanes.* Their glory did not fail in the field of battle when the banners clashed *after they had parted* as the Lord himself, the High King of Heaven, had commanded them.)

The Dream of the Rood (lines 1-3, italics ours):

> *Hwæt!* Ic swefna cyst   secgan wylle,
> *hwæt me gemætte*   to midre nihte,
> *sydpan reordberend*   reste wunedon![8]

(Listen! I wish to tell the best of dreams *that came to me* in the middle of the night, *after the bearers of speech* [men] had gone to their rest.)

These poems have essentially little of theme and subject in common. **Beowulf** is the story of a warrior, *Andreas* and *Fates* are principally religious chronicles, and *Dream* is an almost mystical vision. Also, these passages have more differences in phrasing between them than close similarities. But the rhetorical structures are the same, and, as the italicized phrases show, the key formulas are essentially the same.

First, we cannot escape the opening "Hwæt!" Then, in **Beowulf** and *Andreas* follows the days-of-yore formula, "in geardagum," and "on fyrndagum." The source formula "we have learned" ("þrym gefrunon" in **Beowulf** and "we gefrunan" in *Andreas*) is paralleled by variant formulas in the other two, "Ic þysne sang sidgeomor fand" ("Weary with the journey I made this song") in the *Fates of the Apostles* and "hwæt me gemætte" ("lo, I dreamed") in *The Dream of the Rood.* **Beowulf** and the *Fates* share an identical formula about what is learned—"hu da æþelingas" (how the princes [performed]) in the same position, line 3a. Likewise, **Beowulf**'s "ellen fremedon" (performed

deeds of valor) is paralleled by the *Fates'* "ellen cyddon" (showed their courage), in line 3b—again, the same position. Next we consider the location formula "on earth" or "under heaven." In **Beowulf** it is "weox under wolcnum" (grew under the skies), and in *Andreas* we find "twelfe under tunglum" (twelve under the stars); in *Fates* it is "ofer middangeard" (throughout the middle yard). And, finally, the "since . . . (happened)" formula, which is rendered in **Beowulf** as "syddan ærest weard" (since he first was [found]), is rendered in *Andreas* as "syddan hie gedældon" (since they parted), and in *Dream* as "sydþan reordberend . . . reste wunedon" (after the speech-bearers had gone to rest).

In addition to the phrases in italics that are repeated or paralleled in one or another of the quoted passages, practically every phrase in each of the passages can be matched by a similar formula in several other Old English poems. Our purpose here, however, is to observe not only the verbal similarities but—equally important for illustrating the formulaic tradition of composition—the structural formula for opening a poem. It goes something like this: "Behold, . . . We [or I] have heard . . . in days of yore . . . how princes [or others] performed . . . deeds of glory . . . under the heavens . . . , since [or after] . . . [whatever happened at the beginning of the story or the circumstances of the telling]." This rhetorical pattern can be expanded or contracted as the poet wishes, and formulas selected and woven into the pattern. Although the passages quoted are introductory, the pattern can also be used for summary or transition within a narrative, as can been seen in lines 1769-81, 2384-90, and elsewhere in **Beowulf.**

ELABORATION OF THEMES

In addition to such rhetorical structures, Old English poetry abounded in thematic formulas for everything of consequence in Anglo-Saxon life or story. By "thematic" we mean a nongrammatical contextual relationship of certain kennings, epithets, and symbolic objects. The poet was provided with ready-made formulas to elaborate the battle and its aftermath, sea-journeys, treasure-giving, the joy of the hall, funerals, introductions and farewells, etc. In describing a battle, for instance, the Anglo-Saxon poet would almost inevitably employ at some point the theme of the "beasts of battle."[9] These beasts are the animals that feed upon the bodies of the slain—the wolf, the raven, and the eagle. One of the most famous instances of the theme is found at the end of *The Battle of Brunanburh* (lines 60-65):

> Letan him behindan   hræw bryttian
> saluwigpadan,   þone sweartan hræfn,
> hyrnednebban,   and þane hasewanpadan,
> earn æftan hwit   æses brucan,
> grædigne gudhafoc   and þæt græge deor,
> wulf on wealde.[10]

(They left behind them, to devour the corpses, the dark-coated, swart raven, horn-beaked, and the gray-coated, white-tailed eagle to enjoy the carrion, the greedy war hawk, and that gray beast, the wolf in the forest.)

This passage, with the three beasts of battle—the raven, the eagle, and the wolf—prepares the conclusion of the poem, for the poet is turning from the field. Like all other such formulas, it is amenable to variation of form and function as the poem demands. Probably because there are no fully described pitched battles between men in **Beowulf,** this theme is little used there, but the one full use of the formula is doubly impressive, for it does not describe a present field but is symbolic of the future fall of the Geatish nation, appearing near the end of the poem where the poet prophesies, through the voice of the messenger who announces Beowulf's fall and the dragon's demise, the coming doom of the Geats (lines 3021b-3027):

> Fordon sceall gar wesan
> monig morgenceald   mundum bewunden,
> hæfen on handa,   nalles hearpan sweg,
> wigend weccean,   ac se wonna hrefn
> fus ofer faegum   fela reordian,
> earne secgan,   hu him æt æte speow,
> þenden he wid wulf   wæl reafode.

(Therefore, many a spear, cold in the morning, shall be wound about with fingers, raised in hands; not at all shall the sound of the harp stir the warriors, but instead the dark raven, eager above the fated, shall speak much, shall say to the eagle how it sped him at the feasting when he and the wolf plundered the slaughtered.)

The theme, though rooted in a context of battle description, is clearly more variable in its usefulness than to be merely descriptive; in **Beowulf** the ancient theme has become symbolic in its function as in its nature. For ironic contrast it is joined with the theme of the joys of the hall, whose symbol is the harp. The gladsome sound of the harp is gone, and in its place is the snarling of the animals of the battlefield. Grammatically the passage is constructed on the "nalles . . . ac" (not at all this . . . but that) formulaic pattern. These are only two examples of formulaic themes that abound in **Beowulf** (the "joys of the hall" theme itself appears on several occasions, as in lines 89-98, 491-98, 642-45, 1980-83, and 2262-63, etc.). The sea-voyage themes are twice elaborately done and well illustrate the variety available to the scop within a thematic pattern. Although certain formulas are repeated, and although the structure of the passages is identical, most of the words are different. The structure is simply this: the boat was in the water; the men loaded it and steered it into the sea; there it was urged by the wind, until the time came that the seamen could see the cliffs of the shore. Each of the steps in the pattern is expressed in a formula, and the pattern itself is constructed around an "until . . . that" clause. The similar formulas are italicized. First, Beowulf's journey to Denmark (lines 210-28, italics ours):

> Fyrst ford gewat;   *flota wæs on ydum,*
> bat under beorge.   Beornas gearwe
> on stefn stigon,—   streamas wundon,
> sund wid sande;   secgas bæron
> on bearm nacan   beorhte frætwe,
> gudsearo geatolic;   guman ut scufon,
> weras on wilsid   wudu bundenne.
> Gewat þa ofer wægholm   winde gefysed

> *flota famiheals*   fugle gelicost,
> *od þæt* ymb antid   oþres dogores
> *wundenstefna*   gewaden hæfde,
> *þæt da lidende*   land gesawon,
> brimclifu blican,   beorgas steape,
> side sænæssas;   þa wæs sund liden,
> eoletes æt ende.   þanon up hrade
> Wedera leode   on wang stigon,
> sæwudu sældon,—   syrcan hrysedon,
> gudgewædo;   Gode þancedon
> þaes þe him yþlade   eade wurdon.

(Time passed; *the ship was on the waves,* the boat under the cliff. The warriors eagerly stepped aboard; the currents wound, the sea against the sand; the men bore into the bosom of the ship bright ornaments, splendid battle armor; the warriros on their sought-for journey pushed off the well-made ship. The *foamy-necked floater* departed over the waves, most like a bird, urged on by the wind, *until* in due time on the next day *the ship with the curved prow* had progressed *so that the voyagers* saw the land, the shining sea cliffs, the steep hills, the wide headlands; then was the sea crossed, the travel at an end. Thence the men of the Weders quickly stepped on the land and tied up the ship. Their armor, the weeds of war, rattled; they gave thanks to God that the crossing had been an easy one for them.)

This is surely one of the better-known passages in **Beowulf.** The references made to it often imply that it is full of the rhetoric of sea travel, but actually the description of crossing is confined to lines 216-21: "The foamy-necked floater departed over the waves, most like a bird, urged on by the wind." We are clearly deluded by the famous "foamy-necked floater." Aside from this kenning the only other figure is a rather rare example of an Old English simile, "fugle gelicost" (most like a bird). We turn from this passage with its emphasis on preparation and battle spirit to the second sea voyage, which takes Beowulf and his men home after they have rid Hrothgar's land of monsters (lines 1896-1913, italics ours):

> þa wæs on sande   sægeaþ naca
> hladen herewædum   *hringedstefna,*
> mearum ond madmum;   mæst hlifade
> ofer Hrodgares   hordgestreonum.
> He þæm batwearde   bunden golde
> swurd gesealde,   þæt he sydþan wæs
> on meodubence   maþme þy weorþra,
> yrfelafe.   Gewat him on naca
> drefan deop wæter,   Dena land ofgeaf.
> þa wæs be mæste   merehrægla sum,
> segl sale fæst;   sundwudu þunede;
> no þær wegflotan   wind ofer ydum
> sides getwæfde;   sægenga for,
> *fleat famigheals*   ford ofer yde,
> *bundenstefna*   ofer brimstreamas,
> *þæt hie Geata clifu*   ongitan meahton,
> cuþe næssas;   ceol up geþrang
> lyftgeswenced,   on lande stod.

(*Then the roomy ship* loaded with war weeds *was on the sands—the ring-prowed vessel* loaded with horses and treasure; the mast stood high above Hrothgar's precious hoard goods. He [Beowulf] gave to the boat ward a sword wound with gold so that afterward at the mead bench the guardian was held more worthy because of this treasure, the heriloom. He boarded the ship, to drive through the deep water, he departed the land of the Danes. Then the sea garment, a sail bound with a rope, was at the mast. The sea wood resounded; the wind over the waves did not force the wave floater from its course; the sea traveler went on, the *foamy-necked one* floated onward over the waves, *the well-joined prow* over the sea streams, *until they might see the Geatish cliffs,* the known headlands. The keel, urged by the wind, pressed upward and stood on the land.)

We have a repetition of the "foamy-necked" figure, but the other terms are varied; the ship is "ring-prowed" or "curved-prowed," the ship is "sundwudu," the "wave-floater," and so on. The return voyage is described with considerably more detail than is the voyage in the preceding passage; in addition to describing the loading of the vessel and its arrival "on lande," the poet gives six lines of carefully varied description to the ship, the wind, and the sea. We learn that the ship has a sail, a "sea garment," and we hear the sound of the ship straining against the sea ("sundwudu punede," the sea wood groaned, or resounded). The only sound in the first passage is the grim noise of the rattling of armor. The effect of this is not hard to find: in the first passage all attention is to the coming struggle; here the spirit is one of release.

In addition to elaborate thematic set pieces such as these, scattered throughout *Beowulf* one finds many short tropes, frequently of a moralizing nature. These are often in the form of sentences, such as, "Swa sceal mon don," (So shall a man do, line 1172), or, "Swa he nu git ded" (So He [God] still does, line 1058), in passages illustrating proper conduct in a situation or summarizing the actions of God or the course of fate, over which man has no control. Such gnomic themes are "the uselessness of buried gold" (lines 3058-60, 2275-77, 3167-68), "the dangers of disturbing dragons" (lines 2836-42, 3050-60), and the "unfæge eorl" (the undoomed warrior who may escape fate if his courage avails him, lines 2291-93, 572-73).[11]

Although the various stories intruded into *Beowulf,* such as the Finn episode, the story of Offa, or the story of Hama, have no place in the present discussion, having been considered in our treatment of the background of the poem, in a sense these "digressions" are much like the moral tropes in that they illustrate good and bad behavior, wise and foolish conduct. They are elaborate analogies that, while not exactly formulaic in nature, serve the purposes of shorter formulaic themes. There are other formulaic aspects of *Beowulf,* but these seem to us to be of most significance for the modern reader.

Having surveyed some of the materials of Old English poetry, let us now see how these materials are used in *Beowulf* and what kind of poetry they produce. In the preceding chapter we have seen something of how Old English verse works; its structure is that of balanced building blocks of complementary meter united by alliteration. The smaller formulaic units, as we have seen, form many

of these building blocks, each usually occupying a half line. As anyone familiar with the medieval ballad (or modern ballads, for that matter) knows, much of the ballad is of preformed phrases and whole lines that do not themselves move the poem. These formulas provide a brief stasis in the progression of the narrative and cause the "hitching" effect that is so noticeable in ballads. In *Beowulf* the formula likewise provides the reflection more often than the action, though, as we have seen, Old English poems use a number of formulaic sentences to get the action under way.

Normally the *Beowulf* poet balances an epithet half line with a verb phrase half line, as in lines 2397-2400:

> Swa he nida gehwane   genesen hæfde
> slidra geslyhta,   sunu Ecgdiowes
> ellenweorca,   od done anne dæg
> pe he wid pam wyrme   gewegan sceolde.

(So he each of battles had survived, each terrible conflict, the son of Ecgtheow, each courageous work, until one day that he should meet with the dragon.)

The "he" in line 2397a is balanced by its epithet "sunu Ecgdiowes" in line 2398b. In this brief passage there are two formulas roughly comparable in meaning to "nida gehwane": "sliddra geslyhta" and "ellenweorca," both in the a verses. All the b verses except for lines 2398b are occupied by the verb or adverbial phrases. The verses cannot be read rapidly, for the formulas give a parenthetical effect in their reinforcing role. The movement of the verse is therefore largely incremental.

As we consider the method of the *Beowulf* poet, we realize that the paralleling characteristics of the formula are shared by the other rhetorical elements. We have observed that the themes introduced as ornament parallel or contrast the character or action that they comment upon. An example is the poet's use of the theme of the joys of the harp in the hall as ironic contrast in lines 89-98; it is the very joy of the men and the noise of the harp that brings their catastrophe, for it arouses Grendel. The larger episodes function in much the same way, as the Finn episode comments on Hrothgar's court, and the Sigemund story anticipates Beowulf and the dragon. It is not even beyond the bounds of possibility that, as Tolkien suggested, the two parts of Beowulf, paralleling one another, reflect this fundamental quality of Old English poetry.[12]

It might well seem, from our discussion, that the kind of poetry that the Germanic tradition produced would inevitably be slow, tedious, and dully repetitive. It has, indeed, been argued that *Beowulf* is validly appreciated only as barbaric poetry, possessing merely an unsophisticated irony.[13] Old English poetry was very far from being wholly formulaic, however, and the *Beowulf* poet in particular possessed great resources of poetic vocabulary for variation. He was also capable of dispensing with the elaborate parallel movement of his verse to rush headlong into the action, as in lines 1441-42:

       Gyrede hine Beowulf
eorlgewædum,   nalles for ealdre mearn

(Beowulf then dressed himself in earl's weeds—not at
all did he care for his life.)

Here the formula "nalles for ealdre mearn" does not interrupt Beowulf's quick arming for the fray but for emphasis
is left to line 1442b.

It cannot be denied, however, that the poetry of ***Beowulf***
is quite different from the post-Renaissance English verse
to which we are accustomed. The formulaic nature of the
Old English language results in a certain lack of that precision which we have come to expect from the poetic
imagination. The very nature of compound words seems to
involve a semantic compromise. The effect of ***Beowulf,***
like that of other Old English poems, results from a building of meaning rather than an assertion of it. The poet
swings between ironic under-statement and hyperbole. He
tends frequently to tell us what things are not and what
people did not do, leaving us to supply the positive.

Although it must be admitted that Old English kennings
and epithets frequently clog up the movement of the narrative, in ***Beowulf*** particularly the modifiers tend to be cumulative, each adding a quality or aspect to character or
action. This incremental effect is seen in a long passage already cited, that of Beowulf's sea voyage to Hrothgar's
court. The poet uses in the passage a variety of kennings
for the boat: It is "flota" at line 210, "bat" at line 211, "nacan" (of the ship) at line 214, "wudu bundenne" at line
216, "flota famiheals" at line 218, and "wundenstefna" at
line 220. Now "flota," "bat," and "nacan" do not much
improve on one another, for they all rather nakedly mean
"boat" or "ship." But the poet is at the beginning simply
saying that the boat is there, on the waves in shallow water, being loaded. When the boat begins to move, the poet
selects kennings that focus attention on the ship itself, its
ornament and motion. The poet's imagination has been
awakened. The ship is a craftsman's work, we learn,
"wudu bundenne," well-joined wood. As it moves into the
open sea, the "famiheals" or "foamy-necked" image pictures for us the waves being sliced by the long prow of the
ship. This prow is itself the next image, the curved stem of
"wundenstefna." All the words are kennings for "ship,"
but they tell us, in themselves, something of what is happening. They reflect the changing focus of the narrative.
We could arrange these figures in their order, remove them
from their context, and learn that the "flota" has become
"foamy-necked," that the well-built ship of "wudu bundenne" is now represented by another aspect, its curved
prow—the "wundenstefna," suggestive of the outward
thrust of the ship. When at the end of the journey the ship
is tied to the Danish shore, it becomes "saewudu" or "sea
wood," simply another kenning for "ship" but one that
now has the nuance "seaworthy wood," wood that has
been tried. the incremental effect of the series of images
suggests the progress of the narrative.

In a similar way the repetitive aspect of sentences and
larger patterns can be cumulative and extremely effective.

The first-time reader of ***Beowulf*** is impressed by the twice-
repeated formula of movement when Grendel's approach
to the high-gabled hall of Hrothgar is being described in
lines 702-21a: "Com on wanre niht / scridan sceadugenga"
(There came in the dim night stealthily moving the shadow
goer); "þa com of more / under misthleoþum / Grendel
gongan" (Then came from the moor under the dark mists,
Grendel moving); and, finally, "Com þa to recede / rinc
sidian / dreamum bedæled" (There came then to the hall
that warrior bereft of joy). The effect of the repeated patterns is undeniably powerful, and it is a typical, though
spectacular, example of the ***Beowulf*** poet's method.[14]

The result of incremental aspect of the poetic method is
that the individual epithet or phrase has more emphasis—
more time in the reader's or hearer's consciousness. The
reader or hearer, in short, is required to play a rather active role in the poem, almost a creative one. The tradition
of oral poetry depends on an alert, participating, cooperat-
ing hearer. To a greater extent than with poetry whose tradition is totally literary, poetry that has its origins—in
however dim a past—in the give-and-take between performer and audience depends for the completion of its
meaning upon its audience. Therefore, particularly for
early Germanic poetry, the best possible preparation that
the student can make is to acquaint himself with as many
of the surviving poems as possible, either in the original
or in modern versions. He can then share with the poet a
knowledge of the legends, recognize the context of kennings, and appreciate the unexpected variation.

Notes

1. Francis P. Magoun, Jr., "The Oral Formulaic Character of Anglo-Saxon Poetry," *Speculum* 28 (1952):446-
   67.

2. For a variety of approaches to the evidence on this
   question, the student should consult the works by
   Benson, Creed, Greenfield, Lord, Magoun, Watt, and
   Whallon listed in the Bibliography. We discuss something of the course of this controversy in chapter 10.
   At the core of the problem is the question whether
   the characteristics of the oral formula that Milman
   Parry and Alfred B. Lord observed in twentieth-
   century Balkan poetry composed orally and that they
   also find in the poetry of the *Iliad* and the *Odyssey*
   are also those of the formula of Germanic poetry.
   The scholarly consensus at present is that they are
   not. The syllabic regularity of Greek meter, on which
   Parry's concept of the oral formula is based, has no
   parallel in Germanic poetry. The far greater variety
   of formulaic epithet found in *Beowulf,* which admits
   of far more specific appropriateness to context, sets it
   apart from the more rigidly stereotyped Greek epithet. It would be fair to say that, although every
   scholar today would assume that the formulaic qualities of Old English are of a kind that has its origin in
   nonliterate poetry—i.e., a poetry not only orally
   transmitted but orally created—the great majority of
   scholars would maintain that *Beowulf's* enormous
   variety of epithet would in itself likely preclude oral
   composition of the poem.

3. It is beyond our brief to argue here whether we ought to label as kennings many of the Old English figures usually so called. For the technically accurate claim that most are *kend heiti,* see the discussion by Arthur G. Brodeur in *The Art of Beowulf,* p. 18.

4. For illustration of the variation of which the *Beowulf* poet was capable, see the discussion in ibid. and the appendix of epithets unique to *Beowulf.*

5. For a thorough comparison of the Anglo-Saxon and the Homeric epithet, see William Whallon, *Formula, Character, and Context: Studies in Homeric, Old English, and Old Testament Poetry.*

6. G. P. Krapp, ed., *The Vercelli Book,* in *The Anglo-Saxon Poetic Records,* vol. 2. (New York: Columbia University Press, 1932), p. 51.

7. Ibid., p. 3.

8. Bruce Dickins and A. S. C. Ross, eds., *The Dream of the Rood* (London: Methvem, 1934), p. 20.

9. See discussions of this theme in F. P. Magoun, Jr., "The Theme of the Beasts of Battle in Anglo-Saxon Poetry," *NM* 56 (1955): 81-90; and Adrian Bonjour, "*Beowulf* and the Beasts of Battle," in his *Twelve Beowulf Papers,* pp. 135-46.

10. E. V. K. Dobbie, ed., *The Anglo-Saxon Minor Poems,* in *The Anglo-Saxon Poetic Records,* vol. 6 (New York: Columbia University Press, 1942), pp. 19-20.

11. See chapter 7 for discussion of these themes.

12. J. R. R. Tolkien, "Prefatory Remarks," in J. R. Clark Hall, trans., *Beowulf and the Finnsburg Fragment,* p. xliii.

13. Such is the underlying assumption of Kenneth Sisam in *The Structure of Beowulf.*

14. For a stimulating discussion of the poet's uses of repetition and variation, the reader is referred to Arthur G. Brodeur, *The Art of Beowulf,* pp. 39-70. See our remarks on Brodeur's arguments in chapter 10.

Bernard F. Huppé (essay date 1984)

SOURCE: "Thematic Polarity," in *The Hero in the Earthly City,* State University of New York Press, 1984, pp. 24-45.

[*In the essay below, Huppé asserts that the author of* Beowulf *demonstrates by antithesis the concept of the Christian hero and shows how Beowulf's lack of Christianity reveals the emptiness of his heroic ideals.*]

the contrapuntal narrative method of *Beowulf* demands close attention to the interweaving of the threads that make up the story of the hero. The narrative moves from puzzles to answers which raise further questions. Thus, the poem begins with the puzzle of Scyld and his succession. Although answers are later given, they leave a mystery to be

understood only in the realization that Scyld is an agent of destinal or divine purpose, which man cannot comprehend any more than he can the mystery of death. The function of narrative puzzlement, in short, is thematic.[2]

The epic life of Beowulf unfolds by puzzlement and shadowy recall of the deeds he has done. An ultimate question, however, is not answered. Why does Beowulf, heroically virtuous in death, leave a legacy of worthless gold and a future of unrelieved misery for his people? Although he is the heroic antithesis of Heremod, both leave their people wretched. Why? When Beowulf determines to fight the dragon, why is he filled, not with fear, but with doubt? Why does he have misgivings about transgressing the ancient law when in dying he is aware only of having lived with pious regard to the right uses of the strenth given him for destinal purposes? In short, why does the second part of the poem not move to triumphant affirmation of the glory of Beowulf's heroic death, but rather to lamentation over its waste?

These questions, as with Scyld, can only be answered thematically. The answers to them rest in the meaning that is given to the hero's life, and that meaning is based on the poet's concept of the heroic, which, in turn, must reflect a then-current climate of belief. Thus, it would appear essential to discover what this attitude was, a seemingly impossible task since the date of *Beowulf* has not been determined. It may have been written during the early, missionary stages of Christianity in England when the triumph of the new religion required apology and vigorous defense (seventh century). It may have been written when Christianity was firmly established and English energies were directed, for example, to the conversion of the continental Saxons (eighth century). Finally, it may have been written after the Viking invasions when English intellectual energies would have been responsive to Scandinavian paganism or, conversely, would have been influenced by Scandinavian Christianity (ninth, tenth, or even eleventh centuries).[3]

All these varying dates, however, belong as a whole to the Christian era when the intellectual life of England was dominated by Augustinian and monastic conceptions and constructs. This temporal-intellectual fact provides the opportunity and governs the attempt to recapture some approximate understanding of the preconceptions of an earlier age, the meta-linguistic imperatives that directed the poet's concept of his hero, Beowulf.

In this attempt to rediscover the territory of the poet's mind, we are like the makers of historical maps who plot the routes of communication of a forgotten past. They cannot use the grid of the modern highway system; rather they must disregard the modern to discover obliterated roads leading to obliterated villages, camouflaged and covered by the modern grid. Once we find the ancient road, however, we are met with the puzzle of a road sign pointing in two opposite directions. One directs us to the paganism of the poem that appears to govern its forms and the motivation of its characters. The other points to the Christianity of the poem. The authenticity of the signpost is attested by contemporary evidence. Thus Alcuin, Charlemagne's English school-master, asks the vital question, "Why Ingeld with Christ?"[4] If Alcuin, in the poet's own monastic era, was troubled, surely the modern scholars who began the serious study of **Beowulf** appeared to be on the right track in assuming the poem to be basically Germanic and pagan, with interpolations designed to allow Ingeld to live more comfortably with Christ; that is, to give the basic paganism of the poem the coloring, if not the substance, of Christianity.

This satisfying direction, however, does not suffice in the face of the most recalcitrant of all facts, the poem itself. For Klaeber long ago observed, and modern scholarship is in agreement, that the pagan and Christian threads of the poem are too intertwined to be disentangled. If the Christian threads were removed from the poem, its unity would be destroyed. Thus it may be that our modern perception of what troubled Alcuin is at fault, for it is likely in the context of the Augustinian theory of literature to which he subscribed that Alcuin was no more disturbed by the juxtaposition itself than he would have been in finding God called Jove in a Latin Christian poem. What he was troubled by was not the juxtaposition, rhetorically permissible, but the need *in a monastery* to fashion Christian truths in poetic guise. Augustine had defended the use of literature as providing nourishment for babies in faith—until they could feed on the sturdy meat of doctrine itself. Alcuin, in turn, would not have questioned the use of pagan fable to inculcate Christian truth in neophytes and worldly men, but he might well have questioned the need of such a pedagogic device for monks who would presumably have been both knowledgeable and otherworldly.

The Christian moralizations of **Beowulf** may appear jarringly anachronistic, tangential to, and incompatible with the basic paganism of its story, language, and motivations. However, such a reaction is modern, a signpost hiding the old Janus-faced one which points in the direction of the intertwined existence of pagan and Christian in the poem. There is a reason for the bivalent sign, and this reason may be sought in the literary evidence of English attitudes toward the heroic.

Since we cannot be sure when the poet lived, it seems best to trace this evidence backwards from that expressed in the late tenth, early eleventh centuries, by lfric and in the *Battle of Maldon*. In dealing with ælfric's conception of the hero, we face the problem that his heroes are saints, in particular the kingly martyrs, Oswald and Edmund.[5] These two are first of all saints, and only thus are heroes: they are examples of perfect living and perfect dying. The clash of swords, the bang of shields are missing in their stories—and the loss is essential. The hero, to be anything like Beowulf, must do battle as did Aeneas, one obvious prototype for the medieval hero.

Of prime importance in the conception of a hero like Aeneas is that he served an inner direction. Aeneas is governed by fate, in the Christian interpretation an emblem of divine providence directing man to his true home, the heavenly Jerusalem. But such a hero is not simply driven; he must himself act, and act heroically. It is only through his personal discovery of the right road, frequently after misdirection, that the operation of the divine plan can be seen. The saint, on the other hand, in his actions too clearly exemplifies the operation of divine providence. The saint's life is a miracle and is punctuated by miracles, the embodied evidence of things unseen. The saint is defined as a manifestation of divine purpose, whereas the hero, however superhuman, lives in a frequently strained relationship between himself as human agent and the larger purpose he must learn to serve. Except where his conversion may be involved, the saint knows his way and is devoid of strain in submitting to the will of God.

Thus lfric's saints, though they are heroic, are not Beowulfian heroes simply because they are too exemplary. They are living miracles: not superhuman as Beowulf is, but supra-human. Their battlefields are totally spiritual, and they are divinely, not humanly, motivated. Nothing more clearly illustrates the distinction between saint and hero than lfric's two martyred warrior kings. Oswald's reign is punctuated by a pair of heroic battles, his victory over the heathen Cedwalla and his death and defeat at the hands of the apostate Penda. The battles demand heroic treatment; they are the substance of the epic. But lfric sees Oswald not as a hero, but as a saint, so that the battles are deliberately slighted in favor of the development of the charity of his reign and of the miracles that followed his death. For example, the story of the sick horse who is cured after it wandered over Oswald's place of death is more developed than are both battles put together.

The first battle is described with startling brevity:

> Oswald then raised up a cross to the honor of God before he came to battle and called out to his companions, "Let us kneel before the rood and pray to the Almighty that He protect us against the haughty enemy who wishes to slay us: God himself knows readily that we contend rightfully against this fierce king to protect our people." They all then knelt with Oswald in prayer and afterwards in the early morning went to battle and won the victory as God aided them because of Oswald's faith, and they laid low their enemy, the proud Cedwalla with his great army, he who thought that no army might withstand him.

In essence the battle consists in the raising and worshipping of the cross; the victory is that of God's power and Oswald's faith—no shields are raised, no spears brandished. In the second battle "celebrated" by lfric, high heroic tragedy is implicit in the defeat and slaying of Oswald by the apostate Penda. Yet ælfric, with conscious artistry, erases from the scene all but the motif of Oswald's saintly martyrdom:

> It came to pass that Penda waged war on him, Penda the king of the Mercians who had aided Cedwalla at the slaying sometime before of Oswald's kinsman, Ed-

win the king; and Penda understood nothing about Christ, and all the Mercian people were still unbaptized. They came then to battle at Maserfield and met together until the Christians fell and the heathens approached the holy Oswald. Then he saw the end of his life approach and prayed for his people who there fell in death and commended their souls and himself to God, and thus called out in his dying, "God have mercy on their souls!" Then the heathen king commanded that his head be cut off, and his right arm, and that they be set up as a sign.

Even the background for the action raises Beowulfian expectations of the heroic with the evocation of the motif of vengeance for a kinsman. lfric, however, merely notes as a matter of fact that Penda had been allied with Cedwalla when he slew Oswald's kinsman, Edwin. Apparently, the thought of vengeance is as foreign to Oswald as it was natural for Beowulf to consider vengeance as the highest of duties. ælfric's failure to exploit the possibilities inherent in the motif of vengeance and in the battle is deliberately designed to stress the saintliness of Oswald's character. The organization of lfric's account of the battle suggests that he was conscious of the contrast between saintly and heroic ideals, and that he deliberately plays one against the other, counter-pointing expectations of the heroic against the actuality of saintly conduct.

The death of Edmund, as lfric narrates it, even more clearly exemplifies his conscious disavowal of the heroic and emphasis on the saintly. In the scene, the saintly martyr facing the heathen Hingwar deliberately discards the heroic response to which he is naturally attracted. He rejects it to follow Christ's injunction literally:

> Lo then when Hingwar came, King Edmund stood within his home mindful of the Savior and cast aside his weapons. He wished to imitate the example of Christ who forbade Peter to contend with weapons against the bloodthirsty Jews. Lo the heathens bound and humiliated Edmund shamefully and and beat him with cudgels and then led the confessorking to an earth-rooted tree and tied him thereto with strong bonds and beat him then for a long time with whips; and he always called out between the blows with true faith to the Savior Christ; and the heathens became madly angry because in his faith he called upon Christ for aid. They shot at him then with spears as if in a game until he was all covered with their shafts as if with the bristles of a porcupine, just as Sebastian had been. When Hingwar, the heathen pirate, saw that the noble king would not abandon Christ but with steadfast belief ever called upon Him, he commanded that he be beheaded, and the heathens did so. While still he called upon Christ the heathens drew the saint to slaughter and with one blow cut off his head, and his soul voyaged blessed to Christ.

In this scene ælfric has Edmund deliberately reject the heroic response, a rejection prepared for earlier by juxtaposing Christian and heroic ideals in the king's mind as he deliberates his response to the invasion. True to the patterns of heroic conduct, the king declares his wish not to survive the death of his dear retainers and continues:

> It was never my custom to turn to flight; for if I must I would readily die for my country, and the Almighty God knows that I will never turn from His worship, nor from His true love, whether I live or die.

The king is motivated both by Christian and by heroic ideals, but at the crisis recognizes that they cannot coexist; he rejects heroic death for triumphant martyrdom in imitation of his Master's unheroic surrender to the enemy. His death, even to the image of the porcupine and the heathen game-playing, is made humiliating to reflect the ignominious victory of Christ's Passion and St. Sebastian's martyrdom. Edmund becomes saint and Christian hero in the act of rejecting the heroic.

lfric's awareness of the heroic tradition and his rhetorical use of it for antithesis is anticipated about a century earlier in the Old High German *Ludwigslied*.[6] This poem, written in late 881 or early 882, celebrated the victory of the king of the Franks, Louis, over the Vikings, but the heroic potentials of the subject are realized only as antithesis to the king's Christian triumph through God. The poet concentrates his attention on celebrating Louis as the vicar of God, executing divine purpose. Louis has no personality in the poem except for his relationship to God. The king served God, we are told; indeed when Louis lost his father, God adopted him as His own son, became his foster father. However, for their sins, God visited punishment upon the Franks by permitting the attack of the Vikings, but then called on Louis to defend them: "Louis, my king, help my people." In response Louis gathers his men to face the Northmen; he takes shield and spear, but this heroic gesture is followed by his singing the praise of God. To his saintly battle-cry, his men respond "Kyrie eleison!" The battle begins and victory and honor are immediately awarded to Louis. The potential for the heroic in such a battle is left unrealized except as it provides implicit counterpoint to the tendentiously Christian.

A tradition of rhetorical use of heroic motifs in antithesis to the Christian ideal appears to exist, as is attested by the *Dream of the Rood*, a poem written perhaps as early as the beginning of the eighth century. In it the Cross itself narrates the Crucifixion in terms appropriate to heroic battle:

> I saw mankind's Protector
> most manfully hasten   to ascend me;
> I did not dare   in disobedience
> to bow or crack   though I saw the bounds
> of earth trembling;   truly I had the might
> to fell these foes   —yet I stood fast.
> The young hero prepared   —He was Almighty God—
> great and gallant to ascend   the gallow's abject height,
> wishing as many watched   magnanimously to free mankind.
> Trembling in the Son's clasp   I dared not crouch on the ground
> or fall to earth's boundaries   —I had need to stand fast;
> erected as a cross   I raised the King

> of the heavens above   —I dared not bow.
> They pierced me with dark nails;   on me ap-
>   pear the wounds,
> the gaping blows of hate   —I dared not hurt them
>   in return.
> They besmirched us both;   I was besmeared with
>   the blood
> which poured from the Man's side   after he sur-
>   rendered his soul.

The rhetoric of the passage is complex, involving meta-phorical extension, metonymy, oxymoron, and antithesis. For the present purpose, however, what is important is the metaphor of battle, with Christ pictured as a warrior pre-paring for battle and the Cross as the Lord's retainer, torn between his desire to attack and the compulsion to obedi-ence. The effect of the poet's heroic metaphor is to em-phasize the antithesis between the degradation of the cru-cifixion and the language of heroic battle employed to describe it. His bold rhetoric may be explained as serving the ends of missionary apology. By this hypothesis, the poet would have had the specific intention of engaging the imagination of an audience brought up on heroic poetry and responsive to it, so that they could perceive through the epic diction the higher heroism of the penitential life, the way of the cross.

The heroic, then, would have been employed to celebrate its antithesis, Christian humility. The poet's vision serves as apologia for an ideal in conflict with what was custom-ary in a warrior society. It does so by suggesting that the penitential life has affinities with that of the warrior, who also must suffer privation that he may win triumph and glory; only the definition of what constitutes glory is changed. That is why, in *The Dream of the Rood,* both Christ and Cross appear as soldiers engaged in a conflict with victory as its goal. Like good soldiers, they are abso-lutely obedient to a command that calls upon them not to strike but to endure, not to be heroic but to be humble. The Cross tells the story of the Crucifixion as if he were a warrior who has had placed upon him a soldierly obliga-tion not to be heroic. In so doing, the Cross reveals the tensions inherent in a warrior society, the ultimate values of which have been put in question by the new dispensa-tion that refutes the heroic ideal by redefining glory, the reward of victory. Thus the Cross yearning for heroic battle is enjoined to the higher fortitude of humble suffering in order to gain Christian glory, the crown of victory in the kingdom of Heaven. This reward the Cross promises to all who forego wordly glory to follow the penitential way to heavenly glory.

The currency of the use of the heroic by antithesis to cel-ebrate its opposite is attested in other poems. In *The Won-der of Creation,* of undetermined date, a striking equation is made between the contemplative (monastic) life and the life of fortitude. By redefinition, it claims for Christian contemplation a virtue which in the heroic warrior's defi-nition was his alone. In *Judith,* perhaps of the ninth cen-tury, a battle scene appears celebrating the victory of the

Hebrews over the Assyrians. The narrative mode is heroic: the banners move forward; the shields clash at dawn; the carrion wolf and raven are aroused and the eagle sings the battle song; the warriors advance under their shields, dis-charge arrows, cast spears, draw their swords and attack hand-to-hand. The battle, however, has no part in the Vul-gate source, which expressly states that no battle took place, only the threat of attack and the consequent flight of the Assyrians. Thus the battle scene, rendered in the tradi-tional formulaic patterns of heroic verse, involves an ex-tended use of hysteron-proteron, the thematic function of which is to emphasize the presence of God's hand and to establish the spiritual, providential nature of the Hebrew victory. The Hebrew warriors, like Judith, are the agents of God, His executioners, as it were. Again, the heroic serves as emblem of its antithesis, Christian victory through faith.[7]

The battle in *Judith* is very like the symbolic battles be-tween Abraham and the nine kings in *Genesis A,* a poem unquestionably among the earliest in the Old English po-etic corpus. The account of the battles is lengthy and is characteristically heroic (lines 1960-2095). The northern kings are at first victorious, so that "many a fearful maiden had trembling to go to a stranger's embrace," and the de-fenders perish, "sick with wounds." In a second battle, the kings again attack; "the spears sing, the raven croaks, greedy for prey." The "battleplay" is hard but the kings "possess the place of slaughter." Abraham now gathers a small band, symbolically numbering three hundred and eighteen; he comforts his band by declaring his faith that "the Eternal Lord may easily grant good speed in the spear strife." In the ensuing battle, "Abraham gave war as a ran-som for his nephew [Lot], not the wound gold." Finally, the army of the kings is left to be torn by the carrion birds. This heroic battle scene, however, both echoes and was written against standard interpretation of the Bible, where it was considered to be, as Bede puts it, an emblem of "a very great miracle of divine power." The numbers of the kings and of Abraham's band are symbolic, so that the battle is, in its significance, a psychomachia in which Abra-ham's victory is "symbolic of the Christian soldier's vic-tory over wordly temptation."[8] The poet's heroic battle scenes do not celebrate the memories of heathen poetry; rather by symbolic antithesis they celebrate the triumph of faith. The intended effect was through the use of tradi-tional heroic idiom by antithesis to affirm Christian doc-trine. The figure of Abraham does not evoke the pagan warrior but rather the ideal of Christian faith.

Judging from all this literary evidence, which spans the entire period in which **Beowulf** could have been written, the heroic tradition appears to have been very much alive, however negatively, in the consciousness of the early me-dieval poet and writer.[9] Further, the antithesis between he-roic and Christian ideals, it must be assumed, presented a primary social problem. The strain caused by the coexist-ence of Christian and pagan traditions in a war-like soci-ety may be shown by two examples, one from the court of Theodoric, the other from Charlemagne's court. Theodor-ic's successor, Athalaric, under the influence of his mother, was given clerical training in the arts. This effort, however, was successfully resisted by the unreconstructed nobility who considered such clerkly instruction to be opposed, as Reto Bezzola puts it, "to the spirit of the Ostrogoths." It was not an education, they argued, suitable to "a young king of their race destined for a warrior and heroic career." In short, Christianity was for priests and women, the heroic was for the warrior. The second example comes from a poem by Theodulf, a clerk and poet in Charlemagne's court. He tells how his verses pleased the court except for a certain "Wibrodus heros." He, as Bezzola summarizes, "shook his huge head in a menacing and ferocious manner," until Charlemagne himself was forced to stop him. The strain evident early in Theodoric's court remains in Charlemagne's court in the ninth century in the confrontation between the clerk and the warrior, so significantly termed "heros."[10]

The conflict of ideals would also have presented a basic problem to Christian writers in England from the time of the Conversion until after the Viking invasions. After the Conversion they faced the dilemma of teaching Christianity to an audience brought up with, or vividly remembering, the heroic poetry of their pagan ancestors. Thus we hear of Aldhelm in the seventh century, according to William of Malmesbury, composing secular verses in the accustomed manner, but with the purpose of leading his listeners to doctrinal truth "by interweaving among foolish things, the words of Scripture."[11] In the ninth century, Alcuin, it will be recalled, was aware of the commonplace interweaving of Ingeld with Christ. After the Viking incursions, the English poet, by definition Christian and probably monastic, would have written for a society facing the pagan Vikings whose attack upon Christendom required both prayer and, more importantly, a heroic, warrior-like response. It would have been the task of the poet somehow to reconcile the two ideals of the heroic and the Christian, not merely to use the heroic to serve by rhetorical antithesis as metaphor for penitential fortitude. This is the task, of the poet of *The Battle of Maldon,* and it was also that of the poet of **Beowulf,** as will be argued, whether he wrote at the same time as *The Dream of the Rood* or much later.

The problem these poets faced cannot be glossed over by hypothesizing the side-by-side existence of two cultures, that of the warrior and that of the clerk, in which the heroic poem is simply covered with a veneer of Christian moralization.[12] There may have been in fact a division in society, but the poetry that remains to us is inevitably the product of clerks, that is to say, at that time of monks. Yet, though the poetry is monastic, the heroic in *Maldon* and in **Beowulf** cannot be explained away simply as rhetorical manipulation, as is true of *The Dream of the Rood.* The heroic in the two poems under question cannot be transformed into Christian statement, for example, by allegorization.[13] Rather, the poets were trying, according to my hypothesis, to effect a reconciliation, trying to bring together the split halves of their society. These were great poets writing about what was most profoundly important

in their own times; there could have been nothing more important for them than to deal with the meaning of the Christian soldier in actuality, not merely metaphorically. The dilemma they faced is clear: the only valid life was that led in the *imitatio Christi,* yet meek surrender to the heathen could not have been contemplated in the actual world. lfric was aware of the dilemma and offered a traditional solution: that military (heroic) action with the intention of humble service to Christendom is justified. Thus, in commenting on his metrical version of the biblical Judith, he cites her both as an example of the triumph of humility and as "an example to you men that you with weapons should protect your land against the attacking enemy."[14] One way or another the Christian writers of *Maldon* and **Beowulf** were dealing with the problem of the relation between the parts of the equation, Christian and heroic.

The *Battle of Maldon* is a Christian poem of monastic provenance. In the traditional manner, it narrates a battle in which the English, led by the pious yet heroic Byrhthnoth, were defeated by the heathen Vikings.[15] Two matters are of special interest in the attempt to discover how the poet conceived of the heroic in Byrhthnoth's conduct of the battle. First of all, it should be clear that *Maldon* is a poem, not an historical account to be judged by the principles of accurate representation. In all likelihood, the poet felt free to take what might be called poetic license with the accounts of the battle which he had heard. At any rate, he contrives his narrative so that the death of the hero, Byrhthnoth, appears not as the climax but as the center of his poem, as in ælfric's homilies on Oswald and Edmund. The first half of *Maldon* leads up to his death; the last part narrates the treachery of some of Byrhthnoth's followers and the faithfulness to death of the remainder. In consequence, the poem appears to enclose, to set off Byrhthnoth's dying speech:

> I give Thee thanks,   God of nations,
> for my well-being   here in the world;
> now my greatest need,   Gracious Lord,
> is that You grant   this grace to me
> that now my soul   may ascend to Thee,
> Ruler of angels,   and into your realm
> may come in peace;   upon Thee I call
> to hold it safe   from the devils of hell.

His speech is Edmund-like. He is a martyr turning to God in the full expectation of protection from devils and of eternal life because he is dying in battle against human devils, the Vikings. Yet, as the poet has made clear earlier, Byrhthnoth's own heroic actions contribute in a decisive way to his defeat and death and that of his men, when he recklessly abandons the advantageous position he holds at the ford. Out of heroic pride, *for his ofermode,* Byrhthnoth agrees to permit the Vikings to mass their forces on the shore instead of having to cross the ford singly. Then he taunts them and tempts God:[16]

> Room has been made;   now speed you men
> to give us battle   —God alone knows
> who will be the victor   on the battle-field

Byrhthnoth's action and his speech are governed by an heroic ideal of warrior conduct; in sharpest contrast, his death is pictured as that of a Christian martyr. The antithesis the poet establishes is similar to that found in *The Dream of the Rood* and lfric's homilies, but with a crucial difference. Here the antithesis is embodied in a single Christian hero, Byrhthnoth. Apparently the poet must have felt that in his portrait of Byrhthnoth he had achieved a reconciliation of the antithetical halves of his character. Relying upon a shared climate of belief, he found no need for explanation, so that his reconciliation of the Christian and the heroic must be examined to provide some clue to the concept of the Christian hero that he and his audience held.

Byrhthnoth's heroic recklessness in permitting the Vikings to fight on equal terms may be likened to that of Beowulf's in determining to battle Grendel on even terms by abandoning his sword and armor. Such conduct, however, though it may be appropriate to a pagan hero, seems ill-suited to the character of a Christian hero. The poet is aware of this in equating his heroism with pride, *ofermode*, the sin of Satan who is also given heroic stature in two poems, *Genesis* and *Christ and Satan*. At the same time, however, the poet appears to accept Byrhthnoth's heroic pride as an essential characteristic, in this case, not of a satanic heathen but of a pious Christian warrior. Byrhthnoth's decision to follow heroic precepts in giving away his advantage on the battlefield, accompanied by an heroic boast (*beot*), does not represent a sudden change, but is of a piece with his earlier defiant reply to the Viking messenger's demand for tribute. Here in epic formulas he reveals his heroic resolve (*anræd*):

> Seaman do you hear   what this people say?
> They willingly give   a gift of spears
> to you in battle   and profitless booty
> of poisoned point   of patrimonial sword.
> Viking messenger,   bring to your men
> a loathsome tale   in the telling:
> here in loyalty   a leader with his troop
> stands to keep safe   his native soil,
> the land of his king,   Lord æthelred's
> fields and his folk.   The heathens shall fall
> in battle here;   it seems to me base
> that without battle   you board your ships
> with our treasure   now you have traveled
> the long way here   into our land.
> Without trouble   you'll not gain treasure;
> the point and the edge   will be our appeasement,
> rough battle-play   before we pay tribute.

The heroic resolve of this speech anticipates the heroic pride involved in his giving fighting room to the heathen enemy. In heeding an heroic imperative he becomes responsible for disaster, so that in Byrhthnoth's heroism lies something akin to the tragic flaw. Conversely, he appears also to be governed by faith and Christian piety, as in his thanks to God for victory in his first skirmishes after he had drawn back to give the Vikings room:

> The doughty earl

> was happy and laughed,   gave thanks to heaven
> for the day's labor   the Lord gave him.

As his boast to the Viking messenger leads to his fatal heroic action, this speech of Christian thanksgiving, revealing the steadfastness of his Christian faith and purpose, leads to his dying speech in which as a martyr he expresses his hope of salvation.

In *Maldon,* Christian and heroic exist as antitheses, yet are reconciled in Byrhthnoth. His death as a martyr apparently absolves, for the poet, the fatal flaw of pride in his obeying the dictates of heroic conduct. The poet's line of reasoning is not difficult to follow because it flows from the rudimenatry Christian doctrine of grace. The heroic is human, thus part of man's estate, the result of original sin. But the heroic in Byrhthnoth, the taint of fallen humanity, is absolved because it has been placed in the service of the Faith, and, through grace, becomes good work. In his heroic bravado he falls, but in his death he imitates Christ and becomes a martyr. Because Byrhthnoth's martyrdom is an emblem of Christ's death, it shares in the mystery of grace by which erring humanity is reconciled with God. In the Christian interpretation of the *Aeneid,* the hero serves a divine purpose which he does not recognize; Byrhthnoth in *Maldon,* though flawed by his heroic recklessness, serves God's purpose, which he recognizes. Byrhthnoth's human heroism leads to defeat, but his heroic effort serves Christendom, so that his defeat reveals a high, providential purpose by providing a Christian example of a warrior's holy dying.

Implicit in the poem is the recognition that the human condition requires men to do battle. Such men are likely to be self-reliant, proud of their valor and, in their fallen humanity, heroic. The hero *qua* hero is without grace; his heroism, however, may be redeemed by its service to Christendom, and he may thus achieve the status of the saint through grace, right faith and holy dying. The concept is analogous to that of the *felix culpa,* the sin which through providence becomes the happy redemption. Though the dictates of the heroic lead to the sin of self-reliant pride, the heroic may be transformed in obedience to divine will. The act of doing battle with heathens in the defense of Christendom partakes of the penitential, and if death follows from the act it becomes martyrdom which exculpates the sinfulness of heroic conduct. Thus the battle for the Faith and the martyr's death transform heroic conduct into a model of salvation, and Byrhthnoth's folly is reconciled with his Christian life.

This concept provides an adequate explanation for the heroic in Byrhthnoth but may be of less value in explaining Beowulf, a pagan for whom the heroic imperatives are the essential motivations of his conduct. It is tempting to solve this difficulty by resort to the notion that **Beowulf** essentially conveys a pagan heroic ethic which cannot be explained by recourse to the concept of the Christian hero. In such a view the Christian, as merely external coloring, cannot lead to the heart of the poem. Such a solution will not suffice, however, because the Christianity of **Beowulf** has been shown to be an essential part of its form and structure, although its subject and the motivations of its characters are pagan. It would be naive to assume that the poet was not aware of the paganism of his hero and of his society. It would be equally naive to assume that he would have celebrated a society which lacked the knowledge of the truths of Christianity.[17] The values of such a society, lacking in the saving grace of the theological virtues, he would have deplored.

However, even if a pagan hero were blessed with piety and the cardinal virtues, he could not thereby attain the status of Christian hero, which involves the possession of the three theological virtues of Faith, Hope and Charity. Like Aeneas, the pagan hero in Christian interpretation, may reveal the way in which providential design makes use of the hero, or may even typify the Christian search for the heavenly home.[18] Nonetheless the pagan hero remains a pagan, blind himself to the real meaning of his life. Christian doctrine alone provides the key to such meaning; in and for themselves the epic adventures of a pagan hero can only reveal his limitations and those of his society, for he, without faith, is a blind man leading the blind. Yet this very antithesis between the Christian and pagan understanding of the epic hero provides an hypothesis for the understanding of how **Beowulf** was intended to be read by its Christian audience. The hypothesis assumes that the fictional world of **Beowulf** is pagan, its point of view Christian. From the Christian point of view, the pagan events of the poem reveal the limits of heathen society, the limits of the righteous pagan, and the limits of the heroic ideal.[19] Such Christian revelation is the primary thematic function of the poem.

This hypothesis serves to explain much that is otherwise puzzling in the poem: for one major example, its descending line of mood and action, so that the omens of disaster in the first half of the poem are fulfilled and completed in the last half. After Beowulf returns home and gives his account of his exploits in Denmark, there is a scene of joyous, prosperous amity jarringly concluded without interruption by the twenty-line narrative of ensuing disasters leading to Beowulf's reign, which culminates in the coming of the dragon. Amidst forebodings of disaster, Beowulf decides to revenge the dragon's onslaught and gain the treasure. His mind, however, is darkened by ethical doubt and is filled with memories of past battles. He recalls the tangled net of Higelac's adventures and the internecine Swedish wars in which he became involved. Finally, he recalls the death in grief of ancient Hrethel, fatally unable to solve the dilemma to which his heroic ethic could give no answer: his duty to avenge his son; his duty not to be guilty of the death of his son. In the battle, Beowulf is fatally wounded and averts defeat only through the aid of Wiglaf. In his dying speech, Beowulf places his hope for the future upon the gold he has won. His speech, as he gazes upon the gold, recalls in counterpoint the lament of the last survivor as he looked on the useless treasure he was about to bury, a counterpoint of doom and disaster

which dominates the last part of the poem. After Beowulf's death the mood is further darkened, not so much by grief over his passing as by forebodings of impending doom. The messenger retells the story of Higelac's fatal raid and of the deadly Swedish wars, not to celebrate the hero, but to foretell the disastrous legacy of lordless grief, suffering, and exile that Beowulf will leave to his people.

Further underscoring the dismal view of his death is the contrast between youthful Wiglaf and aged Beowulf. Wiglaf recalls the young Beowulf in Denmark as, concomitantly, Beowulf recalls the aged Hrothgar. Hrothgar, with his self-deceiving trust in the security provided by his power to reward through treasure, has his counterpart in Beowulf, with his equally self-deceiving trust in the security provided his nation by the dragon's treasure. Wiglaf, however, is not the exact counterpart of the young Beowulf. If he were, he would be expected to lighten the oppressive gloom in providing some hope for the future. Such expectation the poet takes pains not to fulfill. Beowulf transfers his kingship to Wiglaf who has proved his heroic quality, but Wiglaf does not respond with the assurance of the young Beowulf. He provides no expected show of determination to emulate his dead hero-king; rather he shares completely in the messenger's sense of inevitable disaster. He refuses to share Beowulf's trust in the dragon's treasure, but agrees that it should again be buried to remain as worthless as it was before. Further, he openly declares that Beowulf's encounter with the dragon was the result of a doomed, reckless heroism, a recklessness which will have the ruin of his people as a consequence. Wiglaf's grief is understandable; the failure of his will to succeed is not. The hope implicit in his heroic youth is not realized. Because he considers Beowulf's death only as a disaster brought about through heroic pride, and because he has no apparent hope for the future, Wiglaf reveals the ineffectual emptiness of his society, the failure of its ideal hero and of the heroic. Far from lightening the darkness, Wiglaf's bright, heroic youth intensifies it. From the cycle of trust in treasure and the heroic response there is no escape. **Beowulf** does not end in tragic celebration of the hero but in lament over the doomed waste of his youth and valor.

The heroic in *Maldon* is represented as a tragic flaw which precipitates disaster but leads through the mystery of the *felix culpa* to the good of redemption through martyrdom. Byrhthnoth's death is the tragic cause for celebration; Beowulf's is not. The heroic in **Beowulf** is self-contained; it is the ethos of a culture, of the heroic past as the poet envisioned it; it must be self-justified because it cannot, as in *Maldon,* appeal to redeeming grace. That is why the last words about Beowulf are about his search for glory, the empty ideal of a pagan, heroic world. To the contrary, the poet's attitude toward the heroic ethos and its goal of glory is Christian and critical.[20] That is why the direction of the poem is inevitably toward doom and disaster unrelieved by any sense of hope and redemption. Beowulf's flaw is tragic precisely because there are no means available to him by which the flaw may be redeemed. Thus his tragedy rests in his inability to rise above the ethos of his society, the mores of revenge and war which govern his actions. In the first part of the poem, in contrast to the aged and ineffectual Hrothgar and to the vigorously evil Heremod, Beowulf appears as a savior, a cleanser of evil; in the last part, Beowulf appears to echo and reflect not beginnings but endings. He has become involved in his world and in the ethos of the feud. Though he remains heroic, his heroism is no more effective than is Hrothgar's helplessness. Like Hrothgar he looks toward the past, as does also the last survivor, lamenting the glory that is gone.

The hero's role, as with Aeneas, is to be an agent of fate, that is, Divine Providence in Christian understanding. The beginning of **Beowulf** introduces the theme of agency in the figure of Scyld who appears mysteriously to succor the Danes and disappears in death into the unknown. His mystery is that of the agent of God by whom he has been sent, though a pagan, to alleviate pagan suffering. Yet, in counterpoint to this Christian understanding of his role is that of his pagan followers who see in him only the mystery of his coming and of his leaving. That is to say, Scyld's pagan followers reveal the limitations of their paganism, the limitations of an understanding lacking the truth of faith.

Beowulf, thus introduced, is also an agent of God, as is seen most clearly in his battles against Grendel and particularly against the mother whom he slays with a giant sword to which he is divinely guided.[21] Beowulf brings back the hilt of this sword upon which is recorded the biblical tale of the downfall of the giants, the race of Cain. One effect of the story is to cast Beowulf in the role of God's avenger who eradicates a residue of Cain's generation of monsters. In turn, Hrothgar, gazing on the hilt, is inspired to utter a homily which reaches to the edges of Christian truth. The homily provides a warning to Beowulf against heroic self-reliance whereby his subsequent actions may be judged.[22] Beowulf's own judgment of himself is clouded. On the one hand, when he determines to attack the dragon he is concerned about having violated the old law; on the other hand, in dying he finds comfort in knowing that he has not violated the code by which he has lived. His wavering between moral doubt and certainty results from his being both righteous and pagan. He strives for the truth but cannot escape from the necessary error of all who are without the grace of knowing through faith. Beowulf's striving for righteousness is blocked by the very ethical code which he has piously observed. He cannot understand his feeling that he has transgressed against the old law because he does not know the new law. He has no referent for righteousness except the heroic code, which has revenge as its most sacred obligation, glory and gold as its ultimate reward.[23] The futility of such a code is made evident in Hrethel's fatal ethical dilemma. From the Christian perspective, to seek revenge is sinful error; thus Hrethel, who accepts revenge as ethical obligation, cannot solve his dilemma because he seeks to find his answer in a false faith.

How Beowulf is himself caught in the iron circle of heroic error is evidenced in his inward determination to avenge the death of his nephew, Heardred, Higelac's son, by securing the death of his slayer, Onela, the Swedish king, who had entrusted Beowulf with the Geatish throne, presumably after appropriate swearing of oaths. Beowulf, however, does not perceive that his secret determination to betray Onela is dishonorable because he feels he is being morally obedient to the sacred and paramount duty of revenge.[24] This appears from his dying assertion that he has not dishonored himself with false oaths. Finally, his reasons for attacking the dragon flow from his allegiance to a false moral ideal. He need not have sought revenge; the dragon would have remained in his barrow unless he were again disturbed. For the hero, however, who strives for the ultimate goal of such abiding glory as Sigemund had attained, revenge is an absolute imperative which takes no count of practicalities. Further, the attack on the dragon holds the promise of another ultimate reward, the treasure, visible evidence of glory. In short, as Wiglaf puts it, Beowulf is driven by "relentless doom" because of his own will he seeks the two goals of worldly men living in error, glory and its visible sign, gold. He is doomed because his will now serves a faulty human end.[25] Before, in Denmark, he served as agent of a merciful design, though without understanding; now as king he serves only himself by seeking a heroic goal. In pursuing gold and glory Beowulf becomes the victim of fate because he has accepted the error of his society, and has lost his youthful role as agent of providence.

Thus the final action of the poem takes place not providentially but fatalistically. This fatalism reveals that Beowulf, governed by the law of revenge, is self-doomed, and it reveals the futility of a society not governed and directed by the goal of salvation. The movement of the poem is downward toward a fatally tragic end. Beowulf and the dragon are the victims, the first in seeking the gold, the other in keeping it, and Beowulf's doomed descent is that of all who lack saving grace. The poem ends, to be sure, with Beowulf's people celebrating him as the mildest of kings and the most worthy of praise. He is worthy of praise, however, as the last words of the poem reveal, because he was "most eager for glory." That is, they praise him in terms that would befit any good pagan hero and apply equally well to Aeneas, to Hector, to Odysseus. Their praise is defined by purely human limitations and specifically lacks any of the Christian overtones of *Maldon*. For in direct contrast to Byrhthnoth, Beowulf in dying reveals no movement toward redemption. His death is completely unlike that of the Christian hero because it lacks the sense of revealed understanding suggested by Byrhthnoth's dying plea that his soul be brought home safely to his God.

Beowulf ends with the death and burial of the hero, which is precisely what might be expected in heroic epic, except that no sense of triumph is imparted.[26] The oddity is in the *Battle of Maldon* where the death of the hero comes at the center of the poem, with the result that his death is not the main point toward which the poem is leading. Rather his death serves to reveal the fulfillment of God's design, of which the hero's death is but part. The real point of *Mal-*

don does not rest in the battlefield death. Conversely, the death of the hero *is* the point of *Beowulf.* The first part of the poem reveals and celebrates the workings of God's hand; the death of the hero reveals the emptiness of Beowulf's heroic life when it serves the hero's own ends of glory rather than God's purpose. His death suggests that the heroic ideal is ineffectual and futile, that its supreme embodiment in a Beowulf or an Aeneas lacks any real dignity when compared with the ideal of the Christian as embodied in Byrhthnoth who serves the Lord in faith. In this implicit contrast, the tragic implications of *Beowulf* may most clearly be realized; its pathos rests in the irony of its conclusion where the Geats celebrate a hero who has left them literally nothing but the legacy of debts to be collected.

To conclude, for the author of *Beowulf* and his audience there can be but one ultimate hero, and he is Christ. Whatever is truly heroic comes from the imitation of Him, and the saint is the true hero. St. Edmund imitated Christ truly and is the saintly hero and martyr. Byrhthnoth is a hero who follows Christ and in so doing redeems that which is merely heroic within him. Beowulf is a hero who lacks Christ and reveals that the heroic in itself is an empty ideal. The contrast suggests the obvious, that *Beowulf* may have served as Christian apologetic, revealing the error of the ancestral way of the English, however eager for glory it was, and, in contrast, suggesting the truth and validity of Christian faith. Thus a central thematic function of *Beowulf* as Christian apologetic is, through the tragedy of its great and virtuous heathen hero, to promote by antithesis the concept of the Christian hero, true to himself in being true to Christ in seeking not glory but salvation. In the poet's intention the hero to emulate is not a Beowulf but a Byrhthnoth.

Notes

1. This chapter has been developed from a paper delivered in 1970 at the Fourth Annual Conference of the Center for Medieval and Early Renaissance Studies, Binghamton, N.Y. which appears in *Concepts of the Hero in the Middle Ages and Renaissance,* edited by Norman Burns and Christopher Reagan (Albany: State University of New York Press, 1975), pp. 1-26. Documentation has been up-dated through 1980 and less exhaustively through 1981.

2. W. F. Bolton, "Boethius and a Topos in Beowulf" (see Chapter One, note 2), illustrates the thematic role of what I have termed "polarity" by examination of the Boethian "topos, 'one of two things,'" showing how for the hero "while the topos expresses a static view, the view is increasingly in error about the situation it observes and summarizes. . . . The pervasive dualism of Beowulf schematizes the conflicts that lie at the surface of the narrative. . . . Tragedy, accordingly, is not reversal of fortune but rather commitment to Fortune's sphere. . . . Beowulf's thrice repeated 'one of two things' predictions in the alternativefatal mode just before each of his three great fights express his grasp of his role in

the world. The poet's concern is not with this world, however, but with man's understanding of it; epistemology is the central concern of *Beowulf,* and in this lie both its basic structure and close affinities with the *Consolation,*" pp. 16 ff. J. D. A. Ogilvy, "Beowulf, Alfred, and Christianity," *Saints, Scholars and Heroes* (see Chapter One, note 2), observes the polarity and concludes that the poet "may have regarded Beowulf as a good pagan, like Dante's Vergil. At any rate, being a good Christian himself, he endowed Beowulf with such Christian virtues as were compatible with the heroic code. When Christian virtue and the code diverged, however—as in the matter of vengeance or of worldly fame—the Christian view came out a poor second (p. 64). Ogilvy is misled, I believe, by his failure to distinguish between the poet's attitude and that of his narrator and his characters. As Joseph Baird, "Unferth the Thyle," *Medium Aevum* 39 (1970): 1-7, cogently observes, "The presence of conscious paganism in a poem has nothing to do with whether or not it is the work of a Christian poet"; rather it is "the *attitude* which he evinces toward this pagan subject matter." *Beowulf,* indeed, splendidly exemplifies the heroic, but it is precisely the heroic which is being examined and found wanting on its own terms.

Barbara Raw, *The Art and Background of Old English Poetry* (New York: St. Martin's Press, 1978), observes the polarity but superimposes on it a modern point-of-view, coming to a somewhat anticlimatic view: "Heroism may be a glorious thing in poetry, but in real life it is seen to lead to nothing but misery. Moreover, by juxtaposing the mythical Beowulf, a type of the heroic ideal, with the real-life events of the digressions, the poet has shown the ideal for what it is: something splendid but impractical," p. 96.

Adelaide Hardy, "Historical Perspective and the 'Beowulf'-poet," *Neophilologus* 63 (1979): 430-49, from an historical perspective attempts an impossible reconciliation of the antitheses: "Through his hero the poet shows that faith in the Ruler of Man has immeasurable value because it inspires the esteemed Germanic ideal of absolute courage and loyalty," 439. To consider that faith is justified by its reconciliation with the heroic is to posit a "historical perspective" which is closer by far to that of "ethical culture" than it is to either Germanic paganism (whatever that may have been) or Augustinian Christianity (whose limits of tolerance are not elastic). Only a resolute modernism could think of a Christian poet finding ultimate value in the ideal of the *comitatus.* It is such a view which leads to her conclusion: "The *Beowulf*-poet has accepted the challenge of conveying in formulaic verse the tension between old and new religions, evoking at the same time continuity through the complex theme of the *comitatus*—a court which is superficially noble, yet essentially ignoble, a vision of the human condition in which men enjoy the warmth and security of close-knit fellowship, yet are essentially alone in their freedom to choose alliance with a God they cannot see or touch" (pp. 445-46). This eloquent and perceptive conclusion cannot fail to evoke a responsive modern reaction; unfortunately, from the perspective of intellectual history, it is simply heretical and no part of an Augustinian frame of reference. A good corrective to Hardy's view is Anne Payne's "The Dane's Prayer to the 'gastbona' in *Beowulf*," *Neuphilologische Mitteilungen* 80 (1979), which provides the right historical perspective on the poet's universality in observing that in his employment of the Christian-heathen polarity, he makes his audience aware that Christianity provides an antidote to the heroic, not a total cure, since man is always liable to mistake the values of the world for those of reality: "The poet was consciously drawing on the Christian-heathen dichotomy for a convenient metaphor to describe a state of mind which he found perpetually possible, perpetually destructive to his own society as well as to the heroic society he writes about" (pp. 508-9). W. F. Bolton, *Alcuin and Beowulf* (New Brunswick, N.J.: Rutgers University Press, 1975), also provides a salutary reminder of what must be borne in mind when assessing the Christian poet's viewpoint on heroic virtue. "Beowulf has virtue, but virtues alone do not make a Christian; on the contrary, Alcuin insists, what makes a Christian—and hence saves a soul—is baptism and faith" (p. 155). Marijane Osborn, "The Great Feud: Scriptural History and Strife in *Beowulf*," *PMLA* 93 (1978): 973-98, argues cogently for the need to maintain "two separate frames of reference" (p. 980), that is, the heroic against Augustine's two worlds.

Finally, it should be noted that J. R. R. Tolkien, "*Beowulf: the Monsters and the Critics*," *Proceedings of the British Academy* 22 (1936): 245-95, marks the beginning of the serious study of the thematics of *Beowulf*, and that Dorothy Whitelock, *The Audience of Beowulf* (Oxford: the Clarendon Press, 1951), has laid the groundwork for our understanding of the intellectual milieu in which the poet wrote.

3. For citations see Douglas Short's bibliography (Chapter One, note 1.) The parameters are given recent illustration. Louise Wright, "*Merewioingas* and the Dating of *Beowulf*: a Reconsideration," *Nottingham Medieval Studies* 42 (1980): 1-6, argues that the word gives a *terminus a quo* of possibly 751, but more likely early 800. Norman Blake, "The Dating of Old English Poetry," *An English Miscellany Presented to W. S. Mackie*, edited by Brian Lee (Cape Town: Oxford University Press, 1977), pp. 14-27, argues for a date in the Alfredian period, and Nicolas Jacob, "Anglo-Danish Relations: Poetic Archaisms and the Date of *Beowulf*: a Reconsideration of the Evidence," *Poetica* 8 (Tokyo, 1977): 23-43, also argues for the ninth century. In two recent books, which I have not had the opportunity to consult, the dating

of *Beowulf* has been reconsidered: Kevin S. Kiernan, *Beowulf and the Beowulf Manuscript* (New Brunswick: Rutgers University Press, 1981) has apparently presented a vigorously-argued dating of the poem in the eleventh century, but we are best advised to consider the matter as still open, a conclusion which follows from the collection of essays by various hands, *The Dating of Beowulf*, edited by Colin Chase (Toronto: University of Toronto Press, 1981). In the light of what I have found in ælfric, Kiernan's dating would suit admirably my thesis that the poet's intellectual milieu is Augustinian, but is not essential to it since, early or late, the viewpoint is traditional and is based on an unchanging theological point of reference. Whatever the immediate context of the poet's own time may be, he remains within the parameters of the Christian view. Kiernan appears also to have presented important observations on the structure of *Beowulf* which, unfortunately must be left for later consideration in the detail they deserve.

4. *Monumenta Alcuina,* edited by Wattenbach and Duemmler (Berlin, 1873), p. 357.

5. Both lives are edited by G. I. Needham, *Lives of Three English Saints* (New York: Methuen, 1966). Translations are my own except where indicated.

6. *Ludwigslied,* edited by T. Schauffer in *Althochdeutsche Litteratur,* 2nd edition (Leipzig, 1900), pp. 119-23.

7. For *The Dream of the Rood, Wonder of Creation* and *Judith* see my *Web of Words* (Albany: State University of New York Press, 1970), pp. 85-88, 103-4, 173-78.

8. See my *Doctrine and Poetry* (Albany: State University of New York Press, 1959): 195-200; 237-38.

9. *Widsith, Deor* and *Beowulf* themselves testify, for example to the lively survival of the "heroic" literary conventions.

10. Reto Bezzola, *Les Origines et la Formation de la Litterature Courtoise en Occident,* Part I (Paris: Champion, 1958), pp. 19-21 and 98.

11. William of Malmesbury, *Gesta Pontificum Anglorum,* Vol. 5, edited by N. Hamilton (London, 1870), p. 38.

12. Just such an attempt is apparently made by Jon Kasik, "The Use of the Term 'Wyrd' in 'Beowulf,'" *Neophilologus* 63 (1979): 128-35. He concludes that his "analysis shows that the *Beowulf*-poet used the term 'Wyrd' in neither a purely pagan nor a purely Christian sense" (p. 132). Although he does examine each example of 'wyrd' in the poem, his conclusion results from the primary critical error of failing to distinguish between a character's use of the term and the author's. Further, he totally ignores the background of intellectual history which must undergird any attempt at semantic analysis. For a somewhat similar attempt, see Adelaide Hardy, note 5 above, and Robert L. Kindrick, "Germanic *Sapientia* and

the Heroic Ethos of *Beowulf,*" *Medievalia et Humanistica* 10 (1981): 1-17, who concludes that *Beowulf* represents a genuine advancement in the development of social consciousness" (p. 14), a comfortable conclusion whatever it may mean. Robert Levine, "Ingeld and Christ: a Medieval Problem," *Viator* 2 (1971): 105-28, solved the problem *ignotum per obscurum* by finding a "compassable ambiguity" (p. 117).

13. M. B. McNamee, "*Beowulf*—an Allegory of Salvation," *Journal of English and Germanic Philology* 59 (1960): 190-207, demonstrates that almost anything can be allegorized, but that it is another matter to show that *Beowulf* is actually allegorical. Charles Donahue, "*Beowulf* and Christian Doctrine: a Reconsideration from a Celtic Stance." *Traditio* 27 (1965): 55-116, although denying that allegory is involved (p. 116), would, however, make Beowulf a kind of type of Christ. His argument fails in not taking into account the downward movement of the poem. For an important study of typology in *Beowulf,* see Margaret Goldsmith, *The Mode and Meaning of Beowulf* (London: Athlone Press, 1970). John Halverson, "*Beowulf* and the Pitfalls of Piety," *The University of Toronto Quarterly* 35 (1965-66): 260-78, with a certain amount of gleeful accuracy smashes the arguments for transforming *Beowulf* through allegory, significantly concluding against "an optimistic view of what happens in *Beowulf,*" that "its power . . . lies precisely in the fact that it represents a world without salvation" (p. 277). Curiously, however, he also considers that it is tragic because it is not Christian, failing again to distinguish the poet from his story.

To conclude, *Beowulf* is not Christian allegory, but this is not to deny what Margaret Goldsmith and recently Sylvia Horowitz, "Beowulf, Samson, David and Christ," *Studies in Medieval Culture* 12 (1978): 17-23, have demonstrated—that biblical typology exists in *Beowulf.* A distinction must be kept in mind, however, as Sylvia Horowitz makes clear in her conclusion that "in Beowulf we have a post-Christ figure who symbolizes Christ in the way that Samson and David did" (p. 22). David and Christ may be typologically similar in being agents of God, but David, through grace, may prefigure Christ; Beowulf cannot. He can, with reservations, symbolize David and through him Christ. Because he is outside grace, a basic limitation is in effect, and when he ceases to act as God's agent, he ceases to typify David. He is the dark mirror in which is reflected both of Augustine's cities; as God's agent in Denmark he typifies the citizen of Jerusalem, as heroic warrior facing the dragon he typifies the citizen of Babylon.

14. *Web of Words,* p. 146. ælfric's adjuration is based on traditional view, for a summary of which see my "The Concept of the Hero," (note 1 above), pp. 24-25, note 10.

15. *The Battle of Maldon,* edited by Eric Gordon (New York: Methuen, 1966).

16. As Morton Bloomfield, "Beowulf, Byrthnoth, and the Judgment of God: Trial by Combat in Anglo-Saxon England," *Speculum* 44 (1969): 547-48, observed. George Clark, "The Hero of *Maldon:* Vir Pius et Strenuus," *Speculum* 44 (1979): 257-82, unconvincingly attempts to show that Byrhthnoth's decision to let the Vikings cross was sensible and thus that Byrhthnoth is an unsullied hero. It should be observed, however, that for the poet, Byrhthnoth was not less a hero because of his heroic pride, which is, indeed, essential to his being an heroic figure. But in finding him a true hero, he does not exonerate him from the Christian condemnation of the heroic ethic; from this he is exonerated through the operation of grace and his conscious service of God. Fred Robinson, "God, Death, and Loyalty in the *Battle of Maldon,*" *J. R. R. Tolkien, Scholar and Story Teller,* edited by Mary Salu and Robert Farrell (Ithaca: Cornell University Press, 1979), pp. 64-75, provides a convenient review of the controversy. He correctly observes "that Maldon was written out of a culture whose fundamental assumptions about God and death were incompatible with a heroic sense of life" (p. 77), but places the reconciliation of Christianity and the heroic (that is, the poet's universality), upon the pivot of the loyalty of Byrhthnoth's doomed men. This appears to me to miss the point of what is argued here and earlier in "Concepts," (see note 1 above) of which he has not taken note.

17. This represents, in essence, the view of Patrick Wormald, "Bede, *Beowulf* and the Conversion of the Anglo-Saxon Aristocracy," *Bede and Anglo-Saxon England,* edited by Robert Farrell (Oxford: British Archaeology Reports, 1978), pp. 32-95. He finds that "the early English Church was, in a sense, dominated by aristocratic values," so that "the coming of Christianity displaced the old Gods, and diverted traditional values into new postures, but it did not change these values" (p. 67). He further considers that the dualism of Christianity and paganism "springs from a fundamental tension within the poet's soul" (p. 67). Tension, however, is not reconciliation of discordant views of value; such reconciliation can be found only in the concept of martyrdom.

18. See *Doctrine and Poetry* (note 8 above), pp. 28-29, 66-67. John Gardner, "Fulgentius' 'Expositio Vergiliana Continentia' and the Plan of *Beowulf:* an Approach to the Poem's Style and Structure," *Papers on Language and Literature* 6 (1970): 227-62, provides an appealing suggestion of the influence of just such Christian allegorization on *Beowulf.*

19. Robert Finnegan, "Beowulf at the Mere (and elsewhere)," *Mosaic* 11, no. 4 (1978): 45-54, makes the point that in *Beowulf* "the characters within the artistic frame" do not have the Christian "perspective and cannot have it" (p. 48). He concludes that the hero "is the good man, manqué from the Christian

point of view, struggling to defeat forces he cannot fully understand with weapons that often do not function at need . . . and becomes increasingly entrammeled in the meshes of the society of which he is part. . . . The society which as king he represents is judged and found wanting" (p. 54). Edmund Reiss, "Nationalism and Cosmopolitanism as Subject and Theme in Medieval Narrative," *Proceedings of the IVth Congress of the International Comparative Literature Association,* edited by François Jost (The Hague: Mouton, 1966) 1: 619-22, finds Augustine's doctrine of the Two Cities reflected in Beowulf: as agent of God he reflects the heavenly, but in his pride when he attacks the dragon he reflects the worldly city.

20. Robert Hanning, "*Beowulf* as Heroic History," *Medievalia et Humanistica,* New Series 5 (1974): 77-102, independently and from a different perspective arrived at conclusions encouragingly similar to my own. *Beowulf,* he cogently argues, "functions as a post-conversion essay in pre-conversion heroic history" (p. 88). Of Beowulf's death he says the poet "completely reverses all tendencies toward harmony in heroic history, and offers instead a soured, ironic version of what has gone on before, embodying a final assessment of a world without God as a world in which time and history are themselves negative concepts"; he further notes that the poet uses "the metaphor of treasure . . . as an image of flawed achievement and human limitation" (p. 94).

21. Robert Morrison, "*Beowulf* 698a: 'frofor ond fultum,'" *Notes and Queries,* New Series 27 (1980): 193-94 in a detailed analysis of the biblical influence on the phrase supplies further evidence for Beowulf's being considered as God's agent in his adventures in Denmark.

22. See Chapter Five note to lines 1705-8.

23. A. J. Bliss, "*Beowulf,* Lines 3074-75," *J. R. R. Tolkien* (see note 16 above), in his analysis of the much-debated curse on the treasure, which he finds symbolic (see Chapter Five, note to lines 3074-75), makes clear Beowulf's flaw. The curse, he states, "symbolizes the corrupting power of the gold (*hæðen gold* as it is called in line 2276), which the poet has described explicitly in lines 2764-66. . . . Far from being arbitrary, the curse is the direct consequence of Beowulf's avarice" (p. 60), and "in lines 2345-47, a verbal reminiscence emphasizes the fact that Beowulf . . . did succumb to arrogance" (p. 61). (See Chapter Five, note to line 2345). Thus, "far from being a hero without tragic flaw' [Arthur Brodeur, *The Art of Beowulf,* p. 105], he is a hero with two tragic flaws." John Gardner, "Guilt and the World's Complexity: the Murder of Ongentheow and the Slaying of the Dragon," *Anglo-Saxon Poetry: Essays in Appreciation for John C. McGalliard,* edited by Lewis Nicholson and Dolores Frese (Notre Dame: Univer-

sity Press, 1975), pp. 14-22, comes to a somewhat similar conclusion (pp. 21-22). Robert Burlin, however, comes to a startlingly different one, in "Inner Weather and Interlace: A Note on the Semantic value of Structure in *Beowulf,*" *Old English Studies in Honor of John C. Pope,* edited by Robert Burlin and Edward Irving (Toronto: University Press, 1974). The poet "does not need to find some flaw—Augustinian or Aristotelian—in his hero or some inherent deficiency in the heroic society he embodies, to envision the death of Beowulf and its consequences." He arrives at this conclusion without effective massing of evidence, as with Bliss, but I suspect that the dichotomy rests on almost inarguable premises. Both feel the force of the poet's "universality," but Burlin, I would venture, feels that such universality is cabined and confined by reference to an historical frame, where I (and I assume Gardner and Bliss) feel that universality is thereby enhanced.

24. Norman Eliason, "Beowulf, Wiglaf and the Wægmundings," *Anglo-Saxon England* 7 (1978): 95-118, puts the matter clearly: "The Wægmundings [through Weohstan] had earned Onela's gratitude. . . . Later when the Swedish king's gratitude was extended to Beowulf [in offering him the throne], we are surely to understand that this was because of Beowulf's connection with the Wægmunding family." Beowulf attacks Onela, however, "to avenge the death of Heardred. . . . The moral is plain: man's transcendent duty is to avenge the killing of his kinsman or his king" (p. 100).

25. Anne Payne, "Three Aspects of Wyrd in *Beowulf,*" *Old English Studies in Honor of John C. Pope* (see note 23), presents the issue with clarity: "The nature of Beowulf's violation puts him in a narrow place where no universal forces reflect and magnify his energies. . . . He is not able to project in this episode an adequate understanding against the challenge, so as to put himself immediately in touch with what he should have done; he is too close to his error," and thus his boast before the dragon battle "is characterized by a desperate search for a comprehensible mode of action and fulfillment" (p. 23). "The heroic code, even if followed at the highest of all ethical levels, is not sufficiently inclusive to materialize clearly the divine order of things for man to follow" (p. 26).

26. Larry Benson, "The Originality of *Beowulf,*" *The Interpretation of Narrative,* edited by Morton Bloomfield (Harvard English Studies 1, Cambridge: Harvard University Press, 1970), places Beowulf's death with accuracy as "an unusual death for a hero, for though heroes must die they die gloriously; their death is their victory. Not so with Beowulf. . . . The poet goes out of his way to stress the futility, the ultimate defeat that Beowulf suffers" (p. 32). See also his "The Pagan Coloring of Beowulf," in *Old En-*

glish Poetry, edited by Robert Creed (Providence, R. I.: Brown University Press, 1967), pp. 193-213.

Stanley B. Greenfield (essay date 1985)

SOURCE: "*Beowulf* and the Judgement of the Righteous," in *Learning and Literature in Anglo-Saxon England,* edited by Michael Lapidge and Helmut Gneuss, Cambridge University Press, 1985, pp. 393-407.

[*In the following essay, Greenfield maintains that the Christian author of* Beowulf *viewed the heroic society of the poem sympathetically and recognized the ethical and social values of that world. Furthermore, Greenfield contends, the poet humanized Beowulf—for example, by making his judgement fallible—in order to elicit a more emotional response from the audience.*]

When Beowulf utters his last words on earth, the poet comments,

> him of hræðre gewat
> sawol secean　　　soðfæstra dom.[1]

(2819b-20)

Despite some critical attempts to find these lines ambiguous, they seem to state unequivocally that the hero's soul has found salvation.[2] Wiglaf seems equally certain that his lord's soul will find its just reward:

> Sie sio bær gearo
> ædre geæfned,　　　þonne we ut cymen,
> ond þonne geferian　　　frean userne,
> leofne mannan,　　　þær he longe sceal
> on ðæs Waldendes　　　wære geðolian.

(3105b-9)

Though Beowulf's other followers, riding about the barrow that is their lord's monument to time, give no testimony as to their belief in his eternal resting-place, they praise him ('as is fitting') in terms of impeccable moral qualities, some of which (in particular the assertion that he is 'manna mildust ond mon(ðw)ærust') are used elsewhere in Old English to describe Christ and saintly men.[3] Towards the end of the first part of the poem, the narrating voice had praised Beowulf's generosity, loyalty to his lord and companions, and restraint in using the 'ample gift' (*ginfæstan gife*) of his strength (2166b-83a). As he lies dying, the hero himself echoes these remarks, feeling that the *Waldend fira* will not be able to reckon him among those unrighteous who sought treacherous quarrels, were false to their oaths or murdered their kinsmen (2737-43). Unfortunately for critical consensus, neither the poet nor any of his characters says that Beowulf had *not* been proud, avaricious or imprudent; and a sizeable number of recent critics, writing about the poet's monument to time, have, in relation to the dragon episode, laid those very charges to his hero's account. Others, in turn, have not been slow in rising to Beowulf's defence, even to seeing him in his last

fight as a Christ figure. Interestingly enough, both critics who read the poem literally and those who read it allegorically or exegetically have included both detractors and defenders of Beowulf.[4]

Not uncoincidentally, there are disparate critical views of the Christian poet's attitude towards his poem's pagan heroic world. Some see the poet condemning that world because it necessarily lacks Christ's redeeming grace; some suggest that it is flawed purely as a socio-economic system, where the underpinnings of gift-giving are wars and social instability. Such views find poet and poem stressing the limits of heroism and the heroic world. On the other hand, some critics find the poet celebrating the heroic values of loyalty, courage and generosity, values consistent with his own Christian ethos.[5]

A few critics have been less moralistic. Shippey, for example, concludes that 'what the poet has done is to create a universe which is lifelike, consistent, a model for emulation, and one seen through a film of antique nostalgia; but which remains at the same time a world the poet and all his contemporaries could properly thank God they did not live in'.[6] (One may be forgiven for wondering, in light of the second half of that sentence, for whom that universe is 'a model for emulation'.) Chickering feels that the poet is asking his audience both to admire and to reject the heroic ideal.[7] Chase suggests that the poet's 'attitude towards heroic culture . . . is neither romantic idealizing nor puritan rejection, but a delicate balance of empathy and detachment'.[8] I am not sure that such contrarieties or balance can coexist comfortably in a work of art, or at least that we can accept them simultaneously. On the other hand, I am not quite ready to accept the 'heretical' view tentatively advanced by Douglas Short, that 'the poet may not have totally harmonized the various aspects of the dragon episode'.[9] Nor am I at all ready to accept what Tripp calls 'subtractive rectifications' of the text of this episode so as to remove inconsistencies and allow Beowulf to emerge 'as the ideal king he is'.[10] Perhaps there is still room to explore this dominant critical controversy of recent years; and I should like to take this opportunity to offer *ofer bronrade* some comments on it—both theoretical and substantive—as part of the *gombe* which this volume pays to Peter Clemoes.

For there to exist such critical disarray in our perceptions of the poem's *gestalt* and the poet's attitude towards hero and heroic world, there must be what Norman Rabkin, in commenting on a similar state of affairs in Shakespeare studies, calls 'centers of energy and turbulence' in the work which we reduce from our several perspectives into 'coded elements of [different] thematic formula[s]'.[11] Of course we recognize that *others'* perceived thematic designs in **Beowulf** are 'either generalized to the point of superficiality, or . . . [are] too narrow to accommodate large segments of the poem'.[12] That our *own* formulations may be far from the proper heat and centre of the poet's or the poem's design is, understandably but regrettably, less apparent to us.

It is not difficult to single out three such volatile centres that have produced negative perceptions of the hero. First, there is Hrothgar's sermon: why should he give this cautionary speech to Beowulf at the height of the young hero's triumph over the kin of Cain, if it is not to be a touchstone by which to judge (adversely) Beowulf's behaviour in the later part of the poem? Secondly, as if to justify Hrothgar's admonition, we find Beowulf's 'prideful' and 'avaricious' speech of lines 2518b-37, in which he asserts that the battle against the dragon is his responsibility alone, and that he will either win the gold or die in the attempt. And third comes Wiglaf's speech of lines 3077-109, in which Beowulf's young kinsman says that now the Geats must suffer *anes willan,* 'for the sake of one', that despite all their advice to shun the dragon their lord *heold on heahgesceap:* here Beowulf's imprudence or obstinacy is made manifest by his own liegeman, a view seemingly reinforced by the messenger's prophecy that Franks and Frisians, or Swedes, will swoop down upon the Geats once the word spreads that their lord is dead.

It is less easy to find *in the text itself* such centres as suggest that the poet is at all antipathetic to the ethical or social values of the heroic world he depicts. The poet is a Christian, true, and he specifically condemns the heathen practice of praying to the *gastbona* for help, a practice which (as he says) assigns one's soul to the fire's embrace. But this custom is mentioned and condemned only once, in lines 175-88; is it enough to sustain the weight of 3182 lines? Though the Geats (as well as the Danes) were historically heathens—and Beowulf is a Geat—*they* are in no way so stigmatized. The argument that the poem's heroic world and its protagonist are flawed because they lack Christ's redeeming grace is really one *ex silentio.* Even the Christian excursus makes no mention of Christ's redemptive power, or of Christ for that matter. The God who governs human and seasonal *edwenden* in the *geardagum* of the narrative setting still rules such change, the 'authenticating voice' reiterates, in the poet's own time.[13] The argument that there is a fatal contradiction at the heart of heroic society, in that a hero-king, who behaves (as he must) with pride and action rather than with discretion and *mensura,* is a liability to his people, ultimately has to admit that 'abstract comments on pride in a king are to be found, not in **Beowulf,** but in early medieval works on kingship'[14]—again an appeal outside the text. The rather different argument that the hero-king who is so good in his rôle usurps the capacity for action from his warriors (hence Beowulf's desertion by his retainers), and thus suggests the limits of heroic society, depends on an assumed causal relationship *never made in the poem* between two facts.[15] And so forth.

On the other hand, John D. Niles, by closely examining Wiglaf's speech about the cowardice of the retainers, has recently made anew a case for the poet's approval of the heroic ethos. His conclusion is worth quoting:

> If the society portrayed in **Beowulf** is weak, its weakness can be ascribed to the too-frequent failure of people to live by the ethics that, when put into practice,

hold society together. The fatal contradiction developed through the narrative of **Beowulf** is nothing inherent in heroic society, feudal society, capitalist or Marxist society, or any other social system. It is lodged within the recalcitrant breasts of human beings who in times of crisis find themselves unable to live up to the ideals to which their lips give assent. The poem does not criticize the hero for being unlike the Geats. It criticizes all of us for not being more like the hero.[16]

If by this time I seem to suggest that I believe the Christian poet looked with kindly eye on his heroic world and saw its ethical and social values (even if not its religious ones) as consonant and coextensive with his own, that is so. If I also give the impression that I perceive King Beowulf as flawed by pride, avarice or imprudence, that is *not* so. My view is that the poet has presented both the hero and his world with more *humanitas* than *Christianitas;* that to make us feel *lacrimae rerum* in his hero's death, he has humanized the 'marvellous' (or monstrous) Beowulf by making him fallible *in judgement* (his only flaw) and historicized his world so that we, the audience, are better able to empathize with the tragic situation, to suffer with Wiglaf and the Geats, even as we stand in awe of the hero who held to his high fate.[17]

As to the poet's attitude towards the heroic ethos, there can be no doubt that he finds loyalty among kin and retainers highly praiseworthy. Consider, for example, the 'voice's' gnomic wisdom in lines 2600b-1 and 2708b-9a: 'sibb æfre ne mæg / wiht onwendan þam ðe wel þenceð' and 'swylc sceolde secg wesan, / ðegn æt ðearfe!'. The heroic ideal of generosity or gift-giving and the value of treasure have, on the other hand, been much disputed. I have had my say elsewhere about the place of gold in the scheme of **Beowulf:** that the poet praises the giving, faults the hoarding.[18] There I observed that 'the contention of critics who would interpret the gold as a temptation to sin and an invitation to spiritual damnation . . . rest[s] . . . on presumed parallels between **Beowulf** and exegetical commentary, based on the assumption of a tacit understanding between poet and audience as to how to listen to or read poetry[19]—that is, it too is an argument not based on the text. In that essay, however, I conceded that the gnomic passage of lines 2764b-6 was something of a stumbling block for my interpretation:

> Sinc eaðe mæg,
> gold on grund(e)   gumcynnes gehwone
> oferhigian,   hyde se ðe wylle.

I could only suggest then that they did not have the same explicit Christian pointing of lines 100-2 of *The Seafarer* and, more tentatively, that they could be omitted (as a possible interpolation) without disturbing at all the metrical contour of the lines in which they are embedded. Now I think there is a better idea.

All the other gnomic or semi-gnomic passages in the second part of the poem (nine made by the 'voice' and two by Wiglaf, as I see them)[20] arise from and are 'natural' concomitants of the action that has been or is being described: they blend that action into universal traditional truth. The usual translation of this passage, with *oferhigian* as 'tempt' or 'overpower' and *hyde* as either 'hide' or 'heed', is quite at odds with the action being described: Wiglaf is viewing the treasure hoard at the command of Beowulf, and is in no way being tempted or overpowered by it, now or later. In line with the other gnomic comments, these words should be universalizing the exposure of the treasure. Peter Clemoes has astutely observed that Anglo-Saxon art, as well as *Beowulf,* 'shows insight into inner forces', and as one example in the poem he cites lines 864b-5:

> hleapan leton,
> on geflit faran   fealwe mearas.

'The men', he comments, 'allowed their steeds to exert their natural tendency, identified as a certain kind of movement (*hleapan*) and as movement in competition (*on geflit faran*).'[21] With these considerations in mind, I think Niles's translation of the gnomic passage quoted above has much to recommend it:

> Given the context of the passage, I take *oferhigian* rather in the sense of "outsmart." The treasure is just about to be brought out into the light, despite the efforts of a previous tribe of men to keep it hidden in the earth forever. *Hydan* means "hide," as it should. The lines amount to no more than a brief aside concerning the futility of burying riches: "Treasure, gold in the ground, can easily outsmart anyone, no matter who hides it!" This is essentially the reading of Bosworth and Toller, s.v. "oferhigian."[22]

This reading makes the passage consistent in kind and context with other such passages, reveals the inner force of treasure (compare below my comment on *lifað,* of the treasure, in 3167b), and reinforces the anti-hoarding theme of Hrothgar's sermon and of elsewhere in the poem.

That the poet has no quarrel with the heroic ideal of revenge may also be debatable. Yet we know the ideal or practice was not interdicted in Anglo-Saxon Christian England, and was even in some cases encouraged.[23] The *Beowulf* poet clearly approves of God's revenge on Cain's descendants in lines 111-14 and on the giants who 'behaved badly' in lines 1688-93. In human feuds he seems to distinguish between rightful actions and *unrihte* ones. Hygelac's Frisian raid was evidently one of the latter:

> syþðan he for wlenco   wean ahsode,
> fæhðe to Frysum.

> (1206-7a)

But Beowulf's revenge on Onela for the Swedish king's killing of Heardred seems to have the poet's tacit approbation, to judge from the tone of lines 2391-6 (and, additionally, from 2390b, 'ðæt wæs god cyning', if that verse refers to Beowulf rather than to Onela). Surely the poet does not fault Beowulf's revenge on Grendel and Grendel's

mother; nor does he, I think, fault the hero's revenge on the dragon when he simply states: 'him ðæs guðcyning, / Wedera þioden wræce leornode' (2335b-6).

A further adverse judgement on the poem's heroic world is embodied in the concept of 'social guilt': feuds and violence are inevitable in a society where gifts must be obtained from someone in order to be given to others as rewards. Thus leaders, especially kings, need to perform deeds of derring-do for the acquisition of material treasures, but in so doing they make bad kings, exposing themselves to death and leaving their people leaderless. A subtle argument, drawn (as Shippey observes) 'from comparative considerations of Beowulf, Hrothgar, Hygelac', and encouraged by the 'interlace' structure of the poem. We

> think that the poet is demonstrating the inadequacy of heroic society; that he sees this the more forcibly for being a Christian; and that his rejection of overt fingerpointing first gives [us] the pleasure of ironic perception, and second shows [us] the glittering insidiousness of heroism, the way it perverts even the best of intentions. This whole approach offers evidently attractive baits, propounding an interesting sociological thesis, rejecting the cult of violence, and making it possible to give the poet immense credit for conscious artistry.[24]

But as with the exegetical critics' approach, this view finds no confirmation in the text: it rests on *our* sense of the poet's perspective, on unproven and unprovable ironies that may well be more modern than medieval.

In turning from consideration of the perspective on the heroic ethos in *Beowulf* to the view of the hero himself, we find, I think, equally tenuous rationales for negative *gestalten.* A brief examination of a short passage in what has been called 'the most influential [essay] in expressing the pejorative view of the hero and heroic society'[25] may not be amiss, for the ways of argument therein can tell us something more about the difficulties of evidential practices and about the questionability of adverse judgements of the hero. This analysis will lead into my own (I hope not so tenuous) arguments for a Beowulf who, in the dragon episode, may be fallible in judgement but is otherwise unexceptionable.

Discussing this episode, Leyerle says that Beowulf 'undertakes precipitant action . . . the last of the foolhardy deeds attributed to him by Wiglaf'.[26] The passage in question is the following:

> hlaford us
> þis ellenweorc   ana aðohtè
> to gefremmane,   folces hyrde,
> forðam he manna mæst   mærða gefremede,
> dæda dollicra,

> (2642b-6a)

Why is Beowulf's undertaking called *foolhardy,* we may ask? Why, indeed, is it the *last* of such deeds? There has been no suggestion of a series of foolhardy deeds in the poem. Beowulf's only action that qualifies for this epithet is his swimming match with Breca, which he admits was a foolish, youthful undertaking. Leyerle seems to have seized on the word *dollicra* in the passage he quotes (though he does not say so), since *dollice* in other contexts means something like that. But *dæda dollicra* is in variation with *mærða*, which in turn goes back to *ellenweorc*—and these terms are anything but pejorative. Whatever the normal meaning of *dollice,* it must have a favourable sense in this series; and we can find support for Klaeber's suggested gloss 'audacious, daring' (more consonant with the tenor of Wiglaf's speech) in the term *dolsceaða* (479a) used by Hrothgar when he says of Grendel's reign of terror 'God eaþe mæg / þone dolsceaða dæda getwæfan!'—hardly 'foolhardy-ravager'. The fact that *dol-*and *dæd* are in alliterative coupling in both lines suggests that the force of formulaic composition may be more powerful than 'normal' word-meaning. The pressure of the hermeneutic circle, I suspect, led Leyerle to the use of this rather dubious bit of evidence.[27]

So too in Leyerle's next paragraph:

> [Beowulf] disdains the use of an adequate force against the dragon:

> Oferhogode ða　　　hringa fengel,
> þæt he þone widflogan　　　weorode gesohte,
> sidan herge.

> (2345-7a)

> The verb *oferhogode* echoes Hrothgar's words *oferhygda dæl* (1740) and *oferhyda ne gym* (1760).

In this argument verbal echo from *within* the poem is used to suggest that, indeed, Beowulf is exemplifying precisely that pride and disdain against which Hrothgar had warned the young hero. But if we look at what Hrothgar is actually saying, we find that the *oferhygd* he cautions against, in both lines 1740 and 1760, is connected with greed, with hoarding, with failure of generosity in gift-giving, and *not* with scorning to have help in battle. In fact, the poet goes on to point out, in the first historical digression of the second part of the poem, that Beowulf has plenty of past credentials to support his decision to move against the dragon:

> 　　　　　forðon he ær fela
> nearo neðende　　　niða gedigde,
> hildehlemma . . .

> (2349b-51a)

This passage, incidentally, would seem to disprove the arguments of the many critics who think that King Beowulf's fifty years of keeping the peace (2732a-6a) means he engaged in *no* human battle clashes.[28]

Lines 1760b-1a might, I suppose, be taken, by changing Klaeber's punctuation, with the verses that follow, 'Nu is þines blæd / ane hwile'; and many critics have also seemed to think that old King Beowulf, like the aged Hrothgar, suffered a decline in his *fortitudo*. But, whereas the Danish king is explicitly characterized in 1886b-7a as one whom old age has deprived of the joys of strength, no such observation is made about Beowulf. We should notice that he still has that *mægen* that overtaxes any sword (2682b-7)—it is surely not a failure in human strength that causes Nægling to break (2680b)! Once again we should recognize that Hrothgar's cautionary comments do not really apply to the Beowulf of the second part of the poem, except for his final generalization about mortality: 'semninga bið, / þæt þec, dryhtguma, deað oferswyðeð' (1767b-7).[29]

Thus far I have tried to indicate that Hrothgar's sermon is no touchstone for a negatively portrayed Beowulf of later days. Let me consider now more briefly the two other 'centers of energy and turbulence' I mentioned earlier.

Beowulf's speech in which he declares he will fight the dragon alone and gain the gold (2518b-37) is the first of these. Since I have considered this previously, I shall only refer the reader to that discussion.[30] The second 'centre' is a combination of Wiglaf's speech in lines 3077-109 with his messenger's preceding harangue in lines 2900-3027. In reviewing this locus, we had best include *all* the speeches, in order, after Beowulf dies and his soul seeks *soðfæstra dom.* When the cowards creep out of the woods and approach Wiglaf, he looks at the *unleofe,* comments that Beowulf threw away the wargear he had equipped them with, and says further that they shall henceforth forgo

> 　　　　　sincþego　　　ond swyrdgifu,
> eall eðelwyn　　　eowrum cynne,
> · · ·
> · · ·　　　syððan æðelingas
> feorran gefricgean　　　fleam eowerne,
> domleasan dæd.　　Deað bið sella . . .

> (2884-5 and 2888b-90)

Then Wiglaf orders his messenger to announce the sad news to the waiting Geats; in his speech the messenger twice states that a time of war and revenge is inevitable once Franks and Frisians on the one hand and Swedes on the other learn of Beowulf's death. Some lines later, after the poet has told about the curse on the gold, Wiglaf again speaks (3077-109) and this time seems to accuse Beowulf of obstinacy in seeking the dragon, of not listening to all their advice for him to leave the dragon alone. From the inconsistencies in these accounts, a critic can select the evidence for either a positive or a negative view of the hero's actions—and so critics have done. Can *all* the evidence, including the difficult curse on the gold, be accounted for in a unified pattern?

That evidence, it seems to me, leads to an emphasis on fate and the interlacing threads that comprise human and societal doom and *dom,* 'glory': the retainers' cowardice that leads to their lord's death, the fact of their lord's death (one would hardly expect the messenger, who must be one of the cowards, to stress his and his comrades' failure to live up to their oaths of allegiance),[31] a force beyond human comprehension (the curse), and a hero's (proper) refusal to abide by his counsellors' (timid) advice to sidestep the dragon's challenge. Wiglaf sums all this up, it should be noted, not by blaming Beowulf for violating kingly *mensura* but, in a tight stylistic 'envelope' that emphasizes the combination of human will and 'determinism' in Beowulf's fate, he says:

> *Heold* on heahgesceap;   hord ys gesceawod,
> grimme gegangen;   wæs þæt gifeðe to swið,
> þe þone [þeodcyning]   þyder *ontyhte*.
>
> (3084-6; my italics)

We may recall young Beowulf's recognition of a similar juxtaposition of human and superhuman in his account of the Breca match, when a sea monster drew him to the depths:

> hwæþre me gyfeðe wearþ,
> þæt ic aglæcan   orde geræhte,
> hildebille;   heaþoræs fornam
> mihtig meredeor   þurh mine hand.
>
> (555b-8)

And the poet's own comment with regard to Beowulf's success in his fight with Grendel's mother:

> ond halig God
> geweold wigsigor;   witig Drihten,
> rodera Rædend   hit on ryht gesced
> yðelice,   syþðan he eft astod.
>
> (1553b-5)

What the **Beowulf** poet thereby achieves in his poem is a miracle of the highest tragic art, wherein man's fate is balanced between his own human will and the power of forces beyond his control. We do not draw practical moral lessons about human behaviour from *Oedipus* or *King Lear;* nor should we scan **Beowulf** either as a mirror for princes or a reverse mirror-image of unkingly or sinful action.

That the hoard *grimme gegangen* is reburied in the earth,

> þær hit nu gen lifað
> eldrum swa unnyt,   swa hi(t æro)r wæs,
>
> (3167b-8)

is something of a small centre of energy and turbulence for interpretation too. The poet does not explicitly say why it is reburied, but the fact that it *will* be given back to earth is first mentioned by the messenger in lines 3010b-17, after he has finished saying that the reasons he has just adduced (old feuds) will lead to resumption of 'sio fæhðo ond se feondscipe', and advised the Geats to hurry to see their dead lord, 'þe us beagas geaf' (3009b). The most likely inferences to be drawn from this juxtaposition are, first, that Beowulf deserves the hoard as a measure of his greatness, and, secondly, that the Geats (by their cowardice and dim prospects for the future) are unworthy of it. I do not recall anyone's having commented on the poet's use of the word *lifað* in 3167b, a strange word applied to gold, and one rendered by most translators, including myself, as 'remains' or the like. Perhaps the verb is being

used in ironic contrast to the dead Beowulf and the soon-to-perish Geats? Perhaps the whole clause suggests that gold has a life of its own: it will reveal itself to those who fight for it (see the gnomic passage considered above) or to those who have God's grace (the thief; lines 3054b-7), but it will live, useless to those who have not the fortitude in *mod* and *mægen* to subjugate *its* life to their own will. Whatever the case, one sure effect of the comment is to make Beowulf's dying remark that he is glad to have won the gold for his people (2794-8) seem impercipient indeed; and *this* irony leads me to the final argument of this paper: that whatever negative impulse throbs through the dragon episode results from the humanization of the hero.

The terms of disapprobation which critics have applied to King Beowulf's behaviour in the dragon fight are all judgemental: proud, avaricious, obstinate, imprudent, rash etc. My term 'fallible (in understanding or perception of events)' carries no such connotations. What I am suggesting is that the hero, who by his very nature has something of the monstrous or marvellous in him,[32] is here made more human, so that the audience will react to his death more feelingly. Not a decline in his *fortitudo,* as I have argued above, but in his *sapientia:* not in what he does, but in what he perceives. And with this humanization the Geatish world he now moves in becomes more historicized than the Danish one of his exploits against the Grendel-kin.

My first remarks will be on the historicization. Attempts to link the Cain-descended monsters of the first part of the poem with the dragon, to see the *wyrm* or *draca* as a satanic figure that is somehow the progeny of Cain, or to see the dragon's feud in the perspective of the scriptural 'Great Feud' between God and his enemies, will not bear close scrutiny.[33] For all the beast's pyrotechnics, the dragon's world, if we can call the setting and action in the latter part of the poem by that term, has no suggestions such as 'Godes yrre bær' (711b—of Grendel), or of a wondrous light shining like heaven's candle (1570-2a—after Beowulf defeats Grendel's mother). To say that the poet had 'no need for further scriptural reference after the two kinfolk of Cain have been destroyed'[34] is begging the question, an admission that there is no textual evidence for the position being argued; but when the same critic continues with 'we have had Hrothgar's warning that calamity continues to come unexpected upon mankind: strife is *always* renewed', we can agree with what precedes the colon, but find no evidence that Hrothgar says what follows it (and we note that the following sentence of additional 'evidence' points outside the text to the 'Exeter Book maximist'). When we read further that 'the advent of another adversary of mankind is inevitable', we may note that although Grendel is called *feond mancynnes* and *mancynnes feond* (164a and 1276a) and *Godes andsaca(n)* (786b and 1682b), the dragon has a rather different set of terms for his designation: *eald uhtsceaða* (2271a), *ðeodsceaða* (2278a and 2688a), *guðsceaða* (2318a), *gearo guðfreca* (2414a), *mansceaða* (2514b) and *attorsceaða* (2839a). The dragon wears his adversarial nature with at least an epithetical difference.

The human feuds in the latter part of the poem are likewise more down-to-earth, more historical than legendary. I have explored elsewhere the force and place of 'history' in providing an epic sense of destiny in this part of the poem,[35] and shall not repeat myself here. This historical world is appropriate for, and lends credence to, Beowulf's humanity.

Beowulf's fallibility is exhibited most obviously in the discrepancy I have already touched on. That discrepancy cannot simply be an inconsistency of the kind Niles cogently argues for as 'the truncated motif' of the 'barbaric style' in which the poem is composed[36]—and Niles does not suggest it is such. It *must* be meant to indicate that the dying Beowulf no longer has the perspicacity he had when he told Hygelac about Freawaru's proposed marriage to Ingeld: he cannot see that his retainers' cowardice will render the treasure useless to his people. This failure is not surprising, perhaps, in view of the fact that Beowulf has always, by virtue of his marvellous abilities, acted alone. Whether his men draw their swords and hack futilely at a charmed-skin Grendel, or wait helplessly by the mere's edge, or flee precipitously into the woods, Beowulf has never counted on them. Even in human battles he seems to have been 'ana on orde' (2498b). No wonder, then, that he says the battle against the dragon is his responsibility alone, and that he cannot now understand the impact of his followers' treachery upon the Geats' future. There is irony here no doubt, but hardly of a judgemental kind. Rather, by Beowulf's fallible understanding we are made to feel the pathos of his self-sacrifice for a nation that cannot profit thereby.

But Beowulf has also misjudged with respect to the 'measure' of the battle, for the man who is his kinsman and retainer *does* help him defeat the foe 'ofer min gemet', as he says (2879a). The very notion that Beowulf *can* be helped this time further humanizes him. That the dragon is a more 'natural' phenomenon than the Grendel-kin, *un*associated with Cain or the Great Feud, is consonant with Wiglaf's being able to help, and creates an irony in that this time, when his followers *could* have helped the hero, they flee. The dying king misjudges again when he believes that Wiglaf can look after his people's needs: both Wiglaf's and his messenger's speeches point up that miscalculation. He who when young had the wisdom to suggest tactfully that Hrothgar's son Hrethric, if he were a worthy heir apparent, might go abroad while a threat to his succession existed (1836-9), now cannot perceive that no ordinary mortal, even one who has fought beyond his measure, is qualified to keep old enemies at bay in the face of the Geat's manifest weakness. How like in (fallible) judgement to us all the epic hero has become, despite his still imposing stature!

This falling-off in Beowulf's 'situational' grasp is revealed at the very start of the dragon episode when the hero, seeing his *gifstol* razed, thinks he may have offended God 'ofer ealde riht' (2330a). The audience, however, knows that his perception of the situation is wrong, that the mon-

ster has been loosed because of the cup's theft; and of course Beowulf later learns 'hwanan sio fæhð aras' (2403b). Though Beowulf has the wisdom to recognize that he will need an iron shield as protection against the dragon's flames, he seems unaware that the bone of the beast's skull is less vulnerable to penetration than its softer underbelly; whereas, for all his inexperience, Wiglaf has the shrewdness to strike lower down.

I shall mention but one further piece of evidence which suggests that old Beowulf but slenderly knows the score/ In accounting for his life, in summing up his record as king, he says, among other things:

$$\text{Ic on earde bad}$$
mælgesceafta,   heold min tela,
ne sohte searoniðas,   ne me swor fela
aða on unriht.

(2736b-9a)

Three hundred and more lines later, the poet comments that Beowulf, like other mortals, did not know how his death would come about:

$$\text{þa he biorges weard}$$
sohte searoniðas.

(3066b-7a)

The formulaic repetition is startling. Is this just a case of non-significant formularity, or is the poet suggesting a further limit on his hero's percipience? Beowulf is obviously referring to *human* relations in giving his righteous reckoning, but the poet seems to indicate that his seeking out of the dragon was also a *searonið*, and the cause of his *worulde gedal*. I realize that this evidence can be interpreted otherwise to support the arguments of those who would see Beowulf as acting improperly in seeking out the dragon; but it, too, is a centre of energy and turbulence that should not be discounted or overlooked.

The reading I have proposed on the controversy over the hero and his world has tried to encompass the most relevant evidence on both sides, and to avoid the pitfalls of the hermeneutic circle (as much as possible) in argumentation. I am not that sanguine about my success on both scores. But I believe my reading is as plausible as any. One can comprehend a Beowulf whose actions in the latter part of the poem reveal him to be a peerless hero still— and action, as Peter Clemoes has observed, defines the agent in this poem[37]—even as his sapiential vulnerability in his final confrontation demarvellizes (rather than indicts) him. The poet has forthrightly placed his hero's soul among those seeking the judgement of the righteous, but has not suggested that the audience judge him self-righteously. Rather, I believe, by revealing a weakness in the aged Beowulf he has somewhat humanized his hero's nature, making him easier of empathetic access to an audience's sensibilities. He helps thus awaken in the reader or listener 'a poignancy, a pathos . . . [which] springs from epic's presentation of man's accomplishments against the background of his mortality, from the implication the hero's fall entails for his people, from a sense of futility in the splendid achievement, a resignation and despair in the face of the limits of life'.[38] The Christian poet, indeed, sees, and aesthetically achieves, a continuity between the *geardagas* of the poem's heroic world and the *windagas* (1062) of his own time.[39] *Life* has its limits, not heroism or the heroic world: this, I think, might have been his answer to Alcuin's abiding question, 'Quid Hinieldus cum Christo?'.[40]

Notes

1. All quotations are from *Beowulf and the Fight at Finnsburg,* ed. F. Klaeber, 3rd ed. (Boston, Mass., 1950).

2. See, e.g., E. G. Stanley, 'Hæþenra Hyht in *Beowulf*', *Studies in Old English Literature in Honor of Arthur G. Brodeur,* ed. S. B. Greenfield (Eugene, Oreg., 1963), pp. 142-3, for a denial of Beowulf's salvation. See J. D. Niles, *Beowulf: the Poem and its Tradition* (Cambridge, Mass., 1983), p. 297, n. 11, for citations to the contrary.

3. See M. P. Richards, 'A Reexamination of *Beowulf* ll. 3180-3182', *ELN* 10 (1973), 163-7.

4. For a summary of bibliography on these positions, see D. D. Short, '*Beowulf* and Modern Critical Tradition', *A Fair Day in the Affections: Literary Essays in Honor of Robert B. White, Jr,* ed. J. D. Durant and M. T. Hester (Raleigh, NC, 1980), pp. 1-22, esp. 9-14.

5. For the first of these views, see, e.g., R. W. Hanning, '*Beowulf* as Heroic History', *Medievalia et Humanistica* n.s. 5 (1974), 77-102; for the second, see H. Berger, Jr, and H. M. Leicester, Jr, 'Social Structure as Doom: the Limits of Heroism in *Beowulf*', *Old English Studies in Honor of John C. Pope,* ed. R. B. Burlin and E. B. Irving, Jr (Toronto, 1974), pp. 37-79; and for the third, see Niles, *Beowulf,* pp. 235-47.

6. T. A. Shippey, *Beowulf* (London, 1978), p. 44.

7. H. D. Chickering, Jr, *Beowulf: a Dual-Language Edition* (Garden City, NY, 1977), pp. 26-7.

8. C. Chase, 'Saints' Lives, Royal Lives, and the Date of *Beowulf*', *The Dating of Beowulf,* ed. C. Chase (Toronto, 1981), pp. 161-71, at 161-2.

9. Short, '*Beowulf* and Modern Critical Tradition', p. 11.

10. R. P. Tripp, Jr, *More About the Fight with the Dragon: Beowulf 2208b-3182, Commentary, Edition, and Translation* (Lanham, Md, 1983), p. ix.

11. N. Rabkin, *Shakespeare and the Problem of Meaning* (Chicago, Ill., 1981), p. 25.

12. Short, '*Beowulf* and Modern Critical Tradition', p. 9.

13. See my essay 'The Authenticating Voice in *Beowulf*', *ASE* 5 (1976), 51-62, at 55-7.

14. J. Leyerle, 'Beowulf the Hero and the King', *Mæ* 34 (1965), 89-102, at 98.

15. Berger and Leicester, 'Social Structure', pp. 64-5.

16. Niles, *Beowulf,* p. 247.

17. On Beowulf's 'marvellous' or monstrous nature, see my essay 'A Touch of the Monstrous in the Hero, or Beowulf Re-Marvellized', *ES* 63 (1982), 294-300, and Niles, *Beowulf,* pp. 3-30. Obviously I am disagreeing with Niles, however, when he says (p. 29): 'In the end, the audience . . . cannot really identify itself with Beowulf the man . . . We know too little of his everyday humanity, his normal human feelings and weaknesses, to be able to see him as an extension of ourselves.'

18. S. B. Greenfield, '"Gifstol" and Goldhoard in *Beowulf*', *Old English Studies in Honor of John C. Pope,* ed. Burlin and Irving, pp. 107-17.

19. *Ibid.* p. 115.

20. The nine by the 'voice' are lines 2275b-7, 2291-3a, 2514b, 2590b-1, 2600-1, 2708b-9a, 2858-9, 3062b-5 and 3174b-7; the two by Wiglaf are lines 2890b-1 and 3077-8. Some of these are discussed T. A. Shippey, 'Maxims in Old English Narrative: Literary Art or Traditional Wisdom?', *Oral Tradition, Literary Tradition: a Symposium,* ed. H. Bekker-Nielsen *et al.* (Odense, 1977), pp. 28-46.

21. P. Clemoes, 'Action in *Beowulf* and our Perception of it', *Old English Poetry: Essays on Style,* ed. D. G. Calder (Berkeley, Calif., 1979), pp. 147-68, at 155.

22. Niles, *Beowulf,* p. 299, n. 6.

23. See D. Whitelock, *The Beginnings of English Society* (Harmondsworth, 1952), pp. 31-3.

24. Shippey, *Beowulf,* pp. 37-8.

25. Short '*Beowulf* and Modern Critical Tradition', p. 10; the essay is Leyerle's (cited above, n. 14).

26. Leyerle, 'Beowulf the Hero', p. 95.

27. I would add that I find no evidence at all in Hrothgar's sermon for Leyerle's contention that the king's speech 'is, in part, a caution against *headlong* action' ('Beowulf the Hero', p. 97; my italics). The only possible referent for Leyerle's remark is Heremod's killing of his table companions; but this action is hardly on the same level as fighting a dragon to revenge one's people and gain treasure for them.

28. Cf. lines 2391-6. Note that Beowulf had survived many battle clashes *since* he had cleansed Hrothgar's hall (2351b-4a). This is clearly not a reference to further monster battles. Lines 2391-6 refer specifically to Beowulf's military support of Eadgils against Onela. Niles is the latest to overlook such evidence; see his *Beowulf,* pp. 252 and 304, n. 5, for bibliographic references to others of like mind.

29. Beowulf's *oferhygd* is often compared to that of Byrhtnoth in *The Battle of Maldon* and that of Roland; but neither of the latter destroys his enemy by his self-sacrifice.

30. '"Gifstol" and Goldhoard' (cited above, n. 18).

31. Still, the messenger echoes Wiglaf's comment about no more treasure-giving by indicating that *all* the hard-won treasure will be buried with Beowulf (3010b-17).

32. See above, n. 17.

33. On the former, see, e.g., my review of D. Williams, *Cain and Beowulf: a Study in Secular Allegory* (Toronto, 1982) in *MP* 81 (1983), 191-4. The 'Great Feud' perspective has been advanced by M. Osborn, 'The Great Feud: Scriptural History and Strife in *Beowulf*', *PMLA* 93 (1978), 973-81.

34. Osborn, 'The Great Feud', p. 979.

35. S. B. Greenfield, 'Geatish History: Poetic Art and Epic Quality in *Beowulf*', *Neophilologus* 47 (1963), 211-17.

36. Niles, *Beowulf,* pp. 167-76.

37. Clemoes, 'Action in *Beowulf*', esp. pp. 155-60.

38. S. B. Greenfield, 'Beowulf and Epic Tragedy', *Studies in Old English Literature in Honor of Arthur G. Brodeur,* ed. Greenfield, p. 104.

39. Cf. above, n. 13.

40. I should like to express my appreciation to Daniel G. Calder and Thelma N. Greenfield for their most helpful comments in the shaping of this paper.

Abbreviations

AAe: Archaeologia Aeliana

AB: Analecta Bollandiana

AntJ: Antiquaries Journal

ArchJ: Archaeological Journal

ASC: Anglo-Saxon Chronicle

ASE: Anglo-Saxon England

ASNSL: Archiv für das Studium der neueren Sprachen und Literaturen

ASPR: The Anglo-Saxon Poetic Records, ed. G. P. Krapp and E. V. K. Dobbie, 6 vols. (New York, 1931-42)

BAR: British Archaeological Reports, British series (Oxford)

BGDSL: Beiträge zur Geschichte der deutschen Sprache und Literatur [Bollandists], *Bibliotheca Hagiographica Latina,* 2 vols. (Brussels, 1899-1901)

BL: British Library manuscript

BN: Bibliothèque Nationale

CA: Current Archaeology

CCSL: Corpus Christianorum, Series Latina (Turnhout)

CM: Continuatio Mediaevalis

CSEL: Corpus Scriptorum Ecclesiasticorum Latinorum (Vienna)

EEMF: Early English Manuscripts in Facsimile (Copenhagen)

EETS: Early English Text Society

e.s.: extra series

o.s. original series

s.s.: supplementary series

EHD: D. Whitelock, *English Historical Documents c. 500-1042,* 2nd ed. (London, 1979)

EHR: English Historical Review

ELN: English Language Notes

EPNS: English Place-Name Society

ES: English Studies

FS: Frühmittelalterliche Studien

HBS: Henry Bradshaw Society Publications

HE: Bede's *Historia ecclesiastica gentis Anglorum*

JBAA: Journal of the British Archaeological Association

JEGP: Journal of English and Germanic Philology

JEH: Journal of Ecclesiastical History

JTS: Journal of Theological Studies

Mæ: Medium ævum

MGH: Monumenta Germaniae Historica

Auct. antiq.: Auctores antiquissimi

Epist.: Epistolae Aevi Carolini

Epist. select.: Epistolae selectae

PLAC: Poetae Latini Aevi Carolini

Script.: Scriptores

Script. rer.Meroving.: Scriptores rerum Merovingicarum

MLR: Modern Language Review

MP: Modern Philology

MS: Mediaeval Studies

NM Neuphilologische Mitteilungen

N&Q: Notes & Queries

OED: Oxford English Dictionary

OEN: Old English Newsletter

PBA: Proceedings of the British Academy

PL: Patrologia Latina, ed. J. P. Migne (Paris, 1841-64)

PMLA: Publications of the Modern Language Association of America

RB: Revue bénédictine

RHE: Revue d'histoire ecclésiastique

SM: Studi medievali

SN: Studia Neophilologica

TPS: Transactions of the Philological Society

YAJ: Yorkshire Archaeological Journal

ZDA: Zeitschrift für deutsches Altertum

Alain Renoir (essay date 1988)

SOURCE: "Oral-Formulaic Context in *Beowulf:* The Hero on the Beach and the Grendel Episode," in *A Key to Old Poems: The Oral-Formulaic Approach to the Interpretation of West-Germanic Verse,* Pennsylvania State University Press, 1988, pp. 107-32.

[*In the essay below, Renoir examines the ways in which the author of* Beowulf *employed the motifs and formulas of oral composition, maintaining that the use of such devices does not necessarily indicate that the poem was composed orally, but only that the poet was well-versed in the traditional methods of oral-formulaic composition.*]

Just as the prominence rightfully granted **Beowulf** by the literary world has naturally turned that poem into a standard against which much Germanic traditional poetry has been at times mistakenly measured, so it has encouraged the most distinguished Anglo-Saxonists and students of oral-formulaic matters to dissect practically every conceivable aspect of its artistry, language, and background; and the vigor with which the operation has been carried out shows no sign of abating. Within the realm of oral-formulaic studies alone, for example, it was indeed **Beowulf** that Magoun first examined when he set out to argue the oral-formulaic quality of Old-English narrative poetry;[1] it was to **Beowulf** that Crowne first turned when he needed an instance of the theme of the hero on the beach outside *Andreas;*[2] it was to **Beowulf** that Lord first turned when he wished to extend to the mediaeval epic the theories which he had elaborated in respect to Homer and South-Slavic poetry;[3] and it was exclusively to **Beowulf** that Creed turned when he argued the fundamental relevance of traditional oral-formulaic elements to the critical interpretation of Old-English poetry.[4] The list could be extended for page after page, but the foregoing examples should suffice to suggest that anyone preparing to examine any portion of **Beowulf** from an oral-formulaic point of view would do well to keep in mind that he or she is about to plow a field which has already been plowed and replowed by the masters. In this light, my only defense against the charge of presumption is that, in the first place, the very eminence of **Beowulf** rules out the possibility of ignoring it in the present study and that, in the second place, the unequivocally obvious nature of the observa-

tions which follow will provide ample proof that I make no claim to any kind of original thinking in this chapter.

Before examining the affective role which oral-formulaic rhetoric plays in the Grendel episode, it seems advisable to remind ourselves of the sequence of events that leads to it as well as of the action that follows immediately thereafter, hence the following outline of the first part of **Beowulf.**

After an initial account of the founding of Denmark's Scylding Dynasty by the mythological Scyld Scefing (1ᵃ-52ᵇ), the narrative traces the royal succession down to King Hrothgar, who decides to advertise the might of his realm by erecting a magnificent hall which he names Heorot (78ᵇ). Here, king and warriors spend much time joyously feasting at night until a troll-like and cannibalistic creature of darkness named Grendel (102ᵇ) takes such vehement exception to the constant uproar of revelry that he submits the hall to a series of murderous attacks which eventually put an end to all nightly occupancy for the next twelve years (147ᵃ). Apparently nonplused by the monster's overpowering savagery, Hrothgar finds no better solution than to bear his grief (147ᵇ) and hold constant but seemingly fruitless meetings with his advisers (171ᵇ-172ᵃ).

Somewhere in the land of the Geats, a physically powerful young man identified as a retainer of King Hygelac (194ᵇ) and whose name we shall later learn to be Beowulf (343ᵇ) hears of this situation (194ᵃ-195ᵇ) and immediately sets sail for Denmark with fourteen companions (215ᵇ-216ᵇ) to free the world from Grendel's depredations. The Geats make land the next day and, after an initially somewhat tense but brief and amicable encounter with a coast guard (234ᵃ-300ᵇ), march to Heorot, where Beowulf announces the purpose of his visit and his determination to fight Grendel alone and unarmed (424ᵇ-440ᵃ), though he will wear a corslet made by Weland himself (455ᵃ). Hrothgar invites the Geats to a banquet, during which Beowulf is in turn taunted by a retainer named Unferth (506ᵃ-528ᵇ) and honored by Queen Wealhtheow's gracious attention (620ᵃ-628ᵃ). The Geats are then left alone to wait for Grendel, who soon breaks into the hall and succeeds in devouring one of them before grappling for life with Beowulf, from whom he escapes mortally wounded, leaving an arm behind (815ᵇ-823ᵃ).

The next day is devoted to celebrations, during which a poet entertains the company by singing a song about Beowulf's exploit (871ᵇ-874ᵃ), which he likens by implication to the deeds of the Germanic heroes Sigemund and Fitela (874ᵇ-900ᵇ) and contrasts to the crimes of a wicked king of old named Heremod (901ᵃ-915ᵇ). During the sumptuous banquet which follows, Hrothgar bestows priceless gifts upon Beowulf (1020ᵃ-1053ᵃ), and the poet sings once again to tell of the heroic death of the Half-Dane leader Hnaef and of that of the Frisian king Finn, who was killed by Hnaef's successor, Hengest (1063ᵃ-1159ᵃ). Wealhtheow then presents Beowulf with a necklace as valuable as the legendary one which Hama once stole from Eormanric

(1197ᵃ-1201ᵃ). That night, a contingent of Danes remains in Heorot, but Grendel's mother attacks to avenge her son and carries off a warrior named Aeshere, who is Hrothgar's dearest companion (1296ᵃ⁻ᵇ).

Early next morning, Beowulf is asked to help with the renewed peril (1376ᵇ-1377ᵃ) and is taken to a pond where Grendel and his mother presumably have their lair and on whose shore the young warrior receives a valuable and tried sword from Unferth (1455ᵃ-1457ᵇ), who seems to have forgotten his earlier antagonism. He then dives into the pond and enters an underwater cave where he kills Grendel's mother beside the body of her dead son, although Unferth's weapon fails him (1522ᵇ-1525ᵃ) and he must use an ancient sword which seems to have been waiting for him there (1557ᵃ-1568ᵇ). Back in Heorot, his accomplishments are praised by Hrothgar, who again contrasts him to Heremod (1709ᵇ) and seizes upon the occasion to deliver a little sermon on the sins of pride, sloth, and covetousness (1724ᵇ-1757ᵇ). On the fourth day, the Geats sail back to their homeland, where Hygelac expresses some surprise at the success of the expedition (1992ᵇ-1997ᵃ).

Sketchy though it be, the foregoing outline illustrates the highly traditional and oral-formulaic nature of the narrative. The names listed therein, for instance, should suffice to alert us to the extent to which the materials belong to the Old-English literary tradition. The mention of Finn, Hnaef, and Hengest takes us to the *Finnsburg Fragment,*[5] which gives a detailed account of part of the action mentioned in **Beowulf;** and Eormanric figures prominently in both *Widsith* and *Deor,* which are generally considered highly representative of the repertory of traditional Old-English poetry. In addition, Weland—the same whose picture on the Franks Casket may be seen by every visitor to the British Museum—plays an important part in the latter, while Hama, Finn, and Hnaef are included in the former, where we also find Hrothgar's political situation described in a manner consonant with the account in **Beowulf.** Outside Old English, the most cursory and random glance at mediaeval German and Scandinavian traditional literature shows that the same kind of observation may be made in respect to the broader Germanic context. The Eormanric of Old-English poetry is central to the German epic cycle of Dietrich von Bern and to the Old-Norse *Thidreks Saga*—both of which include Hama—and the sixteenth-century Low-German *Koninc Ermenrikes Dot* makes it clear that the impetus of his fame was strong enough to carry beyond the Middle Ages. Weland also appears in the *Thidreks Saga* and rates an entire poem in the *Elder Edda.* Sigemund, Heremod, and Eormanric likewise appear in an Eddic poem, known in English as *The Lay of Hyndla,* which also mentions the Scyldings.

Among all these, as well as others whose names have been left out here, Sigemund and Fitela deserve special mention because of their position as the central characters of the *Völsunga Saga.* In addition, the latter's death is commemorated in a special prose link in the *Elder Edda,* while the former is remembered as Siegfried's father in the *Nibelungenlied.* These titles would, of course, have been unknown to the audience of *Beowulf,* especially since the Old-Norse saga and the Middle-High-German epic were both written more than a century after the end of the Anglo-Saxon period, but, as I tried to argue in Chapter 6, specific performances and their titles must have meant very little to the normal audiences of traditional poetry composed orally or in writing according to the canons of oral-formulaic rhetoric. Fortunately, the affective impact which the mention of the two heroes might have had upon such audiences may be inferred from the Old-Norse *Eiríksmál,* which was almost certainly composed in England very soon after 964, when Erik Bloodaxe, recently expulsed King of Northumbria, was slain on the road from Carlisle to York. In order to magnify Erik's posthumous renown in the world, the anonymous author of the poem apparently found it sufficient to show the god Odin asking Sigemund and Fitela themselves to welcome the slain king to Valhalla:

> Sigmundr ok Sinfjotli!   rísið snarliga
> ok gangið   í gøgn grami:
> inn þú bjóð,   ef Eiríkr sé.[6]
>
> (19ᵃ-21ᵇ)

[Sigemund and Fitela! get up quickly and go meet the king: invite him in if he be Erik.]

We may accordingly imagine that, upon hearing Beowulf's exploits extolled in practically the same breath with those of these legendary Volsungs, a traditional Germanic audience would unconsciously have associated the glory of the former with the deeds of the latter, since human nature tends to decree virtue by association as easily as it decrees guilt by the same token.

Just as the names mentioned above place **Beowulf** squarely within the context of the Germanic tradition, so the several motifs recognizable in my outline—that is to say, these narrative situations and actions which transcend a particular story—do the same thing in respect to various episodes. The underwater fight and the depredations performed by a monster against some kind of human dwelling, for instance, have clear analogues in the otherwise vastly different story recounted in the fourteenth-century *Grettis Saga,* and analogues to one or the other episode are found in so many other Old-Norse sagas that Friedrich Klaeber observed that "the points of contact between [these] . . . and the **Beowulf** are unmistakable"[7] and explained the similarities by positing ancient folk legends which were "circulated orally in the North" and "in the course of time . . . were attached to various persons,"[8] including Beowulf. This explanation makes eminent sense, and I should personally hesitate to question its validity. Yet, there is more to be said if we look beyond the Germanic world and into one of the very most familiar episodes of the *Odyssey.* I am referring to the scene, in the ninth book, during which Odysseus kills the Cyclops Polyphemus in his cave just as Beowulf kills Grendel's mother in hers. Michael Nagler, who has analyzed comparatively the respective treatments of both killings, points out that "clearly each poet was dealing with the same theme,"[9] and he thus provides us with a theme likely to hark all the way back to Indo-European times. I must insist, however, that Nagler's analysis detracts in no way from Klaeber's explanation, since there is absolutely no reason why a particular implementation of a theme should not be transmitted in the manner surmised by Klaeber. In this case, the implementation is typically Germanic insofar as it involves Germanic warriors behaving in accordance with Germanic values in a Germanic environment, but the thematic paradigm necessarily antedates the Germanic narrative tradition.

The same argument may be advanced in respect to the fourteenth-century *Hrólfs Saga Kraka,* which deals in part with the legend of the Scyldings and in which the visit of the hero Bothvar Bjarki to the Danish court is so reminiscent of Beowulf's own visit that the taunts which Unferth directs at the hero in the latter are matched by those of some of the king's men in the former and that Bothvar has been said to be "possibly . . . identical with Beowulf himself."[10] But then, we may recall from the discussion of the theme of the singer looking at his sources, in Chapter 6, that precisely the same thing happens to Odysseus under very similar circumstances when he is taunted by Laodamas and Euryalus during his visit to the Phaeacian court. We must accordingly reckon with the probability that what we have here is not only a fact of Germanic legend but also an oralformulaic theme possibly dating back to Indo-European. Similarly, the mention of the singer looking at his sources reminds us that *Beowulf* was the Old-English poem in which Creed identified that particular theme. Yet, had we known the theme from a different source, the mention of a song about the hero's exploit, in my outline, would certainly have alerted us to its presence in the poem. Because they are based on an extremely sketchy outline and can accordingly reveal only the most conspicuous features, the foregoing observations should underscore the fact that the oral-formulaic nature of *Beowulf* is obvious enough to be taken into account not only by experienced scholars but also by readers trying their hand at literary interpretation for the first time.

For the present purpose, another important feature of the poem stands out in the outline. Because the hero and his companions cross the sea twice and he dives into a pond in which he engages in a bloody fight, we may say that the text of the Grendel episode of *Beowulf* is replete with opportunities for the implementation of the theme of the hero on the beach; and the chances are that any ancient or modern audience familiar with Germanic oral-formulaic rhetoric would be cued to watch for that theme the moment when Beowulf orders a ship readied to take him and his companions overseas to rescue Hrothgar (198[b]-207[a]).

In actuality, the expected theme is implemented in its so-called "pure form" in a type-scene which begins with the very next line:

> XVna sum
> sundwudu sohte;   secg wisade,

lagucræftig mon,   landgemyrcu.
>   Fyrst forđ gewat.   Flota wæs on yđum,
> bat under beorge.   Beornas gearwe
> on sfefn stigon;   streamas wundon,
> sund wiđ sande;   secgas bæron
> on bearm nacan   beorhte frætwe,
> guđsearo geatolic . . .

(207[b]-215[a])

[With fourteen others, he went to the boat; the man, a person wise in the ways of the sea, led the way to the shore. Time moved on. The vessel was afloat, the boat beneath the cliff. Without delay, the men embarked at the prow; the currents eddied, the water against the sand; the men carried their shining trappings, their splendid battle-gear into the bosom of the ship.]

Quite clearly we have here an instance of the theme in its so-called pure form: a hero on the beach (208[b]-209[b]) with his retainers (207[b]; 211[b]-215[a]) in the presence of a flashing light, here emanating from the shining equipment to which our attention is called twice in a row (214[b]; 215[a]), as a journey is begun (e.g., 207[b]-208[a]).

This particular occurrence of the theme has little to add to the factual expectations already raised in the audience by the preceding narrative, for nobody is likely to expect the outcome of Beowulf's expedition to be anything but slaughterous and no rhetorical device can do much to make us unconsciously aware of what we already know consciously. Yet, the occurrence has its affective impact, as may be assessed in the light of its immediate context. Until now, the poem has emphasized not only the brute horror of Grendel's slaughterous depredations but also the glaring contrast between the sheer energy of repeated action which they represent and the limp passivity with which the Danes submit to their humiliating plight. Grendel acts upon impulse and wastes no time doing so. No sooner has he discovered that the Danes are intent on spending their nights feasting loudly in the great hall (89[a]: "hludne in healle") than his furor grows out of control in a manner which requires no explanation with those readers who have endured neighbors excessively fond of loud parties at night. Without waiting to consider the ethical implications of violence or even to devise a strategy, he goes into action and bursts into the hall under the cover of darkness. There he finds the human occupants, who have just now wound up that evening's beer party (117[a]: "æfter beorþege") and are already sleeping it off right after the banquet (119[a]: "swefan æfter symble"). Without so much as a hint of pause or hesitation, he grabs thirty of them and is once again on his way home with his booty in five and one-half lines:

>   Wiht unhælo,
> grim ond grædig,   gearo sona wæs,
> reoc and reþe,   ond on ræste genam
> þritig þegna,   þanon eft gewat
> huđe hremig   to ham faran,
> mid þre wælfylle   wica neosan.

(120[b]-125[b])

[The creature of destruction, fierce and ravenous, savage and furious, was quickly ready and grabbed thirty thanes from where they were sleeping; thence he departed to return home, exulting in his booty, to seek his abode with his fill of slaughtered bodies.]

Here, in powerful contrast to the immediately preceding image of the Danes peacefully sleeping in contented repletion, almost every other word suggests either fierce determination (e.g., "reoc and reþe" ["savage and furious"]) or instant action (e.g., "gearo sona wæs" ["was quickly ready"]), and the resulting sense of horrifying enthusiasm is brilliantly capped by the sight of Grendel's exultant delight in his own performance ("huđe hremig" ["exultant in his booty"]). For an audience attuned to oral-formulaic devices, incidentally, the tension of the scene is established at the outset with the mention of the Danes "sleeping after the banquet," for this particular brand of inactivity has been identified as an oral-formulaic theme whose participants are usually about to meet their doom.[11]

Within four lines of Grendel's triumphant departure, the contrast is again impressed upon us when, at sunrise, the surviving Danes gather to assess the damage and find no better course of action than to indulge in loud lamentations (129[a]: "micel morgensweg"). Hrothgar is quintessential of the general paralysis. Whereas the situation obviously calls for action on the leader's part, he can only sit in sorrow (130[b]: "unbliđe sæt") while passively suffering and enduring (131[a-b]: þolode . . . dreah") a fate which obviously has him totally baffled. The poet sums up this situation by remarking that "the struggle was too strong, hateful, and longlasting" (133[b]-134[a] and again 191[b]-192[a]: wæs þæt gewin to strang, / lađ ond longsum").[12] It is no wonder, then, that the next line should show Grendel hurrying in for a return engagement the night after (134[b]-137[a]), and it is characteristic that he should feel absolutely no remorse (136[b]; "ond no mearn fore") for hitting so hard and so often warriors who do nothing to stop him and whose only active concern is to keep out of his way by whatever means (138[a]-143[b]).

Throughout the twelve years that this situation endures, Grendel is always seen doing things that require determination and quick action. Just as he was "quickly ready" to kill on the occasion of his first onslaught and had the stamina to repeat the grisly exploit the following night, so the only rest he ever takes thereafter is when he lies in wait to pounce upon his victims (161[a]: "seomade ond syrede"), and his life is accordingly described as a "constant strife" (154[a]: "singale sæce"). In contradistinction, the Danes are repeatedly seen engaging in activities which require neither determination nor quick action and which, in fact, do not always have definable beginnings and ends. Just as Hrothgar's response to Grendel's first raid was to "sit in sorrow" and to take no action, so the meetings which he presumably calls to find a solution are made to sound like continuous affairs unlikely to produce any serious plan or strategy:

> Monig oft gesæt
> rice to rune;   ræd eahtedon

> hwæt swiđferhđum   selest wære
> wiđ færgryrum   to gefremmanne.

> (171[b]-174[b])

[Many a powerful man sat often in council; they debated as to what might be best for strong-minded men to do in respect to the terror of sudden attacks.]

We are not surprised to learn that, despite these repeated meetings, Hrothgar spends his time continually brooding (190[a]: "singala seađ").

After more than a hundred lines (86[a]-193[b]) devoted primarily to impressing us with the contrast between Grendel's murderous energy and the disastrous passivity of the Danes' response, the account concludes with the statement that Hrothgar could do nothing whatsoever to turn aside the calamity which had been plaguing his people for so many years (189[a]-193[b]). It is at this point that Beowulf enters the poem, and in the space of only five and one-half lines learns of Grendel's depredations, decides to do something to put a stop to them, and has a ship readied to take him to Denmark (194[a]-199[a]). Through the mere act of ordering a boat to be readied, Beowulf accomplishes much more within these five and one-half lines of text and a few seconds of decision-making than Hrothgar and all his Danes have done in the preceding one hundred and eight lines and twelve years of indecision.

The swiftness of the operation is emphasized in two ways. In the first place, we are made to see Beowulf, in radical contrast to Hrothgar, sweeping into immediate action without giving the slightest hint of ever stopping to devise a plan of action or to consider the possible consequences of that action.[13] In the second place, the structure of the passage illustrates a device which might be called "semantic gapping" for lack of a better term. We know that what linguists call "gapping constructions" (e.g., "John saw the dog and Mary the cat" instead of "John saw the dog, and Mary saw the cat")[14] shortens sentences by dropping the repetition of a verb without affecting its semantic function, and they can thus give the action an appearance of rapidity. With what I have called "semantic gapping," an entire unit of meaning is dropped with the same result. A thought whose expression might have required a whole sentence or even several sentences remains unstated, but we nevertheless assume its nature because the rest of the message would be incomplete without it. In the case of the passage under consideration, we should expect the sequence of utterances to make us see Beowulf (a) learning about Grendel's depredations, (b) making up his mind to go fight the monster, and (c) accordingly ordering a ship readied to take him to Denmark. Instead, we are presented with (a) a statement of his learning about Grendel's depredations, (b) a parenthetical digression about his being the strongest man in the world, and (c) a statement of his ordering a ship to be prepared:

> Þæt fram ham gefrægn   Higelaces þegn,
> god mid Geatum,   Grendles dæda;
> se wæs moncynnes   mægenes strengest

on þæm dæge   þysses lifes,
æþele ond eacen.   Het him yðlidan
godne gegyrwan . . .

                                        (194ᵃ-199ᵃ)

[In his homeland, Hygelac's thane, excellent among the Geats, learned about Grendel's deeds; on that day of this life, he was the mightiest in strength among mankind, enormous and noble. He ordered a good ship to be prepared for him . . .]

Not only does the omitted statement speed up the action, but it also drives home from the start the contrast between Beowulf and Hrothgar. Whereas the old Danish king has repeatedly proceeded from information to deliberation and unfailingly stopped short of action, the young Geatish warrior skips over deliberation to charge directly from information into action.

The passage under consideration does more than contrast the energy of youth to the limpness of age; it forces us to look at Beowulf in relation to Grendel. In the first place, its structure plainly matches that of the passage which has introduced Grendel and his original raid some hundred lines earlier. There, we should have expected to be told that the monster (a) learned through firsthand experience that the sounds of nightly Danish revelry in Heorot were revolting to him, (b) made up his mind to take the matter in hand and put an end to the offending noises while treating himself to a good meal, and (c) accordingly moved in on the hall. Instead, exactly as with the passage which introduces Beowulf, the implementation has satisfied our initial and concluding expectations (86ᵃ-98ᵇ and 115ᵃ-116ᵃ) but has replaced the middle one by a parenthetical digression, in this case on Grendel's descent from biblical giants and sundry other monsters. The structure common to both passages is reminiscent of a syllogism whose second premise had been replaced by a statement unconnected to the logical process. In addition, just as we have seen Beowulf introduced as "Hygelac's thane" (194ᵇ) rather than by name, so Grendel is introduced as "the bold demon" (86ᵃ: "se ellengæst") rather than by name. The parallels between the two passages may quite conceivably betoken the use of a common oral-formulaic theme,[15] but they are much too obvious to pass unnoticed. In the second place, the digression at the center of each passage emphasizes precisely the same quality of physical strength in Beowulf and Grendel, respectively: just as the human hero is "the mightiest in strength among mankind" (196ᵃ⁻ᵇ), so his prospective antagonist is a "savage demon" (102ᵃ: "grimma gæst") related to the "giants who struggled against God a long time" (113ᵃ-114ᵃ: "gigantas, þa wið gode wunnon / lange þrage"), and we shall later be reminded that "he was bigger than any other man" (1353ᵃ⁻ᵇ: "he wæs mare þonne ænig man oðer"). In other words, Beowulf is to good what Grendel is to evil. Like the positive and negative of the same picture, the two are perfectly matched, and it is only fitting that, just as the monster always fights "alone against all" (154ᵃ: "ana wið eallum"), so his human opponent should vow to face the giant alone (425ᵇ-426ᵃ: "ana gehegan / ðing wið þyrse").

Positive and negative must perforce adhere to the same structure, but they are nevertheless the opposite of each other. This fact is essential to our grasp of the relationship between Grendel and Beowulf and is impressed upon us immediately after the latter has ordered that a boat be prepared to take him to Denmark. On the very next line (199ᵃ-201ᵇ) the premise missing from the pseudo-syllogism discussed above reappears to tell us how and why he decides to undertake the adventure:

    [Beowulf] cwæð   he guðcyning
ofer swanrade   secean wolde,
mærne þeoden,   þa him wæs manna þearf.

                                        (199ᵇ-201ᵇ)

[(Beowulf) said that he intended to seek the war-king, the famous prince (i.e., Hrothgar), over the swan-road, since he had need of men.]

The statement stands out in our mind because it answers a question to which logic had led us to expect an answer three lines earlier; and it drives home the radical difference between Grendel and Beowulf by stating what we have already assumed: whereas the latter has traveled to Heorot to destroy, the former is about to travel there to mend, and the negative-positive relationship between the two is now clear in every respect.

Against this background the occurrence of the theme of the hero on the beach affects us through three suggestive aspects thereof, even though it adds no major factual information to what we already know. In the first place, it reinforces our expectation of a bloody struggle between Beowulf and Grendel, since we have already noted that the theme usually occurs before a scene of carnage or at least a mention thereof. In the second place, it also reinforces our natural but necessarily tentative expectation that good will triumph over evil, since the hero of the theme usually emerges victorious from the ensuing struggle.[16] In the third place, it lends the whole affair an air of immediacy because the recorded instances of subsequent carnage tend to take place soon after the relevant occurrences of the theme rather than in some vague and distant future;[17] and, within the poem, Beowulf will in fact come face to face with Grendel in fewer than forty-eight hours. Against the information which has ushered in the occurrence of the theme, the cumulative effect of these three suggestive aspects is to initiate a tension which might otherwise not develop until later. Because of the associations which the theme triggers in our mind, the embarkation scene affects us no longer as a mere prelude to a bloody struggle that will eventually take place at a different time in a different location, but rather as an initial step in that struggle. In other words, the counteraction to Grendel's abominable actions has become operative, and the audience is swept along in a chain of events which may no longer be stopped.

Even though fewer than forty-eight hours elapse between the embarkation and the fight with Grendel, over five hundred lines—or nearly a half-hour of listening or reading aloud—intervene between the conclusion of the type-scene (215^a) and the beginning of that fight (739^a), so that we should expect the initial impact of the theme to be considerably, if not totally, blunted by the time the anticipated slaughter finally takes place. Quite on the contrary, the poet has succeeded in repeatedly boosting that impact in such a way as to keep the tension mounting until the very last moment. This narrative feat is accomplished through the recurrence of type-scenes embodying the theme as well as through the periodic appearance of various sources of flashing light which keep the idea of that theme alive in our mind.

The first recurrence takes place, not surprisingly, as the Geats complete their crossing some twenty-four hours later (219$^{a\text{-}b}$). As they near the Danish coast, the very first thing to come within their ken is the line of shining cliffs: ". . . đa liđende land gesawon, / brimclifu blican" (221^a-222^a ["the voyagers caught sight of the land, of the sea-cliffs shining"]). Because associations readily take place in the reader's or listener's mind while remaining unstated in the text, a given implementation of a theme may prove perfectly clear while omitting key elements which have to be supplied by the audience in accordance with the principles outlined earlier in connection with semantic gapping. In the present case, the text makes no mention of the hero, but the initial type-scene has told us only a few lines earlier (207^b-209^a) that Beowulf was leading the expedition, so that we automatically provide the missing element by assuming his unmentioned presence aboard ship, and we accordingly have a perfectly clear implementation of the theme, though not in its so-called "pure form." The affective result is that, as we come within sight of the land where Grendel performs his bloody deeds, we are again presented with an unmistakable instance of a familiar narrative device which signals carnage, and the tension increases accordingly.

Motion-picture and television viewers need not be told that the tension attendant upon an approaching struggle tends to be most keenly felt when the audience is made to see the approach from the respective points of view of both the entity which approaches and that which is approached. This principle is illustrated in a third implementation of the theme of the hero on the beach. We have just now been made to see the telltale flashing light from the point of view of Beowulf and his companions as their ship approaches the cliffs, and we are suddenly made to turn around one hundred and eighty degrees to look from those same cliffs at the Geats landing on the beach. As we do so, we notice from the point of view of a Danish coast guard the shining shields carried by the sailors as they disembark, and we are thus provided with the necessary cue to reconstruct the theme in our mind, although the text makes no explicit mention of the hero, or his retainers, or the voyage, or even the beach, and we must supply these things from the preceding scenes:

> Þa of wealle geseah   weard Scildinga,
> se þe holmclifu   healdan scolde,

beran ofer bolcan   beorhte randas,
fyrdsearu fuslicu.

(229^a-232^a)

[Then from the wall the Scyldings' watchman, he whose duty it was to guard the sea-cliffs, noticed shining shields, the battle-gear at the ready, being carried over the gangway.]

We have thus had three implementations of the theme in a row, and each one has included fewer of the required elements than the one before. We have started out with a neat type-scene incorporating the theme in its "pure form," with explicit mentions of a hero with his retainers, on a beach, at the outset of a journey, in the presence of a flashing light; we have then proceeded to a second implementation in which the expected mention of the hero has been omitted, and we have ended with a third implementation in which everything except the flashing light has been left out. Since all three implementations take place within a mere twenty-five lines and the previous section of the narrative has thoroughly familiarized us with the situation at hand, we deserve scant credit for being able to supply the missing elements on demand. The process, however, is important because, in a manner of speaking, it forces us to participate actively in the composition of the very poem which we are reading or to which we are listening. The principle is a familiar one for anyone acquainted with those Impressionist or Late-Roman paintings which leave out details which our mind supplies because we naturally assume their presence although our eyes do not see them. With literature as with painting, the likely result is that we become so personally involved with the process of creation that we are unwittingly prompted to become part of the action. In the present case, the device further prepares us to associate subsequent flashes of light with the theme of the hero on the beach and thus to keep the affective impetus going.

A well-trained craftsman working within a firm tradition will often implement certain requirements of that tradition without questioning their significance, and we may accordingly doubt that every Greek stonecutter carving eggs and darts around a temple wasted much time pondering the message which each of these would convey to the onlookers. By the same token, it would be difficult to determine whether the **Beowulf**-poet was fully conscious of the affective potential of the theme or whether he was simply implementing it because the situation traditionally called for this particular narrative device. It would likewise be difficult to determine whether subsequent occurrences of a flashing light must be considered conscious attempts at keeping the theme going or simply happen to be here because the contents of the narrative make their presence unavoidable. This compound uncertainty need not affect our interpretation any more than the fact that Molière's Mr. Jourdain never knew that he was speaking prose until his teacher of philosophy enlightened him[18] should prevent us from placing the label of prose on his previous utterances. In addition, we need not be uncertain about what we hear or see on the page, even if we do not know how it came to be there. In the present case, the picture of the shining sea-cliffs is so conspicuous that we cannot miss it, and the flashing quality of the trappings and shields which alert us to the other two occurrences of the theme of the hero on the beach is unmistakably brought out by the repeated use of the adjective "shining" (214[a]; 231[b]: "beorhte").

With these observations in mind, we may now glance at the return journey, which forms a natural companion piece to the journey which we have examined and offers a revealing contrast to the techniques therein. Because Hrothgar has showered upon the Geats all kinds of gifts made of precious metal, the opportunities for calling attention to flashing objects are practically endless, so that we should expect the poet to return to his earlier technique and make repeated use of the adjective "shining" and various equivalents. But the situation is different because Beowulf has killed both Grendel and Grendel's mother and there is no more prospect of immediate slaughter awaiting him at the end of the journey. As a result, the conventions of oral-formulaic rhetoric no longer call for the theme of the hero on the beach, even though the sea that must be sailed and the beaches that must be trod are the very same which we have seen Beowulf and his companions sail and tread at the outset of the adventure.

In this light, it seems worth noting that, as the Geats tread once again the Danish beach where their boat has been waiting for them, the text makes nine separate mentions of situations or objects which ought to be sources of flashing light: Beowulf is "proud with gold" (1881[a]: "gold-wlanc") and "exultant in treasure" (1882[a]: "since hremig"); he and his companions "in bright armor" (1895[a]: "scirhame") are wearing "coats of mail" (1889[b]: "hringnet") and corslets (1890[a]: "leoðosyrcan"); the ship is loaded with "precious things" (1898[a]: "maðmum") and "stored-up treasures" (1899[b]: "hordgestreonum"); and the coast guard receives a "sword bound with gold" (1900[b]-1901[a]: "bunden golde / swurd"), which is compared to a treasure (1902[b]: "maðme"). Yet, only one among the nine includes an explicit reference to the process of emitting light; and that one is the adjective *scirham,* which I have translated as "in bright armor" in keeping with common practice, but whose literal meaning is "with a bright (or clear) covering" and which seems to suggest little beyond the fact that the person thus qualified wears some kind of metal armor.[19] In the other eight cases, the presence or absence of the latent flash is left for us to determine if we think of it. This observation would be unquestionably and totally insignificant if it were not for the fact that the particular lack of explicit formulation to which it calls attention stands in contrast not only with the technique evident in the three implementations of the theme of the hero on the beach discussed above but also with the practice constantly illustrated in subsequent implementations, which will be examined presently.

The extent of this contrast becomes manifest if we read on or listen for only eight more lines to make the homeward crossing with the Geats and share their first sight of the approaching coastline. Except for one detail, the picture evoked is an exact counterpart of the picture which we were asked to imagine when they were shown approaching the Danish coast ("the voyagers caught sight of the land, of the sea-cliffs shining"), and it is likewise conveyed by (a) a statement of what is seen, followed by (b) an appositive which tells us something about what we are seeing: "they could make out the cliffs of the Geats, the familiar promontories" (1911[a]-1912[a]: ". . . hie Geata clifu ongitan meahton, / cuþe næssas"). The missing detail is, of course, the shining quality which made the appearance of the Danish cliffs so striking over sixteen hundred lines earlier and which alerted us to the presence of the theme. We may further wish to note that, as the Geats actually set foot on their homeland, their arrival is observed by a coast guard (1914[a]-1916[b]) just as their arrival in Denmark was observed by a coast guard, but this time the text includes no mention or even suggestion of any kind of flashing equipment. Just as we need only give enough monkeys enough typewriters and we are bound to find a Shakespeare sooner or later, so the foregoing similarities and contrasts could conceivably be attributed to sheer coincidence; but this coincidence would not alter the fact that the key component of the theme of the hero on the beach is stressed when the presence of that theme is required by the conventions of oral-formulaic rhetoric and is either left to our imagination or completely omitted when these conventions no longer require the theme.

The principle formulated above is illustrated over and over again between the landing in Denmark and the fight with Grendel. As the Geats walk away from the beach, our attention is made to focus on the golden boar images gleaming on their helmets:

> Eoforlic scionon
> ofer hleorberan   gehroden golde,
> fah ond fyreheard.
>
>   (303[b]-305[a])

[Boar images adorned with gold gleamed above the cheek-guards, shining and fire-hardened.]

A similar technique comes into play a few lines later, when Beowulf and his companions catch their first glimpse of their goal and the gleaming quality of the great hall is explicitly stressed three times in a row. We are told that it is "gleaming with gold" (308[a]: "goldfah"), that it is "shining" (313[a]: "torht"), and that its radiance is such that it shines "over many lands" (311[a-b]: "lixte se leoma ofer landa fela"). As the Geats pause in front of Heorot, the emphasis falls squarely on the luster of their byrnies (321[b]: "Guðbyrne scan") and the brightness of the iron rings in their corslets (322[b]: "hringiren scir"). Since those flashes which do not occur by the beach occur as the travelers reach the door of Heorot—which we have seen in Chapter 6 to satisfy the same formulaic requirement as a beach—we again have all the components of the theme of the hero on the beach, and it should be noted that the theme thus occurs with particular vigor as we reach the building in which Beowulf will shed Grendel's blood that very night.

No sooner have the Geats crossed the threshold into the hall than the text once again calls attention to the brightness of Beowulf's byrnie (405[b]: "on him byrne scan"). Thus, just as we were earlier made to notice first the shining cliffs as the Geats were approaching the shore and then the shining shields carried by the same Geats as they were landing on the beach, so we have now been made to notice first the gloriously shining hall from the outside as the Geats were approaching it and then the shining byrnie worn by Beowulf as he stands facing Hrothgar inside the hall. We may therefore say that, in similar structural situations, the handling of the theme is remarkably consistent, and I believe that this consistency helps keep the impetus going.

By now, we are so conditioned by occurrences of the theme reiterated in narrative layers superimposed under parallel circumstances and indicated by explicit mentions of various kinds of flashing lights that any subsequent mention of any sort of light is likely to affect us as would another instance of the theme itself. This kind of association is likely to take place, for example, when Beowulf introduces himself to Hrothgar by stating his intention to put an end to the incursions which Grendel regularly makes after the "evening light" (413[b]: "æfenleoht") has died out; and this mention of light appropriately occurs five lines before the summary of an adventure during which the hero encountered and slaughtered several sea monsters (419[a]-424[a]), and ten and one-half lines before his rather truculent request that he may face Grendel in single combat (424[b]-432[b]). The association is again likely to take place when Hrothgar, in his reply to Beowulf, tells of one of Grendel's raids and describes the gory state of Heorot the morning after, "when the day shone" (485[b]: "þonne dæg lixte"); and the same principle applies when the Danes eventually retire for the night and leave the Geats in Heorot to await Grendel's onslaught "after they could no longer see the light of the sun" (648[a-b]: "siððan hie sunnan leoht geseon ne meahton").

In the immediately foregoing cases, semantic gapping has been carried to the extreme insofar as one single component of the theme—even though it has consistently been the key component—has served to keep the momentum of the original impact alive. We should note that, whether this technique be used wittingly or otherwise, it has the effect of forcing the audience into active reading or listening. The cues are perfectly clear, and a properly trained audience has only one way to interpret them, but they nevertheless require interpretation, however automatic and elementary, and the process entails at least some kind of creative involvement on our part. There is no difficulty involved, but neither are we spoonfed a predigested narrative.

The process whereby the impact of the theme of the hero on the beach is sustained in our mind by strategically located mentions of flashing lights is reinforced by three additional implementations thereof which take us all the way to the beginning of the expected bloodshed. The first two depart palpably from the "pure form" of the theme but nevertheless contribute to the tension by keeping the concept of slaughter foremost in our mind. The first of these is found in the reply which Beowulf makes to Unferth's taunts in Heorot and in which he claims to have once killed nine sea monsters (557[b]-558[b] and 574[a]-575[a]) who—in a manner reminiscent of Grendel's way of doing things—had planned on eating him near the bottom of the water (562[a]-564[b]). No sooner had he achieved his victory at sea, he tells us, than "light came from the East, the shining beacon of God" (569[b]-570[a]: "Leoht eastan com, / beorht beacen godes") and the shoreline loomed ahead of him (571[a]-572[a]). Although the hero's retainers are nowhere in sight, we have here a type-scene which includes the other three components of our theme (a sea voyage, a flashing light, and a shoreline), but the order is askew insofar as the expected slaughter is mentioned along with the theme which should normally precede it. The second type-scene occurs a little later in the same reply, as Beowulf proclaims that he will prove more of a match for Grendel than the Danes have ever been. Because he begins this particular part of his speech with a mention of Grendel's unopposed slaughter of Danes (590[a]-601[a]), the order is again askew, and, because he is sitting at a banquet table in Heorot, the usual connection between the action and some kind of boundary between two worlds is missing. Yet, we know that he speaks in the presence of both the Danes and his own companions and that he has arrived and entered the hall just a little earlier, so that we have our theme before us the instant he provides us with the needed flash of light by assuring all present that the long-drawn ordeal will finally be over on the next morning, "when the morning light . . . , the brightly clothed sun will shine from the south" (604[b]-606[b]: "siþþan morgen leoht / . . . , / sunne sweglwered suþan scined").

The last implementation of the theme before the encounter with Grendel deserves special attention, not merely because it takes us to the event which we have been relentlessly approaching with mounting anticipation for more than five hundred lines, but especially because the effectiveness with which it triggers in the audience a sense of absolute terror at the approach of the unknown is unlikely ever to be surpassed in literature. The fact that the Geats have only this day arrived in Denmark has remained fresh in our minds throughout the preceding narrative, and no sooner have the Danes vacated Heorot for the night than we are specifically reminded of the presence of two other components of the theme. Although there is no mention of the boundary between two worlds, we are made to hear the hero stating once more his intentions (677[a]-687[b]) before lying down to rest (688[a]-689[a]) along with his companions (689[b]-690[b]), and the presence of both is stressed one last time when we are told that victory will be granted to all of them through the might of a single one (696[b]-700[a]). It is at this point that, after only a two-line parenthesis to the effect that the outcome of human affairs rests in the hands of God (700[b]-702[a]), we are made to sense Grendel's approach. I am using the verb "to sense" instead of the more usual "to see" because the episode takes place at night and we do not, in fact, see anything at all. Furthermore, we have thus far been given no description of Grendel, although we have seen his bloody work and have gathered that he is an oversized and monstrous creature, so that we cannot even rely on hearsay to imagine in our mind's eye what the darkness of night hides from our actual sight.

This unsettling uncertainty is compounded by the fact that we do not know whence the monster will come. We have learned that he lives in the darkness (87[b]: "þe se in þystrum bad") and keeps to the moors (103[b]: "se þe moras heold"), but this information does not tell us whether he is approaching from the front, the rear, or the side. We must also remember that all previous mentions of Grendel have been outside the time frame of the poem. We have been told that he had come and slaughtered, but *not* that he was coming now, because his incursions had either taken place before the beginning of the story proper or been mentioned by characters in the story who were discussing actions already completed. As already noted, we have been made to imagine the gory spectacle he left behind after each incursion, but the very fact that we could imagine such a spectacle must by definition emphasize the fact that the action was over. In brief, we have thus been made to feel the horror of witnessing the aftermath of slaughter, but we have not felt the terror that comes from imagining ourselves on the targeted spot as the agent of destruction approaches.

This time, however, things are different. Grendel is now coming at us, and we are made to sense his coming inexorably nearer and nearer with each successive statement of his approach:

Com on wanre niht
Scriðan sceadugenga.   Sceotend swæfan,
þa þæt hornreced   healdan scoldon,
ealle buton anum.   Þæt wæs yldum cuþ
þæt hie ne moste,   þa metod nolde,
se scynscaþa   under sceadu bregdan;
ac he wæccende   wraþum on andan
bad bolgenmod   beadwa geþinges.
Ða com of more   under misthleoþum
Grendel gongan,   godes yrre bær;
mynte se manscaða   manna cynnes
sumne besyrwan   in sele þam hean.
Wod under wolcnum   to þæs þe he winreced,
goldsele gumena,   gearwost wisse,
fættum fahne.   Ne wæs þæt forma sið
þat he Hroþgares   ham gesohte;
næfre he on aldordagum   ær ne siþðan
heardran hæle,   healþegnas fand.
Com þa to recede   rinc siðian
dreamum bedæled.   Duru sona onarn,
fyrbendum fæst,   syþðan he hire folmum æthran;
onbræd þa bealohydig,   ða he gebolgen wæs,
recedes muþan.   Raþe æfter þon
on fagne flor   feond treddode,
eode yrremod;   him of eagum stod
ligge gelicost   leoht unfæger.

(702[b]-727[b]).

[The walker in darkness came sweeping through the dark night. The warriors—all but one—slept, those who were there to hold the gabled hall. It was known to men that the demoniac foe could not drag them away under the shadows as long as the Lord did not wish it; but he (i.e., Beowulf), watching in fierce anger, waited with enraged heart for the issue of battle. Then, out of the moor, came Grendel moving under the misty slopes: he bore the wrath of God; the murderous foe intended to ensnare one of the human beings in the high hall. He advanced under the clouds toward the place where he most readily knew the wine-hall, the gold-chamber of men, to stand adorned with gold plates. It was not the first time that he had sought Hrothgar's home; never at any time in his life-days did he come upon harder luck or hardier hall-thanes. The warlike one, deprived of joy, came hastening to the hall. Instantly the door, fastened with fire-forged bands, burst open at the touch of his hands; enraged and intent on destruction, he wrenched the hall's mouth wide open. Quickly thereupon, the attacker stepped on the ornate floor, he moved on with anger in his heart; an ugly light came from his eyes, most like a flame.]

The cumulative impact of these successive pictures of destruction on the move lends the account an affective power which the intended readers or listeners must necessarily feel almost as if they were there, and the techniques behind this descriptive feat have been brilliantly analyzed by Arthur Brodeur[20] and by Greenfield. I am quoting a brief passage from the latter because it neatly sums up the phenomenon and the mechanics of its implementation:

> The . . . scene . . . is a brilliant tableau. The three forces that are soon to be brought into collision in combat are presented here as separated, each with its own attitude and behavior toward the impending event. The walker-in-darkness is on the march, his murderous intentions implicit in the association with night and darkness; the warriors are sleeping, believing that the monster will, if God so wills, have no power to harm them; Beowulf is watching, enraged and anticipating the outcome of battle. These differences are rendered poetically effective by the syntactical, metrical, and rhetorical patterns in which they are rooted.[21]

Two additional observations are called for in relation to the theme of the hero on the beach. The first is that Grendel's crossing of the threshold between his outdoor world of the wild and our own indoor world of comfort and civilization has provided the mention of a boundary which we noted a little earlier as missing, and the sight of the ugly light shining from his eyes provides the last component still needed to complete the theme.[22] The second is that, just as we were earlier made to experience the approach to the Danish shore both from the point of view of the approaching Geats and from that of a coast guard on the shore being approached, so we have now been made to experience Grendel's approach both from the point of view of the target being approached (702[b], 710[a], 720[a]: "com" ["he came"]) and from that of the monster himself (714[a]: "wod" ["he advanced"]).

In addition to providing yet another instance of the consistent manner in which the poet handles separate implementations of the theme under similar circumstances, these observations illustrate once again the affective mastery behind the composition. As we sense Grendel coming upon us through the darkness, we need very little willing suspension of disbelief to experience all the terror attendant upon the apprehension of looming destruction at the hands of the monstrous unknown. As we are made to shift camp and turn around to recognize the target for slaughter which we are now approaching with him, we feel the horror of having become, so to speak, the agent as well as the target of that destruction. For readers or listeners steeped in the oral-formulaic tradition, however, it must be with the mention of the ugly light flashing from Grendel's eyes that the tension reaches its peak. Since Germanic halls were equipped with neither large windows nor night-long illumination, we must imagine the darkness inside Heorot as far too opaque to let us see much of what is going on. We may conceivably have caught a glimpse of Grendel as he sent the door crashing down and his silhouette stood momentarily outlined against the presumably lighter night outside. Yet, since he makes a detour to gulp down a Geat (739[a]-745[a]) before attacking Beowulf, he must by definition move out of the line between the gaping door and whatever position we imagine ourselves occupying, so that the silhouette vanishes instantly into the dark and we can see no more of the monster than do the occupants of the hall. Under these conditions, the only thing they can see is, of course, the ugly light flashing from his eyes. In other words, the exact shape of the monster remains unknown until Beowulf begins grappling for life with him, and the one thing which we are allowed to see is that flash which stands out inescapably against the ambient blackness and happens to be the key component of a theme which has been present with increasing intensity since the beginning of the action and which we associate with impending slaughter. In view of the mystery which surrounds Grendel, incidentally, it is interesting to note that the one thing which Beowulf emphasizes with undisguised pride when he accounts for the event in front of the Danes is the fact that he and his companions "boldly braved the might of the unknown" (959[b]-960[a]: "frecne geneðdon / eafoð uncuþes").

Whether fully intended or partially accidental, the way in which the flashing light is made to stand out against a background of stark blackness is a masterstroke of affective rhetoric insofar as the impact upon the audience comes from the context of the immediate action as well as from the implications of a familiar theme, and the total effect is stronger than the sum of its two parts experienced separately. The handling of the materials is typical, since the poet reveals a decided fondness for making us focus on a small detail which stands for something larger. When the Geats were setting out for Denmark, we were made to look at those small eddies (212[b]-213[a]) which usually take place along the hulls of beached ships as the waves surge forward and then retreat over the sand. As Beowulf and Grendel grapple with each other for life, we are made to focus on the single detail of fingers bursting under the formidable pressure of adversary grip (760[b]: "fingras

burston"); and as Beowulf tears off Grendel's arm, the focus shifts on the very point where the sinews burst and the bones separate as a wound opens at the shoulder joint:

> . . .   him on eaxle weard
> syndolh sweotol,   seonowe onsprungon,
> burston banlocan.
>
> (816[b]-818[a])

[. . . a gaping wound appeared on his shoulder, the sinews sprang apart, the bone-joints burst.]

The merciless nature of the struggle is impressed upon us because, instead of being asked to see the whole scene from a distance, we are forced to concentrate at close range on a few gruesome details which epitomize the action.

The technique so effectively implemented here is that of the close-up on the motion-picture screen. It consists in concentrating on one or two paradigmatic details instead of stretching the field of vision to encompass the entire action; and modern readers may recall that it was precisely this kind of selectivity that Antoine de Saint Exupéry most admired in the art of Joseph Conrad.[23] As a result of these close-ups, the readers or listeners find themselves at the very center of the action rather than merely observing it from a safe distance; and few things are likely to inspire more terror than finding oneself on the very spot where the sinews spring and the bones break, even if our familiarity with the theme of the hero on the beach tells us that the human hero will in all probability emerge victorious from the bloody struggle.

An examination of every flashing light in the poem would belong to a monograph on the subject rather than to a general introduction to oral-formulaic rhetoric, but a cursory glance at two additional occurrences seems warranted to show that the theme of the hero on the beach also occurs in conjunction with the two remaining great crises in Beowulf's life: the fight with Grendel's mother at the bottom of a pond and the hero's ultimate fight, this time with a dragon, near the end of the poem, more than fifty years later. As Beowulf prepares to dive into the pond in pursuit of his enemy, he has just completed the journey from Heorot to the spot where he now stands (1400[b]-1421[b]), he is in the presence of both Geats and Danes (e.g., 1412[a]-1413[b]), he stands on the bank of a body of water (e.g., 1416[b]), and he is given a sword which is described as either ornamented or flashing, depending on how we wish to interpret the adjective "fah" (1459[b]), so that we have here a type-scene which embodies all the elements of the theme. The fight proper takes place at the bottom of the pond but in a cave that acts like a kind of diving bell to keep the water out (1512[b]-1516[a]), so that he is in effect standing by a small underground beach, and the very first thing which he notices is a "firelight, a clear flame, shining brightly" (1516[b]-1517[b]: "fyrleoht . . . / blacne leoman, beorhte scinan"). Furthermore, just as we may recall having heard Beowulf nearly a thousand lines earlier tell of his youthful adventures at sea and claim that he had no sooner killed nine monsters in the water than light flashed from the east (569^b-570^a), so now a light flashes as soon as he has killed Grendel's mother; and the metrical formula which conveys the fact—"Lixte se leoma" (1570^a)—is word-for-word the same which was used to convey the glory of Heorot (311^a) and forms the left-hand hemistich in both cases. If, in addition, we note that Beowulf kills his opponent with a sword which he finds in the cave and we happen to recall that the killing of a man-eating monster in a cave with a weapon found there in the presence of a fire has been identified as a theme of its own,[24] we must once again be impressed by both the density of oral-formulaic elements in the poem and the consistent manner in which they are used.

The presence of the theme of the hero on the beach in connection with Beowulf's last fight is likewise easily detectable. Beowulf and twelve of his warriors have just now made the trip from his home to the dragon's lair (2401^a-2412^a), and he addresses them before going into action alone (2510^a-2537^b). He then advances near the opening of the dragon's cave and stands by a stream which flows from it (2538^a-2546^a) and is "hot with battle-fire" (2547^a: "heaðufyrum hat") and the "dragon's flame" (2549^b: "dracan lege"). Finally, the dragon comes out "burning" (2569^a: "byrnande"), and the fight is on. Because the action is interrupted by an account of two different killings and of some of Beowulf's earlier feats, we do not have a typescene, but we nevertheless have all the components of the theme.

Since the theme usually precedes the hero's victory, the modern reader may feel justifiably puzzled when Beowulf dies of his wounds after having killed the dragon. I believe that the intended audience would probably have reacted quite differently. In the first place, we are warned from the start that the hero will lose his life in the struggle:

> . . .   wyrd [wæs] ungemete neah,
> se ðone gomelan   gretan scolde,
> secean sawle hord,   sundur gedælan
> lif wið lice,   no þon lange wæs
> feorh æþelinges   flæsce bewunden.
>
> (2420^b-2424^b)

[. . . fate was immeasurably near, that which must come to the old man, seek out the soul's treasure, tear the life from the body; not for long would the nobleman's life remain confined in flesh.]

And we are soon reminded of the warning when Beowulf utters a traditional battle boast "for the last time" (2511^a: "niehstan siðe") and addresses his companions likewise "for the last time" (2517^b; "hindeman siðe"). In the second place, Beowulf has to be a very old man, since he was clearly beyond childhood when he fought with Grendel, and we have learned that he subsequently served his own king as well as that king's successor for an unspecified but presumably substantial period before ascending the throne and reigning for fifty years (2208^b-2210^a); and we need not turn to formal statistics to know that old men—even

experienced early-mediaeval monster slayers—stand a poor chance of surviving an encounter with a fire-spewing dragon. In the third place—and this is the real point—Beowulf's death is a victory. Not only does he die in killing a dragon and thereby saving the kingdom from impending destruction, but he wins a treasure for his people in the process. In so doing, he becomes an ideal Germanic king—a "protector of noblemen" (*æðelinga helm*) and a "dispenser of treasure" (*sinces brytta*)—and it is accordingly no wonder that his dying words should be to thank God for the triumph which has been granted him:

> Ic ðara frætwa   frean ealles ðanc,
> wuldurcyninge,   wordum secge,
> ecum dryhtne,   þe ic her on starie,
> þæs ðe ic moste   minum leodum
> ær swyltdæge   swylc gestrynan.
>
> (2794^a-2798^b)

[To the Ruler, to the King of Glory, to the Eternal Lord, I say thanks with words for all of the treasures on which I look here, for the fact that I was permitted to acquire such things for my people before my death-day.]

The foregoing analysis has obviously been superficial, and I may well have interpreted an occasional word—for instance, the adjective *fah*, which I have usually translated as "shining," but which also means "adorned" and various other things—in a way with which other Anglo-Saxonists would disagree and which may differ from the meaning intended by the poet or from that understood by the original audience. Yet, if we accept the premise that the supporting evidence has not been fabricated from scratch, logic requires that we also accept the contention that the theme of the hero on the beach plays a detectable affective role in ***Beowulf***. If we are willing to grant this contention or even to entertain its feasibility, we should then take note of a key aspect of my analysis. Although I mentioned various analogues of ***Beowulf*** and listed the names of certain historical and legendary characters to establish the Germanic quality of the poem, and although Chapter 6 discussed occurrences of the theme in other poems for the sake of defining its nature and the circumstances under which it usually occurs, the analysis proper has relied on absolutely no specific text or person or historical event outside of the poem to inform the interpretation. In so doing, it has departed radically from the more conventional techniques illustrated in the first two chapters with the discussion of Thomas Farber's story of Mad Dog and of Langston Hughes's *I, Too, Sing America*. Of the five kinds of context mentioned at the close of Chapter 1, the historical context has been entirely disregarded, and the empirical context within the text has been repeatedly invoked, while both the empirical context outside the text and the objective context which we ourselves provide have been replaced by the oral-formulaic context in order to provide the subjective context which we ourselves bring to the interpretation.

This kind of one-sided analysis is necessarily incomplete insofar as it leaves out much information which might inform our interpretation. I should personally be much happier if I could also approach the poem as we approached *I, Too, Sing America,* but we have already seen that we can only guess at the locations where composition might have taken place and that the dates proposed vary by several hundred years. This situation further means that we have no means of ascertaining the specific social context within which composition actually took place or what specific oral or written texts constituted the literary luggage of the audience and the poet. Even the facts concerning the historical characters of the poem are too nebulous to afford us much help, so that the oral-formulaic approach provides us with the only empirically ascertainable context likely to inform our interpretation of the text.

My position does not imply that we should not consider the other contexts as well, but that we should keep in mind that they are by definition hypothetical in most respects and occasions. Even Theodore Andersson, who has formulated a particularly brilliant and useful argument in support of what he calls the "Virgilian Heritage" of *Beowulf,* must warn us that we have here a "much less clear-cut case" than with certain Mediaeval-Latin epics, partly because "there is too much evidence to ignore and too little to decide the case to everyone's satisfaction."[25] Nor am I suggesting that the tension which I have pointed out in the Grendel episode can be apprehended exclusively through the oral-formulaic approach, and Edward Irving's classic study of the poem has made it amply clear that we need not be practitioners of that approach—or of any one approach, for that matter—in order to sense the power of the narrative.[26] Professional students of Old English, for example, will know that Robinson, whose approach to the poem is anything but oral-formulaic, calls attention to certain uses of compounds which, very much like what I have called semantic gapping, "seem to achieve their effect by a simple juxtaposing of independent elements, with the reader being left to infer the relationship of the two and their composite meaning."[27]

What I am saying is that, even if we had at our disposal enough external facts to approach *Beowulf* as we do a modern text, we should nevertheless do well to give the oral-formulaic approach its due simply because an understanding of a given rhetorical system is necessary to grasp certain aspects of works composed within that system. In brief, although I emphatically do not believe that the oral-formulaic approach to *Beowulf* should be practiced to the exclusion of any other approach which may contribute to our interpretation, I concur with Creed when he admonishes us not "to ignore the traditional elements which are the very fabric of the poem."[28]

In view of my position, I must emphasize once more that the kind of analysis which I have tried on the Grendel episode does not presuppose that *Beowulf* was composed orally, although it assumes composition by a poet thoroughly versed in the traditional devices of oral-formulaic composition and composing for an intended audience likely to appreciate them. Knowing for certain that the ex-

tant text or an immediate predecessor thereof was composed orally in front of a live audience would undeniably help explain some features which may affect our interpretation in a peripheral way,[29] and knowing for certain that it was composed with pen and ink in the seclusion of a cell would explain others,[30] but I have purposefully steered clear from such concerns in order to concentrate on the main line of affective narrative. If my analysis has clarified any aspect of the episode which we have examined, we may then conclude that, under the conditions stated here, the oral-formulaic approach can provide a key to the interpretation of certain poems regardless of the circumstances under which the act of composition actually took place.

Notes

1. Magoun, "Oral-Formulaic Character," pp. 449-56.

2. Crowne, "Hero on the Beach," p. 368.

3. Lord, *Singer of Tales,* pp. 198-202.

4. Robert P. Creed, "On the Possibility of Criticizing Old English Poetry," *Texas Studies in Literature and Language* 3 (1961): 96-106.

5. *The Finnsburg Fragment* is also known as *The Battle of Finnsburh* (e.g., in the EETS edition) and *The Fight at Finnsburg.* The development of the Finn legend and its relation to *Beowulf* are discussed by Friedrich Klaeber, ed., *Beowulf and the Fight at Finnsburg* (Boston: D. C. Heath, 1941), pp. 230-38.

6. *Eiríksmál,* in E. V. Gordon, *An Introduction to Old Norse* (1927; London: Oxford University Press, 1949), pp. 130-31, with historical introduction on p. 130. One might add that, regardless of the point of view from which we approach *Beowulf,* the various references and allusions therein never appear gratuitous to those who study the text seriously. In a discussion of the "apparently irrelevant description of the mysterious coming of Scyld" at the beginning of the poem, for instance, Edward B. Irving, *Introduction to Beowulf* (Englewood Cliffs, N.J.: Prentice-Hall, 1969), has pointed out that the episode is "furnishing us here with a role model for the hero of the poem" (p. 36).

7. Klaeber, *Beowulf and the Fight at Finnsburg,* p. xviii. The analogues to the Grendel episode are discussed on pp. xiii-xxi. For a complete discussion of these analogues, along with translations of the relevant passages, see Chambers, *Beowulf: An Introduction,* esp. pp. 129-244 and 490-503.

8. Klaeber, *Beowulf and the Fight at Finnsburg,* p. xx.

9. Michael N. Nagler, "*Beowulf* in the Context of Myth," in Niles, *Old English Literature in Context,* p. 145, with analysis running through the essay, pp. 143-55. The episode occurs in *Beowulf,* 1512^b-1590^b, and *Odyssey,* IX, 216-402. In each case, the hero comes from across the sea, goes into a cave where there is a fire and which is the home of a man-eating monster whom he puts out of commission (by killing

Grendel's mother or by blinding Polyphemus) with a weapon that was already in the cave (a sword in *Beowulf* and a stake in the *Odyssey*). Nagler's essay takes its point of departure from Joseph Fontenrose, who, in his *Python: A Study in the Delphic Myth and Its Origins* (Berkeley and Los Angeles: University of California Press, 1959), calls attention to striking relationships between Grendel's mother and certain Indo-European and Near-Eastern myths (p. 526).

10. Klaeber, *Beowulf and the Fight at Finnsburg,* p. xix. Klaeber also notes that "only in the *Hrólfssaga* do we find a story at all comparable to the Grendel part placed in a historical setting comparable to that of the Anglo-Saxon epic. . . . Manifestly the relation of Boðvar to Hrolfr is not unlike that of Beowulf to Hroðgar—both deliver the king from the ravages of a terrible monster, both are his honored champions and friends, Boðvarr the son-in-law, Beowulf the 'adopted son' (946ff., 1175ff.). . . . Boðvar goes from Gautland, whose king is his brother, to the Danish court at Hleiðra; Beowulf goes from the land of the Geats, who are ruled by his uncle Hygelac, to the court of the Danish King at Heorot. Boðvarr makes his entrance at the court in a brusque, self-confident manner and at the feast quarrels with the King's men; Beowulf introduces himself with a great deal of self-reliance tempered, of course, by courtly decorum (407 ff.); also his scornful retort of II. 590ff. is matched by Boðvarr's slighting remarks, 68. 17ff. (para. 9)" (pp. xviii-xix).

11. Harry E. Kavros, "*Swefan æfter Symble:* The Feast-Sleep Theme in *Beowulf,*" *Neophilologus* 65 (1981): 120-28. Edward B. Irving, *A Reading of Beowulf* (New Haven: Yale University Press, 1968 [2d printing, 1969]), accurately notes that, "like almost everything else in the poem, Grendel is most clearly defined and outlined by contrast" (p. 87).

12. Caution requires adding here that I am by no means certain that this statement is intended to reflect the poet's opinion rather than Hrothgar's own, since it bears a close resemblance to what Ann Banfield has termed "represented speech and thought" in her *Unspeakable Sentences: Narration and Representation in the Language of Fiction* (Boston: Routledge and Kegan Paul, 1982), p. 17. Yet, Highley, "Aldor on Ofre," p. 353, calls Hrothgar's behavior "appallingly weak before Grendel."

13. This is not to say that Beowulf is incapable of thinking. As I have stated in my "*Beowulf:* A Contextual Introduction to Its Contents and Techniques," in Felix J. Oinas, ed., *Heroic Epic and Saga* (Bloomington: Indiana University Press, 1978), pp. 99-119, I incline to think that we are meant to see the hero learning how to think as the story moves along, so that he behaves "like most unthinking men of action in the first half of the poem" (p. 109) but eventually turns into "an embodiment of the ideal union of wisdom and action" (p. 111).

14. See, e.g., Winfred P. Lehmann, *Historical Linguistics: An Introduction,* 2d ed. (New York: Holt, Rinehart and Winston, 1973), p. 56.

15. The thematic paradigm, if these occurrences be indeed implementations of a theme, would include (a) some kind of good or bad warrior either experiencing or learning of some action or situation of which he disapproves, (b) a digression on the warrior, with emphasis on his destructive power, and (c) an account of the warrior taking some initial step to put an end to the objectionable action or situation.

16. Carol Jean Wolf, "Christ as Hero on the Beach," notes that "almost invariably, the journey of the hero is either the prelude or the sequel to a triumph" (p. 274).

17. The tendency for the carnage to take place soon after the occurrence of the theme of the hero on the beach is discussed in my "Oral-Formulaic Rhetoric and the Interpretation of Written Texts," in Foley, *Oral Tradition in Literature,* p. 129. See also the discussion of the *Nibelungenlied* in Chapter 9, text to note 9.

18. Molière, *Le Bourgeois Gentilhomme,* in *Théâtre Choisi de Molière,* ed. Ernest Thirion (Paris: Hachette, n.d.), has Mr. Jourdian exclaim, "Par ma foi! il y a plus de quarante ans que je dis de la prose sans que j'en susse rien, et je vous suis le plus obligé du monde de m'avoir appris cela" (II, iv, 654).

19. Joseph Bosworth and T. Northcote Toller, *An Anglo-Saxon Dictionary* (London: Oxford University Press, 1898), translate *scír-ham* as "having bright armor," but translators of the poem are by no means unanimous in this respect. E.g., Lucien Dean Pearson, trans., *Beowulf* (Bloomington: Indiana University Press, 1965), has "bright-mailed" (p. 91); Kevin Crossley-Holland, trans., *Beowulf,* has "in gleaming armour" (p. 83); E. Talbot Donaldson, trans., *Beowulf,* has "in bright armor" (p. 33); Howell D. Chickering, ed. and trans., *Beowulf: A Dual-Language Edition* (Garden City, N.Y.: Anchor Press/ Doubleday, 1977), has "bright-armored" (p. 159). Subsequent translations, however, have been somewhat more circumspect, with Stanley B. Greenfield, trans., *A Readable Beowulf* (Carbondale: Southern Illinois University Press, 1982), using the adjective "bright-clad" (p. 100), which renders the ambiguity inherent in the original, and Marijane Osborn, trans., *Beowulf* (Berkeley and Los Angeles: University of California Press, 1983), using the phrase "in the handsome birnies" (p. 69). Since the instance under discussion is the only recorded occurrence of this compound adjective, the interpretation is necessarily left in part to the individual scholar.

20. Arthur G. Brodeur, *The Art of Beowulf* (Berkeley and Los Angeles: University of California Press, 1960), pp. 88-91. Attention is also called to Adeline Courtney Bertlett, *The Larger Rhetorical Patterns in Anglo-Saxon Poetry* (New York: Columbia University Press, 1935), pp. 49-50. I have discussed the

passage in my "Point of View and Design for Terror in *Beowulf*," *Neuphilologische Mitteilungen* 63 (1962): 154-67.

21. Stanley B. Greenfield, "Grendel's Approach to Heorot: Syntax and Poetry," in Creed, *Old English Poetry*, p. 277.

22. If the adjective *fag* in the phrase "on fagne flor" (725[a]) is construed as *shining*, as is done by many translators, including Greenfield, then the presence of shining light is even more obvious than in my own translation, where I have chosen the adjective *ornate* only to avoid equivocation in respect to my documentation.

23. Antoine de Saint Exupéry, *Wind, Sand and Stars*, trans. Lewis Galantière (New York: Reynal and Hitchcock, 1939), admires the fact that "when Joseph Conrad described a typhoon, he said very little about towering waves, or darkness, or the whistling of the wind. Instead, he took his reader down into the hold of the vessel, packed with emigrant coolies, where the rolling and the pitching of the ship had ripped up and scattered their bags and bundles, burst open their boxes, and flung their humble belongings into a crazy heap . . ." (p. 77).

24. See note 9, Chapter 3, and corresponding text.

25. Theodore M. Andersson, *Early Epic Scenery* (Ithaca, N.Y.: Cornell University Press, 1976), p. 145.

26. Irving, *A Reading of Beowulf*, has analyzed the Grendel episode as one would the product of written rhetoric and produced a superbly sensitive account of its impact (esp. pp. 94-128).

27. Robinson, *Beowulf*, p. 14.

28. Creed, "On the Possibility of Criticizing Old English Poetry," p. 106.

29. E.g., the fact that *Beowulf*, 1999[a]-2183[a], is devoted to a recapitulation of the events of the preceding 1,998 lines would be explained if we assumed oral composition and either (a) the late arrival of a member of the audience for whom the poet would want to sum up the preceding narrative or (b) the interruption of the narrative—which is very long for a one-shot performance, since it takes three and one-half hours to read aloud and would accordingly earn a single performer some sort of laryngitis—and its resumption the next day or a few hours later, thus requiring the kind of summary of previous events to which television audiences are accustomed in programs which are carried on from one day to the next.

30. E.g., the fact that critics have noted possible verbal correspondences between the poem and Virgil's *Aeneid* (see, e.g., Andersson's *Early Epic Scenery*, pp. 146-56) would be explained if we assumed a poet writing in a cell with a copy of Virgil right at hand, or at least with school training in classical Latin.

Stephen S. Evans (essay date 1997)

SOURCE: "The Dating of *Beowulf*," in *The Heroic Poetry of Dark-Age Britain: An Introduction to Its Dating, Composition, and Use as a Historical Source*, University Press of America, Inc., 1997, pp. 41-63.

[*In the following essay, Evans examines the debate concerning the date of composition of* Beowulf *and argues that an oral version (probably composed between 685 and 725) of the poem preceded the earliest written version.*]

It is with no little trepidation that the present study enters the battle that has raged, and continues to rage, over the dating of *Beowulf*. It is clear that a wide array of knowledge and expertise from a variety of disciplines has been brought to bear on the question at hand. That the question remains a subject of often intense debate certainly is not attributable to any lack of interest, nor to a dearth of publications. To begin this particular contribution to the long-running debate,[1] it is best to start with the manuscript itself.

Beowulf is found in the Nowell Codex,[2] the second of two codices that comprise BL MS. Cotton Vitellius A.XV. The Nowell Codex, on folios 94-209 of the manuscript, contains five works in Old English: a homily on St. Christopher (Folios 94-98r), *Wonders of the East* (98v-106), a "letter" from Alexander the Great to Aristotle (107-131), *Beowulf* (132-201), and *Judith* (202-209). The beginning of *Christopher* and a majority of *Judith* already was lost by 1563, when the manuscript came into Lawrence Nowell's possession, for whom the codex is named. A few decades later, it became part of Sir Robert Cotton's library. Shortly before moving to the British Museum in 1753, the codex was damaged during the Cottonian Library fire in 1731, with the tops and outer parts of many of the vellum folios being burnt, along with much of the physical evidence regarding the bindings, and the formatting and composition of the quires. In 1786-87, the two Thorkelin transcripts of the poem were made. Transcript A was made by a copyist who knew no Old English and who was employed by Thorkelin, while Transcript B was made by Thorkelin himself. In a few instances, because of the continued deterioration of the original text that occured after the 1731 fire, these transcripts can provide a clearer reading than that found in the original manuscript.

The first question that needs to be asked is: What can the palaeography of the codex itself tell us about the poem's dating and origins? Neil R. Ker has dated the Nowell Codex to somewhere within the half century surrounding the year 1000 (975 × 1025).[3] Beyond the fact that the manuscript had been in a fire, and that Beowulf's Geatish lord Hygelac is indeed the Chlochilaichus mentioned by Gregory of Tours as having died in a raid against the Frisians in 521, Ker's dating of the extant manuscript is about the only statement on this issue upon which all scholars can agree. Given this state of affairs, it should come as no surprise that recent scholars have continued to hold widely divergent views and reach diametrically opposing conclusions concerning the manuscript's codicology. Of immediate note are the opposing views and conclusions held by Leonard Boyle and Kevin Kiernan.[4]

Using Ker's dating scheme as a foundation, Kiernan has proposed a historical argument to support his claim that *Beowulf* was a product of Cnut's reign in England, and subsequently assigned a *terminus post quem* for the poem at 1016. Kiernan claimed that, due to the Danish genealogy found in the poem's opening lines, the copying of the poem would have been possible only after 1016, "when the genealogical panegyric was a compliment, rather than an insult, to the reigning king".[5] To bolster this argument, he proposed an unusual interpretation of the codicological data contained in the manuscript. Essentially, Kiernan declared that the poem in its present form is actually a composite that had been joined together by a new transitional section (folios 171-178 in Kiernan = 174-181 BL foliation). This transitional section, which includes the poem's section known as "Beowulf's Homecoming" (1888-2199), was composed by two scribes in an effort to join together two other poems they had in their possession: one about Beowulf's fights against Grendel and his mother, and another whose story centered on the battle between the Dragon and an aged Beowulf. According to Kiernan, Scribe B returned to the text at some later date, and washed down and subsequently composed the lines found on folio 179 (BL 182) in a further effort to smooth the transition between the newer segment and the final poem. This and evidence of other scribal revisions and emendations led Kiernan to conclude that the "eleventh gathering, containing Beowulf's homecoming, is palaeographically and codicologically as well as textually transitional".[6] In fact, folio 179, regarded by Kiernan as a palimpsest, and the B scribe's later emendations throughout the text led him to advance the possibility that:

> the *Beowulf* manuscript amounts to an unfinished draft of the poem. As incredible as an extant draft of *Beowulf* may seem to some readers, there is considerable palaeographical and codicological support for the view that the *Beowulf* manuscript in fact preserves for us the last formative stages in the creation of an epic.[7]

For Kiernan, the date of the poem's composition—in the form that is contained in the extant text—and the date of the poem's manuscript are one and the same; the sole manuscript represents the unfinished draft of, quite literally, an epic in the making.

Kiernan's arguments can be contested on several palaeographical and codicological grounds.[8] First, Kiernan's interpretation of the codicological evidence has been countered forcefully and effectively by Leonard Boyle. In his interpretation of the text, Boyle agreed that the A and B scribes did collaborate, but only to the extent of deciding how much of a "copy-text" each would be responsible for copying. According to Boyle, this copy-text contained the same five works in the same sequence as they now are found in the Nowell Codex, and was written in the same format—uniform quires of eight folios each; text frames ruled for twenty lines on each page—as that first selected by both scribes. This was indeed the format used by both scribes during their initial copyings, which were *Beowulf's* beginning quires for Scribe A and *Judith* for Scribe B.[9]

Though several scribal miscalculations on their part threw them "off course" during the course of their copying, both scribes knew exactly the type and amount of modifications that they would be required to make in their textual format in order to get them back in step with the text which lay before them in their "copy-quires".[10] Contrary to Kiernan's claims, the cumulative evidence and reasoning found in Boyle's article make it clear that both scribes were copying a manuscript that contained a version of *Beowulf* exactly like the one that is contained in the Nowell Codex, with the poem beginning on the seventh folio of the fifth quire—a quire of normal four-sheet length—in both the extant manuscript and its antecedent copy.[11] Further, Kiernan's fundamental argument that folio 179 (182) represents a palimpsest, whose purpose was to join together two disparate tales, has been shown to be the least likely of several explanations that would serve to explain the poor condition of that particular folio.[12]

Katherine O'Brien O'Keefe also has objected to Kiernan's findings and methodology, and has dismissed Kiernan's claim that *Beowulf* is a composite poem compiled during Cnut's reign,[13] having found that the amount and style of pointing found in the Nowell Codex is inconsistent with eleventh-century practices. Instead, she discovered that the pointing practices used by both Scribes A and B are consistent with those found in works of the third quarter of the tenth century.[14] These tenth-century practices extend to Quire 11 of the Nowell Codex, the very same quire that constituted the key section of the poem for Kiernan's entire dating scheme. Consequently, she concluded that:

> the pointing of the manuscript does not support Kiernan's contentions either that the manuscript represents work done in the latter part of the first quarter of the eleventh century or that the work of the eleventh quire and the so-called palimpsest of folio 179 (fol. 182) represent contemporary editing. The evidence of the pointing simply cannot sustain such a hypothesis.[15]

More importantly, the findings of Ashley Crandell Amos in her *Linguistic Means of Determining the Dates of Old English Literary Texts* are especially damaging, not only to Kiernan, but to all those scholars who had assigned the poem's composition to either the tenth or eleventh centuries. In that study, Amos conducted an extensive analysis and evaluation of the various linguistic tests that had been developed by Lichenheld, Morsbach, Sarazin, Richter, and others. Because Amos believed that linguistic tests should be applied in the same objective, mechanical manner as in the natural sciences,[16] it is not surprising that her research led her to conclude that "most of the linguistic tests . . . are so limited by qualifications that they do not provide clear, unambiguous, objective evidence with respect to date".[17] However, even given the parameters of her overly-stringent methodology, Amos declared that:

> a poet's metrical practice with respect to alliteration of palatal and velar g is probably a valid chronological criterion, as long as it is recognized that metrical practice is in part a function of personal poetic style, and

that there is no *a priori* reason that a late poet might not adopt an earlier, traditional style.[18]

Keeping in mind the possibility that a late poet might adopt an earlier style, it is nonetheless true that alliteration of palatal and velar g suffers a marked decline as the period progresses, a decline that is evidenced in the poems to which dates readily can be assigned, such as *Maldon* and *Brunanburh*. Thus, while it is true in theory that later poets were free to follow an earlier style that alliterated palatal and velar g, it seems clear that they did not avail themselves of this option in practice. That later poets would have avoided earlier practices in this regard is to be expected, given the importance of alliterative techniques in Anglo-Saxon poetry. As Amos explains, "it is difficult to imagine a late poet depending for functional alliteration on sounds that no longer alliterated in most of his hearers ears".[19] Consequently, the fact remains that it is likely that poems in which velar and palatal g alliterate are older than poems in which they do not, a change that is seen in poems of the tenth century and later.[20] Using this criterion, one can claim that, on the basis of the consistent alliteration of velar and palatal g in *Beowulf*, the poem can be placed with some confidence prior to the beginning of the tenth century. Thus, based on these patterns of alliteration, dating schemes that had assigned the poem's composition to either the tenth or eleventh century are not likely to be valid.

Despite some problems that it shares with other linguistic tests, also important to the discussion at hand is the contention that a useful dating criterion would be where the contraction in words with original hiatus between vowels, or hiatus caused by loss of intervocalic h, j, or w affects the number of syllables in a verse, especially those verses that have only three syllables without the decontracted form of the word assumed to have contracted.[21] Though in fact only the loss of intervocalic h should be seen as an valid chronological indicator,[22] this remains a fundamental point for the dating of *Beowulf* because:

> It has been deemed possible to infer the presence of archaic forms in the text on the basis of metrical considerations, in that certain lines appear not to scan unless they are assumed to have contained older, uncontracted spellings. Theoretically, for example, if the poem was composed before loss of intervocalic h in Old English, a sound-change datable to around the end of the seventh century, the diphthongs produced by the resulting contractions of the affected forms in the course of transmission would require disyllabic scansion. Such disyllabic diphthongs would thus not necessarily be explained by the use of the diction of the Old English poetic tradition. As there does appear to be a higher proportion of such disyllabic diphthongs in *Beowulf* than in other Old English verse, we might have a hint of evidence pointing to early composition, perhaps even within a generation or two of the end of the seventh century.[23]

However, this test is not without its problems,[24] the most notable of which is the claim that "'uncontracted' forms like *heahan* and *doan* were re-formed in late Old English by analogy to the standard inflectional systems, so an 'uncontracted' form could as easily be late as early".[25] This point, first advanced by Randolph Quirk over four decades ago,[26] recently has met with strenuous opposition by Fulk and others.[27] Most damaging to the case for late analogical re-formation is the regularity of spelling of these forms. In other words, to adhere to the assumption that "contractions could be reformed a century or a century and a half later in ways that exactly recapitulate the pre-history of *þeon, fleon, teon, feon,* and *slean* is less probable than to assume that these disyllabic forms are early".[28]

Even if Quirk's contention were valid, since *Beowulf* can be shown to be early on other grounds, then its higher degree of uncontracted forms—a characteristic it shares only with other early texts such as *Guthlac A*—must be seen as retained archaisms and therefore can be attributed directly to its early composition, and not to any late analogical re-formation. At the very least, one could plead that the poem's higher proportion of disyllabic diphthongs should "count for something in placing *Beowulf* earlier than most other poems".[29]

Another piece of evidence clearly demonstrates *Beowulf* to be the earliest of the longer Old English poems. This evidence is the *Beowulf* poet's utter and unequivocal adherence to Kaluza's law,[30] in sharp contrast to all other Old English poems. Briefly, Kaluza's law states that "some metrical positions resolution is governed in part by etymological considerations" that are based on a phonological distinction between long and short inflectional endings in Proto-Germanic.[31] Fulk's analysis of the longer Anglo-Saxon poems in regard to their adherence to Kaluza's law led him to conclude that:

> *Beowulf* is unique in respect to the great ease and regularity of the poet's ability to distinguish long and short endings. The facts about Kaluza's law in *Beowulf* are impressive, as Amos remarks (p.99): out of 108 unambiguous instances there are just 2 exceptions. Such a proportion is unquestionably outside the range of coincidence, and the exceptions are few enough that they are within the statistical range of being due possibly to scribal corruption. No other poem approaches *Beowulf* in this regard.[32]

In fact, the probable explanation as to why later poets avoided using verses of the type in question is that "the metrical value of the vocalic endings was no longer obvious when they were composed"; this in stark contrast to *Beowulf*, whose poet undoubtedly was aware of the distinction in vowel quantities.[33] The difference between *Beowulf* and the other poems in respect to Kaluza's law, both in the regularity with which it is applied and in the frequency of relevant verse types "is so profound that it can hardly be dissociated from the elimination of the phonological distinction between long and short vocalic endings", which would mean that "*Beowulf*, at least, must have been composed before the shortening of the long endings".[34] In other words, the argument's rationale states that:

Observance of Kaluza's law . . . depends upon the maintainence of the original distinctions in vowel quantities. The fidelity of *Beowulf* to the law demonstrates that the poem can only have been composed before the quantitative distinction was lost. The law thus provides a fairly precise *terminus ad quem* for the dating of the poem.[35]

Thus, if *Beowulf* was composed somewhere south of the Humber River—that is, in Mercia or one of the Anglo-Saxon kingdoms in southern England—it could have been composed as late as the first quarter of the eighth century; if composed in the north, its *terminus ad quem* could be a century later. In sum, "*Beowulf* almost certainly was not composed after ca.725 if Mercian in origin, or after ca.825 if Northumbrian".[36] Since it is evident that a Mercian origin is more likely than a Northumbrian one,[37] based upon the poet's use of *nemne* as well as other indicators, it is likely that *Beowulf* was composed prior to ca.725.

Two other arguments based on the text's orthography also serve to confirm the existence of a written exemplar at a date that is far earlier than that of *Beowulf's* extant manuscript. The first of these was advanced long ago by Klaeber in his edition of *Beowulf*. Essentially, Klaeber made a claim for a written exemplar for the poem, whose existence he dated ca.750, based on the orthographic evidence provided by various stray language forms—especially those in an East Anglian dialect—that are found scattered throughout *Beowulf,* a poem written primarily in West Saxon.[38] According to Klaeber, the presence of these stray language forms in the extant manuscript was the result of a long process of copying and recopying a text whose original text had been written in an East Anglian dialect. During this long process of transmission, certain forms were updated while others, whether by simple omission or due to metrical considerations, were not. It was the existence of this medley of spellings in the text that led Klaeber to declare that "the significant coexistence in the manuscript of different forms of one and the same word, without any inherent principle of distribution being recognizable, points plainly to a checkered history of the written text".[39]

However, Klaeber's hypothesis has come under attack recently, notably by Kiernan and J.F. Tuso, who claimed that the various language forms in *Beowulf* were the result of a traditional, conservative poetical diction that employed older language forms with little regard for their specific dialect.[40] While these arguments have managed to weaken Klaeber's claim for an early East Anglian genesis for the poem, they have by no means discredited the hypothesis entirely. In fact, Klaeber's claim has been taken up recently by Sam Newton in a wide-ranging and persuasive work.[41]

A second argument, formulated by C.L. Wrenn, addressed the evident scribal confusion of d for ð (*eth*) and d for þ (*thorn*). Wrenn argued that a number of textual corruptions could be explained as scribal in the process of modernizing a text which used d for sounds that would later be represented by ð or þ.[42] Prior to the eighth century, ð evi-

dently could be employed either as a voiced spirant or as a stop.[43] Based on this evidence, Wrenn concluded that a written exemplar of *Beowulf* must have existed already by the late eighth century, when ð was introduced as a letter.[44] While some of these textual corruptions might be explained by simple mechanical error—a scribe forgetting to cross an *eth*—given the number of instances that this occurs in our text, it seems unlikely that this explanation is entirely satisfactory. In any event, it is almost certain that scribal confusion over d and ð or þ is evidenced at 1.1278 in the poem (which has þeod for deod/dead), a confusion that cannot be attributed to mechanical error (since a *thorn,* which is not crossed, is involved).[45] If this view is correct, Wrenn's argument for an eighth-century exemplar for the *Beowulf* manuscript can be seen to be valid. In fact, Wrenn appears to have been overly cautious in his dating for the introduction for the letter ð. Recent scholarship on the Epinal Glossary has dated this development much earlier than Wrenn had supposed, perhaps even to the seventh century.[46]

In any event, Wrenn's call for an eighth-century exemplar for *Beowulf* has been bolstered recently by Anita Riedinger, who has advanced a compelling argument for an eighth-century date for a written copy of *Beowulf.* In that article,[47] Riedinger sets forth new evidence that demonstrates unequivocally that the author of *Andreas* had before him a copy of *Beowulf* from which he borrowed, often and methodically, during the course of writing *Andreas*. She concludes that it was this methodical, and often verbatim, borrowing of formulaic expressions from *Beowulf* on the part of the *Andreas*-poet that accounts for the striking verbal similarities of the two poems, and not literary convention or a shared oral-formulaic tradition.[48] In fact, Riedinger concluded that "the formulaic relationship between *Beowulf* and *Andreas* is stunning", stating that "I believe that the later poet needed no other technique of composition here than a *Beowulf*-manuscript at his elbow (with his Latin source nearby) and that this explains the very special relationship that scholars long believed existed between these two poems alone".[49]

Scholars have assigned dates to *Andreas'* composition that range from the late-eighth to the late-ninth century, with most dating schemes centering on the early to mid-ninth century.[50] Thus, based on Riedinger's analysis, a written copy of *Beowulf* can be placed in the early ninth century at the latest, or even somewhere in the eighth.

Finally, while not offering absolute and irrefutable proof on their own, there are a few other arguments, uniformly pointing to an early date for the composition of *Beowulf,* that reinforce the conclusions provided by the other types of data. In particular, one argument shows that, in sharp contrast to Anglo-Saxon poems of the tenth century—most notably *Brunanburh* and *Maldon*—there is a marked absence of identifiable Scandinavian loan-words from Viking-Age Britain in *Beowulf.*[51] It is thus unlikely that the material used by the *Beowulf* poet was derived from information obtained by Anglo-Saxon interaction with Vikings of this period. This point is reinforced further by the forms of the names of Scandinavian dynastic figures that are found in *Beowulf*, which, as they stand in the poem, "although etymologically related to their later Northern equivalents, none of these names show any evidence for any Scandinavian sound changes."[52] This point is reinforced yet again by the accuracy with which *Beowulf* presents the names of its Scandinavian dynastic figures, again in sharp contrast to the inept transposition of Scandinavian names found in the *Anglo-Saxon Chronicle*.[53] When taken together, these various indications uniformly suggest that *Beowulf's* composition is unlikely to have been as late as the first part of the ninth century, and was in fact probably earlier.

The initial decades of the eighth century then, or perhaps even a little earlier, is the approximate limit to which most of the orthographic and linguistic evidence of the extant text can carry the argument for a written exemplar. This does not mean that a written version of *Beowulf* could not have existed earlier than the eighth century. Theoretically, there is nothing that would preclude, at least in terms of Anglo-Saxon orthography, a written form for the poem in the seventh century. As Dumville has noted, the Old English language evidently had developed an efficient orthography no later than the 670's, which is the date of the earliest charters and the first works of Aldhelm.[54] Still, it is unlikely that a written copy of *Beowulf* existed prior to c.685, a *terminus a quo* for the composition of *Beowulf* and the other longer poems that is based upon the higher levels of non-contraction that is evidenced in the early glossaries.[55] In sum, while Anglo-Saxon orthography would permit the existence of a copy of *Beowulf* as early as c.670, the orthography of the extant manuscript itself would call for a written exemplar for the poem that is anywhere within the 685-725 period.[56]

An oral form of the poem certainly preceded this 685-725 period, the period in which the poem assumed its written form. As was related in Chapter 3, because of its oral-formulaic nature, the poem could have been the product of a process that might have stretched over several centuries. However, there are several arguments that can be used to establish a more precise period in which the poem and/or its component parts were orally composed. The earliest *terminus a quo* for the poem is based on the one historical fact in the poem upon which scholars can agree: the death of Hygelac, Beowulf's Geatish lord, during a raid against the Frisians. Mentioned in the poem, this event is corroborated by Gregory of Tours in his *Historia Francorum*[57], who dated the death of Chlochilaichus (the Latin form of Hygelac) to around 521. In fact, Gregory's corroboration of this event constitutes our only indisputable external evidence for the poem's composition.

Moreover, the internal evidence of the poem also leads one to believe that the poet assumed a ready knowledge and easy familiarity on the part of his audience of various sixth-century Scandinavian heroes, a knowledge and familiarity that provides "solid internal evidence for placing the poem at a time when these stories were still vivid in the memory of the early Angles and Saxons".[58] Further, it seems that the poet was familiar with pagan ship burials and other funeral practices, and with the material culture of both early Anglo-Saxon England and of Sweden during the seventh century. In fact, the archaeological evidence of Sutton Hoo's grave goods and artifacts—addressed below in Chapter 7—shows a remarkable resemblance to the material goods—most notably to weapons and armor—that *Beowulf* describes in great detail.

While it is evident that some sections of *Beowulf* clearly portray pagan Anglo-Saxon and Scandinavian society, it is equally clear that the poem's "author" was a Christian, both by his references to events in the Bible and by his use of Latin terms that were probably adopted after the coming of Christianity to Britain.[59] Thus, the poem as we have it must be later than 597, the date of Augustine's mission to the island. Still, the degree to which Christianity actually is in evidence in *Beowulf* has been a matter of no little debate. While the arguments of this debate are found elsewhere,[60] the persuasive arguments advanced by William Whallon[61] are of special relevance at this point. Whallon has shown that the knowledge of Christianity exhibited in the poem is rudimentary at best, stating that "the epic knows little of Christianity besides two stories from the first nine chapters of Genesis".[62] Whallon also has shown that the words and phrases for God and the Devil in *Beowulf* need not imply a Christian background for the poem, but could be explained just as easily as deriving from traditional Germanic poetic vocabulary. In fact, "the words *fæder, alwalda,* and *meotod* are as biblical as *pater, omnipotens,* and *fatum* are in the *Aeneid,* and *Beowulf* is to this extent neither Christian nor un-Christian but pre-Christian".[63] From this it should be clear that the *Beowulf* poet is not writing allegory; Beowulf the Hero is not to be equated with Christ the Savior, nor is Hrothgar's "sermon" to Beowulf to be regarded as some type of Germanic accolade of all things Christian. Quite simply, Christianity as a subject was not high on the list of topics that the poet thought needed to be covered. Instead, the main themes and topics presented in *Beowulf* are those associated with heroic society. Thus, it seems reasonable to conclude that:

> The narrator and the important heroes in *Beowulf* speak as if they were superficially Christian. Within the confines of the poem itself, however, the Christianity appears rather elementary in quality; scriptual references are limited to perhaps two stories from Genesis, while references to theology or dogma are virtually impossible to identify with an appreciable degree of confidence. Germanic heroic ideals of conduct control the action of the poem; Christian piety is incidental to it. Without the various pious comments and Christian allusions in the poem, *Beowulf* would remain our finest Germanic poem.[64]

It is likely that *Beowulf,* whose subject matter is centered on a heroic pre-Christian society, acquired whatever Christian trappings it possesses during its oral stage of existence. This acquisition of Christian themes and concepts would have occurred at some point after the conversion of the Anglo-Saxons to the new religion. It was during this specific period that the originally pagan poem incorporated Christian material during the process of being sung by one or more converted oral poets.[65] As a consequence, over the course of several generations, this Christian material became incorporated into the poem with varying degrees of intensity and success, depending on the particular portion of the narrative in question. This uneven treatment of Christian material is evident to anyone familiar with the poem. A likely explanation for this uneven incorporation, and for the poem's other discrepencies as well, can be found in the proposal that *Beowulf* represents a "song amalgam", a joining together of two or more originally distinct songs.[66]

Once joined, these separate tales—most notably the poem's stories regarding the fights at Finnsburg and at Ravenswood[67]—would have retained their usefulness to an oral poet as distinct units of presentation that could be recited before an audience. In any case, because of the poem's general unity, as well as the essentially uniform densities of formulas and formulaic expressions found in the various parts of the poem, it seems likely that this process of amalgamation already had been completed prior to the poem being written down. Thus, the poem in its present form must be seen as a product of an oral, rather than a written tradition, and "the spectre of a 'monkish scribe' tampering with a pre-Christian text, altering a word here and a line there in order to make the heathen king of the Danes sound like a Christian Sunday-School teacher, may be exorcised".[68]

From the above discussion, it is apparent that the dating of *Beowulf* presents no easy task. Still, given the evidence presented, I would propose that some sections of the poem—the ones about Finnsburg and Ravenswood, for example—had their genesis in oral form sometime during the sixth century. This contention is supported by three arguments: first, Gregory's corroboration of Hygelac's death in Frisia; second, by the audience's knowledge of sixth-century Scandinavian heroes; and third, by the poet's familiarity with sixth-century funerary practices and material culture of both the Anglo-Saxons and the Scandinavians.

Beowulf—though more likely its component parts—underwent an extensive modification at the hands of converted oral poets as they attempted to make the poem better suited for a Christian audience. This incremental process of modification and alteration of the pagan poem must have occurred somewhere during the period ca.625x700, and eventually produced the version of *Beowulf* that, with few exceptions, is found in the manuscript. I would propose also that the incorporation of the poem's Christian material occurred during the earlier portion of this period, based upon a degree of sophistication regarding the new religion that only can be described as rudimentary. Further, I would propose that the incorporation of this material occurred at some point before the poem's several component parts were woven into an epic, based on the poem's uneven handling of Christian themes and concepts. This too indicates that the pagan poem's modification and alteration had been effected during the earlier portion of this 625-700 period. It also seems evident that the process of literary amalgamation, which joined together the once-independent component poems comprising the epic, occurred during the latter part of the period, and produced to a great degree the poem as we have it today. However, in light of the uniform densities of formulas and formulaic expressions throughout the epic's various parts, it appears that the amalgamation process essentially was complete before the oral poem was first written down.

The above description of the inception and subsequent evolution of the oral poem, as well as the proposed period in which this process occurred, is attractive for several reasons. First, the 625-700 period is late enough to have allowed sufficient time for Christianity to have taken hold among the Germanic peoples who lived on the island, yet early enough to have allowed for the accurate transmission of sixth-century heroes, societal values, and material culture. Such a time period also is reflected in the elementary quality of the poem's Christianity, and would allow several generations of oral poets enough time to mold *Beowulf* into some semblance of a Christian poem. Further, the proposed dating is late enough to allow for a period spanning several generations in which oral poets would have woven the varied fabrics of the disparate poems into an epic tapestry, though early enough to ensure that any flaws in its manufacture still would be present when eventually it was written down.

Whether the poem existed in a written form prior to the 685x725 period probably will never be resolved to anyone's total satisfaction. Indeed, it might be possible that the present form of the *Beowulf* poem-the epic as it is found in the extant manuscript—never existed until the oral poem was set down in writing.[69] One can state only that ca.685x725 is the earliest date that can be assigned to a written exemplar for the poem, based on the available orthographic and linguistic evidence. This period is attractive for well-known historical and literary reasons that have been presented many times before.[70] For my part, I see no reason for assuming that the poem did not achieve a written form during this 685-725 period, though the location where the poem actually was written down must remain unknown. While such a proposition cannot be verified beyond doubt, it accords well with the arguments and data that have been presented. Certainly, there is nothing that would prohibit this possibility.

In any case, it seems likely that the lines of *Beowulf* known as the "Offa Digression" (1931-62) were inserted into the poem during the reign of Offa of Mercia (757-96) as an obvious compliment to that powerful king and warlord.[71] It is impossible to determine whether this interpolation occurred when the text first was committed to writing or whether these lines were added during the course of later copyings. In this regard, I would conclude that *Hetware* and *Hugas,* the names of two early continental tribes mentioned in **Beowulf,** are written interpolations inserted at a late stage of the manuscript's history. In no way should these terms lead one to place the poem's composition within the tenth century, with a *terminus a quo* of ca.923, as Walter Goffart has done.[72] The same can be said for arguments regarding the term *merewioingas*.[73] They are interpolations and nothing more, and as such are useful only in providing some insight into the poem's various stages of textual history.[74] These interpolations show that the epic was the subject of continued modifications—the extent of which will never be known—even after it had achieved a written form.

Notes

1. For a useful history and overview of the debate, see Colin Chase, "Opinions on the Date of *Beowulf,* 1815-1980", in *The Dating of Beowulf,* edited by Colin Chase (Toronto: University of Toronto Press, 1981), pp.3-8. For a summary of the dates that have been advanced for *Beowulf,* see pp.186-7 (fn.12) in Alain Renoir's *A Key to Old Poems: The Oral-Formulaic Approach to the Interpretation of West-Germanic Verse.* (University Park: Pennsylvania State University Press, 1988). The amount of scholarship that has been generated and subsequently applied to almost every conceivable aspect of *Beowulf,* and especially to the question at hand, is enormous. See Douglas D. Short (ed.), *Beowulf Scholarship: An Annotated Bibliography,* Vol.193 of the Garland Reference Library of the Humanities (New York: Garland Publishing, 1980) or Robert J. Hasenfratz (ed.), *"Beowulf" Scholarship: An Annotated Bibliography, 1979-1990,* Garland Medieval Bibliographies, Vol.14. (New York and London: Garland Publishing, 1993). The sheer volume and scope of this scholarship is overwhelming, and was itself a key factor in establishing the methodology allowing Chapters 4, 5, and 6 to sequence their arguments.

2. The description in the text is based on the one in Leonard E. Boyle's "The Nowell Codex and the Poem of *Beowulf*", in *The Dating of Beowulf,* edited by Colin Chase (Toronto: University of Toronto Press, 1981), p.23. For the study's purposes, Boyle's description is sufficient. For a thorough investigation of BL MS. Cotton Vitellius A.XV, see Kevin Kiernan, *Beowulf and the Beowulf Manuscript* (New Brunswick, N.J.: Rutgers University Press, 1981). See also J. Gerritsen's "British Library Cotton Vitellius A.xv—A Supplementary Description", *English Studies* 69 (1988), pp.293-302 or his "Have with you to Lexington! The *Beowulf* Manuscript and *Beowulf*", in *In Other Words: Transcultural Studies in Philology, Translation, and Lexicography Presented to Prof. Dr. H.H. Meier on the Occasion of his Sixty-fifth Birthday,* (Dordrecht: Foris, 1989), edited by J. Lachlan Mackenzie and Richard Todd, pp.15-34. For the Nowell Codex, see Kemp Malone's *The Nowell Codex: British Museum Cotton Vitellius A.XV. Second Manuscript.* Early English Manuscripts in Facsimile, no.12 (Copenhagen: Rosenkilde and Bagger, 1963).

Unless otherwise stated, all folio numbers in this chapter follow the official numbering of the British Library. The reader should be aware that Kiernan and Boyle use different numbering systems for the foliations of the Beowulf manuscript. Kiernan uses the older numbering found in the manuscript itself and the one employed in both the Zupitza facsimile (EETS 77, 1882) and Klaeber's edition of the poem. Boyle prefers the 1884 numbering accepted as official by the British Library and found in Kemp Malone's facsimile edition (EEMF 12, 1963). The difference results in Boyle's numbers being three more than the reference numbers of Kiernan's.

3. Neil R. Ker, *Catalogue of Manuscripts Containing Anglo-Saxon* (Oxford: Oxford University Press, 1957), MS. no.216. Ker (p.281) dates the manuscript as 's.X/XI, equivalent to 975-1025 (i.e. to within 25 years on either side of 1000).

4. See Kiernan, *Beowulf Manuscript,* especially pp.65-169 and 219-43, and his summary article "The Eleventh-Century Origin of *Beowulf* and the *Beowulf* Manuscript", pp.9-21 in *The Dating of Beowulf,* edited by Colin Chase (Toronto: University of Toronto Press, 1981). In the latter book, see also Boyle's "The Nowell Codex and the Poem of *Beowulf*", pp.23-32. For a quick summary of both sets of arguments, see O'Brien O'Keefe's *Visible Song: Transitional Literacy in Old English Verse,* Cambridge Studies in Anglo-Saxon England, Vol.4 (Cambridge: Cambridge University Press, 1990), at pp.172-74.

5. Kiernan, "Eleventh-Century Origin", p.10.

6. Kiernan, *Beowulf Manuscript,* p.258. The argument is detailed on pp.249-58 and again at pp.271-2.

7. Kiernan, "Eleventh-Century Origin", p.14. This possibility seems incredible. It is impossible to believe that the poem's sole extant manuscript is also its interim rough draft. Kiernan has overstated the capabilities of the two scribes, especially in regard to the poetic sensitivity and linguistic abilities that he attributes to the second one.

In "Anglo-Saxon Scribes and Old English Verse", *Speculum* 67 (1992), pp.805-28, Douglas Moffat saw that too great an emphasis was being placed on the abilities of Anglo-Saxon scribes by scholars such as Eric Stanley, who seemed "willing to equate facility with the language of the exemplar with probable accuracy as a copyist", a position that he thought was not entirely tenable (p.809). Moffat also took aim at Kiernan's unfounded assumptions, declaring (*ibid*) that "far more radical than Stanley in his deference to scribal ability is Kevin Kiernan". Quite simply, such deference to scribal abilities is likely to prove unfounded.

Ironically, these overly optimistic views on scribal ability were, in part, in reaction to the earlier, widely-held scholarly opinion that saw these scribes as incompetent dolts who uniformly mangled the manuscripts that lay before them. For more on this, see Moffat's article (*op.cit.*), pp.806-07.

8. Kiernan's conclusions came under attack almost at once by Boyle in "Nowell Codex". For other opposition, see the reviews by J.D. Niles and Ashley Crandell Amos of *Beowulf and the Beowulf Manuscript*, found in *Speculum* 58 (1983), pp.76-77, and *Review* 4 (1982), pp.335-45 respectively, O'Brien O'Keefe's *Visible Song*, pp.173-74, and Sam Newton's *The Origins of Beowulf and the Pre-Viking Kingdom of East Anglia* (Cambridge, England: D.S. Brewer, 1993), pp.3-5.

Regarding Kiernan's historical argument (*Beowulf Manuscript*, pp.18-23), little need be said here except that West Saxon kings also employed some of the same warriors and kings listed in the poem's opening lines (1-63) as a part of their genealogy since the late ninth century. On this point, see Alexander C. Murray, "*Beowulf*, the Danish Invasions, and Royal Genealogy" and Roberta Frank, "Skaldic Verse and the Date of *Beowulf*" in *The Dating of Beowulf*, edited by Colin Chase (Toronto: University of Toronto Press, 1981), pp.103-05 and 128-29. In essence, it can be argued that the poem's genealogy would have been "panegyric" to either West Saxon or Danish kings. Further, I would credit the scribes with enough common sense to be able to distinguish the difference between the migration-era Danes whom the poem portrayed, and the contemporary Danes who were busy ravaging the countryside.

9. Boyle, "Nowell Codex", p.27.

10. *Ibid*, pp.27-29. Especially useful is his schematic on p.29 showing the relationship between the "Copy-Beowulf" and the "Nowell-Beowulf". Boyle's chart on p.24 clearly presents his view of the divisions and organization of the entire codex. For the differences between Kiernan's and Boyle's views of quire organization, see Newton, *The Origins of Beowulf*, pp.3-4.

11. Despite Kiernan's claims, Quire 5 should be seen as a normal four-sheet quire. As Newton has noted (*ibid*, pp.4-5), the ruling of this quire differed from that of both the preceeding and following folios, reinforcing the impression that it was a normal four-sheet quire. The same conclusion has been reached by: Boyle ("Nowell Codex", p.23); R.D. Fulk ("Dating *Beowulf* to the Viking Age", *Philological Quarterly,* 61 (1982), pp.352-3); and Gerritsen ("Have with you to Lexington!", pp.15-16).

12. See Newton, *ibid* (pp.8-9) and the references cited.

13. Like Kiernan, O'Brien O'Keefe has been accused of having too high a regard for the abilities of Anglo-Saxon scribes, especially in regard to their alleged abilities in the Anglo-Saxon oral poetic tradition. For more on the abilities of these scribes, see Moffat, "Anglo-Saxon Scribes", pp.810-14.

14. In *Visible Song,* O'Brien O'Keefe concluded that "it is quite unlikely that the pointing in *Beowulf* represents eleventh-century practice or was added by the scribes who copied this work" (p.174). Also, she equated the pointing practice evidenced by *Beowulf* with that found in *Solomon and Saturn*, which Ker has dated s.xmed (p.178), while noting that it also likely antedates the copying of the B-text of the *Chronicle* (p.179). It is useful to reiterate that both Scribes A and B used the same scribal practices in regard to pointing in their portions of the manuscript, a fact that indicates, in no uncertain terms, the existence of an earlier written exemplar of the poem's text.

15. *Ibid.,* p.179.

16. As we saw earlier in Chapter 1, this belief really is not a valid one; the social and behavioral sciences employ inductive, probabilistic logic in establishing hypotheses, whose proofs are derived primarily from statistical data. By their very nature, such proofs are relative rather than absolute, and are to some degree always subjective. For further opposition to the application of purely objective, mechanically applied standards to the tests of historical linguistics, see Fulk's *Old English Meter*, especially at pp.6-24, which was written largely in direct response to Amos' strict methodology for evaluating the validity of linguistic tests.

17. Amos, *Linguistic Means*, p.167. The book provides a useful overview, summary, and evaluation of a wide array of linguistic tests. Despite its belief that the methodology of the natural sciences could be applied to historical linguistics, it remains a seminal and valuable work. This is not to imply that Amos felt that all linguistic tests are without value. Amos relates (p.167) that "the syncope and apocope of unaccented vowels, and in particular u-apocope, predate all surviving Old English texts, and thus provide a *terminus a quo* for the literature" in the seventh century or earlier. Further, according to Amos (pp.167-8), other potentially useful dating criteria would be the shortening of the vowel lengthened after the loss of post-consonantal prevocalic h and, in a very limited number of cases, where "the contraction in words with original hiatus between vowels, or hiatus caused by loss of intervocalic h, j, or w affects the number of syllables in a verse". In addition, datable phonological changes can be used to "establish secure dates for those texts in which authorial spelling is preserved (inscriptions, early manuscripts, verses with acronyms)". A final valid criterion would be the lifetime of certain words where it can be determined (p.167).

18. *Ibid.,* p.102.

19. *Ibid.* It is this situation that led Amos to state (p.168) that "Alliterative practice with respect to palatal and velar g is by far the most reliable of the purely metrical tests".

20. *Ibid,* pp.100-102 and p.167. In fact, Colin Chase noted in "Opinions on the Date of *Beowulf*" (p.5, fn.7), in his *The Dating of Beowulf* that this important finding was presented by Amos and several others at the Toronto conference from which *The Dating of Beowulf* was to emerge. Yet, as Chase notes, "this point failed to appear in any of the papers which follow".

21. Amos, *Linguistic Means,* pp.167-8. For more regarding this test, see R.D. Fulk, "West Germanic Parasiting, Siever's Law, and the Dating of Old English Verse", *Studies in Philology* 86 (1989), pp.117-38. For examples of contraction and loss of intervocalic h, j, and w, see Klaeber's *Beowulf,* pp.274-5. Thomas Cable, "Metrical Style as Evidence for the Date for *Beowulf*", in *The Dating of Beowulf,* edited by Colin Chase, pp.77-82 (Toronto: University of Toronto Press, 1981), also viewed (p.81) the higher proportion of disyllabic diphthongs in *Beowulf* as a possible indication for an early composition for the poem.

22. For more on the validity of the loss of intervocalic h as a valid chronological indicator, as opposed to the loss of intervocalic j or w, see Chapter II in Fulk's *Old English Meter.*

23. Newton, *The Origins of Beowulf,* p.13. For Newton's references for this statement, see the works cited (*ibid*) in fnn. 55,56,57, and 58.

24. For a discussion, see Amos' *Linguistic Means,* pp.40-9.

25. *Ibid.,* p.168.

26. Randolph Quirk, "On the Problem of Morphological Suture in Old English", *Modern Language Review* 45 (1950), p.2.

27. For more regarding this opposition, refer to Fulk's *Old English Meter,* at pp.116-21.

28. Thomas Cable, review article of Amos' *Linguistic Means of Determining the Dates of Old English Literary Texts. JEGP* 85 (1986), pp.93-95.

29. Cable, "Metrical Style", p.82.

30. This subject forms the topic of Chapter VI in Fulk's *Old English Meter.* The reader is encouraged to refer to this for a much fuller discussion of Kaluza's Law and its implications for the dating, in both relative and absolute terms, of *Beowulf* and other Old English poetry.

31. *Ibid.,* p.153.

32. *Ibid.,* p.164. While Fulk does admit that most poems do observe the distinction between long and short endings to some degree, he attributes this (*ibid.,* p.165) to the formulaic character of the verses in which this observance is found; usually those involving poetic compounds.

33. *Ibid.,* pp.164-5.

34. *Ibid.,* p.166. No other explanation is really credible. As Fulk explains (*Ibid.,* p.167):

Appendix C demonstrates that the distribution of vocalic endings is irregular, and too complex to have been preserved as consciously archaic language: there must have been a phonological difference between the two types of endings at the time *Beowulf* was composed.

35. *Ibid.,* p.167.

36. *Ibid.,* p.390. The dating arguments and references for the shortening of the long endings are found on pp.381-90.

37. The arguments for this contention, as well as further references, are found in *ibid.,* pp.390-91.

38. For a more detailed look at his arguments and examples, see the introduction to his *Beowulf and the Fight at Finnsburg,* 3d ed. w/supplements (Lexington, Mass.: D.C. Heath & Co., 1950), pp.lxxxi-lxxxviii. As for the poem's date of composition, Klaeber stated that "the only extant manuscript of *Beowulf* was written some two and a half centuries after the probable date of composition" (p.lxxxviii).

39. *Ibid.,* p.lxxxiii.

40. Kiernan, *Beowulf Manuscript,* pp.48-50 and J.F. Tuso, "*Beowulf's* Dialectal Vocabulary and the Kiernan Theory", *South Central Review* 2 (1985), p.3. For other opposition to Klaeber and for details, see Newton, *The Origins of Beowulf,* pp.11-12.

41. Using a wide-ranging and impressive array of evidence, Newton makes a convincing case for an East Anglian genesis for *Beowulf* in his *The Origins of Beowulf.* His book is an important work and one that, in my opinion, will be crucial in any future discussions regarding the dating of *Beowulf.*

42. For a listing of these possible corruptions, see Newton's *The Origins of Beowulf,* p.9 (at fn.35).

43. Ker, *Catalogue of Manuscripts,* p.xxxi.

44. C.L. Wrenn, *Beowulf: With the Finnsburg Fragment,* 3d ed. with revisions and preface by W. F. Bolton (London: Harrap, 1973), p.17. As noted in Newton's *The Origins of Beowulf* (p.9 at fn.35), Wrenn first advanced this proposal in his "The Value of Spelling as Evidence", *Transactions of the Philological Society* (1943), pp.14-27.

45. Newton, *The Origins of Beowulf,* pp.9-10.

46. On this, see Malcolm Parkes, "Palaeographical Commentary", in *The Epinal, Erfurt, Wurden, and Corups Glossaries,* edited by B. Bischoff, et al (Copenhagen: Rosenkilde and Bagger, 1988).

47. Anita R. Riedinger, "The Formulaic Relationship Between *Beowulf* and *Andreas*", in *Heroic Poetry in the Anglo-Saxon Period: Studies in Honor of Jess B. Bessinger, Jr.,* Studies in Medieval Culture XXXII, edited by Helen Damico and John Leyerle (Kalamazoo Michigan: Medieval Institute Publications, 1993), pp.283-312.

48. *Ibid.,* p.299.

49. *Ibid.* Riedinger (*ibid., pp.304-5*) saw it as likely that the *Andreas*-poet employed a written manuscript of *Beowulf,* rather than working from memory. In any case, she concludes (p.305) that "whether the *Andreas*-poet knew *Beowulf* in a written or memorized form, however, it is clear that his source was very close to the version that survives in Cotton Vitellius A.xv".

50. See *ibid,* pp.305-6 for details about the dating schemes advanced for *Andreas.*

51. Newton, *The Origins of Beowulf,* p.14. As Newton relates, both Klaeber (*Beowulf,* p.cxvii) and Roberta Frank ("Skaldic Verse", p.123) had noted *Beowulf's* lack of these Viking-Age Scandinavian loan-words.

52. See *ibid.,* pp.14-15 for the argument and its references.

53. See *ibid.,* pp.15-16 for details and further references.

54. Dumville, "The Uses of Evidence", p.120.

55. Fulk, *Old English Meter,* pp.380-81.

56. *Ibid.,* pp.389-90.

57. Gregory of Tours, *The History of the Franks,* L. Thorpe, tr. (Harmondsworth: Penguin Books, Ltd., 1974), III.3. For more on Hygelac's raid, and the possible interrelationships between the poem and the Frankish sources, see Dorothy Whitelock, *The Audience of Beowulf,* pp.38-54. See also Walter Goffart, "Hetware and Hugas: Datable Anacronisms in *Beowulf*", in *The Dating of Beowulf,* edited by Colin Chase (Toronto: University of Toronto Press, 1981), pp.83-100.

58. Chickering, *Beowulf: A Dual-Language Edition,* p.248.

59. See Newton, *The Origins of Beowulf,* pp.13-14, for an overview and further references pertaining to the two categories of Latin loan-words found in *Beowulf,* and their utility in providing a *terminus ad quem* for the poem.

60. While the debate usually is framed around the question of whether *Beowulf* is essentially a "pagan" or "Christian" poem, Cherniss has suggested that it might be more productive to view the poem's secular elements as "pre-Christian", "Germanic", or "heroic" rather than as either "pagan" or "heathen" (*Ingeld and Christ,* p.125). Cherniss provides (*ibid, pp.125-34*) an overview and summary of the arguments advanced by H.M. Chadwick, Fr. Klaeber, J.R.R. Tolkien, *et alia* regarding the Christianity (or lack thereof) of the poem. It is an issue that has been argued forcefully and cogently by both sides.

61. William Whallon, "The Christianity of *Beowulf*", *Modern Philology* LX (1962), pp.81-94 and "The Idea of God in *Beowulf*" in *Proceedings of the Modern Language Association* LXXX (1965), pp.19-23. These points were brought out later in his *Formula, Character, and Context: Studies in Homeric, Old English, and Old Testament Poetry* (Washington, D.C.: The Center for Hellenic Studies, 1969). In that work, Whallon clearly and effectively showed that most, if not all, of the poem's "Christian" words and motifs could just as easily be explained within a Germanic, pre-Christian context. (See Chapter 4, pp.117-138).

62. Whallon, "The Christianity of *Beowulf*", p.81.

63. Whallon, "The Idea of God in *Beowulf*", p.20.

64. Cherniss, *Ingeld and Christ,* at pp.133 and 149.

65. Robert D. Stevick, "Christian Elements and the Genesis of *Beowulf*", *Modern Philology* LXI (1963), p.88. Like Magoun's article cited above, this article (pp.79-89) should be viewed as seminal in the application of Oral Theory to *Beowulf* studies.

66. John Miles Foley, "*Beowulf* and Traditional Narrative Song: The Potential and Limits of Comparison", in *Old English Literature in Context: Ten Essays,* p.136. As we see below in Chapter 7, these narrative inconsistences are a reflection of the oral-formulaic tradition that is represented by the poem.

67. The Fight at Finnsburg (1068-1159, 874-902) and The Battle of Ravenswood (2922-98) certainly must have had a separate existence apart from the *Beowulf* poem as we now have it. See Nicholas Jacobs, "The Old English Heroic Tradition in the Light of Welsh Evidence", *CMCS* No.2 (Winter 1981), pp.9-20.

68. Cherniss, *Ingeld and Christ,* p.134. In all fairness to the monks, it should be noted, as Dumville has done ("The Uses of Evidence", pp.109-21), that it is quite possible that Anglo-Saxon monks of the seventh and eighth centuries, trained in the Irish tradition, would have had no difficulty whatsoever in copying down any kind of heroic poem, even if the poem's subject matter alluded to a pagan past. Irish monks of the same period who were working in Ireland certainly had no qualms about committing to writing the blatantly pagan poems of the Ulster Cycle. The study, in fact, agrees that the poem's eventual existence in manuscript form is attributable to the efforts of a monastic community (though it is impossible to say precisely which one), and that such an existence may very well antedate the date provided by the orthography of the extant manuscript. The study is attempting to show that the poem as we now have it is the product of an oral tradition and a process of amalgamation that must be seen as a *fait accompli* before the poem was committed to writing.

69. The interaction between the written and oral traditions as the poem was committed to writing might have influenced the bard dictating the text. Elaborating on this point in "From Horseback to Monastic Cell", Opland notes (p.43) that "one of the consequences of the meeting between an oral tradition and writing: the issue may well be a longer and fuller text, a version that could never have any oral existence among the people. *Beowulf* might well be such a product".

70. For the historical arguments, see Dorothy Whitelock, *The Audience of Beowulf*, or Patrick Wormald, "Bede, *Beowulf*, and the Conversion of the Anglo-Saxon Aristocracy", in *Bede and Anglo-Saxon England: Papers in Honour of the 1300th Anniversary of the Birth of Bede*, No.46 *British Archaeological Reports* (Oxford: BAR Publications, 1978), pp.32-95, or Eric John's "*Beowulf* and the Margins of Literacy", *Bulletin of the John Rylands University Library of Manchester* 56 (1973-74), pp.388-422. See also Dumville's wide-ranging historical arguments in his "The Uses of Evidence", pp.109-60. Finally, see M.J. Swanton's comments about the poem and the reign of Offa in his *Crisis and Development*.

71. This is not a novel idea. The digression has long been seen to be an indication for the poem's dating in dating schemes proposed by many scholars. For example, see Whitelock, *Audience*, pp.57-59 and 63-64. For an overview of this subject, see Chase, "Opinions on the Date of *Beowulf*, 1815-1980", p.5.

72. Goffart, "Hetware and Hugas", pp.83-100. *Hetware* is found on lines 2363 and 2916 of the poem; *Hugas* on lines 2502 and 2914. The first term's use in Britain is dated by Goffart to no earlier than the second half of the eighth century, while he assigned a *terminus a quo* of ca.923 for the second one (p.100). The article offers a well-written and thoughtful analysis, and one that has my wholehearted approval with the exception of his specific use of these terms to date the poem's composition to the second quarter of the tenth century. Such a date is simply at odds with the available orthographic and linguistic evidence, as well as with the oral-formulaic process. I would agree that these terms, if they are viewed as items of interpolation into a written text, can be of great use in helping to determine the textual history of the manuscript. However, neither *Hetware* nor *Hugas* can be used in any effort to date the poem's composition *per se*.

73. Louise E. Wright, "*Merewioingas* and the Dating of *Beowulf*: A Reconsideration", *Nottingham Medieval Studies* 24 (1980), provides a helpful summary of the major arguments concerning the term on pp.1-2. She herself assigns a *terminus a quo* for the poem, based on *merewioingas*, to sometime after 751, and possibly as late as the early ninth century (p.5). Again, I would see this as a written interpolation belonging to an earlier stage of the manuscript's textual history than that evidenced by *Hugas*, though not necessarily *Hetware*.

74. One of the major contentions in Swanton's *Crisis and Development* is that *Beowulf* reflects the political conflicts that had arisen between the older (horizontal) and newer (vertical) concepts of kingship and society during the course of the eighth century. During this period, the older concept of the king as *vox populi* was replaced by one which viewed the king as *vox Dei* as one aspect of a general stratification of the political structure and the society at large. For Swanton, this conflict forms a persistent theme throughout the poem, and is an indicator of the period in which the poem was composed.

However, if undercurrents of this eighth-century political/philosophical conflict indeed are present in *Beowulf* (and I am not convinced that this is the case), then the presence of such a theme should be seen as an interpolation to the text, the result of a scribe's or poet's efforts during the latter stages of the poem's history in much the same manner that the incorporation of Christian motifs and themes had been effected during the earlier period of the poem's evolution.

FURTHER READING

Bibliographies

Fry, Donald K. *"Beowulf" and "The Fight at Finnsburh": A Bibliography*. Charlottesville: University Press of Virginia, 1969, 221 p.

Bibliography including extensive subject classifications, compiler's remarks, and notices of reviews.

Short, Douglas D. *"Beowulf" Scholarship: An Annotated Bibliography*. New York: Garland Publishing, 1980, 353 p.

Bibliography offering detailed annotations and a selection of listings dating from 1705 through 1949, and a more comprehensive listing from 1950 through 1978.

Criticism

Clark, George. *Beowulf*. Boston: Twayne Publishers, 1990, 169 p.

Book-length analysis of the poem, including discussion of the heroic nature of the poem, the battles with monsters, and kingship.

Cox, Betty S. *Cruces of "Beowulf."* The Hague: Mouton, 1971, 192 p.

Examination of textual and interpretative issues within the context of the widely-held belief that the poem is a work of art addressed by a Christian poet to a Christian audience.

Earl, James W. "The Necessity of Evil in *Beowulf*." *South Atlantic Bulletin* XLIV, No. 1 (January, 1979): 81-98.

Argues that Grendel functions as an evil creature, but one who serves a positive function in the molding of Hrothgar's moral vision, as well as the moral vision of the poet.

Fajardo-Acosta, Fidel. *The Condemnation of Heroism in the Tragedy of Beowulf: A Study in the Characterization of the Epic.* Studies in Epic and Romance Literature, Vol. 2. Lewiston, N.Y.: The Edwin Mellen Press, 1989, 215 p.

Studies the significance of the name and character of Beowulf and Grendel; of the symbol of the wolf; and of the fratricide motif.

Fulk, R. D., ed. *Interpretations of "Beowulf": A Critical Anthology.* Bloomington: Indiana University Press, 1991, 282 p.

Collection of critical essays dating from the 1920s through the 1980s, focusing on a variety of subjects, including the Christian elements of *Beowulf,* its formulaic structure, its epic nature, and the nature and role of the monsters.

Gulley, Ervene F. "The Concept of Nature in *Beowulf.*" *Thoth* 11, No. 1 (Fall 1970): 16-30.

Studies the concept of nature from the point of view of the Germanic people of the period during which the poem was written, as well as the poet's artistic use of nature. Gulley maintains that within the artistic confines of the poem, nature serves as a source of imagery; connects narrative portions; generates and emphasizes mood and theme; and creates a sense of realism.

Haarder, Andreas. *"Beowulf": The Appeal of a Poem.* Akademisk Forlag, 1975, 340 p.

Provides an extended discussion of the poem's artistic merit.

Hill, John M. *The Cultural World in "Beowulf."* Toronto: University of Toronto Press, 1995, 224 p.

Examines society and culture within the poem, investigating feudal settlements, the temporal world, the jural world, the psychological world, and the concept of honor.

Howlett, David R. "Form and Genre in *Beowulf.*" *Studia Neophilologica* XLVI, No. 2 (1974): 309-25.

Analyzes details within the poem that suggest various sources which may have influenced its form and structure.

Irving, Edward B., Jr. *Rereading "Beowulf."* Philadelphia: University of Pennsylvania Press, 1989, 183 p.

Discusses recent approaches to *Beowulf* and its oral nature; examines its oral modes of characterization and narrative construction; and studies the hall (Heorot) as a unifying symbol within the poem.

Lapidge, Michael. "*Beowulf* and the Psychology of Terror." *Heroic Poetry in the Anglo-Saxon Period: Studies in Honor of Jess B. Bessinger, Jr.,* edited by Helen Damico and John Leyerle, pp. 373-402. Studies in Medieval Culture XXXII. Kalamazoo, Mich.: Western Michigan University, 1993.

Contends that *Beowulf* is not a heroic poem because the poet is less concerned with heroic action than with reflection on human lives and conduct. Investigates

the poet's interest in "the workings of the human mind," particularly his depiction of Grendel and the monster's advancing on the great hall, Heorot.

Lee, Alvin A. *Gold-Hall and Earth-Dragon: "Beowulf" as Metaphor.* Toronto: University of Toronto Press, 1998, 279 p.

Analyzes the way in which the poem's figurative language and verbal structure support the extended metaphor of the poem.

Leyerle, John. "Beowulf the Hero and the King." *Medium Ævum* XXXIV, No. 2 (1965): 89-102.

Demonstrates the way in which the episodes of the poem are connected to create structural unity, and examines the major theme of the poem. Leyerle describes this theme as the contradiction between the heroic code—which praises individual valor—and society's desire to have a king who acts on behalf of the common good, not personal glory.

McNamee, M. B. "*Beowulf*—An Allegory of Salvation?" *JEGP* LIX, No. 2 (April 1960): 190-207.

Examines the evidence supporting the theory that *Beowulf* is a Christian allegory, and argues that viewing the poem in this manner reveals its great artistic unity.

Overing, Gillian R. *Language, Sign, and Gender in "Beowulf."* Carbondale: Southern Illinois University Press, 1990, 137 p.

Investigates the *Beowulf* poet's use of textual effects, metonymy, and kenning; the interlace structure and symbols used in the text; and gender issues— specifically, the way desire operates within the narrative.

Robinson, Fred C. *"Beowulf" and the Appositive Style.* Knoxville: The University of Tennessee Press, 1985, 106 p.

Discusses the appositive style and structure of *Beowulf,* arguing that this style enabled the poet to express from his Christian point of view the pagan heroic life. Robinson explains that grammatical appositions are often called "variations," and consist of poetic compounds, amphiboles, and a variety of narrative devices that are used in a suggestive, rather than an equivocal manner.

Stanley, Eric Gerald. *In the Foreground: "Beowulf."* Rochester, N.Y.: D. S. Brewer, 1994, 273 p.

Examines the poem's critical history, dating, and poetics.

Tietjen, Mary C. Wilson. "God, Fate, and the Hero of *Beowulf.*" *JEGP* LXXI, No. 2 (April 1975): 159-71.

Analyzes the Christian and pagan elements of the poem and asserts that the poet's attitude and tone are both Christian and pagan. The heroic ideal prevails, explains Tietjen, while the Christian notion of grace is also a significant component within the text.

Tripp, Raymond P., Jr. *Literary Essays on Language and Meaning in the Poem Called "Beowulf."* Lewiston, N.Y.: The Edwin Mellen Press, 1992, 300 p.

A selection of essays exploring and elucidating various constructions and specific words, lines, or concepts within the poem.

Additional coverage of *Beowulf* is contained in the following source published by the Gale Group: *Epics for Students.*

Cassiodorus
c. 490-c. 583

(Full name Flavius Magnus Cassiodorus) Latin prose writer and statesman.

INTRODUCTION

Cassiodorus is best known for dedicating himself and his monastery to the preservation of ancient pagan and Christian texts at a time when Italy was threatened by invaders and its intellectual development was deteriorating. Many scholars have described Cassiodorus as poised between the ancient and medieval worlds. His works are typically divided into two periods: those composed before his retirement from public life, including the *Variae Epistolae* and the *History of the Goths*, and those written after he began monastic life, including *Institutiones Divinarum et Saecularium Litterarum.*

BIOGRAPHICAL INFORMATION

Born into a respected senatorial family from southern Italy, Cassiodorus entered public office. After serving as *quaestor*, or private secretary, to Theodoric, the Ostrogothic King of Italy, he held the post of *magister officiorum* from 523 through 526, succeeding Boethius. Under the next king, Ahalaric, he became praetorian prefect, in 533. In 535 and under the rule of another new king, Cassiodorus attempted to establish a theological college in Rome, but the endeavor failed. He retired in 537, devoting himself to religion and scholarship. Byzantine troops took him prisoner in 540 and sent him to Constantinople. He was returned some years later, during the 550s, after the Byzantine Emperor Justinian had captured control of Italy from the Ostrogoths. At this time, Cassiodorus returned to his family's estate and created a hermitage and a monastic institution he named Vivarium. Here Cassiodorus systematized a process by which multiple copies of manuscripts could be transcribed. Under his direction, numerous ancient texts were translated and copied by monks.

MAJOR WORKS

Scholars consider the *Variae* and his *History of the Goths* the most significant works of Cassiodorus's public career. The *Variae*, a twelve-volume work, consists of letters and state documents written and collected by Cassiodorus during his life in office. Widely viewed as perhaps the most important of Cassiodorus's works of his public life, the *History of the Goths* was comprised of twelve books, none of which is now extant. A summary exists in the form of Jordanes' *Getica*. The *History* portrays the Goths favorably and seems to encourage a peaceful relationship between Goths and Romans. During these years Cassiodorus also composed a philosophical treatise on the nature of the soul, *De Anima*, as well as *Chronica*, a survey of world history through the year 519. *Institutiones*, the central work of his retired life, was designed to instruct his monks on sacred, as well as pagan, scholarship. The first portion of this work focuses on the study of Holy Scripture; the second portion deals with a survey of the liberal arts and provides what may be described as a summary of secular scholarship. In addition to editing various translations of ancient texts and an ecclesiastical history, Cassiodorus also wrote a treatise on spelling, *De Orthographia*, designed as a tool for copyists.

CRITICAL RECEPTION

Many modern critics have asserted that Cassiodorus's achievements have been overlooked and they have attempted to rectify that situation by evaluating his career and influence. Jacob Hammer surveys Cassiodorus's life and writings, and notes that Cassiodorus revived Italy's intellectual life when it was in "utter decay." Similarly, S. J. B. Barnish focuses on Cassiodorus' influence, maintaining that both before and after he retired from public life, Cassiodorus used his writings to inspire the lay and religious public in matters concerned with politics, religion, and culture. Taking a different approach, Leslie Webber Jones examines literary and historical references to Cassiodorus and his work from the time of Cassiodorus' death through the late thirteenth century, in an attempt to gauge his influence on later culture. Jones finds that in their preservation of the writings of the Church Fathers and ancient Latin writers, Cassiodorus's works proved to be "extremely useful" to the Middle Ages.

Other critics focus their analyses on Cassiodorus's three major works: the *Variae*, the *Institutiones*, and the *History of the Goths*. In his study of the *Institutiones*, Rand examines the title of the work and various manuscript issues. Rand maintains that Cassiodorus's aim in this work was to nurture the "proper" attitude toward Holy Scripture so that it could be understood and passed on to later generations. Leslie Webber Jones analyzes the content of the work and observes in particular that Cassiodorus was careful to emphasize that secular writers should not be neglected in scriptural study, and that he stressed learning as a way to better understand Scripture. Jones also studies the style and vocabulary of the *Institutiones*, describing the style as wordy, elaborate, and informed by Cassiodorus's desire for balance.

Offering an introduction to the *Variae,* Barnish studies the work's compilation, content, character, and style, as well as its reliability as a historical resource. Its political themes, he notes, include Italy's defense, the relationship between the Goths and the Franks, and diplomacy with Byzantium. The style is ornate and rhythmical and demonstrates Cassiodorus's facility and originality in his use of metaphor and digression, Barnish states. The critic does note that, as history, the work is not entirely reliable, as evidenced by examples of its "overt propaganda." James J. O'Donnell likewise comments on the slant of the *Variae,* arguing that while Cassiodorus praised the virtues of Gothic rule and emphasized its success, he did not intend the work as a polemical treatise. Similarly, Robin Macpherson notes the use of "politic falsehood" in the work, but maintains that this was a practice typical of the institutional world of late Rome. Macpherson also discusses the language of the *Variae,* noting the proliferation of abstract nouns, Cassiodorus's use of simple syntax, and his use of action-nouns.

The Gothic history is of major interest to critics despite the fact that it exists only in excerpts and in Jordanes's summary, *Getica.* Barnish examines Cassiodorus's purpose in writing the *History of the Goths,* as well as the circumstances surrounding Jordanes' composition of his summary. The work, argues Barnish, was designed to celebrate the Goths, their royal lineage, and their political achievements. Arnaldo Momigliano analyzes the way in which the political atmosphere in Italy influenced Cassiodorus's writings, especially the *History of the Goths.* Explaining that there existed an awareness of a possible rebellion against the Gothic government of Ravenna, Momigliano asserts that the *History of the Goths* was intended to advocate pacific coexistence between the Goths and the Romans. Additionally, the critic observes that the political message of the Gothic history reflects that of the *Variae,* which Momigliano describes as the presentation of the "barbarian" government as the "embodiment of civilized justice and wisdom."

PRINCIPAL WORKS

*De Orthographia (treatise)
*Family History of the Cassiodori (history)
Institutiones Divinarum et Saecularium Litterarum [Institutes of Divine and Secular Literature] 2 vols. (treatise)
Chronica (history) 519
De Anima [On the Soul] (philosophy) c. 537
Variae Epistolae 12 vols. (letters, political documents) c. 537
†History of the Goths. 12 vols. (history)

Principal English Translations

The Letters of Cassiodorus: A Condensed Version of the "Variae Epistolae" (translated by T. Hodgkin) 1886

*Date unknown.

†Scholars believe that this work was written before 534 and revised around 551.

CRITICISM

E. K. Rand (essay date 1938)

SOURCE: "The New Cassiodorus," in *Speculum,* Vol. 13, No. 4, October 1938, pp. 433-47.

[*In the following essay, Rand examines textual issues related to Cassiodorus's* Institutiones, *focusing on the work's title; the "archetype" of the various extant manuscripts and the categories into which the manuscripts may be placed; and the history of the earliest manuscript, as well as that of the codices.*]

The significance of Cassiodorus in the history of the transmission of Classical and patristic texts and thus in the history of mediaeval education has long been duly acclaimed. It is he who made sound learning and the copying of books a part of monastic discipline. It is he who saved the ancient Latin authors and the Fathers of the Church for the Middle Ages. He built, of course, on foundations that others had laid.[1] Without his aid, the Church might have somehow transmitted its two-fold culture to the ages to come. But as it is, the credit should go primarily to Cassiodorus for this happy result. He came at the moment when the monastery succeeded the university as the centre of education. In fact he had originally intended with the help of Pope Agapetus (535-536) to establish a kind of Christian university, or theological school, in Rome. Some ten years later he founded instead the monastery of Vivarium on his estate at Scylacium in South Italy. His plans for scholarship were transferred to the new institution and imparted new vigor to whatever had been the scholarly programme of the institutions of St Benedict. It is not often that one can lay one's finger so exactly on an event that sums up initial attempts and precipitates an historical period.

I speak of a 'new Cassiodorus' because Cassiodorus has been made new for me by Mr Mynors's edition of his *Institutiones.*[2] Readers of this work have hitherto resorted to the indispensable, and frequently annoying, *Patrologia Latina* of the Abbé Migne (LXX, 1847 and 1865). The text there given is a reproduction of that by Dom Jean Garet, a Benedictine monk of the Congregation of St Maur (Rouen, 1679). It is astounding that an epoch-making book like the *Institutiones* should have bad no editorial attention during the last two centuries and a half. There have been critical studies of the manuscripts, notably by Usener, Keil, Laubmann, Mortet, Paul Lehmann, Stettner and Van de Vyver. There have been critical editions of other works—the *Chronica* by Mommsen, the *Variae* by Mommsen and Traube. Traube's seminary in 1906, not long before his lamented death, inspired young Paul Lehmann with a devotion to Cassiodorus, which, mingled with his devotion to Traube, has led to most important studies of various aspects of the text and its transmission.[3] But none before Mynors, who is thoroughly conversant with the work of his predecessors, has given us a real text; 'edited from the manuscripts,' as he says, and presented in a small octavo volume, in the elegant style of the Clarendon Press, with introduction, appendices, an *index rerum,* an *index nominum,* and an *index auctorum.* Cassiodorus's work will gain a far wider reading than ever before. The present reader is glad to admit that after a careful perusal of the text, the apparatus, and the discussion of the manuscripts, he has found a new Cassiodorus.

Mr Mynors speaks most modestly of his achievement. He regrets that his knowledge did not permit notes on the subject-matter, and that he could attempt no history of the transmission, 'illustrated from palaeography and from the literature of succeeding centuries.' His 'sole aim' has been 'to establish the relationship of the manuscripts to one another, and to provide at least the materials for a text that can be trusted.' Yet, in so doing, he has laid the foundations for a new study of the influence of Cassiodorus's work on the educational system of the early Middle Ages.

I shall not attempt in the present paper to follow down all the paths of inquiry suggested by Mr Mynors's edition. Let us hope that he himself will pursue them. For the moment I wish to make certain suggestions with regard to the nature and the title of Cassiodorus's work, to the archetype of the manuscripts and the classes into which they fall, to the earliest of the manuscripts, (*B = Bamberg, H.J. iv. 15* [*Patr. 61*], *saec.* VIII), and to a codex closely related to *B,* namely *M (= Paris, Bibliothèque Mazarine 660, saec.* X *in.*).

I

The primary aim of Cassiodorus in the work before us was to inculcate in the monks of Vivarium a proper attitude towards Holy Scripture. He would teach them how to read it, how to understand it, how to treat its text, and how to hand on that text to coming generations. What are the helps in such a task? He describes the important commentators and the Fathers who in their works have furnished incidental comment on the Bible. Nor does he neglect the chance bits of interpretation that may come to the pure in heart, some of the simpler brethren in the monastery, who though not deeply versed in the arts may penetrate the divine meaning directly. There follows a delightful description of the monastery of Vivarium and of the duties and pleasures of its scribes. Such, in brief, are the contents of the first book of **Institutiones.** But the interpreter of Holy Scripture and the scribe that hands on its text need a previous grounding in the ancient liberal arts, which since the fourth century had been an integral part of Christian education. Cassiodorus, therefore, in the second book, treats each art in turn, briefly describing it and giving the titles of the most important books about it, all of which he included, or meant to include, in his monastic library.

The whole work, therefore, constitutes a training in the complete art of reading the Word of God—an art to which human studies lead the way. The two books constitute a two-fold *Einleitung,* or better, a λόγος προτρεπτικός, with bibliographies.

The matter of the title is a vexed question. Mynors cuts through the mass of conflicting testimony and decides (p. liii) for a simple **Institutiones.** This we may use for convenience, as Cassiodorus himself does,[4] but the formal designation on the title-page should tell us the subject of which the 'foundations' or 'principles' are to be discussed. Cassiodorus evidently had in mind the title of Lactantius's work, *Divinae Institutiones,* and Lactantius, as he tells us (I, 1, 12), meant to contrast his treatise with the *institutiones civilis iuris* of the writers on law, i.e., Gaius, Ulpian, and the rest.[5] The title **Institutiones** alone would suggest, in Cassiodorus's day, rather one of the variety of law-books than anything else. It needs amplification in order to describe his undertaking precisely. From the evidence before us, I think we may select as the most likely title to appear at the head of his work, *Institutionum Divinarum et Humanarum Lectionum Libri II.* The word *Lectionum* is an all-important part of it; for this is the essence of the author's bibliographical design.[6]

II

With the same scholarly jealousy with which he would safeguard the texts of Holy Scripture and of the other works that he describes, Cassiodorus had a special copy of his own work made as the original from which further copies should be taken. This we know from the subscription in the oldest manuscript, *B,* which reads: CODEX ARCHETYPUS AD CUIUS EXEMPLARIA SUNT RELIQUI CORRIGENDI. This codex is naturally not *B* itself, with its barbarous errors, but I see no reason for doubting with Mynors (p. x) that this manuscript descended, with however many intermediaries, from Cassiodorus's own codex that bore this inscription.

Another feature of his edition was the presence of certain pictures, notably that of the monastery itself, possibly (though not so probably) one of the author, and of ornamental diagrams for various of the topics discussed in Book II. These may well have multiplied, or have been reduced, or have submitted to fresh decoration at the fancy of scribes, as the copying advanced. But that something of the sort was present in the original copy seems to me, despite Mynors's cautious statement,[7] fairly certain. A profitable and fascinating study of the ornamentation and illustration of the manuscripts of Cassiodorus, in the hope of deducing the character of their archetype,[8] awaits some scholar, let us hope Mr Mynors himself, who is familiar with the art of illumination and with the art of script and with the problems of the text. As no one has more brilliantly shown in recent times than Wilhelm Köhler in his monumental volumes on the School of Tours,[9] these three aspects of the mediaeval book all clamor for attention.[10]

Cassiodorus's *codex archetypus ad cuius exemplaria sunt reliqui corrigendi* was obviously one of the treasures of

Vivarium. It, of course, contained both books of the *Institutiones,* and that work was but the preface to a set of careful texts of the various writings that he mentions in it as indispensable guides in the art of interpreting Holy Scripture and in the pursuit of the liberal arts. At the end of *B* a most significant note appears (p. 163):

> Complexis, quantum ego arbitror, diligenterque tractatis institutionum duobus libris qui breviter divinas et humanas litteras comprehendunt, tempus est ut nunc edificatrices veterum regulas, id est codicem introductorium, legere debemus qui ad sacras litteras nobiliter ac salubriter introducunt.

The work to which Cassiodorus here refers is the volume of *introductores*—Augustine, Ticonius, Adrianus, Eucherius and Junilius—which he had described in the chapter entitled *De Modis Intelligentiae*.[11] Instead of that work, however, *B* contains the *De Metris* of Mallius Theodorus (Keil, *G. L.,* VI, 579), a work not mentioned in the *Institutiones.* The scribe of *B*, therefore, adds this supplement to the *Institutiones,* while omitting the *codex introductorius* and whatever other works followed in the collection of Cassiodorus's works accessible to him.

We should like more evidence of what doubtless occurred in many a monastery—the construction of a library, in whole or in part, on Cassiodorus's model plan. There might well have been such an intention on the part of St Columbanus or his successors at Bobbio. In 1911, Rudolf Beer published the startling theory[12] that Cassiodorus's library itself was transported to Bobbio not long after the foundation of that monastery in 612. Finding that no champion had come out against his novel views,[13] he set them forth with new details in 1913.[14] Criticism came slowly; it took time for critics to recover consciousness after this bolt from the blue.[15] The general tendency at the time of Beer's publications was not to deny; today it is not to believe. But in any event, we may accept without hesitation the statement of His Eminence Giovanni Cardinal Mercati, in his magisterial treatment of the history of Bobbio[16] that Cassiodorus's *Institutiones* may well have served the early librarians of Bobbio—and bibliophiles in general—as a bibliographical guide and as an incentive to look around for good old copies of the works therein recommended.[17] Very few libraries, I imagine, could afford to possess all the books recommended by Cassiodorus, and as we shall see in a moment, even the two books of the *Institutiones* itself had separate traditions.

The *codex archetypus (X)*, I think we may infer, was about as perfect as Cassiodorus could make it. But we can hardly suppose that he lent this treasure to other monasteries for copying. Rather he had a copy *(X¹)* made for that purpose. Its existence is proved by the agreement of the different classes of copies in significant errors. *X* itself may have had some imperfections, but not so many as the common errors found in all of our extant manuscripts. I have counted about a score in Book I and more than twice as many in Book II, not including mistakes in the transcription of Greek words. Some of these, such as matters of

spelling, might have been independently committed. Thus Livy's name is written[18] *libius,* or *lybius,* by the very error against which Cassiodorus warned.[19] In the same way some of the simpler errors of omission occasioned by *homoioteleuta* might have arisen independently.[20] Others go back to a single source, like the number of the quaternions in the codex of the Greek Bible that Cassiodorus had prepared.[21] Again, as C. H. Turner pointed out, there is an apparent lacuna in I, 10, where the author is speaking of the various aids to the understanding of Holy Scripture. The fifth[22] of these consists of the random interpretation of special passages given by the Fathers in their various works, but only three are mentioned before this. It may be, as Mynors hints, that the phrase *quae prius clausa manserunt,* found at the end of the first category (the *introductores*) and likewise the second (the *librorum expositores*), stood at the end of the third (possibly those who treated not whole books but substantial parts of them?) and occasioned the omission of this third section. Whether this is the reason or not, another lacuna meets us in the description of St Ambrose,[23] which seems relatively too short, and in which no main verb is to be found.

From Book II, I will note but two cases. In II, 3, 15 (p. 127, 1), Terence's *Dave ne faceres* becomes *da bene faceres* and in II, 4, 6 (p. 140, 11) for *spheram, id est quinquies* we have *spheramides quinquies.*

Errors like these could hardly have been left in the *codex archetypus ad cuius exemplaria sunt reliqui corrigendi.* The plural *exemplaria* seems to indicate that several reproductions of it were made, from which still others (*reliqui*) were taken;[24] but once more their common errors point to an original *exemplar (X¹),* from which and not from *X* itself the course of copying began.

III

As indicated above,[25] the two books of the *Institutiones* had different histories in their course through the Middle Ages. In fact only two other manuscripts contain both books in the kind of text found in *B - M* (see above, p. 434) and *U (Vat. Urb. lat. 67, saec. XII),* which is a direct copy of *B* made at a time when *B* had received corrections *(B²),* many of which were taken by *U*.[26]

Fortunately, another family of manuscripts is available that contain only Book I and another consisting of those that contain only Book II.[27] For Book I a stemma is presented (p. lvi) which indicates four families, which fall into two main classes; these we may call for clearness *Y* and *Z*. It is plain that these classes are independent one of the other and that though *Y* is in general the better source, it sometimes strays, when *Z* gives the correct reading.[28] It is identified with 'Italy, then Germany.' It is surely Italian and later affected Germany since *B*, written at Monte Cassino or some other Italian scriptorium,[29] was brought up to Bamberg, perhaps by Otto III (A.D. 999) or Henry II (A.D. 1022), as Traube shrewdly guessed.[30]

Under *Z* there are two main branches. *Z¹ (= Θ)* includes two sub-classes. In one *(Z³)* we find *F (Florence, Ashb.*

13, from Beauvais, *saec.* IX) and *V* (*Valenciennes 353*, from St Amand, *saec.* IX) and θ (*St Gall 199, saec.* IX/X). This branch Mynors traces naturally to a centre in Northern France.

Z^2 (= Ξ) has similarly two branches. One includes *C* (*Cassel theol. fol. 29*, from Fulda, *saec.* IX *med.*) and *X* (*Würzburg M. p. th. f. 29* [*Dombibliothek No. 63*] *saec.* X). In the other is *G* (*Wolfenbüttel, Weissenburg 79* [*4163*], *saec.* X *in.*).[31]

This class is obviously German. Fulda and Würzburg might suggest a lineage from the British Isles, an hypothesis that might be strengthened by *H*, were it not for the mixed character of that manuscript.[32] Furthermore, among the codices that contain only fragments or excerpts, although their evidence for the text is rightly found dubious, something may be gleaned from further palaeographical study as to the history of the text. In particular the Munich manuscript *14469* from St Emmeram of Regensburg (Ratisbon), apparently of the early ninth century,[33] might yield such information, while the fragment (p. xvi) in Berlin (*162, saec.* IX/X;*D*), being a Phillipps manuscript, most probably is of French origin. The line of tradition, therefore, may perhaps be traced from Germany back to France rather than either to the British Isles or directly to Italy.

There remains the case of *H* (*Hereford Cathedral Library O. III. 2, saec.* IX^2, from an Insular original), which with two sets of *recentiores* is located in 'France (?), then England,' and put in the stemma (p. lvi) on a line running above the original of Θ (Z^1) and Ξ (Z^2). But whatever the source of its text, this manuscript shows a suspicious concurrence with significant errors of *M* (33, 19; 40, 21). If it took over bad readings from such a source it might well have derived thence the good readings it shows when Θ and Ξ go astray. Or some of these it might have achieved by conjecture—for *H* can emend most audaciously (55, 16). Mynors notes that *H* has little value for the text, though historically important as the ancestor of a type widely spread in the twelfth and following centuries (p. xvi).

Similarly in Book II, the family *B M U* (*Y*) is matched by Σ (*Z*) which seems to be even more useful than Class *Z* in Book I for correcting the errors of *Y*.[34] My list of readings, though not complete, hints at two facts, first that Class *Z* rises in value in Book II and second that the errors of both classes are so patent in quality that the readings of their original X^1 may be deduced with comparative ease.

Class *Z* (Σ) in Book II comprises four manuscripts. From the stemma on p. lvi they apparently form three subclasses, but a study of the apparatus suggests rather that there are but two. Z^1 comprises: (1) *S* (*St Gall 855, saec.* IX). Since Alcuin's *De Rhetorica* is a member of the little corpus that it contains,[35] a French origin may be suspected (see *T*). (2) *L* (*London, Brit. Mus., Harley 2637*, from the Hospital of Nicolaus Cusanus at Cues, *saec.* IX *ex.*). (3) *K* (*Karlsruhe, Augiensis 241, saec.* IX *ex.*), written at Re-

ichenau and copied, as Mynors thinks with high probability, from *L*. Z^2 comprises two manuscripts: (I) *T* (*Berlin 176, Phillipps 1780, saec.* X, from Fleury). This manuscript (cf. *S*) contains Alcuin's *De Rhetorica* with his *De Dialectica* and that of St Augustine. It contains only chapter 1 and 2, but these are enough to show its affiliation with the other manuscript of this class. (2) *O* (*Chartres 130* [*148*], *saec.* X *in.*).

Z^2 is obviously French in origin, and Z^1 may well be.

This part of our survey of the manuscripts suggests that the work of Cassiodorus in the text here under discussion came to France directly from Italy and thence was disseminated in Germany. The question of a line of descent through the British Isles had better be postponed till Professor Beeson's investigation of Insular traits is completed. I refrain from summarizing in stemmata the modifications in those of Mynors that I have proposed. For I offer them not as sure results, but as possible clues for further investigation.

I refrain also from examining the questions raised by the new evidence presented in this edition relating to the transmission of what is called the 'interpolated' text of Book II. The word seems to me a misnomer. I gather, rather, that Cassiodorus himself revised this book, and that later this *revised* text was submitted to both expansion and contraction by some ancient scholar, possibly working under the direction, or with the help, of Cassiodorus himself; his purpose was to combine this introduction to the liberal arts with certain special manuals to form a little *corpus*, or *Handbuch der weltlichen Wissenschaft*. Such a work (called Φ by Mynors) is represented by four manuscripts (pp. xxiv-xxv). It forms the basis of another affair of the same sort (called Δ) of which thirteen manuscripts are listed (pp. xxxi-xxxiv). This, too, is probably ancient. A thorough discussion of the problems that these collections raise would throw a new light on the history of Classical culture in the early Middle Ages. It is noteworthy that the part of the *Institutiones* that is the more interesting for us, the First Book, should receive, at first, less attention than the Second. But while we are more enlightened by the Founder's account of his plans for the new education, his contemporaries and successors, while not neglecting that part of his instruction, found even more necessary his bibliographical aids to the different arts on which the new training depended. In the twelfth century, when such manuals had been multiplied and enlarged, the First Book came to its own again.[36]

But instead of setting a little boat adrift on such a sea, I turn to the manuscripts that I promised to discuss, *B* and *M*.

IV

The *codex Bambergensis*, the oldest and most famous of all the manuscripts of the *Institutiones*, was written in the second half of the eighth century. It is in a script described by Lowe and accepted by everybody else as early Beneventan, though the place of writing is not certainly Monte Cassino.[37] It is at once not far removed from Cassiodorus's archetype on account of its famous subscription and its picture of Vivarium, and yet considerably remote, owing to its barbarous errors. It is corrected by a scribe, B^2, who indulges at times in unfortunate emendations.[38] It would at first appear that this corrector, having no other manuscript—certainly not the original of B—at his disposal, emended out of his own head. U also, as we have seen, is a direct copy, or descendant, from B, since it incorporates various of the 'corrections' of $B^{2.}$ U and B^2, therefore, may probably be ruled out as independent sources for the text of Y.[39]

As for the original of B, two passages in Book I may possibly indicate its length of line. In I, 6, 6, the words *expositas . . . labore* (71 letters and spaces) are written by a contemporary hand in the margin. In I, 16, 3, the words *mavut . . . legat* (36 letters and spaces) are omitted by B U. This looks like a short line of 17-18 letters (four lines being omitted in the first passage and two in the second) of a rather sumptuous original. This suspicion is somewhat strengthened by errors arising from the copying of *scriptura continua*,[40] though such errors do not necessarily presuppose an original in majuscules. In fact it is quite clear that the immediate ancestor of B was in minuscules[41] and probably in minuscules of a cursive character.[42] Obviously one copy at least, and probably more than one, intervened between B and the original X^1 of Vivarium.

Another sign of the remoteness of B is furnished by the other works contained in this manuscript. The *Liber de Metris* of Mallius Theodorus might well have been known to Cassiodorus, though, to the best of my knowledge, he does not mention it in his **Institutiones** or elsewhere,[43] but Gregory of Tours' De cursu stellarum points to France, while Isidore's De natura rerum and the Carmen de eclipsi lunae of that poetical warrior, King Sisebut, Isidore's friend, take us to Spain.[44] One might even imagine that the collection contained in B was put together in Spain, but probably at some time later than Isidore; for as we have, seen, Isidore was not familiar with Book I of the **Institutiones.** Of course Spanish works like those of Isidore and Sisebutus were widely disseminated all over Europe.[45] In some home of learning, therefore, in Spain or elsewhere, whither Cassiodorus and Isidore and Gregory of Tours had penetrated, the collection of which B is a copy was compiled.

V

There is luckily a manuscript, which Victor Mortet first brought into the light,[46] of the same family as B but superior, on the whole, in its text of Book I of the **Institutiones.** This is M (*Paris, Bibliothèque Mazarine 660*), which I examined in the summer of 1937 and of which through the kindness of MM. Lauer, Van Moé, and Le Bossu I have a number of photographs.[47] The description of Mynors (pp. xi-xii), though carefully made, might give

the impression that this is a Beneventan book. Hand A displays 'a good many Beneventan characteristics.' He notes in Hand B, which is 'in a more marked style,' the *te* ligature[48] and the distinction of the hard and soft sounds of *ti* by the use of the ligature with the high cursive *t* for the latter sound.[49]

On turning the pages of M for the first time, I was surprised to find that the script of the first hand, A, did not seem necessarily Beneventan at all. Hand B, however, looked nearer to the type, Hand C which soon followed, proved to be, as Mynors says, more in the style of A, while the hand in Book II seemed surely not merely 'perhaps,' as he cautiously states, that of A again. The identification of this hand is of considerable importance, for while in Book I, M obviously comes from a better source than B, in Book II, on the other hand, 'it is in constant agreement with B—sometimes with B^2—and must be derived from it.' He concludes that M either 'derives its text of Books I and II from different sources, or its parent was a copy of B in which Book I had been carefully corrected from another source.' At least, since the same hand both begins and ends the manuscript in an even flow of script, any such correction or conflation most probably took place before our manuscript was copied. The possibility that M was copied directly from B is of course strengthened if it is true that both M and B are Beneventan books. If they are not, that supposition is not disproved, but it becomes somewhat weaker.

Let us look more precisely at the palaeographical criteria. The ligatures, especially in Hand B, are notably Beneventan, particularly those for *ei, fi, ti* (both kinds), *nt*, and perhaps above all, *ae*.[50] Hand B has some exceptions to the *ti* rule, but here the use of the regular form of *t* in cases of assibilation may be explained by the fact that the letter had already been involved in a ligature with a preceding *c* or *s*.[51] In Hand A, the ligature of the regular form with a descending *i longa* is used for the assibilated form—but for the unassibilated as well[52]—and sometimes the assibilated form appears without either ligature.[53] The cursive ligature is not used. In Hand C, neither ligature appears.

The abbreviations in M agree well enough with what we should expect of an early tenth-century manuscript (I could as readily put it in the latter half of the ninth) in Beneventan script.[54] The usage in general is the same in the three hands. Some eccentricities occur, but such are not surprising at a time when the characteristic Beneventan traits are not yet fixed.[55] The punctuation is simple: a dot alone, or one with an upward curving stroke, for a half-pause; an angle like a small figure 7 slightly tipped down, with a dot above or at the right or without a dot, for a whole pause. The characteristically Beneventan . , . or ' , ' for a whole pause do not occur.[56]

The uncial first lines in Hand A are also impressive.[57] To the best of my knowledge uncials like these do not occur in the early (or the later) Beneventan. The nearest approach that I note in the first volume of Lowe's facsimiles, which come down to the end of the tenth century, is in the hand that Lowe (No. XXVI) calls non-Beneventan in *Bamberg E. III. 4* (*Hist. 6*), *ca* 900 A.D., Victor Vitensis and Eutropius. The other scribe at work in this manuscript has a 'strange Beneventan-like hand' that suggests to Lowe that a Beneventan scribe had wandered north, perhaps to Nonantola.

The ornamentation in *M* is of a competent and systematic sort. Unhappily the gathering that contained the passage which in *B* and some other manuscripts[58] is accompanied by a picture of Vivarium is lost, but elsewhere we find at least elaborate human figures. One (Plate D) gives an impersonation of Rhetoric with two fingers extended in the familiar gesture, and another (fol. 132^v) portrays Music, evidently beating time with clenched fist.[59] Then there is an amazing diversity in the other diagrams that accompany the accounts of the seven liberal arts, with figures of fish, flesh, and fowl and elaborate borders.[60] Nine elaborate initials appear,[61] with enough repetition to suggest that a font of such letters had been devised[62] with an occasional blossoming out into something still more elaborate.[63] These initials are colored in a simple but effective manner with red, blue, green, yellow, and brown.

There is also, for the shorter sections, a minor font of initials, in which a simply outlined letter is filled in with two or three of the colors mentioned. Thus the *C* and the *Q* in Plates A.2 and B.1 have a green centre with red in the outlines of the letter. Finally in the first words of sentences, uncial initials are used by Hand *A*, and excellent uncials they are.[64] This scribe may well have written the uncial lines at the beginning of the main chapters, as well as (later) the titles in red minuscules that precede them.[65] In Hands *B* and *C* these uncial initials are far less carefully made. The scribes followed the instructions of the director, or perhaps the fashion of the manuscript that they were copying, as best they could.

In the more elaborate specimens of ornamentation I seem to see two forces at work. One is native Italian, very possibly of ancient lineage. The bird-forms have a parallel in those of *B,* figured in Lowe's plate of the latter manuscript. The human figures, as in Plate D, suggest an antique prototype.[66] But in one of the initials here shown (Plate B.2) there appears a touch of something different. This initial and the accompanying line of uncials almost look as if they had stepped into our manuscript from a North-French book. The influence from a source like that accounts for the character of the script in Hands *A* and *C.* If we were sure that this manuscript were written at a Beneventan centre, we might regard Hand *B* as a scribe of that place, and Hands *A* and *C* as monks who had wandered down there from the north. But Lowe has made it clear[67] that the two different kinds of script were not cultivated in Beneventan monasteries. When we find them in the same manuscript, it is clear that the non-Beneventan variety is the work of an outsider. Since two of the hands in *M* are of that sort, perhaps Hand *B* came up to a North-Italian monastery from the Beneventan zone.[68] It is more

reasonable, however, to regard the whole book as characteristic of some scriptorium in North Italy where different styles were employed. I fail to see that Hand *B* is any more Beneventan than that of the scribe who wrote the page of a manuscript (No. 202) of Vercelli—and perhaps at Vercelli—reproduced by Ehrle and Liebaert.[69] Some such centre as Vercelli seems the most likely birthplace for manuscript *M.*

Furthermore, we must take into consideration a movement at which I have hinted in my account of the script of Tours[70]—the spread of the 'Martinian' hand. It is a part and the centre of the general progress of Carolingian script, its conquest of the national hands of Spain, the British Isles, Germany, and Italy. Starting from Tours, it shows itself first and most notably in Fleury and in the Franco-Saxon centres of northern France, whence it passes to Fulda, Reichenau, and St Gall, crosses the Alps and appears at Bobbio, Novara, and Vercelli.[71] I venture to suggest that we may see in *M* the traces of this Martinian style. But this history of peaceful penetration is still to be written.

One of the manuscripts of excerpts listed by Mynors (p. xviii) may furnish an important clue to the original of *M.* This too is a codex of Vercelli, No. 183. It is a patristic miscellany, containing from Cassiodorus only chapters 8 and 9 of Book I, in a greatly abbreviated form. From the text shown in the facsimile in Ehrle-Liebaert,[72] we may not determine its class, but the character and the antiquity (*saec.* VIII) of its script suggest the general style of *B.* I am not going so far as to rob some Beneventan centre of that manuscript and locate it in the north. Whether *B* was written in the Beneventan region or not,[73] we have found evidence for believing that a sister-manuscript, or a parent-manuscript, of *B* was somewhere in the north and that *M* descends from that. Such a lineage, rather than a direct descent from *M* is attested by the text of Book I.

But what of Book II? Here the text of *M* is certainly inferior to that in Book I. There is also apparent evidence pointing towards Mynors's conclusion that in Book II, *M* is a direct copy of *B* or a direct descendant from it. His most telling case is II, 5, 1 (p. 143, 4) where *B,* pressed for space at the end of a line, writes the final *s* of *mathesis* above the line. Here *M* has *mathessi.* Among a goodly number of others I will specify merely:

> II, 2, 9 (p. 103, 10) gestarum (*alterum*)] gesitarum *BM* (though *gestarum* [prius] in the same line is given correctly by both).

> II, 2, 9 (p. 103, 17) epilogorum] et pilogorum *B* et philogorum *M* (a reprehensible attempt at emendation!)

> II, 2, 15 (p. 107, 18) deliberatio] deberatio *B M.*

> II, 5, 1 (p. 142, 18) Musis] musit *B* pmusia *M.*[74]

We have already noted the character of the corrections in *B* made by the second band in Book I.[75] It seems fatal to the independence of *M,* therefore, when we find a number of them in the text of that manuscript. Here are a few examples, in addition to those given by Mynors.[76]

II, 3, 6 (p. III, 5) quoniam] quae B^2 *M*.

II, 3, 8 (p. 112, 22) ab omni communione] ab hominis communione B^2 *M p*.

II, 3, 17 (p. 128, 2) iurisperitosque] iurisque peritos B^2 *M*.

II, *Conclusio*, 2 (p. 158, 22) in Deuteronomio] incede uteronomio *B S*. Here, we infer, *M* is correct, and we might infer its independence were not the curious error corrected by B^2, happy for once in his emendation.

Such instances might induce one to regard the case as closed, were it not for a score or so of cases in which *M* seems independent of *B* or B^2 or both, or allied with another source.

II, 2, 4 (p. 99, 7) iuridicialis] iuri iudicialis *M* Σ (*praeter T O*). Here it would seem that an original error of *iudicialis* in the original of *M*, and that of the other class Σ (made independently later by *U*), had been corrected by the addition above the line of *iuri*, which in the descendants of Σ (except *T O*) and in *M* was then incorporated in the text.

II, 3, 14 (p. 121, 16) adhibita] ad avita *B* adhabita *M*. Here it looks as if *M*'s reading (not reported by Mynors) were that of the original of both *M* and *B*, which the latter manuscript still further distorted.

II, 3, 15 (p. 125, 10) ex vi] ex III *B M* (*corr. B^2*). Here we may again congratulate B^2 on an excellent emendation—or an excellent appropriation from another manuscript—and wonder why *M*, if he saw the correction in *B*, did not take it.

II, 3, 15 (p. 125, 20) everrisse] B^2 evertisse Ω. B^2 has surpassed himself here, but with no recognition from *M*.

II, 5, 4 (p. 144, 17) cythar (ar)um] chitarum *B* cytharum *M* Σ. Here again *M* agrees with the other class against the barbarous spelling of *B*, which B^2 did not touch. The parent manuscript X^1 may have been responsible for the easy haplography.

II, 5, 8 (p. 145, 23) hypolydius] ypodus *B U* ypolidus *M* Σ. Again *M* is hardly correcting (or semi-correcting) but reproducing an error of X^1, which *B* makes worse still.

II, *Conclusio*, 7 (p. 162, 13) nimis] nisi *B U om. p*. Here *M* has the right reading, if Mynors's report, as I have no reason to doubt, is complete.

This delicate matter cannot be settled until an absolutely complete collation of *B* and *M* lie before us, but the above instances at least warrant the suspicion that *M*, instead of deriving directly from *B*, comes from another branch of the same class. The errors specified above which it shares with *B* may have been in their common ancestor *Y*, which in general is inferior to *Z* in Book II.[77] Even in the curious error *mathessi* for *mathesis*, the form that misled *M*, might

have existed in *Y* and been reproduced in *B* only by chance at the end of a line. . . .

The whole question needs a fresh sifting, but until that is made, I see no cogent reason for placing *M* in Book II any more than in Book I on an immediate line of descent from *B*.

I hardly need to state once more that if in the present paper certain positions have been taken not quite in line with those of Mynors, my views are presented not as adverse criticism, but as incentives to further investigation in a most fertile field, to which his 'new Cassiodorus' has invited us.

Notes

1. See the important note by Van de Vyver in *Speculum*, VI (1931), 279, n. 4.

2. *Cassiodori Senatoris Institutiones*, edited from the Manuscripts by R. A. B. Mynors (Oxford: Clarendon Press, 1937). Pp. lvi, 193. $4.00. The only defects in printing that I have noted are these: p. 2, under *D:* for 'xxxii' read 'xxxiii' (cf. p. xvi and p. 83, 12, *app.*); p. 77, 8, *app.: facias* lacks the designation of the MS. or MSS in which it is found; Père Delebaye, *Anal. Boll.*, LV (1937), 183, notes *Heliodoram* for *Heliodorum* (p. 80, 24). 'Munich clm.' (p. xvii) is redundant.

3. 'Cassiodorstudien,' *Philologus*, LXXI (1912), 282-299; LXXII (1913), 503-517; 'Die Institutio Oratoria des Quintilianus im Mittelalter,' *ibid.*, LXXXIX (1934), 349-383, on Cassiodorus, p. 350. On p. 515 of the earlier article he speaks of material on the text of the *Institutiones* collected by Th. Stettner. See the latter's article in *Philologus*, LXXXII (1926), 241-242.

4. *De Orthographia*, p. 145, 18 Keil (*G.L.*, VII): 'in primo libro institutionum nostrarum.' But note that he has just described the work exactly (p. 144, 2).

5. Quintilian's *Institutio Oratoria*, 'Training of the Orator,' is a different affair.

6. This he states in his *De Orthographia*, p. 144, 2 (Keil, *G.L.*, VII): 'Institutiones quem ad modum divinae et humanae debeant intellegi lectiones duobus libris . . . inpletas,' and *lectionum* appears in the preface to Book II of the present work (p. 89, 3, 8). True, an ancient author did not always quote the exact title of a work of his when referring to it, but *lectionum* also appears in the *Incipit* of the best manuscripts for Book I (p. 9, 20). Cassiodorus also uses *litterarum* (I, *praef.*, 6 p. 6, 15; 21, 2 p. 60, 22; 27, 2 p. 69, 1) and that appears in the *Explicit* of the manuscripts for Book I (p. 85) and in those of the *capitula* of Book II (p. 93, 11). I should treat *lectionum* (I am forced to a pun) as the *lectio difficilior*. Another variant is *rerum*, found in Class Σ of the manuscripts in the *Explicit* of Book II and in the oldest manuscript. *B*, in the *Explicit* for the entire work (p. 163). These manuscripts are right, however, I think, in giving *hu-*

manarum (cf. *De Orthog., loc. cit.*) instead of *saecularium*, though *saecularium* too appears in Cassiodorus both in the text (I, 21, 2 p. 60, 22; II, *praef.* p. 89, 8)—he also has *liberalium* (I, *praef.*, 6 p. 6, 14)—and in the *Incipit* of the manuscripts for Book II (p. 85; cf. p. 93, 11). V. Mortet, *Rev. de Philol.*, XXIV (1900), 103-110, argues for *Institutiones divinarum et saecularium litterarum*. The title that I would adopt had the approval, if my memory is correct, of Traube.

7. P. xxiv. The picture of Vivarium was not first reproduced by F. Milkau, 'Zu Cassiodor,' *Festschrift Kuhnert*, 1928. It will be found also in G. Pfeilschifter, *Die Germanen im röm. Reich. Theoderich der Grosse* (Mainz, 1910), Abb. 96, from a photograph lent to him by Traube. In Abb. 64 this writer reproduces the portrait of Cassiodorus given by Mommsen and Traube in their edition of the *Variae* (M. G. H., *Auct. Ant.*, XII, 1894, Tab. B) from Leyden, *Vule. 46, saec.* XII.

8. Note incidentally the picture of the *tabernaculum templumque Domini* that Cassiodorus had introduced *depicta subtiliter lineamentis propriis in pandecte Latino corporis grandioris* (I, 5, 2 p. 23, 5). As my friend Bernard M. Peebles reminds me, a copy (North English) of this picture is doubtless preserved in the Codex Amiatinus of the Vulgate. See Dom H. Quentin, *Mémoire sur l'Établissement du Texte de la Vulgote* (Rome, 1922), p. 477, Fig. 77.

9. *Die karolingischen Miniaturen* I. *Die Schule von Tours* (Berlin, 1930 [Teil 1], 1933 [Teil 2]).

10. As Mynors points out (p. xxiii), the picture of the monastery appears not only in *B*, but in *C* and *X*, important members of the German branch of manuscripts of Book I, while *G* and *D* of that branch and θ of the French branch (see p. 72, 23, *app.*) leave spaces for it. Since there are really but two main families of manuscripts (see below, p. 438) the presence of this picture in the archetype seems assured.

11. I, 10, 1 (p. 34). After writing the above, I re-read my friend Lehmann's 'Cassiodorstudien' (see above, p. 433, n. 3) and was glad to find that he had expressed the same view (p. 287). Possibly my 'independent' observation was a reminiscence.

12. 'Bemerkungen über den ältesten Handschriftenbestand des Klosters Bobbio,' *Anzeiger der k. Akad. d. Wiss.* (Vienna), phil.-hist. Kl. XLVIII (1911), No. xi.

13. In 1912, when I had the pleasure of meeting this eminent scholar in Vienna, Beer told me that before publishing he had written to a number of librarians and palaeographers for their criticisms, but that no one had any to offer.

14. *Monumenta Palaeographica Vindobonensia*, II, 15-26.

15. The first, to the best of my knowledge, to speak up was Dom A. Wilmart in *Recherches de science religieuse*, IX (1919), 65, n. 4. A recent attempt to defend Beer's hypothesis has been made by H. Gomoll, 'Zu Cassiodors Bibliothek und ihrem Verhältnis zu Bobbio,' *Zentralblatt für Bibliothekswesen* LIII (1936), 185-189. I am indebted to Mr Peebles for a reference to this article (the conclusions of which he does not accept) and for various emendations of this paper of mine.

16. *M. Tulli Ciceronis De re publica libri e codice rescripto Vaticano latino 5757 phototypice expressi*, Codices e Vaticanis selecti quam simillime expressi iussa Pii XI P. M. consilio et opera curatorum Bibliothecae Apostolicae Vaticanae, Vol. XXIII (Bibl. Apost. Vat. 1934), *Prolegomena*. The *Vivarium* hypothesis is discussed on pp. 14-19.

17. *Op. cit.*, p. 18: 'Anzi nei primi secoli che seguirono fino al X, presso i bibliofili che non mancarono nemmeno allora, le *Istituzioni* di Cassiodoro avranno servito, come una guida bibliografica, a farle apprezzare e cercare dattorno.'

18. I, 17, 1 (p. 55, 16).

19. I, 15, 9 (p. 46, 16). Two manuscripts, *V* and *Q*, corrected this mistake. The latter, *Vat. Pal. lat. 274 saec.* XI, emends with a high hand almost everything in sight.

20. E.g., II, 3, 12 (p. 117, 2); abdicativa <et particulari dedicativa>.

21. I, 14, 4 (p. 41, 8).

22. I, 10, 4 (p. 34).

23. I, 20 (p. 58, 25). I feel like attributing to X^1 (or to various later scribes) the common mediaeval spelling *rethorica* adopted by Mynors throughout. It was not Isidore's spelling (at least not in Lindsay's text).

24. Mr Peebles (who is somewhat inclined to emend *exemplaria* to *exemplar*) finds it difficult to suppose that the *archetypus* was not used for purposes of verification. It, or a careful copy, *ought* to have been so used, but again I cannot believe that it contained as many mistakes as the common errors of all our manuscripts. They prove (to me) the existence of X^2, which somebody (not the busy Cassiodorus, poor man) should have scrupulously collated with the original.

25. P. 437.

26. Some of these may have been taken not from B^2, but some manuscript or manuscripts of the other families (e.g., see Mynors's apparatus for 5, 20; 49, 18; 76, 18). But until *U* is reported fully (see p. xi), it is not worth while to pursue this clue further. See below, p. 447.

27. Since two that contain Book I (*C* and *X*) have at least chapter 1 of Book II, it may be that their original included the entire work.

28. E.g., *Y* is right against *Z* in 4, 23; 31, 11; 39, 21; 47, 7. *Z* is right against *Y* in 20, 23; 64, 18.

29. See below, p. 441, n. 2.

30. *Palaeographische Forschungen,* IV (1904), 11.

31. The manuscript Q (*Vat. Pal. lat. 274, saec.* XI, from Augsburg) should hardly be attached to a higher point on the stemma than the parent of *C, X,* and *G.* As Mynors states (p. xiv) it contains 'innumerable alterations,' i.e., conjectures. It also agrees very often with the second hand in *C,* which may well have been its immediate source.

32. See below.

33. Called 'IXth century' on p. xvii, but '*saec.* VIII-IX' on p. 2.

34. E.g., *Y* is right against *Z* in 90, 16; 104, 24; 106, 3; 111, 4; 142, 5. *Z* is right against *Y* in 89, 5; 91, 1; 100, 3; 104, 1; 105, 17; 122, 9; 128, 7; 130, 2; 140, 7; 153, 9; 156, 21.

35. Another is Mallius Theodorus, *De Metris,* as in *B.* See above, p. 436.

36. One question previously discussed and now definitely answered by this work of Mr Mynors relates to St Isidore's acquaintance with the *Institutiones.* It seems clear that though he did not know the First Book (Lehmann, *op. cit.,* p. 517) he did use the Second. But the attempt to show (p. xxii) that he had the first ('authentic') form of the text at his disposal seems to me dubious. The evidence, which I cannot here discuss, points rather to the presence of the *revised* text, though not to the modified ('interpolated') form found in Φ and Δ.

37. Lowe, *Script. Ben.* (1929), I, No. VIII. Lowe states in his *Ben. Script* (1912), p. 202, that *B* has certain un-Beneventan traits. In this early period, with the paucity of material at our disposal, it is hard to say just what Beneventan is. Lowe now writes me that the manuscript might perhaps have been written elsewhere than in the Beneventan zone—but not at Bobbio.

38. Lowe, *Script. Ben., loc. cit.,* states that the scribe himself makes numerous corrections, and that there are two correcting hands, one of the ninth or tenth century, and one of the eleventh. Mynors does not distinguish between these hands.

39. We should note, however, in both B^2 and *U* certain readings that are identical with those in Class *Z.* Such is the heading DE MODIS INTELLIGENTIAE inserted by B^2 *U Q* after §4 in I, 9 (p. 33, 27), written at that point in the margin by *C* and put after I, 9, 5 (p. 34, 6), where it belongs, by the rest of *Z* (except *G,* which, apparently, omits it). It is not in *B M.* It was apparently omitted by X^1 and then put by the scribe in the margin. By *Y* it was omitted, by Θ it was re-inserted correctly, by Ξ it was left in the margin, at the right place in manuscript *X,* at the wrong place in *C,* and hence was wrongly re-inserted in the book of the type which affected B^2 *U Q.* (Cf. the relation of *Q* and *C;* above, p. 439, n.4). Such a heading might of course have been devised independently; it is its wrong position in B^2 *U Q C* that attests their close connection. Of course one might say that *U* simply copied what he found in *B,* but a number of cases occur where no correction by B^2 is reported, but where *U* agrees with one or more manuscripts of the other main class. I will mention merely: I, *praef.,* 4 (p. 5, 20) Graecia facunda] gr(a)eca facundia *U* Θ C^2 *X Q* [but possibly correctly!]; I, 15, 14 (p. 49, 18); unus quis] unus quisque *U V* $θ^2$ Ξ *Q H;* I, 30, 2 (p. 76, 18): pro maxima] propria Θ proxima *U Q D. Q* is always present in the readings that *U* shares with *Z* against *Y* (*B M*). That an older source is possible, is indicated by the agreement in 76, 18 with *D,* a fragmentary manuscript, *saec.* IX/X.

40. I, *praef.,* 7 (p. 7, 12): debere talia] deberet alia *B* debere alia B^2 *U;* I, 1, 4 (p. 12, 6): qui quamvis] quicquam vis B^1; I, 1, 10 (p. 15, 23) unamquamque rem dum] unam quam qu(a)erendum *B U F E.*

41. E.g., I, 15, 4 (p. 44, 1); ab expositoribus] habet positoribus *B,* where the similarity of *ex* and the ligature & led *B* astray (if *U* is correct here, he either, for once, made an *emendatio palmaris* or borrowed from his *Z* codex); I, 24, 3 (p. 66, 4) fit] sit *B U.*

42. E.g., I, 27, 2 (p. 68, 20): ut quae] aque *B* atquae B^2 et quae *U;* I, 28, 4 (p. 70, 24); suffarcinatus sufascinatus *B U;* I, 32, 3 (p. 80, 11): iam patriae] impatriae *B* (what of *U?*); I, 32, 6 (p. 82, 19) super haec etiam] superectiam *B* super etiam B^2 *U.*

43. In the list of authors cited by Cassiodorus given in Migne, *Patr. Lat.,* LXX, 1459, Mallius Theodorus does not appear, nor is his work cited by A. Franz, *M. Aurelius Cassiodorus Senator* (Breslau, 1872), pp. 80-92. One of the chief manuscripts is a famous Beneventan book, a miscellany of grammatical works (Paris, *B. N. lat. 7350, saec.* VIII), which Lowe (*Script. Ben,* No. IX) finds closely related to *B* in its script.

44. Above, p. 441, n. 1.

45. Some have even argued from the vogue of Sisebutus in South Italy that the Beneventan script itself drew many of its features from the Visigothic. But that spectre has been laid once and for all by Lowe (*Ben. Script,* pp. 104-121).

46. *Revue de Philol.,* XXIV (1900), 103-118.

47. The volume is bound in brown blotched calf later than the time of Cardinal Mazarin, probably of the eighteenth century. It contains two different manuscripts. A. Fols 1-74. Nicolaus Secundinus, trans. of Onesander, *De perfecto imperatore, et al.* A beautiful humanistic book-hand of the end of the fifteenth century. B. Fols 75-142. Cass., *Inst.* Good parchment, 68 leaves, 262×172 mm. One column, 217×143, including side-columns of 5 mm. on either side of script-space. 27 lines for Book I (fols 75-106), 28 for Book II (fols 107-142). Gatherings. I-VIII (fols 75-138), quaternions; IX (fols 139-142), binion. Signatures in centre of lower margin: Q II (fol. 90ᵛ); Q III (fol. 98ᵛ); Q III (fol. 106ᵛ). The fifth gathering, containing from p. 67, 10 *Euangeliorum* to the end of Book I is

lost. No signatures for Book II. Ruling on hair-side 2 O. S.: >><< | >><<. The confronting of ridges between the second and the third and between the sixth and the seventh leaves suggests N. S., but this is here the result of the make-up of the gathering, not of the ruling. In Q. I (>>>< | >><<) the irregularity is probably caused by a second ruling of the third leaf on the recto. Three hands, A. fols 75ʳ-103ᵛ; 107ʳ-142ᵛ (Plates A.1, B.2, C, D). B. fols 104ʳ-105ᵛ, l. 7 *uideam[ur]* (Plates A.2, B.1); C. fols 105ᵛ, l. 7 *[uideam]ur* -106ᵛ (Plate B.1). This is the end of Q. IV, after which Q. V is lost. What hand or hands wrote Q. V we know not. Provenience doubtful. What was apparently a note, or notes, of ownership at the top of fol. 75ʳ is partly erased and partly cut away. Traces may be seen in Plate A.1. (All of the plates are slightly reduced.)

48. Frequent in Beneventan script of the ninth century, less so in the tenth (Lowe, *Ben. Script*, p. 148).

49. The distinction occurs only sporadically in Beneventan books before the end of the ninth century (*ibid.*, p. 305).

50. See Plate B.1, l. 4 (*quae*). It is the first of the forms described by Lowe, *Ben. Script*, p. 142. This, like the similar form in Insular script comes from the union of an open *a* with *e*. See the following pages in Lowe for descriptions of the other ligatures mentioned.

51. Plate A.2, ll. 5-6; *lectione*; l. 7: *questiones*. In the case of *sti*, at least, the form here used is normal. See Lowe, *Ben. Script*, p. 147.

52. Plate B.2.

53. Plate A.1, l. 10: *traditioni.*

54. See the list in Lowe, *Ben. Script*, pp. 174-196.

55. We may note *aūt* as well as *aū* for *autem* (the former Lowe notes as exceptional); dilmi ff for *dilectissimi fratres* (ff is cited by Lowe only from our MS. *B*); nomi for *nomins* (not abbreviated till the eleventh century); &nam for *aeternam*, Plate B.2, l. 8 (t not found in middle of words); t for *tur*, Plates A.2, B.1, C.2 (the figure-2 form does not appear before the eleventh century).

56. On fol. 78ᵛ a square of dots and a triangle ∴ appear, but these, like the four dots in Plate B.2, are the adornments of an *explicit* and an *incipit*, not properly punctuation.

57. Plates A.1, B.2, C.1.

58. See above, p. 436, n. 4.

59. Perhaps in the original the thumb was extended a bit. Cf. Horace, *Carm.*, IV, 6, 35: Lesbium servate pedem meique / poilicis ictum.

60. Specimens in Plates C.2 and D.

61. E.g., Plates A.1, B.2, C.1.

62. The *S* of Plate B.2 reappears on fol. 127, and the same *G* is used on fols 109ʳ, 131ᵛ and 136ʳ.

63. Plate C.1.

64. See Plates A.1, B.2, C.1.

65. In red are such titles in Plates A.1, B.2 and C.1.

66. Once more, a study of the ornamentation of all the manuscripts might well enable us to reconstruct many of the features of the *codex archetypus* of Cassiodorus's work.

67. *Benev. Script*, p. 90.

68. For such cases, see *id.*, p. 91.

69. *Spec. Cod. Lat., sec. ed.* (reprint of 1932), Tab. 10. The script is earlier than that of our book. It is called in the plate *saec.* VIII/IX but in the description (p. XX) it is associated with the style that prevailed in North Italy 'ineunte saeculo IX.' The latter date seems preferable—if not one still a bit later.

70. *Studies in the Script of Tours*, I. *A Survey of the Manuscripts of Tours* (Cambridge, Mass.: Mediaeval Academy of America, 1929), p. 9.

71. A manuscript of Vercelli, *Bibl. d. Chiesa Metropol., 104 (47)*, Augustine, *De Sancta Trinitate, saec.* IX *med.*, described by Dom Wilmart, *Revue Bénédictine*, XLV (1933), 162, is most illuminating in this connection. The first quaternion is in a hand of Tours; the rest of the book is written by two Italian hands that imitate the style of St Martin's.

72. *Spec. Cod. Lat.*, Tab. 9.

73. See above, p. 441.

74. The error of *B*, *t* for *s*, would account for the error of *M* on account of the similarity between a Beneventan (or cursive) *t* with a curved initial stroke and an open *a*.

75. See above, p. 441.

76. P. xix: 90, 13; 132, 4; 156, 21.

77. See above, p. 439.

Jacob Hammer (essay date 1944)

SOURCE: "Cassiodorus, the Savior of Western Civilization," in *Bulletin of the Polish Institute of Arts and Sciences in America*, Vol. 3, No. 1, October, 1944, pp. 369-84.

[*In the essay below, Hammer reviews Cassiodorus's literary achievements, praising him for rejuvenating Western intellectual life when it was in "utter decay."*]

Everybody is familiar with the phrase "forgotten man." I shall speak to-day of a forgotten man, forgotten even by some classicists, a man whose absence is singularly noticeable in Holbrook Jackson's "*Anatomy of Bibliomania.*" And there certainly he ought to have found a place of honor. My forgotten man is Flavius Magnus Aurelius Cassiodorus Senator, 490-583 (?) A.D., a man who stood on the boundary of two worlds, the ancient and medieval, or as some maintain, the Roman and Teutonic. It may even be said that he stood on the confines of the ancient and modern worlds: in the writings of Cassiodorus the word *modernus* occurs for the first time.

To understand his role it is necessary to survey certain problems which had beset the Roman world for several centuries past. For the decline of the Roman Empire was not cataclysmic. The deadly action of financial and economic factors paved the way for the decline long before the deposition of the last emperor of the West in 476 A.D. and long before the invasions of the barbarians began to weaken the once powerful structure of the Roman Empire. Among the causes of the decline may be cited the slow and sure extinction of the middle class, men being compelled by law to follow the occupation of their fathers; a general aversion to military service; a corrupt officialdom, indifferent to the sufferings of the population bled white, for whom the word "freedom" lost its meaning utterly; the weakness, greed and impotence of the central government with its puppet emperors; external troubles caused by the enemies of the empire, including the invasions of the barbarians; and lastly the depreciation of currency.

Some able emperors, it is true, succeeded in stemming the tide for a while. So Septimius Severus, whose military autocracy worked for a short time, only to collapse at the beginning of the third century; so Diocletian, who appointed a co-emperor and two Caesars to help him to share the burden of ruling; so Constantine the Great, who for strategic reasons established another capital in Constantinople. But the price-fixing edict of Diocletian and the public buildings projects of Constantine and the monetary reforms of both produced only an interval of tranquillity, comparable to an Indian summer. Another important point must be added. Roman armies ceased to be composed of Italians, who preferred to mutilate themselves rather than be branded upon entering the army and have their children serve as hereditary soldiers. What is more, the Italians and the Mediterranean nations from the third century on were unable, physically speaking, to cope with the invaders. But armies were needed. In the third century Roman armies were composed of Illyrians and of peoples of Asia Minor. Then the Balkans supplied recruits and it is worth keeping in mind that both Diocletian and Constantine were emperors of Balkan stock. Enlistment had to be opened to all kinds of barbarians, including Huns, but the Teuton element predominated. The Teutons became career men and succeeded in securing positions of the highest authority. You can see how liberal this Roman policy was. Liberal, indeed, but with tragic consequences, because for years the emperors did not realize the danger. When Constantine perceived it, he incorporated the Visigoths in the Empire as "*foederati*," in return for protecting the frontiers and supplying soldiers. They received yearly subsidies, either in grain or money. As Professor Bury says:[1] "Federal relations of this kind are a standing feature of the whole period during which the German people were encroaching upon the provinces of the empire, from the fourth to the sixth century." That such an arrangement revealed a consciousness of deterioration spreading through the life arteries of the Empire, is clear.

Everyone knows that in centuries past the Romans had assailed and destroyed their enemies. Now the opposite was taking place. The defense of the Empire was entrusted to the invaders and I leave it to you to decide whether a state, whose citizens, refuse to protect it and prefer to entrust the defense of their country to former invaders, has a right to survive.

At the end of the fourth century, shortly after the battle of Adrianople (378), which military historians consider the greatest disaster that befell Rome in her battles with the Teutons, the emperor Theodosius fully realized the danger of the Teuton problem. For this battle revolutionized warfare as much as did the invention of gunpowder centuries later. Theodosius entered upon a policy of appeasement and conciliation, hoping to enervate the Goths and stop their migratory habits by keeping them in permanent settlements. But he failed. Even his permanent division of the Empire into two halves, under two separate emperors did not produce the desired results, although both halves were legally a unity, one consul being elected in Rome and another in Constantinople and though laws and edicts were enacted in the name of both emperors. Alaric was now coming into the limelight. Stilicho, the Vandal general of Theodosius, for all his ability could do little to stop him and the pressure of his Visigothic hordes. Now we witness a peculiar spectacle. Stilicho the defender of the Empire was a German; Alaric the aggressor also a German; all this can only show the immense power of a foreign general, who combined in his single person the offices previously separate, the *magister peditum* (commander of infantry) and *magister equitum* (commander of cavalry), blended into the office of *magister utriusque militiae* (commander of both services). If one German had that office, why not another? Alaric wanted it and so did other leaders of the barbarians. To secure that office they did not hesitate to blackmail the government by ravaging parts of the Empire. For to ravage was a means of having their claims granted and of securing new privileges for their people. But in all fairness they did not want the destruction of the empire of which they wished to become a part. It has been pointed out that had Alaric been told that he was seeking to destroy the empire he would have repudiated the idea. And so things went on. The Romans resented the situation: witness the execution of Stilicho (408) and the slaughter of the Goths in Italy in the same year.

An outstanding event in the fifth century was the sack of Rome by Alaric in 410 A.D. This was followed in 455 by another savage pillage of the eternal city by the German tribe of the Vandals, who stowed into the holds of their insatiable ships all the treasures of Rome. During the same century the Empire lost Spain, Britain, Africa and Gaul, all invaded by Germans tribes. Now another danger loomed: the invasions of the Huns into Gaul and Italy. It may sound paradoxical, but it is nevertheless a historical fact that the inroads of the Huns rendered a great service to the Empire. The Huns retarded the dismemberment of the Empire by keeping many German tribes in check on the one hand, and by supplying mercenaries for the so-called Roman army on the other; a blessing in disguise for the Empire and civilization! Let us keep in mind that the provinces ravaged by the Huns would have been devasted by the German tribes anyway.

From 456 to 472 Ricimer, a German general of Suevic extraction, was the real master of the state, who with the help of his mercenaries made and unmade emperors. One thing must be said in his favor. Like his predecessors of German birth, Bauto, Merobaudes, Arbogastes, Stilicho and others, he preferred to be the power behind the throne than to wear the purple himself. He knew that he was a stranger and therefore realized that his rule would lack popular support because an emperor of Roman stock still commanded respect. Nor must the religious factor be ignored: the invaders were Arians, followers of the religious teachings of Arius, who taught that the Son and Spirit were creations of God who was from eternity. Since this was contrary to the teachings of the Catholic Church, they were considered heretics and excluded from communion.

All this time, however, while these German protectors made and unmade the West, there was no interregnum, because the emperor of the East exercised sway, and again I must remind you that these Germans were imperial officials appointed by the emperor.

We now approach a new period. Up to 474 the German protectors of Italy, forming the Empire's armies, lived in barracks and were never actually settled on Italian soil, though their kinsmen had settlements on the frontiers. They now demanded land in Italy and were refused. Under the command of the master of soldiers, Odovacar, they revolted and deposed the last emperor of the West, Romulus Augustulus, in 476. But even Odovacar had no intentions of assuming the purple; he refused, however, to have a puppet emperor. In agreement with Constantinople he became the regent of Italy, thus acknowledging the fact that the Emperor of the East was the sole ruler. An ambiguous letter of the emperor made Odovacar a patrician and he ruled the country as an imperial official. For the time being the East had no power to act.

Again, as in the past, the Romans carried on the administration, while Odovacar and his men did the fighting. The father of our Cassiodorus held high official positions under Odovacar, a Roman dignitary in the service of a barbarian. The reason is simple: Odovacar was an imperial official.

In 488 an important event took place. Theodoric, the King of the Ostrogoths, a master of soldiers, began to cause trouble to the Emperor of the East. To get rid of him the emperor consented to his going to Italy, which he took after three years of bloody fighting and after treacherously murdering Odovacar. Though ruler of Italy *de facto,* he was in relation to the Italians a Roman governor,[2] ap-

pointed by the emperor, or a viceroy, Italy remaining in theory part of the Empire. Though one third of the lands of Italy was given the Ostrogoths, from the legal point of view the Ostrogoths were not citizens. They lived side by side with the Italians to whom the Roman law applied, while the Ostrogoths adhered to their own laws.

Cassiodorus' father, as a Roman official in the service of Odovacar, immediately entered the service of Theodoric, so that there was no break in the administration. For thirty years, during the rule of the illiterate Theodoric Italy flourished and enjoyed prosperity she had known for a century. Theodoric restored buildings, encouraged agriculture and commerce and showed a remarkable capacity for attracting to his service the best men Rome had in those days. For to maintain a proper balance between Roman and German, Catholic and Arian, Christian and Jew, barbarian and cultured, was certainly no easy task. He succeeded and was assisted by such men as Boethius, Symmachus and others and above all by young Cassiodorus, to whom I shall now turn.

Scion of a noble family of Syrian extraction, settled in Southern Italy, he, like other relatives of his, rendered distinguished service to the Empire. Like his father he served Theodoric and this was an event of importance to this king who did not speak Latin fluently. He attained the highest offices, was head of the civil service, then secretary of state, postmaster and consul. His legal training, his character and education were the qualities that assisted him in his heavy task of keeping peace and harmony between two peoples differing widely in education, culture, and above all in religion. To this harmony Cassiodorus contributed a great deal, because he enjoyed the confidence of both the Romans and Ostrogoths. Moreover Theodoric showed cooperation by his attempts to soothe the pride and vanity of the Roman Senate. His slogan was *'civilitas,'* meaning 'good order' or observance of law; that was followed by religious tolerance which existed in the full sense of the word under Theodoric, whose famous saying: "We cannot command religion because no one can be compelled to believe against his will," was surely inspired by Cassiodorus. During this period Cassiodorus had one thing in mind: to save as much of Roman institutions and character as possible. That they needed saving after so many bloody wars goes without saying.

This state of affairs continued until 523, when the emperor of the East began to persecute Arians, an action that found favor with some of the senators in Rome and above all with the clergy. Theodoric's attempts to induce the emperor to stop the persecution failed. He became suspicious, discovered a faction in the Senate favoring reunion with the East and this resulted in the execution of the great Boethius and his father-in-law, Symmachus. What this meant for the relations between Roman and Teuton now is clear. Theodoric's death prevented him from taking measures against Catholics in Italy. But after his death, though Cassiodorus continued to serve his successors, the *'civilitas'* of Theodoric was gone and with it the experiment of blending the two peoples into one, a thing which succeeded, for example, in Spain. Now the tension between Ostrogoths and Romans came to a climax; the Romans hoped to be freed by the emperor of the East Justinian, whose goal was the recovery of the Western part of the Empire and the attainment of religious unity throughout Christendom; the Ostrogoths seeing the ground slipping from under their feet and resenting the romanizing policy of their queen, Amalasuntha, became sulky and vindictive. Amalasuntha was murdered, but Cassiodorus continued in the service of her murderer. Some consider it a blot on his character and indeed it may be so. He may be accused of time serving, but there is no doubt that he believed that a cooperation between Ostrogoth and Roman was the only solution for Italy's ills. If that was his belief, he was right. When the armies of Justinian invaded Italy, they started a war that lasted for twenty years, with the result that the saviors became more hated than the Ostrogoths. The troubles of Italy were not solved, since Cassiodorus lived long enough to hear of the invasion of the Langobards in 568.

Cassiodorus retired from public life. I shall not enter into all the reasons given for his retirement. It seems to me that he realized that his usefulness was a matter of the past and that his dream to build up an independent Italy with German help was shattered. In other words, his policy of appeasement and his secular hopes collapsed. Perhaps the brutal slaughter of Roman senators, held as hostages in Ravenna (538) at the order of Witigis, on whose bandwagon Cassiodorus jumped, opened his eyes; the news of the slaughter of the population of Milan in 539, an act of savagery surpassing all the outrages of the Hun Attila, may have been an additional eye-opener. You see that killing hostages is an ancient sport, though rarely practiced in antiquity. It would seem that for all his learning Cassiodorus was not familiar with the well known statement of Velleius Paterculus, a Roman historian of the first century A.D., who had the following to say on the subject of the Germans: "Germani . . . quod nisi expertus vix credat, in summa feritate versutissimi natumque mendacio genus.[3] To come back to the bloody massacre of Milan, 300,000 adult males were slaughtered there according to the historian Procopius, while all the women were given away as slaves. Even assuming that Procopius exaggerated the number of victims, this shocking act, to quote Professor Bury, "gives us the true measure of the instincts of the Ostrogoths, claimed by some to have been the most promising of the German invaders of the Empire."[4] In this connection I cannot refrain from quoting the statement of the well-known Swedish scholar, Professor Martin P. Nilsson.[5] The Roman Empire, he says "betrayed civilization by providing weapons, first to the barbarians within the Empire, and afterwards to the barbarians without. First it was barbarized by its own people, and in the end was overrun by aliens and subjected to their domination." How right Professor Nilsson is present conditions in Italy seem to indicate.

During his occupation with state affairs Cassiodorus found time for literary pursuits. This is clear from the twelve books of the *Variae,* a collection of letters and state documents, the style of which became the model of European chancelleries in the Middle Ages. The great French naturalist, Buffon, in his inaugural address to the French Academy in 1753, entitled *Discours sur le Style,* made the following pert remark: "Le style est l'homme." I shall apply this remark to Cassiodorus, but with a slight modification: "le style est l'âge." For the *Variae* are our most important source for the legal and political conditions during his period and incidentally reveal the mentality of the author and his interest in the construction of water clocks, sun dials and musical instruments. He also wrote a chronicle, beginning with Adam to the year 519, based on second hand sources. As a whole it is friendly to the Goths. This tendency manifests itself more clearly in his *History of the Goths,* which has come down to us only in excerpts found in the history of Jordanes.

The fact that Cassiodorus attempted to connect the origin of the Goths with Roman history on the one hand, while on the other he aimed to reconcile both nations by pointing out that the new blood that was pouring into Italy was of noble origin, allows only one conclusion that he attempted what we may call "literary appeasement." But just the same he is the one and only author who must be consulted on different problems of German antiquities. Another work, very popular in the Middle Ages, was the *De Anima,* 'On the Soul,' in which he tries to define the soul, its functions and its moral virtues.

It was between the years 538 and 540 that Cassiodorus retired from public life, "repulsis dignitatum sollicitudinibus et curis saecularibus." Rather than enter the service of Justinian, who would have received him with open arms he preferred to become a *vir religiosus* or *conversus,* a monk. He retired to his estate at Scyllacium, the modern Squillace, in Southern Italy. Here he founded a monastery, *Vivarium,* called so from *vivaria,* or fishponds which he had built there while he was governor of Southern Italy. It was an ideal spot, five miles from the sea, at the foot of Mount Moscius (Mascio). It had the advantage of being far away from the theatre of war and was surrounded by vineyards, olive groves and gardens. It furthermore enjoyed a translucent air, sunny winters and cool summers. Above all, the place was self-sufficient, including even baths for the sick. In short *Vivarium* reminds us in every respect of the enchanted spot Horace longed for:

> There every grace that Nature's hand can lend,
> Invite our steps, and all the clime endear . . .

The monastery had two sections. One was inhabited by monks, the other by austere hermits, who wished to be alone. The hermits lived among the sweet recesses of Mount Castellus, a place well fit for people bent upon meditation. The monks lived in *Vivarium* proper, amidst its well watered gardens. From every point of view this was a place favored by nature, climate and all other things that could give stimulus to mental pursuits. It is proper to call *Vivarium* an estate in the best classical tradition; what is more Cassiodorus was an heir of that tradition, following let us say Cicero, who when condemned to political inactivity would retire to the country to devote himself to literary pursuits. And we must keep in mind that Cassiodorus was the last Roman. Here Cassiodorus set out to employ his leisure for the preservation of Divine and Human learning and for its transmission for after ages that entitles him to the eternal gratitude of Europe. Here, too, he assembled a library. As for libraries, a library had its place in the house of every educated Roman. Some of them had libraries even in their villas along the roads they travelled. How much Romans cared for libraries becomes clear from the fact that Varro was the author of a book *"De Bibliothecis,"* "On the Management of Libraries," and that the great architect Vitruvius (VI.4), explicitly recommends that libraries should look to the East, because in rooms that look south or west books are damaged by dampness. During the republican period, men like Lucullus and Aemilius Paullus had considerable libraries. Lucullus specialized in fine copies and permitted scholars to use them. Sulla, too, had a library containing volumes that once belonged to Aristotle. Cicero had a considerable library and employed special help to put it in order and during the imperial period Augustus established two public libraries, excellently organized, with a general director, called *procurator bibliothecarum,* with a staff of trained assistants for both the Latin and Greek divisions. Pliny and Persius had considerable libraries and libraries were found even in public baths. Another famous library was that of Asinius Pollio and the *Bibliotheca Ulpia* founded by Trajan, where the Roman writer Aulus Gellius did his reading. Even cities in Italy and in the provinces had their libraries. What is more we have references in Latin literature to many a fashionable craze for book collecting. Seneca sums up the situation as follows: "a library takes rank with a bathroom as a necessary ornament of the house." All these libraries, however, were built and founded when both prosperity and peace were tolerably established. Thus collecting books by individuals and government agencies was a factor not to be ignored; but again it must be repeated that this assembling of books went on in times of tolerable peace when there was some prospect of an economic future. But when we come down to the period of Cassiodorus we see a different situation. A country torn by wars and repeatedly invaded by barbarians; every destroyed villa and city meant the permanent loss of some valuable manuscripts; literary activity was non-existent and hand in hand with this went a low level of education, perhaps the lowest known to us in Roman history. There were few people who could boast of the education of a Cassiodorus and we must not take too seriously what either Cassiodorus or Bishop Ennodius say about the zeal with which studies were pursued in Rome, even though under the rule of Theodoric the situation improved somewhat. This period must be judged by its products and with sole exception of the writings of Boethius, the literary contributions of this age were absolutely devoid of originality and there were no educators, as in centuries past, in government service, busy to improve the status of teachers and teaching. Now education paraded in a meretricious garment and at best it could train

officials. Hence its limitations are manifest. This being the case one must not wonder that even theological studies at Rome had to share the fate of lay studies and sink to their level. It must not be forgotten that theological studies were never the *forte* of Italy. For great theologians one had to go to Egypt, Africa and elsewhere, outside the peninsula. The great Tertullian was an African; so were Lactantius and St. Augustine; St. Jerome was a Dalmatian and Cassian was a Scythian. There were no institutions in Italy to train theologians and it is clear that something had to be done to remedy the situation. The heritage of the past had to be saved if the present, representing the remnants of the past, was to survive. Cassiodorus did it. Let us keep in mind that it is easier to build and equip libraries and easier to preach education during a period of prosperity. It is quite a different story to do so in a period of moral and intellectual decay and in a country invaded by barbarians and torn by wars. One who undertakes to save the treasures of the past becomes a servant of humanity, endowed with vision; one who tries both to save and to raise the level of education, profane and religious, is a man of foresight, nay, a benefactor of humanity. It does not matter whether this salvaging is done on a large or small scale; it is the result that counts.

Even before his retirement to *Vivarium,* Cassiodorus was well aware of the prevalent low level of education, lay and religious. He was more than aware, nay, deeply perturbed by the fact that there were no public teachers of theology. He must have been equally perturbed by the shortage of books. To remedy the situation, he conceived in 535 the idea which had the blessing of Pope Agapetus, of establishing at Rome a school of biblical studies, like that at Alexandria earlier, when Clement and Origen had taught there, or like the contemporary Hebrew university at Nisibis in Mesopotamia. But this idea never reached the stage of fruition because of wars and political turmoil.

What he failed to accomplish on a large scale in the metropolis he succeeded in achieving on a smaller scale after his retirement. At *Vivarium* he concentrated his efforts to stimulate lay and theological studies and, what is more, to secure the necessary equipment without which studies would have been impossible. He procured manuscripts from every quarter possible, from Italy and Africa and his extensive connections were of great help here. Thus *Vivarium* became a place of refuge for some who cared for religious meditation; for others it became a school, equipped with books and a *scriptorium,* where theological writings and those of pagan antiquity were studied, copied and multiplied. Here, as nowhere else, an intellectual elite, headed by Cassiodorus, took up the study of liberal arts, not as an end, to be sure, but as a means for the reading of the Scriptures. True, this is a restriction, but it must be granted that even so Cassiodorus, for whom the salvation of the soul and spiritual reading were of supreme importance, by placing the classics in the hands of his monks, rendered the greatest service to secular education. He saw clearly that without the study of astronomy, for example, or geography, the full understanding of the Scriptures was well nigh impossible.

Not all monks, however, were expected to be intellectuals. Those who showed interest in horticulture or in tending the sick were permitted to follow their line of interest, but not without preparation. They were referred to books in the library dealing with their respective subjects.

It was at *Vivarium* that Cassiodorus composed his most famous work, the **Institutiones,**[6] in two books. The first dealt with Christian learning, the second with such secular learning as was necessary for the study of the Scriptures. Broadly speaking it is a kind of methodology. The most surprising thing is that we do not find here a condemnation of pagan authors and in this respect he differs from other great theologians. Tertullian and Cassian, for example, had no use for classical authors. St. Jerome and Augustine, though steeped in the classics, warned of their influence. There was a general feeling that the lips that praised Jupiter could not praise Christ. I shall best illustrate my point by quoting Isidore of Seville on the subject:

"Let the monk beware of reading the books of gentiles and heretics. It is better for him to be ignorant of their pernicious doctrines than through making acquaintance with them to be enmeshed in error." You see that Cassiodorus, though a pious Christian, did not share that point of view.

It is from the **Institutiones** of Cassiodorus that we get some of his ideas. Let me quote to you the following: "Read assiduously, diligently return to your reading. For constant and intent meditation is the mother of understanding." Modern educators may well consider this statement.

We also get an idea of the library. It was collected and constantly increased at great expense. The volumes were kept in *armaria,* or presses, in which the books were arranged not according to authors, but to subject matter; we know that the Greek codices were in the eight *armarium.* The *scriptorium* was equipped with sundials to regulate the hours of work and with mechanical lamps, which, through some device invented by Cassiodorus, were automatically filled with oil.

Since subject matter was the medium of classification, the works of the same author were separated and placed in a particular *armarium.* A group of historians or grammarians after being copied were placed together in the same codex; so for example St. Jerome's historical works; so the rhetorical works of Quintilian and others.

Cassiodorus was very particular about the internal and external appearance of the codices and himself collated the most ancient manuscripts of the Bible. He insisted on a correct transcript and put down a set of rules limiting hasty corrections and emendations in the text. Even though the text fails to live up to the rules of grammar and to the Latin usage of his day it must not be tampered with; the same applies to unusual phrases. Credit must be given to Cassiodorus for setting this high standard, for heaven only knows what trouble presumptuous scribes have given to

modern scholars. What a difference between these rules for copying adhered to by the *servi Dei,* "servants of the Lord," as Cassiodorus called his scribes and the copying done by real *servi,* slaves, during the imperial period! No wonder that we hear frequently of *libri mendosi,* badly written books, requiring the *curae secundae,* or proof reading by the author!

Those, however, who introduce corrections ought to do so skilfully, that the added letters may appear to have been inserted by the original scribes. By all this Cassiodorus laid the foundation for text-criticism.

I mentioned his own collation above. He did it in order to encourage his monks and in order to leave them a model. Among other things he added notes in red ink, to facilitate the finding of the commentaries of the Scriptures. For example he used AAA for *Acta Apostolorum et Apocalypsis;* he furthermore marked idioms with "pp" to denote that this was the proper reading, to prevent hasty correction and to take the place of cross reference. Lastly, to insure correctness, he composed a treatise on spelling (**De Orthographia**), when 93 years of age. It contains various rules and examples aiming to teach the coypist how to avoid common mistakes in spelling. One of the most common mistakes in those days was caused by the confusion of "b" and "v".

As far as the external appearance of the codex was concerned, he left to his monks what he calls *species facturarum,* or samples of bindings, prepared by skilful workers. They were gathered in one special codex, to make it easy for future binders to chose the binding they liked most. Title pages were also inserted and a system of punctuation and division into chapters devised for the purpose of facilitating reading and finding the proper place in the book. Blank pages were even left in some of them, to provide space in case some lost work would turn up.

Aside from all this, great literary activity reigned at *Vivarium.* With the asistance of able friends the **Tripartite History** was written, which is actually a translation from the Greek, but served as a textbook of ecclesiastical history for generations to come. Here, too, the *Antiquities of the Jews* of Josephus Flavius were translated into Latin, a work found in almost every medieval library. Also his great commentary on the Psalms belongs to this period.

Time does not permit me to discuss the list of books in the library, about which we are singularly well informed, but the collection was impressive. Through his activity Cassiodorus transmitted to posterity pagan and Christian learning, which would have otherwise perished in these troubled days. If ever there was an instrument of fate,[7] it was Cassiodorus. Through his writings he became a teacher of a later generation of scholars, like Isidore of Seville, Alcuin and others, to say nothing of the great influence his **Institutiones** exerted on education in the Middle Ages. It is only by realizing that the preservation of our heritage is due to the efforts of monastic copyists that we can evaluate what we owe to Cassiodorus. No wonder, then, that the Venerable Bede remarks that Cassiodorus started as a statesman and ended as a *doctor ecclesiae*. He revived intellectual life in a period of utter decay; he gave stimulus to learning; by his liberal attitude he did not kill in his monks that intellectual curiosity which the study of the classics so richly fosters. Professor De Labriolle is right in saying that Cassiodorus "rendered eminent services to the old learning far superior to those to which some ill-informed minds give the honor in the Rule of his contemporary, St. Benedict."[8] By his high standards he left something for later generations to follow; what is more, in a disordered world *Vivarium* was like an oasis giving an example of a well ordered community, leading a well ordered life and devoted to an ideal of salvaging from the wreck of humanity all the treasures of ancient civilization. It is really hard to imagine what turn or what form our civilization would have taken had the monuments of ancient civilization and tradition been destroyed and had Cassiodorus and his community failed to save them. He ought not to be a forgotten man, since to him one may aptly apply Ruskin's famous statement that a "work becomes more noble in proportion to the amount of human energies expressed therein." There are times such as the era we have been handling when two of the functions listed by Sir William Osler as the peculiar functions of writers becomes of the greatest importance, those of transmission and of transmutation. True, we would like to have the third, that of creative writing, but our own age, witnessing as it does the destruction of priceless treasures, calls for a Cassiodorus, nay for many of them. May they appear and the sooner the better!

And now a word in conclusion. I have given you a sombre and dark picture of past events. But of even darker hue is the present picture of Europe in general and of Poland in particular. However, to quote Horace (*Carmina* 2. 10, 17-18), non, si male nunc, et olim sic erit (if things are bad to-day, they will not be ever so). When the victorious forces of light put to flight the powers of darkness and when those spiritual, cultural and moral values which we all hold dear regain their rightful place, then the sacrifices and sufferings of Poland will not be forgotten. To your country, men and women of Poland, both here and under the heel of the oppressor I can apply the words of Rutilius Namatianus (1.139-140), noble words, even though they come from a pagan:

> Illud te reparat, quod cetera regna resolvit:
> Ordo renascendi est, crescere posse malis.

The pagan Rutilius, then, believed in rebirth that thrives upon national sufferings. I do not need to speak here of the calamities and sufferings that fell to the lot of Poland, reborn in 1918 after partitions and national disaster. But the idea of rebirth reminds me of your great national poet, Adam Mickiewicz. Permit me to call him in classical fashion a *vates sacer*, a sacred or inspired bard; as a classicist I cannot but admire an ode of his, written in Latin after the best classical tradition. In a moment of unspeakable mental agony and torture Mickiewicz compared your country to Christ, Christ of Nations. What his sufferings would be to-day one can only guess and one may well ponder to what he would compare Poland if he were living to-day; but on this point one cannot speculate. Be it as it may, with millions of your compatriots, brutally ravaged, pillaged and oppressed, but never suppressed, your country will witness again, as before, the well-merited glory of national resurrection. Of this I am sure. Therefore, to quote an ancient poet again, Vergil (*Aen.* 1.206):

> durate, et vosmet rebus servate secundis

Endure and keep yourselves for brighter days!!

Notes

1. *The Invasion of Europe by the Barbarians*, p. 24.

2. *Cf.* Ferdinand Lot, *Les Invasions Germaniques*, p. 138.

3. Book 2, chap. 118. The judgment of Velleius is shared by a ninth century historian, Einhard, the author of *Vita Caroli Magni*. This is what Einhard has to say (chap. 7): Saxones, sicut omnes fere Germaniam incolentes, et natura feroces et cultui daemonum dediti nostraeque religioni contrarii neque divina neque humana iura vel polluere vel transgredi inhonestum arbitrabantur.

4. *History of the Later Roman Empire*, 2.204.

5. *Imperial Rome*, p. 316.

6. For an excellent edition see Cassiodori Senatoris *Institutiones*, by R. A. B. Mynors (Oxford 1937).

7. See C. Foligno, *Latin Thought During the Middle Ages*, pp. 51-52.

8. *Histoire de la Littérature Latine Chrétienne*, p. 41; English translation by Herbert Wilson, p. 29.

Leslie Webber Jones (essay date 1945)

SOURCE: "Notes on the Style and Vocabulary of Cassiodorus's *Institutiones*," in *Classical Philology*, Vol. XL, No. 1, January, 1945, pp. 24-31.

[In the following essay, Jones reviews the content and aims of Cassiodorus's Institutiones *and comments that the style of the work is elaborate and characterized by Cassiodorus's desire for balance. Jones then analyzes specific examples of the type of vocabulary used in the work.]*

Though many Latin scholars are aware of the unusual importance of Cassiodorus' **Institutiones divinarum et humanarum lectionum,**[1] the difficulties of its style and vocabulary (and even of its syntax) often prevent perfect comprehension. For this reason any light at all on these matters ought to be welcome. It happens that I have been laboring intermittently for several years on an English translation of this very work—its first translation into any language. In the course of my labors I have compiled observations on the style and vocabulary which ought to be useful not merely to those who desire to read the *Institutiones* but also to those who have other interests in this fascinating but vexing period of transition from Classical Latin to Late Latin. I shall submit these observations below.

Before we proceed to a detailed discussion, it will be wise to outline fully the contents of Cassiodorus' work. It was written at some time after 551[2] for the instruction of his monks. It begins with a description of his unsuccessful effort to found a theological school at Rome in conjunction with Pope Agapetus and continues as follows:

> But although my ardent desire could in no way have been fulfilled. . . . I was driven by divine charity to this device, namely, in the place of a teacher to prepare for you under the Lord's guidance these introductory books; through which, in my opinion, the unbroken line of the Divine Scriptures and the compendious knowledge of secular letters might with the Lord's beneficence be related.

In the first of the two books of which the treatise is composed Cassiodorus describes briefly the contents of the nine codices[3] which make up the Old and New Testaments and lists the names of the chief commentators. He proceeds to describe the various means of understanding the Scriptures. Then, after giving an account of the four accepted synods, he carefully cautions scribes and editors to preserve the purity of the sacred text and to abstain from making even plausible emendations.[4] He points out the value of the Scriptures; lists the historians whose works are of value in interpreting them—Eusebius, Rufinus, Socrates, Sozomenus, Theodoritus, Orosius, Marcellinus, Prosper, and several others; and gives brief character sketches of some of the chief Fathers of the Church—Hilary, Cyprian, Ambrose, Jerome, Augustine, and Eugippius. He mentions incidentally, as a colleague and literary helper, the monk Dionysius Exiguus, who settled the date of our present era.[5] After a recapitulation, he provides one chapter on cosmographers and a second on the system of notes which he has used in his manuscripts of the various ecclesiastical commentators. He urges his monks to cultivate learning, not as an end in itself, but as a means toward the better knowledge of the Scriptures.[6] After dealing with secular literature and recommending the study of the classics, he exhorts those of his readers who are not inclined toward literature to spend their time in farming and gardening and to read the manuscripts of the ancient authors on this subject which have been left by him for their perusal—Gargilius Martialis, Columella, and Aemilianus Macer.[7]

He tells us that he sought out and bought manuscripts from northern Africa and other parts of the world[8] and encouraged his monks to copy them with care. He mentions the assembling of a text of Jerome's version of the Scriptures, a *codex grandior littera clariore conscriptus,* which he divided into nine volumes completely revised by himself.

Cassiodorus was especially interested in the copying of manuscripts. His opinion of the nobility of the scribe's work is well shown in the following description:

> I admit that among those of your tasks which require physical effort that of the scribe, if he writes correctly, appeals most to me. . . . Happy his design, praiseworthy his zeal, to preach to men with the hand alone, to loosen tongues with fingers, to give salvation silently to mortals, and to fight against the illicit temptations of the devil with pen and ink. Every word of the Lord written by the scribe is a wound inflicted on Satan. And so, though seated in one spot, with the dissemination of his work he travels through different provinces. . . . O sight glorious to those who contemplate it carefully![9]

One must not infer from the passage quoted that Cassiodorus was interested merely in sacred literature. The greater part of chapter 28 of the first book of the *Institutiones,* for example, is devoted to an argument against neglecting secular writers.

Book i of the *Institutiones* contains, among other things, certain rules of spelling. Thus, for the sake of euphony, Cassiodorus apparently favors assimilation of the prefix *in-*[10] and prefers *quicquam* to *quidquam.* For the avoidance of errors the copyist is instructed to read the works of ancient authors on orthography[11]—Velius Longus; Curtius Valerianus; Papyrianus; "Adamantius Martyrius" on V and B, and other subjects; Eutyches on the rough breathing; and Phocas on genders—works which Cassiodorus had himself collected to the best of his ability.

Our author now goes on to describe the care which he has taken to insure the binding of the sacred codices in covers worthy of their contents, as the householder in the parable provided fitting garments for all who came to his son's wedding feast.[12] He states that he has prepared a single volume containing samples of various sorts of binding and directs one interested in bindings to choose that which seems best.

He continues with an account of the various mechanical devices provided for the convenience of the copyists. For use at night there were mechanical lamps cleverly constructed so as to trim themselves and to provide themselves with a steady supply of oil.[13] There were also water clocks for nights and cloudy days, and sun dials for bright weather.[14]

After a brief discourse on medical works, Book i ends with an admonition of the abbot to the community of monks and a prayer.

Book ii contains a brief account of the seven liberal arts—grammar, rhetoric, dialectic, arithmetic, geometry, music, and astronomy. A complete investigation of the sources of Cassiodorus' information on all these subjects is yet to be made. The extremely short chapter on grammar lists various grammarians and quotes a number of definitions from Donatus. The treatment of rhetoric is based chiefly upon

Cicero's *De inventione* and to a lesser extent upon Fortunatianus; Quintilian is used twice and the author of the *Rhetorica ad Herennium* once. The long chapter on dialectic[15] depends upon several sources: Aristotle's *Categories;* Pseudo-Apuleius' *De interpretatione* (or Martianus Capella); three works by Marius Victorinus—the *De syllogismis hypotheticis,* the *De definitionibus,* and the commentary[16] on Cicero's *Topica;* and two works by Boethius—his translation of Porphyry's *Introduction* and his commentary on Aristotle's *De interpretatione.* The source of most of the treatment of arithmetic remains to be found; Boethius' *De arithmetica* seems to supply a few lines at the beginning, while Eucherius' *Formulae* certainly furnishes a page at the end on the importance of numbers in the Scriptures. The chapter on music lists several works and especially recommends Mutianus' Latin translation of Gaudentius; Varro or Censorinus may be the authority used in the first part of section 9. Little is known of the sources of the chapters on geometry[17] and on astronomy.[18]

The ***Institutiones*** is not written for the learned. Instead of the *affectata eloquentia* which Cassiodorus employs in the official correspondence in his **Variae,**[19] we find "more utility than ornament."[20] The change, however, is only a relative one: the style is still wordy and elaborate, often to the point of obscurity.[21] Superlatives whose force has been lost either partly or completely are common. In less than two pages of text (i. pref. 5-6) we find the following: "most ready masters" (*magistros . . . paratissimos*), "very delicate strength" (*tenuissimas vires*), "most wisely" (*prudentissime*), "a very obscure passage" (*obscurissimo loco*), "a very frequent prayer" (*oratione creberrima*), "most difficult matters" (*res difficillimas*), and "an exceedingly sweet gift" (*suavissimum donum*). Equally frequent in occurrence are two further types of exaggeration—the application of *nimis* ("exceedingly") to the positive or superlative form of an adjective or an adverb without the addition of any emphasis, and the use of stronger words than the context seems to require. Examples follow: "unusually eloquent sermons" (*eloquentissimae nimis omeliae,* i. 1. 8), "a name exceptionally pleasant" (*dictio nimis suavissima,* i. 5. 5), "remarkably profound books" (*libri . . . mirabili profunditate,* i. 6. 3), "anything unsightly" (literally "base": *quicquam turpe,* i. 15. 15), and "the gravest heresy" (literally "most violent," "most furious": *saevissimi erroris,* i. 24. 1).

Without question, the influence of years of official correspondence has caused Cassiodorus not merely to exaggerate but also to cultivate abstract expressions at the expense of concrete and to fall naturally into complicated and unnecessary periphrases. Heaven is described literally as "that sweetness of fatherland" (*in illa suavitate patriae,* i. 28. 5). For the single words "substance" and "reckoning" we have *substantiae ratio* (ii. 3. 9) and *calculi . . . quantitatem* (ii. 4. 7). Most troublesome of all, perhaps, is the type of periphrasis in which two verbs are used instead of one—*probor esse compulsus* for the aorist perfect *compulsus sum* ("I was driven," i. pref. 1) and *reliquisse cognoscor* for the present perfect *reliqui* ("I have left," ii. 2. 10);

monstro, nosco, cerno, and other verbs are commonly used in these expressions.

Despite these shortcomings, Cassiodorus has a genuine feeling for style. His numerous parenthetical expressions, for example, show an endless variety. Thus "as most people hold" (*ut usus habet,* i. 5. 5) becomes, first, "as it seemed to our Fathers" (*sicut et Patribus nostris visum est,* i. 27. 1) and then "as it has been said" (*sicut dictum est,* i. 32. 4) and, finally, "according to the ancients" (*sicut antiqui voluerunt,* ii. 5. 1). His desire for balance often causes him to prefer two adverbs or two adjectives at a time instead of one; such combinations as "with caution and wisdom" (*caute sapienterque,* i. 1. 8) and "very subtle and very concise words" (*suptilissimas . . . ac brevissimas dictiones,* i. 13. 2) are carefully chosen and not at all redundant. His characterizations of authors are concise and effective: Ambrose is called "a clear and very delightful interpreter" (*planus atque suavissimus doctor,* i. 1. 3) and Augustine "a fluent and extremely wary disputant" (*disertus atque cautissimus disputator,* i. 1. 4). His poetic figures are often as pleasing as the two which follow: contemplation, "the mother of understanding" (*mater . . . intelligentiae,* i. pref. 7); and the marks of punctuation, "the paths for thoughts and the beacon-lights for words" (*viae . . . sensuum et lumina dictionum,* i. 15. 12).

One is impressed with the archaic and artificial quality of his rich vocabulary. Highly specialized technical terms abound, particularly in the discussion of the seven liberal arts. Ecclesiastical expressions are varied. The Late Latin words include fifty-three[22] apparent neologisms, none very daring. The translator is often at a loss to determine whether a word is being employed in its Classical or Late Latin sense. He is likely to have a similar difficulty in deciding between Classical and Late Latin syntax.[23]

Since the important aspects of the vocabulary are treated by Sister Mary Gratia Ennis in the invaluable dissertation mentioned in note 21,[24] there is no need for any extended discussion of the matter here. The dissertation, however, is by no means infallible. Some of its English equivalents are infelicitous; others are positively erroneous. I shall discuss below the more important instances in which I have found it necessary to deviate from Ennis' interpretations.[25] In each instance I shall cite, first, the word in question; second, Ennis' description; third, the Latin passage in which the word occurs; fourth, my own English translation; and, fifth, my comments, if any are necessary.

contropabilis.—Ennis (p. 4): "comparative"; not cited in the lexica; a neologism. 75. 21-23:[26] *verba caelestia multiplicat homo, et quadam significatione contropabili, si fas est dicere, tribus digitis scribitur quod virtus sanctae Trinitatis effatur.* Jones: "Man multiplies the heavenly words, and in a certain *metaphorical*[27] sense, if one may so express himself, that which the virtue of the Holy Trinity utters is written by a trinity of fingers." Cassiodorus is describing the work of a scribe. Cf. the late rhetorical usage of the adjective *tropicus* in the sense of "metaphorical," "figurative" (Gellius xiii. 24. 31; Augustine *Contra mendac.* 10).

linealiter.—Ennis (p. 19): "by means of lines"; a word of recent coinage (Mart. Cap.; in Boeth.: *lineariter*). 139. 9-12: *linealis numerus est qui inchoans a monade linealiter scribitur usque ad infinitum, unde alpha ponitur pro designatione linearum, quoniam haec littera unum significat apud Graecos—aaa.* Jones: "A linear number is one which starts from unity[28] and continues *in a straight line* to infinity; for this reason alpha, a letter which, among the Greeks, signifies unity, is used to designate lines—aaa."

clmia.—Ennis (p. 44): "latitude; part of the heavens divided in various ways by astrologers and mathematicians for searching nativities"; extension or generalization of meaning (Ps. Apul., Firm., Serv., Rufin., Mart. Cap., Aug., Petr. Chrys., Isid.); a region (Veg.); a land measure of 60 sq. ft. (Colum.). 156. 4-15: *. . . ex quibus, ut mihi videtur, climata forsitan nosse, horarum spatia comprehendere, lunae cursum pro inquisitione paschali, solis eclipsin, ne simplices aliqua confusione turbentur, qua ratione fiant advertere non videtur absurdum. sunt enim, ut dictum est, climata quasi septem lineae ab oriente in occidentem directae, in quibus et mores hominum dispares et quaedam animalia specialiter diversa nascuntur; quae vocitata sunt a locis quibusdam famosis, quorum primum est Merohis, secundum Sohinis, tertium Catochoras, id est Africa, quartum Rodus, quintum Hellespontus, sextum Mesopontum, septimum Borysthenus.* Jones: ". . . and, lest the untutored be in some way confused, it is in my opinion not unwise to use these *Canons* as a means of learning the *latitudes*[29] perhaps, and of perceiving the measure of the hours, and of observing the nature of the moon's course (in order to determine the date of Easter) and of a solar eclipse. The *latitudes* have been described as seven *lines,* as it were, drawn from the east to the west—lines on which are found different kinds of human beings and certain unusually varied animals;[30] the *latitudes* are named after certain famous places, the first being Meroe,[31] the second Syene,[32] the third the coast[33] (of Africa), the fourth Rhodes, the fifth the Hellespont, the sixth the Black Sea,[34] and the seventh the Borysthenes."[35] Cassiodorus here states explicitly that *climata* are *lines* which bound the various regions of the heavens; he does not state that they are *parts* of the heavens. To say, moreover, as Ennis does, that the *climata* were made "for searching nativities" is to give the wrong emphasis; cf. Cassiodorus' own words eight lines below (156. 23-157. 2): "Other powers which pertain to an acquaintance with the stars—that is, to a knowledge of fate—and which without doubt are contrary to our faith deserve to be ignored in such manner that they may seem not to have been mentioned by writers."

extrinsecus.—Ennis (p. 56): "outside (fig.) without the aid of rhetoric," a change from the material meaning to the mental or moral (Colum.); *lit.:* "on the outside, without" (Varro, Cic., Colum., Sen. ph., Cels., Suet., Apul.). 127. 10-11: *Argumenta ducuntur extrinsecus quae Graeci atechnos, id est artis expertes, vocant, ut est testimonium.* Jones: "*Extrinsic* arguments are those which the Greeks term ατεχνοι, that is, without art,[36] as in the case of evidence." Ennis' rendering is infelicitous if not misleading.

qualitas.—Ennis (p. 104): "quality, nature *in general*" (11.14 and 56.13 are cited); *qualitas* is also cited as a "category" (114. 9) and as a "status" (110. 4). 43. 7-15: *Hebrea vero quaedam nomina hominum vel locorum nulla declinatione frangatis; servetur in eis linguae suae decora sinceritas. illas tantum litteras commutemus, quae vocabuli ipsius possunt exprimere qualitatem, quoniam interpretatione nominis sui unum quodque eorum magno sacramento rei alicuius constat appositum, ut est* Seth, Enoch, Lamech, Noe, Sem Cham *et* Iafeth, Aaron, David *et his similia. locorum autem nomina, ut est* Sion, Choreb, Geon, Hermon *vel his similia, pari devotione linquamus.* Jones: "Do not weaken certain Hebrew names of persons and places by any modification of form;[37] let an integrity proper to their tongue be preserved in them. Let us change only those letters which can express *the grammatical case* of the word, inasmuch as it is generally agreed that every one of these names—*Seth,* for example, *Enoch, Lamech, Noah, Shem, Ham* and *Japheth, Aaron, David,* and the like[38]—has been applied, through an interpretation of the name itself, to some great mystery. Let us with equal piety leave unchanged the names of such places as *Zion, Horeb, Gihon, Hermon,* and the like."[39] Hebrew words whose endings are analogous to those of Latin words are declined by Cassiodorus as if they were Latin: thus, *Saul,* gen. *Saulis* (Mynors, 17. 4); *Helias,* abl. *Helia* (16. 24); *Moyses,* acc. *Moysen* (89. 18); etc. Hebrew words whose endings are not analogous are left unchanged by him: thus, *David,* nom. and acc. (16. 19) and abl. (148. 21); *Adam,* nom. and abl. (56. 27); *Chanaan,* nom. and gen. (41.12); *Bethlehem,* nom. and abl. (59. 20). Though the entire list quoted at 43. 7-15 belongs to this group, none of the words except *David* can be used as evidence, since none occurs in an oblique case in the *Institutiones. Qualitatem* is, of course, not the technical word of Probus or Donatus (see Keil, *op. cit.,* IV, 5 and 373), which indicates either *nomina propria* (names of persons or gods) or *nomina appellativa* (names of animals or things). The use of *qualitas* in the sense of "a grammatical case" seems to be a neologism.

ab adiunctis (argumentum).—Ennis (p. 76): "a form of argument or rhetorical commonplace worded to imply that certain probable but not necessary accessories should be admitted before the transaction in question can be said to have been done or not." 125. 13-19: *effecta argumenta sunt, quae quodammodo ex rebus aliis tracta noscuntur: coniugata—a genere—a forma generis—a similitudine—a differentia—ex contrario—ab adiunctis—ab antecedentibus—a consequentibus—a repugnantibus—a causis—ab effectibus—a comparatione, quae fit a maiore ad minus, a minore ad maius, a pari ad parem.* Jones: "Effected arguments are those which are in a certain measure produced by additional circumstances: arguments from cognate words[40]—from genus—from species—from likeness—from difference—from the opposite—*from analogy*[41]—from anterior circumstances—from posterior circumstances—from contradictory ideas—from causes—from effects—from comparison: of the greater to the lesser, of the lesser to the greater, of equal to equal." *Ab adiunctis* is a difficult phrase, whose meaning must be considered in the light of the first *a coniugatis* (125. 19), a second *a coniugatis* (126. 22), and even an *a coniunctis* (Append., 164. 22 and 165. 26). The first *a coniugatis* is properly defined by Ennis (p. 84) as "a basis of rhetorical argument which rests on the use of terms related by derivation or of similar inflections" (that is, as I put it, "from cognate words or similarity of form"). The second is defined by her (*ibid.*) as "a basis of rhetorical argument which states the proportionate or relative effect of a comparative opposition to a common standard"; my own rather literal translation of Cassiodorus' own definition (126. 22-25) has some points in common: "An argument *from kindred ideas* is a demonstration by means of a comparison of the effect which will arise from something: 'If they drive us forth, they deem that naught will stay them from laying all Hesperia utterly beneath their yoke.'"[42] The use of *a coniugatis* by Cassiodorus in two distinct senses is confusing. Instead of a second occurrence of this phrase, one would have expected something like *a coniunctis*. The argument defined at 126. 22-25 seems to be the opposite of the argument *from contradictory ideas* (which precedes) and follows naturally after the latter. It is probably to be identified with the argument *from analogy* (*ab adiunctis:* 125. 16); cf. Cicero's *Topica* iii. 11 and iv. 18. The *a coniunctis* (164. 22 and 165. 26), which the Φ and Δ manuscripts read instead of *ab adiunctis,* gives us still another meaning; it seems to signify "an argument from a combination of circumstances" (i.e., an argument from a combination of items individually weak which gain force when taken together).

praemium.—Ennis (p. 98): "reward" (in the definition of *iuridicialis,* 100.11), but (p. 102): "penalty, fine, redress" correctly. 100. 11-12: *iuridicialis est in qua aequi et recti natura et praemii aut poenae ratio quaeritur.* Jones: "The juridical position is that in which the nature of the justice and right involved and the reasonableness of the *fine* or punishment are sought." The context requires "fine."

secundae substantiae.—Ennis (p. 107): "species and genus: substances within which, as *species,* the primary substances are included, or those which, as *genera,* include the species." 113. 23-25: *secundae autem substantiae dicuntur in quibus speciebus illae, quae principaliter substantiae primo dictae sunt, insunt atque clauduntur, ut in homine Cicero.* Jones: "Second substances, however, are species within which the above-mentioned primary substances are contained and included, as man, for example, is the species within which Cicero is contained." The second half of Ennis' definition applies to Aristotle's *Categories* 2 a 14 ff. and 2 b 6 ff., but not to Cassiodorus.

tempus.—Ennis (p. 109) fails to give "tense" (of a verb), the meaning required. 95. 18-20: *participium est pars orationis dicta quod partem capiat nominis, partem verbi; recipit enim a nomine genera et casus, a verbo tempora et significationes, ab utroque numeros et figuras.* Jones: "A participle is a part of speech so called because it partakes of the functions of a noun and of a verb; it receives gender and case from the noun, *tense* and meaning from the verb, number and form from both" (cf. Varr., Quint. often, etc.).

diapason simul et diatessaron symphonia.—Ennis (p. 115): "a compound fourth" (in music). 145. 13-15: *diapason simul et diatessaron symphonia est quae constat ex ratione quam habet XXIIII numerus ad octonarium numerum. . . .* Jones: "The interval of the diapason and the diatessaron taken together is that which is arranged in the ratio of 24 to 8. . . ." Ennis' definition is correct, but she fails to note the error in the text of Cassiodorus; the ratio should not be 24 to 8 (a ratio which equals 3 to 1, the interval of the compound fifth described immediately below in 145. 16-17) but rather 24 to 9 (a ratio which equals 8 to 3).

temperamentum.—Ennis (p. 129): "consonance, 144. 21-22 (*proper disposition, moderation:* Cic., Colum., Plin. mai., Plin. min., Tac., Iust., Tert., Vulg.)." 144. 21-145. 2: *symphonia est temperamentum sonitus gravis ad acutum vel acuti ad gravem, modulamen efficiens sive in voce sive in flatu sive in percussione.* Jones: "A consonance [*symphonia*] is *a proper mixing*—productive of euphony in a stringed, wind, or percussion instrument—of a bass sound with a treble or of a treble sound with a bass." The literal meaning suits the context.

I trust that these comments will be of use in the study of an unusual man, who, to be sure, was not the first to introduce into the monastery either the copying of manuscripts or the study of the Scriptures, but whose work was more systematic than that of his predecessors and had more important results. To Cassiodorus more than to anyone else we are indebted for the transformation of the monastery into a theological school and a *scriptorium* for the multiplication of copies of the Scriptures, of the Fathers of the Church and the commentators, and of the great secular writers of antiquity.

Notes

1. On the title see R. A. B. Mynors, *Cassiodori Senatoris Institutiones Edited from the MSS* (Oxford: Clarendon Press, 1937), pp. lii-liii; and E. K. Rand, "The New Cassiodorus," *Speculum,* XIII (1938), 434-35.

2. I shall postpone discussion of my reasons for this date to a later article.

3. (A) Octateuch, (B) Kings (Samuel, Kings, and Chronicles), (C) Prophets (four major, including Daniel, and twelve minor), (D) Psalms, (E) Solomon (Proverbs, Ecclesiastes, Canticles, Wisdom, Ecclesiasticus), (F) Hagiographa (Tobias, Esther, Judith, Maccabees, Esdras), (G) Gospels, (H) Epistles of the Apostles (including that to the Hebrews), (I) Acts of the Apostles and the Apocalypse. The various methods of dividing the Scriptures—those employed by Jerome, Augustine, and the writers of the Septuagint—are discussed in chaps. 12-14.

4. *Inst.* i. 15. Only scholars of the highest standing in both sacred and secular literature are to be allowed to correct sacred texts. Other texts are to be revised only after study of the works of the ancients and after consultation with men proficient in secular literature.

5. The earliest use of Dionysius' system of reckoning occurs in A.D. 562 (*Computus paschalis* in J. P. Migne [ed.], *Patrologia cursus completus, series Latina,* Vol. LXIX, col. 1249; first ascribed to Cassiodorus by Pithoeus).

6. *Inst.* i. 27.

7. *Ibid.* i. 28.

8. *Ibid.* i. 8.

9. *Ibid.* i. 30.

10. *Ibid.* i. 15: *illuminatio, irrisio, immutabilis, impius, improbus.*

11. *Ibid.* i. 30. 2.

12. *Ibid.* i. 30. 3.

13. *Ibid.* i. 30. 4.

14. *Ibid.* i. 30. 5.

15. Martianus Capella is the source of almost all of Appen. A (commonplaces); Boethius' *De diff. top.* is used once.

16. A possible source only.

17. [Boethius'] *De geometria* is the source of the first two sentences. Varro and Censorinus are mentioned incidentally. Boethius' *Euclid* is the source of Appen. C (on geometry).

18. The source of Appen. B (on the four elements) is unknown.

19. The language of the *Variae* is so turgid and bombastic that Thomas Hodgkin (*The Letters of Cassiodorus. . . .* [London, 1886]) feels under no compulsion to reproduce it in its entirety; his translation of each letter is only half as long as Cassiodorus' original and considerably simpler. The Rev. Odo Zimmerman has recently finished a dissertation on the Late Latin vocabulary of the *Variae* (Catholic University of America Press, 1944).

20. This is Cassiodorus' own characterization in *De orthogr.* (in H. Keil [ed.], *Grammatici Latini,* VII [Leipzig, 1880], 144).

21. For a further consideration of Cassiodorus' style see Sister Mary Gratia Ennis, *The Vocabulary of the Institutiones of Cassiodorus with Special Advertence to the Technical Terminology and Its Sources* (Washington, D.C.: Catholic University of America Press, 1939), pp. 147-54. Sister Josephine Suelzer has recently finished a dissertation on the clausulae in Cassiodorus (Catholic University of America Press, 1944).

22. J. L. Heller, in his review of Ennis (*Classical Weekly,* XXXIII [1939], 58), points out that *panaretus* is not a neologism but a word quoted from Jerome. *Qualitas,* on the other hand, as I demonstrate below, seems to be a neologism in the sense of "a grammatical case."

23. There has been no special study of the syntax of the *Institutiones,* but the following works are extremely useful in this connection: E. Löfstedt, *Syntactica: Studien und Beiträge zur historischen Syntax des Lateins* (2 vols.; Lund, 1928-33); F. A. Bieter, *The Syntax of the Cases and Prepositions in Cassiodorus' "Historia ecclesiastica tripertita"* (dissertation, Catholic University of America, 1938); and B. H. Skahill, *The Syntax of the "Variae" of Cassiodorus* (dissertation, Catholic University of America, 1934).

24. Professor Martin R. P. McGuire was kind enough to send me a copy of this dissertation as soon as it was available in 1939. I have found it extremely useful, even though it arrived after I had finished a large part of my translation.

25. For other corrections see Heller's review, cited in n. 22.

26. The numerals in this position throughout the discussion refer to the page and line in which the word occurs in Mynors, *op. cit.*

27. The italics in my translations here and below serve merely to emphasize my own version of the word in question.

28. Unity is not included, for a line is the aggregate of two or more points. 2, 3, 4, 5, 6, etc., are linear numbers.

29. I.e., the *lines* which bound the various regions of the heavens, regions which are divided in various ways by mathematicians.

30. The celestial latitudes are apparently a mere extension of the terrestrial latitudes here described.

31. A city located on the upper Nile, north of Khartoum.

32. A town at the southern extremity of Upper Egypt; now Essouan.

33. Catochoras = . . . "on the coast." Alexandria is meant.

34. Mesopontum: obviously the Black Sea. Eratosthenes, Strabo, and Ptolemy, however, omit this. Eratosthenes and Strabo add Cinnamomifera (south of Meroe) and Ptolemy adds Thule (north of the Borysthenes).

35. The Dnieper River. Isidore iii. 53. 4 takes over the entire sentence.

36. "Empirical"; "which require no art on the orator's part" (Cicero *Top.* iv. 24).

37. Ennis (*op. cit.,* p. 86) cites *declinatio* in this passage under "declension of a noun," which is perhaps the correct meaning. I prefer "modification of form" as a more general term which will include not only inflection but also orthographical changes employed to make Hebrew words conform to Latin rules.

38. These names have the following meanings in Hebrew: "appointed," "dedicated," "destroyer," "rest" (or "wandering"), meaning uncertain, "warm," "extension," "light (?)," "beloved."

39. The meanings are: "lifted up," "desert," "river," "lofty."

40. Or, as in the third example presented in the definition below, from similarity of form.

41. The bare possibility that *ab adiunctis* means "an argument from collateral circumstances" and that the next two items (anterior and posterior circumstances) are subdivisions of this category seems dissipated by the considerations discussed below.

42. *Aeneid* viii. 147-48.

Leslie W. Jones (essay date 1945)

SOURCE: "The Influence of Cassiodorus on Mediaeval Culture," in *Speculum*, Vol. 20, No. 4, October, 1945, pp. 433-42.

[*In the following essay, Jones surveys the literary and cultural impact of Cassiodorus from the years following his death through the end of the thirteenth century, observing that he systematized the process of producing multiple copies of the Scriptures and that he helped to transform the monastery into a theological school.*]

That Flavius Magnus Aurelius Cassiodorus Senator was indeed a remarkable man I hope to make clear in the introduction and notes of my forthcoming translation of his *Institutiones.* [The translation is now in the hands of the publisher.] His career as a statesman and scholar is in its length and industry almost without parallel. From 503 to 539 A.D., [See my translation for a discussion of C.'s dates and for numerous other Cassiodorian problems.] the period during which he held a succession of important political offices under four Ostrogothic rulers—Theodoric, the regent Amalasuentha, Theodahad, and Witigis, he strove to build a strong Italian state with Gothic and Roman elements working together in complementary and harmonious fashion—a dream utterly shattered by the victories of Belisarius. From 539 to 575, the year in which he died at the advanced age of ninety-five, he spent an equal amount of energy commenting on the Christian Scriptures, assembling an important collection of theological and of classical works, and teaching the monks of the two monasteries which he had founded precise rules for the copying of his precious manuscripts.

The second phase of his activities ultimately proved much more important to the world than his political labors. The great merit of his monastic work lay in his determination to utilize the vast leisure of the convent for the preservation of divine and human learning and for its transmission to posterity. Cassiodorus must not of course be considered the first man to have introduced into monasteries either the copying of manuscripts or the study of the Scriptures. The rule of St Pacomius (who died in 346) had already prescribed knowledge of reading and writing and the study of lessons to this end thrice daily,[1] and in his foundations there had also existed a body of monastic copyists.[2] The younger monks alone were copyists in the monastery of St Martin's at Tours.[3] St Jerome in his cell at Bethlehem had

not only shown what great results a single recluse could obtain from patient literary toil, but he had taught grammar to the monks resident there.[4] In Gaul, moreover, there had been famous schools like those at Lérins,[5] and in the rules laid down *ca* 550 by Ferreolus reading and copying were considered suitable for monks who were too weak for harder work.[6] At the same time Cassian and Gregory the Great had rejected the liberal arts as being unnecessary for the study of the Scriptures.[7] It remained for Cassiodorus to make of the monastery a theological school and a *scriptorium* for the multiplication of copies of the Scriptures, of the Fathers of the Church and the commentators, and of the great secular writers of antiquity.[8] His work was more systematic than that of his predecessors and it had more important results. He showed deep insight into the needs of his time. The quality of theological study had seriously declined; the best works of classical literature were no longer being copied; and every movement of the Ostrogothic armies or of the still more savage imperial hordes against a city or even a villa resulted in the destruction of priceless codices.

A critical and complete investigation of the culture of Italy and of Europe in general in the seventh and eighth centuries—a difficult but exceedingly important task—is yet to be made. This article cannot therefore attempt a final evaluation of the extent of Cassiodorus' influence on the culture of the Middle Ages. It is impossible, for example, to trace at present the direct routes by which knowledge of Cassiodorus' monastic program and of his books[9] arrived at other centers. For this reason, moreover, it is impossible to estimate accurately the degree—probably considerable—to which Cassiodorus' cultural program was a model for monastic use.[10] One would like to know, for example, whether the Irish and the Anglo-Saxons of this period were familiar with the entire contents of the *Institutiones;*[11] when and by whom the cultural views of the Irish and the Anglo-Saxons were established and to what extent, if any, these views were modified by this contact; how Cassiodorus' ideas and books moved into central and northern Italy and into France. Countless questions of this type are bound to occur.

Despite these gaps in our knowledge we have considerable evidence for the influence of Cassiodorus on subsequent generations. Thus, the mere list of the more important manuscripts of the *Institutiones* described by *Mynors* (pp. x-xlix) bears eloquent testimony to the wide dissemination of this particular work. A complete account of all the manuscripts of all of Cassiodorus' works would be impressive. In the absence of such an account, however, we shall find it interesting and instructive to consider the detailed evidence which is presented by items other than manuscripts. Let us restrict our survey of Cassiodorus' influence to the period which runs from the time of his death to the end of the thirteenth century[12] and let us begin with the most general references.

In some instances Cassiodorus is mentioned by subsequent writers without reference to any of his works in particular.

Thus Bede states that our author changed from a senator [*sic!*] into a 'doctor' of the Church.[13] Sigebert, a monk at Gembloux in the eleventh century, gives Senator's dates briefly, but nothing else.[14] In the following century the anonymous writer of a *De Scriptoribus ecclesiasticis* mentions our author in his preface without making further use of him,[15] while a library catalogue[16] compiled at Hirsau bears the simple entry *libri Cassiodori Senatoris* without specifying what work or works are meant.[17] During the very same period the *Historia regum Francorum* of the cloister of St -Denis reveals that Cassiodorus Senator and the Bishop Dionysius were famous men who lived in the vicinity of Rome,[18] and the *Historia pontificalis* offers the somewhat misleading information that our author changed from a heathen into a Christian, from a senator into a monk, and from a rhetorician into an ecclesiastical teacher.[19] Around 1241 the *Chronicon* of the monk Alberic of Troisfontaines refers to Cassiodorus as the chancellor of Theodoric.[20] The so-called 'interpolator Hoiensis' who appears in manuscripts of the *Gesta Episcoporum Leodiensium* by Aegidius of Orval inserts Cassiodorus' dates from Sigebert's work of two hundred years before.[21]

There is another group of instances in which subsequent writers have used particular books written by Cassiodorus, but in which the particular work or portion of the work is not mentioned by our modern authorities and cannot therefore be discovered without considerable research—research which is beyond the province of this article.[22] In this group we find as our earliest representatives Aeneas of Paris, in his ninth-century publication *Adversus Graecos,*[23] and an anonymous ecclesiastic, in a letter written between 1074 and 1079 under the name of Bishop Udalricus of Augsburg.[24] The twelfth century provides our remaining examples: Placidus of Nonantola, in his *De honore ecclesiae;*[25] Petrus Cantor, in his ethical work, the *Verbum abbreviatum;*[26] William of Malmesbury, in the *De dictis et factis memoralibus philosophorum;*[27] Alexander Neckam, in the description of waters and springs in his *De naturis rerum;*[28] and, finally, Alain de Lille, in his *Distinctiones.*

Let us now consider the particular works for which we have more precise and definite information. The two books of the *Institutiones* may be considered separately in view of the separate tradition of their manuscripts. Book I is cited in a ninth-century library catalogue of Reichenau, in a later catalogue of St Gall which lists only manuscripts that can be identified with extant books of the ninth century, in an eleventh-century catalogue of Pompuse, and in twelfth-century catalogues of Michelsberg (near Bamberg)[29] and of Reading.[30] There is at least the possibility that the two-fold division of Cassiodorus' *Institutiones* may have influenced a statement made by Virgilius Maro in the seventh century.[31] Lupus of Ferrières mentions the first chapter of Book I in connection with a work written by Jerome.[32] In a letter to Haistulph, archbishop of Mainz, Rabanus Maurus lists Cassiodorus among the authorities whom he has used for his book *De ecclesiasticis ordinibus.*[33] In another letter, written between 835 and 840 to Otgar, also archbishop of Mainz, he quotes chapter 5 on the

difference between *Ecclesiastes* and *Ecclesiasticus.*[34] In a third letter, to the same Otgar, he cites from chapter 5 again a remark of Jerome's on the *Book of Wisdom.*[35] In still another letter (840-842), directed to the Emperor Lothaire, he refers to chapter 3 in connection with one of Jerome's works.[36] In his *Institutio clericorum,* moreover, he also apparently makes use among other sources of the important chapter 28, which treats profane science as the basis of study of the Scriptures.[37] Alcuin's use of Book I is not certain; Alcuin does, however, mention Cassiodorus in his *Versus de sanctis Euboracensis ecclesiae* as being among the authors whose works were present at the school of York.[38] Hildemar, in his *Expositio regulae* (a treatise on Benedict's rule) quotes chapter 15 in its entirety.[39] Sedulius Scottus knows Book I and cites part of a sentence from the preface.[40] An anonymous author who may belong to the ninth century wrote a handbook of Biblical and Patrological knowledge based entirely on this same book.[41] In the eleventh century Berno of Reichenau cites chapter 29 in his letter 11, which criticizes Cassiodorus' *Institutiones* harshly;[42] while Gerard, bishop of Czanád in Hungary, who came from Venice and was trained in Bologna and Chartres, uses chapter 16 in his *Deliberatio supra hymnum trium puerorum.*[43] In the following century Hugo of St Victor employs Cassiodorus' treatment of theology as a model for Books 4-6 of his *Didascalicon;*[44] Sigebert of Gembloux cites chapter 5 (in his *De viris illustribus*) on Bellator's exposition of the *Wisdom of Solomon;*[45] and Radulfus de Diceto quotes from chapter 17 in his *Abbreviationes Chronicorum.*[46]

Book II of the *Institutiones,* Cassiodorus' treatise on the seven liberal arts, is somewhat more widely disseminated. Two copies of it appear in the previously mentioned ninth-century library catalogue of Reichenau; one copy each in a catalogue of the same date from Fulda, in the previously mentioned eleventh-century catalogue of Pompuse, and in four catalogues of the twelfth century—those of St -Amand, Anchin, St -Bertin, and Chartres.[47] Isidore of Seville makes a most extensive use of Book II for all the disciplines treated in his *Etymologies;* he quotes great sections of the text verbatim.[48] It is likely that Alcuin brought this book from England to the continent; in any case he uses it for his discussion of grammar, his discussion of rhetoric, and the chapter *De topicis* of his *Dialogus de dialectica.*[49] Rabanus Maurus employs Cassiodorus' second book as one of the chief sources for his work, the *Institutio clericorum;*[50] he appropriates a sentence on grammar from chapter 1, the definition of rhetoric from chapter 2, the definition of arithmetic and a further large section from chapter 3, the definition of music and a further large section from chapter 5, a part of chapter 6 as the only source for his treatment of geometry, and chapter 7, finally, as the main source for his treatment of astronomy. In the ninth century at least four authors base their works in part upon this same Book II: Aurelian of Moutier-St -Jean (or of Reomé), in his *Musica disciplina;*[51] Regino of Prüm, in his *De armonice institutione;*[52] Erchanbert of Freising, in his commentary on *Donatus* (*minor* and *major*);[53] and the author of the *Quaestiones grammaticae* (a work, apparently dictated by a teacher of grammar, which appears in part of *codex Bernensis 83*).[54] Finally, in the same century or the next, the author of an *Ars geometrica* borrows freely from Cassiodorus' chapter 6.[55]

Cassiodorus' **Commentary on the Psalms**[56] is mentioned in no less than thirteen mediaeval library catalogues: four of the ninth century—those at Reichenau, St Gall, Fontanelles, and St -Riquier; two of the tenth—those at Lorsch and Bobbio; two of the eleventh—those at Liège and Toul (the latter a fragment); and five of the twelfth—those at St -Bertin (a fragment), Chartres (also a fragment), Bec, Corbie, and Michelsberg (near Bamberg). Bede, the first man to mention our author by name, makes considerable use of the commentary in his own *De schematibus et tropis.*[57] Alcuin, who characterizes Cassiodorus as *eximius interpres psalmorum,* is also apparently familiar with it.[58] The monk Hildemar makes frequent citations from it in his own *Expositio regulae*[59] and also mentions it in a letter sent between 841 and 846 to Pacificus, archdeacon of Verona.[60] Their contemporary, Angelomus of Luxeuil, employs the commentary as one of the sources for his own *Enarrationes in libros Regum.*[61] Flodoard of Reims mentions it in one of his great poetical achievements of the following century, the *De triumphis Christi sanctorumque apud Italos.*[62] Notker Labeo, who translated the *Psalms,* Terence's *Andria,* Virgil's *Eclogues,* and several other Classical and early mediaeval works into German *ca* 1000 A.D., finds it secondary only to Augustine's commentary in usefulness.[63] Within the next sixty years no less than three men testify to its worth: Berno of Reichenau, who cites chapter 69 (§1);[64] Bruno of Würzburg, who uses chapters 11 (§§4-8) and 13 of the preface in his own *Expositio psalmorum;*[65] and Durand, Bishop of Troarn, who quotes Cassiodorus on *Psalm 109* in his own *Liber de corpore et sanguine Christi contra Berengarium et eius sectatores.*[66] Ekkehard, in his *Chronicon universale* (written *ca* 1100), also speaks of the excellence of our author's work,[67] while Abelard, writing somewhat later, cites Cassiodorus' remarks on *Psalm 50.*[68] Further mention appears in the *Annales* of St Rudbert in Salzburg[69] and in the *Auctarium Carstense*[70] (both of the twelfth century), and in the chronicle of Sicardus of Cremona[71] and in the annals of Admont[72] (both of the thirteenth century).

The **De anima** occurs in seven mediaeval catalogues: those at St Emmeran's at Regensburg (tenth century), Liège (eleventh century), St -Bertin, Bec, Corbie, Michelsberg (near Bamberg), and St Peter's at Salzburg (all of the twelfth century). It is used frequently by subsequent writers—in the ninth century, for example, by Rabanus Maurus in his *De anima*[73] and by Hincmar in his *De diversa et multiplici animae ratione.*[74]

Cassiodorus' other theological works seem to have had little influence. His **Complexiones in epistulas et acta apostolorum et apocalypsin** was not widely known. Two other works—the **Expositio epistolae quae scribitur ad Romanos unde Pelagianae haereseos pravitatis amovi** and the **Liber titulorum quem de divina scriptura collectum memorialem volui nuncupari**—have been lost.

The **De orthographia** proved to be a useful work. Though it occurs in only two mediaeval catalogues—those of St-Vaast at Arras (eleventh century) and of Anchin (twelfth century)—it is the basis of much of the writing in this field by Isidore,[75] by Alcuin,[76] and, in the twelfth century, by William of Malmesbury.[77]

Cassiodorus' letters (**Variae**) are listed in a single mediaeval library catalogue—the tenth-century catalogue of Lorsch. Most of the extant manuscripts were written in the next five hundred years.[78] In the twelfth century the work is cited by Radulfus de Diceto in his *Abbreviationes chronicorum*[79] and by Giraldus Cambrensis in the parts of his remarkable *Topographia Hibernica* in which he discusses birds[80] and music.[81] At the end of the same century or the beginning of the next the work is cited twice by Alexander Neckam, once in connection with his account of birds.[82]

The **Chronicon** appears in two ninth-century catalogues—one of Reichenau and the other of Würzburg. Apparently unknown to Isidore, Bede, or Paulus Diaconus, it is first cited by Marianus Scottus in the eleventh century,[83] and used somewhat later as the basis for chronicles or annals by Hermannus Contractus (extensively)[84] and by Bernold, a monk of St Blasien.[85] It is known in the twelfth century to the writer of the *Historia pontificalis*[86] and to the author of the annals of Disibodenberg.[87]

The earliest recorded use of any of Cassiodorus' works is the use of his **History of the Goths** around 551 by Jordanes, whose work is a mere résumé of the original, which disappeared entirely in the eight or ninth century.[88]

Two translations produced under Cassiodorus' direction—the so-called **Historia tripartita** and the Vivarian version of Josephus' *Antiquitates*—had a wide influence. The first is listed in fifteen mediaeval catalogues: three of the ninth century—those of Reichenau, St Gall, and Würzburg; one of the tenth—that of Tegernsee; three of the eleventh—those of Toul, St Vaast's at Arras, and Trier; and eight of the twelfth—those of St -Bertin, Bec, Corbie, Michelsberg (near Bamberg), Prüfening, St -Maur de Fossés, an unknown English cloister, and Constance. It is familiar to Isidore[89] and is mentioned by Paulinus of Aquileia in a letter written between 776 and 802.[90] Bishop Adalhard of Corbie had a manuscript copy made *ca* 820.[91] The subsequent use of the work is extensive. Thus in the remaining three-quarters of the ninth century it is employed by the authors of the acts of the Council of Paris (in 825),[92] by Almannus in his *Vita et translatio Helenae,*[93] by Frechulf in his universal chronicle,[94] by Walafrid Strabo in his *De exordiis et incrementis rerum ecclesiasticarum,*[95] by Sedulius Scottus in his *Liber de rectoribus christianis,*[96] by Anastasius Bibliothecarius,[97] and by Hincmar in his *De regis persona et regio ministerio.*[98] Chapters 5 and 45 are cited *ca* 965 A.D. by the author of the *Miracula Sancti Gorgonii* in support of one of his historical incidents (chapter 22).[99] In the eleventh century the work is employed by Marianus Scottus,[100] by Cardinal Humbert (in his work *Adversus simoniacos*),[101] by the author of the second revision of the *Vita III. Willibaldi,*[102] by Manegold of Lautenbach (in his *Liber ad Gebehardum,*[103] by Wido of Osnabrück,[104] and by the anonymous author of the *De unitate ecclesiae conservanda.*[105] In the twelfth it appears in the *Abbreviatio chronicorum* of Radulfus de Diceto,[106] in the *Chronica pontificum et imperatorum Tiburtina*[107] (which corrects the *Historia tripartita*), and in a notice by Wibaldus, bishop of Corbie.[108] Finally, in the thirteenth century, it is the basis of part of the three chronicles written respectively by Sicardus of Cremona,[109] Robert of Auxerre,[110] and Albertus Miliolus.[111]

The translation of the *Antiquitates* is listed in at least fourteen mediaeval catalogues: four of the ninth century—those at Reichenau, St Gall, Fontanelles, and St-Riquier; three of the tenth—those at Lorsch, at an unnamed 'bibliotheca Francogallica,' and at Freising; and seven of the twelfth—those at St -Amand, St-Bertin, Bec, Corbie, Michelsberg (near Bamberg), Durham, and at an unnamed English cloister. Alcuin cites this translation[112] and Frechulf uses it in his universal chronicle.[113] Two centuries later Ekkehard IV shows knowledge of it in his *Casus Sancti Galli,*[114] while Lantbert of Deutz cites it in his *Vita Heriberti.*[115] The *Chronicon Ekkehardi,*[116] William of Malmesbury's *Gesta regum Anglorum,*[117] and the *Gesta abbatum* of Weingarten[118] all make use of it in the twelfth century. In the next century the chronicle of Sicardus of Cremona[119] and the *Chronica imperatorum* of Albertus Miliolus[120] both show knowledge of Josephus and of the *Antiquitates* as well, while actual use of the Vivarian translation is made by Konrad (in his chronicle of Scheier),[121] by Alberic of Troisfontaines,[122] and by the author of the *Chronicon imperatorum et pontificum Bavaricum.*[123]

The record is impressive. At the very least the ***Institutiones*** must have served in many centers as a bibliographical guide and an inspiration to the librarians to look around for good old copies of the works recommended.[124] Second, Book II of the ***Institutiones*** took a place along with the works of Martianus Capella, Boethius, Priscian, and Donatus, as one of the important schoolbooks of the early Middle Ages. Third, several of Cassiodorus' other works—particularly his ***Commentary on the Psalms,*** his ***De anima,*** and his ***De orthographia***—proved to be extremely useful. Fourth, two translations produced under his direction—the so-called ***Historia tripartita*** and the Vivarian version of Josephus' *Antiquitates*—had a wide influence. Fifth, and most important, the manuscripts of Vivarium and of Cassiodorus preserved in sound form for generations to come both the Fathers of the Church and the ancient Latin authors; this two-fold culture might of course have survived somehow without the aid of Cassiodorus but, as it is, the credit should go primarily to him.

Notes

To conserve space I have employed the following abbreviations in citations:

Chapman, St. Benedict.

Dom J. Chapman, *St. Benedict and the VIth century* (London, 1929).

De Orthographia.

Cassiodorus, *De orthographia,* in H. Keil, ed., *Grammatici latini,* VII (Leipzig, 1880).

Franz.

A. M. Franz, *Aurelius Cassiodorus Senator* (Breslau, 1872).

Howell.

W. S. Howell, *The Rhetoric of Alcuin and Charlemagne* (Princeton, Princeton University Press, 1941).

Lehmann.

P. Lehmann, 'Cassiodorstudien,' *Philologus,* LXXI (1912), 278-299; LXXII (1913), 503-517; LXXIII (1914), 253-273; LXXIV (1917), 351-383.

Manitius.

M. Manitius, *Geschichte der lateinischen Literatur des Mittelalters,* I (Munich, 1911), 36-52.

Mercati.

Giovanni Cardinal Mercati, *Marci Tulli Ciceronis De re publica libri e codice rescripto Vaticano latino 5757 phototypice expressi. Codices e Vaticanis selecti quam simillime expressi iussa Pii XI. P. M. consilio et opera ouratorum Bibliothecae Apostolicae Vaticanae,* vol. XXIII (Vatican City, Bib. Apost. Vat., 1934).

Migne, Pat. Lat.

J. P. Migne, ed., *Patrologia cursus completus, Series latina.* 221 vols. (Paris, 1844-1864).

M. G. H.

G. H. Pertz, T. Mommsen, et al., edd., *Monumenta Germaniae Historica* (500-1500). Folio series (Berlin, 1826-96). Quarto series (Berlin, 1876 ff.).

————, *Conc.*

Conciliae.

————, *Ep.*

Epistulae.

————, *SS.*

Scriptores.

Mynors.

R. A. B. Mynors, *Cassiodori Senatoris Institutiones Edited from the MSS.* (Oxford, 1937).

Rand, Founders.

E. K. Rand, *Founders of the Middle Ages* (Cambridge, Mass., 1928), chapter vii.

Roger.

M. Roger *L'enseignement des lettres classiques d'Ausone à Alcuin* (Paris, 1905).

Thiele.

Hans Thiele, 'Cassiodor, seine Klostergründung Vivarium und sein Nachwirkung im Mittelalter,' in *Studien und Mitteilungen zur Geschichte des Benediktiner-Ordens und seiner Zweige*, III. Heft (1932), 378-419.

Van De Vyver.

A. van de Vyver, 'Cassiodore et son oeuvre,' *Speculum*, VI (1931), 244-292.

1. Holstenius, *Cod. regul.*, I (Rome, 1661), 83, §§139-140; cf. §25. I owe this reference and those in notes 5-8 below to *van de Vyver*, 279-280.

2. Cf. Lenain de Tillemont, *Mémoires*, VII (Paris, 1700), 179-180.

3. Sulpicius Severus, *Vita S. Martini*, c. 7.

4. *Apol. adv. Ruf.*, I, 30-31 (*Migne Pat. lat.*, XXIII, col. 421-424), cited by *Rand, Founders*, p. 120.

5. Cf. P. Lahargou, *De Schola Lerinensi* (Paris, 1892).

6. C. 28: *paginam pingat digito, qui Terram non praescribit aratro* (*Franz*, p. 56).

7. Cf. *Roger*, pp. 131-143; 175-187; *Rand, Founders*, p. 234 ff. Cf. also A. Hauck, *Kirchengeschichte Deutschlands*, II (2nd ed., 1912), 61 ff.; Erna Patzelt, *Die Karol. Renaissance* (Vienna, 1924), p. 41 ff.; and *Chapman, St Benedict*, pp. 90-91.

8. Copies of the works of many of these secular writers belonged to the private library of Cassiodorus rather than to the library of Vivarium according to *van de Vyver*, p. 283 and note 5.

9. Both those at Vivarium and those in his own personal library.

10. *Thiele*, pp. 401-417, opposes various exaggerated claims of C.'s influence and holds that C. did not write *the* schoolbook of the Middle Ages and that Vivarium was not *the* model cloister. In his opinion C.'s works were used largely as sources of information and not as inspirations for a plan of monastic cultural training. Even *Thiele*, however (pp. 415-417), admits the considerable importance of Vivarium as a disseminator of historical and classical works.

11. This is uncertain according to *Lehmann*, LXXII (1913), pp. 503-517.

12. The thirteenth century is arbitrarily selected here as a terminus to keep the investigation within reasonable bounds. As any student of the period knows, the number of MSS, belonging to the next two centuries is great. Even for the period selected the evidence presented here is decidedly incomplete. Thus, *Manitius*, our chief authority, himself incomplete, goes through the twelfth century only. The evidence assembled in *Thiele*, pp. 407-417, does not even cite all the material available in *Manitius;* one must also keep Thiele's bias in mind. A complete study of C.'s influence—an obvious *desideratum*—is apparently planned by Mary Stanley, notice of whose projected Oxford University thesis, *The Monastery of Vivarium*

and Its Historical Importance, appeared in the *Revue d'histoire ecclésiastique*, XXXV (1939), p. 674.

13. *Thiele*, p. 411.

14. *M.G.H., SS.*, VI.

15. *Manitius*, III, pp. 313 and 314.

16. All the information on mediaeval library catalogues contained in this entire article is based upon G. Becker, *Catalogi bibliothecarum antiqui* (Bonn, 1885; with additions by G. Meier, *ibid.*, II, 1885, pp. 239-241) and P. Lehmann, *Mittelalterliche Bibliothekskataloge Deutschlands und der Schweiz* (2 vols., Munich, 1918 and 1928). To save space more exact references are not given here.

17. This catalogue is presumably, though not certainly, of the twelfth century.

18. *M.G.H., SS.*, IX.

19. *Ibid.*, XX.

20. *M.G.H., SS.*, XXIII.

21. *Ibid.*, XXV.

22. A single error may also be mentioned here: *Manitius*, III, 1097 (index) lists under C. 'bei Petrus von Cluni . . . 140,' but p. 140 contains no mention of C.

23. *Manitius*, I, 416.

24. *Ibid.*, III, 25.

25. *Ibid.*, III, 50.

26. *Ibid.*, III, 160.

27. *Ibid.*, III, 469.

28. *Ibid.*, III, 784. The work was written at the end of the twelfth or the beginning of the thirteenth century.

29. It must be borne in mind that only tangible evidence is admitted throughout the present account. Failure to be listed in library catalogues (of which there are only a few extant belonging to the earlier Middle Ages) and failure to be quoted in recognizable form or by name are not necessarily proof that a work was either unknown or without influence.

30. *Mynors*, p. xlv and the reference there cited.

31. *Manitius*, I, 125, note 3; *hoc consultissime statuerunt, ut duabus librariis conpositis una fidelium philosophorum libros et altera gentilium scripta contineret.*

32. *M.G.H. Ep.*, VI, 62.

33. *Ibid.*, V, 386.

34. *Ibid.*, V, 427.

35. *Ibid.*, V, 425.

36. *Ibid.*, V, 443.

37. *Franz*, p. 124. As it happens, Rabanus' chapter (Bk. III, chap. 26) may also come directly from Augustine, as *Thiele* believes (p. 413), since C. is quoting Augustine (but only in part).

38. *Thiele,* p. 412. Thiele argues that since C. is mentioned together with Chrysostom and Johannes Damascenus the reference is more probably to C.'s commentary on the *Psalms* and that in any event Alcuin shows little in his work that seems to be influenced by Bk. I.

39. *Thiele,* p. 414.

40. S. Hellman, ed., *Sedulius Scotus, Liber de rectoribus christianis,* in *Quellen u. unters. z. lat. Phil. d. M. A.,* I, 1 (Munich, 1920), pp. 31; 109.

41. *Manitius,* II, p. 793.—See also *Lehmann,* LXXIII (1914), pp. 253-273.—Lehmann points out that *Inst.* I is not used in Rabanus' *Institutio clericorum,* in Notker's *Notatio,* or in Hugo of St Victor's *Libri VII eruditionis didascaliae,* each of which is an important handbook of ecclesiastical instruction. One should note, however, that *Manitius,* III, p. 114, indicates Hugo's debt to C. and that Rabanus does use *Inst.* II as one of his chief sources.

42. *Manitius,* II, pp. 62; 65.

43. *Ibid.,* II, pp. 81; 77; 79.

44. *Ibid.,* III, 114.

45. *Ibid.,* III, 347.

46. *M.G.H., SS.,* XXVII.

47. *Thiele* points out (p. 408) that Bk. II occurs in library catalogues much less frequently than Isidore's *Etymologies* or even Martianus Capella's work.

48. For the details see the apparatus in *Mynors.*—Cf. also *Lehmann,* LXXII (1913), pp. 504-517.

49. *Thiele,* p. 412. Among other things, Thiele quotes Lehmann concerning the sporadic character of Alcuin's use (in his *Rhetoric*) of C.'s *Inst.* or of some work dependent upon C.—For the details see *Howell,* pp. 14; 23-25; 159; 160; and my review of Howell's book in the *American Historical Review,* XLVIII (1943), pp. 305-306.

50. See *Mynor's* apparatus.—Cf. *Thiele,* p. 413.

51. *Manitius,* I, 446.

52. *Ibid.,* I, 698.

53. *Ibid.,* I, 492.

54. *Ibid.,* I, 477.

55. *Ibid.,* II, p. 741.—*Thiele's* statement (p. 416) and his reference (note 110) are both incorrect.

56. A listing of the actual manuscripts of this work and of the remaining works which are described below in this chapter, though bound to be illuminating, is beyond the province of this article.

57. *Thiele,* p. 411.

58. *M.G.H., Ep.,* IV, p. 468.

59. *Thiele,* p. 414.

60. *M.G.H., Ep.,* V, p. 357.

61. *Manitius,* I, p. 420.

62. *Ibid.,* II, pp. 158; 165.

63. *Ibid.,* II, p. 698, note 3.

64. *Ibid.,* II, pp. 62; 65.

65. *Ibid.,* II, p. 78.

66. *Ibid.,* II, p. 117.

67. *M.G.H., SS.,* VI.

68. *Manitius,* III, 112.

69. *M.G.H., SS.,* IX.

70. *Ibid.*

71. *Ibid.,* XXXI.

72. *M.G.H., SS.,* IX.

73. *M.G.H., Ep.,* V, p. 515.

74. *Manitius,* I, 42.

75. *Thiele,* p. 411.

76. *De orthographia,* p. 307.

77. *Manitius,* III, 469.

78. *Ibid.,* I, p. 41.

79. *Ibid.,* III, p. 638.

80. *Ibid.,* III, p. 625, note 5.

81. *Ibid.,* p. 626, note 3.

82. *Ibid.,* p. 786 (birds). For the second citation: *ibid.,* p. 787.

83. *Ibid.,* II, pp. 392; 792. Cf. *M.G.H., SS.,* V.

84. *Manitius,* II, 760-761; *M.G.H., SS.,* V.

85. *Manitius,* III, 405 (Manitius wrongly indexes this reference as 'bei Helmold'); *M.G.H., SS.,* V.

86. *M.G.H., SS.,* XX.

87. *Manitius,* II, 393. *Thiele,* p. 416, erroneously cites *Manitius,* II, 792, and assigns the work to the eleventh century.

88. *Manitius,* I, pp. 212 and 43.

89. *Thiele,* p. 411.

90. *M.G.H., Ep.,* IV, p. 526.

91. *Manitius,* I, p. 407 and note 3.

92. *M.G.H., Conc.,* II.2, pp. 487 ff.

93. A. Ebert, *Allgemeine Geschichte der Literatur des Mittelalters* (Leipzig, 1895), Bd. III, p. 203.

94. Ebert, *op. cit.,* Bd. II, p. 384.

95. *M.G.H., cap.* II, pp. 492 and 505.

96. Edit. of S. Hellman, in *Quellen u. Unters. z. lat. Phil. d. M. A.* (Munich, 1920), Bd. I, p. 207.

97. *Manitius,* I, 685-686.

98. *Thiele,* pp. 415-416.

99. *Manitius,* II., 196.

100. *Ibid.,* p. 392. Cf. *M.G.H., SS.,* V.

101. *Ibid.*, III, p. 24.

102. *M.G.H., SS.,* XV.

103. *Manitius*, III, 27.

104. *Ibid.*, p. 29.

105. *Ibid.*, p. 43. Two passages from the *Hist. trip.* are cited.

106. *M.G.H., SS.,* XXVII.

107. *Ibid.*, XXXI.

108. *Monumenta Corbeiensia*, ep. 167, cited by *Thiele*, p. 416, note 122.

109. *M.G.H., SS.,* 31.

110. *Ibid.*, 26.

111. *Ibid.*, 31.

112. *M.G.H., Ep.,* IV, no. 162.

113. Ebert, *op. cit.*, Bd. II, p. 384.

114. *M.G.H., SS.,* II.

115. *Monitius*, II, 365.

116. *M.G.H., SS.,* VI.

117. *Ibid.*, X.

118. *Ibid.*, XV.

119. *Thiele*, p. 417.

120. *M.G.H., SS.,* XXXI.

121. *M.G.H., SS.,* XVII.

122. *M.G.H., SS.,* XXIII.

123. *M.G.H., SS.,* XXIV.

124. *Mercati* says, p. 18: 'Anzi nei primi secoli che seguirono fino al X, presso i bibliofili che non mancarono nemmeno allora, le *Instituzioni* di Cassiodoro avranno servito, come una guida bibliografica, a farle apprezzare e cercare datorno.' Cf. also *Lehmann*, LXXI (1912), p. 281: 'Mit Recht hat das M. A. deren erstes Buch [of the *Inst.*] als eine literarhistorische Quelle betrachtet und es mehrfach mit Hieronymus, Gennadius u. a. zu einem Corpus vereinigt.' Cf. *Lehmann*, LXXII (1913), p. 507, and LXXIII (1914), p. 253.

Leslie W. Jones (essay date 1947)

SOURCE: "Further Notes Concerning Cassiodorus's Influence on Mediaeval Culture," in *Speculum*, Vol. 22, No. 4, April, 1947, pp. 254-56.

[*In this essay, Jones lists a number of corrections and emendations to his previous essay (see above).*]

That the appearance of my recent article, 'The Influence of Cassiodorus on Mediaeval Culture,' *Speculum*, XX (1945), 433-442, has prompted several friends to send me a few suggestions for its correction and improvement, and many for its amplification is not surprising. One who has the hardihood to attempt to cover a broad field is bound to fall into occasional error. I desire to express here not only my gratitude for the suggestions but the hope that other readers of *Speculum* will let me have further recommendations. Professor Wilhelm Levison of the University of Durham is responsible for the items listed below under p. 436, notes 3a (in part) and 6, and p. 441, line 9 ('bishop'); Professor E. A. Lowe of the Institute for Advanced Study at Princeton for the item listed under p. 442, line 4; Professor Alexander Souter of Oxford for the items listed under p. 439, lines 32-35, and p. 439, line 35, end; and Professor B. M. Peebles of St John's College, Annapolis, for most of those which remain. The list of corrections, improvements, and additions follows. The changes outlined here should also be applied, at least in part, to pp. 47-58 of my recent book, *An Introduction to Divine and Human Readings by Cassiodorus Senator,* a translation with an introduction and notes (New York, Columbia University Press, 1946), where the substance of the *Speculum* article is presented in slightly different form.

P. 434, note 7. Add: Chapman, *St Benedict*, p. 286, has conjectured that St Benedict's community must have embraced the work of MS copying; possibly scribes were among the *artifices* dealt with in the *Rule* (chap. 57). Dom P. Schmitz, in 'Les *Inst.* de C. et sa fondation à Vivarium,' *Revue bénédictine*, LIII (1941), and *L'Histoire de l'ordre de Saint Benoît* (Maredsous, 1942), II, 92, believes that Cassiodorus knew and used the *Rule*.

P. 435, note 1. Add: See Cardinal Schuster's article on the fate of the *codices Vivarienses* in *La Scuola Cattolica* for December 1942.

P. 435, note 3, Add: Relevant here are the findings (largely negative) of J. D. A. Ogilvy, *Books Known to Anglo-Latin Writers from Aldhelm to Alcuin: 670-804* (Cambridge, Mass., The Mediaeval Academy of America, *Studies and Documents No. 2,* 1936), p. 24. See also N. R. Ker's *Mediaeval Libraries of Great Britain* (London, 1941).

P. 436, lines 3-4: Add: The anonymous writer also gives a moderately complete bibliography of Cassiodorus; he mentions six works, one of them a 'liber de viris illustribus,' which is presumably the *Inst.* (at least Book I) and not the *Ordo generis Cassiodoriorum*, which P. Lehmann considers the more probable candidate (*Gnomon*, XII [1936], 273 ff.).

P. 436, note 3a. Add: One should now also consult the three parts of Lehmann's third volume published in 1932-1939 (Augsburg, Eichstätt, Bamberg, by P. Rufs), or, better still, Max Manitius' *HSS antiken Autoren in mittelalterlichen Bibliothekscatalogen* (*Zeitschrift für Bibliothekswesen, Beiblatt 67,* Leipzig, 1935).

P. 436, note 6. Add: John of Salisbury is today recognized as the author of the *Historia pontificalis:* see R. L. Poole's edition, *Ioannis Saresberiensis Historiae Pontificalis quae supersunt* (Oxford, 1927). John's *Policraticus* and *Metalogicus* could also be quoted.

P. 437, line 1. Add: Since the entry in the Pompuse catalogue is merely 'Cassiodori liber I' (Manitius, *HSS* etc.), there is no more than a bare possibility that *Inst.* I is meant.

P. 437, line 2. Add: Additional catalogue entries for *Inst.* I prior to 1300 (from Manitius, *HSS* etc.): Murbach, *s.* ix; Gorize, *s.* xi; Bobbio, *s.* xi; Canterbury, *ca.* 1300. Entries for *Inst.* II (from Manitius, *op. cit.*): Murbach, *s.* ix; Gorize, *s.* xi; Cluny, *s.* xii; St Wandrille, after 823 (only the *De arithmetica;* perhaps not the true *Inst.* II text).

P. 437, note 9. Add: Cf., however, Lehmann below, note 13.

P. 438, line 11. Add: The Anchin catalogue may represent the library of St Amand (see Boutemy, *Revue belge de philologie et d'histoire,* XVIII [1939], 765).

P. 438, line 29. Add: In the twelfth century Hugo of St Victor (in *Didascalicon,* II and III) draws frequently on *Inst.* II, though probably via Isidore (see C. H. Buttimer, *Hugonis de Sancto Victore Didascalicon,* etc., diss., The Catholic Univ. of America, Washington, D. C., 1939).

P. 438. line 32. Add: Is the Fontanelles item identical with the St Wandrille catalogue cited above in the addition to p. 437, line 2?

P. 438, note 1. Add: Buttimer, *op. cit.,* cites no textual parallels in *Didascalicon,* IV-VI except IV, 14 (p. 89, line 24), a reference to Cassiodorus on the Psalms.

P. 438, note 6. Add: On Alcuin (*De rhetorica*) see Ogilvy, *op. cit.* (in the addition to p. 435, note 3), p. 24.

P. 438, note 11. Add: The probable author of the *Quaestiones grammaticae* is Gottschalk (see Dom Lambot in *Revue bénédictine,* XLIV [1932]).

P. 439, line 22. Add: Hugo of St Victor (Buttimer, *op. cit.;* see my addition to p. 438, note 1), and Honorius of Autun, *De luminaribus ecclesiae,* III, xxi (Manitius, *Geschichte der lateinischen Literatur des Mittelalters,* III, p. 373; Migne, *P. L.* 172, 224).

P. 439, line 28, first word. Add: There are catalogues at Passau (903) and Canterbury (*ca.* 1300) according to Manitius, *HSS* etc.

P. 439, lines 32-35. Read: [His] *Complexiones in epistulas et acta apostolorum et apocalypsin* and the *Expositio epistolae quae scribitur ad Romanos unde Pelagianae haereseos pravitates amovi* were not widely known. One other work, the *Liber titulorum quem de divina scriptura collectum memorialem volui nuncupari,* has been lost.

P. 439, line 35, end. Add: The *Expositio* is of course extant under the name of Primasius. The true history of this work and of C.'s share in it has been unravelled with masterly skill by A. Souter in 'Pelagius' Exposition on the Thirteenth Epistle of St Paul,' *Texts and Studies,* edited by Armitage Robinson, Vol. IX, Parts 1-3 (Cambridge 1922, 1926, 1931).

P. 439, line 38, after 'century.' Add: There is also a catalogue of Canterbury of *ca.* 1300 (cited in my addition to p. 439, line 28, above).

P. 439, note 2. Add: See Ogilvy, *op. cit.,* p. 24, for additional examples.

P. 439, note 20. Add: On Alcuin (and Bede) and the *De orthographia* see Ogilvy, *op. cit.,* p. 24.

P. 440, line 2, middle. Add: catalogues from Bec, *s.* xii, and Glastonbury, 1247 (C.'s 'Epistulae').

P. 441, line 9. Change 'bishop of Corbie' to read 'abbot of Corvey.' Add: Honorius of Autun (see my addition to p. 439, line 22, above).

P. 441, note 14. Add: Ogilvy, *op. cit.,* p. 56, states that Alcuin is using Rufinus' translation. There is no inconsistency here, since C's work was never attributed to C. but was attributed to Rufinus in the fifteenth century and later (Manitius, *Geschichte der lateinischen Literatur des Mittelalters,* I, 51-52).

P. 442, lines 4-5 ('Fifth, . . . to come both the'). Change to read: 'Fifth, and most important, in collecting and editing MSS and in having them copied at Vivarium, Cassiodorus attempted to preserve in sound form for generations to come both the. . . .'

M. L. W. Laistner (essay date 1948)

SOURCE: "The Value and Influence of Cassiodorus's Ecclesiastical History," in *Harvard Theological Review,* Vol. XLI, No. 1, January, 1948, pp. 51-67.

[*In the essay below, Laistner analyzes the ecclesiastical history edited by and translated under the direction of Cassiodorus, praising his critical skill in selecting the material to be included in the* Historia Tripartita.]

Most students of history or literature have had at some time the experience of encountering statements or generalizations made by a writer of an earlier generation and then finding them repeated without question by his successors working in the same field of inquiry. What is more, if dissentient voices have been raised, they have often been overlooked or disregarded. The prevailing estimate of Cassiodorus' Ecclesiastical History affords an excellent example of the manner in which erroneous opinions have been repeated *ad nauseam* from one generation to the next, although more than thirty years have passed since two scholars of the first rank, Bidez and Parmentier, provided at least some of the evidence needed for a more just evaluation of Cassiodorus' book. There are two essential questions which seem to call for fresh investigation. The first is concerned with the value and accuracy of the compilation, the second with its diffusion during the Middle Ages and its popularity as a work of reference.[1]

Some years after political conditions had forced Cassiodorus to withdraw from public life, he founded his monastic community at Vivarium in southern Italy. He built up his famous library in order to make possible the study of secular and religious works by his monks; and, as a general guide to their reading, he composed his treatise, **Institutiones,** in two short books, the first devoted to sacred, the second to profane letters.[2] He did not, however, consider the study of only Latin writers to be an adequate preparation for the monastic student. Hence one part of his general plan was to make available in Latin dress Greek works which for one reason or another seemed to him of essential utility. He refers to the Greek books which he caused to be translated, and he names several of the helpers to whom the actual task of translation was entrusted. Amongst the historical works for which he thus assumed a general responsibility was a condensed version of the Ecclesiastical Histories composed by Socrates, Sozomen, and Theodoret. Epiphanius, the translator, was responsible also for Latin renderings of several Greek theological works; otherwise nothing is known about him. Cassiodorus refers twice to the undertaking. He explains its origin and purpose briefly in the Preface, which is certainly from his pen even if his share in compiling the actual history was purely advisory or editorial; and he included an even shorter statement in that chapter of the **Institutiones** (1, 17) where he describes the historical section of his library.

Epiphanius began by turning into Latin the abbreviated version of the three Histories put together a decade or two before by a certain Theodore, Reader at the church of S. Sophia in Constantinople, but Cassiodorus makes no mention of this fact. Theodore's work, although it has never been printed, is still extant in the same manuscript at Venice (Marcianus 344: saec. xiii) which, as far as it goes, contains the best surviving text of Sozomen.[3] From Book 2, chapter 8, however, Epiphanius proceeded independently. There are a few more borrowings from Theodore here and there; after that Epiphanius, with or without the guidance of Cassiodorus, makes his own selections from the Greek originals. The name by which this Latin version became known, *Historia Tripartita,* explains its origin and seems obvious enough; nevertheless it is hard to say when it first came into use. Theodore Lector called his book a *syntaxis* or compilation. Cassiodorus' contemporary, Liberatus of Carthage, obtained material from Epiphanius' version for his account of Nestorianism and Monophysitism; he calls it "the ecclesiastical history lately translated from Greek into Latin."[4] Gregory the Great refers to a passage "in historia Sozomeni"; actually it is in Theodoret, but Gregory's mistake is readily understandable if he was using HT [*Historia Tripartita*]. Isidore of Seville obtained material from HT for his Chronicle and two notices in De viris illustribus, but did not indicate his source. After that evidence is lacking for a long while; but in the ninth century the title, Historia Tripartita, is well established, though by no means in universal use. It is found in the official report of the Synod held at Paris in 825 and it is employed by individual writers, for example, by Amalarius of Metz and Jonas of Orleans. Others, like Ratramnus of Corbie and Hincmar of Rheims, prefer to name the particular Greek author, for instance, "Socrates in his Ecclesiastical History," although they quote the Latin translation. Wahlafrid employs both methods.[5] The library catalogues of the ninth century show a similar variation in usage. Some mention only the three Greek authors and call the book, "Ecclesiastical History," while one lists it as "Tripartite History of Socrates, Sozomen, Theodoret." Whereas the cataloguer at Reichenau with his entry, "Tripartitae II," believed in extreme brevity, his confrère at St. Gall went to the opposite extreme with his, "The Ecclesiastical Histories of Cassiodorus Senator derived from three authors, to wit, Sozomen, Theodoret, and Socrates, twelve books in one volume." Gradually the short title, *Historia Tripartita* (or Tripertita), without mention of either the Greek authors or of Cassiodorus or Epiphanius, became more and more usual, and in the library catalogues of the twelfth century and later it predominates. Yet authors of the twelfth century still introduce quotations from HT with a reference to the Greek historian cited. William of Tyre inserted two considerable passages from Book 6 into his own History, assigning them correctly to Sozomen and Theodoret "in the Tripartite History." John of Salisbury introduced a citation with the comment: "Hence Socrates—not the Socrates of antiquity, but the writer whom Cassiodorus in his *Tripartite History* praises as a historian—remarks."[6]

We may now turn to the first of the two questions which call for reconsideration, the value and accuracy of HT. Adverse judgments on it go back a long way. They are as old as Beatus Rhenanus whose book, Autores Historiae Ecclesiasticae, published at Basel in 1523, contained Rufinus' translation of Eusebius' Ecclesiastical History together with Rufinus' two additional Books and HT. He added the documents in Theodoret in the Greek text, using a manuscript at Basel which is still extant.[7] In modern times the most detailed criticism of HT was made by Adolf Franz whose book on Cassiodorus appeared in 1872. After pointing out that the translator's knowledge of Greek was imperfect, he listed many examples of mistranslations in HT and also examples of careless arrangement in the material selected. As often happens when a notable book on a special topic has appeared, Franz' judgments were adopted more or less without question by subsequent writers. They appear in the standard literary histories of Schanz, Manitius, Bardenhewer, Moricca, and Labriolle, as well as in occasional articles. Manitius asserts that the translator had before him a text marred by many errors, while M. van de Vyver indulges in a little hyperbole when he suggests that a monograph would be necessary to describe the many mistakes of which Epiphanius was guilty.[8] That the critics of HT were neither accurate nor just was first demonstrated by Bidez in 1908 when he published his study of the surviving manuscripts of Sozomen. Three years later Parmentier's admirable edition of Theodoret appeared.

Both of these scholars were fully aware that Epiphanius had from time to time made "boners," which occasionally are even amusing.[9] But they showed that the Greek manuscripts used for HT were superior, and that by the help of Latin manuscripts of HT it is often possible to correct readings where the extant Greek codices differ. What is more, the Latin text can be used to restore the true reading in places where the surviving Greek text is defective or corrupt. In short, a study of the examples listed by Parmentier in his Introduction and a perusal of the apparatus criticus accompanying the text of Theodoret fully demonstrate the injustice of Cassiodorus' modern detractors.

In the Preface to HT Cassiodorus observes that the three Greek writers, in treating the same events, had not all been equally detailed or shown an equal amount of care; hence some parts were better in one author, some in another. Hitherto it has not been noticed that the selection of passages included in HT implies considerable exercise of the critical faculty. This, it can hardly be doubted, was Cassiodorus' own contribution, in other words, his editorial function was real not nominal. Regarded from the point of view of historical accuracy Socrates' book is unquestionably the most valuable and the most accurate of the three. Sozomen, a far better stylist, is more agreeable to read. Theodoret's History with its strongly partisan outlook belongs, like Orosius' History, in spirit though not in form to apologetic rather than to historical literature. This feature, which a modern student would regard as a defect, would appear as a merit to the men of the Middle Ages. Besides, although all three introduce documentary material into their books, Theodoret in this respect is much more lavish than the other two. Examination of the selections in HT leads to a significant result. The excerpts from Socrates, the soundest historian of the three, greatly exceed in number those from Sozomen or Theodoret. In Books 4, 9, and 10 Sozomen comes in a bad third, nor are the extracts from him in Books 7 and 8 numerous. He is in the lead only in Book 6. Not a few of the passages taken from Theodoret are documentary or else contain material which is omitted by Socrates and Sozomen. Theodoret is, for example, the only one of the three to give in full the report of the Council of Sardica (HT 4, 24) or Athanasius' letter to the African bishops concerning the Synod of Rimini (HT 5, 30) or the letter from the Synod of Constantinople to George, bishop of Alexandria (HT 5, 42); and there are other instances of the same thing. Books 11 and 12 of HT come entirely from Socrates who carried the story down to 439. Sozomen appears to have done the same, but the surviving version of his History does not extend beyond 421. One may perhaps surmise that the last section was already missing in the codex used by Epiphanius. Theodoret's account ended with events of the year 428.

If the selection made by Cassiodorus thus shows more care and critical acumen than he has generally been credited with, there was also some excuse for Epiphanius' occasional lapses as a translator. As Parmentier has justly observed, it was no easy task to render into adequate Latin certain of the Greek documents. Many dealt with difficult

and obscure points of dogma, and it is probable that already by the middle of the sixth century corruptions had crept into the Greek text. Besides, why should Epiphanius or Cassiodorus be singled out for special obloquy? Rufinus, whose facilities were better and for whom there was therefore less excuse, was not always an accurate translator. This fact has been recognized but his versions have not been judged as harshly as HT has. And, while it would be invidious to particularize, one could readily point to translations published in our own day which are disfigured not just by verbal infelicities but by errors falsifying the author's meaning. Parmentier rated HT more highly than Bidez. The reason is not far to seek. He consulted three extant manuscripts of HT, whereas Bidez had been content to work with Garet's text as reprinted in Migne's Patrology. But Garet was certainly one of the less distinguished members of the Congregation of St. Maur. Mynors has called Garet's edition of the Institutiones a "disappointing and misleading work." The same estimate may be applied to his edition of HT. It thus becomes evident that some of the criticism levelled against Cassiodorus or Epiphanius should by right be directed at the Benedictine editor. A final judgment on the merits and defects of HT will only be possible when a trustworthy edition based on a collation of the best codices becomes available. In the meantime the evidence scattered through the apparatus criticus of Parmentier's Theodoret is highly significant.

The popularity of HT during the Middle Ages has often been stressed in a general way, but without an adequate investigation of the facts. Even those who, like Thiele, have not been content with generalizations but have taken the trouble to collect some evidence are still misleading because their inquiries have not gone far enough.[10] In the first place all the available evidence seems to point to the conclusion that for several centuries after its composition HT was not widely used. For a long time it could not compare in popularity with Orosius' History or even with Rufinus' version of Eusebius. On the other hand, Rufinus' continuation went no further than A.D. 395, and Jerome's adaptation of Eusebius' Chronicle ends with the year 378. Orosius carried his story down to 419, but his book was not an *ecclesiastical* History; and, moreover, in his later books he concentrated mainly on events in the western half of the Empire. Continuations of Eusebius-Jerome by western chroniclers were many, but the only one which met with lasting success was Prosper's. The Chronicle of Hydatius survives in a single manuscript; the same thing is true of later compilers, like John of Biclaro and Marius of Avenches. Besides, the emphasis in these continuations was wholly or almost wholly on western affairs. The one chronicler who appears to have enjoyed a somewhat wider diffusion and who at the same time gave information about the Byzantine world was Marcellinus Comes.[11] Since HT was the only work in Latin to offer detailed information about the Church in the eastern half of the Empire for forty odd years after the death of Theodosius I, one might have supposed, arguing *a priori,* that its popularity would be ensured from the beginning. Yet the evidence points to a different conclusion. Extant manuscripts copied before c.

900 are scarce, and in library catalogues of the ninth century the book appears only seven times, in four German and three French collections. Obviously at least one manuscript of very early date must have survived, the archetype of the oldest that we now possess, and there may well have been two or three venerable codices. The mere fact, however, that extant manuscripts of early date—there are none of the eighth century—are few shows that HT only made headway very slowly, compared, for instance, with Cassiodorus' commentary on the Psalms.[12] It does not appear to have been much consulted by continental authors of the eighth century, and in England it seems to have been unknown at that period. Levison has noted a reminiscence from HT in Boniface's correspondence, Alcuin cites from it once, and his contemporary, Paulinus of Aquileia was certainly familiar with it.[13] From Alcuin's time on the writers on the Continent betray increasing interest in the book, with the incidental result that it began to receive more attention also in the scriptoria. How is this change of attitude to be explained? The treatises composed in the ninth century, in which quotations from HT occur, suggest a probable answer.

There were two topics which engaged the attention of scholars in that age for which HT supplied useful material—the various doctrinal "errors" of the Greek Church and the duties of rulers coupled with the problem of their relation to the ecclesiastical authority. It is surely no accident that so many citations from HT in the literature of the ninth century are found in works bearing on one or other of these two subjects. The Synod of Paris in 825 addressed itself once more to the task of refuting Iconoclasm. Opposition to it and also to the extreme form of image-worship approved by the Council of Nicaea in 787 had been stated with great fulness a generation before by the Synod of Paris in the so-called Libri Carolini. Doctrinally the position of their author or authors was midway between the two extremes sanctioned and enforced successively by imperial authority in the East. The Libri Carolini are full of quotations from Patristic literature, but I could find no trace of HT. The purpose of the Synod held at Paris is expressly stated: ". . . sententias colligere contra eos qui imagines non solum ab aedibus, sed etiam a sacris vasis indiscrete abolere praesumunt." There follows in the surviving report of the Synod a collectaneum of passages from the Fathers. Included are quotations from Books 1, 2, 6, 9, and 10 of HT. But the Greeks had some sympathisers in the West, notably Claudius of Turin. Against him Jonas of Orleans composed a tract, De cultu imaginum, which again is largely a cento of citations from earlier writers, and again HT supplied some of the ammunition for the verbal battle.[14] Controversy died down for a while, only to flare up afresh when the Patriarch Photius in 866 issued an encyclical. This brought to the fore once again various doctrinal differences between the two Churches, the chief of which now concerned the dogma of the Procession of the Holy Spirit. Pope Nicholas I, who invited the Carolingian divines to reply formally to the Patriarch's charges, had himself cited a passage from "Theodoret" in a letter addressed in the previous year to the Emperor Michael. In

the most penetrating of the works composed in answer to the papal request, Ratramnus of Corbie's Contra Graecorum opposita, passages from HT find a place.[15]

The ideal Christian ruler and the relationship between Temporal and Spiritual Authority were discussed by Smaragdus, Jonas, Hincmar of Rheims, and Sedulius Scottus. Although his use of HT in the tract against Claudius of Turin proves Jonas' familiarity with HT, he does not seem to have consulted it when engaged in writing De institutione regia for the young king Pippin; nor does Smaragdus seem to have known the book. But Hincmar in the short essay, De fide Caroli, quotes episodes from the lives of Ambrose and Theodosius I as narrated in HT.[16] Sedulius made more extensive use of it than any other scholar of the age. He included extracts from it in his Collectaneum, while in his treatise, De rectoribus Christianis, there are, in addition to many brief phrases or reminiscences, eight long quotations from that source. The extended excerpts are what one would have expected in view of the purpose of Sedulius, to write a kind of "Mirror for Princes." They record episodes in the life of Constantine, the virtues of Flaccilla, wife of Theodosius I, and, of course, Theodosius' penance at the behest of Ambrose. A letter of Athanasius bids temporal rulers to learn and to yearn for heavenly things, and Valentinian I replies with suitable modesty when consulted by a bishop on a point of doctrine. Nor are a notable miracle at the siege of Nisibis in 350 and Julian's death in the Persian war forgotten.[17] There are traces of HT in a few other authors of the ninth century. It was one of the historical works used by Freculph of Lisieux for his History. He appears to have been a pupil of Helisachar who from c. 822 was abbot of St. Riquier and who may have taught there at an earlier date. The extant catalogue of St. Riquier, drawn up in 831, lists a copy of HT.[18] We have already seen that Amalarius and Wahlafrid quote from it.[19] Later in the century the papal librarian Anastasius evidently consulted the same copy of HT in the Lateran to which Nicholas I had turned for his quotation when writing to the emperor Michael.[20]

It is thus apparent that by the end of the ninth century HT was well established, and it is not difficult to trace its continued use in the centuries that followed. A few examples must suffice to illustrate the trend and the kind of works for which HT provided useful material. Odo of Cluny relates in his own words the story of Theodosius II's humility towards an arrogant monk of whom Odo dryly observes, "ut credo, non bene compos mentis suae erat." A certain Adalger addressed a brief hortatory tract to a nun, Nonsvinda, for which HT provided suitable exempla. Here and there he indicates his source, but his indebtedness went much further than this; for example, the long description of the controversy between Theodosius I and Ambrose, filling two columns in Migne, is repeated verbatim and without acknowledgment towards the end of this Admonitio.[21] Hagiographers also found Cassiodorus' compilation serviceable, as we see in the Miracula Gorgonii, of which more hereafter, and in Gozwin of Mainz' Passio S. Albani.[22] The numerous writers who contributed, taking one side or the other, to the controversial literature which concerned itself with the Investiture Strife and abuses in the Church, such as simony and the incontinence of the clergy, found HT a handy source for quotations. Passages were taken from Books 2, 7, 9, 10, and 12, some recurring more than once. Thus the story of Paphnutius' intervention at Nicaea in the matter of clerical marriage and its prohibition (HT 2, 14) and the story of Ambrose's election to the see of Milan (HT 7, 8) recur three times.[23] Finally, HT became a normal source of information for historian and chronicler, as can be seen in the works of Marianus Scottus, Sigebert of Gembloux, Otto of Freising, and others of later date.[24] But it is needless to labor the point further; rather one must turn to the even clearer evidence furnished by the catalogues of medieval libraries and by the extant manuscripts of HT.

The lists of medieval libraries containing a copy of HT that are given by Thiele and more recently by Mr. L. W. Jones are incomplete even for the period—down to the end of the twelfth century—to which they confine their attention. Nor, as far as I am aware, has any list of surviving manuscripts ever been drawn up. Yet this is essential evidence. It is more conclusive than many of the quotations or reminiscences found in authors; for it is sometimes impossible to be sure that a medieval writer is citing or repeating a story from the primary source. An example will illustrate this. Among the many miraculous episodes related by Theodoret was one that occurred at the siege of Nisibis in 350 and led to the repulse of the Persian forces under Sapor. The holy Ephrem having prayed from the top of a tower which commanded a view of the besieging army, swarms of mosquitoes and other insects appeared and attacked the Persian elephants and horses, filling the trunks of the one and the eyes and ears of the other. This tale was included in HT (5, 45). Soon after the middle of the tenth century an unknown writer composed a brief work, Miracula S. Gorgonii. This minor piece of hagiography was written to glorify the patron saint of Gorze, a monastery in Lorraine. Its author after relating one of the saint's miracles recalls by way of comparison the miracle at Nisibis. The modern editor of the Miracula and Manitius have assumed that the hagiographer took his story directly from HT, but this is far from certain.[25] He narrates the tale in an abbreviated form and in his own words. But the story had been used by Sedulius in De rectoribus Christianis; and it is known that the library of Gorze in the eleventh century possessed a copy of Sedulius' treatise. This codex is lost but formed the basis for a printed edition issued in 1619. The date of the lost manuscript is uncertain, but it was closely related to an extant manuscript of the late ninth century, so that it too may have been copied at that date or not much later.[26] Thus it is at least an even chance that the hagiographer took his illustration from Sedulius rather than from Cassiodorus. . . .

Notes

1. The following abbreviations have been used throughout: HT = Historia Tripartita; MGH = Monumenta Germaniae Historica; PL = Migne, Patrologia Latina.

2. The best treatment of Cassiodorus' activities at Vivarium is now to be found in the brilliant book, *Les Lettres grecques en Occident,* by Pierre Courcelle (Bibliothèque des écoles françaises d'Athènes et de Rome, Fasc. 159; Paris, de Boccard, 1943), pp. 313-388. Cf. my review in *Classical Philology* for October, 1947.

3. Cf. J. Bidez, *La tradition manuscrite de Sozomène et la Tripartite de Théodore le lecteur* (A. Harnack und C. Schmidt, Texte und Untersuchungen XXXII [1908], Heft 2b), pp. 35 ff.; and generally, O. Bardenhewer, *Geschichte der altkirchlichen Literatur* 5 (1932), pp. 117-118.

4. Cf. Bidez, op. cit., p. 46, where the whole of Theodore's Preface is printed; Liberatus in PL 68, col. 969C.

5. *De exordiis,* chs. 20 and 26 (ed. Knöpfler, pp. 45 and 76-77).

6. PL 201, 403A (from HT 1058B-C) and 309D-310A (from HT 1051D); Policraticus (ed. C. C. Webb) II, 214, 10 ff.

7. L. Parmentier, *Theodoret: Kirchengeschichte* (Die griechischen christlichen Schriftsteller der ersten drei Jahrhunderte, Leipzig, 1911), p. LXVI.

8. M. Manitius, *Geschichte der lateinischen Literatur des Mittelalters I,* p. 51. In the Nachträge published in II, p. 793 he alludes to the work of Bidez and Parmentier, but he does not point out that their researches invalidated his earlier opinion. M. van de Vyver (*Speculum* 6 [1931], pp. 264-265), refers to Bidez in a footnote, but his estimate of HT and the fact that he repeats a mistake in Bidez' book suggest that he had not read it very carefully. On p. 51 Bidez had stated that Epiphanius used Theodore Lector down to Book 2, chapter 3. This was either a slip or a misprint; and on p. 55 he says correctly that Theodore's Syntaxis was followed down to Book 2, chapter 7.

9. For example, the confusion between ᾠδῖσιν and ᾠδαῖς, so that παρθενικαῖς ᾠδῖσιν in HT become *virginum cantibus*! See Parmentier, op. cit. p. LII.

10. See Hans Thiele, *Studien und Mitteilungen zur Geschichte des OSB 50* (1932), pp. 415-417; the information in L. W. Jones, *Divine and Human Readings by Cassiodorus* (Columbia U. P., 1946), pp. 56-57, is also insufficient, being taken from Thiele with some additions from Manitius' third volume. There are many omissions even in M. Manitius, *HSS antiker Autoren in mittelalterlichen Bibliothekskatalogen,* pp. 319-322.

11. The Liber pontificalis, apart from its specialized nature, making any references to eastern affairs merely incidental, only becomes a detailed record from the end of the sixth century. Cf. the judicious summary of Bardenhewer, op. cit. 5, p. 302.

12. M. Courcelle, whose account of Cassiodorus is otherwise so good, is utterly misleading in what he says

about extant manuscripts of these two works. He asserts (op. cit., p. 351 with note 7) that "quantité de manuscrits carolingiens" of HT survive and, in support of this statement, he lists seven. One of these (Sangall. 561) contains saints' lives with, as far as can be judged from Scherrer, at most a few excerpts from HT. Casinensis 302, according to Lowe (Beneventan Script, p. 349), is written partly in ordinary minuscule (saec. x/xi), partly in Beneventan (saec. xi ex.). Vattasso dates Vat. lat. 1970 in the tenth century, while Stevenson, whose dates are less reliable, says of Vat. Pal. 823, "saec. ix vel x." Reifferscheid, on whom M. Courcelle relies, dated Vercelli CI "saec. ix-x" and Naples VI D 18 "saec. x." In short, under the term "carolingien" M. Courcelle lumps together manuscripts varying in date by two centuries or more. He follows a similar procedure in note 2 on the same page when he lists codices of the commentary on Psalms. For the information of the interested reader a more accurate enumeration of truly early manuscripts of that work follows. The dates are not mine but have been assigned by expert palaeographers, Lindsay or Lowe or, in one case, Bruckner: Autun 20A (saec. viii-ix); Durham B.II.20 (saec. viii med.); Laon 26 (saec. ix in.); Munich 14077-78 (saec. ix[1], since Lindsay did not include mss of the later ninth century in his Notae latinae); Paris 12239-41 (saec. viii med.); St. Gall 202 (saec. ix med., period of Grimalt); Schaffhausen, Ministerialbibl. 77 (saec. viii-ix); and Troyes 657 (saec. viii ex.).

13. W. Levison, England and the Continent in the eighth century, p. 141, note 1, points out that I was mistaken in deriving a passage in Bede's commentary on Mark from HT. For Boniface, see ibid., p. 283; Alcuin, PL 101, 97 B-C (=PL 69, 909D-910A): Paulinus, MGH: Epist. IV, 526, 35 ff.

14. MGH: Concilia II, 484, 25-27, with quotations from HT on pp. 487 and 503; PL 106, 345C, 346B, 346C, 349C.

15. MGH: Epistulae VI, 481, 18, quoting from HT 4, 6; PL 121, 307C, 336A, 344B.

16. PL 125, 969B and 974B-D from HT 9, 20-23.

17. See S. Hellmann, *Sedulius Scottus* (Munich, 1906) whose edition of De rectoribus provides full information about Sedulius' sources. For the Collectaneum see ibid., p. 97.

18. G. Becker, *Catalogi bibliothecarum antiqui* 11, 193.

19. See page 53 above and MGH: Epistulae V, 248, 19ff., where Amalarius quotes HT on the subject of the Quartodecimans and Lenten fasting.

20. MGH: Epistulae VII, 419, 25-26 and 421, 3-4; for Nicholas I see above, page 59.

21. PL 133, 535A; 134, 922C, 932B, and particularly 934D-936D (= PL 69, 1145A-1146D).

22. See Manitius, op. cit., II, p. 473, with the references there given.

23. See the excellent index to MGH: Libelli de lite, I-III, where this pamphlet literature has been conveniently collected.

24. Cf. MGH: Scriptores V, 525, 11 ff.; VI, 307 and 310; XX, 200 and 201.

25. MGH: Scriptores IV, 245, 10 ff.; Manitius, op. cit., II, p. 196.

26. See the full discussion in S. Hellmann, op. cit., pp. 12-13.

Arnaldo Momigliano (lecture date 1955)

SOURCE: "Cassiodorus and Italian Culture of His Time," in *Proceedings of the British Academy,* Vol. 41, 1955, pp. 207-45.

[*In the essay below, originally delivered as a lecture, Momigliano studies the political atmosphere in Italy during Cassiodorus's career and demonstrates the ways in which the relationship between the Romans and the Goths influenced Cassiodorus's writings. Momigliano observes that in works such as the* Gothic History, *Cassiodorus intended to support the peaceful coexistence of Goths and Romans.*]

I

When I want to understand Italian history I catch a train and go to Ravenna. There, between the tomb of Theodoric and that of Dante, in the reassuring neighbourhood of the best manuscript of Aristophanes and in the less reassuring one of the best portrait of the Empress Theodora, I can begin to feel what Italian history has really been.[1] The presence of a foreign rule, the memory of an imperial and pagan past, and the overwhelming force of the Catholic tradition have been three determining features of Italian history for many centuries. These three features first joined together when Ravenna became the capital of the Ostrogothic kingdom. The beginnings of Italian history such as we have known it are contemporary with the building of Sant' Apollinare Nuovo, with the martyrdom of Boethius, and with that moving note left by a scion of a great house at the bottom of a manuscript of Macrobius: 'I, the Right Honourable Aurelius Memmius Symmachus, have emended and revised this manuscript in Ravenna with the help of the Right Honourable Macrobius Plotinus Eudoxius.'[2] Notwithstanding the crime, the cruelty, and the enormous destruction, one receives the impression that Italian society in the sixth century was humane and easygoing.[3] I always like to remind myself of that miracle so precisely told by Gregory the Great. Two Goths on their way to Ravenna paid a visit to Bonifatius, Bishop of Ferentium in Etruria. The bishop provided them with a bottle of wine. The more the Goths drank, the more wine there was in the bottle. So the two Goths passed their days in Ravenna drinking, as the Goths are wont to do: 'biberunt ut Gothi'.[4] Bonifatius was a very understanding Italian bishop.

II

Two members of the Italian aristocracy of that time—Boethius and St. Benedict—have been chosen by universal consent to represent and symbolize what is highest in the Italian contribution to mediaeval civilization. Nobody will dispute this choice. Another member of the same aristocracy, Cassiodorus Senator, has been slower in receiving due appreciation. Though his *Institutiones* rank among the formative books of the Middle Ages, he was never an awe-inspiring figure.[5] Dante, who declared the greatness of Boethius and St. Benedict in lines as good as any that he ever wrote, did not mention Cassiodorus. The many references in mediaeval literature do less than justice to his achievements and are sometimes curiously misinformed. One is surprised to see that John of Salisbury in his *Historia Pontificalis* took him to be a recent convert to Christianity: 'Cassiodorus ex gentili Christianus, monachus ex senatore.'[6]

I am quoting John of Salisbury because his statement that Cassiodorus was a convert to Christianity may have some remote connexion with a strange tradition studied thoroughly, but not exhaustively, by Père Delehaye.[7] This tradition seems to go back to the eighth or ninth century and is presented both in a Greek and in a Latin version, but the Latin version depends on the Greek. We are told of three men, Senator, Viator, and Cassiodorus, who lived under the Emperor Antoninus. They were the sons of an officer of Delchemus, King of Sardinia, were baptized by Eusebius, Bishop of Caesarea, took part in a war between Caesarea and Carthage, and finally died the martyr's death in Calabria. Père Delehaye saw that Senator and Cassiodorus derive their names from Cassiodorus Senator, who was born and died in Calabria, while Viator is probably his contemporary, Flavius Viator, consul in 495; the whole legend must have been inspired by an inscription in honour of Viator and Cassiodorus Senator found in Calabria. I would only add that the war between Caesarea and Carthage, in which Cassiodorus and Senator are said to have taken part, may well be a recollection of the war between Justinian Caesar and the Vandals of Carthage. The tradition is worth further examination and shows that a vague memory of Cassiodorus lingered on in the land he loved so well. But this legend also shows that little more than his name was popularly remembered. His reputation as a learned man was always confined to narrow circles and even in these it was never comparable with that of Boethius. Modern scholars also have been slow in taking a real interest in Cassiodorus. We had to wait until 1937 for a critical edition of his *Institutiones,* though when it came it provided our Academy with one of its most distinguished members. The *Historia Tripartita,* inspired, if not actually written, by Cassiodorus, was first critically edited in 1952. The *De anima* is still no man's land, though we have the promise of an edition from America and of a critical commentary from Switzerland. For Cassiodorus's Commentary on the Psalms there is not even the promise of a modern edition, as far as I know.

A man of no heroic character and of no towering intelligence, Cassiodorus hardly appealed to generations for whom nothing less than unconditional heroism and indisputable intellectual greatness counted. We, the members of the race of iron, have learnt to appreciate lesser men—the men who tried to save what could be saved and who did not disdain the task of elementary teaching when elementary teaching was needed. Cassiodorus's recent rise to universal fame is not due to doubtful theories about the survival of the books of Vivarium[8] nor to the equally doubtful theories about the connexion between the *Regula Magistri* and Vivarium:[9] even the alleged discovery of his tomb at Squillace has failed to fire our imagination.[10] The change is simply due to our own recent experience in matters of scholarship and political life. We have learnt again what it means not to be able to consult a book because it was destroyed by war. Our gratitude for the monks who saved our classics in their monasteries has become something more than conventional homage. Indeed monastic life itself has become less alien to the modern scholar's taste: it may become a desirable alternative to the horrors of University committees.

But if the Vivarium period of the life of Cassiodorus is now properly appreciated, not much attention has recently been paid to Cassiodorus as the historian of the Goths. This is no easy subject, for of course we have not his *Gothic History* but only a summary made by Jordanes, and any attempt to define Jordanes's treatment of his source is likely to lead the unwary into trouble.[11] Yet there can be no doubt that Cassiodorus's *Gothic History* is a landmark in the history of Latin historiography and of Late Roman politics. It is about Cassiodorus's *Gothic History* that I feel I can offer a few suggestions this evening. The 'Getica', however, cannot be appreciated in isolation. They emerge as an exceptional, yet timely, work only if they are examined against the background of the literary production of the first part of the sixth century.

III

In the ninth century the chronicler Agnellus could still see in Ravenna a mosaic in which Theodoric was represented between the images of Ravenna and Rome.[12] Rome was a woman with a helmet and a spear, but Ravenna was shown as jumping out of the sea—with a leg still in it—in her desire to meet the king. The whole representation has its iconographical interest into which I need not go, but it also has a plain historical meaning. Ravenna was at the end of both land and sea routes, and these routes pointed to the East. Under Theodoric and his Gothic successors Italy had no control of her seas. Cassiodorus himself says plainly that his king had no fleet of his own: 'Cum nostrum igitur animum frequens cura pulsaret naves Italiam non habere.'[13] Theodoric's last-minute attempt to build up a fleet in Ravenna came to an end with his death.[14] But the Vandals too were no longer so powerful at sea.[15] Organized naval power existed only in the Eastern Empire. This is one of the main facts that explain why Italy again fell under the influence of the Hellenic East. The other fact is, of course, that Africa, Gaul, and Spain in their increasing barbarization had less to give.

We can hardly measure what the loss of Africa to the Vandals meant to the Church in Italy and, more generally, to Italian intellectual life.[16] Since the end of the second century the super-abundant spiritual energies of African Christianity had inspired the Church in the West. These energies were still abundant enough to account for the stubborn resistance to the Arian Vandals and for the amount of apologetic literature thrown into the controversy. But the death of Augustine while besieged by the Vandals had signed the end of the intellectual supremacy of Christian Africa. Nor were Spain and Gaul ready to supply intellectual food of equivalent value. Spain seems to have been as good as lost to creative culture in the first part of the sixth century. Martinus of Bracara, who in the name of Seneca started something of a Renaissance about A.D. 550, was an import from the East.[17] Things were of course not so bad in Gaul. But the circle of Sidonius Apollinaris did not survive *in situ*. If he had a follower it was Ennodius, who, though born in France, lived in Milan and Pavia: Milan, indeed, became a centre of learning that attracted not only Italians, but Gauls.[18] Sidonius's friend, Claudianus Mamertus, also found his follower in Italy rather than in France: his *De statu animae* was one of the sources of Cassiodorus's *De anima*. About A.D. 500 there were only two writers of uncommon stature in France—Avitus, Bishop of Vienne, and Caesarius, Bishop of Arles. Their pastoral activities were absorbed in specifically local problems—which incidentally compelled Caesarius to come to an agreement with King Theodoric. Their strictly theological writing had not sufficient distinction to make a strong impression on Italy. Caesarius's biographer tells us that his hero distributed his sermons in Spain and in Italy.[19] If this is true, they served the pastoral rather than the theological interests of the Italian clergy.

Saint Augustine had of course not exhausted his influence. In dedicating his *De trinitate* to Symmachus, Boethius expressed the hope of being a good pupil of St. Augustine. Eugippius prepared an anthology of St. Augustine for the benefit of those who could not provide themselves with the Saint's *Opera Omnia* and dedicated it to that remarkable woman relative of Boethius, Proba.[20] Proba herself and Galla, Symmachus's daughter, maintained close relations with St. Augustine's follower, Fulgentius of Ruspe.[21] But the theological controversies just then raging with the East in consequence of the *Henotikon* increased the need for recent, up-to-date, theological information. Besides, there was an aspect of St. Augustine's philosophy that the aristocratic circle of Symmachus and Boethius could never make its own: this was his view of Roman history.

Symmachus and Boethius were not prepared to admit that pagan Rome had had little to show but disasters and robberies. They had succeeded in combining a genuine Christian faith with a devotion to all that was pagan in Roman tradition. Quintus Aurelius Memmius Symmachus, the senior leader of this intellectual revival, had chosen Cato as his model, *antiqui Catonis novellus imitator.*[22] He was a descendant of the last defenders of pagan Rome in the fourth century and was only too conscious of his ancestry. His care for the text of Macrobius was not uninfluenced by the circumstance that another Symmachus had been a speaker in Macrobius's *Saturnalia*. He wrote a Roman history in imitation of one of his ancestors, *parentes suos imitatus:* here, too, the model was pagan, if the allusion is to Nicomachus Flavianus's history.[23] Our sixth-century Symmachus is the only writer in antiquity who, to our knowledge, used and quoted the *Scriptores Historiae Augustae*—that mysterious compilation of the fourth century with a marked bias towards paganism and senatorial authority.[24] Another man of the same senatorial group and another descendant from one of the great pagan champions of the fourth century, Vettius Agorius Basilius Mavortius, emended the texts of both Horace and of Prudentius—of the most pagan and of the most Christian Latin poets.[25]

These antiquarians were not frivolous. They were aware that their attempt to combine Christian devotion with pagan tradition could succeed only if it was supported by the strength of Greek thought and by the continuity of imperial tradition. They looked to the East where exciting things seemed to be happening. In Constantinople Priscian was opening new vistas to Latin grammatical studies.[26] In Alexandria the school of Ammonius was making a new effort to harmonize Plato, Aristotle, and Porphyrius and to reconcile all with Christianity.[27] These were intellectual events giving hope to men whose hearts never turned away from the classical past of Greece and Rome. Symmachus was already well known in Constantinople when he went there on a visit.[28] He befriended Priscian and brought back three of his rhetorical works with resounding dedications to himself.[29] Boethius may even have been educated in the East, if, as Courcelle has suggested, he was the son of Boethius, the prefect of Alexandria about 475.[30] Symmachus and Boethius certainly had a large number of oriental connexions which helped to bring about the reconciliation between the Church of Rome and that of Constantinople in 519.[31] In 515 Ennodius, who was a relative of Boethius, was sent to Constantinople to discuss the union of the Churches.[32] Indeed, a woman of their family group, Anicia Juliana, the daughter of the Emperor Olybrius, was in Constantinople to work for the union.[33]

Symmachus encouraged Boethius to make Aristotle and Plato and their commentators known to the West in a Latin translation. But theology no less than philosophy was involved in this effort to capture the latest results of Eastern speculation and to harmonize them with Western tradition. Boethius complained bitterly in some of the prologues of his works about the hostility of those who did not know the meaning of their own words and more particularly of the theologians who disapproved of him.[34] Yet he was not alone in spreading knowledge of the Greek doctrines. At least three other Roman senators are known to have taken an interest in theological controversies. One was the patrician Senarius, a relative of Ennodius, who, as we said, was himself a relative of Boethius; another was Faustus, probably the consul of 490, and the third was Albinus, who later was accused of treason by Theodoric and became the immediate cause of Boethius's fall.[35] At the service of this Italian group Dionysius Exiguus—a Scythian by birth, but a Roman in manners, as Cassiodorus said—passed his life in translating theological, philosophic, and ecclesiological treatises from Greek into Latin.[36]

The mere fact that we find in Constantinople a man of Priscian's distinction shows that the efforts of the Romans to re-establish their cultural contacts with the Greeks were reciprocated by the Greeks themselves. Priscian was no isolated figure in Constantinople as a student of Latin grammar and rhetoric. We know the names and the works of some of his pupils. One of them, Flavius Theodorus, was in the office of the *quaestor sacri palatii* in Constantinople.[37] Priscian's protector, the consul and patrician Julian, is described as equally learned in things Greek and Latin.[38] The compliment is perhaps not undeserved if he was the Julian who is connected with the text of Statius.[39] The Latin interests of the court society of Justin and Justinian were not confined to Roman Law. About 512 John the Lydian started his career of the perfect bureaucrat. The services of this comic figure towards Roman antiquities are well known: among his many boasts there is that of an exceptionally fine knowledge of Latin.[40] A few years later, a man of a quite different calibre and importance, Peter the Patrician, who specialized in the knowledge of the West, wrote his history of the Roman Empire from the death of Caesar to the death of Constantius II.[41] Men of his kind could of course sympathize with the Roman aristocrats of Symmachus's circle and established friendships that were to bear fruit during Justinian's determined struggle to destroy the Ostrogothic kingdom.

In judging this movement both from the Western and from the Eastern side, we must take it for granted that Boethius's *De Consolatione Philosophiae* does not belong to it. However prepared by long meditation in earlier life, *De Consolatione* went beyond anything Boethius had done before: it must have taken the author himself by surprise. Many people have turned to Christianity for consolation. Boethius turned to paganism. His Christianity collapsed—it collapsed so thoroughly that perhaps he did not even notice its disappearance. The God of the Greek philosophers gave peace to his mind. The arrogance with which he had dealt with Christian theology was replaced by a new humility. This may show that his earlier attempt to harmonize philosophy and Christianity was on an unstable basis, but it cannot be a guide to the conscious aims of the Roman group of which he was a member, nor of its Byzantine counterpart.[42]

Nobody of course can say—perhaps even the men involved did not know—when the efforts to bring about a reconciliation between Rome and Constantinople began to imply a covert rebellion against the government of Ravenna. Symmachus, like some of his friends, was wise enough to avoid taking employment under Theodoric in Ravenna. He was content with his Roman honours. Boethius, after hav-

ing long imitated his father-in-law, was persuaded to accept the *magisterium officiorum* in 522. It would have been a mistake in any case. The circumstances made it a tragedy.[43]

IV

Cassiodorus was so little involved in this tragedy that he succeeded Boethius in the *magisterium officiorum*. He had never been a full member of Symmachus's circle. He did not belong to the Roman aristocracy in a full sense. His family had come from the East and had been established in Calabria for four generations. Squillace, *prima urbium Bruttiorum,* was the city he felt his own. One of the *Variae* has a lyrical, almost incongruous, description of the countryside round Squillace that anticipates the famous description of Vivarium in the *Institutiones.*[44] Though Cassiodorus's estate must have been substantial, he went naturally into the civil service as his father and his grandfather had done. He did not take pride in independence as did Symmachus or, to some extent, Boethius. His education was correspondingly different. It is true that at a certain moment of his life he studied dialectics with Dionysius Exiguus, but his training was rhetorical rather than philosophical.[45] Some Greek he certainly knew, but how much is uncertain. In his later years he patronized translations from Greek works such as Josephus's *Jewish Antiquities*[46] and a conflation of the Church histories of Theodoretus, Sozomenus, and Socrates—the so-called *Historia Tripartita.* But as far as we know he did not translate any work himself. Among his contemporaries he has more points in common with the poet Arator than with Symmachus. Arator, too, was a powerful public speaker, who served Theodoric for many years, and later in life entered holy orders.[47] Cassiodorus's name does not appear in the works of Boethius or in those of Ennodius: this is particularly remarkable in the latter case, as Ennodius, though a priest and a relative of Boethius, was in close contact with Ravenna.

On the other hand it is of fundamental importance for the argument I shall soon develop about the History of the Goths to notice that Cassiodorus emphasized his family connexions with Symmachus and Boethius. He never lost an opportunity to celebrate Boethius's family, the Anicii.[48] The most important evidence for Cassiodorus's family pride is his *Ordo generis Cassiodororum,* a sort of family history addressed to Flavius Fufius Petronius Nicomachus Cethegus consul in 504 and probably a member himself of the group of the Anicii. Only an excerpt from the *Ordo generis Cassiodororum* is preserved, but it is enough to show that the original text contained a biography of all the members of the family who had contributed to literature together with a list of their publications.[49] The extract that has come to us preserves the sections or parts of the sections dealing with Cassiodorus himself, with Symmachus and with Boethius. Unfortunately the text is corrupt just at the point that would decide whether Cassiodorus explicitly claimed Boethius and Symmachus as his relatives.[50] But no other reason can easily explain why he included Symmachus and Boethius in the account of his own family. This interpretation is confirmed by a passage of the *Institutiones* in which Cassiodorus mentions Proba as *parens nostra*.[51] We have already had occasion to say that Proba was a close relative of Boethius and Symmachus: she was either Symmachus's daughter or his niece. Her very name Proba shows that she was connected with the Anicii.[52] Admiration for the nobility of the Anicii—and perhaps pride in it—is apparent from what Cassiodorus wrote at length in his *Variae* to celebrate them: he praised them as an almost regal family. It is hardly necessary to point out that the aristocrats of late antiquity gave a very wide interpretation to the term of family when they could claim illustrious relatives. Thus the poet Avitus talks of *nostra familia* with the son of Sidonius Apollinaris, simply because Sidonius had been son-in-law to the Emperor Avitus, who was in some way related to the poet Avitus.[53] One has the impression that there was a far greater desire on Cassiodorus's side to associate himself with the Anicii than on the side of the Anicii to admit Cassiodorus to their kin. Nor was Cassiodorus interested in emphasizing his relationship with the Anicii only before the fall of Boethius. All the evidence we have quoted seems to be later than Boethius's death about 524. Hermann Usener, who was the first editor of the *Ordo generis Cassiodororum* in 1877—and what an admirable editor he was—tried to prove that the *Ordo* had been written before Boethius's death. But Mommsen was in my opinion quite right in refusing to accept this date. The mention of the *Variae* in the *Ordo* and other details point to a date at least as late as 538.[54] The addressee, Cethegus, was still alive and near Cassiodorus in Constantinople in 550.[55]

The points that separated Cassiodorus from the circle of Symmachus and Boethius were of great importance, but one can understand that they alienated Boethius from Cassiodorus rather than vice versa. The intellectual horizon of Boethius included Greeks and Romans, whether pagan or Christian, but excluded the Germans. The Germans were ignored. It is difficult to imagine that Symmachus could be so thorough as his son-in-law in this omission, because he wrote history—and imperial history at that. It is at least arguable that he presented the Emperor Maximinus Thrax as the first Goth on the Roman throne.[56] But we have no further reason to believe that he tried to give a place to the Barbarians in his intellectual world. No doubt Boethius and Symmachus followed with anxious attention the daily movements of their Gothic masters, but they studied and wrote to forget them.

Cassiodorus faced the Goths not only in his daily work of a secretary and administrator but in his own studies. In Rome one could ignore them. In Ravenna he found it necessary to educate them and to give them a past and a future in the history of the Roman world. There were other Latin writers who did not ignore—could not ignore—the Goths. They were the writers of biographies of bishops and abbots and saints. The leaders of the Church were then playing an essential part in trying to reduce the horrors and the hardships of the Barbarian invasions, and

their biographers could not forget this aspect of their activities. Thus Ennodius's life of Bishop Epiphanius and Eugippius's life of Saint Severinus provide invaluable evidence for this aspect of ecclesiastical history.[57] But this was of course a different point of view from that of Cassiodorus. He was not facing the Goths as the Christian representative of the native population; he was working in an exalted position for the Goths in Ravenna.

Day after day Cassiodorus tried to give Roman *dignitas* to the orders of his Barbarian masters. His eloquence, his historical and philosophic knowledge, and even his personal sympathies were transferred into the *Variae* and put into the mouths of the Gothic kings. He was pompous, but there are moments in which even pomposity can serve a serious purpose if it is an endeavour to dignify what is in itself undignified. There can be few other works in the literature of any country comparable with such a sustained effort to present a Barbarian as the embodiment of civilized justice and wisdom. Cassiodorus's zeal was such that the *Variae* became a sort of encyclopaedia: not unfairly German dissertations have been treating them as a document of *Kulturgeschichte*.[58] In his private conversations with Theodoric Cassiodorus was expected to convey the answers of Greek science to the naïve questions of the Barbarian king about natural phenomena.[59] In the *Variae* he tried to give the answers of Roman *civilitas* to the political and administrative problems opened up by the Ostrogothic gettlement in Italy: 'Gothorum laus est civilitas custodita.' To preserve the ancient things—'vetusta servare'—that was the intention Cassiodorus liked to attribute to his masters.[60]

V

In 519 a symbolic event seemed to confirm that the best hopes of peace between Constantinople and Ravenna were going to be realized. Eutharicus, the husband of Amalasuntha, was recognized by Justin as the heir presumptive of Theodoric. He was made a consul and had Justin himself as a colleague: he was the first German to be made a consul during the Ostrogothic rule in Italy. Cassiodorus celebrated the date in a typical Romano-Christian way. He produced a new version of the chronicle of Eusebius-Jerome and brought it up to date, giving the Goths pride of place. Thus the admission of the Gothic prince to the Roman consulship was presented as the beginning of a new period of world history.[61]

Not long afterwards Cassiodorus must have started working on his History of the Goths. He says in the *Ordo generis Cassiodororum* that he started it to please Theodoric, that is before 526. In 533 his work was already finished or rather had progressed far enough to become the object of praise in a letter which King Athalaricus sent to the Roman Senate to announce that Cassiodorus had been made the prefect of the praetorium. Needless to say, the eulogy of Cassiodorus the historian had been written with conspicuous care by Cassiodorus the secretary. Thanks to this indiscretion we know what he wanted to do in his work: 'originem Gothicam historiam fecit esse Romanam'.[62]

This history in twelve books is lost. Jordanes, a man of at least partial Gothic origin, tells us that about 551 he was preparing a survey of Roman history—later to be known as *Romana*—when he was urged by his friend Castalius to interrupt it and to give priority to a compendium of Cassiodorus's **Gothic History.** Jordanes obeyed, but added apologetically that his task was difficult because he had only been able to borrow Cassiodorus's History for three days from Cassiodorus's steward: he admitted, however, that he had already read the book before. 'Ad triduanam lectionem dispensatoris eius beneficio libros ipsos antehac relegi.'[63]

There is certainly something mysterious about this statement. Three days are an impossibly short time to prepare a summary of twelve books. Besides, this passage is stylistically an imitation of Rufinus's Prologue to his translation of Origen's commentary on the letter to the Romans by St. Paul; and Jordanes feels the need for introducing his excuse by *ut not mentiar*—'let me lie not', which makes it doubly suspicious.[64] But if one may well doubt the story of the three days, there is no reason to doubt the main facts. Jordanes was urged to prepare in haste a summary of the History of the Goths, he did his work about 551 and used a copy borrowed from Cassiodorus's own library.[65] Now the year 551 falls within a period of some importance in the relations between Justinian and the Goths. In 550 Matasuntha, Theodoric's granddaughter, now an exile in Constantinople, had married Germanus, a cousin of Justinian.[66] The marriage had been arranged to attract Gothic loyalism. After a few months Germanus died, but a posthumous son of the same name was born to Matasuntha. This is the event with which Jordanes emphatically concludes his work. His line of thought is that Theodoric himself before dying had recommended to his people to 'love the senate and the Roman people, and to make sure of the peace and good will of the Emperor of the East as next after God'.[67] Theodahatus had called upon himself Justinian's wrath by killing Amalasuntha. After Belisarius's expedition and Vitiges's defeat there was only one hope left for the Goths: it was this marriage between Matasuntha and Germanus. Their son was a promise of reconciliation and peace between the two races.

Jordanes does not make any allusion to Narses's expedition which started in 552 with the definite aim of destroying the Ostrogoths for ever. The conclusion of his work is enough to show that he was evidently not a naïve Gothic monk living somewhere in Thrace, as Mommsen conjectured.[68] He did not summarize the Gothic history simply because it flattered his patriotic sentiments. His work had a clear political message. It invited the Goths to cease resistance, but also gave encouragement to those who worked in Constantinople for a *modus vivendi* between Goths and Romans.

The real question which I want to put before you is whether this political message was introduced by Jordanes into Cassiodorus's work or whether it was part of Cassiodorus's original work. In the former hypothesis Jordanes would have summarized Cassiodorus in order to make him serve a new political cause. In the latter hypothesis Jordanes would have summarized Cassiodorus in order to make more easily available for propaganda purposes a work that already contained a political message for the time.

So far as I can see, the almost unanimous opinion of modern scholars is that Cassiodorus concluded his work on the Goths in or before 533 and therefore could not describe the later developments to 551. As a matter of fact, a very substantial section of modern critics believe that he did not even write the history of the reign of Theodoric. Now let me first remind you that although we know that Cassiodorus had already a reputation as an historian of the Goths about 533, we have no reason to think that he stopped working on his *magnum opus* about 533. On this point I find myself in solitary agreement with the Belgian scholar Dom Cappuyns.[69] Between 535 and 550 many things happened to Cassiodorus, but none of them made it impossible for him to give further attention to his Gothic History. About 535 he made his unsuccessful attempt to build up a Christian university in Rome.[70] About 538 he relinquished his position as a *praefectus praetorio,* but remained on good terms with Vitiges.[71] He turned increasingly to religion and wrote *De anima.*[72] In 540 Ravenna was occupied by the Byzantines, and Vitiges was taken prisoner and transferred to Constantinople where he was treated very kindly.[73] We do not know whether Cassiodorus was one of those who followed Vitiges in 540, but in 550 (the date is significant) we learn from a letter of Pope Vigilius that he was an authoritative man in Constantinople.[74] Like Pope Vigilius and Cethegus, to whom he dedicated his **Ordo generis Cassiodororum,** he must have returned to Italy after the promulgation of the pragmatic sanction of 554 that fixed the organization of the reconquered territory.[75] Cassiodorus then was obviously a follower of Justinian even if, like his friends the Pope Vigilius and Cethegus, he did not often see eye to eye with the Emperor. Already in collecting his **Variae** about 538 he had carefully eliminated any piece of writing that might give offence to Justinian; and I do not see why we should rule out that he submitted his work on Gothic history to a similar revision in order to make it compatible with the new situation.

Questions of this sort, however, cannot be argued with *a priori* arguments. What I wish to do is to offer a very simple argument which in my opinion establishes that Cassiodorus really continued his work after 535 until 551 and supported the efforts for a final reconciliation between Goths and Romans under Justinian. My only hesitation in presenting my argument is that it is so simple; one would expect it to have been presented before. It is my considered opinion that Mommsen has already said all the right things about Roman history. I always feel uneasy when I discover that he has not yet said what I am going to say. My argument is this. As I have mentioned, Jordanes concludes his history with the baby Germanus as the new hope for the two nations. But he formulates this hope in a very remarkable way: 'And of them was born a son (also called Germanus) after the death of his father Germanus. This union of the race of the Anicii with the stock of the Amali gives hopeful promise, under the Lord's favour, to both peoples.' 'In quo coniuncta Aniciorum genus cum Amala stirpe spem adhuc utriusque generi domino praestante promittit.'[76]

The marriage of Matasuntha with Justinian's cousin Germanus is presented as a union of the family of the Amali with the family of the Anicii. It is only natural that Matasuntha should represent the Amali—the royal family of the Ostrogoths. But we are not told why Germanus should represent the family of the Anicii rather than the imperial family of Justinian. No doubt, some fact is behind this statement. Perhaps Germanus's mother belonged to the family of the Anicii.[77] But even if there must be some factual basis for this statement, the statement itself remains most extraordinary. The union of a member of the imperial family of Constantinople with a member of the royal family of the Amali is described as a union of the Roman family of the Anicii with the Amali—and no explanation is given. It seems to me clear that this passage is a shortened version of something more circumstantial about the same subject. If this is true, Jordanes summarized his source here as elsewhere—and his source was Cassiodorus.

But the clearest proof of the Cassiodorean origin of the passage is its very content. Nobody except Cassiodorus could represent the union between Matasuntha and Justinian's cousin as a union not of the royal family of Ravenna with the imperial family of Constantinople, but between the Amali and the Anicii. Here, it seems to me, Cassiodorus has put his seal. In all probability he considered himself connected with the family of the Anicii; and his friend Cethegus, next to the Pope the most eminent Italian exile in Constantinople, was very probably a member of the Anician family.[78]

VI

If there is some truth in what I am saying, important consequences follow. When Cassiodorus went to Constantinople he must have carried with him a copy of his **Gothic History.** He kept it up to date and modified it to serve the new situation. When the marriage between Germanus and Matasuntha took place and the preparation for a new expedition against the Goths of Italy was progressing, there were good reasons for bringing the work to a conclusion. His last chapters evidently expressed the hopes of the Italian aristocratic exiles who wanted to go back to Italy with a part to play in the reorganization of the country. They did not contemplate the utter destruction of the Goths—and of so much else—that Narses was soon to perpetrate. They may well have thought that the most advantageous situation for themselves would be one in which enough Goths were left to counterbalance Byzantine influence. Certainly they liked the marriage between Germanus and Matasuntha. By emphasizing the connexion between Germanus and the family of the Anicii Cassiodorus was dis-

creetly calling attention to his friend Cethegus and to himself. After all he had been in the service of the Amalian family for so many years. Thus the new edition of his own *Getica* expressed the opinions and the hopes of the Italian aristocrats who were exiles in Constantinople in 551.

But a work in twelve books was not the most suitable for propaganda. Anyone who felt that Cassiodorus's work could make an impression either on the Goths of Italy or on the Byzantine leaders would have been well advised to take steps for a shortened edition. The next question is whether Cassiodorus himself saw to it that his work should be summarized. This, of course, is not a question that can be answered with certainty. But there are two arguments that point to Cassiodorus's intervention. First, Jordanes admits to having borrowed Cassiodorus's work from Cassiodorus's steward. Cassiodorus must have known how to choose a steward who would not lend the manuscripts of his master's works without his permission. Secondly, there may be something in Jordanes's personality to corroborate this hypothesis. There is no evidence that Jordanes was a monk, as Mommsen suggested, but there is some reason to believe that he was a Gothic Catholic bishop of Italy. Jordanes dedicated his *Romana* to a Vigilius about 551. Now we know that a Bishop Jordanes of Crotone was in Constantinople together with Vigilius, Bishop of Rome, in 550, and we also know that Pope Vigilius was on friendly terms with Cassiodorus.[79] Furthermore part of the manuscript tradition calls Jordanes *episcopus.*[80] The conclusion seems inescapable that the Jordanes who summarized Cassiodorus's **Gothic History** is the Bishop Jordanes who was the friend of Bishop Vigilius who was the friend of Cassiodorus. Jordanes would have borrowed Cassiodorus's work in Constantinople.

This conclusion was already drawn by Jacob Grimm more than a hundred years ago, but after a period of general acceptance it has now been universally abandoned.[81] There is in fact a serious difficulty against the identification of Jordanes's friend Vigilius with the Bishop of Rome. Jordanes calls his friend Vigilius *nobilissimus et magnificus frater,* while we would expect *venerabilis* or *reverendissimus* or *sanctissimus frater,* if he addressed the Bishop of Rome. More generally one can say that Jordanes talks to Vigilius in a way that would be very clumsy if Vigilius were the Pope. However, I am inclined to suspect that Jordanes was a clumsy man: he could hardly keep his Latin together. Either we are prepared to admit that near Cassiodorus there were two Jordanes and two Vigilii, or we must admit that Jordanes was a boorish provincial bishop of Gothic extraction who did not know how to talk to his fellow exile, the Bishop of Rome. If Jordanes was the exiled Gothic Bishop of Crotone one can understand even better why he was selected in a hurry to compile a summary of Cassiodorus's views about the Goths. A last detail may be added. Jordanes addresses his work to his friend Castalius who is living 'near the Goths', *vicinus genti.* This would seem to designate a man living in Italy—precisely the place where the summary could be most useful.

Ranke already suspected in general terms that Jordanes wrote his summary in agreement with Cassiodorus and for political purposes. I rejoice at the idea that if I cannot agree with Mommsen, I have at least Ranke's support.[82]

VII

After von Sybel's dissertation of 1838 and even more after Carl Schirren's distinguished work of 1858, modern scholars have tried various methods to establish what Jordanes owed to Cassiodorus. Two Italian contributions to this discussion, by C. Cipolla in 1893 and by R. Cessi in 1912, should not be forgotten.[83] These researches, however acute, never produced conclusive results, and we can now see that they were vitiated by three wrong assumptions in the matter of style, chronology, and geography. It is true that some of Jordanes's chapters are written in better Latin than others, but it does not follow that what is good comes from Cassiodorus and what is bad was added by Jordanes. No doubt in some cases Jordanes copied literally whole sentences from Cassiodorus, while in other cases he summarized long passages of his source in his own inferior Latin. On the other hand one used to assume that Cassiodorus wrote in the West under Arian kings and therefore one attributed to Jordanes all that in the present text of the *Getica* is definitely anti-Arian and shows an intimate acquaintance with the East.[84] But now we have to reckon with the strong probability that Cassiodorus revised his work in the East when he had become the subject of a Catholic emperor.

Jordanes's own declaration—'I have put in an introduction and a conclusion of my own and have also inserted many things of my own authorship'—is not necessarily false.[85] He probably added the initial quotation from Orosius, the final paragraph, and a few details in the middle. But it is simply impossible to determine exactly the quantity and the quality of his own contributions. What we can say is that in all probability Jordanes's *Getica* reflects Cassiodorus's political ideas as Cassiodorus reformulated them about 550 when the Goths were on the wane.

Books about Gothic history probably existed before Cassiodorus: he himself mentions a source, Ablabius;[86] and if we accept an attractive emendation by W. Meyer to a passage of the *Variae*, Ablabius was a Greek.[87] Furthermore, there was a tradition already well established in the fourth century that *Getae* and *Gothi* were the same people.[88] This made it possible for Cassiodorus to incorporate into his history what Dio Chrysostom and other writers had written on the Getae. There seems to have been also another tradition identifying the Goths with the Scythians.[89] This, too, was exploited by Cassiodorus. He extended the range and respectability of Gothic history by adding what one knew about the Getae and the Scythians. Thus the Goths were shown to have been educated by the divine Zalmoxis and became the wisest of the Barbarians: 'pene omnibus barbaris Gothi sapientiores semper exiterunt'.[90] Goths and Romans were born to help each other. Good Emperors like Theodosius were lovers of peace and of the Goths: *amator pacis generisque Gothorum*. It was a tragedy that the Emperor Valens chose to offend the Goths or that more than once the Goths went their own way without respecting the Romans.[91] Attila's story according to Cassiodorus demonstrated both the advantages of the collaboration between Romans and Goths and the disadvantages of mutual distrust.[92] Applied to contemporary events this lesson of history meant that the only hope for the Goths was the peaceful acceptance of Justinian's rule. But Justinian would be well advised to persevere in a policy of collaboration both with those members of the Gothic aristocracy who were prepared to help and with those Italian aristocrats who knew their Goths by long experience.

What unfortunately we can no longer assess is the scholarly effort of Cassiodorus. Unlike the referendarius Cyprianus and his sons, he was not able to read the Gothic language,[93] but there must have been many people in Ravenna ready to help him if he ever wanted to go beyond his classical sources. It was indeed the first time, as far as we know, that a Roman historian had found himself in the position of writing the history of an alien group ruling Rome. Cassiodorus's work is as epoch-making in its way as Polybius's work had been in its own. He tried to understand the Goths as Polybius tried to understand the Romans. He had an idea of Gothic psychology—of the pride, violence, gratitude to benefactors of these people—which must have been the result of long observation.[94] The first attempt to place the history of the Goths within the framework of Roman history and civilization was also the last great work of Roman historiography. Not long afterwards the Barbarians of the West began to speak for themselves. There are less than forty years in the chronology I have adopted between Cassiodorus's **Gothic History** and the *History of the Franks* by Gregory of Tours.[95]

Cassiodorus's History, if it was not the product of a very critical and independent mind, showed love of knowledge, realism about the present, and a considerable amount of kind and humane feeling.[96] It was meant to help the cause of a peaceful coexistence of Goths and Romans. If my hypothesis is right, we can also say that Cassiodorus remained faithful to his policy of collaboration—for what it was still worth—even on the eve of Narses's expedition. The old universal spirit of Roman tradition was still at work in the last representative of Roman historiography.

Justinian's policy of extermination of the Goths must have come as a deep disappointment to Cassiodorus. Now there was really nothing left for him to do in the world of politics. We shall probably never know whether he had already turned his beloved estate of Squillace into a monastery before going to Constantinople. He certainly concentrated his attention on Vivarium after his return and perhaps became a monk.[97] Though old, he was vigorous enough to start a new life for himself and to open new ways to Latin culture. The task he set himself was to make pagan learning the servant of Christian knowledge. If political life was disintegrating, St. Benedict was there to teach that it was possible to build up new unities of economic and spiritual life in the form of monasteries.[98] Classical scholarship would contribute to monastic life. The cloister would replace the court as a centre of culture.[99] The last chapter in the biography of Cassiodorus is undoubtedly more important than that I have tried to reconstruct on the basis of Jordanes's *Getica*—but it is one on which other members of this Academy can speak more competently than myself.

Notes

1. It will be enough to refer to E. Dyggve, *Ravennatum Palatium Sacrum,* Copenhagen, 1941 (Arkaeol.-Kunsthist. Meddelelser Danske Vidensk. Selskab iii. 2); S. Fuchs, 'Bildnisse und Denkmäler aus der Ostgotenzeit', *Die Antike,* xix, 1943, 109-53; A. M. Schneider, 'Die Symbolik des Theoderichgrabes', *Byz. Zeitschrift,* xli, 1941, 404-5; C. O. Nordström, *Ravennastudien. Ideengesch. und ikonographische Untersuch. über die Mosaiken von Ravenna,* Stockholm, 1953, which has an excellent bibliography; M. Mazzotti, *La Basilica di Sant' Apollinare in Classe,* Studi di Antichità Cristiane, Pontificio Istituto Archeol. Cristiana, Roma, 1954.

2. O. Jahn, 'Ueber die Subscriptionen in den Handschriften römischer Classiker', *Berichte Sächs. Ak. Wiss.* iii, 1851, 347.

3. There is no satisfactory modern account of Italian life in the sixth century. O. Bertolini, *Roma di fronte a Bisanzio e ai Longobardi,* Roma, 1941, provides, however, an excellent introduction to the evidence.

4. *Dialogi,* i. 9, pp. 55-56, ed. Moricca (Fonti per la Storia d'Italia).

5. Cf. A. Franz, *M. Aurelius Cassiodorius Senator,* Breslau, 1872, 122-7; Manitius i-iii, index s.v.; P. Lehmann, 'Cassiodorstudien', *Philologus,* lxxi, 1912, 278-99; lxxii, 1913, 503-17; lxxiii, 1914, 253-73; lxxiv, 1917, 351-83; H. Thiele, 'Cassiodor. Seine Klostergründung Vivarium und sein Nachwirken im Mittelalter', *Studien und Mitteil. z. Geschichte d. Benediktinerordens,* l, 1932, 378-419; L. W. Jones, 'The Influence of Cassiodorus on Medieval Culture', *Speculum,* xx, 1945, 433-42 (cf. ibid., xxii, 1947, 254-6); M. L. W. Laistner, 'The Value and Influence of Cassiodorus' Ecclesiastical History', *Harv. Theol. Rev.* xli, 1948, 51-68; J. J. van den Besselaar, *Cassiodorus Senator,* Haarlem, n.d. [1950], 253-63. L. W. Jones's papers are utilized in his introduction to the translation of the *Institutiones,* New York, 1946, 47-58.

6. *Historia Pontificalis,* ed. R. L.' Poole, Oxford, 1927, p. 2: 'Cassiodorus quoque ex gentili Christianus, monachus ex senatore, ex oratore doctor ecclesie, palmas Christiane militie visas et acceptas a patribus preconatur et sicut previos in cronicis descriptionibus habuit, sic illustres viros huius studii reliquit successores.'

7. P. Delehaye, 'Saint Cassiodore', *Mélanges Fabre,* Paris, 1902, 40-50. Cf. *Acta Sanctorum,* Sept., iv. 349-50.

8. It will be enough to mention: R. Beer, 'Bemerkungen über den ältesten Handschriftenbestand des Klosters Bobbio', *Anz. Phil.-Hist. Klasse Wiener Akad.* xlviii, 1911, 78-104; idem, *Monumenta Palaeogr. Vindobonensia,* ii, 1913, 14-50; W. Weinberger, 'Handschriften von Vivarium', *Miscellanea F. Ehrle,* iv, 1924, 75-88. *Contra:* E. A. Lowe, 'Some Facts about our oldest Latin Manuscripts', *Classical Quarterly,* xix, 1925, 205, and *Codices Latini Antiquiores,* iv, 1947, pp. xx-xxvii, and above all G. Mercati, in *Prolegomena* to *M. Tulli Ciceronis De re publica libri . . . phototypice expressi (Codices e Vaticanis selecti,* xxiii), Città del Vaticano, 1934, 1-174. Cf. R. Devreesse, 'La Bibliothèque de Bobbio et le palimpseste du De Republica', *Bull. Ass. Budè,* 1935, 27-33; F. Blatt, 'Remarques sur l'histoire des traductions latines', *Classica et Mediaevalia,* i, 1938, 226-42; A. Souter, 'Cassiodorus' Library at Vivarium', *Journ. Theol. Studies,* xli, 1940, 46-47; Card. I. Schuster, 'Come finì la biblioteca di Cassiodoro', *La Scuola Cattolica,* lxx, 1942, 409-14; P. Courcelle, *Les Lettres grecques en Occident. De Macrobe à Cassiodore,* 2nd ed., Paris, 1948, 357-88; H. Bloch in his review of E. A. Lowe, *Codices,* iv, *Speculum,* xxv, 1950, 283-7. About the *Amiatinus* I shall only refer to H. Quentin, *Mémoire sur l'établissement du texte de la Vulgate,* Rome, 1922, 438-52; Lowe, *Codices,* iii, 1938, no. 299 with bibl.; Courcelle quoted; M. Cappuyns, *Dict. Hist. Géogr. Eccl.* ii, 1384-8; H. Blum, 'Über den Codex Amiatinus und Cassiodors Bibliothek in Vivarium', *Zentralbl. f. Bibliothekswesen,* lxiv, 1950, 52-57. For a curious detail of the 'Codex Amiatinus' cf. C. Roth, 'The Priestly Laver as a Symbol on Ancient Jewish Coins', *Palest. Explor. Quart.* lxxxiv, 1952, 91-93; other literature in Wattenbach-Levison, *Deutschlands Geschichtsquellen,* i, 1952, 47 n. 32; 75 n. 139, and (for archaeological criticism) in F. Saxl, *Journ. Warburg and Courtauld Inst.* vi, 1943, 15 n. 1.

9. It is impossible and would be superfluous to give here the whole literature on the question whether the *Regula Magistri* was written by Cassiodorus or can at least be associated with Vivarium. Cassiodorus's authorship has not been demonstrated, and the connexion with Vivarium seems to be a vague probability at best. Cf. Dom H. Vanderhoven and F. Masai, *Aux sources du monachisme bénédictin,* i, *Regula Magistri,* Paris-Bruxelles, 1953, with the reviews of H. I. Marrou, *Rev. Étud. Lat.* xxxii, 1954, 414-20; P. Courcelle, *Rev. Étud. Anc.* lvi, 1954, 424-8; and F. Vandenbroucke, *Rev. Bénéd.* lxiv, 1954, 277-82. Among the former papers the following can be singled out *exempli gratia:* J. Pérez de Urbel, *Rev. Hist. Eccl.* xxxiv, 1938, 707-39; A. Genestout, *Rev. d'Ascétique et de Mystique,* xxi, 1940, 51-112; M. Cappuyns, *Recherches de théolog. ancienne et médiévale,* xv, 1948, 209-68, who suggested the name of Cassiodorus; F. Vandenbroucke, ibid. xvi, 1949, 186-226; F. Masai, *Scriptorium,* ii, 1948, 292-6; F. Renner, *Stud. Mitt. Geschichte Benedikt.* lxii, 1950,

87-195; E. Franceschini, *Aevum,* xxiii, 1949, 52-72; idem in *Liber Floridus . . . P. Lehmann gewidmet,* St. Ottilien, 1950, 95-119; O. J. Zimmermann, *Amer. Bened. Review,* i, 1950, 11-36; H. Vanderhoven, *Rev. Hist. Eccl.* xlv, 1950, 707-70; P. Blanchard, *Rev. Bénéd.* lx, 1950, 25-64; F. Vandenbroucke, ibid. lxii, 1952, 216-73. Now see C. Mohrmann, *Vigiliae Christianae,* viii, 1954, 239-51 (with an excellent bibliography), and J. Froger, *Rev. d'Ascétique,* xxx, 1954, 275-88.

10. I know only G. Iacopi, *Brutium,* xxxii, 1953, nos. 3-4, pp. 8-9, a provisional note substantially repeated in Πεπραγμένα του ΘΔιεθνους Βυζαντινολογικου Συνεδριου, i, Athens, 1955, 201-5, that leaves me sceptical. But we must wait for further details. I have not yet seen P. Courcelle, 'Nouvelles recherches sur le monastère de Cassiodore', *Actes du Congrès International d'archéol. chrétienne 1954.* We owe to Courcelle the most important research on 'Le Site du monastère de Cassiodore', *Mélanges École Rome,* lv, 1938, 259-307.

11. The most recent treatments known to me are Wattenbach and Levison, *Deutschlands Geschichtsquellen,* i. 75-81, and F. Giunta, *Jordanes e la cultura dell' alto medio evo,* Palermo, 1952. I understand that a new edition of the text of the *Getica,* which will make use of the ninth-century manuscript noticed by E. Sthamer in the Archivio di Stato of Palermo, is being prepared in England. On the Palermo manuscript cf. *Forschungen und Fortschritte,* v, 1929, 45, and Giunta, pp. 188-202. R. Cessi's suggestion that the second section of the *Anonymus Valesianus* (c. 36-78) goes back to Cassiodorus is not well founded (cf. the ed. of the Anonymus in *Rer. Ital. Script.* xxiv, pp. lxxvii-lxxxviii). F. Rühl's alleged discovery of another excerpt of Cassiodorus's *Gothic History* (*Neue Jahrb, f. Phil.* cxxi, 1880, 549-76) was soon disproved by Th. Mommsen, *Chron. Minora,* ii, *Monum. Germ. Hist.* [*M.G.H.*], xi. 308-22 (*Exordia Scythica*): 'Cassiodori Geticis tantum abest ut auctor usus sit, ut ne Iordanianorum quidem certa indicia deprehendantur.'

12. *Agnelli Liber Pontificalis,* ed. O. Holder-Egger (*M.G.H.*), 94: 'In pinnaculum ipsius loci fuit Theodorici effigies, mire tessellis ornata, dextera manum lanceam tenens, sinistra clipeum, lorica indutus. Contra clipeum Roma tessellis ornata astabat cum asta et galea: unde vero telum tenensque fuit, Ravenna tessellis figurata, pedem dextrum super mare, sinistrum super terram ad regem properans.' E. Dyggve (quoted in n. 1), p. 50.

13. *Variae,* 5. 16. 2.

14. Cf. W. Ensslin, *Theoderich der Grosse,* 1947, 321.

15. The extent to which the Vandals interfered with communications in the western Mediterranean after 500 is still disputed. For an extreme view cf. N. H. Baynes, *Byzantine Studies and Other Essays,* London, 1955, pp. 309-20 (from *J.R.S.* xix, 1929, 230).

More cautious in the same sense: G. Mickwitz, 'Der Verkehr auf dem Westlichen Mittelmeer um 600 n. Chr.', *Wirtschaft und Kultur. Festschrift A. Dopsch,* Leipzig, 1938, 74-83. For the view minimizing Vandal interference: A. R. Lewis, *Naval Power and Trade in the Mediterranean, 500-1100,* Princeton, 1951, 1-30; idem, 'Le Commerce maritime et les navires de la Gaule occidentale (550-570)', *Études Mérovingiennes,* Paris, 1953, 191-9, and to a certain extent C. Courtois, *Les Vandales et l'Afrique,* 1955, 207-9. But Ennodius, *Paneg. Theod.* xiii. 70, and Cassiod. *Variae,* 5. 17, mention troubles, and the existing evidence on the relations between Africa and Gaul (cf. C. Courtois, *Cahiers de Tunisie,* ii, 1954, 127-34) and between Africa and the other Western regions (Courtois, *Les Vandales,* 205, n. 3) is not too clear. Cf. also W. H. C. Frend, 'North Africa and Europe in the Early Middle Ages', *Trans. Royal Hist. Soc.* v. 5, 1955, 61-80.

16. Cf. *inter alia* G.-G. Lapeyre, *Saint-Fulgence de Ruspe,* Paris 1929; W. Pewesin, *Imperium, Ecclesia Universalis, Rom. Der Kampf der afrikanischen Kirche um die Mitte des 6. Jahrh.,* in *Geistige Grundlagen römischer Kirchenpolitik,* Stuttgart, 1937; P. Courcelle, *Histoire littéraire des grandes invasions germaniques,* 151 ff.; C. Courtois, *Victor de Vita et son uvre,* Alger, 1955; Idem, *Les Vandales,* 284 ff. R. R. Bezzola, *Les origines et la formation de la littérature courtoise en Occident,* i, Paris, 1944, 7, seems to me to overrate the Vandals.

17. He came from Pannonia: 'Pannoniis genitus, transcendens aequora vasta Galliciae in gremium divinis nutibus actus' (*Martini Episcopi Bracarensis Opera Omnia,* ed. C. W. Barlow, 1950, p. 283).

18. The new great collective *Storia di Milano,* ii, Fondazione Treccani, Milano, 1954 (*Dalla invasione dei barbari all' apogeo del governo vescovile, 493-1002*), is disappointing about Milan as a centre of learning in Late Antiquity.

19. *Vita Caesarii,* lv, p. 480 (with note), ed. B. Krusch ('Passiones Vitaeque Sanctorum Aevi Merovingici', *M.G.H.*). Cf. M. Dorenkemper, *The Trinitarian Doctrine and Sources of St. Caesarius of Arles,* Fribourg, 1953; G. Bardy, 'L'Attitude politique de saint C. d'A.', *Revue d'histoire de l'église de France,* xxxiii, 1947, 241-57.

20. See the *Epistula ad Probam Virginem* preceding the *Excerpta* (ed. P. Knoell in *Corp. Script. Eccl. Lat.* [*C.S.E.L.*]), where Eugippius says 'cum bibliothecae vestrae copia multiplex integra, de quibus pauca decerpsi, contineat opera, placuit tamen habere decerpta'. Cf. Cassiodorus, *Inst. I* (*div. litt.*), 23: 'hic ad parentem nostram Probam, virginem sacram, ex operibus sancti Augustini valde altissimas quaestiones ac sententias diversasque res deflorans'. Cf. Max Büdinger, 'Eugippius, eine Untersuchung', *Sitz.-Ber. Wiener Akad.* xci, 1878, 804. I may mention here G. Morin, 'Une Compilation antiarienne inédite

sous le nom de S. Augustin issue du milieu de Cassiodore', *Rev. Bénéd.* xxxi, 1914-19, 237-43 (not very cogent).

21. Fulgentius, *Ep.* ii. 16 (*Patr. Lat.* [*P.L.*] lxv. 320); *Vita Fulgentii,* xxv (*P.L.* lxv. 144), edited by G.-G. Lapeyre, Paris, 1929, p. 119. Cf. G.-G. Lapeyre, *Saint Fulgence de Ruspe,* 234-6.

22. So Cassiodorus, *Ordo generis Cassiodororum* ('Anecdoton Holderi') in *Variae* rec. Mommsen, p. v.

23. Cf. the genealogical tree of the Symmachi in Seeck's edition of Q. Aurelius Symmachus, *M.G.H.,* p. xl.

24. Cf. Jordanes, *Getica,* xv. 83, and the discussion by W. Hartke, *Römische Kinderkaiser,* 1951, 427-39. Cf. H. Löwe, 'Von Theoderich dem Groen zu Karl dem Groen', *Deutsches Archiv,* ix, 1952, 354-6.

25. O. Jahn, *Ber. Sächs. Akad.* iii, 1851, 353; J. Sundwall, *Abh. z. Geschichte d. ausgeh. Römertums,* 1919, 139 (about Horace), and M. Schanz, *Gesch. Röm. Lit.* iv. 1, 2nd ed., 258. Sidonius associates Horace and Prudentius in *Ep.* 2. 9. 4.

26. P. Courcelle, *Les Lettres grecques en Occident,* 2nd ed., 307. Cf. J. Martin, *Grillius. Ein Beitrag zur Geschichte der Rhetorik,* Paderborn, 1927 (Studien zur Geschichte und Kultur des Altertums, xiv). Cf. also L. Hahn, 'Zum Sprachenkampf im Römischen Reich bis auf die Zeit Justinians. Eine Skizze', *Philologus,* Suppl. x, 1907, 675-718.

27. The two basic researches are by K. Praechter, 'Richtungen und Schulen im Neuplatonismus', *Genethliakon C. Robert,* Berlin, 1910, 105-56, and 'Christlich-neuplatonische Beziehungen', *Byzant. Zeitschrift,* xxi, 1912, 1-27. Cf. furthermore P. Courcelle, *Les Lettres grecques,* 257 ff.; R. Vancourt, *Les Derniers Commentateurs alexandrins d'Aristote. L'école d'Olympiodore, Étienne d'Alexandrie,* Lille, 1941; H.-D. Saffrey, 'Le chrétien Jean Philopon et la survivance de l'école d' Alexandrie', *Rev. Étud. Grecques,* lxvii, 1954, 396-410.

28. *Gramm. Lat.* iii. 405 Keil: 'Fama quidem antea nobis absentem venerabilem faciebat; nunc autem praesentem veritas supergressum laudes praedicationis ostendit.'

29. Cf. *Gramm. Lat.* iii. 405; notice in this passage a sentence remarkable from the political point of view: 'petimus igitur sapientem eloquentiam vestram ut . . . Romanorum diligentiam vestrorum ad artes suorum alacriorem reddatis auctorum, quibus solis ceteras cum Grais gentes superasse noscuntur.' Cf. in general R. Helm in Pauly-Wissowa, s.v. 'Priscianus', and V. Schurr, quoted below, n. 31.

30. *Les Lettres grecques,* p. 299.

31. Cf. the admirable book by V. Schurr, *Die Trinitätslehre des Boethius im Lichte der skythischen Kontroversen,* Paderborn, 1935, 198. Part of the evidence is given in the following notes. But a fact deserves to be emphasized with Schurr. A corrector of manu-

scripts of Boethius called *Renatus v.s.* appears as the transmitter of a letter by Senarius to Iohannes Diaconus with questions about 'catechumeni', &c. (the reference in n. 35). The same Renatus of Ravenna was apparently in Constantinople about 510 to argue with the monophysite Severus (J. Lebon, *Le Monophysisme sévérien,* Louvain, 1909, p. 46. n. 3, on the evidence of *Severi Antiocheni Liber contra Impium Grammaticum Orat. III Pars Posterior,* Paris, 1933, ed. J. Lebon, ch. 29, p. 72 of the translation). On the background see E. Caspar, *Geschichte des Papsttums,* ii. 149 ff., and A. A. Vasiliev, *Justin the First,* 1950, 160 ff.

32. *Epistulae Romanorum Pontificum,* ed. Thiel, 1868, 755; *Avellana quae dicitur collectio,* ed. O. Günther (*C.S.E.L.*), *Ep.* 115.

33. Cyrilli Scythopolitani, *Vita Sabae,* c. 53, p. 145, ed. Schwartz, 1939; Theophanis *Chronographia,* p. 157, ed. De Boor; *Avellana . . . collectio,* nos. 164, 179, 198 (*C.S.E.L.*). Cf. J. Aschbach, 'Die Anicier', *Sitz.-Ber. Wiener Akad.* lxiv, 1870, 392; E. Schwartz, *Kyrillos von Skythopolis,* 1939, 379-83; E. Stein, *Histoire du Bas-Empire,* 1949, ii, p. 67, n. 1; 172. Cf. also E. Schwartz, 'Publizistische Sammlungen zum acacianischen Schisma', *Abh. Bayer. Akad.* 1934, p. 245, and A. von Premerstein, 'Anicia Juliana im Wiener Dioskorides-Codex', *Jahrb. d. Kunsthist. Sammlungen,* xxiv, 1903, 106-23 (cf. R. Delbrueck, *Die Consulardiptychen,* 1929, 55).

34. *Liber contra Eutychen et Nestorium,* Prooemium.

35. Senarius: *P.L.* lix. 399; A. Wilmart, *Analecta Reginensia* (Studi e Testi, lix, 1933), 170-9. Cf. Avitus, *Ep.* 36 (*P.L.* lix. 252; *M.G.H.* vi. 2, p. 68, ed. Peiper); Ennodius, *Ep.* i. 23, and J. Sundwall, *Abh. zur Geschichte des ausgeh. Römertums,* 153. Faustus: *P.L.* lxiii. 534; E. Schwartz, *Publizistische Sammlungen zum acacianischen Schisma,* 115-17; J. Sundwall, 117. Albinus: *Avellana . . . collectio* (*C.S.E.L.*), *Ep.* 173, p. 629; J. Sundwall, 87. On Senarius, O. Fiebiger, *Denkschr. Wiener Akad.* lxxii, 1944, 2 Abh., 10, is misleading.

36. Cf. Cassiod. *Instit.* i. 23. 2. His work collected in *P.L.* lxvii. Cf. Schanz, iv. 2, 1920, 589; E. Schwartz, *Zeitschr. Savigny-Stift.,* Kan. Abt. xxv, 1936, 1-114; H. Wurm, *Studien u. Texte zur Dekretalen-Sammlung d. Dionysius Exiguus,* Bonn, 1939 (Kanonistische Studien und Texte 16), pp. 10-30, and bibl. there quoted. Cf. also B. Altaner, 'Zum Schrifttum der skythischen (gotischen) Mönche', *Historisches Jahrbuch,* lxxii, 1953, 568-81; H. Steinacker, 'Die römische Kirche und die griechischen Sprachkenntnisse des Frühmittelalters', *Mitt. Inst. Österr. Gesch.* lxii, 1954, 28-66, especially 51 ff., and in general the article by J. Rambaud-Buhot, 'Denys le Petit', *Dict. Droit Canon.* iv, 1949, 1131-51. P. Heck, *Übersetzungsprobleme im frühen Mittelalter,* Tübingen, 1931, must be consulted on the nature of mediaeval translations.

37. The evidence in Schanz, iv. 2. 230.

38. *Inst. Gramm.* ii. 2, Keil 'non minus Graecorum quam Latinorum in omni doctrinae genere praefulgentem'.

39. *Codex Iuliani v.c.* in the subscriptio of Stat. *Theb.* iv, in the Cod. Puteanus. The identification was suggested by F. Vollmer, *Rh. Mus.* li, 1896, 27, n. 1. But cf. R. Helm, Pauly-Wissowa, s.v. 'Priscianus', 2329.

40. E. Stein, *Histoire du Bas-Empire,* ii. 729, 838; A. H. M. Jones, *Journ. Rom. Studies,* xxxix, 1949, 52. For his love of Latin *De Magistr.* iii. 20, 27, and especially the pathetic passage, ii. 12.

41. E. Stein, *Histoire du Bas-Empire,* ii. 723-9. Cf. the telling chapters by John Lydus, *De Magistr.* ii. 25-26. About him cf. also E. Schwartz, 'Zu Cassiodorus und Prokop', *Sitz. Bayer. Akad.* 1939, n. 2—a study of his diplomatic activity; his conclusions are not accepted by Stein, ii. 337, n. 1; 342, n. 2, but the matter deserves further consideration. See O. Veh, *Zur Geschichtsschriebung und Weltauffassung des Prokop von Caesarea,* iii, Bayreuth, 1953, 3-11.

42. It will be enough to register here my disagreement with the admirable essay by F. Klingner on Boethius in *Römische Geisteswelt,* Leipzig, 1943, p. 432.

43. Here again I shall be content to refer to C. H. Coster, 'The Fall of Boethius', *Ann. Inst. Phil. Hist. Orient.* xii, 1952, 45-87, for recent literature, but G. B. Picotti, 'Il senato romano e il processo di Boezio', *Arch. Storico Italiano,* vii. 15, 1931, 205-28, mentions previous Italian work and clears away wrong hypotheses. Coster's theory that Boethius was arrested in 525 and executed in 526 seems to me untenable: it goes against the Anonymus Valesianus and the date at which Cyprianus was still referendarius (*Variae,* 5. 40).

44. *Variae,* 8. 32.

45. *Instit.* i. 23. 2: 'qui [Dionysius] mecum dialecticam legit.' Note his autobiographical remark in *Anecdoton Holderi* 'iuvenis adeo dum . . . laudes Theodorichi regis Gothorum facundissime recitasset'.

46. *Instit.* i. 17. 1: 'Hunc tamen ab amicis nostris, quoniam est subtilis nimis et multiplex, magno labore in libris viginti duobus converti fecimus in Latinum.' On Cassiodorus's knowledge of Greek see the remarks by H. Steinacker, *Mitt. Inst. Österr. Geschichtsforschung,* lxii, 1954, 46, n. 76*a*.

47. Biographical details in Schanz, iv. 2. 392. For his clerical status *Epist. ad Parthenium,* 69; *Epist. ad Vigilium,* 11 (now in Aratoris Subdiaconi *De Actibus Apostolorum,* ed. A. P. McKinlay (*C.S.E.L.*), 1951, p. 152; 4).

48. *Variae,* 10. 11, and 12, 'Anicios quidem paene principibus pares aetas prisca progenuit.' This was written in 535. Significantly enough, the family 'vere dicitur nobilis, quando ab ea actionis probitas non recedit'. After 533 the family of Boethius was mentionable again in Ravenna (Procopius, *B.G.* i (5), 2,

5)—a fact not without importance for the question of the date of the *Ordo generis Cassiodororum;* cf. n. 54.

49. The most recent edition of the text—first published by H. Usener, *Anecdoton Holderi,* Bonn, 1877, and then by Mommsen, *Cassiodori Variae,* p. v—is in J. J. van den Besselaar, *Cassiodorus Senator en zijn Variae,* 1945, p. 206.

50. 'Ordo generis Cassiodororum qui scriptores exstiterint ex eorum progenie vel ex quibus eruditis.' Usener's emendation 'ex civibus eruditis' will not do. Mommsen wavered between 'vel qui eruditi' in his edition of Jordanes, p. xli, and 'vel ex quibus eruditis profecerint' in *Variae,* p. v. The emendation 'vel qui eruditi' would make it certain that Boethius and Symmachus were included in the *Ordo generis Cassiodororum* as relatives, not as teachers. But even if one accepts 'ex quibus eruditis profecerint' it is hard to believe that Boethius was mentioned by Cassiodorus as a teacher. Professor Mynors, whom I consulted on this passage, wrote to me (13. x. 1955): 'Really we have not the needful resources to solve the problem. None of the suggestions so far made seems to me at all on the right lines; if I had to add to their numbers, it would be to supply a verb, which must be in the third person singular: e.g.

> qui scriptores extiterint ex eorum progenie vel ex quibus eruditis <claruerit>

the subject being either *genus* or *progenies* understood, preferably *genus.* I cannot begin to explain why the verb should have fallen out; but when one is dealing with (*a*) a title, (*b*) an excerpt, one cannot be expected to explain omissions as one normally has to when dealing with continuous literary text.' Another conjecture in *Dict. Hist. Géogr. Eccl.* xi, 1367.

51. *Instit.* i. 23. 1: 'ad parentem nostram Probam virginem sacram'.

52. J. Sundwall, *Abhandlungen,* 161; J. J. van den Besselaar, *Cassiodorus Senator en zijn Variae,* pp. 13-14; Seeck, Pauly-Wissowa, s.v. 'Symmachus' ii. 4, 1161.

53. Avitus, *Ep.* 51, p. 80, Peiper (*M.G.H.*).

54. In his edition of the *Variae,* p. xi, Mommsen thought that in the corrupt sentence of the *Anecdoton Holderi:* 'postmodum dehinc magister officiorum et praefuisset', there was an allusion to the dignity of a praefectus praetorio received by C. in 533: this seems to be confirmed by Dom Cappuyns, *Dict. Hist. Géogr. Eccl.* xi, 1368. Van den Besselaar, *Cassiodorus Senator en zijn Variae,* defends Usener's date not very convincingly (p. 5), though one must admit that the present state of the text of the Anecdoton does not allow any certainty about its date. For another suggestion, R. Cessi, *Studi critici preliminari* to his edition of the *Anonymus Valesianus,* pp. cxxxvi-cxxxvii. I was unable to consult R. Anastasi, 'La fortuna di Boezio', *Miscellanea Studi Letteratura Cristiana Antica,* iii, 1951, 93-109, which deals with the *Anecdoton Holderi.*

55. See the text quoted in n. 74. Furthermore Mansi, *Conciliorum Omnium Amplissima Collectio,* ix. 50 and 347. Cf. Sundwall, pp. 107-8.

56. Cf. W. Ensslin, 'Des Symmachus Historia Romana als Quelle für Jordanes', *Sitz. Bayer. Akad.* 1948, no. 3, 5-12. Ensslin has made a powerful case for Symmachus as the chief source of the *Romana.* I may add that, if the thesis on the *Getica* defended in the present lecture is correct, Jordanes's *Romana* also needs reconsideration.

57. Cf. G. M. Cook, *The Life of St. Epiphanius by Ennodius* (transl. and commentary), Washington, 1942. About Eugippius, *Vita S. Severini* (ed. Th. Mommsen *M.G.H.;* transl. and commentary by R. Noll, Linz, 1947). I. Zibermayr, *Noricum, Baiern und Österreich, Lorch als Hauptstadt und die Einführung des Christentums,* Berlin, 1944; F. Kaphan, *Zwischen Antike und Mittelalter,* 2nd ed., München, 1947; E. Schaffran, 'Frühchristentum und Völkerwanderung in den Ostalpen', *Arch. f. Kulturgesch.* xxxvii, 1955, 16-43. Cf. also R. Noll, *Mitt. Inst. Österr. Geschichtsf.* lix, 1951, 440-6.

58. A. Th. Heerklotz, *Die Variae des Cassiodorus Senator als kulturgeschichtliche Quelle,* diss. Heidelberg, 1926. Cf. also G. A. Punzi, *L'Italia del secolo VI nelle Variae di Cassiodoro,* Aquila, 1927. But I recommend the shrewd remarks by E. Sestan, *Stato e Nazione nell' alto Medioevo,* Napoli, 1952, 221-31.

59. *Varia,* 9. 24: 'nam cum esset publica cura vacuatus, sententias prudentium a tuis fabulis exigebat, ut factis propriis se aequaret antiquis. Stellarum cursus, maris sinus, fontium miracula rimator acutissimus inquirebat, ut rerum naturis diligentius perscrutatis quidam purpuratus videretur esse philosophus.'

60. 'Civilitas' in *Variae,* 9. 14. 8. In the same sense 1. 27. 1; 3. 24. 4; 4. 33, 1, &c. 'Vetusta servare', 3. 9. 1; cf. 2. 4.

61. 'Eo anno multa vidit Roma miracula, editionibus singulis stupente etiam Symmacho Orientis legato divitias Gothis Romanisque donatas', &c., ed. Mommsen, *Chronica Minora,* ii, *M.G.H.* xi. 161. Cf. M. Büdinger, 'Die Universalhistorie im Mittelalter', *Denkschr. d. Kais. Akad. Wien,* xlvi, 1900, 26.

62. *Varia,* 9. 25. This passage, as is well known, imitates Justinus's promium to his Summary of the *Historiae Philippicae.*

63. *Getica,* i. 3. The meaning of 'relegi' is not clear to me: it seems to imply that Jordanes had already read Cassiodorus before. Cf. Wattenbach and Levison, i. 77, n. 149; on the interpretation of this passage cf. A. von Gutschmid, *Kleine Schriften,* v, 1894, 331-3, *contra* C. Schirren, *De ratione quae inter Iordanem et Cassiodorum intercedat,* 92-93.

64. This was shown by H. von Sybel, *Allgemeine Zeitschrift für Geschichte,* vii, 1847, 288.

65. The date is approximately fixed by *Romana,* 4: 'in vicensimo quarto anno Iustiniani imperatoris': the

year 24 started on April 550 (Stein, *Histoire du Bas-Empire,* ii. 821, but the reasons given by Stein for dating the *Getica* in the spring of 552 are not cogent). Another suggestion in A. van de Vyver, *Speculum,* vi, 1931, 259, n. 1.

66. Procopius, *B.G.* iii (7), 39, 14; Jordanes, *Getica,* 314.

67. *Getica,* 304.

68. Mommsen, preface to his edition, pp. x-xiv. W. Wattenbach, *Deutschlands Geschichtsquellen,* i, 6th ed., 1893, p. 77, remarked: 'Ich halte es für vollkommen undenkbar, dass ein Mönch in einem Kloster in Mösien ein solches Werk hätte zu Stande bringen, da er das neueste Annalenwerk hätte erhalten und über die politischen Angelegenheiten der Gegenwart hätte schreiben können.' Other not very convincing suggestions in L. Erhardt, *Gött. Gel. Anz.* 1886, 676, n. 1; B. von Simson, *Neues Archiv,* xxii, 1896, 741-7; J. Friedrich, *Sitz. Bayer. Akad.* 1907, 379-442.

69. In the excellent art. *Cassiodore* of Baudrillart, *Dictionn. d'histoire et de géogr. ecclés.* xi, 1949, col. 1366: 'en complétant à Constantinople son ouvrage de 519-22, à l'occasion de la naissance de Germain (551), l'ancien ministre entrevoyait la possibilité d'une restauration romano-gothique . . . Trois années plus tard cette possibilité était irrémédiablement exclue.'

70. *Inst., Praefatio:* 'nisus sum cum beatissimo Agapito papa urbis Romae ut, sicut apud Alexandriam multo tempore fuisse traditur institutum, nunc etiam in Nisibi civitate Syrorum Hebreis sedulo fertur exponi, collatis expensis in urbe Romana professos doctores scholae potius acciperent Christianae'. H. Marrou, 'Autour de la bibliothèque du Pape Agapit', *Mél. d'archéol. et d'hist.* xlviii, 1931, 124-69 (fundamental, but pp. 157-69 are somewhat speculative). About the model cf. J. B. Chabot, 'L'École de Nisibe', *Journ. Asiat.* ix, 8, 1896, 43-93. The preserved inscription of the library (Diehl, *Inscr. Lat. Christ. Vet.* i, 1898) is a monument to Cassiodorus's intentions:

> Sanctorum veneranda cohors sedet ordine [longo]
>   divinae legis mystica dicta docens.
> hos inter residens Agapetus iure sacerdos
>   codicibus pulchrum condidit arte locum.
> gratia par cunctis, sanctus labor omnibus unus,
>   dissona verba quidem, sed tamen una fides.

On the school of Nisbis, cf. also Th. Hermann, *Zeitschr. f. Neutest. Wiss.* xxv, 1926, 89-122.

71. This is shown by the conclusive page of *De anima,* 'Invidit [diabolus] (pro dolor!) tam magnis populis, cum duo essent' (*P.L.* lxx. 1307). The past *essent* does not necessarily imply the end of the Gothic régime: see A. van de Vyver, *Speculum,* vi, 1931, 253.

72. Cassiodorus himself considered *De anima* as the thirteenth book of the *Variae, Expos. in Psalterium* 145 (*P.L.* lxx. 1029). Cf. also *Variae,* 11, praef. 7, and above all the preface to *De anima* itself: 'Dixi propo-

sitiones has non praeceptis regum, quae nuper age-bantur, sed profundis et remotis dialogis convenire' (*P.L.* lxx. 1281). This dates *De anima* about 538-40.

73. Jordanes, *Getica*, 313; Procopius, *B.G.* iii (7), 1. 2.

74. 'nec non et per gloriosum virum patricium Cethegum et religiosum virum item filium nostrum Senatorem aliosque filios nostros commoniti noluistis audire' (Mansi, *Concilior. Omn. Ampliss. Collectio,* ix. 357). Cf. Jaffé, *Regesta Pontificum,* i, 2nd ed., p. 122; Pro-cop. *B.G.* iii (7). 35. 10 (where Cethegus is called Γόθιγος) and Liber Pontific. *Vita Vigilii,* vii (ed. Duchesne, p. 298).

75. Liber Pontific. *Vita Vigilii,* ix (ed. Duchesne, p. 299); Victor Tonnensis, *Chronica,* pp. 203-4, Mommsen, *M.G.H.* xi. Cf. Stein, ii. 669. In *Instit.* i. 17. 2, Cas-siodorus may express some authentic admiration for Justinian, though the words are conventional: they are paralleled by *Variae,* 11. 13. 5 'si Libya meruit per te recipere libertatem'.

76. The manuscript tradition is divided between 'utri-usque generi' and 'utriusque generis' and between 'genus' and 'gens'.

77. As we have seen (n. 33), a branch of the family was in Constantinople. Cf. J. Aschbach, *Sitz. Wien. Ak.* lxiv, 1870, 416-17.

78. This cannot be stated confidently as J. Aschbach, *Sitz. Wien. Ak.* lxiv, 1870, 415, and J. J. van den Besselaar, *Cassiodorus Senator en zijn Variae,* p. 14, do, but Flavius Rufius Petronius Nicomachus Cethe-gus was the son of Petronius Probinus, consul 489 (Ennodius, *Opusc.* 6, p. 314, Vogel), and Petronius-Nicomachus-Probinus are names typical of the Ani-cian groups. As Besselaar rightly says, 'op deze wijze zou men zoowel de opdracht als den inhoud van den "Ordo generis Cassiodororum" beter kunnen verklaren'. About the importance of the Anicii in the Gothic war cf. also Procop. *B.G.* iii (7). 20. 26-31; on Cethegus, ibid. iii (7). 13. 12.

79. Mansi, *Sacrorum Concil. . . . Collectio,* ix. 60 D (A.D. 551): 'cum Dacio Mediolanensi . . . Paschasio Aletrino atque Iordane Crotonensi fratribus et coepis-copis nostris'. Ibid. ix. 716 (A.D. 556): 'directam a vobis relationem, defensore ecclesiae nostrae Iordane deferente, suscipientes satis mirati sumus' (a letter of Pope Pelagius I). The text of the former now in E. Schwartz, 'Vigiliusbriefe', *Sitz. Bayer. Ak.* 1940, 2, p. 14.

80. Manuscripts PVS of *Romana:* 'Incipit liber Iordanis episcopi'. In XZY of the third class of the manu-scripts of the *Getica:* 'episcopus ravenatis civitatis' (or similar expressions). About the 'versus Honorii scholastici ad Iordanem episcopum' (Riese, *Anth. Lat.* 666) I accept Mommsen's suggestion that Jor-danes's name is a later addition (pref. to Jordanes, p. xlvi, but cf. Pauly-Wissowa, s.v. 'Iordanis', col. 1911). Jordanes is called episcopus, also in old cata-logues. See M. Manitius, *Neues Archiv,* xxxii, 1906, 651.

81. Grimm, *Abh. Berlin,* 1846, p. 11; *Kleinere Schriften,* iii, 1866, 182, identified Vigilius with the pope but did not yet know that a Jordanes was mentioned as a bishop of Crotone. The identification of Jordanes with this bishop was suggested by S. Cassel, *Mag-yarische Alterthümer,* Berlin, 1848, 302, n. 1, from Mansi, *Sacrorum Concil . . . Collectio,* ix. 60, quoted above. Mommsen, *Jordanes,* p. xiii, n. 22 is clearly embarrassed: 'quod ut non inepte excogi-tatum est, ita vincitur indiciis plurimis et certissimis originis libellorum Thracicae'. The possibility of identifying Vigilius with the pope had already pre-sented itself to J. E. Metzgerus, *De Jornande,* Alt-dorf, 1690, p. 18.

82. *Weltgeschichte,* iv. 1, 1883, 313-27, a magnificent analysis: 'Jordanes hätte nur den Namen gegeben, durch welchen der eigentliche Ursprung verborgen gehalten werden sollte; er wäre mehr Redaktor als Autor' (p. 327).

83. C. Cipolla, *Memorie Accad. Torino,* ser. 2, xliii. 99-134; R. Cessi, Introd. to his ed. of the *Anonymus Valesianus* (Rer. Ital. Script. 24. 4), pp. lxxxix ff. A survey of opinions on the date of composition of Cassiodorus's Gothic History in Wattenbach and Le-vison, i. 71. F. Altheim, 'Waldleute und Feldleute', *Paideuma,* 1953, p. 427, dates the *Hist. Gothorum* about 526-33. Waitz in *Nachr. Göttingen,* 1865, p. 101, followed by A. Gaudenzi, *Atti e Memorie Depu-tazione . . . Romagna,* 1884-5, 278, thought that Jor-danes was responsible for mistakes about Clovis's family. This is possible, but nobody can tell what mistakes Cassiodorus could make and any inference about the terminal point of Cassiodorus's history would seem to me unjustified.

84. It will be enough to mention one *locus classicus: Getica,* 133, 'sic quoque Vesegothae a Valente im-peratore Arriani potius quam Christiani effecti'.

85. i. 3: 'ad quos et ex nonnullis historiis Grecis et Lati-nis addidi convenientia, initium finemque et plura in medio mea dictione permiscens'. I cannot go into the question of the relation between Jordanes's text and the continuation of the Chronicle of Marcellinus. In any case the answer to this question cannot be deci-sive for our problem whether Jordanes had Cas-siodorus's work before him for the period after The-odoric. But remarks on the connexions of this *auctarium* of Marcellinus preserved in Bodleianus Auct. T. ii. 26 with Cassiodorus are to be found in Courcelle, *Rev. Étud. Anc.* lvi, 1954, 428.

86. *Getica,* 28, 82, 117.

87. *Variae,* 10. 22. 2: 'et abavi (*Ablavi* Meyer) vestri his-torica monimenta recolite'. L. Schmidt, *Geschichte d. deutschen Stämme,* i², 1934, 28, n. 2, does not ac-cept the emendation and altogether minimizes the importance of Ablabius. Sidonius refused to become the historian of the Visigoths: *Ep.* 4. 22.

88. For instance, Orosius, 1. 16, 'Getae illi qui et nunc Gothi.' Cf. *Scr. Hist. Aug.* (Spartianus) *Anton. Carac.*

10; *Geta*, 6. As is well known, the identity of Getae and Gothi was still defended by J. Grimm. The point was elaborated by C. Schirren, *De ratione quae inter Jordanem et Cassiodorium intercedat*, 1858, 54 ff., and before him by S. Cassel, *Magyarische Alterthümer*, 302 ff. 'Getae' instead of 'Gothi' is also found in inscriptions: for instance Dessau, *I.L.S.*, 798.

89. Sidonius Apollinaris, *Panegyr. Aviti*, 403: 'Obstupuere duces pariter Scythicusque senatus'. Cf. 498.

90. *Getica*, 40.

91. *Getica*, 146; cf. 131 ff.

92. *Getica*, 180 ff. The analysis of the sources in M. Schuster, 'Die Hunnenbeschreibungen bei Ammianus, Sidonius und Iordanis', *Wiener Studien*, lviii, 1940, 119-30, is unsatisfactory. Cf. also D. Romano, 'Due storici di Attila: il Greco Prisco e il Goto Jordanes', *Antiquitas*, ii, 1947, 65-71.

93. *Variae*, 8. 21. 7: 'pueri stirpis romanae nostra lingua loquuntur'. Their father was, of course, 'instructus trifariis linguis', *Variae*, 5. 40. 5.

94. A study of this aspect of Jordanes-Cassiodorus in its relation to the methods of ancient historiography would be rewarding. Sections 121-63, 180-229 are particularly interesting. Some good remarks in H. Helbling, *Goten und Wandalen. Wandlung der historischen Realität*, Zürich, 1954, 29-32.

95. Gregory died in 593 or 594, Wattenbach and Levison, i. 101. Cf. J. M. Wallace-Hadrill, *Trans. Royal Hist. Soc.* v, 1, 1951, 35-36.

96. 'Diese Widersprüche und Inkonsequenzen dem Jordanes beizumessen, geht nicht an', L. Schmidt, *Geschichte der deutschen Stämme*, i², 1934, 27.

97. In the preface of *De orthogr.* (*Gramm. Lat.* vii. 144 K.) Cassiodorus speaks of 'conversio mea': 'post commenta psalterii, ubi praestante domino conversionis meae tempore primum studium laboris impendi'. About the meaning of 'conversio' see Kappelmacher in Pauly-Wissowa, s.v. 'Iordanis', col. 1911; J. J. van den Besselaar, *Cassiodorus Senator*, Haarlem, n.d. [1950], 146-51. I am not convinced by C. Mohlberg, *Ephemerides Liturgicae*, xlvii, 1933, 3-12, that the 'Sacramentarium Leonianum' was C.'s prayer-book. Mohlberg is followed by G. de Jerphanion, *Rech. de science religieuse*, xxvi, 1936, 364-6.

98. I may perhaps refer to L. Salvatorelli, *San Benedetto e l'Italia del suo tempo*, Bari, 1929; Dom J. Chapman, *St. Benedict and the Sixth Century*, London, 1929; S. Brechter, 'St. Benedikt und die Antike', *Benedictus der Vater des Abendlandes*, München, 1947, 139-94; Ph. Schmitz, *Histoire de l'Ordre de Saint Benoît*, i, 2nd ed., Maredsous, 1948; G. Aulinger, *Das Humanum in der Regel Benedikts von Nursia*, St. Ottilien, 1950; J. J. van den Besselaar, *Cassiodorus Senator*, Haarlem, n.d. [1950], 134 ff. For anti-ascetic tendencies in the fifth-sixth centuries

notice G. A. Cary, 'A Note on the Mediaeval History of the Collatio Alexandri cum Dindimo', *Class. et Mediaevalia*, xv, 1954, 124-30.

99. Cf. M. Roger, *L'Enseignement des lettres classiques d'Ausone à Alcuin*, Paris, 1905; G. Manacorda, *Storia della scuola in Italia. I, Medioevo*, Milano, 1913; G. Hoerle, *Frühmittelalterliche Mönchs- und Klerikerbildung in Italien*, Freiburg, 1914; F. Ermini, 'La scuola a Roma nel VI° secolo', *Archivum Romanicum*, xviii, 1934, 143-54; B. Gladysz, 'Cassiodore et l'organisation de l'école médiévale', *Collectanea Theologica* (Lwów), xvii, 1, 1936, 51-69; P. Courcelle, 'Histoire d'un brouillon cassiodorien', *Rev. Étud. Anc.* xliv, 1942, 65-86; E. R. Curtius, 'Das mittelalterliche Bildungswesen und die Grammatik', *Romanische Forschungen*, lx, 1947, 1-26; H. I. Marrou, *Histoire de l'éducation dans l'antiquité*, Paris, 1948, 435 ff. Other references in P. Renucci, *L'Aventure de l'humanisme européen au Moyen-Âge*, Paris, 1953, 210-14; R. R. Bolgar, *The Classical Heritage and its Beneficiaries*, Cambridge, 1954, p. 416 (cf. also p. 405). There is much, of course, to learn from A. Viscardi, *Le origini*, 2nd ed., Milano, 1950, and R. Bezzola, *Les origines et la formation de la littérature courtoise en Occident*, i, Paris, 1944. Cf. E. Bickel's review of Mynors's edition of the *Institutiones*, in *Gnomon*, xiv, 1938, 322-8, and E. K. Rand, *Speculum*, xiii, 1938, 438-47.

James J. O'Donnell (essay date 1979)

SOURCE: "The *Variae*," in *Cassiodorus*, University of California Press, 1979, pp. 55-102.

[*In the following essay, O'Donnell analyzes the compilation, content, and character of Cassiodorus's* Variae, *arguing that while Cassiodorus extols the virtues of Gothic rule, the work was not intended as a polemical treatise.*]

The collapse of Ostrogothic Italy in the face of Byzantine reconquest casts a shadow over the most important literary product of Cassiodorus' public career. That career, dated according to the documents in the **Variae**, did not last beyond 537 or 538; his appointment as praetorian prefect had originally been made in 533 in the name of Athalaric under Amalasuintha's influence, but we have seen how that youth died less than a year afterwards, to be followed swiftly to the grave by his murdered mother, leaving Theodahad in control of the kingdom. Theodahad's reign lasted scarcely two years, for it was in 535 that Belisarius set out on the war of reconquest, and by 536 he had advanced as far as Naples and Rome; Gothic dissatisfaction with Theodahad's rule ended in his murder.

If we take the relatively cultured Theoderic and Amalasuintha as the norm of the Amal dynasty, Theodahad was a crude intruder whose efforts to acquire a patina of Roman culture were overshadowed by his murderous instinct for power. But to most of the Goths, Theodahad was an Amal like the rest, given over to the enfeebling pursuits of literature and philosophy and thus incapable of leading the nation in battle; the early successes of Belisarius confirmed this fear, leading to the rise of the more vigorously military Witigis. There was sense, apparently, in this choice of a new leader, for the Goths rallied behind him. He besieged the Byzantine army in Rome in 537, and as late as 539 recaptured Milan. It was not until 540 that Ravenna surrendered and Witigis was captured for delivery to Constantinople.

Even this blow did not put an end to the resistance offered by the Goths in Italy. While Belisarius was absent in the east, the Goths found stability under the leadership of Totila, who ruled for eleven years (longer than any king since Theoderic), capturing Rome twice more from the Byzantine forces. Belisarius himself returned to Italy for several years, without much success; in 550, upon marriage with Mathesuentha, Justinian's nephew Germanus was placed in command of the Byzantine forces, but he died too quickly for the eastern empire to claim him as a representative of the legitimate Gothic line of succession as well as the legitimate imperial power in Italy. At length the eunuch Narses launched a successful campaign in 551, delivering the final defeat to the Goths under their last king, Teias, in 553. The reconquest was thus completed after an eighteen-years' struggle, and Justinian was free to reorganize the imperial administration of Italy; this he did in the so-called Pragmatic Sanction of 554.

Against this dark backdrop, Cassiodorus' career as a statesman came to an end. The years of the Gothic War began with Cassiodorus holding power as the leading civil official in Italy, continued by taking him on a voyage of geographical and intellectual discovery to Constantinople, and concluded by sending him back to his family's estates, no longer a great statesman but only a simple *conversus*, a man who had turned his life to God in the monastic community he had caused to grow up at Squillace. There is no great mine of information in any of his works to reveal to us the secrets of his soul at this period; instead, we are forced to trace with difficulty the external events of his life through these years, seeking acceptable grounds for speculation on what private thoughts may have accompanied them.

The *Variae* is a work in twelve books containing the collected literary products of Cassiodorus' years in office. It contains letters, proclamations, *formulae* for appointments, and edicts in which are recorded the military commands, political appointments, judicial decisions, and administrative orders of the Ostrogothic kingdom; most are written in the name of the reigning kings, but some are in Cassiodorus' name.[1] Most of these documents (about two-thirds of the total) are not datable except by their position in the collection in relation to documents datable on internal grounds. Very frequently dates and names have been excised from the documents as we have them to make them more edifying and (to Cassiodorus' colleagues and

successors in administration) useful. As many of them as can be dated, e.g., appointments to a particular office stated to begin from a specific indiction, can be fixed to three periods: 507-511, 523-527, and 533-537. These, we deduce, are the periods during which Cassiodorus himself was at Ravenna holding office, in the first instance as quaestor, in the second as *magister officiorum,* and in the third as praetorian prefect. We assume that Cassiodorus' activity drafting letters for the king would in each case roughly begin and end with his terms in office, that Cassiodorus was only involved in the literary activity preserved in the *Variae* during those years when he was holding appointive office. This in turn may imply that he did not in fact normally reside at court except when in office; for as we saw in the first chapter, his efforts as a ghostwriter for the king during the last two periods of official activity were supernumerary activities, undertaken as favors because of the high esteem in which his literary style was held. Thus, had he been at court while out of office, he would have been every bit as capable of aiding the quaestorial staff as when holding an official appointment.

We saw in the *Ordo generis* that Cassiodorus entered public life as *consiliarius* (a kind of aide-de-camp for legal affairs) to his father during the latter's term as prefect. In fact, that post was descended from that of the *assessores* in ancient Roman courts, the jurists who sat next to the magistrate on the judicial bench and gave him legal advice on the disposition of cases before him.[2] We know so little of the post in the sixth century that it is only a probable assumption that the holder of the office had to have had some legal training before such an appointment. We have seen, however, that Cassiodorus seems to have been unusually young at the time of his appointment, and it is natural to wonder whether most of his legal education might not have come to him on the job; that a father would be allowed to appoint his own son to assist in this way indicates that it was not a post under severe outside scrutiny.

As a result of the oration in praise of Theoderic that Cassiodorus presented at this time, he received his appointment as quaestor. It seems clear that the post was a reward not merely for the loyalty of a sycophant but also for the talent of a polished rhetorician. For the specific function of the quaestor in this age (as the *Notitia Dignitatum* informs us tersely) was literary: "Under the authority of the quaestor: drafting laws, answering petitions."[3] The *Notitia* adds that the quaestor did not have his own *officium* (bureaucratic staff), but could requisition help from other imperial bureaus as necessary. The formula of appointment emphasizes the quaestor's intimate relationship with the king, since it was he who put the desires of the monarch into words that were both rhetorically effective and legally valid (*Var.* 6.5). Much was indeed made of the importance of rhetoric as a weapon for insuring compliance with decrees by effecting the persuasion of the subjects that the decrees communicated were right and necessary; the quaestor's words should prevail "so that the sword of punishment should be made almost superfluous where the quaestor's eloquence has its way" (*Var.* 6.5.3). Certainly, great store would be set on presenting the commands of the king in as impeccably correct (both rhetorically and legally) and pleasing a fashion as possible. It was for this virtue, as well as the presumed knowledge of the law, that Cassiodorus, the youthful orator, must have been selected.[4] Despite the intellectual demands of the post, the telltale absence of an *officium* marks the quaestorship as the least lofty of the posts carrying the rank of *illustris;* for it is an unchanging rule of bureaucratic government that one's dignity and worth are directly proportionate to the number of underlings on hand to do one's bidding.

It is a subject for much speculation and little certain knowledge, to what extent the role of the quaestor was more important under the Ostrogothic kings than under the late emperors. For it would seem that the quaestor's job was in large measure to put the best face on official pronouncements and to look after the sensibilities of the thin-skinned aristocracy. To these ends every appointment to a high office was accompanied by a letter to the senate announcing the appointment and expressing concern for the senators' desire that their company be augmented by the most worthy candidates.[5] Even if Theoderic was not illiterate, the presence in his retinue of a polished Latin rhetorician was a valuable asset; but we have no way of knowing how far Cassiodorus went in polishing and elaborating the monarch's thoughts. It is possible that Theoderic could understand little more than the gist of most of Cassiodorus' most polished productions; however that may be, it is clear that the eloquence at least, and perhaps a goodly part of the accompanying philosophy about the nobler purposes of the king's rule, are directly attributable to Cassiodorus. We can recall, moreover, that on his appointment to the prefecture by Athalaric, the letter of appointment recalled Theoderic's fondness for laying aside the cares of state and indulging in philosophical conversation with his learned minister (*Var.* 9.24.8). Whether we choose to interpret this statement as exaggerated boasting by Cassiodorus, as evidence of the king's own relatively high level of intellectual ability, or as a carefully colored description of a relationship where a comparatively ignorant king listened in silence, if not awe, to the lectures of his bookish friend, the most important information seems to be that at least Cassiodorus thought of himself as a part-time minister of culture to the Gothic kings; that his literary efforts were sought after is the best and only confirmation that such a view has. One sees, however, that his employment as publicist for the court was good politics for maintaining good relations with the restive aristocracy. Theoderic must have found Cassiodorus a valuable tool for keeping him in contact with a faction in his kingdom that he might otherwise not have known.

Most of the letters written for the king in the *Variae* date to the period of the quaestorship. A total of 187 letters in Books I through V are commonly dated to the 507-511 period, and it is possible that the 72 *formulae* in Books VI and VII were composed at this time. From the first years as *magister officiorum* there are 42 letters written in the name of Theoderic. After Theoderic's death, Cassiodorus remained in office for little more than a year, producing the thirty-three letters of Book VIII and the first thirteen or fourteen letters of Book IX; many of those letters were announcements of the death of Theoderic and other documents related to the transfer of power. The remaining eleven letters in Book IX were written after Cassiodorus' appointment as prefect in 533 and before the death of Athalaric in 534. Book X contains all of the letters written in the names of the various monarchs during the last three years that Cassiodorus spent in office. Many of the first letters are pairs, e.g., one written by Amalasuintha to introduce Theodahad, and one by Theodahad to acknowledge his own appointment. There are only four letters in Amalasuintha's name for the six months between her son's death and her own. Twenty-four letters appear in the name of Theodahad as well as two addressed to the empress Theodora by Theodahad's wife and queen, Gudeliva.[6] Finally, there are only five letters in Witigis' name: a formal announcement of his election to his Gothic subjects, three diplomatic pieces to Byzantine addresses, and one to all his bishops asking their support for a mission to Constantinople.

There was, therefore, a decline in the volume of Cassiodorus' ghostwriting during his term as prefect especially; but it was at this time that he was for the first time entitled to issue decrees in his own name, and these are collected (to a total of 68) in Books XI and XII of the *Variae.*

It is thus of comparatively little importance to the study of the *Variae* to consider Cassiodorus' activity as *magister officiorum,* since in fact no trace of his activities specifically undertaken as a function of that office comes down to us. It can be reconstructed from remarks about the office in Cassiodorian and other sources that the *magister* was something remotely like head of the civil service, involved in all the decisions of the realm insofar as they needed facilitating by the bureaucracy; and he frequently attempted to extend the scope of his action, but was not in fact a major force in the making and execution of policy.[7] In the *Notitia Dignitatum* the *magister* seems to be in charge of certain household troops (but whether this continued under the Goths is to be doubted), the *agentes in rebus* (a courier service largely replaced by Gothic *saiones,* probably under Gothic control), and the four principal bureaus of the court in charge of shuffling papers and pushing pencils: the *scrinia memoriae, dispositionum, epistolarum,* and *libellorum.* The distinction in function between these offices is difficult to recover at this date, though it surely resided in the form and content of the documents with which each was concerned. The *magister officiorum* also had charge of the system of post-horses maintained throughout the realm for official purposes (the *cursus publicus*) and the arsenals.[8] There is some trace in Cassiodorus' own *formula* for the office that the post had something of the functions of a modern ministry of foreign affairs (though his role in meeting foreign ambassadors may have been more a matter of protocol and hospitality than policy) and some authority over provincial governors (**Var.** 6.6). The office seems to have taken over, as time passed, more and more functions once exercised by the praetorian prefect, due in part to the ambition of the holders of the office, in part to a need to relegate routine bureaucratic functions to the *magister* while the bulk of the administrative, judicial, and financial authority remained with the praetorian prefect. We have seen how Athalaric related that Cassiodorus' service in this post was enlivened not only by his frequent assistance to the quaestors but also by his ready assumption of a military command when the shores of Italy seemed menaced and there was no one else at hand to do the job (**Var.** 9.25.9). This glimpse of the practical role of the office under the Goths seems to depict the *magister* as a kind of chief of staff for the whole government, in charge of making things work and taking burdensome administrative tasks away from king and prefect.[9] Of Cassiodorus' own performance in this post, however, this fleeting glimpse is our only direct information.

For Cassiodorus' second extended period out of office, from the end of his term as *magister* in about 527 until his appointment as prefect in 533, we are more poorly informed than for the first. The evidence becomes generous again only when we examine Cassiodorus' performance as praetorian prefect. He was appointed in 533, apparently to take office from the first of September with the beginning of the official year; the letters concerning his appointment are contained in the **Variae,** drafted by their subject. Only at this point, a quarter of a century after Cassiodorus entered public life and almost a decade after Theoderic's death, can we begin to think of him as the leading figure of the Ostrogothic civil government. However useful he may have been as quaestor in publicizing and praising Theoderic's actions for a Roman audience, however skillful a manager of bureaucrats he contrived to be as *magister officiorum,* he was still undeniably outside the narrowest inner circle of power. Not only had he not held the prefecture (though the distinguished Liberius had reached that rank before the age of thirty, while Cassiodorus was nearly fifty in 533), he had not held any of the major portfolios in the financial departments. His actions had been limited in their significance to the government itself, rarely involving intervention in the affairs of the society at large. Even if his influence with Theoderic was as substantial as he himself would have us believe, it could only have been the influence of an adviser, and, to judge by the time he was allowed to spend away from court, an adviser less than vital to the interests of the monarch. And we are not without grounds for supposing that the comparatively hasty departure from office after the change of kings in 526 indicated some reshuffle in the royal cabinet after which Cassiodorus, willingly or not, found himself on the outside once again.

But Amalasuintha, the actual ruler of Italy in her son's regency, did bring back Cassiodorus to the highest rank in 533 and allowed him to publish flowery praise of himself in her son's name. His task can have been anything but easy during these besieged years, but the books of the

Variae dealing with the period give the opposite impression. In Cassiodorus' own books, XI and XII, sounds of war are distant indeed;[10] the letters collected treat all manner of quite ordinary administrative topics. A large part of Book XI is devoted to letters of appointment for posts in Cassiodorus' own *officium;* in the same vein are edicts and letters of instruction to lower officials for the conduct of business under the new prefect—all of Book XI may date from the first few months of Cassiodorus' term. In Book XII there are ordinary matters of tax relief, an obscure property case, some construction orders, and a few more appointments. No fewer than four of the letters there have to do with the appointment of officials and the instructions given them for the procurement of delicacies for the royal table (**Var.** 12.4, 12.11, 12.12, 12.18). Mommsen dated these letters to the period of the prefecture in general, but it is likely that they can be attributed to the reign of Theodahad, who died in 536. For there is not much evidence of contact between Cassiodorus and the martial-minded Witigis (only the five perfunctory letters in his name in Book I), nor is there much reason to think that the new warrior king was much concerned with the consumption of royal delicacies in a peaceful palace—he had to spend too much time with the troops. Theodahad, on the other hand, always appears to have been a man who enjoyed the perquisites of the throne to the fullest.

Because he insists on including only matters of peaceful import and such a substantial body of material on the administrative details of his assumption of office, Cassiodorus gives us a good picture of the functionings of the *officium* of the praetorian prefect at this time. The picture is largely theoretical—that is, confined to a description of how things should run, rather than a record of actual performance. Since similar descriptions survive in the *Notitia Dignitatum* and in the *De magistratibus* of John Lydus, we can perceive the structure and some of the functions of the office at this period.[11]

This snapshot of administrative structure shows how little really did change. There was some shuffling about of minor responsibilities from office to office, but in general the prefecture remained recognizably similar in the last days of the Gothic kingdom to what it had been more than a century before. The office was the only cabinet post to authorize the holder to issue directives in his own name; these included edicts on judicial affairs and price control (e.g., **Var.** 11.12). He also supervised the levying of the annual indiction, or general tax, payable in kind throughout the realm; this levy was so important that it was assigned directly to the prefect for collection rather than to a separate ministry (like the others that dealt chiefly with the royal monetary transactions—*sacrae largitiones*—and estates—*res privatae*). The indictional year began on the first of September, to coincide with the end of the harvest and the beginning of the collection of the tax on that year's crops. Since the entire realm depended on the efficient collection and redistribution of the harvests in the summer and fall before the onset of the winter closed off the seas (by mid-November at the latest) and the world settled down to a long season without economical means of transporation for bulky products, this function of the prefecture was central to the well-being of any government; not only must the troops on the frontier be supplied, but the corps of bureaucrats itself and the royal court had to be the objects of the prefect's efficient (perhaps his most efficient) attention.

The prefect also had important administrative and judicial functions. He appointed and paid provincial governors; and he was authorized to discipline them, as well as to offer direct rescripts to their queries, some of which appear in the last books of the *Variae.* Finally, he was the highest judge of appeal in all legal matters; this was important under the Gothic kingdom, and still more so in the kingdom's last disorganized years, when royal justice was untutored in the ways of Roman law and not easily tracked down sometimes in the camps. To whatever extent the ordinary administration of the kingdom progressed in any ordinary way in the war years, the prefect, as the head of that administration, was a figure on whom much would, or at least could, depend.

As indicated, every praetorian prefect was in a position to issue documents in his own name; moreover, the occupant of the government's highest seat would have access to the records of preceding administrations.[12] A preoccupation with his own literary activity and the availability of copies of the documents that he had produced over the preceding three decades as quaestor and as informal quaestor's helper eventually led Cassiodorus to the notion of publishing a compilation of those documents as a monument to his public career. In the prefaces with which he adorned this compilation (one at the very beginning, and another before Books XI and XII to introduce his own prefectural documents) there are self-effacing apologias. While it is difficult to descry genuine literary motivations behind such a facade (where the urging of friends was introduced as the motive for publication), and indeed while such a facade may not be without some substantially accurate backing, the role of literary vanity in stimulating such a compilation seems undeniable. If from his earliest years Cassiodorus had been praised on all sides for the facility of his pen, it would be difficult for him to avoid thinking fondly of his accumulated literary production at the close of his career.

To impute such a motive to Cassiodorus, however, requires us to think that he did indeed foresee the proximate end of his public career while he was still at Ravenna with access to the files; it is not in the ordinary course of events for a man in his early fifties to be thinking of imminent retirement. There seems, therefore, to be a definite, if completely unstated, air about the *Variae* of a man who realized that one phase of his life was coming to an end. Whether this was connected with a growing desire to turn to a more expressly religious style of life or with shrewd estimates of the inevitability of Gothic defeat and the absorption of Italy into a larger political structure in which Cassiodorus could not or would not find a place, the effect is the same. For all the likelihood, however, that such thoughts were occurring to Cassiodorus at this time, they, like the bloody war going on about him, leave no direct trace on the *Variae.*

For as much as the *Variae* is a document of the career of one statesman, it is also a semiofficial record of the kingdom itself. The original readers of the *Variae* were not so concerned with using it as a source to establish the dates and events of Cassiodorus' life, or even to learn about the affairs of the kingdom. Instead, readers in Italy (or even in the east, if such there were) perusing these pages around 540 would see spread out before them a varnished picture of the successes of the Gothic kingdom in Italy reaching back over three decades. The work covers a full generation of the politics of the kingdom and brings to life again in particular the acts and achievements of the dead and sorely missed founder of the Gothic experiment in government. When we read, for example, the first letter of the *Variae,* in which Theoderic speaks of reconciliation to the emperor Anastasius after a minor skirmish in 508, our attention is riveted on the event itself; to Cassiodorus the editor (as opposed to Cassiodorus the original author) and to his reading public, the letter was a painful reminder of the sad course that events had taken in the years since. In years when Rome was besieged by warring armies, captured and recaptured amid scenes of carnage and destruction, the lofty purposes of Theoderic in encouraging the rebuilding of the ruins of former wars would again evoke an echo of what might have been, what was in fact once beginning to be, before events overtook their shapers. The *formulae* in Books VI and VII, moreover, are a clear demonstration of the state of bureaucratic "normalcy" that once prevailed in the kingdom, whatever their use to future quaestors may have been.

But while the *Variae* is a testament to the virtues of the Gothic kingdom, it is a nonpolemical treatise, threading carefully through the events of the preceding decades, glossing over disturbances past and present, emphasizing only the happy and the successful. Thus the omission of any mention of the sad fate of Boethius and Symmachus may have been conditioned by more than Cassiodorus' own reluctance to reveal seamy details of his own advancement at his kinsmen's expense; the crime for which the two nobles were executed was alleged collusion with the eastern empire. Whether or not they had been guilty and whether Cassiodorus felt remorse at his own inability to alter their fates, that aspect of their lives was not an appropriate subject for inclusion in this dossier of success. In addition to literary vanity, then, this new motive appears for Cassiodorus' choice of literary forms for this work; the documents of past years, edited and selected carefully for innocuousness, had an impersonal ring to them that increased the ability of the work as a whole to mollify inflamed sentiments. If such a work was meant to be read in Constantinople and in Rome and in Campanian villas as well as in Ravenna, it would have been extremely difficult to make the case for the Gothic kingdom in the form of a treatise arguing the case as such; even a revised *Gothic*

History, by virtue of its need to treat all of the historical events serially, would have been inappropriate for leading men's sentiments to reconciliation.[13] Instead, the *Variae* as it stands is a work with which no one in the Mediterranean world had reason to take deliberate exception. Theoderic, Athalaric, Witigis, and the Byzantine rulers appear in these pages without stain on their character, always acting honorably and fairly. The only former starring character in the drama on whom any adverse light is thrown is Theodahad, but even this is most indirect; for in the palmy days of Theoderic's reign, letters were addressed to Theodahad three times, and on two occasions the letters were rebukes for the rapacious behavior of Theodahad's men (*Var.* 4.39, 5.12).[14] In both cases, Theoderic makes explicit the need for his own relatives to maintain higher standards of behavior than others.[15] This hint of disapproval of Theodahad (these two letters could as easily have been omitted) is undoubtedly a quiet rebuke for the man (already dead at the time of compilation) who had been instrumental in the downfall of the kingdom by his murder of Amalasuintha and who had been on the throne when Justinian opened hostilities. In spite of this, acts of his administration are preserved, in large part addresses to the emperor and empress at Constantinople seeking peace and reconciliation. This careful inclusion of initiatives for peace (and the omission of letters, if any there were, of a more belligerent nature) is all part of the attempt to establish and maintain the record of the Ostrogothic kingdom as an enterprise dedicated to the well-being of its people and the empire of which it still confessed itself a part.

We have spoken of the *Variae* as though it were such a dossier without being very clear about the intended audience. Here again the evidence deserts us. Is it likely that this was a composition intended to win the attention of powerful figures in Constantinople? If so, whom? For ultimately only Justinian could reverse the policy of reconquest; and it is difficult to see how much hope Cassiodorus could have entertained of having his treatise reach the emperor at all, much less of having it convince him to abandon a policy for rehabilitating the ancient glories of the empire that he must have seen, at that particular time, as an almost total success. If the work was not directed to the emperor, or to Constantinople, then to whom in Italy could it have been aimed? With what urgency? Those who had lived under the Ostrogoths must have by that time known fairly clearly what that rule was like; indeed, there must have been few Italians alive who could remember the days before Theoderic arrived almost half a century before, and fewer still who could remember the days when emperors ruled the west. Agents of an imperial ideology in Italy in the late 530's must have been men of great faith indeed, since the last years of the emperors in Italy had not been such as would inspire nostalgic yearning in those who had heard their history. In fact, whatever nostalgia for the empire there could have been in Italy at this time depended on what men had heard (and some possibly seen) in the contemporary empire in the east or what had been handed down by traditions from as far back as the grandfathers of the older men of that time.

One possible circumstance of composition needs to be observed, however. Procopius recounts a debate between Belisarius and Gothic ambassadors at Rome in 537 or 538. The arguments advanced by the Goths at this point resemble very closely the kind of position that Cassiodorus takes in the *Variae.*[16] The written work, coming out at just about the same time as the debate Procopius recounts, might then have been meant to appeal to the Roman aristocracy in land already occupied or threatened by Belisarius.

But such speculation aside, what then are we to make of the work itself? In part we must retreat to our notions of Cassiodorus' unquestionable literary vanity, and in part we must confess that he may have felt only very generally that the record was worth establishing precisely "for the record" while it still could be done. In fact, both of these motives are the ones that appear, disguised in rhetorical coloring, in Cassiodorus' own prefaces.

The most extended apology for the work is the initial preface, where these motives must be pursued behind the billowing garments of Cassiodorian rhetoric.[17] Cassiodorus begins by attributing the idea for such a collection to learned men (*diserti*), who thought he should collect the letters "so that posterity might recognize the burdens I undertook for the common good and the conscientious deeds of a man who could not be bought" (*Var.,* Praef. 1). To this, Cassiodorus replies that such publication might subvert the purpose of establishing his own reputation, if what he had written appeared foolish (*insubidum*) to later generations. After quoting Horace's dictum (*Ars poet.* 388) that what is to be published should be held back nine years to give the author ample time for reflection, Cassiodorus elaborates that his literary performance in public documents had been rushed and less than perfect; instead of nine years, Cassiodorus had had scarcely a few hours (*Var.,* Praef. 3-4).[18] He emphasizes for a long paragraph the cares that beset him in office, his solicitousness for the welfare of the people, and the consequent defects of his writing. In such words he purports to decline the suggestion to publish.

But the friendly urgings of learned men (never identified) are reintroduced at substantial length in what amounts to direct quotation. They begin by accepting and repeating with added praise the argument that Cassiodorus has been busy in his function as prefect, and add a reference to his extracurricular activity as quaestor's helper; they praise his lack of corruption, which is compared to his father's integrity, and they add remarks alluding to his intimacy with Theoderic and the long hours spent in conversation with the monarch. They turn the initial argument in on Cassiodorus, insisting that men already know how busy he was, and that if he could produce anything worth reading under such circumstances, his reputation will be doubly enhanced. They add that his work can serve as a teacher for both the well-prepared and the unprepared holders of offices in the *res publica;*[19] moreover, if he does not act, he will allow the acts of his kings to be obliterated in forgetfulness. "Do not, we pray, let those whom you have addressed on their promotions to the rank of *illustris* be overcome forever in silence and obscurity" (*Var.,* Praef. 9). For all this, they ask, "do you still hesitate to publish what you know can be of such great use to others? You are hiding, if we might say so, the mirror in which every future age could examine the quality of your mind" (*Var.,* Praef. 10). The appeal to vanity is capped by a remark that, while sons are often very different from their fathers, "one never finds a man's speech unreflective of his character" (*Var.,* Praef. 10).[20] They conclude that after his earlier successes of a literary nature (the **Laudes** and the **Gothic History** are enumerated), there is no reason why he should resist the persuasion to publish his records.

In the face of such argument, Cassiodorus owns himself a beaten man. "Be merciful, my readers," he pleads, "and if there is any temerity and presumption here, blame these friends rather than me, for I am in complete agreement with my detractors on these points" (*Var.,* Praef. 12). A description of the work's contents then follows.

For Cassiodorus has collected "whatever I have been able to find written (*dictatum*) by me on public business while I held office as quaestor, *magister,* or prefect,"[21] and arrayed the material in twelve books. To protect others from the "unpolished and hasty addresses" that he is conscious of having produced himself all too often in honoring new appointees, he justifies the inclusion of the sixth and seventh books containing the *formulae,* "for my own use, late as it is in my own career, and for my successors who find themselves pressed for time" (*Var.,* Praef. 14).[22]

The contents are reflected in the title, and he devotes the remainder of the preface to explaining his title, *Variae,*[23] which he chose "because we could not use a single style to address such a variety of audiences" (*Var.,* Praef. 15). He identifies three classes of individual readers to whom the individual letters could be addressed, including those "multa lectione satiati," those "mediocri gustatione suspensi," and those last "a litterarum sapore ieiuni"; each must be addressed in a different way "persuasionis causa," so that "it sometimes becomes a kind of artistry, the avoiding of what learned men would praise" (*ibid.*). The preface concludes with a largely artificial and irrelevant attempt to connect these three kinds of audience with the three traditional levels of ancient style (high, middle, low); this particular schematization is not reflected in the letters themselves.

The other preface included in the *Variae,* at the beginning of Book XI before the books of Cassiodorus' own publications from his prefecture, seems to postdate the earliest preface by some time, though it is not necessary to assume that earlier portions of the work had been published separately. The evidence for a lapse of time is the mention only here, and not at the beginning where it might rightly belong, of the addition of the treatise *De anima* to the twelve books of the *Variae;* that treatise is mentioned here in terms that echo the opening lines of the little treatise itself.

The remainder of the second preface consists chiefly of an excuse for not having more in the way of judicial decisions to include. Cassiodorus had, he explains himself, the assistance of one Felix, a young lawyer whose talent he praises highly, who removed much of the burden of such work from Cassiodorus himself. In particular, his help is credited with having enabled Cassiodorus to give fuller and less fatigued attention to the higher affairs of state (*regales curae*). Finally, Cassiodorus drapes this praise of Felix with the further admission of his own deficiencies and the arrogance of any author so bold as to publish such material. Here again the excuses ring truer than at first glance if read carefully.[24]

However successful the prefaces were in their literary intent, they leave open some questions that we would have been glad to have answered. The most pressing is that of the comprehensiveness of the contents. In the passage quoted above, Cassiodorus claims to have included whatever he had been able to find ("quod . . . potui reperire") of those things dictated while he held office as quaestor, *magister,* and prefect. Are we to take this literally? Is this collection a complete anthology of all such surviving documents? If we assume, as we probably must, that Cassiodorus was still in Ravenna and probably still in office at the time of compilation, and then assume that he had access to the files of the court for gathering these documents, do we then accord to this work credit for being a full chronicle of the public acts of the Ostrogothic kingdom for those years? On balance, we cannot.

First, according to our interpretation of the circumstances in which Cassiodorus came to be involved in quaestorial activities during his last two terms of office, he was almost certainly not involved in *all* of the literary activity of the quaestor's office; moreover, for the eleventh and twelfth books, he explicitly states that legal decisions were largely drafted by his aide (his *consiliarius*?). Second, there is an obvious conflict between the express purpose of presenting documents that make either the author or the subject (or preferably both) look good and the claim to have included everything Cassiodorus could find of his compositions. Moreover, a very clear impression comes from reading this work that nothing, nothing whatever, of a controversial nature has been allowed to remain. The most heatedly debated events of the kingdom's history appear indirectly if at all; thus the letter inviting the elder Cassiodorus back to court is itself the major link of evidence in the hypothesis that the prefect Faustus fell from favor as a result of his actions in office at about the time certain of these letters were written; but nowhere is Faustus explicitly criticized.[25] Of course the deaths of Boethius and Symmachus are nowhere hinted at, though they appear as addressees of flattering letters; and one would scarcely know, from the exaggerated formality and courtesy of the diplomatic letters, that there were wars being fought in these years. The nearest one gets to warfare are letters reestablishing peace and letters involving the equipping and mustering of troops (included because they reflected well upon the civil officials involved). Left to ourselves, and convinced that these letters represented a balanced picture of the Ostrogothic kingdom from 507 to 537, we would immediately conclude that so peaceful and so happy a realm never existed on the face of the earth; if our attention were then called to the sounds of war echoing from Italy at the very moment of publication, we would be most disagreeably surprised.

From all that we have said so far in this chapter, therefore, it becomes evident that what we have here is an edited transcript of the public record, not the unexpurgated whole. We have already suggested the main lines of the propagandistic purpose that this work was expected to serve, as is apparent from both the contents themselves and Cassiodorus' own prefaces. It is worth repeating that the only one of the major characters on the scene of Italian politics in the sixth century to appear at all to a disadvantage, and that only indirectly, is the dead and—to both sides—discredited Theodahad.[26] Theoderic, Amalasuintha, and Witigis all used murder as an instrument of policy; but only Theodahad's action was universally, if not reviled, at least disclaimed by 537 or 538. If motives apart from literary vanity are to be accepted for the *Variae,* as I think they must, Cassiodorus' own explicit claim that his purpose was to enshrine the memories of the notables chronicled therein becomes a declaration of that propagandistic intent, a clear enough statement that the work was seen to seek reconciliation, at the price of a little self-inflicted blindness to the seamier side of affairs.

More of this propagandistic purpose appears in the way in which the collection was arranged. To begin with, the only chronological force demonstrably existing in that arrangement was the division between Cassiodorus' terms of office (though this was violated for a purpose with the last two letters of Book V) and the distinction of monarchs under which they were originally written. Thus, as stated before, the first four books contain documents from Cassiodorus' quaestorship under Theoderic (507-511); Book V, except the last two letters postponed from 511, contains the letters from his term as *magister officiorum* while Theoderic was still alive;[27] Books VI and VII, the geographical center of the work, separating Theoderician books from those of his successors, contain the *formulae dignitatum;* Book VIII and the first half (letters 1-13 or 14) of Book IX record events of the remainder of Cassiodorus' term as *magister* (526-527); the remainder of Book IX, terminating in the two letters of his own appointment, contains documents of his term as prefect under Athalaric (533-534); Book X contains the diverse letters, taken in rough chronological order, under the several monarchs of the remainder of that term (534-537/8); and Books XI and XII contain his own letters as prefect (533-537/8).

If the arrangement of letters in the individual books is not strictly chronological, however, there is still a discernible literary pattern.[28] (Cassiodorus himself describes the actual composition of the books as involving conscious *ordinatio* on his part [*Var.,* Praef. 13].) The principle at work is that the positions of honor in each book are at the very beginning and at the end.

Books I, II, VIII, and X all begin with letters addressed to the emperor at Constantinople. In Book I, the letter treats for peace after the skirmishes of 505-508; in the second book, the first letter merely announces the consul for the year (and is followed by the other two letters in the dossier on that particular appointment, to the appointee and to the senate); while Books VIII and X each begin by announcing the succession to the throne of a new ruler, Athalaric in the one case, Theodahad in the other. On the other hand, Books III, IV, V, and IX open with letters to barbarian kings. In Book III, there are four such royal communications, all attempting to keep the peace in Gaul; Book IV begins with two unrelated letters to different kings (of the Thuringians and the Heruli); and Books V and IX begin with isolated letters of that nature.[29] To confirm the importance of the opening spot in each book, there are no letters to Constantinopolitan emperors that do not hold that spot, except in Book X, where no fewer than ten of the book's thirty-five letters are directed to Justinian and five more to Theodora; but this exception proves the rule, since Book X is the only one written under more than one monarch, and the broad chronological outline takes precedence.

Obviously Books XI and XII could not open with addresses to emperors or monarchs; again the chronological motive seems to take over, since Book XI begins with Cassiodorus' collection of letters announcing his own appointment (though he may obviously be using the place of importance to call attention to his own virtues a little more), and Book XII begins with a relatively general set of instructions to various officials.

If emperors only customarily appear in the first spot in a book, barbarian kings can appear elsewhere, but only in one specific location: at the end of a book. Thus Gundobad and Clovis, who are both addressed in letters at the beginning of Book III, also appear as addressees of the letters at the ends of Books I and II, respectively. Furthermore, Transimundus, king of the Vandals, is sent two letters that appear in the *Variae* at the end of Book V. This apparently deliberate positioning of the non-imperial royal letters calls our attention to the last letters in other books, to see by what right they hold that position. The results are at first diverse. Book III ends with a letter to a *comes privatarum* named Apronianus, directing him to welcome an *aquilegus* (water-diviner) coming from Africa; the letter contains a long digression on that special art of divination. Book IV, on the other hand, concludes with a letter to Symmachus, praising his work in reconstructing damaged edifices and particularly commissioning the rebuilding of a theater; then the letter digresses on the nature of the theatrical art, with frequent reference to the science of etymology. Books VI and VII, following the hierarchical order of the offices they describe, conclude with minor offices. The last letter in Book VIII is a directive to one Severus, *vir spectabilis,* to put down riots in connection with rural, apparently pagan, celebrations in the province of Lucania (not far from Squillace), and contains a digression on a miraculous fountain there; the two preceding letters, also to Severus, also digress readily in praise of various amenities of Cassiodorus' home territory. Book IX is completed by the two letters to Cassiodorus on his elevation to the prefecture. Book X, always pedestrian, ends with the distressingly plain letters ascribed to Witigis. In Books XI and XII, Cassiodorus chooses to end his personal books with impersonal documents; in the first case with a general amnesty, very possibly issued at Easter 534 during Cassiodorus' first year in office, while in the second case the last four letters dealt with, and the very last letter is an edict establishing remedies for, famine in northern Italy.

Despite their diversity (their "variousness"), it is possible, I hold, to see clear threads connecting these letters.[30] To begin with, the first several books end on letters carrying as a unifying theme ideas about various arts and sciences. In Books I and II, the letters to German kings are covering letters for gifts of clocks in the one case and a musician in the other (in both cases furnished by Boethius), while Books III and IV deal with the science of divining and the art of theatrics, respectively. Book V's concluding letters show Theoderic, in his last appearance in the *Variae,* at his best in reaching a peaceful settlement of an international disagreement; this is the very virtue that is the last thing for which Theoderic was praised in the *Getica* (*Get.* 58). Books VIII and IX both end with letters on subjects dear to Cassiodorus himself, namely his own home province and his own career's advancement. This self-indulgence is paralleled by the ends of Books XI and XII, both of which show Cassiodorus the prefect to his best advantage, dispensing legal mercy in the indulgence at the end of Book XI, and working diligently to remedy the evils of famine in Italy in Book XII.

Both halves of the *Variae,* therefore, feature letters at the end of each book designed to put the very best possible face on the Ostrogothic kingdom for its sophistication of culture as well as its benevolence in government. The first five books reflect most favorably on Theoderic himself, while the last five books seem to be centered more and more on the person of Cassiodorus himself, a tacit recognition that the kingdom was not so well governed at that epoch as to merit making the later kings heroes in quite the way that Theoderic was. It is even possible to see an ironic twist (or *apologia pro vita sua*) in this transition, perhaps even a hint that with Theoderic gone, Cassiodorus himself was the last guardian of the old values left in the government. If the first letters in each book demonstrate the public grandeur of the kingdom in its negotiations with great monarchs, the last letters give an elegant picture of the whole life of the kingdom and its society. Moreover, by including in these concluding letters the flattering missives to Boethius and Symmachus, Cassiodorus is at least making an attempt to reconcile their mourners to the Gothic kingdom; the praises of his favorite province are couched in a repression of pagan rites that no doubt would please a Byzantine audience still not sure just how fully Christian these people in Italy had remained under Arian rule. And pointing out the amiability of his own administration and his concern for the well-being of the greatest

part of the people allows Cassiodorus to show how a besieged regime merits the acceptance and support of his audience, whether Roman or Gothic, Italian or Byzantine.

The frame placed around each book in this way further conditions reactions to the contents of the whole, giving honorable dealings with foreign powers and correct ideas of civilization at home as the poles between which the affairs of the kingdom are set.[31] The remainder of the contents, for all their variousness, are remarkably true to the overall guidelines thus tacitly set out. This consistency leads us to believe that all the letters in this collection were chosen according to definite limiting criteria.

More letters dealing with appointments to *illustres dignitates* appear in the *Variae* than with any other subject. Some of those honors were virtually empty (cf. the case at *Var.* 2.15-16), but most are real offices by which the civil affairs of the kingdom were administered. Since for all the highest honors there exist letters in the books of *formulae* as well as personal efforts in the rest of the work, we are justified in assuming that not every appointment was treated with the same personal touch. Very many of the families honored with personal letters appointing their members to high office are indeed the greatest families of the Ostrogothic realm; these letters commonly provide an occasion for recalling the virtues of ancestors and relatives who have already served the kingdom well.

After the appointments, the next commonest type of letter in the *Variae* is the decree on a given administrative matter of a more or less routine nature, whether issued spontaneously or in response to a petition. The most common subjects of these documents are private and ecclesiastical lawsuits, with frequent cases involving the conflicting claims to property of feuding heirs or even churches. In one instance, for example, a minor's guardian had apparently accused the youth's brother-in-law of engineering an unfair division of inherited property; the two letters preserved require the parties to come to court and have justice done; a third party is directed to supervise the execution of that justice (*Var.* 1.7-8).[32] Without fail, such cases are adorned in Cassiodorus' letters with the king's solemn promises that he will recognize his duty to protect the weak and secure justice.

Apart from judicial determinations, there is a large collection of royal orders on the interconnected subjects of commerce, transport, taxes, and the grain supply. Here the end in view is the welfare of the people and the establishment of a fair method for providing the fisc with its revenues. Thus, one case agrees to allow the annual payment of the *tertiae* (tax in lieu of land for Gothic settlers) to be lumped together by its payers with taxes already being paid, since their land had been independently declared immune from actual confiscation and the annual payment will continue indefinitely (*Var.* 1.14). In another instance, the bishops and *honorati* of a district left anonymous are charged to cooperate with royal agents in putting an end to speculation in grain that is causing the *possessores* of the region to suffer (*Var.* 9.5). Frequently the topic is of particular interest to the court: once Theoderic is heard complaining about an interruption in the supply of *sacra vestis,* the royal purple cloth (*Var.* 1.2); other letters speak of procuring delicacies for the king's table from those parts of Italy that have special treats to offer.

Such documents provide the most mundane reading in the *Variae.* Scattered throughout the first five books, the last half of Book VIII, and throughout Book IX, they provide the background of ordinary benevolence on which the Gothic rule was based. Taken together with letters ordering an end to various abuses of the public post, they fill up the gaps between the more remarkable discussions. For in addition to these ordinary affairs, three other subjects stand out, two of special interest to a specifically Roman audience.

The topic of most general interest is the succession to the throne. Half of Book VIII is filled with documents of Athalaric's succession, including notifications to virtually every constituency (beginning with the emperor Justin) of the death of Theoderic and the orderly transfer of power. Since Athalaric says when appointing Cassiodorus that there were in fact some military scares at this time, we may assume that these letters served at that time a function analogous to that which the *Variae* was expected to perform a decade later—the self-justification of the Gothic rule.

The two Roman topics have to do specifically with the circus (and circus factions) and the interest that Theoderic had in the rebuilding of structures damaged in Italy's wars. In the last half of the *Variae,* the only document concerning rebuilding is Cassiodorus' own letter ordering repair of the Flaminian Way (*Var.* 12.18). Under Theoderic, however, there had been more leisure and opportunity to attempt (as civilized monarchs should) to repair what Italy had lost, and especially the city of Rome. Twenty-five letters deal with subjects ranging from the ordinary (clearing vegetation from a watercourse [*Var.* 5.38]) to the decorative (mosaics for Ravenna [*Var.* 1.6]) to the strictly cultural (the letter to Symmachus praising his earlier rebuilding efforts and enjoining the reconstruction of the theater of Pompey [*Var.* 4.51]). In one case, Theoderic explicitly allows the use of scattered stonework fallen from ruined buildings in these rebuilding activities, and several other letters involve arrangements for the transportation of materials; clearly the enterprise was one that was both necessary after decades of warfare and neglect and at the same time willingly undertaken. There can be little doubt that such a policy was good politics, since its result would be to associate in the public mind the Gothic regime with the new and refurbished structures it caused to be built throughout Italy. Theoderic's private motives—how much of this was simple expedience, how much royal vanity, and how much a sincere concern for the ancient glories of noble Italy—are hidden from us. Furthermore, the frequent appearance of these letters in the books dating from Theoderic's reign (they exceed 10 percent of the letters in those

five books) may be exaggerated by Cassiodorus' own practice of selection; certainly any letters that he could find in which Theoderic appeared as the dedicated rebuilder of Roman Italy would have a strong claim to inclusion in a collection published shortly after the Gothic siege of Rome sustained by Belisarius. Whatever Theoderic's policy really was, the *Variae* makes it clear that Cassiodorus wanted his king remembered for his unflagging concern for the renovation of Italy's damaged splendor. In this and other respects, Theoderic's reign is made to seem a golden age, and one not long past at that; by implication, it was a golden age recoverable by prudent men.

The other rulers in whose names Cassiodorus wrote do not appear fully enough, or enough to their own advantage, for us to derive a consistent picture of the image that Cassiodorus meant to create for them. It must have been difficult, in the first place, to do this for Athalaric, whom everyone knew to have been in fact a child, and for Theodahad and Witigis afterwards, the documents of whose reigns were too much constrained by circumstance to allow much scope for the display of virtue (though Cassiodorus' selection at least removes almost all the blots from their records, a negative but effective device). Theoderic, on the other hand, does succeed in becoming attached in our minds to an image of the kind of king he was (or was represented to be). Whatever he may have been in real life, the king we meet in the *Variae* was a gentle man, always happy to praise his subjects for their faithful service to his kingdom and, *a fortiori* (and the way in which the logical connection is made to seem obvious is usually the acme of Cassiodorus' art as propagandist), to virtue and justice. When he has reason to reproach his subjects, it is with sorrow rather than anger: the voice is that of a gently chiding father, calmly reviewing the principles of good government, finding them sadly lacking, and quietly but forcefully urging the rectification of the unhappy situation.[33] We are entitled to believe that Theoderic may have been more vigorous in expressing himself when seen in life; but we see him always in the *Variae* as Cassiodorus would paint him for us, or rather for the angry, strident warring parties of the time in which he published his anthology.

In every way, then, the *Variae,* read as a work of contemporary history, presented a picture of life in Italy as it once was—and as it still could be—and which contrasted sharply with the quickly deteriorating reality. There was once a time when a learned king sent erudite directives to his subjects, ruled moderately and justly, and was solicitous of the health and happiness of his kingdom through happy decades. There is not much way of knowing whether this portrait comes close to the truth; but its purpose was not, in fact, objective truth, but the counteraction, by a kind of genteel polemic, of the angry prejudices that were displayed on all sides in the Gothic war. The *Variae* is thus a kind of final effort in the genre of panegyric by Cassiodorus, but panegyric of a considerably more sophisticated form than any of his earlier efforts. Judged as history the book exhibits many faults; but it is a kind of panegyric of the past that has striking and lasting value. That it succeeded in some measure is best remarked by observing how thoroughly our own present ideas about Theoderic and his kingdom have been conditioned by this one work; even if our suspicions are aroused, it is still against this text alone that they can be tested.

A literary analysis of the book (which must be balanced between considering the works as individual documents and as elements in the whole collection) throws further light on the nature of the work and its particular success and failures. Some such analysis has, in the past, been based on attempts to identify the literary genre in which the *Variae* can be formally located.[34] It is valuable to begin such a study of the *Variae* by observing the mixed position it takes between various traditional uses of the epistolary genres. For example, the *Variae* partakes both of the ancient tradition of the literary epistle as practiced by Pliny or Symmachus (the letters of appointment to high office resemble the documents by which the earlier authors had practiced the *religio* of polite society), but at the same time it has the formality of chancery rhetoric of more ordinary royal and imperial documents of the sort that survive in bulk from all ages. In fact, the strictly literary use of the epistolary genres dies out for most of the middle ages, reviving only with the twelfth century; in Cassiodorus, however, two different kinds of letter-writing have been welded together to form a new kind of document. For, in fact, late antique chancery style, such as we know its existence, was not as consciously literary as the letters in the *Variae*. The kind of letter contained in the *Variae* seems almost to have been invented by Cassiodorus to combine business and pleasure. Each individual letter was from the beginning a little piece of propaganda, as well as an instrument of government. Receiving one of Cassiodorus' letters from the royal messenger denoted the favor one found in the eyes of the king, gave opportunity to delight in a pleasing literary style, and for both reasons inspired reflection on the wisdom and cultivation of the magnanimous monarch.

Thus the propagandistic thrust of the *Variae* as a published collection was not something altogether new imposed by artful selection and editing at the time of publication; from the first, these letters had been fulfilling many of the purposes that they were then meant to fill again for a new audience when Cassiodorus published the collection. Furthermore, this idiosyncratically propagandistic use of the royal chancery was a skill at which Cassiodorus was particularly adept, beyond the range of the ordinary quaestor. We should note, moreover, that we only see Theoderic granting benefits (e.g., agreeing to hear a legal case or granting tax relief), never denying them. Requests that the bureaucracy (or even the king) rejected were probably not honored with a royal letter of reply. The image of generosity was thus encouraged with no conscious effort at deception and selection of material, for the *Variae* in fact began with dozens of day-to-day decisions years before.

With the *Variae* there are many different styles, adapted chiefly to the subject of the letter and the occasion of composition. As stated earlier, it is difficult to see a direct relationship between a recipient's level of education or social status and the level of style of the letter addressed to him; nevertheless, there is doubtless substantial tailoring of the more important letters to the individual recipients in a way that is inaccessible to us, since the private details of the relationships between these people (particularly the high potentates of the court) and their king are lost to history. The most obvious cases of this tailoring are the letters to Boethius and Symmachus, where the whole point of the letters is to flatter the aristocrats by asking their advice and assistance on cultural matters; the king wants to show an interest in such affairs, while deferring to the vanity of those who felt themselves the particular guardians of culture. Of a different nature are the letters at the end of Book VIII to Severus, governor of what is now Calabria, in which Cassiodorus goes on at length about the beauty of his home province; similarly, in the extended description of Squillace upon which we drew in Chapter 1 above, Cassiodorus' addressee has obviously come to expect that the good prefect will grow a little long-winded and lyrical when he has the chance to write about his home town.[35] As political documents, these letters in particular may have had some effect in maintaining good relations with the folks back home, but that was undoubtedly minimal compared with the simple literary delight that Cassiodorus would take in the act of composing them. By contrast, when the time came to publish the *Variae*, these descriptions of a happy and fertile country could doubtless also be read as evidence of the prosperity of Italy under the Goths.

The literary resources that went into composing these rhetorical tours de force were considerable. The most famous example, a favorite with all Cassiodorus scholars, is the query directed to the prefect Faustus about a delay in the arrival of the grain supply (*Var.* 1.35). The ships in which the grain is to be transmitted are the focus of the trope, which becomes outright allegory. The king wonders aloud what could cause the delay when such favorable weather attends the season for sailing; could it be, he supposes, the sucking-fish that has fixed its teeth in his ships, or the conch from the Indian Ocean? Perhaps the sailors are themselves made languid by the touch of the stingray. "Truly," the king concludes, "men who cannot move must have suffered some such attack." But then, he adds, the sucking-fish is really procrastinating venality, the bite of the conch really insatiable cupidity, and the stingray is fraudulent pretense. "They manufacture delays with corrupt ingenuity, pretending to encounter adverse conditions." The prefect is then strictly directed to look into this situation quickly and make the needed amends, "lest famine might seem to be born of negligence rather than drought."

This letter also contains one of Cassiodorus' trademarks, discussion of natural phenomena. The effect of the various marine creatures on the ship's course is discussed carefully in view of the behavior of the animals, and the figure stands in close relation to the thing allegorized. This attachment to natural history is one of the commonest themes of Cassiodorus' digressions.[36] He has at least ten such lengthy digressions on subjects ranging from storms and elephants to the production of purple cloth and the production of amber.[37] A large number of these digressions have been shown to derive from the *Hexameron* of Ambrose, including the case discussed in the paragraph, where Cassiodorus was drawing on a similar treatment in Ambrose of the various fish.[38]

It should not be thought that Cassiodorus is not capable of integrating digressive material harmoniously into his work. Two elegant examples demonstrate this. One of the simplest, shortest letters in the collection is a proclamation "to all Goths and Romans and those who command harbors and castles," dating from Cassiodorus' quaestorship (*Var.* 2.19). In an unknown locality, certain slaves have murdered their own master and dishonored the funerary rites. Theoderic is grieved, comparing human behavior to that of birds: "Alas, the pity men abandon is found even among birds. The vulture, who lives on the corpses of other creatures, for all his great size is friendly with lesser birds and protects them from the attacking hawk, beating him away with his wings and gnashing his beak: and yet men cannot spare their own kind" (*Var.* 2.19.2-3). This is more than a zoological metaphor chosen arbitrarily to illustrate the cruelty of men to men; Cassiodorus did not leave the metaphor at that, but instead integrated it neatly with the final statement of Theoderic's judgment: "So let him be food for the vultures, who can cruelly seek the slaughter of his shepherd. Let him find such a sepulcher, who has left his master unburied" (*Var.* 2.19.3). No one, not even Cassiodorus, would call this letter a masterwork of literature; but such a piece, unambitious yet neatly suited to its circumstances, with the verbal details of its metaphorical structure completely worked out and adroitly executed, is perhaps comparable to good lyric poetry for its scope and workmanship, if not for its theme.

It is not, therefore, surprising that Cassiodorus could be as effective and competent in one of his longer efforts with a more consciously literary purpose. The letter to Boethius at the end of Book II, requesting that a musician be found as a gift for Clovis the Frank, is one of the longest letters in the *Variae.* The business of the letter is transacted in a few lines at the beginning and end; the bulk of the text is a little treatise *de musica,* with historical and technical material in abundance. The digression begins with the third sentence of the letter and continues for over 120 printed lines (*Var.* 2.40.2-16). At the end, Cassiodorus calls this little treatise a *voluptuosa digressio,* then gives Boethius his instructions: "Please name the *citharoedus* we have requested from you; he will be another Orpheus, taming the hard hearts of these foreigners [*gentiles*] with sweet music" (*Var.* 2.40.17). But this precisely calls into question the digressiveness of the whole letter. For the theme of the discussion of music has been its capacity to impart peace to the soul, to represent the peace of celestial harmony; and it is precisely peace that is the goal of the gift itself.

In fact, no more competent and learned case could have been made for the suitability of just such a gift at just such a time.

In the same letter there is a parallel case of a well-integrated bit of apparently digressive material, in the story of Odysseus and the Sirens. The familiar tale is repeated, mainly to show the power of music, culminating in Odysseus' successful escape from the Sirens. As Cassiodorus finishes this passage, he has also completed one section of his discourse on the effects that music has on men; he wishes to turn to the music of the Psalter as his next subject. His transition is effected by means of the mythical tale just concluded, turning from the last sentence of the tale to the next topic thus: "He had himself bound to the mast so that he could hear the Sirens' songs with his own ears but still escape the dangers of the sweet voices, prevented as he was from plunging to the foaming waves. In the same way, let us pass from the example of the crafty Ithacan to speak of the Psalter sent from heaven" (*Var.* 2.40.10-11). The transition is not strictly logical, but the neatness of the figure and its integration into the structure of the letter makes it possible, almost inevitable, that we overlook that. Our attention is propelled along happily without being too explicitly bothered about where it is being headed next.

A more doubtful example of the functional utility of rhetorical figures, and a more revealing specimen of Cassiodorus' practice, is a short letter to Faustus, the praetorian prefect, enjoining tax relief for inhabitants of the Cottian Alps suffering from the depredations of marching Gothic armies; to his command Theoderic adds the brief metaphorical statement that "The river continuously scours its channel and sterilizes it, leaving the surrounding country more fertile for its passing" (*Var.* 4.36.2). The figure is a neat one again, offering to modern readers, for example, a new way of considering what the effects of such an army's passing must have been like; it is less certain that Faustus really needed to be told such things. What has happened here, instead, is that the format has become fixed, requiring that every letter to come from Cassiodorus' pen have some literary pretensions.

The apparatus of classical learning is another bit of fretwork added to the more colorless business at hand. It is surprising, however, that there is so little formal classical allusion in the *Variae.* Apart from the silent use of such presumed sources as Ambrose or Pliny for the substance of digressions, there is very little dropping of classical tags, with or without acknowledgment. From the whole work, for example, there are only five explicit mentions of Vergil, three with quotations; and the quotations are not quite verbatim, thus probably from memory.[39] The explicit and implicit allusions in the *Variae* are almost exclusively from Latin literature, with only three allusions to Homeric events to demonstrate any familiarity with Greek legends.

Cassiodorus' other major literary habit is a taste for etymology common in late antiquity and almost extinct today.

That this particular trait was Cassiodorus' own is best seen when he makes extensive use of the science again in his *Expositio Psalmorum,* written far from the dictates of chancery style. One scholar has catalogued etymologies in the *Variae* ranging from the months of the year to musical terms to the names of provinces; as usual in late antique authors, they contain a mixture of fact and fiction.[40]

When all this literary baggage had been collected and Cassiodorus set out to produce one of his little masterpieces, the final effect achieved was neither unpleasing nor ineffective. From the preamble (frequently taking the form of a first premise of a syllogism developed by the letter) through the exposition of the subject (with time out for illuminating digression) to the final determination of the king's will, the line was actually very clear and direct.[41] Brevity is the reigning characteristic of the individual documents. The longest letters are those in which Cassiodorus had a personal interest; the longest in the whole collection is only 154 lines long in the most recent edition.[42] After that, the longest letters are to Boethius to provide a musician for Clovis and to the senate on the merits and ancestry of Cassiodorus' own father (*Var.* 2.40 and 1.4). Few of the other letters run to more than a hundred lines; the average length is approximately thirty-five lines. There is a certain tedium that affects modern readers of the *Variae* for two reasons, one unrelated to the original composition of the letters, the other unrelated to Cassiodorus at all. First, the original letters came to their audience only in small doses; while Cassiodorus argues in his preface that the variousness of the collection makes it read more quickly, even the first readers of the whole work must have felt some discomfort with such a vast collection of short, disconnected letters. But second, the original letters had an attraction that does us little good—that is, their strong topical interest. For us, to whom the events described are long ago and far away, and to whom the individuals are names only a few of which we recognize with any enthusiasm, the main attraction of the work for its contemporary readers is lost. If we can presume for this work, moreover, an audience still in love with rhetoric, the presence of its ornaments in these letters in such liberal and diverse portions was an added attraction of no little merit.

The formal shape of the letters has been altered in the course of compiling the whole collection in two ways that lessen their interest for us but that in fact increased their aesthetic attraction in Cassiodorus' eyes. First, there has been a wholesale deletion of names and dates to increase the timelessness of the letters published. Most names of legates to whom diplomatic letters were entrusted are gone, but in one case the names of two barns involved in a lawsuit have been reduced to "illud et illud" anonymity as well (*Var.* 3.29.2). But by no means are all dates missing, or all names; Cassiodorus the compiler functioned erratically on this one point.

Second, we have also lost the attached *breves* by which were transmitted particular details of the case for many of the more complicated issues treated.[43] In one case the letter preserved in the *Variae* is almost without significant content, merely exhorting the recipient to obey the commands specified in the attached *breves;* in another letter the attachment would have given the list of names of persons affected by the royal action (*Var.* 4.21 and 5.31.1).

Hard linguistic evidence both confirms our estimation of the kind of work this was and gives independent testimony to the level of culture still attained by educated classes of the sixth century. The language of the *Variae* has been studied from several aspects;[44] the sum total of the research demonstrates that the work's ties to Latin literary traditions are as strong in language as in rhetoric and style. Only two Germanic words are used in the whole work, both nouns for specific technical needs (*saio* for the kind of court functionary who replaced the *agens in rebus,* and *carpa* for a fish). There are a great many more words that occur for the first time to our knowledge in Cassiodorus, often formed by adding standard endings to old words to form new nouns (ending in *-or, -tio, -tas, -ius*) and otherwise orthodox in their Latin derivation. Moreover, very many recently coined nouns in *-tio,* adjectives in *-lis,* and adverbs in *-ter* are used. The most characteristic feature is the use of increasingly abstract words to replace existing words; the new words (whether coined by Cassiodorus or drawn by him from the usage of his day) are weaker in force but (superficially) more specific in meaning than classical equivalents. In addition to all of this, there is the importation of numerous Greek words (though none in such a way as to indicate that Cassiodorus himself knew Greek at this time).[45]

In syntax, Cassiodorus similarly represents the trends of the consciously literary language of his age. He runs into occasional trouble on matters of form (his use of the royal "we" is sometimes inconsistent even within a given letter), but he is clearly in command of the language to the extent that anyone was in his age. The vocative case is disappearing, to be replaced by the formal third person (e.g., *magnitudo vestra*), and the general use of demonstrative pronouns is far more abundant than in Caesar and Cicero. But nothing Cassiodorus does is without precedent in Silver or Late Latin, in the church fathers, or in other acceptable representatives of later style. His is a rhetoric of the schools to a fault, resulting in a highly artificial kind of work.[46] There is a tendency, difficult to isolate, to depart from the periodic style in favor of a monotonous alignment of clauses, against the boredom of which the excessive use of consciously flashy figures and language attempts to militate.[47]

Whether chancery style was a cause or an effect of some of these developments in the language is an unanswerable question. Certainly there was generally a shrill respect enunciated by all emperors for literary values that they did not always understand fully. Thus government language becomes characterized in general by euphemism and vagueness.[48] As an author, Cassiodorus does not transcend the literary faults of his environment; rather, he may be said to have attempted to find ways to circumvent them, to make virtues of the vices that had crept into the language he had been taught. The mannered style of late antique rhetoric was a home for him, a way of reacting against the boredom that sets in when an austere style becomes too familiar and thus contemptible.[49]

The most obvious thing about the language of the *Variae*, however, is perhaps the most important for an understanding of the work as a whole; namely that the language is clearly that of Cassiodorus himself, uninfluenced by Gothic elements. This is an important consideration for answering the most important question about the *Variae*, namely the degree to which these letters reflect the actual policies of the Gothic kings in whose names the bulk of the individual letters were written, and how much they simply show Cassiodorus playing with his rhetorical toys. Some scholars are too ready to assume that the letters can be taken as is to reflect the thoughts of the monarch in whose name they were drafted; others too skeptically assume that Theoderic was an illiterate who could scarcely understand the purport of the letters drafted for him, much less appreciate the literary art. It seems, in light of all that we know about Cassiodorus and Theoderic, that a middle position does least violence to the evidence.

There is unquestionably triteness in even the most intellectually central concepts that appear in the *Variae*, and with it further evidence of the evisceration of the natural force of language. It has been traditional to see this process at work in the concept of *civilitas*, which even the most superficial treatments of the *Variae* have distinguished as a central idea of Theoderician government. Indeed, if Theoderic were entirely responsible for the words uttered in his name, the presence of such a concept would be praiseworthy in the policies of a barbarian. But it is Cassiodorus to whom we must assign responsibility for the intellectual framework of the *Variae*, and we can be less lenient with triviality on his part. *Civilitas* is in fact part of a larger scheme of slogans that springs from the whole pattern of denatured language with which Cassiodorus loaded the *Variae*.

For it must be remarked that, for all the literary care that has gone into the *Variae*, the effect is not memorable; there is nothing so well put anywhere in these letters that it would bear remembering. There is everywhere in Cassiodorus a nostalgia for the epigrammatic brilliance of Silver Latin rhetoric, but this emotion is couched in a growing wordiness. Every epigram is taken out, examined from all angles, and belabored to death. In the preface to Book XI of the *Variae*, for example, Cassiodorus quotes a pithy anecdote to Cicero's rhetorical practice: "For that fount of eloquence is said to have declined an invitation to speak by saying that he had not read anything the day before" (*Var.* 11, Praef. 8). In the context of Cassiodorus' preface the remark has point and purpose, for he is pleading for mercy from his audience for the failings of his own ill-considered, hastily-published writings. But Cassiodorus is not content with Cicero's remark; he must elaborate it

through six more sentences. "What can happen to others, if such a marvel of eloquence has to demand the assistance of *auctores*? Talent grows ever rusty unless refreshed by reading." (This sentence in particular is limited to saying just what Cicero has already been quoted as saying, but saying it less memorably.) "The barn is quickly emptied unless replenished by continuous additions. The treasury is readily emptied unless refilled with money." (Illustrating the line of Cicero, Cassiodorus adds two gratuitous analogies.) "So human invention, when it is not stocked with other people's sayings, is quickly exhausted on its own." (He summarizes the main point again, perhaps misunderstanding it slightly—Cicero would have sought ideas, not words, from his reading. "Anything sweet-smelling in our prose is the flower of our studies, which nonetheless withers if cut off from its source, assiduous reading" (*Var.* 11, Praef. 8-9). (Finally a connection back to the thread of the preface's argument is made.)

In part the nature of the documents preserved in the *Variae* is responsible for this rhetorical weakness at the knees. Very many indeed are the royal letters in the *Variae* whose punch is pulled at the last moment with a final qualifier, in particular in legal cases where the facts admit of some doubt and Theoderic wants to circumscribe the effects of his rescript (e.g., *Var.* 2.29.2); in a more modern bureaucratic jargon, if anything goes wrong the monarch must preserve his "deniability" and shift the blame that may result from the case onto the shoulders of a bureaucratic underling.

As a matter of simple language, enervated terminology is everywhere apparent, particularly in certain terms that recur frequently; these words are almost totally devoid of denotative content, but they act as signals of royal approval or disapproval. It is precisely the famous slogan *civilitas* and its parallel terms that provide the best example of this linguistic spinelessness. *Civilitas* itself always refers in Cassiodorus to the actions of a citizen (as etymologically it should, as Cassiodorus would see). Behaving like a good citizen was something that Theoderic wanted to preach to his Goths, whom he was teaching to pay taxes; his remark, "*Civilitas* preserved is an honor for the Goths," was addressed to a Gothic military governor in Sicily (*Var.* 9.14.18).[50]

But Theoderic spoke more often of his own virtues than of his subjects', and in edicts and letters laying down the law, more often of wrongdoing to be avoided than virtue to be practiced. As a king and as a representative of Roman imperial traditions, Theoderic would not prescribe *civilitas* as a model for his own behavior; when he wishes to describe his own magnanimity, the term chosen more often than any other is *humanitas*—whether as a general quality or as a term for specific acts (even used occasionally in the plural in that restricted sense). This slogan is Ciceronian, of course, though it never really caught on in Latin, perhaps precisely because it was too vague and watery for most political purposes. But Cassiodorus must have thought it appropriate for giving a folksy touch to a lofty monarch, assuring the audience he addressed that the king was at heart decent and kind. At any rate, by a rough count *humanitas* and its immediate derivatives appear about as often in the *Variae* as *civilitas* and its derivatives.[51]

A word that appears about four times as often as either of these terms for the kind of behavior one hopes to cultivate is the blanket term for behavior one wants to discourage: *praesumptio*.[52] Etymologically, the term means a taking for oneself of something; in the *Variae* it usually means to do so in an unlawful or wrongful way. In particular it is a term favored in edicts to describe proscribed behavior; it appears eight times (*civilitas* appears twice) in the *Edictum Athalarici* in Book IX, and it appears three times, balanced with three appearances of *humanitas,* in the edict that ends the *Variae* (*Var.* 9.18, 12.28).[53] On the rare occasions in the *Variae* where the word does not refer to wrongdoing, it still has the sense of undertaking something vaguely undesirable; a general getting a new assignment is reminded that youth is benefited by such a task: "Iuvenum siquidem virtus praesumptione laboris animatur . . ." (*Var.* 5.25.1). In another case, the presumption is that of the king, presuming the loyalty and integrity of a fiscal officer (*Var.* 8.23.8).

In the generally negative sense of the *Variae, praesumptio* is often tied to *cupiditas* as effect in action of a cause in spirit.[54] *Praesumptio* can include crimes up to and including murder, but in later life Cassiodorus will use the same word to describe the blunders of scribes (*Inst.* 1.15.6-16). Thus the word has not been strengthened by Cassiodorus in the *Variae* to serve as a strong rebuke against criminal behavior; rather the rebuke has been weakened so far as to be summarized in the equivocal term.[55]

And so the pattern of cliché is complete: *humanitas* is the kind of behavior the king promises on his part; *civilitas* is the behavior he preaches as desirable from his citizens; and *praesumptio* is what he deprecates. These are not the catchwords of a vital political conception or a strong central administration; they are moralistic slogans, slogans that fail to inspire, bits of euphemism that assume definite meanings from being used so often but that in turn at least partially deflate what is being said in the name of verbal nicety.

It is thus in Cassiodorus' clichés that we find the traces of his policies. That the soul of his political purposes was thus entrusted to weak and hackneyed language, fortified with euphemism and shored up with triviality, was not a sign of any great strength of purpose or confidence in execution of design. To what extent this weakness mirrored an insecurity of Theoderic we do not know; it may have been imported gratuitously by Cassiodorus, since we have no certain knowledge of the roles that king and courtier played in drafting these documents and the ideas that lay behind them. But Theoderic was apparently pleased by the fainting language in the documents he was given to sign, and it is certain that in the end the weakness of the kingdom did in fact come to reflect the weakness of the language in which it was extolled. Whether it was Theoderic who got the kind of propaganda he deserved, or whether it was the propoganda that was as ineffectual as the government, we do not know.

In either case, the documents were the same precious little things, rhetorically and literarily self-conscious, meant to please, to edify and (usually) not to offend, and similar in their individual purposes to the purpose to which they would be put when collected into the *Variae.* For their function was nothing less than the justification, in the course of everyday business, of the Ostrogothic rule in Italy, on the grounds of political and imperial legitimacy, and the demonstration of the success of the kingdom when left to its own devices to establish and maintain an orderly society under a humane monarch, in spite of the barbarian origin of its leaders and many of its people. In a sense, therefore, the *Variae* began as panegyric but ended as a serious brief for the constitutional legitimacy of the whole kingdom, carrying the arguments and the supporting evidence in favor of the continued existence of the kingdom within the Roman empire. For the tragedy of the Ostrogothic kingdom is that precisely that subject of so much modern scholarly speculation, the constitutional position of Theoderic, was never clearly established; the Ostrogoths always occupied an ambiguous, delicately balanced position, in danger of overthrow at any time from several directions. In the end, the most fearful power decided to put an end to the ambiguity. As this was happening, Cassiodorus brought a lifetime of statesman's work to bear in this last work, presenting the case for the Ostrogothic kingdom as strongly and diplomatically as he could. But the forces then in motion were too great, too much beyond the control of individuals, to be called back by the voice of reason and the winged words of rhetoric.

As long as we witness Cassiodorus in his public *persona* as spokesman to the Latin literary world of the Ostrogothic kingdom, we are only allowed to see him as a diligent optimistic bureaucrat. His concerns are consistently those worldly problems of the conscientious public servant, diversified only by occasional, touching attempts to maintain as much external pomp of the Roman traditions under the new regime as possible. Thus the last letter we have in the collection written in the name of Theodahad, just before that king's murder and replacement by Witigis, just as Italy began again to know the ravages of war after Belisarius' invasion, is a marvelous, erudite, and even amusing discussion of the condition of certain bronze elephants on the *Via Sacra* at Rome that had fallen into disrepair (*Var.* 10.30).[56] When the king wants to have them repaired, he illuminates his letter with all the hoary legends about the elephant that were handed down from one ancient writer to another (Cassiodorus has what Pliny had, but is independent of him as well). For example, we are told that "a wounded elephant remembers the offense and is said to revenge himself on the perpetrator long afterwards" (*Var.* 10.30.6). Cassiodorus' elephants adore their creator and serve only good princes, opposing evil ones. In the midst of war, the king took time to speak of these things, and he concluded, "Do not let these images perish, since it is Rome's glory to collect in herself by the artisan's skills whatever bountiful nature has given birth to in all the world" (**Var.** 10.30.8).

This hopeless effort to preserve a memento of empire at the heart of Rome epitomizes much of what Cassiodorus had been trying to do for thirty years. There is quixotic nobility about this that weighs disproportionately heavy in any assessment of the virtues and vices of the man. If Cassiodorus was not, for most of his career, the most outstanding figure in the rank-conscious society of Romans at the Gothic court, he was still a consistent presence, loyal and ingenious after his own lights, and clearly still faithful until virtually the very end.

Notes

1. In Books I-X, there are 346 letters, 43 proclamations, 3 edicts, and 8 legal *formulae* (in Books VI-VII, 62 form-letters, 2 proclamations, and all 8 legal *formulae*); in Books XI-XII (in Cassiodorus' own name), 52 letters, 11 proclamations, and 5 edicts.

2. Augustine's friend Alypius was an incorruptible *consiliarius* for a *comes largitionum Italicianarum* at a very early stage in his legal career: Aug., *Conf.* 6.10.16.

3. *Notitia Dignitatum*, Occ. 10.3-5 (ed. Seeck, p. 147).

4. Knowledge of law as a requirement is specified in *Var.* 6.5.4; for other characteristics of the quaestorship, see *Var.* 1.12.2 (it is a "dignitas litterarum"), 1.13.2 (the man must be a *iuridicus*), 5.4.1-2 (his qualities at some length), 8.14.4 (his function as a publicist—cf. the allusion to his status as ghostwriter in 6.5.2, where he is said to make a "gloriosa falsitas"). The ideal quaestor has a degree of moral independence, however, which Cassiodorus shores up with traditional authority at *Var.* 8.13.5: "Renovamus certe dictum illud celeberrimum Traiani: sume dictationem, si bonus fuero, pro re publica et me, si malus, pro re publica in me." But note that this version does not repeat earlier versions surviving from antiquity (Pliny, *Paneg.* 67.8; Victor, *Caes.* 13.9) *ad verbum*, nor do any of those versions refer specifically to the quaestor.

5. As we saw in Chapter I, at this time actual membership in the senate was almost exclusively conferred by appointment to a post of the rank of *illustris*. But see *Var.* 6.11 for an apparent method for conferring the rank—and actual membership in the senate?—without any accompanying duties.

6. Amalasuintha did not marry Theodahad, as some assume, but only associated him to her throne; the phrases she uses include "producere ad sceptra/regnum," and "consors regni" for Theodahad himself; see *Var.* 10.3.2 and 10.4.1 for the latter phrase, which does not imply marriage in Latin. Theodahad was probably already married to Gudeliva, who appears officially as his queen after Amalasuintha's death.

7. Cassiodorus once calls the post of *magister officiorum* "quoddam sacerdotium" (*Var.* 1.12.4).

8. Abuse of the *cursus* is deprecated in *Var.* 4.47 and 5.5. By the sixth century the *cursus clabularis* (ox-drawn wagons for heavy hauling) seems to have been abandoned, leaving only the *cursus velox* (horses and light carts); Jones, *LRE*, 830-834. The Ostrogoths may have maintained arsenals at some of the following sites mentioned in the *Notitia Dignitatum*: Concordia, Verona, Mantua, Cremona, Ticinum, and Lucca.

9. For the *formulae* may in part preserve traditional material about the offices and in part tend to exaggerate the glory of the office for the benefit of the individual to whom the letter is addressed.

10. The famine in the last four letters of Book XII, once thought the result of the Gothic war, is now known to have been meteorological in origin: L. Ruggini, *Economia e società nell' "Italia Annonaria"* (1961), 321-341.

11. T. Hodgkin, *The Letters of Cassiodorus* (1886), 93-114, describes the *officium* of the prefect at length, appending a useful table comparing the pictures given by the *Notitia*, Cassiodorus, and John Lydus. Jones, *LRE*, 586-592, summarizes the material more lucidly; his information on the other details of the prefect's tasks is better than Hodgkin's.

12. *Var.* 1.26.2 shows one generation of bureaucrats referring to their predecessors' files.

13. The great difficulty that Cassiodorus would have faced in finding a way to record all the events of the period 519-551 without offending any of his potential audiences is, to me, another strong argument against Momigliano's claim that he kept the *Gothic History* up to date until 551.

14. Procopius, *De bello gothico* 1.3.2, also knows of Theodahad's avaricious ways.

15. *Var.* 4.39.1-2: ". . . avaritiam siquidem radicem esse omnium malorum, . . . Hamali sanguinis virum non decet vulgare desiderium, quia genus suum conspicit esse purpuratum." *Var.* 5.12.1: "Si iustitiam colere universos et amare praecipimus, quanto magis eos qui nostra proximitate gloriatur, quos omnia decet sub laude gerere, ut regiae possint fulgorem consanguinitatis ostendere. haec est enim indubitata nobilitas, quae moribus probatur ornata: quia pulchrum est commodum famae foeda neglexisse lucra pecuniae." Note the isolation of *fama* as a commendable target for acquisitiveness, where money is not.

16. *De bello gothico* 2.6.14-22.

17. Before even the preface, one scrap of text may be authentic and tantalizing without telling us much. In a single MS of the twelfth century there is transmitted the following elegiac couplet before the preface: "Iure Senator amans offert haec dona magistro / cui plus eloquio nulla metalla placent." (Fridh prints this

on his reconstructed title page as we would a book's dedication.) The use of the single name Senator has the ring of authenticity; that the line is transmitted only in one copy may prove only that it was transcribed (even at considerable remove) from a single original exemplar, a presentation copy for a revered teacher.

18. "Dictio semper agrestis est, quae aut sensibus electis per moram non comitur aut verborum minime proprietatibus explicatur."

19. T. Hodgkin, *The Letters of Cassiodorus* (1886), 136, erred in his note by assuming that a negative has dropped out of this line; he misses the parallel and contrast between *rudes* on the one hand and those *praeparatos* to serve the republic. The text is: "deinde quod rudes viros et ad rem publicam conscia facundia praeparatos labor tuus sine aliqua offensione poterit edocere . . ." (*Var.*, Praef. 8).

20. "Oratio dispar moribus vix potest inveniri." An aged commonplace; cf. Seneca, *Ep.* 114.1: "hoc quod audire vulgo soles, quod apud Graecos in proverbium cessit: talis hominibus fuit oratio qualis vita."

21. Cassiodorus is not likely to have used his terms loosely in bureaucratic connections; *dictatum* recalls precisely the function of the quaestor's office as quoted above ("leges dictandae," see note 3, above), thus canceling any impression this sentence might give that there was an essential connection between the offices held and the documents drafted in the king's name; as mentioned before, the contents of Books I through V and VIII through X are indistinguishable from one another in the sense that the same subjects are treated throughout irrespective of the offices Cassiodorus held at different times.

22. This line probably confirms that Cassiodorus was still on the job as prefect when compiling the *Variae*, and thus in touch with the royal archives (and secretarial assistance). But was he phasing out his activity and thus more at leisure than (as he reminds us throughout these prefaces) was his custom while serving as prefect?

23. "Librorum vero titulum . . . variarum nomine praenotavi;" cf. *Ordo generis*, line 14.

24. Cassiodorus is scrupulous about the inclusion in the *Variae* only of pieces he has himself written; it would have been easy to include some of Felix's work without admitting that someone else had written them.

25. The sequence of letters (*Var.* 3.20, in which Faustus is mentioned as prefect, and *Var.* 3.21, in which he is addressed only as "V.I."—which rank would remain if the office were removed) has inspired suspicion, which then fastens on the sudden appearance of the older Cassiodorus in *Var.* 3.28.

26. The case of Argolicus, urban prefect from 510, is only an apparent exception. Appointed in *Var.* 3.11, recipient of five more letters in Books III and IV, he is rather sharply rebuked in 4.29 for a fairly ordinary-

sounding bit of profiteering in office; he is seen again in 4.42 in unrelated business. Argolicus' reputation was clearly slight enough to be sacrificed to show Theoderic as a corruption-fighting king. By contrast, *Var.* 8.20, appointing Avienus praetorian prefect, cast aspersions on a nameless predecessor in that office (who almost surely must be Abundantius—cf. 5.16, 9.4).

27. One suspects that many letters in Book V, however, may still date from the period 507-511; but this cannot be proven.

28. Note that 2.27 and 4.43, as well as 3.23 and 4.13, are pairs of letters that have gotten separated by inadvertence. Another slip of the compiler is the presence of both 1.39 and 4.6, which are verbally identical descriptions of two similar cases (Cassiodorus was using *formulae* of his own all along, no doubt).

29. *Var.* 9.1 is the only letter to a German king after Theoderic's death; Besselaar, *Cassiodorus Senator en zijn Variae* (1945), 124, points out how this letter, full of threats and recriminations, exemplifies the decline of the policy that Theoderic had pursued towards his neighbors, which had led Cassiodorus, as abridged by Jordanes, to claim that, "nec fuit in parte occidua gens, quae Theoderico, dum adviveret, aut amicitia aut subiectione non deserviret" (*Get.* 58.303).

30. Besselaar, *op. cit.*, 163, identifies the two positions of honor, but claims that elevation of style is more important than addressee. As I show, content takes precedence over style and is on a par with addressee in determining position.

31. The beginning and ending letters are tied together most closely in the first three books, where Books I and II end with letters to Gundobad and Clovis (probably written almost simultaneously) offering attractive bribes furnished by Boethius as bait to win favorable consideration of peace initiatives; Book III begins with the dossier of letters that followed these gifts by some time, in which the motives of diplomacy are more explicit and, as events proved, more hopeless, however noble.

32. These two letters may date to before and after the appearance at court and may be meant to show the workings of the king's justice in some detail. Our view is distorted because we can see only the indictment and/or the execution, never the legal process itself.

33. *Var.* 1.35, the sucking-fish letter (discussed below) is a good example of the gentle chiding at which Theoderic excelled when Cassiodorus wrote the words.

34. The over-sensitive distinction between *Brief* and *Epistel*, which Besselaar, *Cassiodorus Senator en zijn Variae* (1945), 127, applies to Cassiodorus (stemming from theories of A. Diesmann), has been confuted by Å. J. Fridh, *Terminologie et formules dans les "Variae"* (1956), 3-4.

35. Letters that pause to praise Cassiodorus' home province (Lucania et Bruttii) include 3.8, 8.31-33, 9.3-4, 11.39.3 (the first "for example" that comes to his mind), 12.5, and 12.12-15; this probably shows a combination of native bias and a half-random search of the files. See also 2.29-30, clearly pulled from the "Milan" file together, though otherwise unrelated.

36. H. F. A. Nickstadt, *De digressionibus quibus in Variis usus est Cassiodorus* (1921) on the digressions; see also Å J. Fridh, *Terminologie et formules dans les "Variae"* (1956), 18-19.

37. *Var.* 5.2.15 cites Tacitus' *Germania* on the origins of amber.

38. Ambrose, *Hexameron*, 5.10.31; Nickstadt, *op. cit.*, 22-23, showed the connection to Ambrose and listed parallel passages.

39. See Vergil slightly misquoted from memory in *Var.* 5.21.3 and 5.42.11, for example.

40. Besselaar, *Cassiodorus Senator en zijn Variae* (1945), 145-147, identified forty-three uses of etymology (not all noted in Traube's index to Mommsen's edition).

41. On the preamble to the typical letter, see my remarks above and Å. J. Fridh, *Terminologie et formules dans les "Variae"* (1956), 30-59.

42. *Var.* 11.1, in which Cassiodorus announced his own appointment as prefect to the senate.

43. For this practice in the strictly personal letter-writing of late antiquity, see J. F. Matthews, "The Letters of Symmachus," in J. W. Binns, ed., *Latin Literature of the Fourth Century* (1974), 48-99, esp. 63-81. He shows how our valuation of trivia and substance is exactly the reverse of the late antique taste; we think the elegant letters preserved intentionally are trivial, hankering after concrete information that the disdainful ancients consigned to their attached memos.

44. On the language of the *Variae*, see Å J. Fridh, *Terminologie et formules dans les "Variae"* (1956); also his *Études critiques et syntaxiques sur les Variae de Cassiodore* (1950), and his *Contributions à la critique et à l'interprétation des Variae de Cassiodore* (1968), all prolegomena to his Corpus Christianorum edition (1973). There are several dissertations from the Catholic University of America on Cassiodorus; for the *Variae*, see B. H. Skahill, *The Syntax of the Variae of Cassiodorus* (1934); M. J. Suelzer, *The Clausulae in Cassiodorus* (1944, but based on Garet's 1679 text, so compare H. Hagendahl, *La prose métrique d'Arnobe* [1937], 79-83, 257-260); and (best of all) O. J. Zimmermann, *The Late Latin Vocabulary of the Variae of Cassiodorus* (1944).

45. See O. J. Zimmermann, *op. cit.*, for the material in this paragraph. He points out that there was very little afterlife in Latin prose for most of the apparent neologisms in Cassiodorus (only 16 of 129 were ever used again by other authors).

46. Skahill, *op. cit.*, can be squeezed to produce this paragraph.

47. Å. J. Fridh, *Études critiques et syntaxiques . . .* (1950), 82.

48. R. MacMullen, *Traditio*, 18(1962), 364-378. See Besselaar, *Cassiodorus Senator en zijn Variae* (1945), 179, for a table of the frequency of formal verbs, contributing an air of authority and an appropriate number of syllables for a clausula, but little more, in the *Variae* and the *Institutiones*.

49. E. R. Curtius, *European Literature and the Latin Middle Ages* (1953), 273-301, for the mannerist theory of late antique and early medieval Latin.

50. "Gothorum laus est civilitas custodita."

51. By thirty-four times to thirty-one.

52. With its derivatives, *praesumptio* appears about 125 times in the *Variae*.

53. See *incivilitas* equated with *praesumptio*, *Var.* 7.39.2.

54. This is explicitly the case at *Var.* 7.9.3, often implicitly elsewhere.

55. One other term appears as a feeble prod to motivate good behavior: *fama* (cf. note 15, above). A desire for *fama* will preserve one from too much desire for lucre (*Var.* 1.4.8), for it benefits a patrician to seek that "quod et famam vestram possit augere" (*Var.* 2.11.3). This idea is never elevated to the rank of slogan, but it seems to contain a shrewder insight than many other trite expressions of the work. In approving a love of *fama*, however, Cassiodorus was closer to classical antiquity than to the church fathers. Augustine, *De civ. Dei* 5.12-15, was even shrewder than Cassiodorus in observing the way a love of glory replaced (sublimated?) lesser cupidities in the Roman scheme of values.

56. From 535/536; this was probably placed at the end of Theodahad's documents for the reasons enunciated above for placing similar letters at the ends of whole books.

Abbreviations

I. Works By Cassiodorus

Quotations from Cassiodorus' writings are always made from the editions cited below and identified in the ways indicated. In addition to the editions listed below, all of Cassiodorus' works are available in volumes 69 and 70 of *Patrologia Latina*, for the most part in the edition of the Maurist J. Garet (1679).

Chron. Chronica.: Entries cited by year (in the Dionysian reckoning B.C./A.D.) after the edition of Theodor Mommsen, *Abhandlungen der phil.-hist. Classe der kön. sächischen Gesellschaft der Wissenschaften*, 8 (1861), 547-596; reprinted with a shorter preface in *MGH.AA.XI* (Chron. Min. II), 1894. The full preface is in Mommsen, *Gesammelte Schriften*, 7(1909), 668-690.

Comp. Complexiones in Epistulas.: Cited by column and section from *PL* 70.1309-1422, which is a reprint of the edition of Scipio Maffei (Florence, 1721).

De an. De anima.: Cited by chapter and line numbers from the edition of J. W. Halporn, *CCSL* 96 (1973), which reprints Halporn's text published in *Traditio,* 16 (1960) 39-109; but the line numbers are not the same in both editions. Halporn's chapter divisions differ from all previous editions.

De orth. De orthographia.: Cited by page and line from the edition of H. Keil, *Grammatici Latini* (1880), 7.143-210.

Ex. Ps. Expositio Psalmorum.: Cited by Psalm (or, for the preface, by "Praef." and sometimes the chapter thereof) and line numbers from the edition of M. Adriaen, *CCSL* 97-98 (1958).

Get. Getica.: Jordanes' abridgment, titled by him *De origine actibusque getarum,* cited from Mommsen's edition, *MGH.AA.*V (1882), using the chapter and section numbers given there. When I wish to refer to Cassiodorus' original work in twelve books, I call it the *Gothic History.*

Hist. trip. Historia ecclesiastica tripartita.: Cited by book, chapter, and section, from the edition of W. Jacob and R. Hanslik, *CSEL* 71 (1952).

Inst. Institutiones.: Cited by book, chapter, and section, from the edition of R. A. B. Mynors (1937).

Ordo gen. Ordo generis Cassiodororum,: also known as the *Anecdoton Holderi.* Cited by line numbers from the edition given in Appendix I, below.

Var. Variae.: Cited by book, letter, and section, from the edition of Å. J. Fridh, *CCSL* 96 (1973). These references are equally valid for Mommsen's edition, *MGH.AA.*XII (1894).

II. Other Works

AJP: American Journal of Philology.

ALMA: Archivum Latinitatis Medii Aevi (Bulletin Du Cange).

Anon. Vales. Anonymus Valesianus.

BARB: Bulletin de la classe des lettres et des sciences morales et politiques de l'académie royale du Belgique.

CCSL: Corpus Christianorum, Series Latina (Turnhout).

CIG: Corpus Inscriptionum Graecarum.

CIL: Corpus Inscriptionum Latinarum.

CJ: Codex Justinianus.

Courcelle, *LLW:* P. Courcelle, *Late Latin Writers and Their Greek Sources* (1969).

CSEL: Corpus Scriptorum Ecclesiasticorum Latinorum (Vienna).

DA: Dissertation Abstracts (Ann Arbor).

DACL: Dictionnaire d'archéologie chrétienne et de liturgie.

DHGE: Dictionnaire d'histoire et de géographie ecclésiastiques.

Fliche et Martin A. Fliche et V. Martin, eds., *Histoire de l'église.*

HSCP: Harvard Studies in Classical Philology.

IG: Inscriptiones Graecae.

Jones, *LRE:* A. H. M. Jones, *The Later Roman Empire, 284-602* (1964), using pagination of the American edition to refer to the notes.

JRS: Journal of Roman Studies.

JThS: Journal of Theological Studies.

Lowe, *CLA:* E. A. Lowe, *Codices Latini Antiquiores* (1934-1971).

Mansi J. D. Mansi, *Sacrorum Conciliorum Nova et Amplissima Collectio* (1759-1798).

MEFR: Mélanges d'archéologie et d'histoire de l'École Française de Rome.

MGH: Monumenta Germaniae Historica. (AA = Auctores Antiquissimi.)

PBA: Proceedings of the British Academy.

PG: Patrologia Graeca.

PL: Patrologia Latina. (PLS = Patrologiae Latinae Supplementum [ed. A. Hamman].)

PLRE: Prosopography of the Later Roman Empire (ed. Jones, Martindale, and Morris).

Reg. Ben. Regula Benedicti.

Rev. Ben. Revue Bénédictine.

RTAM: Recherches de théologie ancienne et médiévale.

SC: Sources Chrétiennes.

SE: Sacris Erudiri.

Settimane Settimane di Studio del Centro Italiano di Studi sull'Alto Medioevo (Spoleto).

SMRL: Studies in Medieval and Renaissance Latin Language and Literature (The Catholic University of America).

S. J. B. Barnish (essay date 1984)

SOURCE: "The Genesis and Completion of Cassiodorus's *Gothic History,*" in *Latomus: Revue D'Etudes Latines,* Vol. XLIII, No. 2, April-June, 1984, pp. 336-61.

[*In the following essay, Barnish studies Cassiodorus's aims in writing his* Gothic History, *analyzes the circumstances surrounding the work's composition, and discusses how Jordanes came to write his summary of the work.*]

The history which Cassiodorus, one of the leading statesmen and literary figures of sixth century Rome, composed to celebrate the race, lineage, and achievements of his Gothic masters, is now known only through the illiterate epitome made and supplemented by Jordanes. Yet, even the so-called *Getica* are evidence of great value, both for Gothic history, culture, and legend, and for the impression which the barbarians made, or wished to make, on their Italian subjects. Neither that work, nor its original, were written in a political vacuum. In this article, I will investigate the purpose and circumstances with and in which the *History* was begun and ended, and those which prompted Jordanes to write his summary.

When, in 533, writing for king Athalaric, Cassiodorus announced to the Senate his own appointment as praetorian prefect, he praised his work on the *History,* especially the genealogy of the Amal kings. In his complementary address to the Senate, he eulogized the regent, Amalasuintha, by comparing her to a list of Gothic ancestors[1]. A substantial part of the *History* must have been completed by this time. How much? The *Ordo Generis Cassiodororum* tells us that *scripsit praecipiente Theoderico rege historiam Gothicam, originem eorum et loca mores XII libris annuntians.* H. Usener dated the *Ordo Generis* in 521-2[2], but few would now agree. His theory was based on its omission of the *Consolatio Philosophiae* from a list of Boethius' works, implying that Cassiodorus was writing before the philosopher's imprisonment (c. 523-525). As the *Consolatio* was politically controversial, that inference is very doubtful. The most recent editor, J. O'Donnell, dates the *Ordo,* in its original form, to 527-33[3]. I myself prefer M. Cappuyns' date of c. 537[4]. Momigliano has suggested that Cassiodorus' historical labours overlapped the reigns of Theoderic (died in 526) and Athalaric, and were begun in the last years of the former[5]. O'Donnell has argued that the *History* was prompted by the consulship of Theoderic's heir and son-in-law Eutharic, in 519, and must have been completed before his death (c. 522)[6]. His main proof is that the *Getica* record the ancestry and virtues of Eutharic at some length, but refer to his death, so to speak, only in parentheses[7]. The *Gothic History* is seen as the companion piece to Cassiodorus' *Chronicle* of 519. While, in the former, *Originem Gothicam historiam fecit esse Romanam*[8], in the latter, we have "the record of Roman antiquity which is made to culminate in the Gothic prince"[9]. The reference in *Variae* IX.25 to Cassiodorus *ostendens in septimam decimam progeniem stirpem nos habere regalem* has been seen as dating the genealogy after Athalaric's accession, he having only sixteen named ancestors; but the young prince could have been presented as *regalis* even before that event.

I am quite unconvinced by this theory. The notices of Eutharic form the strongest argument. But we should consider how clumsy and inadequate is Jordanes' abbreviation of the *History.* Moreover, praise of Eutharic may still have been very desirable long after his death, to shore up the shaky prestige of his son, Athalaric. As a literary parallel to the twelve book *History,* the *Chronicle* simply will not do. It is jejune and unoriginal, even by the unexacting standards of the genre. Furthermore, the two works differ on important points. Thus, in the *Getica,* the treatment of Ricimer, and his struggle with Anthemius, is much less unfavourable to Ricimer than in the latter[10]. The notices of Aspar's end show a similar inconsistency[11]. The *Chronicle* also records the rumour that Ricimer poisoned Libius Severus. The *Getica* do not[12]. The *Chronicle* represents the battle of Horrea Margi, in which a partly Ostrogothic army defeated Byzantines and their Bulgar federates, and gained possession of Sirmium, as a victory over Bulgars only. The *Getica* give a detailed account, in which the Bulgars are omitted, and the role of the Byzantines is made quite clear[13]. For some of these details and discrepancies, Jordanes may be responsible[14]; but, in general, they indicate a difference in date, and a change of mind, for scholarly or political reasons. It seems likely that the *Chronicle,* allegedly commissioned by Eutharic[15], inspired the Gothic rulers to order, to encourage, the production of the more ambitious *History.*

We can, in fact, suggest a very tentative *terminus post quem* for Cassiodorus' researches. Between his quaestorship, ending in 511/12, and his promotion to *magister officiorum* in 523, he seems to have been absent from the court. Although, when *magister,* his rhetorical talents were used to help out the quaestor's department[16], nothing in the *Variae* can be dated to his time out of office. Had he then been at court, he might well have done some "ghost-writing" for active officials which we would expect to find among his letters[17]. The *Getica* make extensive use of oral, Gothic sources. These would probably have been available to Cassiodorus elsewhere, but the court was the best place for them, and Theoderic himself the most suitable informant on the deeds of his ancestors, and his own career. We should note his conversations with Cassiodorus on "history" and natural philosophy[18]. It is very possible that much of the author's information on northern geography was owed to conversations with guests and envoys at the royal palace[19]. A good deal of the research for the *History* may, then, fall in the period 523-6, and it may well have been commissioned after the death of Eutharic[20].

This inference, however, is far from certain. Cassiodorus may have been too busy with his *History* before 523 to act as a "ghost-writer", though then at court. No one may have required his services in that capacity. Again, he could have been too busy to write history in 523-7, the period of his service as *magister officiorum.* A. van de Wyver suggested that the work was composed between 519 and 523, and between 527 and 533[21]. On the other hand, it has been argued that the phrase in *Variae* IX.25, *subito a litterarum penetralibus eiectus,* describing Cassiodorus' assumption of a military command on Athalaric's accession, implies more than just official letter writing[22]. The immediate context, however, is the account of his aid to the quaestor's office.

If at Rome, Cassiodorus may have done much of his literary research there—it was better equipped than Ravenna. Furthermore, his use of oral sources, as distinct from that made by Jordanes, is rather dubious. Mommsen argued that *Getica* 38, where the author rejects an oral legend with the words *nos enim potius lectioni credimus quam fabulis anilibus consentimus,* shows Cassiodorus to have denied any value to such material[23]. In fact, the passage looks more like an insertion by Jordanes; and, in any case, the author has at least considered one legend. We could support Mommsen from Cassiodorus' own words, *Tetendit se etiam in . . . prosapiem nostram* (sc. *Athalarici), lectione discens quod uix maiorum notitia cana retinebat"*[24]. Once again, however, the words imply that the author had some knowledge of the *notitia cana*. We should remember that large sections of the **History,** those produced by the identification of Goths with Getae and Scythians, will have been totally unknown to Gothic legend. In my opinion, Cassiodorus probably used oral sources in the compilation of the Amal genealogy[25]; and neither of these two passages can possibly exclude the Goths themselves as informants for the most recent events in their history. But certainly, literary sources will have dominated Cassiodorus' work, and could well have been collected before 523.

A further difficulty arises over the *Getica*'s treatment of the Vandals. Mommsen believed this to be hostile[26], which is what we would expect, if the **History** followed Theoderic's quarrel with the Vandal monarch Hilderic, in 523[27]. D. Bradley, however, has argued that most of the references to the Vandals are neutral, one rather favourable, and only two markedly hostile. This suggests a pre-523 date, since the two kingdoms had generally been on good terms, up to then[28]. But the favourable reference (*Get.* 169) commends the system for peaceful succession established by Geiseric. It ignores not only the rebellion of Amalafrida, widow of king Trasamund, in or after 523, but the execution of prince Theoderic, and others, for treason, about 480. The praise, in fact, is very reminiscent of Justinian's diplomacy, which represented his attack on the Vandals as a defence of Geiseric's constitution, overthrown by Geilimer's coup[29]. It is followed by a brief account of that war. I would, therefore, suspect this passage, from *per annorum . . .* onwards, to be a later addition to the **History,** made after the conquest of the Vandals, perhaps by Jordanes, or perhaps by Cassiodorus himself. Of the two really hostile passages, one (168) is a famous character sketch of Geiseric; the other (184) the story of how Huneric horribly mutilated his wife, a Visigothic princess, on suspicion of poisoning, and sent her home, so that *uindictam patris efficacius impetraret.* Bradley notes this passage as a difficulty for his theory, but fails to observe a possible topical reference. As Cassiodorus tells us, Amalafrida, king Theoderic's sister, also suffered on a charge of treason, which, allegedly, was never proved to the satisfaction of the

Goths: *Si successio debebatur alteri, numquid femina in eo ambitu potuit inueniri? . . . Nam etsi quodlibet negotium in tali persona fuisset enatum, nobis debuit intimari . . .* The execution was felt as an insult by *Gothi nostri,* her *parentes.* A threat of vengeance, though not stated, was clearly implied[30].

There are other points of comparison between the *Getica* and the post-522 *Variae* which suggest an origin in that period. Theoderic once received an embassy from the Aestii of the Baltic, bearing gifts of amber. *Variae* V. 2 (of 523-6), replying to them, cites Tacitus (*Germania* 45) on the nature of amber, and its collection by that tribe. *Getica* 36 refers to the same passage, this time on the peaceful character of the Aestii. *Getica* 120 tells of their incorporation into the Ostrogothic empire of Ermanaric; while the letter shows Theoderic as sending them his commands (*aliqua uobis . . . uerbo mandauimus*). With *Getica* 21, however, (*Thyringi equis utuntur eximiis*) we should compare *Variae* IV.1, probably written before 513, praising Thoringian horses. In *Variae* VIII.9, Cassiodorus refers to Gensimund, *toto orbe cantabilis,* who *uiuit semper relationibus.* This hero may be identical with the Gesimund of *Getica* 248; but Jordanes tells us no such story of him as appears in the *Variae.* Still, we should note the implications that Gothic history was at the front of Cassiodorus' mind at this time (526-7), and that it was reaching him in oral form.

I shall argue that Momigliano was probably correct in supposing that Cassiodorus went on adding to the **History.** If so, then these possibly topical passages may be no more than supplements to a work begun, and substantially completed, much earlier. There is, however, a slight indication that it was still unfinished in 533. Both the *Ordo Generis,* and the preface to the *Variae,* give its full length of twelve books, with a touch of pride. Not so the letter to the Senate, although considerable parts must have been in circulation by that time.

A starting date in 523-6 for work on the **History** is of great significance for our understanding of it. Those years were a time of crisis, in which Cassiodorus may well have been required to make political points of some urgency. M. Wes, for instance, has argued that it was commissioned to counter the supposedly anti-Gothic *Roman History* of Symmachus, which he believes to have been published after 519[31]. In fact, however, we know next to nothing of the tone or contents of Symmachus' work[32], and its date is extremely conjectural. Setting this theory aside, we have already noticed the possible effect on the **History** of Vandal relations, and of Athalaric's orphaned state. Wallace-Hadrill, indeed, has suggested that the Amal genealogy was especially needed to impress the pedigree conscious Roman aristocracy[33], whose loyalty was then both much desired, and deeply suspect. Worsening relations with Constantinople may help to explain the discrepancy with the 519 **Chronicle** over Horrea Margi. We should note that, early in the reign of Athalaric, the emperor was putting pressure on the Danube frontier of the Goths[34]. Cassiodorus' praise of the Gothic interest in natural philosophy (*Get.* 69-73) gains a new edge when we recall the charges of magic brought against Boethius in 523[35]. We should observe the general presentation of the Gothic role in Roman politics: usually friends and allies, except when foolish emperors refused their subsidies (*Get.* 89, 270; cf. 134f., 153ff.). Alaric's pious clemency at the sack of Rome is praised (*Get.* 156), as in the **Chronicle.** Theoderic, in his last years, was on doubtful terms with the Catholic Church. Much of the **History,** and some of Cassiodorus' finest writing, must have been devoted to the great alliance of Goths and Romans against Attila, and the battle of the Catalaunian Plains, although Aetius' advice to Thorismud after the fight (*Get.* 216f.) shows that tensions between the races were not ignored. Attila was allegedly stirred up against the Gothic and Roman world through the machinations of Geiseric (*Get.* 184). Honorius had been honoured when his sister became the bride of Athaulf, and the marriage struck terror into the hearths of the barbarians by uniting the Romans and the Goths (*Get.* 160, *quasi adunatam Gothis rem publicam*).

We should also observe the treatment given to the great barbarian *magistri militum.* Ricimer, as we have seen, is awarded high praise; and, so far as we can tell through Jordanes' version, the **History** probably described his part in the election of the Anician emperor Olybrius, while putting the blame for his civil war with the easterner Anthemius on the latter, who thus exhausted Rome (*Get.* 239, but Olybrius' family is not mentioned). The account of Aspar's end seems more sympathetic than the corresponding passages of Jordanes' *Romana,* and the *Chronicle* of Count Marcellinus[36]—he is described as *Gothorum genere clarus,* and (so too in the *Romana*) the detail of his Arianism is omitted. The young Theoderic was a hostage at Byzantium during the years of his ascendancy, and evidently recalled him with respect[37]. But Stilicho, the great enemy of the Senate, is savagely condemned, in a travesty of history. After the Senate and emperor had agreed to use the Goths as federates in the west, Stilicho treacherously attacked them at Pollentia, thereby leading his army to disaster, and causing the sack of Rome. The Goths are thus shown as natural friends of Senate and emperor, and enemies of their enemy. In the post-523 context, we should also remember that Stilicho was of Vandal parentage, not mentioned by Jordanes, and is shown as inviting the Vandals into Gaul (*Get.* 115; cf. *Rom.* 322). Yet, Theoderic's problems in those years, threatened by the hostility of Africa and the eastern empire, were ominously similar to those which had set Stilicho and the Senate at odds. (We should note, though, that the 519 **Chronicle** similarly distorts Pollentia). The praise given to Aetius, and the condemnation of Petronius Maximus (*Get.* 176, 235) also seem to correspond with senatorial feelings[38]. But the former is chiefly shown as the architect of the Romano-Gothic alliance. His murder by Valentinian III is not mentioned; but Cassiodorus' **Chronicle,** like that of Marcellinus, gives it, together with the murder of his ally, Boethius, grandfather of Theoderic's victim. Is this discrepancy due to omission by Jordanes, or to the embarrassing contemporary associations of the Boethian name?

The *Getica* seem to stress at once the legitimacy of Gothic rule in Italy, and its constitutional difference from imperial[39]. Theoderic asks leave from Zeno to go to Italy, and to free the Senate from a *tyrannicum iugum.* If he conquers, *uobis donantibus regnum illud possedeam.* Zeno commends to his care the Senate and people; and, eventually, Theoderic *Zenonemque imp. consultu priuatum abitum suaeque gentis uestitum seponens insigne regio amictu, quasi iam Gothorum Romanorumque regnator, adsumit* (*Get.* 291f., 295)[40]. If this account is Cassiodoran, and belongs to the original period of composition, its insistence on the king's legitimate, imperially appointed position as ruler and protector of the Romans—an insistence made rather at the expense of truth[41]—may have been meant as a sharp reminder to the Senate in those years.

More significant, perhaps, is Theoderic's dying establishment of Athalaric, and charge to the Gothic counts and chieftains: *eisque in mandatis ac si testamentali uoce denuntians, ut regem colerent, senatum populumque Romanum amarent, principemque Orientalem placatum semper propitiumque haberent post deum* (*Get.* 304). However, the succeeding comment that the Goths had peace, during the lives of Athalaric and Amalasuintha, while they kept that command, must either be due to Jordanes, or be a post-535 addition by Cassiodorus—more probably the latter[42]. It has been argued, we should note, that the **History** was carried down no further than Theoderic's invasion of Italy, since the *Getica* are so sketchy in their treatment of his war with Odoacer, and the subsequent events of his reign. But it seems unlikely that Cassiodorus would have stopped short at so interesting a moment; while the *Getica* continue to recall his other work, both in style and content[43].

Even so, it is still possible that many passages in the *Getica,* which we have seen as especially interesting in the context of the period, are, in fact, non-Cassiodoran. The difficulty lies in the transmission of the **History** by Jordanes, who broke off work on his *Romana* in order to write the *Getica,* and did so with unspecified additions of his own[44]. We can expect the two works to have influenced each other. Both, also, have much in common with the *Chronicle* of Count Marcellinus, and its continuation. Mommsen, editing Jordanes, explained the resemblances by arguing that Jordanes epitomized, and made extracts from, the annually updated *Fasti* of Constantinople[45]. He showed echoes of Marcellinus not in the *Romana* only, but also in the *Getica.* Cassiodorus could not have used Marcellinus, whose work finished in 534. As, however, there is no change of tone, the passages involved probably are not owed to Jordanes, and Cassiodorus, therefore, may also have used these *Fasti*[46]. But, by the time that he came to edit Marcellinus, Mommsen believed that Jordanes had drawn directly on him and his continuator for the *Romana,* while still maintaining the *Fasti* as an *ignotus* source, used independently in both works[47]. (Ensslin's theory, enlarged by Wes, that this source was the lost *Roman History* of Symmachus, has been completely refuted by Croke)[48]. Direct use of Marcellinus can also be plausibly argued in the case of the *Getica,* which show some striking verbal resemblances to the **Chronicle,** in the period after 410[49]. Cipolla even held that all the *Getica*'s notices of the last western emperors were added by Jordanes[50].

However, the author takes some care to integrate these with the main theme of his work, showing how the weakness of the western empire gave Euric his chance to expand the Gothic dominions in Gaul (*Get.* 237, 239, 244). Occasionally, there are notable parallels between the *Getica* and Cassiodorus' **Chronicle,** but not the *Romana* or Marcellinus[51]. Moreover, the discrepancies between *Getica, Romana,* and Marcellinus or his continuator, both in the Gothic Wars, and in their pre-476 narratives, are nearly as striking as the resemblances. In the latter area, for instance, we should notice the *Getica*'s variant account of the death of Petronius Maximus (235); its greater detail on the falls of Majorian, Anthemius, and Julius Nepos (236, 238, 241); and its more elegant and rhetorical account of Honoria's invitation to Attila (224). Yet, all these passages have considerable likeness to Marcellinus and the *Romana.* Indeed, at some points, the *Getica* echo Marcellinus more closely than do the *Romana*[52], or even contain material which is in the former, but not in the latter[53]. Again, in all three works, the Italian-born emperor Libius Severus *inuasit* the empire; but in the *Getica,* his rule is *imperium,* in the *Romana* a tyranny[54]. If the Marcellinus-related entries in the *Getica* were all Jordanes' own work, a much closer resemblance between all three would be natural. Many of the correspondences may be due simply to use of a common source, in the Constantinopolitan *Fasti,* which may themselves have had variant versions of events[55]. Some may still derive straight from Marcellinus, through Jordanes only[56]; but I suspect that, even in the *Romana,* Jordanes was independent of him. Thus, to take some parallel passages, Anthemius is *imperator* in Marcellinus, but merely *Caesar* in the *Romana*[57]. Only the *Romana* (238) give the detail that Zeno contrived the murder of Aspar; while, as we have noted, neither *Romana* nor *Getica,* unlike Marcellinus, mention Aspar's Arianism, although Jordanes probably made some anti-Arian additions to the *Getica* (132f., 138). Marcellinus describes Basiliscus as dying *fame;* but the *Romana* have *frigore,* and agree in this with the *Anonymus Valesianus*[58]. However, in the *Romana* in general, as a glance through Mommsen's edition shows, Jordanes was very capable of blending the details from various sources in his brief notices of events.

This may also apply in the *Getica,* where Várady argues for numerous combinations of Marcellinus with the unrelated Cassiodorus[59]. However, we must not only face the discrepancies from the *Romana*[60]; but, remembering that Jordanes' primary business was to summarize the **Gothic History,** we must also ask why he should suddenly have felt that Cassiodorus needed so much supplementing for events which he himself had handled. I believe that Cassiodorus, writing the history of eastern, as well as western,

Goths, turned, as he had not needed to in the **Chronicle,** to an eastern source, and also exploited it for some western events. The *Fasti* were probably used by Marcellinus, as well[61]. Be that as it may, the last years of the western empire had such relevance to the theme of the **History** that Cassiodorus must have given some account of them, and it is natural to suppose that Jordanes, on the whole, reflects him. While we can never be confident that any one of the problematic passages in fact derives from the **History,** we should be reluctant to reject it, and very reluctant to ascribe the general political impression made by this part of the *Getica* to Jordanes, rather than to Cassiodorus.

To turn to the occasion of the *Getica* itself, this work was written probably at Constantinople, and not earlier than the spring of 551[62]. Jordanes tells us that, while he was busy with his chronicle called the *Romana,* a friend, Castalius, asked him to epitomize the **Gothic History** (*Get.* 1, *Rom.* 4). He had some trouble in doing so: *quod nec facultas . . . librorum nobis datur, quatenus eius sensui inseruiamus, sed, ut non mentiar, ad triduanam lectionem dispensatoris eius* (sc. *Cassiodori*) *beneficio libros ipsos antehac relegi. quorum quamuis uerba non recolo sensus tamen et res actas credo me integre retinere. ad quos et ex nonnullis historicis Grecis ac Latinis addedi conuenientia, initiumque finemque et plura in medio mea dictione permiscens.* It is hard to know just how much to make of this last statement; but one part of the *Getica* is certainly Cassiodoran, the main Amal genealogy in 79-81, with its seventeen generations, corresponding to the claim of *Variae* IX.25. As the *Getica* give it, however, it concludes with the two marriages of Theoderic's grand-daughter. Matasuentha, first to king Witigis, then to Germanus, kinsman of Justinian; and with the posthumous child Germanus, whom she bore to the latter. This detail is also given in a second version of the family tree, with an account of the marriage of Matasuentha's parents, Amalasuintha and Eutharic (251-3). The actual narrative of the *Getica* (followed by a rhetorical postscript) ends with the words *Mathesuentham uero iugalem eius fratri suo Germano patricio coniunxit imperator, de quibus post humatum patris Germani natus est filius idem Germanus, in quo coniuncta Aniciorum genus cum Amalorum stirpe spem adhuc utriusque generi domino praestante promittit* (314).

Momigliano has argued that Cassiodorus had revised his **History** down to 551, that the abridgement was made with his approval, and that it reflects the wishes of certain Italian exiles for an Italy in which Goth and Roman could continue to co-exist. He bases this theory on the belief that the *Ordo Generis* shows Cassiodorus to have been related to the Anicians, Boethius and Symmachus. Proud of his connection with such a family, he presented Germanus as an Anician, where an ordinary man, like Jordanes, would simply have stressed his relation to the emperor. Furthermore, we know a Jordanes, bishop of Croton, to have been in Constantinople with Pope Vigilius in 550. Jordanes the author dedicated his *Romana* to a Vigilius; and part of the manuscript tradition calls him bishop, albeit of Ravenna. Cassiodorus and Pope Vigilius were associated at this time; and so too were the Pope and Cethegus, to whom the *Ordo Generis* is dedicated. On the urging of the latter pair, if Procopius' Γόθιγος is a mistake for Cethegus, Justinian prepared the great expedition of Germanus and Narses against Totila[63]. Vigilius later secured the publication of the *Pragmatic Sanction* which set Italian affairs in order, and he and Cethegus must have been the most active and influential of the expatriates[64].

Can this hypothesis be supported by a detailed examination of the text? First, Jordanes describes the **Gothic History** as *ab olim et usque nunc per generationes regesque descendentem.* (*Get.* 1). The phrase *usque nunc* could be translated as "up to the present day"; but it may mean no more than "up to this general period". Next, the crucial hope for the future of the two race: *praestante domino* is a very common Cassiodoran phrase[65], but this is its sole occurrence in Jordanes[66]. A letter of Cassiodorus on an earlier marriage of Amals and Anicii may also give a few slight stylistic parallels: *. . . cuius tempore meruisti coniugem regiae stirpis accipere . . . sed qui nostro iungeris generi . . .*[67]. However, Jordanes' own style was certainly influenced by his reading of Cassiodorus[68]; and we should compare the *item Amalorum stirpe iam diuisa coniunxit* of *Get.* 251, a rather redundant passage, which could well be one of Jordanes' insertions. So too, we cannot depend on Schirren's detection of Cassiodoran language in the *Getica*'s narrative of the Gothic wars. There may, however, be some force in his comparison of *Get.* 305, where Athalaric commends his orphaned state, and mother's widowhood, to Justin, with **Variae** VIII.1, in which Athalaric asks for the emperor's *tuitio*[69].

Did Cassiodorus then, in fact, continue his **History** after the death of Theoderic, its most natural point of conclusion, and go on adding to it up to 551, as a chronicle writer might have done? To judge by the manuscript title, he may have reissued his own *Chronicle* while praetorian prefect, but he did so without chronological extension. Moreover, in *Get.* 81, Jordanes promises *quomodo autem aut qualiter regnum Amalorum distructum est, loco suo, si dominus iubauerit, edicimus.* The promise can hardly be Cassiodoran. Is its fulfilment, therefore, all Jordanes' own? In *Get.* 9, we have a parallel: *. . . Scandzam, unde nobis sermo, si dominus iubauerit, est adsumpturus, quia gens cuius originem flagitas, ab huius insulae gremio . . . erumpens, in terram Europae aduinit: quomodo uero, aut qualiter . . . si dominus donauerit, explanauimus.* There follows a digression, a Tacitean description of Britain, perhaps deriving from Cassiodorus[70]; then (16), *Ad Scandziae insulae situm, quod superius reliquimus, redeamus.* It is certain that Cassiodorus gave an account of the origin and migration of the Goths[71]. Therefore, on this analogy, the *si dominus iubauerit, edicimus* of 81 does not mean that the Gothic War narrative is non-Cassiodoran. It may mean no more than "if my notes and memory hold out".

Moreover, the contents of that narrative differ in tone, perhaps significantly, from those of the *Romana's*. In the latter, Jordanes is contemptuous of Witigis's efforts at the siege of Rome: *per anni spatium quamuis inaedia laborans deludit* (*Rom.* 374). The *Getica* are more respectful: *ut leo furibundus . . . Romanas arces obsidione longa fatigat. sed frustrata eius audacia . . . aufugit* (*Get.* 312). Something may here be due simply to the different requirement of a Gothic history; but the *Getica*'s account is still more what one would expect of Witigis' former praetorian prefect, who had once praised his warlike qualities in a panegyric[72]. This speech was produced for the wedding of Witigis and Matasuentha. The *Romana* (373) describe the union as *plus ui quam amori*. They echo the phrasing of the continuator of Marcellinus; and Procopius also takes what was probably the official Byzantine view[73]. But this aspect of the marriage does not appear in the *Getica*'s notice (311). Sincerity, of course, was hardly expected of a panegyrist. In the *Consolatio Philosophiae,* Boethius both denounced Theoderic, and recalled with pride his recent oration in praise of him. All the same, Cassiodorus might well have found it embarrassing to show the fate of the unfortunate girl in such a light.

Such discrepancies, however, may be due to no more than the carelessness of Jordanes. Furthermore, we are again faced with the problem of the relations of *Getica, Romana,* and Marcellinus' *Chronicle*. Thus, where we read in the continuator, *Rauennamque ingressus Matesuentham nepotem Theoderici sibi sociam in regno plus ui copulat quam amore;* in the *Romana, et priuata coniuge repudiata regiam puellam Maathesuentam . . . plus ui copolat quam amori. dumque ille nouis nuptiis delectatur Rauenna . . .* ; and, in the *Getica, Rauenna profectus, Mathesuentam filiam Amalasuenthae Theoderici quondam regis neptem sibi in matrimonio sociarat. cumque his nouis nuptiis delectatus aulam regiam fouit Rauenna . . .*, Jordanes may basically be reproducing the continuator in both cases, with a few additions, whose differences are of no significance. Alternatively, he may have been excerpting from the *Fasti* of Constantinople, rather more fully than the continuator, but without consistency. We should also notice that the continuator has much information on the Gothic War, especially from 537-40, of which there is no trace in Jordanes. This suggests that either he was using a second source, or else the version, or versions, of the *Fasti* behind Jordanes had already been abbreviated when they reached him.

As in earlier sections, so in the area of the Gothic War, while *Romana* and *Getica* have much general similarity, each have much that is not to be found in the other, including verbal and factual parallels to the continuator. For instance, the *Getica,* and possibly the continuator, give the detail that Ebremud had encamped at Rhegium, or at least in Bruttium, when he decided to go over to Belisarius. The *Romana* do not[74]. *Getica* and continuator echo each other on Belisarius' march into Campania, and the sack of Naples. The *Romana* have a more detailed account, without such resemblances[75]. The *Romana* and continuator echo each other on the murder of Theodahad. The *Getica*'s version is rather different[76]. In general, the *Romana* have the livelier narrative of Witigis' coup, with use of direct speech. The *Getica* give more detail on the stages at Rome and Ravenna, and attribute Gothic suspicion of Theodahad to the surrender of Ebremud. The *Romana,* and, by implication, the continuator, give the loss of Naples as the cause[77]. If the end of the *Getica* were all Jordanes', we would expect fewer discrepancies. It is, therefore, very possible that Cassiodorus updated his history, using, like Jordanes, the *Fasti* of Constantinople, as he had done earlier, but giving them his own flavour, which was preserved for the *Getica* by Jordanes' notes. By the time that he wrote the **Institutiones,** he may have come to know of the continuator[78], but it is unlikely that he made use of him in the **History.**

However, not all in this part of the *Getica* is Cassiodoran. Jordanes probably added the notice of Liberius' expedition to Spain[79] (*Get.* 303), if not the excursus on Visigothic history under Theoderic, and following his death, which it concludes. Again, could Cassiodorus have stated that Athalaric ceded Gallic territory, *quod pater et auus occupasset,* to the Franks, who were threatening war[80]? It was, in fact, Witigis who made this surrender[81]. The problem may arise out of the return to the Burgundians in 533, following an abortive Frankish expedition, of territory annexed by Theoderic—but probably not Eutharic—in 523. During 532-4, the whole of Burgundy was taken over by the Franks. Jordanes' memory of the Cassiodoran narrative may have become confused; but, if so, his confusion seems to represent the affair rather more honestly than does Cassiodorus, in **Variae** XI.1.12. There, the concession appears simply as an act of generosity[82]. Again, *Get.* 313 seems to imply, erroneously, that Witigis was besieged at Ravenna for a very short time: *nec mora ultro se ad partes dedit uictoris.* Is this an insertion by Jordanes, or has he confused some Cassiodoran remark on the progress of the negotiations for surrender? If Cassiodorus dealt with the War at all, he must have mentioned this event.

Should the Germanus Postumus passage be included among these doubtfully Cassiodoran elements? Wagner has pointed out that the child was probably born about the beginning of March, 551. Therefore, the *Getica* were written not long after that date. The *Romana* were carried down into the twentyfourth year of Justinian (*Rom.* 4), which ended on March 31st, 551. The fact that Jordanes' two works coincided so closely in date with Cassiodorus' supposed final addition suggests that that addition is due to Jordanes only[83]. He does not notice that the passage follows a long hiatus in the narrative. The *Getica* bring the Gothic War down only to the surrender of Witigis, though with a notice of later Visigothic affairs. The *Romana* continue with the campaigns against Totila, and with events elsewhere in the Roman world. The discrepancy helps to confirm a Cassiodoran origin for the later *Getica,* if not for this passage, but the coincidence seems to remain. We should not make too much of it, since the date at which either work was completed is rather doubtful. They do not mention the battle of Busta Gallorum, fought at the end of June, 552; but Stein has strongly, though not conclusively, argued that Liberius' expedition (*Get.* 303) did not leave

for Spain until the spring of 552, while the battle between the Lombards and Gepids, of *Rom.* 386, probably occurred about the same time[84]. O'Donnell, on the other hand, has recently asserted that Jordanes' report on Liberius' appointment was only a rumour, and that the *Romana* were written in 551[85]. This glosses over the difficulty of the Lombard battle, and does not leave time for events in Spain, and negotiations between Justinian and the Visigothic rebel, Athanagild[86]. If Stein is right, then the *Romana* were only begun in the twentyfourth year of Justinian, perhaps some months before the *Getica,* while the two were finished a year after the birth of Germanus Postumus.

Again, it has been argued that kinship, through the Anicii, with Boethius and Symmachus, or even kinship of any kind, is not certainly claimed in the *Ordo Generis*[87]; that Germanus' Anician descent was probably on the father's side, which makes the reference to that family less surprising[88]; that, to the ordinary man. Anician descent would have seemed more impressive than a connection with the peasant house of Justin; and that the *spes* may be simply for the two families, rather than the two races[89]. In any case, both there, and elsewhere in the *Getica,* Germanus' imperial kinship is made amply clear[90].

Against this, we should note that Cethegus, the dedicatee of the *Ordo,* probably belonged to the Petronian branch of the Anicii[91]. Despite obscurities in the text, it is hard to see why Boethius and Symmachus should have been mentioned at all, unless they were relatives of Cassiodorus[92]. As far as the *Getica's* use of language goes, there is no reason why *generi* should not be translated as "race", rather than as "family"[93]; and only with that translation does the hope have any significance. Germanus had left two adult and distinguished sons by an earlier marriage; while, about this time, an Amal niece of Theodahad was married off to Audoin, king of the Lombards, and her brother made a Byzantine general[94]. The Anicii themselves still had many representatives. Neither family depended for its survival on Germanus Postumus. The *spem adhuc utriusque generi* is certainly racial and political. Furthermore, I do not believe that the stress on the Anicii, when combined with that forceful phrase, implies no more than a minor piece of imperial propaganda, designed to attract Italian loyalties to the emperor, in the same way that Matasuentha's remarriage was meant to appeal to the Goths[95].

Even if we take this reductive view of the passage, it still comes more naturally from Cassiodorus than from Jordanes. Momigliano's identification of the latter with the bishop of Croton, and of his friend with Pope Vigilius, is untenable. Not only does Jordanes call Vigilius *nouilissime ac magnifice frater,* but he hopes that *quatinus diuersarum gentium calamitate conperta ab omni erumna liberum te fieri cupias et ad deum conuertas . . . estoque toto corde diligens deum et proximum*[96]. The tone is that of a man addressing a worldly superior, but a spiritual inferior, who has not yet experienced *conuersio*[97]. As a *notarius,* however *agramatus* (*Get.* 266), Jordanes would have had to get the titles of great men correct, and to address them as befitted their rank. We should note, however, that he and Vigilius had a common friend in Castalius, described (*Get.* 3) as *uicinus genti* (sc. *Gothorum*), and so, probably, an Italian. Vigilius could have been a relative of the Pope, but the *Romana* have a far more eastern outlook than the *Getica*[98], suggesting that the dedication was to a permanent resident in the east. As for Jordanes himself, in *Get.* 39, he speaks of foolish tales about the Goths current *in nostro urbe*. The general context may be Cassiodoran[99], but the phrase sounds like a reference to Constantinople, and is probably Jordanes' own. Again, in *Get.* 132, he speaks of the eastern churches as *nostrarum partium omnes ecclesias*. The *Getica* contain a number of contemporary references which are personal in form, and almost all relate to the eastern empire[100]. A good many could still derive from Cassiodorus, since they are mostly prompted by events in Gothic or Germanic history; but we should observe how, at *Get.* 50, the Lazi are described as even now guarding the Caspian Gates, *pro munitione Romana;* or, at *Get.* 264, the Gepids' receipt of subsidies, *usque nunc . . . a Romano . . . principe.* In the *Romana,* unlike the continuator of Marcellinus, Jordanes fails to mention Totila's invasion of Lucania, an odd omission for a bishop of Croton[101]. His family was eastern, if partly Gothic, and he himself, before his *conuersio,* had been secretary to an eastern general, of Amal descent (*Get.* 266, 316). We know of several near contemporary easterners, lay or ecclesiastical, who transferred their careers to the west[102], but it is hard to see Jordanes as one of them.

A close concern for the joint future of Ostrogoths and Italian Romans is what we would expect from a westerner. Jordanes may have inserted the Germanus Postumus passage for the benefit of the western Castalius, and without real personal interest; he may have meant the Anician emphasis as a compliment to Cassiodorus; but it is easiest to assume that it was written by an Italian, with some political intent. And, although Jordanes asked Castalius *et si quid parum dictum est et tu, ut uicinus genti, commemoras, adde,* Cassiodorus, in view of the phrasing, is still the likeliest author. Setting aside his probable kinship, Anician blood is more likely to have impressed the Romans than the Constantinopolitans, less dominated by noble families[103]. Anicia Juliana, to whom Germanus may have been closely related, had kept up her connections with the west[104]. Many in Rome must have remembered that she was the granddaughter of Valentinian III, and daughter of the emperor Anicius Olybrius, whose reign, we should notice, does not appear in the *Romana.* A Fl. Anicius Olybrius was probably western consul in 526[105]. But Jordanes' personal opinion of Rome and its aristocracy, in 551-2, is shown by his *illo populo quondam Romano et senatu iam pene ipso nomine cum uirtute sepulto* (*Rom.* 373). Historically, the comment is a fair one[106]; but it hardly suggests either an Italian patriot, or an enthusiast for the greatest senatorial family. Whatever the role of Castalius, Jordanes' initial interest—note his *relegi*—in the **Gothic History** will have been stimulated by his ties with the Goths and Amals, rather than by concern for Italy and its nobility.

Momigliano sees the *Getica* as authorized by Cassiodorus. This, too, is hard to believe. So fastidious a literary artist would scarcely have submitted his *magnum opus* to the incompetent attentions of the *agramatus* Jordanes. Moreover, Jordanes' difficulties in obtaining the work do not indicate the making of an official epitome[107]. Indeed, *antehac relegi* may even imply that the steward's three day loan[108] had occurred some time before Castalius' request. Whatever the case, we must still ask why the work was needed at this moment, and at all. And, if Jordanes "pirated" the **History,** that raises a further question, why the highly political Germanus Postumus passage should have been added to a work apparently not meant for publication.

We seem to know little about the publication and diffusion of books at this period. There are signs that a high class book trade of some kind still existed in Italy, about 500[109], and we may suppose that productions of the chronicle or *Fasti* type found a good popular market. Cassiodorus refers, in the **Institutiones,** to *antiquarii* and *librarii,* fine copyists, lay or monastic, whose work, in the latter case, at least, might circulate *per diuersas prouincias;* but there is no indication that these were concerned with secular, as well as religious writings[110]. Monastic copying, in general, was becoming ever more important[111]. It might even be done for profit, and we have an example from the period of a Gothic clergyman, who was also an *antiquarius,* with a bookshop, or workshop, at Ravenna[112]. When Cassiodorus' contemporary, Arator, brought out his poem *De Actibus Apostolorum,* he gave highly popular recitals in the church of S. Pietro in Vincoli, at Rome. The work had received the approval of Pope Vigilius, who had allowed the recitation, and a copy had been deposited in the papal archives[113]. Presumably, others were sent to Arator's dedicatees, Florianus, and the Gallo-Roman Partenius. Some may have been sold to the general public in Rome, but for them we have no evidence, although the poem was fairly short, and its subject matter likely to appeal to the tastes of the day[114]. Again, when equipping the library of Vivarium, Cassiodorus had to send to Africa for an edition of Cassian and other works. Albinus on music was available only in a Roman library, if the copy had not been carried off *gentili incursione.* He had only hearsay knowledge of the work of Martianus Capella[115]. He owned some, at least, of the philosophical works of Boethius, but then these had special interest for him[116].

Some of these references concern Italy in war-time, or post-war conditions; but we may still ask how large a readership a new, monumental, and sophisticated history could have found, even before the invasion. Marrou has argued that *editio,* in the late Roman world, meant little more than the circulation of one exemplar, from which private friends, or perhaps enterprising *antiquarii,* might make their own copies[117]. *Variae* IX.25 indicates that court and senatorial circles were familiar with the existence, and perhaps with some of the contents, of the **Gothic History,** but then these circles were very small. For Cassiodorus, publication may have implied simply the distribution of a few copies to men of wealth and influence, possibly combined with recitals such as Arator gave[118]. The alliance against Attila, and the battle of the Catalaunian Plains would have made an impressive set-piece for public delivery. Hence, it is quite possible that, when he left Italy, he took with him the only copy of the *History* whose location could be confidently guessed. This would help to explain Castalius' request. We should notice that Jordanes is probably the only author to have made direct use of it, but that the use and manuscript tradition of the *Getica* seem to be entirely western. Yet, this also applies to the *Romana,* and the two works are associated in the best class of manuscripts[119].

Why, though, should an Italian have wanted to read a version of the *Gothic History* at this particular time? Totila had enjoyed great, if not complete, military success, but his erratic attempts to patronize Roman culture, and to win over the senatorial class, had been rather a failure[120]. At the same time, the Romans detested Byzantine troops and administrators[121]. Justinian, however, had obstinately refused to make peace, even on terms which would reduce the Goths to clientship[122], and Totila's position was weak. The Franks had rejected his alliance[123]. The marriage of Germanus and Matasuentha had shaken Gothic loyalties; and, although Germanus' death had meant a set-back for Byzantium, his army had been held together. About the time, perhaps, of the birth of Postumus, Narses was appointed to its command[124]. The final struggle was close, its outcome probable, and either result must have been awaited with dread. Many must have looked back to the days of Theoderic, when Italy was strong, relations with the emperor often peaceful, and Goths and Romans united. Some easterners perhaps despised the Goths, and disregarded the Italians[125], but others may have sympathized. Procopius praises Theoderic's regime with enthusiasm, and is very conscious of the protection which Gothic rule in Gaul and the Balkans had given to the Roman world. Justinian's breaking of their power had destroyed the stability of both regions[126].

Such men may have hoped that Germanus would arrive in Italy both as western emperor, and, by virtue of his marriage, as king of the Goths[127], who had once offered that joint position to Belisarius[128]. W. Wroth suggested that Matasuentha, at Constantinople, struck silver coinage as a monarch in her own right[129]. The literary sources are completely silent on such a plan; but those Goths who deserted Totila, on the news of the marriage, may have supposed Germanus to be coming as their king. Justinian, moreover, often vacillating and secretive in his schemes, may have thought it time enough to declare his kinsman's position after he had won the war. Once Germanus' death had ended the plan, it would have been an indiscretion for any historian to recall it. However, the birth of his son may have revived it for a time, in the minds of the Italian exiles[130], though probably not of the emperor. Amalasuintha, aided by an allegedly Romanophile Gothic general[131], had lately ruled Italy in the name of her young son. Her daughter might now play the same role, with the help of a Byzantine commander. Such a regime would supply the Italian

nobility with wealth, honour and influence in a way that the hated logothetes, representatives of a distant emperor, could not achieve. The commander hoped for may have been Belisarius. He was greatly admired by the Goths; and Procopius, by his denial that Justinian ever meant to send him back to Italy on the death of Germanus, implies that there were rumours of his possible return. Narses' appointment seems to have come as a surprise[132]. By the spring of 552, however, the latter's position must have been fairly secure. The hopes and intrigues of Constantinople will have been reflected in Italy, particularly at Ravenna[133]. Castalius, if a westerner, probably lived in territory firmly controlled by Byzantium, since he could correspond so freely with the east.

In these circumstances, then, Cassiodorus may have started to update and recirculate his *Gothic History.* Both to the Byzantines, and to the Amal legitimists, Totila was a usurper, and his achievements an embarrassment. Hence, perhaps, the narrative gap in the *Getica,* between the surrender of Witigis and the birth of Postumus. Circulation and revision will probably both have been discreet. Cassiodorus was no recluse. He was active in ecclesiastical politics, at least, and may already have been at odds with Justinian over the Three Chapters controversy[134]. He will probably have been conscious that the emperor would take a lot of persuading over Germanus Postumus. Wes sees Narses' appointment as a defeat for the exiles[135]. But, if the *spes utriusque generi* were to be fulfilled, someone would have to campaign in its support. In such a situation, the word *spes* is likely to imply more than just a private hope of the author. However, we should notice that the *Getica* draw no political implications from Matasuentha's remarriage. At some point, the *History* reached Jordanes, who read, and reread it more for the sake of his ties with the Goths and Amals than because of any special concern in the affairs of Italy. Nonetheless, he passed on his knowledge of the work to a politically interested Italian friend, and eventually epitomized it for him, embodying Cassiodorus' latest piece of propaganda, and perhaps attaching the *Romana* to the copy he sent[136]. But the politician author was not now concerned with the Italian circulation of the *History.* Constantinople was the city where you pulled the strings, and it was there that he meant his work to influence opinion.

With this situation, we might find a partial, but useful, analogy in the Laurentian Schism (499-c. 507). Pope Symmachus, in his struggle with his rival Laurentius, was supported by the pamphlet of the learned deacon Ennodius, and enjoyed the favour of cultured senators and churchmen. His followers also produced a quantity of brief, popular propaganda, including forged conciliar acts, and dishonest papal biography[137]. These are generally illiterate in style and grammar, and sometimes differ in their views on such crucial issues as the role of the secular power in ecclesiastical disputes, and the right of lesser men to judge the Pope. Not all, if any, can have been officially authorized, and all seem a world away from the barely comprehensible rhetoric of the elegant Ennodius. He may have met the authors, but they can have had little in common beyond their loyalty to the person of the Pope. Jordanes and Cassiodorus were united only by their interest in the Amal dynasty. Castalius was probably not a man of high rank[138], or of great learning. In general, those in Italy or Byzantium, who were involved in Italian politics around 550, may not always have agreed on their objectives[139]. And, even where they were agreed, they may not have co-operated consciously in their work.

Notes

1. *Variae* IX.25, XI.1 [ed. Th. Mommsen, *Monumenta Germaniae Historica, auctores antiquissimi XII* (Berlin, 1894)].

2. *Anecdoton Holderi* (Bonn, 1877), p. 73f.

3. *Cassiodorus* (Berkeley, etc., 1979), app. 1, p. 265.

4. Art. "Cassiodore", *Dict. d'Histoire et Géographie Ecclésiastique* XI [ed. M. Baudrillart *et al.* (Paris, 1937)], p. 1351, 1367f. The theory is based on a MS variant of *praefectus* for *praefuisset*. O'Donnell doubts the variant, and supposes the *Ordo* to have been interpolated after Cassiodorus' prefecture.

5. *Cassiodorus and Italian Culture of his Time*, in *Proceedings of the British Academy*, 41, 1955, p. 207-45, 217 [also in *Secondo Contributo alla Storia degli Studi Classici* (Rome, 1960); *Studies in Historiography* (London, 1969)]. But contrast his *Cassiodoro*, in *Sesto Contributo*, 2 (Rome, 1980), p. 49, seemingly suggesting composition in 511-23, but not necessarily finished in 526. Mommsen, editing Jordanes, *MGH a.a.V.1* (Berlin, 1882), p. XLI, supposed a date after Theoderic's death.

6. *Cassiodorus*, p. 44-7—finished "in or very shortly after 519".

7. Cf. *Getica* 81, 298f., with 304.

8. *Variae* IX.25.

9. *Cassiodorus*, p. 47.

10. *Getica* 236, 239; *Chron.*, a.471 (ed. Th. Mommsen, *Chronica Minora II, MGH a.a.XI* (Berlin, 1893-4).

11. *Getica* 239; *Chron.*, a.471.

12. *Chron.*, a.464.

13. *Chron.*, a.504; *Getica* 300f.

14. On this problem, see below, p. 344ff.

15. Cf. *Chron.*, praef.

16. Cf. *Variae* IX.24.

17. Cf. O'Donnell, *Cassiodorus*, p. 26f., 42.

18. *Variae* IX.24.

19. Cf. E. Lonnroth, in *Studia Gotica* [ed. U. Hagberg (Stockholm, 1970)], p. 59; Å. Fridh, *ibid.*, p. 68f.

20. Theoderic or Amalasuintha could have served to give information on Eutharic's supposed branch of the Amals.

21. *Cassiodore et son Oeuvre*, in *Speculum*, 6, 1931, p. 244-92, 249.

22. Cf. E. Wattenbach & W. Levison, *Deutsche Geschichtsquellen im Mittelalter*, 1 (Weimar, 1952), p. 72.

23. *MGH a.a.V.*1, p. XXXVIIf. For a survey of the problem, see C. Mierow, *The Gothic History of Jordanes* (Princeton, 1915), p. 20ff. N. Wagner, *Getica: Untersuchungen zum Leben des Jordanes und zur frühen Geschichte der Goten* (Berlin, 1967), p. 64-70, believes Cassiodorus to have used oral sources, but sees (69) no reason why this passage should not be Cassiodoran.

24. *Variae* IX.25. Cf. O'Donnell, *Cassiodorus*, p. 49, n. 21.

25. But contrast Mommsen, *MGH a.a.V.1*, p. XXXVIII, and the debate between Å. Fridh and J. Svennung, *Studia Gotica*, p. 69ff., deriving it from Ablabius.

26. *MGH a.a.V.1.*, p. VIIf.

27. For this, cf. Procopius, *Bell. Vand.* I.9.3ff.

28. *The Composition of the Getica*, in *Eranos*, 64, 1966, p. 67-79, esp. p. 74-9.

29. Cf. Procop., *Bell. Vand.* I.7.29, 9.10-13,19, 16.13.

30. *Variae* IX.1.

31. *Das Ende des Kaisertums im Westen des Römischen Reiches* (The Hague, 1967), p. 170, 174, O'Donnell's recent article, *The Aims of Jordanes*, in *Historia*, 31, 1982, p. 223-40, 236, seems unintentionally to reverse this argument.

32. Wes's reconstruction has been completely demolished by B. Croke, *The Chronicle of Marcellinus* (D. Phil. diss., Oxford, 1978), cap. 5.

33. *The Barbarian West, 400-1000* (London, 1967, 3rd ed.), p. 35.

34. Cf. *Variae* XI.1.

35. Cf. *Consolatio Philosophiae* I.pr.iv.

36. *Romana* 239; COM. MARC., a.417 (ed. Mommsen, *Chron. Min.* II). On the relation of these sources, see below, p. 344ff.

37. Cf. W. Ensslin, *Theoderich der Grosse* (Munich, 1947), p. 29f.; and, for a Theoderican anecdote of Aspar, *Acta Synhod.*, *MGH a.a.XII*, p. 425.

38. Cf. Wes, *op. cit.*, p. 132-5, E. Stein, *Histoire du Bas-Empire*, I (Bruges, 1959), p. 540; but contrast Croke, *diss. cit.*, p. 275.

39. However, the date of 476 for the end of the *Hesperium Romanae gentis imperium* may well be an insertion by Jordanes. The comment on the event appears nearly *uerbatim* in Marcellinus and the *Romana*.

40. *Romana* 348 is similar, but shows Zeno less enthusiastic, and Theoderic more overtly a client.

41. Zeno may have died before he could give his *consultum,* and Theoderic have assumed the kingship before his envoys had returned [cf. *Anonymus Valesianus* 53, 56f., ed. Mommsen, *Chron. Min.* I, *MGH a.a.IX* (Berlin, 1892)].

42. *principemque Orientalem* (which recurs in the comment) and similar phrases, occur twice in the *Variae* (XI.1, XII.20), and in *Get.* 139, 225, 304, 305; but never in the *Romana,* or in passages paralleled by Marcellinus.

43. Cf. C. Cipolla, *Considerazioni sulle Getica di Jordanes,* in *Memorie della R. Accademia di Scienze di Torino,* 2, 43, 1893, p. 97-134, 115f., 129f.

44. See below, p. 347.

45. *MGH a.a.V.1,* p. xxix.

46. *Ibid.,* p. xxxix. But the first edition of the *Chronicle* was carried down only to 518, and, Croke has argued, written shortly after (*diss. cit.,* p. 8f., with n. 2, 11f., 13f.). If so, Cassiodorus could have used it. But J. R. Martindale, *The Prosopography of the Later Roman Empire,* II (Cambridge, 1980), Marcellinus 9, on Cassiod., *Institutiones* I.17.2, suggests first publication c. 527.

47. *Chron. Min.* II, p. 53f.

48. Wes, *op. cit.,* p. 77ff., 110-22, cap. 5; Croke, *diss. cit.,* cap. 5.

49. Cf. Croke, *diss. cit.,* p. 223ff.; L. Várady, *Jordanes-Studien,* in *Chiron,* 6, 1976, p. 441-87, especially 455-80.

50. *Considerazioni,* p. 127.

51. Cf. Várady, *Jordanes-Studien,* p. 470, on *Get.* 236 and Cassiod., *Chron.,* a.457-8.

52. E.g. on the accession and death of Majorian (*Get.* 236 = *Rom.* 335, Com. Marc. a.457.2, 461.2), the death of Anthemius (*Get.* 238f. = *Rom.* 338, Com. Marc. a.472.2), the accession of Nepos, and the fall of Glycerius (*Get.* 239 = *Rom.* 338, Com. Marc. a.474.2).

53. Thus, *Get.* 165f., 172, 181 = Com. Marc., a.411-12, 425, 534, 445.1.

54. Com. Marc., a.461.2 (no judgement beyond *inuasit*), *Get.* 236, *Rom.* 335.

55. Cf. Croke, *diss. cit.,* p. 196—"document (or set of documents)".

56. The comment on the deposition of Romulus Augustulus, and the notice of the reconquest of Africa (*Get.* 172 = Com. Marc., a.534) are likely, but not certain, examples.

57. Com. Marc., a.467.1, *Rom.* 336. The *Getica* (236, 238) have the non-committal *princeps.*

58. Com. Marc., a.476, *Rom.* 343, *Anon. Val.* 43. O'Donnell (*Aims of Jordanes,* p. 237f.), ignoring the *Anon.,* draws the opposite conclusion. All three accounts show marked differences, as well as resemblances.

59. *Jordanes-Studien, loc. cit.*

60. As we shall see, similar arguments suggest that the post-526 section of the *Getica* is mainly Cassiodoran.

61. Cf. Mommsen, *Chron. Min.* I, p. 252, II, p. 46; but contrast Croke, *diss. cit.,* p. 200-205, for some doubts on this.

62. On the problem of date, see below, p. 352f.

63. *Bell. Goth.* III.35.9f.

64. Momigliano, *Cassiodorus,* p. 219-22.

65. For the *Variae,* cf. *MGH a.a.XII,* p. 571. It occurs 24 times in the *Institutiones,* perhaps written c. 560.

66. Compare his *diuino auxilio* (*Rom.* 317), *fauente deo* (*Rom.* 366), and *iubante domino* (*Rom.* 385, *Get.* 75). The latter two are also common in Cassiodorus. Cf. *MGH a.a.XII,* p. 542, 545; O'Donnell, *Cassiodorus,* p. 188.

67. *Variae* X.11.

68. Cf. O'Donnell, *Cassiodorus,* p. 52f.

69. Cf. Cipolla, *Considerazioni,* p. 130f., citing C. Schirren, *De Ratione quae inter Jordanem et Cassiodorium intercedat commentatio* (diss., Dorpat, 1858).

70. Cf. Wagner, *op. cit.,* p. 71-6.

71. Cf. the *Ordo Generis: originem eorum et loca mores . . . annuntians.*

72. *MGH a.a.XII,* p. 465-84, especially 473-6.

73. Com. Marc. (*Auct.*), a.536.7; *Bell. Goth.* I.11.27. . . .

74. *Get.* 308f., *Rom.* 370; Com. Marc. (*Auct.*), a.536.1, perhaps reading *Rhegii* for *regio.*

75. *Get.* 311, *Rom.* 370, Com. Marc. (*Auct.*), a.536.3.

76. *Get.* 310, *Rom.* 372; Com. Marc. (*Auct.*), a.536.5-6, perhaps restoring *eos qui* after *Rauennam.*

77. *Get.* 309f., *Rom.* 371-3, Com. Marc. (*Auct.*), a.536.3-7.

78. Cf. P. Courcelle, *De la 'Regula Magistri',* in *Rev. des Études Anciennes,* 56, 1954, p. 427f.; but contrast Croke, *diss. cit.,* p. 289-94.

79. Cf. below, p. 352f.

80. *Get.* 305, paralleled by *Rom.* 367, but not by Marcellinus.

81. Cf. Procop., *Bell. Goth.* I.13.14-29.

82. Another source of confusion may have been concessions made by the young Amalaric to the Franks and Ostrogoths, after 526. Cf. *Bell. Goth.* I.13.4f.

83. *Op. cit.,* p. 51.

84. *Hist. du Bas-Emp.,* II (Paris, etc., 1949), p. 820f. Cf. p. 534, 601; E. A. Thompson, *The Goths in Spain* (Oxford, 1969), p. 323ff. Momigliano (*Cassiodorus,* p. 233, n. 65), doubts this, but gives no reason.

85. *Liberius the Patrician,* in *Traditio,* 37, 1981, p. 31-72, 66f. Cf. his *Aims of Jordanes,* p. 239f.

86. It is unlikely that Justinian had instigated the revolt, which broke out in 551. Cf. Thompson, *op. cit.,* p. 324—arguments nearly as applicable for 552 as for 551. On Stein's chronology, Liberius had one campaigning season in Spain (*ibid.,* p. 326).

87. Cf. O'Donnell, *Cassiodorus,* p. 271.

88. Cf. Wagner, *op. cit.,* p. 51-6.

89. Cf. Croke, *diss. cit.,* p. 238.

90. Cf. *Get.* 81, 251, 314; Bradley, *The Composition,* p. 69.

91. Cf. Momigliano, *Cassiodorus,* p. 234, n. 78. By this time, the high Roman families formed a small and closely inter-related group.

92. But contrast M. Van Den Hout, *American Journ. Philology,* 69, 1948, p. 233ff. (review).

93. Cf. Bradley, *The Composition,* p. 71, n. 17.

94. *Rom.* 386, PROCOP., *Bell. Goth.* IV.25.11ff. The brother, with the elder sons of Germanus, helped Audoin against the Gepids.

95. Cf. Wagner, *op. cit.,* p. 56, for this view; *Bell. Goth.* III.39.14-21, for the effect of the marriage.

96. Cf. Mommsen, *MGH a.a.V.1,* p. XIV.

97. But Mierow, *op. cit.,* p. 8f., thought it appropriate to the Pope's misfortunes.

98. Cf. Croke, *diss. cit.,* p. 256-9.

99. Cf. Wagner, *op. cit.,* p. 71-6; above, p. 3f., and n. 23.

100. E.g. *Get.* 50, 74, 96, 103, 104, 107, 112, 113, 168, 171f., 264, 267, 273, 303.

101. Cf. Wagner, *op. cit.,* p. 47.

102. Artemidorus, Anthimus, Dionysius Exiguus, Dioscuros, and Theoderic himself, are examples.

103. But note a MS dedicated to Anicia Juliana, with a Greek epigram, honouring her Anician blood. Cf. A. Von Premerstein, *Anicia Iuliana im Wiener Dioskorides-Codex,* in *Jahrbuch der Kunsthistorischen Sammlungen des Allerhöchsten Kaiserhauses,* 24.3, 1903, p. 105-24, 110f.

104. For her correspondence with Pope Hormisdas, see *Collectio Avellana* (ed. O. Guenther, *Corp. Script. Ecc. Lat.,* 35 (Vienna, 1835-8)), nos. 164, 179, 198.

105. Cf. Martindale, *Prosopography,* II, Olybrius 7. Note *Variae* X.11: *Anicios quidem paene principibus pares aetas prisca progenuit.*

106. Cf. Procop., *Bell. Goth.* III.20.26ff., IV.22.4.

107. Cf. B. Baldwin, *The Purpose of the Getica,* in *Hermes,* 107, 1979, p. 489-92, 490f.

108. Várady, *Jordanes-Studien,* p. 449ff., believes *triduanam* to be approximate and conventional; but, anyway, a short time is meant.

109. Cf. B. Bischoff, *Scriptoria e Manoscritti Mediatori di Civiltà,* in *Settimane di Studio del Centro Italiano di Studi sull'Alto Medioevo,* 11, 1963, p. 479-504, 485ff., on luxury copies of Virgil. But the reproduction of established classics is rather different from the large scale publication of new and major books.

110. *Inst.* I.xv.14, xxx.1 [ed. R. A. B. Mynors (Oxford, 1937)].

111. Cf. Bischoff, *Scriptoria,* p. 486.

112. Cf. Cassiod., *Inst.,* I. xxx.1, John Cassian, *Inst.* IV.12, V.39; and, for the Goth, E. A. Lowe, *Codices Latini Antiquiores,* III (Oxford, 1938), no. 298; J. O. Tjäder, *Die Nichtliterarischen Lateinischen Papyri,* II (Stockholm, 1982), p. 96.

113. *Corp. Script. Ecc. Lat.,* 72 [ed. A. McKinley (Vienna, 1951)], p. XXVIII.

114. *Librarii* may have sold the religious poems of Avitus of Vienne, c. 500. Cf. his *Ep.* 52 (ed. R. Peiper, *MGH a.a.VI.2,* p. 80). For a 5th or 6th c. *librarius,* selling scriptures, at least, near S. Pietro in Vincoli, see D. De Bruyne, *Gaudiosus, un vieux libraire Romain,* in *Rev. Bénédictine,* 30, 1913, p. 343ff.

115. *Inst.* I.xxix.2, II.v.10; II.iii.20.

116. *Ibid.,* II.iii.18, iv.7. The *Theodorus antiquarius* who revised a text of Boethius may well have been an official copyist at Constantinople.

117. *La technique de l'édition à l'époque patristique,* in *Vigiliae Christianae,* 3, 1949, p. 208-224. For some doubts, especially for the earlier Roman period, see H. Van Der Valk, *On the Edition of Books in Antiquity, ibid.,* 11, 1957, p. 1-10, Cf., also, G. Bardy, *Copies et éditions au Vᵉ siècle,* in *Rev. des Sciences Religieuses,* 23, 1949, p. 38-52.

118. Mommsen (*Chron. Min.* II, p. 113) held that his *Chronicle,* at least, was meant for a plebeian readership at Rome; but that work is very unambitious.

119. Cf. Mommsen, *MGH a.a.V.1,* p. XLIV-LXX. It is unlikely that Agathias ever knew either *History* or *Getica.* Cf. A. Cameron, *Agathias* (Oxford, 1970), p. 118ff.

120. Cf. Procop., *Bell. Goth.* III.9.7-21, 20.22-31, 31.6-18, 32.6-19, 33.4, IV.22.2f.

121. Cf. *ibid.,* III.1.32f., 4.16, 9.1-5, 7-18, 17.10, 21.12-17.

122. *Ibid.,* IV.24.4f.

123. *Ibid.,* III.37.1f.; though IV.24.9f. indicates a doubtful armistice.

124. For the probable date, cf. Stein, *op. cit.,* II, p. 597, with n. 2; J. B. Bury, *History of the Later Roman Empire,* II (New York, 1958), p. 256, with n. 3.

125. Cf. Cameron, *Agathias,* p. 116ff.

126. *Bell. Goth.* I.1.26-31; III.33.1-9, 24.10-15, IV.24.6-8.

127. Cf. Wes, *op. cit.,* p. 189f.

128. Procop., *Bell. Goth.*, II.29.17-27.

129. *Catalogue of the Coins of the Vandals, Ostrogoths, etc., in the British Museum* (London, 1911), p. xxxvif., 80. The coin forms lack Italian character, but Wroth also suggests Pavia as the possible mint.

130. Cf. Wes, *op. cit.*, p. 191.

131. For the role of Tuluin, cf. *Variae* VIII.9-10.

132. *Bell. Goth.* IV.21.1, 6ff.

133. Note that certain Gothic exiles at Constantinople had once engaged in plots which must have been equally unwelcome to Justinian and to Matasuentha (*Bell. Goth.* IV.27.6, Com. Marc. (*Auct.*), a.540.5. The latter seems to give Witigis and Matasuentha a share in the proclamation of Heldebad, and the revolt of the Goths; but I suspect that the entry has been confused with a.540.3.

134. Cf. A. Cameron, *Cassiodorus Deflated* (reviewing O'Donnell), in *Journ. Roman Studies,* 71, 1981, p. 183-6.

135. *Op. cit.*, p. 191.

136. He also sent the *Getica* to Vigilius (*Rom.* 4).

137. For the influence of the affair on papal biography. cf. L. Duchesne, *Liber Pontificalis,* I (Paris, 1882), p. 213f., 228, 264f. P. Coustant, *Epistulae Romanorum Pontificum,* I (Paris, 1721), appendix, prints the apocrypha. For a survey, see W. T. Townsend, *The so-called Symmachan Forgeries,* in *Journ. Religion,* 13, 1933, p. 165-74.

138. In *Get.* 3, he is addressed as *frater carissime.* Contrast *Rom.* 4, *nouilissime et magnifice frater,* to Vigilius. But note that Castalius and Vigilius were friends.

139. Thus, the continuator of Marcellinus was very possibly an Italian exile at Constantinople, but one with a distinctly anti-Gothic attitude. Cf. Croke, *diss. cit.,* p. 296-300, 303ff., against Momigliano, *Gli Anicii e la Storiografia Latina del VI secolo d.c.,* in *Secondo Contributo,* p. 272f., who would assimilate him to the supposed milieu of Cassiodorus and Jordanes.

Postscript

I must thank Dr. B. Croke for permission to cite his thesis on the *Chronicle* of Count Marcellinus. Some of his arguments on the relation of that work to the *Romana* and *Getica* of Jordanes, and to Symmachus' *Roman History* have recently been published as *A.D. 476: The Manufacture of a Turning Point,* in *Chiron,* 13, 1983, p. 81-119. Readers should also note his *The Misunderstanding of Cassiodorus, Institutiones* I.17.2, in *Classical Quarterly* n.s. 32, 1982, p. 252-6.

S. J. B. Barnish (essay date 1989)

SOURCE: "The Work of Cassiodorus after His Conversion," in *Latomus: Revue D'Etudes Latines,* Vol. XLVIII, No. 1, January-March, 1989, pp. 157-87.

[*In the essay that follows, Barnish argues that many of Cassiodorus's writings, particularly those composed after he retired to his monastery, were designed to influence both the lay and clerical public in matters of politics, religion, and culture.*]

About the end of the year 537, Cassiodorus, former consul, Roman aristocrat, and elder statesman of that Gothic realm on which the mantle of the western empire had fallen, laid down his last office, the praetorian prefecture of Italy. His time was then being devoted to a collection of the documents which he had drafted as a civil servant. These **Variae,** he claimed, were meant as a memorial of his own labours and the virtues of his colleagues, and as a model of style for future administrators of less polished education[1]. This statement can be expanded on. The armies of Justinian were clearly winning their war against the Goths. The fate of the whole native Italian administration, and of such individual collaborators as Cassiodorus was now in doubt. The Byzantines were virtually to abolish the former, and to enquire rigorously into the official frauds and activities of the latter[2]. The collection may have seemed necessary, both as an apologia for the past, and as a piece of advocacy for a separate bureaucracy, even for a continuing Gothic role in Italy in the future.

To these twelve books of letters and *formulae,* with their worldly aims and content, he added, however, a thirteenth, a devotional treatise on the nature of the soul[3]. At the same time, he was already starting work on that giant commentary on the Psalms which, in extreme old age, he was to describe as the first-fruits of his *conversio*[4]. In 533/4, he and other high officials had come close to opposing Pope and emperor over a point of theological politics[5]. He may already have founded the monastery of Vivarium on his ancestral estates at Squillace, as the home for a devout retirement[6]; and, in 550, by now in Constantinople, he acted as go-between for Pope Vigilius in the Three Chapters dispute, and was called by him *religiosum uirum*[7]. Yet, even down to 552, he may have been updating and recirculating his propagandist history of the Goths, with the needs of Italy and his old barbarian masters in mind[8]. We might compare his noble near-contemporaries, the Decian brothers Albinus and Theodorus. The first of these was called *uir religiosus* by Pope Hormisdas in 519; a few years later, he was accused of treason at the court of Theoderic. About the same time, Theodorus, who had turned to a semi-monastic life, was used by Theoderic as envoy to Byzantium in a quarrel which combined religion and secular politics[9].

Conuersio, it seems, then, did not always imply complete withdrawal from the world. Yet, it certainly meant, at least in theory, a profound alteration of interests. J. J. O'Donnell has recently argued that it was a very gradual process for Cassiodorus, but one which meant an increasing loss of interest in public affairs, and ultimately stranded him at Squillace, a pious recluse, all but isolated from the great world, in which he had long played a leading part[10]. In this paper, I hope to show that much of Cassiodorus' writings and activities, both at Constantinople and Vivarium, was meant to influence a wide public, lay and clerical, in concerns of deep importance for the politics, faith and culture of the western Mediterranean world. The interests of the veteran statesman and litterateur may slowly have changed, but for many years they reached far beyond his cloister.

. . . . .

In 544, the emperor Justinian hoped to find a means of reconciliation with the Monophysites and unity in the eastern Church through the condemnation of Theodore of Mopsuestia (d. 428), and of certain writings of Theoderet of Cyrrhus (d. c. 455), and Ibas of Edessa (d. 457), the so-called Three Chapters. These men had been leaders in the Antiochene school of theology; in their exegesis, literal and methodical, opposing the more unrestrained allegorical interpretations of Origen and the Alexandrian tradition; in their Christology, stressing the human nature of Christ. The Nestorians owed much to them, but so too did more orthodox theologians. Directly or by implication, they had been vindicated at Chalcedon; and, in much of the Balkans and the west, where Chalcedon was a touch-stone of orthodoxy and demonstration of papal prestige, Justinian's move was strongly resisted.

The vigorous opposition of the African Church has been seen as an expression of discontent with the effects of the reconquest in 534[11]. The province had experienced military rebellion, acute Moorish raiding, increased taxation, and a slump in overseas trade. The Italians, along whom a bitter war was still raging, had even more reason for complaint[12]; and, as noted, some of Cassiodorus' more secular writing, at least, was directed to their problems. What was his position in the crisis which eventually split their Church until c. 700? His aid to Pope Vigilius, reluctant tool of the emperor, his friends, contacts or associates, and his own compositions all give guidance in this question.

In 550, Vigilius tried to win over the deacons Rusticus (his own nephew) and Sebastianus, rebellious defenders of the Three Chapters. His envoys were three clerics, Cassiodorus, and the patrician Cethegus, formerly *magister officiorum* under the Ostrogoths. The attempt failed, and the deacons were deposed. Those seven clergy who witnessed the sentence included the three former go-betweens and bishop Zacchaeus of Squillace. Zacchaeus was later in 553, to sign the Pope's first *constitutum*, condemning Theodore of Mopsuestia; and, on that, and on another occasion, he was associated with bishop Valentinus of Silva Candida, whom Vigilius had once made his regent in Rome[13]. The Cassiodori are known to have been much involved in the ecclesiastical politics of their home town[14]; and it is at least plausible that the bishop's position as a supporter of Vigilius was closely linked with that of his senatorial neighbour. Cethegus, perhaps related to Cassiodorus, was the dedicatee of his work of family history, the so-called *Ordo Generis Cassiodororum*. He had had to flee from Rome under suspicion of pro-Gothic treason; but, in Byzantium, was twice used by Justinian in efforts to reassure and reconcile the Pope[15]. We may assume that

he was friendly with Vigilius, not an extremist on the Three Chapters, but now solidly the emperor's man. Indeed he and Vigilius joined in urging Justinian to finish off the Ostrogothic king Totila[16]. Cassiodorus is not known to have shared in any of this activity[17]. Religious withdrawal may have been the motive, but it may be that his attitude was more ambivalent than his friend's. This second alternative is borne out by his other contacts.

At some point he read, and was impressed by, the *Institutes* of Junilus, probably written in 542, with their praise of the Nestorian teacher Paul of Edessa, and their introduction to the Antiochene exegesis of his famous school of Christian studies at Nisibis[18]. Junilus, an African civil servant at Constantinople, dedicated his book to the African bishop Primasius of Hadrumetum, initially a strong defender of the Three Chapters in the capital. Primasius' *Quid faciat haereticum*? was praised and twice cited by Cassiodorus in the **Expositio Psalmorum,** and, like his treatise on the Apocalypse, was in the Vivarium library[19]. With it, Cassiodorus cited the recent two books *De Duabus Naturis* of bishop Facundus of Hermiane in Africa, another and more stalwart defender of the Three Chapters at Constantinople. These may have been either a part or the whole of the *Pro Defensione Trium Capitulorum*, dated 547, and were also in the Vivarium library, where two other pieces of propaganda by Facundus may likewise have been copied[20]. In his polemical *Breuiarium Causae Nestorianorum et Eutychianorum,* the deacon Liberatus of Carthage, an official visitor to Rome in 534, made use of a recent Latin translation. This is clearly the *Historia Ecclesiastica Tripartita,* made by Epiphanius, a member of Vivarium, and ordered, and probably overseen by Cassiodorus[21]. He may also have used the *Codex Encyclius* of Chalcedonian letters, which Epiphanius translated at Cassiodorus' behest[22]. Writing between 555 and 566, most probably in 563/6[23], Liberatus may have obtained the works some time before, in Constantinople, or, more likely, have been sent them from Vivarium, as with texts procured from Rome[24]. Since the *Breuiarium* and *Codex Encyclius* occur together in their two best manuscripts[25], Liberatus may even have despatched a complimentary copy of his work to Vivarium. We know the foundation to have had dealings in manuscripts with Africa[26]; and, as we shall see, it probably maintained some contact with the African *monasterium Gillitanum* of abbot Felix, who had been associated with Rusticus and Sebastianus in their opposition to Vigilius at Constantinople.

This group of figures would seem to put Cassiodorus very much in the Three Chapters camp. Is the impression confirmed by the tone and content of his own writings? To take first the **Expositio Psalmorum,** this makes extensive use of the *De Trinitate* and *Tractatus super Psalmos* of Hilary of Poitiers. Facundus repeatedly held up this father as a model for the opposition to Justinian, owing to his resistance to Constantius II during the Arian controversy[27]. By contrast, the **Expositio** makes some use of Origen, and, in general, shares in the Origenistic technique of interpretation so objectionable to the Antiochene school[28]. Origen was a figure of some importance in the Three Chapters controversy. Liberatus tells how Pelagius, papal *apocrisiarius* and later Pope, pressed Justinian into condemning him, thereby striking a blow against Theodore Ascidas, his Origenist rival for imperial favour. Theodore retaliated by moving Justinian against the Three Chapters authors[29]. Not surprisingly, Facundus took strong exception against Origen, but both Pope and emperor also committed themselves irrevocably against him. Justinian's unreservedly hostile treatise is still extant; and Vigilius' condemnation is recalled in the *Institutiones* by Cassiodorus, who, by contrast, advises a cautious use of Origen[30]. Many years later, Pope Pelagius II and the Three Chapters schismatics of Istria still had hostility to Origen in common[31]. At the same time, Cassiodorus did not ignore Antiochene methods. R. Schlieben argues that, while western exegetes usually tended to combine the literal and allegorical approaches, he is still unusual in his close attention to the verbal content and literal and historical meaning of the text. His employment of theological tropology suggests some Antiochene influence, and his use of *diuisiones* to analyse the Psalms recalls the *hypotheses* in the commentary of Theodore of Mopsuestia[32].

The Christology of the work is also important for its relation to the Antiochenes. As studied by O'Donnell, this steers very much a middle course, condemning both the Nestorians and the Eutychian Monophysites. But it also emphasizes the two natures of Christ and the authority of Chalcedon in a way which would not have pleased an emperor who was seeking a compromise with the Monophysites[33]. One Christological exposition, with a lengthy defence of the two natures, begins, we should notice, by citing Hilary, and ends with Facundus' treatise and its dedication to Justinian[34]. As the same time, where Facundus uses Theodore's commentary on Psalm 44 to defend the latter's Christology[35], Cassiodorus avoids outright controversy in his own exegesis. Theodore on the Psalms was, indeed, specifically anathematized by Vigilius' first *Constitutum* and the Fifth Council in 553[36]. Cassiodorus follows them, and, like Theoderet (another commentator on the Psalms), tacitly rejects Theodore, in giving a Christological interpretation to Psalms 15, 21, and 68[37]. Like Facundus, though, he may even make some use of Theodore, as well as Theodoret, on Psalm 44[38]. Theodore's exposition of Psalm 8 had been condemned as tending to divide the two natures, but Cassiodorus may echo it, especially on v. 7, although he concludes with a firmly orthodox statement of Christology.

His attitude, then, seems to distance him from both sides, but especially, perhaps, from the official, for all the *Expositio's* dedication to Vigilius[39]. However, the spirit of the work, as regards the western, if not the eastern Churches, may appear in these words: *propheta populis beatam praedicat unitatem: ut qui se christiana religione constringunt, in una caritatis conuenientia perseuerent. Quod licet ad monachos quidam aptandum esse iudicauerint, nos tamen dicimus ad generalitatis concordiam pertinere, quoniam hoc non tantum monasteriis, sed universae pronun-*

tiatur Ecclesiae . . . non enim reluctor beatis monasteriis dictum, sed nec generalitati aestimo subtrahendum[40]. The comment which follows and develops this theme is noticeably free from the usual condemnation of heretics and schismatics; and it is clear that Cassiodorus did not have his handful of devotees at Vivarium in mind as the sole public.

The *Historia Tripartita* is similar in its attitudes. Much praise of Origen and his exegesis is translated from Socrates[41]. The account of the attacks made on him by Theophilus, who exploited him in the rivalries of his time, recalls Liberatus on the prelude to the Three Chapters quarrel. But the *Historia* has none of that partisan's rejection of Origen[42]; and, as for the imperial attack, Athanasius, whom Justinian had cited against him, is used in his defence[43]. At three points, though, the *Historia* does come close to an unreservedly pro-Three Chapters line. Firstly, in its use of the history of the condemned or suspect Theoderet, whose work on the Psalms, if employed in the *Expositio,* had gone unacknowledged. Secondly, in its adoption from that history of the theme of the Church's independence and superiority when dealing with the emperor. This emerges clearly in the dialogue between Constantius II and Pope Liberius[44], and in the account of Ambrose and the penance of Theodosius, an affair with which Facundus concluded the *Pro Defensione,* presenting it as a model for Justinian[45]. Thirdly, it takes over from Socrates and Theoderet high praise for Theodore of Mopsuestia, though, perhaps significantly, omitting a passage on the anti-allegorical exegesis of his master, Diodore of Tarsus[46]. Gregory the Great may have made some use of the *Historia* in the *Dialogues;* but for this praise he condemned it as contrary to the Fifth Council, by which the Three Chapters had been definitively rejected[47].

Yet, despite this papal ban, some of Epiphanius' work actually served the official side in the Three Chapters schism. Pelagius II was able to cite his version of the *Codex Encyclius* against the Istrian bishops, who were quoting a different, allegedly less accurate rendering, made by Facundus[48]. It may be significant that, in the same letter, he stressed that only Theoderet's attack on Cyril was condemned. There, perhaps, and in the *Historia Tripartita,* we find some reflection of a will to compromise, comparable to the first *constitutum* of Vigilius, signed by Zacchaeus of Squillace, which anathematized Theodore of Mopsuestia only[49].

The *Expositio,* though revised at Vivarium, was mainly a product of Cassiodorus' life at Constantinople. The model for the *Historia Tripartita* was Byzantine, and its materials must at least have been assembled in the capital, wherever the work was done[50]. From the monastery itself, however, we have two more pointers to Cassiodorus' attitude. One of these is quite unambiguous. In the *Institutiones,* he carefully lists the ecumenical councils which have disciplined the Church, and confirmed and defined the true and ancient Christian faith. These are four in number: Nicaea, First Constantinople, First Ephesus, and Chalcedon. Fifth

Constantinople is ignored as totally as the heretical councils of Seleuceia, Rimini, and Second Ephesus[51]. The section, moreover, ends with a warning against those who ignore conciliar prohibitions against the raising of new disputed, and *putant esse laudabile, si quod contra antiquos sapiant, et aliquid noui, unde periti uideantur, inueniant*[52]. The **Institutiones** also recommend the *Codex Encyclius* to the monks, along with the acts of Chalcedon and First Ephesus, as a protection against heretical seductions; and we should recall that its manuscript tradition links it with a pro-Three Chapters corpus which includes the *Breuiarium* of Liberatus[53].

The second pointer is the dedication of the two churches at Vivarium. According to an illustration in the 10th century Würzburg manuscript of **Institutiones** I, one of these was devoted to St. Martin, the other to St. Hilary[54]. Martin, the founder of western monasticism, was a natural choice; and, as we have seen, Cassiodorus had been much influenced by Hilary's exegesis. As a pair, the two might imply anti-Arian attitudes in the monastery, not unlikely in the aftermath of the Gothic wars, and during the Lombard invasions[55]. But, as also seen, Hilary was something of a symbol for the resistance of western churchmen to state pressure; and Martin, with his opposition to Valentinian I and Magnus Maximus, could well have had similar connotations. His cult seems to have been introduced to Rome by the controversial Pope Symmachus (498-514)[56], at whose trial synod the superiority of the Pope to all but divine judgement had been vindicated. Symmachus had also taken a tough line with the emperor during the Acacian schism, an affair which Facundus and others saw as a model of the Three Chapters dispute[57].

If, however, the sympathies of Cassiodorus and his monks were distinctly on the side of the Three Chapters, they probably never impelled them to break off communion with the Popes, in whose suburbicarian territory they lay. Gregory the Great once received an appeal from Cassiodorus' foundation over a dispute with the bishop of Squillace[58]. In the **Institutiones,** even where his outright condemnation of Origen is rejected, Vigilus remains *beatissimus papa*. We might compare the attitude of Mocianus Scholasticus, just possibly identical with the Vivarian translator Mutianus. This probably African friend of Theodore Ascidas and acquaintance of Justinian had strong reservations about the condemnation of the Three Chapters; but in 553, he still criticised their defenders for wantonly creating a new Donatist schism[59].

Such ambivalence, shown here and elsewhere, demonstrates the continuity between Cassiodorus' secular and religious personae. As statesman and civil servant, he had survived four changes of regime and two *coups d'état*. He had worked first for the harmonious administration of Italy by Goths and Romans, then for some kind of reconciliation between the two races and the eastern empire. At no point can he clearly be seen either to have compromised his integrity, or to have become irrevocably identified with any one party. Inertia, the flexibility of a smooth politi-

cian, or sincere open-mindedness and dislike of faction? The **De Anima's** enigmatic little lament, *Inuidit (sc. diabolus), pro dolor, tam magnis populis, cum duo essent,* may confirm the more favourable alternative[60]. So too, the entry in his *Chronicle* for 514, his consular year, in which he seem to take credit for the end of the Laurentian schism. Again, as a religious scholar, he showed himself relatively tolerant in the use of heretical techniques and writings, though with suitable warnings and expurgations[61]. In general, though, we should see him as a representative of the vocal provincial and upper-class opposition to the growing absolutism of imperial rule in Church and state[62].

When Cassiodorus withdrew from Constantinople to Squillace, was he necessarily cutting himself off, as O'Donnell supposes, from the political and intellectual currents of the Mediterranean world? He may thereafter have travelled little, if at all[63]; but, at first sight, this belief still seems rather implausible. Generations of his family had used their estates as a power-base from which they had played a leading part in southern Italy and Sicily, and had joined in the wider politics of imperial and barbarian courts[64]. Squillace was not the world's end. Under Athalaric, it received an inconvenient number of official visitors, and the monks of Vivarium were later urged to show their charity to the traveller[65]. Under Byzantine rule, the deep south of Italy may have taken on a new importance. Carthage and Ravenna were now provincial capitals in the same empire, and the sailing route between the two passed close to Squillace. It also touched Syracuse. Sicily had long been an island of great senatorial estates, and the last representatives of that aristocracy in the west seem to have hung on there, in close touch with Constantinople[66]. A monastery at Taormina seems to have been linked with Vivarium—perhaps another Cassiodorian foundation on ancestral property[67]. Increasingly, too, the island was one of great church domains, belonging to the sees of Rome and Ravenna, and ever more important in the provisioning of mainland Italy. Bruttium, likewise, had its papal estates; and, though the peninsula produced little but cattle and timber, Cassiodorus noted the commercial merits of its situation, with its coasts open to both east and west[68]. Catanzaro, on its best southerly crossing point, and near Squillace, seems to have received its first development in the early 7th century[69]. Did Cassiodorus exploit, or hope to exploit, the geographical advantages of his foundation?

Of all physical labour, he wrote to his monks, *antiquariorum mihi studia . . . plus placere, quod et mentem suam relegendo scripturas diuinas salutariter instruunt et Domini praecepta scribendo longe lateque disseminant . . . tot enim uulnera Satanas accipit, quot antiquarius Domini uerba describit. uno itaque loco situs, operis sui disseminatione per diuersas prouincias uadit; in locis sanctis legitur labor ipsius; audiunt populi unde se a praua uoluntate conuertant, et Domino pura mente deseruiant; operatur absens de opere suo. nequeo dicere uicissitudinem illum de tot bonis non posse percipere, si tamen non cupiditatis ambitu sed recto studio talia noscatur efficere*[70].

If these words are to be taken seriously, he must have hoped that Vivarium would prove almost a religious publishing concern, serving the needs of the popular preacher, as well as the scholar or dévot, over a wide area. That they should be so taken is suggested by the central place which he gave to manuscript copying in the life of his monks. Better endowed, perhaps, than many of their contemporaries, they were freed by the rents of their *coloni* from the necessity of agricultural labour. Only the less academic-minded brethren might use it as a substitute for the intellectual service of God[71]. The copyists and editors were supplied with excellent advice, encouragement, and manuals, with skilled illuminators and book-binders, with self-replenishing oil-lamps of their founder's own invention[72]. He seems virtually to have introduced the methods and standards of the professional and secular *antiquarius* to his community[73]. *Scriptoria,* of course, dated back to the earliest days of western monasticism, but in no other house does their importance seem to have been so emphasised[74]. We might contrast Eugippius' foundation of St. Severinus at Castellum Lucullanum near Naples, known to Cassiodorus, and equal or second only to Vivarium as a centre for learning and the diffusion of texts. Its probable rule, compiled from Basil, Cassian, and the *Regula Magistri,* makes not the smallest mention of such pursuits[75].

Was Cassiodorus' hope fulfilled? How soon, and how far afield, were the manuscripts of his house distributed? It is not easy to say of any individual work that it, or its archetype was, or may possibly have been written at Vivarium[76]. Still, through listing texts that may arguably so derive, we can yet gain some cumulative evidence for Cassiodorus' influence, even though certainty in individual cases may be impossible.

The papal libraries of Rome are the clearest early beneficiaries. We have already noticed the *Codex Encyclius* and the *Historia Tripartita* as texts available to late 6th century Popes, although the works associated with the former suggest that its ultimate survival is not due to Rome. Perhaps they arrived as formal presentation copies, like Arator's *De Actibus Apostolorum*[77]. Other texts made the same journey: Vivarian volumes of the Bible, destined, maybe, to end up in remote Northumbria; Ps. Epiphanius on the Song of Songs; a corpus of Trinitarian works; and perhaps a corpus on the canonical epistles, another of Jerome, Gennadius and Augustine, and a copy of Eugippius' excerpts from Augustine[78]. Vivarium may also have played a part in the diffusion of the *Regula Magistri,* via a Roman *scriptorium,* but the work did not travel far afield at an early date[79].

Courcelle has argued forcibly that the Lateran library, not Bobbio, was the chief intermediary between Vivarium and the culture of Carolingian Europe[80], and for some texts this must be true. Yet, although the dispersal of the Lateran collection was well under way by the mid 7th century, the list of writings composed or attested at Vivarium and known in northern Italy is so long, and begins so early that I suspect some to have travelled there direct from

Squillace in the late 6th and early 7th centuries. The north made 6th to 7th century copies of Cassiodorus' speeches and *Complexiones*[81]. 6th to 7th century fragments of the Vivarian Josephus, from a northern copy, are preserved at Milan[82]. Of other Vivarian texts, a 7th century copy of Julius Honorius was in Verona, by the 8th century, at latest; and Gargilius Martialis was transcribed, probably in the north, c. 600[83]. (These may, of course, have been independently available in that area.) Junilus reached the north in a probably Vivarian text, not later than 800, and perhaps as early as the 6th century[84]. Mutianus' translation of Chrysostom on Hebrews may also have been palimpsested in the north c. 800[85]. *Institutiones* I was already popular enough in the north in the early 8th century to be abridged there, perhaps at Vercelli[86]; while the *Historia Tripartita* was in use there by the end of that century.

The latter text was than in the library of Paulinus, Patriarch of Aquileia[87]. That see had played a leading part in the Three Chapters schism, and we should ask whether Vivarium was used as a centre of schismatic propaganda. We have seen that the Istrians may have had their own, African text, superior from their point of view, of the *Codex Encyclius*[88]. Facundus they certainly owned. A 6th century copy of the *Pro Defensione* and *Contra Mocianum* was produced at a northern *scriptorium,* probably at Verona. (Significantly, texts of the Acts of Chalcedon, and of other works useful to the Three Chapters defenders, were also copied there[89].) Like the *Complexiones* manuscript, this may be a case of the rapid reproduction of a Vivarian archetype, but Cassiodorus' monastery cannot be definitely shown to have possessed the *Contra Mocianum*[90]. Moreover, the high quality of these manuscripts reminds us that Vivarium and Castellum Lucullanum were not the only competent *scriptoria* then working in Italy[91]. Despite the turmoils of the Gothic wars—Verona finally surrendered to the Byzantines only in 562—and Lombard invasions, the north still maintained its own cultural and religious activity. In view of such disturbances, and of alternative sources, it is interesting that so much Vivarian material should have found its way there—a sign, perhaps, of the care which the monastery took to circulate its copies; but it is also notable that this material was probably on the whole non-controversial. This agrees with our picture of a Cassiodorus who did not wish to exacerbate the quarrel, despite his support for the Three Chapters.

Do his links with Africa, following his return from Constantinople, give a similar impression[92]? During the latter part of Justinian's reign, African partisans of the Three Chapters were mostly in prison or in hiding, and the exchange of polemic literature, though not impossible, was far from easy[93]. Liberatus' copies of the *Historia Tripartita* and *Codex Encyclius* may or may not have been obtained from Vivarium; Facundus' writings continued to reach Italy, and perhaps Vivarium; and the *Monasterium Gillitanum* used the Dionysian *Easter Tables*[94]. In view of its abbot Felix's prominence at Constantinople, of Cassiodorus' friendship with Dionysius Exiguus[95], and of Vivarium's use of the *Tables,* the earliest known, to produce the *Computus Paschalis* in 562[96], Squillace seems the likeliest source for this acquisition. However, Dionysius and the African bishop Fulgentius of Ruspe (d. 533) had probably had a common friend in Eugippius[97]. The *Tables* could therefore have reached Africa earlier, independently of Cassiodorus. A similar problem arises over a Spanish *florilegium,* anti-Priscillianist and anti-Arian, apparently first compiled c. 600. This includes (a) an extract from Junilus; (b) four of Boethius' theological works; (c) a probably African corpus of anti-Arian texts[98]. Cassiodorus knew of Boethius' *Tractates,* as the *Ordo Generis* testifies, but he did not recommend them in the *Institutiones,* and they may not have been at Vivarium. The Junilus and Boethius may, then, have reached Spain either straight from Vivarium, or from Vivarium via Africa, or straight from Africa[99]. Boethius, too, was probably linked with Dionysius, and so, indirectly with African circles, and his Chalcedonian work may have interested Three Chapters defenders equally in Italy and Africa[100]. Considering Cassiodorus' expected consignments of Africa codices, it seems highly probable that he maintained friendships formed in Constantinople with the Africans, and likely that he sent them Vivarian manuscripts, but we can say little of their nature. The books he was awaiting seem to have been non-controversial[101], and his copies of the *Pro Defensione* and Primasius, if not of Liberatus, were probably acquired at the capital[102].

As for contacts nearer home, Cassiodorus probably had dealings in manuscripts with Castellum Lucullanum. The archetype of the 7th century Anglo-Saxon Echternach Gospels may have been corrected by Cassiodorus himself, using a text from the library of Eugippius which was said to have belonged to Jerome[103]. The *Institutiones,* with their praise of Eugippius, could well have been sent to his house[104]. To it, J. Fontaine has suggested, Isidore of Seville owed his early text of *Institutiones* II[105]. Lowe ascribed our oldest manuscript of "Ambrosiaster" on the Epistles to Castellum Lucullanum, where it was corrected in 570. However, a copy of the work was probably at Vivarium, and the text has an addition from another Vivarian piece, Rufinus' translation of Origen on Romans[106]. Probably in the late 6th century, the Campanian Dulcitius of Aquinum corrected a text of Hilary's *De Trinitate* and *Contra Arianos*—perhaps a significant choice—in accordance with the principles of the *Institutiones*[107]. The medical writers recommended by Cassiodorus also seem to have circulated in the south, and may have influenced the school of Salerno[108]. Finally, Schwartz was inclined to attribute the *Collectio Sangermanensis* corpus of Liberatus, the *Codex Encyclius,* and other Three Chapters material to a southern, rather than a northern *scriptorium,* though not, in its present form, to Vivarium itself[109].

Institutiones II may not have been the only Vivarian work to reach Spain. Junilus, and Boethius' *Tractates,* we have noted as possibilities. There are signs that Isidore also knew the *Expositio Psalmorum,* the *De Orthographia,* some of the grammatical treatises[110], the *Historia Tripartita*[111], and even the *Variae* and *De Anima*[112]. He probably

had the Boethian version of Euclid's *Geometry,* known to have been at Vivarium[113]. A Spanish compilation, dated c. 550-750, of Pelagian and other exegesis of the Epistles may well be his work, and certainly uses Cassiodorus' revision of Pelagius, as well as African material of the school of Fulgentius[114]. He has read, or at least knew of, the works of Primasius, Facundus, and perhaps Rusticus, and was firmly on the side of the Three Chapters[115].

So long a list suggests the possibility that Cassiodorus was sending manuscripts directly to Spain. His old colleague and acquaintance Liberius had commanded Justinian's expedition there in 552, and he could well have had younger successors with a similar past in Gothic affairs. The *Variae* would have been of peculiar interest to them. However, African or other non-Vivarian sources must remain an equal possibility[116]. It is worth remarking that Isidore's own work achieved a rapid circulation in Gaul and northern Italy during the 7th century[117].

The career of Venantius Fortunatus, and Arator's dedication of the *De Actibus Apostolorum* to Parthenius show the existence of cultural contacts between mid-late 6th century Gaul and Italy. 7th century Gaul may be the source of a compilation which included both books of the *Institutiones,* and from which the important Bamberg manuscript is descended, though Spain seems the likelier origin[118]. Either Spain or Gaul may have transmitted the Vivarian Josephus to Ireland in the 7th century, and the *Institutiones* perhaps as early as 600. There the latter influenced the grammarian Asper; and possibly, in its bipartite structure, the mysterious Virgilius Maro[119].

Fontaine has also suggested Constantinople as a source for Isidore's text of *Institutiones* II: Cassiodorus had sent his old acquaintances an early copy of the book, and this, or a descendant, was brought to Spain by Leander[120]. Whatever the truth of this, it is quite likely that the author maintained literary connections with the capital. When writing the *Institutiones,* he referred to the African émigré Priscian, assuming him to have written in Greek. This error was later corrected, and the library acquired a text of the grammarian, which was used in the *De Orthographia*[121]. Constantinople seems the likeliest source for this manuscript (though Syracuse and Africa cannot be ruled out): perhaps a return present for a copy of the *Institutiones* which was raising some Byzantine eye-brows[122]. Following the first draft of the *Institutiones,* Vivarium seems also to have gained a number of manuscripts of Boethius[123]. Constantinople and the circle of Priscian appear to have played an important part in the diffusion of his works[124]. Moreover, Vigilius' nephew Rusticus, working in the capital in 563-5, seems to have used a text of the letters of Isidore of Pelusium which was closely related to that employed by the possibly south-Italian, even Vivarian editor of the *Collectio Sangermanensis.* The collection of Three Chapters texts which Rusticus himself produced was probably being used in the Verona *scriptorium* by the end of the century[125], and we have noticed his *Contra Acephalos* as a possible traveller to Spain. There is, indeed, some palaeographical evidence for the transmission of Greek and Latin manuscripts, legal, theological, and other, from the east to Italy, and even as far as Gaul, in the later 6th century. Among these may have been a text of Malalas' _Chronicle_, which was used for book-binding by a 14th century south Italian scribe[126]. We should remember Cassiodorus' recommendation of the _Chronicle_ of Marcellinus, and his suggestion that his monks might find words to continue it[127].

Of all the Vivarian texts, those which achieved the widest early circulation seem to have been the _Codex Encyclius_, the **Historia Tripartita,** and the **Institutiones,** the last sometimes further adapted for profane learning[128]. We cannot say how often the despatch of a Vivarian manuscript was a response, by sale or gift, to a specific request, and how often an unsolicited present to a distant friend, or ecclesiastical superior[129]. (Earlier in the century, Eugippius seems to have shared in the exchange of texts amongst a religious and aristocratic circle[130].) What does seem evident is that, after all, the monastery did not withdraw completely from the Three Chapters dispute, although it was far less deeply involved than Verona. At the same time, its work in propaganda was balanced not by straightforward exegesis and theology, but by an educational text, keyed to religious purposes. This, as also the interpolations and collections from other sources associated with some manuscripts of **Institutiones** II[131], was not very advanced in character. The **Variae** and **Expositio,** which would have instructed in a more sophisticated way, figure little and doubtfully in our list. Such a demand, probably typical of the day[132], says little for the level of cultural attainments in the western Mediterranean[133]; but it does suggest that people felt their deficiencies, particularly, perhaps, in the secular arts, that they might look far afield to supply them, and that Vivarium had some reputation as a source. The **Expositio** shows that, at Constantinople, and even at Ravenna, Cassiodorus' concern for secular and religious politics was already rivalled by his educational labours. We should look more closely at them, and at the public to which they were directed.

Cassiodorus describes to his readers how he came to write the **Institutiones**[134]: _Cum studia saecularium litterarum magno desiderio feruere cognoscerem, ita ut multa pars hominum per ipsa se mundi prudentiam crederet adipisci, grauissimo sum, fateor, dolore permotus ut Scripturis diuinis magistri publici deessent, cum mundani auctores celeberrima procul dubio traditione pollerent. nisus sum cum beatissimo Agapito papa urbis Romae, ut, sicut apud Alexandriam multo tempore fuisse traditur institutum, nunc etiam in Nisibi ciuitate Syrorum Hebreis_ (sic) _sedulo fertur exponi, collatis expensis in urbe Roma professos doctores scholae potius acciperent Christianae, unde et anima susciperet aeternam salutem et casto atque purissimo eloquio fidelium lingua comeretur._ As war made this plan impossible, _ad uicem magistri introductorios uobis libros istos . . . conficerem; per quos, sicut aestimo, et Scripturarum diuinarum series et saecularium litterarum compendiosa notitia . . . panderetur . . . utilitas uero inesse magna cognoscitur, quando per eos discitur unde et salus animae et saecularis eruditio prouenire monstratur._

This preface raises a number of questions[135]. Did he and Agapitus intend their foundation to educate clergy and _conuersi_ only, or laymen too, who were still active in the world; to balance the secular schools, or to replace them? How closely did they take Nisibis as a model? How closely were Vivarium and the **Institutiones** designed as a substitute for the failed school? Could the **Institutiones** also have been addressed to that wider public which might once have attended it? How far was their stress on subordinate but serviceable profane learning a positive valuation; and how far was it consistent with the traditions of aristocratic and monastic Christianity in the west?

His strange apparent error _Hebreis_ makes me wonder how much, despite Junilus, Cassiodorus really knew about Nisibis[136]. However, even if his accurate information was slight, that school may still deserve a glance, and yield some points of comparison. Its students, who perhaps then numbered over 1000, seem to have been initially instructed in basic grammar and letters, with elementary dogmatic, exegetical and liturgical studies. Thereafter, they might move on to a higher course, perhaps involving advanced grammar, with rhetoric and philosophy, although these were still strictly subordinated to religious ends, and sophisticated exegesis and theology must have been included. Like Vivarium, the school had its _scriptorium_, which probably had an important effect in the evolution of written Syriac. Again like Vivarium, Nisibis (and its precursor Edessa) produced many translations, from Greek to Syriac, and from Syriac to Persian. Those made at Edessa may have included a version of Aristotle. Not strictly a monastery, as Vivarium was, Nisibis attracted monks, and had a semi-monastic discipline. Pupils who had finished their education may often have gone out as teachers to surrounding villages and monasteries, themselves perhaps founding their own schools of monastic type. Yet doctors from the town may have been allowed to attend its medical lectures, and it could well have been intended for the education of layman, in addition to monks and clergy[137].

If so, we should contrast Facundus, where he deplores the lack of theological schools, in words which may have influenced Cassiodorus' preface: _Solae in contemptu sunt diuinae litterae, quae nec suam scholam nec magistros habeant, et de quibus peritissime disputare credat, qui numquam didicit_[138]. The passage is clearly a hit at the lay theologians Zeno and Justinian; but the context, using analogies from the specialised traditions of various crafts, urges the complete separation of Church and state. The schools which Facundus favoured, I think, have been for churchmen only.

Augustine's _De Doctrina Christiana,_ to which the **Institutiones** are largely indebted, lays great stress on the use of rhetorical skills, suitably adapted by the Christian preacher or controversialist[139]. Although Nisibis had a considerable output of sermons, funeral orations and religious poetry, this possibility is not really taken up by Cassiodorus. The Ciceronian principle of the three levels of style and persuasion, to which he had once paid lip-service[140], does not

feature in the *Institutiones*. There is no sign of Augustine's serious concern to fit it to the needs of the Christian
congregation, a concern which must have played its part in
the birth of the *sermo humilis* of the early Middle Ages[141].
His monks were expected to do something towards the
conversion of their *coloni,* and the value of the oratorical
skills of memory and elocution for liturgical chants and
readings was also stressed[142]. He disapproved, however, of
wandering monks[143], and cannot have meant his flock to go
round the countryside like the near-contemporary Italian
abbot Equitius, that travelling preacher, with the scriptures
stuffed in his saddle-bags[144]. In book I, he emphasises the
use which the preacher might make of texts produced by
his *scriptorium*[145]; but, in II, there is generally very little
concern to integrate the functions of the secular studies
with religious life. On the contrary, the arts of rhetoric are
valued chiefly for their use in the secular world[146].

So too, where Augustine justifies the discipline of dialectic
as useful in religious controversy, Cassiodorus, in the *Institutiones,* at least, takes no such trouble[147]. Geometry is
useful to the surveyor, and astronomy to the farmer or
sailor[148]; though it is notable that the Vivarian *Computus
Paschalis* makes no use of the recommended literature on
the latter science[149]. Again, we should contrast Augustine.
Anyone using book II alone, as many did, especially in
editions shorn of much of their devout preface[150], would
have got the impression that the arts and sciences were to
be given in value almost independent of scripture[151].
Worldly utility apart, they might have been seen as ornaments to life, like the elegant polymathic digressions which
are so marked a feature of the *Variae*[152]. (In book I, Columella is recommended as much for style as for agricultural information[153].) However, they are also a means of
spiritual discipline, whetting the intellect, aiding the control of the body, and, above all, leading to the praise of the
creator by the intelligent contemplation of his works[154].

Such an impression would, of course, have been exaggerated. The two books of the *Institutiones* were planned as a
pair[155], and it was stressed that the second was needed if
those brethren who had not enjoyed the blessing of a classical education were to understand the fathers, and to make
the most of the scriptures recommended in the first[156]. The
Expositio Psalmorum shows a similar tension between its
aims and practice; it forms the educational complement to
the *Institutiones,* and embodies Cassiodorus' repeated
conviction that secular wisdom derived from the Jews; it
is genuinely devotional and theological; yet it often treats
the monks' most cherished biblical texts as a quarry and
advanced training manual of rhetorical figures, logic, and
other learning[157]. The structure of the Psalms is handled as
if they were secular and Ciceronian orations[158]. The principles were, again, taken from Augustine, but they were
used with a confident enthusiasm which Augustine did not
allow himself[159]. Cassiodorus carefully began and ended
the *Expositio* with a demonstration of the categorical syllogism[160]. The final example, drawn out from *omnis spiri-
tus laudet dominum,* leads into a summary of the Psalms
as replete with every kind of rhetorical trope and learned

discipline: *Ecce de grammatica et de etymologiis, de schematibus, de arte rhetorica, de topicis, de arte dialectica,
de definitionibus, de musica, de geometria, de astronomia
et de propriis lectionibus legis diuinae, seriem refertam
esse monstrauimus . . . ut qui talia legerint, gratanter ag-
noscant et qui adhuc rudes sunt, planissime dicta sine offensione percipiant.* Not only are the Psalms God's tool
for educating men; but, the context implies, their learning
and rhetoric are human tools for praising God, and even,
we find elsewhere, for defending him[161]. The catalogue just
quoted ends, though, with the *lex diuina;* and the *Expositio* returns, in its conclusion and prayer, to the Psalms as a
means of Bible-orientated devotion, and to an address to
the masters of sacred learning[162]. Yet, for all such efforts at
integration, it often strikes the reader as a work of literary
criticism, rather than of direct devotion and interpretation.
Much in it has small relevance to a student concerned with
the Psalms primarily for their religous content, as we
would expect of a monk. But, for those anxious to advance in practical eloquence and general education, while
simultaneously increasing their piety and religious knowledge, it might have been intended to form an acceptable
substitute for Cicero.

Such, perhaps, were the students whom Cassiodorus and
Agapitus had once hoped to train at Rome; and I think it
possible that an audience there, or at least beyond the
cloister, was still aimed at in the *Institutiones*. Even in the
later 6th century, Rome and other Italian towns still had
their educated men and teachers[163]. In *Institutiones* I, the
coming of Christ in judgement is likened to the coming of
the city prefect of Rome with carriage and heralds, as if to
an event familiar to the readers[164]. Another revealing passage may be the extensive praise given to Dionysius Exiguus: friend and fellow-student of Cassiodorus, skilled Gre-
cian and dialectician, an austere monk who yet moved
sociably and affably in the highest Roman circles[165]. Did
Cassiodorus hope that some of the readers would take him
for a model? Again, in book II, he refers to a treatise of
Albinus, *De Musica: quam in bibliotheca Romae nos habuisse atque studiose legisse retinemus. qui si forte gentili
incursione sublatus est, habetis Gaudentium . . .*[166]. This
is a puzzling passage. Gaudentius was an author translated
at Vivarium[167], which seems to imply that Cassiodorus is
addressing his flock alone. However, he does not refer to
efforts being made to procure the Albinus text, as was
done with others. His readers were, then, seemingly meant
to consult the *De Musica* in Rome, if possible; and Vivarian monks were not supposed to travel[168]. Possibly the
translation of Gaudentius was being put into circulation at
Rome. The *Institutiones* are, of course, intended primarily
for Vivarium—both books, especially the first, have many
references, bibliographical and other, to that community.
But we have only to look at the *Variae* and *Expositio* to
see that Cassiodorus did not necessarily mean his work to
serve a single public[169].

When considering this educational programme, however,
we should again bear in mind that the second book of the
Institutiones, the dry, technical digest, which did little to

explain or justify its content, probably circulated more widely than the first; that there is small evidence for the *Expositio* outside Vivarium before the 8th century; and that none of these works can be shown to have reached Rome[170]. Cassiodorus' public, even his monastic public[171], was seemingly most interested in his manual of secular studies. A religious bibliography they could, perhaps, have provided for themselves; and, anyway, its utility, where the books were not available, would have been small[172]. And, if few read Cicero, fewer still were prepared to accept the Psalms as an adequate or proper substitute.

It is, perhaps, easy to exaggerate the anti-intellectual, anti-classical strain in western monasticism and religious life[173]. Jerome seems to have thought a sound rhetorical education commendable for an intended Gallo-Roman monk, and authorship a proper aim. According to Rufinus—hardly an unbiassed source—he taught classical literature at Bethlehem, and kept his monks busy on lucrative copies of Cicero[174]. Sulpicius Severus engaged in much sophisticated literary activity at Primuliacum, as did Paulinus at Nola[175]. Lérins housed generations of traditionally educated men, and may even have had its own school, in which the classical texts were still used[176]. Vivarium was only the latest in a long line of country residences where Roman aristocrats, pagan and Christian, enjoyed a leisured and cultivated retirement[177]. Remembering its fish-ponds, perhaps we should see Cassiodorus as, if not the last of the Romans, at least as the last of the *piscinarii!* C. 527, as *magister officiorum,* he had tried to check the tendency of the Bruttian gentry to desert the towns for their rural estates. In a last and moving defence of civic society in the ancient world, he included an appeal for the liberal studies which flourished only in its competitive atmosphere[178]. After the failure of his plan for an urban school with a difference in Rome itself, Vivarium and the *Institutiones* seem an almost deliberate attempt to transpose the ancient education to the rural setting whose attractions had partly caused the decay of the cities which had formed it. And, both at Rome and Squillace, he was attempting another transposition. The theory of the Jewish derivation of classical culture[179] was an ancient commonplace; but, as he handled it, it became almost an equivalent to his *Gothic History.* By using the old identification of Goths, Getae and Scythians, he had brought his political masters into the familiar framework of Graeco-Roman history[180]: *Originem Gothicam historiam fecit esse Romanam*[181]. He now tried to move classical culture and its origins into the Judaeo-Christian frame-work. None of these endeavours had much impact in his own day.

If, as the *Expositio* and *Institutiones* suggest, he still took pleasure in the technicalities of the old culture for their own sake, did he still delight in its literature? He has sometimes, and misleadingly, been credited with its transmission, even with making a formal place for it in the monastic life[182]. Only once, however, does he overtly recommend a classical author for more than information; few literary texts seem to have been on his shelves[183]; and, to judge by the preface to the *Institutiones,* it was Christian learning which he saw as endangered, or at least as undervalued, by comparison with traditional studies[184]. Yet though, like Augustine, he sometimes has to defend the propriety of using profane learning[185], there is none of that prickly and apologetic attitude to the old authors which we find in the *De Doctrina Christiana*[186]. Jerome is praised for his use of the *gentilium exempla* to point his arguments and ornament his style[187]; Cicero is praised and cited freely and by name, although the oratorical quotations are perhaps at second-hand; Josephus is called 'almost a second Livy'[188]; Vergil is treated with peculiar affection and respect in a charming and important passage of the *Institutiones*[189]. Following an Augustinian defence of secular studies, it exhorts the more academic monks to the pursuit of God by intellectual means; the less to the rustic pleasures of farming and gardening.

Quod si alicui fratrum, ut meminit Vergilius, "Frigidus obstiterit circum praecordia sanguis", ut nec humanis nec diuinis litteris perfecte possit erudiri, aliqua tamen scientiae mediocritate suffultus eligat certe quod sequitur; "Rura mihi et rigui placeant in uallibus amnes", quia nec ipsum est a monachis alienum hortos colere, agros exercere et pomorum fecunditate gratulari. legitur enim in psalmo cxxvii: "Labores fructuum tuorum manducabis; beatus es et bene tibi erit"[190]. The poet whose works had been almost a Bible to the last pagan nobles is here paired with the psalmist[191]: something which recalls both the two-fold structure of the *Institutiones,* and those senators in the Gothic period who edited both a pagan and a Christian text[192]. It is also reminiscent of the early 6th century African author Fulgentius, who saw Vergil as unconsciously grasping Christian truths, and compared passages from the *Aeneid* with the Psalms[193]. I wonder how many of Cassiodorus' readers would have taken his allusions a few lines further, recognizing in the monk of the first class *felix qui potuit rerum cognoscere causas;* in the second *fortunatus et ille deos qui nouit agrestes*[194].

Would a monk who had read the *Institutiones,* and noted these quotations and indirect commendations, have been the readier to read, preserve, and even copy such texts of the literary classics as might come his way[195]? In contrast with the precepts of Isidore of Seville, whose own attitude was hardly consistent, if he was not directed to read such works, neither was he forbidden them[196]. In the *Expositio* also, he could find praise of a secular author: Aristotle is honoured for his collection of the topics of rhetorical argument, and their presence in every kind of profane literature is celebrated. To read and consider them, *religio nulla condemnat, quoniam innoxie requiritur, quidquid litteris sacris non probatur aduersum*[197]. Monte Cassino itself may have shared in the spirit of Vivarium. Probably about this time, one of the brethren, Marcus, praised and recounted Benedict's foundation of the site, using elegiacs of some elegance, with a classical vocabulary, and at least one echo of the *Georgics,* in a context similar to that of Cassiodorus[198].

At the same time, if Cassiodorus' attitude to the old literature and disciplines was less negative than Augustine's, it was still far from positive. He stood very remote from Basil of Caesarea, who was prepared to use every genre of pagan writing in the first stage of a moral and Christian education[199]. The difference is, perhaps, symptomatic of the cultural and religious gulf between east and west. Another symptom is the contrasting impact of Vivarium and Nisibis. Men of the great Nestorian school consciously applied Aristotelian methods to Christian hermeneutics and theology. Their achievement in these and many other disciplines was great and original, and their influence extensive in the near east[200]. Their *alma mater* was to produce learned men and works well into the 8th century, at least, and had many off-shoots and rivals. The Jacobite Monophysites had comparable institutions[201]. As for Vivarium, its history cannot be traced beyond the time of Gregory the Great, a Pope who would probably have held the educational approach of Cassiodorus in deep suspicion[202]. The founder of this tiny institution, in extreme old age, was forced to busy himself with an elementary guide to orthography for willing, but barely literate disciplines[203]; and it is notorious that, like his great contemporaries, Boethius and Benedict, he had small influence on European culture until the Carolingian renaissance.

Nonetheless, we should not use hindsight to condemn his work as unfitted to his day, and clearly doomed to rapid failure. As we have seen, Vivarian handbooks may have been in some demand; and, at least in Ireland and Visigothic Spain, they had their influence in the 7th century[204]. As for Vivarium itself, the preface to the **De Orthographia** should not, perhaps, be taken at face value. Cassiodorus had a special affection for the *amantissimos orthographos* whom he was compiling, and his description of the demand for the work may be partly a conventional *topos*[205]. It can be put into perspective by the Leningrad patristic corpus studied by O. Dobiache-Rojdestvensky. In contents, calligraphy, spacing and orthography, this manuscript is thoroughly consistent with Cassiodorus' prescriptions and a Vivarian origin. In general, its quality is very high. Only the last copyist to work on it committed more than a very occasional infringement of the spelling rules[206]. Perhaps he was a beginner; and perhaps it was at him, or at his instructors in or outside Vivarium—for, like so many textbooks, it requires some capacity in its public to read, if not to write, intelligently—that the **De Orthographia** was partly aimed.

There are other pointers which indicate that intellectual pursuits were not confined to the founder, or even to his handful of translators. Hand in hand with the outflow of Vivarian manuscripts went new accessions for the library, and the re-editing of texts in their light. The original draft of the **Institutiones** is probably lost to us under Cassiodorus' own revisions[207]. Of the recensions of book II on its own, the earliest archetype (Ω, giving Mynors' form I) was itself late, as shown by a reference to the compilation of the Donatus-Sacerdos codex[208]. The two later editions (archetypes Φ and Δ) were both probably made at Vivarium. In the first case, this is suggested by the association of the *Computus Paschalis;* in the second by that of

the *Ordo Generis,* and by its use of the **Expositio Psalmorum**[209]. Where Ω has hearsay references to Martianus Capella, Φ completely omits the references, but interpolates extracts[210]. It was probably therefore even later than Ω, but based on an earlier edition, as indicated by the uncorrected reference to Priscian. This reference also suggests that it was not the work of the author himself, despite a first-person expanded description of the Donatus-Sacerdos codex[211]. Δ does not derive directly from Φ, but may be similarly based. Its copyist may have read Martianus, but did not have him to hand, and passed over him in favour of Quintilian, with a cavalier *reliqua qui uoluerit in alio quaerat uolumine, nam ego descriptor ad potiora discurrens reliquorum oblitus sum, aut fors neglexi*[212]. In this, and in the numerous Boethian additions and substitutions made by ΦΔ, we can see a considerable import to Vivarium of texts recommended by the founder[213]. These were then read with comprehension, and used with some degree of critical intelligence by the monks.

Δ gives us the most favourable impression of the intellectual level at the monastery. Its copyist had read the **Expositio,** and applied its principles as Cassiodorus would have wished[214]. He had read Cicero's *De Inuentione,* recommended and used by Cassiodorus[215]; he may have read Dionysius on music, in the Greek original[216]; his interpolations, indeed, frequently show some knowledge of Greek, and even, perhaps, of the works of Ammonius[217]. This should not surprise us, in view of the numerous Greek texts, often classical, copied in those parts in the early middle ages[218]. Despite his translation programme, Cassiodorus had even left and catalogued some Greek manuscripts for his monks, including a Septuagint, which they were to use in correcting Latin versions of the Bible[219]. Finally, the Latin style of both the Φ and the Δ interpolators is reasonably good, almost Cassiodorian[220]. In view both of the extracts which they added, and of the didactic corpora associated with their editions, particularly Φ, it seems very possible that they were producing export copies, destined for a public with access to few of the books named.

There is another pointer to the level of Vivarian scholarship. Cassiodorus had worked on an expurgated edition of a Pelagian commentary on Romans (Ps. Primasius)[221]. This was completed by his monks, using texts of Tyconius and Eucherius which he had recommended, to cover the whole of the Epistles. Since the **Institutiones,** although updated to cover the **De Orthographia,** refer to this project as still in the future[222], it may well have been carried out after Cassiodorus' death. Furthermore, an anonymous reader of the Ps. Rufinus included in the Leningrad codex noticed that this was a Pelagian treatise, disguised as a work of anti-Arian orthodoxy, and advised other students to replace it in the volume with Augustine's *De Vera Religione,* a text attested at Vivarium. This recommendation, and the high standard of spelling and grammar, suggest a Vivarian gloss, though it is unlikely to be, as Dobiache-Rojdestvensky thought, the hand of Cassiodorus himself[223]. It is another sign that the monks were at least following up the interests of their master with intelligence, though without the self-confident scholarship which had produced his dehereticated commentary[224]. We should also note that with the *Codex Encyclius* is associated not only a pro-Three Chapters, but an anti-Pelagian corpus of texts[225]. In similar vein, they may have produced an anti-Arian compilation[226], perhaps a response to the establishment of the Lombards at Benevento in 571, on the edge of Campania, with which Vivarium had cultural contact.

The level of such activity may not be high, but it is far from negligible. It indicates very strongly that Cassiodorus had inspired or fostered a particular interest both in religious studies, and in the secular disciplines of grammar, rhetoric and logic; and also that his house continued to serve with intelligence similar interests in the world outside, perhaps as late as the papacy of Gregory the Great[227]. These, after all, were the monks whose eagerness for learning the *Institutiones* had actually restrained, and for whom the *Expositio Psalmorum* had been copied in three parts, to satisfy their demands on the library[228].

Our picture of Cassiodorus, then, shows a man who, during his long life as a *conuersus,* was concerned with far more than the progress of his own soul, or even the affairs of his little community; who, while very slowly withdrawing from religious and political controversies which he may always have found distasteful[229], remained alert to the needs and requests, religious and intellectual, of that part of the Mediterranean which his Gothic masters had once dominated[230]. Hardly a "remote don", then; and, if an "ineffectual don", ineffectual neither during his own life, nor a century and a half after his death[231]. Following Italy's brief cultural dark age in the 7th century, those powers of imagination and receptivity which he had once deployed as politician, exegete and educator, were to help in the recovery associated with Charlemagne and the later Lombards, in many ways the heirs of Theoderic[232].

Notes

1. *Variae,* praef. 1, 8-10, 14; on date, cf. J. J. O'Donnell, *Cassiodorus* (Berkeley, 1979), 104.

2. Cf. Procopius, *Wars,* VII.i.32; xxi.14; *Anec.,* xxiv.9.

3. Cf. *Var.,* XI, praef. 7; *Expositio Psalmorum,* ad cxlv. 2, ed. M. Adriaen, *CCSL,* 97-8; O'Donnell, 114.

4. *De Orthographia,* praef. 1 (ed. H. Keil, *Gramm. Lat.,* VII).

5. Cf. John II, *ep.,* ed. E. Schwartz, *Acta Conc. Oec.,* IV.2, 206-10; L. Duchesne, *L'Église au VIe Siècle* (Paris, 1925), 87 ff.

6. Cf. O'Donnell, 189-93.

7. *Ep. ad Rusticum et Sebastianum,* 18 (Schwartz, *ACO,* IV.1, 193 = Mansi, *Conc.,* IX, 357).

8. Cf. my *Genesis and Completion of Cassiodorus' Gothic History,* in *Latomus,* 43 (1984), 336-61, esp. 347 ff., defending, with reservations, Momigliano's controversial theory on the *Getica,* in *Proc. Brit. Acad.,* 41 (1955), 207-45.

9. For Albinus' religious character, see *Collectio Avellana,* 173; for Theodorus, Fulgentius Ruspensis, *ep.,* 6. Both had held the consulship and praetorian prefecture. For comparisons with Cassiodorus, see A. Van de Vyver, *Cassiodore et son uvre,* in *Speculum,* 6 (1931), 244-92, 256; L. W. Jones, *An Introduction to Divine and Human Readings by Cassiodorus Senator* (New York, 1946), 23 ff.

10. *Cassiodorus,* 115, 135, 177, 220 f., 233 f. For doubts, see Averil Cameron's review: *Cassiodorus Deflated,* in *JRS,* 71 (1981), 183-6.

11. Cf. Averil Cameron, *Byzantine Africa—the Literary Evidence,* in *Excavations at Carthage, 1978,* VII (ed. J. H. Humphrey, Michigan Univ., 1982), 29-62, 45.

12. Cf., especially, the speech given to Totila by Procopius, *Wars,* VII.xxi.12 ff.

13. Mansi, IX.359 (= *ACO,* IV.1.194); 106. He signed the *Constitutum* on behalf of the handless Valentinus. At the excommunication of Theodore Ascidas (*PL,* 69.62), the two are referred to together by Vigilius. Bp. Jordanes of Croton, another participant, is probably not the author of the *Getica.*

14. Cf. Gelasius, in *Ep. Pont. Rom. Gen.,* ed. A. Thiel, I.452.

15. Procop., *Wars,* III.xiii. 12; *ACO,* IV.1.185 f., 198 f. (= Mansi, IX.363 f., 347, 349).

16. Procop., III.xxxv.9-10.

17. But does Procopius' Ἰταλοῖς πολλοῖς τε αχί λογιμωτάτοις include him?

18. Cf. Cassiod., *Institutiones,* I, praef. 1; on Junilus' date and name, T. Honoré, *Tribonian* (London, 1978), 238 f.

19. Junilus, *Inst.,* praef. (*PL,* 68.15 f.); Cassiod., *E. Ps.,* cxviii, 2; cxxxviii, concl.; *Inst.,* I, ix.4.

20. *E. Ps.,* cxxxviii, concl.; cf. Galland, *PL,* 67.521; Van de Vyver, *Spec.,* 6, 273 and n. 2. I.-M. Clément and R. Vander Plaatse, introduction to Facundus, *CCSL,* 90A, viii ff., argue for a textual corruption of this passage: a marginal note was added by Cassiodorus to record the copying of the *duos libellos, Contra Mocianum* and *Ep. Fidei Catholicae.*

21. *Breu.,* praef., *ACO,* II.5, 98 f. (= *PL,* 68.965). On Cassiodorus' share in the *Hist. Tri.,* see M. Laistner, *The Value and Influence of Cassiodorus' Ecclesiastical History,* in *Harvard. Theol. Rev.,* 41 (1948), 51-68, 55 f.; R. Hanslik, *CSEL,* 71, xiii ff., and in *Philologus,* 115 (1971), 107-13; A. Momigliano, *Sesto Contributo alla Storia* (Rome, 1980), 501.

22. Cf. Schwartz, *ACO,* II.5, xxii on *Breu.,* xv, though Liberatus does not specify that he is using a translation.

23. Cf. E. Stein, *Histoire du Bas-Empire,* II (Paris, 1949), 680 ff.; P. Peeters, in *An. Bolland.,* 55 (1937), 374 f., against Schwartz, *ACO,* IV.2, xvi f. Liberatus wrote following a journey, most likely his return from exile

either after the death of his bishop Reparatus in 562, or when Justin II recalled the Chalcedonian bishops at the end of 565.

24. Cameron, in *Excavations,* 46, takes the latter view, but argued for the former in *JRS,* 71, 185. Against Schwartz's conjecture that Liberatus actually wrote at Vivarium (*ACO,* II.5, xxii), see Peeters, in *An. Boll.,* 55 (1937), 375. Roman texts: see Schwartz, *ACO,* II.5, xvi.

25. Schwartz, *ibid.,* 1 ff.

26. Cf. *Inst.,* I.viii.9, xxix.2.

27. *Pro Def.,* X.vi.5-14 (cf. I.iv.20 f., XII.3.24); *Contra Mocianum,* 17, 49, 64; *Ep. Fidei Cath.,* 52 f.

28. Cf. O'Donnell, 144-7, 153-7: "as resolutely and monolithically allegorical a commentary as was ever written".

29. *Breu.,* xxiii f.

30. *Pro. Def.,* I.ii.3 f.; *ACO,* III.189-214; *Inst.,* I.i.8 f. The Origenist revival of 537-43 seems to have been another attempt at compromise with the Monophysites.

31. *Ep.,* 3, *MGH Epp.,* II, app. 3, p. 466. On Pelagius' authorship, see J. Petersen, *The Dialogues of Gregory the Great* (Toronto, 1984), 184 f.

32. *Cassiodors Psalmenexegese* (Göppingen, 1979), 36 ff., 109 f., 120 f.

33. *Op. cit.,* 166-72; cf. Schlieben, 181 f.

34. *E. Ps.,* cxxxviii, 1 and concl.

35. *Pro Def.,* IX.i.5 ff.; cf. H. Kihn, *Theodor von Mopsuestia und Junilius Africanus als Exegeten* (Freiburg im Breisgau, 1860), 458 ff. He also sees Junilus as influenced by Theodore.

36. *Const.,* xx, xxiii, xxv, Mansi, IX, 76-9; *Conc.,* V, actio, iv, 25, 29; 30, 82 (*ACO,* IV.1). For Theodore's commentary, see the edition of R. Devreesse, in *Studi e Testi,* 93 (1939), and the translation of (?) Julian of Eclanum, ed. L. de Coninck and M. J. d'Hont, in *CCSL,* 88A (1977).

37. Like Theoderet (*PG,* 80.964), Cassiodorus uses Ps. 15 for an attack on Apollinarist teaching; compare them also on Ps. 44, vv. 9, 13, 15.

38. On 44.10, Cassiodorus seems to use and take further Theodore's remarks on ivory; note also the stress they both lay on the daughters of kings, not commented on by Theoderet.

39. The *pater apostolice* of *E. Ps.,* praef., 1.121 (lineation as in *CCSL,* 97) is fairly certainly Vigilius; but I disagree with Schlieben (4 ff.) that this must date the work before the Pope's anti-Three Chapters *iudicatum* of April 11th, 548. Compare Facundus' dedication to Justinian of a hostile treatise.

40. *E. Ps.,* cxxxii, ad init.; cf. Schlieben, 170.

41. *Hist. Tri.,* VI.20; VII.2.19 f.; VIII.8.9 f.; IX.38.24; X.7-13.

42. With X.11.4 contrast *Breu.,* xxiv.

43. With X.11.10 f. contrast *ACO,* III.198.

44. *Hist. Tri.,* V.17. The exile of Pope by emperor, with which the dispute ends, will have had resonances, in view of the fate of Silverius.

45. *Ibid.,* IX.30 (cf., esp., 30.10); *Pro Def.,* XII.v.9-14.

46. X.3.34; omission from Socrates VI.3.

47. *Reg. Ep.,* VII.31 (*MGH*), a muddled reference, but with verbal reminiscence of the text. On the *Dialogues,* cf. Petersen, 121; the index to A. de Vogüé's ed. (*Sources Chrét.,* Paris, 1980), III, 296. Gregory may even have used Theoderet's *Historia Religiosa* himself (Petersen, 181-4).

48. *MGH, Epp.,* II, p. 465; cf. S. Baluze in Mansi, VII, 777-84; P. Courcelle, *Les Lettres Grecques en Occident de Macrobe à Cassiodore* (Paris, 1948), 362 f. Schwartz, *ACO,* II.5, xvi, denies that Facundus translated the *CE* in full.

49. *Epp.,* II, 464 ff. (note the citation of Theoderet against Theodore of Mopsuestia on the Song of Songs); Mansi, IX.61-106.

50. Cf. O'Donnell, 193; Cameron, in *JRS,* 71, 185. Theodore Lector may have inspired the *Hist. Tri.,* and been used in it.

51. *Inst.,* I.xi.1; cf. O'Donnell, 171. As the passage was never altered in revision, I cannot accept Schlieben (6 f.) that it merely dates the work before the council. Nor can I accept P. Lehmann's argument [*Cassiodorstudien, Erforschung des Mittelalters,* II (Stuttgart, 1959), 42 f.] that westerners generally ignored the council. He is unaware of Greg. Mag., *Reg. Ep.,* VII.31; while in III.10 and IV.33, which he cites, the Pope is trying to reconcile Three Chapters sympathizers.

52. There may be some resemblance here to Liberatus' judgement on the quarrel of Pelagius and Theodore Ascidas.

53. *Inst.,* I.xxiii.4; cf. above 160, and Schwartz, *ACO,* II.5.xx ff., on the *Collectio Sangermanensis.*

54. Cf. P. Courcelle, *Nouvelles Recherches sur le Monastère de Cassiodore,* in *Actes du Vᵉ Congrès Internat. d'Arch. Chrét.* (Rome, 1957), 511-28, 525 ff., rejecting *MS Bamberg HJ.iv.15*'s substitution of Januarius for Hilary.

55. Cf. P. Riché, *Education and Culture in the Barbarian West* (tr. Contreni, Columbia, 1976), 161, and below, 186.

56. On the Martinian cult in Italy, see P. Courcelle, *Le Site du Monastère de Cassiodore,* in *MAH* 55 (1938), 259-307, 284 ff., 293 f. But contrast O. von Simson, *Sacred Fortress*² (Princeton, 1987), 83, 87, on S. Apollinare Nuovo.

57. *Pro Def.,* XII.4 uses it to defend the independence of church from state. Note the inclusion of Acacian

schism documents in a pro-Three Chapters collection from north Italy. On its paradoxical inclusion of the anti-Symmachan *Laurentian fragment,* cf. E. Schwartz, *Abh. Bayer. Akad., ph.-hist. abt.,* N.F. 10, 263.

58. *Reg. Ep.,* VII.32 (cf. 30).

59. Cf. Facundus, *Contra Mocianum,* 2-10. On the date, cf. Stein, II, 824 ff.; on the identification, based apparently on no more than similar names, cf. Baronius, *Ann. Ecc.,* s.a. 562, followed by Galland, *PL,* 67.853, and M. Cappuyns, *Cassiodore* in *Dict. d'Hist. et Géog. Ecc.,* XI, 1360.

60. *De An.,* xviii; for a discussion, cf. O'Donnell, 127 ff.

61. In addition to use of Origen and the Antiochenes, note commendations of Cassian, Ticonius, the Origenist Didymus, and Cassiodorus' expurgation of a Pelagian commentary on Romans—*Inst.,* I.xxix.2 (cf. praef. 7, *E. Ps.,* cxviii, 28); ix.4; x.1; v.2.

62. On this, cf. Averil Cameron, *Procopius and the Sixth Century* (London, 1985), esp. chap. 14. For the increasingly hard line on Church-state relations taken by Facundus, cf. R. A. Markus, in *Studies in Church History,* 3, 146.

63. Cf. Cappuyns, in *DHGE,* XI, 1362 f.

64. Cf. Cassiod., *Var.,* I.3-4; IX.24-5.

65. *Var.,* XII.15 (cf. VIII.32); *Inst.,* I.xxviii.7; xxix.1.

66. Cf. T. S. Brown, *Gentlemen and Officers* (London, 1984), 27 ff. These included Cethegus and his descendants.

67. Cf. Gregory, *Reg. Ep.,* VII.30, Jones, *Introduction,* 43. For a Cassiodorus as (?) governor of Sicily, see *Var.,* I.3.

68. Cf. *Reg. Ep.,* IX.124 ff.; *Var.,* VIII.31.

69. Cf. P. Loiocano, in *Boll. d'Arte,* 28 (1934-5), 174-85.

70. *Inst.,* I.xxx.1.

71. *Inst.,* I.xxxii.2; xxviii.5 ff. Even the less intelligent were given a corpus of agronomists. Monks tended to regard field-work as a distracting second-best, for stupid individuals or poor foundations; cf. *Reg. Magistri,* 1, lxxxvi; *Reg. Benedicti,* xlviii, lxvi.

72. *Inst.,* I.xv.1-15; xxx, 1-4, *De Orthographia.*

73. Cf. A. Pettrucci, *Scrittura e Libro nell'Italia Altomedievale,* in *Studi. Med.,* X/2 (1969), 157-213, 184 ff.

74. Cf. Riché, 119 ff.; for copying at Marmoutier, Sulpic, Sev., *V. Martini,* 10.5-8. Note that the older monks were devoted entirely to prayer.

75. Ed. by Villegas and de Vogüé, *CSEL,* 87. On the monastery's culture cf. Riché, 160 f., below, 171. For MS copying there and at nearby monasteries, cf. M. Gorman, *Eugippius and the Origins of the MS Tradition of St. Augustine's De Genesi ad Litteram,* in *Rev. Bén.,* 93 (1983), 7-30, 11 f.: "it is remarkable

how many of the oldest subscriptions which are to be found in Latin manuscripts refer to Eugippius and Naples".

76. Note Petrucci's criticism of such conjectures in *Studi Med.,* X/2, 182 f., n. It also applies to much larger centres, Rome itself, and, to some degree, Verona; cf. E. A. Lowe, *Codices Latini Antiquiores,* IV, xviii ff.

77. *CSEL,* 72, p. xxviii.

78. Cf. Courcelle, *Lettres,* 356-62, 364-73. Did the last two (*Bamberg IV.21* and *Vatic. Lat. 3375*) come from Vivarium, or straight from Castellum Lucullanum? Both are attested at Vivarium; but these products of the same southern *scriptorium* could well be Neapolitan in origin; cf. Gorman, in *Rev. Bén.,* 93, 9-12, 29 f.

79. Cf. A. Mundó, in *Rev. Bén.,* 71 (1961), 388, n. 2; A. de Vogüé, ed. of the *Reg. Mag.,* I (Paris, 1964), 126, 149 f.

80. *Lettres,* 373-82; for a refutation of Beer on Bobbio, cf., e.g., *ibid.,* 343-56; Lowe, *CLA,* IV, xxvi f.

81. *CLA,* nos. 342, 496. The speeches may have been disseminated from Ravenna; the political implications of the copy are interesting.

82. Cf. *CLA,* 304; O'Donnell, 246; F. Blatt, *The Latin Josephus,* I (Copenhagen, 1958), 26.

83. *CLA,* 477, 404. Against Courcelle, 348, Lowe believes the Gargilius to be northern, and, at IV, xix f., is inclined to ascribe the Honorius to Verona. Note also *CLA,* 398, Sacerdos-Vivarian according to Courcelle, but, for Lowe, 5th c., palimpsested at Bobbio.

84. Cf. O'Donnell, 247 and n. 36, on *St. Gall,* 908, which Lowe (*CLA,* 965) believes to have been written perhaps at Bobbio in the 7th to 8th century, and rewritten c. 800 in northern Italy or Switzerland.

85. Cf. Lowe, *An Uncial (Palimpsest) MS of Mutianus,* in *JThS,* 29 (1928), 29-33.

86. *CLA,* 469; cf. R. Mynors, ed. of *Institutiones,* xviii; O'Donnell, 244 f.

87. Paulinus, *MGH Epp.,* IV, p. 526, cites directly *Hist. Tri.,* VI.27.5; cf. L. W. Jones, *The Influence of Cassiodorus on Mediaeval Culture,* in *Speculum,* 20 (1945), 433-42, 440.

88. Cf. above, n. 48, contrasting Baluze and Schwartz.

89. *CLA,* 506 (cf. 8, 490, 509); contrast Cappuyns, in *DHGE,* XI, 1398; Courcelle, *Lettres,* 378. On the aims and products of this *scriptorium,* see further C. H. Turner, *Ecc. Occid. Mon. Iuris Antiquiss.* II (Oxford, 1907), viii f.; Schwartz, *ACO,* I.5.2, ii f.

90. But cf. above, n. 20. Clément and Vander Plaatse in fact support Courcelle on the Vivarian transmission of Facundus to Verona.

91. But, by contrast with Lowe, Petrucci, in *Studi Med.,* X/2, 187, takes an unfavourable view of its quality.

92. For a possible parallel, where Three Chapters and cultural contacts between Italy and Africa were combined, cf. S. Lusuardi Siena, in *Archeologia Medievale,* 12 (1985), 306 f., on the mosaics of Luni cathedral, with Mansi, IX, 718 f.

93. Cf. Facundus, *C. Moc.,* 1 f., 7; Stein, II, 679 ff.

94. Cf. R. L. Poole, *The Earliest Use of the Easter Cycle of Dionysius,* in *EHR,* 33 (1918), 57-62, 210-13; but I cannot agree with him that the *Felix abbas Ghyllitanus* who updated the cycle c. 627 was really abbot at Squillace. Textual variants for *Scyllitanus* show no really comparable corruptions.

95. Cf. *Inst.,* 1.xxii.2 f.

96. Cf. Lehmann, *Erforschung,* II, 41-55.

97. Cf. *PL,* 67.345, 908 ff. Eugippius was a dedicatee of Dionysius, and a correspondent of Ferrandus, biographer of Fulgentius, and another Three Chapters defender.

98. On *Karlsruhe Aug. XVIII,* cf. M. Laistner, *Antiochene Exegesis in W. Europe during the Middle Ages,* in *Harvard Theol. Rev.,* 40 (1947), 20-31, 24; K. Künstle, *Forschungen zur Christlichen Litteratur- und Dogmengeschichte,* I.4 (Mainz, 1900), 13 ff., 23, 137 and passim. But did the Junilus belong to the original recension? The extract is associated with ones from Isidore, Alcuin and Irish canons, but so too are extracts from 5th-6th c. Spanish councils.

99. On cultural contact between Africa and Visigothic Spain, cf. J. Fontaine, *Isidore de Séville et la Culture Classique dans l'Espagne Wisigothique,* II (Paris, 1959), 853-8; R. Collins, *Early Mediaeval Spain* (London, 1983), 59 f. Note Ildefonsus, *PL,* 96.200, the migration to Spain from Africa, c. 570, of abbot Donatus, with a large library.

100. Note his position, c. 518, in the controversy over the Theopaschite formula for compromise with the Monophysites, which Justinian supported (*unus ex Trinitate carne passus est*). He and Dionysius held very similar Theopaschite views; cf. V. Schurr, *Die Trinitatslehre des Boethius* (Paderborn, 1935), chap. 3, esp. 198-228; H. Chadwick, *Boethius* (Oxford, 1981), 185 ff., 212 f. Chadwick (201) believes him to have been "almost certainly in contact with Fulgentius". Cassiodorus treated the formula with suspicion in 533/4, but seems to have used it in the *E. Ps.;* cf. above, n. 5; Schlieben, 179 ff., on *E. Ps.,* praef. 13, lines 38 ff.; xiii, 3; 1v, 11. It was affirmed at the fifth council (canon 10), and discussed by Facundus (*Pro Def.,* I.i.1, iii).

101. Cf. *Inst.,* I.viii.9; xxix.2.

102. If, however, we accept Clément and Vander Plaatse, then he must have received Facundus' *Ep. Fidei Catholicae,* dated in 568/9.

103. Cf. D. Chapman, *Cassiodorus and the Echternach Gospels,* in *Rev. Bén.,* 28 (1911), 283-95, 288 ff.; Van de Vyver, *Spec.,* 6, 282 f.

104. I.xxiii.1.

105. *Isidore,* III, 1176. On the date of Isidore's copy of *Inst.* II, see Mynors, p. xxii.

106. *CLA,* 374A; cf. *Inst.,* I.viii.2, 10, 12; A. Souter, *A Study of Ambrosiaster* (Cambridge, 1905), 4, 12 f.

107. On *CLA,* 1507 (*Vindob. 2160*), cf. Van de Vyver, *Spec.,* 6, 281; Jones, *Introduction,* 27 f.; Riché, 160 f.

108. Cf. Courcelle, *Lettres,* 382-8, suggesting Monte Cassino as intermediary.

109. *ACO,* II.5, xv, xviii f., xxii. He argues that the *Collectio's* abridgement of the *CE* is too clumsy to be Vivarian.

110. Cf. Fontaine, I, 143, n. 4, 199 f., 246, n. 4, 311, n. 2, 438; III, 1175; Lehmann, *Cassiodorstudien,* 60-5.

111. Cf. Th. Mommsen, *MGH, Chron. Min.,* II, 395; Lehmann, 60.

112. With *Var.,* III.51, cf. *Et.,* 18.27-41; with II.40.11-14, *Et.* 3.22.6-9; with I.35.2, *Et.* 5.33.11 and *De Natura Rerum* 4.4; with *De An.,* xi, lines 76-80 (*CCSL,* 96), cf. *Et.,* 11.1.34. If, though, Isidore knew the *Variae,* it is surprising that he apparently used so informative a work so little. A common source on circuses may be indicated by Servius, *ad Georg.,* III.18, *ad Aen.,* VIII.36. Cf. Fontaine, I, 416, 434 f., for a parallel; but note that if Isidore used the *E. Ps.,* he did so very infrequently.

113. With the interpolations in Mynors, 169 ff. (Isidore probably did not have this interpolated text), cf. *Etymologiae,* 3.12.1-2, 7—more parallels than Mynors notes. On the translation at Vivarium, cf. *Inst.,* II.v.3; *E. Ps.,* xcvi, 4. There was, though, at least one other Latin Euclid extant; cf. D. Pingree, in *Boethius,* ed. M. Gibson (Oxford, 1981), 157 ff.

114. Cf. A. Souter, *The Earliest Latin Commentaries on the Epistles of St. Paul* (Oxford, 1927), 210 f., on *CLA,* 527 (Paris, *Bibl. Nat. Lat.,* 653).

115. Cf. *De Viris Illustribus,* ix, xviii f., xxv (ed. C. Codoñer Merino); note no mention of Liberatus.

116. Note that Isidore knew neither the *Gothic History,* nor the *Getica.*

117. Cf. B. Bischoff, *Mittelalterliche Studien* (Stuttgart, 1966), 174 ff.

118. Cf. E. K. Rand, *The New Cassiodorus,* in *Speculum,* 13 (1938), 433-47, 442, noting works of Isidore, Sisebut and Greg. Tur., in *Bamberg HJ iv.15,* on which cf. Mynors, x f. The collection must have returned to Italy by the late 8th c.

119. Cf. L. Holtz, in *Columbanus and Merovingian Monasticism,* ed. H. B. Clarke and M. Brennan (Oxford, 1981), 139, 142 ff., 146 f. Jones, in *Spec.,* 20; 437, suggests the link with Virgilius, whom Holtz, 137-41, convincingly shows to have worked c. 650, in Ireland, not Toulouse.

120. *Isidore,* III, 1176.

121. Cf. Mynors, xxviii f., on II.i.1.

122. Isodore, though, had a corrected copy. If Fontaine is right, we must then assume that the embarrassed author hastily sent an improved version east again.

123. Cf. Mynors, xxvii f., xxxvii f.; A. Van de Vyver, *Les Institutiones de Cassiodore et sa Fondation à Vivarium,* in *Rev. Bén.,* 53 (1941), 59-88, 70 f., 74; P. Courcelle, *Histoire d'un Brouillon Cassiodorien,* in *Rev. des Ét. Anc.,* 44 (1942), 65-86, 69, 79-86.

124. Cf. Chadwick, 27, 255 ff. It is curious that Cassiodorus apparently had no contact with this circle when in Byzantium.

125. Cf. Schwartz, *ACO,* II.5, xxi f., 146; I.5.2, iii; II.4, xvi-xx.

126. Cf. E. A. Lowe, in *Studies in Honour of A. M. Albareda,* ed. S. Prete (New York, 1961), 279-89; J. Irigoin, *L'Italie Méridionale et la Tradition des Textes Antiques,* in *Jahrb. Österreich. Byzantinisk,* 18 (1969), 37-55, 42 f. Note also Courcelle, *Lettres,* 399, n. 2, on late 6th c. western knowledge of Ps. Dionysius.

127. *Inst.,* I.xvii.2. There is, though, no reason to see *CLA,* 233 a-b, Jerome, Marcellinus and his continuator, though Italian, as a Vivarian corpus; cf. B. Croke, *Marcellinus on Dara,* in *Phoenix,* 38 (1984), 77-88, 78, n. 5-6.

128. Cf. Mynors, ix f., xxv, xxviii.

129. Riché (163) supposes that *Inst.,* I.xxx.i, *si tamen non cupiditatis ambitu sed recto studio talia noscatur efficere,* warns the monks against working for profit only, rather than profit at all; I disagree. Did Cassiodorus have only his own monks in mind? Note *Reg. Benedicti,* lvii; *Reg. Magistri,* lxxxv, on the sale of monastic products; and cf. Cassian, *Inst.,* V, 39; Rufinus, *PL,* 21.591, for MSS.

130. Cf. S. T. Stevens, *The Circle of Bishop Fulgentius,* in *Traditio,* 38 (1982), 327-41, 331 f.

131. On these, cf. Mynors, xxv ff., xxxvi ff.

132. Cf. Irigoin, 40 f., 61, comparing the technical productions of s. Italy with the northern texts palimpsested at Bobbio.

133. But we might contrast larger scale encyclopaedic works: the 6th c. popularity of Martianus' *De Nuptiis;* Helpidius' compilation in Cassiodorian Ravenna (on which cf. G. Billanovich, *Ann. del Univ. Cathol. del S. Cuore,* a. 1955-6, 75-81); and the *Etymologiae* of Isidore.

134. *Inst.,* praef. 1; on the translation, cf. G. Fiaccadori, *Cassiodorus and the School of Nisibis,* in *Dumbarton Oaks Papers,* 39 (1985), 135 ff., against R. Macina, *Cassiodore et l'École de Nisibe,* in *Le Muséon,* 95 (1982), 131-66, 135 ff.

135. Cf. O'Donnell, 184 f.

136. Kihn, 210, n. 1, would read *hebraice,* suggesting that Cassiodorus saw Hebrew and Syriac as identical; Mynors records no variants; Fiaccadori points out that enemies of the Nestorians frequently called them Jews; Macina (151 ff., 156 ff.) argues that the school offered proselytizing instruction to Jews, and renders *Hebreis* as a dative. Kihn's suggestion (210 f.) that the educational method of the *Institutiones* actually derived primarily from Nisibis ignores the great and obvious influence of Augustine's *De Doctrina Christiana.*

137. Important sources are: *Barhadbšăbba 'Arbaya,* ed. A. Scher, *Patr. Or.,* 4, esp. 375-93, and ed. F. Nau, *ibid.,* 9, 594 ff., 620 ff., and the *Histoire Nestorienne (Chron. of Seert),* ed. A Scher and P. Dib, *ibid.,* 5, 273 f., 328; 7, 114 ff., 121, 133 ff.; 13, 507 ff. For studies, see esp. A. Vööbus, *History of the School of Nisibis (CSCO,* 266, *subs.,* 26, 1965), *passim*—13-24 for Edessa, 96-115, 143-7, 177-209 for Nisibis; also Scher, *PO,* 4, 398 f.; Kihn, 198-210; D. Wallace-Hadrill, *Christian Antioch* (Cambridge, 1982), 45 ff.; R. Nelz, *Die theologischen Schulen der mörgenlandischen Kirchen* (Bonn, 1916), 93-108; and, less impressed than Nelz and Scher by the element of secular learning, J.-B. Chabot, *L'École de Nisibe,* in *J. Asiat.,* ser. 9.8 (1896), 43-93.

138. *Pro Def.,* XII.iv, 12.

139. Cf., esp., IV.2-4, 12-19.

140. Cf. *Var.,* praef. 16 ff.

141. Cf. *De Doctr.,* IV.10-25; E. Auerbach, *Literary Language and its Public* (London, 1965), 35 ff. Note Augustine, *De Opere Monachorum,* xviii, for monks composing sermons.

142. *Inst.,* I.xxxii.2, II.ii. 16.

143. *Inst.,* I.xxv.2; *E. Ps.,* cxxxii, 1.

144. Greg. Mag., *Dial.,* I.4.

145. I.xxx.1.

146. Cf. II.ii.1, 4 f., iii.2. The spirit is that of Ennodius' Rhetoric: *qui nostris seruit studiis mox imperat orbi (Paraenesis Didascalia).*

147. Cf. *De Doctr.,* II.31.

148. *Inst.,* II.vi.1, vii.4.

149. Cf. M. Stanley, *The Monastery of Vivarium* (B. Litt. diss., Oxford, 1939), 157; *De Doctr.,* II.29.46.

150. Cf. O'Donnell, 252; Mynors, xxvii f.

151. Cf. Fontaine, II, 844, for the effect on Isidore.

152. Note, though, *E. Ps.,* viii, 9, against the frivolous *curiositas* of pagan philosophers.

153. I.xxviii.6.

154. Cf. II.iii.22, on the disciplines in general; v. 11 on geometry; but contrast iv.8, defending arithmetic as useful in theological, especially biblical, numerology.

155. Contrast Courcelle, in *RÉA,* 44, 74 f.

156. Cf. I, praef., 3, 5-6, xxvii. 1-2.

157. Cf. O'Donnell, 157-62.

158. Cf. U. Hahner, *Cassiodors Psalmenkommentar* (Munich, 1973), 65-71, 91-4; note esp. *E. Ps.,* vi, div., 2, and concl. Cf., also, Schlieben, 29 ff.; J.-M. Courtès, *Figures et Tropes dans le Psautier de Cassiodore,* in *Rev. Ét. Lat.,* 42 (1964), 361-75, 374.

159. Cf. *De Doctr.,* IV.6.10, 7, 20.39-42.

160. *E. Ps.,* i, 2, cl, 6.

161. In *E. Ps.,* cxxxviii, concl., lines 506 ff., Cassiodorus shows how syllogistic argument should be used in Christological dispute against those who *se maximos dialecticos uideri uolunt.*

162. *E. Ps.,* cl, concl., esp., lines 237 ff.

163. Cf. Riché, 140-5; Brown, 79.

164. I.xxxii.5.

165. I.xxxiii.2 f. I do not believe that *interueniat pro nobis qui nobiscum orare consueuerat* must imply that Dionysius was ever resident at Vivarium; cf. Cappuyns, *DHGE,* XI, 1361.

166. II.v.10. Should *habuisse* be rendered *owned,* or *had the use of?* If the former, it is strange that Cassiodorus was so ill informed on the fate of his own library; if the latter, it is strange that he should have given no more specific a location.

167. II.v.1.

168. But I.xxx.2 suggests that they might search out needed texts for themselves. Those mentioned however, are not ones to whose location Cassiodorus himself had a clue, and the search need not have involved travelling for the monks.

169. Cf. above, 157, 161 f.; Schlieben, 168 ff. Even as individual pieces, many of the *Variae* must have been meant for an audience wider than their official recipients.

170. But another suggestion by Fontaine for Isidore's *Inst.,* II is a present to Leander from Gregory the Great (*Isidore,* III, 1176).

171. The inclusion of the *Computus Paschalis* suggests that the Φ corpus (see below) of *Inst.,* II and related educational texts was meant for a religous house.

172. *Inst.,* II would be more useful than I in isolation; did Cassiodorus mean Vivarium to supplement I with copies of the texts recommended there?

173. For one statement of this view, see Riché, 86-105, 113 ff.

174. Rufinus, *PL,* 21.591 f.; Jerome, *ep.,* 125.6, 18, a letter quoted in *Inst.,* I.xxxii.4. Note unreserved praise for the education which Rusticus' religious mother gave her son; contrast Ennodius, 431 (*MGH*), *Vita Caesarii,* I.9.

175. Cf. C. Stancliffe, *St. Martin and his Hagiographer* (Oxford, 1983), 34 f.

176. Cf. P. Courcelle, *Nouveaux Aspects de la Culture Lérinienne,* in *Rev. Ét. Lat.,* 46 (1968), 379-409, 404 ff.—rather speculative.

177. Cf. P. Brown, *Augustine of Hippo* (London, 1969), 115 f.; J. Fontaine, in *Epektasis, Mél. J. Danielou,* ed. J. Fontaine and C. Kannengeisser (Beauchesne, 1972), 571-95, and *L'Aristocratie Occidentale devant le Monachisme,* in *Riv. Stor. e Lett. Religiosa,* 15 (1979), 28-53. However, we should note how deeply the Benedictine-type monastery, with its stern discipline in obedience and humility, and its liturgical *opus Dei,* differs from the ancient model. We know nothing of the daily routine at Vivarium; but the house may have formed a link between the life of, say, Cassiciacum, and of Monte Cassino.

178. *Var.,* VIII.31; contrast *Inst.,* I.xxxii.3.

179. Cf. *E. Ps.,* praef. 15, vi, 2, xxxiii, 10; *Inst.,* praef. 6, I.iv.2.

180. Cf. Momigliano, in *PBA,* 41, 223.

181. *Var.,* IX.25.5.

182. Against this, cf. O'Donnell, 219 f., 238 f.

183. Cf. *Ibid.,* 219, n. 54, perhaps overstated.

184. Cf. P. Brown, 267 f., on the *De Doctr.:* Augustine also assumed the survival of the old culture, but, unlike Cassiodorus, 'felt under no obligation to perpetuate his attitude (of detachment from it) by creating an education of his own'.

185. Cf. *Inst.,* praef. 6, I.xxvii.1; xxviii.3 f.

186. Cf. *De Doctr.,* II.25-7, 40-2 (note the quotation in *Inst.,* I.xxviii.4); R. A. Markus, *Christianity in the Roman World* (London, 1974), 138 ff., 160 f., and in *Latin Literature in the Fourth Century,* ed. J. Binns (London, 1974), chap. 1, esp. 11 ff.

187. *Inst.,* I.xxi.1.

188. *Inst.,* II.ii.6 f., 10, 13, 15; iii.14, 15; I.xvii.1 (cf. Jerome, *ep.,* 22.35.8, *Graecus Livius*); Livy was an author of peculiar significance for the late Roman nobility.

189. For Augustine's varying attitudes to, and use of Vergil, cf. H. Hagendahl, *Augustine and the Latin Classics* (Göteborg, 1967), II, chap. 2, esp. 437 ff., on his *interpretatio Christiana.*

190. I.xxviii.5, quoting *Georg.,* II.484 f., perhaps influenced by Jerome's quotation of I.108-10 in *ep.,* 125.11. Vergil is cited or echoed many times in both *Inst.* and *E. Ps.,* though never by name in the latter, which gives a much more allegorical interpretation to Ps. cxxvii, 2.

191. *E. Ps.,* viii, concl., has a comparable dualism.

192. Cf. Markus, in Binns, 14 f. Fl. Turcius Rufius Apronianus Asterius edited Vergil (in 494) and Sedulius; Fl. Vettius Agorius Basilius Mavortius, Horace and Prudentius.

193. See *De Continentia Virgiliana* (transl. L. G. Whitbread, *Fulgentius the Mythographer,* Ohio State Univ., 1971), 7-10, 19, 21. *Aen.,* I.2 is compared with Ps. 1, 1; the triton episode in *Aen.,* VI allegorised and compared with Ps. 50, 19/51, 17.

194. *Georg.,* II.490, 493.

195. Bobbio's record is not good, but not only pagan texts were palimpsested, and at least the *Mediceus* Vergil was preserved. On palimpsesting in general, see E. A. Lowe, *Codices Rescripti,* in *Studi e Testi,* 235 (1964), 67-114, esp. 69-76. Of all classical authors, grammarians were most likely to survive, even being copied over Christian texts. On the effect even of Isidore's second-hand citations from the classics, cf. Fontaine, I, 741 ff.

196. Cf. Van de Vyver, in *Spec.,* 6, 279; Isidore, *Sent.,* 3.13, distinctly Augustinian in spirit. Contrast *Et.,* 8.6.8, which Fontaine sees as going even beyond Cassiodorus in positive acceptance of pagan culture; cf. *Isidore,* II.vi, chap. 3, esp. 802-6.

197. *E. Ps.,* cxliv, 21.

198. *PL,* 80.183-6; cf. *Georg.,* II.82. On Marcus, cf. A. Pantoni, *L'Acropoli di Montecassino e il Primitivo Monasterio di San Benedetto* (Montecassino, 1980), 81 ff., 97, n. 3; but he has also been dated to the Carolingian period.

199. Πρὸς τους Νεους. ii.5-iii, vii, x; cf. the remarks of N. G. Wilson, *St. Basil on Greek Literature* (London, 1975), 9 ff. Note, though, that Basil has a moral education in mind; Augustine's and Cassiodorus's is mainly technical.

200. Cf. Vööbus, 20 ff. (Edessa), 171, 188 ff., 203-9 (Nisibis); on Aristotle at Nisibis / Edessa, and in the eastern Church, Wallace-Hadrill, 47, 107 ff.

201. Cf. Vööbus, 318-26; Chabot, 65, 80-92.

202. Cf. Fontaine, *Isidore,* I, 33 f., III, 1175, on the dedication of the *Moralia.*

203. *De Orth.,* praef.; cf. O'Donnell, 229-33.

204. The two Irishmen, Asper and Virgilius, the former writing with a devout and monastic flavour, replacing Donatus' quotations from Vergil with the Psalms, the latter using classical learning without reference to the Church, may reflect the ambivalence of Cassiodorus' work; cf. Holtz, 140 f., 144-8.

205. Cf. T. Janson, *Latin Prose Prefaces* (Stockholm, 1964), 114 ff.; but note that Cassiodorus' preface reverses the convention of incompetent writer and learned recipient.

206. *Le codex Q. v. I.6-10 de la Bibliothèque Publique de Léningrad,* in *Speculum,* 5 (1930), 21-48, approved by Lowe, *CLA,* 1614; though cf. Courcelle, *Lettres,* 349, on the dangers of some of these criteria for attribution. C. Nordenfalk, *Die Spätantiken Zierbuchstaben* (Stockholm, 1970), 184-8 hesitantly agrees on Vivarian origin, while remarking that the illumina-

tors of the MS must have been rather ahead of their time. D. Ganz in *Columbanus,* 169 f., n. 36, doubts both the Vivarian origin and the unity of the MS; but note that its texts apparently show great similarity in script. On spelling, note that the Prudentius MS, *CLA,* 331, described by Dobiache-Rojdestvensky as its twin, has been condemned as the work of a copyist who barely knew Latin; cf. G. Pascal, in *Riv. Ital. Filol. Class.,* 13 (1905), 77, J. Bergman, ed. of Prudentius, *CSEL 61,* XXXIII.

207. Cf. the references to the Donatus-Sacerdos codex, and the *De Orth.:* II.i.2 f.; I, praef., 9, xv.10; xxx.2.

208. Being probably related to the *Bambergensis* (cf. Mynors, xxi, on Σ), Ω may be later than the *De Orth.,* too.

209. Cf. Courcelle, in *RÉA,* 44, 71 ff.; but note that, of 13 MSS, only the 10th c. *Rheims, 975* and *Karlsruhe Aug., 106* have the *Ordo,* the former as an 11th c. interpolation. With the interpolation to II.ii.3 (Mynors, 98), cf. *E. Ps.,* xxxv, 6; and note Mynors, xxxvii, on similar *marginalia* in Δ.

210. II.iii.20 (cf. ii. 17); interpolation at i.3.

211. Cf. above, 173, Mynors, xxviii f. Van de Vyver, *RB,* 53, 60 ff., gives this and other arguments, and I have generally followed his unravelling of this textual and chronological cats-cradle.

212. Mynors, 96. *Descriptor* is probably not Cassiodorus' reference to himself. Nowhere else does he use the word, or display so slap-dash a manner.

213. Cf. Van de Vyver, in *RB,* 53, 71 f., 74 f., and esp. Courcelle, in *RÉA,* 44, 78-83, 85; also above, n. 168.

214. Cf. above, 184 and n. 209.

215. II.ii.6, 10; interpolation at Mynors, 97.

216. Cf. the *marginalis,* Mynors, xxxviii. This is probably the Dionysius 150 of *P.-W.,* V (1905), 993.

217. Greek glosses, translations and numbers at Mynors, 91, 95, 98-103, 105-7, 110, 112 f., 115, 120, 123 f., 133, 136, 142, 144-6, 146, 151, 154 ff., 167; on Ammonius, cf. Van de Vyver, in *RB,* 53, 75. Owing to this knowledge of Greek, which few non-Italian Carolingian scholars would have had, and the other considerations noted, I cannot agree with Pingree (above, n. 113) that Δ was made at Corbie in the 8th c. The Boethian *Geometry* inserted was available at Vivarium; cf. *Inst.,* II.vi.3; *E. Ps.,* xcvi, 4; Courcelle, in *RÉA,* 44, 71 ff. But Mynors, xxxix, suspects the 8th c.; note his impression of Δ as "a late and rather bad text . . . worked over and expanded by an efficient redactor".

218. Cf. Irigoin, passim, esp. 49 ff. We should allow for the effects on the south of prolonged Byzantine rule; but the MS traditions of the southern Ps. Phocylides and Diodorus Siculus, at least, go back to the period of uncial use.

219. *Inst.,* I.xiv.4; xv.11 (cf. viii.15; xxv.2).

220. Cf. Van de Vyver, in *RB*, 53, 75.

221. Cf. O'Donnell, 218; A. Souter, *The Commentary of Pelagius on the Epistles of Paul*, in *Proc. Brit. Acad.*, 2 (1905-6), 409-39.

222. I.viii.1.

223. *Spec.*, 5, 31, 34-7. The style seems to me too clumsy for Cassiodorus, and Petrucci (*Studi Med.*, X/2, 183, n., cf. 180) observes that it is too carelessly written to agree with his prescriptions on *marginalia*.

224. O'Donnell, 218, detects a similar lack of confidence in their continuation of that work.

225. Cf. Schwartz, *ACO*, II.5, xix f., although he judges the latter material in the *Collectio Sangermanensis* to be an irrelevant Carolingian addition. Pelagianism had historical links with Nestorius, Theodore of Mopsuestia and the Antiochene school, and was still affecting Gaul and Italy c. 490-530.

226. Cf. G. Morin, in *Rev. Bén.*, 31 (1914), 237-43; Van de Vyver, in *Spec.*, 6, 290, n.; Cappuyns, in *DHGE*, XI, 1382.

227. Courcelle, in *RÉA*, 44, 73 f., conjectures that this was the date of the Φ recension.

228. Cf. *Inst.*, I, praef., 5 f. (though 7 warns those who believe divine inspiration a substitute for learning); *E. Ps.*, praef., lines 29-38.

229. O'Donnell, 228, contrasts the more militantly Chalcedonian theology of the *Expositio* with that of the late *Complexiones*.

230. We might compare the declining, but still substantial volume of goods carried by the western Mediterranean trade-routes in the late 6th c.; cf. D. Whitehouse, *Papers of the British School at Rome*, 53 (1985), 185; M. d' Agostino and F. Marazzi, *Archeologia Medievale*, 12 (1985), 16-24; S. J. Keay, in *Papers in Iberian Archaeology*, ed. T. Blagg, R. Jones and S. J. Keay (Oxford, 1984), 564 f., and *Late Roman Amphorae in the Western Mediterranean* (Oxford, 1984), 427 f.

231. Cf. Courcelle, *Lettres*, 399 f.

232. Cf. H. Löwe, *Von Cassiodor zu Dante* (Berlin, etc., 1973), chap. 2; P. A. B. Llewellyn, *The Popes and the Constitution in the 8th c.*, in *English Hist. Rev.*, 101 (1986), 42-67, 55 ff.; note also above, n. 81.

Addenda

To p. 168. Gregory the Great may well have used the *Expositio* in his *Magna Moralia*, but perhaps obtained his copy at Constantinople. With *E. Ps.* xxxvii, 6, cf. *Moralia* IX.83; with 1, 7, XI.70; with ciii, 26 f., XXXIV.39, II.31; with cvi, 40, XIX.27.

To p. 172. The *De Vitiis et Figuris* of Julian of Toledo was much influenced by the *Expositio*. With *E. Ps.* lxxiv, 7, xxi, 7, xxxix, 16, cf. *De Vitiis* (ed. W. M. Lindsay) III.7, 9, VI.83; perhaps also with cxxxviii, 12, 16, cf.

III.7. In contrast with Isidore (cf. Fontaine, II, 795), Julian seems to have sought out many rhetorical *exempla* for himself from the Bible.

To p. 173. C. 610, a fine Greek text of Dioscorides (*MS Neap. Gr. 1*) was produced at Rome or further south in Italy. Closely related to the famous Vienna Dioscorides, it may thus be linked with the Romano-Byzantine aristocracies; cf. G. Cavallo in *I Bizantini in Italia*, ed. V. von Falkenhausen (Milan, 1982), 502. G. Fiaccadori has suggested to me that it has features in common with the possibly Vivarian Latin MS, *Leningrad Q.v.I.6-10*, discussed at 184.

To p. 183. In *Società Romana e Impero Tardoantico* IV, ed. A. Giardina (Bari, 1986), 184 f., A. Petrucci suggests that the *Institutiones'* model of the single-codex corpus of texts was very influential, at least down to the Carolingian period.

To p. 184. D. Shanzer (*Riv. di Fil.* 112 (1984), 298 f.) argues that a better text of Martianus than the one used by Φ was available in the early 8th c.: therefore Φ cannot be much earlier. This confirms the suspicions of Mynors and Pingree; but, in view of the corpora of 5th to 6th c. compositions associated with ΦΔ, a contrast with other MSS of the *Inst.*, I remain unconvinced.

Robin Macpherson (essay date 1989)

SOURCE: "Zeitgeist," in *Rome in Involution: Cassiodorus's "Variae" in Their Literary and Historical Setting*, Poznan, 1989, pp. 151–63.

[*In the essay below, Macpherson comments on the historical accuracy of the* Variae *and analyzes the language and style of the work, stating that its tone suited the tastes of the upper classes.*]

I. THROUGH THE PRISM

In the *Variae* Cassiodorus depicts the exemplary character of the brother-courtiers Cyprian and Opilio: they appear with a symmetric perfection which reflects their moral perfection:

> He, Opilio, allied and joined himself to his brother's virtues in such a manner that it is uncertain . . . as to who should derive more praise from the other. One honours his friendships with true faith, but a great trustworthiness belongs to promises made by the other. One is also devoid of greed, while the other is proven to be alien to cupidity. Hence they know how to be loyal to their kings, since they show no treachery to their fellows".[1]

Boethius tells us that the pair brought false accusations against him, Opilio in order to extricate himself from impending disgrace "on account of frauds . . . innumerable" during his term of office. Had Opilio not attacked him, he would the very day after have been driven from Ravenna by the king, branded on the forehead like a common criminal.[2]

Similar contradiction arises with the great official Parthenius, Master of Offices to the Frankish king. Arator's letter to him is in the most glowing terms: Parthenius, whose name, Arator avers, aptly betokened his virgin modesty,[3] had deigned to befriend him while they were both at Ravenna; and under Parthenius' guidance Arator had been introduced to the delights of Caesar's writings and of poetry both secular and divine. It was Parthenius, indeed, who had urged Arator to undertake the versification of the Scriptures; and now Arator had come to dedicate to his old friend his huge versification of Acts.

Another picture emerges from what Gregory of Tours has to say: that he was malodorous in more ways than one, that he killed wife and friend, and that only a few years after Arator's letter (which dates from 544) he was himself killed by a mob outraged by his fiscal exactions (548). Two different pictures thus exist, which scarcely seem to be of the same man.[4]

If Cassiodorus in his eulogy of the brother-courtiers was indulging in politic falsehood, such behaviour was not confined to court: Late-Roman literati in general tend to impart a formal sheen to their correspondents.[5] Yet in his preface to the *Variae* Cassiodorus himself claims that he has bestowed "true praise" on high dignitaries, has painted them with the "colour of historical reality". He continues: the *Variae* are the "mirror" of his mind, where all posterity may examine him: speech not in keeping with character is scarcely to be found, for the offspring of the heart's inner sanctum is thought to belong to its creator even more truly than a man's posterity.[6] Elsewhere he describes an advocate as employing a translucency of eloquence, such as fittingly emanates from a pure conscience; for his oratory as an advocate was a sort of mirror of his moral code, and there could be no greater testimony to his mind than an inspection of the quality of his words.[7] The content and tone of the utterance were both sure indicators of character.[8] Indeed even posture and bearing could be reliable pointers: a man always remains in honour, if not only his voice be tranquil but he be commended by a most serene aspect.[9]

> In the face and in the voice we learn the mores of the officials serving us. If the face is tranquil, or if it is in a modest tone of voice that the petition is made, then we believe that the cases at hand are most deserving: for whatever is said in a state of turmoil is not in our opinion justice. . . .[10]

Cyprian and Opilio would have cultivated their speech and their appearance to a consummate degree; Cyprian himself was so distinguished in this respect that he had been sent on diplomatic missions to Byzantium.[11] This curious externalism, so typical of the *Variae,* was a general feature of the period. It was the product of an education which existed despite—indeed even in reaction to—a larger social

reality; its extremely stereotyped character imparted a lustre to men of all moral hues.

Just as high officials and great nobles were exposed but momentarily to the resounding fanfare of laudation which Late-Roman rhetoric largely was, with its galaxy of splendid words such as *lux, splendor, iubar, decus, serenitas, claritas, radius, coruscare, rutilare, fulmen, aura, fax, lampas, lumen, gloria, laus, praeconia, tituli, insignia, micare, ornamentum,* so their integrity may often have been as continuous as the limelight which was upon them.

In the *Variae* the following remark is to be found: "It is a great testimony to a man's life not to be called 'famous' (*clarum*) as much as 'most famous' (*clarissimum*), since almost everything is believed to be excellent in a man who is denoted by such a splendid superlative (*tanti fulgoris superlativo nomine vocitatur*)".[12] Much of the Late-Roman institutional world came to assume a strange, optical quality, the degree of distortion or exactitude differing according to position.[13]

II. Abstract Nouns in Late Latin

In the Latin of Late Antiquity the predilection for hypotaxis, characteristic of the literary prose of the Classical Period at the beginning of our era, was waning, in favour of simpler syntax, often supported by strings of particles such as *enim* and *nam* ("for").[14] With the shift away from the complex periodic sentence structure the force of the meaning tends to be entrusted less to the verb than to increasingly prolix clusters of nouns.

In the proliferation of abstract nouns in Late Latin a number of interrelated factors may be discerned. Firstly, the incisiveness of Classical Latin, which had so facilitated reasoning upon the facts,[15] was compensated for in Late Latin by what might be termed a new sensitivity; Late Latin was a language of abstract nouns, and even though many new coinages are semantic equivalents to Golden Age vocabulary, they tend to have a certain baroque exuberance about them. The lack of verbal economy in Late Latin—and the *Variae* in particular—can often be explained in terms of aesthetic change: a newfound need to shield from the factual world. The age favoured words such as *districtio* ("severity"), *interminatio* ("threat"), *nimietas* ("exorbitance"), *oblocutio* ("reproach"), *depraedatio, hostilitas, incivilitas, indisciplinatio* etc., most of them not earlier than the third century and all of them in the *Variae.*[16]

Much can be said concerning the enormous predilection of Late Latin for abstract titulature at the cost of the personal pronoun. Such abstracts are found on occasion in the classics and even in Cicero's correspondence, but their ubiquitousness in Late Latin, whether in bureaucracy, official ceremony and protocol, epistolography, or even strictly religious writings, can be attributed to a newly-felt need for "protective padding".[17]

There existed a more or less clear gradation of titles, each appertaining to certain levels of eminence, ranging from the *nostra/vestra serenitas* or *mansuetudo* of the emperor, through *celsitudo* or *sublimitas* or *magnitudo* of high- or middle-level dignitaries, to *devotio tua* of executive officers. So the system is crystallised in the *Variae*.[18]

The use of abstract nouns in Late Latin was, therefore, largely conditioned by the fastidious tastes of the upper classes, who chose to distance themselves from the factual world, to subject it to a screen of abstracts, of impressions bland and innocuous.[19] Many abstract nouns of Late Latin are found already in the Golden Age, but it is only in Late Antiquity that they occur in superabundance; most of them stem from the adjective (*carus/caritas*), and Late Latin had a predilection for stringing them together in long segments: their cumbersomeness, the greater time needed to read, write, or speak them, was hardly compatible with the highly versatile, almost excessively organising structure of Classical Latin, at its zenith as a synthetic language.

The values and sensitivities of Late Antiquity could to a large extent be articulated by means of a newly emerging pattern of "key vocabulary", words which though already available in the language's lexical store had remained comparatively in the background.[20] In many cases, however, new abstract nouns were needed, coined according to principles of analogy—*Trinitas, puritas, profunditas, moralitas, resurrectio, sanctificatio, pollutio, dilectio, manifestatio, afflictio, illuminatio, adunatio. . . .*[21]

Given the need for euphony, it is not surprising that writers of this period thought very much in terms of words for "pleasantness" and "sweetness". To a sober traditionalist like the elder Symmachus the word *mel* ("honey") would have been no more than a metaphor for stylistic excellence:[22] with Christian writers, especially epistolers, it becomes one of the most frequent metaphors for spirituality, especially when manifest in the written word. To *mel*, whether in general or epistolary contexts, can be added *dulcedo* ("sweetness"), *suavitas* ("pleasantness"), *favus* and *nectar*,[23] or words denoting refreshment (*fons, irrigare, refrigerare*), nourishment (*ubertas, cibus, pastus, lac*), and satiety.[24] Such language was not considered appropriate for Late-Roman government, but it is the ubiquitous currency of Christians in social or more specifically spiritual contexts, whether one thinks of Paulinus of Nola or the frocked Sidonius, of Ruricius, of Ennodius when he is speaking less as an aristocrat and more as a representative of the Church, or of the later Cassiodorus, when he became "converted" from the world. Such words preserve their frequency for centuries to come, and their popularity is clearly connected with the momentous cultural upheavals of the era.

This new Latin reflects cultural change rather than any decline in technical mastery as such. Late-Latin epistolers such as Sidonius and to an even greater degree Avitus of Vienne testify to the sophistication and extreme subtlety of nuance in a cultural backwater of Europe at a very late period. It was a world in which men chose no longer to be endowed with simple earthy names such as *Naevius* or *Balbus*, derived as often as not from physical blemishes, but rather with the splendid apparel of *Asterius, Celestinus, Orientius, Fulgentius*, or of virtues, such as *Constantius*, or of Biblical names, such as *Petrus* or *Johannes*.

III. THE ECLIPSE OF THE INDIVIDUAL

One scholar has noted that the widespread substitution in Late Greek of the simple verb by a paraphrase consisting of an action-noun (perhaps of the "-*esis*" -type) and subsidiary verb could only be at the expense of the dynamic element of speech—the verb.[25] A similar phenomenon was widely at work in Latin. Ennodius, like any other Roman of his age, could express himself with the words "*me ad amicitiae custodiam . . . compellis*" ("you coerce . . . me into the preservation of friendship"), where the Classical Age would perhaps have preferred a construction with the verb *custodire*.[26] In the *Variae* the action-noun is a salient feature: "*Manifestatio est conscientiae bonae praesentiam iusti principis expetisse*" ("It is the manifestation of a good conscience to have sought out the presence of a just prince"), for example, when "*Manifestat conscientiam bonam qui. . . .*" would have been more likely in the Classical Age—in any case *manifestatio*, like many other words in -*atio* used in the *Variae,* is postclassical.[27] Elsewhere in the *Variae* occurs the phrase "*consiliorum participatione*" ("by the participation in counsels"), while *participatio* is first found in the third century and the classical would perhaps have had "*consilia participando*" ("by participating in counsels").[28]

The observation has been made that the development of the action-noun out of the verb—for example: cremate - cremation, participate - participation, visit - visitation, *imitari Deum* ("to imitate God") - *imitatio Dei* ("imitation of God")—"implies institutionalization, solidity, durability". "The step of forming the noun means that there has been some trend towards abstraction, systematization, classification perhaps; the thing is becoming more of an institution—a higher degree of reflection, formalization, than its verb".[29]

Nor is it the action-noun alone that would seem to point to a world of institutions, an essentially static world. Abstracts of the type -*tas,* derived from adjectives, can in their own way become institutions, such as *caritas* and *puritas* in the moral sphere, *Trinitas* in the religious, and *spectabilitas* in the sociopolitical.

The world of Late Antiquity was very highly institutionalised in not only the political and legal spheres, with its wealth of abstracts pertaining to ceremony of state, legal processes, political and administrative functions, but also those of morality and religion; while time and again those virtues pertaining to emperors and high officials coincide with those of the Church.[30] Men's acts tended to be significant only insofar as they conformed to an institutionalised pattern of behaviour, in the performance of roles,[31] while the actors themselves came to be remarkable only to the degree to which they embodied moral ideals. Virtues in the form of abstract nouns become ubiquitous.

With such a manner of perception dominant it is not surprising that people were seen less in terms of any indefinable, quintessential individuality than of such ideal attributes. With the ubiquitous custom of substituting for the names of emperors, officials, nobles, and churchmen abstract phrases such as "Your Serenity", "Your Piety", it is seen how people have actually become their attributes. A whole book has been devoted to these abstracts as they occur in the *Variae,* in such profusion and density are they to be found there.[32]

This predilection for virtues conceived of in isolation, in abstract-noun form, is closely linked to the enormous frequency in Late Antiquity (especially in the context of official decrees) of *semper* ("always", "ever"): if people and their ideals are synonymous in more ways than one, then a certain constancy and inevitability may be said to govern their behaviour.[33]

A world of ideals is also a world of platitudes, statements of a general, usually moralising nature; and the writers of the age were much given to these: here also there was much occasion for the use of *semper.*[34]

Closely linked to these developments, whereby qualities in each individual were made to stand for him, is the widespread occurrence—especially in the fifth and sixth centuries—of words such as *insignia* and *tituli* to refer to moral attainments, on the analogy of titles and insignia of office.[35]

But *tituli* and *insignia* occur in a literal sense to the same extent as the figurative, and are an aspect of the Later Empire's highly pronounced morality of office and position, the role-playing that is such a feature of the time: "by virtue of our ecclesiastical rank (*per titulum ecclesiasticum*) we have renounced our sins", writes Ennodius.[36]

This externalism is linked to developments in art, especially imperial art: from the fourth century onwards figures of authority come to be portrayed more and more in terms of the external trappings of their authority.[37] Mediaeval art is also well-known for the most painstaking care bestowed on reproducing the exact details of paraphernalia, costume, or gesture of the temporal and spiritual great, leaving us with no idea of what the outstanding figures of the time actually looked like.[38]

The predilection for, indeed engrossment with jewels, is a salient feature of the Late-Roman and Early-Mediaeval West, concomitant with a love of insignia, and this fascination for such inanimate objects may be seen as having far-reaching implications with regard to the perception of human beings. Here a fragment (quoted at length below, in the following chapter) from Cassiodorus' panegyric to Vitigis and Matasuentha is especially relevant.

Another aspect of this general trend is the applying of metaphors to people directly. On his epitaph Senarius, Theoderic's faithful minister, describes himself as "voice of kings, salvation's tongue, pact's advocate, avenue to peace, wrath's bounds, friendship's seed, war's flight, discord's foe . . .".[39] A letter of appointment in the *Variae* uses similar language: "Therefore you will be the security of the drowsing, the fortifying of homesteads, the protection of barriers. . . ." In this latter instance the transition from imperial coins ("Public Safety" and the like) is clear enough, while the language of both quotes makes it quite unambiguous that persons are denoted, no longer the mere representatives of *pax* and *securitas,* but their symbols.[40]

Venantius Fortunatus, contemporary of Pope Gregory, is an interesting proponent of this idealising world. After receiving his education at Ravenna he made his way to Gaul, where his poetry in honour of royalty, saintly dignitaries, and things venerable refreshed those who chose to forget the sordid world which his neighbour, Gregory of Tours, depicts. The poetry never descends even for one moment from the lofty ideals of sanctity, tranquillity, and Platonic love; it tends thus to be rather monotonous, with the constant recurrence of a very limited number of concepts and sentiments. A desultory look through the poems would reveal the word *semper.* Every feature of Venantius' world is frozen in the image of eternity. Even Frankish royalty, no matter how unsavoury their actual lives, appear enshrined in the crystalline rigidity of the poet's thought-world.[41]

Any individuality assigned to these monarchs by Venantius is negligible; the usual repertoire of royal virtues seems to be applied to them indiscriminately. Venantius tends to address them in symbolic terms, such as *speculum* ("mirror"), *lux* ("light"), *dulcedo* ("sweetness"), *honos* ("honour"), *caput* ("head"), *decus* ("grace"), *salus* ("salvation"), *apex* ("pinnacle"), *bonitas* ("goodness"), *ornatus, ornamentum* ("adornment"), *spes* ("hope"), *flos* ("flower"), *fons* ("fount"), *regimen* ("rule").[42]

The subjects of honorific addresses in Late Antiquity—without underestimating the formalism of earlier ages—fail to come to life, can scarcely be visualised as individuals. Venantius' poems to living people are no more than a kaleidoscope of stock virtues and topoi, apparently with no personal touch. This honorific idiom seems to have been matched by a corresponding perception of individuals and lent itself very well to the "optical ambivalence" discussed elsewhere.[43]

Very similar in implication is the predilection in Latin of and after the first century AD[44] for *nomina agentis* of the type ending in ". . . *tor*", ". . . *sor*", ". . . *trix*". In the *Variae* there are some fifty postclassical coinages of this type.[45] Such nouns had always been frequent in the Republic, but mainly to designate technical functions or operations (*e.g. accusator*).[46] Under the Empire, however, there is a considerable proliferation of these nouns resulting from stylistic needs as well as semantic necessity.[47] These stylistic creations "crystallize a fact, quality, *etc.* Contrast *e.g.* the effect of '*qui primus opes adcumulavit*' ('who was the first to amass wealth') and of '*opum primus adcumulator*' ('first amasser of wealth'). The latter expression has an air of finality, characterizing the self-made millionaire once and for all".[48] Apart from being compact and economical, such words make an action, whether done once or habitually, into an aspect of the doer's identity, an inseparable attribute of his. Naturally they are well-suited to morally charged contexts such as invective or Christian sermon: with words such as *fornicatores* sinners are branded forever.[49] In panegyric also and in the language of liturgy such words are well-favoured: *Preserver of the Human Race, Saviour.* . . . When used instead of verbal phrases of the type "*he who preserves* . . .", such words are, by their being nouns, emancipated from the temporal sphere and freeze the very substance of reality.

All the linguistic features described above seem to point in one direction, the eclipse of the individual behind a role, an ideal, an image, in an institutional world conceived of as static and changeless. In art people came to be depicted in terms of their social status, their *tituli* and *insignia*, rather than of any facial or psychological traits. In the literature of the Middle Ages surprisingly little in the way of biography or anecdotes has survived, and the men that do appear are not real men at all, but merely types.[50] It is argued that this is how men were actually perceived.

Hagiography and the collections of correspondence of churchmen hardly clash with this picture. In the centuries after 400 literarcy in the West became increasingly the preserve of clerics and monks, exclusively so by about 600. The literary language thus came to be the exclusive property of a special section of society, and as such exclusively reflecting its specific values; and even though the Church Fathers were largely responsible for an increase in the amount of actual vocabulary in this language, this did not offset a basic conceptual one-sidedness.

The simplicity, matter-of-factness, and unselfconscious familiarity of Cicero's correspondents and of the letters preserved, for example, in Suetonius' biographies of the Caesars[51] had in the course of the Empire gradually been replaced by a distant formalism. The acceptance of Christianity, nominal or otherwise, by an ever-growing proportion of the literary classes merely facilitated the development of this stereotyped literary language. It is noteworthy that for all their protestations of affection, epistolers of the Late-Roman West seldom insert their addressee's name in the body of the letter, while the highly personal *praenomen* seems to have all but disappeared from the written language. Not surprisingly, writers for whom Christian *caritas* ("love") was the central mystery possessed a style characterised—especially at the level of *clausulae*—by fixity, monotony, uniformity, at the cost of freedom;[52] the proponents of *caritas* certainly claimed that this language represented the "mirror" of the soul, the outpourings of an exuberant heart,[53] yet the fact remains that their correspondence consisted mostly of slight variations on the same few themes.

Writing about the final arrogation of classical culture in the West by the Church one scholar could remark:

A time had dawned and would long endure when the leading classes of society possessed neither education nor books nor even a language in which they could have expressed a culture rooted in their actual living conditions. There was a learned language . . . There was a language of general culture.[54]

It is significant that when in the early-ninth century Einhard came to write the biography of that larger-than-life monarch Charlemagne, whose greatness extended far beyond the sphere of sanctity, he was reduced to piecing together tesserae from Suetonius' *Lives of the Caesars*, written in the second century.[55]

Between 600 and 1100 the word *humanitas* was used nearly always in a derogatory sense, "human frailty", the merely carnal, whereas in Antiquity it had meant "philanthropy" or "kindness" or else denoted the breadth of outlook associated with a classical education.[56]

In the art of Antiquity the great tradition of Roman portrait busts reaches its zenith of "wart-and-all" naturalism in the third century. Thereafter in this and most other genres of art individual physical peculiarities tend to pale away before a transcendental which irradiates all.[57] Later, in the art of the Mediaeval West, there is hardly any social or human realism: its effect is often derived from the juxtaposition of contrasts—God and Man, powerful and small; the unseen world is all-important.

In Late Antiquity the mimetic tradition of representation, which had been dominant throughout the classical eras of Greece and Rome, came to be undermined, its place being largely taken over by symbolic representation, as though an alternative to mimesis.

Notes

1. 248.11-15.

2. *De Consol. Phil.* I.4 (Peiper pp. 12.53-13.59); *PLRE* 2. "Opilio 4", "Cyprianus 2".

3. Arator, *Epistula ad Parthenium*. It seems strange for such a quality to be officially eulogised; *cf. Var.* 250.12; CIL 9.1596.

4. See generally, *PLRE* 2. "Parthenius 3".

5. *Cf.* Enn. 314.29ff; contrast *Liber Pontificalis* 53.3-5.

6. 4.19-27.

7. *Var.* 157.1-5.

8. *Var.* 155.31-2.

9. *Var.* 245.18-20. The idea of the correspondence of face, words, mind, and mores, was, admittedly, already very ancient.

10. *Var.* 183.7-13; and *cf.* 82.24-6.

11. *Var.* 167.7-8.

12. *Var.* 221.14-17.

13. *Cf.* also *Var.* VII.35. O'Donnell (*op. cit.* 5) calls the Ostrogothic Kingdom "a looking-glass world".

14. Cf: Var. VIII. 26. 3-4; X. 31. 2-3; A. J. Fridh, *Études critiques et syntaxiques sur les Variae de Cassiodore* (Göteborg 1950) 62–82. Indeed, sentences could be presented without any conjunction at all: cf. E., 12. 9-13; CDLVIII iv-vii, pp. 318-9; cf. Fronto, *Ad Marcum Caesarem et Invicem*, III. 12 (Van den Hout, p. 44), advocating such a repetition. A desultry look through the preambles of the *Variae* or of the *Novellae* of the *Theodosian Code* would reveal a predilection for expressing the generalities twice over by means of two cola side by side in parataxis: e. g. *NMarc.* IV, p.191. 26-8; *NMai.* IV, p.161. 5-6; *Var.* 124. 32-3; 126. 2-3. Apropos the *Variae*, O'Donnell (op. cit. 96) speaks of "a nostalgia for the epigrammatic brilliance of Silver Latin rhetoric".

15. So Auerbach (1953) 89.

16. *Cf.* also perhaps Jordanes p. 91.1, for the rather colourless *"terribilitate"* instead of *"terrore"* to denote the Huns.

17. *Cf.* also H. F. Muller, *L' époque mérovingienne. Essai de synthèse de philologie et d' histoire* (New York 1945) 161. See also below, pp. 157-8.

18. *Cf.* Fridh (1956), *passim*.

19. For a few examples more exquisite in both nuance and euphony, *cf. cervicositas, flexibilitas, numerositas, oficiositas,* all in O. J. Zimmerman, *The Late Latin Vocabulary of the Variae of Cassiodorus* (Washington 1944). *Cf.* also A. J. Fridh, *Contributions à la critique et l' interprétation des Variae de Cassiodore,* Göteborg 1968, 33f.

20. Discussed below, pp.16-24.

21. All these items are specifically Christian, or, as with *profunditas* or *puritas,* are creations of the Late-Antique World in general.

22. E. g. p. 16. 24.

23. *Cf.* Paulinus of Nola, Ep. 21. 6; Sid., 153. 6-8; *V. Honorati* c. 22, PL 50. 1261B-C *"blanda . . . dulcia . . . mel . . . dulcendinis"*; Victor Vitensis, p. 4. 8-10, etc.

24. E. g. Prudentius, *Cathermerinon* IV. 33; Sid., 108. 27-8; *Fausti aliorumque epistulae,* MGH (Aa) VIII. 271. 22-7; Enn., 18. 12–14; LXXIX; V. Caesarii I.52, P. 477; Cassiod., Instit. I.17.1; 20; *Epp. Austrasicae* 12, p.127 (dynamius). Such language is infrequent in Symmachus, e. g. P. 110.18.

25. H. Zilliacus, 'Zur Umschreibung des Verbums in spätgriechischen Urkunden', *Eranos* 54 (1956) 160-6.

26. 288. 25-6; *cf.* Symm., *Ep.* II.9, "ad conciliationem gratiae", for the more classical ad conciliandam gratiam.

27. *Var.* 220.12.

28. 246. 31. For other examples, *cf.* 179.31, "diligentiae suae districtione", for districta diligentia; 317.31, "captivationis"; 127.22, "decoctione"; 371.17, "inroratione"; 126.8; 258.15, 27, "obiectio"; 29.31,

"reparatio"; 290.1, "sequestratione"; 23.4; 377.16, "subreptionibus"; 192.17, "visitatio". All these words are cited by Zimmerman (*op. cit.* 17-25) as being of "recent coinage"; *cf.* generally H. Roseń, 'The Mechanisms of Latin Nominalisation', in *Aufstieg und Niedergang* II, *Principat,* ed H. Temporini and W. Haase, 29.1, pp. 178-211 (Berlin and New York 1983).

29. D. Daube, *Roman Law: Linguistic, Social, and Philosophical Aspects,* (Edinburgh 1969), Lecture 2, "The Action Noun", 45, 11.

30. See back, pp. 37-40; Fichtenau, op. cit. passim.

31. *Cf.* MacMullen (1964) 435-8.

32. *Cf.* Frindh (1956). The gradual eclipse of the vocative case in Late Latin is doubtless also relevant (O'Donnell, *op. cit.* 95).

33. For examples from imperial decrees, see back, p. 34.

34. E. g. Paulinus of Pella, *Eucharisticon,* 540, *"instabilis semper generaliter aevi".*

35. *Cf.* Enn., 105.19-20, 138.20; 186.17; *Var.* 48.17; 82.26-7; *AL* II.2.1376.6; 1385.6; 1411.13; 1414.14; 1430.7; 1445.7; 1516.3. Words such as *gemmae* are regularly used in this metaphorical way (see pp. 192-7). For the same static perception in a different context, cf. Enn., 78.10 (a herb is plucked) *"et ad dotem manuum hamanarum nobile germen adiungitur":*— the plant is perceived as the permanent endowment of the hands.

36. 16.30; *cf.* also *Var.* 301.19-20, "We have changed our rule of living (*propsitum*) along with our office", words put into Theodahad's mouth at his accession.

37. *Cf.* MacMullen (1964) 445-450; also Salvian, *De Gubern. Dei* IV.33, p. 42.7, "When a man changes his garments, he immediately changes his rank".

38. See generally C. Morris, *The Discovery of the Individual, 1050–1200* (London 1972); Ullmann, *op. cit.* esp. 43f; A. Grabar, 'Plotin et Les Origines de l'Esthétique Médiévale' (*Cahiers Archéologiques I,* 1945), at p. 19.

39. Quoted in full, MGH *Variae, Index Nominum,* "Senarius".

40. 206.31-2; *cf.* 21.6-7; 117.24-5; 178.22-3; 179.6-8; *cf.* Sid. *Ep.* 1X.4.1, p. 153.5; *AL* I. 1.689; *ILS* 1259, "*Paulina. . . fomes pudoris, castitatis vinculum amorque purus et fides caelo sata . . . munus deorum"*; V. Caesarii I. 45, p. 474. 22-4; Agnellus, *Lib. Pontif. Eccles. Ravenn.,* c. 114 (poem); Venantius, *Appendix* V.10. p. 279, *"florum flos florens".*

41. E. g. Avitus, *Appendix XV,* p. 191 (attributable to Venantius), in honour of Austregilde, described by Gregory of Tours (*HF* V. 36) as "wicked".

42. E. g. *Carmina VI.* 1A.23, 27, p.130; X.8.5-6, p. 241; *Appendix V,* p. 279.

43. See above, pp. 151-3.

44. See A. Weische, *Studien zur politischen Sprache der römischen Republik* (Münster 1966), 105–111.

45. Zimmermann, op. cit. 1f, 28-32.

46. See Weische, op. cit. 105; also F. T. Cooper, *Word-Formation in the Roman Sermo Plebeius* (N. Y. 1895) 58-70.

47. I am indebted to the late Prof. F. R. D. Goodyear, formerly of London University, for sending me details of works relevant to the present paragraph, as well as for elucidating his own views on this phenomenon in Silver Latin.

48. F. R. D. Goodyear, *The Annals of Tacitus, Book I, Chapters 1-54,* (Cambridge 1972) 221 (the translations of the Latin phrases are the present author's); cf. ibid. 121,236; also F. Kuntz, *Die Sprache de Tacitus und die Tradition der lateinischen Historikersprache* (Heidelberg 1962) 106-110; A. A. Draeger, *Über Syntax und Stil des Tacitus* (3rd ed. Leipzig 1882) 3f.

49. Weische, op. cit. 109f.

50. Ullman, op. cit. 43f.

51. *E. g. V. Augusti* cc. 69; 71; 87; *V. Tiberii* 21. The Latin epistolers of the Late Empire were influenced above all by stylistic canons laid down by Pliny and Fronto, who had written with a view to publication.

52. Cf. Hagendahl 1952 37: *"La richesse en formes métriques de la prose ciceronnienne, sa variété et sa liberté sont remplacées par un systéme fixe, caractérisé par la pauvreté en formes, la monotonie, et le manque de liberté. Plus les soins que consacre un auteur au rythme sont grands, et plus la tendance à l' uniformisation du rythme est forte".*

53. E. g. Paulinus of Nola, *Epp.* 13.2, *PL* 61.208; 21.6, *PL* 61.253C.

54. Auerbach (1965) 255.

55. Morris, *op. cit.* 8.

56. Ullman, *op. cit.* 7ff; *cf.* Morris, *op. cit.* 10.

57. See Grabar (1945) 19.

Abbreviations

AE: Année Épigraphique.

AJ: F. F. ABBOTT AND A. C. JOHNSON, *Municipal Administration in the Roman Empire.*

AL: ANTHOLOGIA LATINA.

Amm: AMMIANUS MARCELLINUS.

BG PROCOPIUS, *De Bello Gothico.*

CA: COLLECTIO AVELLANA.

CC: Corpus Christianorum.

CIL: CORPUS INSCRIPTIONUM LATINARUM.

CIust: CODEX IUSTINIANUS.

CM: CHRONICA MINORA.

CSEL: Corpus Scriptorum Ecclesiasticorum Latinorum.

CTh: CODEX THEODOSIANUS.

Enn: ENNODIUS.

FIRA FONTES IURIS ROMANI ANTEIUSTINIANI.

FS: INSCHRIFTENSAMMLUNG ZUR GESCHICHTE DER OSTGERMANEN I, *ed.* O. Fiebiger and L. Schmidt.

HF: GREGORY OF TOURS, *History of the Franks.*

IHC: INSCRIPTIONES HISPANIAE CHRISTIANAE, *ed.* A. Hübner.

ILS: INSCRIPTIONES LATINAE SELECTAE.

JRS: Journal of Roman Studies.

LRE A. H. M. Jones, *The Later Roman Empire,* Oxford 1964.

MGH: (Aa) Monumenta Germaniae Historica, *Auctores Antiquissimi*—to be distinguished from other series, above all *Scriptores Rerum Merowingicarum (Scr. Rer. Merow.).*

MRLC: MOSAICARUM ET ROMANARUM LEGUM COLLATIO, *ed.* J. Baviera, FIRA.

NAnth: *Novella Divi Anthemii Augusti (see* CODEX THEODOSIANUS).

NMai: *Novella Divi Maioriani Augusti (ibidem).*

NMarc: *Novella Divi Marciani Augusti (ibidem).*

NTheo: *Novella Divi Theodosii Augusti (ibidem).*

NVal: *Novella Divi Valentiniani Augusti (ibidem).*

OS Th. MOMMSEN, *Ostgotische Studien.*

PL: Patrologia Latina (J. P. Migne).

PLRE: 2 J. R. MARTINDALE, *The Prosopography of the Later Roman Empire,* Vol. 2.

PW: A. Pauly, G. Wissowa, W. Kroll, Real-Encyclopaedie der klassischen Altertumswissenschaft.

SC: Sources Chrétiennes.

Sid: SIDONIUS APOLLINARIS.

Sirm: SIRMONDIAN CONSTITUTIONS.

Symm: SYMMACHUS.

TLL: *Thesaurus Linguae Latinae.*

Var: CASSIODORUS, *Variae.*

S. J. B. Barnish (essay date 1992)

SOURCE: An introduction to The *"Variae"* of Magnus Aurelius Cassiodorus Senator, translated by S. J. B. Barnish, Liverpool University Press, 1992, pp. ix-xxxv.

[In the excerpt below, Barnish offers an overview of the Variae, *discussing its style, its reliability as a source of historical information, and various manuscript issues.]*

. . . B. The Variae

1. The Compilation

Our most important documents for the history of Gothic rule in Italy are the *Variae* of Cassiodorus: twelve books, comprising 468 letters, edicts and model letters (*formulae*), which the author drafted, between 506 and 538, for Theoderic, Athalaric, Amalasuintha, Theodahad, Witigis, and the Senate, and in his own person as Praetorian Prefect of Italy. In the case of those written for monarchs, he was acting as, or for, the Quaestor, chief legal expert and official publicist.[1] He apparently compiled the *Variae* in 537/8, near the harassed end of his service as Prefect, while war was raging, and Witigis was besieging the Byzantine commander Belisarius in Rome. In a long and conventionally self-deprecatory Preface, he claimed a range of motives for this work: to satisfy the demands of friend—a standard apology; to supply models of official eloquence for future administrators, himself among them; to ensure immortality for those praised in the letters; to strengthen respect for the laws; and to provide a mirror of his own character. The title *Variae* reflects the varieties of rhetorical style which the letters show. A verse couplet dedicated the collection to an unnamed rhetorician: '[Cassiodorus] Senator offers these gifts of love and duty to the master whom no gold pleases more than eloquence.'

The claims and suggestions of the Preface are a useful starting-point when considering the *Variae*. Official education is a plausible motive. Cassiodorus' later commentary on the psalms (*Expositio Psalmorum*) and his *Institutiones* show a deep concern for rhetorical training. His near contemporary John Lydus, a middle ranking career bureaucrat in Constantinople, was awarded a state teaching post for his general learning and skill in Latin. In the early medieval west, formulary collections of legal and chancery documents were common; the *Variae* are an early example of the genre. An inscription from the territory of Timgad in Numidia repeats a sentence from VII.7, the formula of appointment for the Prefect of the Watch at Rome. This suggests that the collection was read and used by the provincial administrators of Justinian. A Boethius, probably related to Cassiodorus, served as Praetorian Prefect of Africa in 560.[2]

As a compilation, the *Variae* can also be read as an apology, both for the Gothic regime, and for the Roman aristocracy which had served it. (Justinian's officials were to penalise the Romans for abuses of power under the Goths.[3]) There is something almost defiant in Cassiodorus' inclusion of 67 letters from his own Prefectural administration. Perhaps, too, he was advocating either a continuing Gothic role in Italy, a revival of the western empire, or a combination of the two. About the time the *Variae* were published, he probably also collected and published his formal panegyrics on Gothic royalties.[4] While Ravenna was under

siege in 540, the Goths offered the rule of the western empire to Belisarius. Many *formulae* in the *Variae* (e.g. VII.42) suggest an expectation that the Gothic administration would continue; but VI.6, at least, may describe imperial practices obsolete under the Goths. Some of the Roman senators praised in the collection probably remained loyal to the Goths; others had transferred their allegiance, and one, Fidelis, may already have been serving as Justinian's Praetorian Prefect of Italy, in rivalry with Cassiodorus.

Politically significant themes, such as the defence of Italy, relations between Goths and Franks, and diplomacy with Byzantium are also prominent. Moreover, both in general and in detail, the *Variae* may imply a critique of the growing cultural and religious intolerance of Justinian's regime. (Cf. II.27, X.26.) The emperor, furthermore, was at odds with the Senate of Constantinople, which probably hoped for a greater share in government, and a leading role in the choice of the emperor. Controversy of this kind may lie behind the fall of Boethius in Italy, the *Nika* riots of 532 in Constantinople, and an anonymous Greek dialogue on political science.[5] In the context of such debate, Cassiodorus gives a model of courteous relations between monarch and Senate; he depicts the Senate as a galaxy of learned, talented statesmen, which embodies the traditions of Rome; but he seldom shows it acting corporately, to devise or execute policy, and he makes it clear that it played no part in the choice of rulers for Italy.

In these political circumstances, his favourable picture of senators, tribesmen and Gothic monarchs should not be taken on trust. (He is well able to gild or ignore decay; cf. note 14 to VIII.33.) However, the image is far from ideal. Corruption, brutality and inefficiency among Goths and Romans, and the impotence of the monarch are often shown or hinted at, sometimes illustrating, perhaps, the political struggles of Cassiodorus and his family (III.8, III.21, III.27-28, III.46). A policy not of racial integration, but of an uneasy partnership, with the Goths forming Sidonius' 'privileged military class' against the civilian Romans, is also plain to view (III.13). Gothic rulers seem to stand above the two races, to hold an unequal balance between them, and to owe their authority to this position. (The emperors had treated the military and civilian hierarchies similarly.) Between the lines, indeed, we see these monarchs manoeuvering with difficulty to enforce their will and restrain disorder among the jostling pride and interests of Roman and Gothic barons. The land-grabbing of Theodahad is not ignored, and the drunkenness of Athalaric is hinted at; as too, perhaps, the murder of Amalasuintha (X.5, X.20-21, XI.1.4-5).

Cassiodorus must, however, have selected only a minority of his letters, and certain omissions are striking. Some of these may be on literary grounds. Cassiodorus must have drafted many letters of appointment for Consuls and ministers which are not included. Thus, Liberius' appointment as Praetorian Prefect of Gaul is missing; the high praise he receives elsewhere in the *Variae* (II.16, XI.1.16f.) suggests that the motive for this was not political. In the Preface, the author claims that over hasty compositions caused him embarrassment. Another factor is the composition of his public: there is much on the administration of Gaul, little on Pannonia or Spain; the Gallic and Italian aristocracies were closely linked (cf. II.1, III.18).

More significant is silence on the internal strife of Theoderic's last years, which brought Cassiodorus back to court as Master of the Offices, replacing his fallen kinsman Boethius. Instead, the building of a fleet to defend Italy from foreign threats is given prominence, and Boethius features only in much earlier letters. Amalasuintha's murder of her Gothic opponents, to which Cassiodorus may have owed his promotion to the Italian Prefecture, is also missing. Of such conflicts, we have only the occasional hint, although one of his major tasks must have been their favourable public presentation. Did he rewrite the letters he included?[6] For extensive political revision there was probably no time: careless syntax, incorrect titles and arrangement, and the incomplete adaptation of letters of *formulae* (e.g. XI.36) confirm the complaints of the Preface; the royal formulary books VI-VII are more carefully written.[7] Yet, like the letter collections of the younger Pliny or the elder Symmachus (written c. A.D. 100-110 and 364-402), the *Variae* were perhaps intended to coat with plaster the more conspicuous cracks in their society. Style, however, appears in the Preface as Cassiodorus' main concern: the study of his literary form will give a deeper understanding of his aims.

2. THE CHARACTER OF THE VARIAE[8]

Cassiodorus gave the *Variae* a character partly formulaic, partly timeless and literary. Some persons—especially envoys, although these were often high in rank—are referred to not by name, but as X and Y (*illum et illum*). Dates have been removed, save for the occasional internal reference to the tax year (indiction), and figures for money and commodities have often disappeared. Official protocols, with the full titles due to sender and recipient have been abbreviated to short rubrics (not always accurate); presumably, this must have detracted from their value as secretarial models. We should contrast the Merovingian protocols in some of the *Epistulae Austrasicae,* private and official letters, probably compiled for chancery instruction c.600. A document which Cassiodorus' predecessor as Quaestor probably drafted in 507 is also typical: 'King Flavius Theodericus to the Senate of the City of Rome, Tamer of the World, Head and Restorer of Liberty'.[9] Except in the *formulae* of VI-VII and XI.17-34, there is a very rough and unreliable chronological arrangement, but the order of the letters is determined partly by literary considerations: for instance, set-piece documents, particularly diplomatic, begin and end the books. Sometimes, though, we find a string of letters of similar date and subject, and may surmise that portions of an official file (e.g. on the administration of Gaul) have been included without much disturbance.

The letters differ greatly in size, content, and elaboration. In Å. Fridh's text, the average length is some 30 lines, but the range is between 5 and 140. Formally, the majority convey administrative measures, legal rulings and edicts, or announcements of appointments. The last of these usually include miniature panegyrics on the more eminent ministers, and remarks on their offices. Resembling the speeches of a university's Public Orator, they are literary equivalents to the illuminations found in the late empire's *Register of State Dignities (Notitia Dignitatum).*[10] They usually come in pairs (e.g. I.3-4), one for the honorand, the other for the Senate, notifying it of the appointment and requesting confirmation. The legal and administrative types often include digressive, belletristic essays: set-piece descriptions (*ekphrases*) of public works and spectacles are frequent; so too accounts of the liberal arts and cultural inventions; also (recalling Vergil), the wealth, landscapes and natural phenomena of Italy, especially the author's native south. Digressions are generally addressed to men of learning and social distinction, and must usually affirm a bond between recipient and sender, as similar private letters would do; sometimes, though, they are included in rebukes to the erring or negligent.

Letters of the more elaborate type are probably over represented in the collection. But, short or long, the majority are prefaced by, and mixed with general reflections on the conduct and duties of monarchs, subjects and administrators, which too often resemble the woolly platitudes of Jane Austen's Mr Collins. From these principles, the measure conveyed is deduced, although sometimes the proem is so stylised as to seem almost irrelevant. In a substantial minority of cases, morality is illustrated by digressive analogies, drawn usually from nature, but now and then from political or Biblical history.[11] We get the impression of an urge to justify and explain, which has been devalued almost to an irrational habit, and is coupled with a high level of generality.

The style, in general, is highly ornate: formulaic, rhythmical, repetitive, given to internal rhyme, and studded with antitheses, paradoxes, exclamations and rhetorical questions. Abstract nouns and passive or impersonal verbs are very numerous; so too are causal and conclusive conjunctions, particles, and adverbs, words in which Latin is far richer than English. *Constat,* forms of *probari* and *videri,* and superlatives are commonplace, indeed are often almost meaningless; many words, phrases and inflections are introduced largely for the sake of rhythm and euphony. To give variety, neologisms are created, and old words given new uses. In the combination of stock phrases, or the accumulation of clauses, the syntax may become confused, and a paratactic arrangement of clauses is often preferred to a subordinate—signs, perhaps, of hasty writing and compilation.[12]

By comparison with other late Latin letters, the *Variae* make easy reading: Cassiodorus is less dry, compressed, and elliptical than Symmachus or his own contemporary, bishop Ennodius of Pavia, less recherché in vocabulary than Sidonius or Ennodius. Even so, his later *Institutiones,* a guide to the world of learning, intended partly for monastic readers, is generally plainer and more comprehensible, designed to instruct, more than to impress. The *De Anima,* appended to the *Variae,* seems to be transitional in manner as well as matter.[13]

Connoisseurs would have seen his letters as studded with rhetorical conceits and figures like a meadow jewelled with flowers. The stock vocabulary of symbols, metaphors, and abstract qualities has lately been compared to heraldic blazonry.[14] The ancients had always exploited history and nature for moral *exempla,* and this may have been especially so in late antiquity, a culture fascinated by type, symbol and allegory. The great men of the realm seem identified with virtues, vices, skills and offices (cf. Preface, 14); their array has as little individuality as the saints and prophets who look down in mosaic from the walls of Theoderic's church of S.Apollinare Nuovo at Ravenna. Cassiodorus' ekphrastic descriptions are often vivid and instructive—thus, V.1 gives a remarkable word-picture of the play of light on a pattern-welded German sword. However, they lack the precision of those in Pliny's letters which lie behind their tradition, and they sometimes leave us doubtful if the author has seen the object he describes. Even in the less relevant descriptions, the object, and men's response to it, are given an exemplary turn, and a moral or religious purpose seems never far away. (For instance, with VIII.33, contrast Pliny, *Ep.* IV.30 and VIII.8.)

Literary allusions and echoes are probably numerous. (No thorough scrutiny has yet been made, but I have noted a few instances.) Despite the many pious expressions of the *Variae,* especially those letters which the Catholic Cassiodorus drafted in his own right, rather than for Arian rulers, secular classics are more alluded to than the scriptures. In this, there is some contrast with the *De Anima,* discussed below, but the general avoidance of Christian discourse seems comparable to the non-religious *Novels* of the last western emperors. On natural disasters, Cassiodorus speaks less of divine vengeance, than of physical causes, as in XII.25.[15] Now and then, however, Christian miracles and morality are introduced, and may even be used to condemn traditional Roman practices (V.42, VIII.33). A digression addressed to the Christian philosopher Boethius combines classical and biblical allusions, and concludes with a passage of near Christian mysticism (II.40). While the ancient Roman title of Patrician is traced back to the priesthoods of early Rome (VI.2), in the next *formula* the prototype of the Praetorian Prefect is the Patriarch Joseph (VI.3).

On practicalities, the letters are not always very instructive: the technical exposition of law and administration features less than in the official correspondence of Symmachus (Book X, *Relationes*), or of Pliny (Book X). In one letter (XI.14), such is Cassiodorus' absorption in his rhetoric that the official point is all but omitted: administration has become a vestigial frame for verbal landscape-painting. Most letters, however, are quite brief; and sometimes oral messages were sent, or accounts, lists, and detailed instructions were attached in *breves,* a practice familiar from private and literary epistolography. But, in general, we do not get so sure a grasp on the diplomacy and administration of the regime as papal correspondence gives us for the sixth century Roman Church.

The late Roman upper classes linked themselves privately by elegant correspondence,[16] but it seems a strange mode for official business. Was it peculiar to Cassiodorus? His Latin is not mere bureaucratese, but it has much in common with chancery style in the late antique world. So too his moralising proems. Ancient rulers believed it important to use persuasion; and late Roman laws, which give the best comparisons to the *Variae,* often show a similar rhetorical structure: they move from the moral *arenga* to an exposition of the situation (*narratio* or *expositio*), thence to a decision (*dispositio*) and measures of enforcement (*sanctio* or *corroboratio*).[17] Examples can be conveniently studied in the imperial *Novels* and *Sirmondian Constitutions* attached to the *Theodosian Code:* some of these go straight to the point, and the *arenga* is almost lacking; others come close to rivalling the wordiest *Variae.*[18] Evidently, much depended on the time, taste and talents of the drafting officer; sometimes, perhaps, of the monarch himself; sometimes, too, on his political position. Verbose edicts of consolation to men afflicted by flood, famine or earthquake probably had a long imperial history, although Cassiodorus gives the sole surviving examples.[19] An edict of the emperor Julian, a talkative intellectual, with special need to justify himself, included an extensive essay on funerary rites; it was eventually reduced to a much briefer law.[20] The short law-code called the *Edict of Theoderic*[21] is far more straight-forward and usefully informative than the *Edict of Athalaric* (IX.18). The Cassiodorian piece, though, was probably designed for a different end: not to provide a handy legal compendium for judges, but to shore up the shaky moral and political authority of the regime. Hence its rather artificial twelve-part structure, recalling the *Twelve Tables* that were the foundation of Roman law.[22]

Cassiodorus' originality lies in his elaborate use of metaphor and digression, an importation, perhaps, to the official world from sermons, secular declamations, and sermonising private letters.[23] From a tradition of private letters which goes back to Pliny, he has adopted his descriptions of scenery or natural wonders, and his miniature panegyrics; both have their parallels in the correspondence of Sidonius in late fifth century Gaul. Epistolary panegyric was also in vogue with the contemporary Byzantine bureaucracy, as shown by examples in the *De Magistratibus* of John Lydus.[24] 'A flow of the most genial impertinence', George Gissing affectionately called Cassiodorus' digressions; but there may be more to them than learned light relief.

The ascendancy of the Graeco-Roman ruling classes was based on their mastery of rhetoric and associated learning. To civilian administrators, it gave an éclat to parallel the soldier's glory.[25] East and west, this tradition was increasingly threatened, whether by social mobility, declining education, Christian values, or the contempt of warrior élites; not surprisingly, men reaffirmed it, deliberately showing its virtues in the work of government. Rhetoric, indeed, had traditionally a moral, as well as a practical function, and we shall see that the *Variae* may have been designed to educate the ruling class in the values of its role and the purposes of the state. As Cassiodorus wrote, 'the knowledge of literature is glorious, since it purifies our morals—something of prime importance for mankind; as a secondary matter, it supplies us with eloquence' (III.33.3; cf. III.6.3-5, 11.4-5, IX.21.8, 24.8). The virtues of prudence and integrity inculcated may seem tediously banal, but he occasionally reveals something of the moral dilemmas and special obligations of high office (XII.5.1-2,9, XI.16).[26]

The rule of law, as both a natural and social phenomenon, and the chief end of politics, is a common theme of the *Variae*. A key word is *civilitas*. In classical usage, this had implied a ruler's correct demeanour towards his subjects, and still did so for Sidonius and for Cassiodorus' contemporary, bishop Avitus of Vienne. In the *Variae*, as in writings of Ennodius and Pope Gelasius (492-6), it more usually denotes the duty of subjects towards each other, decent social behaviour, and respect for law; 'civilisation' and 'good order' are sometimes possible translations. By his use of natural and cultural history, Cassiodorus seems to root *civilitas* in a garden of natural law and social progress.[27]

Men of the sixth century liked to theorise about government and society,[28] and Cassiodorus gave to his picture of men at work in their secular society a theoretical dimension which combined Bible-based theology with classical philosophy. The *De Anima*, he claimed, was an afterthought; but it also formed the thirteenth book of the *Variae*, was similar in length to the others, was probably published and long joined with them in manuscript, and was allegedly composed by request of the same friends. There, the digressions of the *Variae* expand into the nature and destiny of the soul, which has made the marvellous discoveries necessary to earthly society, and perceives and understands the divinely ordered universe (XI, praef.7, *De An.* i, iv, *Expositio Psalmorum,* cxlv.2).[29] The four cardinal virtues, which figure largely in the *Variae,* are given a social emphasis, and are complemented by a more spiritual or intellectual trio (vii). Prayer and meditation close the treatise. St Augustine's *On Order* may lie behind the concept; we might also compare the thirteen books of his *Confessions,* of which the last four turn from autobiography to associated meditation and theology. Boethius' *Consolation of Philosophy* likewise moves from political autobiography to the religious philosophy of the cosmos, and is copiously illustrated with natural analogies. In their original form, the mosaics of S.Apollinare Nuovo probably showed Theoderic's family and courtiers in solemn procession from the palace at Ravenna to the throne of Christ,[30] to this Cassiodorus gives a literary parallel.

To develop a Christian version of the rhetorical training for public life, while retaining classical elements, was a major concern for Cassiodorus.[31] In his *On the Duties of the Clergy* (c.390), St Ambrose had replaced Cicero's *On Duties,* articulating practice and ideals for the servants of God in the Latin Church. Despite the Stoic and Platonic tradition, of which Boethius was the last, belated representative,[32] Roman secular officials had always lacked an ideology of service formulated with such clarity; the *Variae* and *De Anima* seem a half deliberate response to their need.

Boethius saw it as his consular duty to translate Greek philosophy for his fellow citizens.[33] He also hoped to play the philosopher statesman at Theoderic's court, and both he and Cassiodorus may have been influenced by the orator and philosopher Themistius (317-88), counsellor to successive emperors. Roman arms had not restrained the barbarians; Roman culture might yet do so.[34] Cassiodorus celebrated the instruction he had given to Theoderic (IX.24.8). In his lost *Gothic History,* he apparently depicted a legendary sage Dicineus. This alien had given the Goths political counsel, and had taught them logic, natural philosophy, and finally religion; their understanding of nature gave them laws and moral standards. In Dicineus, did Cassiodorus idealise his own aims and achievement at the court of Ravenna?[35]

In the tenth century, the emperor Constantine Porphyrogenitus was to write of the ceremonies of his court, 'Hereby may the imperial power be exercised with due rhythm and order; may the empire thus represent the harmony and motion of the universe as it comes from its creator; and may it thus appear to our subjects in a more solemn majesty, and so be the more acceptable to them and the more admirable in their eyes . . .'[36] Supported by the *De Anima,* the *Variae* display this governmental mirror of the cosmos.

When not acting as Quaestor, Cassiodorus was sometimes called on to help out the Quaestor of the day with his compositions. In theory, Quaestors were men of rhetorical skill; but it seems that his talents were regarded as exceptional by successive rulers. (At a lower level, John Lydus similarly lent his talents around the Praetorian Prefecture of the East.) We have, in fact, a few documents probably drawn up by other Theoderican Quaestors which support this impresssion: the Latin is a chancery style similar to Cassiodorus's, but the letters seem much shorter and plainer than he would have made them. The rhetorical declamations of Ennodius are the work of a skilled and learned orator, and have some general resemblance to the *Variae:* for instance, a new pupil is introduced into a school of rhetoric like a new minister to the Senate. However, they show little of the Cassiodorian digressive technique, which Theoderic himself may well have enjoyed (cf. IX.24.8, and note).[37]

We should compare another Quaestor of the time, Justinian's great jurist Tribonian. The prefaces which he devised for his master's *Novels,* and which ceased when he died, often include lengthy historical digressions, reassurances to a doubtful public that radical reforms really followed Roman tradition. For the reforms themselves, though, he was probably not responsible—they were the work of Justinian and his Prefect John the Cappadocian; and some he may even have opposed.[38] Allusions to history long past are infrequent in the *Variae*—their history is contemporary—and the political thrust is rather different. The Ostrogothic rulers tried to change as little as possible. Cassiodorus could not prove them Romans, although *exempla* from Roman history may have been more frequent in their formal panegyrics. Instead, he seems to assure educated Roman gentlemen that they were not lawless, arbitrary, and uncultivated despots, that they observed natural justice, and differed from other tribesmen, who lacked their noble-savage traditions, and the educating grace of residence in Italy. Pope Gregory the Great (590-604) was to write, 'this is the difference between tribal kings and emperors of the Romans, the fact that tribal kings are lords of slaves, but emperors of the Romans lords of free men'.[39] Cassiodorus' task was to show the Goths as defenders of freedom under the law, and of civilised values, who honoured and employed gentlemen of humane education; the term 'barbarian' is never applied to them.[40] To read Theoderic's letters to the recovered provinces of Gaul and Pannonia (III.17 and 23) is to meet again the Caesar Constantius in 296, as a medallion depicts him, delivering London from rebels and barbarians, and 'restoring the eternal light' of Rome.[41]

If the execution was the work of Cassiodorus, what of the policy? Procopius tells of cultural tension between Romans and barbarians in Italy.[42] The honours given by Theoderic to Boethius, then translating Greek philosophy into Latin, were conferred in 521-2, when Cassiodorus was out of office, and suggest royal awareness of the problem. If the *Variae* portray Theoderic, Amalaberga, Amalasuintha and Theodahad as 'philosophers in purple'—a phrase perhaps taken from Themistius[43]—the image need not have been foisted on them by Cassiodorus who helped to shape it. Many emperors had worn a double mask of soldier and intellectual, and other barbarian rulers employed Roman rhetoricians among their leading counsellors. The political, if not the cultural, tone of the reign had been set at least as early as 500, when Theoderic visited Rome in a generous and impressive but tactful triumph: citizens, clergy and senators found their religious sensibilities reassured, and their political traditions confirmed.[44] Cassiodorus enjoyed unusually long periods in high office, but these total fifteen years at most; the Ostrogothic state down to the fall of Ravenna, lasted for some forty. As with Tribonian, the influence he must have had is hard to disinter from documents in which every decision and appointment is presented, at least to the casual eye, in similar style, through all changes of political weather and regime.

One quaestor of Theoderic apparently altered a general pardon to make it still more inclusive,[45] and two non-Cassiodorian Ostrogothic documents also shed light on the independence of official draftsmen. One of these is a formal directive sent by Theoderic to a council of bishops set up to try Pope Symmachus; the other seems to reproduce the words of the king on which the first was based.[46] The Quaestor of the day improved his master's Latin and the structure of his remarks; he eliminated biblical references, and a not very relevant historical anecdote; in general, he produced a blander discourse, less lively and forceful, but more coherent, and less biassed. At the same time, he followed Theoderic's general gist, and sometimes closely echoed it. In the same way, Tribonian's laws may express the personality of Justinian with more elegance than the emperor could command.[47] The Symmachus case, however, was one of great political importance, in which the Quaestor's work would have been closely monitored; on lesser occasions, or where flexibility was needed, he may have been allowed a freer hand. As noted earlier, between the lines of the *Variae,* we can sometimes read a criticism of the monarch.

Cassiodorus sometimes likens secular offices to the priesthood, and the overall impression left by the *Variae* is of governmental liturgies, compiled in a secular Sacramentary: their stereotyped sentiments and instructions correspond to prayers and ritual actions, their metaphors and digressions to pulpit oratory. Popes contemporary with Cassiodorus did much to shape the liturgy of the Roman Church, and the age was one of sacred texts, religious and secular: the law codes of Theodosius II and Justinian mirror the scrolls and jewelled codexes in the mosaics of the Ravenna churches, or the great Bible[48] produced by Cassiodorus' monks at Vivarium.

Modern readers tend to dislike the repetitious habit of the *Variae:* ideas are worked to death by an author who did not know when to stop. Some ancients would have agreed: Quintilian wrote c. A.D. 90, 'In our passion for words we paraphrase what might be said in plain language, repeat what we have already said at sufficient length, pile up a number of words where one would suffice, and regard allusion as better than directness of speech.'[49] But repetition is an important liturgical element, a fact of which Cassiodorus shows some appreciation in his commentary on the Psalms. He might also be compared to a musician, composing multiple variations on a theme. With his varied repetitions, his use of paradox and antithesis, his careful, sonorous rhythms, his lengthy periods, paratactically organised, and his display of curious learning, he has his closest English counterpart in Sir Thomas Browne. Rooted in Roman liturgies of the fifth to seventh centuries, the old Book of Common Prayer also conveys the flavour of his more religious moralising and his simpler sentences (cf. XI.2). The style of the letters won the respect of the novelist George Gissing; while Gibbon, though outwardly contemptuous, at least paid them the compliment of paraphrase.

3. The Variae as Separate Documents

What congregations heard these chants of the state liturgy, as each was separately sung? One audience, of course, was the person or persons to whom they were immediately directed. An edict on simony in episcopal elections was to be engraved on marble, and placed in the atrium of St Peter's; another general edict was to be read in the Senate, then formally posted (or proclaimed) in public places and assemblies for thirty days (IX.15-16, IX.18-20).[50] A letter to a provincial governor regulating a country fair was to be read to the people there, then posted up (VIII.33). No such document would have been easily understood by an ordinary person, and the last is an essay of great literary pretensions. Doubtless, the governor was properly impressed, but we may surmise larger educated audiences. An unauthorised circulation among the educated is sometimes attested for private letters and declamations, before they were published in collections.[51] One recipient of a specially elaborate letter summoned an assembly of the cultured and eminent in his province for a formal recitation.[52] Official assemblies of provincial notables probably continued in Ostrogothic Italy, and I would guess that Cassiodorus' letters were distributed or recited at such gatherings. XII.25 was designed to reassure anxious subjects, rather than his deputy.

Some documents, at least, will probably have been publicised before they left the palace or reached the relevant official. Cassiodorus certainly did not intend the royal directives which he drafted to himself as Praetorian Prefect for his eyes only. To judge by imperial precedent, copies of edicts would routinely have been posted outside the royal residence where they had been produced. Among the duties of the Quaestor may have been the public declamation, before their despatch, of decrees and rescripts he had drafted, a practice which saved the monarch's credit if they were challenged.[53] Formal diplomatic letters may often have been recited in council; so too, perhaps, set-piece rebukes (e.g. I.2, 35) which displayed the monarch's cultivation, but which the recipient would hardly have publicised. Public shame, as well as honour, could be conveyed by letter, although learned digression might soften reproof (e.g. V.42). Many office holders, like John Lydus, must have dangled their letters of appointment before the public eye; indeed, they may have displayed them formally on their desks.[54] The letter to the honorand, and its twin to the Senate usually cover rather different ground, as if the Senate were expected to hear them both.

Moreover, some leading Goths and their followers will have been literate in Latin; and those whose style and grammar were shaky may yet have appreciated an elegant author, as did Jordanes, whose *Getica* abridged Cassiodorus' *Gothic History*. At Naples in 535, two trained rhetoricians of the city apparently persuaded a popular assembly of Goths and Romans to resist the Byzantines.[55] The *Gothic History* may likewise have been aimed at both races: to impress on blue-blooded senators, and proud Gothic chieftains the dignity and antiquity of the Amal house, whose pre-eminence was recent and precarious.[56] Probably, then, at least so long as Cassiodorus was active at court, most Roman, and some Gothic notables in state and society will have been exposed to a sequence of letters, building up the desired image of their monarchs.

What, though, of the non-élite? How far did the *Variae* resemble the ivory diptychs and silver-ware which Consuls and emperors presented to a chosen few?[57] In the Preface, Cassiodorus claims to have adapted his style to his audience; but, though the style does often vary, the education and status of the recipient was not always a criterion.[58] Most barbarians, and even Romans of the day would have found even the simpler letters hard to understand. (Interpreters had to be provided for a learned letter on amber [V.2], sent to Estonia!) As so often in ritual, the language and ideas are meant to be heard widely, but are intelligible mainly to a few. Goths will have depended on Romans, and the unlearned on their social betters, to interpret what concerned them; relations of dependency and respect may thereby have been strengthened or created. The Lucanian peasants at the fair of St Cyprian, whom Cassiodorus disciplined and threatened (VIII.33), were the distant ancestors of those whom Carlo Levi met in his exile beyond Eboli in 1935. They had received nothing from Rome except the tax collector, and radio speeches, irrelevant and incomprehensible. How much in common had the audiences of Athalaric and Mussolini?

4. The Variae as an Historical Source: a Caution

Even where suspicious silences and overt propaganda cannot be detected, the *Variae* must be used with caution. Next to the imperial laws, they are our fullest source for the administrative workings of the late, particularly the western empire. They may, indeed, be too full a source, shedding strong light on a very restricted region and period. During the fifth century, great political changes had taken place in the west, while the volume of new legislation declined sharply, ceasing altogether in Italy from 476. Hence, we cannot always tell when features of government encountered in the *Variae* had arisen, and how far Odoacer and his successors dealt with novel situations by new arrangements. So too with administrative politics: the light cast by Cassiodorus hardly extends beyond his tenures of office. Hence, certain letters may mark new drives against private violence or official corruption, for which he and his masters should be given some credit—or they may be common form.

5. The Variae: Text and Editions; Selection, Dating and Translation

More than a hundred manuscripts of the *Variae* survive. Those which Th. Mommsen used in his edition (below), he divided into six classes, stemming principally from a lost archetype. This archetype may be identical with a manuscript which probably also contained the archetype of the *De Anima*, attested in a ninth century catalogue from Lorsch.[59] The *Variae* archetype came to be divided into two parts, the second commencing with letter VII.41, and wholly or partially transmitted by Classes 3-5. Class 6 is the only one to give a complete text, but it is mainly a composite, drawn from Classes 1, 4, and 5. The two best manuscripts are, for the first part, *Codex Leidensis Vulcanianus* 46 in Class 2, written at Fulda c.1170; for the second part, *Codex Bruxellensis* 10018-10019 in Class 4, also of the 12th century. *Leidensis,* whose attractive drawings of Cassiodorus and Theoderic are reproduced in Mommsen's edition, contains I.1 to VII.41, and alone gives the dedicatory couplet. *Bruxellensis* runs from VII.42 to the end, and is the only member of its class to give VII.42-47.[60]

The *editio princeps* of the complete *Variae* appeared in 1533, the work of M. Accursius. In many libraries, the only edition available is likely to be the mediocre one of J.P. Migne, *Patrologia Latina,* vol. 69, based on that of the Maurist J. Garet (1679). Th. Mommsen's edition of 1894 (*MGH AA* XII) is a monument of scholarship, which put the text and chronology of the letters on a sound footing. It includes some additional documents relevant to Theoderic's relations with the Church of Rome, and L. Traube's edition of the fragments of Cassiodorus' panegyrics. The introduction is important for text, dates, and orthography; while the indexes, especially Traube's index of words and things, which includes remarks on textual readings, word usage, grammar and syntax, make the edition vital for research. In 1973, Å. Fridh edited the text in *CCSL,* vol.96. Based on deep study of late antique Latin, and adding a manuscript unknown to Mommsen, this edition offers some textual improvements, and cannot be ignored. It also has indexes of scriptural and other citations (to be used with caution), a bibliography, and Halporn's appended edition of the *De Anima.* However, it is marred by a throng of misprints, and the index of names and things is very inadequate, being confined to the title rubrics. The only English translation published is that of 1886 by T. Hodgkin, *The Letters of Cassiodorus.* In this, the contents of many letters are only noted; others are 'condensed.' Hodgkin was a learned authority on Ostrogothic Italy, but lacked literary sympathy for Cassiodorus, and worked from Garet's inferior text. He provided a lengthy introduction and notes, but these are frequently misleading, knowledge of the late Roman world having advanced considerably since his day. Consultation of his work is sometimes worthwhile, although it will often prove dangerous or frustrating.

The *Variae* have much to interest the political, social, economic, religious, and cultural historian; a selection with something for each was hard to make. To focus on Cassiodorus' career, interests, and way of life, with those of his family connections, seemed the least unsatisfactory solution; at least it fulfills one of the author's intentions. The section below, 'Cassiodorus and his Kindred in the Variae', shows why each letter was chosen for translation.

Like all translators, I have had to compromise between a rebarbatively literal rendering, and one so free that it would neither guide the student through the original, nor convey its formal qualities. I have tended to break up Cassiodorus' lengthier sentences, and have sometimes substituted the active for the passive voice. Cassiodorus commonly uses honorific plurals ('the royal we'), but does not do so with consistency, or confine them to royalty; I have altered

them to the singular. In general, though, I have tried to stick closely to the text, even translating many words which were probably added more for rhythm than for meaning. The dearth of causal and conclusive expressions in English has given an inevitable and misleading monotony to the start of many sentences and clauses. Latin is also a language far more economical than English, and Cassiodorus less prolix than translation makes him seem.

In dating the *Variae,* I have used Mommsen's work as my foundation, but have sometimes had to refine or question his chronology, and have found an invaluable supplement in Krautschick's recent study. . . .

Notes

1. On this office, see Honoré, 8f., 136, 201; Harries.

2. *Corpus Inscriptionum Latinarum,* VIII, 2297; cf. Macpherson, 181; but both texts may be modelled on an earlier one.

3. Procopius, *Wars* VII.i.32.

4. On the character of these, see MacCormack, 1975, 187-91, 1981, ch.8.

5. Cf. Averil Cameron, 247-53.

6. Cf. Ward-Perkins, 116.

7. Cf. Vidén, 140-4.

8. On this, see especially Zimmermann, Fridh, 1956, O'Donnell, ch.3, Vidén, ch.3-4, Macpherson, part 4; on Cassiodorus' political concepts and terminology, Reydellet, ch.5, Teillet, ch.8.

9. *MGH AA* XII, 392.

10. Examples are illustrated in Cornell and Matthews, 202f.

11. Other types of structure are used. A moral (or digression) may end, rather than start a letter, e.g. XII.20; a letter may move in a circle, from moral to matter to moral, e.g. I.25, I.27, III.20; or from matter to moral (or digression), and back to matter, e.g. VIII.33, XI.14, XII.15.

12. Cf. Fridh, 1956, 81f.

13. Cf. Halporn, *CCSL* vol.96, 513ff.

14. Cf. Roberts, ch. 2-3, Macpherson, 182.

15. Cf. Leopold.

16. Cf. Matthews, 1974.

17. See Fridh, 1956, 39-59; Benner, 1-25; Vidén, 120-53.

18. *Constitution* 8, an Easter-tide amnesty for prisoners, published at Constantinople in 386, may have influenced XI.40 on the same subject; cf. Macpherson, 174-9.

19. Cf. Leopold.

20. Julian, *Ep.* 56; *C.Th.,* IX.17.5, a.363; compare Valentinian III's Quaestor in *Novel* 23.

21. This code is sometimes claimed as the work of the Visigoth Theoderic II (453-66); I disagree.

22. Even in less rhetorical codes and edicts of the period, the laws stated may be less important than the action of stating them; cf. Wormald (2).

23. Some of his bestiary morality is shared with the sermon-based *Hexaemeron* of St Ambrose; St Jerome gives good examples of analogy in the homiletic letter, e.g. 125.2-4.

24. III.29f.

25. Cf. Sidonius, *Ep.* VIII.2, Gregory of Tours, *Life of the Fathers,* ix.1.

26. Readers 1500 years hence may well find the high minded editorials of our more intellectual newspapers equally platitudinous!

27. Cf. Reydellet, 193f.

28. Cf. Averil Cameron, ch.14.

29. Cf. Halporn, *CCSL* vol.96, 505, 510-13, O'Donnell, ch.4.

30. Cf.MacCormack, 1981, 238-9.

31. Cf. Barnish, 1989, 174-83. Ennodius 452 (*Opusc.* 6) seems a comparable project.

32. Cf. Matthews, 1981, 35-8.

33. *In Categorias Aristotelis* II, J.P. Migne, *Patrologia Latina* 64, c.201 B.

34. Cf. Sidonius, *Panegyric on Avitus,* 489-518, *Ep.* VIII.2.2, 3.3.

35. Jordanes, *Getica* 67-72; like a Praetorian Prefect, Dicineus was given 'almost regal power' by the king.

36. *De Caerimoniis,* praef.D, tr. E. Barker. Compare the interpretation of the money-system [I.10], and the elaborate symbolism of chariot-races [III.51], long closely linked with imperial ceremony.

37. The closest parallel may be Ennodius 8 (*Opusc.*7), a directive probably drafted for archbishop Laurentius of Milan, in 501. Also, with II.14, cf. 239 (*Dictio* 17).

38. See Honoré, 58ff., 244f.; Maas.

39. *Reg.Ep.* XI.4; cf. ibid. XIII.32, Wormald, 126ff.

40. Tribonian did a similar job for his low-born emperor.

41. Illustrated by Cornell and Matthews, 172. Compare also king Euric of the Visigoths in 476, using the declamations of his Roman counsellor Leo to restrain 'arms by laws' in his newly conquered territory (Sidonius, *Ep.* VIII.3.3).

42. *Wars* V.i.33, ii.1: chauvinist Goths claimed that Theoderic had wisely kept his tribe illiterate; cf. Wormald (1), 97ff.

43. IX.24.8, Themistius, *Or.* 34.viii.34; cf. Procopius, *Wars* V.iii.1, vi.10.

44. *Anonymus Valesianus,* 65-9.

45. Ennodius, 80.135 (*Opusc.*3).

46. *MGH AA* XII, 424f.

47. Cf. Honoré, 26ff.

48. The probable ancestor of the famous Anglo-Saxon *Codex Amiatinus.*

49. *Inst. Or.* VIII, praef. 24 (Loeb translation).

50. Cf. *Anonymus Valesianus* 69: a royal address to the people of Rome engraved on bronze, and publicly displayed.

51. Symmachus, *Ep.* II.12, 48; Sidonius, *Ep.* IX. 7.

52. Synesius, *Ep.* 100/101.

53. Procopius, *Anecdota* 14.2-3.

54. *De Mag.* III.29f.; cf. Cornell and Matthews, 202.

55. Procopius, *Wars* V.viii.29-42.

56. Cf. Wallace-Hadrill, 35; Heather. The Amals are given noticeably more prominence in letters to the Senate (IX.24.4-5, XI.1.19) than to barbarians (e.g. IV.1.1).

57. Cf. Matthews, 1975, 112, 244; Roberts, 90-111, 121, 125-9.

58. Cf. O'Donnell, 73f., 87.

59. Interestingly, some *De Anima* manuscripts so derived may be linked with the Palace School at Aachen; did Carolingian officials also know the *Variae*?

60. These remarks are based on Mommsen's and Fridh's prefaces to the *Variae,* and on Halporn's to the *De Anima.*

References and Abbreviations

References to the *Variae* in bold type are to texts translated in this volume, e.g. Preface, or VIII.33; references in plain type are to those which are omitted.

CCSL: Corpus Christianorum, Series Latina

CSEL: Corpus Scriptorum Ecclesiae Latinorum

C.Th.: Theodosian Code

JRS: Journal of Roman Studies

MGH: Monumenta Germaniae Historica

MGH AA MGH: Auctores Antiquissimi

PBSR: Papers of the British School at Rome

PLRE II: Prosopography of the Later Roman Empire, vol.II.

RBPh: Revue Belge de Philologie et d'Histoire

FURTHER READING

Criticism

Andersson, Theodore M. "Cassiodorus and the Gothic Legend of Ermanaric." *Euphorion* 57, No. 1 (1963): 28-43.

Studies the historical accuracy of the account of the legend of Ermanaric as it is found in Jordanes's summary of Cassiodorus's *Gothic history.*

Heather, Peter. "Cassiodorus and the Rise of the Amals: Genealogy and the Goths under Hun Domination." *Journal of Roman Studies* 79 (1989): 102-28.
Attempts to determine the historical accuracy of Cassiodorus's account of Amal genealogy and to assess the reliability of the possible sources used by Cassiodorus.

Hodgkin, Thomas. Introduction to *The Letters of Cassiodorus, Being a Condensed Translation of the "Variae Epistolae" of Magnus Aurelius Cassiodorus Senator,* pp. 1-67. London: Henry Frowde, 1886.
Detailed overview of Cassiodorus's life and works, with commentary on the *Variae, Chronica,* and the *History of the Goths.*

Jones, Leslie Webber. Introduction to *An Introduction to Divine and Human Readings,* by Cassiodorus Senator, translated by Leslie Webber Jones, pp. 3-63. New York: Octagon Books, 1966.
Biographical account of Cassiodorus, followed by an assessment of his influence on the Middle Ages and a discussion of manuscripts and editions of the work.

Leopold, John W. "*Consolando per edicta:* Cassiodorus, *Variae,* 4, 50, and Imperial Consolations for Natural Catastrophes." *Latomus* 45, No. 4 (December-November 1986): 816-36.
Argues that the portion of the *Variae* dedicated to the discussion of the eruption of Mount Vesuvius is an example of imperial concern for those who have suffered a natural catastrophe.

Mynors, R. A. B. Introduction to *Cassiodorus Senatoris: Institutiones,* edited by R. A. B. Mynors, pp. ix-lv. Oxford: Clarendon Press, 1937.
Reviews the manuscripts containing various portions of the *Institutiones;* lists the printed editions of the work.

Viden, Gunhild. *The Roman Chancery Tradition: Studies in the Language of Codex Theodosianus and Cassiodorus's "Variae". Studia Graeca et Latina Gothoburgensia* XLVI, 1984, 168 p.
Uses the *Variae* and other texts to examine the development of the official language of the Roman Empire in its eastern and western parts.

Zimmerman, O. J. *The Late Latin Vocabulary of the "Variae" of Cassiodorus.* Washington, D.C.: Catholic University of America, 1944, 277 p.
Discusses the importance of and difficulty in interpreting the letters of the *Variae* and examines its vocabulary, including neologisms, words of foreign origin, Late Latin words and their meanings, words endowed by Cassiodorus with a new meaning, and administrative technical words.

Mansur Abu'l Qasem Ferdowsi
c. 935-c. 1020

Persian poet.

INTRODUCTION

Ferdowsi's major work, the *Shah-Nama,* or "Book of Kings," is comprised of over 50,000 verses and recounts the history of Persia from its creation to the Arab invasion. The work encompasses sections that scholars have described as mythological, legendary, and quasi-historical, with each portion covering a different era. In its length and heroic focus, the *Shah-Nama* has often been compared to the *Iliad.* Because of its sweeping scope and depiction of Iranian beliefs and values, the poem has been revered as a national treasure that continues to serve as a touchstone for Iranian cultural identity.

BIOGRAPHICAL INFORMATION

Very little is known about the life of Ferdowsi. Even his real name remains a mystery; "Ferdowsi" is his poetical name, and means "paradisal." He was born into a family of land owners near Tus, in eastern Iran. Scholars believe that he composed the *Shah-Nama* over thirty years, between 980 and 1010, and that he based it on a tenth-century prose compilaton. Ferdowsi presented the poem as a gift to Sultan Mahmud of Ghazna, but, according to legend, Ferdowsi was deeply dissatisfied with his reward and wrote a savage satire against Mahmud. The *Shah-Nama,* Ferdowsi's masterpiece, became the model for most later Muslim epic poetry. It was also read and appreciated by western authors and served as the inspiration for Matthew Arnold's *Sohrab and Rustum.* Another work, *Yusuf and Zulayka,*was at one time attributed to Ferdowsi, but today that attribution is disputed by scholars.

MAJOR WORKS

The *Shah-Nama* comprises fifty chapters which narrate the story of fifty Persian kings and queens, from the legendary Kayumard to the fall of te Sassanian dynasty in the year 641. Beginning with the creation of the world, the narrative proceeds by relating the means by which primordial kings conceived the basic tenets of civilization. Next follows description of the reigns of numerous shahs, interspersed with the intermittent appearance of the prince Rostram, the greatest of the *Shah-Nama*'s heroes. Rostram faces a number of natural as well as supernatural challenges. In his battle with Esfandiyar, Rostram briefly escapes death, but endures the shame of having slain a great

Manuscript illumination of the poem depicting Gourdez receiving Sohrab in his tent.

hero, while Esfandiyar dies before ruling Iran, but leaves the world with an untarnished reputation. Seyavash is another outstanding hero, who rejects his father's demands and is subsequently killed by his enemies. While he experiences spiritual triumph, he nevertheless succumbs to physical defeat. Ferdowsi continues tracing the line of monarchial succession through the reign of Yazdegerd, under whose rule the Iranian empire fell to the Arab invaders. Given its focus on dynastic succession, one of the most prominent themes of the *Shah-Nama* is the nature of kingship. Ferdowsi places great emphasis on the divine sanction of Iran's monarchs, as well as on God's favoring of Iran over other nations. The *Shah-Nama* also highlights the malevolent nature of the universe, and of fate. Through the deeds of its heroes, the poem also examines the immortality of noble actions.

CRITICAL RECEPTION

Critics approach the *Shah-Nama* from a variety of angles. Some focus on Ferdowsi's goals, methods, and influences, while other critics study the themes and structure. Still others discuss individual stories or characters within the larger work. G. E. Von Grunebaum examines Ferdowsi's motivation to compose the *Shah-Nama*, arguing that the poet strove to create Iranian unity by revealing the "oneness" of the nation's past. Given this goal, Von Grunebaum states, the elements Ferdowsi chose to eliminate from the historical sources available to him are significant. Von Grunebaum finds that the philosophical and artistic flaw of the work is the lack of a unified view of the past. Similarly, Reuben Levy observes that Ferdowsi's main objective is to relate the story of his fatherland. Levy further contends that the work is unified through the theme of the hostile nature of the universe. G. M. Wickens identifies kingship as one of the main themes of the *Shah-Nama* and maintains that, although the work contains all the necessary components of dramatic form, it lacks the formal structure of great drama. William L. Hanaway analyzes the structure and language of the *Shah-Nama*, concluding that the work is structured according to four major dynastic divisions and is characterized by plain language and economy of imagery. He observes, too, a tension between Ferdowsi's desire to use rhetorical devices and figurative language, and the need to keep the listener's attention fixed on the poem's heroic action. In her structural analysis, Olga M. Davidson demonstrates the influence of the oral tradition on the *Shah-Nama*, asserting that a rich tradition of recitation helped to shape the poem and explains the variety of interpolations in various manuscripts. Jerome W. Clinton surveys the major themes in the poem, and notes that several themes are recurrent—the immortality of heroic deeds, the inevitability of fate, and the divine sanction enjoyed by the monarchy. Clinton further observes that Ferdowsi does not present a perfect monarchy, despite its divine backing, and states that in stories such as those of Rostram and Esfandiyar, the poet explores this theme. A number of other critics, like Clinton, examine particular stories or characters from the *Shah-Nama*. James Atkinson describes the story of Suhráb as both beautiful and interesting, but comments that Ferdowsi is unable to portray such emotions as love, passion, or despair. Minoo S. Southgate discusses the fatalism of the Suhráb story, observing that Ferdowsi's fatalism is not fully borne out by his characters. In his examination of the Seyavash story, Dick Davis focuses on the symmetry and economy of the narrative. Davis also argues that Ferdowsi's own interest in a character is influences the psychological depth with which that character is portrayed—a depth, notes Davis, that is not typically found in epic poetry. In addition to his discussion of the Seyavash story, Davis also examines elements of Zoroastrianism (the Persian national religion) within the larger work, stating that Ferdowsi exhibits a distinctly Zoroastrian suspicion of appearances and physical reality. Von Grunebaum similarly identifies elements of Zoroastrianism in Ferdowsi's usage of traditional myths, but contends that the poet downplayed the doctrines of Zoroastrianism that would offend a Muslim audience. Von Grunebaum further explains that although Ferdowsi himself was a Muslim, pride in Persia's national past is inextricable from pride in the ancestral religion of Zoroastrianism in the *Shah-Nama*. Anna Krasnowolska challenges critics who find in the *Shah-Nama* a Zoroastrian dualistic view of life, stating that textual analysis does not support such a contention. Krasnowolska maintains that in Ferdowsi's depiction of conflicts between two branches of the same tribe, and in his portrayal of events from a movable perspective, the poet presents his view that nothing is "black and white," and that God transcends good and evil.

PRINCIPAL WORKS

Shah-Nama ["Book of Kings"] c. 980–c.1010

Principal English Translations

The Shahnama (translated by A. G. and E. Warner) 1905-12
The Shah-Namah of Fardusi (translated by Alexander Rogers) 1973

CRITICISM

James Atkinson (essay date 1814)

SOURCE: A preface to *Suhráb and Rustam: A Poem from the "Shāh Nāmah" of Firdausī*. 1814. Reprint. Scholars' Facsimiles and Reprints, 1972, pp. l-xxv.

[*In the following essay, Atkinson prefaces the translation of the Suhráb story from the* Shah-Nama *with a biographical sketch of Ferdowsi and a general overview of the poem. Atkinson praises the poet's descriptions and his flowing verse.*]

The **Shahnamu,** from which the Poem of Soohrab is taken, comprises the history and achievements of the ancient Kings of Persia from Kuyomoors, down to the invasion and conquest of that empire by the Saracens, during the reign of Yuzdjird, in 636. It is replete with heroic and chivalrous adventures, which are written with great strength of genius and fervor of imagination. Of Abool Qasim Firdousee, the author of this celebrated work, little is satisfactorily known. He was born at Toos, a city of Khorasan, about the year 950. The following circumstances respecting the origin of the Poem and the life of the Poet, are chiefly derived from the Preface to the copy of the *Shahnamu* which was collated in the year of the Hijree 829, nearly 400 years ago, by order of Bayisunghur Buhadoor Khan. It appears from that Preface that Yuzdjird, the last King of the Sassanian race, took considerable pains in collecting all the chronicles, histories, and traditions, connected with Persia and the Sovereigns of that country, from the time of Kuyomoors to the accession of the Khoosroos, which by his direction were digested and brought into one view, and formed the book known by the name of Siyurool Moolook, or the Bastan-namu. When the followers of Moohummud overturned the Persian monarchy, this work was found in the plundered library of Yuzdjird. The Preface above alluded to minutely traces its progress, through different hands in Arabia, Ethiopia, and Hindoostan. The chronicle was afterwards continued to the time of Yuzdjird. In the tenth century, one of the Kings of the Samanian dynasty directed Duqeeqee to versify that extensive work, but the Poet only lived to finish a thousand distichs, having been assassinated by his own slave. Nothing further was done till the reign of Sooltan Mahmood Subooktugeen, in the beginning of the eleventh century. That illustrious conqueror with the intention of augmenting the glories of his reign, projected a history of the Kings of Persia, and ordered the literary characters of his court conjointly to prepare one from all accessible records. While they were engaged upon this laborious undertaking, a romantic accident, which it is unnecessary to describe, furnished the Sooltan with a copy of the Bastan-namu, the existence of which was till then unknown to him. From this work Mahmood selected seven Stories or Romances, which he delivered to seven Poets to be composed in verse, that he might be able to ascertain the merits of each competitor. The Poet Unsuree, to whom the story of Roostum and Soohrab was given, gained the palm, and he was accordingly engaged to arrange the whole in verse.

Firdousee was at this time at Toos, his native city, where he cultivated his poetical talents with assiduity and success. He had heard of the attempt of Duqeeqee to versify the history of the Kings of Persia, and of the determination of the reigning King, Mahmood, to patronize an undertaking which promised to add lustre to the age in which he lived. Having fortunately succeeded in procuring a copy of the Bastannamu, he pursued his studies with unremitting zeal, and soon produced that part of the Poem in which the battles of Zohak and Fureedoon are described. The performance was universally read and admired, and it was not long before his fame reached the ears of the Sooltan, who immediately invited him to his Court.

When Firdousee arrived at Ghuzneen, the success of Unsuree in giving a poetical dress to the Romance of Roostum and Soohrab, was the subject of general observation and praise.[1] Animated by this proof of literary taste, he commenced upon the story of the battles of Isfundiyar and Roostum, and having completed it, he embraced the earliest opportunity of getting that Poem presented to the Sooltan, who had already seen abundant evidence of the transcendent talents of the author. Mahmood regarded the production with admiration and delight. He, without hesitating a moment, appointed him to complete the *Shahnamu,* and ordered his chief Minister[2] to pay him a thousand misqals for every thousand distichs, and at the same time honored him with the surname of Firdousee, because that he had diffused over his Court the delights of paradise.[4] Unsuree liberally acknowledged the superiority of Firdousee's genius, and relinquished the undertaking without apparent regret.

The Minister, in compliance with the injunctions of Mahmood, offered to pay the sums as the work went on; but Firdousee preferred waiting till he had completed his engagement, and receiving the whole at once, as he had long indulged the hope of being able to do something of importance for the benefit of his native city.

It appears that Firdousee was of an independent spirit, and not of that pliant disposition which was necessary to satisfy the expectations and demands of the proud Wuzeer, who offended at his unbending manners, did every thing in his power to ruin his interest with the King. Several passages in his Poems were extracted and invidiously commented upon, as containing sentiments contrary to the principles of the true Faith! It was alleged that they proved him to be an impious philosopher, a schismatic, and a follower of Ulee. But in spite of all that artifice and malignity could frame, the Poet rose in the esteem of the public. Admiration followed him in the progress of the work, and presents were showered upon him from every quarter. The Poems were at length completed. The composition of sixty thousand couplets[5] appears to have cost him the labour of thirty years. The Sooltan was fully sensible of the value and excellence of that splendid monument of geniusand talents, and proud of being the patronizer of a work which promised to perpetuate his name, he ordered an elephant-load of gold to be given to the author. But the malignity of the Minister was unappeased, and he was still bent upon the degradation and ruin of the Poet. Instead of the elephant-load of gold, he sent to him 60,000 silver dirhums![6] Firdousee was in the public bath at the time, and when he found that the bags contained only silver, he was so enraged at the insult offered to him, that on the spot he gave 20,000 to the keeper of the bath, 20,000 to the seller of refreshments, and 20,000 to the slave who brought them. "The Sooltan shall know," he said, "that I did not bestow the labour of thirty years on a work, to be rewarded with dirhums!" When this circumstance came to the knowledge of the King he was exceedingly exasperated at the disgraceful conduct of the Minister, who had, however, artifice and ingenuity enough to exculpate himself, and to cast all the blame upon the Poet. Firdousee was charged with disrespectful and insulting behaviour to his Sovereign; and Mahmood, thus stimulated to resentment, and not questioning the veracity of the Minister, passed an order that the next morning he should be trampled to death under the feet of an elephant. The unfortunate Poet, panic-struck and in the greatest consternation heard of the will of the Sooltan. He immediately hurried to the presence, and falling at the feet of the King, begged for mercy, at the same time pronouncing an elegant euloguim on the glories of his reign, and the innate generosity of his heart. The King touched by his agitation, and respecting the brilliancy of his talents, at length condescended to revoke the order.

But the wound was deep and not to be endured without a murmur. He went home and wrote a Satire against Mahmood, with all the bitterness of reproach which insulted merit could devise, and instantly fled from the court. He passed some time at Mazinduran and afterwards took refuge at Bagdad, where he was in high favour with the Caliph Ul Qadur Billah, in whose praise he added a thousand couplets to the **Shahnamu,** and for which he received a robe of honor, and 60,000 deenars. He also wrote a poem called Joseph during his stay in that city.

Mahmood at length became acquainted with the falsehood and treachery of the Wuzeer, whose cruel persecution of the unoffending Poet had involved the character and reputation of his Court in disgrace. His indignation was extreme, and the Minister was banished for ever from his presence. Anxious to make all the reparation in his power for the injustice he had been guilty of, he immediately dispatched to Bagdad, a present of 60,000 deenars, and a robe of state, with many apologies for what had happened. But Firdousee did not live to be gratified by this consoling acknowledgment. He had returned to his friends at Toos, where he died before the present from the King arrived. His family however scrupulously devoted it to the benevolent purposes which the Poet had originally intended, viz. the erection of public buildings, and the general improvement of his native city.

This brief biographical notice is the sum of all that is known of the great Firdousee. The Poet seems to have lived to a considerable age. When he wrote the Satire against Mahmood, according to his own account, he was more than seventy.

> When Charity demands a bounteous dole,
> Close is thy hand, contracted as thy soul:
> Now seventy years have marked my long career,
> Nay more, but age has no protection here!

Probably about ten years elapsed during his sojourn at Mazinduran and Bagdad, after he quitted the Court of Ghuzneen, so that he must have been at least eighty when he died. It appears from several parts of the Satire that a period of thirty years were employed in the composition of the **Shahnamu,** from which it must be inferred that he had been engaged upon that work long before the accession of Mahmood to the throne, for that Monarch survived Firdousee ten years, and the period of his reign was only thirty-one. Although there be nothing in the preceding memoir to indicate that the poet had commenced versifying the Bastan-namu nine years before the reign of Mahmood, the circumstance can hardly be questioned. All Oriental Biography is so vague, metaphorical, and undetermined, that there is always great difficulty in arriving at the simplest fact, yet it is not at all probable that the

round number of thirty years was falsely assumed by the poet. Notwithstanding the turn which is given by the Preface just mentioned, to the cause of Firdousee's disappointment, in referring it to the rancour of the Minister, the conduct of Mahmood was in the highest degree ungrateful and insulting. He well knew that the Minister sent dirhums instead of the elephant-load of gold, and still he suffered himself to be flattered and cajoled into petty resentment against the man who had, in the opening verses of the Poem, immortalized his name. The present of 60,000 deenars which he afterwards sent to Bagdad seems at any rate to shew that he felt some stings of conscience and that he wished to recover from the disgrace which attached to him, as a patron of literature, from so dishonorable a transaction.

The **Shahnamu** is the finest production of the kind which Oriental Nations can boast. The general character of Persian verse is well known to be excess of ornament and inflation of style, but the language of Firdousee combines a great portion of the energy and grace of western poetry. His descriptions are generally powerful, though sometimes diffuse and tedious. His verse is exquisitely smooth and flowing, and never interrupted by harsh forms of construction. He is the sweetest and most sublime poet of Persia. In epic grandeur he is above all, and in the softer passions he is far superior to Jamee or Hafiz. He is besides the easiest to be understood.

The author of the **Shahnamu** has usually been called the Homer of the East, but certainly not from any consideration of placing the Greek and Persian together in the same scale of excellence. Sir W. Jones in his Essay on the Poetry of the Eastern Nations, does "not pretend to assert that the Poet of Persia is equal to that of Greece; but there is certainly," he observes "a very great resemblance between the works of those extraordinary men; both drew their images from Nature herself, without catching them only from reflexion, and painting in the manner of the modern poets, the likeness of a likeness; and both possessed, in an eminent degree, the rich and creative invention which is the very soul of Poetry." There is another resemblance, which is however unconnected with their comparative merits; the heroic Poems of Firdousee are held exactly in the same estimation in the East, with reference to the works of other poets, as those of Homer are in the West. Like Homer too he describes a rude age, when personal strength and ferocious courage were chiefly valued, and when the tumultuous passions of the mind had not been softened and harmonized by civilization, or brought under the control of reason and reflexion. Firdousee is also as much the father of Persian Poetry as Homer is of the Greek; but it would be sacrilege to draw a dritical comparison between the **Shahnamu** and the Iliad!

It has been observed by Dr. Hurd in his Letters on Chivalry and Romance, that "there is a remarkable correspondence between the manners of the old heroic times as painted by their great Romancer Homer, and those which are represented to us in the modern books of knight-errantry." The correspondence is however infinitely more striking between the manners described by Firdousee, and those of the age of European Chivalry. It is well known that the Moors carried into Spain the Fictions and Romances of Arabia and Persia. Most of our best tales are derived from the same source, but it was not till the 12th Century that Romances of Chivalry began to amuse and delight the Western world. Although the *Roman de la Rose* was the first considerable work of the kind in verse, the Poem which gave life and character to all succeeding tales of Chivalry was the Orlando Innamorato of Boyardo, afterwards improved and paraphrased by Berni. To this production we are indebted for the Orlando Furioso of Ariosto. The **Shahnamu** was finished early in the eleventh century, gathered from the tales and legends, for ages traditionally known throughout the East, and there are Camillas, and Bradamantes in it as valiant and beautiful as in Virgil or Ariosto. In the following Poem the reader will be struck with many resemblances to the classical compositions of the West.

The story of Soohrab is a fair specimen of Firdousce's powers as a Poet. It is perhaps one of the most beautiful and interesting in the **Shahnamu.** Had the Poet been able to depict the nicer varieties of emotion and passion, the more refined workings of the mind under the influence of disappointment, love, and despair, the poem would have been still more deserving of praise. But, as Johnson observes of Milton, "he knew human nature only in the gross, and had never studied the shades of character, nor the combinations of concurring, or the perplexity of contending passions;" yet is there much to admire. Sir William Jones, had planned a tragedy of Soohrab, and intended to have arranged it with a Chorus of the Magi, or Fire-worshipers, but it was found unfinished at the time of his death.[7]

Respecting the work now offered to the public it may be necessary to say a few words. The rules of poetical translation are now pretty generally understood, and even in European languages, which are not essentially dissimilar in idiom and imagery, considerable latitude of expression is always allowed. Those who best know the peculiarities of the Persian will acknowledge how requisite it is to adopt a still greater freedom of interpretation in conveying Eastern notions into English verse. I have consequently paid more attention to sentiments than words. The translation is much shorter than the original, having avoided all the repetitions and redundancies which I could not preserve with any degree of success. The Persian reader may be of opinion, that a closer adherence to the descriptions and amplifications of the original would have given a better view of the merits of the author, but I was not desirous of hazarding the experiment. The-progress of the tale would have been interrupted, and unnecessarily protracted to double the extent. One unsuccessful attempt is a sufficient beacon. Some years ago Mr. Champion published a volume containing a translation in English verse of the first parts of the **Shahnamu.** I have never been able to procure a copy of that work and can only judge of its mer-

its from the copious extracts which are inserted in Waring's Tour to Sheeraz (London edition). They are much too diffuse, and possess little of the spirit of Firdousee. Specimens of the Persian Poet liave also been translated into French by Wallenburg. Hammer, the conductor of the periodical work published in Germany, called mines of the East, has recently given to the world a translation of one of the Tales, Khoosroo and Sheereen, with the original annexed, adjusted from the only two manuscript copies which he could obtain. In proposing to publish an entire translation, with the text, which he calculates will occupy ten years! Hammer laments the scarcity of valuable MSS, and indeed it seems quite impossible that, in Europe, he can ever have the opportunities and advantages required in an Editor of such an extensive work. The text which he publishes may consequently be taken from one that has no greater claim to correctness than those commonly circulated in the East. The translation he has given appears to be quite literal, and is written in the same measure as the Persian,[8] to which language, the German is said to have a great affinity, and may in consequence bear repetition and diffusion. The English language, on the contrary, is too concise, vigorous, and comprehensive to admit of the prolixity of detail and flowery amplification of the Persian, and I am of opinion that a literal translation of Firdousee would never be read with pleasure or satisfaction.

Some apology may be demanded for the length of the notes. I was anxious to illustrate the Poem by analogous passages from our own poets, as well as to shew that the chaster productions of the East are more meritorious, and more closely resemble those of the West, than has been commonly imagined. With what success the reader must decide.

The original text, now first printed, is taken from a manuscript corrected under the superintendence of the learned Mr. Lumsden, Professor of the Arabic and Persian languages in the College of Fort William, and kindly lent to me by that gentleman with the laudable view of promoting the diffusion of Oriental literature. It was carefully collated from twenty seven manuscript copies, by a body of natives of acknowledged acquirements, whom he had selected for the purpose of preparing a complete Edition of the **Shahnamu,** which it was calculated would be comprised in eight folio volumes. The first volume appeared in 1811, but the publication of the second, which will contain the story of Soohrab, has been suspended. When we consider that at present all the manuscripts of the **Shahnamu** extant are so exceedingly incorrect, and many of them with interpolations and omissions to the extent of from ten to twenty thousand verses, the importance of the work, liberally undertaken to rescue the great Poet of Persia for ever from the ignorance and vanity of transcribers, may be supposed to ensure its completion. I trust that nothing may occur to operate against the final accomplishment of this desirable object. It will be as highly creditable to the industry and erudition of the Editor, as it is peculiarly worthy of the patronage and munificence of the Honorable Court of Directors, under whose fostering care and protection the languages and literature of Asia have been studied with such distinguished success.

Notes

1. A singular anecdote is also related in the same Preface. When our author reached the capital, he happened to pass near a garden where Unsuree, Usjudee, and Furrokhee were seated. The Poets observed him approach, and at once agreed that if the stranger chanced to have any taste for poetry, which they intended to put to the test, he should be admitted to their friendship. Firdousee joined them and hearing their proposal, promised to exert his powers. Unsuree commenced with an extemporaneous verse:

   The light of the moon to thy splendor is weak,
   Usjudee rejoined:
   The rose is eclipsed by the bloom of thy cheek;
   Then Furrokhee:
   Thy eye-lashes dart thro' the folds of the joshun.[3]
   And Firdousee:
   Like the javelin of Gu in the battle with Poshun.

   The Poets were astonished at the readiness of the stranger and ashamed at being totally ignorant of the story of Gu and Poshun, which Firdousee related as described in the Bastan-namu. They immediately treated him with the greatest kindness and respect.

2. Uhmud Mymundee.

3. Joshun, armour.

4. Firdous signifies paradise.

5. In a dissertation called Yaminee it is said that the ancient Poet Rodukee, who flourished half a century before Firdousee, had written one million and three hundred verses!!!

6. This conduct is more than paralleled by the Cardinal Farnese. Annibale Caracci devoted eight years of study and labour in painting the series of pictures in the Farnese Gallery at Rome, which do honor to his name and country, and when he expected to be rewarded with the munificence which they merited, he received little more than 200£ and to add to the indignity, the amount is said to have been sent to him in copper money!

7. It is very extraordinary how this great Orientalist could have mistaken the Story so far as the following view of it, at the end of his History of Nadir Shah, demonstrates: "Rustem, voyageant *sous un nom emprunte,* avoit trouve *le moyen de seduire une jeune princesse,* à qui la honte fit ensuite exposer le fruit de cet *amour infortuni.* Sohareb, c'est le nom de cet enfant abandonné, ne conoissant point ses parens, entre au service d'Afrasiab, est avance par ce roi aux premieres charges de l'Armée, et enfin envoyé pour combattre Rustem, qui ne le reconnoit pour son fils qu'après Tavoir mortellment blessé."

   Traite sur la Porsie Orientale.

8. The same as Anstey's Bath Guide.

G. E. Von Grunebaum (essay date 1955)

SOURCE: "Firdausî's Concept of History," in *Islam: Essays in the Nature and Growth of a Cultural Tradition,* Routledge and Kegan Paul, Ltd., 1955, pp. 168-84.

[*In the following essay, Von Grunebaum studies Ferdowsi's portrayal of Persian history, arguing that the poet's aim was to generate a feeling of national unity by portraying the "oneness" of Iran's past.*]

It is only when it is drawing to its close or even after it has passed away that a creative age will receive that literary representation that will be felt thenceforth to constitute the valid embodiment of its spirit, its aspirations, and its self-interpretation. *Iliad* and *Odyssey* follow rather than accompany the efflorescence of the civilization that has come to be known, for them, as Homeric. Virgil sings the mission of Rome at the very moment when, to him, this mission has been accomplished and when, to us, stagnation and decline are about to set in. Camões finishes the *Lusiad* only a few years before the Portuguese fight and lose their last battle to extend their possessions overseas. The glory of the Samanids was paling when Firdausî undertook his work; it had been a memory for almost a generation when he completed it. Yet it is the Samanid period in which the **Shâh-Nâmah** belongs, whose dreams it lent body and whose spirit it immortalized without ever devoting a single verse to honoring its deeds.

The Samanid century had created the language which Firdausî perfected and canonized; it had cultivated a sober and balanced taste in literary expression—jejune but graceful, fond of movement but careful of the bizarre, artful without artificiality. And it had fostered the spreading through all of north and east Persia of an interest in the national past. Or rather it had, through the encouragement of the court, made this interest that had always been there respectable in the Islamized circles of educated Iranian society, and had, by seeking to draw political strength from historical memories of pre-Arab achievement, Sassanian and older, actualized the latent national sentiment and, as it were, created the need for a national past to dignify the present through the demonstration of its direct descent from the Golden Age of Iran. And this national continuity was to be personified in the unbroken chain of legitimate rulers from the first man to the uncertain sovereigns of the day.

The period wanted for a compendium of the past, not necessarily complete in the pedantic sense of the word, but complete inasmuch as the nation cared or needed to remember. Firdausî's success is primarily due to his tact in collecting and selecting. Clearly his sense of relevance was in tune with contemporary judgment. The very uncertainties of his attitude toward history must have helped to make his presentation universally acceptable—especially since he was at one with his generation in his valuations and took pride in what they prized. Firdausî was a man of considerable information, but he was not a learned poet. In the light of later epics his style is simple and his vocabulary limited, his imagery pellucid and his narrative direct. Just as Homer could never be matched, in the eyes of the Greeks, by the Homeridae be it only for the comparative insignificance of their themes that were developed to fill in gaps of the Homeric narrative proper, nor by the sometimes powerful and sometimes painful but always clever efforts of the Hellenistic epigoni, even so did Firdausî's standing remain untouched by an Asadî the Younger who dealt with a saga cycle neglected by the **Shâh-Nâmah,** or by a Nizâmî, whose presentation of Alexander is perhaps more interesting than Firdausî's but who no longer cared for storytelling as such and who deliberately dimmed the understandability of his verse.

It has been pointed out[1] that only since the beginning of the nineteenth century has historiography claimed the right to treat of any historical theme which it feels able to inform. The earlier historian of the West—and we may add, of the East as well—found his theme solely in his own period or rather in that segment of the past that was still felt to be alive. It does not matter that this past may extend backward to the very creation of the world; the fact remains that it is studied and presented not for its own sake but as an integral part of the consciousness of the historian's contemporaries.

Thus the **Shâh-Nâmah** articulates the memories and associations of a past that was at the back of the period's consciousness of itself.[2] It is true that in all likelihood Firdausî amplified and modified what he knew to be the collective memories of his time; it is also true that he organized and rigidified those memories. Nonetheless it is unmistakable that he never ceases to speak but of what is near and emotionally effective because of its nearness. Countless years have passed since the treachery of time removed first one and then the next royal line from sight. Yet those ancient kings and heroes continue to live in the minds of their subjects' descendants as examples or simply as people whose problems and responses are their own. And Firdausî's casual anachronisms tend to weld tighter the circle that holds together the living and the dead.

Firdausî supplemented the more or less official construction of history as it was transmitted by the Sassanian *Book of Rulers,* or *Xvaδ[âγ-Nâmaγ,* from other presentations going back to Sassanian times. Apart from the *Book of the Chiefs of Sakistân,* mentioned by Mas'ûdî (d. 956)[3] and used in its (lost) translation by Ibn al-Muqaffa' (d. 757) for 'Tabarî's (d. 923) report of Persian dynastic history,[4] Firdausî could rely on not a few Pahlavî monographs, as we would call them now, on personages and episodes of the Iranian past. He completed his material by delving deep into the "oceans" of saga and legend, into popular romances that had not found their way into authoritative compilations. For his purpose the nature of his sources was perhaps less important than their range. He achieved that integration of Sîstânî (Sakistânî) and Zâbulî traditions in the main current of Iranian tradition that the Sassanian historians and romancers had failed to accomplish—pro-

vided, of course, they ever intended a synthesis of this kind.[5] By allowing his narrative to roam over the vast expanse from Kâbul and Zâbul and Sijistân through the Persian heart lands to the Caspian Sea at Mâzandarân and again northward across the Oxus into the Turanian plains, Firdausî united in a fairly consistent whole the essential memories of that area which his contemporaries were prepared to think of as the lands of Iran. It is true that the lines along which the several traditions are riveted together remain for the most part easily discernible. But this may have been less so for the contemporaries. And in any event, Firdausî succeeded in laying down the frontiers of a Greater Iran (as compared with the political entities that had existed on its soil during the more than three centuries preceding his time) and in consolidating them on the foundation of a common past. The **Shâh-Nâmah** allowed every Iranian to share in the memories of every section of his country as in a personal possession. It helped the national consciousness to revert to a patriotism with which provincial loyalties could readily merge.

In the light of Firdausî's determination to create or revive a feeling for the oneness of Greater Iran through the realization of the oneness of its past, his omissions of available materials assume especial significance. It is almost immediately obvious that, of the three strands of tradition that were alive in Firdausî's century or that had been at work in the written evidence at his disposal, he follows almost exclusively the national, not to say nationalistic, which had been given final form under the Sassanians. The popular traditions, from which Firdausî borrowed a great deal, also seem to have fitted in with the national view of history, at least in spirit. The third strand, the priestly tradition that had been elaborated as early as the Arsacid period, Firdausî left largely aside. Where it can be traced, as in the story of Darius, it appears somewhat incongruously side by side with the national, and it may be assumed that the juxtaposition is due not to Firdausî himself but to his sources.

Firdausî devotes considerable space to the mythical kings; as a matter of fact he begins his tale with the world's creation. But he makes no mention of Zoroastrian and pre-Zoroastrian lore on the origin of earth and man, being satisfied with a concise *aperçu* of the conventional Muslim view. The national tradition did, of course, operate with the philosophical concepts animating the priestly tradition. The Sassanians, especially in their later days, affected a strictly religious outlook. The two traditions differ in emphasis and in the valuation of individual events and rulers—they represent different phases of theological thought; and the national tradition bears the marks of that romantic love of the past that had grown stronger during the last two hundred years of Persian independence.[6]

Firdausî does not eliminate the basic dualism that pervades the narrative of his sources. Without entering into theological disquisitions regarding the fundamental conflict between dualistic Zoroastrianism and monistic Islam, or regarding the individual tenets of the old religion, he allows mythical events to retain their significance in terms of the dualistic conflict between good and evil, Ormizd and Ahriman.[7] In general, Firdausî is content to play down such features of the old faith as would directly offend the Muslim reader. He is anxious to avoid giving the impression that the Zoroastrians worshiped the fire, and he relegates to the background the "incestuous" marriage between brother and sister.

Zoroastrianism as represented in the *Bundahishn* assigns to the world a duration of twelve thousand years. The first three thousand, it existed unnoticed by the evil principle. After the initial conflict Ahriman agrees to a period of nine thousand years for the combat with Ormizd. The first third of this period, Ahriman has the upper hand; in the second the wills of Ahriman and Ormizd are intermingled; in the third Ahriman is reduced to impotence.[8] This concept of cosmic history as the frame of human history which is made meaningful within the larger sphere by man's participation on the side of one or the other of the eternal antagonists remained active well into the period of Arab domination. The thirty-third chapter of the *Bundahishn* tells of the misfortunes that befell *Êrânshahr* in the several millennia. The first three (of the six millennia here accounted for) carry the history of man from the first attack of the Evil Spirit on the first man to the appearance of Zoroaster. The fourth millennium witnesses the rise of the pure religion, the reign of Alexander, the period of the provincial lords (καδαγ xvαδ[âγ, *mulûk at-tawâ'if*), the rule of the Sassanians, and the Arab conquest. At some future date after a short year of Byzantine occupation of Iran, Mazdasnian Persia will rise once more. Then the fifth millennium will begin, and after it the sixth will bring the end of the world with the appearance of the *Sôshyans,* the Savior.[9]

Firdausî tacitly dropped this construction; or it may be more accurate to say that he secularized it. The fight of Good and Evil is real to him, but as a Muslim he identifies the Good Principle, or Ormizd, with Allâh, the One, the Creator, and reduces the stature of Ahriman to that of a *dêv* or of the koranic Iblîs. Firdausî at various points speaks of the youth or the rejuvenation of the world, but this renewal no longer is tied to the sequence of cosmological events; rather it is connected with a change of dynasties or merely with the advent of a new ruler. Any chronological link with cosmic process has disappeared. Firdausî's world grows young, not because as time wears on the victory of the Good Principle approaches, but because a model king has put an end to a bad reign—he will bring about a new era of social and administrative progress, and he will mature into a sage and become a spiritual guide for his people.[10]

Zoroastrianism had dominated the last great age of Iranian history. Pride in the ancestral religion was inseparable from pride in the Persian past. But as a Muslim, Firdausî had to dissociate himself from the national faith and to avoid the psychological and the practical conflict of divided religious loyalties as best he could. As his contemporaries did not accuse him of being a crypto-Magian, it is likely that the coexistence of two conflicting prides was too common in his day to be accounted scandalous.

The concept underlying the national tradition was, from a Muslim's point of view, more readily defensible. In it the glory of the past stood firm, no matter what the religious allegiance of the ruler. The emotional conflict arose when the Arabs, the soldiers of the Prophet's successor, vanquished the legitimate sovereigns of Iran in the name of the new faith. As a Persian, Firdausî was irremediably humiliated by the Sassanian defeat; as a Muslim he should have felt elated at a development that had brought the true faith to his people and to himself. So the national tradition ended in a melancholy key. All through the Samanid century and its national revival the foreign faith was pushing back the indigenous religion. What to the contemporaries may have appeared as portents of a quickening of Mazdaean life soon proved of mere local or denominational significance. The sectarian movement of Ibn abî Zakariyyâ at-Tammâmî[11] broke down shortly after its start in A.D. 931, and the great effort of the Zoroastrian orthodoxy to codify its heritage that led to the compilation of the *Dênkart* in tenth-century Baghdâd resulted in nothing but a precarious consolidation of the faith, unable to prevent the further decline of the "Magian" community.[12] And religious conditions had not become sufficiently stabilized to compel Firdausî to adjust himself to that double self-identification which an unqualified assent to the national past would have required. To this division within himself we owe such beautiful passages as Bârbad's elegy for Husrav Parvêz[13] or the prophetic letter written by Rustam to his brother on the eve of his decisive defeat by the Arabs with its prediction of the downfall of Persia and all she stands for.[14] After he has told of the murder of the last king and the punishment of his assassin, Firdausî concludes his narrative perhaps somewhat too dryly:

> . . . Since then
> Hath been the epoch of 'Umar, made known
> The Faith, and to a pulpit changed the throne.[15]

Four hundred years have passed; now, in Firdausî's time, the period of oppression is coming to its end. But was it really ending when a Turkish ruler actually controlled most of Iran?

The Muslim idea of history was at one with the Zoroastrian in viewing the life of mankind as a process of limited duration. The coming of Islam was the climax of the sequence of happenings, and the world was now to be confronted in the relatively near future with the Last Judgment. The total number of years allotted to man in history was not fixed by doctrine and, since it was established without reference to cosmic events known to take place at definite points of time, variations would not matter. But Islam did, of course, reject unquestioningly any suggestion of an *apokatastasis* to introduce another, though identical, sequence of human history. The conception of religion and empire as "sisters," as it is developed by Firdausî in the

Sassanian tradition,[16] had become an integral part of Muslim political theory, where we find it often expounded directly on the basis of Persian sources[17] and where it was destined to survive throughout the Middle Ages. Despite affinities of this kind, the Muslim concept of history with its devaluation of all pre-Islamic phases, its implied Arabism and open contempt for superseded truth was essentially incompatible with both the concepts that had been shaped by Persian tradition. Firdausî might have had hopes for a Muslim-Persian empire, but as long as this had not become a reality the painful conflict of the values inherent in the two traditions could not be reconciled. The bleak pragmatism of an older contemporary of his, whose name, Abû Bakr al-Qûmisî, bespeaks his Iranian descent and who proposed to rate any historical period solely for its material prosperity,[18] may possibly be ascribed to a feeling of hopeless inability to resolve the clash of traditions except by discarding them both.

The unresolved conflict of the concepts of history, in fact, their almost clumsy juxtaposition is characteristic of the realities of Firdausî's age. Persian national sentiment had to appropriate both the Zoroastrian past and the Muslim present as effective motivations. If it had been a political factor under the Samanids, which is not too certain, it had ceased to count when the Ghaznavids took over. The "brokenness" of the Persian intellectual's response to his historical situation was tolerable at a time when conditions excluded his nation from effective power.[19]

Firdausî's somewhat passive attitude toward the conflicting traditions was not necessarily typical of his Persian contemporaries. The Samanid vizier, Bal'amî, writing in 963, succeeds much better than does the poet in coordinating Muslim and Persian lore. His method consists in synchronizing the Persian king-list and the list of koranic or biblical prophets. He quotes contradictory traditions with respect to the total duration of this world without committing himself. In a passage added by Bal'amî to the 'Tabarî text which he is translating and condensing, the beginning of the world is given in astronomical terms and metaphysical time thus definitely transformed into historical time.[20] Thus the evolution of what was to become the Arab and the Persian wings of the Muslim Empire could be shown at any given stage. The Ihwân as-Safâ[21] record a line of thought according to which the world was to come to its end on November 19, 1047,[22] and which is based on a parallelism of cosmic change and changes of political power on earth.[23] Ismâ'îlî ideology of the period, too, insists on the double role, cosmic and historical, of the imâm, without, however, setting a definite term to the life of this world. History is, in part at least, articulated by prefiguration—the Ismâ'îl of the Old Testament prefigured the imâm of this name, the imâm Ja'far acts out what was prefigured by the patriarch Jacob.[24]

Firdausî is alone among the major contemporary students of history in that he seems to be utterly unable to extract any general ideas from the developments which he presents in such masterly fashion. The outlook characteristic of the period is that of the Hellenistic age, which looked upon history, the magistra vitae as Cicero was to say, largely as a collection of exempla. Miskawaih (d. 1030) at least pretends to deal with history for its didactic value. He entitles his work The Experiences of the Nations and assumes that the present generation may learn from the lessons of the past. Tauhîdî (d. 1023) displays the same didactic motivation with regard to his own interest in history,[25] and the tradition of this attitude continues to the close of the Middle Ages, to Tâj ad-Dîn Subkî (d. 1370)[26] and Ibn Haldûn (d. 1406). Firdausî does not seem to have professed this view. His comments on the events which he narrates are confined to melancholy observations on the inevitability of change, which must not be dignified out of proportion by ascribing them to a tragic feeling of life. For nothing is farther from Firdausî than that conflict between the concatenation of events and the individual's compulsion to realize the values governing his own existence, or that clash of law and conscience, of freedom and necessity, which are the essence of tragedy.[27] When Firdausî mentions change it is with the implied sentiment that change is for the worse; the transitoriness of greatness makes its value questionable; human ambition and human achievement kindle pride and may yield fame, but the treachery of time, the raib az-zamân of the Koran, stultifies human success, and fate ever tends to underline the essential futility of man's works—those very works that make up the glory which the poet sings.

Even as a collection of facts has a useful life longer than an interpretative synthesis of the same facts that will be significant in terms of the synthesizer's age, so has Firdausî's unintegrated presentation of his nation's memories retained the stimulating usefulness of factual materials where a thoroughly integrated presentation would long have become solely an object of study and perhaps of edification and aesthetic enjoyment. The facts still carry, even where the formative power of the poet falters. The most cursory comparison of the **Shâh-Nâmah** with the kindred efforts of Virgil and particularly of Camões demonstrates immediately Firdausî's lack of a unified view of his nation's past except, of course, for such as is inherent in mere chronological or dynastic sequence.[28] This failing, which is both philosophical and artistic, did, however, manifestly further Firdausî's ultimate purpose, viz., the strengthening and consolidating of an Iranian national consciousness through the common possession by all of Iran of a body of history that would justify collective pride even when the present would not seem to justify it. And this pride would be the double pride of political leadership once held and cultural superiority still retained and ennobled by the adoption of the revealed faith of Islam. By leaving to his people the sum total of their relevant collective experience, he allows each subsequent generation to find its own meaning in the past. No final interpretation of the heritage is presumed; no one tradition is preferred to the exclusion of any other vital mode of self-perception. The glittering beauty in which Firdausî presented the heroes of the past has kept them alive in the minds of the Persians to this very day. Persia did not have the sense of a specific mission in Firdausî's time, so she did not demand a definite and exclusive interpretation of herself in her past. When she regained this sense of mission under the early Safavids, her Muslim present had grown out of a centuries-old Muslim past which, in turn, had come to be felt to blend with the more remote and not-yet-Muslim past. And today a revised Iranian nationalism avails itself in its historical self-interpretation (although with the more systematic claims of scientific aspirations) of the same past that Firdausî portrayed with such superb artistry and such philosophical casualness.

The historical object reveals itself only through the contexts in which we place it and capture it. Firdausî gives his object a peculiar richness of perspective by carelessly multiplying the contexts, that is, the traditions. Camões and Virgil are greater than Firdausî in their comprehensive and unifying *Sinngebung* of their nations' histories, which makes the present the consummation of the past; but Firdausî preserved better than they the multiple interpretability of the historical process, which allows every age to keep alive the past by finding itself in it.

EXCURSUS

A NOTE ON KIND AND FORM OF THE SHÂH-NÂMAH

The kinship of the **Shâh-Nâmah** with the *Aeneid* or the *Lusiad* is more limited in its form than in its intent. In fact, in terms of the Western contemporary of Firdausî, whose literary categories would be more or less patterned on a tradition transmitted or formulated by Isidore of Seville (d. 636), the **Shâh-Nâmah** might not have passed as poetry at all. For Isidore states: *Officium autem poetae in eo est ut ea, quae vere gesta sunt, in alias species obliquis figurationibus cum decore aliquo conversa transducat. Unde et Lucanus* [the author of the *Pharsalia*, A.D. 39-65] *ideo in numero poetarum non ponitur, quia videtur historias composuisse.*[29]

From the viewpoint of composition we might be inclined to classify the **Shâh-Nâmah** as a *chanson de geste* rather than as an epic, which term, to the Occidental student, inevitably suggests a work in the line of the "great" tradition from Homer to Milton. The interest in poeticized history, part chronicle and part romance, was almost equally strong in medieval Europe and in medieval Iran. Firdausî's approach to his subject reminds one to some extent of that displayed by the authors of the *chansons de geste* that belong to the Crusade cycle. This cycle has been described as consisting of (1) une section entièrement fabuleuse; (2) une section rigoureusement historique; and (3) une section semi-historique[30]—a classification which could *mutatis mutandis* be meaningfully applied to the matter of the **Shâh-Nâmah**.

The similarity of taste extends to the form as well. The medieval epic in the "vulgar" tongues of Europe shows the same preference as the Persian for narrative in rhyming pairs of comparatively short lines. It may be noted that the rise and rule of the rhyme are among the most striking

common characteristics of medieval literature East and West, as contrasted with its "premedieval" models and antecedents.

In this connection the observation is called for that a *chanson de geste* is little else but a *kâr-Nâmak,* or book of deeds or *gesta,* in poetical form. *Praxis,* as the individual "deed" of the hero in the *spätantike* life-tale of a philosopher, saint, or martyr; and *kâr,* as the individual "deed" of the heroized prince on his road to kingship in the Pahlavî narrative of Artaχshêr-ê Pâβaγân, are, the first very likely an antecedent, but both, curious parallels to the etymological origin and function of the French term. E. R. Curtius[31] points out that the Spanish priest, Juvencus, in the preface of his *Evangeliorum libri IV,* defines his program by saying (vs. 19): *"mihi carmen erunt Christi vitalia gesta."* Curtius continues: "In diesem Vers war ein Anhaltspunkt für die mittelalterliche Auffassung des Epos gegeben: die Taten (*gesta*) eines Helden zu versifizieren."

Although for the sake of classification the **Shâh-Nâmah** should be placed with the *chansons de geste* rather than with the Great Tradition, certain affinities of its presentation with the style and the clichés of that very Tradition must not be overlooked. Even as it has been possible to demonstrate, for example, the survival into Arabic times of the ancient rhetorical pattern for the city panegyric[32] as well as that of the *Ubi sunt qui ante nos* motif[33]—the same could be shown, e.g., for the *topos* of the "praise of poetry"[34] and for that of the *Lustort*[35]—so the survival of other stylistic habits of late antiquity could be documented in Firdausî. The *spätantike* stylistic clichés traced by Curtius in the *Chanson de Roland*[36] could as easily be traced in the **Shâh-Nâmah**.

Persian theory has not found the epic its proper place. Shams-i Qais (who completed his work in 1232/3) is representative when he confines himself to consideration of the prosodical appearance of the *mathnawî* (literally: couplet[-poem]), as epic narrative is called in Persian where the term is chosen solely for its metrical characteristics. These characteristics Shams-i Qais illustrates by an example from the **Shâh-Nâmah,** concluding his exposition with the remark: "This kind, *nau',* is used for extensive tales and long stories which it would be impossible to compose on one and the same rhyme throughout."[37] His contemporary, Diyâ' ad-Dîn Ibn al-Athîr (d. 1234), is the only Arab theorist to refer to the Persian epic. He sees poetry as separated from prose composition, *kitâba,* by three peculiarities: meter, a different choice of words, and limitation in length. But with regard to this last point he feels constrained to make one qualification: "I found that the Persians, *al-'ajam,* excel the Arabs in this point; for their poet [!] records a [kind of] book(s) composed in poetry from beginning to end. It is a detailed presentation, *sharh,* of stories and events, *ahwâl.* Nenetheless it is exceedingly eloquent [the text has both *fasâha* and *balâgha*] in the language of the people." Firdausî's **Shâh-Nâmah** is an unsurpassed specimen of this kind, which deals in 60,000 verses with the history of the Persians. "It is the Koran of those people." Despite the general inferiority of Persian to Arabic letters, in this one respect the Arabs have nothing to match Persian achievement.[38]

The origin of the meter of the **Shâh-Nâmah**—a hendecasyllabic line with four *ictus*—has been followed back to the Arsacid period. Rhymed pairs of such lines occur in the Turfan Fragments and in the *Great Bundahishn*. The meter was taken over by the Arabs in pre-Islamic times and developed in accordance with their quantitative prosody. Persian prosodical theory of the Islamic period repatriated the meter under its Arabic name, *mutaqârib*—there is no evidence of a native name.

It is to be noted, however, that the Pahlavî specimens of the hendecasyllabic verse are not to be found in historical narrative but in a sample of *Rangstreitliteratur* and in religious poetry. As we do not know whether the *Xvaδ[âγ-Nâmaγ* was written in verse or in prose, we cannot decide who first selected the *mutaqârib* as the vehicle of an extensive "historical" narrative. Nöldeke has pointed out, with reference to a *mutaqârib* couplet by Abû Shukûr of Balh (*fl.* 941/42), that already some time before Daqîqî and Firdausî the *mutaqârib* had been employed for epic presentation and that, besides, the style of this epic had developed certain fixed forms that had had their roots in Pahlavî narrative.[39] If the use of the *mutaqârib* originated with a poet of the post-Pahlavî period, his choice is all the more remarkable since the octosyllabic variety of the other principal meter of the Persian epic, the *hazaj*, actually had been used in Pahlavî for historical narrative. In fact, the so-called *Great Bundahishn*[40] contains five lines (two of which rhyme) that deal with the exposure of a newborn prince, Kavât, in a chest on a river and his discovery by one Urav who brought him up in his home—the very motif that was spun out to considerable length by Firdausî[41] when he recorded the youth of the future king Dârâb. The octosyllabic verse (with occasional rhyme) had also been used in the apocalyptic prophecies of the *Zhâmâsp-Nâmaαγ*.[42] Equally remarkable is the disregard shown by Daqîqî of the hexasyllabics used with such great skill and effect by the poet of the *Ayâδγâr-ê Zarêrân*,[43] although (1) its contents were incorporated in the **Shâh-Nâmah;** (2) it anticipates such peculiarities of the **Shâh-Nâmah** as the hyperbolic imagery; and (3) not a few individual lines of Daqîqî's are nothing but recastings of specific passages of the *Zarêr Book*.[44] The joining of two octosyllabic (and hendecasyllabic) lines to a rhymed pair or, in the language of Arabo-Persian prosody, the joining of two such lines into one verse with rhyming hemistichs, must have been widely practiced by the end of the Sassanian period, since the Arabs took over this form, later called *muzdawij*, as early as *ca.* A.D. 700.[45]

The occurrence in the **Shâh-Nâmah** of classical or post-classical stylistic devices and clichés is readily ascertained. It is, of course, much more difficult to reconstruct the road on which these clichés found their way into tenth-century Persia than to retrace that which connects their Hellenistic-Roman sources with the pertinent clichés of the *Chanson*

de Roland. It may, however, be tentatively suggested that the *Alexander Romance,* which was translated into Pahlavî directly from the Greek toward the end of the Sassanian period,[46] played a significant part in the history of this transmission. Nöldeke has pointed out[47] that the main contents of the *Romance* may have already been incorporated in the *Xvaδâγ-Nâmaγ*. In any case, passages such as **Shâh-Nâmah,** VI, 1787-89 (Alexander goes to Darius as his own ambassador), VI, 1805-7 (Alexander's letter to his new subjects), and VII, 1810-12/C 1286-87 (Alexander's letter to Roxane's mother) are but "amplifications" of *Pseudo-Callisthenes* II, 14; II, 21; and II, 22, respectively.[48] **Shâh-Nâmah,** VI, 1801-3, the meeting of Alexander with the dying Darius, is closely modeled on *Pseudo-Callisthenes* II, 20, where the Greek narrative is almost completely in so-called "epic choliambs" of twelve syllables with four (or five) principal *ictus*,[49] a verse that rather provokes comparison with Firdausî's couplets of hendecasyllabic lines with four *ictus*. While it would be rash to base on a passage of this kind any conclusions as to the reasons for Daqîqî's selection of the *mutaqârib* for historical narrative, the similarity of the two meters (which may well have been reflected in the Pahlavî translation of the *Alexander Romance*) should at least be noted pending further investigations. Such investigations would also have to take into account the development of the (Greek and Latin) hendecasyllabic verse ("Elfsilbler") that was to be employed so widely in Byzantine literature, even as it should not be forgotten that the *Chanson de Roland,* for example, is composed in decasyllabic couplets of alliterative verse.

Notes

1. By E. Schwartz, "Geschichtschreibung und Geschichte bei den Hellenen," *Die Antike,* XII (1928), 14; reprinted in *Gesammelte Schriften,* I (Berlin, 1938), 67.

2. Precedent goes back as far as the Zam Yasht (Yasht 19) of the Avesta where, §§21-87, a long list of mythical rulers and heroes is presented in whom the *Xvarenah*, the divine *Machiglanz*, manifested itself; cf. H. S. Nyberg, *Die Religionen des alten Iran* (Leipzig, 1938), p. 72.

3. *Murûj ad-dahab,* ed. Barbier de Meynard and Pavet de Courteille (Paris, 1861-77), II, 118.

4. Cf. A. Christensen, *Les Kayanides, Danske Videnskabernes Selskab, Hist.-fil. Meddelelser,* XIX/2 (1931), p. 143.

5. Two Sogdian fragments of episodes of the (Sijistânî) Rustam story are extant. They were published with translation by E. Benveniste, *Textes sogdiens* (Paris, 1940), pp. 134-36 (No. 13 I, II). On p. 134, Benveniste connects the fragments with Rustam's battle against the *dêvs* of Mâzandarân; but the *Shâh-Nâmah* has a completely different version of the events. The origin of the Sogdian narrative remains obscure. So does the relation of its form to that of the *Shâh-Nâmah*. In 1913, W. Barthold suggested rather

vaguely that the introduction of the Rustam cycle in the epic dates back to the times of the Arsacids or the Sassanians; cf. *Zeitschrift der deutschen morgenländischen Gesellschaft,* XCVIII (1944), 134.[1]

6. The priestly tradition found itself embarrassed by the failure of the Achaemenids to embrace Zoroastrianism. On the question of their Zoroastrian affiliations, I agree with the negative verdict of E. Benveniste, *The Persian Religion According to the Chief Greek Texts* (Paris, 1929), pp. 34-49, and more particularly of Nyberg, *op. cit.,* pp. 355-74. Firdausî's detachment from the priestly tradition may be reflected in his designation of the two ministers, *dastûr,* of Darius who become his murderers, as *môbads,* or priests (VI, 1800, vss. 315-16/C [=ed. Turner Macan, Calcutta, 1829] 1280). Whether or not Firdausî's source here mirrors an actual antagonistic attitude of the Zoroastrian clergy to the Achaemenid dynasty we do not seem to have any means of investigating, although the assumption does not appear too probable. Mary Boyce, *Serta Cantabrigiensia* (Wiesbaden, 1954), pp. 45-52, makes a judicious attempt to follow the "secular" (oral) tradition from its inception in Achaemenid times to its condification under the Sassanians.

7. Cf., e.g., *Shâhnâmah* (Teheran, 1313-15/1934-36), I, 33, vss. 186-87 (trans. A. G. and E. W. Warner [London, 1905-25], I, 139), where Firdausî comments on the *dêv*'s action in causing snakes to grow out of Zohâk's shoulders:

The purpose of the foul Dív shrewdly scan:
Had he conceived perchance a secret plan
To rid the world of all the race of man?

8. A. Christensen, *Les Types du premier homme et du premier roi dans l'histoire légendaire des Iraniens,* I (Stockholm, 1917), p. 15; cf. also Christensen, *Les Gestes des rois dans les traditions de l'Iran antique* (Paris, 1936), pp. 24-27.

The first three thousand years that really mark a period before the actual creation of the world constitute a Zoroastrian addition to an originally Zervanistic scheme; cf. Benveniste, *Persian Religion,* pp. 109-10. In Nyberg's interpretation (*op. cit.,* p. 21), the universe was first created as *mênôk,* transcendent reality, in a state of perfection in which it remained for three thousand years until it was transferred by the creator into the state that is called *gêtîk,* or earthly reality.

9. Cf. *Kayanides,* pp. 61-64.

10. For the model king, cf. *Gestes,* p. 75.

11. Cf. Bêrûnî, *Chronology,* ed. trans. E. Sachau, text (Leipzig, 1878), p. 213, translation (London, 1879), p. 196. For anti-Islamic prophecies in connection with this revolt, cf. A. Z. Validi Togan, *Ibn Fadlân's Reisebericht* (Leipzig, 1939), pp. xxi, xxvi-xxvii.

12. For both events, cf. Nyberg, *op. cit.,* pp. 3, 14, 35.

13. *Shâh-Nâmah,* IX, 2930-33/C 2041-42 (Warners' translation, IX, 29-32).

14. *Shâh-Nâmah,* IX, 2965-71/C 2062-65 (Warners' translation, IX, 74-78).

15. *Shâh-Nâmah,* IX, 3016, vs. 833/C 2095 (Warners' translation, IX, 121).

16. Cf. the passage just quoted in the text.

17. Cf. Ibn Qutaiba (d. 889), *'Uyûn al-ahbâr* (Cairo, 1343-49/1925-30), I, 13; trans. J. Horovitz, *Islamic Culture,* IV (1930), 197; *Murûj,* II, 162; Abû Manşûr Tha'âlibî, *Histoire des rois des Perses,* ed. trans. H. Zotenberg (Paris, 1900), p. 483. F. Rosenthal, *Journal of the American Oriental Society,* LXX (1950), 181-82, shows conclusively that the author is identical with the well-known philologist (d. 1038); C. Brockelmann, *Geschichte der arabischen Litteratur,* I (Weimar, 1898-1902), 342, and *GAL,* Suppl. (Leiden, 1937-42), I, 581-82, should be corrected accordingly. The *Histoire* was written before 1021.

18. Tauhîdî, *Muqâbasât* (Cairo, 1347/1929), pp. 143-44.

19. Cf. Nöldeke's judgment of the strength of Iranian national feeling under Mahmûd in: W. Geiger and E. Kuhn, *Grundriss der iranischen Philologie* (Strassburg, 1896-1904), II, 154. 'Utbî considers it a barbarism when Mahmûd's vizier, Fadl b. Ahmad (deposed in 1010/11), makes Persian the language of the royal chancellery; his successor, Hasan Maimandî, restores Arabic as the official language (*loc. cit.,* n. 3).

20. *Chronique de Tabarî,* traduite sur la version persane de Bal'amî par H. Zotenberg (Paris, 1867-74), I, 2-3; for the integration of Persian in Muslim tradition, cf., e.g., I, 100 ff.

21. *Rasâ'il* (Bombay, 1305-6), IV, 194.

22. Cf. P. Casanova, *Journal asiatique,* 1915, 5-17, esp. pp. 6-7.

23. Tauhîdî, *Risâla fî 'l-'ulûm* (in: *Risâlatâni* [Constantinople, 1301/1884], p. 207), speaks of the expectation of an early end of the world that is cherished in Sûfî circles, but it cannot be made out whether the Sûfîs in question are Persians.

24. Cf. W. Ivanow, *Ismaili Tradition concerning the Rise of the Fatimids* (London, 1942), pp. 232, 244, 248, 250, 255, 259-60, 266, 296-97. The Ismâ'îlî concept of history, dubbed "historiosophie" by H. Corbin (*Eranos Jahrbuch,* XIX [1951], 251), is designed to account for the permanence of history in terms of a (practically) unending sequence of cycles that receive their rhythm from the alternation of periods of unveiling, *kashf,* and periods of concealment, or veiling, *satr.* Meta-physical time is connected with mundane history in the particular cycle in which we find ourselves, through the Adam of our cycle who is identical with the "historical" Adam of Bible and Koran. His fall necessitated the instituting of a new Era of Concealment (in which we are still living). This fall was induced by the eternal Satan, whose functional perpetuity ties together our cycle with the

one preceding it. Also, the fall itself is meaningful only when seen as a *descensus* from the happy state of the end-time of the last cycle; it is essentially an error of judgment on Adam's part with regard to the structure of the time in which he finds himself placed. There is no evidence in the *Shâh-Nâmah* that Firdausî was moved by what from the Sunnite as well as the modern occidental viewpoint must be called the anti-historical outlook of the Ismâ'îliyya. For this outlook, cf. especially the studies of H. Corbin, *ibid.,* XIX (1951), 181-246; XX (1952), 149-217; and his "Étude préliminaire" to his and M. Mo'în's edition of Nâsir-i Khusraw's *Jâmi' al-hikmatain* (Teheran and Paris, 1953), *passim* and particularly pp. 123-26.

25. *Kitâb al-imtâ' wa'l-mu'ânasa* (Cairo, 1939-44), III, 150. Actually it is Ibn Sa'dân, vizier 983/4-985/6, who is expounding to Tauhîdî the idea of the instructiveness of the past with relation to the future.

26. *Tabaqât ash-Shâfi'iyya* (Cairo, 1323-24/1905-6), I, 184. In a characteristic passage Yâqût (d. 1229), *Mu-'jam al-buldân,* ed. F. Wüstenfeld (Leipzig, 1866-73), I, 2, quotes Koran 22:45, "Have they not traveled about in the land so as to have hearts to understand with and ears to hear with? For it is not the eyes which are blind, but blind are the hearts which are in the breasts," and adds, "This [pericope] is an upbraiding of him who travels through the lands without taking an example [from what he sees] and who looks upon the past generations without feeling restrained." (The somewhat similar *âya,* Koran 47:11, could also be taken as an indication of God's self-revelation in history.)

27. For a discussion of different views of the nature of the tragic, cf. A. Weber, *Das Tragische und die Geschichte* (Hamburg, 1942), esp. pp. 40-44. Max Scheler's (d. 1928) approach seems particularly fruitful. He sees in the tragic a *Daseinstatbestand,* owing to which *Kausalitätsverlauf* and *Wertverwirklichung* will find themselves in a conflict that cannot be resolved. E. R. Curtius, *Europäische Literatur und lateinisches Mittelalter* (Berne, 1948), p. 175, expresses this view: "Altes Heldenepos und tragische Daseinssicht gibt es nur bei den Griechen; in später Gestaltung bei den Persern, den Germanen, den Kelten und den in der Kreuzzugsära zum nationalen Sendungsbewusstsein erwachten Franzosen."[1]

28. See Excursus.

29. *Etymologiae* viii. 7, 10. E. R. Curtius, *op. cit.,* pp. 451-52 (=*Zeitschrift für romanische Philologie,* LVIII [1938], 470), has pointed out that the first sentence recurs *verbatim* in Lactantius (d. after 313) *Divinae Institutiones* i. 11, 24. Servius (*fl. ca.* 400) *ad Aeneidem* i. 382, who voices the same opinion, adds the verdict on Lucan. Petronius, *Satyricon,* chap. 118, contains a passage which is generally believed to have been directed against Lucan: "It is not a question of recording real events in verse; historians can do that far better. The free spirit of genius must

plunge headlong into allusions and divine interpositions, and rack itself for epigrams coloured by mythology, so that what results seems rather the prophecies of an inspired seer than the exactitude of a statement made on oath before witnesses" (trans. Michael Heseltine [London and New York, 1913]). It is easy to see which parts of the *Shâh-Nâmah* Petronius would have accepted as poetry and which he would have considered "versified" history somewhat after the manner in which Aristotle, *Poetics* IX, 2 (1451*b*), declined to accept a "versified Herodotus" as poetry.

30. A. Hatem, *Les Poèmes épiques des Croisades* (Paris, 1932), p. ix.

31. *Zeitschrift für romanische Philologie,* LXIV (1944), 251.

32. Cf. G. E. von Grunebaum, *Journal of the American Oriental Society,* LXIV (1944), 61-65.

33. Cf. C. H. Becker, *Islamstudien* (Leipzig, 1924-32), I, 501-19, for the Eastern, E. Gilson, *Les Idées et les lettres* (Paris, 1932), pp. 9-38, for the Western, development of the *topos* that goes back to the *diatribe* of the Cynics, and beyond it to Isa. 33:18 (cf. also Apoc. Bar. 3:16-19; I Cor. 1:19-20), as pointed out by Gilson, pp. 12-13 and 31. Further examples of transitions of Greek themes and genres into Arabic literature have been listed by this author, *Journal of the American Oriental Society,* LXII (1942), 291-92.

34. For its history in medieval Europe, cf. Curtius, *Europ. Mittelalter,* pp. 533 ff.

35. As indicated by this writer, *Journal of Near Eastern Studies,* IV (1945), 145, n. 67; for the Western development, cf. again Curtius, *op. cit.,* pp. 200-3. The cliché has also entered Byzantine literature, where it occurs, e.g., in the epic of Digenes Akritas.

36. *Zeitschrift für romanische Philologie,* LXIV (1944), 273-78. Curtius' observations, *ibid.,* LVIII (1938), 215-32, should also be considered in this connection. Cf., e.g., on p. 229 the short list of elements which were taken over by the *Chanson de Roland* from ancient epic tradition: "(1) Hervorhebung der Wohlgestalt des Helden; (2) abstrakt typisierende Landschaftschilderung; (3) Tötung von Ross und Reiter mit einem Streich; (4) Vorbereitung der Tragik durch Vordeutungen des Dichters, Omina und Träume."

37. *Al-Mu'jam fî ma'âyîr ash'âr al-'Ajam,* ed. Muhammad Qazvînî (Leiden and London, 1909), p. 290.

38. *Al-Mathal as-sâ'ir* (Cairo, 1312), p. 324. On the other hand, Ibn al-Athîr's contemporary, Yâqût (d. 1226), *op. cit.,* IV, 733-34, apologizes for telling the story of Bahrâm Gôr's master-shot, as it is a *qissa min hurâfât al-Furs,* "one of the silly stories of the Persians."

39. "Persische Studien" II, in *Sitzungsberichte der Wiener Akademie, phil.-hist. Cl.,* CXXVI (1892), Abh. 12, p. 13; cf. also *Grundriss,* II, 149.

40. Ed. B. T. Anklesaria (Bombay, 1918), pp. 231^{13}-32^2, as read and interpreted by H. W. Bailey, *Bulletin of the London School of Oriental and African Studies,* VII (1933-35), 760.

41. *Shâh-Nâmah,* VI, 1759-61/C 1249-50.

42. In the case of this book, it is likely that the author deliberately patterned his verse on the verse of the (lost) Avestan Vahman Yasht; cf. Benveniste, *Revue de l'histoire des religions,* CVI (1932), 366 ff.

43. Sassanian *Bearbeitung* of an Arsacid work; cf. Benveniste, *Journal asiatique,* CCXX (1932), 291.

44. These have been pointed out by Benveniste, *op. cit.,* pp. 262, n. 2, 271, 275-81, 282; for further literature on the *Zarêr Book* and its connections with the *Shâh-Nâmah,* cf. Nöldeke, *Nationalepos,* pp. 134-35, and p. 135, n. 5.

45. A good survey of Pahlavî poetry is found in A. Christensen, *Heltedigtning og Fortaellingslitteratur hos Iranerne i Oldtiden* (Copenhagen, 1935), pp. 32-37; for the *muzdawij,* cf. this author, *Journal of Near Eastern Studies,* III (1944), 9-13.[1]

46. Cf. Th. Nöldeke, "Beiträge zur Geschichte des Alexanderromans," *Denkschriften der Wiener Akademie, phil.-hist. Cl.,* XXXVIII/5 (1890), pp. 14-16, 34.

47. *Ibid.,* p. 34.

48. Ed. W. Kroll (Berlin, 1926).

49. The lines were composed *ca.* A.D. 200; cf. Pauly-Wissowa, *Realenzyklopädie,* IX, 679. H. Kuhlmann, "De Pseudo-Callisthenis carminibus choliambicis" (Diss., Münster i. W., 1912), does not contribute to the solution of our problem. The "Matrical Discourse upon Alexander" which C. Hunnius, *Das syrische Alexanderlied* (Diss., Göttingen, 1904), dates between 628 and 637, uses the dodecasyllabic verse (three units of four syllables each) customary with the Syriac homilies.

Reuben Levy (essay date 1967)

SOURCE: A prologue to *The Epic of the Kings: "Shah-Nama," the National Epic of Persia,* by Ferdowsi, translated by Reuben Levy, revised by Amin Banani, Routledge and Kegan Paul, Ltd., 1967, pp. xv-xxvi.

[*In the essay below, Levy offers an overview of Ferdowsi's* Shah-Nama, *commenting on its form and style and praising, in particular, the poet's skill in his laments for Persia's fallen kings and heroes.*]

Before the land of Iran was converted to its present religion of Islam, or Mohammadanism, it had for many centuries followed the doctrines of Zoroaster. His religion, known in the West as Zoroastrianism or Mazdaism, had a literature of its own, which concerned itself largely, as might be expected, with doctrinal and ritual matters. But in its later stages there had also grown up a small body of secular works, of which some at least dealt with the history of the land, its monarchs and heroes.

The conquest of Persia by the Mohammadan Arabs, an event which took place in the years after 636 of the Christian era, wrought a profound change not only in the religion of the people but in its language and literature. The older Pahlavi script was displaced by the Arabic alphabet, and the older language, while remaining basically Indo-European, was blended with a great number of Arabic words relating not only to the new religion and the new worship, of which the sacred language was Arabic, but also to everyday life. In a measure it was a precursor of what happened to the Saxon vocabulary after the conquest of England by the Normans.

THE SHAH-NAMA AND ITS AUTHOR

Of the writers in the new Persian, the Iranians themselves look upon seven as outstanding, and of these the earliest and most linked with national sentiment is the poet known as Ferdowsi, author of the ***Shāh-nāma*** [Vowels are pronounced as in Italian: ä, i and u are long, representing the long vowels which occur in the English words 'father', 'chief', and 'rule', while a, e, and o are short, as in 'cat', 'egg', and 'lot'.] (literally 'King-book', i.e. 'The Book of Kings'). This work provides a more or less connected story, told in metrical and rhymed verse, of the Iranian Empire, from the creation of the world down to the Mohammadan conquest, and it purports to deal with the reigns of fifty kings and queens, the section devoted by the poet to each bearing little relationship to the length of his or her reign.

The author himself is normally spoken of by his poetical name of 'Ferdowsi (or Ferdausi)', i.e. the 'Paradisal', whose honorific title was Abo'l-Qāsem. His personal name is unknown and the dates of his birth and death are both conjectural, though the latter probably took place at some time between the years 1020 and 1025 of the Christian era. He came from the neighbourhood of Tus in the province of Khorāsān and appears to have been a member of a family not wealthy but which owned a certain amount of land that they cultivated themselves. They belonged in fact to the 'Dehqān' class, which seems to have been the depository of national and local tradition and which educated some, at any rate, of its sons.

THE ORIGINS OF THE SHAH-NAMA

Ferdowsi had in his possession a prose book on the history of the Persian kings, and possibly also one in verse, but it was not until middle life that he began his own poem which, from beginning to end, took him about thirty-five years. He was not continuously employed at it and this is known from the fact that here and there he tells us what his age was at the time when he was composing some particular episode. This enables us to deduce that the various portions of the work were not done in the order in which they appear in the final form of the Shāh-nāma. His method was to select episodes as the fancy took him and he, or a redactor, later put them together in the chronological order of the reigns.

THE CONTENTS OF THE SHAH-NAMA

As a whole the work is a collection of episodes, providing a fairly continuous story of the Iranian Empire from before the creation of the world down to Iran's submergence under the Muslim Arabs. The material was of ancient origin and much of it had been stored up in the minds of *Dehqāns,* who were able to refresh their memories from records written in Pahlavi [Middle Persian] or in Arabic prose translations. Ferdowsi indeed did not invent the legends he put into verse form; in other words, he was not a fiction-writer drawing on his imagination for the central characters or the actual plots of his stories. They were established parts of the national tradition. But he elaborated what he found already in existence and he himself composed the innumerable speeches he put into the mouths of his heroes, as well as the many long letters written at the dictation of the kings and other principal characters.

The narrative begins with the creation of the world 'out of nothing' and continues by narrating how the primordial kings invented the crudely conceived basic requirements of civilization. During the reign of Jamshid, who was king for seven hundred years, there appeared, born of a family with Arab blood in its veins, the monster Zahhāk, who was finally overcome by Kāva the Blacksmith, whose famous banner was for long the palladium of the Iranians. Another great character who appears in the primeval era is Faridun, whose division of the earth between his three sons, Iraj, Tur, and Salm, leads to the murder of Iraj by the other two, and, hence, to the long feud between Tur (Turān) and Iran.

Manuchehr it was who avenged the blood of his father Iraj; then later in his reign appears the warrior Sām. His son Zāl fell in love with Rudāba, by whom he became the father of the prince Rostam, mightiest of all the heroic figures who enter upon the scene in the *Shāh-nāma.* He makes his appearance intermittently during a number of reigns which between them cover a space of over three centuries. Born in the reign of Manuchehr he does not die until Goshtāsp is on the throne of Iran, when he is killed, treacherously, in vengeance for having caused the death, howbeit involuntarily, of the Shāh Esfandiyār. Even in his last moments the hero had strength enough to slay the miserable wretch who had betrayed him.

It was during the reign of the inept Shāh Kāvus that most of Rostam's heroic feats occurred, and also his combat with his son Sohrāb, who died tragically by his hand. During that reign also the war between Iran and Turān flared up with renewed strength. This was in part due to a quarrel between Kāvus and his son Siyāvush, who fled to the court of the Turanian king Afrāsiyāb. For a time all had gone well with the fugitive prince, to whom Afrāsiyāb had given his daughter in marriage, but then the Turanian king

became offended with him and had him murdered. The need to avenge his death therefore became imperative. Key Khosrow, the son of Siyāvush, had grown to manhood in Turān and been with difficulty rescued from it. It was he who brought the war to a successful conclusion, Afrāsiyāb being killed after a long pursuit.

It is here that the romance of Bizhan and Manizha is inserted into the narrative.

After Key Khosrow there ascended the throne the Shāh Lohrāsp, member of a parallel branch of the Kaiānid dynasty. In his reign occur most of the adventures of his son Goshtāsp, who became the lover and husband of the daughter of the Caesar of Rum, i.e. Eastern Rome. It was in Goshtāsp's reign that Zoroaster introduced his new religion, being supported by the Shāh's son, Esfandiyār. He was kept from the throne long after his succession was due and was slain in the end by Rostam, who had to employ magic to achieve his aim.

The reigns of Dārā and Dārāb, both of which names represent Darius, are followed by that of Sekandar [Alexander] with the accounts of his more or less mythical adventures. Then comes Ardashir, with whom the narrative enters the historical period of the Sasanian Shahs, though it is interspersed with much that is romantic and legendary. Interest is chiefly concentrated on Bahrām Gur, one of the favourite heroes of Persian romantic poetry, and on Kasrā (Khosrow) regarded as the paragon of kingly wisdom. To another Bahrām, known as Chubin, who revolts against Kasrā, is devoted a lengthy portion of the Shāh-nāma and much attention is given also to the fall of the second Khosrow and the rise of his son Shiruy (Qobād).

With sympathetic detail the poet describes the fall of the Iranian Empire under its last Shah, Yazdegerd, after his army, led by a second Rostam, had been defeated by the Arab invaders at the battle of Qādesiya. Then the long story is brought to its close in a brief section containing some dates which purport to give the author's age at the time of his putting the finishing touches to the work.

THE CHARACTER OF THE SHAH-NAMA

The various episodes which compose the narrative are strung together very loosely, for, as we have seen, they were not composed in the chronological sequence proper to a work of history. The whole can be likened to a vast canvas on which the great heroes of Iran's past are depicted against the background of the poet's beloved country. From the nature of the work it cannot be an exact portrayal, for it begins from before the creation of the world and describes the careers of the Shahs who reigned during the era of myth and legend. Nevertheless it took the place of history with the audiences who listened to the stories recited to them; they were not concerned with the fact that no one could have been an eyewitness to the scenes described to them or could have been close to them in time.

There is in the *Shāh-nāma* an amalgamation of the Persian equivalents of chapters in the book of Genesis, the

Odyssey, Paradise Lost, Chaucer's Canterbury Tales and Shakespeare. It is indeed astonishing how often the vocabulary of Shakespeare suits the incidents described in the Persian epic. Drama, comedy, tragedy—all are here. Nature has a conspicuous and felicitous place in the *Shāh-nāma.* Tree lore has a prominent part. The vast scene of operations is bathed in a wondrous light.

In two types of passages Ferdowsi's art is often at its highest: the laments for the fallen kings and heroes, and the descriptions of sunrise. Perhaps Ferdowsi has intended an organic artistic link between these two themes that like a great antiphony run through the whole of the *Shāh-nāma.* The endless procession of death is punctuated by the recurrent birth of the source and symbol of all life itself. For the technical solution to the difficult task of treating repetitive material Ferdowsi borrows a prevalent and highly-regarded art form, namely theme and variations, and proves himself a consummate master. The full range of poetic arts are brought into play so that no two sunrises are described in the same terms and the same manner and no two laments are identical. There is an unsentimental pathos and a measured humanity in these laments. They often contain some of the profoundest lines in the whole poem.

But the poet's main object is to tell the story of his fatherland. We are stirred by the constant clash of arms, more particularly caused by the attacks and counter-attacks that throughout the passage of time recurred between Iran and its enemies, the most formidable of whom was Turān, the great national antagonist. The air is nearly always filled with the dust of battle, the roll of drums of war or the clash of heavy mace on steel helmet when a warrior meets his adversary in single combat.

Yet there are intervals for peaceful pursuits, when the monarchs, their coronets firmly attached to their heads, play polo or go hunting the onager—their favourite game—or the gentle gazelle. Following on triumphs in the field of battle or the hunting ground they seat themselves before huge trays laden with viands of every kind, being waited on by moon-cheeked maids who are constantly at hand with flagons of red wine. From time to time they engage in amorous dalliance.

The events and characters described suffer no terrestrial limitations as they range over land and sky, though it is only rarely that anything is said of adventure by sea. In this connection it may be said that Ferdowsi was as little trammelled by the facts of geography as was Shakespeare. Territories separated by vast stretches of road are traversed in an instant or else brought for convenience into close proximity. Monarchs dictate their behests to the whole world from the height of their thrones and proclaim themselves the direct instruments of God's will. The prehistoric kings, and heroes such as Rostam, live and wage war for hundreds of years. Throughout the whole poem the struggle with the national foes is associated with the struggle between good and evil, where the good must in the long run gain the upper hand.

FERDOWSI AND THE ART OF TRAGIC EPIC

Ferdowsi's main object is to preserve the 'history' of his fatherland, but the sum of the *Shāh-nāma*'s artistic worth outweighs the inherent shortcomings of the poet's conscious scheme. Broadly conceived, it belongs to the epic genre. But it is not a formal epic as the *Aeneid* or the *Lusiad.* Rather, it has the spontaneity of the *Iliad* and its episodic character reveals its kinship with the *chançons de geste.* More than any of its kindred poems, however, the *Shāh-nāma* is beset with paradoxes and conflicts. Paradoxes that are the protein of its art and the source of tragic nobility. If there is a unifying theme in the *Shāh-nāma* it is no simple 'wrath of Achilles', but the malevolence of the universe. Yet Ferdowsi is no passive fatalist. He has an abiding faith in a just Creator, he believes in the will of man, the need for his efforts, and the worth of his good deeds.

The pervading paradox of human existence is refracted and made particular in episodes and lives of mortals who, prism-like, reflect the light and shadow of character, the changes of moods and motives, and the many psychic levels of personality. In the strength, variety, and sometimes profundity of its characterization—often achieved with such economy of means—the *Shāh-nāma* is remarkable in the annals of classical literature. Very few of its many protagonists are archetypes. Alas, all too many of its noblest heroes are prey to the basest of human motives. And even the vilest among them have moments of humanity. Although outwardly many a character defies all natural bounds, none is exempt from the inner reality of human nature. The goodness of the best is possible and the evil of the most wretched is not incredible.

Nowhere is this depth of characterization more evident than in the person of Rostam, the foremost of Iranian heroes. He is essentially a man of the arena. Chivalrous, intensely loyal, pious, fearless, steel-willed and obdurate, he is nevertheless subject to occasional moods of disenchantment and indifference accompanied by gargantuan gluttony. He has a mystic reverence for the crown of Iran that inspires him to all his heroic feats. But he is quick to take offence and, at the slightest bruise to his ego or threat to his independent domain, wealth or power, he reacts with the full fury and resentment of a local dynast. For all his 'active' temperament he can be very wordy and didactic. When the occasion demands he is wise, temperate and resourceful. Of the more than three hundred years of his life, so lovingly recounted by Ferdowsi, only one night is spent in the amorous company of a woman. It serves the purpose of siring the ill-fated Sohrāb. For the rest, he is infinitely more devoted to his horse. Sometimes he is unable to rein his pride, which results in the two monstrous deeds of his life—and shapes the final tragedy of his life.

It is partly this depth of characterization that enhances and ennobles the tragic episodes of the *Shāh-nāma.* Jamshid the priest-king, world-orderer, and the giver of knowledge and skills, is the victim of his own hybris. The tragedy of Sohráb is not merely in the horror of filicide but in the fear and vanity of Rostam and the repulsed tender premonitions of Sohráb. The tragedies of Iraj and Siyávush evoke the cosmic anguish and the inconsolable pity of the guileless and the pure, ravaged by the wicked. Forud and Bahrám are the promise of sweet and valorous youth cut down by the senselessness of war. Esfandiyár is rent by the conflict of his formal loyalties and his piety and good sense. But it is his vanity and ambition that send him to his doom. Nor is this moving sense of the tragic reserved for the Iranians alone. Pirán, the hoary Turánian noble, shows compassion to captive Iranians and risks his own life to protect them only, in the end, to lose it for remaining loyal to his sovereign. Even the villainous Afrásiyáb—a prisoner of his evil nature—is pitiable and tragic in the helpless moments of self-awareness.

Ferdowsi has no set formulae for tragedy, yet in the early and mythical part of the *Shāh-nāma* an inexorable divine justice seems to balance most of the scales. Iraj and Siyávush are restored and triumphant in Manuchehr and Key-Khosrow, Rostam is reconciled to his fate as the price for the slaying of Sohráb and Esfandiyár, and Afrásiyáb cannot escape his share. The tragic impact of the *Shāh-nāma,* however, is not simply the sum of its tragic episodes. It pervades the encompassing conception of the work, and the sources of it are to be found in the conscious and unconscious paradoxes that form the personality, the emotional and the intellectual outlook of Ferdowsi.

The overriding tragic fact of the poet's life is that the glory of which he sings is no more. But this is not to say that the *Shāh-nāma* is a defiant nostalgic lament. The intellectual horizon of Ferdowsi is that of a rational and devout Muslim. Mohammad and Zoroaster are venerated as if they were of the same root, but Ferdowsi's pride in Iran is his constant muse. His concept of history is thoroughly Islamic, but there is no Augustinian righteous indignation in him. The cumulative emotional tensions of his 'history' are unresolved. Even in his stark treatment of the final reigns of the Sásánian empire, when the succession of evil, tyranny, rapacity, treachery and chaos is unrelieved by any sign of grace, he cannot quite bring himself to a condemnation of the Iranian empire. The only possible catharsis is in the contemplation of the ideal of justice, essential in Islam—yet already far detached from the realities of his time. Nor is the holocaust so distant as the fall of the Sásánians. Ferdowsi was undoubtedly inspired by the renascent Iranism of the Sámánid epoch and may have even conceived of his masterwork as an offering to that illustrious house, only to witness its demise at the hand of the Turkic Ghaznavids. The bitterness of the mythical Iranian-Turánian epic struggle that permeates the *Shāh-nāma* and gives it its dramatic tension is largely the pressing phenomenon of the poet's own time. Thus he has experienced a re-enactment of the final tragedy of his poem. The necessity of dedicating the *Shāh-nāma* to the very Turkic destroyer of the Iranian Sámánids must have been a

bitter and demeaning fact. Much of the traditional denunciatory epilogue addressed to Mahmud of Ghazna may be accretions of later times, but the tone is true.

The tensions and contradictions in the experience of the poet that are reflected in the tragic paradoxes of the *Shāh-nāma* and are a source of validity, profundity, and universality of its art, are not all conscious or external. The interactions of his innate character, his inculcated traits, his social position, his changing environment, and the nature of his creative genius, all fail to achieve a synthesis. Instead, they fashion a personality marred by unresolved intellectual conflicts and spiritual anguish.

He belongs to the class of *dehqāns,* or landed gentry, and has an inherited sense of expectation of privilege, which is embittered by gradual impoverishment. He is not yet free of the impulses of generosity and noble detachment that sometimes flourish in the serene and self-assured middle plateaux of wealth and power of a social class; but he is already afflicted with the material obsessions, if not greed and avarice, that characterize the periods of rise and fall of those classes. Thus he seeks, and needs, the patronage and the emoluments of the Ghaznavid court, yet he is too proud, too detached and too dedicated to his 'uncommercial' art to secure that patronage in the accepted mode of the day. He is contemptuous of the servility and the parasitic existence of the court poets, of the artificiality of their panegyric verse, of the ignobleness of their self-seeking and mutual enmity, yet he is not without the artist's vanity, envy and acrimony and, occasionally, he succumbs to the temptation of proving himself in their terms.

Ferdowsi's genuine compassion for the poor and the wronged, his remarkable and persistent sense of social justice, his courageous and vocal condemnation of irresponsibility of rulers, his altruism and idealism—in short, his profound humanity—account for some of the most moving and ennobling passages in the *Shāh-nāma* and endow it with a consistent integrity. At the same time he had the conservative impulses of the *dehqān.* His yearning for legitimacy, his outrage at disregard of position, his abhorrence of anarchy, his fear of heresy, and his dread of unruly mobs provide the narrative with moments of eerie drama and Jeremiah-like visions and nightmares of the apocalypse.

However much may be said of the formal and philosophical diffuseness of the *Shāh-nāma,* it is transcendentally successful as a true epic. In that sense only a comparison with the Iliad can be meaningful and instructive. In their origin, nature and functions as well as in form and content, there are arresting similarities between the two poems. This is not to say that the likenesses outnumber the differences. The *Shāh-nāma* is, of course, the product of a much later and more self-conscious age, and it draws from a vast fund of literary conventions and clichés of 'Near Eastern' cultures. But the *Shāh-nāma* and the Iliad partake of the fundamental mysteries of epic as art. They both represent the instantly and eternally triumphant attempts of conscious art to immortalize the glory and the identity of a people. It does not matter that neither Homer nor Ferdowsi were the very first to attempt such a task in their cultures. It is the supreme elixir of their art which accomplished the miracle. They ennobled the natural epic without losing its spontaneity. Furthermore, they did so at a time when the cement of past associations was crumbling and the common identity of their peoples was in danger of effacement. Thus by their creations Homer and Ferdowsi succeeded at once in immortalizing the past and bequeathing the future to the language and life of their nation.

The western reader of the *Shāh-nāma* will learn much—and may gain in enjoyment—by some comparison of its similarities and differences with the Iliad. Although Ferdowsi works with a number of written and even 'literate' sources, at least in the first half of the Shāh-nāma, as in the Iliad the roots of oral tradition are close to the surface. Both poems employ a simple, facile metre and their rhyme schemes are suited to the long narrative and aid in memorizing. The heroes in both epics are affixed with appropriate epithets and are easily recognizable even without mention of their names. Both poems make use of a certain amount of repetition to assist recapitulation. Episodes of battle and heroism are modulated by sequences of chase, ostentatious banquets and idyllic revels, and ceremonious councils and parleys. Semi-independent sub-episodes are interspersed to vary the mood and relieve the tedium of the narrative. Of these, several romances in the *Shāh-nāma,* particularly those of Zāl and Rudāba and of Bizhan and Manizha in their exquisite lyricism, poignant intimacy and self-contained perfection, have no peers in the Iliad. Both poets lavish masterful attention upon the details of the martial life—the description of armours and weapons, the personal and near magical love of the heroes for their mounts and their armour, etc.—that breed and sustain a sense of epic involvement. Both poems abound in little warm human touches that evoke pathos and enhance the evolving drama.

Transcending these more or less formal similarities are the fundamental parallels of human behaviour under similar relationships and social conditions and the recognizable range of human types in the Iliad and the *Shāh-nāma.* The affinities of the indispensable hero Rostam with Achilles; of the capricious, covetous, apprehensive and envious monarch Key Kāvus with Agamemnon; of the stolid and martial Giv with Ajax; of the wily and wise Pirān with Odysseus; of the dutiful and sacrificial Gudarz with Hector; of the impetuous and handsome Bizhan with Paris; of the youthful, loyal and pathetic Bahrām with Patroklos; of the impulsive, sensuous and beautiful Sudāba with Helen; of the adoring, meek and resigned Farangis with Hecuba; are only a few of the evocative suggestions of artistic kinship between the two epics. In the fragile social order depicted in the Iliad and in the first half of the *Shāh-nāma* tension and strife are never far from the surface. But Ferdowsi has endowed his cosmos with a higher morality and thus the lapses of his heroes are more grave and aweful.

In addition to mortal humans both epics are peopled by several supernatural orders of goodly spirits, demons and magical creatures who intervene in the affairs of men and profoundly affect their fate. But the God of *Shāh-nāma* is the unknowable God of Zoroastrians, Jews, Christians and Muslims. Unlike the deities of the Iliad He is not implicated in the struggle of the mortals though he is constantly evoked and beseeched. Only twice does an angel intervene to alter the course of battle. At other times there is only indirect confirmation of the righteous and chastisement of the wayward. On the other hand prophetic dreams count for more in the *Shāh-nāma.* Fate is the unconquerable tyrant of both poems, but in the *Shāh-nāma* it is sometimes unravelled by the stars, robbing the drama of its mystery.

The *Shāh-nāma* is inordinately longer than the Iliad. Essentially it is made in two segments: the mythical first half and the 'historical' second half. The psychological and artistic seam cannot be concealed. The fundamental affinities with the Iliad are primarily true of the first half. But even there the unity of theme, the limitation of action and time, the rapid devolution of the 'plot', the resolution of the conflict and the uncanny proportions of the Iliad are missing. Ferdowsi's 'historical' mission undoubtedly scatters the artistic impact of the *Shāh-nāma* and diffuses the focus of its aesthetic concept. But the wrath of Achilles', after all, is not the sole catalyst of Homer's art. The validity and viability of the Iliad rests in its general relevance to the human situation. In this sense the artistic 'flaw' of the *Shāh-nāma* is more than made up by, and perhaps makes for, its greater universality. Thus in the *Shāh-nāma* we come across characters who have no counterparts in the Iliad, and one must cull the whole of Greek mythology, mystery and drama for parallels. Jamshid, the primal priest-king, the divinely inspired creator of civilization, the bringer of world order, whose hybris causes his fall and plunges mankind into evil and darkness. Zahhāk, the grotesque tyrant, the personification of irrational and demonic forces who grips the world in a thousand-year reign of terror. Kāva, the rebellious *vox populi* triumphant in a just cause. Faridun, the ideal and wise king, compassionate pastor of his people. Siyāvush, the tragic guileless youth, maligned, helpless and martyred. Key-Khosrow, the messiah-king, avenger and restorer. Every one of them is a focal realization of a master figure in the history of man's existence and aspirations.

It is this universality together with its faithful and unresolved reflection of the human paradox that is the essence of *Shāh-nāma*'s art and the cause of its timelessness; for it permits every generation to seek its own resolution.

G. M. Wickens (essay date 1972)

SOURCE: "The Imperial Epic of Iran: A Literary Approach," in *Iranian Civilization and Culture,* edited by Charles J. Adams, McGill University, 1972, pp. 133-44.

[*In the essay that follows, Wickens examines the portion of the* Shah-Nama *dedicated to the Sasanid period of Iran's history, offering a synopsis of this section and emphasizing its dramatic form and themes.*]

Many of the ideas presented here have undoubtedly been maturing in my mind since I was first compelled, some thirty-four years ago, to read a portion of the **Shāh-nāmah** not for its own splendid sake but as a tool on which to practice my elementary grasp of the Persian language. They are thus very personal ideas, very much a part of my life; but they have been sharpened and brought to the point of public utterance as the result of several recent discussions on literary and related matters with my colleague and friend, Dr. Rivanne Sandler. It is, therefore, only fitting that I make at this point a grateful, if necessarily somewhat imprecise acknowledgement of Dr. Sandler's part in this enterprise. She may yet have other things to say on her own account, or we may say them in collaboration; but meanwhile, the following speculations are offered in their own right as a tribute to some of the imperfectly appreciated versatilities of Iran's great singer of the royal saga.

Like most other works of Persian literature, the **Shāh-nāmah** has received very little analysis in purely literary terms, and even less in the context of really modern literary criticism. It is of course a commonplace among students of Persian literature that, in Iran itself, the traditional literary 'appreciation' is confined to generalities or to technicalities of exegesis, prosody and figurative style, or tends to pass rapidly into biographical and anecdotal narrative. In the case of the **Shāh-nāmah,** moreover, the would-be modern critic's problems are compounded by a virtually unique element—namely the work's long-standing pious prestige as the classic literary affirmation of the Iranian sense of identity, particularly as that identity reveals itself in a consciousness of historic destiny embodied in both a royal personage and a masterly wielding of the Persian speech-form as such. Even a readable and valuable work like *Firdawsī w shi'r-i ū*, published in 1346 s./1967 by that eminent man-of-letters Mujtabā Mīnuvī, still very largely concerns itself with such aspects as these to the virtual exclusion of any validly literary analysis.

Non-Iranian evaluation (which of course connotes primarily Western studies) is in even less satisfactory case. At least no one can doubt that the Iranian tradition itself is one of both reverence and delight; but it would be next to impossible to point to a single Western scholar who has either approached the work with real respect or laid it aside with keen pleasure. All have at times commented on what they felt to be its inordinate length, its wearisome repetitions, its stock situations, its stylized language, its dullness and lack of humour—and so on and so forth. Those who have at least taken the work at all seriously (like Windischmann, or Geiger or Noeldeke, or their few modern successors like Wolff) have looked upon it primarily as a text for critical source research or as a component in comparative studies in language or history or mythology. Perhaps the most favourable treatment the work has received in the West has been at the hands of art histori-

ans, who have valued it—along with Nizāmī's *Khamsah*—for the superb illustrations that have often accompanied the best manuscripts. Virtually no one, however, up to and including Reuben Levy's 1967 précis in prose, has treated the work as a great piece of literature, much less as literature to be assessed in literary terms.

In this paper it is hoped to make some small beginning towards a literary appraisal of what might be termed Iran's 'royal work' *par excellence.* It might be appropriate for several reasons to base myself primarily, though not exclusively, on the early Sasanid period, specifically the reigns of Ardashīr I and his son Shāpūr I. In the first place, this was the portion I was obliged to read all those years ago in 1937; and I have read it many times since, so it is perhaps the one on which my thoughts about literary matters in the **Shāh-nāmah** have been most concentrated over the years. Secondly, it is—as most people will surely agree—far from being one of the most obviously literary portions of the **Shāh-nāmah;** for it is only loosely woven of threads that ostensibly neither match nor contrast—among them, rather flat narrative, both factual and apocryphal, from the historical period, grotesque magic and fantasy from the realm of the timeless, and didactic material that is of classic social significance but, by any immediate standards, of only limited literary merit. If such a portion of the work can plausibly be shown to contain several features of genuine literary significance, the case will have been fairly adequately suggested for the rest. My final reason for this choice is that the early Sasanid period is perhaps peculiarly fitted for consideration on this occasion, being—like the present—one of the notable ages of Iranian national resurgence after a lengthy period of decline and stagnation.

At this point it would be well to summarize the themes of the main subdivisions of this portion.

At the opening of the narrative for this period, the five hundred years following Darius' death and Alexander's succession are dismissed in a few lines; and we are told how the true royal stock survived in hardship and obscurity until a descendant, working as a shepherd in south Persia, is recognized as kingly by his master in a dream and married to the latter's daughter. From this union is born Ardashr, who is sent by his grandfather to the Parthian court of Ardavān for his education and advancement. Before long, Ardashīr offends Ardavān by surpassing the Parthian ruler's sons in his accomplishments; and he also attracts Ardavān's mistress, who, in her roles as royal confidant and treasurer, keeps him informed of Ardavan's anxieties and initiatives for his family's succession. When matters become dangerously critical, she aids Ardashīr, materially and otherwise, to make his escape back to Fārs. Ardavān pursues them without success, and in subsequent battles he is progressively reduced to the support of his immediate family and entourage, while more and more forces gather to Ardashīr. Ardavān is finally killed and his line almost obliterated on the male side. As the first of his many struggles to maintain himself. Ardashīr now engages in a long-drawn war with the Kurds, at length obtaining victory.

There follows here the episode of the Worm of Kirmān. A Worm found in an apple is reared by a girl of poor family. Eventually it becomes an enormous dragon in whose service the girl and her family achieve great power. Ultimately, the Worm presents a serious threat to Ardashīr, who is not only at first defeated but finds his homeland attacked and plundered in his rear by other enemies as well. At last he obtains access to the Worm, disguised as a grateful merchant come to pay tribute; he kills the creature by feeding it a diet of molten metal and goes on to defeat and kill its cohorts in battle. On the site of the Worm's stronghold, as one of his many measures to restore and strengthen the Zoroastrian faith, he erects a fire temple and makes provision for worship in the old religion.

At this date begins officially Ardashīr's reign of 'forty years and two months,' and he establishes his court in Ctesiphon, near the modern Baghdad. He now seeks in marriage the daughter of his old enemy Ardavān, primarily so that she can be induced to reveal the whereabouts of her father's great treasure. Whatever her own feelings towards him, she is pressed to kill him by her elder brother, who has escaped to India and now sends her poison and reproachful admonitions to use it forthwith. King-favouring fate intervenes before the Shāh drinks the poison; and when her treachery becomes apparent, Ardashīr gives orders for her to be killed despite her claim to be now pregnant by him and his own keen desire for an heir. But his loyal first minister, conscious of the desperate need for established succession, shelters the girl in his own home. In a macabre side-incident, this faithful servant avoids scandal by castrating himself and depositing in the royal treasury a sealed and dated receptacle containing his manhood. Shāpūr I is born of Ardavān's daughter, and is eventually recognized (a very common occurrence in the epic) by his father from among several youths playing in a polo match. Ardavān's daughter, still alive, is forgiven and restored to a position of honour.

At this point, Ardashīr, anxious like Ardavān before him, sends to an Indian sage for advice on the future and for some encouragement to believe he will soon find rest from his constant struggles against enemies. The answer comes that peace and tranquility may be expected only when Ardashīr's line is joined with that of Mihrak, one of the several treacherous rivals the Shāh has had to eliminate in the course of his rise to power. Ardashīr is outraged and vows to seek out and kill the one child of Mihrak, a daughter, who has hitherto eluded him. Fate once again intervenes, and the heir-apparent Shāpūr accidentally meets and falls in love with Mihrak's daughter, who is living in obscurity with a village headman's family. From their union is born Ohrmazd, and he is reared secretly until (once again) his grandfather picks him out at a polo match by his kingly skill and daring. The Shāh accepts the workings and wisdom of fate, recalling that since Ohrmazd's conception he

has known peace and contentment as promised by the Indian seer. Here follows a long, and classic passage on Ardashīr's political sagacity and administrative ability; then an encomium upon Ardashīr by a certain Kharrād; next a discourse on the ultimate faithlessness of fate, at least in its dealings with human beings as individuals; Ardashīr's last injunction to Shāpūr before dying; and finally a short section in praise of God and in commendation of the poet's prospective patron, Mahmūd of Ghaznah.

Shāpūr's historically eventful reign of thirty-two-odd years is dealt with in about one-seventeenth of the space given to his father. There is a passage of conventional exhortation to the great administers of the realm, and an account of Shāpūr's wars with the Romans and the capture of their general. Peace comes at last.

So much for a bare synopsis of the material in this section of the *Shāh-nāmah,* some mere three percent of the whole work. In what ways may one interpret this section as a piece of work revealing a high degree of literary skill? The *Shāh-nāmah* is commonly referred to, at least in the West, as an epic: in Iran itself there is no genuine, indigenous word for the genre to which this work might loosely be said to belong. However, as there is no clear agreement, even in the West, on the essential nature of the epic, and since the *Shāh-nāmah* is in all sorts of ways in a class apart—in both Persian and world literature—the term epic is not altogether enlightening; but it is convenient and handy, and there seems little point in trying seriously to replace it. However, one feature the work displays quite unmistakably, in the first place, is the tension of great drama—a tension, moreover, not only of language and the confrontation of persons with persons or with events, but one of overall conception. At no point in this vast cavalcade are we in any serious doubt that the true line of kingship, as distinct from the individual kings, will survive—certainly until the coming of Islām, and perhaps even beyond that. At the lowest mechanical level, to demonstrate this theorem is the avowed purpose of the work as a whole. But on a higher literary plane also, throughout the course of the narrative, the bearer of kingship is constantly recognized, helped and protected by a whole series of figures—some of them gigantic and heroic and enduring like Rustam, others obscure and ephemeral (shepherds and boatmen are the commonest representatives from among the people), while still others—though ostensibly folk figures—carry a shadowy suggestion of the supernatural and the angelic. Of course, for any with what Firdawsī would call clarity of eye and heart, the true king carries around him a royal aura, the *farr,* that is both physically and psychologically palpable. Nevertheless, if all is due to come out right in the long run, there are many tragic failures along the way, and even more frequent examples of the royal figure's veritable human nature threatening to impede the ultimate success of his cause, to say nothing of instances where his weaknesses help it along. In many and varied ways, this long line of princes interacts (to use the modern terminology) with the end-purpose of fate and of their own loyal followers, but by no means do they always dovetail with it. These rulers are, in other words, realistically enough conceived to be often unwise, headstrong and hubristic—sometimes almost comically so. A few are almost constantly thus (e.g. Kay Kā'us), some only in spells (like Ardashīr), while others begin well and end irrevocably badly (like Jamshīd). From one point of view, the whole massive sub-epic of Rustam is a prolonged instance of such dramatic tensions, though it has many subordinate tensions besides.

Let us consider some examples of this sort of situation as they work themselves out in the cases of Ardashīr I and Shāpūr I. Dramatic tension, often associated with irony and humour, will be my main concern, but I shall seize the opportunity to touch briefly on several other literary and related features which seem to me to have been largely ignored by others so far. It may be that I shall attempt too much, and so produce a measure of mental and emotional congestion; but I would plead that it is in a good, and even a desperate, cause; and I certainly propose to develop each of these ideas elsewhere, as suitable opportunities arise, in more disciplined and rigorous categories.

The opening passage, where the defeated royal line endures centuries of poverty and obscurity in India and Iran, is a low-key masterpiece of Firdawsī's technique. Not only do we here have tension, but also—lightly but significantly introduced—the constantly present feature of dramatic irony: we ourselves know the true identity of these honest labourers, but virtually nobody else does, and even they themselves seem at times but dimly aware of their royal heritage and destiny. Even when the action starts to move again, the unknown prince is still busily playing his natural (if symbolic) part as a shepherd. When he takes service under the landowner who finally recognizes him in a vision, there are no heavy, mechanical portents, only the simple—practically colloquial—question: 'Could you use a hired hand, passing this way, down on his luck?' . . .

And when, after consecutive dreams revealing the young man's, or his descendants', glorious future of temporal and spiritual power, the landowner summons him, there is still no forcing of the action: 'He ordered the head-shepherd should come to him from the flocks, on a day of wind and snow; who came to him, panting, in his cloak—the woollen garment filled with snow, his heart with fear.' Anyone who has spent a winter's day among the nomads of Iran will appreciate this as a vignette of high artistry (even in my version); but it is more—it holds off the great movements of fate, forcing them to play themselves out in the business of daily living. Again, as Bābak tries to persuade the young man to speak of his background and family (for even inspired dreams must be tested in the *Shāh-nāmah*), the shepherd is silent and ultimately speaks, in very restrained language, only after obtaining a sworn guarantee for his security. No instant recognitions here, no ringing declarations, no bold decisions. And Bābak, despite his tearful joy at confirming the survival of the true royal line, is nevertheless abruptly practical in his dismissal of the smelly young shepherd to the bath . . .

before proceeding further. Throughout the poem royalty is associated, in high symbolic drama, with a pastoral aristocracy, and there is no indignity in honest labour in such pursuits, but the earthy realities of the pastoral life are never ignored.

Even later, when the royal figure has married Bābak's daughter and lives (somewhat improbably) in elegance and splendour, there is no rapid restoration of the right order of things. All must work itself out through human motivation, even where humanity is at its weakest. When Ardashīr is born and grows to young manhood, he is sent by his wise old grandfather to the Parthian court of Ardavān in North Persia. (As an aside, we may here point out other subordinate tensions in the work, such as the fruitful ones between grandfathers and grandsons: those between fathers and sons—of which Rustam and Suhrāb offer the best-known example—are often highly destructive.) Now Ardashīr is sent at Ardavān's own request, for the latter has heard of his 'accomplishments and wisdom.' Preceding lines also dwell on his appearance and his true descent, and in later passages other gifts are mentioned. The decisive action is sprung by none of these aids to greatness, but rather, by the natural often unbridled, urges of a young man in high health and prideful spirits. The ironies and tensions lie thick hereabouts, though never obtruded. Here are a few.

The old grandfather, whatever his secret knowledge and his high hopes for his grandson, is on excellent and respectful terms with the Parthian usurper, who is in effect precipitating his own downfall by his desire to embellish his court with gallant youths like Ardashīr. Again, Ardavān persuades Bābak to relinquish his beloved grandson with vows (which he inevitably, because of Ardashīr's nature, will not be able to keep) to treat him exactly as one of his own sons. The grandfather, on his side, plays a part entirely in character by giving the young prudent advice about his conduct, which Ardashīr at the time may well intend to follow, but which—if actually put into practice— would effectively rule out his future greatness as purposed by fate. For the moment, at any rate, all goes well; and the ironies are evident, as they should be, only in the reflection of what follows. Neither Ardavān's figure and character nor those of his family are at this time presented in anything but a dignified and generous light: their only real defect is that fate cannot be on their side, for they are not of the true royal line. (Only much later do two mysterious young men speak of Ardashīr as having escaped 'the palate and the breath of the dragon'; but this is less a designation of Ardavān's character than a clear casting of him for the malevolent role in a quasi-cosmic drama.)

When the crucial quarrel erupts between Ardashīr and Ardavān—over the fact that the former not only surpasses Ardavān's son on the hunting-field, but refuses graciously to back down and even calls the Parthian prince a liar who makes false claims—Ardashīr is sent to be Ardavān's head groom and odd-job man . . .

This is not quite 'clogs to clogs in three generations' (as the old Lancashire saying has it), but it is a sufficiently

ironical come-down to make what follows not merely plausible but inevitable. Ardashīr chafes and plots (as the poet
puts it, his head is 'full of alchemy'), and he complains to
his grandfather, who writes back, still very much in character: 'O youth, little-wise, part-ripe . . . you are his ser-
vitor, not his relative; he showed not you the enmity in
malice that you have shown yourself by your unwisdom!'
But he sends him money and supplies and bids him lie
low in hopes that time will heal the quarrel. Ardashīr goes
his own way, putting his mind now to *nayrang w awrand*,
the 'craft and deceit' without which even fate cannot bring
the royal aspirant to his rightful end, and which are in no
way seen as a detraction from his character or his felicitous auspices. Outwardly he lulls suspicions by adopting
the life-style of a frivolous playboy.

The events that follow, leading to the ultimate confrontation, are brought about and directed, however, not by any
scheming on Ardashīr's part but by the resourcefulness of
Ardavān's girl-Friday, Gulnār—one of a line of remarkable female characters that form one of the poem's most
striking features. This spirited girl's one weakness is a
passionate obsession with Ardashīr (which gives Firdawsī
the opportunity to write some rarely tender and emotional
lines. Ardashīr, by contrast, is cool and detached, even
peevish—a mood set by his first words when he awakes to
find her at his pillow: 'Where have you sprung from?'
. . .

So much for her weakness, but in all other respects she is
calm, intelligent, practical and strong-minded. It is no accident that the great Ardavān not only needs her constantly
by him, but is described as unable to begin his day unless—another supreme irony!—she shows her auspicious
face at his bedside each morning. At any rate, she establishes a liaison with Ardashīr at considerable risk to herself, she skilfully manages Ardavān's affairs while keeping
Ardashīr fully informed of them and of her master's
troubles and anxieties, and she plots and plans and urges
various courses of action. Eventually she brings the critical news that astrologers, employed by Ardavān, have
forecast the affliction of a great man in consequence of the
revolt of a subordinate destined for greatness. (No ominous judgments of this kind, astrological or otherwise, are
ever couched in the **Shāh-nāmah,** in anything but vague—
and sometimes ironically reassuring—terms.) This, she indicates, is Ardashīr's moment, but he greets her—totally
in character, but with what must be seen as an ironic resistance to destiny—with the following words: 'Can't you do
without Ardavān for a single day?' . . .

she has been absent for three days, busily following the
full cycle of the astrological processes. Even when she
convinces him that it is now or never, he is clearly 'lost'
rather than grateful, and promises her a share of his greatness if only she will accompany him on the flight to Fārs.
She, poor girl, needs no urging, staying only to say, 'I will
never leave you so long as I live!' . . .

she hastens back to her quarters to organize all the material and other necessities for the escape. One of the most

significant silences in the work touches her eventual fate,
for she drops out of the narrative completely after playing
her usual important role on the return journey. Like Homer,
Firdawsī sometimes nods, but his shuttling back and forth
of his *personae* is normally very skilful and thorough. Accordingly, I think we must regard this fade-out as deliberate, a further stroke in delineating the character of Ardashīr himself.

In this portion of the work there are four major feminine
figures: this girl; Ardavān's daughter (who, after marriage
to Ardashīr, tries to poison him); Mihrak's daughter (who
secretly marries Shāpūr); and Haftvād's daughter (the girl
who finds the Worm in the apple). The characters and the
actions of these women illuminate not only Firdawsī's
skilful management of the fundamental tensions between
the sexes, but also his ability to pass to and fro between
delicate irony and outright comedy—I say this in the belief that the humorous side of the poet's work has hitherto
been underestimated, if not virtually ignored. We have
seen how Ardavān's daughter, in peril of her life, still
manages to circumvent Ardashīr's hot-tempered decree,
and this for his own ultimate and inevitable good—one of
the most fateful events in the whole work, for the true line
is about to die out. In the cases of Gulnār and Mihrak's
daughter, however, the events—though almost as porten-
tous—are more lightly handled. On his flight from Ardavān's court, Ardashīr (supported as he is by all sorts of
earthly and supernatural phenomena, including a spectral
ram—a sort of pastoral symbol of his *farr*) is, as usual, in
danger of committing all manner of fateful imprudences,
including that of delaying for rest and refreshment. Two
mysterious young men exhort him to press on, and for the
first time, even if in an ironically misguided context, he
begins to feel his authority. Turning to Gulnār, as though
the idea of halting had been hers, he says sharply: 'Mark
these words!' . . .

and on several occasions throughout his subsequent career
(notably after the two events he has done his utmost to
thwart, i.e., the birth of his heir, and the marriage of that
heir to Mihrak's daughter), he will seize the opportunity to
read back at some length, to both fate and his loyal followers, the moral in all that has come to pass so won-
drously.

The first encounter of Shāpūr with Mihrak's daughter
strikes an even more absurd note. In her disguise as a village maiden, she is drawing water from a well. The enam-
oured Shāpūr orders one of his retinue to relieve her, and
when the man fails to raise the bucket, shouts: 'O half a
woman! Did not a woman wield this pail and wheel and
rope, raising no little water from the well, where you are
full of toil and call for help?' He then tries his own hand,
barely succeeding; and this domesticated version of the
drawing of Excalibur enables each young person to recognize the other as royal. Yet the girl, whose royal title is
only partial, emerges—humanly speaking—as the victor in
the exchange. While Shāpūr blusters and puffs over the
pail, she sits to one side and smiles. When he covers his

embarrassment with an abrupt, brief outburst to the effect that she must be something more than ordinary to cope so easily with the bucket, she counters with an elegant reply, fully delineating his identity and qualities and suggesting that the water will now turn to milk by the grace of his intervention. All in all, she is shown as not only most beautiful, but stronger and wittier than the man she will marry. It is important to realize, however, that the royal figure remains great on an entirely different scale from the purely human; and the use of these gifted, but ultimately less than ideal, human instruments to bring out the essential greatness of royalty (or sometimes of sainthood) is a staple of Persian literature. Gulnār (the ex-mistress of a hated rival, and a girl whom some would regard as a forward, bossy hussy), Ardavān's daughter (of part-impure stock, and a would-be poisoner), and Mihrak's daughter (a show-off and descended from a traitor)—all these parallel, in one way or another, that classic female figure in Persian literature, Zulaykhā, Potiphar's wife, who (driven by unlawful passions) demonstrates Joseph's inner greatness by contrast and relief. Yet, at the human level, few poets have missed the formal beauty and the pathetic dignity of the Zulaykhā figure, rather than of Joseph, so that—while he may be virtuous—it is she who, by an only seeming paradox, becomes the symbol of the helpless self-sacrificing mystic. Similarly in the *Shāh-nāmah.*

In the case of Haftvād's daughter, the Worm-girl, there is no direct confrontation with the royal line, and here Firdawsī builds his tensions, and displays his literary skills generally, in a somewhat different manner. Broadly speaking, the effects are achieved by emphasizing at the outset, and reminding us throughout, that the girl who rises to ultimately sinister fortune and power is, originally and essentially, a hardworking, natural, kindly person. Likewise, what eventually becomes a monstrous and baleful dragon is but a gradually developed projection, again with frequent flashbacks, from a rather cute, helpless, tiny creature. Even the girl's father, who soon becomes a boastful layabout and finally a tyrant, is depicted at first as a natural victim of life's handicaps and of other men's greed and callousness.

To make these points somewhat clearer, it is worth quoting the low-key opening passages from this fantastic episode at some length:

> A town there was, cramped, the people numerous, each person's eating by effort only; many girls there were therein, seeking their bread without fulfillment. On one side the mountains came closer, and thither they would all go together, each carrying cotton weighed out by measure and a spindle-case of poplar-wood. At the gates they would gather, striding from the city towards the mountains. Their food they pooled in common, in eating there was neither more nor less. There was no talk there of sleeping or eating, for all their efforts and endeavours were towards their cotton. In the evening homeward they would return, their cotton to a long thread turned. In that city, having nothing but of serene disposition, was a man named Haftvād . . . who had but one beloved daughter . . .

The action opens one day, at the lunch-break, again most unportentously, or at least with such portents as are realized later to be delicately ironical:

> . . . It befell that this girl of good fortune had seen on the road, and swiftly picked up, an apple cast down from its tree by the wind. (Now hear this marvellous tale!) That fair-cheeked one, into the fruit biting, saw a worm lodged inside; with her fingers she lifted it from the apple and gently placed it in her spindle-case. Then, taking up her cotton from the case, she said: "In the name of the Lord, with no mate or companion, I today by the Star of the Apple-Worm will show you a terrible prodigy of spinning!" All the girls took to merriment and laughter, open-cheeked and silvery of teeth. So she spun twice what she would spin in a day, and marked its quantity on the ground . . .

So is laid the foundation of the family's enormous wealth and authority throughout the land, until even the up-and-coming Ardashīr feels threatened. But events move with anything but unnatural swiftness. The girl constantly increases her intake of cotton and her output of thread, while feeding the Worm bigger pieces of apple and other delicacies and moving it to ever more spacious quarters as it grows bigger and more strikingly beautiful. Her parents are pleased, but at a loss. They wonder if she has, as they put it, 'become sister to a fairy-being,' and Firdawsī begins a series of skilfully ambivalent references to her: 'spellbinding' (*pur-fusūn*) as against 'industrious' (*pur-hunar*), and so on. There is as yet no clear suggestion of evil, not even of evil of which the agents themselves are unaware, merely the suspicion of some supernatural or magical intervention. When she tells her parents how matters stand, they are 'augmented in brightness' (*rawshanā'ī*), a term the poet always uses in auspicious and rational contexts. Yet, in the very next line we meet a bad omen ironically arising from what is taken to be a good one: 'Haftvād took this affair for a good sign, giving no further thought in his mind to work, and talking of nothing but the Star of the Worm.' Like Mr. Micawber in his Australian days, he becomes a man of substance and a local wiseacre. Eventually the regional governor falls foul of him, still through no fault of his own, thinking to put down and rob this newly-risen one 'of evil stock.' (In using this latter term, Firdawsī again preserves a measure of ambiguity, for *bad-nizhād* could also be rendered merely as 'baseborn': the whole series of shifting degrees of pejorative connotation is, of course, fully comprehensible only within the poet's own social and literary ambiance.) The outcome is victory for Haftvād, who betakes himself with his mascot the Worm, and his great treasure and retinue, to one of those mountain-top fortresses which often figure as the great focal points of Persian literature and Iranian history.

Even at this point the Worm continues to be described in terms that present him as a creature of impressive beauty. The daughter, now become the Worm's chief keeper and executive agent, is still spoken of as 'serene' or 'cheerful' (hereafter there is no specific mention of her, though we may presume her destruction together with that of her monstrous pet); and Haftvād himself continues to be spoken of, in terms that are at least neutral and possibly even complimentary, as a 'combative captain.' Or again, 'And such was *illustrious* Haftvād's fortress that the wind dared not to move around it.' Only when hostilities are initiated by Ardashīr, do we begin to hear a different note: for example, one of Haftvād's seven sons is described, in a threefold denunciation, as 'impudent, a doer of evil, ill-natured.' Even so, after sharp fighting, the upstart Haftvād is still in a position to spare Ardashīr's life when he has him at his mercy, albeit he does so insultingly, warning him that he is out of his depth, Shāh though he be, in tangling with the domination of the Worm. In his dejection Ardashīr is counselled, by two more of the mysterious young men we have referred to earlier, as to the true nature of the Worm and the conditions on which alone he can hope to subdue it: 'A worm you call him, but within his skin there lives a warlike devil, shedding blood . . . You, in battle with the Worm and with Haftvād, will not be adequate if you swerve from Justice.' Ardashīr's undoubted success in this venture may be attributed, by reference to these words, to his *subsequent* record as a just and efficient ruler. But this is to miss a characteristic *leitmotiv* of the **Shāh-nāmah:** we are no longer dealing at this point in normal human motivation, and that type of dramatic tension is suddenly snapped: what the Shāh is being told is that he is face to face with the fatal and the supernatural, and the Justice he is to put himself in service to is not so much that of the ministry and the courtroom as the eternal archetype, the ultimate principle of all Being and Doing.

To emphasize this point perhaps, Ardashīr says: 'So be it! My dealings with them, for good and evil, lie with you,' and the two young men are by his side throughout the operation of his stratagem to kill the Worm. As if to escape the relatively undramatic, or melodramatic, situation into which he has now come, Firdawsī makes much less of the foregone dénouement than of the wealth of incident leading up to it: Ardashīr's disguising himself and a small band of followers as merchants, their accumulation of goods of all kinds, their departure for the fortress and the arrangements made to keep in communication with the main force of the royal army, the approach—with subservience and blandishments—to Haftvād's retinue, the initiatives to make the Worm's staff drunk and to take over their duties—and so on. When the climax comes, it is brief and has elements of both the comic and the pathetic: 'When from the wine-cup their minds were drunken, came the World-Lord with his sponsors, bringing lead and a brazen cauldron; and a fire he lit, all in the white of day. (When it came that Worm's feeding-time, its nourishment was of boiling lead.) Towards the pit, Ardashīr the hot lead carried, and the Worm gently raised its head. They saw his tongue, coloured like a cymbal, thrust out as when he earlier rice would eat. Down, the hero poured the lead, and in the pit the Worm lost all its strength. From its gullet there arose a rattle, at which the pit and land around did tremble.' That's all there is: in the common phrase, 'It's all over bar the shouting'—and, of course, the fighting.

On the present occasion, time does not allow a lengthier development of our theme that Firdawsī—no matter where his variegated materials came from or how unreliable they may be as history—was a supreme literary and linguistic artist in the use he made of them. We have seen him developing a wide range of characters and throwing these characters into tensions of personality and of role, both with each other and vis-à-vis fate itself. We have seen also how he controls the rate and force of his action so as to ensure the maximum use of dramatic effect. And finally, we have seen how he shades off a melodramatic situation until it becomes firmly integrated in the commonplace; and how he relieves, for those who will accept such relief, solemnity and high drama with the ironical, and sometimes even with the comic. In all of these technical virtuosities, however, the most significant thing is perhaps that he operates, despite his virile and athletic style, not as a teller of tales or an epic poet, but as a dramatist. This may well seem a rash statement to make in reference to a culture which—at least until modern times and under Western influence—has never developed a genuine, full-blown drama as such. But I would suggest that we have in the **Shāh-nāmah** all the elements of the dramatic form except the formal structure itself, and that this can be supplied by little more than a typographical rearrangement and a little judicious editorial cutting. By this means some of the most important themes in the work could be set out in such a way as to alternate between dramatically significant speeches by the *personae* and commentary by the poet and/or others. If that should make you think of the Greek drama on the one hand and Bertolt Brecht on the other, that may only go to indicate the timelessness and the topical relevance of the first great figure in the literature of Islamic Persia.

Minoo S. Southgate (essay date 1974)

SOURCE: "Fate in Firdawsī's 'Rustam vam Suhrāb'," in *Studies in Art and Literature of the Near East*, edited by Peter J. Chelkowski, University of Utah, 1974, pp. 149-59.

[In the essay below, Southgate maintains that Ferdowsi uses the story of Suhrāb to emphasize the inevitability of fate but stresses that the author's fatalistic view is not shared by all of his characters.]

In a recent study of Matthew Arnold's "Sohrab and Rustum," Hasan Javadi observes that Arnold's version of the story is more fatalistic than Firdawsī's. Javadi admits that fate is not absent from Fardawsī, but declares that its force "is lessened by the Persian poet's concern to present the catastrophe partially as the result of cunningly motivated human action." According to Javadi, "The treason of a man, the tyrant Afrasiab, deadly foe of Rustum, is actually responsible for the fight between father and son."[1]

Comparing the two treatments of the story, I find Firdawsī's version no less fatalistic than Arnold's. Indeed, proportionately, those of Firdawsī's lines which express fatal-istic sentiments far exceed Arnold's. But Firdawsī's belief in fate and his tragic view of human life find expression in an epic poem which must include action; and in order to have characters who act, the poet has had to create a sem-blance of free will, and of a cause-and-effect relationship between the events. Beyond the surface action, however, the poet points to Providence as the true mover of the events. Fate takes its course, careless of mankind. Caught in the mesh of ambititon, enmity, and rivalries of great men, Suhrāb is led to meet his death at his father's hand. But the sound and fury signifies nothing. The innocent Su-hrāb dies, leaving his father to bear his guilt and loss for the rest of his life, while the treacherous Afrāsiyāb and Hūmān go unpunished. Thus, the narrative itself serves as an objective correlative for the poet's belief in fate and his contention that man is unable to comprehend God's ways.

Absorbed in the intricate and complex action of "Rustam va Suhrāb," the reader can easily miss its philosophy and moral. I believe that Firdawsī was aware of this danger, and, as I shall attempt to demonstrate, he tried to direct the audience in its response to the poem.

In the opening line of "Rustam va Suhrāb," Firdawsī intro-duces the poem as a tragic tale and anticipates the audi-ence's negative response to Rustam, who, in this episode of the *Shāhnāmah,* fails to maintain his heroic and moral stature:

> It is a tale full of tears;
> the tender heart will be angered against Rustam.[2]

This anger is to be expected of an audience who, ignorant of the working of Providence behind the events, holds the protagonists responsible for their deeds, and, as such, passes judgment upon them. Won by Suhrāb's youthful enthusiasm, his courage, and especially his magnanimity in his glorious death scene when he forgives those who caused his death, the audience recoils from Rustam, who, faced with an uncommonly strong adversary, resorts to treachery unworthy of a hero of his stature. But the poet warns against this reaction, and, in the opening section of "Rustam va Suhrāb"[3] (from now on called the prologue) he directs the audience to see, beyond the surface story, Providence guiding the events in its inscrutable way. Events that seem to result from the characters' deliberate planning are in reality effected by Fate. The poem's tragic climax is an outcome of Fate rather than moral flaws in the characters.

The prologue contains the philosophic core of the poem. Here the poet sees man as placed in a callous universe, prey to destructive forces. But the poet's voice is calm as he reflects on life and death, on fate and fortune, and on the ultimately incomprehensible nature of these matters. The tone is that of a Boethius, led out of error by Lady Philooosphy, reflecting calmly, and accepting the order of things, Indeed, the prologue is imbued with conventional consolatory *topoi.* Having considered man's uncertain fate

in this life, his inability to comprehend God's ways, and his helplessness before death, the poet urges the audience to turn their hearts away from the world, to think of salva-tion, and, in resignation to God's will, to accept His righ-teousness through faith.

The poet's fatalistic position and his didactic philosophy in the prologue find expression in the remaining sections of the poem and especially near its end. Similarly, the pro-logue's symbolic imagery foreshadows the tragic climax of the poem:

> If, rising as if from nowhere, a hard gale
> pluck the unripe orange to the ground,
> should it be called righteous or unjust?
> Is it to be praised or to be blamed?[4]

In these lines the poet poses a question to the audience which is angered against Rustam. The imagery emphasizes the poet's fatalistic outlook. The hard gale (Rustam), put into motion by forces not his own, is innocent of the de-struction of the unripe orange (the young Suhrāb). The same fatalistic attitude is present in the imagery of the fol-lowing lines in the prologue:

> Once lit, it is no wonder if,
> burning, the fire consume
> that which is sound and whole—
> the young shoot risen from the old root.
> Death's breath is a fierce fire
> that dreads neither the young, nor old.[5]

Demanding the kind of order he can comprehend, pre-sumptuously making God after his own image and judging him by human standards, man finds God's ways unjust. Man cannot accept his own mortality. The poet, on the other hand, accepts the necessity of death, finds man's protest against death unreasonable, and his attempt to solve the riddle of death fruitless:

> If death is just, why call it unjust?
> Why such a clamor over what is just?
> This shall remain a mystery to your soul.
> Through this curtain you must not go.
> All arrive at the voracious gate,
> and the gate reopens to none.[6]

The poet finds consolation in the possibility of a better lot in the next world:

> Departing you may find a better place
> when you come to rest in the other world.[7]

He bids the audience to accept God's ways:

> Imbue your heart with the fire of faith.
> Question not his ways, for you are but a slave.[8]

And, employing consolatory *topoi,* he ends the prologue, urging the reader to reject the world and think of his sal-vation:

> The young shall not set his heart upon mirth,
> for death does not come solely from age.

> When death spurs hard the courser of Fate,
> you must not tarry, but depart in haste. . . .
>
> Devote yourself to worship and prayer,
> and be ever mindful of the Last Day.
> You cannot fathom the mystery of God's ways,
> unless your soul is of the devil's company.
> Let this be your goal that you end your days
> in resignation to the divine will.[9]

The prologue with its imagery, fatalistic philosophy, and consolatory *topoi* foreshadows the content of the rest of the poem, and its thematic movement (from action—implied in symbolic imagery—to philosophical meditation and consolation) is roughly paralleled by the rest of the poem.

A summary of the plot will demonstrate how the poem's intricate and suspenseful action can divert attention from its philosophy and moral. In "Rustam va Suhrāb," on the human level the action results from the conflicting intentions of Tahmīnah and Zhandahrazm, Suhrāb's mother and uncle, who want to unite Suhrāb with his father, and Afrāsiyāb, the shāh of Turan, who schemes to prevent this union. The poet's task in making Rustam's failure to recognize his son credible is a hard one. Rustam, it seems, does not even associate the name *Suhrāb* with his son born of his union with Tahmīnah, his wife of one night. Although the poet does not explicitly state this, it seems that Tahmīnah has intentionally kept Rustam in the dark about Suhrāb's progress, for fear of losing her son. When Suhrāb demands to know the identity of his father, she says:

> If your father learns that you have thus
> surpassed all the mighty warriors,
> he will at once call you unto him,
> wounding your mother's heart with pain.[10]

She also has kept Suhrāb's parentage secret to protect him from Afrāsiyāb, Rustam's enemy. When Suhrāb declares his intention to find his father, defeat Kāvūs, the shāh of Iran, and make Rustam king in his place, Tahmīnah advises him to conceal his parentage from Afrāsiyāb. However, the latter, who knows Suhrāb is Rustam's son, provides the youth with a great army headed by Hūmān. Knowing that confronting Suhrāb, Kāvūs will seek Rustam's aid, Afrāsiyāb rightly concludes that if father and son face each other in battle, whichever is killed, he himself will prosper. He instructs Hūmān to hide Rustam's identity from Suhrāb. Tahmīnah, on the other hand, requests Suhrāb's uncle, Zhandahrazm, who knows Rustam, to accompany her son on his expedition and make his father known to him.

Crossing the border of Iran, Suhrāb defeats Hujīr, the keeper of a fortress, and takes his prisoner. Later, when Suhrāb's host faces Kāvūs shāh's army, in one of his most vivid passages, Firdawsī paints a detailed picture of the marvelous splendor of Kāvūs shāh's camping ground. Suhrāb looks from a hill top. Colorful tents, splendid stan-

dards with fabulous coats of arms, gorgeously bedecked with gems, dazzle the eye. Suhrāb points out each Iranian nobleman to Hujīr and asks his name, hoping to learn which one is Rustam. Hujīr, having tasted Suhrāb's prowess and seeking to protect Rustam, conceals Rustam's identity. The only man who knows both Rustam and Suhrāb and could effect their union is Zhandahrazm. Ironically, he is killed by Rustam, who at night visits Suhrāb's camp in disguise.

Thus, father and son face each other in combat. Moved by his adversary's youth, Rustam addresses Suhrāb:

> Pity for you moves my heart.
> I do not want to pluck your life.
> With such shoulder and neck, you surpass the Turks,
> and none is your equal in Iran.[11]

To these words Suhrāb responds with affection. He asks his adversary to tell him truly who he is:

> I suspect you to be the great Rustam,
> from the seed of the renowned Nayram.[12]

But Rustam conceals his identity, and the poet does not explain why he does so. Ignorant of the unnaturalness of their act, father and son fight to the point of exhaustion:

> Then they stood apart, one from the other,
> the father in anguish, the son full of pain.
> (Oh world! your deeds are inscrutable;
> you break, and you make whole.)
> In neither of the two could love stir,
> Reason was absent, so love hid her face.
> The beasts know their young:
> the fish in the sea, the zebra in the field.
> But man, blinded by wrath and greed,
> Cannot tell his son from his foe.[13]

The argument that when reason is ruled by passion the law of nature fails to operate is more accurately applicable to Rustam, for Suhrāb is moved by a son's natural affection for his father. Before the second combat Suhrāb speaks to Hūmān about Rustam:

> His breast, his shoulders, and his neck resemble mine—
> as if the omniscient measured us both the same. . . .
>
> I find manifest the signs my mother gave.
> My heart too is somewhat stirred by love.
> I suspect him to be Rustam himself,
> for there are not many warriors like him.
> God forbid that I fight my father,
> and shamelessly combat him face to face.[14]

Rustam has none of these misgivings:

> . . . Rustam like a fierce lion
> arrayed himself in Babr-i bayān.
> His head full of wrath, his heart seeking revenge,
> proudly he marched to the field.[15]

Suhrāb tries to dissuade Rustam from war:

As if together they had spent the night in mirth,
he said to Rustam, his lips full of laughter,
"How was your night, and how your morning?
Why have you set your heart upon war?
Drop this war-club and this sword of wrath,
and put to silence the harp of discord.
Let us sit together and make merry.
Let wine erase sadness from our looks.
Let us swear before the mighty God,
repent from war, and make peace. . . .

Oft I have sought to learn your name.
Say who you are, for others do not reveal.[16] . . .

Are you not the renowned Rustam,
the Son of Dastān and the mighty Sām?"[17]

Rustam replies:

O thou seeking for fame. . . .
This was not our tale yesterday.
We swore to meet again in war.
By fine words I shan't be deceived.[18]

As the poet anticipates in the prologue, the audience comes to resent Rustam for obstinately thwarting Suhrāb's peace overtures. Later, the great hero of the *Shāhnāmah*, overpowered by Suhrāb in a wrestling combat, dissuades him from killing him by claiming that among the Persians it is not the custom to take advantage of the first fall.[19] The next day, however, overpowering Suhrāb, he knows no such custom:

Lightly he drew the keen blade,
and pierced the breast of the brave youth.[20]

Firdawsī uses the story of Suhrāb to illustrate the inevitability of fate. The poet's fatalistic attitude, however, is not fully shared by his characters. They act on the basis of the belief that they can cause and control the events. For example, Tahmūnah, Suhrāb's mother, in her long lament blames herself for not accompanying Suhrāb on his expedition; a step which, she believes, would have averted the tragedy.[21] Characters consider themselves and others responsible for what occurs. Thus, Rustam upbraids Hūmān for deceiving Suhrāb, and seeks to avenge Suhrāb's death on Hujīr who also misled his son. Later, holding himself responsible for Suhrāb's death, he seeks to take his own life. The contention that man is responsible for his deeds and must be punished for his wrongdoings cannot exist without a belief in free will. In the poem, however, side by side with this outlook, the characters express a fatalistic attitude toward life. For example, when the young Suhrāb, confident and proud, launches on his ambitious plan to conquer Iran and give its kingship to Rustam, he takes no heed of fate. But, wounded mortally, he holds fate responsible for his downfall and says to Rustam:

Fortune gave you the sword to end my life. . . .

You are innocent, for it was this Hump-backed,
who raised me high, and of a sudden slew me.[22]

Later, having learned that Rustam is his father, he says:

It was the destined decree of the stars,
that I should die at my father's hand.[23]

Other characters also express a belief in fate. Speaking of the forthcoming war against Suhrāb, Rustam says:

Such a task is not formidable,
unless Good Fortune is slumbering.[24]

To Suhrāb he says:

Let us fight, the end shall be none else
but was intended and decreed by God.[25]

How is the characters' apparent belief in fate to be reconciled with their pursuit of the active life? An examination of the characters' fatalistic utterances in context will reveal that they generally resort to a fatalistic attitude in hardship, as a means to console themselves or others. Their fatalistic lines are commonplaces of folk philosophy rather than expressions of a true belief in fate. Thus, when having mortally wounded his son, Rustam intends to take his own life, old Gūdarz begs him to hold his hand, for nothing he can do will change what is to be:

If it is destined that he shall live,
he will remain, and you with him.
But if he is to part from this world,
observe well, for who is immortal?
We are all but death's quarry,
the crowned, and the helmeted head.[26]

Likewise, to alleviate Rustam's sense of guilt, Kāvūs remarks:

Fortune aroused him with his host,
that he might meet his death at your hand.[27]

Unlike his characters, the poet's belief in predestination revealed in the prologue and at crucial points in the rest of the poem carries the weight of a consistent philosophy. Uninvolved in the action, the poet views the events from his Olympian seat. Regarded from this height, man ceases to be the self-propelled actor. Commenting on Suhrāb's fruitless efforts to identify his father, the poet remarks:

In vain you try to master and change the world,
for the Ruler set its course long ago.
Destiny had determined otherwise;
one cannot but do as it decrees.
Setting your heart on this transient world,
you shan't reap aught but poison and pain.[28]

When Rustam prays to God to increase his strength that he may defeat Suhrāb, the poet comments:

He sought victory and grandeur,
not knowing his lot from the sun and moon:
How Good Fortune was to leave his side,
and snatch the crown from his head.[29]

He begins the section on Suhrāb's death with these words:

Once more they tied the horses firmly,
Evil Fortune circling overhead.[30]

And, finally, when Suhrāb falls, the poet comments:

The brave youth's back was bent,
His time was at hand, his strength failed.[31]

Like its prologue, the poem abounds in consolatory *topoi*. Fearing death, Rustam instructs his brother to console his father, Dastān:

Tell him. . . .
Rustam's time has ended.
It was the decree of the pure God,
that he meet his death at a youth's hand.[32]

Console my mother's heart and say
God had alloted me this fate.
She shall not mourn my death eternally, . . .

for none remains for ever in this world.
If you remain on earth a thousand years,
You still shall meet death, this common end.
Observe Jamshīd, the mighty sovereign,
and Tahmūres, the slayer of giants.
There was no king like them in the world,
but they at last went to their Maker.
The world they owned passed to other hands.
I too must follow that road. . . .

Young or old we belong to death;
none remains in this world for ever.[33]

Consolatory passages occur frequently near the end of the poem, especially in the section that follows Suhrāb's death, in the words of the noblemen who try to console the bereaved Rustam. The poet's own comments at the end of the poem recall his words in the prologue. Once more he declares God's ways to be inscrutable:

Locked is the secret and locked it shall remain.
Do not search in vain for the key.
None knows how to open the gate.
Waste not your life in this quest.[34]

As in the prologue, he emphasizes the transitory nature of worldly felicity:

This is the way of Fortune:
In one hand holding a crown, in the other a noose.
The ruler rejoicing in his crown and throne,
is suddenly snatched, encircled in the noose.
Why must you set your love upon the world,
since you must join in the march of death?[35]

And, finally, like Rustam who

In the end made patience his way. . . .[36]

the audience is instructed to resign itself to the divine will. Thus, in its philosophy the poem reaches the same conclusion as the prologue; and, it is possible that Firdawsī, fearing that the plot would divert attention from the poem's

philosophy and moral, wrote the prologue after the completion of "Rustam va Suhrāb" and added it to the poem in order to insure the right response from his audience.

Notes

1. "Matthew Arnold's 'Sohrab and Rustam' and Its Persian Original," *Review of National Literatures*, II, No. 1 (Spring, 1971), 69.

2. Unless indicated otherwise, references to "Rustam va Suhrāb" are to: Firdawsī, *Shāhnāmah*, Vol. II (Tehran: Yahūdā Burūkhīm, n.d.). Hereafter, Burūkhīm. Translations mine.

3. Burūkhīm, 11. 1-21.

4. *Ibid.*, 11. 3-4.

5. *Ibid.*, 11. 10-13.

6. *Ibid.*, 11. 5-7.

7. *Ibid.*, 1. 8.

8. *Ibid.*, 1. 17.

9. *Ibid.*, 11. 13-14, 18-20.

10. *Ibid.*, 11. 158-59.

11. *Ibid.*, 11. 904-5.

12. *Ibid.*, 1. 909.

13. *Ibid.*, 11. 923-27.

14. *Ibid.*, 11. 1057, 1959-61.

15. My source for these lines (not found in the Burūkhīm edition) is: Hakīm Abū al-Qāsim Firdawsī, *Shāhnāmah* (Tehran: Amīr Kabī, 1963), p. 115. Lines are not numbered in this edition.

16. These two lines are found in MS C only. See the Burūkhīm edition, II, 498, n. 9.

17. Burūkhīm, 11. 1068-72, 1077.

18. *Ibid.*, 11. 1078-79.

19. *Ibid.*, 11. 1099-1105.

20. *Ibid.*, 1. 1152.

21. *Ibid.*, 1. 1425-27.

22. *Ibid.*, 11. 1157-58.

23. *Ibid.*, 1, 1211.

24. *Ibid.*, 1. 479.

25. *Ibid.*, 1. 1081.

26. *Ibid.*, 11. 1254-56.

27. *Ibid.*, 1. 1339.

28. *Ibid.*, 11. 788-90.

29. *Ibid.*, 11. 1124-25.

30. *Ibid.*, 1. 1145.

31. *Ibid.*, 1. 1150.

32. Found in MS C only. See the Burūkhīm edition, II, 496, n. 3.

33. Burūkhīm, 11. 1035-36, 1041-44, 1047.

34. *Ibid.,* 11. 1455-56.

35. *Ibid.,* 11. 1324-26.

36. *Ibid.,* 1. 1329.

Anna Krasnowolska (essay date 1977)

SOURCE: "About the 'Black-and-White Thread' in *Šāh-Nāme*," in *Folia Orientalia,* Vol. XVIII, 1977, pp. 219-31.

[*In the essay that follows, Krasnowolska examines the contention that the* Shah-Nama *reflects Ferdowsi's dualistic view of life, maintaining that there is insufficient evidence to support this argument. Rather, Ferdowsi presents his story from a flexible point of view in order to demonstrate that events can be observed from many angles and that nothing is "black and white."*]

Comments about the structure of Ferdousi's **Šāh-nāme** have not been until now, very numerous. They were rather occasional and chiefly included into the more general descriptions of this great poem.

Among the scholars who wrote on this subject chiefly the Russians tried to connect the composition of the poem with its author's view of reality. However, the solution proposed by Bertels[1] and followed, among the others, by Starikov[2], Gafurov[3], partly by Braginskiy[4], and also by such non-Russian scholars as e.g. Rypka[5] and Machalski[6] can raise certain doubts and does not seem to be based on firm foundations. At the same time, being plain and suggestive, Bertels' idea is particularly suitable for a wide popularisation.

Bertels writes: "Ferdousi has created a strikingly clear composition basing the whole of his poem on an idea which is not Moslem but Zoroastrian—the idea of the fight of two principles: Good and Evil, the righteous god Ormuzd and the dark army of Ahriman"[7]. And later on: "In this way all the [. . .] parts [of the poem] stringed on the two threads—black and white, interweave with one another and form a close unity"[8].

According to Bertels, the fight of the two opposite moral principles is supposed to be the leitmotif of the whole book, in which the part of good is represented by Iran, and the powers of evil take the shape of its succesive political enemies, the most important of them being the neighbouring Turan:

". . . for a long time Turan takes the part of one who realizes the evil intentions of Ahriman"[9].

Starikov: "Turan in the **Šāhname** is the kingdom, or more exactly the sphere of influence of Ahriman"[10]; and later on: "The conception of a struggle of good and evil found its incarnation and realization in the fight of Iran and Turan"[11].

Starikov speaks of Ahriman in such a manner, as if he were an always present and really acting character of the epic, and the hidden mover of history: "All the efforts of Ahriman in order to kill the hero [.e. *Rostam*] failed. Ahriman prepares a finishing stroke for him . . ."[12].

The attribution of the Mazdaean convictions to Ferdousi and the interpretation of his book as a story about a series of succesive stages of the fight between good and evil must lead to the conclusion about the generally optimistic implication of the work and its obvious drift towards a happy end. This conclusion stands in contradiction with the significance of the facts and is the source of difficulties for the above mentioned adherents of the dualistic interpretation of the poem. The juxtaposition of two passages from Rypka's work may illustrate these difficulties:

"But there are still other factors that bring unity into this immense mass of verse . . . [one of them is] the contrast between Good and Evil, and the final victory of the former[13], also expressed in the religious dualism Ormuzd—Ahriman and thus resolving a priori the ever-old struggle between Iran and Turan"[14].

Later on Rypka writes about the lack of unity in the poet's view on history: "He conceals the antithesis of these two views [Moslem and Zoroastrian] by a slight touch of melancholy, evoked in him by the instability of things which always, in his opinion, show a tendence towards the less favourable, more wicked"[15].

The careful analysis of the text does not provide sufficient proofs which would allow to impute to Ferdousi the dualistic view of life and still less, to see in it the main principle of the composition of his poem.

The Iranian epic in its synthetic form, such as recorded by Ferdousi, developed gradually from the mythical passages, some of which belong to the old common Indo-Iranian heritage[16]. The fragments composing the cycle of Turanian wars can be partly found already in this oldest layer. Its central plot, the vengeance for the killing of *Siyāvuš,* can be found in Avestan *Yašts.* More details on the Turanians are provided by the Pahlavi texts[17].

It appears from these passages that the antagonists in the original version are neither the two anthropomorphised cosmical principles nor even two peoples ethnically differentiated, but rather two formerly closely connected tribes, or even two clans of the same tribe (if we decide to treat the terms *Kavi* and *Tura* as designations of family affiliation). In the literary tradition their conflict is enlarged to the dimension of a dramatic event. The myth of the common origin of the two antagonists is recorded in a Middle Persian text (Bd. 31, 9-14). According to the preserved fragments, the pre-Zoroastrian tale of the revenge for *Siyāvuš* was not strongly marked by any ethical notions. This tale was always connected with a set of very old myths of cosmogony and fertility. The myths of this category are usually ethically indifferent, which is proved by the ambivalent meaning of murder in them. The main villain of the epic, *Afrāsiyāb* Avestan *Franrasyan* has many features of a demon of drought[18]. His marriage with the holy goddess of the earth, *Spandarmaz* in a very ancient mythical fragment reconstructed by Benveniste[19] indicates it distinctly.

No doubt the epic tradition has been incorporated into the Zoroastrian dualistic system, and the fighting parties found their own places within the two opposing worlds. But this must have happened relatively late, as an effect of the intensive efforts of the learned dasturs, aming at classification and unification of the religious and mythical tradition.

Thus the dualistic interpretation of the epic, based on one of the meanings present in its background, is possible, but only as one among many ways of interpretation. We do not know how deeply could such a dualized version penetrate into the oral tradition, existing and developing parallelly with the written one, but having a wider social resonance. At any rate Ferdousi seems to continue the older version. The dualistic interpretation of *Šāh-nāme* by the European scholars seems to be based rather on the general knowledge of Zoroastrian literature than on a careful analysis of the text itself.

Let us look at the facts. Wikander comparing some passages of *Šāh-nāme* and *Mahābhārata* states:

"Le Mbh traite d'une grande mais brève campagne, qui, pendant 18 jours, met aux prises deux groupes de cousins princiers; dans le ShN, il s'agit d'une phase importante d'une lutte séculaire entre Iran at Touran"[20].

Putting in opposition a struggle of the two branches of the same family and a struggle of two nations which are strange to each other, Wikander ignores the fact that, similar to the Indian epic, the Iranian and Turanian kings of Ferdousi are relations, too.

The enmity and duty of revenge (*kin*) arose among them because of a fratricide that took place in the family of *Feridun*[21]. Ferdousi shows their conflict as a gradual increase of strangeness and hostility as the time goes by and the range of vendetta gets wider and wider.

The common origin of the antagonists is not treated by the author as an accidental fact. On the contrary, the fact of this kinship is constantly present in the heroes' consciousness, and exerces a considerable influence on their deeds.

In the first stage of the conflict the awareness of its origin is very strong in both parties. Several efforts are repeated in order to restore the peace and to demarcate the borderline between Iran and Turan[22]. When a calamity of drought and hunger emerges as a consequence of their wars, both parties feel equally guilty[23]. As the years go by, the memory of relationship gets weaker, but it never disappears completely.

The historical ties of blood are often renewed by the mixed marriages. Here the plot is seen from an Iranian perspective: the Iranian men marry Turanian women, but it never happens vice versa.

Thus, the kings of Iran and Turan have common ancestors, the great mythical heroes, and also a large part of common history. They are perfectly aware of this:

> az iraj; ke bi gonāh košte šod   ze maɣz-e bozo-
> rgān χerad gašte šod
> ze turān be irān jodā'i nabud   ke bā kin o jang
> āšnā'i nabud

"When *Iraj* was murdered without guilt, reason went out from the heads of the nobles. There was no separation between Turan and Iran till they were not acquainted with hatred and war"[24].

Just as in *Avesta* where they worship the same gods, in the *Šāh-nāme* Iranians and Turanians are confessors of one religion: *Afrāsiyāb* prays in a fire-temple built by his grandfather *Feridun* in Kondoz[25] (according to *Šahrastānīhā-ī Erān* he himself built one in Zrang)[25], the Turanians use the same epithets to describe God as Iranians do. When they speak of God, they seem to refer to a reality common to both[27].

Iranians and Turanians represent the same culture, both material and spiritual, and the same hierarchy of values. The problem of language difference appears for the first time relatively late, i.e. in the tale of *Siyāvuš*[28].

According to the above mentioned authors, Turan is supposed to be the sphere of influence of Ahriman. In this case its inhabitants should show some demonical or supernatural qualities. This is not the case, however. It is true, that Iblis appears several times and lures some of the heroes, as the usurper *Zahhak* who is of Arab origin or *Key Kā'us,* the legitimate ruler of Iran. But there is only one passage in which the devil gets into touch with a Turanian character (i. e. the king of China) it is the fragment of Daqiqi[29] and Ferdousi clearly keeps distance from it. In the declarations of the poem's characters about both Iranian and Turanian heroes we often meet with an expression that Ahriman has "changed" or "led astray" somebody's mind. This expression cannot be considered as literally as Starikov would like it. Some of the Turanians, as *Bidarafš* or *Afrāsiyāb* himself, are gifted with a magical power, but it is also the case for some of the Iranians, as well (*Feridun, Key Xosrou,* and, first of all, *Zāl*).

There exists in the *Šāh-nāme* a very particular type of a hero, emerging from time to time in the course of history: it is a very young and noble-minded idealist, who, acting against the official policy, tries to restore the unity of the fighting parties. All his efforts result in failure: he comes into conflict with his own environment and perishes in tragic circumstances. Paradoxically, the death of such a hero makes the split still deeper and gives an occasion for a new cycle of revenge. This type of hero is represented by *Iraj*, whose murder began the whole conflict, by the Turanian *Aɣriras*, brother of *Afrāsiyāb* and, most perfectly, by *Siyāvuš*. Some qualities similar to the heroes of this group are to be found in *Siyāmak, Sohrāb Forud* and *Sorχe*.

The Turanian *Pirān* is a unique character and cannot be classified in any way. As a friend of the Iranian prince *Siyāvuš* and at the same time as a loyal subject of *Afrāsiyāb* and the chief of his army, he remains a puzzle for his fellow-characters[30]. After the death of *Pirān Key Xosrou* explains his "metamorphosis" in this way:

> *čonān mehrabān bud dežχim šod va z-u šahr-e irān por az bim šod*
> *mar u-rā bebord ahraman del ze degar gune piš andar āvard pāy*
> *jāy*

> "He had been so kind, but he became malignant and spread terror all over the country of Iran, Ahriman has displaced his heart and he chose another path"[31].

In fact, the personality of *Pirān* is much more complex. After the death of *Siyāvuš Pirān* fights the Iranians and refuses to take their side. He is also bound by the duty of bloody revenge for his sons and brothers. In spite of all this, he still makes some friendly gestures towards the Iranians: he rescues the life of *Bižan*[32] and tries to save that of *Bahrām*[33], he proposes to spare the unnecessary bloodshed ending the war by a duel[34]. *Pirān* understands the futility of the war in which he is involved:

> *miyān-e niyā o nabere do šāh nadānam šerā bāyad in kine gāh*

> "This hostility between the two kings, grandfather and grandson—I do not know what is it for"[35][36].

The Turanians motives to consider themselves as the offended side of the conflict are as valid as those of the Iranians. *Pašang*, preparing a new war after the death of *Manučehr*, says:

> *ke bā mā ce kardand irāniyān bādi rā bebastand yek yek miyān*

> "[Look] what have the Iranians done to us: they have all girded their waists to do evil"[38].

Often the Iranians prove to be just as cruel and cunning as they believe the Turanians to be e.g., *Key Ka'us* violates the peace concluded by *Siyāvuš*[37]; *Rostam* rules Turan for six years: murdering and looting he draws upon him the hate of inhabitants[38], the slying of *Siyāvuš*, bearing signs of a ritual murder[39] is reproduced mirror-like by the Iranians in the act of revenge on the innocent coeval of *Sijāvuš*, the Turanian prince *Sorχe*[40].

The emergence of a split between the two branches of the house of *Feridun* is not a unique phenomenon of this kind described in the **Šāh-nāme**. Ferdousi presents the origin of another analogical conflict: the ruling dynasty and the house of *Sām*, closely connected together for a very long

time, start a war because of killing *Esfandiyār* by *Rostam*. This initiates a chain of revenges, brought promptly to an end, because of the extinction of the Sistān family[41]. The river of Hirmand, until now not very important in the topography of the epic, begins to play a major role of a border river, comparable to that of Jeyhun in the Turanian conflict.

From the facts quoted above it can be seen already that the depicted situation is far from conforming to any black-and-white pattern. What is more, Ferdousi is able to present the many-layered nature of reality due to his technique of narration. He uses a movable point of view which enables him to show events from different angles.

The characters and facts are seen most frequently through the eyes of the Iranians who evaluate them and comment upon them. From time to time, however, the action switches to the Turanian side, bringing the Turanian characters to the foreground. Now and again (e.g. the story of *Sohrāb*, that of *Siyāvuš* or of *Bižan and Maniže*) the author follows an Iranian hero to the country of his adversaries. The Turanians are in such cases observed more systematically in their everyday activities. Just as in the case of the description of internal conflicts (e.g. *Goštāsp—Esfandiyār* and *Esfandiyār—Rostam*) Ferdousi relates sometimes the controversies between Iran and Turan by confronting their different points of view. This effect is frequently achieved by quoting dialogues and letters (e.g. *Gudarz—Pirān*)[42], or by switching repeatedly the focus of the action from one side of the scene to the other. This type of narration predominates for instance in the description of the wars in the tale of *Kāmus-e Kašāni*[43].

The development of action on the Iranian side can be followed by the reader in the continuous way, with all the motivations and consequences of the events; on the other hand the proper Turanian story is shown in a haphazard way, as if by a kind of windows, opened to us from time to time by using the above mentioned technique. The procedure of changing the point of view may be compared metaphorically to the crossing of the Jeyhun river which is not only a frontier line in the geographical meaning but also a symbolical border limiting the reader's horizon. Therefore it is not possible to reconstruct a coherent picture of the history and the inner relations in Turan. These insights suggest, however, that there is a fundamental similarity between the two worlds, and that the attitudes of the Turanians are as diversified as those of the Iranians.

The author usually puts the opinions about the events and persons into the mouths of his characters[44] and he himself is keeping distance from them. His own estimating commentary is relatively scarce. Sometimes it takes a form of some short characterisation of a personage appearing for the first time, such as that of a Turanian hero, *Pilsam*:

> *ze pirān yeki bud kahtar be sāl barādar bod u-rā o farroχ hamāl*
> *kojā pilsam bud nām-e javān yeki por honar o roušan ravān*

"*Pirān* had a brother younger than himself, but equally fortunate. The youth whose name was *Pilsam* was full of virtues and clearheaded"[45].

The larger passages in which Ferdousi expresses his views and convictions on his own behalf usually do not occur in the course of the narrative, but rather on its margins: they signal a beginning or end of any broader autonomous portion of the text and they often contain reflections of a more general character.

It can be said that the method consisting in confronting of opposite solutions or of many different aspects of the same situation is one of the main principles of composition of Ferdousi's text. This confrontation is often put discretly enough to confuse the reader. Braginskiy[46] has already pointed to the phenomenon of a whole underground current existing in the **Šāh-nāme**. He analyses it on the example of a passage about Mazdak's insurrection. The opinion of Braginskiy is that this stratification of the text is due to the presence of a hidden social bias coded in the **Šāh-nāme**. It seems, however, that the phenomenon is of a more general nature: it consists of a perpetual dissonance between the two coexisting levels of the depicted reality: the stereotype and its actual realisation. The stereotype consists of a general scheme of action with a precised definition of parts assigning to the characters' particular places in the hierarchy and in the social arrangements. At the same time it represents a postulated ideal situation. The whole pathetic and ceremonial ornamentation underlined by an archaic language functions in this strata. On this level the personalities presented in the book may be considered nothing but multiplications of one standard pattern. But the actual realisation contradicts the traditional patterns and modifies them incessantly. Particular individualities of the characters and some striking, untypical situations emerge from below the "official" layer of the text. The hero's personality is shaped by a number of historical, psychological and social factors. He undergoes some conflicts because of fulfilling at the same time several parts which exclude themselves respectively. (e.g. *Pirān, Forud*) or fulfilling his part in a manner different from the postulated one (*Key Kā'us, Iraj*). Thus for instance the kings whose deeds cannot be respectful in any way are refered to by the author with veneration, while being sharply criticized by their subjects.

So far as the dualistic scheme can belong somehow to the surface strata of the book, the deeper current blows it up systematically. The authors who try to deduce Ferdousi's philosophy from a stiff and superficial generalisation fall into contradiction with the full of meaning facts as those quoted above (pp. 223-7). Thus the question arises how the creative method of Ferdousi and his literary vision of the world is connected with his personal philosophy. Also those scholars[47] who wrote about Ferdousi's outlook on life building their conclusions on the basis of the analysis of some aphorisms and maxims torn out of their context in **Šāh-nāme** could not render justice to this complex problem.

First of all, it is important to remember that the author's own reflections should be distinguished from those given through the mouths of his characters. The former can be regarded as a manifestation of Ferdousi's real attitudes; the latter should be treated with more prudence, seeing always the context in which they appear and the personality of the speaker. Of course, the characters' views will be partly identical with those of the author. What is more, these ideas which are particularly often repeated in the text in many different circumstances, may also be treated as a part of Ferdousi's own views.

Secondly, the author's metaphysical, ethical and historiosophic conceptions are expressed not only by the direct declarations, but also on a higher level of textual organisation. The higher and the lower level complement each other continually and we must take them both equally into consideration. When the author confronts without a comment contradictory rights of two persons, he is conscious of the two manners of argumentation and puts himself above them, without declaring himself openly in favour of any side.

The introduction to **Šāh-nāme** (*Āyāz-e ketāb*)[48] may be regarded as the principal declaration of Ferdousi's convictions and as the key to the whole book. From this short text Ferdousi's concept of God can be deduced, and, indirectly, his concept of history as well. Thus, God is "beyond all names, signs and conceptions", he is "the artist who is above his creations"[49]. He escapes all descriptions, because reason can make concepts only out of the visible world.[50] Another attribute of God, which often appears within the epic itself is a consequent enlargement of the preceeding attributes: God is "beyond good and evil", or he is even the "giver" or "creator" of good and evil[51]. Such concept of God implies the relativity of human ethical notions and, therefore, excludes any simplified black-and-white dualism. In the course of his introduction Ferdousi says that in spite of his imperfection and lacking the necessary means, the man should worship God with these means which are given to him i.e. with his reason, soul and language, looking for the way of truth and scrupulously inquiring into God's decrees[52]. This postulate was put by Ferdousi at the beginning of his exposition of history; that makes us believe that the poet treated history as a revelation to decipher, the meaning and rules of which are known only by the Supreme Consciousness.

At the same time Ferdousi, as the author of the book, assumes towards his imaginary world the part analogical to that which God plays towards his creation. The consciousness of the author creates in the world of his epic rules and regularities unknown to his characters, because he is above their limitations and outside the inner time sequence of the book.

Notes

1. Ye. E. Bertels, *Ferdovsi i yego tvorčestvo* [in:] *Ferdovsi* 934-1934, Leningrad 1934, pp. 92-118 and *Ferdousi* [in:] *Istoriya persidskotadzikskoy literatury,* Moskva 1960, pp. 169-238.

2. A. A. Starikov, *Firdousi i yego poema Šahname* [in:] Firdousi, *Šahname* (translation), ed. I. B. Banu, A. Lahuti, Moskva 1957, pp. 169-238.

3. B. Gafurov, *Firdousi-slava i gordost' mirovoy kultury* [introd. to] Firdousi, *Šāh-nāme*, perevod s farsi, Moskva 1972, pp. 5-18.

4. I. S. Braginskiy, *K izučeniyu Šahname*, [in:] *Iz istorii tadžikskoy i persidskoy literatur,* Moskva 1972, pp. 243-302.

5. I. Rypka, *History of the Iranian Literature*, Dordrecht 1968, pp. 154-162.

6. F. Machalski, *Firdausi i jego "Szāh-nāme"*, Kraków 1970, p. 35.

7. *Ferdovsi i yego tvorčestvo*, p. 102.

8. *Ibid.*, p. 103.

9. *Ferdousi*, p. 223.

10. *Op. cit.*, 565.

11. *Ibid.*, p. 566.

12. *L. cit.*

13. In this quotation and the next one spacing by the author of this paper.

14. *Op. cit.*, p. 159.

15. *Ibid.*, p. 161.

16. Cf. J. Darmesteter, *Points de contact entre le* Mahābhārata *et le* Shāhnāmeh, Journal Asiatique 2, 1887, pp. 38-75; S. Wikander, *Sur le fond commun indo-iranien des épopées de la Perse et de l'Inde,* La Nouvelle Clio 1-2, 1949, pp. 310-329; M. Molé, *Deux notes sur le* Rāmāyana [in:] *Hommages a G. Dumézil,* Bruxelles 1960, p. 140-150.

17. The Avestan and Middle Persian passages concerning the Turanians are listed e.g. by: E. Herzfeld, *Zoroaster and his World,* vol. II, Princeton 1947, pp. 704-720 (*Anrān-Turān*); also A. Christensen, *Les Kayanides,* Kobenhavn 1932, pp. 85-91 and J. Darmesteter, *Etudes Iraniennes,* vol. II, Paris 1883, pp. 225-231.

18. E. Benveniste, *Le témoignage de Théodore bar Kōnay sur le zoroastrisme,* Le Monde Oriental 1932-33, pp. 170-215. For a general scheme of the Indo-Iranian myths of fertility and drought see G. Widengren, *Les religions de l'Iran,* Paris 1968, pp. 59 ff.

19. *Op. cit.*, pp. 192-200.

20. *Op. cit.*, p. 312.

21. *Feridun,* v. 400 ff; vol. I, pp. 103 f. (All the quotations according to the edition of A. Ye. Bertels and A. Nušin, *Šāh-nāme-ye Ferdousi,* vol. I-IX, Moskva 1960-1971).

22. *Nouzar* 30-35, vol. II, p. 45; *Keyqobād* 124 ff, vol. II, p. 70.

23. *Nouzar* 20-30, vol. II, p. 44 f.

24. *Siyāvuš* 808, vol III, p. 54; Cf. *Nouzar* 71, vol. II, p. 11; *Siyāvuš* 2305, vol. III, p. 150; *Davāzdah row* 158-9, vol. V, p. 95; *Jang-e bozorg* 2365, vol. V, p. 376.

25. *Jang-e bozorg* 215-17, vol. V, p. 248.

26. Benveniste, *op. cit.,* p. 194.

27. Cf. the opening sentences of the letters—of *Afrāsiyāb* (*Siyāvuš* 1144-46, vol. III, p. 74) and *Pirān* (*Davāzdah row* 1109-10, vol. V, p. 148).

28. *Siyāvuš* 1350, vol. III, p. 88. T. Kowalski in his *Studia nad* Šāh-nāme, (vol. I, Kraków 1952, pp. 243-258) quotes many examples for the similarities and differences of culture between Iran and Turan in *Šāh-nāme,* believing that Ferdousi describes the iranized Turks of his days, confusing them with some historical Iranian people.

29. *Soxan-e Daqiqi* 97 ff., vol. VI, p. 71.

30. *Pirān* is a puzzle for the scholars, too. E. g. Braginskiy (*op. cit.,* p. 301) believes that the heroes formerly belonging to the Saka epic tradition were afterwards devided between the two parties: some of them, as *Rostam,* became Iranians; the others, as *Pirān,* are to be found among the Turanians, but still bear some traces of their original righteousness.

31. *Dawāzdah rox* 2400, vol. V, p. 222.

32. *Bižan o Maniže* 379 ff, vol. V, pp. 31 f.

33. *Forud-e Siyavuš* 1510-17, vol. IV p. 106.

34. *Davāzdah rox* 1164-68, vol. V, p. 151 f.

35. *Ibid.*, 1460, p. 168.

36. *Nouzar* 73, vol. II, p. 11.

37. *Siyāvuš* 940 ff, vol. III, p. 62.

38. *Ibid.*, 2973 ff, p. 194.

39. The death of *Siyāvuš,* who was murdered "like a sheep" (*ču gusfand*) continues the mythical theme of the Primeval Ox (about the identity of *gao spenta* and *gusfand*—J. Duchesne-Guillemin, *Miettes iraniennes* [in:] *Hommages a G. Dumézil,* Bruxelles 1960, p. 98 f). Cf. also: M. Skladankowa, *Irańska wersja legendy o umeczonym bogu,* Przeglad Humanistyczny 78, 1970, pp. 61-75.

40. *Siyāvuš* 2746 ff., vol. III, p. 180.

41. *Rostam o Esfandiyār,* vol. VI, pp. 216-321.

42. *Davāzdah rox,* vol. V.

43. Vol. IV.

44. Cf. different opinions about *Afrāsiyāb: Nouzar* 83-4, vol. II, p. 11; *Siyāvuš* 573-6, vol. III, p. 40.

45. *Siyāvuš* 2252, vol. III, p. 147.

46. *Op. cit.,* p. 259 ff.

47. J. C. Coyajee, *Theology and philosophy in Firdausi,* Journal of the K. R. Cama Oriental Institute 33, 1939, p. 1-36. Cf. also relevant chapters in: Kowalski, *op. cit.* (p. 189-216); H. Massé, *Firdousi et l'épopée nationale,* Paris 1935 (p. 227-261).

48. Vol. I, p. 12-13.

49. *Ibid.*, v. 4.

50. *Ibid.,* v. 8.

51. Cf. e.g.: *Manučehr* 1644, vol. I, p. 248: *Davāzdah rox* 985, vol. V, p. 141; *Rostam-Esfandiyār* 1125, vol. VI, p. 286.

52. *Ayāz-e ketāb* 11-13. vol. I, p. 12.

Jerome W. Clinton (essay date 1987)

SOURCE: An introduction to *The Tragedy of Sohráb and Rostám from the Persian National Epic, the "Shahname" of Abol-Qasem Ferdowsi,* translated by Jerome W. Clinton, University of Washington Press, 1987, pp. xiii-xxv.

[*In the following essay, Clinton reviews the structure and themes of the* Shah-Nama, *observing that the work is unified by its focus on dynastic succession.*]

The story of Sohráb is just one small portion of the vast compilation of stories that make up the Iranian national epic commonly known as the **Shahname,** or Book of Kings. The **Shahname** traces the history of the Iranian nation from the first mythological shah, Kiumars, down to the defeat and death of the last Sassanian emperor, Yazdegerd III, at the hands of the Arab armies of Islam in the middle of the seventh century A.D.

The events narrated in the first two-thirds of the **Shahname,** tales both heroic and romantic, belong to a mythical or legendary time. In the last third, these events are set in historical times, and stories are introduced from the biography of Alexander the Great and from the history of the Parthian and Sassanian dynasties (247 B.C.-A.D. 651). But the style of presentation does not change. Historical figures and events are presented as the stuff of myth and legend.

The **Shahname** does not begin as Homeric epics do "in the midst of things," but with the appearance of the first shah, Kiumars. Mankind seems to have existed before him, but as an undifferentiated species. The formation of human society required the shaping presence of a shah. And other shahs, most notably Jamshid, the Iranian Solomon, provide human society with those things—fire, tools, agriculture, and the various crafts—that raise men and women above the level of beasts. The history of the Iranian nation from that point on assumes the existence of a divinely chosen ruler. Indeed, while there are a number of recurrent themes in the **Shahname,** such as the immortality of noble deeds, the malignancy of fate, and its inevitability, and the persistent hostility and envy of Iran's neighbors, the theme that underlies all of these is that God prefers Iran to other nations, and sustains it through the institution of monarchy. So long as there is a shah, there will be an Iran. When Yazdegerd III is slain in A.D. 652, the Iran of the **Shahname** comes to an end.

As the continuous thread that holds this vast compilation together is dynastic succession, so the principal figures

that people its tales are Iran's shahs and the members of their court. Like Malory's *Le Morte d'Arthur,* its focus is that of the court and its concerns to the exclusion of the world outside. War and feasting, hunting and feats of strength and skill, courtly intrigue and struggles for succession to the throne are the events and themes of its narratives. Moreover, these same subjects are the sources of incident and imagery as well, not the everyday concerns of farmers, herdsmen, artisans or traders, nor the details of domestic life. Each day dawns with the sun as an invincible warrior advancing over the mountains to put the armies of night to flight with his shining blade. The coming of spring is seen in the palace garden where the blossoming flowers are described as precious gems or rich brocade. Armies on the move seem to pass through a landscape devoid of life and character until they encounter the goal of their march—another army, a fortress, a fortified city.

Although the Divinity's support for Iranian monarchy is a central constant of the **Shahname,** its ideology is not a naïve and enthusiastic monarchism. Abol-Qasem Ferdowsi (d. ca. 1025), who gave the **Shahname** its present form, was not a panegyrist who presented idealizations of the ruler for the admiration of royal sponsors and their followers. He was as realistic about the limitations of individual monarchs as was Shakespeare. Many of the greatest tales in the epic are as much concerned with the dilemmas of the monarchial state as they are its inevitability. In the story translated here, for example, Sohráb must be killed, even though he is Rostám's son, because he has sworn to overthrow Shah Kavús and set his father on the throne. This violates both the sanctity of the shah and the principle of divine selection. And the reason that Rostám, Iran's foremost hero, must be the one who kills his son is that he has been slack in his loyalty to the shah, albeit with good reason. He has repeatedly saved the shah from the consequences of his rash and foolish actions. Still, Kavús remains remarkably ungrateful and even threatens Rostám's life when he is slow to respond to the shah's summons. But in the end, both familial bonds and personal dignity must be sacrificed to instant and unwavering obedience to even so unworthy a shah as Kavús.

In the next tale, Kavús places his own son, Siyavosh, in the untenable position of having to choose between obeying his father or honoring an oath taken before God. When Siyavosh chooses the latter, he, too, is destroyed. Kavús, who by his action has deprived Iran of a loyal and exemplary prince and condemned his country to a protracted conflict with Turán, escapes punishment completely. As the prologue to the story of Sohráb says, the ways of the Creator are mysterious, God exacts a high price for his support of the Iranian nation.

THE HISTORY OF THE "*SHAHNAME*"

It is virtually impossible to put a date to the origins of a national epic tradition. Yet one can say with confidence that many of the stories that make up the **Shahname** are of great, if undetermined, antiquity. Herodotus tells us that in the time of Darius, the accounts of Iran's kings and heroes were celebrated in story and song. And many of the characters and events that appear in the *Shahname* appear as well in the Zoroastrian scripture, the Avesta, which dates from the time of Cyrus and Darius, some 2,500 years ago. We also know that this national epic tradition was an active and vital one, and that stories from it circulated widely in several languages and in a number of versions. From time to time monarchs sponsored recensions of these stories that attempted to bring together the versions of the various stories that had become current in different parts of the vast Iranian empire. We know of one such recension that was prepared at the behest of the Sassanian monarch Khosrow Anushirvan in the mid sixth century A.D. Another dates from just after the accession of Yazdegerd III in the mid seventh century. However, while these versions may be said to have had official sanction, none became the sole and authoritative text. On the contrary, it is clear that the stories were transmitted both orally and in writing, in prose and poetry, and in several languages down to the late tenth century, when the greatest poet of the national epic, Abol-Qasem Ferdowsi, undertook the task of producing a new and comprehensive poetic rendering of the whole work.

Ferdowsi was able to draw upon a wide variety of sources. The Sassanian recension was surely one of them, but probably in an Arabic translation, or, rather, in a variety of translations. The Iranian epic materials were rendered into Arabic by many scholars and in many ways after the Islamic conquest of the seventh century. Ferdowsi also seems to have had access to an extensive store of oral material, to a prose recension in the Persian of his day, and, possibly, to untranslated Middle Persian texts. These sources have now largely vanished, in part because of the success of Ferdowsi's work.

During the thirty-five years that he devoted to this task, Ferdowsi was as much a scholar and editor as he was a poet and author. He not only gave the *Shahname* what was to become its definitive poetic form, he also determined which stories from among the many that made up the tradition would be included, and in which versions. In the first few decades after the Ferdowsian recension of the *Shahname* began to circulate, other poets gave poetic form to chapters of the national epic that they felt he had slighted—perhaps motivated as much by a desire to imitate his success as to "correct" his version—but these never came to enjoy the currency of his work, and many are known to us only by name.[1]

In the *Shahname,* Ferdowsi at times speaks of his own role as that of one who has given new life to tales that had long fallen into oblivion: "These stories, long grown old, will be renewed / By me, and men will tell them everywhere" (3:6:9).[2] And he clearly thought of himself as a reviver of a tradition that had come to be disregarded. The reason for this decline of the national tradition is the Arab conquest of the seventh century, and the subsequent spread

of Islam. The national epic was so deeply identified with the royal court that when that court was overthrown and Iran's shahs were replaced by rulers who spoke a different language, had entirely different cultural traditions, and were militant advocates of an entirely new religion, the decline of the *Shahname* was an inevitable consequence. Ferdowsi alludes to this profound cultural transformation brought about by the spread of Islam to Iran and its effects upon the Iranian tradition in a famous passage toward the close of the poem. The commander of the Iranian army, who was decisively defeated by the Arab forces at Qadesiya, reads Iran's fortunes in the stars and predicts both the coming defeat of his army and the ultimate decline of the Iranian nation:

> They'll set the *minbar* level with the throne,
> And name their children Omar and Osman.
> Then will our heavy labors come to ruin.
> Oh, from this height a long descent begins.
> You'll see no throne or court or diadem;
> The stars will smile upon the Arab host.
> And after many days a time will come
> When one unworthy wears the royal robes. . . .
>
> Then men will break their compact with the truth
> And crookedness and lies will be held dear.

> (9:318:88-91, 97)

The Iranian tradition declined for nearly two centuries until Iranian dynasties, beginning with the Samanids in the late ninth century, once more gained ascendancy over Central Asia and the Iranian plateau, land that had traditionally been the heart of Iran's empire. Although they were now themselves Muslims, and Arabic had permeated their language and culture, they made the revival of Persian poetry and the Iranian national epic a conscious policy. The Samanids, like Iranian monarchs before them, sponsored the preparation of a comprehensive prose recension of the text, and encouraged an eminent poet of the time, Daqiqi (d. ca. 980), to turn it into poetry. When he died before the task was completed, or even well begun, it fell to Ferdowsi to finish the work. In the process, he revived the stories of the *Shahname* and made them current. For this reason, Ferdowsi is revered in Iran as much for his service to Iranian culture as for his genius as a poet. His reward was that immortality of reputation that he had so accurately predicted:

> And when this famous book shall reach its end,
> Throughout the land my praises will be heard.
> From that day on I shall not die, but live,
> For I'll have sown my words both far and wide.

> (9:382:863-64)

THE "*SHAHNAME*" AFTER FERDOWSI

The development of the text of the *Shahname* does not stop with Ferdowsi, however, for it was never seen as a sacred book that must be preserved with immaculate textual exactitude. Our earliest manuscript of the *Shahname* was discovered recently in Florence—where it had been miscatalogued as a Koran commentary—and dates from 1216, two centuries after Ferdowsi completed his work. It is the first volume of a two-volume set, and contains only the first half of the text's 50,000 couplets. The next oldest manuscript, and the first to contain the complete text, is that of the British Museum, which was copied in 1276. The British Museum manuscript served as the basis for the only attempt in modern times to make a critical edition, that of the Soviet Academy of Sciences, which was begun in 1960 and completed eleven years later. As close as the British Museum manuscript is to the Florence manuscript, it differs from it in ways that cannot simply be explained as scribal error. The choice of words in individual lines frequently differs between the two manuscripts, each has numerous lines not found in the other, and the sequence of incidents in stories may also vary. In short, it appears that even at this early date the text had begun to be affected by other versions of the stories and the personalities of the scribes and poets who transmitted it.

From the fourteenth century on, many manuscripts, some clearly identified as recensions, not simple copies, and all somewhat fuller than their predecessors, were produced. To give only one example of how the text has grown, Sohráb's tale, which contains 1,050 couplets in the earliest manuscripts, has grown to 1,459 couplets in the nineteenth-century manuscript edited by Jules Mohl, from which both his own translation into French was made, and that of Arthur George and Edmond Warner's into English. The changes most often amplify the story rather than alter events or characterization, but sometimes they seem to have been made with the intention of adapting a story to the expectations of its audience. In later versions of the tale, Tahminé and Rostám are given a proper, Islamic-style wedding, for instance, not simply allowed to co-habit as mutually consenting adults.

The tales are also recited and elaborated upon in Iranian coffeehouses, and there are, in addition, popular, oral versions that circulate widely, and that often contain startling differences from the manuscript versions of the text. Sohráb becomes a daughter in one, and in another he is not slain at all. The **Shahname** tradition, in short, is still one of continuing currency and vitality.

The Cultural Importance of the "*Shahname*"

The **Shahname** has had a sustained and vital influence within its cultural tradition comparable to that of the Old Testament or Homer's works within theirs. It depicts the beliefs and values of Iranian society as they were before the coming of Islam, and so has helped to mark them as distinctive within the complex mix of elements that make up Islamic culture. Its heroes embody ideals of personal conduct that are still current, and its vision of Iranian society as one that is sustained by a divinely sanctioned monarchy pervades the whole course of Iranian history. For nearly a thousand years, the **Shahname** has also served poets and historians as a source of illustrative incident, a reference grammar of narrative technique, and a glossary

of human motivation. It has provided compelling challenges to artists in every generation. Medieval miniatures, modern painting, and sculpture have drawn their subject matter from it. The *Shahname* was both the first literary text to be illustrated, and the one whose illustration produced some of the greatest monuments of Islamic bookmaking and illustration. The influence of the **Shahname** on Iranian cultural life has been simply incalculable. It is one of the two or three most important works in a long and unusually rich literary tradition.

Nor has the **Shahname**'s influence been restricted to that of the Iranian nation alone, anymore than has Homer's to Greece. Ferdowsi's recension of the **Shahname** appeared just as Persian poetry was undergoing the remarkable efflorescence that allowed it first to rival and then to supersede Arabic poetry in the eastern Islamic world. Persian poetry was widely read and imitated in courts from Istanbul to Delhi, and exerted a formative influence on poetry in both Ottoman Turkish and Urdu.

The Language of the "*Shahname*"

The language of the **Shahname** is called New or Modern Persian to distinguish it from two earlier stages of the language: (1) Old Persian, a contemporary and cousin of Sanskrit and Avestan, and (2) Middle Persian, the language, or group of languages, that was current in Iran from roughly the time of Alexander to the Islamic invasion. The term New Persian is misleading in that it is used to designate the language throughout the entire thousand-year period of classical Persian literature. The language of contemporary Iran is known as Modern Persian. It would be more accurate to say that the language of the **Shahname,** and of classical poetry generally, is a special poetic dialect of Persian that has the same relationship to the language of today's Iran that Shakespeare's language does to the English we speak. The language of the **Shahname** represents an early and special form of this dialect. It retains a number of words and grammatical forms from Middle Persian that would have seemed archaic even to Ferdowsi's contemporaries, and is also virtually free of words borrowed from Arabic, even though Arabic loans words were common in the poetic dialect in use in the court.

The poetic form of the **Shahname** is a rhyming couplet of roughly ten syllables. The nearest equivalent to the Persian couplet in English is the heroic couplet. In both, the poetic unit is a pair of lines, marked by rhyme, and usually by syntactic divisions as well. The principal difference between the two is that in Persian, enjambment is virtually unheard of. While a sentence may run on for three lines, or even more on rare occasions, each clause of that sentence ends with the line. For example:

> Rostám, when he looked on her angel face,
> And saw in her a share of every art,
> And that she'd given him some news of Rakhsh,
> He saw no end to this that was not good.

The other striking difference between the two is that Persian poetic meters are based exclusively on syllable length.

Syllables are measured as short . . . , long . . . , or over-long . . . , and various combinations of these units make up the feet from which the many Persian meters are composed. Each meter has a name, and that of the meter of the **Shahname,** and, indeed, of most heroic poems in Persian, is *motaqareb*. This meter is composed of three feet of . . . (short + long + long) and one of . . . (short + long). . . . Because the unit of measure is length not number, and a single overlong syllable may be counted as two syllables, the length of a line of *motaqareb* may vary from eight to eleven syllables although ten is the most common. Of the twenty-eight lines that make up the prologue of the poem, seventeen have ten syllables, five have eleven, three have nine, and three have eight. Stress is not included as a part of the metrical system. There are four or five stresses per line, but the placement of these stresses varies from foot to foot.

Rhyme in Persian is essentially what it is in English. Persian, however, has a preference for multiple rhymes, for a rhyme that consists of a sequence of two or more syllables. Moreover, Persian has a strong predilection for syntactic and phonetic parallels between the two lines that make up a couplet. Here are the first three couplets of the poem by way of example:

> ágar tónd bádi bár ayad ze kónj
> be khák áfkanad nárasidé torónj
>
> setámkaré khanímesh ár dad*gár*
> honarmánd danímesh ár bí hon*ár*
>
> ágar márg dádast bí*dad chíst*
> ze dád in hame báng o fary*ád chíst*
>
> What if a fierce and vagrant wind springs up,
> And casts a green unripened fruit to earth.
> Shall we call this a tyrant's act, or just?
> Shall we consider it as right or wrong?
> If death is just, how can this not be so?
> Why then lament and wail at what is just?

In the second couplet each word in the second line has the same number of syllables as the word parallel to it in the first, and there is a sequence of four syllables in the middle of the line that differs only in the consonant that begins them (*khanimesh ar, danimesh ar*). And the rhyme of the third couplet is a phrase of two syllables. . . .

Notes

1. The relation of Ferdowsi to the Iranian national epic tradition has been reviewed most recently and authoritatively by Olga M. Davidson in "The Crown-Bestower in the Iranian Book of Kings," *Studia Iranica*, vol. 10, Papers in Honor of Professor Mary Boyce (Leiden: E. J. Brill, 1985), see particularly pt. 2: "The Authority and Authenticity of Ferdowsi's Book of Kings." The development of the epic tradition after Ferdowsi's completion of his work is reviewed in various places, most recently and best in William L. Hanaway, "The Iranian Epics" in *Heroic*

Epic and Saga, ed. Felix J. Oinas (Bloomington: University of Indiana Press, 1978).

2. All references to the text are to the edition prepared by Ye. E. Bertel's et al., eds., *Shāh-nāme,* 9 vols. (Moscow: AN SSSR, 1960-71). This abbreviation means volume 3, page 6, line 9. All translations are my own.

William L. Hanaway (essay date 1988)

SOURCE: "Epic Poetry," in *Persian Literature,* edited by Ehsan Yarshater, Bibliotheca Persica, 1988, pp. 96-108.

[*In the essay below, Hanaway discusses Persian national epic poetry in general and the* Shah-Nama *in particular, focusing on the poem's language and the nature of its heroes. Hanaway also comments on the movement from epic to romance that occurred in the literature of medieval Persia after the* Shah-Nama.]

Persian epic poetry is both extensive and little known. The following discussion will attempt to introduce this poetry by touching on several areas of literary and cultural interest. Beginning with a definition of epic poetry, it will move on to examine some of the background of the Persian national epic and then will focus on Ferdowsi's **Shāh-nāma** itself. The nature of the heroes and the language of the epic will be discussed, and the shift from epic to romance that took place in medieval Persian literature after the **Shāh-nāma** will be examined. Finally a word will be said about the place of **Shāh-nāma** in the Persian literary tradition.

Epic poetry in its oldest form is oral poetry, and from this unwritten form the literary epic evolved. In the present context an epic poem is understood to be an extended narrative, focusing on the deeds of high-ranking persons, with the interest generally revolving around the adventures of a few kings and great heroes. Thus it is a poetry of action, reflecting a court-centered society. Nevertheless, epic poetry always has a close connection with a particular people for whom it has a profound meaning. Likely to embody the history, the ideals, and the values of a people, it is often a cohesive force in ethnic or national consciousness. It can formulate a people's cultural and spiritual heritage and objectify it in a manner which appeals to the heart as much as to the mind. Persian epic poetry fits all of these requirements perfectly, although what survives of it today is not oral but literary. Doubtlessly a long tradition of oral poetry lies behind this, but it is a tradition lost to us today.

As Persian epic poetry is explored in terms of the above characteristics, the discussion will then focus on Ferdowsi's **Shāh-nāma,** its antecedents, and its descendants. The **Shāh-nāma** is closer than any other work in Persian literature to our definition of epic poetry and is thus the most useful pivot for a general discussion. Other works will be mentioned against the background of the **Shāh-nāma.**

To understand better this poetry and the way it fits into the framework of Persian literature, some general background information is necessary. Paradoxically, we have far more material available from the Iranian epic tradition than we have epic poetry embodying this material. Furthermore, the greater part of what remains to us of the epic tradition was written down in Islamic times by Muslim writers for Muslim audiences. This religio-cultural setting obviously influenced what was set down and how it was presented. Regardless of when they were written down, however, these stories, legends, motifs, beliefs, and attitudes have their roots deep in the past, and this past shows itself in ways both obvious and subtle. Some of these ways will be discussed later, but first, the main sources of Persian epic poetry must be considered.

The deepest roots lie in ancient Indo-European and Indo-Iranian traditions, and the traditions of the Iranians as they developed into a nation. The sources of this national tradition are often difficult to identify, but we can be reasonably certain that traces of myths and practices stemming from the common period of the Indo-Europeans can be seen in the Avesta and in the epic poetry that survives. It is probably from those times that the accounts of Jamshid, Faredun, Hōshang, Kay Khosrow, and others who play important roles in the *Shāh-nāma* have their origin.

As the Iranians moved onto the plateau that is now their homeland, they brought with them old myths and legends. In the process of territorial expansion and settlement, battles fought with the indigenous peoples also left their mark in the Iranians' memory, and accounts of these were preserved in oral tradition. Assuming that there was oral epic poetry even in this early period, it is likely that these stories existed simultaneously in several different versions. In a tradition of oral epic poetry, the concept of a "correct" version of a story, a canonized variant to be preferred over all others does not, cannot, exist. In orally transmitted epics, the story is recreated with each telling; only with the invention of writing did the concept of a fixed text develop.

In addition to ancient memories and traditions, another major source of Persian epic poetry is prehistoric religious tradition, from Zoroastrianism and other pre-Islamic religions. It is not certain how long the Iranians had been settled on the plateau when Zarathushtra appeared as a prophet in the sixth century B.C., or earlier. This would give at least fifteen hundred years for episodes from that period to work their way into the national legend and the material that Ferdowsi used as his source.

As the Iranians wandered onto the plateau, some of them began to shift from nomadism to agriculture. This development implied a more settled life, the growth of villages, and a change in their view of the world. It must have been during these transitional times that one of the great motifs of Persian epic poetry began to emerge: the theme of Iran versus Turan. In the *Shāh-nāma* we see a late and confused form of this theme, cast in terms of Iranians versus Turks, with the Oxus River forming the boundary between the two hostile peoples. The wars between these peoples occupy such a large part of the *Shāh-nāma* that they must reflect older and deeper oppositions, possibly beginning with the age-old animosity between nomads and settled people. Zoroastrianism contributed religious and ethical dimensions to this conflict, and it is no surprise that such opposition, growing out of conflicting social and religious systems, was also seen as a struggle between the forces of good and evil. In the entire national legend the Iranians have no more bitter enemies than the Turanians.

Along with national and religious traditions, a third major element entering into Persian epic poetry can be called the popular tradition. This consists of legends, stories, traditions, and fantasies about persons and places, real or imagined, that form a part of a nation's culture but are not necessarily part of the mainstream of the national tradition and its heroes. Many stories from popular tradition are grafted onto great figures in the national tradition. The sources of the popular tradition are found all over the world and are productive even today.

With some idea of the principal elements that go into Persian epic poetry, we may now turn to the major example of that poetry. The *Shāh-nāma* is an epic poem of some fifty thousand lines, written over a period of about thirty years and completed around A.D. 1000 by Abul's-Qāsem Ferdowsi, a member of the landed gentry from the village of Tus, a few miles north of Meshed in eastern Iran. It is written in rhyming couplets in the *motaqāreb* meter: . . . Ferdowsi displays great pride in his work and takes pains to tell us that he has written this poem as a monument that will endure the ravages of time. It should be stressed that the *Shāh-nāma* is a carefully created literary epic and not a product of the oral tradition, although there is certainly much from that tradition in it.

The epic falls into natural divisions of an introduction and fifty sections of unequal length, each devoted to the reign of a king. The fifty reigns are grouped chronologically into four major dynastic divisions—the Pishdadians, the Kayanians, the Parthians, and the Sasanians—and form a chronicle of the Iranian people from the creation of the world to the Arab conquest of Iran. Overlapping the first two dynastic divisions is a special cycle of tales integrated into the mainstream of the narrative. This is the so-called Seistan cycle, part of a much larger cycle of stories originating in eastern Iran and devoted to the exploits of the great hero Rostam and his descendants. Thus it can be said that Ferdowsi cast a considerable portion, but not all, of the national legend into the form of an epic poem. The parts that he left out will be discussed later.

The *Shāh-nāma* is a poem of action. The characteristic pursuits of the Iranian nobles are hunting, feasting, and war—three closely related activities. In hunting for sport, the aggressive drives of the warrior are directed toward animals, thus satisfying the desire for action and conflict while reducing the risks involved. Feasting, with its erotic overtones, represents the other side of the coin, where the urge to violence is sublimated. Since the heroes of the *Shāh-nāma* are free of the administrative duties of kingship, they have little else to do but hunt, drink, and fight, and thus pass their time alternating between excesses of violent action and, as it were, violent indolence. They never flag in their pursuit of personal honor and glory. The kings, on the other hand, fulfill a different role and hence tend to behave with a greater degree of decorum and gravity.

We recall that it is the rule for epic poetry to focus on the deeds of a great hero. The conventions of the epic, however, allow for little psychological development in the characters, with the result that the heroes of the *Shāh-nāma* are born, not made. Cast in the heroic mold from birth, the hero's life is merely the working-out of its predestined nature. The great hero of the *Shāh-nāma* is Rostam, and his career is no exception to this rule. Descended from a long line of Seistani rulers tracing their lineage back to the mythical hero Keresāspa, Rostam, like many heroes in world literature, was born by cesarian section and showed astounding prowess practically from his first day. He matured much more quickly than other boys of his age, and while still a youth, he killed an elephant singlehandedly. Entering into a lifetime of heroic behavior, he fearlessly met all challengers, natural and supernatural. He was independent in the rule of his own territory but subservient to the ruling monarch of Iran. After a long and splendid career of service to several kings, he met an ignominious and unheroic death.

According to Northrup Frye's definition, the epic hero's power of action is superior in degree to other men's but not superior to the natural environment. In this respect too Rostam is a typical hero, endowed with superhuman strength and endurance but still subject to fatigue, the pain of wounds, and the normal human emotions of anger and love. He is not immune to the rigors of old age, and he cannot fly through the air, control the elements, or make himself invisible. Because of these limitations, we can easily identify with Rostam as a human being. If he is more powerful than we, he still cannot challenge nature or the gods, nor can we. If Rostam's pride sometimes interferes with his good sense, who of us can claim never to have had this happen? As an epic hero, Rostam is solid and dependable, with a clear idea of his own importance in the general scheme of things.

Rostam and his royal masters are not the only characters in the epic, at least in the legendary parts. While the majority of the actors are human and most of the action motivated by human concerns, supernatural agents are present as well. *Divs* (demons) are a common breed of the latter. Rostam is captured and carried off by a *div* named Akvān in a very peculiar episode, and in a famous series of adventures the great hero rids the province of Mazanderan of these creatures.

One of the most spectacular of the supernatural creatures is the Simorgh, a mythical bird who nourishes Rostam's father and protects Rostam himself. This bird, with its healing powers and its protective attitude toward great heroes, may embody a very old Iranian or Indo-Iranian belief. In his well-known battle with Esfandiyār, Rostam faces an enemy who seems to be his match. In desperation Rostam summons the Simorgh, who provides him with the magical means of killing his enemy. Such aid is not given without recompense, however, and the direct result of Rostam's victory is his own death at the hands of his brother later on.

The most pervasive of the supernatural forces is God, and He too intervenes on behalf of the hero. When Rostam is fighting Sohrāb in their tragic conflict, Rostam is hard-pressed by his adversary. Although earlier he had prayed that God take some of his excessive power from him, now he prays for added strength. The ironic result is that Rostam is victorious, only to learn, as his heroic opponent lay dying, that he has killed his own son.

One might object here that Rostam is something less than a real hero because, when he is hard-pressed, he can call upon supernatural help. There are two dimensions to this problem, one literary and the other moral. First, Rostam is an epic hero, and the job of epic heroes is to win. He does not indulge in scruples, mainly because they are irrelevant here. This is not to say that he is amoral, but only that he is required by epic convention to win, and win by whatever means necessary. Second is the moral dimension. We have seen that in both instances when Rostam is forced to call upon nonhuman help, the aid comes, but a price is exacted in return. In the one case Rostam kills his own son, and in the other he subsequently loses his own life, just as the Simorgh predicted he would if he accepted the means to kill Esfandiyār. The epic hero will win by any means, but he must also win at any cost, and in Rostam's case the cost of winning is the greatest price a person can pay.

The world of the *Shāh-nāma* is centered in Iran and extends outward in all directions. As the action flows in and out like the tide, it surges over much of the then-known world. The geographical scope of the epic is vast. Hunting expeditions and wars carry the heroes far beyond the boundaries of Iran to encounter Arabs, Byzantines, Central Asians, Chinese, Indians, and other non-Iranian peoples. Long journeys and marches are frequent; prolonged absence from home is the rule for heroes. With all of this variety, however, local color plays almost no role at all. Other than the numerous depictions of sunrise and sunset, nature is hardly described. Whether the action is in Arabia or China, the only variable is the enemy, and the terrain and climate might not exist for all we know.

It must not be thought that the whole *Shāh-nāma* is concerned with the exploits of Rostam, for historical material is present in generous measure as well. As mentioned earlier, the epic is divided into four major dynastic sections, and by the end of the second dynasty Rostam is dead and the Seistan cycle has come to an end. The last two sections, on the Parthians and Sasanians, bring the narrative out of the mythical and legendary eras and into historical periods.

The section on the Parthians is very short, while that on the Sasanians is relatively long, taking up roughly one-half of the epic. Here we are given a great deal of historical information on the Sasanians and their principal enemy, the Byzantines, plus, among other things, the amorous adventures of Bahrām Gor, the romance of Khosrow and Shirin, the story of Bahrām Chobin, and a number of throne speeches of ethical content. From this it is evident that the *Shāh-nāma* combines different kinds of material: mythical, legendary, epic, historical, ethical, and romantic.

It is worth noting that in Iran, today's audience is interested only in the earlier part of the **Shāh-nāma** and not in the Parthians and Sasanians. They rightly sense that with the death of Rostam, the truly epic part of the **Shāh-nāma** ends, and what remains is essentially a historical account with no hero to give it focus. To satisfy their audiences and prolong their sessions, the storytellers now interpolate various other tales from the Seistan cycle into their narratives of the **Shāh-nāma.** It is thus mainly the Seistan cycle that provides the true epic heroes, while the latter part of the narrative purports to give us history.

To the extent that the **Shāh-nāma** presents a linear sequence of events, many of which are linked by the process of cause and effect, and also conveys much information, it does constitute a work of history as well as an epic poem. In fact, **Shāh-nāma** means "Book of Kings," and this may be regarded as a generic as well as a specific title. Before Ferdowsi's time there was a long tradition of writing **Shāh-nāma**s, stretching back to the late Sasanian period when an official chronicle called "Book of Kings" was compiled. The intention of this latter work clearly seems to have been historical.[1]

Along with the historical material in the **Shāh-nāma,** however, there is much that falls outside of historical time. Some events described are not susceptible to any sort of verification, and with others the narrative time cannot be historical. What does it mean to us, for example, that Rostam lived several hundred years? What is the real significance of his battle with Esfandiyār? These events have a different kind of meaning for us from those connected with Khosrow II and the Byzantines. We cannot accept as true Ferdowsi's explanation of how material culture developed in the world. Nor could those who explained material culture by the myth in the **Shāh-nāma** understand the history of the world as a process. Thus the **Shāh-nāma** contains not only different kinds of material, but different modes of thought as well, and the tension that exists among these modes of thought is only resolved by the synthetic vision that the poet has imposed on his material.

Turning now to a different sort of question, that of the language of the epic, we see that the **Shāh-nāma,** like much epic poetry, is written in relatively plain language. In this case, the Persian is considered simple for two reasons: it contains a very low percentage of Arabic loanwords, and it is relatively free of rhetorical devices and complicated figurative language. These two qualities are linked: for

technical reasons, it is quite difficult to write highly figured poetry in Persian while severely restricting the Arabic which can be drawn upon. The question is, why should the language of the **Shāh-nāma** be this way? The traditional answer gives Ferdowsi great credit as a nationalist but little credit as a poet. Since great nationalists do not necessarily make great poets, a different answer will be suggested below.

Ferdowsi's images are succinct and appropriate. He rarely piles image upon image, and he seldom employs extended metaphors requiring several lines. An example will help make this clear. At one point, Ferdowsi has an enemy general say to his men before battle:[2]

> We will make the air like a spring cloud;
> We will rain arrows upon them.

The Persian is richer than the English, but the point comes through in translation. He uses the image of a spring cloud to express a threat to the Persians. In the first half-line we are presented with the unqualified image of a spring cloud, which might carry with it associations of abundant rain, revivification, and movement. But these are immediately eliminated by the second half-line, which focuses the image on the rain alone. We now understand that the rain will consist of arrows and that it will bring death rather than new life. It is appropriate that this image is used by an enemy, for how could an Iranian, whose new year commences with the vernal equinox, ever ironically link spring with death? Beginning with a common military cliché, *tir bārān* (raining arrows), Ferdowsi lifts it out of an anonymous and moribund state to endow it with a new freshness and create an image that goes directly to the point.

In contrast to this economy of imagery, the writers of later epics and romances tend to be more prodigal. Images in a long series or large conglomerations are characteristic of these works, as is a more general use of imagery altogether; thus, they depend on figurative writing rather than on precise description. Here then lies one of the basic differences between the epic and other kinds of narrative poetry.

This distinction leads us back to our question of why there are so few similes and metaphors in Ferdowsi's epic language compared with other Persian poetry of his time. The answer lies in the tension which exists between the need to use rhetorical devices and figurative language to render vivid the action of the heroes, and the seductive dangers inherent in the use of such language—seductive because in poetry of heroic action, the listener's attention must remain fixed on that action. The meaning of the event lies in its action. If the action is described in figurative and suggestive language, flights of associations are started up in the listener's mind, associations which add new dimensions and nuances. These in turn divert the mind to contemplation and interpretation and away from the speed, the sequences, the actions and reactions that are the stuff of this poetry. In this respect, Persian epic poetry is not autonomous. It demands the imaginative participation of the listener, as any Tehran storyteller will affirm. It will not, however, bear the kind of imaginative extension which comes with the reading of lyric poetry. The lines of epic poetry should ring like a sword on a shield, or a hammer on an anvil, not like a carillon in a bell tower.

In this sparing and very precise use of imagery I believe we can understand some of Ferdowsi's success. He knew well how to control his language in order to achieve a desired effect. He used epic language with his raw material and produced epic poetry, while others, with no less appropriate material at their disposal, were not able to restrict themselves to the linguistic leanness of the master. Precisely this ability contributes in large measure to his poetic stature.

The language and form of the *Shāh-nāma* had a profound effect on how the remaining material from the national legend—those stories not included in the *Shāh-nāma*—were preserved for posterity. The Persian national legend was enormously broad in scope and in Ferdowsi's time undoubtedly contained much material now lost to us. Hints of such material may be gained from Sogdian, Armenian, Middle Persian, and Arabic sources. All was not lost, however, for we have the numerous post-*Shāh-nāma* epics and traditional romances to supplement these hints. In outward form the later epics closely resemble the *Shāh-nāma* and are written in the same meter and rhyming couplets; traditional romances are in prose for the most part, although in some of them the verse original shows through the thin spots.

As mentioned above, imposed upon the main narrative of the *Shāh-nāma* is a cycle of stories about a family of heroes residing in Seistan who were descended from Keresāspa. Ferdowsi treats the life and adventures of Sām, his son Zāl, and Zāl's son Rostam, all members of this Seistan family. After Rostam's death there is little news of the rest of the family in the *Shāh-nāma,* yet many stories must have been current in medieval Persia, because for four or five hundred years after Ferdowsi's death, tales of the other members of the Seistan family were put into verse on the model of the *Shāh-nāma,* and thus saved from oblivion.

The earliest of the post-*Shāh-nāma* epics, completed about a half-century later, is Asadi Tusi's *Garshāsp-nāma,* which describes the deeds of Garshāsp, a descendant of the legendary King Jamshid. Likewise we have in verse the adventures of Sām, of Rostam's son Farāmarz, of his grandson Borzu, and of various other relations such as Jahāngir, Bahman, Āzarbarzin, Kush, and of one woman, Bānu Goshasp. She is a daughter of Rostam who marries the mighty Giv, son of Godarz. Both of them are prominent figures in the *Shāh-nāma.* They fall into such violent domestic strife that Rostam has to intervene and bring about peace. Their son is Bizhan, whose love for the Turanian Manizha gets him into deep trouble, and he must be rescued by Rostam.

The most extensive of the later epics is the *Borzu-nāma,* of which some manuscripts are equal in size to the *Shāh-nāma.* Borzu is the son of Sohrāb, but he is not mentioned in the latest edition of the *Shāh-nāma.* The Seistan family comes to an end with Borzu's son Shahryār, whose life is described in the *Shahryār-nāma.* Nor does this exhaust the post-*Shāh-nāma* epics, as there are several others concerned with lesser figures.

While all of these works share the epic characteristic of being focused on the deeds of one hero, they differ from the *Shāh-nāma* in their conception of the hero and the nature of his actions. This divergence from the essence of epic poetry (which also includes language, as indicated above) increased over time. The seeds of change can be seen even in the *Garshāsp-nāma,* the closest chronologically to the *Shāh-nāma.* By the time of the *Sām-nāma* of Khwāju Kermāni, written in the fifteenth century, the shift from epic to romance was complete.

The reasons for this change are not known at present; the best one can do is describe the nature of the change and hope this will provide a clue to its causes. What happened, in brief, was that one set of heroic models was substituted for another. Characters who appear in the *Shāh-nāma* as typical but minor epic figures, Sām or Farāmarz for example, are changed when they appear as the central characters of a later epic. In the case of the prose romances, we find the substitution of characters such as Dārāb, Firuz Shāh, and Khorshid Shāh for the Kayanian kings of Ferdowsi's epic.

Our admiration for the older epic heroes is based on their superhuman strength and courage and the patriotic service to which these are put. In this case the poet, the reciter, and the audience are drawn together by a collective memory of the national past. One function of this past is to set norms for the future, thus binding together the whole span of Iranian civilization in a unity of values.

As the epic hero changed to a romantic hero, the relations binding together the poet, the reciter, and the audience also changed. In Frye's terms, the powers of action of the romantic hero are superior in degree both to ours and to the natural environment. Thus, our admiration for the romantic hero is based on our desire to escape from everyday life into a fabulous world of adventure and idealized love, a world where everything turns out well, a world where the passions of mortals are magnified but where, in the process, the characters have lost their human vulnerability. The result is a hero once removed from those we can identify with as we do with an epic hero. The romantic vision of the past sets no norms for the future, and the audience is merely entertained by the stories, having little sense of participation in shared values which have formed his civilization across the centuries.[3]

Keeping in mind this very general picture of the shift from epic to romance, we may suggest some possible reasons for such a change. One could argue, for example, that after Ferdowsi's death there was a general decline in the epic spirit, which might be linked in some fashion to social and intellectual changes in the Iranian cultural area. This point of view, however, would be very difficult to defend. Alternatively, one could suggest that the writers of romances and their audiences had always been present, and that Ferdowsi was an exception. This proposition would be much easier to defend, and would better account for the evidence. No doubt there are other ways to explain the rapid disappearance of epic poetry after Ferdowsi, but any explanation must take into account the long pre-*Shāh-nāma* tradition of oral romance in Persia, a tradition which continued in full force until the twentieth century.

Finally, something should be said about the place of epic poetry within Islamic Persian literature. From one perspective, the *Shāh-nāma* stands out as a towering monument in the literary tradition. As we examine it more closely, we see that, like many monuments, over the years it has developed an extremely complex relationship with its surroundings. For one thing, the *Shāh-nāma* stands at the end of the oral epic tradition in Persian literature. Oral transmission of epic poetry went on after A.D. 1000 to be sure, but its status would never be the same, since a literary tradition now ran parallel to it. Furthermore, the existence of the *Shāh-nāma* galvanized others to write down those parts of the national legend that Ferdowsi had left out. As we have seen, these later epics looked something like the *Shāh-nāma,* but were quite different in language and spirit. In fact they form a major link between the epic and the romance traditions of medieval Persia.

The *Shāh-nāmā,* while incorporating elements of earlier romances such as *Khosrow and Shirin,* had a strong influence on subsequent romance writing. In the verse romances such as *Vis and Rāmin* and those of Nezāmi, the weight of the *Shāh-nāma* is felt everywhere: in the language, in the presentation of battle scenes and descriptions of warriors and heroes, in the description of sunrise and sunset, and in the very structure of the works themselves, where such standard epic elements as single combats and long overseas journeys appear frequently. Much the same can be said of the epic's influence on the traditional prose romances where, in addition to the above, direct quotations from Ferdowsi are frequent.

Beyond the direct influence of the *Shāh-nāma* on the writing of later epics and romances, a large category of pseudo-epics was directly inspired by it. These historical or religious pieces are modeled on the form of the *Shāh-nāma* but are unlike it in the use of language and in epic spirit. The historical pseudo-epics are very numerous. For example, Hamdallāh Mostowfi brought the *Shāh-nāma* up to his own period of the fourteenth century with his *Zafar-nāma.* Many of the pseudo-epics were written about the lives of the Moghul emperors, and the practice was continued into the nineteenth century with the *George-nāma,* produced in India in honor of a visit by the British monarch.

Religious pseudo-epics are also numerous. They are for the most part concerned with the battles and successes of Mohammad and 'Ali. Here the epic form has been used to mold historical and religious material, from a very particular Iranian point of view. The result is a linking of 'Ali, Mohammad, and other religious figures prominent in the Shi'ite tradition, to the older Iranian epic heroes. This brings the religious events in question under a strong Iranian light, and presents them squarely within the tradition of epic-romantic narrative poetry.

While the *Shāh-nāma* had a powerful literary effect in subsequent centuries, it also had and continues to have a powerful psychological effect on the Iranian people through its patriotic and nationalistic sentiments. Since these are extraliterary matters, they will not be discussed here beyond observing that Ferdowsi was able to formulate the national ideals and values of the Iranians in a manner which had no parallel in their literature. His achievement was such, however, that the *Shāh-nāma* can be enjoyed as epic poetry for its own sake by those unaffected by its patriotic and nationalistic appeals. Its literary and symbolic values combine to make it a true monument, with a life of its own and a message for us all.

Notes

1. See also p. 10 (Ed.).

2. *Shāh-nāma,* ed. E. Bertels (Moscow, 1960-), vol. 4, 229, l. 316.

3. See chap. 8 on romances (Ed.).

Bibliography

Frye, N. *Anatomy of Criticism* (Princeton, 1971).

Jauss, H. "Levels of Identification of Hero and Audience," *New Literary History* 5 (1974): 283-317.

Merkelbach, R. "Inhalt und Form in symbolischen Erzählungen der Antike," *Eranos Jahrbuch* 35 (1966): 145-75.

Safā, Z. *Hamāsa Sarā'i dar Irān* (Tehran, 1954).

Dick Davis (essay date 1992)

SOURCE: An introduction to *The Legend of Seyavash,* by Ferdowsi, translated by Dick Davis, Penguin Books, 1992, pp. ix-xxvii.

[*In the following essay, Davis studies the plot and themes of the* Shah-Nama, *focusing in particular on the Sasanian bias of the later portions of the text, including the story of Seyavash. Davis observes that the authority of God and King in the text are of major importance, but are exceeded in significance by the authority of the father over the son.*]

The Legend of Seyavash is a section of **The Shahnameh,** written by the Persian poet Ferdowsi (*c.* 940-*c.* 1020). **The Shahnameh** bears approximately the same relation to Persian culture as the works of Homer do to ancient Greek culture. Coming at the virtual beginning of the recorded literature, it is seen as a massive and masterly work and, in some sense, as a touchstone for everything subsequent to it. It is also considered a uniquely accurate icon of the culture that it defines and, by influencing the notion of self-identity it bequeaths to its people, that it moulds. As Alessandro Bausani has written, Ferdowsi has been regarded by modern Persians as 'the symbol of Persianness, the father of his country',[1] and, though this may be less generally true since the Islamic Revolution of 1979, the remark still has a broad validity to it.

As with Homer's work, the style of the poem indicates a long oral tradition behind the written version we now read (however, Ferdowsi's relation to his sources is more clearly spelt out than Homer's, and we know that the majority of them were written, though many of these, particularly those related to the earlier sections of the poem, must ultimately have been based on the oral tradition); as with Homer's works, the subject matter is largely the heroic history of the people celebrated in the poem.

We are dealing, then, with a national epic. But it is a national epic far vaster in scope than any of its Western equivalents, concerned as it is with the history of Iran[2] from the creation of the world to the Arab/Islamic conquest of the country in the seventh century AD. Perhaps the only works of comparable scope in world literature are the Indian epics, the *Mahabharata* and *Ramayana*. In sheer size, if nothing else, Ferdowsi's achievement is extraordinary, and it has been estimated that **The Shahnameh** is probably the longest poem (some 50,000 lines—very long lines at that, approximately equal to the length of a heroic couplet in English) known to have been substantially completed by one man.[3] The Seyavash episode translated here is a little over 2,500 lines, and it therefore represents only a small portion of the poem, though it is certainly one of its best-known and best-written episodes.

It is usual to divide **The Shahnameh** (for convenience's sake: these are divisions made by modern commentators, not by the poet himself) into three sections—the mythological section, with which the poem opens, the legendary section, and the quasi-historical section, with which it closes. The mythological section is in many ways more like a cosmogony than an epic, recalling, for a Western reader, Hesiod rather than Homer: it details the creation of the world and of the first man, the origin of evil and of human strife, and the discovery/invention of the arts of civilization. The first man is also the first king of the world—a Persian Adam called Keyumars—and it is significant that, though Ferdowsi was undoubtedly a sincere Muslim, he begins his poem in this way (with a king and a figure from Persian myth), rather than by drawing on the version of the world's and man's creation offered in the Koran.

The middle, legendary section of the poem (from which our story is taken) is the one that corresponds most closely to Western notions of epic poetry. More or less constant

warfare between Iran and its northern neighbour Turan is described;[4] and the overt values the poem promotes are those typical of epic poetry the world over—fierce loyalty to tribe and king, bravery, military prowess and the ability to trick the enemy (the epithet of one of the heroes is the equivalent of Odysseus' 'guileful'). In this section Ferdowsi inherits an amalgamation of two quite separate epic traditions—that of the Iranians and that of the inhabitants of Sistan (approximately south-western Afghanistan). The family that rules Sistan is nominally subject to the Iranian royal family and provides them with their main champions; there is, however, a constant and subtle rivalry between the two clans and it is this rivalry which generates many of the best-known stories of the poem. The great hero of Sistan is Rostam (made famous in the West by Matthew Arnold's version of the story of Sohrab and Rostam, in which Rostam inadvertently kills his son)[5] and Rostam is seen as the counsellor, champion and saviour of the Iranian kings. Some of these kings can act with extraordinary foolishness (e.g. Kavus, who is the king during the Seyavash episode) or malevolence (e.g. Goshtasp, who tries to have Rostam enslaved), and when there is such a conflict the reader's sympathy is always directed towards Rostam rather than towards his nominal overlord. The overt value of loyalty to the king come what may still prevails, but much of the poem's human interest arises from the poet's/audience's perception of how difficult it can be to maintain such loyalty, given the nature of some of the kings who demand it. Late on in the poem a king asks his advisor, 'Who is the most desperate of men?', and the answer is, 'A good man whose king is a fool', the remark neatly encapsulating the problem many of the poem's heroes face, including our hero Seyavash.

It is in this legendary section of the poem that we realize that our modern Western perception of Iran/Persia differs radically from the one offered by Ferdowsi. The poet is utilizing the ethnic inheritance of the Iranian people, originally a tribe or tribes inhabiting central Asia who descended on to the Iranian plateau and into modern Persia at some time before the beginning of recorded history. The landscape of much of **The Shahnameh** is the grassy steppe of central Asia, not the arid desert of central Persia, and almost all the place-names mentioned in the first two thirds of the poem are not now within the confines of Iran. In the section here translated we read of Merv (now in southern Russia) and Balkh (now in northern Afghanistan), and the border between 'Iran' and 'Turan' is the river Oxus, now deep within Russian territory. The place-names we associate with Persia—Fars, Shiraz (or its old name Estakhr), Hamadan, Esfahan, Yazd—are virtually absent until the last third of the poem and only appear with any frequency in the last section. In the first two thirds the centre of Persian civilization and influence is seen as what is now the extreme north-eastern corner of the country, Khorasan, where the poet was born, which then extended deep into Russian and Afghan territory. Fars (Pars, from which we derive the word Persia), which the West, as a result of the ancient Greek obsession with the Achaemenid empire, has always seen as the cradle of Persian civilization, does not appear in the poem except as a distant province until just before the advent of Alexander the Great.

The 'historical' section of the poem does not correspond very closely to the West's notions of Persian history either. The Achaemenids are virtually absent; Alexander (Eskandar) is half-Persian, having been born from a Greek princess and a Persian royal father; the Seleucids and Parthians, who between them ruled Iran for about five hundred years, are hardly mentioned. The vast majority of the lines dealing with the history of Iran after the conquest by Eskandar are concerned with the Sasanians, the dynasty destroyed by the Arab invasion in the 640s, and via whom Ferdowsi must have received most of his sources. The great heroic figure of the closing section of the poem is the Sasanian king Anushirvan the Just, who is balanced, in the legendary portion of the poem, by the exemplary king Khosrow (the son of Seyavash).

The Sasanian bias of the later portions of the poem has also radically affected the way in which the mythological and legendary sections are presented. In a way, it is the Sasanian version of the Iranian identity and history which Ferdowsi inherits and to a large extent transmits. This is especially noticeable in two areas—religion and politics. The Sasanian religion was a modified form of Zoroastrianism, a faith deriving from the prophet Zoroaster, who probably lived in Iran at some time in the seventh century BC, though a date much earlier than this is claimed by some, notably by the distinguished scholar of ancient Iranian religions, Mary Boyce. For our purposes the most important aspect of Zoroastrianism is its dualism: the universe is a battleground between the forces of good and evil, both being represented by a divine principle—Ahura Mazda for the good (and light) and Ahreman for the evil (and darkness). The soul of man is a microcosm of the universal battlefield and each man must choose between the contending forces. A Zoroastrian heretic, Mani, gave the West the Manichean religion, which developed the Zoroastrian dualism into a system that ended by rejecting the physical world as belonging to the realm of Ahreman, the realm of the spirit being that of Ahura Mazda.

Though such an extreme rejection of physical reality is not part of the original Zoroastrian message, a suspicion of appearances and physical reality as being somehow less 'good' (even less 'true') than the spiritual realm left its legacy to later Zoroastrianism and, via his Sasanian sources, on Ferdowsi's poem. Ferdowsi's poem has, in contrast with almost all other epics, an urgently ethical cast to it, and this derives in large part from the notion that the true battle, of which all other battles are, as it were, emblems in transient physical reality, is that being waged between good and evil. As important as the physical battles with swords and spears in Ferdowsi's work are the inward ones that take place in the souls of the heroes, and this is particularly true in what are probably the two finest stories of the poem—those of Seyavash and Esfandyar. This inwardness at the poem's high points is something that sharply demarcates it from the notion of the he-

roic we derive from Homer: Erich Auerbach's famous remarks about 'clearly outlined, brightly and uniformly illuminated men and things [that] stand out in a realm where everything is visible' characterizing Homeric epic are quite beside the point for Ferdowsi's poem. In the poem's greatest episodes we feel that Ferdowsi is interested primarily in moral, inward and often hidden, rather than physical heroism, and one of his favourite verbs is a word describing mental 'writhing', the torments of conscience and regret. The overwhelming duty of the poem's heroes is to do what is right, and this rightness is not necessarily consonant with the victory of one's own side in battle or the survival of one's own people, as is the case in a more straightforward heroic poem. Further, failure in the 'real' physical world is not incompatible with triumph in the moral and spiritual world—as is the case with Seyavash, who triumphs spiritually only to be destroyed physically. Again we are far removed from the world of Homer, where failure is failure pure and simple, or even that of so ethical a poet as Virgil, for whom Aeneas' spiritual triumph must also mean literal physical triumph.

The second significant legacy of the Sasanian world-view to the poem is the central importance given to the notion of kingship, a legacy passed on to much of subsequent Persian culture, arguably largely by means of *The Shahnameh* itself. This notion of the central importance of the 'Great King' we know to have been important to the Achaemenids too—it was largely how the Greeks defined their difference from the Persians, and in writers like Herodotus and Xenophon we can see the kind of appalled fascination with which the Greeks regarded this Persian phenomenon. But it was with the Sasanians, who derived from the old Achaemenid centre of Iran, Fars, and who seem consciously to have revived Achaemenid claims to imperial glory, that it entered into its most complex and theologically sanctioned development. The Great King was the representative of Ahura Mazda on earth; he ruled by divine right and possessed a glory unique to kings (the royal *farr*) conferred on him by God. The Sasanian kings ruled in seclusion from their people, surrounded by an aura of divine power. To rebel was to rebel against God. The very survival of the country was dependent on the survival of the king and his family and when a new king acceded to the throne the world itself was seen as renewed. All this *The Shahnameh* faithfully reflects, and the very name of the poem (which means 'King-Book') indicates the centrality of this concept to the work.

The weight of such authority, both secular and spiritual, might be thought to have a monolithic and deadening effect on the values of the poem. But in reality almost the contrary is true. The demands on a subject's allegiance are indeed overwhelming, but they are often split between contradictory claims. What the king demands and what God or the conscience (or even simple common sense) demand should theoretically be one and the same thing, but they are frequently at variance, and this delemma of loyalty is faced at one time or another by most of the poem's heroes.

The claims of God and king are shadowed by a third source of authority, that of the father over the son. It is a striking fact that in the three best-known stories of the legendary section of the poem—those of Sohrab, Seyavash and Esfandyar—a son is killed as a direct result of his father's actions. Rostam kills his son Sohrab in ignorance and with his own hands; Kavus and Goshtasp (the fathers of Seyavash and Esfandyar respectively) make demands on their sons which they cannot in all conscience fulfil. Seyavash rejects his father's demand and throws himself on the mercy of his country's traditional enemies who ultimately kill him; Esfandyar reluctantly attempts to fulfil his father's order that he enslave Rostam and is killed in the process. The fact that Rostam does not know it is his own son whom he kills in combat (on the orders of king Kavus) is what enables him to kill him at all; but the message that the episode conveys, that the father kills the son, is one that is then repeated in the stories of Seyavash and Esfandyar, whose fathers are ultimately responsible for their deaths even though they are not their immediate cause. In the *Farsnameh* of Ebn Balkhi, a prose work written in the twelfth century and reproducing some of the same material as Ferdowsi's **Shahnameh,** Seyavash's father, Kavus, exclaims after his son's death, 'It was I who killed the pure-souled Seyavash, not Afrasyab', and though Ferdowsi's Kavus is too unaware of his own folly to say such a thing, the audience draws the same conclusion. When Esfandyar is slain in **The Shahnameh,** his dying words blame his father, and not the actual opponent in combat who has dealt him the death-blow (Rostam), for his death, and his whole family unite with him in ascribing the blame to Goshtasp.

Seyavash and Esfandyar are presented almost entirely as victims of others' machinations, and Sohrab too is Rostam's victim albeit an unintended one. Similarly many of the kings' champions—and this is especially true of the poem's greatest champion, Rostam—are presented as the victims of their kings' machinations and/or foolishness, and, indeed, Rostam's family is finally wiped out by the Iranian royal family. Beside the weight of authority demanding absolute obedience (the authority of God, king and father), a different ethic emerges, which centres on a sympathy for the victims of such authority. We cannot doubt that we are meant to sympathize with Seyavash in his conflict with his king and father Kavus, and with Rostam in his conflict with the king Goshtasp, who tries to enslave him. The poem's depiction of authority is profoundly ambiguous: it is seen as a prerequisite of organized human life in general, and of the survival of the Iranian nation in particular, but it is also considered the cause of human tragedy and suffering, and the various embodiments of authority in the poem are among its least attractive characters. This questioning seems, in a baffled way, even to extend to the authority of God/Fate itself—and Ferdowsi's comments *in propria persona* at various points in his poem where he has to record the tragic death of a character he admires hint at this; one of the most striking of these comments occurs after Seyavash is killed, when the poet says

in effect that he can't imagine what God can be thinking of by arranging matters thus.

Ferdowsi finished **The Shahnameh** in 1010 and claimed to have spent most of his adult life working on the poem—a claim which, given its vast length, is entirely believable. This means that the poem was written in the latter half of the tenth century and the opening years of the eleventh and though, dealing as it does with prehistoric and quasi-historic material, its roots extend into the distant past, it is also a product specifically of its own time.

Since the Arab/Muslim conquest of Iran in the mid seventh century the country had been part of the Islamic caliphate ruled first from Damascus, under the Umayyads (661-750), and then from Baghdad, under the Abbasids. The Abbasid revolt against Umayyad rule drew particular strength from Khorasan, and many Persians were involved in the movement. Nevertheless, though it is true that Persians were no longer the wholly peripheral people they had been under the Umayyads and that they had great influence at the Abbasid court (for example through the Barmecide family of civil servants), Iran was at first still seen as a group of provinces subject to an Arab, and therefore alien, family's rule. During the later Abbasid period, within which Ferdowsi's lifetime fell, the eastern provinces especially began to achieve something like *de facto* independence of Baghdad, though they were still nominally subject to the caliph there. Under the Samanids—client kings of the Abbasid caliphate—in particular, who ruled in the north-east, a Persian cultural renaissance began to take place. The language of the court became Persian rather than Arabic, and, most importantly, Persian became the language of court poetry. The Samanid princes prided themselves on their Persian identity and encouraged a local and national antiquarianism that emphasized the length and uniqueness of the Persian past. Ferdowsi belonged to the *dehqan* (small landed gentry) class, which was seen as a repository of local tradition and legend and he records during the course of his poem how he conscientiously collected the stories of his country's past, how a particular history that had been recently commissioned was given to him as a major source, and how he sought out those who could pass on oral traditions to him. One reason that Khorasan (rather than the Fars of the Achaemenids) is the cradle of Persian civilization in **The Shahnameh** is that the poem was written there and drew on local tradition.

The Shahnameh was a direct product of the reappearance of a sense of Persian ethnic identity and, as with most epics, the people celebrated are defined as being in conflict with their neighbours, with whom they do not share ethnicity. The first act of human evil in the poem is carried out by an Arab, who seizes power from the Persian king, Jamshid, and the poem ends with the conquest of Iran by the victorious Arab armies of Islam. But if the poem is framed by an ambiguous hostility to Arab civilization (ambiguous because though it destroyed Persian independence it also brought Islam, considered by virtually all of Ferdowsi's contemporary fellow-countrymen as the true religion, to the country), most of it is taken up with the rivalry between Iran and its northern neighbour, Turan, whose inhabitants are Turks. Unfortunately for Ferdowsi the Samanid renaissance of independent Persian culture was short-lived, and eastern Iran was conquered during the poet's lifetime by Mahmud of Ghazni (in Afghanistan), an ethnic Turk. The prestige of Persian culture had spread to Mahmud's court and he was an assiduous patron of Persian poetry; nevertheless, it is difficult to see how he could have been particularly interested in a poem like *The Shahnameh,* which celebrated countless Persian victories over the Turks and which usually cast the Turks as evil and their kings as representatives of the evil principle of the universe, Ahreman. And, indeed, the legends concerning Ferdowsi's presentation of his poem to his new ruler record that Mahmud was singularly unimpressed by it and that Ferdowsi retired to his village in Khorasan a neglected and embittered man. Some manuscripts of *The Shahnameh* include a satire, which may or may not be genuine, on Mahmud and his stinginess toward the poet. All the manuscripts contain passages in which Ferdowsi proclaims his pride in his achievement, and all include passages lamenting his lack of reward for his life's work.

Though the Seyavash story is a more or less self-contained narrative, framed by comments from the poet *in propria persona* (Ferdowsi's normal way of showing when an episode begins and ends), it is also a section of the continuing narrative of the poem as a whole, and a brief summary of the events in *The Shahnameh* prior to the opening of the Seyavash episode will make parts of the story plainer.

The poem opens with praise of God, wisdom, the prophet Muhammad, the caliph Ali and Sultan Mahmud of Ghazni, from whom Ferdowsi clearly hoped for patronage, together with a short section on how he came by his main written source, and one on his predecessor, the poet Daqiqi. We then pass to the creation of the world, to the first king, Keyumars, and his struggle against the forces of evil represented by demons. This struggle is carried on by his descendants Hushang, Tahmoures and Jamshid. Jamshid is a Promethean figure who introduces the arts of civilization to mankind and who thinks that his power rivals God's. His hubris is punished by the arrival of the Arab demon-king Zahhak, who kills Jamshid and sets up a reign of great rapacity and cruelty; snakes grow from his shoulders and the only food they will accept is the brains of young Persians. Zahhak is overthrown by a popular uprising led by the blacksmith Kaveh, and Kaveh's blacksmith's apron becomes the banner of the legendary Persian kings. Kaveh is joined by the prince Faridun, who rules the world with justice. Faridun divides his inheritance between his three sons, Tur, Salm and Iraj. Tur is given Asia, Salm the West, and the youngest, Iraj, is given the land of Iran. Tur and Salm plot against their brother, who is represented as a naive and well-meaning innocent, and kill him. Manuchehr, a grandson of Iraj, avenges his grandfather's murder and rules in Iran. From this time on Iran and Turan (ruled by Tur and his descendants, in particular the king Afrasyab, who is king of Turan during the Seyavash episode) are

more or less perpetually at war. During the reign of the weak and corrupt Persian king Nozar, Afrasyab invades and pillages Iran, and Nozar is killed. There is an interregnum during which Rostam and his father Zal more or less run the country; finally they invite Qobad to be king. Qobad restores the country's fortunes, driving out Afrasyab and his forces and ruling justly and well. However, Qobad's son is the incompetent and rash king Kavus, who is Seyavash's father and the king of Iran when our story opens.

Ferdowsi devotes more space to the reign of Kavus than to that of any other monarch, with the possible exception of Anushirvan the Just.[6] That he should give such a flawed and unsatisfactory king such prominence in his poem is a strong indication that we should not consider it a work written wholly in praise of kings and the notion of kingship, as it has often been regarded. Indeed, the most interesting and aesthetically telling episodes of the poem[7] virtually all deal with weak, evil or corrupt kings, and the Seyavash story is no exception.

The irascible instability of Kavus's character has already been demonstrated at least four times before the opening of the Seyavash episode. Contrary to the advice of his ministers he attacks Mazanderan, the home of demons under their leader the *Div-e Sepid* ('The White Demon'). The *Div-e Sepid* captures Kavus, and Rostam has to be sent to rescue him. Kavus also goes courting, and is imprisoned by his new father-in-law, the king of Hamaveran. Again, Rostam has to be sent to rescue him. Kavus then decides to build himself a flying machine, drawn aloft by eagles—this crashes in enemy territory and again Rostam is sent to bring the hapless king home. Rostam has a further reason to resent Kavus's authority: when Rostam had inadvertently mortally wounded his own son Sohrab, Kavus was in possession of a drug that could have saved the boy; he refused to give it to Rostam partly because he was afraid of Sohrab's prowess if he lived, but partly in order to punish Rostam for what Kavus considered the hero's insufficiently humble demeanour. By the time the Seyavash story opens Kavus has been firmly established in the audience's mind as foolish and short-tempered, often well-meaning but equally often vindictive, alternately vacillating and headstrong.

The Seyavash story is constructed with great symmetry and economy: there are two tests of the prince's integrity, both of which he passes successfully, and there are two plots against his life—the first fails and the second succeeds. The first test is against his sexual integrity, when his stepmother queen Sudabeh[8] attempts to seduce him. His resistance to Sudabeh's wiles and her subsequent fury against him remind a Western reader of the Hippolytus/Phaedra story and, as with Hippolytus, his integrity has something of an anguished adolescent flight from sexuality about it.[9] Having passed unscathed through the metaphorical fire of Sudabeh's passion for him, he is then required to pass through a literal mountain of fire in order to prove his innocence, which of course he is able to do. In order to get away from the corrupt atmosphere of the court he asks permission to lead the Persian armies against the invading forces of Turan, whom he defeats with the help of Rostam. He concludes a treaty with the king of Turan, Afrasyab, and takes hostages as a token of Afrasyab's good conduct. The second and far more important test of his integrity comes when his king and father, Kavus, orders him to send the hostages to the Persian court where they will be killed. Seyavash feels unable to do this in good conscience and throws himself on the mercy of his country's enemies. Afrasyab welcomes him, and marries him first to the daughter of his chief minister and then to his own daughter. But the plot by Sudabeh against Seyavash at the Persian court is paralleled by a plot by Afrasyab's brother against Seyavash at the Turanian court. Sexually unsuccessful with Seyavash, Sudabeh accuses him of sexual treachery; Afrasyab's brother was the commander of the armies of Turan defeated by Seyavash and, militarily unsuccessful against Seyavash, he accuses him of military treachery, of planning a military coup. Seyavash is unable to refute the calumny, largely because of his innocent trust in those who have plotted against him, and is killed. His second wife, the daughter of Afrasyab, is pregnant with the future king, Kay Khosrow, and is saved by Afrasyab's minister, Piran. Kay Khosrow is brought up in secret, escapes to Iran and eventually returns to avenge his father's murder. The story sounds and is fairly complex, but one is never aware of strain as one reads—the poet keeps the various characters in play with an ease which is so practised and elegant as to seem instinctive, and in the unfolding of events he is able to embody with force and emotional conviction the ethical preoccupations that run through so much of his poem.

In a work of the length of **The Shahnameh** it is only natural that one should feel that the poet's interest is quickened more by some episodes than by others. As Ferdowsi's sources no longer exist it is often difficult to guess whether a particularly strong delineation is the result of his own interest or whether it is something he has inherited. However, there are histories[10] roughly contemporary with Ferdowsi's poem which deal with much the same material, and when we compare their treatment of particular incidents with Ferdowsi's we do notice a difference. The poet is clearly more interested in stories that emphasize moral heroism than are the historians, and a concomitant of this is that he lavishes attention on episodes that deal with inward conflict—whether it be conflict within Iran itself between different sources of power, within the royal family, or within a given hero's soul and conscience. He is also far more interested in something that approaches the Western notion of tragedy—the notion of noble souls ineluctably destroyed partly by flaws in their own characters and partly by external events over which they have no control. The tragic and ethical aspects of episodes are, in the writings of his historian near-contemporaries, firmly subordinated to dynastic and national concerns. In Ferdowsi's work, however, they often seem completely to take over the foreground of the poet's—and thus his audience's—consciousness, and the dynastic concerns, while

always present as a ground bass, become temporarily subordinate. In the Seyavash story the hero chooses to side with his country's enemy and his conscience rather than with his own country and what he sees as evil; his notion of the right is supranational, and while he does figure in the work of the historians it is only in Ferdowsi's poem, among extant texts, that the ethical, tragic and quasi-mystical implications of his decisions are explored with such earnestness and in such depth.

It is not normally to epic, among literary genres, that we look for psychological truth: the characters of epic tend to be types, icons, rather than individuals, and while we may feel that we 'know' Odysseus or Hector we do not expect the same psychological subtlety and intensity from their delineations as we do from the creations of, say, Henry James or Proust. In Ferdowsi too we can see a broad, rather than detailed, portrayal of character in most cases, and often the demands of plot will mean that a character's implied inward nature will shift slightly from episode to episode. A good example of this is the character of Sudabeh, Seyavash's stepmother: in the first episode in which she appears (when Kavus goes to her country in order to court her) she is portrayed as a loving, loyal consort; in the Seyavash episode she is a scheming hypocrite. It might be possible to construct a satisfactory psychological profile for her (e.g. her propensity to deceit is there from the beginning, as she deceives her father to save her husband), but it would probably be a wasted effort; her 'character' shifts as the course of the episodes in which she figures demands. Another example from our current story is the character of the king of Turan, Afrasyab: nowhere in the poem is he presented as ethically attractive; however, in the Seyavash episode he is much less unattractive than elsewhere in the poem and his attentive concern for Seyavash's safety is presented as genuine. This is clearly in order to contrast him with his brother Garsivaz and with king Kavus, who are the real villains of the piece.

But one way of recognizing Ferdowsi's particular interest in a character is, I would suggest, the way that he does in fact give him or her a psychological depth and reality beyond that which we expect from the personages of epic. We have already seen how the complex character of Kavus is treated with considerable consistency throughout the many episodes in which he figures. Arguably the same is true of the poem's most famous hero, Rostam, and Seyavash's is a startlingly plausible psychological portrait—as is perhaps appropriate for a character whose outward acts are so governed by inward, ethical preoccupations.

Seyavash's psychological reality is related to the theme of filicide and fatherly oppression that runs through the poem, in that he is presented as a character simultaneously in search of and in flight from his father. He is not brought up by his real father, Kavus, but by a surrogate father, Rostam; when he returns to Kavus's court he is not familiar with his father's true character (as the audience by this time is) and mistakenly trusts him when advised to visit

Sudabeh in the harem. When his conscience does rebel against his true father's advice (that the hostages from Turan be sent to the Persian court where they will be murdered), his instinct is to turn to his surrogate father, Rostam. But Rostam has been relieved of his command and is not available to the prince. Seyavash turns instead to Piran, the counsellor of Afrasyab, who advises him repeatedly to think of Afrasyab as a father, and Piran too is described as his father. Seyavash's progress can be seen as a turning from father-figure to father-figure (Kavus, Rostam, Piran, Afrasyab); as he is betrayed by his Iranian father Kavus, so he is betrayed by his Turanian 'father' Afrasyab; as the Iranian 'father' Rostam is absent when most needed, so the Turanian 'father' Piran is absent when most needed. His search for an adequate father who will both protect him and support him ethically is reflected in the overriding claims of his anguished superego, which demands absolute ethical integrity from him and finally leads him to trust the most potent but also most absent father of all, God—who, like his earthly fathers, proves unwilling or unable to prevent his death. If all this sounds far too twentieth-century and Western an interpretation, we should remember that Freud claimed to have discovered nothing new and that everything he had to offer was present in the works of the poets before him. Indeed it may well be that one of the characteristics of a great narrative poet is exactly this intuitive ability to reproduce and reveal psychologically compelling behaviour that appears to transcend cultural and temporal boundaries.

By the time one reaches the end of the Seyavash story, however, it is not perhaps the psychological aspect of it that has proved the most compelling. The story begins with the stuff of romance—a foreign girl of royal blood is found as a fugitive and is introduced into the king's harem. From this story-book beginning the tale turns realistic, particularly with the introduction of Sudabeh. She too, as a scheming stepmother, could be considered a figure from fairy-tale and romance, but her portrait has a fierce plausibility about it, largely because of the words she is given to speak, which establish her in the audience's mind as a potent, menacing reality. Seyavash's reactions to her and to his various 'fathers' continue this vein of realism, but it begins to dissolve with his trial by fire, and by the time he reaches Turan a strong supernatural element has taken over the tale. The emphasis shifts from the psychological to the 'spiritual' and supernatural, and this is particularly noticeable as soon as Seyavash has become established in Turan. He knows he is going to be killed unjustly, he prophesies the manner of his death and its results and he claims knowledge of the future and of God's will. The story becomes mythical rather than realistic, spiritual rather than psychological.

This mythical, spiritual side to the story was clearly a component from the beginning, or at least considerably preceded Ferdowsi's version. It is known that laments for the martyrdom of Seyavash were sung in central Asia before Ferdowsi ever put pen to paper, and such memorials have been performed up to the twentieth century in various parts of Iran. To an outsider the episode has strong similarities with the story of the martyrdom of Hosayn which is such a prominent feature of the beliefs of Shia Islam; in both cases a young and noble leader who is the hope of his people is cut down in his prime as a result of evil machinations against him; in both cases the victim is a symbol of triumph by martyrdom in that the future will vindicate the rights of the deceased. The shared emotional atmosphere of the two stories is a prominent feature of the Persian cultural experience and has had a lasting effect on Persian artistic expression.

A clue as to the possible mythical origins of the story may be found in the imagery Ferdowsi employs in his version. Like many epic writers, Ferdowsi is not a poet who particularly delights in startling or original imagery, and most of his tropes are formulae distributed apparently haphazardly throughout the poem as a whole. But the Seyavash episode is something of an exception to this rule, unified as it is by a series of images that run throughout the whole tale and which are rare elsewhere in the poem. The images are those of fire and water and, in particular, of fire and water as challenges to the hero. The most famous episode of the story, and the one that most attracted the miniaturists who embellished later manuscripts of *The Shahnameh*, is Seyavash's trial by fire after Sudabeh accuses him of the attempt on her chastity. But the trope occurs with some regularity throughout the whole tale; shortly before his death Seyavash dreams of being caught between fire and water; when Piran dreams of the birth of Kay Khosrow, Seyavash's son, the image is of a candle being lit from the sun; when Garsivaz deceitfully promises to help Seyavash he says he will put out the king's fire of wrath by the water of his advice. The reader will notice other examples of the image. Most interesting is the way the two elements are often associated, even when this can only be done by some contortion. A telling example of this is the description given of Seyavash's clothes when he emerges from the trial by fire unscathed: it is said that if the fire he had passed through had been water, his clothes would not have been wet. It may be that this rather peculiar image is a trace indicating that there were—at some point in the preliterate development of the story—two trials, one by fire and one by water. There is in any case a passage through water later in the poem: in the same way that Seyavash passes through fire after the attempt on his sexual integrity by Sudabeh, he passes through water (when he crosses the Oxus to enter the territory of Turan) after the attempt on his military integrity by his father (when ordered to hand over the hostages to their deaths). The story appears in origin to be one involving rites of passage, symbolized by passing through fire and water, to a higher spiritual state, culminating in the destruction of the body and the triumph of the spirit, the latter symbolized by the new generation as embodied in the hero's son, the unworldly Khosrow. The importance of fire and water in the beliefs of Zoroastrianism cannot be discounted here, but the story seems to refer back to an even more 'universal', perhaps shamanistic, period in which heroes representing the growth of the human soul in spiritual awareness are put to ritual spiritual and physical tests.

The Shahnameh has been known to the West, at least by name, since the seventeenth century, but it was only with the late-eighteenth-century orientalist Sir William Jones[11] that the poem was seriously read and studied in the West. Jones translated parts of the poem into Latin and planned a tragedy based on the Sohrab and Rostam episode. A verse translation of some episodes (into heroic couplets) was made by Joseph Champion in the late eighteenth century, and another into the same medium by James Atkinson in the early nineteenth (Atkinson also produced a shortened prose version of the entire mythological and legendary sections of the poem, ending with the appearance of Eskandar). Editions were produced first in Calcutta (where Jones had been a judge) and then in Leyden, and the first attempt at a complete translation into a European language was that by the German orientalist, Mohl. Mohl was an acquaintance of the Goncourt brothers and was resident in Paris in the middle years of the nineteenth century.[12] His (prose) translation was into French and was printed *en face* with his edition of the poem, which was not superseded until well into this century. Though modern scholarship has considerably revised Mohl's view of the text, and though a few errors can be found in his translation, his work is a quite remarkable monument of scholarship considering the limited materials at his disposal. His translation, which is vigorous and frequently provides very persuasive solutions to difficult parts of the text, can still be consulted with great profit.

A complete verse translation into Italian was made by Pizzi in the late nineteenth century. Pizzi's version was in 'versi sciolti', unrhymed hendecasyllabics, the Italian equivalent of blank verse, and in the Edwardian period a blank verse translation of the whole poem into English was begun by George and Edmond Warner, to be finally completed in 1925. It is perhaps unfortunate that this version can legitimately be called a 'Warner Brothers' epic, as it well lives up to the negative connotations the phrase suggests, though there are fine compensating moments in among the Edwardian Wardour Street diction. The most recent (prose) translation which covers the whole poem (though only by omitting considerable portions of it, including more than half of the Seyavash episode) is that by Reuben Levy, first published in 1967. Levy's view of the poem seems to have been that it was essentially a work about military prowess and kingly glory and, from the point of view of the themes prominent in the Seyavash episode, his translation has little to recommend it. Its advantage, however, is that it does take the reader from **The Shahnameh**'s beginning to its end, but Levy had an almost unerring instinct for missing out the most interesting parts of the poem. The most recent, and easily the most attractive, verse translation of any part of the poem is Jerome Clinton's version of the Sohrab and Rostam story (1987).

Atkinson's and Champion's verse versions are in heroic couplets, the Warners' and Clinton's in blank verse. After some hesitation I have chosen blank verse as the medium for the translation which follows. My hesitation came from the fact that **The Shahnameh** in the original is written in couplets that correspond fairly closely in length to the English heroic couplet, which would therefore seem to be an obvious form to use for the translation of the poem. Another perhaps irrelevant but nevertheless beguiling consideration was the fact that out of all Western authors, Ferdowsi most often sounds like Racine. It is true that there are vast differences—the compactness and relentless focus of Racine are largely absent from Ferdowsi—but Ferdowsi's interest in anguished conflicts of duty and passion and his brilliant handling of the rhetorical tirade can feel extremely Racinian to a Western reader. It was tempting to imagine Sudabeh's or Afrasyab's speeches in some kind of English equivalent of the Racinian couplet. I was swayed, however, by the fact that the relatively little heroic verse there is in English is usually in blank verse and that the heroic couplet has, in this language, traditionally been reserved for romance, social comment or satire—it has become for us a homely and immediate, or comforting and charming, medium. Despite the great rhymed versions by Pope and Dryden of Homer and Virgil, attempts at the spaciousness and sublimity of epic have traditionally been made in blank verse, and it is perhaps worth remembering that blank verse was expressly invented—by Surrey—for the translation of epic into English. (The numbering of the lines does not correspond to the Persian original text; it is simply intended to help the reader refer to parts of the poem more easily. The subheadings were probably inserted by early copyists and not by Ferdowsi, which may explain why they do not appear consistently throughout the text.)

In preparing this translation my main authority has been the recent edition of the text of the story edited by Mojtaba Minovi (Tehran, 1984); I have also on occasion consulted the Moscow edition of the complete poem (eds. Bertel's *et al.*, Moscow, 1966-71) and Mohl's edition (reprinted Paris, 1976). My translation was unfortunately completed before I was able to consult the new edition of the Seyavash portion of the text edited by Khaleghi-Motlagh. Of previous translations I have found the most useful to be Mohl's, followed by that of George and Edmond Warner, though the texts used by both often differ considerably from recent recensions. I have also at times had reference to the Arabic translation of the poem by Bondari. As this translation precedes by over a hundred years all extant Persian language manuscripts of the poem and seems to be based on a very conservative text, it has often been used by scholars as an arbiter between rival versions in Persian manuscripts. . . .

Notes

1. '*i Persiani attuali lo considerano il simbolo dell'iranismo, il padre della patria*' (*Letteratura persiana*, Milan, 1960, p. 589)

2. Whether the name 'Iran' or 'Persia' should be used is a question that can arouse considerable anger. The Western usage of Iran stems from the decree by Reza

Shah in 1935 that this (the name of the country in Persian) was how the country was to be known: until then, the English name had always been Persia. The egregious ignorance demonstrated by this attempt to tell other people how to speak their own languages ('Persia' is a word in the English language just as 'Alman' [Germany] and 'Lahestan' [Poland] are words in the Persian language) may have been deplorable, nevertheless it has had its effect and 'Iran' is now almost universally used. In the translation of *Seyavash* I have on the whole used 'Iran' and 'Iranian' though occasionally I give 'Persia' and 'Persian' (as a translator of Homer might use both 'Hellas/Hellenic' and 'Greece/Greek').

3. Some one thousand lines are by Ferdowsi's predecessor Daqiqi: Ferdowsi took over the task of writing the poem when Daqiqi was murdered by a slave. Daqiqi had begun *in medias res* (with the advent of Zoroastrianism), but Ferdowsi begins at the beginning, with the creation of the world. Daqiqi's portion is therefore an episode embedded in the middle of what is overwhelmingly Ferdowsi's poem.

4. If this name looks vaguely familiar to a Western reader, it is probably because of Puccini's *Turandot*, a word which is a corruption of the Persian '*turandokht*', meaning 'girl (princess) of Turan', Turan being central Asia.

5. Perhaps because of Arnold's poem this has been the most frequently translated episode of *The Shahnameh*. The best English translation is that by Jerome Clinton (University of Washington Press, Seattle, 1987).

6. Kavus is succeeded by his grandson Khosrow. However, for most of Khosrow's 'reign' Kavus is still alive and Khosrow refers back to him as the ultimate authority. When Kavus dies Khosrow is crowned again, as if confirming that it is only then that he does really become king, and a couple of lines later he announces his intention to abdicate. If we count Kavus's reign as lasting till his death, Ferdowsi gives him more space than any other king; if we count it only until Khosrow becomes regent, he is still one of the most extensively treated kings of the poem.

7. e.g. the stories of Zahhak and Kaveh; Kavus, Rostam and Sohrab; Goshtasp, Rostam and Esfandyar.

8. It is unfortunate for a modern audience that the only significant female character in the Seyavash episode is Sudabeh, who is a lustful, scheming and vindictive stepmother. Though *The Shahnameh*, as an epic poem, records a primarily male world, it does, in fact, include very sympathetic portraits of women—in particular Manizheh and Gordiyeh, both of whom display loyalty and heroism when the menfolk who might be expected to display such virtues fail. The Turanian princess Manizheh defies Afrasyab to protect her Iranian lover Bizhan, keeping him alive when Afrasyab has him thrown into a dark well, and she has become for Persian myth the archetype of loyalty

in adversity. Gordiyeh opposes her brother Bahram Chubineh in his attempt to wrest the Iranian throne from the legitimate heir Khosrow Parviz, and her spirited speeches in defence of the poem's epic values are among the most moving and eloquent in the whole work.

9. A closer parallel for Ferdowsi and his original Islamic audience would be the story of Yusuf and Zuleikha from the Koran (Joseph and Potiphar's wife in the Bible); again an attempt is made on the chastity of a young man seen as a spiritual hero/victim, and when her overtures are rejected the scorned woman accuses the young man before her husband of having tried to seduce/rape her. Interestingly enough, there is an eleventh-century Persian poem on the Yusuf and Zuleikha story which used to be ascribed to Ferdowsi, though scholars now reject the attribution: it may be that it was its broad similarity to parts of Ferdowsi's treatment of the Seyavash story that led to the ascription in the first place.

10. Specifically the Histories of Tabari (about a century before Ferdowsi's work, and therefore available to him as a source) and of Tha'alebi (about fifty years after Ferdowsi's work).

11. 'Persian Jones', as he was called, author of the first Persian grammar in English (1771) and the first man to suggest the existence of the Indo-European family of languages including Latin, Greek, Persian and Sanskrit—the intuition that such a relationship existed is said to have come to him while reading *The Shahnameh*.

12. It was largely from Mohl's French version that Matthew Arnold learnt of the Sohrab and Rostam story, though he seems also to have known Atkinson's version.

Olga M. Davidson (essay date 1994)

SOURCE: "Ferdowsi's Oral Poetic Heritage," in *Poet and Hero in the Persian "Book of Kings,"* Cornell University Press, 1994, pp. 58-72.

[*In the essay below, Davidson analyzes the oral tradition from which Ferdowsi drew the* Shah-Nama *and in which the text figured as a recitation piece. Davidson contends that the* Shah-Nama *was shaped by the creativity of its oral tradition.*]

The composite picture of an assembly of *mōbad*s, whose coming together literally constitutes Ferdowsi's "source-book" by way of their collective recitation, can be supplemented by individual pictures, recurring throughout the *Shāhnāma*, of individual recitation. Here too, as in the composite picture, the idea of an archetypal book can be combined with the idea of performance, wherever Ferdowsi claims that he heard a given story from a reciter, who in turn got it from an "ancient book": . . .

Now, O aged singer,
What did the book of the Truthful
     say
return to the time of the Ash-
     kanians.
that the reciter recollected from an-
     cient times?

VII 115.46-47

In one case, the reciter is described as having special affinities not only with the archetypal book but also with the
family of the main hero of the *Shāhnāma,* Rostam. The
hero Sām, Rostam's grandfather, is described as an ancestor of the family of the reciter himself, so that the source
of the oral tradition, the performer, is directly linked to the
subject of that same tradition, the hero: . . .

There was an old man whose name
     was Āzādsarv,
His heart was full of wisdom, his
     head full of words,
Who had the Book of Kings,
He traced his ancestry back to Sām,
     son of Narimān
I will now say what I found out
     from him;
If I remain in this fleeting world,
I will finish this ancient book
who was in Marv with Ahmad son
     of Sahl.
and his speech full of ancient tradi-
     tions.
who had the images and portraits of
     *pahlavān*s.
and knew much about the battles of
     Rostam.
I will weave the words together,
     one to another.
and if my soul and intellect guide
     me,
and leave to this world a story.

VI 322.1-7

With reference to the second of these two examples, it has
been argued on chronological grounds that Ferdowsi could
not actually have heard his predecessor perform epic.[1] We
have already seen, however, that the medium of performance, as an authority, is just as stylized in the *Shāhnāma*
as is the medium of the book. What is essential, therefore,
in the reference to Āzādsarv is that his authority is envis-
aged as a performance that was heard, just as any living
oral performance can be heard. Such a stylized reference
to authority, then, affirms that the medium of performance
is intrinsic to Ferdowsi's own poetry, which presents itself
as part of a continuum in oral tradition.[2]

The point remains that the Book of Kings, where it is described as the possession of a performer heard by Ferdowsi, is a visible sign of that performer's authority, parallel with other visible signs such as an ancestry actually
shared with the lineage of a principal hero. The final authority is not in the book itself but in the actual *perfor-*

mance of the poem. Even the preface of the prose *Shāh-
nāma* acknowledges the authoritativeness of performance,
which is then immediately tied in with the concept of
"book."

Whatever we discuss of this book must be told from
statements of the *dehqān*s, for this kingdom was in
their hands and they know the affairs and proceedings,
whether good or bad, and whether more or less. Therefore we must go by what they say. Consequently, whatever we learn concerning them has been collected from
their books.[3]

Till recent times, in fact, the *Shāhnāma* has survived by
way of performance in oral tradition—albeit indirectly,
since it has assumed the format of prose. Mary Ellen Page
has made a study of the professional storytelling, *naqqāli*,
of the *Shāhnāma* as it is performed in the Iran of recent
times.[4] The word for the professional storyteller is *naqqāl*,
meaning literally 'transmitter'.[5] Granted, the format of this
transmission of the *Shāhnāma* is prose, but the ubiquitous
conceit of the *naqqāl* is that he is indeed performing Ferdowsi's *Shāhnāma*.[6]

The traditional social context for such performances was a
setting of coffee- and tea-houses. Adam Olearius describes
such a coffee-house in his account, dated A.D. 1631-32, of
the main square in Isfahan.

Kahweh chane is ein Krug in welchem die Taback-
schmäucher und *Kahweh* Wassertrincker sich finden
lassen. In solchen drenen Kruegen finden sich auch Po-
eten und Historici welche ich mitten im Gemache auff
hohen Stuelen sitzen gesehen und allerhand Historien
Fabeln und erdichtete Dinge erzehlenhoeren. Im erze-
hlen phantasiren sie wie mit einem Stoecklein gleich
die so aus der Taschen spielen.

The coffee-house is an inn in which smokers of to-
bacco and drinkers of coffee-water are found. In such
inns are also found poets and historians whom I have
seen sitting inside on high stools and have heard telling
all manner of legends, fables, poeticized things. While
narrating they conjure up images by gestures with a
little wand, much as magicians play tricks.[7]

A typical performance by a *naqqāl* lasts for about ninety
minutes.[8] He uses a *tumār* 'prompt-book' which contains
highly compressed thematic summaries of his own repertoire. A study of such a *tumār* shows that it is not a text to
be adhered to but rather a skeletal outline of a story—a
story that the *naqqāl* may expand or compress, even shift
around with variations of theme; the decision is up to the
performer, whose primary need is to keep his hold over
the audience.[9] The *tumār*s of different *naqqāl*s covering a
parallel stretch of narrative vary in much the same way.[10]
The *naqqāl* can of course diverge from his *tumār* as he or
his audience wishes.[11]

There are of course profound variations between Ferdowsi's verse *Shāhnāma* and the prose retellings of the *Shāh-
nāma* tradition. For example, whereas the reign of Bahman
is covered in about two hundred distichs in Ferdowsi's

Shāhnāma, it takes up forty-eight pages in one *naqqāl's tumār* and roughly a month's length of actual retelling in successive daily performances.[12] Yet the conceit of the *naqqāl,* as we have noted, is that he is indeed performing the *Shāhnāma* of Ferdowsi.

There is a comparable conceit among the South Slavic poets, the *guslars* studied by Parry and Lord. The *guslar* will say that he performs the song that he has learned exactly as it has always been performed. For example, Lord quotes from an interview with the *guslar* Suleyman Makić:

> *Interviewer:* "Could you still pick up a song today?"
>
> *Suleyman:* "I could."
>
> *I:* "For example, if you heard me sing a song, let's say, could you pick it up right away?"
>
> *S:* "Yes, I could sing it for you right away the next day."
>
> *I:* "If you were to hear it just once?"
>
> *S:* "Yes, by Allah, if I were to hear it once to the *gusle.*"
>
> *I:* "Why not until the next day? . . . What do you think about in those two days? Isn't it better to sing it right away than later, when you might forget it after so long a time?"
>
> *S:* "It has to come to one. One has to think . . . how it goes, and then little by little it comes to him, so that he won't leave anything out. . . . One couldn't sing it like that all the way right away."
>
> *I:* "Why couldn't you, when it is possible the second or third day afterwards?"
>
> *S:* "Anybody who can't write can't do it."
>
> *I:* "All right, but when you've learned my song would . . . you sing it exactly as I do?"
>
> *S:* "I would."
>
> *I:* "You wouldn't add anything . . . nor leave anything out?"
>
> *S:* "I wouldn't . . . by Allah I would sing it just as I heard it. . . . It isn't good to change or add."[13]

This conceit notwithstanding, the fieldwork of Parry and Lord has established that no two performances, even of the "same" song by the same *guslar,* are ever identical.

In the case of Persian poetic traditions, it is important to note that the narratives of Ferdowsi and of any given *naqqāl* can converge point-for-point—as well as diverge. And such thematic convergences between Ferdowsi and a *naqqāl* are in effect no different from the convergences between any two different *naqqāls.* It is as if Ferdowsi too were a *naqqāl*—the definitive *naqqāl*—of the *Shāhnāma* tradition.[14]

Occasionally a *naqqāl* will recite some of Ferdowsi's actual verses.[15] Again this may be a matter of convergence, not derivation. After all, there can be found, in a given *naqqāl's tumār,* verses in *mutaqārib* meter that are not

even attested in the canonical version of Ferdowsi's *Shāhnāma.*[16] In fact, when the *naqqāl* introduces his story, he can use rhymed prose or a combination of poetry and rhymed prose,[17] and sometimes there is even a melody.[18] Thus the traditional format of a *naqqāl's* introduction may reveal vestigial aspects of an earlier stage in the art-form of the *naqqāl* when his medium was indeed all poetry.[19]

But the crucial indication of the *naqqāl's* independence from Ferdowsi's *Shāhnāma* lies in the fact that there is much narrative material attested in the *naqqāl's* oral traditions that is not attested in any of the literary epics so far known.[20] Many of the themes found in later literary epics such as the *Garshāspnāma* appear as an integral part of the *naqqāl's* narrative repertoire.[21] For example, the Garshāsp stories will be included in the *naqqāl's* story-line where it would have been chronologically appropriate for the *Shāhnāma* to include it. Nöldeke condemns these later epics as not folklore but invention: "It is a common opinion that a great deal of popular epic has been preserved in those poems. It might sound a little bold if I flatly deny that and declare the contents of those narratives to be essentially a free fancy of the respective authors."[22] Similarly, Mohl claims that the epics after Ferdowsi's *Shāhnāma* are not only artless but also simply a matter of filling in lacunae left by Ferdowsi, with no pride in authorship.[23] There can only be a limited number of ultimate poets, however, and what is worthy of special note is the sheer mass of poetic compositions that deal with material beyond Ferdowsi and which usually take a verse from Ferdowsi as a point of departure.

These considerations bring us to one of the major problems confronting the "scientific method" of editing Ferdowsi's *Shāhnāma.* The manuscripts seem to be full of "interpolations," sometimes massive ones, from other literary epics; at other times it is impossible to establish the provenience of the "interpolation." But it can now be seen, from the perspective of studies centering on the *naqqāl* traditions of the *Shāhnāma,* that such interpolations may correspond to actual conventions of *performance.* In other words, the divergences of manuscripts in this regard may be parallel to divergences in performance, since the *tumār* allows the *naqqāl* to expand or compress during any performance in patterns of thematic variations that are clearly parallel to those of the manuscripts. And, as noted, the *naqqāl* can diverge from his *tumār.*

Thus the *Shāhnāma* tradition has survived till recent times, albeit indirectly, as a medium still dynamic, still alive. It could theoretically generate an infinite number of performances—provided that the *naqqāl* is still there to perform and the audience is there to listen. In this light, we may call into doubt the theory that there were gaps in the story-line of the Book of Kings—gaps that had to be filled with Ferdowsi's "Phantasie."[24] From what we can see even from the *naqqāl* traditions, there was a seemingly endless reservoir of narrative traditions standing ready to be filled in at any point in the retelling of the Book of Kings. And just as the *naqqāl* testifies that he is indeed performing

Ferdowsi's **Shāhnāma,** so also Ferdowsi himself testifies that he is "translating" the Pahlavi Book of Kings.

After comparing what the poem says about itself with the external evidence about Middle and New Persian poetry, we may now isolate characteristics of oral poetry as formulated in current scholarship. The fieldwork on oral poetics by Parry and Lord corroborated Parry's earlier work on the crystallized traditions of ancient Greek epic as they survived in the Homeric *Iliad* and *Odyssey.* For our present purposes, the most important aspect of the findings of Parry and Lord is their observation that the formal building blocks of oral poetry consists of what they call *formulas.*

Parry's working definition of the formula had been as follows: "A group of words which is regularly employed under the same metrical conditions to express a given essential idea."[25] This definition, devised by Parry on the basis of his work on Homeric poetry, before he even started work on the living poetry of the South Slavic tradition, has proved enduring despite the need of one small adjustment. Ironically, this adjustment has been prompted at least partly by the evidence of Homeric poetry itself: it has recently been shown that the metrical conditions of the formula can vary, although this variation itself is systematic.[26] Thus it may be useful to revise the phrase "under the same metrical conditions" to read instead "under fixed metrical conditions." The phrase "to express a given essential idea" is crucial, since this aspect of Parry's definition has often been undervalued or even missed altogether. It is important to stress that, for Parry, the formula is not simply a phrase that is repeated for its metrical utility.[27] Rather, the formula is the expression of a traditional *theme.* To quote Parry, "The formulas in any poetry are due, so far as their ideas go, to the theme, their rhythm is fixed by the verse-form, but their art is that of the poets who made them and of the poets who kept them."[28] The word "theme," according to Lord's working definition is "a subject unit, a group of ideas, regularly employed by the singer, not merely in any given poem, but in the poetry as a whole."[29] In other words, the Parry-Lord definition of oral poetry is founded on the proposition that the traditional formula is a direct expression of the traditional theme; in oral poetry, there is a formulaic *system* that corresponds to a thematic *system.*[30]

In a 1977 book by Ruth Finnegan, however, which purports to present the overall subject of oral poetry to the general reader, this basic aspect of the Parry-Lord definition of the formula goes unmentioned.[31] She consistently treats formula as if it were merely a repeated phrase, repeated simply for its metrical utility. In discussing Homeric epithets, for example, she writes that they "are often combined with other formulaic phrases—repeated word-groups—which have the right metrical qualities to fit the [given] part of the line."[32] In the same context, she quotes Parry for support: "In composing [the poet] will do no more than put together for his needs phrases which he has often heard or used himself, and which, grouping them-

selves *in accordance with a fixed pattern of thought* [emphasis mine], come naturally to make the sentence and the verse."[33] We see here that Parry is saying much more than Finnegan, however; the formula is not just a phrase that the poet is free to choose according to his metrical needs,[34] since the formulas are regulated by the traditional themes of the poet's composition. By contrast, Finnegan seems to assume that *formulas* and *themes* are separate ingredients in the poet's repertoire: "*As well as* formulaic phrases and sequences [emphasis mine], the bard has in his repertoire a number of set themes which he can draw on to form the structure of his poem."[35] Working on the assumption that formulas are simply stock phrases repeated to fill metrical needs, Finnegan offers the following criticism of the Parry-Lord theory of oral poetry: "Does it really add to our understanding of the style or process of composition in a given piece to name certain repeated patterns of words, sounds or meanings as 'formulae'? Or to suggest that the characteristic of oral style is that such formulae are 'all-pervasive' (as in Lord 1960, p. 47)?"[36] In light of what I have adduced from the writings of Parry and Lord, I find this criticism unfounded; if the formula is the building-block of a system of traditional oral poetic expression, then I cannot find fault with Lord's observation that the formulas are "all-pervasive" in oral poetry.

Another important point of disagreement between Finnegan and Lord is her insistence that, on the basis of what we know of oral poetry in such cultures as that of the Bantu of South Africa (both Zulu and !Xhosa), the oral poet can both *compose* poetry and *write it down.*[37] It is tempting, of course, to extend such findings to medieval European poetry, where the fundamentals of what is freely acknowledged as oral poetry are preserved and transmitted by *literati* in the context of a vigorous scribal tradition. Finnegan's point of contention with Lord provides ammunition for medievalists who have argued that an Old English poem like the *Beowulf* cannot be considered oral poetry on the basis of the formulas that we find as its building-blocks, simply because we can find comparable levels of formulaic behavior in other Old English poems which were clearly written compositions and some of which were even translations from Latin originals. As one expert concludes, "To prove that an Old English poem is formulaic is only to prove that it is an Old English poem, and to show that such work has high or low percentage of formulas reveals nothing about whether or not it is literate composition, though it may tell us something about the skill with which a particular poet uses tradition."[38]

An important challenge to such a position has been proposed by Michael Zwettler: applying the work of the medievalist H. J. Chaytor,[39] Zwettler suggests that, even when an Old English poem is written down, it is not meant to be read by an individual but performed before an audience.[40] In other words, as Zwettler points out, there is no such thing as an "audience of readers" in medieval European poetry.[41] To quote Chaytor: "The whole technique . . . presupposed . . . a hearing, not reading public."[42] The rules of this poetry, written or not, are those of oral poetry.

Zwettler extends this principle to pre-Islamic Arabic poetry, and I for my part hope to extend it here to the New Persian poetry of Ferdowsi. So long as I can argue that the building-blocks of his *Shāhnāma* are functional formulas, I can also argue that his poetry is based on the rules of oral poetry.

In the appendix to this book, using as a test case a randomly selected passage, I show that every word in this given passage can be generated on the basis of parallel phraseology expressing parallel themes. The degree of regularity and economy[43] in the arrangement of phraseology is clearly suggestive of formulaic language. Moreover, the regularity extends to the actual variation of phraseology. This factor may well be an important additional clue to the formulaic nature of Ferdowsi's *Shāhnāma.* As Parry and Lord had noticed in their South Slavic fieldwork *each new performance/recomposition of a song involved variation in the deployment of formulas.* This principle has been applied successfully by Michael Zwettler in his study of classical Arabic poetry.[44] He extends the observations of the Romance philologist Ramón Menéndez-Pidal, who has drawn attention to the fact that three of the earliest manuscript versions of the *Chanson de Roland* do not share a single identical verse with each other.[45] He had inferred from this and other such facts that this kind of poetry, which Zwettler rightly equates with oral poetry, is "a poetry that lives through variants."[46] "How ironic," Zwettler writes, "that scholars of Arabic poetry have so often cast doubt upon the 'authenticity' or 'genuineness' of this or that verse, poem, or body of poems, or, sometimes, of pre-Islamic poetry in general, because they have found it impossible to establish an 'original version'."[47] The same irony, as we shall see, applies to scholars of Persian poetry. Zwettler goes on to say that

> the multiplicity of variants and attributions and of formulaic phrases and elements attested for the great majority of classical Arabic poems may undermine our confidence in ever establishing an "author's original version"—as indeed it should! But they ought to convince us that we do have voluminous record of a genuine and on-going oral poetic tradition (even if in its latest stages), such as no other nation can match in breadth of content and scrupulosity of collection and documentation.[48]

The conscientiousness of those who preserved all these variants in their editions is a reflection of an attitude that we also witness in the context of Islamic oral transmission, or *hadīth,* and Zwettler insists that the editors' quest for authenticity by way of examining and collecting all variants was due not so much to any need of determining the author but to the desire of recovering the authentic poetic traditions of Bedouin poetry.[49]

An analogous principle of variation, I propose, can also be applied to the text tradition of the *Shāhnāma.*[50] A systematic and exhaustive application, of course, is at this point impossible, since there is no available centralized collection of all the variants as could be collected from the entire textual tradition. Such a collection would be a monumental task indeed. Still, the limited experiment of formulaic analysis that I present in the appendix illustrates the principle of compositional variation as reflected by textual variation. The examples could be multiplied by the hundreds, even thousands, and by then we would start to see clearly that there are legitimate formulaic variants attested for vast portions of the *Shāhnāma.* We may postpone for later any questions about how these considerations may affect our evaluation of the standard Moscow edition. What is important is that even a preliminary test reveals such patterns of variation in the text of the *Shāhnāma*—the surest available sign that we are dealing with the heritage of oral poetry.

We must note, however, an essential difference between the patterns of variation in the textual tradition of the *Shāhnāma,* as revealed by its textual transmission, and in the Arabic poetry studied by Zwettler. In the case of the Arabic evidence, the variants seem to have been collected *while* the given poem was evolving into a fixed text in the process of continual performance/recomposition. In the case of the *Shāhnāma,* on the other hand, the variants seem to have gone on accumulating even *after* the composition had become a fixed text by way of writing. This fact alone suggests that, side by side with the written transmission of the text, the oral transmission of poetry continued as well. Each new performance must have entailed recomposition, and the oral poetry must have continually influenced the text.

This means that we cannot reconstruct with any absolute certainty the original composition of Ferdowsi, because of its susceptibility to recomposition with each new performance in a living oral tradition. All we can say about the original is that, if it is capable of being recomposed, it too must be a product of oral composition. And the continual recomposition on the level of form was matched by recomposition on the level of content, leading to new accretions that are anachronistic to the patterns of earlier layers.[51] We may even compare the accretion of Muslim elements in the Arab pre-Islamic poetic traditions studied by Zwettler:

> We must consider the alleged "inconsistencies," "anachronisms" and "Islamic emendations" that do crop up in our received texts and have so frequently been adduced as proof of the "corruption" of the tradition. Such phenomena as the introduction of post-Islamic expressions or neologisms into archaic poems, elimination of pagan theophoric names or substitution of the name *Allāh,* allusions to Qur'ānic passages or Islamic concepts or rituals, and so on, can all legitimately be seen as a natural result of the circumstance that versions of those poems were derived from oral renditions performed by Muslim renderants conditioned now to the sensibilities of Muslim audiences.[52]

Similarly, we find the accretion and eventual dominance of Shī'ite elements in the poetry of Ferdowsi, which seems to show traces of an earlier Sunni patronage.[53] But even if we cannot reconstruct the original composition, its authority or authenticity as tradition could survive the countless accretions and reshapings of each recomposition in performance. That is the true nature of oral poetry.

Let us imagine going back in time to a point where the oral tradition of the *Shāhnāma* was still in *mutaqārib* verse. At such a point, the formal and thematic variations of performance/composition in oral poetry would surely have affected the manuscript tradition of Ferdowsi's *Shāhnāma*. Even as late as in the era of Bāysonghor Mirza (died A.D. 1433), it seems that no definitive edition was possible, because the extant manuscripts were clearly no better than *tumārs* would be in recent times for the purpose of deciding what is definitive and what is not. The song must have existed in performance. Even though Nöldeke yearns for the attestation of the original "critically revised" copy of the *Shāhnāma* commissioned by Bāysonghor in A.D. 1425,[54] he realizes that he would be disappointed if it suddenly came to light: "How," he asks, "could the Persian bel-esprit in those times—only such can be thought of, if it were not simply copyists—have managed to accomplish a great and purely philological work somewhat critically?"[55] The point is, if no copy could be definitive and preemptive even as late as 1425, it may be that each copy was, at least in part, a reflection of traditions in *performance.*

Nöldeke says that redactors in the era of Bāysonghor could not be "scientific" about consulting other manuscripts, for they had no Aristophanes, no Zenodotus, no Aristarchus in the Timurid court.[56] The princely libraries were full of manuscripts of the *Shāhnāma* such as the one described as "a fine looking, beautifully written, and very defective copy" (to quote from a contemporary evaluation).[57] How, we may ask, were such copies of the *Shāhnāma* "defective"? Is there a trace here of a contemptuous attitude on the part of those better versed than others in the performance of poetry? In Nöldeke's own words, there exists no "final touch" for Ferdowsi's *Shāhnāma.*[58]

As if to console himself, Nöldeke adds: "We are not really worse off than with the text of Homer."[59] But the Homeric analogy in fact leads back to the factor of performance in the constitution of the text of any poetry that is built on an oral tradition. Since Nöldeke's days, new discoveries have emerged about the factor of performance as it affects the canonical text of Homer. It now appears that even the Homeric text is replete with variants that are to be attributed not to textual inconsistencies but rather to actual formulaic alternatives.[60] So also with the textual tradition of Ferdowsi's *Shāhnāma* in its present form: as even Nöldeke concedes, it is replete with "various genuine versions" of given passages.[61] In other words, a given passage may have two or more textual variants that are not a matter of one genuine reading and one or more corrupt or interpolated readings, but rather of two or more traditional alternatives, either or any of which would be acceptable to the discerning audience of Ferdowsi's *Shāhnāma.*

It is now possible to imagine how Ferdowsi's *Shāhnāma* could survive and prevail, albeit with accretions and modi-

fications, if we allow that everything in it is traditional. In his own lifetime, Mohl had an ever-growing intuition that Ferdowsi invented nothing, and he says so most forcefully: "The more one studies the work of Ferdowsi, the more one is convinced, I believe, that he invented nothing and that he was content to restore in brilliant hues the traditions that formed the popular stories of Persia."[62]

For Ferdowsi, the writing down of his composition would make permanent his appropriation of living poetic traditions. For a typical oral poet, by contrast, appropriation could ordinarily be achieved only in the context of performance. But even if Ferdowsi's book, *his* Book of Kings, constitutes a more lasting way of establishing appropriation of his composition, it is nevertheless not a frozen text, like some Pahlavi book. To put it schematically, we could say that the survival of Ferdowsi's *Shāhnāma* depends not so much on the writing down of the composition as on the Persian nation's general approval of the writing down of the performance of the composition. And the approval of Persian audiences through the ages could happen only if the *Shāhnāma* were traditional, that is, if it conformed to the rules of composition-in-performance. It could even be claimed that the survival of the *Shāhnāma,* in the context of countless performances for countless audiences steeped in oral poetry, is the best argument for its own essence as oral poetry. It is also, of course, the best argument against the notion that the poetic form and overall content of the *Shāhnāma* were in any sense an invention of Ferdowsi.

If, however, we accept the idea that the medium of the *Shāhnāma* is that of traditional oral poetry, we should expect that it will be subject to accretions and modifications in the context of each new performance. Thus the recording of an original composition by Ferdowsi, in the process of its textual transmission, would be continually subject to interference from the concurrent process of oral transmission in performance, since each performance in oral poetry entails recomposition. Thus the *Shāhnāma* really could not ever become a completely fixed text until the oral tradition died altogether. The manuscripts of the *Shāhnāma* seem to reflect a period when oral poetry had not yet died, so that editors are left to struggle with the textual variants that are not just a matter of textual transmission. As we have seen, it seems that some variants are also a matter of oral transmission.

The archetypal fixed text of Ferdowsi's *Shāhnāma* can never be recreated, since it would be impossible to decide in any given instance which of, say, two "genuine" variants was actually composed by Ferdowsi. To understand the full creative range of the *Shāhnāma* tradition, it would be more important to have an edition that lists all variants, since many of these will be a matter of *composition/ performance,* not *text.*

If indeed textual variants arise from the perpetuation of the *Shāhnāma* in performance, we need just the opposite of the so-called critical Moscow edition (1960-1971) of Y.

E. Bertels and his colleagues.[63] This edition strips Ferdow-si's **Shāhnāma** to its bare bones (50,000-odd distichs), selecting variants essentially on textual grounds by comparing "superior" and "inferior" manuscripts. It is based essentially on five manuscripts:

(1) L. = ms. Add. Or. 21103 of the British Museum, London, dated A.D. 1276, the oldest extant ms. at the time that the work on the Moscow edition was proceeding; contains the preface of Abu Mansur.

(2) I = ms. 329 of the National Public Library of St. Petersburg, dated A.D. 1333 and the second oldest ms. after L.

(3) IV = ms. S.1654 of the Oriental Institute of the Academy of Sciences, St. Petersburg, dated A.D. 1445; contains the preface of Abu Mansur.

(4) VI = ms. S.822 of the Oriental Institute of the Academy of Sciences, St. Petersburg, dated A.D. 1450.

(5) K = ms. S.40 of the Dār al-Kutub al-Misrīya, Cairo, dated A.D. 1394,[64] utilized only in volumes IV-IX of the Moscow edition; contains the preface of Abu Mansur.

In view of the fact that there are about 500 extant manuscripts of Ferdowsi's **Shāhnāma,**[65] and especially in view of all the variations in manuscript readings, the restriction of the editorial field of vision to five manuscripts is a bold move indeed. The Moscow editors' confidence in this particular 1 percent of manuscript evidence was based primarily on two facts: that this particular manuscript family was singularly old and that this family inherits the "older preface," that is, the preface of Abu Mansur.

But we have already seen that the "older" preface of Abu Mansur, no matter how valuable it is for understanding the history of early Persian prose, cannot be directly linked to the composition of Ferdowsi's **Shāhnāma.** Even on textual grounds, there is a contextual gap between the poetry of Ferdowsi and this particular preface, in marked contrast with the preface of the recension of Bāysonghor.[66]

The latter recension of Bāysonghor, transmitted in a vast family of manuscripts, represents our "vulgate": the Calcutta edition (Macan 1829) follows it closely, and this edition, collated with the eclectic Paris edition of Mohl (1838-1878), is the basis for the incomplete Leiden edition of Vullers (1877-1884) and the completed Tehran edition of Nafisi-Vullers (1934-1936). But the recension of Bāysonghor is late: the preface is dated A.D. 1425, in marked contrast to the preface of Abu Mansur, dated A.D. 957. In view of this contrast, the Moscow editors of the **Shāhnāma** considered the Bāysonghor recension inferior, as opposed to the recension represented by the family of manuscripts L, I, IV, VI, and K, a recension that seems to have had affinities to the preface of Abu Mansur. Guided by the reasoning that a more recent recension must be inferior to an older recension, the Moscow editors as a matter of policy

rejected variant readings stemming from the Bāysonghor recension. They also eliminated readings that could not be verified from the collective testimony of the old family of manuscripts that they had isolated, thereby reducing the corpus of the **Shāhnāma** to 48,617 distichs, to which are added in the appendix another 1,486 distichs, deemed probably spurious. We may appreciate the extent of this textual reduction by comparing the number of distichs in the Calcutta edition, 55,204.

But the basic principle of the Moscow edition, that the older group of manuscripts is by necessity closer to the "original," is open to question. If, as I claim, the many variations in the textual transmission of the **Shāhnāma** are due at least in part to the rich repertoire of concurrent oral poetic traditions, then each attested variation must be judged on its own merits, regardless of its textual provenience.

Moreover, the Moscow edition's dependence on the manuscript family L, I, IV, VI, and K, *to the exclusion of others,* must now be brought in line with the discovery of yet another manuscript of the **Shāhnāma:**

> F = ms. Cl.III.24 (G.F.3) of the Biblioteca Nazionale Centrale, Florence, dated A.D. 1217.

Here, then, is a document considerably older than L, which in turn is dated A.D. 1276 and which had been for the Moscow editors the oldest extant manuscript of the **Shāhnāma.** As Angelo Michele Piemontese, the discoverer of F, has demonstrated, this manuscript, two centuries away from the traditional date of the completion of Ferdowsi's **Shāhnāma,** is replete with valuable new readings that are not to be found in the manuscript family of L;[67] there are also about two hundred "new" distichs attested—distichs that have not been known to exist before.[68] This is not to say that F is closer to the "original" than L simply by virtue of being older than L. Moreover, this is not to discredit L and its family, as opposed to F. Rather, the point is simply that the editorial field of vision cannot be restricted to the family of L.

In fact, the preface of F is clearly in the same tradition that we find attested in the much later preface of the Bāysonghor recension.[69] Even more important, the actual variants that we find in F correspond far more closely to those of the Bāysonghor recension than to those of L and its family.[70] Thus, ironically, the Calcutta edition and its offshoots, most notably the Paris edition of Mohl and the Tehran edition of Nafisi-Vullers, contain "genuine" aspects of the **Shāhnāma** tradition that have been neglected by the "critical" Moscow edition.[71] What we need is an edition of the **Shāhnāma** that accounts for all the variants, each of which may be a reflex of variation in the oral tradition. In addition, we need a concordance that would include all variants that are demonstrably not just a matter of textual corruption or editorial tampering. With the aid of such an ideal edition and ideal concordance, we could demonstrate more rigorously both the power and the flexibility of the oral tradition as it was kept alive in Ferdowsi's **Shāh-nāma.**

Even without such ideal aids, however, we can already begin to appreciate the qualities of oral tradition in the poetry of the **Shāhnāma.** As I hope I have demonstrated, there is enough evidence, both in the **Shāhnāma** and in the history of Persian poetry before and after this monumental composition, to show that the creative power of a rich oral tradition produced and then maintained the authority of the national poem of the Persians.

Notes

1. See Shahbazi 1991.133.

2. I therefore disagree with Shahbazi's inference, ibid., on the basis of such examples as the anachronism just mentioned, that Ferdowsi was literally copying from earlier sources in earlier books whenever he introduces a narrative with such phrases as "So I have heard from the aged *dehqān.*" Such an inference simply displaces to a previous poet what Ferdowsi is doing in the present, that is, claiming a previous performance as the authority for what is "now" written in his book. Even in terms of the inference, the hypothetical previous poet would still be doing exactly the same thing. I maintain that, even if Ferdowsi follows the tradition of earlier books when he bases the authority of his written word on the authority of a continuum of performances that precede him, we have no reason to doubt that he could have direct access to that same continuum—and in fact that he could be part of it.

3. Minorsky 1964.269.

4. Page 1977.

5. Ibid. 4. For a survey of the contexts of the root *naqala,* see ibid. 16.

6. Ibid. 224. She adds at p. 2, paraphrasing Maranda and Maranda 1971.12: "Once the reworking of the tradition ceases to be meaningful to the audience, the tradition will disappear despite written versions."

7. Olearius 1656 [1971].558.

8. Page 1977.55.

9. Cf. also the work of Smith 1979 on Indian oral epic traditions where pictures are used to prompt as well as explain the narrative.

10. Page 1977.134-151.

11. For examples, see ibid. 140, 142, 146, 277.

12. Ibid. 143.

13. Lord 1960.26-27.

14. Cf. Page 1977.150, where she describes Ferdowsi's *Shāhnāma* as "one recension of a work which continues being told today."

15. Ibid. 67.

16. See, e.g., ibid. 73.

17. See ibid. 67.

18. Ibid. 118, n1. For comparable forms of expression in other cultures, where song, poetry, and prose are combined, see, e.g., Nagy 1990a.47, esp. n47.

19. Cf. Zumthor 1972.99-100 on the phenomenon of *dérimage* in Old French poetic traditions.

20. Page 1977.128; see, e.g., the details of the Sohrāb story at pp. 135-139.

21. Ibid. 128.

22. Nöldeke 1930.209.

23. Mohl 1838.liv.

24. Hansen, 1954, 116.

25. Parry 1971.272.

26. See Nagy 1990b.18-35.

27. Cf. Parry 1971.304.

28. Ibid. 272.

29. Lord 1938.440; see also Lord 1974.206-207.

30. For a useful survey of recent scholarship on the interrelationship of formula and theme, see Cantilena 1982.41-73. On p. 56, he offers this summary: "Ogni formula, dalla più stereotipa alla più consapevolmente usata, è motivata semanticamente."

31. Finnegan 1977.

32. Ibid. 59.

33. Parry 1971.270.

34. Cf. Finnegan 1977.62: "He can select what he wishes from the common stock of formulae, and can choose slightly different terms that fit his metre . . . and vary the details."

35. Ibid. 64.

36. Ibid. 71.

37. Ibid. 70, citing the work on Bantu oral poetry by Opland 1971.

38. Benson 1966.336.

39. Chaytor 1967.10-13 and chapters 4 and 6.

40. Zwettler 1978.15-19.

41. Ibid.

42. Chaytor 1967.13.

43. For this concept, see Lord 1960.53.

44. Zwettler 1978.

45. Menéndez-Pidal 1960.60-63; cf. Zumthor 1972.40-41.

46. Zwettler 1978.189.

47. Ibid.

48. Ibid. 212.

49. Ibid. 203.

50. Cf. Pearsall 1984.126-127, with reference to fifteenth-century English manuscript production: "The surviving manuscripts of a poem like *Beves of Hamptoun* make it clear that each act of copying was to a large extent an act of recomposition, and not an episode in a process of decomposition from an ideal

form." On the notion of *mouvance,* where the text is reconstituted with the production of each new copy, see Zumthor 1984.160. For an editorial application of this principle, see the exemplary work of Pickens 1978.

51. Such a possibility is emotionally and sarcastically resisted by Minavi 1972.110.

52. Zwettler 1978.221.

53. Cf. Shahbazi 1991.52.

54. Nöldeke 1930.125-126.

55. Ibid. 126.

56. Ibid.

57. Testimony by way of M. Lumsden, appendix 5, Nöldeke 1930.126.

58. Ibid.

59. Ibid. 127.

60. Cf. Muellner 1976.57-62.

61. Nöldeke 1930.125.

62. Mohl IV p. ii: "Plus on étudiera l'oeuvre de Firdousi, plus on se convaincra, je crois, qu'il n'a rien inventé, et qu'il s'est contenté de revêtir de son brillant coloris les traditions qui formaient l'histoire populaire de la Perse."

63. For a brief history of this edition, see Yarshater 1988.viii-ix. On the principles governing the new edition of Khaleghi-Motlagh (1988), see Yarshater 1988.x-xi.

64. On the problems in dating this manuscript, see Yarshater 1988.ix.

65. See Piemontese 1980.11-12, n27.

66. See ibid. 32-34.

67. See ibid. esp. 218-221.

68. Ibid. 222-226.

69. Ibid. 31-34; cf. Shahbazi 1991.4, n9 (paraphrase of this preface at 5-6).

70. Piemontese 1980.218-219.

71. Ibid. 194, 219. In n145 of p. 219, for example, Piemontese cites cases where the readings of the Florence manuscript vindicate the adopted readings of (1) the Calcutta edition as against the Moscow and Tehran editions, (2) the Paris edition of Mohl as against the Moscow and Tehran editions, and (3) the Paris edition and the Manuscripts I, IV, VI of the Moscow edition as against the Tehran edition and the preferred manuscript L of the Moscow edition. Khaleghi-Motlagh (1988) takes into account the evidence of the Florence manuscript. See also Yarshater 1988.viii-xi.

Jerome W. Clinton (essay date 1999)

SOURCE: An introduction to *In the Dragon's Claws: The Story of Rostram and Esfandiyar from the Persian "Book of Kings"* by Abolqasem Ferdowsi, Mage Publishers, 1999, pp. 9-23.

[*In the following essay, Clinton follows his outline of the* Shah-Nama's *themes with an analysis of the story of Rostram and Esfandiyar as it reflects the recurring themes of the work as a whole—ambivalence toward the demands of heroism and a critical attitude toward monarchy.*]

The story of Rostam and Esfandiyār is taken from the ***Shahnameh,*** or *Book of Kings,* a long narrative poem in Persian that was given its present form by Abolqasem Ferdowsi (AD 932-1025). The many heroic tales that fill the ***Shahnameh*** (Book of kings) are drawn from the history and mythology of Iran, and some of them at least were recited at the courts of Cyrus and Darius in the sixth century BC. In the course of the centuries that followed, these epic tales were gathered together into a book from time to time, but none of these earlier collections has survived. In the tenth century, one such recension, in prose, came into the hands of Ferdowsi, a minor noble who lived in the city of Tus near present-day Mashhad. Although Ferdowsi was a Muslim, he was devoted to the ancient traditions of Iran and feared that they would be lost as Islamic culture became ever more deeply rooted in Iran. To help forestall this, he set himself the task of retelling all the tales of the ***Shahnameh*** in poetry so that they would be remembered and passed on. The labor took him thirty-five years, but the result was a masterly work, nearly 50,000 couplets in length, that has enjoyed enormous popularity throughout the Persian speaking world for a millennium. It was discovered by European scholars in the eighteenth century and eventually translated into all the major languages of Europe.

Ferdowsi also assumed that in giving poetic life to these tales he would assure the survival of his own name as well.

> When this my famous book shall reach its end,
> My praises will be heard throughout the land.
> From this day on I shall not die, but live,
> For I'll have sown my words both far and wide.

In this he was successful beyond his wildest dreams. No name resonates more powerfully in the history of Iranian culture than that of its greatest poet, Abolqasem Ferdowsi.

In its length and its concentration on heroic action the ***Shahnameh*** resembles the western epic tradition, but in other important respects it differs substantially from Homer, Virgil and their imitators. It begins, for instance, not "in the midst of things" as does the *Iliad,* but with the creation of the world and the appearance of the first shah. The many and varied stories that make up the ***Shahnameh*** are joined together not by the force of a single hero like Odysseus, nor by the movement toward a single climactic event, such as the fall of Troy, but by the dynastic history of the Iranian court. This long and vivid history ends when that sequence of rulers does; that is, with the Arab, Islamic invasion of the seventh century AD that replaced the Iranian shahanshah ("emperor") with an Islamic caliph.

Since the focus of the tales is the life of the royal court, one finds little mention in the ***Shahnameh*** of the life of ordinary people such as farmers, shepherds or craftsmen. In this it resembles Malory's tales of King Arthur and the knights of the round table more than it does Homer or Virgil. As in the court of Arthur as well, a single god, called Izad or Yazdān, rules over the universe of the *Shahnameh,* not the celestial college of the Greeks and Romans. The horse riding *pahlavāns* ("heroes") of the Persian court battle each other using lances, shields and heavy maces much as did the knights of King Arthur's round table.

The events of the *Shahnameh* stretch across many generations and so are not tailored to the life span of a single hero. However, the principal figures in its dramas live as long as Biblical patriarchs, and one in particular, Rostam, endures for nearly nine centuries. Rostam is the last and greatest of a family of heroes from the Iranian province of Sistān, and he is a central presence in several of its finest stories. His death, which takes place just after the events of the present tale, and as a result of them, concludes the purely legendary portion of the *Shahnameh.* In the last third, the tales are peopled with figures from historical times. One portion draws heavily on a fictional biography of Alexander the Great, who conquered all of present-day Iran and parts of Central Asia and North India in the fourth century BC. The last sequence of stories is a similarly fictionalized account of the history of the Parthian and Sasanian dynasties (247 BC-AD 651) who ruled in Iran between the time of Alexander's death and the rise of Islam. The style of presentation does not change; however, historical figures and events are presented as the stuff of myth and legend.

In the world of the *Shahnameh,* humankind seems to have existed before the first shah but as an undifferentiated species. The formation of human society required the shaping presence of a divinely appointed ruler. Other shahs, most notably Hushang and Jamshid, the Iranian Solomon, provided human society with those gifts—fire, tools, agriculture and the various crafts—that raise men and women above the level of beasts. In other traditions these gifts that distinguish and sustain human society are gifts from the gods. In the *Shahnameh* it is Iran's shahs who provide them, or, rather, it is through them that Yazdān, the sole god of pre-Islamic Iranian religious belief, gives them to mankind.

While there are a number of recurrent themes in the *Shahnameh,* such as the immortality of noble deeds, the malignancy and inevitability of fate, and the persistent hostility and envy of Iran's neighbors, the theme that underlies all of these is that God prefers Iran to other nations and sustains it through the institution of the shah. So long as His chosen shah sits upon the throne, Iran will endure. When Shah Yazdegerd III is slain in AD 652, the Iran of the *Shahnameh* comes to an end. Other epics use a single dominant hero, like Odysseus, Aeneas or Roland, or a single, epochal event—the destruction of Troy, the founding of Rome or the defeat of the Saracens—to provide dramatic unity. In the *Shahnameh* it is the enduring institution of monarchy that stitches all its stories together.

Although the Divinity's support for Iranian monarchy is a central constant of the *Shahnameh,* its ideology is not a naïve and enthusiastic monarchism. Ferdowsi was not a panegyrist who presented idealizations of the ruler for the admiration of the royal sponsors and their followers. He was as realistic about the limitations of individual monarchs as was Shakespeare. Many of the greatest tales in the epic, like *Rostam and Esfandiyār,* explore the terrible consequences that result when a bad or foolish shah sits upon the throne.

THE PERSIAN LANGUAGE

Persian belongs to the Indo-European family of languages and has strong similarities to the major languages of Europe—the words for father, mother and brother, for instance, are *pedar, mādar* and *barādar.* Old Persian, one of the court languages of Cyrus and Darius, was a contemporary of Sanskrit and closely resembled it. Middle Persian languages had wide currency in Central Asia and the Iranian plateau from the time of Alexander in the fourth century BC to the rise of Islam in the seventh century AD. Modern Persian evolved in the Islamic period from these Middle Persian languages. Its grammar and syntax is Persian, but it contains a large vocabulary of Arabic. The *Shahnameh* is written in a slightly archaized form of this language that is virtually free of Arabic loanwords. Since the ninth century Modern Persian has been written in a modified form of the Arabic alphabet.

Persian and Persian literature first came to the West as a result of the European conquest of India. For centuries Central Asian Muslims, whose literary and administrative language was Persian, ruled in India. When European merchants and adventurers became interested in India in the seventeenth century, they learned Persian in order to trade and rule. Then as now the principal texts for teaching the language were literary, and many of those who learned Persian for practical reasons came to value it as a source of pleasure and a focus of scholarship. One of the principal fruits of this scholarship was the "discovery" of the *Shahnameh,* or *Book of Kings* and its translation into the major languages of Europe. In the nineteenth century the English rulers replaced Persian with English as the language of education and administration in India, but Persian continued as a major language there until well into the twentieth century.

THE STORY OF ROSTAM AND ESFANDIYAR

For a work that is usually described as one of the greatest stories of the Iranian national epic, the story of Rostam and Esfandiyār displays a surprisingly modern skepticism about the values we associate with the epic. In the world of the *Shahnameh,* monarchy enjoys divine sanction and society's most admired virtues are embodied in heroes like Rostam and Esfandiyār, yet the story expresses a profound ambivalence about the demands of heroism and is sharply critical of a monarch who exploits the courage and loyalty of his heroes to further his own selfish ends. The climactic event of the story is the battle between Rostam and Esfandiyār, yet the two heroes do not view themselves as natural enemies. On the contrary, they fight each other against their own wishes and in violation of their own best interests. Moreover, theirs is a battle in which the roles of victor and vanquished seem to have been reversed. Although it is Esfandiyār who dies, the outcome is as tragic for the ancient hero as it is for the young prince. Esfandiyār loses his life and fails in his ambition to rule Iran as a consequence, but he dies with his reputation unsullied and confident that his actions in this world will be judged favorably by God in the next. Rostam gains only a brief respite from defeat and death, and does so at the cost of enduring shame for having slain the only Iranian hero whose virtues and accomplishments approach his own. The one person who may be said to gain by this tragedy, Shah Goshtāsp, pays a heavy price for his triumph as well. The defeat and death of his son lets him sit more easily on his throne, but as a result of it he loses the esteem of his own people, alienates his courtiers and brings disgrace on his family. His victory is a pyrrhic one.

While the narrative focus of the story is the slowly escalating tension between Esfandiyār and Rostam, a tension that explodes in their final tragic confrontation, the engine that drives their struggle is the conflict between Esfandiyār and his father over which of them will rule Iran. The seed of that conflict is in the shah's inability to understand and value his son, not in any failure of loyalty on his son's part. However, it is the son who will suffer the consequences of this, not the father.

As a young man, Goshtāsp was so resentful of his father's reluctance to abdicate in his favor that he was willing to lead the army of Iran's enemy to the west, Rome (Byzantium), against him. When Esfandiyār as a young prince distinguishes himself in a battle against Arjāsp, the ruler of Turān, Iran's hostile neighbor to the north, and so wins the loyalty and admiration of the army, Goshtāsp assumes that his son is as ambitious for rule as he himself was. When an envious courtier, Gorazm, accuses Esfandiyār of plotting against the shah, Goshtāsp believes him and has his son thrown in prison despite his plea that he is innocent. The irony in this is that Esfandiyār is cut from another pattern than the shah, and more nearly resembles his loyal and heroic uncle, Zarir, with whom he is often compared. Initially, at least, he is animated by simple loyalty and virtue, and does not covet his father's throne. Goshtāsp cannot see this and so abandons him to the prison fortress of Gombadān, and rides off to Zābolestān for a long visit with Rostam.

When Arjāsp and his ally, the Khāqān of China, learn that the shah has left his capital and that Iran's greatest hero is in prison, they launch a second invasion and quickly overrun the country. Only then does Goshtāsp recognize his error, and wishing both to make amends and save his rule, he sends his counselor, Jāmāsp, to release Esfandiyār and to promise him the throne if he will drive Arjāsp and his army out of Iran. Jāmāsp, however, does not mention the shah's offer but attempts to win Esfandiyār's support by speaking of the devastation his sisters and brothers have suffered at the hands of their enemies. At first Esfandiyār is unmoved by his pleas—none of his brothers and sisters have shown concern for his own suffering. When he learns that the one brother whom he loves, Farshidvard, has been brutally slain, the news stirs him to action at last. He shatters his bonds, too impatient to wait for the blacksmiths to do so, and sets out to rid Iran of the invading forces.

When Esfandiyār has defeated Arjāsp's army, Goshtāsp himself formally promises to yield his place to him, if he will first rescue his sisters from captivity in the enemy's capital—a fortress encircled with a brass wall. He gives him a royal crown as proof of his good intention and also presents him to the army as his heir. These are the promises that Esfandiyār alludes to when he confronts his father in court. If Goshtāsp now fears his son's eagerness to replace him on the throne, he has only himself to blame.

As the present story opens, Esfandiyār has returned in triumph from his campaign against Turān, where he freed his sisters, beheaded Arjāsp, and captured both Arjāsp's family and his treasury. His expectation is that Goshtāsp will now honor his promise and abdicate in his favor, but his father says and does nothing. Esfandiyār's explosive first scene is fueled by legitimate frustration, but it leads him to make a fatal error. In the heat of his anger and resentment he vows that if his father will not now make him shah, he will overthrow him and seize the throne by force: "I swear by great Yazdān, / Who holds the heavens up, I'll crown myself / Despite my royal father's wish" (11-12). In the world of the *Shahnameh,* challenges to royal authority invariably lead to the challenger's death, even when, as is true here, the threat is more rhetorical than real. This one moment of hotheaded rebelliousness is enough to assure Esfandiyār's destruction. It seems both cruel and unfair that a lapse in obedience that is so brief, and so justified, should be his death warrant. But fate, as Ferdowsi reminds us on many occasions, is as capricious as it is implacable.

In the event, the actual danger to Goshtāsp's monarchy vanishes with the morning sun. It is late and Esfandiyār is drunk when he makes his threat. He apparently thinks better of his angry words the next day and does not confront his father immediately, but only after several days' delay. His manner when he does is not threatening but earnest and pleading. Goshtāsp, forewarned of his son's anger, is able to smoothly deflect his protests by acknowledging their truth and insisting that he still intends to honor his promise. However, he says, there is one final task that Esfandiyār must undertake before he can be crowned. He must journey to Zābol and there humble its ruler, the legendary hero Rostam, for having shown an insulting reluctance to honor Iran's new royal line by attending them at court. Where Esfandiyār's first two tasks were both urgent and honorable, as were his earlier efforts to disseminate the new faith of Zoroastrianism, this new commission is neither. For centuries Rostam has performed heroic services for the shahs of Iran. Whatever his offense, he deserves better than this brutal insult. Esfandiyār knows this, and he senses that his father's intention is to do him some injury, not Rostam. His suspicions are well founded. Earlier, Goshtāsp, hearing of his son's frustration, had cast his horoscope and learned that Esfandiyārwas fated to die by Rostam's hand in Zābol. Although he cannot remedy that fate, he chooses neither to warn his son nor to delay his fatal encounter with Rostam but sends him off to blindly provoke the great hero's anger.

Even though he does not know what fate awaits him in Zābolestān, Esfandiyār would rather retire from the court than accept this commission. Once the shah orders him to do so, however, he has no choice but to obey. Both loyalty and ambition have been offered as motives for his decision to obey his father, but Esfandiyār's motive runs deeper than either of these. As a pious Zoroastrian he believes that the commands of his father, the shah, have the force of divine decree. If he disobeys him, he will suffer eternal torments in the afterlife. Once Goshtāsp has spoken, Esfandiyār has no choice but to raise an army and depart.

The shah's insistence that Rostam submit to having his hands and feet shackled, and that he make the journey to the court on foot, like a slave, comes as a terrible shock to Rostam. He is baffled by this show of hostility from a court that he has served so long and so well. He is more than willing to come to the court to receive whatever chastisement is his due, but, as Goshtāsp has surely anticipated, he is too proud to make the journey to the court on foot and with fetters on his hands and feet. The humiliation of this would be unendurable to him personally, and it also would have terrible consequences both for his own family and for his kingdom. To yield to such a disgrace would negate all that Rostam has been and done throughout his long life.

> I'll look upon your face with joyful heart
> And gladly do whatever you command.
> But not these chains! Shackles are shame, defeat,
> An ugly stain upon my family's name.
> While I'm alive, no one will ever see
> Me bound with chains. My soul insists on this.

> (516-518)

Esfandiyār has willingly endured shackles, and worse, at the shah's hands, but Rostam will not do so. The old hero does not feel himself threatened by the fires of eternal torment should he disobey the shah, or if he does, the destruction of his good name seems a heavier punishment. He cannot bring himself to obey a command that is both unreasonable and unjust even if it does come from the shah. In doing so, he too becomes a threat to the state, and, by the logic of the *Shahnameh*, he must be punished as well.

Esfandiyār deeply admires Rostam and is sympathetic to his sense of being ill used by the court. He has himself already suffered a more painful humiliation at the hands of his father than he would now, in his father's name, inflict

upon Rostam. He attempts to mitigate the harshness of his father's command, promising that once they are at the court he will intercede with the shah on Rostam's behalf; yet if Rostam will not yield, he knows that he has no choice. He must obey the shah's command to the letter. Should he allow Rostam to approach the court mounted and free, as Rostam suggests, and not led by "a rope about his arms . . . on foot and running," like a slave, then his action will be counted by his father as outright disobedience. Goshtāsp, in short, has phrased his commission so that it will create an irresolvable conflict between Rostam and Esfandiyār.

Rostam welcomes Esfandiyār to Zābol with great warmth and admiration, and seems eager to befriend him. Esfandiyār cannot respond in kind, although he feels drawn to the ancient warrior. He must hide the very real affection and admiration he feels for him in order to carry out his father's wishes. There is a poignant moment, one of several, that shows what feelings Esfandiyār has been obliged to hide behind the mask of royal agent. It takes place just after the first, unsatisfactory encounter of the two heroes on the bank of the Hirmand River which marks the border between Iran and Sistan. Rostam has returned alone to his court to await Esfandiyār's invitation to dine, and Esfandiyār ponders how to continue their debate. He decides not to invite Rostam to eat with him because sharing a meal would draw them closer, and he anticipates that ties of friendship with Rostam will ultimately cause him pain. He muses aloud to his brother, Pashutan, whose principal function is to be the recipient of such confidences.

> . . . We thought this was an easy task,
> But it's proved hard indeed. I have no wish
> To visit Rostam in his home, nor has
> He any need to see me here. Should he
> Not choose to come, I will not send for him.
> If one of us should breathe his last while here,
> His death will sear the heart of him who's left.
> A closer friendship would increase that grief.

> (541-544)

His words may seem cool, even harsh at first, but Esfandiyār believes that he himself is invincible and assumes that the heart that will be wounded will be his own. It is the thought of his own grief at Rostam's death that he finds unbearable. Such glimpses behind the mask that Goshtāsp has obliged him to wear reveal him to be an essentially decent man who is constrained by his piety and loyalty to betray his own instincts.

The exchanges between them inevitably become increasingly acrimonious as each tries, and fails, to persuade the other to his view. For the reader, as for Esfandiyār, there is a painful irony in Rostam's pleading with him to be more reasonable. Esfandiyār would gladly accept Rostam's conditions, but as his father's agent he must reject them. Nor, out of loyalty, can he reveal what his true thoughts and feelings are. He also knows that Goshtāsp only wishes him ill, but he cannot say this either. Indeed, when Rostam accuses Goshtāsp of perfidy Esfandiyār must appear to turn a deaf ear to Rostam and even defend the shah.

Hear me! . . .
I will not disobey the shah's command,
Not for a crown or throne. I find in him
Whatever's good or evil in this world.
My hell and heaven are contained in him.

(858-860)

When, at last, they meet in battle, Rostam, at first, comes perilously close to defeat, but through the magical intervention of Simorgh he triumphs over Esfandiyār, although "triumph" is surely the wrong word here. Their combat ends in the death of Esfandiyār, but the outcome is as tragic for the ancient hero as it is for the young shah. Esfandiyār loses his life and fails in his ambition to rule Iran. He must look to receive the reward of his virtue in heaven, not on earth. Rostam gains a brief respite from defeat and death but does so at the cost of enduring shame for having slain a brave and virtuous prince. Moreover, he does not see himself as in any sense the victor in a battle. His only role has been to act as fate's instrument in slaying Esfandiyār with the deadly arrow made of tamarisk wood.

I was the agent of the tamarisk; that's all.
I am what's dark and dismal in this tale.

(1441)

Rostam's role in this drama is, of course, more complex than this. He is obliged here to reprise the role he played in the death of his own son, Sohrāb. There are differences, of course. Sohrāb explicitly threatened to overthrow the shahs of both Iran and Turān, while Esfandiyār's challenge to his father, as we have seen, is only in his father's mind. Rostam was unaware that the young challenger he faced was his son until too late, while he is all too aware of Esfandiyār's identity and of the consequences his death will have for him. But the central fact of Rostam's killing a young hero who challenges royal authority, and of making a terrible personal sacrifice in order to preserve a bad ruler, remains unchanged. He has been absent from the central events of the **Shahnameh** quite literally for centuries. Now he has been called back to perform this terrible and onerous task. It is as though this is the price he must pay for his unique strength and skill, for enjoying Fate's favor throughout his long life.

His death follows closely on that of the young hero he slays and, indeed, is precipitated by it. The final chapter of Esfandiyār's life brings Rostam's life to its end as well. Rostam's presence, and the many similarities between these two remarkable and virtuous heroes, who serve two such deplorable rulers, seems meant to remind us of the terrible consequences of linking human frailty to divine right.

The final resolution of the tale returns the court of Iran to a state of order and security. Bahrām-Ardashir replaces his father as the acknowledged heir to the throne. Rostam is forgiven for not having shown proper respect to the court and reestablished in his rule of Zābolestān. Yet one is left with the sense of the world turned upside down, of the

good being punished while the evil are rewarded. Each of the two heroes has in his own time been the chief prop and support of Iran and its shahs, and neither has done anything to threaten the security of the state. Bahman is in no sense the man his father was, and Shah Goshtāsp is the least admirable of rulers, a moral leper who is the real villain of the story. He provokes his son's anger by lying to him and forces him to fight Rostam, knowing he will be killed. He is the first and only shah to murder his own child, and he is condemned for his actions by the nobles of his court and his own family. He also goads Rostam into a fatal show of rebellion. Like Kay Kāvus, the foolish and arrogant shah whom Rostam served, Goshtāsp is so terrible a ruler for his country that we cannot help but question God's wisdom in choosing him. Worse yet, he is not punished for his sins.

I believe that questioning God's wisdom in choosing and supporting Goshtāsp as shah is precisely what Ferdowsi wishes us to do. He is no revolutionary. He accepts monarchy as the system that God has chosen to order human society. But in this magnificent and painful tale he has chosen to reveal to us the dark and shadowy side of that system. A bad monarch can be the enemy of all that is most admirable, and peace and security have been won here at a price that may be too heavy for society to bear. There is a bitter irony in the words that conclude the story of Rostam and Esfandiyār:

The story of Esfandiyār has reached
Its end at last. Long may the *shahriyār* live!
His heart forever freed of care, the times
Obedient to his command. May he
Rejoice upon his famous throne, a rope
Around the necks of those who wish him ill.

(1664-1666)

FURTHER READING

Criticism

Clinton, Jerome W. "The Tragedy of Suhrāb." *Logos Islamikos: Studia Islamica in honorem Georgii Michaelis Wickens,* edited by Roger M. Savory and Dionisius A. Agius, pp. 63-77. Papers in Medieval Studies 6. Toronto: Pontifical Institute of Mediaeval Studies, 1984.

    Offers a literary analysis of the story of Suhrāb, examining in particular the theme of filicide.

Davis, Dick. *Epic and Sedition: The Case of Ferdowsi's* "Shāhnāmeh." Fayetteville: The University of Arkansas Press, 1992, 222 p.

    Book-length analysis of the poem and its themes.

Hanaway, William L., Jr. "The Iranian Epics." *Heroic Epic and Saga: An Introduction to the World's Great Folk Ep-*

ics, edited by Felix J. Oinas, pp. 76-98. Bloomington: Indiana University Press, 1978.

> Surveys the form, structure, language, style, and content of the *Shah-nama* and comments on the influence of the work on later Persian literature.

Krasnowolska, Anna. "Rostam Farroxzād's Prophecy in *Šāh-nāme* and the Zoroastrian Apocalyptic Texts." *Folia Orientalia* XIX (1978): 173-84.

> Examines the prophecy in the *Shah-Nama* alluding to the decline of Zoroastrianism.

Additional coverage of Ferdowsi is contained in the following source published by the Gale Group: *Epics for Students.*

How to Use This Index

The main references

Calvino, Italo
1923-1985 .... **CLC 5, 8, 11, 22, 33, 39, 73; SSC 3**

list all author entries in the following Gale Literary Criticism series:

BLC = *Black Literature Criticism*
CLC = *Contemporary Literary Criticism*
CLR = *Children's Literature Review*
CMLC = *Classical and Medieval Literature Criticism*
DA = *DISCovering Authors*
DAB = *DISCovering Authors: British*
DAC = *DISCovering Authors: Canadian*
DAM = *DISCovering Authors: Modules*
      DRAM: Dramatists Module; **MST:** *Most-Studied Authors Module;*
      MULT: Multicultural Authors Module; **NOV:** *Novelists Module;*
      POET: Poets Module; **POP:** *Popular Fiction and Genre Authors Module*
DC = *Drama Criticism*
HLC = *Hispanic Literature Criticism*
LC = *Literature Criticism from 1400 to 1800*
NCLC = *Nineteenth-Century Literature Criticism*
NNAL = *Native North American Literature*
PC = *Poetry Criticism*
SSC = *Short Story Criticism*
TCLC = *Twentieth-Century Literary Criticism*
WLC = *World Literature Criticism, 1500 to the Present*

The cross-references

See also CANR 23; CA 85-88;
obituary CA116

list all author entries in the following Gale biographical and literary sources:

AAYA = *Authors & Artists for Young Adults*
AITN = *Authors in the News*
BEST = *Bestsellers*
BW = *Black Writers*
CA = *Contemporary Authors*
CAAS = *Contemporary Authors Autobiography Series*
CABS = *Contemporary Authors Bibliographical Series*
CANR = *Contemporary Authors New Revision Series*
CAP = *Contemporary Authors Permanent Series*
CDALB = *Concise Dictionary of American Literary Biography*
CDBLB = *Concise Dictionary of British Literary Biography*
DLB = *Dictionary of Literary Biography*
DLBD = *Dictionary of Literary Biography Documentary Series*
DLBY = *Dictionary of Literary Biography Yearbook*
HW = *Hispanic Writers*
JRDA = *Junior DISCovering Authors*
MAICYA = *Major Authors and Illustrators for Children and Young Adults*
MTCW = *Major 20th-Century Writers*
SAAS = *Something about the Author Autobiography Series*
SATA = *Something about the Author*
YABC = *Yesterday's Authors of Books for Children*

Literary Criticism Series
Cumulative Author Index

Aksenov, Vassily
See Aksyonov, Vassily (Pavlovich)
Akst, Daniel 1956- .... **CLC 109**
See also CA 161
Aksyonov, Vassily (Pavlovich) 1932-
.... **CLC 22, 37, 101**
See also CA 53-56; CANR 12, 48, 77
Akutagawa, Ryunosuke 1892-1927
.... **TCLC 16**
See also CA 117; 154
Alain 1868-1951 .... **TCLC 41**
See also CA 163
Alain-Fournier .... **TCLC 6**
See also Fournier, Henri Alban
See also DLB 65
Alarcon, Pedro Antonio de 1833-1891
.... **NCLC 1**
Alas (y Urena), Leopoldo (Enrique Garcia)
1852-1901 .... **TCLC 29**
See also CA 113; 131; HW 1
Albee, Edward (Franklin III) 1928- . **CLC 1,
2, 3, 5, 9, 11, 13, 25, 53, 86, 113; DA;
DAB; DAC; DAM DRAM, MST; DC
11; WLC**
See also AITN 1; CA 5-8R; CABS 3;
CANR 8, 54, 74; CDALB 1941-1968;
DA3; DLB 7; INT CANR-8; MTCW 1, 2
Alberti, Rafael 1902-1999 .... **CLC 7**
See also CA 85-88; 185; CANR 81; DLB
108; HW 2
Albert the Great 1200(?)-1280 ..... **CMLC 16**
See also DLB 115
Alcala-Galiano, Juan Valera y
See Valera y Alcala-Galiano, Juan
Alcayaga, Lucila Godoy
See Godoy Alcayaga, Lucila
Alcott, Amos Bronson 1799-1888 ... **NCLC 1**
See also DLB 1, 223
Alcott, Louisa May 1832-1888 . **NCLC 6, 58,
83; DA; DAB; DAC; DAM MST, NOV;
SSC 27; WLC**
See also AAYA 20; CDALB 1865-1917;
CLR 1, 38; DA3; DLB 1, 42, 79, 223;
DLBD 14; JRDA; MAICYA; SATA 100;
YABC 1
Aldanov, M. A.
See Aldanov, Mark (Alexandrovich)
Aldanov, Mark (Alexandrovich)
1886(?)-1957 .... **TCLC 23**
See also CA 118; 181
Aldington, Richard 1892-1962 .... **CLC 49**
See also CA 85-88; CANR 45; DLB 20, 36,
100, 149
Aldiss, Brian W(ilson) 1925- ...... **CLC 5, 14,
40; DAM NOV; SSC 36**
See also CA 5-8R; CAAS 2; CANR 5, 28,
64; DLB 14; MTCW 1, 2; SATA 34
Alegria, Claribel 1924- .... **CLC 75; DAM
MULT; HLCS 1; PC 26**
See also CA 131; CAAS 15; CANR 66;
DLB 145; HW 1; MTCW 1
Alegria, Fernando 1918- .... **CLC 57**
See also CA 9-12R; CANR 5, 32, 72; HW
1, 2
Aleichem, Sholom .... **TCLC 1, 35; SSC 33**
See also Rabinovitch, Sholem
Aleixandre, Vicente 1898-1984
See also CANR 81; HLCS 1; HW 2
Alepoudelis, Odysseus
See Elytis, Odysseus
Aleshkovsky, Joseph 1929-
See Aleshkovsky, Yuz
See also CA 121; 128
Aleshkovsky, Yuz .... **CLC 44**
See also Aleshkovsky, Joseph
Alexander, Lloyd (Chudley) 1924- .. **CLC 35**

See also AAYA 1, 27; CA 1-4R; CANR 1,
24, 38, 55; CLR 1, 5, 48; DLB 52; JRDA;
MAICYA; MTCW 1; SAAS 19; SATA 3,
49, 81
Alexander, Meena 1951- .... **CLC 121**
See also CA 115; CANR 38, 70
Alexander, Samuel 1859-1938 .... **TCLC 77**
Alexie, Sherman (Joseph, Jr.) 1966-
.... **CLC 96; DAM MULT**
See also AAYA 28; CA 138; CANR 65;
DA3; DLB 175, 206; MTCW 1; NNAL
Alfau, Felipe 1902- .... **CLC 66**
See also CA 137
Alfred, Jean Gaston
See Ponge, Francis
Alger, Horatio Jr., Jr. 1832-1899 ... **NCLC 8,
83**
See also DLB 42; SATA 16
Algren, Nelson 1909-1981 .... **CLC 4, 10, 33;
SSC 33**
See also CA 13-16R; 103; CANR 20, 61;
CDALB 1941-1968; DLB 9; DLBY 81,
82; MTCW 1, 2
Ali, Ahmed 1910- .... **CLC 69**
See also CA 25-28R; CANR 15, 34
Alighieri, Dante
See Dante
Allan, John B.
See Westlake, Donald E(dwin)
Allan, Sidney
See Hartmann, Sadakichi
Allan, Sydney
See Hartmann, Sadakichi
Allen, Edward 1948- .... **CLC 59**
Allen, Fred 1894-1956 .... **TCLC 87**
Allen, Paula Gunn 1939- ..... **CLC 84; DAM
MULT**
See also CA 112; 143; CANR 63; DA3;
DLB 175; MTCW 1; NNAL
Allen, Roland
See Ayckbourn, Alan
Allen, Sarah A.
See Hopkins, Pauline Elizabeth
Allen, Sidney H.
See Hartmann, Sadakichi
Allen, Woody 1935- .... **CLC 16, 52; DAM
POP**
See also AAYA 10; CA 33-36R; CANR 27,
38, 63; DLB 44; MTCW 1
Allende, Isabel 1942- . **CLC 39, 57, 97; DAM
MULT, NOV; HLC 1; WLCS**
See also AAYA 18; CA 125; 130; CANR
51, 74; DA3; DLB 145; HW 1, 2; INT
130; MTCW 1, 2
Alleyn, Ellen
See Rossetti, Christina (Georgina)
Allingham, Margery (Louise) 1904-1966
.... **CLC 19**
See also CA 5-8R; 25-28R; CANR 4, 58;
DLB 77; MTCW 1, 2
Allingham, William 1824-1889 ..... **NCLC 25**
See also DLB 35
Allison, Dorothy E. 1949- .... **CLC 78**
See also CA 140; CANR 66; DA3; MTCW
1
Allston, Washington 1779-1843 ...... **NCLC 2**
See also DLB 1, 235
Almedingen, E. M. .... **CLC 12**
See also Almedingen, Martha Edith von
See also SATA 3
Almedingen, Martha Edith von 1898-1971
See Almedingen, E. M.
See also CA 1-4R; CANR 1
Almodovar, Pedro 1949(?)- .... **CLC 114;
HLCS 1**
See also CA 133; CANR 72; HW 2
Almqvist, Carl Jonas Love 1793-1866
.... **NCLC 42**

Alonso, Damaso 1898-1990 .... **CLC 14**
See also CA 110; 131; 130; CANR 72; DLB
108; HW 1, 2
Alov
See Gogol, Nikolai (Vasilyevich)
Alta 1942- .... **CLC 19**
See also CA 57-60
Alter, Robert B(ernard) 1935- .... **CLC 34**
See also CA 49-52; CANR 1, 47
Alther, Lisa 1944- .... **CLC 7, 41**
See also CA 65-68; CAAS 30; CANR 12,
30, 51; MTCW 1
Althusser, L.
See Althusser, Louis
Althusser, Louis 1918-1990 .... **CLC 106**
See also CA 131; 132
Altman, Robert 1925- .... **CLC 16, 116**
See also CA 73-76; CANR 43
Alurista 1949-
See Urista, Alberto H.
See also DLB 82; HLCS 1
Alvarez, A(lfred) 1929- .... **CLC 5, 13**
See also CA 1-4R; CANR 3, 33, 63; DLB
14, 40
Alvarez, Alejandro Rodriguez 1903-1965
See Casona, Alejandro
See also CA 131; 93-96; HW 1
Alvarez, Julia 1950- .... **CLC 93; HLCS 1**
See also AAYA 25; CA 147; CANR 69;
DA3; MTCW 1
Alvaro, Corrado 1896-1956 .... **TCLC 60**
See also CA 163
Amado, Jorge 1912- .... **CLC 13, 40, 106;
DAM MULT, NOV; HLC 1**
See also CA 77-80; CANR 35, 74; DLB
113; HW 2; MTCW 1, 2
Ambler, Eric 1909-1998 .... **CLC 4, 6, 9**
See also CA 9-12R; 171; CANR 7, 38, 74;
DLB 77; MTCW 1, 2
Amichai, Yehuda 1924-2000 . **CLC 9, 22, 57,
116**
See also CA 85-88; CANR 46, 60; MTCW
1
Amichai, Yehudah
See Amichai, Yehuda
Amiel, Henri Frederic 1821-1881 .. **NCLC 4**
Amis, Kingsley (William) 1922-1995 . **CLC 1,
2, 3, 5, 8, 13, 40, 44, 129; DA; DAB;
DAC; DAM MST, NOV**
See also AITN 2; CA 9-12R; 150; CANR 8,
28, 54; CDBLB 1945-1960; DA3; DLB
15, 27, 100, 139; DLBY 96; INT
CANR-8; MTCW 1, 2
Amis, Martin (Louis) 1949- ... **CLC 4, 9, 38,
62, 101**
See also BEST 90:3; CA 65-68; CANR 8,
27, 54, 73; DA3; DLB 14, 194; INT
CANR-27; MTCW 1
Ammons, A(rchie) R(andolph) 1926-
.... **CLC 2, 3, 5, 8, 9, 25, 57, 108; DAM
POET; PC 16**
See also AITN 1; CA 9-12R; CANR 6, 36,
51, 73; DLB 5, 165; MTCW 1, 2
Amo, Tauraatua i
See Adams, Henry (Brooks)
Amory, Thomas 1691(?)-1788 .... **LC 48**
Anand, Mulk Raj 1905- . **CLC 23, 93; DAM
NOV**
See also CA 65-68; CANR 32, 64; MTCW
1, 2
Anatol
See Schnitzler, Arthur
Anaximander c. 610B.C.-c. 546B.C.
.... **CMLC 22**
Anaya, Rudolfo A(lfonso) 1937- .... **CLC 23;
DAM MULT, NOV; HLC 1**
See also AAYA 20; CA 45-48; CAAS 4;
CANR 1, 32, 51; DLB 82, 206; HW 1;
MTCW 1, 2

Andersen, Hans Christian 1805-1875
.. **NCLC 7, 79; DA; DAB; DAC; DAM MST, POP; SSC 6; WLC**
See also CLR 6; DA3; MAICYA; SATA 100; YABC 1

Anderson, C. Farley
See Mencken, H(enry) L(ouis); Nathan, George Jean

Anderson, Jessica (Margaret) Queale 1916-
.... **CLC 37**
See also CA 9-12R; CANR 4, 62

Anderson, Jon (Victor) 1940- . **CLC 9; DAM POET**
See also CA 25-28R; CANR 20

Anderson, Lindsay (Gordon) 1923-1994
.... **CLC 20**
See also CA 125; 128; 146; CANR 77

Anderson, Maxwell 1888-1959 ...... **TCLC 2; DAM DRAM**
See also CA 105; 152; DLB 7, 228; MTCW 2

Anderson, Poul (William) 1926- ..... **CLC 15**
See also AAYA 5, 34; CA 1-4R, 181; CAAE 181; CAAS 2; CANR 2, 15, 34, 64; CLR 58; DLB 8; INT CANR-15; MTCW 1, 2; SATA 90; SATA-Brief 39; SATA-Essay 106

Anderson, Robert (Woodruff) 1917-
.... **CLC 23; DAM DRAM**
See also AITN 1; CA 21-24R; CANR 32; DLB 7

Anderson, Sherwood 1876-1941 .... **TCLC 1, 10, 24; DA; DAB; DAC; DAM MST, NOV; SSC 1; WLC**
See also AAYA 30; CA 104; 121; CANR 61; CDALB 1917-1929; DA3; DLB 4, 9, 86; DLBD 1; MTCW 1, 2

Andier, Pierre
See Desnos, Robert

Andouard
See Giraudoux, (Hippolyte) Jean

Andrade, Carlos Drummond de ..... **CLC 18**
See also Drummond de Andrade, Carlos

Andrade, Mario de 1893-1945 ...... **TCLC 43**

Andreae, Johann V(alentin) 1586-1654
.... **LC 32**
See also DLB 164

Andreas-Salome, Lou 1861-1937 .. **TCLC 56**
See also CA 178; DLB 66

Andress, Lesley
See Sanders, Lawrence

Andrewes, Lancelot 1555-1626 .... **LC 5**
See also DLB 151, 172

Andrews, Cicily Fairfield
See West, Rebecca

Andrews, Elton V.
See Pohl, Frederik

Andreyev, Leonid (Nikolaevich) 1871-1919
.... **TCLC 3**
See also CA 104; 185

Andric, Ivo 1892-1975 .... **CLC 8; SSC 36**
See also CA 81-84; 57-60; CANR 43, 60; DLB 147; MTCW 1

Androvar
See Prado (Calvo), Pedro

Angelique, Pierre
See Bataille, Georges

Angell, Roger 1920- .... **CLC 26**
See also CA 57-60; CANR 13, 44, 70; DLB 171, 185

Angelou, Maya 1928- ... **CLC 12, 35, 64, 77; BLC 1; DA; DAB; DAC; DAM MST, MULT, POET, POP; PC 32; WLCS**
See also AAYA 7, 20; BW 2, 3; CA 65-68; CANR 19, 42, 65; CDALBS; CLR 53; DA3; DLB 38; MTCW 1, 2; SATA 49

Anna Comnena 1083-1153 .... **CMLC 25**

Annensky, Innokenty (Fyodorovich) 1856-1909 .... **TCLC 14**

See also CA 110; 155

Annunzio, Gabriele d'
See D'Annunzio, Gabriele

Anodos
See Coleridge, Mary E(lizabeth)

Anon, Charles Robert
See Pessoa, Fernando (Antonio Nogueira)

Anouilh, Jean (Marie Lucien Pierre) 1910-1987 .... **CLC 1, 3, 8, 13, 40, 50; DAM DRAM; DC 8**
See also CA 17-20R; 123; CANR 32; MTCW 1, 2

Anthony, Florence
See Ai

Anthony, John
See Ciardi, John (Anthony)

Anthony, Peter
See Shaffer, Anthony (Joshua); Shaffer, Peter (Levin)

Anthony, Piers 1934- ... **CLC 35; DAM POP**
See also AAYA 11; CA 21-24R; CANR 28, 56, 73; DLB 8; MTCW 1, 2; SAAS 22; SATA 84

Anthony, Susan B(rownell) 1916-1991
.... **TCLC 84**
See also CA 89-92; 134

Antoine, Marc
See Proust, (Valentin-Louis-George-Eugene-) Marcel

Antoninus, Brother
See Everson, William (Oliver)

Antonioni, Michelangelo 1912- .... **CLC 20**
See also CA 73-76; CANR 45, 77

Antschel, Paul 1920-1970
See Celan, Paul
See also CA 85-88; CANR 33, 61; MTCW 1

Anwar, Chairil 1922-1949 .... **TCLC 22**
See also CA 121

Anzaldua, Gloria (Evanjelina) 1942-
See also CA 175; DLB 122; HLCS 1

Apess, William 1798-1839(?) .... **NCLC 73; DAM MULT**
See also DLB 175; NNAL

Apollinaire, Guillaume 1880-1918 . **TCLC 3, 8, 51; DAM POET; PC 7**
See also CA 152; MTCW 1

Appelfeld, Aharon 1932- .. **CLC 23, 47; SSC 42**
See also CA 112; 133; CANR 86

Apple, Max (Isaac) 1941- .... **CLC 9, 33**
See also CA 81-84; CANR 19, 54; DLB 130

Appleman, Philip (Dean) 1926- .... **CLC 51**
See also CA 13-16R; CAAS 18; CANR 6, 29, 56

Appleton, Lawrence
See Lovecraft, H(oward) P(hillips)

Apteryx
See Eliot, T(homas) S(tearns)

Apuleius, (Lucius Madaurensis) 125(?)-175(?) .... **CMLC 1**
See also DLB 211

Aquin, Hubert 1929-1977 .... **CLC 15**
See also CA 105; DLB 53

Aquinas, Thomas 1224(?)-1274 ... **CMLC 33**
See also DLB 115

Aragon, Louis 1897-1982 . **CLC 3, 22; DAM NOV, POET**
See also CA 69-72; 108; CANR 28, 71; DLB 72; MTCW 1, 2

Arany, Janos 1817-1882 .... **NCLC 34**

Aranyos, Kakay
See Mikszath, Kalman

Arbuthnot, John 1667-1735 .... **LC 1**
See also DLB 101

Archer, Herbert Winslow
See Mencken, H(enry) L(ouis)

Archer, Jeffrey (Howard) 1940- ..... **CLC 28; DAM POP**
See also AAYA 16; BEST 89:3; CA 77-80; CANR 22, 52; DA3; INT CANR-22

Archer, Jules 1915- .... **CLC 12**
See also CA 9-12R; CANR 6, 69; SAAS 5; SATA 4, 85

Archer, Lee
See Ellison, Harlan (Jay)

Arden, John 1930- ..... **CLC 6, 13, 15; DAM DRAM**
See also CA 13-16R; CAAS 4; CANR 31, 65, 67; DLB 13; MTCW 1

Arenas, Reinaldo 1943-1990 . **CLC 41; DAM MULT; HLC 1**
See also CA 124; 128; 133; CANR 73; DLB 145; HW 1; MTCW 1

Arendt, Hannah 1906-1975 .... **CLC 66, 98**
See also CA 17-20R; 61-64; CANR 26, 60; MTCW 1, 2

Aretino, Pietro 1492-1556 .... **LC 12**

Arghezi, Tudor 1880-1967 .... **CLC 80**
See also Theodorescu, Ion N.
See also CA 167; DLB 220

Arguedas, Jose Maria 1911-1969 ... **CLC 10, 18; HLCS 1**
See also CA 89-92; CANR 73; DLB 113; HW 1

Argueta, Manlio 1936- .... **CLC 31**
See also CA 131; CANR 73; DLB 145; HW 1

Arias, Ron(ald Francis) 1941-
See also CA 131; CANR 81; DAM MULT; DLB 82; HLC 1; HW 1, 2; MTCW 2

Ariosto, Ludovico 1474-1533 .... **LC 6**

Aristides
See Epstein, Joseph

Aristophanes 450B.C.-385B.C. ..... **CMLC 4; DA; DAB; DAC; DAM DRAM, MST; DC 2; WLCS**
See also DA3; DLB 176

Aristotle 384B.C.-322B.C. ... **CMLC 31; DA; DAB; DAC; DAM MST; WLCS**
See also DA3; DLB 176

Arlt, Roberto (Godofredo Christophersen) 1900-1942 ..... **TCLC 29; DAM MULT; HLC 1**
See also CA 123; 131; CANR 67; HW 1, 2

Armah, Ayi Kwei 1939- ..... **CLC 5, 33, 136; BLC 1; DAM MULT, POET**
See also BW 1; CA 61-64; CANR 21, 64; DLB 117; MTCW 1

Armatrading, Joan 1950- .... **CLC 17**
See also CA 114; 186

Arnette, Robert
See Silverberg, Robert

Arnim, Achim von (Ludwig Joachim von Arnim) 1781-1831 .... **NCLC 5; SSC 29**
See also DLB 90

Arnim, Bettina von 1785-1859 ..... **NCLC 38**
See also DLB 90

Arnold, Matthew 1822-1888 .... **NCLC 6, 29, 89; DA; DAB; DAC; DAM MST, POET; PC 5; WLC**
See also CDBLB 1832-1890; DLB 32, 57

Arnold, Thomas 1795-1842 .... **NCLC 18**
See also DLB 55

Arnow, Harriette (Louisa) Simpson 1908-1986 .... **CLC 2, 7, 18**
See also CA 9-12R; 118; CANR 14; DLB 6; MTCW 1, 2; SATA 42; SATA-Obit 47

Arouet, Francois-Marie
See Voltaire

Arp, Hans
See Arp, Jean

Arp, Jean 1887-1966 .... **CLC 5**
See also CA 81-84; 25-28R; CANR 42, 77

Arrabal
See Arrabal, Fernando
Arrabal, Fernando 1932- .. **CLC 2, 9, 18, 58**
See also CA 9-12R; CANR 15
Arreola, Juan Jose 1918- ...... **SSC 38; DAM MULT; HLC 1**
See also CA 113; 131; CANR 81; DLB 113; HW 1, 2
Arrian c. 89(?)-c. 155(?) .... **CMLC 43**
See also DLB 176
Arrick, Fran .... **CLC 30**
See also Gaberman, Judie Angell
Artaud, Antonin (Marie Joseph) 1896-1948
...... **TCLC 3, 36; DAM DRAM; DC 14**
See also CA 104; 149; DA3; MTCW 1
Arthur, Ruth M(abel) 1905-1979 .... **CLC 12**
See also CA 9-12R; 85-88; CANR 4; SATA 7, 26
Artsybashev, Mikhail (Petrovich) 1878-1927
.... **TCLC 31**
See also CA 170
Arundel, Honor (Morfydd) 1919-1973
.... **CLC 17**
See also CA 21-22; 41-44R; CAP 2; CLR 35; SATA 4; SATA-Obit 24
Arzner, Dorothy 1897-1979 .... **CLC 98**
Asch, Sholem 1880-1957 .... **TCLC 3**
See also CA 105
Ash, Shalom
See Asch, Sholem
Ashbery, John (Lawrence) 1927- . **CLC 2, 3, 4, 6, 9, 13, 15, 25, 41, 77, 125; DAM POET; PC 26**
See also CA 5-8R; CANR 9, 37, 66; DA3; DLB 5, 165; DLBY 81; INT CANR-9; MTCW 1, 2
Ashdown, Clifford
See Freeman, R(ichard) Austin
Ashe, Gordon
See Creasey, John
Ashton-Warner, Sylvia (Constance)
1908-1984 .... **CLC 19**
See also CA 69-72; 112; CANR 29; MTCW 1, 2
Asimov, Isaac 1920-1992 .... **CLC 1, 3, 9, 19, 26, 76, 92; DAM POP**
See also AAYA 13; BEST 90:2; CA 1-4R; 137; CANR 2, 19, 36, 60; CLR 12; DA3; DLB 8; DLBY 92; INT CANR-19; JRDA; MAICYA; MTCW 1, 2; SATA 1, 26, 74
Assis, Joaquim Maria Machado de
See Machado de Assis, Joaquim Maria
Astley, Thea (Beatrice May) 1925- . **CLC 41**
See also CA 65-68; CANR 11, 43, 78
Aston, James
See White, T(erence) H(anbury)
Asturias, Miguel Angel 1899-1974 ... **CLC 3, 8, 13; DAM MULT, NOV; HLC 1**
See also CA 25-28; 49-52; CANR 32; CAP 2; DA3; DLB 113; HW 1; MTCW 1, 2
Atares, Carlos Saura
See Saura (Atares), Carlos
Atheling, William
See Pound, Ezra (Weston Loomis)
Atheling, William, Jr.
See Blish, James (Benjamin)
Atherton, Gertrude (Franklin Horn)
1857-1948 .... **TCLC 2**
See also CA 104; 155; DLB 9, 78, 186
Atherton, Lucius
See Masters, Edgar Lee
Atkins, Jack
See Harris, Mark
Atkinson, Kate .... **CLC 99**
See also CA 166
Attaway, William (Alexander) 1911-1986
.... **CLC 92; BLC 1; DAM MULT**
See also BW 2, 3; CA 143; CANR 82; DLB 76

Atticus
See Fleming, Ian (Lancaster); Wilson, (Thomas) Woodrow
Atwood, Margaret (Eleanor) 1939- . **CLC 2, 3, 4, 8, 13, 15, 25, 44, 84, 135; DA; DAB; DAC; DAM MST, NOV, POET; PC 8; SSC 2; WLC**
See also AAYA 12; BEST 89:2; CA 49-52; CANR 3, 24, 33, 59; DA3; DLB 53; INT CANR-24; MTCW 1, 2; SATA 50
Aubigny, Pierre d'
See Mencken, H(enry) L(ouis)
Aubin, Penelope 1685-1731(?) .... **LC 9**
See also DLB 39
Auchincloss, Louis (Stanton) 1917- . **CLC 4, 6, 9, 18, 45; DAM NOV; SSC 22**
See also CA 1-4R; CANR 6, 29, 55, 87; DLB 2; DLBY 80; INT CANR-29; MTCW 1
Auden, W(ystan) H(ugh) 1907-1973 . **CLC 1, 2, 3, 4, 6, 9, 11, 14, 43, 123; DA; DAB; DAC; DAM DRAM, MST, POET; PC 1; WLC**
See also AAYA 18; CA 9-12R; 45-48; CANR 5, 61; CDBLB 1914-1945; DA3; DLB 10, 20; MTCW 1, 2
Audiberti, Jacques 1900-1965 .... **CLC 38; DAM DRAM**
See also CA 25-28R
Audubon, John James 1785-1851 . **NCLC 47**
Auel, Jean M(arie) 1936- .... **CLC 31, 107; DAM POP**
See also AAYA 7; BEST 90:4; CA 103; CANR 21, 64; DA3; INT CANR-21; SATA 91
Auerbach, Erich 1892-1957 .... **TCLC 43**
See also CA 118; 155
Augier, Emile 1820-1889 .... **NCLC 31**
See also DLB 192
August, John
See De Voto, Bernard (Augustine)
Augustine 354-430 ...... **CMLC 6; DA; DAB; DAC; DAM MST; WLCS**
See also DA3; DLB 115
Aurelius
See Bourne, Randolph S(illiman)
Aurobindo, Sri
See Ghose, Aurabinda
Austen, Jane 1775-1817 ..... **NCLC 1, 13, 19, 33, 51, 81; DA; DAB; DAC; DAM MST, NOV; WLC**
See also AAYA 19; CDBLB 1789-1832; DA3; DLB 116
Auster, Paul 1947- .... **CLC 47, 131**
See also CA 69-72; CANR 23, 52, 75; DA3; DLB 227; MTCW 1
Austin, Frank
See Faust, Frederick (Schiller)
Austin, Mary (Hunter) 1868-1934 . **TCLC 25**
See also CA 109; 178; DLB 9, 78, 206, 221
Averroes 1126-1198 .... **CMLC 7**
See also DLB 115
Avicenna 980-1037 .... **CMLC 16**
See also DLB 115
Avison, Margaret 1918- .... **CLC 2, 4, 97; DAC; DAM POET**
See also CA 17-20R; DLB 53; MTCW 1
Axton, David
See Koontz, Dean R(ay)
Ayckbourn, Alan 1939- .... **CLC 5, 8, 18, 33, 74; DAB; DAM DRAM; DC 13**
See also CA 21-24R; CANR 31, 59; DLB 13; MTCW 1, 2
Aydy, Catherine
See Tennant, Emma (Christina)
Ayme, Marcel (Andre) 1902-1967 .. **CLC 11; SSC 41**
See also CA 89-92; CANR 67; CLR 25; DLB 72; SATA 91

Ayrton, Michael 1921-1975 .... **CLC 7**
See also CA 5-8R; 61-64; CANR 9, 21
Azorin .... **CLC 11**
See also Martinez Ruiz, Jose
Azuela, Mariano 1873-1952 . **TCLC 3; DAM MULT; HLC 1**
See also CA 104; 131; CANR 81; HW 1, 2; MTCW 1, 2
Baastad, Babbis Friis
See Friis-Baastad, Babbis Ellinor
Bab
See Gilbert, W(illiam) S(chwenck)
Babbis, Eleanor
See Friis-Baastad, Babbis Ellinor
Babel, Isaac
See Babel, Isaak (Emmanuilovich)
Babel, Isaak (Emmanuilovich) 1894-1941(?)
.... **TCLC 2, 13; SSC 16**
See also Babel, Isaac
See also CA 104; 155; MTCW 1
Babits, Mihaly 1883-1941 .... **TCLC 14**
See also CA 114
Babur 1483-1530 .... **LC 18**
Baca, Jimmy Santiago 1952-
See also CA 131; CANR 81, 90; DAM MULT; DLB 122; HLC 1; HW 1, 2
Bacchelli, Riccardo 1891-1985 .... **CLC 19**
See also CA 29-32R; 117
Bach, Richard (David) 1936- .... **CLC 14; DAM NOV, POP**
See also AITN 1; BEST 89:2; CA 9-12R; CANR 18, 93; MTCW 1; SATA 13
Bachman, Richard
See King, Stephen (Edwin)
Bachmann, Ingeborg 1926-1973 ..... **CLC 69**
See also CA 93-96; 45-48; CANR 69; DLB 85
Bacon, Francis 1561-1626 .... **LC 18, 32**
See also CDBLB Before 1660; DLB 151, 236
Bacon, Roger 1214(?)-1292 .... **CMLC 14**
See also DLB 115
Bacovia, George .... **TCLC 24**
See also Bacovia, G.; Vasiliu, Gheorghe
See also DLB 220
Badanes, Jerome 1937- .... **CLC 59**
Bagehot, Walter 1826-1877 .... **NCLC 10**
See also DLB 55
Bagnold, Enid 1889-1981 ..... **CLC 25; DAM DRAM**
See also CA 5-8R; 103; CANR 5, 40; DLB 13, 160, 191; MAICYA; SATA 1, 25
Bagritsky, Eduard 1895-1934 .... **TCLC 60**
Bagrjana, Elisaveta
See Belcheva, Elisaveta
Bagryana, Elisaveta 1893-1991 .... **CLC 10**
See also Belcheva, Elisaveta
See also CA 178; DLB 147
Bailey, Paul 1937- .... **CLC 45**
See also CA 21-24R; CANR 16, 62; DLB 14
Baillie, Joanna 1762-1851 .... **NCLC 71**
See also DLB 93
Bainbridge, Beryl (Margaret) 1934- . **CLC 4, 5, 8, 10, 14, 18, 22, 62, 130; DAM NOV**
See also CA 21-24R; CANR 24, 55, 75, 88; DLB 14, 231; MTCW 1, 2
Baker, Elliott 1922- .... **CLC 8**
See also CA 45-48; CANR 2, 63
Baker, Jean H. .... **TCLC 3, 10**
See also Russell, George William
Baker, Nicholson 1957- . **CLC 61; DAM POP**
See also CA 135; CANR 63; DA3; DLB 227
Baker, Ray Stannard 1870-1946 .. **TCLC 47**
See also CA 118
Baker, Russell (Wayne) 1925- .... **CLC 31**

See also BEST 89:4; CA 57-60; CANR 11, 41, 59; MTCW 1, 2

Bakhtin, M.
See Bakhtin, Mikhail Mikhailovich

Bakhtin, M. M.
See Bakhtin, Mikhail Mikhailovich

Bakhtin, Mikhail
See Bakhtin, Mikhail Mikhailovich

Bakhtin, Mikhail Mikhailovich 1895-1975
.... **CLC 83**
See also CA 128; 113

Bakshi, Ralph 1938(?)- .... **CLC 26**
See also CA 112; 138

Bakunin, Mikhail (Alexandrovich)
1814-1876 .... **NCLC 25, 58**

Baldwin, James (Arthur) 1924-1987 . **CLC 1, 2, 3, 4, 5, 8, 13, 15, 17, 42, 50, 67, 90, 127; DA; DAB; DAC; DAM MST, MULT, NOV, POP; DC 1; SSC 10, 33; WLC**
See also AAYA 4, 34; BW 1; CA 1-4R; 124; CABS 1; CANR 3, 24; CDALB 1941-1968; DA3; DLB 2, 7, 33; DLBY 87; MTCW 1, 2; SATA 9; SATA-Obit 54

Bale, John 1495-1563 .... **LC 62**
See also DLB 132

Ballard, J(ames) G(raham) 1930- .... **CLC 3, 6, 14, 36, 137; DAM NOV, POP; SSC 1**
See also AAYA 3; CA 5-8R; CANR 15, 39, 65; DA3; DLB 14, 207; MTCW 1, 2; SATA 93

Balmont, Konstantin (Dmitriyevich)
1867-1943 .... **TCLC 11**
See also CA 109; 155

Baltausis, Vincas
See Mikszath, Kalman

Balzac, Honore de 1799-1850 .. **NCLC 5, 35, 53; DA; DAB; DAC; DAM MST, NOV; SSC 5; WLC**
See also DA3; DLB 119

Bambara, Toni Cade 1939-1995 ..... **CLC 19, 88; BLC 1; DA; DAC; DAM MST, MULT; SSC 35; WLCS**
See also AAYA 5; BW 2, 3; CA 29-32R; 150; CANR 24, 49, 81; CDALBS; DA3; DLB 38; MTCW 1, 2; SATA 112

Bamdad, A.
See Shamlu, Ahmad

Banat, D. R.
See Bradbury, Ray (Douglas)

Bancroft, Laura
See Baum, L(yman) Frank

Banim, John 1798-1842 .... **NCLC 13**
See also DLB 116, 158, 159

Banim, Michael 1796-1874 .... **NCLC 13**
See also DLB 158, 159

Banjo, The
See Paterson, A(ndrew) B(arton)

Banks, Iain
See Banks, Iain M(enzies)

Banks, Iain M(enzies) 1954- .... **CLC 34**
See also CA 123; 128; CANR 61; DLB 194; INT 128

Banks, Lynne Reid .... **CLC 23**
See also Reid Banks, Lynne
See also AAYA 6

Banks, Russell 1940- ... **CLC 37, 72; SSC 42**
See also CA 65-68; CAAS 15; CANR 19, 52, 73; DLB 130

Banville, John 1945- .... **CLC 46, 118**
See also CA 117; 128; DLB 14; INT 128

Banville, Theodore (Faullain) de 1832-1891
.... **NCLC 9**

Baraka, Amiri 1934- . **CLC 1, 2, 3, 5, 10, 14, 33, 115; BLC 1; DA; DAC; DAM MST, MULT, POET, POP; DC 6; PC 4; WLCS**
See also Jones, LeRoi

See also BW 2, 3; CA 21-24R; CABS 3; CANR 27, 38, 61; CDALB 1941-1968; DA3; DLB 5, 7, 16, 38; DLBD 8; MTCW 1, 2

Barbauld, Anna Laetitia 1743-1825
.... **NCLC 50**
See also DLB 107, 109, 142, 158

Barbellion, W. N. P. .... **TCLC 24**
See also Cummings, Bruce F(rederick)

Barbera, Jack (Vincent) 1945- .... **CLC 44**
See also CA 110; CANR 45

Barbey d'Aurevilly, Jules Amedee 1808-1889
.... **NCLC 1; SSC 17**
See also DLB 119

Barbour, John c. 1316-1395 .... **CMLC 33**
See also DLB 146

Barbusse, Henri 1873-1935 .... **TCLC 5**
See also CA 105; 154; DLB 65

Barclay, Bill
See Moorcock, Michael (John)

Barclay, William Ewert
See Moorcock, Michael (John)

Barea, Arturo 1897-1957 .... **TCLC 14**
See also CA 111

Barfoot, Joan 1946- .... **CLC 18**
See also CA 105

Barham, Richard Harris 1788-1845
.... **NCLC 77**
See also DLB 159

Baring, Maurice 1874-1945 .... **TCLC 8**
See also CA 105; 168; DLB 34

Baring-Gould, Sabine 1834-1924 . **TCLC 88**
See also DLB 156, 190

Barker, Clive 1952- ..... **CLC 52; DAM POP**
See also AAYA 10; BEST 90:3; CA 121; 129; CANR 71; DA3; INT 129; MTCW 1, 2

Barker, George Granville 1913-1991
.... **CLC 8, 48; DAM POET**
See also CA 9-12R; 135; CANR 7, 38; DLB 20; MTCW 1

Barker, Harley Granville
See Granville-Barker, Harley
See also DLB 10

Barker, Howard 1946- .... **CLC 37**
See also CA 102; DLB 13, 233

Barker, Jane 1652-1732 .... **LC 42**

Barker, Pat(ricia) 1943- .... **CLC 32, 94**
See also CA 117; 122; CANR 50; INT 122

Barlach, Ernst (Heinrich) 1870-1938
.... **TCLC 84**
See also CA 178; DLB 56, 118

Barlow, Joel 1754-1812 .... **NCLC 23**
See also DLB 37

Barnard, Mary (Ethel) 1909- .... **CLC 48**
See also CA 21-22; CAP 2

Barnes, Djuna 1892-1982 ... **CLC 3, 4, 8, 11, 29, 127; SSC 3**
See also CA 9-12R; 107; CANR 16, 55; DLB 4, 9, 45; MTCW 1, 2

Barnes, Julian (Patrick) 1946- .... **CLC 42; DAB**
See also CA 102; CANR 19, 54; DLB 194; DLBY 93; MTCW 1

Barnes, Peter 1931- .... **CLC 5, 56**
See also CA 65-68; CAAS 12; CANR 33, 34, 64; DLB 13, 233; MTCW 1

Barnes, William 1801-1886 .... **NCLC 75**
See also DLB 32

Baroja (y Nessi), Pio 1872-1956 .... **TCLC 8; HLC 1**
See also CA 104

Baron, David
See Pinter, Harold

Baron Corvo
See Rolfe, Frederick (William Serafino Austin Lewis Mary)

Barondess, Sue K(aufman) 1926-1977
.... **CLC 8**
See also Kaufman, Sue
See also CA 1-4R; 69-72; CANR 1

Baron de Teive
See Pessoa, Fernando (Antonio Nogueira)

Baroness Von S.
See Zangwill, Israel

Barres, (Auguste-) Maurice 1862-1923
.... **TCLC 47**
See also CA 164; DLB 123

Barreto, Afonso Henrique de Lima
See Lima Barreto, Afonso Henrique de

Barrett, (Roger) Syd 1946- .... **CLC 35**

Barrett, William (Christopher) 1913-1992
.... **CLC 27**
See also CA 13-16R; 139; CANR 11, 67; INT CANR-11

Barrie, J(ames) M(atthew) 1860-1937
.... **TCLC 2; DAB; DAM DRAM**
See also CA 104; 136; CANR 77; CDBLB 1890-1914; CLR 16; DA3; DLB 10, 141, 156; MAICYA; MTCW 1; SATA 100; YABC 1

Barrington, Michael
See Moorcock, Michael (John)

Barrol, Grady
See Bograd, Larry

Barry, Mike
See Malzberg, Barry N(athaniel)

Barry, Philip 1896-1949 .... **TCLC 11**
See also CA 109; DLB 7, 228

Bart, Andre Schwarz
See Schwarz-Bart, Andre

Barth, John (Simmons) 1930- .. **CLC 1, 2, 3, 5, 7, 9, 10, 14, 27, 51, 89; DAM NOV; SSC 10**
See also AITN 1, 2; CA 1-4R; CABS 1; CANR 5, 23, 49, 64; DLB 2, 227; MTCW 1

Barthelme, Donald 1931-1989 . **CLC 1, 2, 3, 5, 6, 8, 13, 23, 46, 59, 115; DAM NOV; SSC 2**
See also CA 21-24R; 129; CANR 20, 58; DA3; DLB 2, 234; DLBY 80, 89; MTCW 1, 2; SATA 7; SATA-Obit 62

Barthelme, Frederick 1943- .... **CLC 36, 117**
See also CA 114; 122; CANR 77; DLBY 85; INT 122

Barthes, Roland (Gerard) 1915-1980
.... **CLC 24, 83**
See also CA 130; 97-100; CANR 66; MTCW 1, 2

Barzun, Jacques (Martin) 1907- ..... **CLC 51**
See also CA 61-64; CANR 22

Bashevis, Isaac
See Singer, Isaac Bashevis

Bashkirtseff, Marie 1859-1884 ..... **NCLC 27**

Basho
See Matsuo Basho

Basil of Caesaria c. 330-379 .... **CMLC 35**

Bass, Kingsley B., Jr.
See Bullins, Ed

Bass, Rick 1958- .... **CLC 79**
See also CA 126; CANR 53, 93; DLB 212

Bassani, Giorgio 1916- .... **CLC 9**
See also CA 65-68; CANR 33; DLB 128, 177; MTCW 1

Bastos, Augusto (Antonio) Roa
See Roa Bastos, Augusto (Antonio)

Bataille, Georges 1897-1962 .... **CLC 29**
See also CA 101; 89-92

Bates, H(erbert) E(rnest) 1905-1974
..... **CLC 46; DAB; DAM POP; SSC 10**
See also CA 93-96; 45-48; CANR 34; DA3; DLB 162, 191; MTCW 1, 2

See also CA 170
Benjamin, David
See Slavitt, David R(ytman)
Benjamin, Lois
See Gould, Lois
Benjamin, Walter 1892-1940 .... TCLC 39
See also CA 164
Benn, Gottfried 1886-1956 .... TCLC 3
See also CA 106; 153; DLB 56
Bennett, Alan 1934- .... CLC 45, 77; DAB;
DAM MST
See also CA 103; CANR 35, 55; MTCW 1,
2
Bennett, (Enoch) Arnold 1867-1931
.... TCLC 5, 20
See also CA 106; 155; CDBLB 1890-1914;
DLB 10, 34, 98, 135; MTCW 2
Bennett, Elizabeth
See Mitchell, Margaret (Munnerlyn)
Bennett, George Harold 1930-
See Bennett, Hal
See also BW 1; CA 97-100; CANR 87
Bennett, Hal .... CLC 5
See also Bennett, George Harold
See also DLB 33
Bennett, Jay 1912- .... CLC 35
See also AAYA 10; CA 69-72; CANR 11,
42, 79; JRDA; SAAS 4; SATA 41, 87;
SATA-Brief 27
Bennett, Louise (Simone) 1919- ..... CLC 28;
BLC 1; DAM MULT
See also BW 2, 3; CA 151; DLB 117
Benson, E(dward) F(rederic) 1867-1940
.... TCLC 27
See also CA 114; 157; DLB 135, 153
Benson, Jackson J. 1930- .... CLC 34
See also CA 25-28R; DLB 111
Benson, Sally 1900-1972 .... CLC 17
See also CA 19-20; 37-40R; CAP 1; SATA
1, 35; SATA-Obit 27
Benson, Stella 1892-1933 .... TCLC 17
See also CA 117; 155; DLB 36, 162
Bentham, Jeremy 1748-1832 .... NCLC 38
See also DLB 107, 158
Bentley, E(dmund) C(lerihew) 1875-1956
.... TCLC 12
See also CA 108; DLB 70
Bentley, Eric (Russell) 1916- .... CLC 24
See also CA 5-8R; CANR 6, 67; INT
CANR-6
Beranger, Pierre Jean de 1780-1857
.... NCLC 34
Berdyaev, Nicolas
See Berdyaev, Nikolai (Aleksandrovich)
Berdyaev, Nikolai (Aleksandrovich)
1874-1948 .... TCLC 67
See also CA 120; 157
Berdyayev, Nikolai (Aleksandrovich)
See Berdyaev, Nikolai (Aleksandrovich)
Berendt, John (Lawrence) 1939- .... CLC 86
See also CA 146; CANR 75, 93; DA3;
MTCW 1
Beresford, J(ohn) D(avys) 1873-1947
.... TCLC 81
See also CA 112; 155; DLB 162, 178, 197
Bergelson, David 1884-1952 .... TCLC 81
Berger, Colonel
See Malraux, (Georges-)Andre
Berger, John (Peter) 1926- .... CLC 2, 19
See also CA 81-84; CANR 51, 78; DLB 14,
207
Berger, Melvin H. 1927- .... CLC 12
See also CA 5-8R; CANR 4; CLR 32;
SAAS 2; SATA 5, 88
Berger, Thomas (Louis) 1924- . CLC 3, 5, 8,
11, 18, 38; DAM NOV
See also CA 1-4R; CANR 5, 28, 51; DLB
2; DLBY 80; INT CANR-28; MTCW 1, 2

Bergman, (Ernst) Ingmar 1918- .... CLC 16,
72
See also CA 81-84; CANR 33, 70; MTCW
2
Bergson, Henri(-Louis) 1859-1941 . TCLC 32
See also CA 164
Bergstein, Eleanor 1938- .... CLC 4
See also CA 53-56; CANR 5
Berkoff, Steven 1937- .... CLC 56
See also CA 104; CANR 72
Bermant, Chaim (Icyk) 1929- .... CLC 40
See also CA 57-60; CANR 6, 31, 57
Bern, Victoria
See Fisher, M(ary) F(rances) K(ennedy)
Bernanos, (Paul Louis) Georges 1888-1948
.... TCLC 3
See also CA 104; 130; DLB 72
Bernard, April 1956- .... CLC 59
See also CA 131
Berne, Victoria
See Fisher, M(ary) F(rances) K(ennedy)
Bernhard, Thomas 1931-1989 .... CLC 3, 32,
61
See also CA 85-88; 127; CANR 32, 57;
DLB 85, 124; MTCW 1
Bernhardt, Sarah (Henriette Rosine)
1844-1923 .... TCLC 75
See also CA 157
Berriault, Gina 1926-1999 ..... CLC 54, 109;
SSC 30
See also CA 116; 129; 185; CANR 66; DLB
130
Berrigan, Daniel 1921- .... CLC 4
See also CA 33-36R; CAAE 187; CAAS 1;
CANR 11, 43, 78; DLB 5
Berrigan, Edmund Joseph Michael, Jr.
1934-1983
See Berrigan, Ted
See also CA 61-64; 110; CANR 14
Berrigan, Ted .... CLC 37
See also Berrigan, Edmund Joseph Michael,
Jr.
See also DLB 5, 169
Berry, Charles Edward Anderson 1931-
See Berry, Chuck
See also CA 115
Berry, Chuck .... CLC 17
See also Berry, Charles Edward Anderson
Berry, Jonas
See Ashbery, John (Lawrence)
Berry, Wendell (Erdman) 1934- .. CLC 4, 6,
8, 27, 46; DAM POET; PC 28
See also AITN 1; CA 73-76; CANR 50, 73;
DLB 5, 6, 234; MTCW 1
Berryman, John 1914-1972 . CLC 1, 2, 3, 4,
6, 8, 10, 13, 25, 62; DAM POET
See also CA 13-16; 33-36R; CABS 2;
CANR 35; CAP 1; CDALB 1941-1968;
DLB 48; MTCW 1, 2
Bertolucci, Bernardo 1940- .... CLC 16
See also CA 106
Berton, Pierre (Francis Demarigny) 1920-
.... CLC 104
See also CA 1-4R; CANR 2, 56; DLB 68;
SATA 99
Bertrand, Aloysius 1807-1841 .... NCLC 31
Bertran de Born c. 1140-1215 .... CMLC 5
Besant, Annie (Wood) 1847-1933 ... TCLC 9
See also CA 105; 185
Bessie, Alvah 1904-1985 .... CLC 23
See also CA 5-8R; 116; CANR 2, 80; DLB
26
Bethlen, T. D.
See Silverberg, Robert
Beti, Mongo . CLC 27; BLC 1; DAM MULT
See also Biyidi, Alexandre
See also CANR 79
Betjeman, John 1906-1984 ..... CLC 2, 6, 10,
34, 43; DAB; DAM MST, POET

See also CA 9-12R; 112; CANR 33, 56;
CDBLB 1945-1960; DA3; DLB 20;
DLBY 84; MTCW 1, 2
Bettelheim, Bruno 1903-1990 .... CLC 79
See also CA 81-84; 131; CANR 23, 61;
DA3; MTCW 1, 2
Betti, Ugo 1892-1953 .... TCLC 5
See also CA 104; 155
Betts, Doris (Waugh) 1932- ..... CLC 3, 6, 28
See also CA 13-16R; CANR 9, 66, 77;
DLBY 82; INT CANR-9
Bevan, Alistair
See Roberts, Keith (John Kingston)
Bey, Pilaff
See Douglas, (George) Norman
Bialik, Chaim Nachman 1873-1934
.... TCLC 25
See also CA 170
Bickerstaff, Isaac
See Swift, Jonathan
Bidart, Frank 1939- .... CLC 33
See also CA 140
Bienek, Horst 1930- .... CLC 7, 11
See also CA 73-76; DLB 75
Bierce, Ambrose (Gwinett) 1842-1914(?)
.... TCLC 1, 7, 44; DA; DAC; DAM
MST; SSC 9; WLC
See also CA 104; 139; CANR 78; CDALB
1865-1917; DA3; DLB 11, 12, 23, 71, 74,
186
Biggers, Earl Derr 1884-1933 .... TCLC 65
See also CA 108; 153
Billings, Josh
See Shaw, Henry Wheeler
Billington, (Lady) Rachel (Mary) 1942-
.... CLC 43
See also AITN 2; CA 33-36R; CANR 44
Binyon, T(imothy) J(ohn) 1936- ..... CLC 34
See also CA 111; CANR 28
Bion 335B.C.-245B.C. .... CMLC 39
Bioy Casares, Adolfo 1914-1999 .. CLC 4, 8,
13, 88; DAM MULT; HLC 1; SSC 17
See also CA 29-32R; 177; CANR 19, 43,
66; DLB 113; HW 1, 2; MTCW 1, 2
Bird, Cordwainer
See Ellison, Harlan (Jay)
Bird, Robert Montgomery 1806-1854
.... NCLC 1
See also DLB 202
Birkerts, Sven 1951- .... CLC 116
See also CA 128; 133; 176; CAAE 176;
CAAS 29; INT 133
Birney, (Alfred) Earle 1904-1995 . CLC 1, 4,
6, 11; DAC; DAM MST, POET
See also CA 1-4R; CANR 5, 20; DLB 88;
MTCW 1
Biruni, al 973-1048(?) .... CMLC 28
Bishop, Elizabeth 1911-1979 .... CLC 1, 4, 9,
13, 15, 32; DA; DAC; DAM MST,
POET; PC 3
See also CA 5-8R; 89-92; CABS 2; CANR
26, 61; CDALB 1968-1988; DA3; DLB
5, 169; MTCW 1, 2; SATA-Obit 24
Bishop, John 1935- .... CLC 10
See also CA 105
Bishop, John Peale 1892-1944 .... TCLC 103
See also CA 107; 155; DLB 4, 9, 45
Bissett, Bill 1939- .... CLC 18; PC 14
See also CA 69-72; CAAS 19; CANR 15;
DLB 53; MTCW 1
Bissoondath, Neil (Devindra) 1955-
.... CLC 120; DAC
See also CA 136
Bitov, Andrei (Georgievich) 1937- .. CLC 57
See also CA 142
Biyidi, Alexandre 1932-
See Beti, Mongo
See also BW 1, 3; CA 114; 124; CANR 81;
DA3; MTCW 1, 2

See also CA 105; CANR 22; DLB 120; DLBY 83

Boucicault, Dion 1820-1890 .... **NCLC 41**

Bourget, Paul (Charles Joseph) 1852-1935 .... **TCLC 12**
See also CA 107; DLB 123

Bourjaily, Vance (Nye) 1922- ...... **CLC 8, 62**
See also CA 1-4R; CAAS 1; CANR 2, 72; DLB 2, 143

Bourne, Randolph S(illiman) 1886-1918 .... **TCLC 16**
See also CA 117; 155; DLB 63

Bova, Ben(jamin William) 1932- .... **CLC 45**
See also AAYA 16; CA 5-8R; CAAS 18; CANR 11, 56; CLR 3; DLBY 81; INT CANR-11; MAICYA; MTCW 1; SATA 6, 68

Bowen, Elizabeth (Dorothea Cole) 1899-1973 .... **CLC 1, 3, 6, 11, 15, 22, 118; DAM NOV; SSC 3, 28**
See also CA 17-18; 41-44R; CANR 35; CAP 2; CDBLB 1945-1960; DA3; DLB 15, 162; MTCW 1, 2

Bowering, George 1935- .... **CLC 15, 47**
See also CA 21-24R; CAAS 16; CANR 10; DLB 53

Bowering, Marilyn R(uthe) 1949- ... **CLC 32**
See also CA 101; CANR 49

Bowers, Edgar 1924-2000 .... **CLC 9**
See also CA 5-8R; CANR 24; DLB 5

Bowie, David .... **CLC 17**
See also Jones, David Robert

Bowles, Jane (Sydney) 1917-1973 .... **CLC 3, 68**
See also CA 19-20; 41-44R; CAP 2

Bowles, Paul (Frederick) 1910-1999 . **CLC 1, 2, 19, 53; SSC 3**
See also CA 1-4R; 186; CAAS 1; CANR 1, 19, 50, 75; DA3; DLB 5, 6; MTCW 1, 2

Box, Edgar
See Vidal, Gore

Boyd, Nancy
See Millay, Edna St. Vincent

Boyd, William 1952- .... **CLC 28, 53, 70**
See also CA 114; 120; CANR 51, 71; DLB 231

Boyle, Kay 1902-1992 .... **CLC 1, 5, 19, 58, 121; SSC 5**
See also CA 13-16R; 140; CAAS 1; CANR 29, 61; DLB 4, 9, 48, 86; DLBY 93; MTCW 1, 2

Boyle, Mark
See Kienzle, William X(avier)

Boyle, Patrick 1905-1982 .... **CLC 19**
See also CA 127

Boyle, T. C. 1948-
See Boyle, T(homas) Coraghessan

Boyle, T(homas) Coraghessan 1948- ... **CLC 36, 55, 90; DAM POP; SSC 16**
See also BEST 90:4; CA 120; CANR 44, 76, 89; DA3; DLBY 86; MTCW 2

Boz
See Dickens, Charles (John Huffam)

Brackenridge, Hugh Henry 1748-1816 .... **NCLC 7**
See also DLB 11, 37

Bradbury, Edward P.
See Moorcock, Michael (John)
See also MTCW 2

Bradbury, Malcolm (Stanley) 1932- .... **CLC 32, 61; DAM NOV**
See also CA 1-4R; CANR 1, 33, 91; DA3; DLB 14, 207; MTCW 1, 2

Bradbury, Ray (Douglas) 1920- ... **CLC 1, 3, 10, 15, 42, 98; DA; DAB; DAC; DAM MST, NOV, POP; SSC 29; WLC**

See also AAYA 15; AITN 1, 2; CA 1-4R; CANR 2, 30, 75; CDALB 1968-1988; DA3; DLB 2, 8; MTCW 1, 2; SATA 11, 64

Bradford, Gamaliel 1863-1932 ..... **TCLC 36**
See also CA 160; DLB 17

Bradley, David (Henry), Jr. 1950- . **CLC 23, 118; BLC 1; DAM MULT**
See also BW 1, 3; CA 104; CANR 26, 81; DLB 33

Bradley, John Ed(mund, Jr.) 1958- . **CLC 55**
See also CA 139

Bradley, Marion Zimmer 1930-1999 .... **CLC 30; DAM POP**
See also AAYA 9; CA 57-60; 185; CAAS 10; CANR 7, 31, 51, 75; DA3; DLB 8; MTCW 1, 2; SATA 90; SATA-Obit 116

Bradstreet, Anne 1612(?)-1672 ..... **LC 4, 30; DA; DAC; DAM MST, POET; PC 10**
See also CDALB 1640-1865; DA3; DLB 24

Brady, Joan 1939- .... **CLC 86**
See also CA 141

Bragg, Melvyn 1939- .... **CLC 10**
See also BEST 89:3; CA 57-60; CANR 10, 48, 89; DLB 14

Brahe, Tycho 1546-1601 .... **LC 45**

Braine, John (Gerard) 1922-1986 .... **CLC 1, 3, 41**
See also CA 1-4R; 120; CANR 1, 33; CD-BLB 1945-1960; DLB 15; DLBY 86; MTCW 1

Bramah, Ernest 1868-1942 .... **TCLC 72**
See also CA 156; DLB 70

Brammer, William 1930(?)-1978 ..... **CLC 31**
See also CA 77-80

Brancati, Vitaliano 1907-1954 ...... **TCLC 12**
See also CA 109

Brancato, Robin F(idler) 1936- .... **CLC 35**
See also AAYA 9; CA 69-72; CANR 11, 45; CLR 32; JRDA; SAAS 9; SATA 97

Brand, Max
See Faust, Frederick (Schiller)

Brand, Millen 1906-1980 .... **CLC 7**
See also CA 21-24R; 97-100; CANR 72

Branden, Barbara .... **CLC 44**
See also CA 148

Brandes, Georg (Morris Cohen) 1842-1927 .... **TCLC 10**
See also CA 105

Brandys, Kazimierz 1916- .... **CLC 62**

Branley, Franklyn M(ansfield) 1915- .... **CLC 21**
See also CA 33-36R; CANR 14, 39; CLR 13; MAICYA; SAAS 16; SATA 4, 68

Brathwaite, Edward (Kamau) 1930- .... **CLC 11; BLCS; DAM POET**
See also BW 2, 3; CA 25-28R; CANR 11, 26, 47; DLB 125

Brautigan, Richard (Gary) 1935-1984 . **CLC 1, 3, 5, 9, 12, 34, 42; DAM NOV**
See also CA 53-56; 113; CANR 34; DA3; DLB 2, 5, 206; DLBY 80, 84; MTCW 1; SATA 56

Brave Bird, Mary 1953-
See Crow Dog, Mary (Ellen)
See also NNAL

Braverman, Kate 1950- .... **CLC 67**
See also CA 89-92

Brecht, (Eugen) Bertolt (Friedrich) 1898-1956 .... **TCLC 1, 6, 13, 35; DA; DAB; DAC; DAM DRAM, MST; DC 3; WLC**
See also CA 104; 133; CANR 62; DA3; DLB 56, 124; MTCW 1, 2

Brecht, Eugen Berthold Friedrich
See Brecht, (Eugen) Bertolt (Friedrich)

Bremer, Fredrika 1801-1865 .... **NCLC 11**

Brennan, Christopher (John) 1870-1932 .... **TCLC 17**
See also CA 117; DLB 230

Brennan, Maeve 1917-1993 .... **CLC 5**
See also CA 81-84; CANR 72

Brent, Linda
See Jacobs, Harriet A(nn)

Brentano, Clemens (Maria) 1778-1842 .... **NCLC 1**
See also DLB 90

Brent of Bin Bin
See Franklin, (Stella Maria Sarah) Miles (Lampe)

Brenton, Howard 1942- .... **CLC 31**
See also CA 69-72; CANR 33, 67; DLB 13; MTCW 1

Breslin, James 1930-
See Breslin, Jimmy
See also CA 73-76; CANR 31, 75; DAM NOV; MTCW 1, 2

Breslin, Jimmy .... **CLC 4, 43**
See also Breslin, James
See also AITN 1; DLB 185; MTCW 2

Bresson, Robert 1901(?)-1999 .... **CLC 16**
See also CA 110; 187; CANR 49

Breton, Andre 1896-1966 . **CLC 2, 9, 15, 54; PC 15**
See also CA 19-20; 25-28R; CANR 40, 60; CAP 2; DLB 65; MTCW 1, 2

Breytenbach, Breyten 1939(?)- . **CLC 23, 37, 126; DAM POET**
See also CA 113; 129; CANR 61; DLB 225

Bridgers, Sue Ellen 1942- .... **CLC 26**
See also AAYA 8; CA 65-68; CANR 11, 36; CLR 18; DLB 52; JRDA; MAICYA; SAAS 1; SATA 22, 90; SATA-Essay 109

Bridges, Robert (Seymour) 1844-1930 .... **TCLC 1; DAM POET; PC 28**
See also CA 104; 152; CDBLB 1890-1914; DLB 19, 98

Bridie, James .... **TCLC 3**
See also Mavor, Osborne Henry
See also DLB 10

Brin, David 1950- .... **CLC 34**
See also AAYA 21; CA 102; CANR 24, 70; INT CANR-24; SATA 65

Brink, Andre (Philippus) 1935- ...... **CLC 18, 36, 106**
See also CA 104; CANR 39, 62; DLB 225; INT 103; MTCW 1, 2

Brinsmead, H(esba) F(ay) 1922- ..... **CLC 21**
See also CA 21-24R; CANR 10; CLR 47; MAICYA; SAAS 5; SATA 18, 78

Brittain, Vera (Mary) 1893(?)-1970 . **CLC 23**
See also CA 13-16; 25-28R; CANR 58; CAP 1; DLB 191; MTCW 1, 2

Broch, Hermann 1886-1951 .... **TCLC 20**
See also CA 117; DLB 85, 124

Brock, Rose
See Hansen, Joseph

Brodkey, Harold (Roy) 1930-1996 .. **CLC 56**
See also CA 111; 151; CANR 71; DLB 130

Brodsky, Iosif Alexandrovich 1940-1996
See Brodsky, Joseph
See also AITN 1; CA 41-44R; 151; CANR 37; DAM POET; DA3; MTCW 1, 2

Brodsky, Joseph 1940-1996 .... **CLC 4, 6, 13, 36, 100; PC 9**
See also Brodsky, Iosif Alexandrovich
See also MTCW 1

Brodsky, Michael (Mark) 1948- ...... **CLC 19**
See also CA 102; CANR 18, 41, 58

Brome, Richard 1590(?)-1652 .... **LC 61**
See also DLB 58

Bromell, Henry 1947- .... **CLC 5**
See also CA 53-56; CANR 9

Bromfield, Louis (Brucker) 1896-1956 .... **TCLC 11**
See also CA 107; 155; DLB 4, 9, 86

Broner, E(sther) M(asserman) 1930-
.... CLC 19
See also CA 17-20R; CANR 8, 25, 72; DLB
28
Bronk, William (M.) 1918-1999 ...... CLC 10
See also CA 89-92; 177; CANR 23; DLB
165
Bronstein, Lev Davidovich
See Trotsky, Leon
Bronte, Anne 1820-1849 .... NCLC 4, 71
See also DA3; DLB 21, 199
Bronte, Charlotte 1816-1855 ..... NCLC 3, 8,
33, 58; DA; DAB; DAC; DAM MST,
NOV; WLC
See also AAYA 17; CDBLB 1832-1890;
DA3; DLB 21, 159, 199
Bronte, Emily (Jane) 1818-1848 .. NCLC 16,
35; DA; DAB; DAC; DAM MST, NOV,
POET; PC 8; WLC
See also AAYA 17; CDBLB 1832-1890;
DA3; DLB 21, 32, 199
Brooke, Frances 1724-1789 .... LC 6, 48
See also DLB 39, 99
Brooke, Henry 1703(?)-1783 .... LC 1
See also DLB 39
Brooke, Rupert (Chawner) 1887-1915
..... TCLC 2, 7; DA; DAB; DAC; DAM
MST, POET; PC 24; WLC
See also CA 104; 132; CANR 61; CDBLB
1914-1945; DLB 19; MTCW 1, 2
Brooke-Haven, P.
See Wodehouse, P(elham) G(renville)
Brooke-Rose, Christine 1926(?)- ..... CLC 40
See also CA 13-16R; CANR 58; DLB 14,
231
Brookner, Anita 1928- . CLC 32, 34, 51, 136;
DAB; DAM POP
See also CA 114; 120; CANR 37, 56, 87;
DA3; DLB 194; DLBY 87; MTCW 1, 2
Brooks, Cleanth 1906-1994 ...... CLC 24, 86,
110
See also CA 17-20R; 145; CANR 33, 35;
DLB 63; DLBY 94; INT CANR-35;
MTCW 1, 2
Brooks, George
See Baum, L(yman) Frank
Brooks, Gwendolyn 1917-2000 . CLC 1, 2, 4,
5, 15, 49, 125; BLC 1; DA; DAC; DAM
MST, MULT, POET; PC 7; WLC
See also AAYA 20; AITN 1; BW 2, 3; CA
1-4R; CANR 1, 27, 52, 75; CDALB 1941-
1968; CLR 27; DA3; DLB 5, 76, 165;
MTCW 1, 2; SATA 6
Brooks, Mel .... CLC 12
See also Kaminsky, Melvin
See also AAYA 13; DLB 26
Brooks, Peter 1938- .... CLC 34
See also CA 45-48; CANR 1
Brooks, Van Wyck 1886-1963 .... CLC 29
See also CA 1-4R; CANR 6; DLB 45, 63,
103
Brophy, Brigid (Antonia) 1929-1995 . CLC 6,
11, 29, 105
See also CA 5-8R; 149; CAAS 4; CANR
25, 53; DA3; DLB 14; MTCW 1, 2
Brosman, Catharine Savage 1934- ... CLC 9
See also CA 61-64; CANR 21, 46
Brossard, Nicole 1943- .... CLC 115
See also CA 122; CAAS 16; DLB 53
Brother Antoninus
See Everson, William (Oliver)
The Brothers Quay
See Quay, Stephen; Quay, Timothy
Broughton, T(homas) Alan 1936- ... CLC 19
See also CA 45-48; CANR 2, 23, 48
Broumas, Olga 1949- .... CLC 10, 73
See also CA 85-88; CANR 20, 69
Brown, Alan 1950- .... CLC 99
See also CA 156

Brown, Charles Brockden 1771-1810
.... NCLC 22, 74
See also CDALB 1640-1865; DLB 37, 59,
73
Brown, Christy 1932-1981 .... CLC 63
See also CA 105; 104; CANR 72; DLB 14
Brown, Claude 1937- .... CLC 30; BLC 1;
DAM MULT
See also AAYA 7; BW 1, 3; CA 73-76;
CANR 81
Brown, Dee (Alexander) 1908- . CLC 18, 47;
DAM POP
See also AAYA 30; CA 13-16R; CAAS 6;
CANR 11, 45, 60; DA3; DLBY 80;
MTCW 1, 2; SATA 5, 110
Brown, George
See Wertmueller, Lina
Brown, George Douglas 1869-1902
.... TCLC 28
See also CA 162
Brown, George Mackay 1921-1996 . CLC 5,
48, 100
See also CA 21-24R; 151; CAAS 6; CANR
12, 37, 67; DLB 14, 27, 139; MTCW 1;
SATA 35
Brown, (William) Larry 1951- .... CLC 73
See also CA 130; 134; INT 133
Brown, Moses
See Barrett, William (Christopher)
Brown, Rita Mae 1944- ...... CLC 18, 43, 79;
DAM NOV, POP
See also CA 45-48; CANR 2, 11, 35, 62;
DA3; INT CANR-11; MTCW 1, 2
Brown, Roderick (Langmere) Haig-
See Haig-Brown, Roderick (Langmere)
Brown, Rosellen 1939- .... CLC 32
See also CA 77-80; CAAS 10; CANR 14,
44
Brown, Sterling Allen 1901-1989 ..... CLC 1,
23, 59; BLC 1; DAM MULT, POET
See also BW 1, 3; CA 85-88; 127; CANR
26; DA3; DLB 48, 51, 63; MTCW 1, 2
Brown, Will
See Ainsworth, William Harrison
Brown, William Wells 1813-1884 .. NCLC 2,
89; BLC 1; DAM MULT; DC 1
See also DLB 3, 50
Browne, (Clyde) Jackson 1948(?)- .. CLC 21
See also CA 120
Browning, Elizabeth Barrett 1806-1861
. NCLC 1, 16, 61, 66; DA; DAB; DAC;
DAM MST, POET; PC 6; WLC
See also CDBLB 1832-1890; DA3; DLB
32, 199
Browning, Robert 1812-1889 . NCLC 19, 79;
DA; DAB; DAC; DAM MST, POET;
PC 2; WLCS
See also CDBLB 1832-1890; DA3; DLB
32, 163; YABC 1
Browning, Tod 1882-1962 .... CLC 16
See also CA 141; 117
Brownson, Orestes Augustus 1803-1876
.... NCLC 50
See also DLB 1, 59, 73
Bruccoli, Matthew J(oseph) 1931- .. CLC 34
See also CA 9-12R; CANR 7, 87; DLB 103
Bruce, Lenny .... CLC 21
See also Schneider, Leonard Alfred
Bruin, John
See Brutus, Dennis
Brulard, Henri
See Stendhal
Brulls, Christian
See Simenon, Georges (Jacques Christian)
Brunner, John (Kilian Houston) 1934-1995
.... CLC 8, 10; DAM POP
See also CA 1-4R; 149; CAAS 8; CANR 2,
37; MTCW 1, 2
Bruno, Giordano 1548-1600 .... LC 27

Brutus, Dennis 1924- .... CLC 43; BLC 1;
DAM MULT, POET; PC 24
See also BW 2, 3; CA 49-52; CAAS 14;
CANR 2, 27, 42, 81; DLB 117, 225
Bryan, C(ourtlandt) D(ixon) B(arnes) 1936-
.... CLC 29
See also CA 73-76; CANR 13, 68; DLB
185; INT CANR-13
Bryan, Michael
See Moore, Brian
Bryan, William Jennings 1860-1925
.... TCLC 99
Bryant, William Cullen 1794-1878 . NCLC 6,
46; DA; DAB; DAC; DAM MST,
POET; PC 20
See also CDALB 1640-1865; DLB 3, 43,
59, 189
Bryusov, Valery Yakovlevich 1873-1924
.... TCLC 10
See also CA 107; 155
Buchan, John 1875-1940 ... TCLC 41; DAB;
DAM POP
See also CA 108; 145; DLB 34, 70, 156;
MTCW 1; YABC 2
Buchanan, George 1506-1582 .... LC 4
See also DLB 152
Buchheim, Lothar-Guenther 1918- ... CLC 6
See also CA 85-88
Buchner, (Karl) Georg 1813-1837 . NCLC 26
Buchwald, Art(hur) 1925- .... CLC 33
See also AITN 1; CA 5-8R; CANR 21, 67;
MTCW 1, 2; SATA 10
Buck, Pearl S(ydenstricker) 1892-1973
.. CLC 7, 11, 18, 127; DA; DAB; DAC;
DAM MST, NOV
See also AITN 1; CA 1-4R; 41-44R; CANR
1, 34; CDALBS; DA3; DLB 9, 102;
MTCW 1, 2; SATA 1, 25
Buckler, Ernest 1908-1984 .. CLC 13; DAC;
DAM MST
See also CA 11-12; 114; CAP 1; DLB 68;
SATA 47
Buckley, Vincent (Thomas) 1925-1988
.... CLC 57
See also CA 101
Buckley, William F(rank), Jr. 1925- . CLC 7,
18, 37; DAM POP
See also AITN 1; CA 1-4R; CANR 1, 24,
53, 93; DA3; DLB 137; DLBY 80; INT
CANR-24; MTCW 1, 2
Buechner, (Carl) Frederick 1926- .... CLC 2,
4, 6, 9; DAM NOV
See also CA 13-16R; CANR 11, 39, 64;
DLBY 80; INT CANR-11; MTCW 1, 2
Buell, John (Edward) 1927- .... CLC 10
See also CA 1-4R; CANR 71; DLB 53
Buero Vallejo, Antonio 1916-2000 . CLC 15,
46
See also CA 106; CANR 24, 49, 75; HW 1;
MTCW 1, 2
Bufalino, Gesualdo 1920(?)- .... CLC 74
See also DLB 196
Bugayev, Boris Nikolayevich 1880-1934
.... TCLC 7; PC 11
See also Bely, Andrey
See also CA 104; 165; MTCW 1
Bukowski, Charles 1920-1994 .. CLC 2, 5, 9,
41, 82, 108; DAM NOV, POET; PC 18
See also CA 17-20R; 144; CANR 40, 62;
DA3; DLB 5, 130, 169; MTCW 1, 2
Bulgakov, Mikhail (Afanas'evich) 1891-1940
. TCLC 2, 16; DAM DRAM, NOV; SSC
18
See also CA 105; 152
Bulgya, Alexander Alexandrovich 1901-1956
.... TCLC 53
See also Fadeyev, Alexander
See also CA 117; 181
Bullins, Ed 1935- .... CLC 1, 5, 7; BLC 1;

See also CA 104; 155; DLB 20, 225; MTCW 2

Campbell, Thomas 1777-1844 ...... **NCLC 19**
See also DLB 93; 144

Campbell, Wilfred .... **TCLC 9**
See also Campbell, William

Campbell, William 1858(?)-1918
See Campbell, Wilfred
See also CA 106; DLB 92

Campion, Jane .... **CLC 95**
See also AAYA 33; CA 138; CANR 87

Camus, Albert 1913-1960 ..... **CLC 1, 2, 4, 9, 11, 14, 32, 63, 69, 124; DA; DAB; DAC; DAM DRAM, MST, NOV; DC 2; SSC 9; WLC**
See also CA 89-92; DA3; DLB 72; MTCW 1, 2

Canby, Vincent 1924- .... **CLC 13**
See also CA 81-84

Cancale
See Desnos, Robert

Canetti, Elias 1905-1994 . **CLC 3, 14, 25, 75, 86**
See also CA 21-24R; 146; CANR 23, 61, 79; DA3; DLB 85, 124; MTCW 1, 2

Canfield, Dorothea F.
See Fisher, Dorothy (Frances) Canfield

Canfield, Dorothea Frances
See Fisher, Dorothy (Frances) Canfield

Canfield, Dorothy
See Fisher, Dorothy (Frances) Canfield

Canin, Ethan 1960- .... **CLC 55**
See also CA 131; 135

Cannon, Curt
See Hunter, Evan

Cao, Lan 1961- .... **CLC 109**
See also CA 165

Cape, Judith
See Page, P(atricia) K(athleen)

Capek, Karel 1890-1938 .. **TCLC 6, 37; DA; DAB; DAC; DAM DRAM, MST, NOV; DC 1; SSC 36; WLC**
See also CA 104; 140; DA3; MTCW 1

Capote, Truman 1924-1984 ..... **CLC 1, 3, 8, 13, 19, 34, 38, 58; DA; DAB; DAC; DAM MST, NOV, POP; SSC 2; WLC**
See also CA 5-8R; 113; CANR 18, 62; CDALB 1941-1968; DA3; DLB 2, 185, 227; DLBY 80, 84; MTCW 1, 2; SATA 91

Capra, Frank 1897-1991 .... **CLC 16**
See also CA 61-64; 135

Caputo, Philip 1941- .... **CLC 32**
See also CA 73-76; CANR 40

Caragiale, Ion Luca 1852-1912 .... **TCLC 76**
See also CA 157

Card, Orson Scott 1951- .... **CLC 44, 47, 50; DAM POP**
See also AAYA 11; CA 102; CANR 27, 47, 73; DA3; INT CANR-27; MTCW 1, 2; SATA 83

Cardenal, Ernesto 1925- ...... **CLC 31; DAM MULT, POET; HLC 1; PC 22**
See also CA 49-52; CANR 2, 32, 66; HW 1, 2; MTCW 1, 2

Cardozo, Benjamin N(athan) 1870-1938
.... **TCLC 65**
See also CA 117; 164

Carducci, Giosue (Alessandro Giuseppe) 1835-1907 .... **TCLC 32**
See also CA 163

Carew, Thomas 1595(?)-1640 . **LC 13; PC 29**
See also DLB 126

Carey, Ernestine Gilbreth 1908- ..... **CLC 17**
See also CA 5-8R; CANR 71; SATA 2

Carey, Peter 1943- .... **CLC 40, 55, 96**
See also CA 123; 127; CANR 53, 76; INT 127; MTCW 1, 2; SATA 94

Carleton, William 1794-1869 .... **NCLC 3**

See also DLB 159

Carlisle, Henry (Coffin) 1926- .... **CLC 33**
See also CA 13-16R; CANR 15, 85

Carlsen, Chris
See Holdstock, Robert P.

Carlson, Ron(ald F.) 1947- .... **CLC 54**
See also CA 105; CANR 27

Carlyle, Thomas 1795-1881 . **NCLC 70; DA; DAB; DAC; DAM MST**
See also CDBLB 1789-1832; DLB 55; 144

Carman, (William) Bliss 1861-1929
.... **TCLC 7; DAC**
See also CA 104; 152; DLB 92

Carnegie, Dale 1888-1955 .... **TCLC 53**

Carossa, Hans 1878-1956 .... **TCLC 48**
See also CA 170; DLB 66

Carpenter, Don(ald Richard) 1931-1995
.... **CLC 41**
See also CA 45-48; 149; CANR 1, 71

Carpenter, Edward 1844-1929 ...... **TCLC 88**
See also CA 163

Carpentier (y Valmont), Alejo 1904-1980
.... **CLC 8, 11, 38, 110; DAM MULT; HLC 1; SSC 35**
See also CA 65-68; 97-100; CANR 11, 70; DLB 113; HW 1, 2

Carr, Caleb 1955(?)- .... **CLC 86**
See also CA 147; CANR 73; DA3

Carr, Emily 1871-1945 .... **TCLC 32**
See also CA 159; DLB 68

Carr, John Dickson 1906-1977 .... **CLC 3**
See also Fairbairn, Roger
See also CA 49-52; 69-72; CANR 3, 33, 60; MTCW 1, 2

Carr, Philippa
See Hibbert, Eleanor Alice Burford

Carr, Virginia Spencer 1929- .... **CLC 34**
See also CA 61-64; DLB 111

Carrere, Emmanuel 1957- .... **CLC 89**

Carrier, Roch 1937- .... **CLC 13, 78; DAC; DAM MST**
See also CA 130; CANR 61; DLB 53; SATA 105

Carroll, James P. 1943(?)- .... **CLC 38**
See also CA 81-84; CANR 73; MTCW 1

Carroll, Jim 1951- .... **CLC 35**
See also AAYA 17; CA 45-48; CANR 42

Carroll, Lewis -1898 ... **NCLC 2, 53; PC 18; WLC**
See also Dodgson, Charles Lutwidge
See also CDBLB 1832-1890; CLR 2, 18; DLB 18, 163, 178; DLBY 98; JRDA

Carroll, Paul Vincent 1900-1968 ...... **CLC 10**
See also CA 9-12R; 25-28R; DLB 10

Carruth, Hayden 1921- .... **CLC 4, 7, 10, 18, 84; PC 10**
See also CA 9-12R; CANR 4, 38, 59; DLB 5, 165; INT CANR-4; MTCW 1, 2; SATA 47

Carson, Rachel Louise 1907-1964 . **CLC 71; DAM POP**
See also CA 77-80; CANR 35; DA3; MTCW 1, 2; SATA 23

Carter, Angela (Olive) 1940-1992 .... **CLC 5, 41, 76; SSC 13**
See also CA 53-56; 136; CANR 12, 36, 61; DA3; DLB 14, 207; MTCW 1, 2; SATA 66; SATA-Obit 70

Carter, Nick
See Smith, Martin Cruz

Carver, Raymond 1938-1988 .... **CLC 22, 36, 53, 55, 126; DAM NOV; SSC 8**
See also CA 33-36R; 126; CANR 17, 34, 61; DA3; DLB 130; DLBY 84, 88; MTCW 1, 2

Cary, Elizabeth, Lady Falkland 1585-1639
.... **LC 30**

Cary, (Arthur) Joyce (Lunel) 1888-1957
.... **TCLC 1, 29**

See also CA 104; 164; CDBLB 1914-1945; DLB 15, 100; MTCW 2

Casanova de Seingalt, Giovanni Jacopo 1725-1798 .... **LC 13**

Casares, Adolfo Bioy
See Bioy Casares, Adolfo

Casely-Hayford, J(oseph) E(phraim) 1866-1930 ..... **TCLC 24; BLC 1; DAM MULT**
See also BW 2; CA 123; 152

Casey, John (Dudley) 1939- .... **CLC 59**
See also BEST 90:2; CA 69-72; CANR 23

Casey, Michael 1947- .... **CLC 2**
See also CA 65-68; DLB 5

Casey, Patrick
See Thurman, Wallace (Henry)

Casey, Warren (Peter) 1935-1988 ... **CLC 12**
See also CA 101; 127; INT 101

Casona, Alejandro .... **CLC 49**
See also Alvarez, Alejandro Rodriguez

Cassavetes, John 1929-1989 .... **CLC 20**
See also CA 85-88; 127; CANR 82

Cassian, Nina 1924- .... **PC 17**

Cassill, R(onald) V(erlin) 1919- .... **CLC 4, 23**
See also CA 9-12R; CAAS 1; CANR 7, 45; DLB 6

Cassiodorus, Flavius Magnus c. 490(?)-c. 583(?) .... **CMLC 43**

Cassirer, Ernst 1874-1945 .... **TCLC 61**
See also CA 157

Cassity, (Allen) Turner 1929- ...... **CLC 6, 42**
See also CA 17-20R; CAAS 8; CANR 11; DLB 105

Castaneda, Carlos (Cesar Aranha) 1931(?)-1998 .... **CLC 12, 119**
See also CA 25-28R; CANR 32, 66; HW 1; MTCW 1

Castedo, Elena 1937- .... **CLC 65**
See also CA 132

Castedo-Ellerman, Elena
See Castedo, Elena

Castellanos, Rosario 1925-1974 ..... **CLC 66; DAM MULT; HLC 1; SSC 39**
See also CA 131; 53-56; CANR 58; DLB 113; HW 1; MTCW 1

Castelvetro, Lodovico 1505-1571 .... **LC 12**

Castiglione, Baldassare 1478-1529 ..... **LC 12**

Castle, Robert
See Hamilton, Edmond

Castro (Ruz), Fidel 1926(?)-
See also CA 110; 129; CANR 81; DAM MULT; HLC 1; HW 2

Castro, Guillen de 1569-1631 .... **LC 19**

Castro, Rosalia de 1837-1885 . **NCLC 3, 78; DAM MULT**

Cather, Willa -1947
See Cather, Willa Sibert

Cather, Willa Sibert 1873-1947 ..... **TCLC 1, 11, 31, 99; DA; DAB; DAC; DAM MST, NOV; SSC 2; WLC**
See also Cather, Willa
See also AAYA 24; CA 104; 128; CDALB 1865-1917; DA3; DLB 9, 54, 78; DLBD 1; MTCW 1, 2; SATA 30

Catherine, Saint 1347-1380 .... **CMLC 27**

Cato, Marcus Porcius 234B.C.-149B.C.
.... **CMLC 21**

See also DLB 211

Catton, (Charles) Bruce 1899-1978 . **CLC 35**
See also AITN 1; CA 5-8R; 81-84; CANR 7, 74; DLB 17; SATA 2; SATA-Obit 24

Catullus c. 84B.C.-c. 54B.C. .... **CMLC 18**
See also DLB 211

Cauldwell, Frank
See King, Francis (Henry)

Caunitz, William J. 1933-1996 .... **CLC 34**
See also BEST 89:3; CA 125; 130; 152; CANR 73; INT 130

Causley, Charles (Stanley) 1917- ...... **CLC 7**
See also CA 9-12R; CANR 5, 35; CLR 30; DLB 27; MTCW 1; SATA 3, 66

Caute, (John) David 1936- .. **CLC 29; DAM NOV**
See also CA 1-4R; CAAS 4; CANR 1, 33, 64; DLB 14, 231

Cavafy, C(onstantine) P(eter) 1863-1933 .... **TCLC 2, 7; DAM POET**
See also Kavafis, Konstantinos Petrou
See also CA 148; DA3; MTCW 1

Cavallo, Evelyn
See Spark, Muriel (Sarah)

Cavanna, Betty .... **CLC 12**
See also Harrison, Elizabeth Cavanna
See also JRDA; MAICYA; SAAS 4; SATA 1, 30

Cavendish, Margaret Lucas 1623-1673 .... **LC 30**
See also DLB 131

Caxton, William 1421(?)-1491(?) .... **LC 17**
See also DLB 170

Cayer, D. M.
See Duffy, Maureen

Cayrol, Jean 1911- .... **CLC 11**
See also CA 89-92; DLB 83

Cela, Camilo Jose 1916- .... **CLC 4, 13, 59, 122; DAM MULT; HLC 1**
See also BEST 90:2; CA 21-24R; CAAS 10; CANR 21, 32, 76; DLBY 89; HW 1; MTCW 1, 2

Celan, Paul .... **CLC 10, 19, 53, 82; PC 10**
See also Antschel, Paul
See also DLB 69

Celine, Louis-Ferdinand .. **CLC 1, 3, 4, 7, 9, 15, 47, 124**
See also Destouches, Louis-Ferdinand
See also DLB 72

Cellini, Benvenuto 1500-1571 .... **LC 7**

Cendrars, Blaise 1887-1961 ..... **CLC 18, 106**
See also Sauser-Hall, Frederic

Cernuda (y Bidon), Luis 1902-1963 .... **CLC 54; DAM POET**
See also CA 131; 89-92; DLB 134; HW 1

Cervantes, Lorna Dee 1954-
See also CA 131; CANR 80; DLB 82; HLCS 1; HW 1

Cervantes (Saavedra), Miguel de 1547-1616 .... **LC 6, 23; DA; DAB; DAC; DAM MST, NOV; SSC 12; WLC**

Cesaire, Aime (Fernand) 1913- .. **CLC 19, 32, 112; BLC 1; DAM MULT, POET; PC 25**
See also BW 2, 3; CA 65-68; CANR 24, 43, 81; DA3; MTCW 1, 2

Chabon, Michael 1963- .... **CLC 55**
See also CA 139; CANR 57

Chabrol, Claude 1930- .... **CLC 16**
See also CA 110

Challans, Mary 1905-1983
See Renault, Mary
See also CA 81-84; 111; CANR 74; DA3; MTCW 2; SATA 23; SATA-Obit 36

Challis, George
See Faust, Frederick (Schiller)

Chambers, Aidan 1934- .... **CLC 35**
See also AAYA 27; CA 25-28R; CANR 12, 31, 58; JRDA; MAICYA; SAAS 12; SATA 1, 69, 108

Chambers, James 1948-
See Cliff, Jimmy
See also CA 124

Chambers, Jessie
See Lawrence, D(avid) H(erbert Richards)

Chambers, Robert W(illiam) 1865-1933 .... **TCLC 41**
See also CA 165; DLB 202; SATA 107

Chamisso, Adelbert von 1781-1838 .... **NCLC 82**

See also DLB 90

Chandler, Raymond (Thornton) 1888-1959 .... **TCLC 1, 7; SSC 23**
See also AAYA 25; CA 104; 129; CANR 60; CDALB 1929-1941; DA3; DLB 226; DLBD 6; MTCW 1, 2

Chang, Eileen 1920-1995 .... **SSC 28**
See also CA 166

Chang, Jung 1952- .... **CLC 71**
See also CA 142

Chang Ai-Ling
See Chang, Eileen

Channing, William Ellery 1780-1842 .... **NCLC 17**
See also DLB 1, 59, 235

Chao, Patricia 1955- .... **CLC 119**
See also CA 163

Chaplin, Charles Spencer 1889-1977 .... **CLC 16**
See also Chaplin, Charlie
See also CA 81-84; 73-76

Chaplin, Charlie
See Chaplin, Charles Spencer
See also DLB 44

Chapman, George 1559(?)-1634 .... **LC 22; DAM DRAM**
See also DLB 62, 121

Chapman, Graham 1941-1989 .... **CLC 21**
See also Monty Python
See also CA 116; 129; CANR 35

Chapman, John Jay 1862-1933 ...... **TCLC 7**
See also CA 104

Chapman, Lee
See Bradley, Marion Zimmer

Chapman, Walker
See Silverberg, Robert

Chappell, Fred (Davis) 1936- .... **CLC 40, 78**
See also CA 5-8R; CAAS 4; CANR 8, 33, 67; DLB 6, 105

Char, Rene(-Emile) 1907-1988 ... **CLC 9, 11, 14, 55; DAM POET**
See also CA 13-16R; 124; CANR 32; MTCW 1, 2

Charby, Jay
See Ellison, Harlan (Jay)

Chardin, Pierre Teilhard de
See Teilhard de Chardin, (Marie Joseph) Pierre

Charlemagne 742-814 .... **CMLC 37**

Charles I 1600-1649 .... **LC 13**

Charriere, Isabelle de 1740-1805 . **NCLC 66**

Charyn, Jerome 1937- .... **CLC 5, 8, 18**
See also CA 5-8R; CAAS 1; CANR 7, 61; DLBY 83; MTCW 1

Chase, Mary (Coyle) 1907-1981 .... **DC 1**
See also CA 77-80; 105; DLB 228; SATA 17; SATA-Obit 29

Chase, Mary Ellen 1887-1973 .... **CLC 2**
See also CA 13-16; 41-44R; CAP 1; SATA 10

Chase, Nicholas
See Hyde, Anthony

Chateaubriand, Francois Rene de 1768-1848 .... **NCLC 3**
See also DLB 119

Chatterje, Sarat Chandra 1876-1936(?)
See Chatterji, Saratchandra
See also CA 109

Chatterji, Bankim Chandra 1838-1894 .... **NCLC 19**

Chatterji, Saratchandra -1938 ..... **TCLC 13**
See also Chatterje, Sarat Chandra
See also CA 186

Chatterton, Thomas 1752-1770 .... **LC 3, 54; DAM POET**
See also DLB 109

Chatwin, (Charles) Bruce 1940-1989 .... **CLC 28, 57, 59; DAM POP**

See also AAYA 4; BEST 90:1; CA 85-88; 127; DLB 194, 204

Chaucer, Daniel -1939
See Ford, Ford Madox

Chaucer, Geoffrey 1340(?)-1400 . **LC 17, 56; DA; DAB; DAC; DAM MST, POET; PC 19; WLCS**
See also CDBLB Before 1660; DA3; DLB 146

Chavez, Denise (Elia) 1948-
See also CA 131; CANR 56, 81; DAM MULT; DLB 122; HLC 1; HW 1, 2; MTCW 2

Chaviaras, Strates 1935-
See Haviaras, Stratis
See also CA 105

Chayefsky, Paddy .... **CLC 23**
See also Chayefsky, Sidney
See also DLB 7, 44; DLBY 81

Chayefsky, Sidney 1923-1981
See Chayefsky, Paddy
See also CA 9-12R; 104; CANR 18; DAM DRAM

Chedid, Andree 1920- .... **CLC 47**
See also CA 145

Cheever, John 1912-1982 ... **CLC 3, 7, 8, 11, 15, 25, 64; DA; DAB; DAC; DAM MST, NOV, POP; SSC 1, 38; WLC**
See also CA 5-8R; 106; CABS 1; CANR 5, 27, 76; CDALB 1941-1968; DA3; DLB 2, 102, 227; DLBY 80, 82; INT CANR-5; MTCW 1, 2

Cheever, Susan 1943- .... **CLC 18, 48**
See also CA 103; CANR 27, 51, 92; DLBY 82; INT CANR-27

Chekhonte, Antosha
See Chekhov, Anton (Pavlovich)

Chekhov, Anton (Pavlovich) 1860-1904 ...... **TCLC 3, 10, 31, 55, 96; DA; DAB; DAC; DAM DRAM, MST; DC 9; SSC 2, 28, 41; WLC**
See also CA 104; 124; DA3; SATA 90

Chernyshevsky, Nikolay Gavrilovich 1828-1889 .... **NCLC 1**

Cherry, Carolyn Janice 1942-
See Cherryh, C. J.
See also CA 65-68; CANR 10

Cherryh, C. J. .... **CLC 35**
See also Cherry, Carolyn Janice
See also AAYA 24; DLBY 80; SATA 93

Chesnutt, Charles W(addell) 1858-1932 ..... **TCLC 5, 39; BLC 1; DAM MULT; SSC 7**
See also BW 1, 3; CA 106; 125; CANR 76; DLB 12, 50, 78; MTCW 1, 2

Chester, Alfred 1929(?)-1971 .... **CLC 49**
See also CA 33-36R; DLB 130

Chesterton, G(ilbert) K(eith) 1874-1936 ..... **TCLC 1, 6, 64; DAM NOV, POET; PC 28; SSC 1**
See also CA 104; 132; CANR 73; CDBLB 1914-1945; DLB 10, 19, 34, 70, 98, 149, 178; MTCW 1, 2; SATA 27

Chiang, Pin-chin 1904-1986
See Ding Ling
See also CA 118

Ch'ien Chung-shu 1910- .... **CLC 22**
See also CA 130; CANR 73; MTCW 1, 2

Child, L. Maria
See Child, Lydia Maria

Child, Lydia Maria 1802-1880 . **NCLC 6, 73**
See also DLB 1, 74; SATA 67

Child, Mrs.
See Child, Lydia Maria

Child, Philip 1898-1978 .... **CLC 19, 68**
See also CA 13-14; CAP 1; SATA 47

Childers, (Robert) Erskine 1870-1922 .... **TCLC 65**
See also CA 113; 153; DLB 70

55; DLB 52; INT CANR-23; JRDA; MAI-
CYA; MTCW 1, 2; SATA 10, 45, 83

Corn, Alfred (DeWitt III) 1943- ..... **CLC 33**
See also CA 179; CAAE 179; CAAS 25;
CANR 44; DLB 120; DLBY 80

Corneille, Pierre 1606-1684 ... **LC 28; DAB;**
DAM MST

Cornwell, David (John Moore) 1931-
.... **CLC 9, 15; DAM POP**
See also le Carre, John
See also CA 5-8R; CANR 13, 33, 59; DA3;
MTCW 1, 2

Corso, (Nunzio) Gregory 1930- .. **CLC 1, 11**
See also CA 5-8R; CANR 41, 76; DA3;
DLB 5, 16; MTCW 1, 2

Cortazar, Julio 1914-1984 .. **CLC 2, 3, 5, 10,**
13, 15, 33, 34, 92; DAM MULT, NOV;
HLC 1; SSC 7
See also CA 21-24R; CANR 12, 32, 81;
DA3; DLB 113; HW 1, 2; MTCW 1, 2

Cortes, Hernan 1484-1547 .... **LC 31**

Corvinus, Jakob
See Raabe, Wilhelm (Karl)

Corwin, Cecil
See Kornbluth, C(yril) M.

Cosic, Dobrica 1921- .... **CLC 14**
See also CA 122; 138; DLB 181

Costain, Thomas B(ertram) 1885-1965
.... **CLC 30**
See also CA 5-8R; 25-28R; DLB 9

Costantini, Humberto 1924(?)-1987 . **CLC 49**
See also CA 131; 122; HW 1

Costello, Elvis 1955- .... **CLC 21**

Costenoble, Philostene
See Ghelderode, Michel de

Cotes, Cecil V.
See Duncan, Sara Jeannette

Cotter, Joseph Seamon Sr. 1861-1949
.... **TCLC 28; BLC 1; DAM MULT**
See also BW 1; CA 124; DLB 50

Couch, Arthur Thomas Quiller
See Quiller-Couch, SirArthur (Thomas)

Coulton, James
See Hansen, Joseph

Couperus, Louis (Marie Anne) 1863-1923
.... **TCLC 15**
See also CA 115

Coupland, Douglas 1961- .... **CLC 85, 133;**
DAC; DAM POP
See also AAYA 34; CA 142; CANR 57, 90

Court, Wesli
See Turco, Lewis (Putnam)

Courtenay, Bryce 1933- .... **CLC 59**
See also CA 138

Courtney, Robert
See Ellison, Harlan (Jay)

Cousteau, Jacques-Yves 1910-1997 . **CLC 30**
See also CA 65-68; 159; CANR 15, 67;
MTCW 1; SATA 38, 98

Coventry, Francis 1725-1754 .... **LC 46**

Cowan, Peter (Walkinshaw) 1914- .. **SSC 28**
See also CA 21-24R; CANR 9, 25, 50, 83

Coward, Noel (Peirce) 1899-1973 . **CLC 1, 9,**
29, 51; DAM DRAM
See also AITN 1; CA 17-18; 41-44R;
CANR 35; CAP 2; CDBLB 1914-1945;
DA3; DLB 10; MTCW 1, 2

Cowley, Abraham 1618-1667 .... **LC 43**
See also DLB 131, 151

Cowley, Malcolm 1898-1989 .... **CLC 39**
See also CA 5-8R; 128; CANR 3, 55; DLB
4, 48; DLBY 81, 89; MTCW 1, 2

Cowper, William 1731-1800 .... **NCLC 8, 94;**
DAM POET
See also DA3; DLB 104, 109

Cox, William Trevor 1928- .. **CLC 9, 14, 71;**
DAM NOV
See also Trevor, William

See also CA 9-12R; CANR 4, 37, 55, 76;
DLB 14; INT CANR-37; MTCW 1, 2

Coyne, P. J.
See Masters, Hilary

Cozzens, James Gould 1903-1978 .... **CLC 1,**
4, 11, 92
See also CA 9-12R; 81-84; CANR 19;
CDALB 1941-1968; DLB 9; DLBD 2;
DLBY 84, 97; MTCW 1, 2

Crabbe, George 1754-1832 .... **NCLC 26**
See also DLB 93

Craddock, Charles Egbert
See Murfree, Mary Noailles

Craig, A. A.
See Anderson, Poul (William)

Craik, Dinah Maria (Mulock) 1826-1887
.... **NCLC 38**
See also DLB 35, 163; MAICYA; SATA 34

Cram, Ralph Adams 1863-1942 ... **TCLC 45**
See also CA 160

Crane, (Harold) Hart 1899-1932 ... **TCLC 2,**
5, 80; DA; DAB; DAC; DAM MST,
POET; PC 3; WLC
See also CA 104; 127; CDALB 1917-1929;
DA3; DLB 4, 48; MTCW 1, 2

Crane, R(onald) S(almon) 1886-1967
.... **CLC 27**
See also CA 85-88; DLB 63

Crane, Stephen (Townley) 1871-1900
..... **TCLC 11, 17, 32; DA; DAB; DAC;**
DAM MST, NOV, POET; SSC 7; WLC
See also AAYA 21; CA 109; 140; CANR
84; CDALB 1865-1917; DA3; DLB 12,
54, 78; YABC 2

Cranshaw, Stanley
See Fisher, Dorothy (Frances) Canfield

Crase, Douglas 1944- .... **CLC 58**
See also CA 106

Crashaw, Richard 1612(?)-1649 .... **LC 24**
See also DLB 126

Craven, Margaret 1901-1980 .... **CLC 17;**
DAC
See also CA 103

Crawford, F(rancis) Marion 1854-1909
.... **TCLC 10**
See also CA 107; 168; DLB 71

Crawford, Isabella Valancy 1850-1887
.... **NCLC 12**
See also DLB 92

Crayon, Geoffrey
See Irving, Washington

Creasey, John 1908-1973 .... **CLC 11**
See also CA 5-8R; 41-44R; CANR 8, 59;
DLB 77; MTCW 1

Crebillon, Claude Prosper Jolyot de (fils)
1707-1777 .... **LC 1, 28**

Credo
See Creasey, John

Credo, Alvaro J. de
See Prado (Calvo), Pedro

Creeley, Robert (White) 1926- . **CLC 1, 2, 4,**
8, 11, 15, 36, 78; DAM POET
See also CA 1-4R; CAAS 10; CANR 23,
43, 89; DA3; DLB 5, 16, 169; DLBD 17;
MTCW 1, 2

Crews, Harry (Eugene) 1935- .... **CLC 6, 23,**
49
See also AITN 1; CA 25-28R; CANR 20,
57; DA3; DLB 6, 143, 185; MTCW 1, 2

Crichton, (John) Michael 1942- **CLC 2, 6,**
54, 90; DAM NOV, POP
See also AAYA 10; AITN 2; CA 25-28R;
CANR 13, 40, 54, 76; DA3; DLBY 81;
INT CANR-13; JRDA; MTCW 1, 2;
SATA 9, 88

Crispin, Edmund .... **CLC 22**
See also Montgomery, (Robert) Bruce
See also DLB 87

Cristofer, Michael 1945(?)- .. **CLC 28; DAM**
DRAM
See also CA 110; 152; DLB 7

Croce, Benedetto 1866-1952 .... **TCLC 37**
See also CA 120; 155

Crockett, David 1786-1836 .... **NCLC 8**
See also DLB 3, 11

Crockett, Davy
See Crockett, David

Crofts, Freeman Wills 1879-1957 . **TCLC 55**
See also CA 115; DLB 77

Croker, John Wilson 1780-1857 ... **NCLC 10**
See also DLB 110

Crommelynck, Fernand 1885-1970 . **CLC 75**
See also CA 89-92

Cromwell, Oliver 1599-1658 .... **LC 43**

Cronin, A(rchibald) J(oseph) 1896-1981
.... **CLC 32**
See also CA 1-4R; 102; CANR 5; DLB 191;
SATA 47; SATA-Obit 25

Cross, Amanda
See Heilbrun, Carolyn G(old)

Crothers, Rachel 1878(?)-1958 ..... **TCLC 19**
See also CA 113; DLB 7

Croves, Hal
See Traven, B.

Crow Dog, Mary (Ellen) (?)- .... **CLC 93**
See also Brave Bird, Mary
See also CA 154

Crowfield, Christopher
See Stowe, Harriet (Elizabeth) Beecher

Crowley, Aleister .... **TCLC 7**
See also Crowley, Edward Alexander

Crowley, Edward Alexander 1875-1947
See Crowley, Aleister
See also CA 104

Crowley, John 1942- .... **CLC 57**
See also CA 61-64; CANR 43; DLBY 82;
SATA 65

Crud
See Crumb, R(obert)

Crumarums
See Crumb, R(obert)

Crumb, R(obert) 1943- .... **CLC 17**
See also CA 106

Crumbum
See Crumb, R(obert)

Crumski
See Crumb, R(obert)

Crum the Bum
See Crumb, R(obert)

Crunk
See Crumb, R(obert)

Crustt
See Crumb, R(obert)

Cruz, Victor Hernandez 1949-
See also BW 2; CA 65-68; CAAS 17;
CANR 14, 32, 74; DAM MULT, POET;
DLB 41; HLC 1; HW 1, 2; MTCW 1

Cryer, Gretchen (Kiger) 1935- .... **CLC 21**
See also CA 114; 123

Csath, Geza 1887-1919 .... **TCLC 13**
See also CA 111

Cudlip, David R(ockwell) 1933- ...... **CLC 34**
See also CA 177

Cullen, Countee 1903-1946 ...... **TCLC 4, 37;**
BLC 1; DA; DAC; DAM MST, MULT,
POET; PC 20; WLCS
See also BW 1; CA 108; 124; CDALB
1917-1929; DA3; DLB 4, 48, 51; MTCW
1, 2; SATA 18

Cum, R.
See Crumb, R(obert)

Cummings, Bruce F(rederick) 1889-1919
See Barbellion, W. N. P.
See also CA 123

Cummings, E(dward) E(stlin) 1894-1962
...... **CLC 1, 3, 8, 12, 15, 68; DA; DAB;**

DAC; DAM MST, POET; PC 5; WLC
See also CA 73-76; CANR 31; CDALB
1929-1941; DA3; DLB 4, 48; MTCW 1,
2

Cunha, Euclides (Rodrigues Pimenta) da
1866-1909 .... **TCLC 24**
See also CA 123

Cunningham, E. V.
See Fast, Howard (Melvin)

Cunningham, J(ames) V(incent) 1911-1985
.... **CLC 3, 31**
See also CA 1-4R; 115; CANR 1, 72; DLB
5

Cunningham, Julia (Woolfolk) 1916-
.... **CLC 12**
See also CA 9-12R; CANR 4, 19, 36;
JRDA; MAICYA; SAAS 2; SATA 1, 26

Cunningham, Michael 1952- .... **CLC 34**
See also CA 136

Cunninghame Graham, R. B.
See Cunninghame Graham, Robert
(Gallnigad) Bontine

Cunninghame Graham, Robert (Gallnigad)
Bontine 1852-1936 .... **TCLC 19**
See also Graham, R(obert) B(ontine) Cun-
ninghame
See also CA 119; 184; DLB 98

Currie, Ellen 19(?)- .... **CLC 44**

Curtin, Philip
See Lowndes, Marie Adelaide (Belloc)

Curtis, Price
See Ellison, Harlan (Jay)

Cutrate, Joe
See Spiegelman, Art

Cynewulf c. 770-c. 840 .... **CMLC 23**

Czaczkes, Shmuel Yosef
See Agnon, S(hmuel) Y(osef Halevi)

Dabrowska, Maria (Szumska) 1889-1965
.... **CLC 15**
See also CA 106

Dabydeen, David 1955- .... **CLC 34**
See also BW 1; CA 125; CANR 56, 92

Dacey, Philip 1939- .... **CLC 51**
See also CA 37-40R; CAAS 17; CANR 14,
32, 64; DLB 105

Dagerman, Stig (Halvard) 1923-1954
.... **TCLC 17**
See also CA 117; 155

Dahl, Roald 1916-1990 ..... **CLC 1, 6, 18, 79;**
DAB; DAC; DAM MST, NOV, POP
See also AAYA 15; CA 1-4R; 133; CANR
6, 32, 37, 62; CLR 1, 7, 41; DA3; DLB
139; JRDA; MAICYA; MTCW 1, 2;
SATA 1, 26, 73; SATA-Obit 65

Dahlberg, Edward 1900-1977 . **CLC 1, 7, 14**
See also CA 9-12R; 69-72; CANR 31, 62;
DLB 48; MTCW 1

Daitch, Susan 1954- .... **CLC 103**
See also CA 161

Dale, Colin .... **TCLC 18**
See also Lawrence, T(homas) E(dward)

Dale, George E.
See Asimov, Isaac

Dalton, Roque 1935-1975
See also HLCS 1; HW 2

Daly, Elizabeth 1878-1967 .... **CLC 52**
See also CA 23-24; 25-28R; CANR 60;
CAP 2

Daly, Maureen 1921-1983 .... **CLC 17**
See also AAYA 5; CANR 37, 83; JRDA;
MAICYA; SAAS 1; SATA 2

Damas, Leon-Gontran 1912-1978 ... **CLC 84**
See also BW 1; CA 125; 73-76

Dana, Richard Henry Sr. 1787-1879
.... **NCLC 53**

Daniel, Samuel 1562(?)-1619 .... **LC 24**
See also DLB 62

Daniels, Brett
See Adler, Renata

Dannay, Frederic 1905-1982 . **CLC 11; DAM**
POP
See also Queen, Ellery
See also CA 1-4R; 107; CANR 1, 39; DLB
137; MTCW 1

D'Annunzio, Gabriele 1863-1938 .. **TCLC 6,**
40
See also CA 104; 155

Danois, N. le
See Gourmont, Remy (-Marie-Charles) de

Dante 1265-1321 .... **CMLC 3, 18, 39; DA;**
DAB; DAC; DAM MST, POET; PC 21;
WLCS
See also Alighieri, Dante
See also DA3

d'Antibes, Germain
See Simenon, Georges (Jacques Christian)

Danticat, Edwidge 1969- .... **CLC 94**
See also AAYA 29; CA 152; CANR 73;
MTCW 1

Danvers, Dennis 1947- .... **CLC 70**

Danziger, Paula 1944- .... **CLC 21**
See also AAYA 4; CA 112; 115; CANR 37;
CLR 20; JRDA; MAICYA; SATA 36, 63,
102; SATA-Brief 30

Da Ponte, Lorenzo 1749-1838 ...... **NCLC 50**

Dario, Ruben 1867-1916 ..... **TCLC 4; DAM**
MULT; HLC 1; PC 15
See also CA 131; CANR 81; HW 1, 2;
MTCW 1, 2

Darley, George 1795-1846 .... **NCLC 2**
See also DLB 96

Darrow, Clarence (Seward) 1857-1938
.... **TCLC 81**
See also CA 164

Darwin, Charles 1809-1882 .... **NCLC 57**
See also DLB 57, 166

Daryush, Elizabeth 1887-1977 .... **CLC 6, 19**
See also CA 49-52; CANR 3, 81; DLB 20

Dasgupta, Surendranath 1887-1952
.... **TCLC 81**
See also CA 157

Dashwood, Edmee Elizabeth Monica de la
Pasture 1890-1943
See Delafield, E. M.
See also CA 119; 154

Daudet, (Louis Marie) Alphonse 1840-1897
.... **NCLC 1**
See also DLB 123

Daumal, Rene 1908-1944 .... **TCLC 14**
See also CA 114

Davenant, William 1606-1668 .... **LC 13**
See also DLB 58, 126

Davenport, Guy (Mattison, Jr.) 1927-
.... **CLC 6, 14, 38; SSC 16**
See also CA 33-36R; CANR 23, 73; DLB
130

Davidson, Avram (James) 1923-1993
See Queen, Ellery
See also CA 101; 171; CANR 26; DLB 8

Davidson, Donald (Grady) 1893-1968
.... **CLC 2, 13, 19**
See also CA 5-8R; 25-28R; CANR 4, 84;
DLB 45

Davidson, Hugh
See Hamilton, Edmond

Davidson, John 1857-1909 .... **TCLC 24**
See also CA 118; DLB 19

Davidson, Sara 1943- .... **CLC 9**
See also CA 81-84; CANR 44, 68; DLB
185

Davie, Donald (Alfred) 1922-1995 ... **CLC 5,**
8, 10, 31; PC 29
See also CA 1-4R; 149; CAAS 3; CANR 1,
44; DLB 27; MTCW 1

Davies, Ray(mond Douglas) 1944- . **CLC 21**
See also CA 116; 146; CANR 92

Davies, Rhys 1901-1978 .... **CLC 23**
See also CA 9-12R; 81-84; CANR 4; DLB
139, 191

Davies, (William) Robertson 1913-1995
.... **CLC 2, 7, 13, 25, 42, 75, 91; DA;**
DAB; DAC; DAM MST, NOV, POP;
WLC
See also BEST 89:2; CA 33-36R; 150;
CANR 17, 42; DA3; DLB 68; INT
CANR-17; MTCW 1, 2

Davies, Walter C.
See Kornbluth, C(yril) M.

Davies, William Henry 1871-1940 .. **TCLC 5**
See also CA 104; 179; DLB 19, 174

Da Vinci, Leonardo 1452-1519 ... **LC 12, 57,**
60

Davis, Angela (Yvonne) 1944- .... **CLC 77;**
DAM MULT
See also BW 2, 3; CA 57-60; CANR 10,
81; DA3

Davis, B. Lynch
See Bioy Casares, Adolfo; Borges, Jorge
Luis

Davis, B. Lynch
See Bioy Casares, Adolfo

Davis, H(arold) L(enoir) 1894-1960 . **CLC 49**
See also CA 178; 89-92; DLB 9, 206; SATA
114

Davis, Rebecca (Blaine) Harding 1831-1910
.... **TCLC 6; SSC 38**
See also CA 104; 179; DLB 74

Davis, Richard Harding 1864-1916
.... **TCLC 24**
See also CA 114; 179; DLB 12, 23, 78, 79,
189; DLBD 13

Davison, Frank Dalby 1893-1970 ... **CLC 15**
See also CA 116

Davison, Lawrence H.
See Lawrence, D(avid) H(erbert Richards)

Davison, Peter (Hubert) 1928- .... **CLC 28**
See also CA 9-12R; CAAS 4; CANR 3, 43,
84; DLB 5

Davys, Mary 1674-1732 .... **LC 1, 46**
See also DLB 39

Dawson, Fielding 1930- .... **CLC 6**
See also CA 85-88; DLB 130

Dawson, Peter
See Faust, Frederick (Schiller)

Day, Clarence (Shepard, Jr.) 1874-1935
.... **TCLC 25**
See also CA 108; DLB 11

Day, Thomas 1748-1789 .... **LC 1**
See also DLB 39; YABC 1

Day Lewis, C(ecil) 1904-1972 . **CLC 1, 6, 10;**
DAM POET; PC 11
See also Blake, Nicholas
See also CA 13-16; 33-36R; CANR 34;
CAP 1; DLB 15, 20; MTCW 1, 2

Dazai Osamu 1909-1948 . **TCLC 11; SSC 41**
See also Tsushima, Shuji
See also CA 164; DLB 182

de Andrade, Carlos Drummond 1892-1945
See Drummond de Andrade, Carlos

Deane, Norman
See Creasey, John

Deane, Seamus (Francis) 1940- ..... **CLC 122**
See also CA 118; CANR 42

de Beauvoir, Simone (Lucie Ernestine Marie
Bertrand)
See Beauvoir, Simone (Lucie Ernestine
Marie Bertrand) de

de Beer, P.
See Bosman, Herman Charles

de Brissac, Malcolm
See Dickinson, Peter (Malcolm)

de Campos, Alvaro
See Pessoa, Fernando (Antonio Nogueira)

See also AAYA 23; CDBLB 1832-1890; DA3; DLB 21, 55, 70, 159, 166; JRDA; MAICYA; SATA 15

Dickey, James (Lafayette) 1923-1997 .. **CLC 1, 2, 4, 7, 10, 15, 47, 109; DAM NOV, POET, POP**
See also AITN 1, 2; CA 9-12R; 156; CABS 2; CANR 10, 48, 61; CDALB 1968-1988; DA3; DLB 5, 193; DLBD 7; DLBY 82, 93, 96, 97, 98; INT CANR-10; MTCW 1, 2

Dickey, William 1928-1994 .... **CLC 3, 28**
See also CA 9-12R; 145; CANR 24, 79; DLB 5

Dickinson, Charles 1951- .... **CLC 49**
See also CA 128

Dickinson, Emily (Elizabeth) 1830-1886 . **NCLC 21, 77; DA; DAB; DAC; DAM MST, POET; PC 1; WLC**
See also AAYA 22; CDALB 1865-1917; DA3; DLB 1; SATA 29

Dickinson, Peter (Malcolm) 1927- . **CLC 12, 35**
See also AAYA 9; CA 41-44R; CANR 31, 58, 88; CLR 29; DLB 87, 161; JRDA; MAICYA; SATA 5, 62, 95

Dickson, Carr
See Carr, John Dickson

Dickson, Carter
See Carr, John Dickson

Diderot, Denis 1713-1784 .... **LC 26**

Didion, Joan 1934- . **CLC 1, 3, 8, 14, 32, 129; DAM NOV**
See also AITN 1; CA 5-8R; CANR 14, 52, 76; CDALB 1968-1988; DA3; DLB 2, 173, 185; DLBY 81, 86; MTCW 1, 2

Dietrich, Robert
See Hunt, E(verette) Howard, (Jr.)

Difusa, Pati
See Almodovar, Pedro

Dillard, Annie 1945- . **CLC 9, 60, 115; DAM NOV**
See also AAYA 6; CA 49-52; CANR 3, 43, 62, 90; DA3; DLBY 80; MTCW 1, 2; SATA 10

Dillard, R(ichard) H(enry) W(ilde) 1937- .... **CLC 5**
See also CA 21-24R; CAAS 7; CANR 10; DLB 5

Dillon, Eilis 1920-1994 .... **CLC 17**
See also CA 9-12R, 182; 147; CAAE 182; CAAS 3; CANR 4, 38, 78; CLR 26; MAICYA; SATA 2, 74; SATA-Essay 105; SATA-Obit 83

Dimont, Penelope
See Mortimer, Penelope (Ruth)

Dinesen, Isak -1962 . **CLC 10, 29, 95; SSC 7**
See also Blixen, Karen (Christentze Dinesen)
See also MTCW 1

Ding Ling .... **CLC 68**
See also Chiang, Pin-chin

Diphusa, Patty
See Almodovar, Pedro

Disch, Thomas M(ichael) 1940- .. **CLC 7, 36**
See also AAYA 17; CA 21-24R; CAAS 4; CANR 17, 36, 54, 89; CLR 18; DA3; DLB 8; MAICYA; MTCW 1, 2; SAAS 15; SATA 92

Disch, Tom
See Disch, Thomas M(ichael)

d'Isly, Georges
See Simenon, Georges (Jacques Christian)

Disraeli, Benjamin 1804-1881 . **NCLC 2, 39, 79**
See also DLB 21, 55

Ditcum, Steve
See Crumb, R(obert)

Dixon, Paige
See Corcoran, Barbara

Dixon, Stephen 1936- .... **CLC 52; SSC 16**
See also CA 89-92; CANR 17, 40, 54, 91; DLB 130

Doak, Annie
See Dillard, Annie

Dobell, Sydney Thompson 1824-1874 .... **NCLC 43**
See also DLB 32

Doblin, Alfred .... **TCLC 13**
See also Doeblin, Alfred

Dobrolyubov, Nikolai Alexandrovich 1836-1861 .... **NCLC 5**

Dobson, Austin 1840-1921 .... **TCLC 79**
See also DLB 35; 144

Dobyns, Stephen 1941- .... **CLC 37**
See also CA 45-48; CANR 2, 18

Doctorow, E(dgar) L(aurence) 1931- .... **CLC 6, 11, 15, 18, 37, 44, 65, 113; DAM NOV, POP**
See also AAYA 22; AITN 2; BEST 89:3; CA 45-48; CANR 2, 33, 51, 76; CDALB 1968-1988; DA3; DLB 2, 28, 173; DLBY 80; MTCW 1, 2

Dodgson, Charles Lutwidge 1832-1898
See Carroll, Lewis
See also CLR 2; DA; DAB; DAC; DAM MST, NOV, POET; DA3; MAICYA; SATA 100; YABC 2

Dodson, Owen (Vincent) 1914-1983 .... **CLC 79; BLC 1; DAM MULT**
See also BW 1; CA 65-68; 110; CANR 24; DLB 76

Doeblin, Alfred 1878-1957 .... **TCLC 13**
See also Doblin, Alfred
See also CA 110; 141; DLB 66

Doerr, Harriet 1910- .... **CLC 34**
See also CA 117; 122; CANR 47; INT 122

Domecq, H(onorio Bustos)
See Bioy Casares, Adolfo

Domecq, H(onorio) Bustos
See Bioy Casares, Adolfo; Borges, Jorge Luis

Domini, Rey
See Lorde, Audre (Geraldine)

Dominique
See Proust, (Valentin-Louis-George-Eugene-) Marcel

Don, A
See Stephen, SirLeslie

Donaldson, Stephen R. 1947- . **CLC 46, 138; DAM POP**
See also CA 89-92; CANR 13, 55; INT CANR-13

Donleavy, J(ames) P(atrick) 1926- ... **CLC 1, 4, 6, 10, 45**
See also AITN 2; CA 9-12R; CANR 24, 49, 62, 80; DLB 6, 173; INT CANR-24; MTCW 1, 2

Donne, John 1572-1631 .... **LC 10, 24; DA; DAB; DAC; DAM MST, POET; PC 1; WLC**
See also CDBLB Before 1660; DLB 121, 151

Donnell, David 1939(?)- .... **CLC 34**

Donoghue, P. S.
See Hunt, E(verette) Howard, (Jr.)

Donoso (Yanez), Jose 1924-1996 .. **CLC 4, 8, 11, 32, 99; DAM MULT; HLC 1; SSC 34**
See also CA 81-84; 155; CANR 32, 73; DLB 113; HW 1, 2; MTCW 1, 2

Donovan, John 1928-1992 .... **CLC 35**
See also AAYA 20; CA 97-100; 137; CLR 3; MAICYA; SATA 72; SATA-Brief 29

Don Roberto
See Cunninghame Graham, Robert (Gallnigad) Bontine

Doolittle, Hilda 1886-1961 ...... **CLC 3, 8, 14, 31, 34, 73; DA; DAC; DAM MST, POET; PC 5; WLC**
See also H. D.
See also CA 97-100; CANR 35; DLB 4, 45; MTCW 1, 2

Dorfman, Ariel 1942- ..... **CLC 48, 77; DAM MULT; HLC 1**
See also CA 124; 130; CANR 67, 70; HW 1, 2; INT 130

Dorn, Edward (Merton) 1929-1999 . **CLC 10, 18**
See also CA 93-96; 187; CANR 42, 79; DLB 5; INT 93-96

Dorris, Michael (Anthony) 1945-1997 .... **CLC 109; DAM MULT, NOV**
See also AAYA 20; BEST 90:1; CA 102; 157; CANR 19, 46, 75; CLR 58; DA3; DLB 175; MTCW 2; NNAL; SATA 75; SATA-Obit 94

Dorris, Michael A.
See Dorris, Michael (Anthony)

Dorsan, Luc
See Simenon, Georges (Jacques Christian)

Dorsange, Jean
See Simenon, Georges (Jacques Christian)

Dos Passos, John (Roderigo) 1896-1970 ..... **CLC 1, 4, 8, 11, 15, 25, 34, 82; DA; DAB; DAC; DAM MST, NOV; WLC**
See also CA 1-4R; 29-32R; CANR 3; CDALB 1929-1941; DA3; DLB 4, 9; DLBD 1, 15; DLBY 96; MTCW 1, 2

Dossage, Jean
See Simenon, Georges (Jacques Christian)

Dostoevsky, Fedor Mikhailovich 1821-1881 .... **NCLC 2, 7, 21, 33, 43; DA; DAB; DAC; DAM MST, NOV; SSC 2, 33; WLC**
See also DA3

Doughty, Charles M(ontagu) 1843-1926 .... **TCLC 27**
See also CA 115; 178; DLB 19, 57, 174

Douglas, Ellen .... **CLC 73**
See also Haxton, Josephine Ayres; Williamson, Ellen Douglas

Douglas, Gavin 1475(?)-1522 .... **LC 20**
See also DLB 132

Douglas, George
See Brown, George Douglas

Douglas, Keith (Castellain) 1920-1944 .... **TCLC 40**
See also CA 160; DLB 27

Douglas, Leonard
See Bradbury, Ray (Douglas)

Douglas, Michael
See Crichton, (John) Michael

Douglas, (George) Norman 1868-1952 .... **TCLC 68**
See also CA 119; 157; DLB 34, 195

Douglas, William
See Brown, George Douglas

Douglass, Frederick 1817(?)-1895 . **NCLC 7, 55; BLC 1; DA; DAC; DAM MST, MULT; WLC**
See also CDALB 1640-1865; DA3; DLB 1, 43, 50, 79; SATA 29

Dourado, (Waldomiro Freitas) Autran 1926- .... **CLC 23, 60**
See also CA 25-28R; 179; CANR 34, 81; DLB 145; HW 2

Dourado, Waldomiro Autran 1926-
See Dourado, (Waldomiro Freitas) Autran
See also CA 179

Dove, Rita (Frances) 1952- ...... **CLC 50, 81; BLCS; DAM MULT, POET; PC 6**
See also BW 2; CA 109; CAAS 19; CANR 27, 42, 68, 76; CDALBS; DA3; DLB 120; MTCW 1

Dye, Richard
See De Voto, Bernard (Augustine)
Dylan, Bob 1941- .... **CLC 3, 4, 6, 12, 77**
See also CA 41-44R; DLB 16
E. V. L.
See Lucas, E(dward) V(errall)
Eagleton, Terence (Francis) 1943- . **CLC 63, 132**
See also CA 57-60; CANR 7, 23, 68; MTCW 1, 2
Eagleton, Terry
See Eagleton, Terence (Francis)
Early, Jack
See Scoppettone, Sandra
East, Michael
See West, Morris L(anglo)
Eastaway, Edward
See Thomas, (Philip) Edward
Eastlake, William (Derry) 1917-1997 . **CLC 8**
See also CA 5-8R; 158; CAAS 1; CANR 5, 63; DLB 6, 206; INT CANR-5
Eastman, Charles A(lexander) 1858-1939
.... **TCLC 55; DAM MULT**
See also CA 179; CANR 91; DLB 175; NNAL; YABC 1
Eberhart, Richard (Ghormley) 1904-
.... **CLC 3, 11, 19, 56; DAM POET**
See also CA 1-4R; CANR 2; CDALB 1941-1968; DLB 48; MTCW 1
Eberstadt, Fernanda 1960- .... **CLC 39**
See also CA 136; CANR 69
Echegaray (y Eizaguirre), Jose (Maria Waldo) 1832-1916 ... **TCLC 4; HLCS 1**
See also CA 104; CANR 32; HW 1; MTCW 1
Echeverria, (Jose) Esteban (Antonino)
1805-1851 .... **NCLC 18**
Echo
See Proust, (Valentin-Louis-George-Eugene-) Marcel
Eckert, Allan W. 1931- .... **CLC 17**
See also AAYA 18; CA 13-16R; CANR 14, 45; INT CANR-14; SAAS 21; SATA 29, 91; SATA-Brief 27
Eckhart, Meister 1260(?)-1328(?) .. **CMLC 9**
See also DLB 115
Eckmar, F. R.
See de Hartog, Jan
Eco, Umberto 1932- .... **CLC 28, 60; DAM NOV, POP**
See also BEST 90:1; CA 77-80; CANR 12, 33, 55; DA3; DLB 196; MTCW 1, 2
Eddison, E(ric) R(ucker) 1882-1945
.... **TCLC 15**
See also CA 109; 156
Eddy, Mary (Ann Morse) Baker 1821-1910
.... **TCLC 71**
See also CA 113; 174
Edel, (Joseph) Leon 1907-1997 . **CLC 29, 34**
See also CA 1-4R; 161; CANR 1, 22; DLB 103; INT CANR-22
Eden, Emily 1797-1869 .... **NCLC 10**
Edgar, David 1948- . **CLC 42; DAM DRAM**
See also CA 57-60; CANR 12, 61; DLB 13, 233; MTCW 1
Edgerton, Clyde (Carlyle) 1944- ..... **CLC 39**
See also AAYA 17; CA 118; 134; CANR 64; INT 134
Edgeworth, Maria 1768-1849 ... **NCLC 1, 51**
See also DLB 116, 159, 163; SATA 21
Edmonds, Paul
See Kuttner, Henry
Edmonds, Walter D(umaux) 1903-1998
.... **CLC 35**
See also CA 5-8R; CANR 2; DLB 9; MAI-CYA; SAAS 4; SATA 1, 27; SATA-Obit 99

Edmondson, Wallace
See Ellison, Harlan (Jay)
Edson, Russell .... **CLC 13**
See also CA 33-36R
Edwards, Bronwen Elizabeth
See Rose, Wendy
Edwards, G(erald) B(asil) 1899-1976
.... **CLC 25**
See also CA 110
Edwards, Gus 1939- .... **CLC 43**
See also CA 108; INT 108
Edwards, Jonathan 1703-1758 ..... **LC 7, 54; DA; DAC; DAM MST**
See also DLB 24
Efron, Marina Ivanovna Tsvetaeva
See Tsvetaeva (Efron), Marina (Ivanovna)
Ehle, John (Marsden, Jr.) 1925- ..... **CLC 27**
See also CA 9-12R
Ehrenbourg, Ilya (Grigoryevich)
See Ehrenburg, Ilya (Grigoryevich)
Ehrenburg, Ilya (Grigoryevich) 1891-1967
.... **CLC 18, 34, 62**
See also CA 102; 25-28R
Ehrenburg, Ilyo (Grigoryevich)
See Ehrenburg, Ilya (Grigoryevich)
Ehrenreich, Barbara 1941- .... **CLC 110**
See also BEST 90:4; CA 73-76; CANR 16, 37, 62; MTCW 1, 2
Eich, Guenter 1907-1972 .... **CLC 15**
See also CA 111; 93-96; DLB 69, 124
Eichendorff, Joseph Freiherr von 1788-1857
.... **NCLC 8**
See also DLB 90
Eigner, Larry .... **CLC 9**
See also Eigner, Laurence (Joel)
See also CAAS 23; DLB 5
Eigner, Laurence (Joel) 1927-1996
See Eigner, Larry
See also CA 9-12R; 151; CANR 6, 84; DLB 193
Einstein, Albert 1879-1955 .... **TCLC 65**
See also CA 121; 133; MTCW 1, 2
Eiseley, Loren Corey 1907-1977 ...... **CLC 7**
See also AAYA 5; CA 1-4R; 73-76; CANR 6; DLBD 17
Eisenstadt, Jill 1963- .... **CLC 50**
See also CA 140
Eisenstein, Sergei (Mikhailovich) 1898-1948
.... **TCLC 57**
See also CA 114; 149
Eisner, Simon
See Kornbluth, C(yril) M.
Ekeloef, (Bengt) Gunnar 1907-1968
.... **CLC 27; DAM POET; PC 23**
See also CA 123; 25-28R
Ekelof, (Bengt) Gunnar
See Ekeloef, (Bengt) Gunnar
Ekelund, Vilhelm 1880-1949 .... **TCLC 75**
Ekwensi, C. O. D.
See Ekwensi, Cyprian (Odiatu Duaka)
Ekwensi, Cyprian (Odiatu Duaka) 1921-
.... **CLC 4; BLC 1; DAM MULT**
See also BW 2, 3; CA 29-32R; CANR 18, 42, 74; DLB 117; MTCW 1, 2; SATA 66
Elaine .... **TCLC 18**
See also Leverson, Ada
El Crummo
See Crumb, R(obert)
Elder, Lonne III 1931-1996 .... **DC 8**
See also BLC 1; BW 1, 3; CA 81-84; 152; CANR 25; DAM MULT; DLB 7, 38, 44
Eleanor of Aquitaine 1122-1204 .. **CMLC 39**
Elia
See Lamb, Charles
Eliade, Mircea 1907-1986 .... **CLC 19**
See also CA 65-68; 119; CANR 30, 62; DLB 220; MTCW 1

Eliot, A. D.
See Jewett, (Theodora) Sarah Orne
Eliot, Alice
See Jewett, (Theodora) Sarah Orne
Eliot, Dan
See Silverberg, Robert
Eliot, George 1819- . **NCLC 4, 13, 23, 41, 49, 89; DA; DAB; DAC; DAM MST, NOV; PC 20; WLC**
See also CDBLB 1832-1890; DA3; DLB 21, 35, 55
Eliot, John 1604-1690 .... **LC 5**
See also DLB 24
Eliot, T(homas) S(tearns) 1888-1965 . **CLC 1, 2, 3, 6, 9, 10, 13, 15, 24, 34, 41, 55, 57, 113; DA; DAB; DAC; DAM DRAM, MST, POET; PC 5, 31; WLC**
See also AAYA 28; CA 5-8R; 25-28R; CANR 41; CDALB 1929-1941; DA3; DLB 7, 10, 45, 63; DLBY 88; MTCW 1, 2
Elizabeth 1866-1941 .... **TCLC 41**
Elkin, Stanley L(awrence) 1930-1995
.... **CLC 4, 6, 9, 14, 27, 51, 91; DAM NOV, POP; SSC 12**
See also CA 9-12R; 148; CANR 8, 46; DLB 2, 28; DLBY 80; INT CANR-8; MTCW 1, 2
Elledge, Scott .... **CLC 34**
Elliot, Don
See Silverberg, Robert
Elliott, Don
See Silverberg, Robert
Elliott, George P(aul) 1918-1980 .... **CLC 2**
See also CA 1-4R; 97-100; CANR 2
Elliott, Janice 1931-1995 .... **CLC 47**
See also CA 13-16R; CANR 8, 29, 84; DLB 14; SATA 119
Elliott, Sumner Locke 1917-1991 ... **CLC 38**
See also CA 5-8R; 134; CANR 2, 21
Elliott, William
See Bradbury, Ray (Douglas)
Ellis, A. E. .... **CLC 7**
Ellis, Alice Thomas .... **CLC 40**
See also Haycraft, Anna (Margaret)
See also DLB 194; MTCW 1
Ellis, Bret Easton 1964- ... **CLC 39, 71, 117; DAM POP**
See also AAYA 2; CA 118; 123; CANR 51, 74; DA3; INT 123; MTCW 1
Ellis, (Henry) Havelock 1859-1939
.... **TCLC 14**
See also CA 109; 169; DLB 190
Ellis, Landon
See Ellison, Harlan (Jay)
Ellis, Trey 1962- .... **CLC 55**
See also CA 146; CANR 92
Ellison, Harlan (Jay) 1934- . **CLC 1, 13, 42; DAM POP; SSC 14**
See also AAYA 29; CA 5-8R; CANR 5, 46; DLB 8; INT CANR-5; MTCW 1, 2
Ellison, Ralph (Waldo) 1914-1994 ... **CLC 1, 3, 11, 54, 86, 114; BLC 1; DA; DAB; DAC; DAM MST, MULT, NOV; SSC 26; WLC**
See also AAYA 19; BW 1, 3; CA 9-12R; 145; CANR 24, 53; CDALB 1941-1968; DA3; DLB 2, 76, 227; DLBY 94; MTCW 1, 2
Ellmann, Lucy (Elizabeth) 1956- .... **CLC 61**
See also CA 128
Ellmann, Richard (David) 1918-1987
.... **CLC 50**
See also BEST 89:2; CA 1-4R; 122; CANR 2, 28, 61; DLB 103; DLBY 87; MTCW 1, 2
Elman, Richard (Martin) 1934-1997
.... **CLC 19**

See also CA 17-20R; 163; CAAS 3; CANR 47

Elron
See Hubbard, L(afayette) Ron(ald)

Eluard, Paul .... **TCLC 7, 41**
See also Grindel, Eugene

Elyot, Sir Thomas 1490(?)-1546 .... **LC 11**

Elytis, Odysseus 1911-1996 ...... **CLC 15, 49, 100; DAM POET; PC 21**
See also CA 102; 151; MTCW 1, 2

Emecheta, (Florence Onye) Buchi 1944- . **CLC 14, 48, 128; BLC 2; DAM MULT**
See also BW 2, 3; CA 81-84; CANR 27, 81; DA3; DLB 117; MTCW 1, 2; SATA 66

Emerson, Mary Moody 1774-1863
.... **NCLC 66**

Emerson, Ralph Waldo 1803-1882 . **NCLC 1, 38; DA; DAB; DAC; DAM MST, POET; PC 18; WLC**
See also CDALB 1640-1865; DA3; DLB 1, 59, 73, 223

Eminescu, Mihail 1850-1889 .... **NCLC 33**

Empson, William 1906-1984 .. **CLC 3, 8, 19, 33, 34**
See also CA 17-20R; 112; CANR 31, 61; DLB 20; MTCW 1, 2

Enchi, Fumiko (Ueda) 1905-1986 ... **CLC 31**
See also CA 129; 121; DLB 182

Ende, Michael (Andreas Helmuth) 1929-1995 .... **CLC 31**
See also CA 118; 124; 149; CANR 36; CLR 14; DLB 75; MAICYA; SATA 61; SATA-Brief 42; SATA-Obit 86

Endo, Shusaku 1923-1996 .... **CLC 7, 14, 19, 54, 99; DAM NOV**
See also CA 29-32R; 153; CANR 21, 54; DA3; DLB 182; MTCW 1, 2

Engel, Marian 1933-1985 .... **CLC 36**
See also CA 25-28R; CANR 12; DLB 53; INT CANR-12

Engelhardt, Frederick
See Hubbard, L(afayette) Ron(ald)

Engels, Friedrich 1820-1895 .... **NCLC 85**
See also DLB 129

Enright, D(ennis) J(oseph) 1920- . **CLC 4, 8, 31**
See also CA 1-4R; CANR 1, 42, 83; DLB 27; SATA 25

Enzensberger, Hans Magnus 1929- . **CLC 43; PC 28**
See also CA 116; 119

Ephron, Nora 1941- .... **CLC 17, 31**
See also AITN 2; CA 65-68; CANR 12, 39, 83

Epicurus 341B.C.-270B.C. .... **CMLC 21**
See also DLB 176

Epsilon
See Betjeman, John

Epstein, Daniel Mark 1948- .... **CLC 7**
See also CA 49-52; CANR 2, 53, 90

Epstein, Jacob 1956- .... **CLC 19**
See also CA 114

Epstein, Jean 1897-1953 .... **TCLC 92**

Epstein, Joseph 1937- .... **CLC 39**
See also CA 112; 119; CANR 50, 65

Epstein, Leslie 1938- .... **CLC 27**
See also CA 73-76; CAAS 12; CANR 23, 69

Equiano, Olaudah 1745(?)-1797 .... **LC 16; BLC 2; DAM MULT**
See also DLB 37, 50

ER .... **TCLC 33**
See also CA 160; DLB 85

Erasmus, Desiderius 1469(?)-1536 ..... **LC 16**

Erdman, Paul E(mil) 1932- .... **CLC 25**
See also AITN 1; CA 61-64; CANR 13, 43, 84

Erdrich, Louise 1954- .... **CLC 39, 54, 120; DAM MULT, NOV, POP**
See also AAYA 10; BEST 89:1; CA 114; CANR 41, 62; CDALBS; DA3; DLB 152, 175, 206; MTCW 1; NNAL; SATA 94

Erenburg, Ilya (Grigoryevich)
See Ehrenburg, Ilya (Grigoryevich)

Erickson, Stephen Michael 1950-
See Erickson, Steve
See also CA 129

Erickson, Steve 1950- .... **CLC 64**
See also Erickson, Stephen Michael
See also CANR 60, 68

Ericson, Walter
See Fast, Howard (Melvin)

Eriksson, Buntel
See Bergman, (Ernst) Ingmar

Ernaux, Annie 1940- .... **CLC 88**
See also CA 147; CANR 93

Erskine, John 1879-1951 .... **TCLC 84**
See also CA 112; 159; DLB 9, 102

Eschenbach, Wolfram von
See Wolfram von Eschenbach

Eseki, Bruno
See Mphahlele, Ezekiel

Esenin, Sergei (Alexandrovich) 1895-1925
.... **TCLC 4**
See also CA 104

Eshleman, Clayton 1935- .... **CLC 7**
See also CA 33-36R; CAAS 6; CANR 93; DLB 5

Espriella, Don Manuel Alvarez
See Southey, Robert

Espriu, Salvador 1913-1985 .... **CLC 9**
See also CA 154; 115; DLB 134

Espronceda, Jose de 1808-1842 .... **NCLC 39**

Esquivel, Laura 1951(?)-
See also AAYA 29; CA 143; CANR 68; DA3; HLCS 1; MTCW 1

Esse, James
See Stephens, James

Esterbrook, Tom
See Hubbard, L(afayette) Ron(ald)

Estleman, Loren D. 1952- .... **CLC 48; DAM NOV, POP**
See also AAYA 27; CA 85-88; CANR 27, 74; DA3; DLB 226; INT CANR-27; MTCW 1, 2

Euclid 306B.C.-283B.C. .... **CMLC 25**

Eugenides, Jeffrey 1960(?)- .... **CLC 81**
See also CA 144

Euripides c. 485B.C.-406B.C. ..... **CMLC 23; DA; DAB; DAC; DAM DRAM, MST; DC 4; WLCS**
See also DA3; DLB 176

Evan, Evin
See Faust, Frederick (Schiller)

Evans, Caradoc 1878-1945 .... **TCLC 85**

Evans, Evan
See Faust, Frederick (Schiller)

Evans, Marian
See Eliot, George

Evans, Mary Ann
See Eliot, George

Evarts, Esther
See Benson, Sally

Everett, Percival 1956-
See Everett, Percival L.

Everett, Percival L. 1956- .... **CLC 57**
See also Everett, Percival
See also BW 2; CA 129

Everson, R(onald) G(ilmour) 1903- . **CLC 27**
See also CA 17-20R; DLB 88

Everson, William (Oliver) 1912-1994
.... **CLC 1, 5, 14**
See also CA 9-12R; 145; CANR 20; DLB 212; MTCW 1

Evtushenko, Evgenii Aleksandrovich
See Yevtushenko, Yevgeny (Alexandrovich)

Ewart, Gavin (Buchanan) 1916-1995
.... **CLC 13, 46**
See also CA 89-92; 150; CANR 17, 46; DLB 40; MTCW 1

Ewers, Hanns Heinz 1871-1943 .... **TCLC 12**
See also CA 109; 149

Ewing, Frederick R.
See Sturgeon, Theodore (Hamilton)

Exley, Frederick (Earl) 1929-1992 ... **CLC 6, 11**
See also AITN 2; CA 81-84; 138; DLB 143; DLBY 81

Eynhardt, Guillermo
See Quiroga, Horacio (Sylvestre)

Ezekiel, Nissim 1924- .... **CLC 61**
See also CA 61-64

Ezekiel, Tish O'Dowd 1943- .... **CLC 34**
See also CA 129

Fadeyev, A.
See Bulgya, Alexander Alexandrovich

Fadeyev, Alexander .... **TCLC 53**
See also Bulgya, Alexander Alexandrovich

Fagen, Donald 1948- .... **CLC 26**

Fainzilberg, Ilya Arnoldovich 1897-1937
See Ilf, Ilya
See also CA 120; 165

Fair, Ronald L. 1932- .... **CLC 18**
See also BW 1; CA 69-72; CANR 25; DLB 33

Fairbairn, Roger
See Carr, John Dickson

Fairbairns, Zoe (Ann) 1948- .... **CLC 32**
See also CA 103; CANR 21, 85

Fairman, Paul W. 1916-1977
See Queen, Ellery
See also CA 114

Falco, Gian
See Papini, Giovanni

Falconer, James
See Kirkup, James

Falconer, Kenneth
See Kornbluth, C(yril) M.

Falkland, Samuel
See Heijermans, Herman

Fallaci, Oriana 1930- .... **CLC 11, 110**
See also CA 77-80; CANR 15, 58; MTCW 1

Faludy, George 1913- .... **CLC 42**
See also CA 21-24R

Faludy, Gyoergy
See Faludy, George

Fanon, Frantz 1925-1961 . **CLC 74; BLC 2; DAM MULT**
See also BW 1; CA 116; 89-92

Fanshawe, Ann 1625-1680 .... **LC 11**

Fante, John (Thomas) 1911-1983 .... **CLC 60**
See also CA 69-72; 109; CANR 23; DLB 130; DLBY 83

Farah, Nuruddin 1945- . **CLC 53, 137; BLC 2; DAM MULT**
See also BW 2, 3; CA 106; CANR 81; DLB 125

Fargue, Leon-Paul 1876(?)-1947 ... **TCLC 11**
See also CA 109

Farigoule, Louis
See Romains, Jules

Farina, Richard 1936(?)-1966 .... **CLC 9**
See also CA 81-84; 25-28R

Farley, Walter (Lorimer) 1915-1989
.... **CLC 17**
See also CA 17-20R; CANR 8, 29, 84; DLB 22; JRDA; MAICYA; SATA 2, 43

Farmer, Philip Jose 1918- .... **CLC 1, 19**
See also AAYA 28; CA 1-4R; CANR 4, 35; DLB 8; MTCW 1; SATA 93

Farquhar, George 1677-1707 . **LC 21; DAM DRAM**
See also DLB 84

Farrell, J(ames) G(ordon) 1935-1979 . **CLC 6**
See also CA 73-76; 89-92; CANR 36; DLB 14; MTCW 1

Farrell, James T(homas) 1904-1979 . **CLC 1, 4, 8, 11, 66; SSC 28**
See also CA 5-8R; 89-92; CANR 9, 61; DLB 4, 9, 86; DLBD 2; MTCW 1, 2

Farren, Richard J.
See Betjeman, John

Farren, Richard M.
See Betjeman, John

Fassbinder, Rainer Werner 1946-1982
.... **CLC 20**
See also CA 93-96; 106; CANR 31

Fast, Howard (Melvin) 1914- . **CLC 23, 131; DAM NOV**
See also AAYA 16; CA 1-4R, 181; CAAE 181; CAAS 18; CANR 1, 33, 54, 75; DLB 9; INT CANR-33; MTCW 1; SATA 7; SATA-Essay 107

Faulcon, Robert
See Holdstock, Robert P.

Faulkner, William (Cuthbert) 1897-1962
..... **CLC 1, 3, 6, 8, 9, 11, 14, 18, 28, 52, 68; DA; DAB; DAC; DAM MST, NOV; SSC 1, 35, 42; WLC**
See also AAYA 7; CA 81-84; CANR 33; CDALB 1929-1941; DA3; DLB 9, 11, 44, 102; DLBD 2; DLBY 86, 97; MTCW 1, 2

Fauset, Jessie Redmon 1884(?)-1961
.... **CLC 19, 54; BLC 2; DAM MULT**
See also BW 1; CA 109; CANR 83; DLB 51

Faust, Frederick (Schiller) 1892-1944(?)
.... **TCLC 49; DAM POP**
See also CA 108; 152

Faust, Irvin 1924- .... **CLC 8**
See also CA 33-36R; CANR 28, 67; DLB 2, 28; DLBY 80

Fawkes, Guy
See Benchley, Robert (Charles)

Fearing, Kenneth (Flexner) 1902-1961
.... **CLC 51**
See also CA 93-96; CANR 59; DLB 9

Fecamps, Elise
See Creasey, John

Federman, Raymond 1928- .... **CLC 6, 47**
See also CA 17-20R; CAAS 8; CANR 10, 43, 83; DLBY 80

Federspiel, J(uerg) F. 1931- .... **CLC 42**
See also CA 146

Feiffer, Jules (Ralph) 1929- ... **CLC 2, 8, 64; DAM DRAM**
See also AAYA 3; CA 17-20R; CANR 30, 59; DLB 7, 44; INT CANR-30; MTCW 1; SATA 8, 61, 111

Feige, Hermann Albert Otto Maximilian
See Traven, B.

Feinberg, David B. 1956-1994 .... **CLC 59**
See also CA 135; 147

Feinstein, Elaine 1930- .... **CLC 36**
See also CA 69-72; CAAS 1; CANR 31, 68; DLB 14, 40; MTCW 1

Feldman, Irving (Mordecai) 1928- ... **CLC 7**
See also CA 1-4R; CANR 1; DLB 169

Felix-Tchicaya, Gerald
See Tchicaya, Gerald Felix

Fellini, Federico 1920-1993 .... **CLC 16, 85**
See also CA 65-68; 143; CANR 33

Felsen, Henry Gregor 1916-1995 .... **CLC 17**
See also CA 1-4R; 180; CANR 1; SAAS 2; SATA 1

Fenno, Jack
See Calisher, Hortense

Fenollosa, Ernest (Francisco) 1853-1908
.... **TCLC 91**

Fenton, James Martin 1949- .... **CLC 32**
See also CA 102; DLB 40

Ferber, Edna 1887-1968 .... **CLC 18, 93**
See also AITN 1; CA 5-8R; 25-28R; CANR 68; DLB 9, 28, 86; MTCW 1, 2; SATA 7

Ferdowsi, Mansur Abu'l Qasem c. 935-c. 1020 .... **CMLC 43**

Ferguson, Helen
See Kavan, Anna

Ferguson, Niall 1967- .... **CLC 134**

Ferguson, Samuel 1810-1886 .... **NCLC 33**
See also DLB 32

Fergusson, Robert 1750-1774 .... **LC 29**
See also DLB 109

Ferling, Lawrence
See Ferlinghetti, Lawrence (Monsanto)

Ferlinghetti, Lawrence (Monsanto) 1919(?)-
.... **CLC 2, 6, 10, 27, 111; DAM POET; PC 1**
See also CA 5-8R; CANR 3, 41, 73; CDALB 1941-1968; DA3; DLB 5, 16; MTCW 1, 2

Fern, Fanny 1811-1872
See Parton, Sara Payson Willis

Fernandez, Vicente Garcia Huidobro
See Huidobro Fernandez, Vicente Garcia

Ferre, Rosario 1942- .... **SSC 36; HLCS 1**
See also CA 131; CANR 55, 81; DLB 145; HW 1, 2; MTCW 1

Ferrer, Gabriel (Francisco Victor) Miro
See Miro (Ferrer), Gabriel (Francisco Victor)

Ferrier, Susan (Edmonstone) 1782-1854
.... **NCLC 8**
See also DLB 116

Ferrigno, Robert 1948(?)- .... **CLC 65**
See also CA 140

Ferron, Jacques 1921-1985 ... **CLC 94; DAC**
See also CA 117; 129; DLB 60

Feuchtwanger, Lion 1884-1958 .... **TCLC 3**
See also CA 104; 187; DLB 66

Feuillet, Octave 1821-1890 .... **NCLC 45**
See also DLB 192

Feydeau, Georges (Leon Jules Marie) 1862-1921 ..... **TCLC 22; DAM DRAM**
See also CA 113; 152; CANR 84; DLB 192

Fichte, Johann Gottlieb 1762-1814
.... **NCLC 62**
See also DLB 90

Ficino, Marsilio 1433-1499 .... **LC 12**

Fiedeler, Hans
See Doeblin, Alfred

Fiedler, Leslie A(aron) 1917- . **CLC 4, 13, 24**
See also CA 9-12R; CANR 7, 63; DLB 28, 67; MTCW 1, 2

Field, Andrew 1938- .... **CLC 44**
See also CA 97-100; CANR 25

Field, Eugene 1850-1895 .... **NCLC 3**
See also DLB 23, 42, 140; DLBD 13; MAICYA; SATA 16

Field, Gans T.
See Wellman, Manly Wade

Field, Michael 1915-1971 .... **TCLC 43**
See also CA 29-32R

Field, Peter
See Hobson, Laura Z(ametkin)

Fielding, Henry 1707-1754 ... **LC 1, 46; DA; DAB; DAC; DAM DRAM, MST, NOV; WLC**
See also CDBLB 1660-1789; DA3; DLB 39, 84, 101

Fielding, Sarah 1710-1768 .... **LC 1, 44**
See also DLB 39

Fields, W. C. 1880-1946 .... **TCLC 80**
See also DLB 44

Fierstein, Harvey (Forbes) 1954- ... **CLC 33; DAM DRAM, POP**
See also CA 123; 129; DA3

Figes, Eva 1932- .... **CLC 31**
See also CA 53-56; CANR 4, 44, 83; DLB 14

Finch, Anne 1661-1720 .... **LC 3; PC 21**
See also DLB 95

Finch, Robert (Duer Claydon) 1900-
.... **CLC 18**
See also CA 57-60; CANR 9, 24, 49; DLB 88

Findley, Timothy 1930- . **CLC 27, 102; DAC; DAM MST**
See also CA 25-28R; CANR 12, 42, 69; DLB 53

Fink, William
See Mencken, H(enry) L(ouis)

Firbank, Louis 1942-
See Reed, Lou
See also CA 117

Firbank, (Arthur Annesley) Ronald 1886-1926 .... **TCLC 1**
See also CA 104; 177; DLB 36

Fisher, Dorothy (Frances) Canfield 1879-1958 .... **TCLC 87**
See also CA 114; 136; CANR 80; DLB 9, 102; MAICYA; YABC 1

Fisher, M(ary) F(rances) K(ennedy) 1908-1992 .... **CLC 76, 87**
See also CA 77-80; 138; CANR 44; MTCW 1

Fisher, Roy 1930- .... **CLC 25**
See also CA 81-84; CAAS 10; CANR 16; DLB 40

Fisher, Rudolph 1897-1934 . **TCLC 11; BLC 2; DAM MULT; SSC 25**
See also BW 1, 3; CA 107; 124; CANR 80; DLB 51, 102

Fisher, Vardis (Alvero) 1895-1968 .... **CLC 7**
See also CA 5-8R; 25-28R; CANR 68; DLB 9, 206

Fiske, Tarleton
See Bloch, Robert (Albert)

Fitch, Clarke
See Sinclair, Upton (Beall)

Fitch, John IV
See Cormier, Robert (Edmund)

Fitzgerald, Captain Hugh
See Baum, L(yman) Frank

FitzGerald, Edward 1809-1883 ...... **NCLC 9**
See also DLB 32

Fitzgerald, F(rancis) Scott (Key) 1896-1940
.... **TCLC 1, 6, 14, 28, 55; DA; DAB; DAC; DAM MST, NOV; SSC 6, 31; WLC**
See also AAYA 24; AITN 1; CA 110; 123; CDALB 1917-1929; DA3; DLB 4, 9, 86; DLBD 1, 15, 16; DLBY 81, 96; MTCW 1, 2

Fitzgerald, Penelope 1916- .. **CLC 19, 51, 61**
See also CA 85-88; CAAS 10; CANR 56, 86; DLB 14, 194; MTCW 2

Fitzgerald, Robert (Stuart) 1910-1985
.... **CLC 39**
See also CA 1-4R; 114; CANR 1; DLBY 80

FitzGerald, Robert D(avid) 1902-1987
.... **CLC 19**
See also CA 17-20R

Fitzgerald, Zelda (Sayre) 1900-1948
.... **TCLC 52**
See also CA 117; 126; DLBY 84

Flanagan, Thomas (James Bonner) 1923-
.... **CLC 25, 52**
See also CA 108; CANR 55; DLBY 80; INT 108; MTCW 1

Flaubert, Gustave 1821-1880 .. **NCLC 2, 10, 19, 62, 66; DA; DAB; DAC; DAM MST, NOV; SSC 11; WLC**
See also DA3; DLB 119

Flecker, Herman Elroy
See Flecker, (Herman) James Elroy
Flecker, (Herman) James Elroy 1884-1915
.... **TCLC 43**
See also CA 109; 150; DLB 10, 19
Fleming, Ian (Lancaster) 1908-1964 . **CLC 3,
30; DAM POP**
See also AAYA 26; CA 5-8R; CANR 59;
CDBLB 1945-1960; DA3; DLB 87, 201;
MTCW 1, 2; SATA 9
Fleming, Thomas (James) 1927- ..... **CLC 37**
See also CA 5-8R; CANR 10; INT CANR-
10; SATA 8
Fletcher, John 1579-1625 .... **LC 33; DC 6**
See also CDBLB Before 1660; DLB 58
Fletcher, John Gould 1886-1950 .. **TCLC 35**
See also CA 107; 167; DLB 4, 45
Fleur, Paul
See Pohl, Frederik
Flooglebuckle, Al
See Spiegelman, Art
Flora, Fletcher 1914-1969
See Queen, Ellery
See also CA 1-4R; CANR 3, 85
Flying Officer X
See Bates, H(erbert) E(rnest)
Fo, Dario 1926- .... **CLC 32, 109; DAM
DRAM; DC 10**
See also CA 116; 128; CANR 68; DA3;
DLBY 97; MTCW 1, 2
Fogarty, Jonathan Titulescu Esq.
See Farrell, James T(homas)
Follett, Ken(neth Martin) 1949- .... **CLC 18;
DAM NOV, POP**
See also AAYA 6; BEST 89:4; CA 81-84;
CANR 13, 33, 54; DA3; DLB 87; DLBY
81; INT CANR-33; MTCW 1
Fontane, Theodor 1819-1898 .... **NCLC 26**
See also DLB 129
Foote, Horton 1916- .... **CLC 51, 91; DAM
DRAM**
See also CA 73-76; CANR 34, 51; DA3;
DLB 26; INT CANR-34
Foote, Shelby 1916- ... **CLC 75; DAM NOV,
POP**
See also CA 5-8R; CANR 3, 45, 74; DA3;
DLB 2, 17; MTCW 2
Forbes, Esther 1891-1967 .... **CLC 12**
See also AAYA 17; CA 13-14; 25-28R; CAP
1; CLR 27; DLB 22; JRDA; MAICYA;
SATA 2, 100
Forche, Carolyn (Louise) 1950- ..... **CLC 25,
83, 86; DAM POET; PC 10**
See also CA 109; 117; CANR 50, 74; DA3;
DLB 5, 193; INT 117; MTCW 1
Ford, Elbur
See Hibbert, Eleanor Alice Burford
Ford, Ford Madox 1873-1939 . **TCLC 1, 15,
39, 57; DAM NOV**
See also Chaucer, Daniel
See also CA 104; 132; CANR 74; CDBLB
1914-1945; DA3; DLB 162; MTCW 1, 2
Ford, Henry 1863-1947 .... **TCLC 73**
See also CA 115; 148
Ford, John 1586-(?) .... **DC 8**
See also CDBLB Before 1660; DAM
DRAM; DA3; DLB 58
Ford, John 1895-1973 .... **CLC 16**
See also CA 187; 45-48
Ford, Richard 1944- .... **CLC 46, 99**
See also CA 69-72; CANR 11, 47, 86; DLB
227; MTCW 1
Ford, Webster
See Masters, Edgar Lee
Foreman, Richard 1937- .... **CLC 50**
See also CA 65-68; CANR 32, 63
Forester, C(ecil) S(cott) 1899-1966 . **CLC 35**
See also CA 73-76; 25-28R; CANR 83;
DLB 191; SATA 13

Forez
See Mauriac, Francois (Charles)
Forman, James Douglas 1932- .... **CLC 21**
See also AAYA 17; CA 9-12R; CANR 4,
19, 42; JRDA; MAICYA; SATA 8, 70
Fornes, Maria Irene 1930- . **CLC 39, 61; DC
10; HLCS 1**
See also CA 25-28R; CANR 28, 81; DLB
7; HW 1, 2; INT CANR-28; MTCW 1
Forrest, Leon (Richard) 1937-1997 . **CLC 4;
BLCS**
See also BW 2; CA 89-92; 162; CAAS 7;
CANR 25, 52, 87; DLB 33
Forster, E(dward) M(organ) 1879-1970
..... **CLC 1, 2, 3, 4, 9, 10, 13, 15, 22, 45,
77; DA; DAB; DAC; DAM MST, NOV;
SSC 27; WLC**
See also AAYA 2; CA 13-14; 25-28R;
CANR 45; CAP 1; CDBLB 1914-1945;
DA3; DLB 34, 98, 162, 178, 195; DLBD
10; MTCW 1, 2; SATA 57
Forster, John 1812-1876 .... **NCLC 11**
See also DLB 144, 184
Forsyth, Frederick 1938- .... **CLC 2, 5, 36;
DAM NOV, POP**
See also BEST 89:4; CA 85-88; CANR 38,
62; DLB 87; MTCW 1, 2
Forten, Charlotte L. .... **TCLC 16; BLC 2**
See also Grimke, Charlotte L(ottie) Forten
See also DLB 50
Foscolo, Ugo 1778-1827 .... **NCLC 8**
Fosse, Bob .... **CLC 20**
See also Fosse, Robert Louis
Fosse, Robert Louis 1927-1987
See Fosse, Bob
See also CA 110; 123
Foster, Stephen Collins 1826-1864 . **NCLC 26**
Foucault, Michel 1926-1984 . **CLC 31, 34, 69**
See also CA 105; 113; CANR 34; MTCW
1, 2
**Fouque, Friedrich (Heinrich Karl) de la
Motte** 1777-1843 .... **NCLC 2**
See also DLB 90
Fourier, Charles 1772-1837 .... **NCLC 51**
Fournier, Pierre 1916- .... **CLC 11**
See Gascar, Pierre
See also CA 89-92; CANR 16, 40
Fowles, John (Philip) 1926- . **CLC 1, 2, 3, 4,
6, 9, 10, 15, 33, 87; DAB; DAC; DAM
MST; SSC 33**
See also CA 5-8R; CANR 25, 71; CDBLB
1960 to Present; DA3; DLB 14, 139, 207;
MTCW 1, 2; SATA 22
Fox, Paula 1923- .... **CLC 2, 8, 121**
See also AAYA 3; CA 73-76; CANR 20,
36, 62; CLR 1, 44; DLB 52; JRDA; MAI-
CYA; MTCW 1; SATA 17, 60
Fox, William Price (Jr.) 1926- .... **CLC 22**
See also CA 17-20R; CAAS 19; CANR 11;
DLB 2; DLBY 81
Foxe, John 1516(?)-1587 .... **LC 14**
See also DLB 132
Frame, Janet 1924- . **CLC 2, 3, 6, 22, 66, 96;
SSC 29**
See also Clutha, Janet Paterson Frame
France, Anatole .... **TCLC 9**
See also Thibault, Jacques Anatole Francois
See also DLB 123; MTCW 1
Francis, Claude 19(?)- .... **CLC 50**
Francis, Dick 1920- ...... **CLC 2, 22, 42, 102;
DAM POP**
See also AAYA 5, 21; BEST 89:3; CA 5-8R;
CANR 9, 42, 68; CDBLB 1960 to Present;
DA3; DLB 87; INT CANR-9; MTCW 1,
2
Francis, Robert (Churchill) 1901-1987
.... **CLC 15**
See also CA 1-4R; 123; CANR 1

Frank, Anne(lies Marie) 1929-1945
.... **TCLC 17; DA; DAB; DAC; DAM
MST; WLC**
See also AAYA 12; CA 113; 133; CANR
68; DA3; MTCW 1, 2; SATA 87; SATA-
Brief 42
Frank, Bruno 1887-1945 .... **TCLC 81**
See also DLB 118
Frank, Elizabeth 1945- .... **CLC 39**
See also CA 121; 126; CANR 78; INT 126
Frankl, Viktor E(mil) 1905-1997 .... **CLC 93**
See also CA 65-68; 161
Franklin, Benjamin
See Hasek, Jaroslav (Matej Frantisek)
Franklin, Benjamin 1706-1790 . **LC 25; DA;
DAB; DAC; DAM MST; WLCS**
See also CDALB 1640-1865; DA3; DLB
24, 43, 73
**Franklin, (Stella Maria Sarah) Miles
(Lampe)** 1879-1954 .... **TCLC 7**
See also CA 104; 164
Fraser, (Lady) Antonia (Pakenham) 1932-
.... **CLC 32, 107**
See also CA 85-88; CANR 44, 65; MTCW
1, 2; SATA-Brief 32
Fraser, George MacDonald 1925- ..... **CLC 7**
See also CA 45-48, 180; CAAE 180; CANR
2, 48, 74; MTCW 1
Fraser, Sylvia 1935- .... **CLC 64**
See also CA 45-48; CANR 1, 16, 60
Frayn, Michael 1933- .... **CLC 3, 7, 31, 47;
DAM DRAM, NOV**
See also CA 5-8R; CANR 30, 69; DLB 13,
14, 194; MTCW 1, 2
Fraze, Candida (Merrill) 1945- .... **CLC 50**
See also CA 126
Frazer, J(ames) G(eorge) 1854-1941
.... **TCLC 32**
See also CA 118
Frazer, Robert Caine
See Creasey, John
Frazer, Sir James George
See Frazer, J(ames) G(eorge)
Frazier, Charles 1950- .... **CLC 109**
See also AAYA 34; CA 161
Frazier, Ian 1951- .... **CLC 46**
See also CA 130; CANR 54, 93
Frederic, Harold 1856-1898 .... **NCLC 10**
See also DLB 12, 23; DLBD 13
Frederick, John
See Faust, Frederick (Schiller)
Frederick the Great 1712-1786 .... **LC 14**
Fredro, Aleksander 1793-1876 .... **NCLC 8**
Freeling, Nicolas 1927- .... **CLC 38**
See also CA 49-52; CAAS 12; CANR 1,
17, 50, 84; DLB 87
Freeman, Douglas Southall 1886-1953
.... **TCLC 11**
See also CA 109; DLB 17; DLBD 17
Freeman, Judith 1946- .... **CLC 55**
See also CA 148
Freeman, Mary E(leanor) Wilkins 1852-1930
.... **TCLC 9; SSC 1**
See also CA 106; 177; DLB 12, 78, 221
Freeman, R(ichard) Austin 1862-1943
.... **TCLC 21**
See also CA 113; CANR 84; DLB 70
French, Albert 1943- .... **CLC 86**
See also BW 3; CA 167
French, Marilyn 1929- .... **CLC 10, 18, 60;
DAM DRAM, NOV, POP**
See also CA 69-72; CANR 3, 31; INT
CANR-31; MTCW 1, 2
French, Paul
See Asimov, Isaac
Freneau, Philip Morin 1752-1832 .. **NCLC 1**
See also DLB 37, 43
Freud, Sigmund 1856-1939 .... **TCLC 52**

Garnett, David 1892-1981 .... CLC 3
See also CA 5-8R; 103; CANR 17, 79; DLB
34; MTCW 2

Garos, Stephanie
See Katz, Steve

Garrett, George (Palmer) 1929- . CLC 3, 11,
51; SSC 30
See also CA 1-4R; CAAS 5; CANR 1, 42,
67; DLB 2, 5, 130, 152; DLBY 83

Garrick, David 1717-1779 ...... LC 15; DAM
DRAM
See also DLB 84

Garrigue, Jean 1914-1972 .... CLC 2, 8
See also CA 5-8R; 37-40R; CANR 20

Garrison, Frederick
See Sinclair, Upton (Beall)

Garro, Elena 1920(?)-1998
See also CA 131; 169; DLB 145; HLCS 1;
HW 1

Garth, Will
See Hamilton, Edmond; Kuttner, Henry

Garvey, Marcus (Moziah, Jr.) 1887-1940
.... TCLC 41; BLC 2; DAM MULT
See also BW 1; CA 120; 124; CANR 79

Gary, Romain .... CLC 25
See also Kacew, Romain
See also DLB 83

Gascar, Pierre .... CLC 11
See also Fournier, Pierre

Gascoyne, David (Emery) 1916- ..... CLC 45
See also CA 65-68; CANR 10, 28, 54; DLB
20; MTCW 1

Gaskell, Elizabeth Cleghorn 1810-1865
.. NCLC 70; DAB; DAM MST; SSC 25
See also CDBLB 1832-1890; DLB 21, 144,
159

Gass, William H(oward) 1924- . CLC 1, 2, 8,
11, 15, 39, 132; SSC 12
See also CA 17-20R; CANR 30, 71; DLB
2, 227; MTCW 1, 2

Gassendi, Pierre 1592-1655 .... LC 54

Gasset, Jose Ortega y
See Ortega y Gasset, Jose

Gates, Henry Louis, Jr. 1950- .... CLC 65;
BLCS; DAM MULT
See also BW 2, 3; CA 109; CANR 25, 53,
75; DA3; DLB 67; MTCW 1

Gautier, Theophile 1811-1872 . NCLC 1, 59;
DAM POET; PC 18; SSC 20
See also DLB 119

Gawsworth, John
See Bates, H(erbert) E(rnest)

Gay, John 1685-1732 . LC 49; DAM DRAM
See also DLB 84, 95

Gay, Oliver
See Gogarty, Oliver St. John

Gaye, Marvin (Penze) 1939-1984 .... CLC 26
See also CA 112

Gebler, Carlo (Ernest) 1954- .... CLC 39
See also CA 119; 133

Gee, Maggie (Mary) 1948- .... CLC 57
See also CA 130; DLB 207

Gee, Maurice (Gough) 1931- .... CLC 29
See also CA 97-100; CANR 67; CLR 56;
SATA 46, 101

Gelbart, Larry (Simon) 1928- ... CLC 21, 61
See also Gelbart, Larry
See also CA 73-76; CANR 45

Gelbart, Larry 1928-
See Gelbart, Larry (Simon)

Gelber, Jack 1932- .... CLC 1, 6, 14, 79
See also CA 1-4R; CANR 2; DLB 7, 228

Gellhorn, Martha (Ellis) 1908-1998
.... CLC 14, 60
See also CA 77-80; 164; CANR 44; DLBY
82, 98

Genet, Jean 1910-1986 . CLC 1, 2, 5, 10, 14,
44, 46; DAM DRAM

See also CA 13-16R; CANR 18; DA3; DLB
72; DLBY 86; MTCW 1, 2

Gent, Peter 1942- .... CLC 29
See also AITN 1; CA 89-92; DLBY 82

Gentile, Giovanni 1875-1944 .... TCLC 96
See also CA 119

Gentlewoman in New England, A
See Bradstreet, Anne

Gentlewoman in Those Parts, A
See Bradstreet, Anne

George, Jean Craighead 1919- .... CLC 35
See also AAYA 8; CA 5-8R; CANR 25;
CLR 1; DLB 52; JRDA; MAICYA; SATA
2, 68

George, Stefan (Anton) 1868-1933 . TCLC 2,
14
See also CA 104

Georges, Georges Martin
See Simenon, Georges (Jacques Christian)

Gerhardi, William Alexander
See Gerhardie, William Alexander

Gerhardie, William Alexander 1895-1977
.... CLC 5
See also CA 25-28R; 73-76; CANR 18;
DLB 36

Gerstler, Amy 1956- .... CLC 70
See also CA 146

Gertler, T. .... CLC 134
See also CA 116; 121

Ghalib .... NCLC 39, 78
See also Ghalib, Hsadullah Khan

Ghalib, Hsadullah Khan 1797-1869
See Ghalib
See also DAM POET

Ghelderode, Michel de 1898-1962 ... CLC 6,
11; DAM DRAM
See also CA 85-88; CANR 40, 77

Ghiselin, Brewster 1903- .... CLC 23
See also CA 13-16R; CAAS 10; CANR 13

Ghose, Aurabinda 1872-1950 .... TCLC 63
See also CA 163

Ghose, Zulfikar 1935- .... CLC 42
See also CA 65-68; CANR 67

Ghosh, Amitav 1956- .... CLC 44
See also CA 147; CANR 80

Giacosa, Giuseppe 1847-1906 .... TCLC 7
See also CA 104

Gibb, Lee
See Waterhouse, Keith (Spencer)

Gibbon, Lewis Grassic 1901-1935 .. TCLC 4
See also Mitchell, James Leslie

Gibbons, Kaye 1960- ...... CLC 50, 88; DAM
POP
See also AAYA 34; CA 151; CANR 75;
DA3; MTCW 1; SATA 117

Gibran, Kahlil 1883-1931 . TCLC 1, 9; DAM
POET, POP; PC 9
See also CA 104; 150; DA3; MTCW 2

Gibran, Khalil
See Gibran, Kahlil

Gibson, William 1914- . CLC 23; DA; DAB;
DAC; DAM DRAM, MST
See also CA 9-12R; CANR 9, 42, 75; DLB
7; MTCW 1; SATA 66

Gibson, William (Ford) 1948- . CLC 39, 63;
DAM POP
See also AAYA 12; CA 126; 133; CANR
52, 90; DA3; MTCW 1

Gide, Andre (Paul Guillaume) 1869-1951
.... TCLC 5, 12, 36; DA; DAB; DAC;
DAM MST, NOV; SSC 13; WLC
See also CA 104; 124; DA3; DLB 65;
MTCW 1, 2

Gifford, Barry (Colby) 1946- .... CLC 34
See also CA 65-68; CANR 9, 30, 40, 90

Gilbert, Frank
See De Voto, Bernard (Augustine)

Gilbert, W(illiam) S(chwenck) 1836-1911
.... TCLC 3; DAM DRAM, POET
See also CA 104; 173; SATA 36

Gilbreth, Frank B., Jr. 1911- .... CLC 17
See also CA 9-12R; SATA 2

Gilchrist, Ellen 1935- ..... CLC 34, 48; DAM
POP; SSC 14
See also CA 113; 116; CANR 41, 61; DLB
130; MTCW 1, 2

Giles, Molly 1942- .... CLC 39
See also CA 126

Gill, Eric 1882-1940 .... TCLC 85

Gill, Patrick
See Creasey, John

Gilliam, Terry (Vance) 1940- .... CLC 21
See also Monty Python
See also AAYA 19; CA 108; 113; CANR
35; INT 113

Gillian, Jerry
See Gilliam, Terry (Vance)

Gilliatt, Penelope (Ann Douglass) 1932-1993
.... CLC 2, 10, 13, 53
See also AITN 2; CA 13-16R; 141; CANR
49; DLB 14

Gilman, Charlotte (Anna) Perkins (Stetson)
1860-1935 ... TCLC 9, 37; SSC 13
See also CA 106; 150; DLB 221; MTCW 1

Gilmour, David 1949- .... CLC 35
See also CA 138, 147

Gilpin, William 1724-1804 .... NCLC 30

Gilray, J. D.
See Mencken, H(enry) L(ouis)

Gilroy, Frank D(aniel) 1925- .... CLC 2
See also CA 81-84; CANR 32, 64, 86; DLB
7

Gilstrap, John 1957(?)- .... CLC 99
See also CA 160

Ginsberg, Allen 1926-1997 ... CLC 1, 2, 3, 4,
6, 13, 36, 69, 109; DA; DAB; DAC;
DAM MST, POET; PC 4; WLC
See also AAYA 33; AITN 1; CA 1-4R; 157;
CANR 2, 41, 63; CDALB 1941-1968;
DA3; DLB 5, 16, 169; MTCW 1, 2

Ginzburg, Natalia 1916-1991 ..... CLC 5, 11,
54, 70
See also CA 85-88; 135; CANR 33; DLB
177; MTCW 1, 2

Giono, Jean 1895-1970 .... CLC 4, 11
See also CA 45-48; 29-32R; CANR 2, 35;
DLB 72; MTCW 1

Giovanni, Nikki 1943- ...... CLC 2, 4, 19, 64,
117; BLC 2; DA; DAB; DAC; DAM
MST, MULT, POET; PC 19; WLCS
See also AAYA 22; AITN 1; BW 2, 3; CA
29-32R; CAAS 6; CANR 18, 41, 60, 91;
CDALBS; CLR 6; DA3; DLB 5, 41; INT
CANR-18; MAICYA; MTCW 1, 2; SATA
24, 107

Giovene, Andrea 1904- .... CLC 7
See also CA 85-88

Gippius, Zinaida (Nikolayevna) 1869-1945
See Hippius, Zinaida
See also CA 106

Giraudoux, (Hippolyte) Jean 1882-1944
.... TCLC 2, 7; DAM DRAM
See also CA 104; DLB 65

Gironella, Jose Maria 1917- .... CLC 11
See also CA 101

Gissing, George (Robert) 1857-1903
.... TCLC 3, 24, 47; SSC 37
See also CA 105; 167; DLB 18, 135, 184

Giurlani, Aldo
See Palazzeschi, Aldo

Gladkov, Fyodor (Vasilyevich) 1883-1958
.... TCLC 27
See also CA 170

Glanville, Brian (Lester) 1931- .... CLC 6
See also CA 5-8R; CAAS 9; CANR 3, 70;
DLB 15, 139; SATA 42

Glasgow, Ellen (Anderson Gholson)
1873-1945 .... **TCLC 2, 7; SSC 34**
See also CA 104; 164; DLB 9, 12; MTCW
2

Glaspell, Susan 1882(?)-1948 . **TCLC 55; DC
10; SSC 41**
See also CA 110; 154; DLB 7, 9, 78, 228;
YABC 2

Glassco, John 1909-1981 .... **CLC 9**
See also CA 13-16R; 102; CANR 15; DLB
68

Glasscock, Amnesia
See Steinbeck, John (Ernst)

Glasser, Ronald J. 1940(?)- .... **CLC 37**

Glassman, Joyce
See Johnson, Joyce

Glendinning, Victoria 1937- .... **CLC 50**
See also CA 120; 127; CANR 59, 89; DLB
155

Glissant, Edouard 1928- . **CLC 10, 68; DAM
MULT**
See also CA 153

Gloag, Julian 1930- .... **CLC 40**
See also AITN 1; CA 65-68; CANR 10, 70

Glowacki, Aleksander
See Prus, Boleslaw

Gluck, Louise (Elisabeth) 1943- . **CLC 7, 22,
44, 81; DAM POET; PC 16**
See also CA 33-36R; CANR 40, 69; DA3;
DLB 5; MTCW 2

Glyn, Elinor 1864-1943 .... **TCLC 72**
See also DLB 153

Gobineau, Joseph Arthur (Comte) de
1816-1882 .... **NCLC 17**
See also DLB 123

Godard, Jean-Luc 1930- .... **CLC 20**
See also CA 93-96

Godden, (Margaret) Rumer 1907-1998
.... **CLC 53**
See also AAYA 6; CA 5-8R; 172; CANR 4,
27, 36, 55, 80; CLR 20; DLB 161; MAI-
CYA; SAAS 12; SATA 3, 36; SATA-Obit
109

Godoy Alcayaga, Lucila 1889-1957
..... **TCLC 2; DAM MULT; HLC 2; PC
32**
See also BW 2; CA 104; 131; CANR 81;
HW 1, 2; MTCW 1, 2

Godwin, Gail (Kathleen) 1937- .... **CLC 5, 8,
22, 31, 69, 125; DAM POP**
See also CA 29-32R; CANR 15, 43, 69;
DA3; DLB 6, 234; INT CANR-15;
MTCW 1, 2

Godwin, William 1756-1836 .... **NCLC 14**
See also CDBLB 1789-1832; DLB 39, 104,
142, 158, 163

Goebbels, Josef
See Goebbels, (Paul) Joseph

Goebbels, (Paul) Joseph 1897-1945
.... **TCLC 68**
See also CA 115; 148

Goebbels, Joseph Paul
See Goebbels, (Paul) Joseph

Goethe, Johann Wolfgang von 1749-1832
. **NCLC 4, 22, 34, 90; DA; DAB; DAC;
DAM DRAM, MST, POET; PC 5; SSC
38; WLC**
See also DA3; DLB 94

Gogarty, Oliver St. John 1878-1957
.... **TCLC 15**
See also CA 109; 150; DLB 15, 19

Gogol, Nikolai (Vasilyevich) 1809-1852
.... **NCLC 5, 15, 31; DA; DAB; DAC;
DAM DRAM, MST; DC 1; SSC 4, 29;
WLC**
See also DLB 198

Goines, Donald 1937(?)-1974 . **CLC 80; BLC
2; DAM MULT, POP**

See also AITN 1; BW 1, 3; CA 124; 114;
CANR 82; DA3; DLB 33

Gold, Herbert 1924- .... **CLC 4, 7, 14, 42**
See also CA 9-12R; CANR 17, 45; DLB 2;
DLBY 81

Goldbarth, Albert 1948- .... **CLC 5, 38**
See also CA 53-56; CANR 6, 40; DLB 120

Goldberg, Anatol 1910-1982 .... **CLC 34**
See also CA 131; 117

Goldemberg, Isaac 1945- .... **CLC 52**
See also CA 69-72; CAAS 12; CANR 11,
32; HW 1

Golding, William (Gerald) 1911-1993
. **CLC 1, 2, 3, 8, 10, 17, 27, 58, 81; DA;
DAB; DAC; DAM MST, NOV; WLC**
See also AAYA 5; CA 5-8R; 141; CANR
13, 33, 54; CDBLB 1945-1960; DA3;
DLB 15, 100; MTCW 1, 2

Goldman, Emma 1869-1940 .... **TCLC 13**
See also CA 110; 150; DLB 221

Goldman, Francisco 1954- .... **CLC 76**
See also CA 162

Goldman, William (W.) 1931- ..... **CLC 1, 48**
See also CA 9-12R; CANR 29, 69; DLB 44

Goldmann, Lucien 1913-1970 .... **CLC 24**
See also CA 25-28; CAP 2

Goldoni, Carlo 1707-1793 .... **LC 4; DAM
DRAM**

Goldsberry, Steven 1949- .... **CLC 34**
See also CA 131

Goldsmith, Oliver 1728-1774 . **LC 2, 48; DA;
DAB; DAC; DAM DRAM, MST, NOV,
POET; DC 8; WLC**
See also CDBLB 1660-1789; DLB 39, 89,
104, 109, 142; SATA 26

Goldsmith, Peter
See Priestley, J(ohn) B(oynton)

Gombrowicz, Witold 1904-1969 ... **CLC 4, 7,
11, 49; DAM DRAM**
See also CA 19-20; 25-28R; CAP 2

Gomez de la Serna, Ramon 1888-1963
.... **CLC 9**
See also CA 153; 116; CANR 79; HW 1, 2

Goncharov, Ivan Alexandrovich 1812-1891
.... **NCLC 1, 63**

Goncourt, Edmond (Louis Antoine Huot) de
1822-1896 .... **NCLC 7**
See also DLB 123

Goncourt, Jules (Alfred Huot) de 1830-1870
.... **NCLC 7**
See also DLB 123

Gontier, Fernande 19(?)- .... **CLC 50**

Gonzalez Martinez, Enrique 1871-1952
.... **TCLC 72**
See also CA 166; CANR 81; HW 1, 2

Goodman, Paul 1911-1972 .... **CLC 1, 2, 4, 7**
See also CA 19-20; 37-40R; CANR 34;
CAP 2; DLB 130; MTCW 1

Gordimer, Nadine 1923- .... **CLC 3, 5, 7, 10,
18, 33, 51, 70, 123; DA; DAB; DAC;
DAM MST, NOV; SSC 17; WLCS**
See also CA 5-8R; CANR 3, 28, 56, 88;
DA3; DLB 225; INT CANR-28; MTCW
1, 2

Gordon, Adam Lindsay 1833-1870
.... **NCLC 21**
See also DLB 230

Gordon, Caroline 1895-1981 ...... **CLC 6, 13,
29, 83; SSC 15**
See also CA 11-12; 103; CANR 36; CAP 1;
DLB 4, 9, 102; DLBD 17; DLBY 81;
MTCW 1, 2

Gordon, Charles William 1860-1937
See Connor, Ralph
See also CA 109

Gordon, Mary (Catherine) 1949- .. **CLC 13,
22, 128**
See also CA 102; CANR 44, 92; DLB 6;
DLBY 81; INT 102; MTCW 1

Gordon, N. J.
See Bosman, Herman Charles

Gordon, Sol 1923- .... **CLC 26**
See also CA 53-56; CANR 4; SATA 11

Gordone, Charles 1925-1995 .... **CLC 1, 4;
DAM DRAM; DC 8**
See also BW 1, 3; CA 93-96, 180; 150;
CAAE 180; CANR 55; DLB 7; INT 93-
96; MTCW 1

Gore, Catherine 1800-1861 .... **NCLC 65**
See also DLB 116

Gorenko, Anna Andreevna
See Akhmatova, Anna

Gorky, Maxim 1868-1936 ... **TCLC 8; DAB;
SSC 28; WLC**
See also Peshkov, Alexei Maximovich
See also MTCW 2

Goryan, Sirak
See Saroyan, William

Gosse, Sir Edmund (William) 1849-1928
.... **TCLC 28**
See also CA 117; DLB 57, 144, 184

Gotlieb, Phyllis Fay (Bloom) 1926- . **CLC 18**
See also CA 13-16R; CANR 7; DLB 88

Gottesman, S. D.
See Kornbluth, C(yril) M.; Pohl, Frederik

Gottfried von Strassburg fl. c. 1210-
.... **CMLC 10**
See also DLB 138

Gould, Lois .... **CLC 4, 10**
See also CA 77-80; CANR 29; MTCW 1

Gourmont, Remy (-Marie-Charles) de
1858-1915 .... **TCLC 17**
See also CA 109; 150; MTCW 2

Govier, Katherine 1948- .... **CLC 51**
See also CA 101; CANR 18, 40

Goyen, (Charles) William 1915-1983
.... **CLC 5, 8, 14, 40**
See also AITN 2; CA 5-8R; 110; CANR 6,
71; DLB 2; DLBY 83; INT CANR-6

Goytisolo, Juan 1931- ... **CLC 5, 10, 23, 133;
DAM MULT; HLC 1**
See also CA 85-88; CANR 32, 61; HW 1,
2; MTCW 1, 2

Gozzano, Guido 1883-1916 .... **PC 10**
See also CA 154; DLB 114

Gozzi, (Conte) Carlo 1720-1806 ... **NCLC 23**

Grabbe, Christian Dietrich 1801-1836
.... **NCLC 2**
See also DLB 133

Grace, Patricia Frances 1937- .... **CLC 56**
See also CA 176

Gracian y Morales, Baltasar 1601-1658
.... **LC 15**

Gracq, Julien .... **CLC 11, 48**
See also Poirier, Louis
See also DLB 83

Grade, Chaim 1910-1982 .... **CLC 10**
See also CA 93-96; 107

Graduate of Oxford, A
See Ruskin, John

Grafton, Garth
See Duncan, Sara Jeannette

Graham, John
See Phillips, David Graham

Graham, Jorie 1951- .... **CLC 48, 118**
See also CA 111; CANR 63; DLB 120

Graham, R(obert) B(ontine) Cunninghame
See Cunninghame Graham, Robert
(Gallnigad) Bontine
See also DLB 98, 135, 174

Graham, Robert
See Haldeman, Joe (William)

Graham, Tom
See Lewis, (Harry) Sinclair

Graham, W(illiam) S(idney) 1918-1986
.... **CLC 29**
See also CA 73-76; 118; DLB 20

Graham, Winston (Mawdsley) 1910-
.... **CLC 23**
See also CA 49-52; CANR 2, 22, 45, 66;
DLB 77

Grahame, Kenneth 1859-1932 ..... **TCLC 64;
DAB**
See also CA 108; 136; CANR 80; CLR 5;
DA3; DLB 34, 141, 178; MAICYA;
MTCW 2; SATA 100; YABC 1

Granovsky, Timofei Nikolaevich 1813-1855
.... **NCLC 75**
See also DLB 198

Grant, Skeeter
See Spiegelman, Art

Granville-Barker, Harley 1877-1946
.... **TCLC 2; DAM DRAM**
See also Barker, Harley Granville
See also CA 104

Grass, Guenter (Wilhelm) 1927- . **CLC 1, 2,
4, 6, 11, 15, 22, 32, 49, 88; DA; DAB;
DAC; DAM MST, NOV; WLC**
See also CA 13-16R; CANR 20, 75, 93;
DA3; DLB 75, 124; MTCW 1, 2

Gratton, Thomas
See Hulme, T(homas) E(rnest)

Grau, Shirley Ann 1929- . **CLC 4, 9; SSC 15**
See also CA 89-92; CANR 22, 69; DLB 2;
INT CANR-22; MTCW 1

Gravel, Fern
See Hall, James Norman

Graver, Elizabeth 1964- .... **CLC 70**
See also CA 135; CANR 71

Graves, Richard Perceval 1945- ..... **CLC 44**
See also CA 65-68; CANR 9, 26, 51

Graves, Robert (von Ranke) 1895-1985
.... **CLC 1, 2, 6, 11, 39, 44, 45; DAB;
DAC; DAM MST, POET; PC 6**
See also CA 5-8R; 117; CANR 5, 36; CD-
BLB 1914-1945; DA3; DLB 20, 100, 191;
DLBD 18; DLBY 85; MTCW 1, 2; SATA
45

Graves, Valerie
See Bradley, Marion Zimmer

Gray, Alasdair (James) 1934- .... **CLC 41**
See also CA 126; CANR 47, 69; DLB 194;
INT 126; MTCW 1, 2

Gray, Amlin 1946- .... **CLC 29**
See also CA 138

Gray, Francine du Plessix 1930- ... **CLC 22;
DAM NOV**
See also BEST 90:3; CA 61-64; CAAS 2;
CANR 11, 33, 75, 81; INT CANR-11;
MTCW 1, 2

Gray, John (Henry) 1866-1934 ..... **TCLC 19**
See also CA 119; 162

Gray, Simon (James Holliday) 1936-
.... **CLC 9, 14, 36**
See also AITN 1; CA 21-24R; CAAS 3;
CANR 32, 69; DLB 13; MTCW 1

Gray, Spalding 1941- ... **CLC 49, 112; DAM
POP; DC 7**
See also CA 128; CANR 74; MTCW 2

Gray, Thomas 1716-1771 ...... **LC 4, 40; DA;
DAB; DAC; DAM MST; PC 2; WLC**
See also CDBLB 1660-1789; DA3; DLB
109

Grayson, David
See Baker, Ray Stannard

Grayson, Richard (A.) 1951- .... **CLC 38**
See also CA 85-88; CANR 14, 31, 57; DLB
234

Greeley, Andrew M(oran) 1928- .... **CLC 28;
DAM POP**
See also CA 5-8R; CAAS 7; CANR 7, 43,
69; DA3; MTCW 1, 2

Green, Anna Katharine 1846-1935
.... **TCLC 63**
See also CA 112; 159; DLB 202, 221

Green, Brian
See Card, Orson Scott

Green, Hannah
See Greenberg, Joanne (Goldenberg)

Green, Hannah 1927(?)-1996 .... **CLC 3**
See also CA 73-76; CANR 59, 93

Green, Henry 1905-1973 .... **CLC 2, 13, 97**
See also Yorke, Henry Vincent
See also CA 175; DLB 15

Green, Julian (Hartridge) 1900-1998
See Green, Julien
See also CA 21-24R; 169; CANR 33, 87;
DLB 4, 72; MTCW 1

Green, Julien .... **CLC 3, 11, 77**
See also Green, Julian (Hartridge)
See also MTCW 2

Green, Paul (Eliot) 1894-1981 .... **CLC 25;
DAM DRAM**
See also AITN 1; CA 5-8R; 103; CANR 3;
DLB 7, 9; DLBY 81

Greenberg, Ivan 1908-1973
See Rahv, Philip
See also CA 85-88

Greenberg, Joanne (Goldenberg) 1932-
.... **CLC 7, 30**
See also AAYA 12; CA 5-8R; CANR 14,
32, 69; SATA 25

Greenberg, Richard 1959(?)- .... **CLC 57**
See also CA 138

Greene, Bette 1934- .... **CLC 30**
See also AAYA 7; CA 53-56; CANR 4; CLR
2; JRDA; MAICYA; SAAS 16; SATA 8,
102

Greene, Gael .... **CLC 8**
See also CA 13-16R; CANR 10

Greene, Graham (Henry) 1904-1991
... **CLC 1, 3, 6, 9, 14, 18, 27, 37, 70, 72,
125; DA; DAB; DAC; DAM MST, NOV;
SSC 29; WLC**
See also AITN 2; CA 13-16R; 133; CANR
35, 61; CDBLB 1945-1960; DA3; DLB
13, 15, 77, 100, 162, 201, 204; DLBY 91;
MTCW 1, 2; SATA 20

Greene, Robert 1558-1592 .... **LC 41**
See also DLB 62, 167

Greer, Germaine 1939- .... **CLC 131**
See also AITN 1; CA 81-84; CANR 33, 70;
MTCW 1, 2

Greer, Richard
See Silverberg, Robert

Gregor, Arthur 1923- .... **CLC 9**
See also CA 25-28R; CAAS 10; CANR 11;
SATA 36

Gregor, Lee
See Pohl, Frederik

Gregory, Isabella Augusta (Persse)
1852-1932 .... **TCLC 1**
See also CA 104; 184; DLB 10

Gregory, J. Dennis
See Williams, John A(lfred)

Grendon, Stephen
See Derleth, August (William)

Grenville, Kate 1950- .... **CLC 61**
See also CA 118; CANR 53, 93

Grenville, Pelham
See Wodehouse, P(elham) G(renville)

Greve, Felix Paul (Berthold Friedrich)
1879-1948
See Grove, Frederick Philip
See also CA 104; 141, 175; CANR 79;
DAC; DAM MST

Grey, Zane 1872-1939 . **TCLC 6; DAM POP**
See also CA 104; 132; DA3; DLB 212;
MTCW 1, 2

Grieg, (Johan) Nordahl (Brun) 1902-1943
.... **TCLC 10**
See also CA 107

Grieve, C(hristopher) M(urray) 1892-1978
.... **CLC 11, 19; DAM POET**

See also MacDiarmid, Hugh; Pteleon
See also CA 5-8R; 85-88; CANR 33;
MTCW 1

Griffin, Gerald 1803-1840 .... **NCLC 7**
See also DLB 159

Griffin, John Howard 1920-1980 .... **CLC 68**
See also AITN 1; CA 1-4R; 101; CANR 2

Griffin, Peter 1942- .... **CLC 39**
See also CA 136

Griffith, D(avid Lewelyn) W(ark)
1875(?)-1948 .... **TCLC 68**
See also CA 119; 150; CANR 80

Griffith, Lawrence
See Griffith, D(avid Lewelyn) W(ark)

Griffiths, Trevor 1935- .... **CLC 13, 52**
See also CA 97-100; CANR 45; DLB 13

Griggs, Sutton (Elbert) 1872-1930 . **TCLC 77**
See also CA 123; 186; DLB 50

Grigson, Geoffrey (Edward Harvey)
1905-1985 .... **CLC 7, 39**
See also CA 25-28R; 118; CANR 20, 33;
DLB 27; MTCW 1, 2

Grillparzer, Franz 1791-1872 . **NCLC 1; DC
14; SSC 37**
See also DLB 133

Grimble, Reverend Charles James
See Eliot, T(homas) S(tearns)

Grimke, Charlotte L(ottie) Forten
1837(?)-1914
See Forten, Charlotte L.
See also BW 1; CA 117; 124; DAM MULT,
POET

Grimm, Jacob Ludwig Karl 1785-1863
.... **NCLC 3, 77; SSC 36**
See also DLB 90; MAICYA; SATA 22

Grimm, Wilhelm Karl 1786-1859 . **NCLC 3,
77; SSC 36**
See also DLB 90; MAICYA; SATA 22

**Grimmelshausen, Johann Jakob Christoffel
von** 1621-1676 .... **LC 6**
See also DLB 168

Grindel, Eugene 1895-1952
See Eluard, Paul
See also CA 104

Grisham, John 1955- .. **CLC 84; DAM POP**
See also AAYA 14; CA 138; CANR 47, 69;
DA3; MTCW 2

Grossman, David 1954- .... **CLC 67**
See also CA 138

Grossman, Vasily (Semenovich) 1905-1964
.... **CLC 41**
See also CA 124; 130; MTCW 1

Grove, Frederick Philip .... **TCLC 4**
See also Greve, Felix Paul (Berthold
Friedrich)
See also DLB 92

Grubb
See Crumb, R(obert)

Grumbach, Doris (Isaac) 1918- ...... **CLC 13,
22, 64**
See also CA 5-8R; CAAS 2; CANR 9, 42,
70; INT CANR-9; MTCW 2

Grundtvig, Nicolai Frederik Severin
1783-1872 .... **NCLC 1**

Grunge
See Crumb, R(obert)

Grunwald, Lisa 1959- .... **CLC 44**
See also CA 120

Guare, John 1938- . **CLC 8, 14, 29, 67; DAM
DRAM**
See also CA 73-76; CANR 21, 69; DLB 7;
MTCW 1, 2

Gudjonsson, Halldor Kiljan 1902-1998
See Laxness, Halldor
See also CA 103; 164

Guenter, Erich
See Eich, Guenter

Guest, Barbara 1920- .... **CLC 34**

See also CA 25-28R; CANR 11, 44, 84; DLB 5, 193

Guest, Edgar A(lbert) 1881-1959 . **TCLC 95**
See also CA 112; 168

Guest, Judith (Ann) 1936- .... **CLC 8, 30; DAM NOV, POP**
See also AAYA 7; CA 77-80; CANR 15, 75; DA3; INT CANR-15; MTCW 1, 2

Guevara, Che .... **CLC 87; HLC 1**
See also Guevara (Serna), Ernesto

Guevara (Serna), Ernesto 1928-1967
.... **CLC 87; DAM MULT; HLC 1**
See also Guevara, Che
See also CA 127; 111; CANR 56; HW 1

Guicciardini, Francesco 1483-1540 ... **LC 49**

Guild, Nicholas M. 1944- .... **CLC 33**
See also CA 93-96

Guillemin, Jacques
See Sartre, Jean-Paul

Guillen, Jorge 1893-1984 ..... **CLC 11; DAM MULT, POET; HLCS 1**
See also CA 89-92; 112; DLB 108; HW 1

Guillen, Nicolas (Cristobal) 1902-1989
.... **CLC 48, 79; BLC 2; DAM MST, MULT, POET; HLC 1; PC 23**
See also BW 2; CA 116; 125; 129; CANR 84; HW 1

Guillevic, (Eugene) 1907- .... **CLC 33**
See also CA 93-96

Guillois
See Desnos, Robert

Guillois, Valentin
See Desnos, Robert

Guimaraes Rosa, Joao 1908-1967
See also CA 175; HLCS 2

Guiney, Louise Imogen 1861-1920 . **TCLC 41**
See also CA 160; DLB 54

Guiraldes, Ricardo (Guillermo) 1886-1927
.... **TCLC 39**
See also CA 131; HW 1; MTCW 1

Gumilev, Nikolai (Stepanovich) 1886-1921
.... **TCLC 60**
See also CA 165

Gunesekera, Romesh 1954- .... **CLC 91**
See also CA 159

Gunn, Bill .... **CLC 5**
See also Gunn, William Harrison
See also DLB 38

Gunn, Thom(son William) 1929- . **CLC 3, 6, 18, 32, 81; DAM POET; PC 26**
See also CA 17-20R; CANR 9, 33; CDBLB 1960 to Present; DLB 27; INT CANR-33; MTCW 1

Gunn, William Harrison 1934(?)-1989
See Gunn, Bill
See also AITN 1; BW 1, 3; CA 13-16R; 128; CANR 12, 25, 76

Gunnars, Kristjana 1948- .... **CLC 69**
See also CA 113; DLB 60

Gurdjieff, G(eorgei) I(vanovich) 1877(?)-1949 .... **TCLC 71**
See also CA 157

Gurganus, Allan 1947- . **CLC 70; DAM POP**
See also BEST 90:1; CA 135

Gurney, A(lbert) R(amsdell), Jr. 1930-
.... **CLC 32, 50, 54; DAM DRAM**
See also CA 77-80; CANR 32, 64

Gurney, Ivor (Bertie) 1890-1937 .. **TCLC 33**
See also CA 167

Gurney, Peter
See Gurney, A(lbert) R(amsdell), Jr.

Guro, Elena 1877-1913 .... **TCLC 56**

Gustafson, James M(oody) 1925- . **CLC 100**
See also CA 25-28R; CANR 37

Gustafson, Ralph (Barker) 1909- ... **CLC 36**
See also CA 21-24R; CANR 8, 45, 84; DLB 88

Gut, Gom
See Simenon, Georges (Jacques Christian)

Guterson, David 1956- .... **CLC 91**
See also CA 132; CANR 73; MTCW 2

Guthrie, A(lfred) B(ertram), Jr. 1901-1991
.... **CLC 23**
See also CA 57-60; 134; CANR 24; DLB 212; SATA 62; SATA-Obit 67

Guthrie, Isobel
See Grieve, C(hristopher) M(urray)

Guthrie, Woodrow Wilson 1912-1967
See Guthrie, Woody
See also CA 113; 93-96

Guthrie, Woody .... **CLC 35**
See also Guthrie, Woodrow Wilson

Gutierrez Najera, Manuel 1859-1895
See also HLCS 2

Guy, Rosa (Cuthbert) 1928- .... **CLC 26**
See also AAYA 4; BW 2; CA 17-20R; CANR 14, 34, 83; CLR 13; DLB 33; JRDA; MAICYA; SATA 14, 62

Gwendolyn
See Bennett, (Enoch) Arnold

H. D. .... **CLC 3, 8, 14, 31, 34, 73; PC 5**
See also Doolittle, Hilda

H. de V.
See Buchan, John

Haavikko, Paavo Juhani 1931- . **CLC 18, 34**
See also CA 106

Habbema, Koos
See Heijermans, Herman

Habermas, Juergen 1929- .... **CLC 104**
See also CA 109; CANR 85

Habermas, Jurgen
See Habermas, Juergen

Hacker, Marilyn 1942- ..... **CLC 5, 9, 23, 72, 91; DAM POET**
See also CA 77-80; CANR 68; DLB 120

Haeckel, Ernst Heinrich (Philipp August) 1834-1919 .... **TCLC 83**
See also CA 157

Hafiz c. 1326-1389(?) .... **CMLC 34**

Hafiz c. 1326-1389 .... **CMLC 34**

Haggard, H(enry) Rider 1856-1925
.... **TCLC 11**
See also CA 108; 148; DLB 70, 156, 174, 178; MTCW 2; SATA 16

Hagiosy, L.
See Larbaud, Valery (Nicolas)

Hagiwara Sakutaro 1886-1942 .... **TCLC 60; PC 18**

Haig, Fenil
See Ford, Ford Madox

Haig-Brown, Roderick (Langmere) 1908-1976 .... **CLC 21**
See also CA 5-8R; 69-72; CANR 4, 38, 83; CLR 31; DLB 88; MAICYA; SATA 12

Hailey, Arthur 1920- .... **CLC 5; DAM NOV, POP**
See also AITN 2; BEST 90:3; CA 1-4R; CANR 2, 36, 75; DLB 88; DLBY 82; MTCW 1, 2

Hailey, Elizabeth Forsythe 1938- .... **CLC 40**
See also CA 93-96; CAAS 1; CANR 15, 48; INT CANR-15

Haines, John (Meade) 1924- .... **CLC 58**
See also CA 17-20R; CANR 13, 34; DLB 212

Hakluyt, Richard 1552-1616 .... **LC 31**

Haldeman, Joe (William) 1943- ...... **CLC 61**
See also Graham, Robert
See also CA 53-56, 179; CAAE 179; CAAS 25; CANR 6, 70, 72; DLB 8; INT CANR-6

Hale, Sarah Josepha (Buell) 1788-1879
.... **NCLC 75**
See also DLB 1, 42, 73

Haley, Alex(ander Murray Palmer) 1921-1992 . **CLC 8, 12, 76; BLC 2; DA; DAB; DAC; DAM MST, MULT, POP**
See also AAYA 26; BW 2, 3; CA 77-80; 136; CANR 61; CDALBS; DA3; DLB 38; MTCW 1, 2

Haliburton, Thomas Chandler 1796-1865
.... **NCLC 15**
See also DLB 11, 99

Hall, Donald (Andrew, Jr.) 1928- .... **CLC 1, 13, 37, 59; DAM POET**
See also CA 5-8R; CAAS 7; CANR 2, 44, 64; DLB 5; MTCW 1; SATA 23, 97

Hall, Frederic Sauser
See Sauser-Hall, Frederic

Hall, James
See Kuttner, Henry

Hall, James Norman 1887-1951 ... **TCLC 23**
See also CA 123; 173; SATA 21

Hall, Radclyffe -1943
See Hall, (Marguerite) Radclyffe
See also MTCW 2

Hall, (Marguerite) Radclyffe 1886-1943
.... **TCLC 12**
See also CA 110; 150; CANR 83; DLB 191

Hall, Rodney 1935- .... **CLC 51**
See also CA 109; CANR 69

Halleck, Fitz-Greene 1790-1867 ... **NCLC 47**
See also DLB 3

Halliday, Michael
See Creasey, John

Halpern, Daniel 1945- .... **CLC 14**
See also CA 33-36R; CANR 93

Hamburger, Michael (Peter Leopold) 1924-
.... **CLC 5, 14**
See also CA 5-8R; CAAS 4; CANR 2, 47; DLB 27

Hamill, Pete 1935- .... **CLC 10**
See also CA 25-28R; CANR 18, 71

Hamilton, Alexander 1755(?)-1804
.... **NCLC 49**
See also DLB 37

Hamilton, Clive
See Lewis, C(live) S(taples)

Hamilton, Edmond 1904-1977 .... **CLC 1**
See also CA 1-4R; CANR 3, 84; DLB 8; SATA 118

Hamilton, Eugene (Jacob) Lee
See Lee-Hamilton, Eugene (Jacob)

Hamilton, Franklin
See Silverberg, Robert

Hamilton, Gail
See Corcoran, Barbara

Hamilton, Mollie
See Kaye, M(ary) M(argaret)

Hamilton, (Anthony Walter) Patrick 1904-1962 .... **CLC 51**
See also CA 176; 113; DLB 191

Hamilton, Virginia 1936- ..... **CLC 26; DAM MULT**
See also AAYA 2, 21; BW 2, 3; CA 25-28R; CANR 20, 37, 73; CLR 1, 11, 40; DLB 33, 52; INT CANR-20; JRDA; MAICYA; MTCW 1, 2; SATA 4, 56, 79

Hammett, (Samuel) Dashiell 1894-1961
.... **CLC 3, 5, 10, 19, 47; SSC 17**
See also AITN 1; CA 81-84; CANR 42; CDALB 1929-1941; DA3; DLB 226; DLBD 6; DLBY 96; MTCW 1, 2

Hammon, Jupiter 1711(?)-1800(?) . **NCLC 5; BLC 2; DAM MULT, POET; PC 16**
See also DLB 31, 50

Hammond, Keith
See Kuttner, Henry

Hamner, Earl (Henry), Jr. 1923- .... **CLC 12**
See also AITN 2; CA 73-76; DLB 6

Hampton, Christopher (James) 1946-
.... **CLC 4**
See also CA 25-28R; DLB 13; MTCW 1

See also CA 49-52; CAAS 17; CANR 1, 33, 87; DLB 53

Hood, Thomas 1799-1845 .... **NCLC 16**
See also DLB 96

Hooker, (Peter) Jeremy 1941- .... **CLC 43**
See also CA 77-80; CANR 22; DLB 40

hooks, bell .... **CLC 94; BLCS**
See also Watkins, Gloria Jean
See also MTCW 2

Hope, A(lec) D(erwent) 1907- ..... **CLC 3, 51**
See also CA 21-24R; CANR 33, 74; MTCW 1, 2

Hope, Anthony 1863-1933 .... **TCLC 83**
See also CA 157; DLB 153, 156

Hope, Brian
See Creasey, John

Hope, Christopher (David Tully) 1944-
.... **CLC 52**
See also CA 106; CANR 47; DLB 225; SATA 62

Hopkins, Gerard Manley 1844-1889
.... **NCLC 17; DA; DAB; DAC; DAM MST, POET; PC 15; WLC**
See also CDBLB 1890-1914; DA3; DLB 35, 57

Hopkins, John (Richard) 1931-1998 . **CLC 4**
See also CA 85-88; 169

Hopkins, Pauline Elizabeth 1859-1930
.... **TCLC 28; BLC 2; DAM MULT**
See also BW 2, 3; CA 141; CANR 82; DLB 50

Hopkinson, Francis 1737-1791 .... **LC 25**
See also DLB 31

Hopley-Woolrich, Cornell George 1903-1968
See Woolrich, Cornell
See also CA 13-14; CANR 58; CAP 1; DLB 226; MTCW 2

Horace 65B.C.-8B.C. .... **CMLC 39**
See also DLB 211

Horatio
See Proust, (Valentin-Louis-George-Eugene-) Marcel

Horgan, Paul (George Vincent O'Shaughnessy) 1903-1995 ...... **CLC 9, 53; DAM NOV**
See also CA 13-16R; 147; CANR 9, 35; DLB 212; DLBY 85; INT CANR-9; MTCW 1, 2; SATA 13; SATA-Obit 84

Horn, Peter
See Kuttner, Henry

Hornem, Horace Esq.
See Byron, George Gordon (Noel)

Horney, Karen (Clementine Theodore Danielsen) 1885-1952 .... **TCLC 71**
See also CA 114; 165

Hornung, E(rnest) W(illiam) 1866-1921
.... **TCLC 59**
See also CA 108; 160; DLB 70

Horovitz, Israel (Arthur) 1939- ..... **CLC 56; DAM DRAM**
See also CA 33-36R; CANR 46, 59; DLB 7

Horton, George Moses 1797(?)-1883(?)
.... **NCLC 87**
See also DLB 50

Horvath, Odon von
See Horvath, Oedoen von
See also DLB 85, 124

Horvath, Oedoen von 1901-1938 .. **TCLC 45**
See also Horvath, Odon von; von Horvath, Oedoen
See also CA 118

Horwitz, Julius 1920-1986 .... **CLC 14**
See also CA 9-12R; 119; CANR 12

Hospital, Janette Turner 1942- .... **CLC 42**
See also CA 108; CANR 48

Hostos, E. M. de
See Hostos (y Bonilla), Eugenio Maria de

Hostos, Eugenio M. de
See Hostos (y Bonilla), Eugenio Maria de

Hostos, Eugenio Maria
See Hostos (y Bonilla), Eugenio Maria de

Hostos (y Bonilla), Eugenio Maria de
1839-1903 .... **TCLC 24**
See also CA 123; 131; HW 1

Houdini
See Lovecraft, H(oward) P(hillips)

Hougan, Carolyn 1943- .... **CLC 34**
See also CA 139

Household, Geoffrey (Edward West)
1900-1988 .... **CLC 11**
See also CA 77-80; 126; CANR 58; DLB 87; SATA 14; SATA-Obit 59

Housman, A(lfred) E(dward) 1859-1936
... **TCLC 1, 10; DA; DAB; DAC; DAM MST, POET; PC 2; WLCS**
See also CA 104; 125; DA3; DLB 19; MTCW 1, 2

Housman, Laurence 1865-1959 ...... **TCLC 7**
See also CA 106; 155; DLB 10; SATA 25

Howard, Elizabeth Jane 1923- .... **CLC 7, 29**
See also CA 5-8R; CANR 8, 62

Howard, Maureen 1930- .... **CLC 5, 14, 46**
See also CA 53-56; CANR 31, 75; DLBY 83; INT CANR-31; MTCW 1, 2

Howard, Richard 1929- .... **CLC 7, 10, 47**
See also AITN 1; CA 85-88; CANR 25, 80; DLB 5; INT CANR-25

Howard, Robert E(rvin) 1906-1936 . **TCLC 8**
See also CA 105; 157

Howard, Warren F.
See Pohl, Frederik

Howe, Fanny (Quincy) 1940- .... **CLC 47**
See also CA 117; CAAE 187; CAAS 27; CANR 70; SATA-Brief 52

Howe, Irving 1920-1993 .... **CLC 85**
See also CA 9-12R; 141; CANR 21, 50; DLB 67; MTCW 1, 2

Howe, Julia Ward 1819-1910 .... **TCLC 21**
See also CA 117; DLB 1, 189, 235

Howe, Susan 1937- .... **CLC 72**
See also CA 160; DLB 120

Howe, Tina 1937- .... **CLC 48**
See also CA 109

Howell, James 1594(?)-1666 .... **LC 13**
See also DLB 151

Howells, W. D.
See Howells, William Dean

Howells, William D.
See Howells, William Dean

Howells, William Dean 1837-1920 . **TCLC 7, 17, 41; SSC 36**
See also CA 104; 134; CDALB 1865-1917; DLB 12, 64, 74, 79, 189; MTCW 2

Howes, Barbara 1914-1996 .... **CLC 15**
See also CA 9-12R; 151; CAAS 3; CANR 53; SATA 5

Hrabal, Bohumil 1914-1997 ...... **CLC 13, 67**
See also CA 106; 156; CAAS 12; CANR 57; DLB 232

Hroswitha of Gandersheim c. 935-c. 1002
.... **CMLC 29**
See also DLB 148

Hsi, Chu 1130-1200 .... **CMLC 42**

Hsun, Lu
See Lu Hsun

Hubbard, L(afayette) Ron(ald) 1911-1986
.... **CLC 43; DAM POP**
See also CA 77-80; 118; CANR 52; DA3; MTCW 2

Huch, Ricarda (Octavia) 1864-1947
.... **TCLC 13**
See also CA 111; DLB 66

Huddle, David 1942- .... **CLC 49**
See also CA 57-60; CAAS 20; CANR 89; DLB 130

Hudson, Jeffrey
See Crichton, (John) Michael

Hudson, W(illiam) H(enry) 1841-1922
.... **TCLC 29**
See also CA 115; DLB 98, 153, 174; SATA 35

Hueffer, Ford Madox
See Ford, Ford Madox

Hughart, Barry 1934- .... **CLC 39**
See also CA 137

Hughes, Colin
See Creasey, John

Hughes, David (John) 1930- .... **CLC 48**
See also CA 116; 129; DLB 14

Hughes, Edward James
See Hughes, Ted
See also DAM MST, POET; DA3

Hughes, (James) Langston 1902-1967
. **CLC 1, 5, 10, 15, 35, 44, 108; BLC 2; DA; DAB; DAC; DAM DRAM, MST, MULT, POET; DC 3; PC 1; SSC 6; WLC**
See also AAYA 12; BW 1, 3; CA 1-4R; 25-28R; CANR 1, 34, 82; CDALB 1929-1941; CLR 17; DA3; DLB 4, 7, 48, 51, 86, 228; JRDA; MAICYA; MTCW 1, 2; SATA 4, 33

Hughes, Richard (Arthur Warren)
1900-1976 .... **CLC 1, 11; DAM NOV**
See also CA 5-8R; 65-68; CANR 4; DLB 15, 161; MTCW 1; SATA 8; SATA-Obit 25

Hughes, Ted 1930-1998 . **CLC 2, 4, 9, 14, 37, 119; DAB; DAC; PC 7**
See also Hughes, Edward James
See also CA 1-4R; 171; CANR 1, 33, 66; CLR 3; DLB 40, 161; MAICYA; MTCW 1, 2; SATA 49; SATA-Brief 27; SATA-Obit 107

Hugo, Richard F(ranklin) 1923-1982
.... **CLC 6, 18, 32; DAM POET**
See also CA 49-52; 108; CANR 3; DLB 5, 206

Hugo, Victor (Marie) 1802-1885 ... **NCLC 3, 10, 21; DA; DAB; DAC; DAM DRAM, MST, NOV, POET; PC 17; WLC**
See also AAYA 28; DA3; DLB 119, 192; SATA 47

Huidobro, Vicente
See Huidobro Fernandez, Vicente Garcia

Huidobro Fernandez, Vicente Garcia
1893-1948 .... **TCLC 31**
See also CA 131; HW 1

Hulme, Keri 1947- .... **CLC 39, 130**
See also CA 125; CANR 69; INT 125

Hulme, T(homas) E(rnest) 1883-1917
.... **TCLC 21**
See also CA 117; DLB 19

Hume, David 1711-1776 .... **LC 7, 56**
See also DLB 104

Humphrey, William 1924-1997 .... **CLC 45**
See also CA 77-80; 160; CANR 68; DLB 212

Humphreys, Emyr Owen 1919- ...... **CLC 47**
See also CA 5-8R; CANR 3, 24; DLB 15

Humphreys, Josephine 1945- .... **CLC 34, 57**
See also CA 121; 127; INT 127

Huneker, James Gibbons 1857-1921
.... **TCLC 65**
See also DLB 71

Hungerford, Pixie
See Brinsmead, H(esba) F(ay)

Hunt, E(verette) Howard, (Jr.) 1918- . **CLC 3**
See also AITN 1; CA 45-48; CANR 2, 47

Hunt, Francesca
See Holland, Isabelle

Hunt, Kyle
See Creasey, John

Hunt, (James Henry) Leigh 1784-1859
.... **NCLC 1, 70; DAM POET**
See also DLB 96, 110, 144

Jakes, John (William) 1932- . CLC 29; DAM
NOV, POP
See also AAYA 32; BEST 89:4; CA 57-60;
CANR 10, 43, 66; DA3; DLBY 83; INT
CANR-10; MTCW 1, 2; SATA 62

James, Andrew
See Kirkup, James

James, C(yril) L(ionel) R(obert) 1901-1989
.... CLC 33; BLCS
See also BW 2; CA 117; 125; 128; CANR
62; DLB 125; MTCW 1

James, Daniel (Lewis) 1911-1988
See Santiago, Danny
See also CA 174; 125

James, Dynely
See Mayne, William (James Carter)

James, Henry Sr. 1811-1882 .... NCLC 53

James, Henry 1843-1916 .... TCLC 2, 11, 24,
40, 47, 64; DA; DAB; DAC; DAM MST,
NOV; SSC 8, 32; WLC
See also CA 104; 132; CDALB 1865-1917;
DA3; DLB 12, 71, 74, 189; DLBD 13;
MTCW 1, 2

James, M. R.
See James, Montague (Rhodes)
See also DLB 156

James, Montague (Rhodes) 1862-1936
.... TCLC 6; SSC 16
See also CA 104; DLB 201

James, P. D. 1920- .... CLC 18, 46, 122
See also White, Phyllis Dorothy James
See also BEST 90:2; CDBLB 1960 to
Present; DLB 87; DLBD 17

James, Philip
See Moorcock, Michael (John)

James, William 1842-1910 ...... TCLC 15, 32
See also CA 109

James I 1394-1437 .... LC 20

Jameson, Anna 1794-1860 .... NCLC 43
See also DLB 99, 166

Jami, Nur al-Din 'Abd al-Rahman
1414-1492 .... LC 9

Jammes, Francis 1868-1938 .... TCLC 75

Jandl, Ernst 1925- .... CLC 34

Janowitz, Tama 1957- . CLC 43; DAM POP
See also CA 106; CANR 52, 89

Japrisot, Sebastien 1931- .... CLC 90

Jarrell, Randall 1914-1965 .. CLC 1, 2, 6, 9,
13, 49; DAM POET
See also CA 5-8R; 25-28R; CABS 2; CANR
6, 34; CDALB 1941-1968; CLR 6; DLB
48, 52; MAICYA; MTCW 1, 2; SATA 7

Jarry, Alfred 1873-1907 . TCLC 2, 14; DAM
DRAM; SSC 20
See also CA 104; 153; DA3; DLB 192

Jawien, Andrzej
See John Paul II, Pope

Jaynes, Roderick
See Coen, Ethan

Jeake, Samuel, Jr.
See Aiken, Conrad (Potter)

Jean Paul 1763-1825 .... NCLC 7

Jefferies, (John) Richard 1848-1887
.... NCLC 47
See also DLB 98, 141; SATA 16

Jeffers, (John) Robinson 1887-1962 . CLC 2,
3, 11, 15, 54; DA; DAC; DAM MST,
POET; PC 17; WLC
See also CA 85-88; CANR 35; CDALB
1917-1929; DLB 45, 212; MTCW 1, 2

Jefferson, Janet
See Mencken, H(enry) L(ouis)

Jefferson, Thomas 1743-1826 .... NCLC 11
See also CDALB 1640-1865; DA3; DLB
31

Jeffrey, Francis 1773-1850 .... NCLC 33
See also DLB 107

Jelakowitch, Ivan
See Heijermans, Herman

Jellicoe, (Patricia) Ann 1927- .... CLC 27
See also CA 85-88; DLB 13, 233

Jemyma
See Holley, Marietta

Jen, Gish .... CLC 70
See also Jen, Lillian

Jen, Lillian 1956(?)-
See Jen, Gish
See also CA 135; CANR 89

Jenkins, (John) Robin 1912- .... CLC 52
See also CA 1-4R; CANR 1; DLB 14

Jennings, Elizabeth (Joan) 1926- ..... CLC 5,
14, 131
See also CA 61-64; CAAS 5; CANR 8, 39,
66; DLB 27; MTCW 1; SATA 66

Jennings, Waylon 1937- .... CLC 21

Jensen, Johannes V. 1873-1950 ..... TCLC 41
See also CA 170

Jensen, Laura (Linnea) 1948- .... CLC 37
See also CA 103

Jerome, Jerome K(lapka) 1859-1927
.... TCLC 23
See also CA 119; 177; DLB 10, 34, 135

Jerrold, Douglas William 1803-1857
.... NCLC 2
See also DLB 158, 159

Jewett, (Theodora) Sarah Orne 1849-1909
.... TCLC 1, 22; SSC 6
See also CA 108; 127; CANR 71; DLB 12,
74, 221; SATA 15

Jewsbury, Geraldine (Endsor) 1812-1880
.... NCLC 22
See also DLB 21

Jhabvala, Ruth Prawer 1927- . CLC 4, 8, 29,
94, 138; DAB; DAM NOV
See also CA 1-4R; CANR 2, 29, 51, 74, 91;
DLB 139, 194; INT CANR-29; MTCW 1,
2

Jibran, Kahlil
See Gibran, Kahlil

Jibran, Khalil
See Gibran, Kahlil

Jiles, Paulette 1943- .... CLC 13, 58
See also CA 101; CANR 70

Jimenez (Mantecon), Juan Ramon
1881-1958 .... TCLC 4; DAM MULT,
POET; HLC 1; PC 7
See also CA 104; 131; CANR 74; DLB 134;
HW 1; MTCW 1, 2

Jimenez, Ramon
See Jimenez (Mantecon), Juan Ramon

Jimenez Mantecon, Juan
See Jimenez (Mantecon), Juan Ramon

Jin, Ha
See Jin, Xuefei

Jin, Xuefei 1956- .... CLC 109
See also CA 152; CANR 91

Joel, Billy .... CLC 26
See also Joel, William Martin

Joel, William Martin 1949-
See Joel, Billy
See also CA 108

John, Saint 7th cent. - .... CMLC 27

John of the Cross, St. 1542-1591 .... LC 18

John Paul II, Pope 1920- .... CLC 128
See also CA 106; 133

Johnson, B(ryan) S(tanley William)
1933-1973 .... CLC 6, 9
See also CA 9-12R; 53-56; CANR 9; DLB
14, 40

Johnson, Benj. F. of Boo
See Riley, James Whitcomb

Johnson, Benjamin F. of Boo
See Riley, James Whitcomb

Johnson, Charles (Richard) 1948- ... CLC 7,
51, 65; BLC 2; DAM MULT

See also BW 2, 3; CA 116; CAAS 18;
CANR 42, 66, 82; DLB 33; MTCW 2

Johnson, Denis 1949- .... CLC 52
See also CA 117; 121; CANR 71; DLB 120

Johnson, Diane 1934- .... CLC 5, 13, 48
See also CA 41-44R; CANR 17, 40, 62;
DLBY 80; INT CANR-17; MTCW 1

Johnson, Eyvind (Olof Verner) 1900-1976
.... CLC 14
See also CA 73-76; 69-72; CANR 34

Johnson, J. R.
See James, C(yril) L(ionel) R(obert)

Johnson, James Weldon 1871-1938
...... TCLC 3, 19; BLC 2; DAM MULT,
POET; PC 24
See also BW 1, 3; CA 104; 125; CANR 82;
CDALB 1917-1929; CLR 32; DA3; DLB
51; MTCW 1, 2; SATA 31

Johnson, Joyce 1935- .... CLC 58
See also CA 125; 129

Johnson, Judith (Emlyn) 1936- .. CLC 7, 15
See also Sherwin, Judith Johnson
See also CA 25-28R; 153; CANR 34

Johnson, Lionel (Pigot) 1867-1902
.... TCLC 19
See also CA 117; DLB 19

Johnson, Marguerite (Annie)
See Angelou, Maya

Johnson, Mel
See Malzberg, Barry N(athaniel)

Johnson, Pamela Hansford 1912-1981
.... CLC 1, 7, 27
See also CA 1-4R; 104; CANR 2, 28; DLB
15; MTCW 1, 2

Johnson, Robert 1911(?)-1938 ...... TCLC 69
See also BW 3; CA 174

Johnson, Samuel 1709-1784 . LC 15, 52; DA;
DAB; DAC; DAM MST; WLC
See also CDBLB 1660-1789; DLB 39, 95,
104, 142

Johnson, Uwe 1934-1984 . CLC 5, 10, 15, 40
See also CA 1-4R; 112; CANR 1, 39; DLB
75; MTCW 1

Johnston, George (Benson) 1913- ... CLC 51
See also CA 1-4R; CANR 5, 20; DLB 88

Johnston, Jennifer (Prudence) 1930- . CLC 7
See also CA 85-88; CANR 92; DLB 14

Joinville, Jean de 1224(?)-1317 ... CMLC 38

Jolley, (Monica) Elizabeth 1923- ... CLC 46;
SSC 19
See also CA 127; CAAS 13; CANR 59

Jones, Arthur Llewellyn 1863-1947
See Machen, Arthur
See also CA 104; 179

Jones, D(ouglas) G(ordon) 1929- ..... CLC 10
See also CA 29-32R; CANR 13, 90; DLB
53

Jones, David (Michael) 1895-1974 ... CLC 2,
4, 7, 13, 42
See also CA 9-12R; 53-56; CANR 28; CD-
BLB 1945-1960; DLB 20, 100; MTCW 1

Jones, David Robert 1947-
See Bowie, David
See also CA 103

Jones, Diana Wynne 1934- .... CLC 26
See also AAYA 12; CA 49-52; CANR 4,
26, 56; CLR 23; DLB 161; JRDA; MAI-
CYA; SAAS 7; SATA 9, 70, 108

Jones, Edward P. 1950- .... CLC 76
See also BW 2, 3; CA 142; CANR 79

Jones, Gayl 1949- ... CLC 6, 9, 131; BLC 2;
DAM MULT
See also BW 2, 3; CA 77-80; CANR 27,
66; DA3; DLB 33; MTCW 1, 2

Jones, James 1921-1977 .... CLC 1, 3, 10, 39
See also AITN 1, 2; CA 1-4R; 69-72;
CANR 6; DLB 2, 143; DLBD 17; DLBY
98; MTCW 1

Keates, Jonathan 1946(?)- .... **CLC 34**
See also CA 163

Keaton, Buster 1895-1966 .... **CLC 20**

Keats, John 1795-1821 .... **NCLC 8, 73; DA;
DAB; DAC; DAM MST, POET; PC 1;
WLC**
See also CDBLB 1789-1832; DA3; DLB
96, 110

Keble, John 1792-1866 .... **NCLC 87**
See also DLB 32, 55

Keene, Donald 1922- .... **CLC 34**
See also CA 1-4R; CANR 5

Keillor, Garrison .... **CLC 40, 115**
See also Keillor, Gary (Edward)
See also AAYA 2; BEST 89:3; DLBY 87;
SATA 58

Keillor, Gary (Edward) 1942-
See Keillor, Garrison
See also CA 111; 117; CANR 36, 59; DAM
POP; DA3; MTCW 1, 2

Keith, Michael
See Hubbard, L(afayette) Ron(ald)

Keller, Gottfried 1819-1890 .. **NCLC 2; SSC
26**
See also DLB 129

Keller, Nora Okja 1965- .... **CLC 109**
See also CA 187

Kellerman, Jonathan 1949- . **CLC 44; DAM
POP**
See also BEST 90:1; CA 106; CANR 29,
51; DA3; INT CANR-29

Kelley, William Melvin 1937- .... **CLC 22**
See also BW 1; CA 77-80; CANR 27, 83;
DLB 33

Kellogg, Marjorie 1922- .... **CLC 2**
See also CA 81-84

Kellow, Kathleen
See Hibbert, Eleanor Alice Burford

Kelly, M(ilton) T(errence) 1947- ..... **CLC 55**
See also CA 97-100; CAAS 22; CANR 19,
43, 84

Kelman, James 1946- .... **CLC 58, 86**
See also CA 148; CANR 85; DLB 194

Kemal, Yashar 1923- .... **CLC 14, 29**
See also CA 89-92; CANR 44

Kemble, Fanny 1809-1893 .... **NCLC 18**
See also DLB 32

Kemelman, Harry 1908-1996 .... **CLC 2**
See also AITN 1; CA 9-12R; 155; CANR 6,
71; DLB 28

Kempe, Margery 1373(?)-1440(?) .. **LC 6, 56**
See also DLB 146

Kempis, Thomas a 1380-1471 .... **LC 11**

Kendall, Henry 1839-1882 .... **NCLC 12**
See also DLB 230

Keneally, Thomas (Michael) 1935- .. **CLC 5,
8, 10, 14, 19, 27, 43, 117; DAM NOV**
See also CA 85-88; CANR 10, 50, 74; DA3;
MTCW 1, 2

Kennedy, Adrienne (Lita) 1931- .... **CLC 66;
BLC 2; DAM MULT; DC 5**
See also BW 2, 3; CA 103; CAAS 20;
CABS 3; CANR 26, 53, 82; DLB 38

Kennedy, John Pendleton 1795-1870
.... **NCLC 2**
See also DLB 3

Kennedy, Joseph Charles 1929-
See Kennedy, X. J.
See also CA 1-4R; CANR 4, 30, 40; SATA
14, 86

Kennedy, William 1928- . **CLC 6, 28, 34, 53;
DAM NOV**
See also AAYA 1; CA 85-88; CANR 14,
31, 76; DA3; DLB 143; DLBY 85; INT
CANR-31; MTCW 1, 2; SATA 57

Kennedy, X. J. .... **CLC 8, 42**
See also Kennedy, Joseph Charles
See also CAAS 9; CLR 27; DLB 5; SAAS
22

Kenny, Maurice (Francis) 1929- .... **CLC 87;
DAM MULT**
See also CA 144; CAAS 22; DLB 175;
NNAL

Kent, Kelvin
See Kuttner, Henry

Kenton, Maxwell
See Southern, Terry

Kenyon, Robert O.
See Kuttner, Henry

Kepler, Johannes 1571-1630 .... **LC 45**

Kerouac, Jack ..... **CLC 1, 2, 3, 5, 14, 29, 61**
See also Kerouac, Jean-Louis Lebris de
See also AAYA 25; CDALB 1941-1968;
DLB 2, 16; DLBD 3; DLBY 95; MTCW
2

Kerouac, Jean-Louis Lebris de 1922-1969
See Kerouac, Jack
See also AITN 1; CA 5-8R; 25-28R; CANR
26, 54; DA; DAB; DAC; DAM MST,
NOV, POET, POP; DA3; MTCW 1, 2;
WLC

Kerr, Jean 1923- .... **CLC 22**
See also CA 5-8R; CANR 7; INT CANR-7

Kerr, M. E. .... **CLC 12, 35**
See also Meaker, Marijane (Agnes)
See also AAYA 2, 23; CLR 29; SAAS 1

Kerr, Robert .... **CLC 55**

Kerrigan, (Thomas) Anthony 1918- . **CLC 4,
6**
See also CA 49-52; CAAS 11; CANR 4

Kerry, Lois
See Duncan, Lois

Kesey, Ken (Elton) 1935- ... **CLC 1, 3, 6, 11,
46, 64; DA; DAB; DAC; DAM MST,
NOV, POP; WLC**
See also AAYA 25; CA 1-4R; CANR 22,
38, 66; CDALB 1968-1988; DA3; DLB
2, 16, 206; MTCW 1, 2; SATA 66

Kesselring, Joseph (Otto) 1902-1967
.... **CLC 45; DAM DRAM, MST**
See also CA 150

Kessler, Jascha (Frederick) 1929- ..... **CLC 4**
See also CA 17-20R; CANR 8, 48

Kettelkamp, Larry (Dale) 1933- ..... **CLC 12**
See also CA 29-32R; CANR 16; SAAS 3;
SATA 2

Key, Ellen (Karolina Sofia) 1849-1926
.... **TCLC 65**

Keyber, Conny
See Fielding, Henry

Keyes, Daniel 1927- ..... **CLC 80; DA; DAC;
DAM MST, NOV**
See also AAYA 23; CA 17-20R, 181; CAAE
181; CANR 10, 26, 54, 74; DA3; MTCW
2; SATA 37

Keynes, John Maynard 1883-1946
.... **TCLC 64**
See also CA 114; 162, 163; DLBD 10;
MTCW 2

Khanshendel, Chiron
See Rose, Wendy

Khayyam, Omar 1048-1131 .... **CMLC 11;
DAM POET; PC 8**
See also DA3

Kherdian, David 1931- .... **CLC 6, 9**
See also CA 21-24R; CAAS 2; CANR 39,
78; CLR 24; JRDA; MAICYA; SATA 16,
74

Khlebnikov, Velimir .... **TCLC 20**
See also Khlebnikov, Viktor Vladimirovich

Khlebnikov, Viktor Vladimirovich 1885-1922
See Khlebnikov, Velimir
See also CA 117

Khodasevich, Vladislav (Felitsianovich)
1886-1939 .... **TCLC 15**
See also CA 115

Kielland, Alexander Lange 1849-1906
.... **TCLC 5**

See also CA 104

Kiely, Benedict 1919- .... **CLC 23, 43**
See also CA 1-4R; CANR 2, 84; DLB 15

Kienzle, William X(avier) 1928- .... **CLC 25;
DAM POP**
See also CA 93-96; CAAS 1; CANR 9, 31,
59; DA3; INT CANR-31; MTCW 1, 2

Kierkegaard, Soren 1813-1855 .... **NCLC 34,
78**
See also CA 147; 151

Kieslowski, Krzysztof 1941-1996 .. **CLC 120**
See also CA 147; 151

Killens, John Oliver 1916-1987 .... **CLC 10**
See also BW 2; CA 77-80; 123; CAAS 2;
CANR 26; DLB 33

Killigrew, Anne 1660-1685 .... **LC 4**
See also DLB 131

Killigrew, Thomas 1612-1683 .... **LC 57**
See also DLB 58

Kim
See Simenon, Georges (Jacques Christian)

Kincaid, Jamaica 1949- .... **CLC 43, 68, 137;
BLC 2; DAM MULT, NOV**
See also AAYA 13; BW 2, 3; CA 125;
CANR 47, 59; CDALBS; CLR 63; DA3;
DLB 157, 227; MTCW 2

King, Francis (Henry) 1923- ...... **CLC 8, 53;
DAM NOV**
See also CA 1-4R; CANR 1, 33, 86; DLB
15, 139; MTCW 1

King, Kennedy
See Brown, George Douglas

King, Martin Luther, Jr. 1929-1968
...... **CLC 83; BLC 2; DA; DAB; DAC;
DAM MST, MULT; WLCS**
See also BW 2, 3; CA 25-28; CANR 27,
44; CAP 2; DA3; MTCW 1, 2; SATA 14

King, Stephen (Edwin) 1947- ..... **CLC 12, 26,
37, 61, 113; DAM NOV, POP; SSC 17**
See also AAYA 1, 17; BEST 90:1; CA 61-
64; CANR 1, 30, 52, 76; DA3; DLB 143;
DLBY 80; JRDA; MTCW 1, 2; SATA 9,
55

King, Steve
See King, Stephen (Edwin)

King, Thomas 1943- .. **CLC 89; DAC; DAM
MULT**
See also CA 144; DLB 175; NNAL; SATA
96

Kingman, Lee .... **CLC 17**
See also Natti, (Mary) Lee
See also SAAS 3; SATA 1, 67

Kingsley, Charles 1819-1875 .... **NCLC 35**
See also DLB 21, 32, 163, 190; YABC 2

Kingsley, Sidney 1906-1995 .... **CLC 44**
See also CA 85-88; 147; DLB 7

Kingsolver, Barbara 1955- .... **CLC 55, 81,
130; DAM POP**
See also AAYA 15; CA 129; 134; CANR
60; CDALBS; DA3; DLB 206; INT 134;
MTCW 2

Kingston, Maxine (Ting Ting) Hong 1940-
...... **CLC 12, 19, 58, 121; DAM MULT,
NOV; WLCS**
See also AAYA 8; CA 69-72; CANR 13,
38, 74, 87; CDALBS; DA3; DLB 173,
212; DLBY 80; INT CANR-13; MTCW
1, 2; SATA 53

Kinnell, Galway 1927- ... **CLC 1, 2, 3, 5, 13,
29, 129; PC 26**
See also CA 9-12R; CANR 10, 34, 66; DLB
5; DLBY 87; INT CANR-34; MTCW 1, 2

Kinsella, Thomas 1928- .... **CLC 4, 19, 138**
See also CA 17-20R; CANR 15; DLB 27;
MTCW 1, 2

Kinsella, W(illiam) P(atrick) 1935- . **CLC 27,
43; DAC; DAM NOV, POP**
See also AAYA 7; CA 97-100; CAAS 7;
CANR 21, 35, 66, 75; INT CANR-21;
MTCW 1, 2

Kueng, Hans 1928-
See Kung, Hans
See also CA 53-56; CANR 66; MTCW 1, 2

Kumin, Maxine (Winokur) 1925- .... **CLC 5,
13, 28; DAM POET; PC 15**
See also AITN 2; CA 1-4R; CAAS 8;
CANR 1, 21, 69; DA3; DLB 5; MTCW
1, 2; SATA 12

Kundera, Milan 1929- . **CLC 4, 9, 19, 32, 68,
115, 135; DAM NOV; SSC 24**
See also AAYA 2; CA 85-88; CANR 19,
52, 74; DA3; DLB 232; MTCW 1, 2

Kunene, Mazisi (Raymond) 1930- .. **CLC 85**
See also BW 1, 3; CA 125; CANR 81; DLB
117

Kung, Hans 1928- .... **CLC 130**
See also Kueng, Hans

Kunikida, Doppo 1869(?)-1908 ..... **TCLC 99**
See also DLB 180

Kunitz, Stanley (Jasspon) 1905- . **CLC 6, 11,
14; PC 19**
See also CA 41-44R; CANR 26, 57; DA3;
DLB 48; INT CANR-26; MTCW 1, 2

Kunze, Reiner 1933- .... **CLC 10**
See also CA 93-96; DLB 75

Kuprin, Aleksander Ivanovich 1870-1938
.... **TCLC 5**
See also CA 104; 182

Kureishi, Hanif 1954(?)- .... **CLC 64, 135**
See also CA 139; DLB 194

Kurosawa, Akira 1910-1998 ... **CLC 16, 119;
DAM MULT**
See also AAYA 11; CA 101; 170; CANR 46

Kushner, Tony 1957(?)- .... **CLC 81; DAM
DRAM; DC 10**
See also CA 144; CANR 74; DA3; DLB
228; MTCW 2

Kuttner, Henry 1915-1958 .... **TCLC 10**
See also CA 107; 157; DLB 8

Kuzma, Greg 1944- .... **CLC 7**
See also CA 33-36R; CANR 70

Kuzmin, Mikhail 1872(?)-1936 ..... **TCLC 40**
See also CA 170

Kyd, Thomas 1558-1594 .... **LC 22; DAM
DRAM; DC 3**
See also DLB 62

Kyprianos, Iossif
See Samarakis, Antonis

La Bruyere, Jean de 1645-1696 .... **LC 17**

Lacan, Jacques (Marie Emile) 1901-1981
.... **CLC 75**
See also CA 121; 104

**Laclos, Pierre Ambroise Francois Choderlos
de** 1741-1803 .... **NCLC 4, 87**

La Colere, Francois
See Aragon, Louis

Lacolere, Francois
See Aragon, Louis

La Deshabilleuse
See Simenon, Georges (Jacques Christian)

Lady Gregory
See Gregory, Isabella Augusta (Persse)

Lady of Quality, A
See Bagnold, Enid

**La Fayette, Marie (Madelaine Pioche de la
Vergne Comtes** 1634-1693 .... **LC 2**

Lafayette, Rene
See Hubbard, L(afayette) Ron(ald)

La Fontaine, Jean de 1621-1695 .... **LC 50**
See also MAICYA; SATA 18

Laforgue, Jules 1860-1887 . **NCLC 5, 53; PC
14; SSC 20**

Lagerkvist, Paer (Fabian) 1891-1974
.... **CLC 7, 10, 13, 54; DAM DRAM,
NOV**
See also Lagerkvist, Par
See also CA 85-88; 49-52; DA3; MTCW 1,
2

Lagerkvist, Par .... **SSC 12**
See also Lagerkvist, Paer (Fabian)
See also MTCW 2

Lagerloef, Selma (Ottiliana Lovisa)
1858-1940 .... **TCLC 4, 36**
See also Lagerlof, Selma (Ottiliana Lovisa)
See also CA 108; MTCW 2; SATA 15

Lagerlof, Selma (Ottiliana Lovisa)
See Lagerloef, Selma (Ottiliana Lovisa)
See also CLR 7; SATA 15

La Guma, (Justin) Alex(ander) 1925-1985
.... **CLC 19; BLCS; DAM NOV**
See also BW 1, 3; CA 49-52; 118; CANR
25, 81; DLB 117, 225; MTCW 1, 2

Laidlaw, A. K.
See Grieve, C(hristopher) M(urray)

Lainez, Manuel Mujica
See Mujica Lainez, Manuel
See also HW 1

Laing, R(onald) D(avid) 1927-1989 . **CLC 95**
See also CA 107; 129; CANR 34; MTCW 1

Lamartine, Alphonse (Marie Louis Prat) de
1790-1869 . **NCLC 11; DAM POET; PC
16**

Lamb, Charles 1775-1834 ... **NCLC 10; DA;
DAB; DAC; DAM MST; WLC**
See also CDBLB 1789-1832; DLB 93, 107,
163; SATA 17

Lamb, Lady Caroline 1785-1828 . **NCLC 38**
See also DLB 116

Lamming, George (William) 1927- .. **CLC 2,
4, 66; BLC 2; DAM MULT**
See also BW 2, 3; CA 85-88; CANR 26,
76; DLB 125; MTCW 1, 2

L'Amour, Louis (Dearborn) 1908-1988
.... **CLC 25, 55; DAM NOV, POP**
See also AAYA 16; AITN 2; BEST 89:2;
CA 1-4R; 125; CANR 3, 25, 40; DA3;
DLB 206; DLBY 80; MTCW 1, 2

Lampedusa, Giuseppe (Tomasi) di 1896-1957
.... **TCLC 13**
See also Tomasi di Lampedusa, Giuseppe
See also CA 164; DLB 177; MTCW 2

Lampman, Archibald 1861-1899 .. **NCLC 25**
See also DLB 92

Lancaster, Bruce 1896-1963 .... **CLC 36**
See also CA 9-10; CANR 70; CAP 1; SATA
9

Lanchester, John .... **CLC 99**

Landau, Mark Alexandrovich
See Aldanov, Mark (Alexandrovich)

Landau-Aldanov, Mark Alexandrovich
See Aldanov, Mark (Alexandrovich)

Landis, Jerry
See Simon, Paul (Frederick)

Landis, John 1950- .... **CLC 26**
See also CA 112; 122

Landolfi, Tommaso 1908-1979 .. **CLC 11, 49**
See also CA 127; 117; DLB 177

Landon, Letitia Elizabeth 1802-1838
.... **NCLC 15**
See also DLB 96

Landor, Walter Savage 1775-1864 . **NCLC 14**
See also DLB 93, 107

Landwirth, Heinz 1927-
See Lind, Jakov
See also CA 9-12R; CANR 7

Lane, Patrick 1939- .. **CLC 25; DAM POET**
See also CA 97-100; CANR 54; DLB 53;
INT 97-100

Lang, Andrew 1844-1912 .... **TCLC 16**
See also CA 114; 137; CANR 85; DLB 98,
141, 184; MAICYA; SATA 16

Lang, Fritz 1890-1976 .... **CLC 20, 103**
See also CA 77-80; 69-72; CANR 30

Lange, John
See Crichton, (John) Michael

Langer, Elinor 1939- .... **CLC 34**
See also CA 121

Langland, William 1330(?)-1400(?) .. **LC 19;
DA; DAB; DAC; DAM MST, POET**
See also DLB 146

Langstaff, Launcelot
See Irving, Washington

Lanier, Sidney 1842-1881 .... **NCLC 6; DAM
POET**
See also DLB 64; DLBD 13; MAICYA;
SATA 18

Lanyer, Aemilia 1569-1645 .... **LC 10, 30**
See also DLB 121

Lao-Tzu
See Lao Tzu

Lao Tzu fl. 6th cent. B.C.- .... **CMLC 7**

Lapine, James (Elliot) 1949- .... **CLC 39**
See also CA 123; 130; CANR 54; INT 130

Larbaud, Valery (Nicolas) 1881-1957
.... **TCLC 9**
See also CA 106; 152

Lardner, Ring
See Lardner, Ring(gold) W(ilmer)

Lardner, Ring W., Jr.
See Lardner, Ring(gold) W(ilmer)

Lardner, Ring(gold) W(ilmer) 1885-1933
.... **TCLC 2, 14; SSC 32**
See also CA 104; 131; CDALB 1917-1929;
DLB 11, 25, 86; DLBD 16; MTCW 1, 2

Laredo, Betty
See Codrescu, Andrei

Larkin, Maia
See Wojciechowska, Maia (Teresa)

Larkin, Philip (Arthur) 1922-1985 .. **CLC 3,
5, 8, 9, 13, 18, 33, 39, 64; DAB; DAM
MST, POET; PC 21**
See also CA 5-8R; 117; CANR 24, 62; CD-
BLB 1960 to Present; DA3; DLB 27;
MTCW 1, 2

**Larra (y Sanchez de Castro), Mariano Jose
de** 1809-1837 .... **NCLC 17**

Larsen, Eric 1941- .... **CLC 55**
See also CA 132

Larsen, Nella 1891-1964 ... **CLC 37; BLC 2;
DAM MULT**
See also BW 1; CA 125; CANR 83; DLB
51

Larson, Charles R(aymond) 1938- . **CLC 31**
See also CA 53-56; CANR 4

Larson, Jonathan 1961-1996 .... **CLC 99**
See also AAYA 28; CA 156

Las Casas, Bartolome de 1474-1566 . **LC 31**

Lasch, Christopher 1932-1994 ...... **CLC 102**
See also CA 73-76; 144; CANR 25; MTCW
1, 2

Lasker-Schueler, Else 1869-1945 .. **TCLC 57**
See also CA 183; DLB 66, 124

Laski, Harold J(oseph) 1893-1950 . **TCLC 79**

Latham, Jean Lee 1902-1995 .... **CLC 12**
See also AITN 1; CA 5-8R; CANR 7, 84;
CLR 50; MAICYA; SATA 2, 68

Latham, Mavis
See Clark, Mavis Thorpe

Lathen, Emma .... **CLC 2**
See also Hennissart, Martha; Latsis, Mary
J(ane)

Lathrop, Francis
See Leiber, Fritz (Reuter, Jr.)

Latsis, Mary J(ane) 1927(?)-1997
See Lathen, Emma
See also CA 85-88; 162

Lattimore, Richmond (Alexander) 1906-1984
.... **CLC 3**
See also CA 1-4R; 112; CANR 1

Laughlin, James 1914-1997 .... **CLC 49**
See also CA 21-24R; 162; CAAS 22; CANR
9, 47; DLB 48; DLBY 96, 97

Laurence, (Jean) Margaret (Wemyss)
1926-1987 . **CLC 3, 6, 13, 50, 62; DAC;
DAM MST; SSC 7**

See also CA 5-8R; 121; CANR 33; DLB
53; MTCW 1, 2; SATA-Obit 50
Laurent, Antoine 1952- .... **CLC 50**
Lauscher, Hermann
See Hesse, Hermann
Lautreamont, Comte de 1846-1870
.... **NCLC 12; SSC 14**
Laverty, Donald
See Blish, James (Benjamin)
Lavin, Mary 1912-1996 . **CLC 4, 18, 99; SSC
4**
See also CA 9-12R; 151; CANR 33; DLB
15; MTCW 1
Lavond, Paul Dennis
See Kornbluth, C(yril) M.; Pohl, Frederik
Lawler, Raymond Evenor 1922- ..... **CLC 58**
See also CA 103
Lawrence, D(avid) H(erbert Richards)
1885-1930 ... **TCLC 2, 9, 16, 33, 48, 61,
93; DA; DAB; DAC; DAM MST, NOV,
POET; SSC 4, 19; WLC**
See also CA 104; 121; CDBLB 1914-1945;
DA3; DLB 10, 19, 36, 98, 162, 195;
MTCW 1, 2
Lawrence, T(homas) E(dward) 1888-1935
.... **TCLC 18**
See also Dale, Colin
See also CA 115; 167; DLB 195
Lawrence of Arabia
See Lawrence, T(homas) E(dward)
Lawson, Henry (Archibald Hertzberg)
1867-1922 .... **TCLC 27; SSC 18**
See also CA 120; 181; DLB 230
Lawton, Dennis
See Faust, Frederick (Schiller)
Laxness, Halldor .... **CLC 25**
See also Gudjonsson, Halldor Kiljan
Layamon fl. c. 1200- .... **CMLC 10**
See also DLB 146
Laye, Camara 1928-1980 .. **CLC 4, 38; BLC
2; DAM MULT**
See also BW 1; CA 85-88; 97-100; CANR
25; MTCW 1, 2
Layton, Irving (Peter) 1912- ...... **CLC 2, 15;
DAC; DAM MST, POET**
See also CA 1-4R; CANR 2, 33, 43, 66;
DLB 88; MTCW 1, 2
Lazarus, Emma 1849-1887 .... **NCLC 8**
Lazarus, Felix
See Cable, George Washington
Lazarus, Henry
See Slavitt, David R(ytman)
Lea, Joan
See Neufeld, John (Arthur)
Leacock, Stephen (Butler) 1869-1944
.... **TCLC 2; DAC; DAM MST; SSC 39**
See also CA 104; 141; CANR 80; DLB 92;
MTCW 2
Lear, Edward 1812-1888 .... **NCLC 3**
See also CLR 1; DLB 32, 163, 166; MAI-
CYA; SATA 18, 100
Lear, Norman (Milton) 1922- .... **CLC 12**
See also CA 73-76
Leautaud, Paul 1872-1956 .... **TCLC 83**
See also DLB 65
Leavis, F(rank) R(aymond) 1895-1978
.... **CLC 24**
See also CA 21-24R; 77-80; CANR 44;
MTCW 1, 2
Leavitt, David 1961- ... **CLC 34; DAM POP**
See also CA 116; 122; CANR 50, 62; DA3;
DLB 130; INT 122; MTCW 2
Leblanc, Maurice (Marie Emile) 1864-1941
.... **TCLC 49**
See also CA 110
Lebowitz, Fran(ces Ann) 1951(?)- .. **CLC 11,
36**
See also CA 81-84; CANR 14, 60, 70; INT
CANR-14; MTCW 1

Lebrecht, Peter
See Tieck, (Johann) Ludwig
le Carre, John .... **CLC 3, 5, 9, 15, 28**
See also Cornwell, David (John Moore)
See also BEST 89:4; CDBLB 1960 to
Present; DLB 87; MTCW 2
Le Clezio, J(ean) M(arie) G(ustave) 1940-
.... **CLC 31**
See also CA 116; 128; DLB 83
Leconte de Lisle, Charles-Marie-Rene
1818-1894 .... **NCLC 29**
Le Coq, Monsieur
See Simenon, Georges (Jacques Christian)
Leduc, Violette 1907-1972 .... **CLC 22**
See also CA 13-14; 33-36R; CANR 69;
CAP 1
Ledwidge, Francis 1887(?)-1917 ... **TCLC 23**
See also CA 123; DLB 20
Lee, Andrea 1953- .. **CLC 36; BLC 2; DAM
MULT**
See also BW 1, 3; CA 125; CANR 82
Lee, Andrew
See Auchincloss, Louis (Stanton)
Lee, Chang-rae 1965- .... **CLC 91**
See also CA 148; CANR 89
Lee, Don L. .... **CLC 2**
See also Madhubuti, Haki R.
Lee, George W(ashington) 1894-1976
.... **CLC 52; BLC 2; DAM MULT**
See also BW 1; CA 125; CANR 83; DLB
51
Lee, (Nelle) Harper 1926- . **CLC 12, 60; DA;
DAB; DAC; DAM MST, NOV; WLC**
See also AAYA 13; CA 13-16R; CANR 51;
CDALB 1941-1968; DA3; DLB 6;
MTCW 1, 2; SATA 11
Lee, Helen Elaine 1959(?)- .... **CLC 86**
See also CA 148
Lee, Julian
See Latham, Jean Lee
Lee, Larry
See Lee, Lawrence
Lee, Laurie 1914-1997 .... **CLC 90; DAB;
DAM POP**
See also CA 77-80; 158; CANR 33, 73;
DLB 27; MTCW 1
Lee, Lawrence 1941-1990 .... **CLC 34**
See also CA 131; CANR 43
Lee, Li-Young 1957- .... **PC 24**
See also CA 153; DLB 165
Lee, Manfred B(ennington) 1905-1971
.... **CLC 11**
See also Queen, Ellery
See also CA 1-4R; 29-32R; CANR 2; DLB
137
Lee, Shelton Jackson 1957(?)- ..... **CLC 105;
BLCS; DAM MULT**
See also Lee, Spike
See also BW 2, 3; CA 125; CANR 42
Lee, Spike
See Lee, Shelton Jackson
See also AAYA 4, 29
Lee, Stan 1922- .... **CLC 17**
See also AAYA 5; CA 108; 111; INT 111
Lee, Tanith 1947- .... **CLC 46**
See also AAYA 15; CA 37-40R; CANR 53;
SATA 8, 88
Lee, Vernon .... **TCLC 5; SSC 33**
See also Paget, Violet
See also DLB 57, 153, 156, 174, 178
Lee, William
See Burroughs, William S(eward)
Lee, Willy
See Burroughs, William S(eward)
Lee-Hamilton, Eugene (Jacob) 1845-1907
.... **TCLC 22**
See also CA 117
Leet, Judith 1935- .... **CLC 11**
See also CA 187

Le Fanu, Joseph Sheridan 1814-1873
.... **NCLC 9, 58; DAM POP; SSC 14**
See also DA3; DLB 21, 70, 159, 178
Leffland, Ella 1931- .... **CLC 19**
See also CA 29-32R; CANR 35, 78, 82;
DLBY 84; INT CANR-35; SATA 65
Leger, Alexis
See Leger, (Marie-Rene Auguste) Alexis
Saint-Leger
**Leger, (Marie-Rene Auguste) Alexis
Saint-Leger** 1887-1975 . **CLC 4, 11, 46;
DAM POET; PC 23**
See also CA 13-16R; 61-64; CANR 43;
MTCW 1
Leger, Saintleger
See Leger, (Marie-Rene Auguste) Alexis
Saint-Leger
Le Guin, Ursula K(roeber) 1929- .... **CLC 8,
13, 22, 45, 71, 136; DAB; DAC; DAM
MST, POP; SSC 12**
See also AAYA 9, 27; AITN 1; CA 21-24R;
CANR 9, 32, 52, 74; CDALB 1968-1988;
CLR 3, 28; DA3; DLB 8, 52; INT CANR-
32; JRDA; MAICYA; MTCW 1, 2; SATA
4, 52, 99
Lehmann, Rosamond (Nina) 1901-1990
.... **CLC 5**
See also CA 77-80; 131; CANR 8, 73; DLB
15; MTCW 2
Leiber, Fritz (Reuter, Jr.) 1910-1992
.... **CLC 25**
See also CA 45-48; 139; CANR 2, 40, 86;
DLB 8; MTCW 1, 2; SATA 45; SATA-
Obit 73
Leibniz, Gottfried Wilhelm von 1646-1716
.... **LC 35**
See also DLB 168
Leimbach, Martha 1963-
See Leimbach, Marti
See also CA 130
Leimbach, Marti .... **CLC 65**
See also Leimbach, Martha
Leino, Eino .... **TCLC 24**
See also Loennbohm, Armas Eino Leopold
Leiris, Michel (Julien) 1901-1990 ... **CLC 61**
See also CA 119; 128; 132
Leithauser, Brad 1953- .... **CLC 27**
See also CA 107; CANR 27, 81; DLB 120
Lelchuk, Alan 1938- .... **CLC 5**
See also CA 45-48; CAAS 20; CANR 1, 70
Lem, Stanislaw 1921- .... **CLC 8, 15, 40**
See also CA 105; CAAS 1; CANR 32;
MTCW 1
Lemann, Nancy 1956- .... **CLC 39**
See also CA 118; 136
Lemonnier, (Antoine Louis) Camille
1844-1913 .... **TCLC 22**
See also CA 121
Lenau, Nikolaus 1802-1850 .... **NCLC 16**
L'Engle, Madeleine (Camp Franklin) 1918-
.... **CLC 12; DAM POP**
See also AAYA 28; AITN 2; CA 1-4R;
CANR 3, 21, 39, 66; CLR 1, 14, 57; DA3;
DLB 52; JRDA; MAICYA; MTCW 1, 2;
SAAS 15; SATA 1, 27, 75
Lengyel, Jozsef 1896-1975 .... **CLC 7**
See also CA 85-88; 57-60; CANR 71
Lenin 1870-1924
See Lenin, V. I.
See also CA 121; 168
Lenin, V. I. .... **TCLC 67**
See also Lenin
Lennon, John (Ono) 1940-1980 . **CLC 12, 35**
See also CA 102; SATA 114
Lennox, Charlotte Ramsay 1729(?)-1804
.... **NCLC 23**
See also DLB 39
Lentricchia, Frank (Jr.) 1940- .... **CLC 34**
See also CA 25-28R; CANR 19

See also CA 77-80; CANR 14, 32, 57

Malory, (Sir) Thomas 1410(?)-1471(?)
.. **LC 11; DA; DAB; DAC; DAM MST;
WLCS**
See also CDBLB Before 1660; DLB 146;
SATA 59; SATA-Brief 33

Malouf, (George Joseph) David 1934-
.... **CLC 28, 86**
See also CA 124; CANR 50, 76; MTCW 2

Malraux, (Georges-)Andre 1901-1976
..... **CLC 1, 4, 9, 13, 15, 57; DAM NOV**
See also CA 21-22; 69-72; CANR 34, 58;
CAP 2; DA3; DLB 72; MTCW 1, 2

Malzberg, Barry N(athaniel) 1939- .. **CLC 7**
See also CA 61-64; CAAS 4; CANR 16;
DLB 8

Mamet, David (Alan) 1947- . **CLC 9, 15, 34,
46, 91; DAM DRAM; DC 4**
See also AAYA 3; CA 81-84; CABS 3;
CANR 15, 41, 67, 72; DA3; DLB 7;
MTCW 1, 2

Mamoulian, Rouben (Zachary) 1897-1987
.... **CLC 16**
See also CA 25-28R; 124; CANR 85

Mandelstam, Osip (Emilievich)
1891(?)-1938(?) .... **TCLC 2, 6; PC 14**
See also CA 104; 150; MTCW 2

Mander, (Mary) Jane 1877-1949 .. **TCLC 31**
See also CA 162

Mandeville, John fl. 1350- .... **CMLC 19**
See also DLB 146

Mandiargues, Andre Pieyre de .... **CLC 41**
See also Pieyre de Mandiargues, Andre
See also DLB 83

Mandrake, Ethel Belle
See Thurman, Wallace (Henry)

Mangan, James Clarence 1803-1849
.... **NCLC 27**

Maniere, J.-E.
See Giraudoux, (Hippolyte) Jean

Mankiewicz, Herman (Jacob) 1897-1953
.... **TCLC 85**
See also CA 120; 169; DLB 26

Manley, (Mary) Delariviere 1672(?)-1724
.... **LC 1, 42**
See also DLB 39, 80

Mann, Abel
See Creasey, John

Mann, Emily 1952- .... **DC 7**
See also CA 130; CANR 55

Mann, (Luiz) Heinrich 1871-1950 .. **TCLC 9**
See also CA 106; 164, 181; DLB 66, 118

Mann, (Paul) Thomas 1875-1955 .. **TCLC 2,
8, 14, 21, 35, 44, 60; DA; DAB; DAC;
DAM MST, NOV; SSC 5; WLC**
See also CA 104; 128; DA3; DLB 66;
MTCW 1, 2

Mannheim, Karl 1893-1947 .... **TCLC 65**

Manning, David
See Faust, Frederick (Schiller)

Manning, Frederic 1887(?)-1935 .. **TCLC 25**
See also CA 124

Manning, Olivia 1915-1980 .... **CLC 5, 19**
See also CA 5-8R; 101; CANR 29; MTCW
1

Mano, D. Keith 1942- .... **CLC 2, 10**
See also CA 25-28R; CAAS 6; CANR 26,
57; DLB 6

Mansfield, Katherine -1923 . **TCLC 2, 8, 39;
DAB; SSC 9, 23, 38; WLC**
See also Beauchamp, Kathleen Mansfield
See also DLB 162

Manso, Peter 1940- .... **CLC 39**
See also CA 29-32R; CANR 44

Mantecon, Juan Jimenez
See Jimenez (Mantecon), Juan Ramon

Manton, Peter
See Creasey, John

Man Without a Spleen, A
See Chekhov, Anton (Pavlovich)

Manzoni, Alessandro 1785-1873 ... **NCLC 29**

Map, Walter 1140-1209 .... **CMLC 32**

Mapu, Abraham (ben Jekutiel) 1808-1867
.... **NCLC 18**

Mara, Sally
See Queneau, Raymond

Marat, Jean Paul 1743-1793 .... **LC 10**

Marcel, Gabriel Honore 1889-1973 . **CLC 15**
See also CA 102; 45-48; MTCW 1, 2

March, William 1893-1954 .... **TCLC 96**

Marchbanks, Samuel
See Davies, (William) Robertson

Marchi, Giacomo
See Bassani, Giorgio

Margulies, Donald .... **CLC 76**
See also DLB 228

Marie de France c. 12th cent. - .... **CMLC 8;
PC 22**
See also DLB 208

Marie de l'Incarnation 1599-1672 ..... **LC 10**

Marier, Captain Victor
See Griffith, D(avid Lewelyn) W(ark)

Mariner, Scott
See Pohl, Frederik

Marinetti, Filippo Tommaso 1876-1944
.... **TCLC 10**
See also CA 107; DLB 114

Marivaux, Pierre Carlet de Chamblain de
1688-1763 .... **LC 4; DC 7**

Markandaya, Kamala .... **CLC 8, 38**
See also Taylor, Kamala (Purnaiya)

Markfield, Wallace 1926- .... **CLC 8**
See also CA 69-72; CAAS 3; DLB 2, 28

Markham, Edwin 1852-1940 .... **TCLC 47**
See also CA 160; DLB 54, 186

Markham, Robert
See Amis, Kingsley (William)

Marks, J
See Highwater, Jamake (Mamake)

Marks-Highwater, J
See Highwater, Jamake (Mamake)

Markson, David M(errill) 1927- ..... **CLC 67**
See also CA 49-52; CANR 1, 91

Marley, Bob .... **CLC 17**
See also Marley, Robert Nesta

Marley, Robert Nesta 1945-1981
See Marley, Bob
See also CA 107; 103

Marlowe, Christopher 1564-1593 ..... **LC 22,
47; DA; DAB; DAC; DAM DRAM,
MST; DC 1; WLC**
See also CDBLB Before 1660; DA3; DLB
62

Marlowe, Stephen 1928-
See Queen, Ellery
See also CA 13-16R; CANR 6, 55

Marmontel, Jean-Francois 1723-1799 . **LC 2**

Marquand, John P(hillips) 1893-1960
.... **CLC 2, 10**
See also CA 85-88; CANR 73; DLB 9, 102;
MTCW 2

Marques, Rene 1919-1979 ... **CLC 96; DAM
MULT; HLC 2**
See also CA 97-100; 85-88; CANR 78;
DLB 113; HW 1, 2

Marquez, Gabriel (Jose) Garcia
See Garcia Marquez, Gabriel (Jose)

Marquis, Don(ald Robert Perry) 1878-1937
.... **TCLC 7**
See also CA 104; 166; DLB 11, 25

Marric, J. J.
See Creasey, John

Marryat, Frederick 1792-1848 .... **NCLC 3**
See also DLB 21, 163

Marsden, James
See Creasey, John

Marsh, Edward 1872-1953 .... **TCLC 99**

Marsh, (Edith) Ngaio 1899-1982 ...... **CLC 7,
53; DAM POP**
See also CA 9-12R; CANR 6, 58; DLB 77;
MTCW 1, 2

Marshall, Garry 1934- .... **CLC 17**
See also AAYA 3; CA 111; SATA 60

Marshall, Paule 1929- . **CLC 27, 72; BLC 3;
DAM MULT; SSC 3**
See also BW 2, 3; CA 77-80; CANR 25,
73; DA3; DLB 33, 157, 227; MTCW 1, 2

Marshallik
See Zangwill, Israel

Marsten, Richard
See Hunter, Evan

Marston, John 1576-1634 .... **LC 33; DAM
DRAM**
See also DLB 58, 172

Martha, Henry
See Harris, Mark

Marti (y Perez), Jose (Julian) 1853-1895
.... **NCLC 63; DAM MULT; HLC 2**
See also HW 2

Martial c. 40-c. 104 .... **CMLC 35; PC 10**
See also DLB 211

Martin, Ken
See Hubbard, L(afayette) Ron(ald)

Martin, Richard
See Creasey, John

Martin, Steve 1945- .... **CLC 30**
See also CA 97-100; CANR 30; MTCW 1

Martin, Valerie 1948- .... **CLC 89**
See also BEST 90:2; CA 85-88; CANR 49,
89

Martin, Violet Florence 1862-1915
.... **TCLC 51**

Martin, Webber
See Silverberg, Robert

Martindale, Patrick Victor
See White, Patrick (Victor Martindale)

Martin du Gard, Roger 1881-1958
.... **TCLC 24**
See also CA 118; DLB 65

Martineau, Harriet 1802-1876 ..... **NCLC 26**
See also DLB 21, 55, 159, 163, 166, 190;
YABC 2

Martines, Julia
See O'Faolain, Julia

Martinez, Enrique Gonzalez
See Gonzalez Martinez, Enrique

Martinez, Jacinto Benavente y
See Benavente (y Martinez), Jacinto

Martinez Ruiz, Jose 1873-1967
See Azorin; Ruiz, Jose Martinez
See also CA 93-96; HW 1

Martinez Sierra, Gregorio 1881-1947
.... **TCLC 6**
See also CA 115

Martinez Sierra, Maria (de la O'LeJarraga)
1874-1974 .... **TCLC 6**
See also CA 115

Martinsen, Martin
See Follett, Ken(neth Martin)

Martinson, Harry (Edmund) 1904-1978
.... **CLC 14**
See also CA 77-80; CANR 34

Marut, Ret
See Traven, B.

Marut, Robert
See Traven, B.

Marvell, Andrew 1621-1678 . **LC 4, 43; DA;
DAB; DAC; DAM MST, POET; PC 10;
WLC**
See also CDBLB 1660-1789; DLB 131

Marx, Karl (Heinrich) 1818-1883 . **NCLC 17**
See also DLB 129

Masaoka Shiki .... **TCLC 18**
    See also Masaoka Tsunenori
Masaoka Tsunenori 1867-1902
    See Masaoka Shiki
    See also CA 117
Masefield, John (Edward) 1878-1967
    .... **CLC 11, 47; DAM POET**
    See also CA 19-20; 25-28R; CANR 33;
    CAP 2; CDBLB 1890-1914; DLB 10, 19,
    153, 160; MTCW 1, 2; SATA 19
Maso, Carole 19(?)- .... **CLC 44**
    See also CA 170
Mason, Bobbie Ann 1940- . **CLC 28, 43, 82;
    SSC 4**
    See also AAYA 5; CA 53-56; CANR 11, 31,
    58, 83; CDALBS; DA3; DLB 173; DLBY
    87; INT CANR-31; MTCW 1, 2
Mason, Ernst
    See Pohl, Frederik
Mason, Lee W.
    See Malzberg, Barry N(athaniel)
Mason, Nick 1945- .... **CLC 35**
Mason, Tally
    See Derleth, August (William)
Mass, William
    See Gibson, William
Master Lao
    See Lao Tzu
Masters, Edgar Lee 1868-1950 ...... **TCLC 2,
    25; DA; DAC; DAM MST, POET; PC
    1; WLCS**
    See also CA 104; 133; CDALB 1865-1917;
    DLB 54; MTCW 1, 2
Masters, Hilary 1928- .... **CLC 48**
    See also CA 25-28R; CANR 13, 47
Mastrosimone, William 19(?)- .... **CLC 36**
    See also CA 186
Mathe, Albert
    See Camus, Albert
Mather, Cotton 1663-1728 .... **LC 38**
    See also CDALB 1640-1865; DLB 24, 30,
    140
Mather, Increase 1639-1723 .... **LC 38**
    See also DLB 24
Matheson, Richard Burton 1926- ... **CLC 37**
    See also AAYA 31; CA 97-100; CANR 88;
    DLB 8, 44; INT 97-100
Mathews, Harry 1930- .... **CLC 6, 52**
    See also CA 21-24R; CAAS 6; CANR 18,
    40
Mathews, John Joseph 1894-1979 . **CLC 84;
    DAM MULT**
    See also CA 19-20; 142; CANR 45; CAP 2;
    DLB 175; NNAL
Mathias, Roland (Glyn) 1915- .... **CLC 45**
    See also CA 97-100; CANR 19, 41; DLB
    27
Matsuo Basho 1644-1694 .... **LC 62; DAM
    POET; PC 3**
Mattheson, Rodney
    See Creasey, John
Matthews, (James) Brander 1852-1929
    .... **TCLC 95**
    See also DLB 71, 78; DLBD 13
Matthews, Greg 1949- .... **CLC 45**
    See also CA 135
Matthews, William (Procter, III) 1942-1997
    .... **CLC 40**
    See also CA 29-32R; 162; CAAS 18; CANR
    12, 57; DLB 5
Matthias, John (Edward) 1941- .... **CLC 9**
    See also CA 33-36R; CANR 56
Matthiessen, F(rancis) O(tto) 1902-1950
    .... **TCLC 100**
    See also CA 185; DLB 63
Matthiessen, Peter 1927- .. **CLC 5, 7, 11, 32,
    64; DAM NOV**

    See also AAYA 6; BEST 90:4; CA 9-12R;
    CANR 21, 50, 73; DA3; DLB 6, 173;
    MTCW 1, 2; SATA 27
Maturin, Charles Robert 1780(?)-1824
    .... **NCLC 6**
    See also DLB 178
Matute (Ausejo), Ana Maria 1925- . **CLC 11**
    See also CA 89-92; MTCW 1
Maugham, W. S.
    See Maugham, W(illiam) Somerset
Maugham, W(illiam) Somerset 1874-1965
    .... **CLC 1, 11, 15, 67, 93; DA; DAB;
    DAC; DAM DRAM, MST, NOV; SSC
    8; WLC**
    See also CA 5-8R; 25-28R; CANR 40; CD-
    BLB 1914-1945; DA3; DLB 10, 36, 77,
    100, 162, 195; MTCW 1, 2; SATA 54
Maugham, William Somerset
    See Maugham, W(illiam) Somerset
Maupassant, (Henri Rene Albert) Guy de
    1850-1893 . **NCLC 1, 42, 83; DA; DAB;
    DAC; DAM MST; SSC 1; WLC**
    See also DA3; DLB 123
Maupin, Armistead 1944- .... **CLC 95; DAM
    POP**
    See also CA 125; 130; CANR 58; DA3;
    INT 130; MTCW 2
Maurhut, Richard
    See Traven, B.
Mauriac, Claude 1914-1996 .... **CLC 9**
    See also CA 89-92; 152; DLB 83
Mauriac, Francois (Charles) 1885-1970
    .... **CLC 4, 9, 56; SSC 24**
    See also CA 25-28; CAP 2; DLB 65;
    MTCW 1, 2
Mavor, Osborne Henry 1888-1951
    See Bridie, James
    See also CA 104
Maxwell, William (Keepers, Jr.) 1908-
    .... **CLC 19**
    See also CA 93-96; CANR 54; DLBY 80;
    INT 93-96
May, Elaine 1932- .... **CLC 16**
    See also CA 124; 142; DLB 44
Mayakovski, Vladimir (Vladimirovich)
    1893-1930 .... **TCLC 4, 18**
    See also CA 104; 158; MTCW 2
Mayhew, Henry 1812-1887 .... **NCLC 31**
    See also DLB 18, 55, 190
Mayle, Peter 1939(?)- .... **CLC 89**
    See also CA 139; CANR 64
Maynard, Joyce 1953- .... **CLC 23**
    See also CA 111; 129; CANR 64
Mayne, William (James Carter) 1928-
    .... **CLC 12**
    See also AAYA 20; CA 9-12R; CANR 37,
    80; CLR 25; JRDA; MAICYA; SAAS 11;
    SATA 6, 68
Mayo, Jim
    See L'Amour, Louis (Dearborn)
Maysles, Albert 1926- .... **CLC 16**
    See also CA 29-32R
Maysles, David 1932- .... **CLC 16**
Mazer, Norma Fox 1931- .... **CLC 26**
    See also AAYA 5; CA 69-72; CANR 12,
    32, 66; CLR 23; JRDA; MAICYA; SAAS
    1; SATA 24, 67, 105
Mazzini, Guiseppe 1805-1872 .... **NCLC 34**
McAlmon, Robert (Menzies) 1895-1956
    .... **TCLC 97**
    See also CA 107; 168; DLB 4, 45; DLBD
    15
McAuley, James Phillip 1917-1976 . **CLC 45**
    See also CA 97-100
McBain, Ed
    See Hunter, Evan
McBrien, William (Augustine) 1930-
    .... **CLC 44**
    See also CA 107; CANR 90

McCabe, Patrick 1955- .... **CLC 133**
    See also CA 130; CANR 50, 90; DLB 194
McCaffrey, Anne (Inez) 1926- .... **CLC 17;
    DAM NOV, POP**
    See also AAYA 6, 34; AITN 2; BEST 89:2;
    CA 25-28R; CANR 15, 35, 55; CLR 49;
    DA3; DLB 8; JRDA; MAICYA; MTCW
    1, 2; SAAS 11; SATA 8, 70, 116
McCall, Nathan 1955(?)- .... **CLC 86**
    See also BW 3; CA 146; CANR 88
McCann, Arthur
    See Campbell, John W(ood, Jr.)
McCann, Edson
    See Pohl, Frederik
McCarthy, Charles, Jr. 1933-
    See McCarthy, Cormac
    See also CANR 42, 69; DAM POP; DA3;
    MTCW 2
McCarthy, Cormac 1933- .... **CLC 4, 57, 59,
    101**
    See also McCarthy, Charles, Jr.
    See also DLB 6, 143; MTCW 2
McCarthy, Mary (Therese) 1912-1989
    ..... **CLC 1, 3, 5, 14, 24, 39, 59; SSC 24**
    See also CA 5-8R; 129; CANR 16, 50, 64;
    DA3; DLB 2; DLBY 81; INT CANR-16;
    MTCW 1, 2
McCartney, (James) Paul 1942- ..... **CLC 12,
    35**
    See also CA 146
McCauley, Stephen (D.) 1955- .... **CLC 50**
    See also CA 141
McClure, Michael (Thomas) 1932- .. **CLC 6,
    10**
    See also CA 21-24R; CANR 17, 46, 77;
    DLB 16
McCorkle, Jill (Collins) 1958- .... **CLC 51**
    See also CA 121; DLB 234; DLBY 87
McCourt, Frank 1930- .... **CLC 109**
    See also CA 157
McCourt, James 1941- .... **CLC 5**
    See also CA 57-60
McCourt, Malachy 1932- .... **CLC 119**
McCoy, Horace (Stanley) 1897-1955
    .... **TCLC 28**
    See also CA 108; 155; DLB 9
McCrae, John 1872-1918 .... **TCLC 12**
    See also CA 109; DLB 92
McCreigh, James
    See Pohl, Frederik
McCullers, (Lula) Carson (Smith) 1917-1967
    .. **CLC 1, 4, 10, 12, 48, 100; DA; DAB;
    DAC; DAM MST, NOV; SSC 9, 24;
    WLC**
    See also AAYA 21; CA 5-8R; 25-28R;
    CABS 1, 3; CANR 18; CDALB 1941-
    1968; DA3; DLB 2, 7, 173, 228; MTCW
    1, 2; SATA 27
McCulloch, John Tyler
    See Burroughs, Edgar Rice
McCullough, Colleen 1938(?)- .... **CLC 27,
    107; DAM NOV, POP**
    See also CA 81-84; CANR 17, 46, 67; DA3;
    MTCW 1, 2
McDermott, Alice 1953- .... **CLC 90**
    See also CA 109; CANR 40, 90
McElroy, Joseph 1930- .... **CLC 5, 47**
    See also CA 17-20R
McEwan, Ian (Russell) 1948- .. **CLC 13, 66;
    DAM NOV**
    See also BEST 90:4; CA 61-64; CANR 14,
    41, 69, 87; DLB 14, 194; MTCW 1, 2
McFadden, David 1940- .... **CLC 48**
    See also CA 104; DLB 60; INT 104
McFarland, Dennis 1950- .... **CLC 65**
    See also CA 165
McGahern, John 1934- .. **CLC 5, 9, 48; SSC
    17**

See also CA 17-20R; CANR 29, 68; DLB 14, 231; MTCW 1

McGinley, Patrick (Anthony) 1937- . **CLC 41**
See also CA 120; 127; CANR 56; INT 127

McGinley, Phyllis 1905-1978 .... **CLC 14**
See also CA 9-12R; 77-80; CANR 19; DLB 11, 48; SATA 2, 44; SATA-Obit 24

McGinniss, Joe 1942- .... **CLC 32**
See also AITN 2; BEST 89:2; CA 25-28R; CANR 26, 70; DLB 185; INT CANR-26

McGivern, Maureen Daly
See Daly, Maureen

McGrath, Patrick 1950- .... **CLC 55**
See also CA 136; CANR 65; DLB 231

McGrath, Thomas (Matthew) 1916-1990
.... **CLC 28, 59; DAM POET**
See also CA 9-12R; 132; CANR 6, 33; MTCW 1; SATA 41; SATA-Obit 66

McGuane, Thomas (Francis III) 1939-
.... **CLC 3, 7, 18, 45, 127**
See also AITN 2; BEST 89:2; CA 49-52; CANR 5, 24, 49; DLB 2, 212; DLBY 80; INT CANR-24; MTCW 1

McGuckian, Medbh 1950- ... **CLC 48; DAM POET; PC 27**
See also CA 143; DLB 40

McHale, Tom 1942(?)-1982 .... **CLC 3, 5**
See also AITN 1; CA 77-80; 106

McIlvanney, William 1936- .... **CLC 42**
See also CA 25-28R; CANR 61; DLB 14, 207

McIlwraith, Maureen Mollie Hunter
See Hunter, Mollie
See also SATA 2

McInerney, Jay 1955- .. **CLC 34, 112; DAM POP**
See also AAYA 18; CA 116; 123; CANR 45, 68; DA3; INT 123; MTCW 2

McIntyre, Vonda N(eel) 1948- .... **CLC 18**
See also CA 81-84; CANR 17, 34, 69; MTCW 1

McKay, Claude . **TCLC 7, 41; BLC 3; DAB; PC 2**
See also McKay, Festus Claudius
See also DLB 4, 45, 51, 117

McKay, Festus Claudius 1889-1948
See McKay, Claude
See also BW 1, 3; CA 104; 124; CANR 73; DA; DAC; DAM MST, MULT, NOV, POET; MTCW 1, 2; WLC

McKuen, Rod 1933- .... **CLC 1, 3**
See also AITN 1; CA 41-44R; CANR 40

McLoughlin, R. B.
See Mencken, H(enry) L(ouis)

McLuhan, (Herbert) Marshall 1911-1980
.... **CLC 37, 83**
See also CA 9-12R; 102; CANR 12, 34, 61; DLB 88; INT CANR-12; MTCW 1, 2

McMillan, Terry (L.) 1951- ...... **CLC 50, 61, 112; BLCS; DAM MULT, NOV, POP**
See also AAYA 21; BW 2, 3; CA 140; CANR 60; DA3; MTCW 2

McMurtry, Larry (Jeff) 1936- . **CLC 2, 3, 7, 11, 27, 44, 127; DAM NOV, POP**
See also AAYA 15; AITN 2; BEST 89:2; CA 5-8R; CANR 19, 43, 64; CDALB 1968-1988; DA3; DLB 2, 143; DLBY 80, 87; MTCW 1, 2

McNally, T. M. 1961- .... **CLC 82**

McNally, Terrence 1939- .. **CLC 4, 7, 41, 91; DAM DRAM**
See also CA 45-48; CANR 2, 56; DA3; DLB 7; MTCW 2

McNamer, Deirdre 1950- .... **CLC 70**

McNeal, Tom .... **CLC 119**

McNeile, Herman Cyril 1888-1937
See Sapper
See also CA 184; DLB 77

McNickle, (William) D'Arcy 1904-1977
.... **CLC 89; DAM MULT**
See also CA 9-12R; 85-88; CANR 5, 45; DLB 175, 212; NNAL; SATA-Obit 22

McPhee, John (Angus) 1931- .... **CLC 36**
See also BEST 90:1; CA 65-68; CANR 20, 46, 64, 69; DLB 185; MTCW 1, 2

McPherson, James Alan 1943- . **CLC 19, 77; BLCS**
See also BW 1, 3; CA 25-28R; CAAS 17; CANR 24, 74; DLB 38; MTCW 1, 2

McPherson, William (Alexander) 1933-
.... **CLC 34**
See also CA 69-72; CANR 28; INT CANR-28

Mead, George Herbert 1873-1958 . **TCLC 89**

Mead, Margaret 1901-1978 .... **CLC 37**
See also AITN 1; CA 1-4R; 81-84; CANR 4; DA3; MTCW 1, 2; SATA-Obit 20

Meaker, Marijane (Agnes) 1927-
See Kerr, M. E.
See also CA 107; CANR 37, 63; INT 107; JRDA; MAICYA; MTCW 1; SATA 20, 61, 99; SATA-Essay 111

Medoff, Mark (Howard) 1940- .. **CLC 6, 23; DAM DRAM**
See also AITN 1; CA 53-56; CANR 5; DLB 7; INT CANR-5

Medvedev, P. N.
See Bakhtin, Mikhail Mikhailovich

Meged, Aharon
See Megged, Aharon

Meged, Aron
See Megged, Aharon

Megged, Aharon 1920- .... **CLC 9**
See also CA 49-52; CAAS 13; CANR 1

Mehta, Ved (Parkash) 1934- .... **CLC 37**
See also CA 1-4R; CANR 2, 23, 69; MTCW 1

Melanter
See Blackmore, R(ichard) D(oddridge)

Melies, Georges 1861-1938 .... **TCLC 81**

Melikow, Loris
See Hofmannsthal, Hugo von

Melmoth, Sebastian
See Wilde, Oscar (Fingal O'Flahertie Wills)

Meltzer, Milton 1915- .... **CLC 26**
See also AAYA 8; CA 13-16R; CANR 38, 92; CLR 13; DLB 61; JRDA; MAICYA; SAAS 1; SATA 1, 50, 80

Melville, Herman 1819-1891 ... **NCLC 3, 12, 29, 45, 49, 91, 93; DA; DAB; DAC; DAM MST, NOV; SSC 1, 17; WLC**
See also AAYA 25; CDALB 1640-1865; DA3; DLB 3, 74; SATA 59

Menander c. 342B.C.-c. 292B.C. .. **CMLC 9; DAM DRAM; DC 3**
See also DLB 176

Menchu, Rigoberta 1959-
See also HLCS 2

Menchu, Rigoberta 1959-
See also CA 175; HLCS 2

Mencken, H(enry) L(ouis) 1880-1956
.... **TCLC 13**
See also CA 105; 125; CDALB 1917-1929; DLB 11, 29, 63, 137, 222; MTCW 1, 2

Mendelsohn, Jane 1965- .... **CLC 99**
See also CA 154

Mercer, David 1928-1980 .... **CLC 5; DAM DRAM**
See also CA 9-12R; 102; CANR 23; DLB 13; MTCW 1

Merchant, Paul
See Ellison, Harlan (Jay)

Meredith, George 1828-1909 . **TCLC 17, 43; DAM POET**
See also CA 117; 153; CANR 80; CDBLB 1832-1890; DLB 18, 35, 57, 159

Meredith, William (Morris) 1919- ... **CLC 4,**

13, 22, 55; **DAM POET; PC 28**
See also CA 9-12R; CAAS 14; CANR 6, 40; DLB 5

Merezhkovsky, Dmitry Sergeyevich 1865-1941 .... **TCLC 29**
See also CA 169

Merimee, Prosper 1803-1870 .. **NCLC 6, 65; SSC 7**
See also DLB 119, 192

Merkin, Daphne 1954- .... **CLC 44**
See also CA 123

Merlin, Arthur
See Blish, James (Benjamin)

Merrill, James (Ingram) 1926-1995 . **CLC 2, 3, 6, 8, 13, 18, 34, 91; DAM POET; PC 28**
See also CA 13-16R; 147; CANR 10, 49, 63; DA3; DLB 5, 165; DLBY 85; INT CANR-10; MTCW 1, 2

Merriman, Alex
See Silverberg, Robert

Merriman, Brian 1747-1805 .... **NCLC 70**

Merritt, E. B.
See Waddington, Miriam

Merton, Thomas 1915-1968 ... **CLC 1, 3, 11, 34, 83; PC 10**
See also CA 5-8R; 25-28R; CANR 22, 53; DA3; DLB 48; DLBY 81; MTCW 1, 2

Merwin, W(illiam) S(tanley) 1927- . **CLC 1, 2, 3, 5, 8, 13, 18, 45, 88; DAM POET**
See also CA 13-16R; CANR 15, 51; DA3; DLB 5, 169; INT CANR-15; MTCW 1, 2

Metcalf, John 1938- .... **CLC 37**
See also CA 113; DLB 60

Metcalf, Suzanne
See Baum, L(yman) Frank

Mew, Charlotte (Mary) 1869-1928 . **TCLC 8**
See also CA 105; DLB 19, 135

Mewshaw, Michael 1943- .... **CLC 9**
See also CA 53-56; CANR 7, 47; DLBY 80

Meyer, Conrad Ferdinand 1825-1905
.... **NCLC 81**
See also DLB 129

Meyer, June
See Jordan, June

Meyer, Lynn
See Slavitt, David R(ytman)

Meyer-Meyrink, Gustav 1868-1932
See Meyrink, Gustav
See also CA 117

Meyers, Jeffrey 1939- .... **CLC 39**
See also CA 73-76; CAAE 186; CANR 54; DLB 111

Meynell, Alice (Christina Gertrude Thompson) 1847-1922 .... **TCLC 6**
See also CA 104; 177; DLB 19, 98

Meyrink, Gustav .... **TCLC 21**
See also Meyer-Meyrink, Gustav
See also DLB 81

Michaels, Leonard 1933- ... **CLC 6, 25; SSC 16**
See also CA 61-64; CANR 21, 62; DLB 130; MTCW 1

Michaux, Henri 1899-1984 .... **CLC 8, 19**
See also CA 85-88; 114

Micheaux, Oscar (Devereaux) 1884-1951
.... **TCLC 76**
See also BW 3; CA 174; DLB 50

Michelangelo 1475-1564 .... **LC 12**

Michelet, Jules 1798-1874 .... **NCLC 31**

Michels, Robert 1876-1936 .... **TCLC 88**

Michener, James A(lbert) 1907(?)-1997
. **CLC 1, 5, 11, 29, 60, 109; DAM NOV, POP**
See also AAYA 27; AITN 1; BEST 90:1; CA 5-8R; 161; CANR 21, 45, 68; DA3; DLB 6; MTCW 1, 2

Mickiewicz, Adam 1798-1855 .... **NCLC 3**

Middleton, Christopher 1926- .... CLC 13
See also CA 13-16R; CANR 29, 54; DLB 40

Middleton, Richard (Barham) 1882-1911
.... TCLC 56
See also CA 187; DLB 156

Middleton, Stanley 1919- .... CLC 7, 38
See also CA 25-28R; CAAS 23; CANR 21, 46, 81; DLB 14

Middleton, Thomas 1580-1627 .... LC 33; DAM DRAM, MST; DC 5
See also DLB 58

Migueis, Jose Rodrigues 1901- .... CLC 10

Mikszath, Kalman 1847-1910 .... TCLC 31
See also CA 170

Miles, Jack .... CLC 100

Miles, Josephine (Louise) 1911-1985 . CLC 1, 2, 14, 34, 39; DAM POET
See also CA 1-4R; 116; CANR 2, 55; DLB 48

Militant
See Sandburg, Carl (August)

Mill, John Stuart 1806-1873 ... NCLC 11, 58
See also CDBLB 1832-1890; DLB 55, 190

Millar, Kenneth 1915-1983 .. CLC 14; DAM POP
See also Macdonald, Ross
See also CA 9-12R; 110; CANR 16, 63; DA3; DLB 2, 226; DLBD 6; DLBY 83; MTCW 1, 2

Millay, E. Vincent
See Millay, Edna St. Vincent

Millay, Edna St. Vincent 1892-1950
... TCLC 4, 49; DA; DAB; DAC; DAM MST, POET; PC 6; WLCS
See also CA 104; 130; CDALB 1917-1929; DA3; DLB 45; MTCW 1, 2

Miller, Arthur 1915- ..... CLC 1, 2, 6, 10, 15, 26, 47, 78; DA; DAB; DAC; DAM DRAM, MST; DC 1; WLC
See also AAYA 15; AITN 1; CA 1-4R; CABS 3; CANR 2, 30, 54, 76; CDALB 1941-1968; DA3; DLB 7; MTCW 1, 2

Miller, Henry (Valentine) 1891-1980 . CLC 1, 2, 4, 9, 14, 43, 84; DA; DAB; DAC; DAM MST, NOV; WLC
See also CA 9-12R; 97-100; CANR 33, 64; CDALB 1929-1941; DA3; DLB 4, 9; DLBY 80; MTCW 1, 2

Miller, Jason 1939(?)- .... CLC 2
See also AITN 1; CA 73-76; DLB 7

Miller, Sue 1943- .... CLC 44; DAM POP
See also BEST 90:3; CA 139; CANR 59, 91; DA3; DLB 143

Miller, Walter M(ichael, Jr.) 1923- .. CLC 4, 30
See also CA 85-88; DLB 8

Millett, Kate 1934- .... CLC 67
See also AITN 1; CA 73-76; CANR 32, 53, 76; DA3; MTCW 1, 2

Millhauser, Steven (Lewis) 1943- ... CLC 21, 54, 109
See also CA 110; 111; CANR 63; DA3; DLB 2; INT 111; MTCW 2

Millin, Sarah Gertrude 1889-1968 . CLC 49
See also CA 102; 93-96; DLB 225

Milne, A(lan) A(lexander) 1882-1956
. TCLC 6, 88; DAB; DAC; DAM MST
See also CA 104; 133; CLR 1, 26; DA3; DLB 10, 77, 100, 160; MAICYA; MTCW 1, 2; SATA 100; YABC 1

Milner, Ron(ald) 1938- ..... CLC 56; BLC 3; DAM MULT
See also AITN 1; BW 1; CA 73-76; CANR 24, 81; DLB 38; MTCW 1

Milnes, Richard Monckton 1809-1885
.... NCLC 61
See also DLB 32, 184

Milosz, Czeslaw 1911- .... CLC 5, 11, 22, 31, 56, 82; DAM MST, POET; PC 8; WLCS
See also CA 81-84; CANR 23, 51, 91; DA3; MTCW 1, 2

Milton, John 1608-1674 .... LC 9, 43; DA; DAB; DAC; DAM MST, POET; PC 19, 29; WLC
See also CDBLB 1660-1789; DA3; DLB 131, 151

Min, Anchee 1957- .... CLC 86
See also CA 146

Minehaha, Cornelius
See Wedekind, (Benjamin) Frank(lin)

Miner, Valerie 1947- .... CLC 40
See also CA 97-100; CANR 59

Minimo, Duca
See D'Annunzio, Gabriele

Minot, Susan 1956- .... CLC 44
See also CA 134

Minus, Ed 1938- .... CLC 39
See also CA 185

Miranda, Javier
See Bioy Casares, Adolfo

Miranda, Javier
See Bioy Casares, Adolfo

Mirbeau, Octave 1848-1917 .... TCLC 55
See also DLB 123, 192

Miro (Ferrer), Gabriel (Francisco Victor) 1879-1930 .... TCLC 5
See also CA 104; 185

Mishima, Yukio 1925-1970 .. CLC 2, 4, 6, 9, 27; DC 1; SSC 4
See also Hiraoka, Kimitake
See also DLB 182; MTCW 2

Mistral, Frederic 1830-1914 .... TCLC 51
See also CA 122

Mistral, Gabriela
See Godoy Alcayaga, Lucila

Mistry, Rohinton 1952- .... CLC 71; DAC
See also CA 141; CANR 86

Mitchell, Clyde
See Ellison, Harlan (Jay); Silverberg, Robert

Mitchell, James Leslie 1901-1935
See Gibbon, Lewis Grassic
See also CA 104; DLB 15

Mitchell, Joni 1943- .... CLC 12
See also CA 112

Mitchell, Joseph (Quincy) 1908-1996
.... CLC 98
See also CA 77-80; 152; CANR 69; DLB 185; DLBY 96

Mitchell, Margaret (Munnerlyn) 1900-1949
.... TCLC 11; DAM NOV, POP
See also AAYA 23; CA 109; 125; CANR 55; CDALBS; DA3; DLB 9; MTCW 1, 2

Mitchell, Peggy
See Mitchell, Margaret (Munnerlyn)

Mitchell, S(ilas) Weir 1829-1914 .. TCLC 36
See also CA 165; DLB 202

Mitchell, W(illiam) O(rmond) 1914-1998
.... CLC 25; DAC; DAM MST
See also CA 77-80; 165; CANR 15, 43; DLB 88

Mitchell, William 1879-1936 .... TCLC 81

Mitford, Mary Russell 1787-1855 .. NCLC 4
See also DLB 110, 116

Mitford, Nancy 1904-1973 .... CLC 44
See also CA 9-12R; DLB 191

Miyamoto, (Chujo) Yuriko 1899-1951
.... TCLC 37
See also CA 170, 174; DLB 180

Miyazawa, Kenji 1896-1933 .... TCLC 76
See also CA 157

Mizoguchi, Kenji 1898-1956 .... TCLC 72
See also CA 167

Mo, Timothy (Peter) 1950(?)- . CLC 46, 134
See also CA 117; DLB 194; MTCW 1

Modarressi, Taghi (M.) 1931- .... CLC 44
See also CA 121; 134; INT 134

Modiano, Patrick (Jean) 1945- .... CLC 18
See also CA 85-88; CANR 17, 40; DLB 83

Moerck, Paal
See Roelvaag, O(le) E(dvart)

Mofolo, Thomas (Mokopu) 1875(?)-1948
.... TCLC 22; BLC 3; DAM MULT
See also CA 121; 153; CANR 83; DLB 225; MTCW 2

Mohr, Nicholasa 1938- .... CLC 12; DAM MULT; HLC 2
See also AAYA 8; CA 49-52; CANR 1, 32, 64; CLR 22; DLB 145; HW 1, 2; JRDA; SAAS 8; SATA 8, 97; SATA-Essay 113

Mojtabai, A(nn) G(race) 1938- .... CLC 5, 9, 15, 29
See also CA 85-88; CANR 88

Moliere 1622-1673 .... LC 10, 28; DA; DAB; DAC; DAM DRAM, MST; DC 13; WLC
See also DA3

Molin, Charles
See Mayne, William (James Carter)

Molnar, Ferenc 1878-1952 . TCLC 20; DAM DRAM
See also CA 109; 153; CANR 83

Momaday, N(avarre) Scott 1934- .... CLC 2, 19, 85, 95; DA; DAB; DAC; DAM MST, MULT, NOV, POP; PC 25; WLCS
See also AAYA 11; CA 25-28R; CANR 14, 34, 68; CDALBS; DA3; DLB 143, 175; INT CANR-14; MTCW 1, 2; NNAL; SATA 48; SATA-Brief 30

Monette, Paul 1945-1995 .... CLC 82
See also CA 139; 147

Monroe, Harriet 1860-1936 .... TCLC 12
See also CA 109; DLB 54, 91

Monroe, Lyle
See Heinlein, Robert A(nson)

Montagu, Elizabeth 1720-1800 .... NCLC 7

Montagu, Mary (Pierrepont) Wortley 1689-1762 .... LC 9, 57; PC 16
See also DLB 95, 101

Montagu, W. H.
See Coleridge, Samuel Taylor

Montague, John (Patrick) 1929- .... CLC 13, 46
See also CA 9-12R; CANR 9, 69; DLB 40; MTCW 1

Montaigne, Michel (Eyquem) de 1533-1592
.... LC 8; DA; DAB; DAC; DAM MST; WLC

Montale, Eugenio 1896-1981 . CLC 7, 9, 18; PC 13
See also CA 17-20R; 104; CANR 30; DLB 114; MTCW 1

Montesquieu, Charles-Louis de Secondat 1689-1755 .... LC 7

Montessori, Maria 1870-1952 ..... TCLC 103
See also CA 115; 147

Montgomery, (Robert) Bruce 1921(?)-1978
See Crispin, Edmund
See also CA 179; 104

Montgomery, L(ucy) M(aud) 1874-1942
.... TCLC 51; DAC; DAM MST
See also AAYA 12; CA 108; 137; CLR 8; DA3; DLB 92; DLBD 14; JRDA; MAICYA; MTCW 2; SATA 100; YABC 1

Montgomery, Marion H., Jr. 1925- .. CLC 7
See also AITN 1; CA 1-4R; CANR 3, 48; DLB 6

Montgomery, Max
See Davenport, Guy (Mattison, Jr.)

Montherlant, Henry (Milon) de 1896-1972
.... CLC 8, 19; DAM DRAM
See also CA 85-88; 37-40R; DLB 72; MTCW 1

Mulock, Dinah Maria
See Craik, Dinah Maria (Mulock)
Munford, Robert 1737(?)-1783 .... **LC 5**
See also DLB 31
Mungo, Raymond 1946- .... **CLC 72**
See also CA 49-52; CANR 2
Munro, Alice 1931- .. **CLC 6, 10, 19, 50, 95;**
DAC; DAM MST, NOV; SSC 3; WLCS
See also AITN 2; CA 33-36R; CANR 33,
53, 75; DA3; DLB 53; MTCW 1, 2; SATA
29
Munro, H(ector) H(ugh) 1870-1916
See Saki
See also CA 104; 130; CDBLB 1890-1914;
DA; DAB; DAC; DAM MST, NOV; DA3;
DLB 34, 162; MTCW 1, 2; WLC
Murdoch, (Jean) Iris 1919-1999 .. **CLC 1, 2,**
3, 4, 6, 8, 11, 15, 22, 31, 51; DAB; DAC;
DAM MST, NOV
See also CA 13-16R; 179; CANR 8, 43, 68;
CDBLB 1960 to Present; DA3; DLB 14,
194, 233; INT CANR-8; MTCW 1, 2
Murfree, Mary Noailles 1850-1922 .. **SSC 22**
See also CA 122; 176; DLB 12, 74
Murnau, Friedrich Wilhelm
See Plumpe, Friedrich Wilhelm
Murphy, Richard 1927- .... **CLC 41**
See also CA 29-32R; DLB 40
Murphy, Sylvia 1937- .... **CLC 34**
See also CA 121
Murphy, Thomas (Bernard) 1935- . **CLC 51**
See also CA 101
Murray, Albert L. 1916- .... **CLC 73**
See also BW 2; CA 49-52; CANR 26, 52,
78; DLB 38
Murray, Judith Sargent 1751-1820
.... **NCLC 63**
See also DLB 37, 200
Murray, Les(lie) A(llan) 1938- .... **CLC 40;**
DAM POET
See also CA 21-24R; CANR 11, 27, 56
Murry, J. Middleton
See Murry, John Middleton
Murry, John Middleton 1889-1957
.... **TCLC 16**
See also CA 118; DLB 149
Musgrave, Susan 1951- .... **CLC 13, 54**
See also CA 69-72; CANR 45, 84
Musil, Robert (Edler von) 1880-1942
.... **TCLC 12, 68; SSC 18**
See also CA 109; CANR 55, 84; DLB 81,
124; MTCW 2
Muske, Carol 1945- .... **CLC 90**
See also Muske-Dukes, Carol (Anne)
Muske-Dukes, Carol (Anne) 1945-
See Muske, Carol
See also CA 65-68; CANR 32, 70
Musset, (Louis Charles) Alfred de 1810-1857
.... **NCLC 7**
See also DLB 192
Mussolini, Benito (Amilcare Andrea)
1883-1945 .... **TCLC 96**
See also CA 116
My Brother's Brother
See Chekhov, Anton (Pavlovich)
Myers, L(eopold) H(amilton) 1881-1944
.... **TCLC 59**
See also CA 157; DLB 15
Myers, Walter Dean 1937- .... **CLC 35; BLC**
3; DAM MULT, NOV
See also AAYA 4, 23; BW 2; CA 33-36R;
CANR 20, 42, 67; CLR 4, 16, 35; DLB
33; INT CANR-20; JRDA; MAICYA;
MTCW 2; SAAS 2; SATA 41, 71, 109;
SATA-Brief 27
Myers, Walter M.
See Myers, Walter Dean
Myles, Symon
See Follett, Ken(neth Martin)

Nabokov, Vladimir (Vladimirovich)
1899-1977 ..... **CLC 1, 2, 3, 6, 8, 11, 15,**
23, 44, 46, 64; DA; DAB; DAC; DAM
MST, NOV; SSC 11; WLC
See also CA 5-8R; 69-72; CANR 20;
CDALB 1941-1968; DA3; DLB 2; DLBD
3; DLBY 80, 91; MTCW 1, 2
Naevius c. 265B.C.-201B.C. .... **CMLC 37**
See also DLB 211
Nagai Kafu 1879-1959 .... **TCLC 51**
See also Nagai Sokichi
See also DLB 180
Nagai Sokichi 1879-1959
See Nagai Kafu
See also CA 117
Nagy, Laszlo 1925-1978 .... **CLC 7**
See also CA 129; 112
Naidu, Sarojini 1879-1943 .... **TCLC 80**
Naipaul, Shiva(dhar Srinivasa) 1945-1985
.... **CLC 32, 39; DAM NOV**
See also CA 110; 112; 116; CANR 33;
DA3; DLB 157; DLBY 85; MTCW 1, 2
Naipaul, V(idiadhar) S(urajprasad) 1932-
...... **CLC 4, 7, 9, 13, 18, 37, 105; DAB;**
DAC; DAM MST, NOV; SSC 38
See also CA 1-4R; CANR 1, 33, 51, 91;
CDBLB 1960 to Present; DA3; DLB 125,
204, 206; DLBY 85; MTCW 1, 2
Nakos, Lilika 1899(?)- .... **CLC 29**
Narayan, R(asipuram) K(rishnaswami)
1906- . **CLC 7, 28, 47, 121; DAM NOV;**
SSC 25
See also CA 81-84; CANR 33, 61; DA3;
MTCW 1, 2; SATA 62
Nash, (Frediric) Ogden 1902-1971 . **CLC 23;**
DAM POET; PC 21
See also CA 13-14; 29-32R; CANR 34, 61;
CAP 1; DLB 11; MAICYA; MTCW 1, 2;
SATA 2, 46
Nashe, Thomas 1567-1601(?) .... **LC 41**
See also DLB 167
Nashe, Thomas 1567-1601 .... **LC 41**
Nathan, Daniel
See Dannay, Frederic
Nathan, George Jean 1882-1958 .. **TCLC 18**
See also Hatteras, Owen
See also CA 114; 169; DLB 137
Natsume, Kinnosuke 1867-1916
See Natsume, Soseki
See also CA 104
Natsume, Soseki 1867-1916 ...... **TCLC 2, 10**
See also Natsume, Kinnosuke
See also DLB 180
Natti, (Mary) Lee 1919-
See Kingman, Lee
See also CA 5-8R; CANR 2
Naylor, Gloria 1950- ... **CLC 28, 52; BLC 3;**
DA; DAC; DAM MST, MULT, NOV,
POP; WLCS
See also AAYA 6; BW 2, 3; CA 107; CANR
27, 51, 74; DA3; DLB 173; MTCW 1, 2
Neihardt, John Gneisenau 1881-1973
.... **CLC 32**
See also CA 13-14; CANR 65; CAP 1; DLB
9, 54
Nekrasov, Nikolai Alekseevich 1821-1878
.... **NCLC 11**
Nelligan, Emile 1879-1941 .... **TCLC 14**
See also CA 114; DLB 92
Nelson, Willie 1933- .... **CLC 17**
See also CA 107
Nemerov, Howard (Stanley) 1920-1991
.. **CLC 2, 6, 9, 36; DAM POET; PC 24**
See also CA 1-4R; 134; CABS 2; CANR 1,
27, 53; DLB 5, 6; DLBY 83; INT CANR-
27; MTCW 1, 2
Neruda, Pablo 1904-1973 . **CLC 1, 2, 5, 7, 9,**
28, 62; DA; DAB; DAC; DAM MST,
MULT, POET; HLC 2; PC 4; WLC

See also CA 19-20; 45-48; CAP 2; DA3;
HW 1; MTCW 1, 2
Nerval, Gerard de 1808-1855 . **NCLC 1, 67;**
PC 13; SSC 18
Nervo, (Jose) Amado (Ruiz de) 1870-1919
.... **TCLC 11; HLCS 2**
See also CA 109; 131; HW 1
Nessi, Pio Baroja y
See Baroja (y Nessi), Pio
Nestroy, Johann 1801-1862 .... **NCLC 42**
See also DLB 133
Netterville, Luke
See O'Grady, Standish (James)
Neufeld, John (Arthur) 1938- .... **CLC 17**
See also AAYA 11; CA 25-28R; CANR 11,
37, 56; CLR 52; MAICYA; SAAS 3;
SATA 6, 81
Neumann, Alfred 1895-1952 .... **TCLC 100**
See also CA 183; DLB 56
Neville, Emily Cheney 1919- .... **CLC 12**
See also CA 5-8R; CANR 3, 37, 85; JRDA;
MAICYA; SAAS 2; SATA 1
Newbound, Bernard Slade 1930-
See Slade, Bernard
See also CA 81-84; CANR 49; DAM
DRAM
Newby, P(ercy) H(oward) 1918-1997
.... **CLC 2, 13; DAM NOV**
See also CA 5-8R; 161; CANR 32, 67; DLB
15; MTCW 1
Newlove, Donald 1928- .... **CLC 6**
See also CA 29-32R; CANR 25
Newlove, John (Herbert) 1938- .... **CLC 14**
See also CA 21-24R; CANR 9, 25
Newman, Charles 1938- .... **CLC 2, 8**
See also CA 21-24R; CANR 84
Newman, Edwin (Harold) 1919- ..... **CLC 14**
See also AITN 1; CA 69-72; CANR 5
Newman, John Henry 1801-1890 . **NCLC 38**
See also DLB 18, 32, 55
Newton, (Sir)Isaac 1642-1727 ...... **LC 35, 52**
Newton, Suzanne 1936- .... **CLC 35**
See also CA 41-44R; CANR 14; JRDA;
SATA 5, 77
Nexo, Martin Andersen 1869-1954
.... **TCLC 43**
Nezval, Vitezslav 1900-1958 .... **TCLC 44**
See also CA 123
Ng, Fae Myenne 1957(?)- .... **CLC 81**
See also CA 146
Ngema, Mbongeni 1955- .... **CLC 57**
See also BW 2; CA 143; CANR 84
Ngugi, James T(hiong'o) .... **CLC 3, 7, 13**
See also Ngugi wa Thiong'o
Ngugi wa Thiong'o 1938- . **CLC 36; BLC 3;**
DAM MULT, NOV
See also Ngugi, James T(hiong'o)
See also BW 2; CA 81-84; CANR 27, 58;
DLB 125; MTCW 1, 2
Nichol, B(arrie) P(hillip) 1944-1988 . **CLC 18**
See also CA 53-56; DLB 53; SATA 66
Nichols, John (Treadwell) 1940- ..... **CLC 38**
See also CA 9-12R; CAAS 2; CANR 6, 70;
DLBY 82
Nichols, Leigh
See Koontz, Dean R(ay)
Nichols, Peter (Richard) 1927- .. **CLC 5, 36,**
65
See also CA 104; CANR 33, 86; DLB 13;
MTCW 1
Nicolas, F. R. E.
See Freeling, Nicolas
Niedecker, Lorine 1903-1970 ... **CLC 10, 42;**
DAM POET
See also CA 25-28; CAP 2; DLB 48
Nietzsche, Friedrich (Wilhelm) 1844-1900
.... **TCLC 10, 18, 55**
See also CA 107; 121; DLB 129

Nievo, Ippolito 1831-1861 .... **NCLC 22**

Nightingale, Anne Redmon 1943-
See Redmon, Anne
See also CA 103

Nightingale, Florence 1820-1910 .. **TCLC 85**
See also DLB 166

Nik. T. O.
See Annensky, Innokenty (Fyodorovich)

Nin, Anais 1903-1977 .... **CLC 1, 4, 8, 11, 14, 60, 127; DAM NOV, POP; SSC 10**
See also AITN 2; CA 13-16R; 69-72; CANR 22, 53; DLB 2, 4, 152; MTCW 1, 2

Nishida, Kitaro 1870-1945 .... **TCLC 83**

Nishiwaki, Junzaburo 1894-1982 .... **PC 15**
See also CA 107

Nissenson, Hugh 1933- .... **CLC 4, 9**
See also CA 17-20R; CANR 27; DLB 28

Niven, Larry .... **CLC 8**
See also Niven, Laurence Van Cott
See also AAYA 27; DLB 8

Niven, Laurence Van Cott 1938-
See Niven, Larry
See also CA 21-24R; CAAS 12; CANR 14, 44, 66; DAM POP; MTCW 1, 2; SATA 95

Nixon, Agnes Eckhardt 1927- .... **CLC 21**
See also CA 110

Nizan, Paul 1905-1940 .... **TCLC 40**
See also CA 161; DLB 72

Nkosi, Lewis 1936- . **CLC 45; BLC 3; DAM MULT**
See also BW 1, 3; CA 65-68; CANR 27, 81; DLB 157, 225

Nodier, (Jean) Charles (Emmanuel) 1780-1844 .... **NCLC 19**
See also DLB 119

Noguchi, Yone 1875-1947 .... **TCLC 80**

Nolan, Christopher 1965- .... **CLC 58**
See also CA 111; CANR 88

Noon, Jeff 1957- .... **CLC 91**
See also CA 148; CANR 83

Norden, Charles
See Durrell, Lawrence (George)

Nordhoff, Charles (Bernard) 1887-1947
.... **TCLC 23**
See also CA 108; DLB 9; SATA 23

Norfolk, Lawrence 1963- .... **CLC 76**
See also CA 144; CANR 85

Norman, Marsha 1947- .... **CLC 28; DAM DRAM; DC 8**
See also CA 105; CABS 3; CANR 41; DLBY 84

Normyx
See Douglas, (George) Norman

Norris, Frank 1870-1902 .... **SSC 28**
See also Norris, (Benjamin) Frank(lin, Jr.)
See also CDALB 1865-1917; DLB 12, 71, 186

Norris, (Benjamin) Frank(lin, Jr.) 1870-1902
.... **TCLC 24**
See also Norris, Frank
See also CA 110; 160

Norris, Leslie 1921- .... **CLC 14**
See also CA 11-12; CANR 14; CAP 1; DLB 27

North, Andrew
See Norton, Andre

North, Anthony
See Koontz, Dean R(ay)

North, Captain George
See Stevenson, Robert Louis (Balfour)

North, Milou
See Erdrich, Louise

Northrup, B. A.
See Hubbard, L(afayette) Ron(ald)

North Staffs
See Hulme, T(homas) E(rnest)

Norton, Alice Mary
See Norton, Andre
See also MAICYA; SATA 1, 43

Norton, Andre 1912- .... **CLC 12**
See also Norton, Alice Mary
See also AAYA 14; CA 1-4R; CANR 68; CLR 50; DLB 8, 52; JRDA; MTCW 1; SATA 91

Norton, Caroline 1808-1877 .... **NCLC 47**
See also DLB 21, 159, 199

Norway, Nevil Shute 1899-1960
See Shute, Nevil
See also CA 102; 93-96; CANR 85; MTCW 2

Norwid, Cyprian Kamil 1821-1883
.... **NCLC 17**

Nosille, Nabrah
See Ellison, Harlan (Jay)

Nossack, Hans Erich 1901-1978 .... **CLC 6**
See also CA 93-96; 85-88; DLB 69

Nostradamus 1503-1566 .... **LC 27**

Nosu, Chuji
See Ozu, Yasujiro

Notenburg, Eleanora (Genrikhovna) von
See Guro, Elena

Nova, Craig 1945- .... **CLC 7, 31**
See also CA 45-48; CANR 2, 53

Novak, Joseph
See Kosinski, Jerzy (Nikodem)

Novalis 1772-1801 .... **NCLC 13**
See also DLB 90

Novis, Emile
See Weil, Simone (Adolphine)

Nowlan, Alden (Albert) 1933-1983 . **CLC 15; DAC; DAM MST**
See also CA 9-12R; CANR 5; DLB 53

Noyes, Alfred 1880-1958 .... **TCLC 7; PC 27**
See also CA 104; DLB 20

Nunn, Kem .... **CLC 34**
See also CA 159

Nwapa, Flora 1931- .... **CLC 133; BLCS**
See also BW 2; CA 143; CANR 83; DLB 125

Nye, Robert 1939- . **CLC 13, 42; DAM NOV**
See also CA 33-36R; CANR 29, 67; DLB 14; MTCW 1; SATA 6

Nyro, Laura 1947- .... **CLC 17**

Oates, Joyce Carol 1938- . **CLC 1, 2, 3, 6, 9, 11, 15, 19, 33, 52, 108, 134; DA; DAB; DAC; DAM MST, NOV, POP; SSC 6; WLC**
See also AAYA 15; AITN 1; BEST 89:2; CA 5-8R; CANR 25, 45, 74; CDALB 1968-1988; DA3; DLB 2, 5, 130; DLBY 81; INT CANR-25; MTCW 1, 2

O'Brien, Darcy 1939-1998 .... **CLC 11**
See also CA 21-24R; 167; CANR 8, 59

O'Brien, E. G.
See Clarke, Arthur C(harles)

O'Brien, Edna 1936- .... **CLC 3, 5, 8, 13, 36, 65, 116; DAM NOV; SSC 10**
See also CA 1-4R; CANR 6, 41, 65; CDBLB 1960 to Present; DA3; DLB 14, 231; MTCW 1, 2

O'Brien, Fitz-James 1828-1862 .... **NCLC 21**
See also DLB 74

O'Brien, Flann .... **CLC 1, 4, 5, 7, 10, 47**
See also O Nuallain, Brian
See also DLB 231

O'Brien, Richard 1942- .... **CLC 17**
See also CA 124

O'Brien, (William) Tim(othy) 1946- . **CLC 7, 19, 40, 103; DAM POP**
See also AAYA 16; CA 85-88; CANR 40, 58; CDALBS; DA3; DLB 152; DLBD 9; DLBY 80; MTCW 2

Obstfelder, Sigbjoern 1866-1900 .. **TCLC 23**
See also CA 123

O'Casey, Sean 1880-1964 ... **CLC 1, 5, 9, 11, 15, 88; DAB; DAC; DAM DRAM, MST; DC 12; WLCS**
See also CA 89-92; CANR 62; CDBLB 1914-1945; DA3; DLB 10; MTCW 1, 2

O'Cathasaigh, Sean
See O'Casey, Sean

Occom, Samson 1723-1792 .... **LC 60**
See also DLB 175; NNAL

Ochs, Phil(ip David) 1940-1976 ...... **CLC 17**
See also CA 185; 65-68

O'Connor, Edwin (Greene) 1918-1968
.... **CLC 14**
See also CA 93-96; 25-28R

O'Connor, (Mary) Flannery 1925-1964
. **CLC 1, 2, 3, 6, 10, 13, 15, 21, 66, 104; DA; DAB; DAC; DAM MST, NOV; SSC 1, 23; WLC**
See also AAYA 7; CA 1-4R; CANR 3, 41; CDALB 1941-1968; DA3; DLB 2, 152; DLBD 12; DLBY 80; MTCW 1, 2

O'Connor, Frank .... **CLC 23; SSC 5**
See also O'Donovan, Michael John
See also DLB 162

O'Dell, Scott 1898-1989 .... **CLC 30**
See also AAYA 3; CA 61-64; 129; CANR 12, 30; CLR 1, 16; DLB 52; JRDA; MAICYA; SATA 12, 60

Odets, Clifford 1906-1963 .... **CLC 2, 28, 98; DAM DRAM; DC 6**
See also CA 85-88; CANR 62; DLB 7, 26; MTCW 1, 2

O'Doherty, Brian 1934- .... **CLC 76**
See also CA 105

O'Donnell, K. M.
See Malzberg, Barry N(athaniel)

O'Donnell, Lawrence
See Kuttner, Henry

O'Donovan, Michael John 1903-1966
.... **CLC 14**
See also O'Connor, Frank
See also CA 93-96; CANR 84

Oe, Kenzaburo 1935- .... **CLC 10, 36, 86; DAM NOV; SSC 20**
See also CA 97-100; CANR 36, 50, 74; DA3; DLB 182; DLBY 94; MTCW 1, 2

O'Faolain, Julia 1932- ... **CLC 6, 19, 47, 108**
See also CA 81-84; CAAS 2; CANR 12, 61; DLB 14, 231; MTCW 1

O'Faolain, Sean 1900-1991 .... **CLC 1, 7, 14, 32, 70; SSC 13**
See also CA 61-64; 134; CANR 12, 66; DLB 15, 162; MTCW 1, 2

O'Flaherty, Liam 1896-1984 ...... **CLC 5, 34; SSC 6**
See also CA 101; 113; CANR 35; DLB 36, 162; DLBY 84; MTCW 1, 2

Ogilvy, Gavin
See Barrie, J(ames) M(atthew)

O'Grady, Standish (James) 1846-1928
.... **TCLC 5**
See also CA 104; 157

O'Grady, Timothy 1951- .... **CLC 59**
See also CA 138

O'Hara, Frank 1926-1966 ...... **CLC 2, 5, 13, 78; DAM POET**
See also CA 9-12R; 25-28R; CANR 33; DA3; DLB 5, 16, 193; MTCW 1, 2

O'Hara, John (Henry) 1905-1970 .... **CLC 1, 2, 3, 6, 11, 42; DAM NOV; SSC 15**
See also CA 5-8R; 25-28R; CANR 31, 60; CDALB 1929-1941; DLB 9, 86; DLBD 2; MTCW 1, 2

O Hehir, Diana 1922- .... **CLC 41**
See also CA 93-96

Ohiyesa
See Eastman, Charles A(lexander)

Okigbo, Christopher (Ifenayichukwu) 1932-1967 . **CLC 25, 84; BLC 3; DAM**

See also CA 45-48; CANR 2, 32, 63; DA3;
DLB 113; HW 1, 2; MTCW 1, 2

Pulitzer, Joseph 1847-1911 .... **TCLC 76**
See also CA 114; DLB 23

Purdy, A(lfred) W(ellington) 1918- .. **CLC 3,
6, 14, 50; DAC; DAM MST, POET**
See also CA 81-84; CAAS 17; CANR 42,
66; DLB 88

Purdy, James (Amos) 1923- ... **CLC 2, 4, 10,
28, 52**
See also CA 33-36R; CAAS 1; CANR 19,
51; DLB 2; INT CANR-19; MTCW 1

Pure, Simon
See Swinnerton, Frank Arthur

Pushkin, Alexander (Sergeyevich) 1799-1837
.... **NCLC 3, 27, 83; DA; DAB; DAC;
DAM DRAM, MST, POET; PC 10; SSC
27; WLC**
See also DA3; DLB 205; SATA 61

P'u Sung-ling 1640-1715 ...... **LC 49; SSC 31**

Putnam, Arthur Lee
See Alger, Horatio Jr., Jr.

Puzo, Mario 1920-1999 ...... **CLC 1, 2, 6, 36,
107; DAM NOV, POP**
See also CA 65-68; 185; CANR 4, 42, 65;
DA3; DLB 6; MTCW 1, 2

Pygge, Edward
See Barnes, Julian (Patrick)

Pyle, Ernest Taylor 1900-1945
See Pyle, Ernie
See also CA 115; 160

Pyle, Ernie 1900-1945 .... **TCLC 75**
See also Pyle, Ernest Taylor
See also DLB 29; MTCW 2

Pyle, Howard 1853-1911 .... **TCLC 81**
See also CA 109; 137; CLR 22; DLB 42,
188; DLBD 13; MAICYA; SATA 16, 100

Pym, Barbara (Mary Crampton) 1913-1980
.... **CLC 13, 19, 37, 111**
See also CA 13-14; 97-100; CANR 13, 34;
CAP 1; DLB 14, 207; DLBY 87; MTCW
1, 2

Pynchon, Thomas (Ruggles, Jr.) 1937-
. **CLC 2, 3, 6, 9, 11, 18, 33, 62, 72, 123;
DA; DAB; DAC; DAM MST, NOV,
POP; SSC 14; WLC**
See also BEST 90:2; CA 17-20R; CANR
22, 46, 73; DA3; DLB 2, 173; MTCW 1,
2

Pythagoras c. 570B.C.-c. 500B.C. . **CMLC 22**
See also DLB 176

Q
See Quiller-Couch, SirArthur (Thomas)

Qian Zhongshu
See Ch'ien Chung-shu

Qroll
See Dagerman, Stig (Halvard)

Quarrington, Paul (Lewis) 1953- .... **CLC 65**
See also CA 129; CANR 62

Quasimodo, Salvatore 1901-1968 .... **CLC 10**
See also CA 13-16; 25-28R; CAP 1; DLB
114; MTCW 1

Quay, Stephen 1947- .... **CLC 95**
Quay, Timothy 1947- .... **CLC 95**
Queen, Ellery .... **CLC 3, 11**
See also Dannay, Frederic; Davidson,
Avram (James); Deming, Richard; Fair-
man, Paul W.; Flora, Fletcher; Hoch, Ed-
ward D(entinger); Kane, Henry; Lee,
Manfred B(ennington); Marlowe, Stephen;
Powell, Talmage; Sheldon, Walter J.; Stur-
geon, Theodore (Hamilton); Tracy,
Don(ald Fiske); Vance, John Holbrook

Queen, Ellery, Jr.
See Dannay, Frederic; Lee, Manfred
B(ennington)

Queneau, Raymond 1903-1976 ...... **CLC 2, 5,
10, 42**

See also CA 77-80; 69-72; CANR 32; DLB
72; MTCW 1, 2

Quevedo, Francisco de 1580-1645 ..... **LC 23**
Quiller-Couch, SirArthur (Thomas)
1863-1944 .... **TCLC 53**
See also CA 118; 166; DLB 135, 153, 190

Quin, Ann (Marie) 1936-1973 .... **CLC 6**
See also CA 9-12R; 45-48; DLB 14, 231

Quinn, Martin
See Smith, Martin Cruz

Quinn, Peter 1947- .... **CLC 91**

Quinn, Simon
See Smith, Martin Cruz

Quintana, Leroy V. 1944-
See also CA 131; CANR 65; DAM MULT;
DLB 82; HLC 2; HW 1, 2

Quiroga, Horacio (Sylvestre) 1878-1937
.... **TCLC 20; DAM MULT; HLC 2**
See also CA 117; 131; HW 1; MTCW 1

Quoirez, Francoise 1935- .... **CLC 9**
See also Sagan, Francoise
See also CA 49-52; CANR 6, 39, 73;
MTCW 1, 2

Raabe, Wilhelm (Karl) 1831-1910 . **TCLC 45**
See also CA 167; DLB 129

Rabe, David (William) 1940- . **CLC 4, 8, 33;
DAM DRAM**
See also CA 85-88; CABS 3; CANR 59;
DLB 7, 228

Rabelais, Francois 1483-1553 .... **LC 5, 60;
DA; DAB; DAC; DAM MST; WLC**

Rabinovitch, Sholem 1859-1916
See Aleichem, Sholom
See also CA 104

Rabinyan, Dorit 1972- .... **CLC 119**
See also CA 170

Rachilde
See Vallette, Marguerite Eymery

Racine, Jean 1639-1699 . **LC 28; DAB; DAM
MST**
See also DA3

Radcliffe, Ann (Ward) 1764-1823 . **NCLC 6,
55**
See also DLB 39, 178

Radiguet, Raymond 1903-1923 ..... **TCLC 29**
See also CA 162; DLB 65

Radnoti, Miklos 1909-1944 .... **TCLC 16**
See also CA 118

Rado, James 1939- .... **CLC 17**
See also CA 105

Radvanyi, Netty 1900-1983
See Seghers, Anna
See also CA 85-88; 110; CANR 82

Rae, Ben
See Griffiths, Trevor

Raeburn, John (Hay) 1941- .... **CLC 34**
See also CA 57-60

Ragni, Gerome 1942-1991 .... **CLC 17**
See also CA 105; 134

Rahv, Philip 1908-1973 .... **CLC 24**
See also Greenberg, Ivan
See also DLB 137

Raimund, Ferdinand Jakob 1790-1836
.... **NCLC 69**
See also DLB 90

Raine, Craig 1944- .... **CLC 32, 103**
See also CA 108; CANR 29, 51; DLB 40

Raine, Kathleen (Jessie) 1908- .... **CLC 7, 45**
See also CA 85-88; CANR 46; DLB 20;
MTCW 1

Rainis, Janis 1865-1929 .... **TCLC 29**
See also Plieksans, Janis
See also CA 170; DLB 220

Rakosi, Carl 1903- .... **CLC 47**
See also Rawley, Callman
See also CAAS 5; DLB 193

Raleigh, Richard
See Lovecraft, H(oward) P(hillips)

Raleigh, Sir Walter 1554(?)-1618 ...... **LC 31,
39; PC 31**
See also CDBLB Before 1660; DLB 172

Rallentando, H. P.
See Sayers, Dorothy L(eigh)

Ramal, Walter
See de la Mare, Walter (John)

Ramana Maharshi 1879-1950 .... **TCLC 84**

Ramoacn y Cajal, Santiago 1852-1934
.... **TCLC 93**

Ramon, Juan
See Jimenez (Mantecon), Juan Ramon

Ramos, Graciliano 1892-1953 .... **TCLC 32**
See also CA 167; HW 2

Rampersad, Arnold 1941- .... **CLC 44**
See also BW 2, 3; CA 127; 133; CANR 81;
DLB 111; INT 133

Rampling, Anne
See Rice, Anne

Ramsay, Allan 1684(?)-1758 .... **LC 29**
See also DLB 95

Ramuz, Charles-Ferdinand 1878-1947
.... **TCLC 33**
See also CA 165

Rand, Ayn 1905-1982 ..... **CLC 3, 30, 44, 79;
DA; DAC; DAM MST, NOV, POP;
WLC**
See also AAYA 10; CA 13-16R; 105; CANR
27, 73; CDALBS; DA3; DLB 227;
MTCW 1, 2

Randall, Dudley (Felker) 1914-2000 . **CLC 1,
135; BLC 3; DAM MULT**
See also BW 1, 3; CA 25-28R; CANR 23,
82; DLB 41

Randall, Robert
See Silverberg, Robert

Ranger, Ken
See Creasey, John

Ransom, John Crowe 1888-1974 . **CLC 2, 4,
5, 11, 24; DAM POET**
See also CA 5-8R; 49-52; CANR 6, 34;
CDALBS; DA3; DLB 45, 63; MTCW 1,
2

Rao, Raja 1909- .... **CLC 25, 56; DAM NOV**
See also CA 73-76; CANR 51; MTCW 1, 2

Raphael, Frederic (Michael) 1931- .. **CLC 2,
14**
See also CA 1-4R; CANR 1, 86; DLB 14

Ratcliffe, James P.
See Mencken, H(enry) L(ouis)

Rathbone, Julian 1935- .... **CLC 41**
See also CA 101; CANR 34, 73

Rattigan, Terence (Mervyn) 1911-1977
.... **CLC 7; DAM DRAM**
See also CA 85-88; 73-76; CDBLB 1945-
1960; DLB 13; MTCW 1, 2

Ratushinskaya, Irina 1954- .... **CLC 54**
See also CA 129; CANR 68

Raven, Simon (Arthur Noel) 1927- . **CLC 14**
See also CA 81-84; CANR 86

Ravenna, Michael
See Welty, Eudora

Rawley, Callman 1903-
See Rakosi, Carl
See also CA 21-24R; CANR 12, 32, 91

Rawlings, Marjorie Kinnan 1896-1953
.... **TCLC 4**
See also AAYA 20; CA 104; 137; CANR
74; CLR 63; DLB 9, 22, 102; DLBD 17;
JRDA; MAICYA; MTCW 2; SATA 100;
YABC 1

Ray, Satyajit 1921-1992 . **CLC 16, 76; DAM
MULT**
See also CA 114; 137

Read, Herbert Edward 1893-1968 .... **CLC 4**
See also CA 85-88; 25-28R; DLB 20, 149

Read, Piers Paul 1941- .... **CLC 4, 10, 25**
See also CA 21-24R; CANR 38, 86; DLB
14; SATA 21
Reade, Charles 1814-1884 .... **NCLC 2, 74**
See also DLB 21
Reade, Hamish
See Gray, Simon (James Holliday)
Reading, Peter 1946- .... **CLC 47**
See also CA 103; CANR 46; DLB 40
Reaney, James 1926- . **CLC 13; DAC; DAM
MST**
See also CA 41-44R; CAAS 15; CANR 42;
DLB 68; SATA 43
Rebreanu, Liviu 1885-1944 .... **TCLC 28**
See also CA 165; DLB 220
Rechy, John (Francisco) 1934- ..... **CLC 1, 7,
14, 18, 107; DAM MULT; HLC 2**
See also CA 5-8R; CAAS 4; CANR 6, 32,
64; DLB 122; DLBY 82; HW 1, 2; INT
CANR-6
Redcam, Tom 1870-1933 .... **TCLC 25**
Reddin, Keith .... **CLC 67**
Redgrove, Peter (William) 1932- . **CLC 6, 41**
See also CA 1-4R; CANR 3, 39, 77; DLB
40
Redmon, Anne .... **CLC 22**
See also Nightingale, Anne Redmon
See also DLBY 86
Reed, Eliot
See Ambler, Eric
Reed, Ishmael 1938- . **CLC 2, 3, 5, 6, 13, 32,
60; BLC 3; DAM MULT**
See also BW 2, 3; CA 21-24R; CANR 25,
48, 74; DA3; DLB 2, 5, 33, 169, 227;
DLBD 8; MTCW 1, 2
Reed, John (Silas) 1887-1920 .... **TCLC 9**
See also CA 106
Reed, Lou .... **CLC 21**
See also Firbank, Louis
Reese, Lizette Woodworth 1856-1935 . **PC 29**
See also CA 180; DLB 54
Reeve, Clara 1729-1807 .... **NCLC 19**
See also DLB 39
Reich, Wilhelm 1897-1957 .... **TCLC 57**
Reid, Christopher (John) 1949- ...... **CLC 33**
See also CA 140; CANR 89; DLB 40
Reid, Desmond
See Moorcock, Michael (John)
Reid Banks, Lynne 1929-
See Banks, Lynne Reid
See also CA 1-4R; CANR 6, 22, 38, 87;
CLR 24; JRDA; MAICYA; SATA 22, 75,
111
Reilly, William K.
See Creasey, John
Reiner, Max
See Caldwell, (Janet Miriam) Taylor
(Holland)
Reis, Ricardo
See Pessoa, Fernando (Antonio Nogueira)
Remarque, Erich Maria 1898-1970
. **CLC 21; DA; DAB; DAC; DAM MST,
NOV**
See also AAYA 27; CA 77-80; 29-32R;
DA3; DLB 56; MTCW 1, 2
Remington, Frederic 1861-1909 ... **TCLC 89**
See also CA 108; 169; DLB 12, 186, 188;
SATA 41
Remizov, A.
See Remizov, Aleksei (Mikhailovich)
Remizov, A. M.
See Remizov, Aleksei (Mikhailovich)
Remizov, Aleksei (Mikhailovich) 1877-1957
.... **TCLC 27**
See also CA 125; 133
Renan, Joseph Ernest 1823-1892 . **NCLC 26**
Renard, Jules 1864-1910 .... **TCLC 17**
See also CA 117

Renault, Mary -1983 .... **CLC 3, 11, 17**
See also Challans, Mary
See also DLBY 83; MTCW 2
Rendell, Ruth (Barbara) 1930- ...... **CLC 28,
48; DAM POP**
See also Vine, Barbara
See also CA 109; CANR 32, 52, 74; DLB
87; INT CANR-32; MTCW 1, 2
Renoir, Jean 1894-1979 .... **CLC 20**
See also CA 129; 85-88
Resnais, Alain 1922- .... **CLC 16**
Reverdy, Pierre 1889-1960 .... **CLC 53**
See also CA 97-100; 89-92
Rexroth, Kenneth 1905-1982 ... **CLC 1, 2, 6,
11, 22, 49, 112; DAM POET; PC 20**
See also CA 5-8R; 107; CANR 14, 34, 63;
CDALB 1941-1968; DLB 16, 48, 165,
212; DLBY 82; INT CANR-14; MTCW
1, 2
Reyes, Alfonso 1889-1959 . **TCLC 33; HLCS
2**
See also CA 131; HW 1
Reyes y Basoalto, Ricardo Eliecer Neftali
See Neruda, Pablo
Reymont, Wladyslaw (Stanislaw)
1868(?)-1925 .... **TCLC 5**
See also CA 104
Reynolds, Jonathan 1942- .... **CLC 6, 38**
See also CA 65-68; CANR 28
Reynolds, Joshua 1723-1792 .... **LC 15**
See also DLB 104
Reynolds, Michael S(hane) 1937- ... **CLC 44**
See also CA 65-68; CANR 9, 89
Reznikoff, Charles 1894-1976 .... **CLC 9**
See also CA 33-36; 61-64; CAP 2; DLB 28,
45
Rezzori (d'Arezzo), Gregor von 1914-1998
.... **CLC 25**
See also CA 122; 136; 167
Rhine, Richard
See Silverstein, Alvin
Rhodes, Eugene Manlove 1869-1934
.... **TCLC 53**
Rhodius, Apollonius c. 3rd cent. B.C.-
.... **CMLC 28**
See also DLB 176
R'hoone
See Balzac, Honore de
Rhys, Jean 1890(?)-1979 .... **CLC 2, 4, 6, 14,
19, 51, 124; DAM NOV; SSC 21**
See also CA 25-28R; 85-88; CANR 35, 62;
CDBLB 1945-1960; DA3; DLB 36, 117,
162; MTCW 1, 2
Ribeiro, Darcy 1922-1997 .... **CLC 34**
See also CA 33-36R; 156
Ribeiro, Joao Ubaldo (Osorio Pimentel)
1941- .... **CLC 10, 67**
See also CA 81-84
Ribman, Ronald (Burt) 1932- .... **CLC 7**
See also CA 21-24R; CANR 46, 80
Ricci, Nino 1959- .... **CLC 70**
See also CA 137
Rice, Anne 1941- . **CLC 41, 128; DAM POP**
See also AAYA 9; BEST 89:2; CA 65-68;
CANR 12, 36, 53, 74; DA3; MTCW 2
Rice, Elmer (Leopold) 1892-1967 .... **CLC 7,
49; DAM DRAM**
See also CA 21-22; 25-28R; CAP 2; DLB
4, 7; MTCW 1, 2
Rice, Tim(othy Miles Bindon) 1944-
.... **CLC 21**
See also CA 103; CANR 46
Rich, Adrienne (Cecile) 1929- .. **CLC 3, 6, 7,
11, 18, 36, 73, 76, 125; DAM POET; PC
5**
See also CA 9-12R; CANR 20, 53, 74;
CDALBS; DA3; DLB 5, 67; MTCW 1, 2
Rich, Barbara
See Graves, Robert (von Ranke)

Rich, Robert
See Trumbo, Dalton
Richard, Keith .... **CLC 17**
See also Richards, Keith
Richards, David Adams 1950- .... **CLC 59;
DAC**
See also CA 93-96; CANR 60; DLB 53
Richards, I(vor) A(rmstrong) 1893-1979
.... **CLC 14, 24**
See also CA 41-44R; 89-92; CANR 34, 74;
DLB 27; MTCW 2
Richards, Keith 1943-
See Richard, Keith
See also CA 107; CANR 77
Richardson, Anne
See Roiphe, Anne (Richardson)
Richardson, Dorothy Miller 1873-1957
.... **TCLC 3**
See also CA 104; DLB 36
Richardson, Ethel Florence (Lindesay)
1870-1946
See Richardson, Henry Handel
See also CA 105; DLB 230
Richardson, Henry Handel .... **TCLC 4**
See also Richardson, Ethel Florence
(Lindesay)
See also DLB 197
Richardson, John 1796-1852 .... **NCLC 55;
DAC**
See also DLB 99
Richardson, Samuel 1689-1761 .... **LC 1, 44;
DA; DAB; DAC; DAM MST, NOV;
WLC**
See also CDBLB 1660-1789; DLB 39
Richler, Mordecai 1931- ..... **CLC 3, 5, 9, 13,
18, 46, 70; DAC; DAM MST, NOV**
See also AITN 1; CA 65-68; CANR 31, 62;
CLR 17; DLB 53; MAICYA; MTCW 1,
2; SATA 44, 98; SATA-Brief 27
Richter, Conrad (Michael) 1890-1968
.... **CLC 30**
See also AAYA 21; CA 5-8R; 25-28R;
CANR 23; DLB 9, 212; MTCW 1, 2;
SATA 3
Ricostranza, Tom
See Ellis, Trey
Riddell, Charlotte 1832-1906 .... **TCLC 40**
See also CA 165; DLB 156
Ridge, John Rollin 1827-1867 ..... **NCLC 82;
DAM MULT**
See also CA 144; DLB 175; NNAL
Ridgway, Keith 1965- .... **CLC 119**
See also CA 172
Riding, Laura .... **CLC 3, 7**
See also Jackson, Laura (Riding)
Riefenstahl, Berta Helene Amalia 1902-
See Riefenstahl, Leni
See also CA 108
Riefenstahl, Leni .... **CLC 16**
See also Riefenstahl, Berta Helene Amalia
Riffe, Ernest
See Bergman, (Ernst) Ingmar
Riggs, (Rolla) Lynn 1899-1954 .... **TCLC 56;
DAM MULT**
See also CA 144; DLB 175; NNAL
Riis, Jacob A(ugust) 1849-1914 .... **TCLC 80**
See also CA 113; 168; DLB 23
Riley, James Whitcomb 1849-1916
.... **TCLC 51; DAM POET**
See also CA 118; 137; MAICYA; SATA 17
Riley, Tex
See Creasey, John
Rilke, Rainer Maria 1875-1926 . **TCLC 1, 6,
19; DAM POET; PC 2**
See also CA 104; 132; CANR 62; DA3;
DLB 81; MTCW 1, 2
Rimbaud, (Jean Nicolas) Arthur 1854-1891
.... **NCLC 4, 35, 82; DA; DAB; DAC;
DAM MST, POET; PC 3; WLC**

See also DA3

Rinehart, Mary Roberts 1876-1958
.... **TCLC 52**
See also CA 108; 166

Ringmaster, The
See Mencken, H(enry) L(ouis)

Ringwood, Gwen(dolyn Margaret) Pharis
1910-1984 .... **CLC 48**
See also CA 148; 112; DLB 88

Rio, Michel 19(?)- .... **CLC 43**

Ritsos, Giannes
See Ritsos, Yannis

Ritsos, Yannis 1909-1990 .... **CLC 6, 13, 31**
See also CA 77-80; 133; CANR 39, 61;
MTCW 1

Ritter, Erika 1948(?)- .... **CLC 52**

Rivera, Jose Eustasio 1889-1928 .. **TCLC 35**
See also CA 162; HW 1, 2

Rivera, Tomas 1935-1984
See also CA 49-52; CANR 32; DLB 82;
HLCS 2; HW 1

Rivers, Conrad Kent 1933-1968 .... **CLC 1**
See also BW 1; CA 85-88; DLB 41

Rivers, Elfrida
See Bradley, Marion Zimmer

Riverside, John
See Heinlein, Robert A(nson)

Rizal, Jose 1861-1896 .... **NCLC 27**

Roa Bastos, Augusto (Antonio) 1917-
.... **CLC 45; DAM MULT; HLC 2**
See also CA 131; DLB 113; HW 1

Robbe-Grillet, Alain 1922- ... **CLC 1, 2, 4, 6,**
8, 10, 14, 43, 128
See also CA 9-12R; CANR 33, 65; DLB
83; MTCW 1, 2

Robbins, Harold 1916-1997 ... **CLC 5; DAM**
NOV
See also CA 73-76; 162; CANR 26, 54;
DA3; MTCW 1, 2

Robbins, Thomas Eugene 1936-
See Robbins, Tom
See also CA 81-84; CANR 29, 59; DAM
NOV, POP; DA3; MTCW 1, 2

Robbins, Tom .... **CLC 9, 32, 64**
See also Robbins, Thomas Eugene
See also AAYA 32; BEST 90:3; DLBY 80;
MTCW 2

Robbins, Trina 1938- .... **CLC 21**
See also CA 128

Roberts, Charles G(eorge) D(ouglas)
1860-1943 .... **TCLC 8**
See also CA 105; CLR 33; DLB 92; SATA
88; SATA-Brief 29

Roberts, Elizabeth Madox 1886-1941
.... **TCLC 68**
See also CA 111; 166; DLB 9, 54, 102;
SATA 33; SATA-Brief 27

Roberts, Kate 1891-1985 .... **CLC 15**
See also CA 107; 116

Roberts, Keith (John Kingston) 1935-
.... **CLC 14**
See also CA 25-28R; CANR 46

Roberts, Kenneth (Lewis) 1885-1957
.... **TCLC 23**
See also CA 109; DLB 9

Roberts, Michele (B.) 1949- .... **CLC 48**
See also CA 115; CANR 58; DLB 231

Robertson, Ellis
See Ellison, Harlan (Jay); Silverberg, Robert

Robertson, Thomas William 1829-1871
.... **NCLC 35; DAM DRAM**

Robeson, Kenneth
See Dent, Lester

Robinson, Edwin Arlington 1869-1935
. **TCLC 5, 101; DA; DAC; DAM MST,**
POET; PC 1

See also CA 104; 133; CDALB 1865-1917;
DLB 54; MTCW 1, 2

Robinson, Henry Crabb 1775-1867
.... **NCLC 15**
See also DLB 107

Robinson, Jill 1936- .... **CLC 10**
See also CA 102; INT 102

Robinson, Kim Stanley 1952- .... **CLC 34**
See also AAYA 26; CA 126; SATA 109

Robinson, Lloyd
See Silverberg, Robert

Robinson, Marilynne 1944- .... **CLC 25**
See also CA 116; CANR 80; DLB 206

Robinson, Smokey .... **CLC 21**
See also Robinson, William, Jr.

Robinson, William, Jr. 1940-
See Robinson, Smokey
See also CA 116

Robison, Mary 1949- .... **CLC 42, 98**
See also CA 113; 116; CANR 87; DLB 130;
INT 116

Rod, Edouard 1857-1910 .... **TCLC 52**

Roddenberry, Eugene Wesley 1921-1991
See Roddenberry, Gene
See also CA 110; 135; CANR 37; SATA 45;
SATA-Obit 69

Roddenberry, Gene .... **CLC 17**
See also Roddenberry, Eugene Wesley
See also AAYA 5; SATA-Obit 69

Rodgers, Mary 1931- .... **CLC 12**
See also CA 49-52; CANR 8, 55, 90; CLR
20; INT CANR-8; JRDA; MAICYA;
SATA 8

Rodgers, W(illiam) R(obert) 1909-1969
.... **CLC 7**
See also CA 85-88; DLB 20

Rodman, Eric
See Silverberg, Robert

Rodman, Howard 1920(?)-1985 ...... **CLC 65**
See also CA 118

Rodman, Maia
See Wojciechowska, Maia (Teresa)

Rodo, Jose Enrique 1872(?)-1917
See also CA 178; HLCS 2; HW 2

Rodriguez, Claudio 1934- .... **CLC 10**
See also DLB 134

Rodriguez, Richard 1944-
See also CA 110; CANR 66; DAM MULT;
DLB 82; HLC 2; HW 1, 2

Roelvaag, O(le) E(dvart) 1876-1931
.... **TCLC 17**
See also Rolvaag, O(le) E(dvart)
See also CA 117; 171; DLB 9

Roethke, Theodore (Huebner) 1908-1963
...... **CLC 1, 3, 8, 11, 19, 46, 101; DAM**
POET; PC 15
See also CA 81-84; CABS 2; CDALB 1941-
1968; DA3; DLB 5, 206; MTCW 1, 2

Rogers, Samuel 1763-1855 .... **NCLC 69**
See also DLB 93

Rogers, Thomas Hunton 1927- .... **CLC 57**
See also CA 89-92; INT 89-92

Rogers, Will(iam Penn Adair) 1879-1935
.... **TCLC 8, 71; DAM MULT**
See also CA 105; 144; DA3; DLB 11;
MTCW 2; NNAL

Rogin, Gilbert 1929- .... **CLC 18**
See also CA 65-68; CANR 15

Rohan, Koda
See Koda Shigeyuki

Rohlfs, Anna Katharine Green
See Green, Anna Katharine

Rohmer, Eric .... **CLC 16**
See also Scherer, Jean-Marie Maurice

Rohmer, Sax .... **TCLC 28**
See also Ward, Arthur Henry Sarsfield
See also DLB 70

Roiphe, Anne (Richardson) 1935- . **CLC 3, 9**

See also CA 89-92; CANR 45, 73; DLBY
80; INT 89-92

Rojas, Fernando de 1465-1541 .... **LC 23;**
HLCS 1

Rojas, Gonzalo 1917-
See also HLCS 2; HW 2

Rojas, Gonzalo 1917-
See also CA 178; HLCS 2

Rolfe, Frederick (William Serafino Austin
Lewis Mary) 1860-1913 .... **TCLC 12**
See also CA 107; DLB 34, 156

Rolland, Romain 1866-1944 .... **TCLC 23**
See also CA 118; DLB 65

Rolle, Richard c. 1300-c. 1349 ..... **CMLC 21**
See also DLB 146

Rolvaag, O(le) E(dvart)
See Roelvaag, O(le) E(dvart)

Romain Arnaud, Saint
See Aragon, Louis

Romains, Jules 1885-1972 .... **CLC 7**
See also CA 85-88; CANR 34; DLB 65;
MTCW 1

Romero, Jose Ruben 1890-1952 ... **TCLC 14**
See also CA 114; 131; HW 1

Ronsard, Pierre de 1524-1585 ...... **LC 6, 54;**
PC 11

Rooke, Leon 1934- . **CLC 25, 34; DAM POP**
See also CA 25-28R; CANR 23, 53

Roosevelt, Franklin Delano 1882-1945
.... **TCLC 93**
See also CA 116; 173

Roosevelt, Theodore 1858-1919 .... **TCLC 69**
See also CA 115; 170; DLB 47, 186

Roper, William 1498-1578 .... **LC 10**

Roquelaure, A. N.
See Rice, Anne

Rosa, Joao Guimaraes 1908-1967 . **CLC 23;**
HLCS 1
See also CA 89-92; DLB 113

Rose, Wendy 1948- . **CLC 85; DAM MULT;**
PC 13
See also CA 53-56; CANR 5, 51; DLB 175;
NNAL; SATA 12

Rosen, R. D.
See Rosen, Richard (Dean)

Rosen, Richard (Dean) 1949- .... **CLC 39**
See also CA 77-80; CANR 62; INT
CANR-30

Rosenberg, Isaac 1890-1918 .... **TCLC 12**
See also CA 107; DLB 20

Rosenblatt, Joe .... **CLC 15**
See also Rosenblatt, Joseph

Rosenblatt, Joseph 1933-
See Rosenblatt, Joe
See also CA 89-92; INT 89-92

Rosenfeld, Samuel
See Tzara, Tristan

Rosenstock, Sami
See Tzara, Tristan

Rosenstock, Samuel
See Tzara, Tristan

Rosenthal, M(acha) L(ouis) 1917-1996
.... **CLC 28**
See also CA 1-4R; 152; CAAS 6; CANR 4,
51; DLB 5; SATA 59

Ross, Barnaby
See Dannay, Frederic

Ross, Bernard L.
See Follett, Ken(neth Martin)

Ross, J. H.
See Lawrence, T(homas) E(dward)

Ross, John Hume
See Lawrence, T(homas) E(dward)

Ross, Martin
See Martin, Violet Florence
See also DLB 135

Ross, (James) Sinclair 1908-1996 .. **CLC 13;**
DAC; DAM MST; SSC 24

See also CA 73-76; CANR 81; DLB 88

Rossetti, Christina (Georgina) 1830-1894 .... **NCLC 2, 50, 66; DA; DAB; DAC; DAM MST, POET; PC 7; WLC**
See also DA3; DLB 35, 163; MAICYA; SATA 20

Rossetti, Dante Gabriel 1828-1882 . **NCLC 4, 77; DA; DAB; DAC; DAM MST, POET; WLC**
See also CDBLB 1832-1890; DLB 35

Rossner, Judith (Perelman) 1935- .... **CLC 6, 9, 29**
See also AITN 2; BEST 90:3; CA 17-20R; CANR 18, 51, 73; DLB 6; INT CANR-18; MTCW 1, 2

Rostand, Edmond (Eugene Alexis) 1868-1918 ...... **TCLC 6, 37; DA; DAB; DAC; DAM DRAM, MST; DC 10**
See also CA 104; 126; DA3; DLB 192; MTCW 1

Roth, Henry 1906-1995 ... **CLC 2, 6, 11, 104**
See also CA 11-12; 149; CANR 38, 63; CAP 1; DA3; DLB 28; MTCW 1, 2

Roth, Philip (Milton) 1933- . **CLC 1, 2, 3, 4, 6, 9, 15, 22, 31, 47, 66, 86, 119; DA; DAB; DAC; DAM MST, NOV, POP; SSC 26; WLC**
See also BEST 90:3; CA 1-4R; CANR 1, 22, 36, 55, 89; CDALB 1968-1988; DA3; DLB 2, 28, 173; DLBY 82; MTCW 1, 2

Rothenberg, Jerome 1931- .... **CLC 6, 57**
See also CA 45-48; CANR 1; DLB 5, 193

Roumain, Jacques (Jean Baptiste) 1907-1944 .... **TCLC 19; BLC 3; DAM MULT**
See also BW 1; CA 117; 125

Rourke, Constance (Mayfield) 1885-1941 .... **TCLC 12**
See also CA 107; YABC 1

Rousseau, Jean-Baptiste 1671-1741 ..... **LC 9**

Rousseau, Jean-Jacques 1712-1778 . **LC 14, 36; DA; DAB; DAC; DAM MST; WLC**
See also DA3

Roussel, Raymond 1877-1933 .... **TCLC 20**
See also CA 117

Rovit, Earl (Herbert) 1927- .... **CLC 7**
See also CA 5-8R; CANR 12

Rowe, Elizabeth Singer 1674-1737 .... **LC 44**
See also DLB 39, 95

Rowe, Nicholas 1674-1718 .... **LC 8**
See also DLB 84

Rowley, Ames Dorrance
See Lovecraft, H(oward) P(hillips)

Rowling, J(oanne) K. 1966(?)- ...... **CLC 137**
See also AAYA 34; CA 173; CLR 66; SATA 109

Rowson, Susanna Haswell 1762(?)-1824 .... **NCLC 5, 69**
See also DLB 37, 200

Roy, Arundhati 1960(?)- .... **CLC 109**
See also CA 163; CANR 90; DLBY 97

Roy, Gabrielle 1909-1983 .... **CLC 10, 14; DAB; DAC; DAM MST**
See also CA 53-56; 110; CANR 5, 61; DLB 68; MTCW 1; SATA 104

Royko, Mike 1932-1997 .... **CLC 109**
See also CA 89-92; 157; CANR 26

Rozewicz, Tadeusz 1921- . **CLC 9, 23; DAM POET**
See also CA 108; CANR 36, 66; DA3; DLB 232; MTCW 1, 2

Ruark, Gibbons 1941- .... **CLC 3**
See also CA 33-36R; CAAS 23; CANR 14, 31, 57; DLB 120

Rubens, Bernice (Ruth) 1923- .. **CLC 19, 31**
See also CA 25-28R; CANR 33, 65; DLB 14, 207; MTCW 1

Rubin, Harold
See Robbins, Harold

Rudkin, (James) David 1936- .... **CLC 14**

See also CA 89-92; DLB 13

Rudnik, Raphael 1933- .... **CLC 7**
See also CA 29-32R

Ruffian, M.
See Hasek, Jaroslav (Matej Frantisek)

Ruiz, Jose Martinez .... **CLC 11**
See also Martinez Ruiz, Jose

Rukeyser, Muriel 1913-1980 . **CLC 6, 10, 15, 27; DAM POET; PC 12**
See also CA 5-8R; 93-96; CANR 26, 60; DA3; DLB 48; MTCW 1, 2; SATA-Obit 22

Rule, Jane (Vance) 1931- .... **CLC 27**
See also CA 25-28R; CAAS 18; CANR 12, 87; DLB 60

Rulfo, Juan 1918-1986 ..... **CLC 8, 80; DAM MULT; HLC 2; SSC 25**
See also CA 85-88; 118; CANR 26; DLB 113; HW 1, 2; MTCW 1, 2

Rumi, Jalal al-Din 1297-1373 ...... **CMLC 20**

Runeberg, Johan 1804-1877 .... **NCLC 41**

Runyon, (Alfred) Damon 1884(?)-1946 .... **TCLC 10**
See also CA 107; 165; DLB 11, 86, 171; MTCW 2

Rush, Norman 1933- .... **CLC 44**
See also CA 121; 126; INT 126

Rushdie, (Ahmed) Salman 1947- ... **CLC 23, 31, 55, 100; DAB; DAC; DAM MST, NOV, POP; WLCS**
See also BEST 89:3; CA 108; 111; CANR 33, 56; DA3; DLB 194; INT 111; MTCW 1, 2

Rushforth, Peter (Scott) 1945- .... **CLC 19**
See also CA 101

Ruskin, John 1819-1900 .... **TCLC 63**
See also CA 114; 129; CDBLB 1832-1890; DLB 55, 163, 190; SATA 24

Russ, Joanna 1937- .... **CLC 15**
See also CA 5-28R; CANR 11, 31, 65; DLB 8; MTCW 1

Russell, George William 1867-1935
See Baker, Jean H.
See also CA 104; 153; CDBLB 1890-1914; DAM POET

Russell, (Henry) Ken(neth Alfred) 1927- .... **CLC 16**
See also CA 105

Russell, William Martin 1947- .... **CLC 60**
See also CA 164; DLB 233

Rutherford, Mark .... **TCLC 25**
See also White, William Hale
See also DLB 18

Ruyslinck, Ward 1929- .... **CLC 14**
See also Belser, Reimond Karel Maria de

Ryan, Cornelius (John) 1920-1974 ... **CLC 7**
See also CA 69-72; 53-56; CANR 38

Ryan, Michael 1946- .... **CLC 65**
See also CA 49-52; DLBY 82

Ryan, Tim
See Dent, Lester

Rybakov, Anatoli (Naumovich) 1911-1998 .... **CLC 23, 53**
See also CA 126; 135; 172; SATA 79; SATA-Obit 108

Ryder, Jonathan
See Ludlum, Robert

Ryga, George 1932-1987 ...... **CLC 14; DAC; DAM MST**
See also CA 101; 124; CANR 43, 90; DLB 60

S. H.
See Hartmann, Sadakichi

S. S.
See Sassoon, Siegfried (Lorraine)

Saba, Umberto 1883-1957 .... **TCLC 33**
See also CA 144; CANR 79; DLB 114

Sabatini, Rafael 1875-1950 .... **TCLC 47**

See also CA 162

Sabato, Ernesto (R.) 1911- .... **CLC 10, 23; DAM MULT; HLC 2**
See also CA 97-100; CANR 32, 65; DLB 145; HW 1, 2; MTCW 1, 2

Sa-Carniero, Mario de 1890-1916 . **TCLC 83**

Sacastru, Martin
See Bioy Casares, Adolfo

Sacastru, Martin
See Bioy Casares, Adolfo

Sacher-Masoch, Leopold von 1836(?)-1895 .... **NCLC 31**

Sachs, Marilyn (Stickle) 1927- .... **CLC 35**
See also AAYA 2; CA 17-20R; CANR 13, 47; CLR 2; JRDA; MAICYA; SAAS 2; SATA 3, 68; SATA-Essay 110

Sachs, Nelly 1891-1970 .... **CLC 14, 98**
See also CA 17-18; 25-28R; CANR 87; CAP 2; MTCW 2

Sackler, Howard (Oliver) 1929-1982 .... **CLC 14**
See also CA 61-64; 108; CANR 30; DLB 7

Sacks, Oliver (Wolf) 1933- .... **CLC 67**
See also CA 53-56; CANR 28, 50, 76; DA3; INT CANR-28; MTCW 1, 2

Sadakichi
See Hartmann, Sadakichi

Sade, Donatien Alphonse Francois, Comte de 1740-1814 .... **NCLC 47**

Sadoff, Ira 1945- .... **CLC 9**
See also CA 53-56; CANR 5, 21; DLB 120

Saetone
See Camus, Albert

Safire, William 1929- .... **CLC 10**
See also CA 17-20R; CANR 31, 54, 91

Sagan, Carl (Edward) 1934-1996 .. **CLC 30, 112**
See also AAYA 2; CA 25-28R; 155; CANR 11, 36, 74; DA3; MTCW 1, 2; SATA 58; SATA-Obit 94

Sagan, Francoise .... **CLC 3, 6, 9, 17, 36**
See also Quoirez, Francoise
See also DLB 83; MTCW 2

Sahgal, Nayantara (Pandit) 1927- .. **CLC 41**
See also CA 9-12R; CANR 11, 88

Said, Edward W. 1935- .... **CLC 123**
See also CA 21-24R; CANR 45, 74; DLB 67; MTCW 2

Saint, H(arry) F. 1941- .... **CLC 50**
See also CA 127

St. Aubin de Teran, Lisa 1953-
See Teran, Lisa St. Aubin de
See also CA 118; 126; INT 126

Saint Birgitta of Sweden c. 1303-1373 .... **CMLC 24**

Sainte-Beuve, Charles Augustin 1804-1869 .... **NCLC 5**

Saint-Exupery, Antoine (Jean Baptiste Marie Roger) de 1900-1944 .. **TCLC 2, 56; DAM NOV; WLC**
See also CA 108; 132; CLR 10; DA3; DLB 72; MAICYA; MTCW 1, 2; SATA 20

St. John, David
See Hunt, E(verette) Howard, (Jr.)

Saint-John Perse
See Leger, (Marie-Rene Auguste) Alexis Saint-Leger

Saintsbury, George (Edward Bateman) 1845-1933 .... **TCLC 31**
See also CA 160; DLB 57, 149

Sait Faik .... **TCLC 23**
See also Abasiyanik, Sait Faik

Saki .... **TCLC 3; SSC 12**
See also Munro, H(ector) H(ugh)
See also MTCW 2

Sala, George Augustus .... **NCLC 46**

Saladin 1138-1193 .... **CMLC 38**

Salama, Hannu 1936- .... **CLC 18**

Salamanca, J(ack) R(ichard) 1922- . **CLC 4, 15**
 See also CA 25-28R

Salas, Floyd Francis 1931-
 See also CA 119; CAAS 27; CANR 44, 75, 93; DAM MULT; DLB 82; HLC 2; HW 1, 2; MTCW 2

Sale, J. Kirkpatrick
 See Sale, Kirkpatrick

Sale, Kirkpatrick 1937- .... **CLC 68**
 See also CA 13-16R; CANR 10

Salinas, Luis Omar 1937- .... **CLC 90; DAM MULT; HLC 2**
 See also CA 131; CANR 81; DLB 82; HW 1, 2

Salinas (y Serrano), Pedro 1891(?)-1951
 .... **TCLC 17**
 See also CA 117; DLB 134

Salinger, J(erome) D(avid) 1919- . **CLC 1, 3, 8, 12, 55, 56, 138; DA; DAB; DAC; DAM MST, NOV, POP; SSC 2, 28; WLC**
 See also AAYA 2; CA 5-8R; CANR 39; CDALB 1941-1968; CLR 18; DA3; DLB 2, 102, 173; MAICYA; MTCW 1, 2; SATA 67

Salisbury, John
 See Caute, (John) David

Salter, James 1925- .... **CLC 7, 52, 59**
 See also CA 73-76; DLB 130

Saltus, Edgar (Everton) 1855-1921 . **TCLC 8**
 See also CA 105; DLB 202

Saltykov, Mikhail Evgrafovich 1826-1889
 .... **NCLC 16**

Samarakis, Antonis 1919- .... **CLC 5**
 See also CA 25-28R; CAAS 16; CANR 36

Sanchez, Florencio 1875-1910 .... **TCLC 37**
 See also CA 153; HW 1

Sanchez, Luis Rafael 1936- .... **CLC 23**
 See also CA 128; DLB 145; HW 1

Sanchez, Sonia 1934- .. **CLC 5, 116; BLC 3; DAM MULT; PC 9**
 See also BW 2, 3; CA 33-36R; CANR 24, 49, 74; CLR 18; DA3; DLB 41; DLBD 8; MAICYA; MTCW 1, 2; SATA 22

Sand, George 1804-1876 ... **NCLC 2, 42, 57; DA; DAB; DAC; DAM MST, NOV; WLC**
 See also DA3; DLB 119, 192

Sandburg, Carl (August) 1878-1967 . **CLC 1, 4, 10, 15, 35; DA; DAB; DAC; DAM MST, POET; PC 2; WLC**
 See also AAYA 24; CA 5-8R; 25-28R; CANR 35; CDALB 1865-1917; CLR 67; DA3; DLB 17, 54; MAICYA; MTCW 1, 2; SATA 8

Sandburg, Charles
 See Sandburg, Carl (August)

Sandburg, Charles A.
 See Sandburg, Carl (August)

Sanders, (James) Ed(ward) 1939- . **CLC 53; DAM POET**
 See also CA 13-16R; CAAS 21; CANR 13, 44, 78; DLB 16

Sanders, Lawrence 1920-1998 .... **CLC 41; DAM POP**
 See also BEST 89:4; CA 81-84; 165; CANR 33, 62; DA3; MTCW 1

Sanders, Noah
 See Blount, Roy (Alton), Jr.

Sanders, Winston P.
 See Anderson, Poul (William)

Sandoz, Mari(e Susette) 1896-1966 . **CLC 28**
 See also CA 1-4R; 25-28R; CANR 17, 64; DLB 9, 212; MTCW 1, 2; SATA 5

Saner, Reg(inald Anthony) 1931- ...... **CLC 9**
 See also CA 65-68

Sankara 788-820 .... **CMLC 32**

Sannazaro, Jacopo 1456(?)-1530 .... **LC 8**

Sansom, William 1912-1976 .... **CLC 2, 6; DAM NOV; SSC 21**
 See also CA 5-8R; 65-68; CANR 42; DLB 139; MTCW 1

Santayana, George 1863-1952 ...... **TCLC 40**
 See also CA 115; DLB 54, 71; DLBD 13

Santiago, Danny .... **CLC 33**
 See James, Daniel (Lewis)
 See also DLB 122

Santmyer, Helen Hoover 1895-1986 . **CLC 33**
 See also CA 1-4R; 118; CANR 15, 33; DLBY 84; MTCW 1

Santoka, Taneda 1882-1940 .... **TCLC 72**

Santos, Bienvenido N(uqui) 1911-1996
 .... **CLC 22; DAM MULT**
 See also CA 101; 151; CANR 19, 46

Sapper .... **TCLC 44**
 See also McNeile, Herman Cyril

Sapphire
 See Sapphire, Brenda

Sapphire, Brenda 1950- .... **CLC 99**

Sappho fl. 6th cent. B.C.- .... **CMLC 3; DAM POET; PC 5**
 See also DA3; DLB 176

Saramago, Jose 1922- .... **CLC 119; HLCS 1**
 See also CA 153

Sarduy, Severo 1937-1993 .... **CLC 6, 97; HLCS 1**
 See also CA 89-92; 142; CANR 58, 81; DLB 113; HW 1, 2

Sargeson, Frank 1903-1982 .... **CLC 31**
 See also CA 25-28R; 106; CANR 38, 79

Sarmiento, Domingo Faustino 1811-1888
 See also HLCS 2

Sarmiento, Felix Ruben Garcia
 See Dario, Ruben

Saro-Wiwa, Ken(ule Beeson) 1941-1995
 .... **CLC 114**
 See also BW 2; CA 142; 150; CANR 60; DLB 157

Saroyan, William 1908-1981 .. **CLC 1, 8, 10, 29, 34, 56; DA; DAB; DAC; DAM DRAM, MST, NOV; SSC 21; WLC**
 See also CA 5-8R; 103; CANR 30; CDALBS; DA3; DLB 7, 9, 86; DLBY 81; MTCW 1, 2; SATA 23; SATA-Obit 24

Sarraute, Nathalie 1900-1999 .. **CLC 1, 2, 4, 8, 10, 31, 80**
 See also CA 9-12R; 187; CANR 23, 66; DLB 83; MTCW 1, 2

Sarton, (Eleanor) May 1912-1995 .... **CLC 4, 14, 49, 91; DAM POET**
 See also CA 1-4R; 149; CANR 1, 34, 55; DLB 48; DLBY 81; INT CANR-34; MTCW 1, 2; SATA 36; SATA-Obit 86

Sartre, Jean-Paul 1905-1980 .... **CLC 1, 4, 7, 9, 13, 18, 24, 44, 50, 52; DA; DAB; DAC; DAM DRAM, MST, NOV; DC 3; SSC 32; WLC**
 See also CA 9-12R; 97-100; CANR 21; DA3; DLB 72; MTCW 1, 2

Sassoon, Siegfried (Lorraine) 1886-1967
 . **CLC 36, 130; DAB; DAM MST, NOV, POET; PC 12**
 See also CA 104; 25-28R; CANR 36; DLB 20, 191; DLBD 18; MTCW 1, 2

Satterfield, Charles
 See Pohl, Frederik

Satyremont
 See Peret, Benjamin

Saul, John (W. III) 1942- ..... **CLC 46; DAM NOV, POP**
 See also AAYA 10; BEST 90:4; CA 81-84; CANR 16, 40, 81; SATA 98

Saunders, Caleb
 See Heinlein, Robert A(nson)

Saura (Atares), Carlos 1932- .... **CLC 20**
 See also CA 114; 131; CANR 79; HW 1

Sauser-Hall, Frederic 1887-1961 ..... **CLC 18**

 See also Cendrars, Blaise
 See also CA 102; 93-96; CANR 36, 62; MTCW 1

Saussure, Ferdinand de 1857-1913
 .... **TCLC 49**

Savage, Catharine
 See Brosman, Catharine Savage

Savage, Thomas 1915- .... **CLC 40**
 See also CA 126; 132; CAAS 15; INT 132

Savan, Glenn 19(?)- .... **CLC 50**

Sayers, Dorothy L(eigh) 1893-1957
 .... **TCLC 2, 15; DAM POP**
 See also CA 104; 119; CANR 60; CDBLB 1914-1945; DLB 10, 36, 77, 100; MTCW 1, 2

Sayers, Valerie 1952- .... **CLC 50, 122**
 See also CA 134; CANR 61

Sayles, John (Thomas) 1950- . **CLC 7, 10, 14**
 See also CA 57-60; CANR 41, 84; DLB 44

Scammell, Michael 1935- .... **CLC 34**
 See also CA 156

Scannell, Vernon 1922- .... **CLC 49**
 See also CA 5-8R; CANR 8, 24, 57; DLB 27; SATA 59

Scarlett, Susan
 See Streatfeild, (Mary) Noel

Scarron
 See Mikszath, Kalman

Schaeffer, Susan Fromberg 1941- .... **CLC 6, 11, 22**
 See also CA 49-52; CANR 18, 65; DLB 28; MTCW 1, 2; SATA 22

Schary, Jill
 See Robinson, Jill

Schell, Jonathan 1943- .... **CLC 35**
 See also CA 73-76; CANR 12

Schelling, Friedrich Wilhelm Joseph von 1775-1854 .... **NCLC 30**
 See also DLB 90

Schendel, Arthur van 1874-1946 .. **TCLC 56**

Scherer, Jean-Marie Maurice 1920-
 See Rohmer, Eric
 See also CA 110

Schevill, James (Erwin) 1920- .... **CLC 7**
 See also CA 5-8R; CAAS 12

Schiller, Friedrich 1759-1805 . **NCLC 39, 69; DAM DRAM; DC 12**
 See also DLB 94

Schisgal, Murray (Joseph) 1926- ...... **CLC 6**
 See also CA 21-24R; CANR 48, 86

Schlee, Ann 1934- .... **CLC 35**
 See also CA 101; CANR 29, 88; SATA 44; SATA-Brief 36

Schlegel, August Wilhelm von 1767-1845
 .... **NCLC 15**
 See also DLB 94

Schlegel, Friedrich 1772-1829 ...... **NCLC 45**
 See also DLB 90

Schlegel, Johann Elias (von) 1719(?)-1749
 .... **LC 5**

Schlesinger, Arthur M(eier), Jr. 1917-
 .... **CLC 84**
 See also AITN 1; CA 1-4R; CANR 1, 28, 58; DLB 17; INT CANR-28; MTCW 1, 2; SATA 61

Schmidt, Arno (Otto) 1914-1979 ..... **CLC 56**
 See also CA 128; 109; DLB 69

Schmitz, Aron Hector 1861-1928
 See Svevo, Italo
 See also CA 104; 122; MTCW 1

Schnackenberg, Gjertrud 1953- ...... **CLC 40**
 See also CA 116; DLB 120

Schneider, Leonard Alfred 1925-1966
 See Bruce, Lenny
 See also CA 89-92

Schnitzler, Arthur 1862-1931 . **TCLC 4; SSC 15**
 See also CA 104; DLB 81, 118

37, 60; DAB; DAM DRAM, MST; DC 7
See also CA 25-28R; CANR 25, 47, 74;
CDBLB 1960 to Present; DA3; DLB 13,
233; MTCW 1, 2

Shakey, Bernard
See Young, Neil

Shalamov, Varlam (Tikhonovich)
1907(?)-1982 .... **CLC 18**
See also CA 129; 105

Shamlu, Ahmad 1925- .... **CLC 10**

Shammas, Anton 1951- .... **CLC 55**

Shandling, Arline
See Berriault, Gina

Shange, Ntozake 1948- ... **CLC 8, 25, 38, 74,**
126; BLC 3; DAM DRAM, MULT; DC
3
See also AAYA 9; BW 2; CA 85-88; CABS
3; CANR 27, 48, 74; DA3; DLB 38;
MTCW 1, 2

Shanley, John Patrick 1950- .... **CLC 75**
See also CA 128; 133; CANR 83

Shapcott, Thomas W(illiam) 1935- . **CLC 38**
See also CA 69-72; CANR 49, 83

Shapiro, Jane .... **CLC 76**

Shapiro, Karl (Jay) 1913- . **CLC 4, 8, 15, 53;**
PC 25
See also CA 1-4R; CAAS 6; CANR 1, 36,
66; DLB 48; MTCW 1, 2

Sharp, William 1855-1905 .... **TCLC 39**
See also CA 160; DLB 156

Sharpe, Thomas Ridley 1928-
See Sharpe, Tom
See also CA 114; 122; CANR 85; DLB 231;
INT 122

Sharpe, Tom .... **CLC 36**
See Sharpe, Thomas Ridley
See also DLB 14

Shaw, Bernard
See Shaw, George Bernard
See also BW 1; MTCW 2

Shaw, G. Bernard
See Shaw, George Bernard

Shaw, George Bernard 1856-1950 . **TCLC 3,**
9, 21, 45; DA; DAB; DAC; DAM
DRAM, MST; WLC
See also Shaw, Bernard
See also CA 104; 128; CDBLB 1914-1945;
DA3; DLB 10, 57, 190; MTCW 1, 2

Shaw, Henry Wheeler 1818-1885 . **NCLC 15**
See also DLB 11

Shaw, Irwin 1913-1984 .... **CLC 7, 23, 34;**
DAM DRAM, POP
See also AITN 1; CA 13-16R; 112; CANR
21; CDALB 1941-1968; DLB 6, 102;
DLBY 84; MTCW 1, 21

Shaw, Robert 1927-1978 .... **CLC 5**
See also AITN 1; CA 1-4R; 81-84; CANR
4; DLB 13, 14

Shaw, T. E.
See Lawrence, T(homas) E(dward)

Shawn, Wallace 1943- .... **CLC 41**
See also CA 112

Shea, Lisa 1953- .... **CLC 86**
See also CA 147

Sheed, Wilfrid (John Joseph) 1930- . **CLC 2,**
4, 10, 53
See also CA 65-68; CANR 30, 66; DLB 6;
MTCW 1, 2

Sheldon, Alice Hastings Bradley
1915(?)-1987
See Tiptree, James, Jr.
See also CA 108; 122; CANR 34; INT 108;
MTCW 1

Sheldon, John
See Bloch, Robert (Albert)

Sheldon, Walter J. 1917-
See Queen, Ellery
See also AITN 1; CA 25-28R; CANR 10

Shelley, Mary Wollstonecraft (Godwin)
1797-1851 .... **NCLC 14, 59; DA; DAB;**
DAC; DAM MST, NOV; WLC
See also AAYA 20; CDBLB 1789-1832;
DA3; DLB 110, 116, 159, 178; SATA 29

Shelley, Percy Bysshe 1792-1822 . **NCLC 18,**
93; DA; DAB; DAC; DAM MST,
POET; PC 14; WLC
See also CDBLB 1789-1832; DA3; DLB
96, 110, 158

Shepard, Jim 1956- .... **CLC 36**
See also CA 137; CANR 59; SATA 90

Shepard, Lucius 1947- .... **CLC 34**
See also CA 128; 141; CANR 81

Shepard, Sam 1943- ... **CLC 4, 6, 17, 34, 41,**
44; DAM DRAM; DC 5
See also AAYA 1; CA 69-72; CABS 3;
CANR 22; DA3; DLB 7, 212; MTCW 1,
2

Shepherd, Michael
See Ludlum, Robert

Sherburne, Zoa (Lillian Morin) 1912-1995
.... **CLC 30**
See also AAYA 13; CA 1-4R; 176; CANR
3, 37; MAICYA; SAAS 18; SATA 3

Sheridan, Frances 1724-1766 .... **LC 7**
See also DLB 39, 84

Sheridan, Richard Brinsley 1751-1816
.. **NCLC 5, 91; DA; DAB; DAC; DAM**
DRAM, MST; DC 1; WLC
See also CDBLB 1660-1789; DLB 89

Sherman, Jonathan Marc .... **CLC 55**

Sherman, Martin 1941(?)- .... **CLC 19**
See also CA 116; 123; CANR 86

Sherwin, Judith Johnson 1936-
See Johnson, Judith (Emlyn)
See also CANR 85

Sherwood, Frances 1940- .... **CLC 81**
See also CA 146

Sherwood, Robert E(mmet) 1896-1955
.... **TCLC 3; DAM DRAM**
See also CA 104; 153; CANR 86; DLB 7,
26

Shestov, Lev 1866-1938 .... **TCLC 56**

Shevchenko, Taras 1814-1861 .... **NCLC 54**

Shiel, M(atthew) P(hipps) 1865-1947
.... **TCLC 8**
See also Holmes, Gordon
See also CA 106; 160; DLB 153; MTCW 2

Shields, Carol 1935- ...... **CLC 91, 113; DAC**
See also CA 81-84; CANR 51, 74; DA3;
MTCW 2

Shields, David 1956- .... **CLC 97**
See also CA 124; CANR 48

Shiga, Naoya 1883-1971 .... **CLC 33; SSC 23**
See also CA 101; 33-36R; DLB 180

Shikibu, Murasaki c. 978-c. 1014 . **CMLC 1**

Shilts, Randy 1951-1994 .... **CLC 85**
See also AAYA 19; CA 115; 127; 144;
CANR 45; DA3; INT 127; MTCW 2

Shimazaki, Haruki 1872-1943
See Shimazaki Toson
See also CA 105; 134; CANR 84

Shimazaki Toson 1872-1943 .... **TCLC 5**
See also Shimazaki, Haruki
See also DLB 180

Sholokhov, Mikhail (Aleksandrovich)
1905-1984 .... **CLC 7, 15**
See also CA 101; 112; MTCW 1, 2; SATA-
Obit 36

Shone, Patric
See Hanley, James

Shreve, Susan Richards 1939- .... **CLC 23**
See also CA 49-52; CAAS 5; CANR 5, 38,
69; MAICYA; SATA 46, 95; SATA-Brief
41

Shue, Larry 1946-1985 .... **CLC 52; DAM**
DRAM
See also CA 145; 117

Shu-Jen, Chou 1881-1936
See Lu Hsun
See also CA 104

Shulman, Alix Kates 1932- .... **CLC 2, 10**
See also CA 29-32R; CANR 43; SATA 7

Shuster, Joe 1914- .... **CLC 21**

Shute, Nevil .... **CLC 30**
See also Norway, Nevil Shute
See also MTCW 2

Shuttle, Penelope (Diane) 1947- .... **CLC 7**
See also CA 93-96; CANR 39, 84, 92; DLB
14, 40

Sidney, Mary 1561-1621 .... **LC 19, 39**

Sidney, SirPhilip 1554-1586 . **LC 19, 39; DA;**
DAB; DAC; DAM MST, POET; PC 32
See also CDBLB Before 1660; DA3; DLB
167

Siegel, Jerome 1914-1996 .... **CLC 21**
See also CA 116; 169; 151

Siegel, Jerry
See Siegel, Jerome

Sienkiewicz, Henryk (Adam Alexander Pius)
1846-1916 .... **TCLC 3**
See also CA 104; 134; CANR 84

Sierra, Gregorio Martinez
See Martinez Sierra, Gregorio

Sierra, Maria (de la O'LeJarraga) Martinez
See Martinez Sierra, Maria (de la
O'LeJarraga)

Sigal, Clancy 1926- .... **CLC 7**
See also CA 1-4R; CANR 85

Sigourney, Lydia Howard (Huntley)
1791-1865 .... **NCLC 21, 87**
See also DLB 1, 42, 73

Siguenza y Gongora, Carlos de 1645-1700
.... **LC 8; HLCS 2**

Sigurjonsson, Johann 1880-1919 .. **TCLC 27**
See also CA 170

Sikelianos, Angelos 1884-1951 ..... **TCLC 39;**
PC 29

Silkin, Jon 1930- .... **CLC 2, 6, 43**
See also CA 5-8R; CAAS 5; CANR 89;
DLB 27

Silko, Leslie (Marmon) 1948- .. **CLC 23, 74,**
114; DA; DAC; DAM MST, MULT,
POP; SSC 37; WLCS
See also AAYA 14; CA 115; 122; CANR
45, 65; DA3; DLB 143, 175; MTCW 2;
NNAL

Sillanpaa, Frans Eemil 1888-1964 .. **CLC 19**
See also CA 129; 93-96; MTCW 1

Sillitoe, Alan 1928- .. **CLC 1, 3, 6, 10, 19, 57**
See also AITN 1; CA 9-12R; CAAS 2;
CANR 8, 26, 55; CDBLB 1960 to Present;
DLB 14, 139; MTCW 1, 2; SATA 61

Silone, Ignazio 1900-1978 .... **CLC 4**
See also CA 25-28; 81-84; CANR 34; CAP
2; MTCW 1

Silver, Joan Micklin 1935- .... **CLC 20**
See also CA 114; 121; INT 121

Silver, Nicholas
See Faust, Frederick (Schiller)

Silverberg, Robert 1935- .... **CLC 7; DAM**
POP
See also AAYA 24; CA 1-4R; 186; CAAE
186; CAAS 3; CANR 1, 20, 36, 85; CLR
59; DLB 8; INT CANR-20; MAICYA;
MTCW 1, 2; SATA 13, 91; SATA-Essay
104

Silverstein, Alvin 1933- .... **CLC 17**
See also CA 49-52; CANR 2; CLR 25;
JRDA; MAICYA; SATA 8, 69

Silverstein, Virginia B(arbara Opshelor)
1937- .... **CLC 17**
See also CA 49-52; CANR 2; CLR 25;
JRDA; MAICYA; SATA 8, 69

See also Queen, Ellery
See also CA 81-84; 116; CANR 32; DLB 8;
DLBY 85; MTCW 1, 2
Sturges, Preston 1898-1959 .... **TCLC 48**
See also CA 114; 149; DLB 26
Styron, William 1925- .. **CLC 1, 3, 5, 11, 15,
60; DAM NOV, POP; SSC 25**
See also BEST 90:4; CA 5-8R; CANR 6,
33, 74; CDALB 1968-1988; DA3; DLB
2, 143; DLBY 80; INT CANR-6; MTCW
1, 2
Su, Chien 1884-1918
See Su Man-shu
See also CA 123
Suarez Lynch, B.
See Bioy Casares, Adolfo; Borges, Jorge
Luis
Suassuna, Ariano Vilar 1927-
See also CA 178; HLCS 1; HW 2
Suckling, John 1609-1641 .... **PC 30**
See also DAM POET; DLB 58, 126
Suckow, Ruth 1892-1960 .... **SSC 18**
See also CA 113; DLB 9, 102
Sudermann, Hermann 1857-1928 . **TCLC 15**
See also CA 107; DLB 118
Sue, Eugene 1804-1857 .... **NCLC 1**
See also DLB 119
Sueskind, Patrick 1949- .... **CLC 44**
See also Suskind, Patrick
Sukenick, Ronald 1932- ...... **CLC 3, 4, 6, 48**
See also CA 25-28R; CAAS 8; CANR 32,
89; DLB 173; DLBY 81
Suknaski, Andrew 1942- .... **CLC 19**
See also CA 101; DLB 53
Sullivan, Vernon
See Vian, Boris
Sully Prudhomme 1839-1907 .... **TCLC 31**
Su Man-shu .... **TCLC 24**
See also Su, Chien
Summerforest, Ivy B.
See Kirkup, James
Summers, Andrew James 1942- ...... **CLC 26**
Summers, Andy
See Summers, Andrew James
Summers, Hollis (Spurgeon, Jr.) 1916-
.... **CLC 10**
See also CA 5-8R; CANR 3; DLB 6
**Summers, (Alphonsus Joseph-Mary
Augustus) Montague** 1880-1948
.... **TCLC 16**
See also CA 118; 163
Sumner, Gordon Matthew .... **CLC 26**
See also Sting
Surtees, Robert Smith 1803-1864 . **NCLC 14**
See also DLB 21
Susann, Jacqueline 1921-1974 .... **CLC 3**
See also AITN 1; CA 65-68; 53-56; MTCW
1, 2
Su Shih 1036-1101 .... **CMLC 15**
Suskind, Patrick
See Sueskind, Patrick
See also CA 145
Sutcliff, Rosemary 1920-1992 .... **CLC 26;
DAB; DAC; DAM MST, POP**
See also AAYA 10; CA 5-8R; 139; CANR
37; CLR 1, 37; JRDA; MAICYA; SATA
6, 44, 78; SATA-Obit 73
Sutro, Alfred 1863-1933 .... **TCLC 6**
See also CA 105; 185; DLB 10
Sutton, Henry
See Slavitt, David R(ytman)
Svevo, Italo 1861-1928 .... **TCLC 2, 35; SSC
25**
See also Schmitz, Aron Hector
Swados, Elizabeth (A.) 1951- .... **CLC 12**
See also CA 97-100; CANR 49; INT 97-
100
Swados, Harvey 1920-1972 .... **CLC 5**

See also CA 5-8R; 37-40R; CANR 6; DLB
2
Swan, Gladys 1934- .... **CLC 69**
See also CA 101; CANR 17, 39
Swanson, Logan
See Matheson, Richard Burton
Swarthout, Glendon (Fred) 1918-1992
.... **CLC 35**
See also CA 1-4R; 139; CANR 1, 47; SATA
26
Sweet, Sarah C.
See Jewett, (Theodora) Sarah Orne
Swenson, May 1919-1989 ..... **CLC 4, 14, 61,
106; DA; DAB; DAC; DAM MST,
POET; PC 14**
See also CA 5-8R; 130; CANR 36, 61; DLB
5; MTCW 1, 2; SATA 15
Swift, Augustus
See Lovecraft, H(oward) P(hillips)
Swift, Graham (Colin) 1949- .... **CLC 41, 88**
See also CA 117; 122; CANR 46, 71; DLB
194; MTCW 1
Swift, Jonathan 1667-1745 ... **LC 1, 42; DA;
DAB; DAC; DAM MST, NOV, POET;
PC 9; WLC**
See also CDBLB 1660-1789; CLR 53;
DA3; DLB 39, 95, 101; SATA 19
Swinburne, Algernon Charles 1837-1909
... **TCLC 8, 36; DA; DAB; DAC; DAM
MST, POET; PC 24; WLC**
See also CA 105; 140; CDBLB 1832-1890;
DA3; DLB 35, 57
Swinfen, Ann .... **CLC 34**
Swinnerton, Frank Arthur 1884-1982
.... **CLC 31**
See also CA 108; DLB 34
Swithen, John
See King, Stephen (Edwin)
Sylvia
See Ashton-Warner, Sylvia (Constance)
Symmes, Robert Edward
See Duncan, Robert (Edward)
Symonds, John Addington 1840-1893
.... **NCLC 34**
See also DLB 57, 144
Symons, Arthur 1865-1945 .... **TCLC 11**
See also CA 107; DLB 19, 57, 149
Symons, Julian (Gustave) 1912-1994
.... **CLC 2, 14, 32**
See also CA 49-52; 147; CAAS 3; CANR
3, 33, 59; DLB 87, 155; DLBY 92;
MTCW 1
Synge, (Edmund) J(ohn) M(illington)
1871-1909 . **TCLC 6, 37; DAM DRAM;
DC 2**
See also CA 104; 141; CDBLB 1890-1914;
DLB 10, 19
Syruc, J.
See Milosz, Czeslaw
Szirtes, George 1948- .... **CLC 46**
See also CA 109; CANR 27, 61
Szymborska, Wislawa 1923- .... **CLC 99**
See also CA 154; CANR 91; DA3; DLB
232; DLBY 96; MTCW 2
T. O., Nik
See Annensky, Innokenty (Fyodorovich)
Tabori, George 1914- .... **CLC 19**
See also CA 49-52; CANR 4, 69
Tagore, Rabindranath 1861-1941 .. **TCLC 3,
53; DAM DRAM, POET; PC 8**
See also CA 104; 120; DA3; MTCW 1, 2
Taine, Hippolyte Adolphe 1828-1893
.... **NCLC 15**
Talese, Gay 1932- .... **CLC 37**
See also AITN 1; CA 1-4R; CANR 9, 58;
DLB 185; INT CANR-9; MTCW 1, 2
Tallent, Elizabeth (Ann) 1954- .... **CLC 45**
See also CA 117; CANR 72; DLB 130
Tally, Ted 1952- .... **CLC 42**

See also CA 120; 124; INT 124
Talvik, Heiti 1904-1947 .... **TCLC 87**
Tamayo y Baus, Manuel 1829-1898 . **NCLC 1**
Tammsaare, A(nton) H(ansen) 1878-1940
.... **TCLC 27**
See also CA 164; DLB 220
Tam'si, Tchicaya U
See Tchicaya, Gerald Felix
Tan, Amy (Ruth) 1952- . **CLC 59, 120; DAM
MULT, NOV, POP**
See also AAYA 9; BEST 89:3; CA 136;
CANR 54; CDALBS; DA3; DLB 173;
MTCW 2; SATA 75
Tandem, Felix
See Spitteler, Carl (Friedrich Georg)
Tanizaki, Jun'ichiro 1886-1965 .. **CLC 8, 14,
28; SSC 21**
See also CA 93-96; 25-28R; DLB 180;
MTCW 2
Tanner, William
See Amis, Kingsley (William)
Tao Lao
See Storni, Alfonsina
Tarantino, Quentin (Jerome) 1963-
.... **CLC 125**
See also CA 171
Tarassoff, Lev
See Troyat, Henri
Tarbell, Ida M(inerva) 1857-1944 . **TCLC 40**
See also CA 122; 181; DLB 47
Tarkington, (Newton) Booth 1869-1946
.... **TCLC 9**
See also CA 110; 143; DLB 9, 102; MTCW
2; SATA 17
Tarkovsky, Andrei (Arsenyevich) 1932-1986
.... **CLC 75**
See also CA 127
Tartt, Donna 1964(?)- .... **CLC 76**
See also CA 142
Tasso, Torquato 1544-1595 .... **LC 5**
Tate, (John Orley) Allen 1899-1979 . **CLC 2,
4, 6, 9, 11, 14, 24**
See also CA 5-8R; 85-88; CANR 32; DLB
4, 45, 63; DLBD 17; MTCW 1, 2
Tate, Ellalice
See Hibbert, Eleanor Alice Burford
Tate, James (Vincent) 1943- .... **CLC 2, 6, 25**
See also CA 21-24R; CANR 29, 57; DLB
5, 169
Tauler, Johannes c. 1300-1361 ..... **CMLC 37**
See also DLB 179
Tavel, Ronald 1940- .... **CLC 6**
See also CA 21-24R; CANR 33
Taylor, Bayard 1825-1878 .... **NCLC 89**
See also DLB 3, 189
Taylor, C(ecil) P(hilip) 1929-1981 ... **CLC 27**
See also CA 25-28R; 105; CANR 47
Taylor, Edward 1642(?)-1729 .... **LC 11; DA;
DAB; DAC; DAM MST, POET**
See also DLB 24
Taylor, Eleanor Ross 1920- .... **CLC 5**
See also CA 81-84; CANR 70
Taylor, Elizabeth 1912-1975 .... **CLC 2, 4, 29**
See also CA 13-16R; CANR 9, 70; DLB
139; MTCW 1; SATA 13
Taylor, Frederick Winslow 1856-1915
.... **TCLC 76**
Taylor, Henry (Splawn) 1942- .... **CLC 44**
See also CA 33-36R; CAAS 7; CANR 31;
DLB 5
Taylor, Kamala (Purnaiya) 1924-
See Markandaya, Kamala
See also CA 77-80
Taylor, Mildred D. .... **CLC 21**
See also AAYA 10; BW 1; CA 85-88;
CANR 25; CLR 9, 59; DLB 52; JRDA;
MAICYA; SAAS 5; SATA 15, 70
Taylor, Peter (Hillsman) 1917-1994 . **CLC 1,**

See also BW 1, 3; CA 124; 89-92; CANR 80; DLB 48, 76

Tolstoi, Aleksei Nikolaevich
See Tolstoy, Alexey Nikolaevich

Tolstoy, Alexey Nikolaevich 1882-1945 .... **TCLC 18**
See also CA 107; 158

Tolstoy, Count Leo
See Tolstoy, Leo (Nikolaevich)

Tolstoy, Leo (Nikolaevich) 1828-1910 . **TCLC 4, 11, 17, 28, 44, 79; DA; DAB; DAC; DAM MST, NOV; SSC 9, 30; WLC**
See also CA 104; 123; DA3; SATA 26

Tomasi di Lampedusa, Giuseppe 1896-1957
See Lampedusa, Giuseppe (Tomasi) di
See also CA 111

Tomlin, Lily .... **CLC 17**
See also Tomlin, Mary Jean

Tomlin, Mary Jean 1939(?)-
See Tomlin, Lily
See also CA 117

Tomlinson, (Alfred) Charles 1927- .. **CLC 2, 4, 6, 13, 45; DAM POET; PC 17**
See also CA 5-8R; CANR 33; DLB 40

Tomlinson, H(enry) M(ajor) 1873-1958 .... **TCLC 71**
See also CA 118; 161; DLB 36, 100, 195

Tonson, Jacob
See Bennett, (Enoch) Arnold

Toole, John Kennedy 1937-1969 .... **CLC 19, 64**
See also CA 104; DLBY 81; MTCW 2

Toomer, Jean 1894-1967 .. **CLC 1, 4, 13, 22; BLC 3; DAM MULT; PC 7; SSC 1; WLCS**
See also Pinchback, Eugene; Toomer, Eugene; Toomer, Eugene Pinchback; Toomer, Nathan Jean; Toomer, Nathan Pinchback
See also BW 1; CA 85-88; CDALB 1917-1929; DA3; DLB 45, 51; MTCW 1, 2

Torley, Luke
See Blish, James (Benjamin)

Tornimparte, Alessandra
See Ginzburg, Natalia

Torre, Raoul della
See Mencken, H(enry) L(ouis)

Torrence, Ridgely 1874-1950 .... **TCLC 97**
See also DLB 54

Torrey, E(dwin) Fuller 1937- .... **CLC 34**
See also CA 119; CANR 71

Torsvan, Ben Traven
See Traven, B.

Torsvan, Benno Traven
See Traven, B.

Torsvan, Berick Traven
See Traven, B.

Torsvan, Berwick Traven
See Traven, B.

Torsvan, Bruno Traven
See Traven, B.

Torsvan, Traven
See Traven, B.

Tournier, Michel (Edouard) 1924- ... **CLC 6, 23, 36, 95**
See also CA 49-52; CANR 3, 36, 74; DLB 83; MTCW 1, 2; SATA 23

Tournimparte, Alessandra
See Ginzburg, Natalia

Towers, Ivar
See Kornbluth, C(yril) M.

Towne, Robert (Burton) 1936(?)- .... **CLC 87**
See also CA 108; DLB 44

Townsend, Sue .... **CLC 61**
See also Townsend, Susan Elaine
See also AAYA 28; SATA 55, 93; SATA-Brief 48

Townsend, Susan Elaine 1946-
See Townsend, Sue
See also CA 119; 127; CANR 65; DAB; DAC; DAM MST; INT 127

Townshend, Peter (Dennis Blandford) 1945- .... **CLC 17, 42**
See also CA 107

Tozzi, Federigo 1883-1920 .... **TCLC 31**
See also CA 160

Tracy, Don(ald Fiske) 1905-1976(?)
See Queen, Ellery
See also CA 1-4R; 176; CANR 2

Traill, Catharine Parr 1802-1899 . **NCLC 31**
See also DLB 99

Trakl, Georg 1887-1914 ..... **TCLC 5; PC 20**
See also CA 104; 165; MTCW 2

Transtroemer, Tomas (Goesta) 1931- .... **CLC 52, 65; DAM POET**
See also CA 117; 129; CAAS 17

Transtromer, Tomas Gosta
See Transtroemer, Tomas (Goesta)

Traven, B. (?)-1969 .... **CLC 8, 11**
See also CA 19-20; 25-28R; CAP 2; DLB 9, 56; MTCW 1

Treitel, Jonathan 1959- .... **CLC 70**

Trelawny, Edward John 1792-1881 .... **NCLC 85**
See also DLB 110, 116, 144

Tremain, Rose 1943- .... **CLC 42**
See also CA 97-100; CANR 44; DLB 14

Tremblay, Michel 1942- .... **CLC 29, 102; DAC; DAM MST**
See also CA 116; 128; DLB 60; MTCW 1, 2

Trevanian .... **CLC 29**
See also Whitaker, Rod(ney)

Trevor, Glen
See Hilton, James

Trevor, William 1928- . **CLC 7, 9, 14, 25, 71, 116; SSC 21**
See also Cox, William Trevor
See also DLB 14, 139; MTCW 2

Trifonov, Yuri (Valentinovich) 1925-1981 .... **CLC 45**
See also CA 126; 103; MTCW 1

Trilling, Diana (Rubin) 1905-1996 . **CLC 129**
See also CA 5-8R; 154; CANR 10, 46; INT CANR-10; MTCW 1, 2

Trilling, Lionel 1905-1975 ..... **CLC 9, 11, 24**
See also CA 9-12R; 61-64; CANR 10; DLB 28, 63; INT CANR-10; MTCW 1, 2

Trimball, W. H.
See Mencken, H(enry) L(ouis)

Tristan
See Gomez de la Serna, Ramon

Tristram
See Housman, A(lfred) E(dward)

Trogdon, William (Lewis) 1939-
See Heat-Moon, William Least
See also CA 115; 119; CANR 47, 89; INT 119

Trollope, Anthony 1815-1882 .. **NCLC 6, 33; DA; DAB; DAC; DAM MST, NOV; SSC 28; WLC**
See also CDBLB 1832-1890; DA3; DLB 21, 57, 159; SATA 22

Trollope, Frances 1779-1863 .... **NCLC 30**
See also DLB 21, 166

Trotsky, Leon 1879-1940 .... **TCLC 22**
See also CA 118; 167

Trotter (Cockburn), Catharine 1679-1749 .... **LC 8**
See also DLB 84

Trotter, Wilfred 1872-1939 .... **TCLC 97**

Trout, Kilgore
See Farmer, Philip Jose

Trow, George W. S. 1943- .... **CLC 52**
See also CA 126; CANR 91

Troyat, Henri 1911- .... **CLC 23**
See also CA 45-48; CANR 2, 33, 67; MTCW 1

Trudeau, G(arretson) B(eekman) 1948-
See Trudeau, Garry B.
See also CA 81-84; CANR 31; SATA 35

Trudeau, Garry B. .... **CLC 12**
See also Trudeau, G(arretson) B(eekman)
See also AAYA 10; AITN 2

Truffaut, Francois 1932-1984 .. **CLC 20, 101**
See also CA 81-84; 113; CANR 34

Trumbo, Dalton 1905-1976 .... **CLC 19**
See also CA 21-24R; 69-72; CANR 10; DLB 26

Trumbull, John 1750-1831 .... **NCLC 30**
See also DLB 31

Trundlett, Helen B.
See Eliot, T(homas) S(tearns)

Truth, Sojourner 1797(?)-1883 ..... **NCLC 94**

Tryon, Thomas 1926-1991 . **CLC 3, 11; DAM POP**
See also AITN 1; CA 29-32R; 135; CANR 32, 77; DA3; MTCW 1

Tryon, Tom
See Tryon, Thomas

Ts'ao Hsueh-ch'in 1715(?)-1763 .... **LC 1**

Tsushima, Shuji 1909-1948
See Dazai Osamu
See also CA 107

Tsvetaeva (Efron), Marina (Ivanovna) 1892-1941 .... **TCLC 7, 35; PC 14**
See also CA 104; 128; CANR 73; MTCW 1, 2

Tuck, Lily 1938- .... **CLC 70**
See also CA 139; CANR 90

Tu Fu 712-770 .... **PC 9**
See also DAM MULT

Tunis, John R(oberts) 1889-1975 .... **CLC 12**
See also CA 61-64; CANR 62; DLB 22, 171; JRDA; MAICYA; SATA 37; SATA-Brief 30

Tuohy, Frank .... **CLC 37**
See also Tuohy, John Francis
See also DLB 14, 139

Tuohy, John Francis 1925-
See Tuohy, Frank
See also CA 5-8R; 178; CANR 3, 47

Turco, Lewis (Putnam) 1934- .... **CLC 11, 63**
See also CA 13-16R; CAAS 22; CANR 24, 51; DLBY 84

Turgenev, Ivan 1818-1883 ..... **NCLC 21, 37; DA; DAB; DAC; DAM MST, NOV; DC 7; SSC 7; WLC**

Turgot, Anne-Robert-Jacques 1727-1781 .... **LC 26**

Turner, Frederick 1943- .... **CLC 48**
See also CA 73-76; CAAS 10; CANR 12, 30, 56; DLB 40

Tutu, Desmond M(pilo) 1931- .... **CLC 80; BLC 3; DAM MULT**
See also BW 1, 3; CA 125; CANR 67, 81

Tutuola, Amos 1920-1997 ..... **CLC 5, 14, 29; BLC 3; DAM MULT**
See also BW 2, 3; CA 9-12R; 159; CANR 27, 66; DA3; DLB 125; MTCW 1, 2

Twain, Mark 1835-1910 ..... **TCLC 6, 12, 19, 36, 48, 59; SSC 34; WLC**
See also Clemens, Samuel Langhorne
See also AAYA 20; CLR 58, 60, 66; DLB 11, 12, 23, 64, 74

Tyler, Anne 1941- . **CLC 7, 11, 18, 28, 44, 59, 103; DAM NOV, POP**
See also AAYA 18; BEST 89:1; CA 9-12R; CANR 11, 33, 53; CDALBS; DLB 6, 143; DLBY 82; MTCW 1, 2; SATA 7, 90

Tyler, Royall 1757-1826 .... **NCLC 3**
See also DLB 37

Tynan, Katharine 1861-1931 .... **TCLC 3**
See also CA 104; 167; DLB 153

Tyutchev, Fyodor 1803-1873 .... **NCLC 34**

Tzara, Tristan 1896-1963 ..... **CLC 47; DAM POET; PC 27**
See also CA 153; 89-92; MTCW 2

Uhry, Alfred 1936- . **CLC 55; DAM DRAM, POP**
See also CA 127; 133; DA3; INT 133

Ulf, Haerved
See Strindberg, (Johan) August

Ulf, Harved
See Strindberg, (Johan) August

Ulibarri, Sabine R(eyes) 1919- .... **CLC 83; DAM MULT; HLCS 2**
See also CA 131; CANR 81; DLB 82; HW 1, 2

Unamuno (y Jugo), Miguel de 1864-1936 . **TCLC 2, 9; DAM MULT, NOV; HLC 2; SSC 11**
See also CA 104; 131; CANR 81; DLB 108; HW 1, 2; MTCW 1, 2

Undercliffe, Errol
See Campbell, (John) Ramsey

Underwood, Miles
See Glassco, John

Undset, Sigrid 1882-1949 .... **TCLC 3; DA; DAB; DAC; DAM MST, NOV; WLC**
See also CA 104; 129; DA3; MTCW 1, 2

Ungaretti, Giuseppe 1888-1970 .. **CLC 7, 11, 15**
See also CA 19-20; 25-28R; CAP 2; DLB 114

Unger, Douglas 1952- .... **CLC 34**
See also CA 130

Unsworth, Barry (Forster) 1930- ... **CLC 76, 127**
See also CA 25-28R; CANR 30, 54; DLB 194

Updike, John (Hoyer) 1932- . **CLC 1, 2, 3, 5, 7, 9, 13, 15, 23, 34, 43, 70; DA; DAB; DAC; DAM MST, NOV, POET, POP; SSC 13, 27; WLC**
See also CA 1-4R; CABS 1; CANR 4, 33, 51; CDALB 1968-1988; DA3; DLB 2, 5, 143, 227; DLBD 3; DLBY 80, 82, 97; MTCW 1, 2

Upshaw, Margaret Mitchell
See Mitchell, Margaret (Munnerlyn)

Upton, Mark
See Sanders, Lawrence

Upward, Allen 1863-1926 .... **TCLC 85**
See also CA 117; 187; DLB 36

Urdang, Constance (Henriette) 1922-
.... **CLC 47**
See also CA 21-24R; CANR 9, 24

Uriel, Henry
See Faust, Frederick (Schiller)

Uris, Leon (Marcus) 1924- .... **CLC 7, 32; DAM NOV, POP**
See also AITN 1, 2; BEST 89:2; CA 1-4R; CANR 1, 40, 65; DA3; MTCW 1, 2; SATA 49

Urista, Alberto H. 1947-
See Alurista
See also CA 45-48, 182; CANR 2, 32; HLCS 1; HW 1

Urmuz
See Codrescu, Andrei

Urquhart, Guy
See McAlmon, Robert (Menzies)

Urquhart, Jane 1949- .... **CLC 90; DAC**
See also CA 113; CANR 32, 68

Usigli, Rodolfo 1905-1979
See also CA 131; HLCS 1; HW 1

Ustinov, Peter (Alexander) 1921- ...... **CLC 1**
See also AITN 1; CA 13-16R; CANR 25, 51; DLB 13; MTCW 2

U Tam'si, Gerald Felix Tchicaya
See Tchicaya, Gerald Felix

U Tam'si, Tchicaya
See Tchicaya, Gerald Felix

Vachss, Andrew (Henry) 1942- ..... **CLC 106**
See also CA 118; CANR 44

Vachss, Andrew H.
See Vachss, Andrew (Henry)

Vaculik, Ludvik 1926- .... **CLC 7**
See also CA 53-56; CANR 72; DLB 232

Vaihinger, Hans 1852-1933 .... **TCLC 71**
See also CA 116; 166

Valdez, Luis (Miguel) 1940- . **CLC 84; DAM MULT; DC 10; HLC 2**
See also CA 101; CANR 32, 81; DLB 122; HW 1

Valenzuela, Luisa 1938- .... **CLC 31, 104; DAM MULT; HLCS 2; SSC 14**
See also CA 101; CANR 32, 65; DLB 113; HW 1, 2

Valera y Alcala-Galiano, Juan 1824-1905
.... **TCLC 10**
See also CA 106

Valery, (Ambroise) Paul (Toussaint Jules) 1871-1945 .. **TCLC 4, 15; DAM POET; PC 9**
See also CA 104; 122; DA3; MTCW 1, 2

Valle-Inclan, Ramon (Maria) del 1866-1936 .... **TCLC 5; DAM MULT; HLC 2**
See also CA 106; 153; CANR 80; DLB 134; HW 2

Vallejo, Antonio Buero
See Buero Vallejo, Antonio

Vallejo, Cesar (Abraham) 1892-1938
...... **TCLC 3, 56; DAM MULT; HLC 2**
See also CA 105; 153; HW 1

Valles, Jules 1832-1885 .... **NCLC 71**
See also DLB 123

Vallette, Marguerite Eymery 1860-1953
.... **TCLC 67**
See also CA 182; DLB 123, 192

Valle Y Pena, Ramon del
See Valle-Inclan, Ramon (Maria) del

Van Ash, Cay 1918- .... **CLC 34**

Vanbrugh, Sir John 1664-1726 .... **LC 21; DAM DRAM**
See also DLB 80

Van Campen, Karl
See Campbell, John W(ood, Jr.)

Vance, Gerald
See Silverberg, Robert

Vance, Jack .... **CLC 35**
See also Vance, John Holbrook
See also DLB 8

Vance, John Holbrook 1916-
See Queen, Ellery; Vance, Jack
See also CA 29-32R; CANR 17, 65; MTCW 1

Van Den Bogarde, Derek Jules Gaspard Ulric Niven 1921-1999 .... **CLC 14**
See also CA 77-80; 179; DLB 19

Vandenburgh, Jane .... **CLC 59**
See also CA 168

Vanderhaeghe, Guy 1951- .... **CLC 41**
See also CA 113; CANR 72

van der Post, Laurens (Jan) 1906-1996
.... **CLC 5**
See also CA 5-8R; 155; CANR 35; DLB 204

van de Wetering, Janwillem 1931- . **CLC 47**
See also CA 49-52; CANR 4, 62, 90

Van Dine, S. S. .... **TCLC 23**
See also Wright, Willard Huntington

Van Doren, Carl (Clinton) 1885-1950
.... **TCLC 18**
See also CA 111; 168

Van Doren, Mark 1894-1972 .... **CLC 6, 10**
See also CA 1-4R; 37-40R; CANR 3; DLB 45; MTCW 1, 2

Van Druten, John (William) 1901-1957
.... **TCLC 2**
See also CA 104; 161; DLB 10

Van Duyn, Mona (Jane) 1921- ..... **CLC 3, 7, 63, 116; DAM POET**
See also CA 9-12R; CANR 7, 38, 60; DLB 5

Van Dyne, Edith
See Baum, L(yman) Frank

van Itallie, Jean-Claude 1936- .... **CLC 3**
See also CA 45-48; CAAS 2; CANR 1, 48; DLB 7

van Ostaijen, Paul 1896-1928 .... **TCLC 33**
See also CA 163

Van Peebles, Melvin 1932- .... **CLC 2, 20; DAM MULT**
See also BW 2, 3; CA 85-88; CANR 27, 67, 82

Vansittart, Peter 1920- .... **CLC 42**
See also CA 1-4R; CANR 3, 49, 90

Van Vechten, Carl 1880-1964 .... **CLC 33**
See also CA 183; 89-92; DLB 4, 9, 51

Van Vogt, A(lfred) E(lton) 1912-2000 . **CLC 1**
See also CA 21-24R; CANR 28; DLB 8; SATA 14

Varda, Agnes 1928- .... **CLC 16**
See also CA 116; 122

Vargas Llosa, (Jorge) Mario (Pedro) 1936-
..... **CLC 3, 6, 9, 10, 15, 31, 42, 85; DA; DAB; DAC; DAM MST, MULT, NOV; HLC 2**
See also CA 73-76; CANR 18, 32, 42, 67; DA3; DLB 145; HW 1, 2; MTCW 1, 2

Vasiliu, Gheorghe 1881-1957
See Bacovia, George
See also CA 123; DLB 220

Vassa, Gustavus
See Equiano, Olaudah

Vassilikos, Vassilis 1933- .... **CLC 4, 8**
See also CA 81-84; CANR 75

Vaughan, Henry 1621-1695 .... **LC 27**
See also DLB 131

Vaughn, Stephanie .... **CLC 62**

Vazov, Ivan (Minchov) 1850-1921 . **TCLC 25**
See also CA 121; 167; DLB 147

Veblen, Thorstein B(unde) 1857-1929
.... **TCLC 31**
See also CA 115; 165

Vega, Lope de 1562-1635 ... **LC 23; HLCS 2**

Vendler, Helen (Hennessy) 1933- .. **CLC 138**
See also CA 41-44R; CANR 25, 72; MTCW 1, 2

Venison, Alfred
See Pound, Ezra (Weston Loomis)

Verdi, Marie de
See Mencken, H(enry) L(ouis)

Verdu, Matilde
See Cela, Camilo Jose

Verga, Giovanni (Carmelo) 1840-1922
.... **TCLC 3; SSC 21**
See also CA 104; 123

Vergil 70B.C.-19B.C. .... **CMLC 9, 40; DA; DAB; DAC; DAM MST, POET; PC 12; WLCS**
See also Virgil
See also DA3; DLB 211

Verhaeren, Emile (Adolphe Gustave) 1855-1916 .... **TCLC 12**
See also CA 109

Verlaine, Paul (Marie) 1844-1896 . **NCLC 2, 51; DAM POET; PC 2, 32**

Verne, Jules (Gabriel) 1828-1905 .. **TCLC 6, 52**
See also AAYA 16; CA 110; 131; DA3; DLB 123; JRDA; MAICYA; SATA 21

Very, Jones 1813-1880 .... **NCLC 9**
See also DLB 1

Vesaas, Tarjei 1897-1970 .... **CLC 48**

See also CA 104; 132; CDALB 1929-1941; DA3; DLB 9, 102; DLBD 2, 16; DLBY 85, 97; MTCW 1, 2

Wolfe, Thomas Kennerly, Jr. 1930-
See Wolfe, Tom
See also CA 13-16R; CANR 9, 33, 70; DAM POP; DA3; DLB 185; INT CANR-9; MTCW 1, 2

Wolfe, Tom .... **CLC 1, 2, 9, 15, 35, 51**
See also Wolfe, Thomas Kennerly, Jr.
See also AAYA 8; AITN 2; BEST 89:1; DLB 152

Wolff, Geoffrey (Ansell) 1937- .... **CLC 41**
See also CA 29-32R; CANR 29, 43, 78

Wolff, Sonia
See Levitin, Sonia (Wolff)

Wolff, Tobias (Jonathan Ansell) 1945-
.... **CLC 39, 64**
See also AAYA 16; BEST 90:2; CA 114; 117; CAAS 22; CANR 54, 76; DA3; DLB 130; INT 117; MTCW 2

Wolfram von Eschenbach c. 1170-c. 1220
.... **CMLC 5**
See also DLB 138

Wolitzer, Hilma 1930- .... **CLC 17**
See also CA 65-68; CANR 18, 40; INT CANR-18; SATA 31

Wollstonecraft, Mary 1759-1797 ... **LC 5, 50**
See also CDBLB 1789-1832; DLB 39, 104, 158

Wonder, Stevie .... **CLC 12**
See also Morris, Steveland Judkins

Wong, Jade Snow 1922- .... **CLC 17**
See also CA 109; CANR 91; SATA 112

Woodberry, George Edward 1855-1930
.... **TCLC 73**
See also CA 165; DLB 71, 103

Woodcott, Keith
See Brunner, John (Kilian Houston)

Woodruff, Robert W.
See Mencken, H(enry) L(ouis)

Woolf, (Adeline) Virginia 1882-1941
. **TCLC 1, 5, 20, 43, 56, 101; DA; DAB; DAC; DAM MST, NOV; SSC 7; WLC**
See also Woolf, Virginia Adeline
See also CA 104; 130; CANR 64; CDBLB 1914-1945; DA3; DLB 36, 100, 162; DLBD 10; MTCW 1

Woolf, Virginia Adeline
See Woolf, (Adeline) Virginia
See also MTCW 2

Woollcott, Alexander (Humphreys)
1887-1943 .... **TCLC 5**
See also CA 105; 161; DLB 29

Woolrich, Cornell 1903-1968 .... **CLC 77**
See also Hopley-Woolrich, Cornell George

Woolson, Constance Fenimore 1840-1894
.... **NCLC 82**
See also DLB 12, 74, 189, 221

Wordsworth, Dorothy 1771-1855 . **NCLC 25**
See also DLB 107

Wordsworth, William 1770-1850 . **NCLC 12, 38; DA; DAB; DAC; DAM MST, POET; PC 4; WLC**
See also CDBLB 1789-1832; DA3; DLB 93, 107

Wouk, Herman 1915- .. **CLC 1, 9, 38; DAM NOV, POP**
See also CA 5-8R; CANR 6, 33, 67; CDALBS; DA3; DLBY 82; INT CANR-6; MTCW 1, 2

Wright, Charles (Penzel, Jr.) 1935- . **CLC 6, 13, 28, 119**
See also CA 29-32R; CAAS 7; CANR 23, 36, 62, 88; DLB 165; DLBY 82; MTCW 1, 2

Wright, Charles Stevenson 1932- .. **CLC 49; BLC 3; DAM MULT, POET**

See also BW 1; CA 9-12R; CANR 26; DLB 33

Wright, Frances 1795-1852 .... **NCLC 74**
See also DLB 73

Wright, Frank Lloyd 1867-1959 .. **TCLC 95**
See also AAYA 33; CA 174

Wright, Jack R.
See Harris, Mark

Wright, James (Arlington) 1927-1980
.... **CLC 3, 5, 10, 28; DAM POET**
See also AITN 2; CA 49-52; 97-100; CANR 4, 34, 64; CDALBS; DLB 5, 169; MTCW 1, 2

Wright, Judith (Arundell) 1915-2000
.... **CLC 11, 53; PC 14**
See also CA 13-16R; CANR 31, 76, 93; MTCW 1, 2; SATA 14

Wright, L(aurali) R. 1939- .... **CLC 44**
See also CA 138

Wright, Richard (Nathaniel) 1908-1960
. **CLC 1, 3, 4, 9, 14, 21, 48, 74; BLC 3; DA; DAB; DAC; DAM MST, MULT, NOV; SSC 2; WLC**
See also AAYA 5; BW 1; CA 108; CANR 64; CDALB 1929-1941; DA3; DLB 76, 102; DLBD 2; MTCW 1, 2

Wright, Richard B(ruce) 1937- .... **CLC 6**
See also CA 85-88; DLB 53

Wright, Rick 1945- .... **CLC 35**

Wright, Rowland
See Wells, Carolyn

Wright, Stephen 1946- .... **CLC 33**

Wright, Willard Huntington 1888-1939
See Van Dine, S. S.
See also CA 115; DLBD 16

Wright, William 1930- .... **CLC 44**
See also CA 53-56; CANR 7, 23

Wroth, LadyMary 1587-1653(?) .... **LC 30**
See also DLB 121

Wu Ch'eng-en 1500(?)-1582(?) .... **LC 7**

Wu Ching-tzu 1701-1754 .... **LC 2**

Wurlitzer, Rudolph 1938(?)- ... **CLC 2, 4, 15**
See also CA 85-88; DLB 173

Wyatt, Thomas c. 1503-1542 .... **PC 27**
See also DLB 132

Wycherley, William 1641-1715 ..... **LC 8, 21; DAM DRAM**
See also CDBLB 1660-1789; DLB 80

Wylie, Elinor (Morton Hoyt) 1885-1928
.... **TCLC 8; PC 23**
See also CA 105; 162; DLB 9, 45

Wylie, Philip (Gordon) 1902-1971 .. **CLC 43**
See also CA 21-22; 33-36R; CAP 2; DLB 9

Wyndham, John .... **CLC 19**
See also Harris, John (Wyndham Parkes Lucas) Beynon

Wyss, Johann David Von 1743-1818
.... **NCLC 10**
See also JRDA; MAICYA; SATA 29; SATA-Brief 27

Xenophon c. 430B.C.-c. 354B.C. .. **CMLC 17**
See also DLB 176

Yakumo Koizumi
See Hearn, (Patricio) Lafcadio (Tessima Carlos)

Yamamoto, Hisaye 1921- ...... **SSC 34; DAM MULT**

Yanez, Jose Donoso
See Donoso (Yanez), Jose

Yanovsky, Basile S.
See Yanovsky, V(assily) S(emenovich)

Yanovsky, V(assily) S(emenovich) 1906-1989
.... **CLC 2, 18**
See also CA 97-100; 129

Yates, Richard 1926-1992 .... **CLC 7, 8, 23**
See also CA 5-8R; 139; CANR 10, 43; DLB 2, 234; DLBY 81, 92; INT CANR-10

Yeats, W. B.
See Yeats, William Butler

Yeats, William Butler 1865-1939 ... **TCLC 1, 11, 18, 31, 93; DA; DAB; DAC; DAM DRAM, MST, POET; PC 20; WLC**
See also CA 104; 127; CANR 45; CDBLB 1890-1914; DA3; DLB 10, 19, 98, 156; MTCW 1, 2

Yehoshua, A(braham) B. 1936- . **CLC 13, 31**
See also CA 33-36R; CANR 43, 90

Yellow Bird
See Ridge, John Rollin

Yep, Laurence Michael 1948- .... **CLC 35**
See also AAYA 5, 31; CA 49-52; CANR 1, 46, 92; CLR 3, 17, 54; DLB 52; JRDA; MAICYA; SATA 7, 69

Yerby, Frank G(arvin) 1916-1991 .... **CLC 1, 7, 22; BLC 3; DAM MULT**
See also BW 1, 3; CA 9-12R; 136; CANR 16, 52; DLB 76; INT CANR-16; MTCW 1

Yesenin, Sergei Alexandrovich
See Esenin, Sergei (Alexandrovich)

Yevtushenko, Yevgeny (Alexandrovich) 1933-
. **CLC 1, 3, 13, 26, 51, 126; DAM POET**
See also CA 81-84; CANR 33, 54; MTCW 1

Yezierska, Anzia 1885(?)-1970 .... **CLC 46**
See also CA 126; 89-92; DLB 28, 221; MTCW 1

Yglesias, Helen 1915- .... **CLC 7, 22**
See also CA 37-40R; CAAS 20; CANR 15, 65; INT CANR-15; MTCW 1

Yokomitsu, Riichi 1898-1947 .... **TCLC 47**
See also CA 170

Yonge, Charlotte (Mary) 1823-1901
.... **TCLC 48**
See also CA 109; 163; DLB 18, 163; SATA 17

York, Jeremy
See Creasey, John

York, Simon
See Heinlein, Robert A(nson)

Yorke, Henry Vincent 1905-1974 .... **CLC 13**
See also Green, Henry
See also CA 85-88; 49-52

Yosano Akiko 1878-1942 .. **TCLC 59; PC 11**
See also CA 161

Yoshimoto, Banana .... **CLC 84**
See also Yoshimoto, Mahoko

Yoshimoto, Mahoko 1964-
See Yoshimoto, Banana
See also CA 144

Young, Al(bert James) 1939- . **CLC 19; BLC 3; DAM MULT**
See also BW 2, 3; CA 29-32R; CANR 26, 65; DLB 33

Young, Andrew (John) 1885-1971 ..... **CLC 5**
See also CA 5-8R; CANR 7, 29

Young, Collier
See Bloch, Robert (Albert)

Young, Edward 1683-1765 .... **LC 3, 40**
See also DLB 95

Young, Marguerite (Vivian) 1909-1995
.... **CLC 82**
See also CA 13-16; 150; CAP 1

Young, Neil 1945- .... **CLC 17**
See also CA 110

Young Bear, Ray A. 1950- ... **CLC 94; DAM MULT**
See also CA 146; DLB 175; NNAL

Yourcenar, Marguerite 1903-1987 . **CLC 19, 38, 50, 87; DAM NOV**
See also CA 69-72; CANR 23, 60, 93; DLB 72; DLBY 88; MTCW 1, 2

Yuan, Chu 340(?)B.C.-278(?)B.C. . **CMLC 36**

Yurick, Sol 1925- .... **CLC 6**
See also CA 13-16R; CANR 25

Literary Criticism Series
Cumulative Topic Index

This index lists all topic entries in Gale's *Classical and Medieval Literature Criticism, Contemporary Literary Criticism, Literature Criticism from 1400 to 1800, Nineteenth-Century Literature Criticism,* and *Twentieth-Century Literary Criticism.*

CMLC Cumulative Nationality Index

CMLC Cumulative Title Index

Title Index

Title Index

Title Index